CONFLICT OF LAWS: FEDERAL, STATE, AND INTERNATIONAL PERSPECTIVES

REVISED SECOND EDITION

Andreas F. Lowenfeld

*Herbert and Rose Rubin Professor
of International Law
New York University School of Law*

2002

This publication is designed to provide accurate and authoritative information in regard to the subject matter covered. It is sold with the understanding that the publisher is not engaged in rendering legal, accounting, or other professional services. If legal advice or other expert assistance is required, the services of a competent professional should be sought.

LexisNexis, the knowledge burst logo, and Michie are trademarks of Reed Elsevier Properties Inc, used under license. Matthew Bender is a registered trademark of Matthew Bender Properties Inc.

Copyright © 2002 Matthew Bender & Company, Inc., a member of the LexisNexis Group.
All Rights Reserved.

No copyright is claimed in the text of statutes, regulations, and excerpts from court opinions quoted within this work. Permission to copy material exceeding fair use, 17 U.S.C. § 107, may be licensed for a fee of 10¢ per page per copy from the Copyright Clearance Center, 222 Rosewood Drive, Danvers, Mass. 01923, telephone (978) 750-8400.

ISBN 0-8205-5488-X

LIBRARY OF CONGRESS CATALOGING IN PUBLICATION DATA

Lowenfeld, Andreas F., 1930-
    Conflict of laws: federal, state, and international perspectives / Andreas F. Lowenfeld — 2d ed. 2002 Reprint
       p. cm. — — (Casebook series)
  Includes index.
  ISBN 0-8205-5488-X
  1. Conflict of Laws—United States— 2. Conflict of laws
  I. Title. II. Series: Casebook series (New York, N.Y.)
KF410.L69 1998   97-53263
340.9—DC21   CIP

Editorial Offices
744 Broad Street, Newark, NJ 07102 (973) 820-2000
201 Mission St., San Francisco, CA 94105-1831 (415) 908-3200
www.lexis.com

To Elena

Acknowledgements

My greatest debt goes to my colleague, Professor Linda J. Silberman. For nearly three decades we have learned from each other, taught together, and debated the issues reflected in this book. I regret that the book did not turn out to be a joint effort, as we once contemplated, but her influence is pervasive, even more in the second than in the first edition.

My own interest in Conflict of Laws was awakened by Professor Paul A. Freund, who, though better known as a scholar in Constitutional Law, was a most stimulating teacher in conflict of laws, with a fine (and early) appreciation of true and false conflicts, genuine and spurious interests, and the demands and concerns of an ever-changing federal system. Professors David Cavers and Willis Reese were never formally my teachers, but by their writings and personal contacts (if that word is permissible in this context) they were a source of inspiration to me as to a whole generation of tillers in their field.

My interest in the relation between Conflict of Laws and International Law, demonstrated particularly in Chapter 10 but in a real sense throughout this book was stimulated first by Professor Henry de Vries, my first employer; subsequently by Professors Abram Chayes and Thomas Ehrlich, my colleagues at the U.S. Department of State and fellow authors of a text on the International Legal Process; and more recently by Professor Louis Henkin, the Chief Reporter for the Restatement (Third) of the Foreign Relations Law of the United States. Many of the issues explored in connection with that project, in which I was privileged to be involved as an Associate Reporter, are reflected in these pages. I hope that I benefited from Professor Henkin's insistence that it is possible to write about law with elegance as well as precision, and that the attempt to do so is always worth the effort.

Until I began to teach from earlier versions of the present volume, I taught both from Reese and Rosenberg and from Cramton, Currie and Kay (and their predecessors); while my approach and emphasis are somewhat different, I have benefited from both of these fine books in developing my own materials. More than most fields of the law, conflict of laws has seen the influence of legal scholars. I struggled with the question of how much to include the writings of my colleagues in a book whose length already strained the tolerance of the publishers. I hope they will forgive me if I have not quoted—or even cited—as much as I might have done; I do want, however, to acknowledge my debt, and that of all teachers of the subject, to the writings of Baade, Brilmayer, D. Currie, Hancock, Hay, Herzog, Juenger, Korn, Leflar, Martin, Scoles, Sedler, Trautman, von Mehren, and Weintraub. Lawrence Collins was kind enough to review portions of the manuscript dealing with English procedure.

I am grateful to Ms. Mary L. B. Betts, who worked with me as a student assistant to develop my first set of materials on transnational conflicts, and later joined me in organizing and teaching a seminar in international litigation that explores many of the problems covered in this book. Also, I want to acknowledge my debt to my colleague, Dean John E. Sexton, who already an accomplished teacher and writer on Civil Procedure and other subjects, attended my course in Conflict of Laws regularly for a full semester, completing, as he said, his own legal education but contributing to mine as well.

I am, of course, in debt to all of my students, who have helped me shape my ideas as to both substance and method. I am particularly grateful to Rachel Ascher, Gianluca Bacchiocchi, Hilary Foulkes, Robin Jo Frank, Frederick S. Harris, Deborah Kolodner, Liam Murphy, Arthur Russell, Lawranne Stewart, Charles Stockmeyer, and Michael S. Straus, who helped in various stages of preparation of this volume while they were students at New York University Law School. I am also grateful to New York University Law School, my professional home for more than three decades, and particularly to the N.Y.U. Law Center Foundation, which supported my work with several summer research grants.

Finally, I belong to the vanishing species that puts pen to paper, rather than processing words or accessing computers. All the greater my gratitude to my secretaries, Elizabeth Sheehan, Rose F. Jacobs, and W. Lee Baer, each of whom, at different times, coped with the process of transforming a manuscript into a book.

Note on Arrangement of the Book

This book is, in the first instance, an anthology of reported judicial decisions, but more attention (and space) has been devoted to the Notes and Questions than is typical in American law school case books. In principle, the Notes and Questions are designed to provide the agenda for a one-hour class, but as will be obvious, quite often a topic breaks down in such a way that two class hours' worth of reading precedes a set of Notes and Questions, and that these in turn provide material for two hours' worth of discussion. It is not, of course, expected that all of the notes or questions will be taken up in class, and instructors will want to add their own perspective, and their own questions, to the class discussion. Experience has shown, however, that indication in advance that particular questions will be focused on leads both to better preparation and to better class discussion.

There is no inevitability to the sequence of the chapters; within each chapter, however, the sequence tends to be chronological by topic, though not perfectly so. In those chapters that contain extended comparative and international materials, these are generally placed at the end, so that they may be omitted without impairing the flow. The author's recommendation would be to include at least some of these materials, however, even at the cost of skipping some other topic, because they add a dimension—not only to conflict of laws but to the study of law generally—that is often missing in American law schools.

Footnotes and internal citations in the reproduced cases have been freely omitted without special indication. Where footnotes in reproduced materials are retained they are presented with their original numbers. Footnotes introduced by letters are those of the author. The Documents Supplement is an integral part of the book, and should always be at hand.

Preface to the Second Edition

Preparing the second edition of any book, but particularly of a law book, always presents a dilemma. Should one rethink the whole presentation, or just bring the first edition up to date? The present text, completed a dozen years after the first edition, does some of each. The basic organization is retained, and the choice of law materials (chapters 1-4) are not significantly changed. Though guest statutes and wrongful death limitations do not play as significant a role as they did thirty years ago, it was in the context of controversy over those laws that the American "conflicts revolution" took place, and I believe a step by step account of that revolution is essential to understanding of choice of law today.

The latest edition of one of the other casebooks on conflict of laws omits *Babcock v. Jackson*, on the ground that it has been overtaken by later decisions. I believe that is a mistake. Both in terms of historical development and in terms of intellectual analysis, I think *Babcock*, as well as *Kilberg*, remain essential sources for the student of conflict of laws, American style. I have also found that the *Knickerbocker* series of imaginary cases developed by Professor Cavers in the early 1960's remain not only entertaining but instructive for law students. I usually appoint two students to represent each of the professor/judges in the *Knickerbocker* series, and come back to them throughout the course.

I have never been quite sure where or when to take up the question of time bar, which occurs in the context of choice of law, (e.g., *Mack Trucks* and *Bournias*), constitutional control (e.g., *Wells* and now *Sun Oil*), and *Erie* (e.g., *Guaranty Trust*). One topic that has become more significant in recent years is the interpretation and application of statutes of repose. I have added a section to Chapter 2 on this topic, focused around certification by the Federal Court of Appeals to the Supreme Court of Connecticut of the question of application of an Oregon statute of repose.

When the first edition of this book was published, the Supreme Court had just decided *Phillips Petroleum Co. v. Shutts*, which indicated some reconsideration of *Allstate Insurance Co. v. Hague*. Chapter 5 follows this development with the second round of the controversy over natural gas leaseholds, *Sun Oil v. Wortman*, suggesting that the venture by the Supreme Court into control of choice of law by state courts does not go very far.

Chapter 6, on the *Erie* question, continues to fascinate both teachers and students. The major new case, *Gasperini*, is certainly worth studying in the context of vertical (i.e., federal/state) conflicts, and as some of the questions following the opinion suggest, it may soon develop horizontal complications as well.

The Supreme Court's approach to judicial jurisdiction, which had encompassed only one international case at the time of the first edition, soon encountered *Asahi*, which seems to have added another dimension, or at least another way of looking at the question of the nonresident defendant. Whether "reasonableness" as a distinct line of inquiry is limited to foreign country defendants is not yet clear as these lines are written. But the hope that unreasonableness—i.e., "tag jurisdiction"—might be phased out was dashed in *Burnham*.

Not much has changed in the field of recognition of judgments, though as of 1998 the United States is actively engaged at the Hague Conference in an effort to develop a multilateral judgments convention, possibly by year 2000.

The greatest change in this book shows up in Chapter 9, focused on Family Law. We have more experience now with the Uniform Child Custody Jurisdiction Act and its federal analogue, the Parental Kidnapping Prevention Act. And as child support has come more and more to be seen as a national problem, both state and federal efforts have been undertaken to overcome the traditional obstacles presented by our federal system. Also, equitable distribution of marital property has become widespread, and brought with it differing approaches to the movement of people and property across state lines. Finally, the possibility of same-sex marriage, while not yet a large-scale phenomenon in the United States, has commanded wide commentary in the context of choice of law and full faith and credit, and is briefly treated at the end of Chapter 9. One could build an entire course around family law and conflict of laws. The hope here is merely to suggest the lines of inquiry, and to acquaint some of the non-specialists with the current ferment in this area.

The interaction of public and private international law was addressed in this book well before others picked it up. It continues to be fertile ground for practitioners and judges. In the *Insurance Antitrust* case, the Supreme Court finally accepted a case involving regulation of international economic activity, and that case is the principal addition to Chapter 10.

A result of all these developments is that the book has become fatter (dare I say richer?). If one wanted to cover all of the material, one would need about 64 hours. I think, however, that the book is suitable for both a 3 times-a-week (42 hour) or a 4 times-a-week (56 hour) course. One could skip family law, or international law, or judicial jurisdiction without destroying the continuity. I would not recommend omitting *Erie*, because that topic, quite apart from its inherent fascination, is much more comprehensible after one has been exposed to choice of law than it is to first-year students, no matter how ably they are taught.

Altogether, conflict of laws continues to stimulate me, and I hope some of this stimulation is communicated in the Notes and Questions scattered throughout the book. To me, conflict of laws offers the opportunity to think about nearly all facets of law, and to demonstrate—as students never fully believe—that we deal not in rules, but in ideas.

A.F.L.
December 1997

TABLE OF CONTENTS

Part I
Choice of Law

Chapter 1. Before the Revolution: A Survey of Black Letter Rules

§ 1.01 Torts: The Place of Injury	1
Alabama Great Southern RR. Co. v. Carroll (1892)	1
Horn v. North British Railway Co. (1878)	6
Notes and Questions	11
§ 1.02 Contracts	14
[A] The American Rule: Place of Contract	14
Milliken v. Pratt (1878)	14
[B] The Traditional English Rule: The Proper Law	17
Notes and Questions	18
§ 1.03 Property	20
[A] The Situs of Real Property	20
In Re Estate of Mary E. Barrie (1949)	20
[B] The Role of Domicile	25
White v. Tennant (1888)	25
In Re Estate of Evan Jones (1921)	28
Notes and Questions	32
§ 1.04 Public Policy	34
Loucks v. Standard Oil Co. (1918)	34
Notes and Questions	38

Chapter 2. Maneuvering Within the Traditional Rules

§ 2.01 Escape Devices	41
[A] Renvoi	41
In Re Annesley (1926)	41
University of Chicago v. Dater (1936)	46
In Re Schneider's Estate (1950)	48
[B] Characterization	52
Haumschild v. Continental Casualty Company (1959)	52
Mertz v. Mertz (1936)	58
Levy v. Daniels' U-Drive Auto Renting Co. (1928)	61
Notes and Questions	62
§ 2.02 Substance and Procedure	66
Levy v. Steiger (1919)	66
Grant v. McAuliffe (1953)	67

In Re Cohn (1944)	71
Notes and Questions	72
§ 2.03 Special Problems of Statutes of Limitations	75
Bournias v. Atlantic Maritime Co. (1955)	75
West v. Theis (1908)	79
Mack Trucks, Inc. v. Bendix-Westinghouse Automotive Air Brake Co. (1966)	81
Notes and Questions	87
§ 2.04 Time Bar a Generation Later: Of Discovery Rules and Statutes of Repose	91
Baxter v. Sturm, Roger & Co., Inc. (U.S. Ct. App. 1993)	92
Baxter v. Sturm, Roger & Co., Inc. (Sup. Ct. Conn.) (1994)	95
Baxter v. Sturm, Roger & Co., Inc. (U.S. Ct. App.) (1994)	98
Further Notes and Questions	99

Chapter 3. Modern American Conflicts Analysis: Torts

§ 3.01 The Range of Modern Thinking	103
Cavers, Adams v. Knickerbocker: Five Imaginary Cases (1965)	104
Notes and Questions	125
§ 3.02 Lex Loci Discarded	129
Kilberg v. Northeast Airlines (1961)	129
Pearson v. Northeast Airlines, Inc. (1962)	135
Notes and Questions	141
§ 3.03 The Search for a Theory	145
Babcock v. Jackson (1963)	145
Notes and Questions	150
§ 3.04 The New York Experience	152
Dym v. Gordon (1965)	152
Kell v. Henderson (1965)	160
Macey v. Rozbicki (1966)	162
Farber v. Smolack (1967)	165
Notes and Questions	168
§ 3.05 Denouement in New York	173
Tooker v. Lopez (1969)	173
Neumeier v. Kuehner (1972)	181
Notes and Questions	187
§ 3.06 Traveling Around the Country: Still More on Guest Statutes	190
Cipolla v. Shaposka (1970)	190
Foster v. Leggett (1972)	192
Labree v. Major (1973)	193
Milkovich v. Saari (1973)	194
Notes and Questions	199
§ 3.07 Do the Neumeier Rules Fit All Sizes? Another Look at the New York Court of Appeals	204

Schultz v. Boy Scouts of America, Inc. (1985)	205
Notes and Questions	214
§ 3.08 Variations on the Law of Torts	215
Uninsured Motorist Insurance	215
Worker's Compensation	216
No-fault Compensation	216
Schulze v. Illinois Highway Transportation Co. (1981)	218
Kurent v. Farmers Insurance of Columbus, Inc. (1991)	221
Cooney v. Osgood Machinery, Inc. (1993)	225

Chapter 4. Modern Conflicts Thinking and Intentional Acts

§ 4.01 Choice of Law with Regard to Contracts	231
[A] Interstate Contracts and Governmental Interests	232
Lilienthal v. Kaufman (1964)	232
Bernkrant v. Fowler (1961)	239
Notes and Questions	242
[B] The Most Significant Relationship	246
Auten v. Auten (1954)	246
Haag v. Barnes (1961)	249
Notes and Questions	252
§ 4.02 Party Autonomy and Conflict of Laws	256
[A] Express Choice of Law	256
Siegelman v. Cunard White Star (1955)	259
Pisacane v. Italia S. p. A. di Navigazione (1963)	271
Southern Int'l Sales v. Potter & Brumfield Div. (1976)	272
Notes and Questions	274
[B] Choice of Forum Clauses	278
1. As Implying a Choice of Law	278
Tzortzis and Sykias v. Monark Line A/B (1968)	279
Cie. Tunisienne de Navigation S.A. v. Cie. D'Armement Maritime S.A. (1970)	282
2. As Conferring and Ousting Jurisdiction of Courts	290
Unterweser Reederei G.m.b.H. v. Zapata Off-Shore Company (1968)	290
The Bremen et al. v. Zapata Off-Shore Co. (1972)	294
Carvalho v. Hull, Blyth (Angola) Ltd. (1979)	302
Notes and Questions	306
[C] Agreements to Arbitrate	312
Gilbert v. Burnstine (1931)	313
Scherk v. Alberto Culver (1974)	315
Mitsubishi Motors v. Soler Chrysler-Plymouth, Inc. (1985)	322
Notes and Questions	331
§ 4.03 Donative Transfers and Conflict of Laws	337
[A] Inter Vivos vs. Testamentary Transfers	338

Wyatt v. Fulrath (1965)	338
Notes and Questions	343
[B] Party Autonomy and State Interests	346
Estate of Clark (1968)	346
The Lanari Estate	351
Maccoun/Watts v. Lanari/Meyer (1964)	351
Watts v. Swiss Bank Corporation (1970)	354
Matter of Bauer (1964)	356
Notes and Questions	359

Part II
The Constitution and Conflict of Laws

Chapter 5. The Constitution and Choice of Law

§ 5.01 The Transitory Action and the Obligation to Provide a Forum	367
Hughes v. Fetter (1951)	367
First National Bank of Chicago v. United Airlines (1952)	371
Wells v. Simonds Abrasive Co. (1953)	374
Notes and Questions	377
§ 5.02 The Rise and Fall of Supreme Court Supervision over Choice of Law	381
[A] Home Town Justice Struck Down	382
Home Insurance Company v. Dick (1930)	382
[B] The Intersection of Full Faith and Credit and Due Process	385
Alaska Packers Association v. Industrial Accident Commission (1935)	386
Pacific Employers Insurance Co. v. Industrial Accident Commission (1939)	389
[C] Forum Law and Out-of-State Contracts (1954)	392
Watson v. Employers Liability Assurance Corporation (1954)	392
Clay v. Sun Insurance Office, Ltd. (1964)	395
Notes and Questions	397
§ 5.03 The Supreme Court Reconsiders Its Role in Choice of Law	401
Allstate Insurance Co. v. Hague (1981)	402
Notes and Questions	417
§ 5.04 The Supreme Court and Choice of Law after *Allstate*	421
Phillips Petroleum Co. v. Shutts (1985)	421
Wortman v. Sun Oil Co. (1988)	422

Chapter 6. Federal Courts and Conflict of Laws—Diversity Jurisdiction and the Erie Question

§ 6.01 Diversity Jurisdiction and the Applicable Law	431
Swift v. Tyson (1842)	432

Erie Railroad Co. v. Tompkins (1938)	435
Notes and Questions	439
§ 6.02 Erie and Choice of Law	444
Sampson v. Channell (1940)	444
Klaxon Company v. Stentor Elec. Mfg. Co. (1941)	449
Notes and Questions	450
§ 6.03 Erie and The Federal Judicial System	454
[A] Interest Analysis Again?	454
[B] The Effect of Transfer on Choice of Law	457
Van Dusen v. Barrack (1964)	457
Notes and Questions	461
§ 6.04 One More Look at the Substance/Procedure Puzzle	470
Gasperini v. Center for Humanities, Inc. (1996)	471
Notes and Questions	480

PART III
Jurisdiction and Judgments

Chapter 7. Jurisdiction of Courts and Choice of Law

§ 7.01 Modern Notions of "Fair Play"	486
International Shoe Co. v. Washington (1945)	486
McGee v. International Life Insurance Co. (1957)	491
Notes and Questions	493
§ 7.02 The Interplay Between Jurisdiction and Choice of Law	498
Hanson v. Denckla (1958)	498
Coast Lines Ltd. v. Hudig & Veder Chartering N.V. (1972)	509
Notes and Questions	515
§ 7.03 Activity as the Basis for Judicial Jurisdiction	519
[A] The Split Tort	520
[B] Split Torts and Claims for Indemnity	521
The West Coast Machinery Case (1972)	522
[C] Sales Contracts	524
State ex rel. White Lumber Sales, Inc. v. Sulmonetti (1968)	526
§ 7.04 The Supreme Court Rethinks Judicial Jurisdiction	531
World-Wide Volkswagen Corp v. Woodson (1980)	531
Keeton v. Hustler Magazine, Inc. (1984)	546
Notes and Questions	551
§ 7.05 International Controversies	559
[A] General vs. Specific Jurisdiction	559
Helicopteros Nacionales de Colombia, S.A. v. Hall (1984)	559
[B] The Question of Reasonableness	565

Asahi Metal Industry Co. v. Superior Court (1987)	565
Notes and Questions	573
§ 7.06 Property as the Basis for Judicial Jurisdiction	578
[A] The Rise and Fall of Quasi in Rem Jurisdiction	578
Shaffer v. Heitner (1977)	580
Intermeat, Inc. v. American Poultry Inc. (1978)	596
Notes and Questions	600
[B] The Effect of *Shaffer* on Transient Jurisdiction	610
Burnham v. Superior Court (1990)	610
Notes and Questions	618
§ 7.07 Judicial Jurisdiction in the European Community	620
Bier v. Mines de Potasse d'Alsace S.A. (1976)	622
Tessili v. Dunlop A.G. (1977)	625
Ivenel v. Schwab (1982)	627
Notes and Questions	631

Chapter 8. Recognition and Enforcement of Foreign Judgments

§ 8.01 Recognition of Judgments Within the United States	637
[A] Res Judicata and Full Faith and Credit	637
1. A Penny's Worth of Res Judicata	637
2. A First Glance at the Full Faith and Credit Clause	638
Fauntleroy v. Lum (1908)	639
Notes and Questions	642
[B] Full Faith and Credit and State Interest	647
Yarborough v. Yarborough (1933)	647
Magnolia Petroleum Co. v. Hunt (1943)	655
Industrial Commission of Wisconsin v. McCartin (1947)	661
Thomas v. Washington Gas Light Co. (1980)	663
Notes and Questions	666
[C] Full Faith and Credit and Jurisdiction of the Rendering Court	674
Baldwin v. Iowa State Traveling Men's Association (1931)	675
Durfee v. Duke (1963)	676
Notes and Questions	679
§ 8.02 Recognition of Foreign Country Judgments	684
[A] Comity	684
Hilton v. Guyot (1895)	684
Johnston v. Compagnie Generale Transatlantique (1926)	694
Notes and Questions	696
[B] Foreign Country Judgments and the Question of Jurisdiction	702
Somportex, Ltd. v. Philadelphia Chewing Gum Corporation (U.K. 1968)	703
Somportex, Ltd. v. Philadelphia Chewing Gum Corporation (U.S. 1971)	708

Notes and Questions	714
§ 8.03 Recognition of Judgments and Awards by Treaty	718
[A] The European Convention on Jurisdiction and Judgments	718
Elefanten Schuh GmbH v. Jacqmain (1981)	721
Etablissements Rohr S.A. v. Ossberger (1981)	726
Notes and Questions	728
[B] The United Nations Convention on Recognition and Enforcement of Foreign Arbitral Awards	734
Parsons and Whittemore Overseas Co., Inc. v. Société Générale de l'Industrie du Papier RAKTA (1974)	736
Soc. Audi-NSU Auto Union, A.G. v. S.A. Adelin Petit (1979)	742
Notes and Questions	744

Chapter 9. Conflict of Laws and Family Law

Introduction: The State's Interest in Marriage: Two Thousand Years of History	747
§ 9.01 Ex Parte Divorce: Jurisdiction and the Full Faith and Credit Clause	749
Williams v. North Carolina (I) (1942)	749
Williams v. North Carolina (II) (1945)	758
Notes and Questions	763
§ 9.02 Bilateral Divorce: Res Judicata and Full Faith and Credit	768
[A] Within the United States	768
Sherrer v. Sherrer (1948)	768
Notes and Questions	774
[B] Foreign Country Divorce	779
Rosentiel v. Rosentiel (1965)	780
The Caribbean Caper	785
Further Notes and Questions	789
§ 9.03 Economic Incidents of Divorce	793
[A] The "Non-Final" Judgment	794
Lynde v. Lynde (1901)	794
[B] "Divisible Divorce"	796
Estin v. Estin (1948)	796
Simons v. Miami Beach First National Bank (1965)	800
Notes and Questions	803
[C] Equitable Distribution	808
In re Marriage of Whelchel	810
Day v. Day	814
Notes and Questions	817
[D] Family Support as a National Problem	819
Notes and Questions about UIFSA	822
§ 9.04 Child Custody: Jurisdiction, Modification and Recognition of Judgments	825
[A] The Traditional View	826

May v. Anderson	826
Notes and Questions	831
[B] Legislative Change: UCCJA and PKPA	832
Brock v. District Court (1980)	834
Glanzner v. State of Missouri, Department of Social Services (1992)	836
Further Notes and Questions	842
[C] The International Dimension	845
1. Under the UCCJA	845
2. The Hague Child Abduction Convention	846
Friedrich v. Friedrich (1996)	847
§ 9.05 Marriage, Public Policy, and Conflict of Laws	854
[A] Capacity to Marry	855
In re May's Estate (1953)	855
Wilkins v. Zelichowski (1958)	858
In re Dalip Singh Bir's Estate (1948)	859
Notes and Questions	861
[B] Same Sex Marriages and the Federal System	862
Notes and Questions	863

Part IV
International Law and Conflict of Laws

Chapter 10. Conflict of Laws on the Interational Stage

Introduction	869
§ 10.01 Conflict of Laws on the International Stage	871
Lauritzen v. Larsen (1953)	871
Romero v. International Terminal Operating Co. (1959)	878
McCulloch v. Sociedad Nacional Marineros de Honduras (1963)	881
Hellenic Lines Ltd. v. Rhoditis (1970)	884
Notes and Questions	887
§ 10.02 Public Policy in an International Context	893
Holman v. Johnson (1775)	893
Government of India v. Taylor (1955)	895
Regazzoni v. K. C Sethia (1944) Ltd. (1958)	899
Notes and Questions	904
§ 10.03 Jurisdiction to Prescribe	908
United States v. Aluminum Co. of America (1945)	909
United States v. Imperial Chemical Industries Ltd. (1952)	911
British Nylon Spinners, Ltd. v. Imperial Chemical Industries, Ltd. (1955)	914
Kahn-Freund, *An English Commentator on the Nylon Patent Cases* (1955)	921
Notes and Questions	922
§ 10.04 More on "Subject Matter Jurisdiction," Jurisdiction to Prescribe, and Conflict of Laws	927

   Schoenbaum v. Firstbrook (1968) 927
   Leasco Data Processing Equipment Corporation v. Maxwell (1972) 930
  Notes and Questions 937
   Timberlane Lumber Co. v. Bank of America, N.T. & S.A. (1976) 943
   Mannington Mills, Inc. v. Congoleum Corp. (1979) 950
  Further Notes and Questions 956
   The Insurance Antitrust Case 960
   Hartford Fire Ins. Co. v. California (1993) 962
  Notes and Questions on the Insurance Antitrust Case 969
§ 10.05 True Conflicts in International Relations 971
  [A] The Fruehauf Case 971
   (1) Background 971
   (2) *Fruehauf Corporation v. Masssardy* (1965) 973
  Notes and Questions 975
  [B] The Siberia-Western Europe Pipeline 977
   (1) Background 977
   (2) A Clash of Wills (1982) 978
  Further Notes and Questions 979
§ 10.06 The Act of State Doctrine 981
  Banco Nacional de Cuba v. Sabbatino (1964) 982
  Sociedad Minera El Teniente S.A. v. A.G. Norddeutsche Affinerie (1973) 993
  Notes and Questions 1001

PART I

CHOICE OF LAW

CHAPTER 1

BEFORE THE REVOLUTION: A SURVEY OF BLACK LETTER RULES

In the first chapter, the subject of choice of law—not the whole of conflict of laws but a good part of it—is introduced with a first lap around the track. The cases in this section do not present answers, at least not answers necessarily valid in the last decades of the twentieth century. But they illustrate, with one or two cases on each topic, the tensions between rules and approach, certainty and justice, jurisdiction-selection and issue-selection, that will recur throughout the book.

---

§ 1.01 Torts: The Place of Injury

ALABAMA GREAT SOUTHERN RAILROAD CO. v. CARROLL

Alabama Supreme Court
97 Ala. 126, 11 So. 803 (1892)

MCCLELLAN, J.

The plaintiff W. D. Carroll is, and was at the time of entering into the service of the defendant, the Alabama Great Southern Railroad Company, and at the time of being injured in that service, a citizen of Alabama. The defendant is an Alabama corporation operating a railroad extending from Chattanooga in the State of Tennessee through Alabama to Meridian in the State of Mississippi. At the time of the casualty complained of, plaintiff was in the service of the defendant in the capacity of brakeman on freight trains running from Birmingham, Alabama, to Meridian, Mississippi, under a contract which was made in the State of Alabama. The injury was caused by the breaking of a link between two cars in a freight train which was proceeding from Birmingham to Meridian. The point at which the link broke and the injury was suffered was in the State of Mississippi. The evidence tended to show that the link which broke was a defective link and that it was in a defective condition when the train left Birmingham. . . . The evidence went also to show that the defect in this link consisted in or resulted from its having been bent while cold, that this tended to weaken the iron and in this instance had cracked the link somewhat on the outer curve of the bend, and that the link broke at the point of this crack. It was shown to be the duty of certain employees of defendant stationed along its line to inspect the links attached to cars to be put in trains or forming the couplings between cars in trains at Chattanooga, Birmingham, and some points between Birmingham and the place where this link broke, and also that it was the duty of the conductor of freight trains and the other train-men to maintain such inspection as occasion afforded throughout the runs or trips of such trains; and the evidence affords ground for inference that there was a negligent omission on the part of such employees to perform this duty, or if performed, the failure to discover the defect in and to remove this link was the result of negligence.

The foregoing statement of facts, either proved or finding lodgment in the tendencies of the evidence, together with the evidence of the law of Mississippi, as to the master's liability for injuries sustained by an employee in his service, will suffice for the consideration and determination of the question which is of chief importance in this case, namely, whether the defendant is liable at all on the facts presented by this record for an injury sustained by the defendant in the State of Mississippi. The affirmative of this inquiry is sought to be rested and maintained upon two distinct propositions. In the first place, it is insisted that the negligence which one aspect of the evidence tends to establish is that of the defendant in respect of a duty which the law imposes upon the master and which whether performed or undertaken to be performed in the particular instance by the hand of the master or by the hand of one to whom he had delegated its performance is yet to be taken as being performed or attempted to be performed by the master himself, in such sort that the employer is responsible for its misperformance or non-performance whereby injury results to one of his employees under the doctrine of the common-law and wholly irrespective of statutory provisions. . . . [But the evidence is] clear upon every aspect of the testimony, . . . that the use of that link in coupling the foreign car to the defendant's train and also in its use throughout the voyage from Chattanooga into Mississippi was due to the negligence of employees of the defendant who were charged by it with the duty of inspecting the link before and at the time of incorporating the foreign car into this train and at the several points in Alabama where inspectors were stationed . . . and also of the train-men charged with the duty of inspection as the train was en route. There is no pretense that the defendant had not been sufficiently careful in the selection of these inspectors or that they were incompetent. It is not pretended that they were insufficient in number or stationed at points too widely separated along the line. There is no such idea advanced as that the defendant was negligent in the purchasing of links of adequate strength, and supplying them to these inspectors and to trains generally; or that there was any necessity for the continued use of this link upon a discovery of its defective condition; but on the contrary it is affirmatively shown that the defendant purchased and supplied its trains and employees with all necessary links of good quality and perfect condition to be used in its trains, to supply the places of links which became defective from use, and to substitute for defective links coming to this road with foreign cars. The only negligence, in other words and in short, which finds support by direction or inference in any tendency of the evidence, is that of persons whose duty it was to inspect the links of the train, and remove such as were defective and replace them with others which were not defective. This was the negligence not of the master, the defendant, but of fellow-servants of the plaintiff, for which at common-law the defendant is not liable. . . .

This being the common-law applicable to the premises as understood and declared in Alabama, it will be presumed in our courts as thus declared to be the common-law of Mississippi, unless the evidence shows a different rule to have been announced by the Supreme Court of the State as being the common-law thereof. The evidence adduced here fails to show any such thing; but to the contrary it is made to appear from the testimony of Judge Arnold and by the decisions of the Supreme Court of Mississippi which were introduced on the trial below that that court is in full accord with this one in this respect. Indeed, if any thing, those decisions go further than this court has ever gone in applying the doctrine of fellow-servants to the exemption of railway companies from liability to one servant for injuries resulting from the negligence of another, holding in one case that a hostler whose only duty it was *to supply an engine* with sufficient sand before turning it over to the engineer to go on the road is a fellow-servant of the engineer for whose negligent failure to supply the same the company would not be liable.—*L. & N. R. R. Co. v. Petty,* 67 Miss. 255; in another, that a section foreman and a laborer working under him were fellow-servants in such sort that their common master would not be liable for the negligence of the former in attempting to repair a fishbar which he ought to have discarded and applied for a new one.—*Lagrave v. Mobile & Ohio R. R. Co.,* 67 Miss. 532; and in yet another case, that a section foreman and train-man are fellow-servants in respect of the negligence of the former unknown to the company *in failing to keep the track in repair,* and that an engineer on a passing train who was injured in consequence could not recover against common employer.—*N. O. J. & G. N. R. R. Co. v. Hughes,* 49 Miss. 258; and the doctrine of this case is said by Mr. McKinney to be "substantially the rule recognized by the English common-law decisions." McKinney on Fellow-servants, p. 82 § 29.

Proceeding therefore on the presumptions we are authorized to indulge and also on the evidence adduced in this case as to the law of Mississippi in this connection, and upon the testimony most favorable to the plaintiff as to the cause of his injuries, we feel entirely safe in declaring that plaintiff has shown no cause of action under the common-law as it is understood and applied both here and in Mississippi.

It is, however, further contended that the plaintiff, if his evidence be believed, has made out a case for the recovery sought under the Employer's Liability Act of Alabama, it being clearly shown that there is no such, or similar law of force in the State of Mississippi. Considering this position in the abstract, that is dissociated from the facts of this particular case which are supposed to exert an important influence upon it, there can not be two opinions as to its being unsound and untenable. So looked at, we do not understand appellee's counsel even to deny either the proposition or its application to this case, that there can be no recovery in one State for injuries to the person sustained in another unless the infliction of the injuries is actionable under the law of the State in which they were received. Certainly this is the well established rule of law subject in some jurisdictions to the qualification that the infliction of the injuries would also support an action in the State where the suit is brought, had they been received within that State. . . .

But it is claimed that the facts of this case take it out of the general rule and authorize the courts of Alabama to subject the defendant to the payment of damages under section 2590 of the Code, although the injuries counted on were sustained in Mississippi under circumstances which involved no liability on the defendant by the laws of that State.

This insistence is in the first instance based on that aspect of the evidence which goes to show that the negligence which produced the casualty transpired in Alabama, and the theory that wherever the consequence of that negligence manifested itself, a recovery can be had in Alabama. We are referred to no authority in support of this proposition, and exhaustive investigation on our part has failed to disclose any. There are at least two well considered cases against it, one of which involved an effort to recover for personal injuries sustained in Alabama under circumstances which afforded no cause of action in Alabama in the courts of Tennessee *where the causal negligence occurred* and where also had the negligence manifested itself in the results complained of there, the plaintiff would have been entitled to recover. . . . In the other case the precise point here under consideration was brought before the Supreme Court of Mississippi, in an action instituted in that State sounding in damages for fatal injuries inflicted upon plaintiff's intestate in the State of Tennessee. It was insisted that inasmuch as the death of the deceased resulted from the negligent failure of a train dispatcher in Mississippi to give requisite orders to the trainmen at a certain point in Tennessee, the rights of the parties were determinable by the laws of Mississippi the place of the disastrous negligent omission. But the court held to the contrary, saying: "The right of the appellee is determinable by the laws of Tennessee, in which State the killing of her husband occurred. The view that no recovery could be had here, except for a result traceable to an omission of duty in Mississippi is unfounded. Physical force proceeding from this State and inflicting injury in another State might give rise to an action in either State, and *vice versa* but the omission of duty in Mississippi cannot transfer a consequence of it manifested physically in another State to Mississippi. . . ."

The position of the Mississippi court appears to us to be eminently sound in principle and upon logic. It is admitted, or at least cannot be denied, that negligence of duty unproductive of damnifying results will not authorize or support a recovery. Up to the time [the] train passed out of Alabama no injury had resulted. For all that occurred in Alabama, therefore, no cause of action whatever arose. The fact which created the right to sue, the injury without which confessedly no action would lie anywhere, transpired in the State of Mississippi. It was in that State, therefore, necessarily that the cause of action, if any, arose; and whether a cause of action arose and existed at all or not must in all reason be determined by the law which obtained at the time and place when and where the fact which is relied on to justify a recovery transpired. Section 2590 of the Code of Alabama had no efficiency beyond the lines of Alabama. It cannot be allowed to operate upon facts occurring in another State so as to evolve out of them rights and liabilities which do not exist under the law of that State which is of course paramount in the premises. Where the facts occur in Alabama and a liability becomes fixed in Alabama, it may be enforced in another State having like enactments, or whose policy is not opposed to the spirit of such enactments, but this is quite a different matter. This is but enforcing the statute upon facts to which it is applicable all of which occur within the territory for the government of which it was enacted. Section 2590 of the Code, in other words is to be interpreted in the light of universally recognized principles of private international or interstate law, as if its operation had been expressly limited to this State and as if its first line read as follows: "When a personal injury is *received in Alabama* by a servant or employee," &c., &c. The negligent infliction of an injury here under statutory circumstances creates a right of action here, which, being transitory, may be enforced in any other State or country the comity of which admits of it; but for an injury inflicted elsewhere than in Alabama our statute gives no right of recovery, and the aggrieved party must look to the local law to ascertain what his rights are. Under that law this plaintiff had no cause of action, as we have seen, and hence he has no rights which our courts can enforce, unless it be upon a consideration to be presently adverted to. We have not been inattentive to the suggestions of counsel in this connection, which are based upon that rule of the statutory and common criminal law under which a murderer is punishable where the fatal blow is delivered, regardless of the place where death ensues.—*Green v. State,* 66 Ala. 40. This principle is patently without application here. There would be some analogy if the plaintiff had been stricken in Alabama and suffered in Mississippi, which is not the fact. There is, however, an analogy which is afforded by the criminal law, but which points away from the conclusion appellee's counsel desire us to reach. This is found in that well established doctrine of criminal law, that where the unlawful act is committed in one jurisdiction or State and takes effect—produces the result which it is the purpose of the law to prevent, or, it having ensued, punish for—in another jurisdiction or State, the crime is deemed to have been commited and is punished in that jurisdiction or State in which the result is manifested, and not where the act was committed.

Another consideration—that referred to above—it is insisted, entitles this plaintiff to recover here under the Employer's Liability Act for an injury inflicted beyond the territorial operation of that act. This is claimed upon the fact that at the time plaintiff was injured he was in the discharge of duties which rested on him by the terms of a contract between him and defendant which had been entered into in Alabama, and, hence, was an Alabama contract, in connection with the facts that plaintiff was and is a citizen of this State, and the defendant is an Alabama corporation. These latter facts—of citizenship and domicile respectively of plaintiff and defendant—are of no importance in this connection, it seems to us, further than this: they may tend to show that the contract was made here, which is not controverted, and if the plaintiff has a cause of action at all, he, by reason of them, may prosecute it in our courts. They have no bearing on the primary question of existence of a cause of action, and as that is the question before us, we need not further advert to the fact of plaintiff's citizenship or defendant's domicile.

The contract was that plaintiff should serve the defendant in the capacity of a brakeman on its freight train between Birmingham, Alabama, and Meridian, Mississippi, and should receive as compensation a stipulated sum for each trip from Birmingham to Meridian and return. The theory is that the Employer's Liability Act became a part of this contract; that the duties and liabilities which it prescribes became contractual duties and liabilities, or duties and liabilities springing out of the contract, and that these duties attended upon the execution whenever its performance was required—in Mississippi as well as in Alabama—and that the liability prescribed for a failure to perform any of such duties attached upon such failure and consequent injury wherever it occurred, and was enforceable here because imposed by an Alabama contract notwithstanding the remission of duty and the resulting injury occurred in Mississippi, under whose laws no liability was incurred by such remission. . . .

If this argument is sound, and it is sound if the duties and liabilities prescribed by the act can be said to be contractual duties and obligations at all, it would lead to conclusions the possibility of which has not hitherto been suggested by any court or law writer, and which, to say the least, would be astounding to the profession. . . . [For instance: if every Alabama contract made since passage of the statute in 1885 were governed by the statute regardless of the place of injury, every contract made prior to passage of the statute would be exempt from the statute and the fellow servant rule would be a defense even for injuries in Alabama; further, contracts for service partly in Alabama might be entered into in adjoining states to avoid application of the Alabama statute. Moreover, if the present defendant is under a contractual obligation to compensate plaintiff for his injuries, that obligation might be enforced in Mississippi, notwithstanding the Mississippi law to the contrary.] These considerations demonstrate the infirmity of plaintiff's position in this connection, and serve to show the necessity and propriety of the conclusion we propose to announce on this part of the case. That conclusion is, that the duties and liabilities incident to the relation between the plaintiff and the defendant which are involved in this case, are not imposed by and do not rest in or spring from the contract between the parties. . . .

It is the purpose of the statute and must be the limit of its operation to govern persons standing in the relation of master and servants to each other in respect of their conduct in certain particulars within the State of Alabama. Mississippi has the same right to establish governmental rules for such persons within her borders as Alabama; and she has established rules which are different from those of our law. And the conduct of such persons toward each other is, when its legality is brought in question, to be adjudged by the rules of the one or the other States as it falls territorially within the one or the other. The doctrine is like that which prevails in respect of other relations, as that of man and wife. Marriage is a contract. The entering into this contract raises up certain duties and imposes certain liabilities in all civilized countries. What these duties and liabilities are at the place of the contract are determinable by the law of that place; but when the parties go into other jurisdictions, the relation created by the contract under the laws of the place of its execution will be recognized, but the personal duties, obligations and liabilities incident to the relation are such as exist under the law of the jurisdiction in which an act is done or omitted as to the legality, effect or consequence of which the question arises. It might as well be said where there is a marriage in Alabama and the parties remove to Mississippi, and the wife there makes a contract which is void in Mississippi but valid under our statute, and subsequently they return to Alabama, that our courts will enforce that contract, or if such husband while in Mississippi does an act which is innocuous and lawful in that State, but which if done here would entail liability upon him, and the parties afterwards return here, that the liability imposed by our laws could be enforced here, because the parties entered into the contract here, as that a master is liable here for conduct towards his servant which was proper, or at least involved no liabilty, where it took place, simply because the contract which created the relation was entered into in this State. The whole argument is at fault. The only true doctrine is that each sovereignty, state or nation, has the exclusive power to finally determine and declare what acts or omission in the conduct of one to another, whether they be strangers or sustain relations to each other which the law recognizes, as parent and child, husband and wife, master and servant, and the like, shall impose a liability in damages for the consequent injury, and the courts of no other sovereignty can impute a damnifying quality to an act or omission which afforded no cause of action where it transpired. . . .

The foregoing views will suffice to indicate the grounds of our opinion that the rights of this plaintiff are determinable solely by the law of the State of Mississippi, and of our conclusion that upon no aspect or tendency of the evidence as to the circumstances under which the injury was sustained and as to the laws of Mississippi obtaining in the premises was the plaintiff entitled to recover.

. . .

For the error in refusing to instruct the jury to find for the defendant if they believed the evidence, the judgment is reversed and the cause will be remanded.

HORN v. NORTH BRITISH RAILWAY CO.

Scottish Court of Sessions
5 R. 1055, 15 Sc. L. R. 707 (1878)

LORD JUSTICE–CLERK.

In this case we propose to deal to-day only with the bill of exceptions. The motion for a new trial will come to be afterwards considered.

The son of the pursuer was killed in the course of a journey from Kirkcaldy[a] to London by the North British, North-Eastern, and Great Northern lines of railway. The accident which caused

---

[a] A city on the north shore of the Firth of Forth, birthplace of Adam Smith and Robert Adam.

his death took place at Morpeth,[b] on the North-Eastern line. He was travelling with a ticket issued by the North British stationmaster at Kirkcaldy in the name of that company only, and which bore to be a voucher for conveyance from Kirkcaldy to London. The jury found that the death of Henry Horn junior, the pursuer's son, was caused by the fault of the defenders, and they mention two specific causes which led to the accident. They accordingly found for the pursuer, and assessed the damages at £700; and they divided that sum into £550 as compensation for pecuniary loss, and £150 as *solatium* for wounded feelings.

In the course of the trial the presiding Judge—Lord Gifford—had occasion to lay down two propositions in point of law, which are the subject of the present bill of exceptions. These two propositions were, first, "that fault of the servants or employees of the North-Eastern Railway Company, which the jury may think caused the death of Henry Horn, was, in the sense of the issue, the fault of the defenders;" and the second was, "that if the death of Henry Horn junior was caused by the fault of the defenders, the jury in assessing the amount of damages are entitled to award to the pursuer, not only compensation for any pecuniary loss he has suffered through the death of his son, but also *solatium* for wounded feelings." The defenders excepted to these two rulings.

Now, these exceptions undoubtedly raise some questions of very considerable general importance. In regard to the first of them, viz., that the servants of the North-Eastern Company in regard to this matter must be held as in a question with the pursuer to have been the servants of the North British Company, I am of opinion that the law laid down by Lord Gifford is right. If an action had been brought by Henry Horn junior himself—if he had survived and had brought an action for injuries received on this occasion—I have no doubt that in a question with him the servants of the North-Eastern Company must have been considered as the servants of the North British Company, with whom his contract was made. The latter company had contracted to convey him from Kirkcaldy to London, and the officials of the North-Eastern Company were, as far as he was concerned, merely the hands by whom the contract was in course of being fulfilled. . . .

It is said, however, that the father was not a party to the contract, and could not sue either for implement or for breach, and that is quite true; but this is not an action of that nature. It is an action for a wrong done to the father by reason of a fault committed by the defenders in the course of the execution of a contract with the son. If that fault and its consequences give rise to an action by the father, it must needs be the fault of the defenders, and they are responsible for it.

It is true that the father sues here in his own right and for his own loss, but the action is not an ordinary suit for patrimonial injury. The same loss which is libelled here, or part of it, might have been sustained by a collateral relation or by a stranger, but it would have conferred no right of action. Moreover, it is only because the son, if he had survived, would have had a right of action against the company that the father was entitled to sue the same persons in respect of the same act. So much is this the nature of the claim by a parent for the loss of his child, or a child for the loss of a parent, that when this principle of liability was introduced into the law of England by Lord Campbell's Act, it was expressly enacted that an action by the father or the wife or child of the deceased, should be brought against the same parties who would have been liable to the deceased, had he survived. In our law, in which the principle has been long recognised, although not strictly a derivative or representative right, the title of the father is a

---

[b] A town in England north of Newcastle-upon-Tyne.

corollary or adjunct to the primary right of the deceased, and, although differing in its incidents, has and must have the same foundation.

. . . I am of opinion that . . . this claim cannot be dissociated from the original and primary wrong, and that if the servants of the defenders caused the death of the deceased they also caused the injury to the father.

. . .

The second exception raises a question of very considerable general interest, or one which might be so if the circumstances under which it arose were such as to give it weight, and it is substantially this—that because Henry Horn was killed in England on the North-Eastern line the right of the father to recover here must be measured by his right to recover in England—that is to say, must be measured by Lord Campbell's Act, and that he is not entitled therefore to payment in name of *solatium,* because under Lord Campbell's Act no such payment would be allowed. I think that the whole argument on this matter proceeds upon a fallacy. The grounds on which it has been maintained have not been very clearly discriminated. It is not quite clear whether the rule contended for be that founded on the place of performance or that founded on the *locus delicti.* But I am of opinion that neither applies here.

The rule by which the law of the place of performance is applied to the incidents of a contract is an exception from the general rule, that the law of a contract is that of the place where it is made; and it is not an exception which is universally applicable; it is only applicable where it may reasonably be inferred from the contract that the parties in contracting had in view the law of the place of fulfilment of the contract. There are many differences between the laws of reparation in different countries which make it impossible to apply the law of the place where a contract is to be performed universally. In Savigny's work on Private International Law many illustrations of that doctrine will be found.

First, as to the place of performance—There is no place of performance stipulated in this contract. Is the place of performance London? Clearly not. The execution of the contract was to be completed there, but the contract was to be executed during the whole course of the journey. The law of one place was not considered more than another. According to this view the law of England would have ruled if the accident had taken place at Dunbar.[c]

Secondly, the *lex loci delicti* cannot rule this question. The law of the place where the breach of contract occurred cannot determine the consequences of the breach of it, because such cannot be assumed to have been the intention of the parties to it. In the course of the execution of a contract of carriage from Southampton to Bombay it might happen that a steamer was wrecked in the Red Sea, through the fault of the carrier; but the *locus delicti* would hardly furnish the law by which the carrier's liability would be determined. The general rule in such contracts, in which performance is to take place in a variety of places, is that the law of the place of the contract was contemplated; and such was the ratio of the judgment in the case of *Shand v. Peninsular and Oriental Company.*[d]

The present case, however, is probably clearer. The question is, what elements of damage shall enter into the amount of reparation claimed in this action. I think the *lex fori* must determine that matter, and it is hard to see what other test could be applied. This is a competent and relevant action brought according to our own forms in the Courts in Scotland, concluding, *inter alia,*

---

[c] A historic Scottish town east of Edinburgh, where Mary Stuart, Queen of Scots, took refuge on several occasions.

[d] 3 Moore's Privy Co. Reps. (N.S.) 272 (1865).

for *solatium*. It is said that we cannot entertain the demand, because, if the action had been brought in England the English Courts could not have awarded *solatium,* as the case could only have been tried under Lord Campbell's Act, which does not admit of such a claim. But if that be a sound proposition it would follow that if the accident had taken place at Dunbar the English Courts, had the contracting railway company been English, would have been bound to entertain the claim for *solatium,* which they have no power to do. This matter savours more of the remedy than of the right. It might be that the law of the country in which the cause of action arose denied the civil remedy altogether; but in a competent action under Lord Campbell's Act the English Courts would not listen to such a plea. Thus, in the case quoted to us from the English books, in which action was brought by one man against another for an assault committed in Naples, Mr Justice Wightman ruled that the law of England, and not the law of Naples, must regulate, because the remedy given by the law of Naples was criminal only.[e] In like manner, if two Neapolitans had quarrelled in London and one brought his action of damages for assault in the Neapolitan Courts, the latter could not have entertained the action, seeing that their law admits of no such remedy. This is a question as to what the elements of damage were which the jury were entitled to take into account in returning their verdict. I think that is a question for the Court in which the case was tried, and that the ruling of the Judge was right.

I do not think there is anything else embraced in these exceptions upon which it is necessary that I should make any observations. The ground is varied in expression in each of them, but I think substantially I have gone over the whole of it.

On the whole matter, I am of opinion that the law laid down was correct, and that the bill of exceptions must be refused.

LORD ORMIDALE.

. . .

The pursuer maintains that the defenders are liable to him because they, by issuing to his son at Kirkcaldy a ticket from that town to London, *via* the North-Eastern Railway among others, contracted to convey him in safety throughout the whole journey. That the defenders would be under that liability *ex contractu* in any question with the pursuer's son, had he, in place of being killed, been merely injured, is, I think, free from doubt, and, indeed, was not disputed. . . .

But do the decisions referred to, or the principle given effect to by them, apply to the present case, keeping in view that the pursuer, who has obtained a verdict for damages, was not a party or privy to the contract between his son and the defenders. The defenders contracted with the pursuer's son to carry him safely from Kirkcaldy to London, but the pursuer was not, in any way, a party to that contract. It does not appear that the defenders, or the person who acted for them in issuing the ticket to the deceased at Kirkcaldy, even knew of the existence of the pursuer, and neither does it appear that the pursuer was aware at the time that his son had obtained a through ticket from Kirkcaldy to London. Nor does the pursuer sue as the executor, or in any other way as representing his son. He sues exclusively in his own right. And, if so, it is difficult to see how his action can lie on the basis of contract. He had certainly no contract himself with the defenders; and if his claim is not, and could not have been made as the executor, or otherwise

---

[e] Apparently a reference to Scott v. Lord Seymour, 1 H. & C. 219, 159 Eng. Rep. 865 (Ex. Ch. 1862). Justice Wightman said that, at least as between British subjects, an action would lie in England for an assault and battery in Naples even if the law of Naples gave no civil remedy for such act; the other justices in the case expressed doubt on the point.

as representing his son, I must own my inability to understand how the present defenders can be sued by him on the ground of contract.

. . .

Supposing, then, that the contract which was entered into between the deceased and the defenders cannot avail the present pursuer, the question remains, whether his action is maintainable *ratione delicti*. I am not to dispute that it might, if the defenders had been the parties who had committed the delict; for the principle *culpa tenet suos auctores* would on that assumption have applied. But, according to any view I can take of the case as it is presented to the Court, I do not see how the delict can be said to have been committed by the North British Railway Company. That might be so in respect of the contract; but the pursuer not being a party or privy to the contract it cannot avail him. He must shew that *de facto* the defenders committed the *culpa* or tort in respect of which he sues for damages. But the jury by their verdict have found that the death of the pursuer's son was "owing to the defective state of the North-Eastern Railway." [I would allow the defenders' exceptions.]

LORD GIFFORD.

I happened to be the Judge who tried the issue in this case, and at the trial, according to the best judgment which I could then form on the very short argument which I then heard, I was of opinion that in a question between the pursuer and the North British Railway Company any fault leading or contributing to the accident on the part of the servants of the North-Eastern Railway, on which line the accident occurred, was in law, and in the sense of the issue, the fault of the defenders, that is, the fault of the North British Company, and that whether the fault related to the state of the North-Eastern line, or whether it related to the conduct of the train itself. I accordingly so directed the jury, and it was this direction which gave rise to the first exception, and to several of the subsequent ones, which all raise under various forms of expression what is substantially the same question. . . .

After the very full argument which we have heard upon the bill of exceptions I still remain of the opinion which I expressed at the trial, although, looking to the difference of opinion which has occurred on the bench, I must feel that the case is a difficult one. I think that, assuming the fault to have occurred wholly in England and on the line of the North-Eastern Company, by the fault either in the North-Eastern line itself or in the conduct of the train in passing over it, still for that fault the North British Company are liable to the pursuer. . . .

Now, if an action laid upon fault or on tort lies at the instance of an injured passenger against the company who issued the ticket, though the servants of another company were solely to blame, it is difficult to see how the same kind of action should not lie against the same defenders at the instance of the relatives of a passenger who was killed.

In Lord Campbell's Act, 9th and 10th Vict. c. 93, which introduced into England the same action at the instance of the relatives of a party killed, which was always competent by the common law of Scotland, it is enacted that the action is to be directed against the party who would have been answerable to the deceased himself had he survived. Of course this Act is not binding in Scotland, but it seems in accordance with the common sense of the case, and it would be very anomalous if the statutory action in England should lie against one party, and the common law in Scotland, of the very same nature, should lie against a different party altogether and on totally different grounds. Suppose that in the present case the late Mr Horn, instead of taking his ticket from Kirkcaldy to London, had taken his ticket in London from London to Kirkcaldy, such ticket being issued, of course, by the Great Northern Company, and suppose that he had been killed at Morpeth in the same circumstances as he actually was, then under Lord Campbell's Act, as amended by 27 and 28 Vict. c. 95, his father would have had an action for reparation which must have been directed not against the North-Eastern Railway, but against the Great Northern. Why should the rule be different in Scotland? I do not think any good reason can be given. I think in both countries the rule is the same,—the issuer of the through ticket is liable to the father just in the same way as he would have been to the deceased himself. I am therefore of opinion that the exceptions founded on the view that the North British Company are not liable at all ought to be disallowed. If the action had been at the instance of the late Henry Horn himself, suing the North British Company for the loss of a limb, the action would have lain, and the fault of the North-Eastern would have been in law the fault of the North British. I think the rule is the same in an action at the instance of the father.

The other exceptions are founded upon the plea that the present case must be decided according to the law of England and not according to the law of Scotland, because the accident occurred in Northumberland. This view would necessarily lead to the result that the action should have been laid upon Lord Campbell's Act alone, because that is the only statute which gives such an action in England, and the same view leads to this result, that as Lord Campbell's Act confines the reparation to pecuniary loss directly sustained, and excludes all *solatium* for wounded feelings, so the verdict of the jury must be reduced by £150, being the amount of *solatium* which the jury have awarded.

I am of opinion that the present action must be regarded by the law of Scotland and not by the law of England. The present action is not laid upon Lord Campbell's Act but upon common law. Lord Campbell's Act is not applicable to Scotland, which is expressly excluded from its operation, and if I am right in holding that the North British Railway Company is the proper defender in this action, I think it follows that the action could not properly be laid on Lord Campbell's Act. I think the action would have been competently laid supposing the accident to have happened (in exactly the same circumstances as those in which it actually took place) before Lord Campbell's Act had been passed, or as if Lord Campbell's Act and the amending Act had never been passed at all. An action like the present, not laid upon contract directly, but upon negligence arising in the course of the execution of a contract, is a common law action brought in the common law Courts of Scotland and founded upon Scotch law. I think that action is competent, and that leads to the result which your Lordship in the chair has stated, that in awarding damages, if the action is competent and the defender is the proper defender, the jury must necessarily go by the law of Scotland. I concur in that result. In like manner, if the through ticket had been issued in London, and the late Henry Horn had been killed in Scotland, then in any action in London against the Great Northern Company, laid on Lord Campbell's Act, the present pursuer could not have recovered *solatium* in the English Courts, although the accident in the case supposed had occurred in Scotland.

NOTES AND QUESTIONS

(1) Before exploring the various techniques of the choice of law process, consider why a court should ever undertake the process at all.

(a) Is the choice of law process a search for justice? For the better law?

(b) Or does it have to do with relations among states? Does *A* want to apply *B*'s law so that in corresponding cases *B* will apply *A*'s law?

(c) Should the choice of law process be used to uphold transactions? To defeat them? To carry out the will of the parties?

(2) What other motives might there be for a court to apply a law other than its own?

(a) To discourage (prevent?) forum shopping?

(b) To advance law reform?

(3)(a) Are the answers to the preceding questions of general application? Would you expect a different approach to contract questions from those applicable to tort? What about issues of public law, such as antitrust, securities regulation, or criminal law?

(b) Would you think the considerations are the same with respect to the preceding questions if the issue is

(i) Alabama vs. Mississippi law?

(ii) Alabama vs. Federal law?

(iii) Alabama vs. British law?

(iv) Alabama vs. Afghanistan law?

(c) Would you think that principles of conflict of laws should be neutral, e.g., a place of accident rule that favors plaintiff today, defendant tomorrow? Or could one establish principles that favor, say, injured workers rather than employers, borrowers rather than lenders, and so on?

(d) If conflict of laws is largely judge-made, would you think that the preceding suggestion violates the basic tenets of democracy? More than the common law generally does?

(4) Turning to *Alabama Great Southern R.R. v. Carroll,* note the arguments made, and not made, on behalf of plaintiff:

(a) Plaintiff tries to persuade the court that the fellow servant rule doesn't apply because the wrong was a breach of duty of the master, not of the servant. On the merits, the argument fails; but it is not so foolish. What is the source of the court's conclusion that the duty was that of the inspector, not of the railroad itself, and that the inspector was a fellow-employee? Mississippi law? Alabama law? The "common" law? If the latter, could you show that Mississippi decisions had departed from that law?

(b) The court cites several Mississippi cases to confirm that Mississippi really does adhere to the fellow servant rule, and apparently to refute plaintiff's assertion to the contrary. Would research into Mississippi's choice of law rules have been worthwhile? Suppose, for example, that Mississippi's interpretation of the fellow servant rule is just as the court tells us, but Mississippi would look for its source of law in this case to the place of the negligent act; or that it would not apply its law to a case having so many Alabama elements. Would this knowledge be helpful to plaintiff? Decisive in his favor?

(c) The court says, at page 4, that Alabama's Employer's Liability Act "cannot be allowed to operate upon facts occurring in another state. . . ." Why not? Is it suggested that Mississippi would be offended if the railroad had to compensate Mr. Carroll for his injuries? Or is the court simply suggesting that if the legislature had wanted to write into the statute ". . . regardless of the place of injury . . ." it would have done so? Could it have done so?

(d) The suggestion that this might be a contract case is regarded by the court as even more unsound—". . . astounding to the profession" (p. 5). Why is that? Suppose Mr. Carroll had been sleeping at the switch in Meridian, and a supervisor had said "you're fired." Carroll then brings a suit for wrongful discharge in Alabama against the railroad. Must Mississippi law be applied to that suit? If not, in what way is the actual case different?

(e) Throughout this book we will see courts talking about "public policy," often without a clear idea where it came from. Here, however, there has been a clear statement of the Alabama legislature repudiating the fellow servant rule. Why does that not tell the court that the fellow servant rule is against Alabama's public policy? If the court cannot bring itself to apply Alabama law, should it dismiss the action without prejudice?

(5) One more question inspired by *Alabama Great Southern R.R. v. Carroll,* though not raised in the actual case, is worth raising at this stage, at least by way of preview:

If the decision stands for the proposition that the governing law in this accident case is the law of the place of accident, how far does that proposition extend?

(a) Suppose the issue arises whether Mr. Carroll is in fact an employee; suppose, for instance, he sells sandwiches on the train.^f

(b) Suppose Mr. Carroll dies, and the issue arises whether his brother has standing to bring a wrongful death action, or whether Sally is really his widow.

(c) Suppose the railroad raises the defense of the statute of limitations. Given the basic proposition, must all of these questions be resolved under Mississippi law?

(6)(a) Does the Scottish court, fourteen years earlier, do a better job than the Alabama court?

(b) Why isn't Lord Ormidale right? (i) There cannot be a contract claim because plaintiff (the father of the deceased) didn't even know his son was traveling and certainly was not a party to any contract; and (ii) there cannot be a tort claim because the defendant, North British, committed no act of negligence. Do the other justices answer his points?

(c) The majority's conclusion that this is really a tort claim seems persuasive; but what is the source of law of this characterization?

(d) Why is *solatium* an issue governed by lex fori?

(7)(a) Lord Gifford, in his second crack at this case, says here the ticket was bought in Scotland and suit is in Scotland, so the place of the accident doesn't matter; correspondingly, if the ticket had been bought in London and suit brought in London for an accident in Scotland, there would be no *solatium.* Do you agree?

(b) How about varying Lord Gifford's hypothetical: Suppose ticket in London, accident in Scotland, suit in Scotland, or ticket in London, accident in England, suit in Scotland?

(c) What would the Alabama Supreme Court have done with the *Horn* case?

---

^f Note that in its discussion at pp. 2–3 of the case of the hostler (a person who takes care of locomotives after a trip), the court says that Mississippi cases on definition of fellow servants have gone further than Alabama cases did before the statute was enacted.

§ 1.02 Contracts

[A] The American Rule: Place of Contract

MILLIKEN v. PRATT

Massachusetts Supreme Judicial Court
125 Mass. 374 (1878)

The plaintiffs are partners doing business in Portland, Maine, under the firm name of Deering, Milliken & Co. The defendant is, and has been since 1850, the wife of Daniel Pratt, and both have always resided in Massachusetts. In 1870, Daniel, who was then doing business in Massachusetts, applied to the plaintiffs at Portland for credit, and they required of him, as a condition of granting the same, a guaranty from the defendant to the amount of five hundred dollars, and accordingly he procured from his wife the following instrument:

> Portland, January 29, 1870. In consideration of one dollar paid by Deering, Milliken & Co., receipt of which is hereby acknowledged, I guarantee the payment to them by Daniel Pratt of the sum of five hundred dollars, from time to time as he may want—this to be a continuing guaranty. Sarah A. Pratt.

This instrument was executed by the defendant two or three days after its date, at her home in Massachusetts, and there delivered by her to her husband, who sent it by mail from Massachusetts to the plaintiffs in Portland; and the plaintiffs received it from the post-office in Portland early in February, 1870.

The plaintiffs subsequently sold and delivered goods to Daniel from time to time until October 7, 1871, and charged the same to him, and, if competent, it may be taken to be true, that in so doing they relied upon the guaranty. Between February, 1870, and September 1, 1871, they sold and delivered goods to him on credit to an amount largely exceeding $500, which were fully settled and paid for by him. This action is brought for goods sold from September 1, 1871, to October 7, 1871, inclusive, amounting to $860.12, upon which he paid $300, leaving a balance due of $560.12. The one dollar mentioned in the guaranty was not paid, and the only consideration moving to the defendant therefor was the giving of credit by the plaintiffs to her husband. Some of the goods were selected personally by Daniel at the plaintiffs' store in Portland, others were ordered by letters mailed by Daniel from Massachusetts to the plaintiffs at Portland, and all were sent by the plaintiffs by express from Portland to Daniel in Massachusetts, who paid all express charges. The parties were cognizant of the facts.

By a statute of Maine, duly enacted and approved in 1866, it is enacted that "the contracts of any married woman, made for any lawful purpose, shall be valid and binding, and may be enforced in the same manner as if she were sole." The statutes and the decisions of the court of Maine may be referred to.

Payment was duly demanded of the defendant before the date of the writ, and was refused by her.

The Superior Court ordered judgment for the defendant; and the plaintiffs appealed to this court.

GRAY, C. J.

The general rule is that the validity of a contract is to be determined by the law of the State in which it is made; if it is valid there, it is deemed valid everywhere, and will sustain an action in the courts of a State whose laws do not permit such a contract. . . . Even a contract expressly prohibited by the statutes of the State in which the suit is brought, if not in itself immoral, is not necessarily nor usually deemed so invalid that the comity of the State, as administered by its courts, will refuse to entertain an action on such a contract made by one of its own citizens abroad in a State the laws of which permit it. . . .

If the contract is completed in another State, it makes no difference in principle whether the citizen of this State goes in person, or sends an agent, or writes a letter, across the boundary line between the two States. As was said by Lord Lyndhurst, "If I, residing in England, send down my agent to Scotland, and he makes contracts for me there, it is the same as if I myself went there and made them." *Pattison v. Mills,* 1 Dow & Cl. 342, 363. So if a person residing in this State signs and transmits, either by a messenger or through the post-office, to a person in another State, a written contract, which requires no special forms or solemnities in its execution, and no signature of the person to whom it is addressed, and is assented to and acted on by him there, the contract is made there, just as if the writer personally took the executed contract into the other State, or wrote and signed it there; and it is no objection to the maintenance of an action thereon here, that such a contract is prohibited by the law of this Commonwealth. . . .

The guaranty, bearing date of Portland, in the State of Maine, was executed by the defendant, a married woman, having her home in this Commonwealth, as collateral security for the liability of her husband for goods sold by the plaintiffs to him, and was sent by her through him by mail to the plaintiffs at Portland. The sales of the goods ordered by him from the plaintiffs at Portland, and there delivered by them to him in person, or to a carrier for him, were made in the State of Maine. . . . The contract between the defendant and the plaintiffs was complete when the guaranty had been received and acted on by them at Portland, and not before. . . . It must therefore be treated as made and to be performed in the State of Maine.

The law of Maine authorized a married woman to bind herself by any contract as if she were unmarried. . . . The law of Massachusetts, as then existing, did not allow her to enter into a contract as surety or for the accommodation of her husband or of any third person. . . . Since the making of the contract sued on, and before the bringing of this action, the law of this Commonwealth has been changed, so as to enable married women to make such contracts. . . .

The question therefore is, whether a contract made in another State by a married woman domiciled here, which a married woman was not at the time capable of making under the law of this Commonwealth, but was then allowed by the law of that State to make, and which she could not lawfully make in this Commonwealth, will sustain an action against her in our courts.

It has been often stated by commentators that the law of the domicil, regulating the capacity of a person, accompanies and governs the person everywhere. But this statement, in modern times at least, is subject to many qualifications; and the opinions of foreign jurists upon the subject, the principal of which are collected in the treatises of Mr. Justice Story and of Dr. Francis Wharton on the Conflict of Laws, are too varying and contradictory to control the general current of the English and American authorities in favor of holding that a contract, which by the law of the place is recognized as lawfully made by a capable person, is valid everywhere, although the person would not, under the law of his domicil, be deemed capable of making it.

. . .

Mr. Justice Story, in his Commentaries on the Conflict of Laws, after elaborate consideration of the authorities, arrives at the conclusion that "in regard to questions of minority or majority, competency or incompetency to marry, incapacities incident to coverture, guardianship, emancipation, and other personal qualities and disabilities, the law of the domicil of birth, or the law of any other acquired and fixed domicil, is not generally to govern, but the *lex loci contractus aut actus,* the law of the place where the contract is made, or the act done;" or as he elsewhere sums it up, "although foreign jurists generally hold that the law of the domicil ought to govern in regard to the capacity of persons to contract; yet the common law holds a different doctrine, namely, that the *lex loci contractus* is to govern." Story Confl. §§ 103, 241. So Chancellor Kent, although in some passages of the text of his Commentaries he seems to incline to the doctrine of the civilians, yet in the notes afterwards added unequivocally concurs in the conclusion of Mr. Justice Story. 2 Kent Com. 233 note, 458, 459 & note.

. . .

The principal reasons on which continental jurists have maintained that personal laws of the domicil, affecting the status and capacity of all inhabitants of a particular class, bind them wherever they may go, appear to have been that each State has the rightful power of regulating the status and condition of its subjects, and, being best acquainted with the circumstances of climate, race, character, manners, and customs, can best judge at what age young persons may begin to act for themselves, and whether and how far married women may act independently of their husbands; that laws limiting the capacity of infants or of married women are intended for their protection, and cannot therefore be dispensed with by their agreement; that all civilized States recognize the incapacity of infants and married women; and that a person, dealing with either, ordinarily has notice, by the apparent age or sex, that the person is likely to be of a class whom the laws protect, and is thus put upon inquiry how far, by the law of the domicil of the person, the protection extends.

. . .

On the other hand, it is only by the comity of other states that laws can operate beyond the limit of the state that makes them. In the great majority of cases, especially in this country, where it is so common to travel, or to transact business through agents, or to correspond by letter, from one state to another, it is more just, as well as more convenient, to have regard to the law of the place of the contract, as a uniform rule operating on all contracts of the same kind, and which the contracting parties may be presumed to have in contemplation when making their contracts, than to require them at their peril to know the domicil of those with whom they deal, and to ascertain the law of that domicil, however remote, which in many cases could not be done without such delay as would greatly cripple the power of contracting abroad at all.

As the law of another state can neither operate nor be executed in this state by its own force, but only by the comity of this state, its operation and enforcement here may be restricted by positive prohibition of statute. A state may always by express enactment protect itself from being obliged to enforce in its courts contracts made abroad by its citizens, which are not authorized by its own laws. Under the French code, for instance, which enacts that the laws regulating the status and capacity of persons shall bind French subjects, even when living in a foreign country, a French court cannot enforce a contract made by a Frenchman abroad, which he is incapable of making by the law of France. See Westlake, §§ 399, 400.

It is possible also that in a state where the common law prevailed in full force, by which a married woman was deemed incapable of binding herself by any contract whatever, it might be inferred that such an utter incapacity, lasting throughout the joint lives of husband and wife, must be considered as so fixed by the settled policy of the state, for the protection of its own citizens, that it could not be held by the courts of that state to yield to the law of another state in which she might undertake to contract.

But it is not true at the present day that all civilized states recognize the absolute incapacity of married women to make contracts. The tendency of modern legislation is to enlarge their capacity in this respect, and in many states they have nearly or quite the same powers as if unmarried. In Massachusetts, even at the time of the making of the contract in question, a married woman was vested by statute with a very extensive power to carry on business by herself, and to bind herself by contracts with regard to her own property, business and earnings, and, before the bringing of the present action, the power had been extended so as to include the making of all kinds of contracts, with any person but her husband, as if she were unmarried. There is therefore no reason of public policy which should prevent the maintenance of this action.

Judgment for the plaintiffs.

[B] The Traditional English Rule: The Proper Law

Until 1990, the English choice of law approach with respect to contracts was based on search for the "proper law of the contract." As set out in the leading English treatise on conflict of laws:

> The term "proper law of a contract" means the system of law by which the parties intended the contract to be governed, or, where their intention is neither expressed nor to be inferred from the circumstances, the system of law with which the transaction has its closest and most real connection.[a]

It is evident that the proper law approach is less rigid than the traditional American approach, and more hospitable to carrying out the intention of the parties, even when that intention is not expressly stated. Also, the place of contracting and place of performance, the traditional American determinants of the applicable law, are not independently significant, but may be relevant in determining the "system of law with which the transaction has its closest and most real connection." Once the proper law has been determined, it is supposed to govern all aspects of the controversy concerning a contract, including formation of the contract, material or intrinsic validity, and interpretation of its terms.

Many countries whose legal system developed under strong English influence, such as Canada and Australia, have continued to follow the "proper law" approach. The reason for qualifying the statement about England itself as "until 1990" is that in that year the United Kingdom adhered to the EEC Convention on the Law Applicable to Contractual Obligations, known as the Rome Convention.[b] The Rome Convention does not constitute a major departure from the prior English

---

[a] Dicey & Morris, *The Conflict of Laws* (10th ed. 1980) Rule 145.
[b] Documents Supplement p. 44.

approach, in that it also gives great freedom to the parties to choose the applicable law, and in the absence of such choice looks to the law of the country with which the contract is most closely connected, but it is more complicated, and draws in significant part from civil, as contrasted with common law sources. We shall return to the Rome Convention in Chapter 4. For the time being, it is useful only keep in mind that the traditional American approach was not an inevitable product of the common law.

NOTES AND QUESTIONS

(1)(a) The court in *Milliken v. Pratt* says the question for decision is "Where was the contract concluded?" Is that the right question? Should it perhaps have asked "Whom is the Married Women's Protective Act trying to protect?" Or "What is the interest of Masachusetts in this case?"

(b) Assuming the court did ask the right question, is its answer correct? Isn't it clear that Mrs. Pratt never left home?

(2)(a) If the arguments of the court in the third paragraph of the opinion, p. 15, *supra,* are less than convincing, is the result nevertheless correct? What other approaches would you suggest to arrive at the same result?

(b) Suppose Mr. Pratt used two suppliers for his store—Deering and Milliken from Portland, and Cabot & Sons from Boston. Both were willing to give him credit, provided his wife guaranteed his debts; in both cases he said he would have to speak to his wife, and the salesman said, "That's quite all right. Just have her sign this form and mail it back to us." When Mr. Pratt runs into difficulty, he falls behind on both accounts, and both Milliken and Cabot bring suit against the wife, who evidently has assets. It seems that the Massachusetts court would rule against the Massacusetts plaintiff, but for the Maine plaintiff. Does that surprise you? Does it suggest some value to preservation of interstate transactions not pertinent to intrastate transactions? Reconsider this point after reading *Lilienthal v. Kaufman,* p. 232, *infra*

(c) Suppose the law is kept the same but the facts are reversed, so that a Massachusetts supplier gives credit to the Maine retailer subject to his wife's guarantee, mailed back to Boston from Portland. Suit, as in the actual case, is brought in Massachusetts. What result would you expect?

(d) One difficulty with reading *Milliken v. Pratt* more than a century after it was decided is that married women's disability laws, fast fading even in 1878, seem very much out of place today. But suppose the relevant law were a truth-in-lending statute that voided a credit transaction if full disclosure had not been made in prescribed form.[c] Seller says, "Never mind. This contract was made in Maine, which has no such law." Is *Milliken* a satisfactory model?

(3)(a) In a sense, the preceding questions have raised the fundamental issue for the law of contracts—freedom and sanctity of contract vs. protection for weaker parties. Different jurisdictions at different times have given differing answers to this question; conflict of laws cases present the task of choosing among these answers, though usually in a kind of hidden agenda. Watch for it throughout the materials on contracts and analogous transactions.

---

[c] See, e.g., the former Illinois Consumer Finance Act, Ill. Ann. Stat. ch. 74, § 37. As revised, the Act provides that only the inadequately disclosed finance charges are subject to forfeiture. 205 ILCS 670/20. Under the Massachusetts Consumer Credit Cost Disclosure Act, Mass. Gen. L. Ch. 140D § 32, the borrower is entitled to recover twice the amount of any finance charges paid without proper disclosure, up to $1,000.

§ 1.02   CHOICE OF LAW   □   19

(b) The first *Restatement of the Conflict of Laws,* published in 1934, with Joseph Henry Beale as Reporter, adopted the law of the place of contracting for most, though not all, purposes:[*]

§332. Law Governing Validity of Contract.

The law of the place of contracting determines the validity and effect of a promise with respect to

(a) capacity to make the contract;

(b) the necessary form, if any, in which the promise must be made;

(c) the mutual assent or consideration, if any, required to make a promise binding;

(d) any other requirements for making a promise binding;

(e) fraud, illegality, or any other circumstances which make a promise void or voidable;

(f) except as stated in § 358, the nature and extent of the duty for the performance of which a party becomes bound;

(g) the time when and the place where the promise is by its terms to be performed;

(h) the absolute or conditional character of the promise.

§ 358. Law Governing Performance.

The duty for the performance of which a party to a contract is bound will be discharged by compliance with the law of the place of performance of the promise with respect to:

(a) the manner of performance;

(b) the time and locality of performance;

(c) the person or persons by whom or to whom performance shall be made or rendered;

(d) the sufficiency of performance;

(e) excuse for non-performance.

On the basis of the three cases studied so far, plus your knowledge of the law of contracts in general, would you regard these rules as satisfactory?

(c) English law, as pointed out above, has long had a quite different rule. Would you find the English rule, as set forth in Dicey,[d] more attractive? More, or less likely to lead to certainty of result?

(d) Note that the English rule assumed that the parties can determine the law to govern their transaction. Beale, Holmes, Learned Hand, and other Americans of their generation, regarded that attitude not only as undesirable, but as based on a logical fallacy, because only law could give effect to intent of parties, not vice versa.[e] Putting the issue of desirability of so-called "party autonomy" off for later, would you be troubled by the logical flaw?

---

[*] Copyright © by American Law Institute. Reprinted by permission.

[d] *Dicey on Conflict of Laws,* with rules, comments and examples, is in some way similar to Restatements in the United States, though it does not bear the approval of a Council and Institute as Restatements do.

The term "proper law" was used in the first edition, published in 1896, and defined substantially as in the tenth edition with respect to intent, or fair inference of intent, of the parties. (R. 143). The reference to "the system of law with which the transaction has its closest and most real connection" when intent could not be inferred was introduced in the eighth edition (1967).

[e] See, e.g., J. H. Beale, *The Conflict of Laws,* 1079–80 (1935). See also L. Hand in *E. Gerli & Co. v. Cunard S.S. Co.,* 48 F.2d 115, 117 (2d Cir. 1931), quoted in Chapter 4, at p. 256 note b, *infra.*

§ 1.03 Property

[A] The Situs of Real Property

IN RE ESTATE OF MARY E. BARRIE

Iowa Supreme Court
240 Iowa 431, 35 N.W.2d 658 (1949)
cert. denied, 338 U.S. 815 (1949)

HAYS, J.

. . .

Mary E. Barrie, domiciled in Whiteside County, Illinois, died owning real and personal property in Illinois and real property in Tama County, Iowa. The instrument in question was offered for probate in Whiteside County, Illinois. Although first admitted to probate, it was later denied probate after the Illinois Supreme Court had ruled that said instrument had been revoked by cancellation and that decedent died intestate.

Thereafter the instrument was offered for probate in Tama County, Iowa, by one of the beneficiaries named therein. To the petition for probate, decedent's heirs at law filed objections based upon the judgment of the Illinois Supreme Court, to the effect that the said last will and testament had been revoked. Objectors assert that this judgment is conclusive upon the Iowa courts. Proponent's motion to strike said objections for the reason that they do not constitute a valid basis for denying probate, being overruled by the trial court, this appeal was taken.

The instrument offered for probate was duly signed by decedent and witnessed by two witnesses. By the terms thereof all property was to be converted into cash and distributed to the named beneficiaries, including appellants. When found, after the death of decedent, the instrument had the word "void" written across its face in at least five places, including the attestation clause. Also, upon the cover and upon the envelope containing same appears the word "void" written with the name "M. E. Barrie" and "Mary E. Barrie." The Illinois court found that the writing of the word "void" on the instrument, as above related, constituted a revocation by cancellation within the purview of the Illinois Revised Statutes, 1945, chapter 3, section 197. This statute provides for the revocation of a will, ". . . (a) by burning, cancelling, tearing, or obliterating it by the testator."[a]

No question is raised as to the due execution of the instrument either under the Illinois or the Iowa statutes. No question is raised as to the testamentary capacity of decedent, nor is it claimed by the objectors that there has been a revocation under the Iowa statute, section 633.10, Code of 1946.[b] The question before this court for determination may be stated thus, "Is the judgment of the Illinois court, holding that said instrument had been revoked and that decedent died intestate, conclusive and binding upon the Iowa courts?"

---

[a] The lower court in Illinois had admitted the will, upon testimony by a handwriting expert that the word "void" written on the will was not in the handwriting of Miss Barrie. (A guardian had had access to her house in her last days.) The Supreme Court of Illinois reversed, finding the testimony of the handwriting expert unconvincing. *In re Barrie's Will,* 393 Ill. 111, 65 N.E.2d 433 (1946).

[b] Section 633.10 read, at the time, as follows:

Revocation-Cancellation. Wills can only be revoked in whole or in part by being canceled or destroyed by the act or direction of the testator, with the intention of so revoking them, or by the execution of subsequent wills. When done by cancellation, the revocation must be witnessed in the same manner as the making of a new will.

Section 604.3, Code of 1946, provides:

> The district court of each county shall have original and exclusive jurisdiction to:
>
> 1. Probate the wills . . . of nonresidents of the state who die leaving property within the county subject to administration. . . .

Decedent was a nonresident of the state and died owning property in Tama county which was subject to administration. Clearly the district court of Tama county has original jurisdiction to probate this instrument unless the Illinois judgment has the effect of nullifying or modifying said statute.

. . .

Upon the general question as to the validity, operation, effect, etc. of a will by which property is devised, there are certain well-established and generally recognized rules, and which definitely differentiate between movable (personal) and immovable (real) property. We are only concerned with immovables in the instant case. . . .

The general rule as stated in Story on Conflict of Laws, Eighth Ed., page 651, is, "the doctrine is clearly established at the common law, that the law of the place where the property [speaking of real (immovable) property] is locally situate is to govern as to the capacity or incapacity of the testator . . . the forms and solemnities to give the will or testament its due attestation and effect." 4 Page on Wills 688, section 1633, states the rule: "The general rule . . . is that the validity, operation, effect, etc., of a will by which real property is devised is determined by the law of the place where the land is situated." Restatement of the Law, Conflict of Laws, section 249, states: "The validity and effect of a will of an interest in land are determined by the law of the state where the land is." Upon the specific question as to revocation of a will, 2 Beale, Conflict of Laws, section 250.1, page 972, states: "The revocation of a will is governed by the law of the state of situs of the land." Restatement of the Law, Conflict of Laws, section 250, says: "The effectiveness of an intended revocation of a will of an interest in land is determined by the law of the state where the land is."

. . .

Under the above-stated rule Iowa courts are free to place their construction, interpretation and sanction upon the will of a nonresident of the state who dies owning real property within the state. . . .

Does a different rule pertain where instead of being admitted to probate in the domicile state probate is denied? We think not. It is generally held that the full faith and credit provision of the Constitution of the United States, Article IV, section 1, does not render foreign decrees of probate conclusive as to the validity of a will as respects real property situated in a state other than the one in which the decree was rendered, nor does the doctrine of res adjudicata or estoppel by judgment apply. See *Robertson v. Pickrell*, 109 U. S. 608 [1883], where the court said the probate established nothing beyond the validity of the will in that state, and while conclusive there, the full faith and credit clause and the Act of Congress enacted pursuant thereto did not require that they shall have any greater force and efficacy in other courts than in the courts of the state from which they were taken, but only such faith and credit as by law and usage they had there.

. . .

In *In re Estate of Barrie,* 331 Ill. App. 443, 447, 73 N.E.2d 654, 656 [1947], where the question was as to the right of the county court to permit the removal of the original will in question from its files, the court said:

> The title to and disposition of real estate either by deed or will is governed by the law of the state where the land is situated. Mary E. Barrie owned real estate located in Iowa, and the disposition of this real estate is governed by the laws of that state. Any order denying that will admission to probate in Illinois does not affect the title of her real estate located in any other state.

. . .

Section 633.49, Code of 1946, provides:

> A last will and testament executed without this state, in the mode prescribed by the law, either of the place where executed or of the testator's domicile, shall be deemed to be legally executed, and shall be of the same force and effect as if executed in the mode prescribed by the laws of this state, provided said last will and testament is in writing and subscribed by the testator.

This statute has not been before this court, so far as the writer of this opinion can find. It is clearly a modification of the common law and should not be extended to include matters not clearly included therein. It specifically deals with the formalities in the execution of the will, and nothing more. No question of execution is here involved. That the legislature might have waived the common-law rule as applicable to revocations as well as to the formal execution, as it has done, cannot be denied. However, the legislature has not seen fit to do so.

. . .

Assuming the instrument creates an equitable conversion of the realty into personalty, that fact is immaterial to the question before this court since the question presupposes the existence of a formally valid will executed by a competent testator. . . .

We hold that the Illinois judgment denying probate to the will in question is not conclusive and binding upon the courts of this state in so far as the disposition of the Iowa real estate is concerned; that the objections filed to the petition do not constitute a basis for denying probate of the will and the appellant's motion to strike should have been sustained. Reversed and remanded for an order in accordance herewith.

OLIVER, BLISS, GARFIELD, and WENNERSTRUM, JJ., concur.

SMITH, J. (dissenting)

I am unable to agree with the majority opinion. It perpetuates an anomalous confusing legal situation which our own statutes seem clearly designed to remove and which judicial thinking should seek a way to avoid. The importance of the question involved justifies, even requires, a statement of the grounds of dissent.

Appellant has litigated in the state of decedent's domicile the very issue it presents here, viz.: Is the instrument in question her will or did decedent die intestate? The Illinois court held there had been a revocation. *In re Barrie's Will,* 393 Ill. 111, 65 N.E.2d 433 [1946]. Unfortunately the method of revocation adopted by decedent does not comply with our revocation statute though recognized in Illinois.

I. Appellant claims (and the majority opinion holds) the Illinois decision does not render the question res adjudicata here because, as to real estate, at common law the "lex loci rei sitae" (the law of the place where a thing is situated) governs as to "the forms and solemnities" necessary to give a will "its due attestation and effect," citing Story on Conflict of Laws, Eighth Ed., 652, and other texts; and because, since decedent owned Iowa land, the question whether she had effectively revoked the instrument can be relitigated here and must be determined under our laws relating to domestic wills.

No contention is or could be made that this would be true if her Iowa property was personalty only. 15 C. J. S., Conflict of Laws, section 18f. The proposition is based squarely on decedent's ownership of real estate in Iowa. The distinction is significant of the historical situation (now nonexistent) out of which it arose—the fact that wills devising real estate were originally solely cognizable by courts of law, while testaments bequeathing personal property were within the exclusive jurisdiction of the ecclesiastical courts. . . . The requirements necessary to give the former instruments validity as conveyances of real estate naturally became considered subject to the common law "lex loci rei sitae," while those which only bequeathed personalty were subject to or followed the rule of testator's domicile, "mobilia sequuntur personam,"—movables (personalty) follow the person.

The courts and text writers who adhere to this ancient distinction overlook the profound effect of modern probate statutes that have entirely eliminated any old differences in formal requirements and solemnities as to mode of execution (and revocation) and probate procedure between "wills of personalty" and "wills of realty," as they were formerly referred to. We no longer speak of "wills of real estate" as something apart or different from "wills of personal property." The term "will" has come to include "testament." All must conform to the same statutory standards.

. . .

II. Our own statutes seem definitely to have done away with the rule of "lex loci" (or "lex sitae" as it is sometimes referred to) in determining whether a foreign decedent has died testate or intestate, or whether a given instrument is or is not his will.

It should be emphasized the rule is still valid in ascertaining what *effect* is to be given the instrument *once it has been found to be a will.* But we are not concerned here with the interpretation or construction or legal effect of the document in question. Before that question is reached it must first be established that it is in fact the will of Mary E. Barrie, which fact the Illinois courts have denied. Many of the cases cited by text writers in support of the rule relate to matters of *construction* and *legal effect* and not to the method of execution. We are concerned here only with the rule as applied to the "forms and solemnities" required in the execution and revocation of wills. . . .

In the face of our statutes it is difficult to see how we can hold the lex loci rei sitae determines the right of probate in this state of a document offered as the foreign will of a testator owning real estate in Iowa. By the express language of section 633.49 the law of his domicile or of the place where the will was executed must govern as to the manner of its execution. And where, in the jurisdiction of his domicile, probate has been granted or denied in proceedings in solemn form, we should hold the status of the instrument to be res adjudicata.

. . .

III. It is true of course that Code section 633.49 refers to *execution* and not directly to *revocation;* and we have here a document, held in Illinois to be nontestamentary, because of *revocation* and not because of any defect in original *execution.* In other words, we have an instrument not merely "executed" but also *revoked* "without this state, in the mode prescribed by the law . . . of the testator's domicile."

But revocation is merely the converse of execution. The power to execute implies the power to revoke. A will can no longer be said to be *executed* after it has been *revoked*. Whether an instrument is a will is determined not only by the manner of its execution but also by the manner of its attempted revocation. Both acts are a part of the testamentary process. It is unthinkable that our legislature intended to require recognition of the laws of another jurisdiction in the matter of one and not of the other.

. . .

The purpose of both Code sections 633.33[c] and 633.49 must have been to abolish or minimize confusion and conflict between states in the matter of handling wills. Foreign ownership of property has become common. Owners of property in different jurisdictions should not be required in making and revoking their wills to do more than comply with the law of their own domiciles, or with the law of the jurisdiction where the instrument is drawn or revoked. . . .

IV. I conclude we are required under Code section 633.49, in connection with other statutes I have cited, to determine the status of the offered instrument *by the law of decedent's domicile*. If there had been no determination of the question in Illinois the issue would of course have to be adjudicated in Iowa. The Iowa court, in that event, would have to construe and apply the Illinois statutes on execution and revocation and decide *by that standard* whether the document was the will of decedent.

But that issue has been adjudicated. The Illinois court has spoken. The judgment of a probate court, within the scope of its jurisdiction, is conclusive upon the parties, just as is the judgment of any other court.

. . .

There is nothing sacrosanct about the "lex loci" any more than about any other common-law rule. Our statute provides:

> The rule of the common law, that statutes in derogation thereof are to be strictly construed, has no application to this code. Its provisions and all proceedings under it shall be liberally construed with a view to promote its objects and assist the parties in obtaining justice.

Code of 1946, section 4.2.

Undoubtedly our will statutes are in derogation of the common law in many respects, not least of which is the abolition of all differences between wills and testaments as regards the method of their execution. Code section 633.49 is clearly in derogation of lex loci rei sitae as to *execution* of foreign wills. Its purpose is obvious. The majority opinion would construe it narrowly and technically by limiting the word "executed" to its strict and more common meaning—the performance of the acts by which the instrument is brought into being, specifically the signing and witnessing of it according to statutory requirements.

But ambiguity, justifying interpretation of a statute is not simply that arising from the meaning of particular words. It includes such as may arise in respect of the general scope and meaning of the statute when all its provisions are examined.

---

[c] Stating that a will probated in any other state or city shall be admitted to probate in this state . . . on the production of a copy of the will and the original record of probate.

It is not a strained construction therefore to say that anything done to the instrument by the testator affecting its status as a will is to be considered in determining whether he has finally *executed* it. And when our statute speaks of a will "executed without this state, in the mode prescribed by the law" of testator's domicile and provides that the instrument "shall be deemed to be legally *executed,* and shall be of the same force and effect as if *executed* in the mode prescribed by the laws of this state," we should construe it as requiring us to recognize the validity of a revocation by the testator, consummated in a mode recognized by the law of his domicile. Any other construction would render the statute impotent as to an important part of the very mischief it was plainly designed to remedy.

With apologies to the court and the profession for the (perhaps unnecessary) length of this dissent, I would affirm the decision of the trial court.

MANTZ, C. J., and HALE and MULRONEY, JJ., join in this dissent.

[B] The Role of Domicile

WHITE v. TENNANT

West Virginia Supreme Court
31 W. Va. 790, 8 S.E. 596 (1888)

SNYDER, JUDGE:

This is a suit brought December, 1886, in the Circuit Court of Monongalia county by William L. White and others against Emrod Tennant, administrator of Michael White deceased and Lucinda White, the widow of said Michael White, to set aside the settlement and distribution made by the administrator of the personal estate of said decedent, and to have the same settled and distributed according to the laws of the State of Pennsylvania, which State it is claimed was the domicile of said decedent at the time of his death. The plaintiffs are the brothers and sisters of the decedent, who died in this State intestate. On October 28, 1887, the court entered a decree dismissing the plaintiffs' bill, and they have appealed.

The sole question presented for our determination is, whether the said Michael White at the time of his death, in May, 1885, had his legal domicile in this State or in the State of Pennsylvania. It is admitted to be the settled law, that the law of the State, in which the decedent had his domicile at the time of his death, will control the succession and distribution of his personal estate.

. . .

The material facts in the case at bar are as follows: Joseph S. White, the father of the plaintiffs and Michael White, died intestate in Monongalia county seized of a tract of about 240 acres of land, of which about forty acres lay in Greene county, Pa., the whole constituting but one tract or farm. The mansion-house in which the father resided was located on the West Virginia side of the farm, and there was also a dwelling-house generally occupied by tenants on the Pennsylvania part of the farm. After the death of the father, his widow and the plaintiffs remained together and occupied the home-farm, residing in the mansion-house in West Virginia. Michael White several years before his death married the defendant, Lucinda White, a daughter of the defendant, Emrod Tennant, and about that time purchased a farm on Day's run, in Monongalia county, some fifteen miles from the home-place, to which he moved, and at which he and his wife resided. It is conceded, that Michael was born and had his domicile in West Virginia all his life, until about April 1, 1885.

In the winter of 1884–85, Michael sold his Day's run farm, and then rented or made an arrangement with his mother and brothers and sisters, the plaintiffs, to occupy the forty acres of the home-farm, in which he still had an undivided interest, and to live in the house on said forty acres in Greene county, Pa. He was to give to the purchaser the possession of his Day's run farm on April 1, 1885, and to have possession of the Pennsylvania house and forty acres at the same time. In March, 1885, he moved part of his household-goods into the Pennsylvania house, and put them into one of the rooms by permission of the tenant, who then occupied it, and who did not vacate it until between the middle and last of March, 1885. About the same time he moved an organ and some grain to the old homestead, until he could get possession of the Pennsylvania house.

On the morning of April 2, 1885, he finally left the Day's run house with the remainder of his goods and his wife, he having no children, with the declared intent and purpose of making the Pennsylvania house his home that evening. He with his team, wife and goods and live-stock passed into the State of Pennsylvania several miles before he reached said house and continued in said State thence to said Pennsylvania house, where they arrived that evening about sundown, and then and there unloaded their goods and put them in the house, setting up one bed and turning the fowls and other live-stock loose at the house.

The said house had been vacated for several days. It was a damp, cool day, and the house was found to be damp and uncomfortable. The wife was complaining of feeling unwell, and in consequence of that fact and the uncomfortable condition of the house, on the invitation of her brother-in-law and others of the family who then resided at the mansion-house, but a short distance therefrom, the said Michael and his wife went to the mansion-house in West Virginia to stay all night and return in the morning. Before leaving the Pennsylvania house the wife had gotten out of the buggy at the house, and the said Michael after putting into it his household-goods locked the door and took the key with him. On the following morning, the wife still feeling unwell, and the brother who was to return the team, which they had used in moving their goods, having taken sick, the wife after going to the Pennsylvania house to milk returned to the mansion-house, and Michael took the team back to Day's run.

On the return of Michael from this trip he found his wife so sick with typhoid fever, that it was impossible to move her, in consequence of which both he and she remained at the mansion-house,—she because she was unable to get away, and he to wait on her,—but he went daily over to the Pennsylvania house to look after it, and to feed his stock there, calling it his "home." In ten or fifteen days, and before the wife had sufficiently recovered to leave her bed, Michael was attacked with typhoid fever, and about ten days thereafter died intestate in the same house. The wife recovered, and the defendant, Emrod Tennant, her father, administered on the estate of Michael, taking out letters of administration in Monongalia county, W. Va. The administrator settled his accounts before a commissioner of said county, and distributed the estate according to the laws of West Virginia; that is, by paying over to the widow the whole personal estate remaining after the payment of the debts of the decedent. It is admitted, that, if the distribution had been according to the laws of the State of Pennsylvania, the wife would have been entitled to the one half only of said estate, and the plaintiffs would have been entitled to the other half.

As the law of the State, in which the decedent had his domicile at the time of his death, must govern the distribution of his estate, the important question is, where, according to the foregoing facts, was the domicile of Michael at the time of his death? It is unquestionable, that prior to the 2d day of April, 1885, his domicile was and had been in the State of West Virginia. Did he on that day or at any subsequent day change his domicile to the State of Pennsylvania? According to the authorities hereinbefore cited, if it is shown, that a person has entirely abandoned his former domicile in one State with the intention of making his home at a fixed place in another State with no intention of returning to his former domicile and then establishes a residence in the new place for any period of time, however brief, that will be in law a change of domicile, and the latter will remain his domicile until changed in like manner.

The facts in this case conclusively prove, that Michael White, the decedent, abandoned his residence in West Virginia with the intention and purpose not only of not returning to it, but for the expressed purpose of making a fixed place in the State of Pennsylvania his home for an indefinite time. This fact is shown by all the circumstances as well as by his declarations and acts. He had sold his residence in West Virginia and surrendered its possession to the purchaser, and thereby made it impossible for him to return to it and make it his home. He rented a dwelling in Pennsylvania, for which he had no use except to live in and make it his home. In addition to all this, he had moved a part of his household goods into this house, and then, on the 2d of April, 1885, he with his family and the remainder of his goods and stock finally left his former home and the State of West Virginia, and moved into the State of Pennsylvania to his house in that State, and there put his goods in the house, and turned his stock loose on the premises. At the time he left his former home on that morning, and while he was on the way to his new home, his declared purpose and intention were to make that his home from that very day, and to occupy it that night. He arrived in Pennsylvania and at his new home with that intention; and it was only after he arrived there and for reasons not before known, which had no effect to change his purpose of making that his future home, that he failed to remain there from that time. There was no change in his purpose, except that after he arrived at his new home and unloaded and left his property there, he concluded on account of the condition of the house and the illness of his wife, that it would be better to go with his wife to remain one night with his relatives and return the next morning.

When he left his former home without any intention of returning and in pursuance of that intention did in fact move with his family and effects to his new home with the intention of making it his residence for an indefinite time, it is my opinion, that, when he and his wife arrived at his new home, it became *eo instanti* his domicile, and that his leaving there under the circumstances with the intention of returning the next day did not change the fact. The concurrence of his intention to make the Pennsylvania house his permanent residence with the fact, that he had actually abandoned his former residence and moved to and put his goods in the new one, made the latter his domicile. According to the authorities hereinbefore referred to he must of necessity have had a domicile somewhere. If he did not have one in Pennsylvania, where did he have one? The fact, that he left the Pennsylvania house, after he had moved to it with his family and goods, to spend the night, did not revive his domicile at his former residence on Day's run, because he had sold that, and left it without any purpose of returning there. By going from his new home to the house of his relatives to spend the night he certainly did not make the house thus visited his domicile; therefore, unless the Pennsylvania house was on the evening of April 2, 1885, his domicile, he was in the anomalous position of being without a domicile anywhere, which, as we have seen, is a legal impossibility; and, that house having become his domicile, there is nothing in this case to show, that he ever did in fact change or intend to change it or to establish a domicile elsewhere.

It follows, therefore, that that house remained his domicile up to and at the time of his death; and, that house being in the State of Pennsylvania, the laws of that State must control the distribution of his personal estate notwithstanding the fact, that he died in State of West Virginia.

For these reasons the decree of the Circuit Court must be reversed, and the cause must be remanded to that court to be there further proceeded in according to the principles announced in this opinion and the rules of courts of equity.

IN RE ESTATE OF EVAN JONES

Iowa Supreme Court
192 Iowa 78, 182 N.W. 227 (1921)

FAVILLE, J.

The decedent, Evan Jones, was a native of Wales. When he was about 33 years of age, he came to America as an immigrant. This was in 1883. He came over on the same ship with the wife and children of one David P. Jones. At that time, David P. Jones was living in Oskaloosa, Iowa, to which place the decedent went. After the death of David P. Jones, the decedent married his widow, who subsequently died, in January, 1914. The decedent, Evan Jones, was a coal miner, an industrious, hard-working, thrifty Welshman, who accumulated a considerable amount of property. In 1896, he was naturalized in the district court of Wapello County, Iowa, and thereafter voted at elections. The reason for his leaving Wales at the time he did was because of bastardy proceedings which had been instituted against him by the mother of the appellant. In 1915, the decedent disposed of his property, which then consisted of two farms and some city real estate. He was advised by his banker to leave the greater part of his money in a bank at Ottumwa until he got to Wales, and did so deposit it. He purchased a draft for about $2,000, and left some $20,000 on deposit in the bank, and also a note and mortgage for collection, and left with the banker the address of a sister in Wales, stating that he intended to live with said sister. He sailed from New York on May 1, 1915, on the ill-fated Lusitania, and was drowned when that boat was sunk by a German submarine on May 7, 1915. The Lusitania was a vessel of the Cunard line, flying the British flag. Thereafter, the brothers and sisters of the decedent secured the appointment of an administrator in Wapello County, Iowa. Various proceedings were had, which finally resulted in the trial of the issues in this cause.

I. The question for our determination in this case is whether or not, under the facts stated, the domicile of the decedent at the time of his death was in Wapello County, Iowa, or in Wales. If his domicile at the time that the Lusitania sank was legally in Wales, then it is conceded by all the parties that, under the laws of the British Empire, the appellant, as his illegitimate child, would have no interest in his estate. On the other hand, if the decedent at said time legally had his domicile in Wapello County, Iowa, then the property passed to the appellant as his sole heir, under the laws of this state.

For the purposes of the present discussion, it may be conceded that the evidence is sufficient to justify a finding that the appellant was the child of the decedent, and had been so recognized and declared to such an extent as to satisfy the requirements of Code Section 3385.

It may also be conceded, for present purposes, that it is established by the evidence in the case that the decedent had, by acts and declarations, evidenced a purpose to leave his home in Iowa permanently, and to return to his native country, Wales, for the purpose of living there the remainder of his life.

The question of what constitutes domicile has often been passed upon by the courts, but the cases are so unlike in their facts that precedents to aid us in the determination of this precise question are difficult to find.

[The court cites numerous authorities distinguishing between domicile of origin, domicile of choice, and domicile by operation of law.]

In the instant case, we have to deal only with the first two kinds of domicile: that is, domicile of origin and domicile of choice. Applying these general definitions to the facts of this case, the domicile of origin of Evan Jones was in Wales, where he was born, and the domicile of choice was Wapello County, Iowa. The question that concerns us is, Where was his domicile for the purpose of descent of personal property on the 7th day of May, 1915, when the Lusitania was sunk off the western coast of the British Isles?

The matter of the determination of any person's domicile arises in different ways, and is construed by the courts for a variety of different purposes. Apparent inconsistencies occur in the authorities, because of the failure to clearly preserve the distinctions to be made by reason of the purpose for which the determination of one's domicile is being legally ascertained. The question frequently arises where it becomes important to determine the domicile for the purpose of taxation, or for the purpose of attachment, or for the levy of execution, or for the exercise of the privilege of voting, or in determining the statute of limitations, or in ascertaining liability for the support of paupers, and perhaps other purposes. Definitions given in regard to the method of ascertaining the domicile for one purpose are not always applicable in ascertaining the domicile for another purpose. Some of the courts have made the broad assertion that a person can have only one domicile. . . . Confusion has frequently arisen because of a failure to distinguish between domicile and residence.

Generally speaking, it is an established rule that a person can have but one domicile *at the same time for the same purpose*. In any event, it is the uniform holding that a person can have only one domicile for the purpose of descent of personal property. . . .

In the instant case, we are concerned only in the matter of the domicile of the decedent, Evan Jones, as it affects the question of the descent of his personal estate. An examination of the record satisfies us that the evidence is sufficient to amply justify a finding that the said decedent disposed of his property in Wapello County, Iowa, and converted the same into money or securities, and left Wapello County, Iowa, with the present intention of abandoning his domicile there, and without any present intention of returning thereto, and also with the express intention of returning to his native country, Wales, to make his permanent home there. Or, in the language of the books, decedent's intention was to abandon his domicile of choice and return to his domicile of origin. He died *in itinere*. . . .

At the outset, it is obvious that, under the circumstances of the instant case, the domicile of the decedent at the time of his death must, in any event, be determined by the assumption of a fiction. All will agree that the decedent did not have a domicile on the Lusitania. In order to determine his domicile, then, one of two fictions must be assumed: either that he retained the Iowa domicile until one was acquired in Wales, or that he acquired a domicile in Wales the instant he abandoned the Iowa domicile and started for Wales, with the intent and purpose of residing there. Which one of these fictions shall we assume, for the purpose of determining the disposition of his personal property? This question first came before the courts at an early day, long before our present easy and extensive methods of transportation, and at a time before the present ready movement from one country to another. At that time, men left Europe for the western continent or elsewhere, largely for purposes of adventure, or in search of an opportunity for the promotion of commerce. It was at a time before the invention of the steamboat and before the era of the oceanic cable. Men left their native land, knowing that they would be gone for long periods of time, and that means of communication with their home land were infrequent, difficult, and slow. The traditions of their native country were strong with these men. In the event of death while absent, they desired that their property should descend in accordance with the laws of the land of their birth. Many such men were adventurers, who had the purpose and intent to eventually return to the land of their nativity. There was a large degree of patriotic sentiment connected with the first announcement of the rules of law in the matter of the estates of such men. The idea found expression in the phrase, "Once an Englishman, always an Englishman," and in the kindred declaration, "A man must intend to become a Frenchman instead of an Englishman." *Moorhouse v. Lord,* 10 H. L. C. 272. This popular and patriotic idea was expressed in the familiar lines of Sir Walter Scott:

> Breathes there the man with soul so dead
>   Who never to himself hath said,
> "This is my own, my native land;"
> Whose heart hath ne'er within him burned,
>   As home his footsteps he hath turned,
> From wand'ring on a foreign strand?

Many men, especially of English birth, became traders in the American colonies or in India. The Englishman of that day was a firm believer in the law of primogeniture, and desired that his estate should descend according to the established laws of his native land.

These reasons, which were, to an extent at least, historical and patriotic, found early expression in the decisions of the courts on the question of domicile. The general rule was declared to be that a domicile is retained until a new domicile has been actually acquired. At an early time, however, an exception was engrafted upon this rule to the effect that, *for the purposes of succession,* a party abandoning a domicile of *choice,* with the intent to return to his domicile of *origin,* regains the latter the instant that the former domicile is abandoned.

It will be observed that this exception involves two elements: First, that the party is seeking to return from a domicile of choice to a domicile of origin; and second, that the question arises in a case involving succession to an estate. It is apparent that this exception to the general rule grew out of the conditions that we have before suggested, and was a recognition of the desire on the part of the English trader in distant lands to have his estate administered according to the laws of the land of his birth.

. . .

In 1834, Mr. Justice Story wrote the first edition of his great work on the *Conflict of Laws.* In it he stated (Section 47):

> If a man has acquired a new domicile different from that of his birth, and he removes from it with an intention to resume his native domicile, the latter is reacquired, even while he is on his way, *in itinere;* for it reverts from the moment the other is given up.

§ 1.03   CHOICE OF LAW   31

In Section 48, he said:

> A national character, acquired in a foreign country by residence, changes when the party has left the country *animo non revertendi,* and is on his return to the country where he had his antecedent domicile. And especially if he be *in itinere* to his native country with that intent, his native domicile revives while he is yet *in transitu;* for the native domicile easily reverts. The moment a foreign domicile is abandoned, the native domicile is reacquired.

This pronouncement by Mr. Justice Story has been frequently referred to by the courts, both English and American, in discussing this question, and has been the basis for decisions, particularly in the English courts.

[The court cites numerous cases of reversion of domicile of origin, and two that suggest that such a rule depends on retaining one's original allegiance.]

It is true that the question of domicile is not to be determined by the question of citizenship; but, when we are assuming the fiction that the domicile of origin reverts immediately upon the abandonment of a domicile of choice, and assume that fiction *because of native allegiance* to the land of one's birth, then the basis for the fiction and assumption is destroyed when it appears that the party has renounced his native allegiance and has secured citizenship in the land of his domicile of choice. The reason for the rule having failed, the rule fails also.

. . .

Perhaps no better case could be found than the instant case, to illustrate the effect of the adoption of the exception to the general rule. The decedent in this case had not only acquired a domicile in the United States, but had become a citizen of this country. Under the general rule, if he had abandoned his domicile in Iowa with the intention of acquiring a domicile in Norway or in France, and had been on the ill-fated Lusitania, it would have been universally held that the domicile in Iowa was still retained. No one will dispute that proposition. But because, although a citizen of the United States, residing here for many years, he was *en route* to Wales, the land of his birth, instead of to some other country, it is contended that he acquired a domicile in *that* country instantly upon abandoning his domicile in Iowa. If some native of Iowa had done exactly what the decedent did,—had disposed of his property, with the avowed and declared intention of abandoning his domicile in Iowa and of securing one in Wales, and had accompanied Jones on his trip, and had gone down on the same boat,—his estate would have been administered according to the laws of the state of Iowa, because he had not yet acquired a new domicile anywhere else; while Jones's estate, under the theory of the English rule, would be administered according to the laws of Wales, because he happened to have been born in that country. If such a rule is to be applied as between different states of the Union, with our freedom of movement between the various states, it would lead to very startling results. The laws of the states differ greatly in regard to descent. There is no logical reason why the rule should not be applied between different states of the Union as readily as between different governments. Under such a doctrine, if applied between the various states of the Union, if a man had been born in the state of New York, and at an early age had removed to Iowa, and had lived in this commonwealth for many years, had voted here, and had become familiar with our laws, and should finally decide to remove to New York to live, and should die *in itinere,* he would be regarded as domiciled in New York. If, however, under identical circumstances, he intended to remove to Massachusetts, he would be regarded as domiciled in Iowa. What good reason is there why "native allegiance" to the state of New York, where he was born, should be the determining factor which would prevail in such an instance? One reason that is persuasive why such a rule should not be adopted is that a person who in these days abandons his domicile of origin and acquires a legal domicile in another jurisdiction is, presumably, at least, familiar with the laws of the jurisdiction of the latter domicile, and there is, to say the least, as strong a presumption that he desires his estate to be administered according to the laws of that jurisdiction as of the jurisdiction of the domicile of origin. While there may have been a good reason for the establishment of the English rule at the time and under the conditions under which it was announced, we do not believe that any good reason exists for the recognition of such a rule under the circumstances disclosed in this case. The general rule that a domicile, once legally acquired, is retained until a new domicile is secured, and that, in the acquisition of such new domicile, the fact and the intention must concur, it seems to us is a rule of universal and general application, and there is neither good logic nor substantial reason for the application of an exception to that rule in the case where the party is *in itinere* toward the domicile of origin. . . . We believe that the general rule is the better rule, and that the exception laid down by Story and followed by the English courts should not be recognized, either as between the states of the Union or between this country and a foreign country, under the facts disclosed in this case.

It therefore follows that the domicile of the decedent was in the state of Iowa until a new domicile had been actually acquired in Wales. No such domicile having been acquired at the time of his death, his personal estate must be administered according to the laws of Iowa. . . .

We have examined the record, and hold that the appellant was legally recognized as the child of the decedent, as required by our statute and the decisions of this court, and is his lawful heir.

If follows that the judgment of the trial court must be, and the same is,

Reversed.

NOTES AND QUESTIONS

(1) The search for a rule to cover questions of property runs into a number of problems at the outset:

(a) Is a contract concerning property to be classified under contracts or under property? The cases in this introductory chapter as well as in succeeding chapters tend to exclude contractual transactions from the discussion of choice of law with respect to property, and to concentrate on succession upon death, trusts and analogous dispositions, and gifts, but the distinction is not inevitable.

(b) Should all property be treated alike, or should there be distinct rules for immovable property? What about intangible property, such as shares of stock, bank accounts, or claims?

(c) Should the rules be the same for voluntary as for involuntary transfers—e.g., for a will as contrasted with intestacy?

(d) Perhaps the hardest question, should the law distinguish between inter vivos and testamentary dispositions?

(2) The *Barrie* case shows both rigidity and flexibility in response to the preceding questions.

(a) The rule that as to real property, the law of the situs governs, seems to come through very clearly. But even that rule is not absolute under the Iowa statute, § 633.49, which, at least as to formal validity of a will, permits application of the law of the testator's domicile, or the law of the place of execution, as well as the law of Iowa. Note that this statute is not a neutral rule, like that in *Alabama Great Southern R.R. v. Carroll*, which would favor a plaintiff one day, a defendant the next. The Iowa "borrowing statute" is designed to sustain wills challenged on formal grounds, and since the will needs to pass only one of several possible tests, the statute clearly expresses a preference for testamentary succession rather than intestacy. More of preferences later.

(b) Why is § 633.49 not the answer to the court's problem, as the dissent argues? Would the distinction between execution and revocation apply equally to revocation by operation of law? Suppose, for example, a man domiciled in Illinois with real property in Illinois and Iowa makes a will leaving all his property to his parents. Thereafter he marries, and subsequently he dies. By the law of Illinois a marriage (with exceptions not here relevant) revokes a prior will;[d] by Iowa law, it does not.[e] Would the court that decided the *Barrie* case hold that the parents inherit the Iowa property, even though the widow takes the Illinois property?

(3) Apart from the debate between the majority and dissent about how to construe section 633.49, the nephews (i.e., those who would benefit from invalidity of the will) have a number of arguments:

(a) As a matter of choice of law, they could argue (1) for the law of the domicile (which apparently would prevail if the case involved personal property), or (2) for the law of the place of execution and/or revocation.

(b) In addition, they could claim that (3) the issue of validity of the will is *res judicata,* or (4) that the Iowa court was bound by the Full Faith and Credit Clause of the U.S. Constitution[f] to recognize the judgment of the Illinois court.

(c) If the first two arguments are not wholly persuasive, why aren't (3) and (4) conclusive? If the Full Faith and Credit clause is really limited as the court's citation to *Robertson v. Pickrell* suggests,[g] what principle of constitutional, common, or natural law do you think accounts for such a limitation on the plain meaning of the Constitutional text? Would you expect the same limitation to apply with respect to probate of a will of personal property? What other kinds of "public acts, records, and judicial proceedings" would you expect to be similarly excluded?

(d) Coming down from the Constitutional plateau, one thing seems clear: Miss Barrie either revoked her will, or she did not. The inconsistent results in the two states cannot possibly both reflect her intentions. Putting aside the duplication of litigation which is probably inevitable with assets of a decedent in different states, isn't the doctrine of *res judicata* designed precisely to avoid logically inconsistent results, such as in the *Barrie* cases? Even if the laws are different— and *res judicata* as to legal determinations is questionable anyhow—why isn't the factual determination governed by *res judicata*?

---

[d] See 3 Ill. Ann. Stat. § 46, repealed (in pertinent part) by § 46 of 1965 Probate Act. The current law, 755 ILCS Ann. Stat. 5/4–7 provides for revocation of a will through change in marital status of the testator only in cases of dissolution of a marriage.

[e] 46 Iowa Code Ann. § 633.284, formerly § 633.10 Code of 1946, Note b, p. 20, *supra*.

[f] Article IV, § 1, Documents Supplement, p. 4.

[g] The case involved an action of ejectment from District of Columbia real estate. Plaintiff claimed title through a will probated in Virginia, and the Supreme Court held that proof of probate in that state did not establish a transfer of title to land in the District.

(4) One's instinct in *Barrie* is that Illinois, as the testatrix's domicile, might have been a more rational point of reference for the court than the situs of the property. The *White* and *Jones* cases suggest that domicile, too, may be an arbitrary concept, at least for those persons who move around.

(a) Are *White v. Tennant* and *Estate of Jones* consistent with each other?

(b) Suppose poor Mr. Jones had made it to a lifeboat and had been rescued, only to die of exposure three days later in a British hospital. Would the case have come out differently?

(c) Would you expect all issues that relate to domicile to be decided the same way? Suppose, for example, West Virginia imposed an estate tax based on the value of personal property left by persons domiciled in the state at the time of their death. Would the *White* case come out the same way—i.e., no tax due?[h]

(d) What about the actual outcome of the two cases? In *White,* the wife who has lived these many years with Michael in a state where she could expect to succeed to his property if she survived him, loses half her inheritance. In *Jones,* one's sympathy may be with the illegitimate child (who must have been 32 years old when Mr. Jones died and 38 when the case was decided). But isn't it true that though she never left Britain, probably had never seen her father, and could not take under English law, she here benefits from a law to which she had no attachment?

(5) Speaking of English law, should the Iowa court have inquired:

(a) Whether Great Britain would consider Mr. Jones to be a British domiciliary;

(b) How a British court would decide this case?

These questions are explored further in the next chapter. For the moment, note only that (a) and (b) are not the same question stated in different words, but are quite distinct questions.

---

§ 1.04 Public Policy

LOUCKS v. STANDARD OIL CO.

New York Court of Appeals
224 N.Y. 99, 120 N.E. 198 (1918)

CARDOZO, J.

The action is brought to recover damages for injuries resulting in death. The plaintiffs are the administrators of the estate of Everett A. Loucks. Their intestate, while traveling on a highway

---

[h] Compare the first *Restatement of Conflict of Laws* (1934):

§ 9. DOMICIL

Domicil is the place with which a person has a settled connection for certain legal purposes, either because his home is there, or because that place is assigned to him by the law.

with the second Restatement (1971):

§ 11. Domicil

(1) Domicil is a place, usually a person's home, to which the rules of Conflict of Laws sometimes accord determinative significance because of the person's identification with that place.

(2) Every person has a domicil at all times and, at least for the same purpose, no person has more than one domicil at a time.

in the state of Massachusetts, was run down and killed through the negligence of the defendant's servants then engaged in its business. He left a wife and two children, residents of New York. A statute of Massachusetts (R. L. ch. 171, § 2, as amended by L. 1907, ch. 375) provides that "if a person or corporation by his or its negligence, or by the negligence of his or its agents and servants while engaged in his or its business, causes the death of a person who is in the exercise of due care, and not in his or its employment or service, he or it shall be liable in damages in the sum of not less than $500, nor more than $10,000, to be assessed with reference to the degree of his or its culpability, or that of his or its servants, to be recovered in an action of tort commenced within two years after the injury which caused the death by the executor or administrator of the deceased; one-half thereof to the use of the widow and one-half to the use of the children of the deceased, or if there are no children, the whole to the use of the widow, or if there is no widow, the whole to the use of the next of kin." The question is whether a right of action under that statute may be enforced in our courts.

(1) "The courts of no country execute the penal laws of another" (*The Antelope,* 10 Wheat. 66, 123). The defendant invokes that principle as applicable here. Penal in one sense, the statute indisputably is. The damages are not limited to compensation; they are proportioned to the offender's guilt. A minimum recovery of $500 is allowed in every case. But the question is not whether the statute is penal in some sense. The question is whether it is penal within the rules of private international law. A statute penal in that sense is one that awards a penalty to the state, or to a public officer in its behalf, or to a member of the public, suing in the interest of the whole community to redress a public wrong (*Huntington v. Attrill,* 146 U. S. 657, 668; *Huntington v. Attrill,* 1893 A. C. 150, 156). . . .

The purpose must be, not reparation to one aggrieved, but vindication of the public justice. . . . The Massachusetts statute has been classified in some jurisdictions as penal, and in others as remedial. Connecticut, Rhode Island and Vermont put it in the first category . . . and some of the Federal courts put it in the second. . . . The courts of Massachusetts have said that the question is still an open one. . . .

We think the better reason is with those cases which hold that the statute is not penal in the international sense. On that branch of the controversy, indeed, there is no division of opinion among us. It is true that the offender is punished, but the purpose of the punishment is reparation to those aggrieved by his offense. . . . The common law did not give a cause of action to surviving relatives. . . . In the light of modern legislation, its rule is an anachronism. Nearly everywhere, the principle is now embodied in statute that the next of kin are wronged by the killing of their kinsman. The family becomes a legal unit, invested with rights of its own, invested with an interest in the continued life of its members, much as it was in primitive law (Maine, Ancient Law, pp. 121, 122, 178; 1 Pollock & Maitland, History of English Law, p. 24; Holmes, The Common Law, p. 342). The damages may be compensatory or punitive according to the statutory scheme (See 8 Ruling Case Law, title Death, sec. 120, where statutes are collated). In either case, the plaintiffs have a grievance above and beyond any that belongs to them as members of the body politic. They sue to redress an outrage peculiar to themselves.

We cannot fail to see in the history of the Massachusetts statutes a developing expression of this policy and purpose. The statutes have their distant beginnings in the criminal law. To some extent the vestiges of criminal forms survive. But the old forms have been filled with a new content. The purpose which informs and vitalizes them is the protection of the survivors. They are moods and phases, the particular and varying expression, of a tendency in legislation as general as the common law. They are not to be viewed in isolation, apart from the stream of events. At first, the remedy was given only when the wrongdoer was a common carrier (St. 1840, ch. 80). That statute goes back to 1840, antedating Lord Campbell's Act in England (St. 9 & 10 Vict. ch. 93, 1846). The remedy was by indictment and fine, the fine being payable to the widow and next of kin. If there were no survivors of the prescribed class, there could be no indictment (*Comm. v. B. & A. R. R. Co.,* 121 Mass. 36). The reason was that even then the dominant purpose was reparation to the family. But later an alternative remedy by civil action at the suit of the executor or administrator became available even against carriers. . . . Then other statutes gave a civil remedy against other wrongdoers, and a civil remedy exclusively. Some statutes were confined to cases where the defendant was the employer of the decedent. . . . Finally there came one which gave a remedy against all persons who had not otherwise been made liable (R. L. ch. 171, § 2). That is the statute sued on. The remedy is civil; it is an action of tort.

Through all this legislation there runs a common purpose. . . . It is penal in one element and one only: the damages are punitive. The courts of Massachusetts do not give punitive damages even for malicious torts except by force of statute. . . . That may have led them to emphasize unduly the penal element in such recoveries. But the punishment of the wrongdoer is not designed as atonement for a crime; it is solace to the individual who has suffered a private wrong. This is seen in many tokens. The employer may be innocent himself. Smart money will still be due in proportion to his servant's negligence. That is a distribution of burdens more characteristic of torts than crimes. But even more significant is the distribution of benefits. All the statutes are *in pari materia.* All or none are penal in the international sense. . . . Under all, liability is conditioned upon the existence of a widow or of next of kin. Under some, there must be proof also that the next of kin were dependent on the decedent's wages for support (R. L. ch. 106, § 73). That restriction brings the dominant purpose into clear relief as reparation to those aggrieved. . . . The executor or administrator who sues under this statute is not the champion of the peace and order and public justice of the commonwealth of Massachusetts. He is the representative of the outraged family. He vindicates a private right.

(2) Another question remains. Even though the statute is not penal, it differs from our own. We must determine whether the difference is a sufficient reason for declining jurisdiction.

A tort committed in one state creates a right of action that may be sued upon in another unless public policy forbids. That is the generally accepted rule in the United States. . . . It is not the rule in every jurisdiction where the common law prevails. In England it has been held that the foreign tort must be also one by English law. . . . That is certainly not the rule with us. But there are some decisions in death cases which suggest a compromise. They say that jurisdiction will be refused unless the statutes of the two states are substantially the same. That is an approach to the English rule. But then they say that if substantial correspondence exists, it is the right of action under the foreign statute, and not the statute of the forum, which our courts will enforce. To that extent, there is a departure from the English rule. There is little doubt about the wisdom of the departure. What is subject to criticism, is the approach. The question is whether the enforcement of a right of action for tort under the statutes of another state is to be conditioned upon the existence of a kindred statute here. Support for the restriction is supposed to be found in four cases in this court.

. . .

[The court summarizes the cases, the first one of which said that New York law did not apply abroad, and that a wrongful death statute must exist at the place of the accident in order to give rise to a cause of action. The succeeding cases misinterpreted this case to require a correspondence between the foreign and the New York statute in order for New York to entertain the action.]

No case has yet arisen in which the statutes were so dissimilar that acceptance or rejection of the rule was necessary to a decision. The time has come to re-examine its foundations.

A foreign statute is not law in this state, but it gives rise to an obligation, which, if transitory, "follows the person and may be enforced wherever the person may be found". . . . The plaintiff owns something, and we help him to get it. . . . We do this unless some sound reason of public policy makes it unwise for us to lend our aid. "The law of the forum is material only as setting a limit of policy beyond which such obligations will not be enforced there". . . . Sometimes, we refuse to act where all the parties are non-residents. . . . That restriction need not detain us: in this case all are residents. If aid is to be withheld here, it must be because the cause of action in its nature offends our sense of justice or menaces the public welfare . . . Our own scheme of legislation may be different. We may even have no legislation on the subject. That is not enough to show that public policy forbids us to enforce the foreign right. A right of action is property. If a foreign statute gives the right, the mere fact that we do not give a like right is no reason for refusing to help the plaintiff in getting what belongs to him. We are not so provincial as to say that every solution of a problem is wrong because we deal with it otherwise at home. Similarity of legislation has indeed this importance: its presence shows beyond question that the foreign statute does not offend the local policy. But its absence does not prove the contrary. It is not to be exalted into an indispensable condition. The misleading word "comity" has been responsible for much of the trouble. It has been fertile in suggesting a discretion unregulated by general principles (Beale, *Conflict of Laws,* § 71). The sovereign in its discretion may refuse its aid to the foreign right. From this it has been an easy step to the conclusion that a like freedom of choice has been confided to the courts. But that, of course, is a false view (*Cuba R. R. Co. v. Crosby,* [222 U.S. 473], 478). The courts are not free to refuse to enforce a foreign right at the pleasure of the judges, to suit the individual notion of expediency or fairness. They do not close their doors unless help would violate some fundamental principle of justice, some prevalent conception of good morals, some deep-rooted tradition of the common weal.

This test applied, there is nothing in the Massachusetts statute that outrages the public policy of New York. We have a statute which gives a civil remedy where death is caused in our own state. We have thought it so important that we have now imbedded it in the Constitution (Const. art. 1, § 18). The fundamental policy is that there shall be some atonement for the wrong. Through the defendant's negligence, a resident of New York has been killed in Massachusetts. He has left a widow and children who are also residents. The law of Massachusetts gives them a recompense for his death. It cannot be that public policy forbids our courts to help in collecting what belongs to them. We cannot give them the same judgment that our law would give if the wrong had been done here. Very likely we cannot give them as much. But that is no reason for refusing to give them what we can. We shall not make things better by sending them to another state, where the defendant may not be found, and where suit may be impossible. Nor is there anything to shock our sense of justice in the possibility of a punitive recovery. The penalty is not extravagant. It conveys no hint of arbitrary confiscation. . . . It varies between moderate limits according to the defendant's guilt. We shall not feel the pricks of conscience if the offender pays the survivors in proportion to the measure of his offense. We have no public policy that prohibits exemplary damages or civil penalties. We give them for many wrongs. To exclude all penal actions would be to wipe out the distinction between the penalties of public justice and the remedies of private law. Finally, there are no difficulties of procedure that stand in the way. We have a statute authorizing the triers of the facts, when statutory penalties are sued for, to fit the award to the offense (Code Civ. Pro. § 1898). The case is not one where special remedies established by the foreign law are incapable of adequate enforcement except in the home tribunals.

We hold, then, that public policy does not prohibit the assumption of jurisdiction by our courts, and that this being so, mere differences of remedy do not count. . . .

The fundamental public policy is perceived to be that rights lawfully vested shall be everywhere maintained. At least, that is so among the states of the Union. . . .

The judgment of the Appellate Division should be reversed, and the order of the Special Term affirmed.

NOTES AND QUESTIONS

(1)(a) Judge Cardozo starts out by quoting Chief Justice Marshall's one-liner in *The Antelope*, "The courts of no country execute the penal laws of another."[a] Why should this be so?

(b) Would you be shocked to learn that *The Antelope* was about slavery, and that the quoted sentence justified a decision under which plaintiffs, claiming on behalf of Spanish and Portuguese slave owners, were permitted to repossess African slaves found on board a Venezuelan vessel brought into a United States harbor? Marshall wrote that although the slave trade was "contrary to the law of nature," it had at one time been a universal practice and could not be pronounced "repugnant to the law of nations."[b] Should Justice Marshall have held the trade in slaves contrary to the public policy of the forum? Or would that exceed the bounds of judicial propriety?[c]

(c) What do you think Cardozo would have done with this case?

(2)(a) Coming back to *Loucks v. Standard Oil*, the problem, strangely enough, is not the $10,000 damage limitation—that comes later.[d] In *Loucks*, it is the defendant who objects to applying Massachusetts law to a Massachusetts accident, because that law provides for a minimum recovery and makes the compensation depend in part on the degree of defendant's culpability. Why should that be against public policy?

---

[a] *The Antelope*, 23 U.S. (10 Wheat.) 66 at 123 (1825).

[b] 25 U.S. (10 Wheat.) at 120. "Whatever might be the answer of a moralist to this question," Marshall went on, "a jurist must search for its legal solution. . . ." *Id.* at 121.

[c] The U.S. Attorney General, William Wirt, as well as Francis Scott Key, urged that the slaves be freed, and Marshall acknowledged that "we ought not to be surprised if . . . even courts of justice should in some instances, have carried the principle of suppression [of the slave trade] further than a more deliberate consideration of the subject would justify." *Id.* at 116. He himself, however, (for a unanimous court that included Story) wrote that "this court must not yield to feelings which might reduce it from the path of duty, and must obey the mandate of the law." *Id.* at 114. Having set out this principle, however, Marshall held that only a small number of the claims of ownership had been established. In the result 39 of the 281 Africans on board were identified as "Spanish" and subsequently sold into slavery; the remainder were set free and transported to Liberia.

[d] See *Kilberg v. Northeast Airlines Inc.*, § 3.02, *infra*.

§ 1.04   CHOICE OF LAW   □   39

(b) Suppose the Massachusetts statute were more explicit, and required the court or jury (i) to establish the monetary value of plaintiff's injury; and (ii) to fix a fine in cases of serious injury, payable to the family of the deceased. Would Judge Cardozo draw the line there?

(3)(a) As we will see, the *Loucks* case is quoted in all kinds of contexts, whenever one side says the applicable choice of law rule points to the law of *X*, and the other side urges application of the law of the forum, or at least dismissal of the case. Is the public policy claim, then, a threat to the fundamental conception underlying the entire subject of conflict of laws?[e]

(b) Here, as we saw, the effort of Standard Oil was to persuade the New York court not to entertain a cause of action. Could the same argument be made to urge a court to refuse to entertain a defense, for instance a wrongful death limitation? Or would that be worse? In the first case, presumably, plaintiff could still bring suit in Massachusetts if New York dismissed her claim; in the second case, plaintiff would get a judgment that could not be secured at the place whose law ought to apply.

(c) Judge Cardozo does not altogether exclude resorting to public policy in choice of law cases. So long as choice of law is governed by fixed rules, such as "this action in tort will be governed by the law of *X,* the place of injury," some kind of safety or escape valve is necessary, if there is no way of knowing what values *X* will have. But for the law of *X* not to be applied, Cardozo says, that law must violate "some fundamental principle of justice" (p. 37, *supra*). What kind of law might that be? Could it ever include the law of a sister state of the United States?[f]

(d) The following case came before the New York Court of Appeals in 1938, when Cardozo was no longer on that court:

> Plaintiff, a German national, entered into an employment contract with Defendant, a German company, for services to be performed for three years from January 1932. Plaintiff alleged that in June 1933, defendants discharged him, solely because he was a Jew, and he claimed damages. Defendant asserted that the contract was made and was to be performed in Germany, and under the laws of that country in effect after April 1933, persons of non-Aryan descent could not be employed in the kind of position for which plaintiff had been hired. Plaintiff moved to strike the defense. What result?[g]

(4) In a well-known article published in 1956, Professors Paulsen and Sovern concluded that "[t]he principal vice of the public policy concepts is that they provide a substitute for analysis."[h] Would you expect that as analysis becomes more refined, for example focusing on particular issues rather than on cases as a whole[i] or as various interests of states, and links between states,

---

[e] Compare Paulsen and Sovern, *Public Policy in the Conflict of Laws,* 56 Colum. L. Rev. 969, at 971 (1956).

[f] Judge Goodrich wrote:

> As among our states, the right of the courts of one state refusing to apply the law of another because the second state's rule shocks the morals of the forum, is one to make the judicious grieve . . . A mutual tolerance for each other's little idiosyncrasies does not seem a great deal to ask from members of a family of states which have so much in common as we have. Such mutual tolerance is all that is necessary in order to get rid of the public policy argument altogether in Conflict of Laws among the states of this country. . . . As among ourselves and foreign nations, the case is not so strong.

Goodrich, *Foreign Facts and Local Fancies,* 25 Va. L. Rev. 26 at 35 (1938).

[g] The Court of Appeals denied the motion and upheld the defense, stating that it was not competent to review the actions of a foreign government within its own territory, "however objectionable." *Holzer v. Deutsche Reichsbahn-Gesellschaft,* 277 N.Y. 274, 14 N.E.2d 798 (1938).

[h] Paulsen & Sovern, *"Public Policy" on the Conflict of Laws,* 56 Colum. L. Rev. 969, at 1016 (1956)

[i] See, e.g., p. 125, question (2)(c); *Babcock v. Jackson,* p. 145 *infra* at 149.

occurrences, and parties are taken into account, public policy is less likely to intrude on the choice of law process? Consider this question as you follow the development from vested rights (see the last paragraph of *Loucks*) through various escape devices (Chapter 2) to the various modern theories disclosed and debated in Chapter 3.

(5) The suggestion that emerges from the preceding discussion is that public policy has a place in choice of law cases concerning slavery, racial discrimination, torture, and similar issues, but not in respect to differences about solutions to legal problems such as how to compensate accident victims. What about subjects that do not sharply pit good against evil, but involve deeply felt social and moral beliefs, such as marriage, divorce, abortion, homosexuality, and incest? We return to this subject in Chapter 9.

CHAPTER 2

MANEUVERING WITHIN THE TRADITIONAL RULES

§ 2.01 Escape Devices

As the brief survey in Chapter 1 has disclosed, none of the "black letter" rules proposed for solution of choice of law problems was fully convincing. Still, it seemed that courts preferred—or thought they were obliged—to search for the jurisdiction whose substantive rules could provide the source for resolution of the controversy before them. If the action were one in tort, the search pointed to the place of injury; if it were in contract, probably to the place of execution (though that was not inevitable) or perhaps to the place of performance or to the "proper law." For property cases, the courts seemed to look to the law applicable at the situs, at least for immovable property, perhaps to the law of the domicile of the donor (decedent) for other kinds of property. Finally, domicile itself seemed to depend on a definition combining a physical fact—presence of a person in a state or nation, with a metaphysical question—did the person intend to remain in that place.

Needless to say, these rules are at most a beginning, not an end to inquiry. But any system of rules might lead to unjust or unwanted results. The conflict of laws developed a series of devices—not doctrines but tools—to ameliorate the rigidity of the black letter system. These devices introduced flexibility either into what the court did with the law of the jurisdiction to which its first reference pointed, or into the process by which it began the search for a source of law.

[A] Renvoi

IN RE ANNESLEY

Chancery Division
[1926] Ch. 692

On January 16, 1924, Mrs. Sybil Annesley died at the Château de Quillebaudy at Orthez in France, in which country she had lived ever since the year 1866.[1]

She was married in the year 1860 to an army officer, Mr. James O'Donel Annesley, whose domicil was English. Until 1866 they lived together at Bath, but in that year they went to reside at Pau, which continued to be their habitual place of residence until the husband died in July, 1884. From that date it was open to Mrs. Annesley to adopt a domicil of choice. After her husband's death she continued to reside at Pau, where her mother also lived; but they occupied

---

[1] It appears to have been undisputed that her domicil of origin was English.

separate establishments. There is no indication that at this time she either owned or took a lease of any residence at Pau; but it was her normal and habitual place of residence.

In 1897 she bought the Château de Quillebaudy, some forty kilometres distant from Pau, where she had a small farm; and there she resided continuously until her death there in 1924. She was then over eighty years of age. Her visits to England were few, the only ones which are clearly established in the evidence, apart from a visit when one of her daughters was married in 1892, are some four in number for short periods, in 1903, 1907, 1911 and 1913. That she did not return after that date may well have been due to the war and to advancing years.

There is no doubt that the château was her home. In her correspondence she alludes to it as such. It was her only home. She never since 1866 had any place of residence in England. According to the evidence of her daughter, Mrs. Davidson, her mother frequently expressed to her dislike of England and the English people, and stated that she never wished to live anywhere but in France, and that she desired to reside in France until she died. At her death a paper was found in which she declared that she wished to be buried in France or in Germany, the latter being the country in which her husband (who in fact died there) was buried.

Mrs. Annesley never took the steps prescribed by art. 13 of the French Civil Code[a] with a view to obtaining a formal French domicil according to French law, but a printed form of application for this purpose was found among her papers. It was not filled up. So far as concerns fixing a date for its coming into her possession, all we know is that it was accompanied by a letter from a M. Maisonnier written some time during the war. Neither document is forthcoming.

She owned immovable property in France only.

She owned movable property both in England and in France. Most of her money was trust money, which was credited to her in England, where she had two banking accounts. On these she used to draw cheques and pay them into her banking account at Pau.

On November 20, 1919, she executed a holograph will in the French language. By it, after stating that her two daughters had their share exceeding two-thirds of her property assured by her marriage settlement, Mrs. Davidson's marriage settlement, and her English will, she disposed of the property which she possessed in France. She disposed of Quillebaudy and a pecuniary legacy in favour of a friend. Other immovable property she gave to two servants. She gave specific legacies of French investments to three other servants. The residue of her movable property she gave to the Rev. René Troyte, coupled with a request to pay the duties on the previous gifts and to make donations to certain local charities. It does not appear what were the contents of the English will referred to. It may be a reference to the will next mentioned, for it would appear from the correspondence that she had (at some date earlier than November 25, 1919) instructed Mr. Mellersh, her lawyer in England, to draw her will.

On December 13, 1919, she executed in France a will in English form. It revokes all former testamentary dispositions and purports to dispose of all her real and personal estate. The five servants named in the French will all take benefits under the English will. Pecuniary legacies

---

[a] Article 13 of the French Civil Code read as follows:

An alien, admitted by the government to establish his domicil in France, shall enjoy all civil rights, so long as he continues to reside there.

The Article was generally interpreted as requiring authorization to establish a French domicile, usually from the local mairie or prefecture, but in some cases also by implication, as where a public job was offered to the alien. The Article was repealed in 1927.

are given to certain friends. By cl. 4 the real estate and residuary personal estate are given on trust for sale; out of the proceeds a sum is to be set aside and invested to produce a small annuity, a further sum of 4300*l*. is to be set aside and invested as a trust legacy. By cl. 5 the ultimate residue is given to her daughter, Miss Annesley, absolutely. Clause 8 runs as follows:

> I declare that although I have lived in France for many years and own the house and grounds which I now occupy it has not been and is not my intention to abandon my domicil of origin namely England and I have not made any application under article 13 of the French Civil Code or otherwise for a decree to fix my domicil in France nor have I done anything to become a naturalised subject of France and I intend to remain a British subject.

On July 4, 1921, Mrs. Annesley executed in France a codicil in English form, by which she stated, in cl. 4: "I confirm my said will in all respects as altered by this codicil, and in particular I confirm cl. 8 of my said will as though such clause were set out in this codicil." The summons asked whether the domicil of the testatrix at the time of her death was French or English: (*a*) for purposes of English law; (*b*) for purposes of French law.

It was admitted that if the domicil was French for purposes of French law the testatrix could only dispose of one-third of her personal property, because she left two children surviving her. The testatrix by her will purported to dispose of the whole of her personal property.

RUSSELL J. stated the facts and continued: The first question to be decided is whether the domicil of the testatrix was English or French. But for the fact that Mrs. Annesley took no steps to obtain a formal French domicil according to French law, and both in her will and in a codicil to it declared that it was not her intention to abandon her domicil of origin—namely, England, there could not I conceive be any room for doubt as to the position according to English law. She died having acquired a French domicil of choice. To use the language of Lord Westbury in *Udny v. Udny*[1] Mrs. Annesley fixed voluntarily her sole residence in France, with an intention of continuing to reside there for an unlimited time. The domicil flows from the combination of fact and intention, the fact of residence and the intention of remaining for an unlimited time. The intention required is not an intention specifically directed to a change of domicil, but an intention of residing in a country for an unlimited time. The above recited facts in my opinion clearly establish both the necessary fact and the necessary intention.

Those who seek to establish an English domicil naturally place much reliance on the declarations in her will and codicil. They contend that we have here two statements made at different times by the lady herself, that she had never intended and did not intend to abandon her English domicil, and that in the face of these statements it is impossible for the Court to hold that a French domicil of choice had in fact or in law arisen. The contention is a tempting one to accede to in view of the fact that the finding of an English domicil would solve sundry other knotty points of difficulty which lurk in the background. But I feel unable to accede to it.

It must I think be conceded that domicil cannot depend upon mere declaration, though the fact of the declaration having been made must be one of the elements to be weighed in arriving at a conclusion on the question of domicil. But if a particular domicil clearly emerges from a consideration of the other relevant facts, a declaration of intention to retain some other domicil will not suffice to destroy the result of those facts. If (as I think she had) Mrs. Annesley had by the factum of long residence and by her animus manendi acquired before the date of her

---

[1] L. R. 1 H. L. Sc. 441, 458.

codicil a French domicil of choice, her statement that she never intended to abandon her English domicil will not prevent the acquisition of a French domicil of choice, unless weighing the statement with the other relevant facts the Court comes to the conclusion that the animus manendi had not been established.

. . . The question of her domicil must be determined not by her statement alone, but by a consideration of all the relevant facts. Upon such consideration I have come to the conclusion and decide that according to English law she died domiciled in France.

It was however contended that assuming that all the relevant facts do establish a French domicil, yet in the particular case it was according to English law impossible for Mrs. Annesley to have acquired a French domicil—because not having taken the steps prescribed by art. 13 of the Civil Code she was not and could not be a domiciled Frenchwoman in the eyes of the law of France. In other words the proposition is that no one can, according to English law, acquire a domicil of choice in a foreign country unless that person has also acquired a domicil there according to the law of the foreign country. [The court reviews a series of decisions of English courts, some agreeing, some disagreeing, with the proposition stated.]

In the result I prefer to adopt the view stated by Lindley M.R. in *In re Martin*[3] and I hold that the question whether Mrs. Annesley died domiciled in France must be answered by ascertaining whether she had abandoned her English domicil and had acquired a French domicil of choice in accordance with the requirements of English law—namely, by the factum of residence coupled with the animus manendi, and that regardless of the question whether she had or had not complied with the formalities required by French law to be carried out by her before she could rank in its eyes as a domiciled Frenchwoman.

I accordingly decide that the domicil of the testatrix at the time of her death was French. French law accordingly applies, but the question remains: what French law? According to French municipal law, the law applicable in the case of a foreigner not legally domiciled in France is the law of that person's nationality, in this case British. But the law of that nationality refers the question back to French law, the law of the domicil; and the question arises, will the French law accept this reference back, or *renvoi,* and apply French municipal law?

Upon this question arises acute conflict of expert opinion. Two experts took the view that the *renvoi* would not be accepted, but that a French Court would distribute the movables of the testatrix in accordance with English municipal law. One expert equally strongly took the view that a French Court would accept the *renvoi* and distribute in accordance with French municipal law. I must come to a conclusion as best I can upon this question of fact upon the evidence after considering and weighing the reasons given by each side in support of their respective views. It is a case rather of views expressed by the experts as to what the French law ought to be, than what it is. Although there is in France no system of case law such as we understand it here—the decisions of higher Courts not being binding upon inferior tribunals—yet I think I must pay some attention to the fact that this question of *renvoi* has at different times come for consideration before the Cour de Cassation, the highest Court in France, and each time with the same result—namely, the acceptance of the *renvoi* and the application of the French municipal law. It is true that the Cour de Cassation is quite free to take the opposite view on a future occasion, but it has never done so. I refer to the cases which were discussed and expounded before me—namely, the *Forgo* case[2] in 1882, and the *Soulié* case[3] in 1910. In the former case,

---

[3] [1900] p. 211, 227.

[2] Clunet (1883), 64.

[3] Clunet (1910), 888.

a decision of the Cour de Cassation, the *renvoi* was accepted, and French municipal law was applied to the disposition of the estate of a Bavarian national domiciled de facto in France (but not domiciled there according to French law), because according to Bavarian law the law of the domicil or usual residence was applicable. The *Forgo* case gave rise to grave differences of opinion among French jurists and was followed by many conflicting decisions in lower Courts, some favouring the "Théorie du Renvoi," others against it. The matter again came under the consideration of the branch of the Cour de Cassation entitled Chambre de Requêtes, one of whose functions is to decide whether or not an appeal to the Cour de Cassation should be allowed to proceed. That was the *Soulié* case, in which the Court below had held that French municipal law governed the succession to the movable property of an American subject who had died in France with a de facto domicil in that country. The Chamber declined to allow an appeal to the Cour de Cassation to proceed. This decision, coming as it did after the grave differences of opinion which resulted from the *Forgo* case, strikes me as of great importance. As is pointed out in a note to the report in Clunet it shows that the Supreme Court persists with energy in its former view, notwithstanding the views of text writers to the contrary.

In these circumstances, and after careful consideration of the evidence of the experts called before me, I have come to the conclusion that I ought to accept the view that according to French law the French Courts, in administering the movable property of a deceased foreigner who, according to the law of his country, is domiciled in France, and whose property must, according to that law, be applied in accordance with the law of the country in which he was domiciled, will apply French municipal law, and that even though the deceased had not complied with art. 13 of the Code.

The result is that as regards her English personal estate and her French movable property the testatrix in this case had power only to dispose of one-third thereof by her will.

Speaking for myself, I should like to reach the same conclusion by a much more direct route along which no question of *renvoi* need be encountered at all. When the law of England requires that the personal estate of a British subject who dies domiciled, according to the requirements of English law, in a foreign country shall be administered in accordance with the law of that country, why should this not mean in accordance with the law which that country would apply, not to the propositus, but to its own nationals legally domiciled there? In other words, when we say that French law applies to the administration of the personal estate of an Englishman who dies domiciled in France, we mean that French municipal law which France applies in the case of Frenchmen. This appears to me a simple and rational solution which avoids altogether that endless oscillation which otherwise would result from the law of the country of nationality invoking the law of the country of domicil, while the law of the country of domicil in turn invokes the law of the country of nationality, and I am glad to find that this simple solution has in fact been adopted by the Surrogates' Court of New York.[1]

---

[1] *Matter of Tallmadge*, 109 Misc. 696, 181 N.Y. Supp. 336 (Surr. Ct. 1919).

UNIVERSITY OF CHICAGO v. DATER

Michigan Supreme Court
277 Mich. 658, 270 N.W. 175 (1936)

In November, 1928, negotiations were commenced to secure a loan in the sum of $75,000 on a piece of property in Chicago. The property was owned by George R. Dater and John R. Price of Benton Harbor, Michigan, and they appointed H. S. Gray, an attorney of Benton Harbor, as their agent in the matter. Plaintiff agreed to make the loan if it could be assured that the title was good. A trust deed and certain promissory notes were drawn up with George R. Dater and Nellie E. Dater, his wife, and John R. Price and Clara A. Price, his wife, as parties of the first part and the Chicago Title & Trust Company, as trustee and as party of the second part. The notes were payable in the city of Chicago and at such place as the legal holder might appoint. The trust mortgage and notes were sent by mail to the Benton Harbor State Bank for the signature of the parties involved. The papers were signed in Benton Harbor, Michigan, about December 8, 1928, and mailed to plaintiff's agent in the city of Chicago where the trust deed was placed on record, then it was found that there were some objections to certain delinquent taxes of 1927. Further negotiations followed and finally on January 3, 1929, and after the tax objections were cleared in the title, the loan was actually made and the money paid over by check made payable to Mr. and Mrs. Dater and Mr. and Mrs. Price and cashed in Chicago, Illinois.

January 29, 1929, John R. Price died and it is conceded that Mrs. Price became the actual and record owner of at least one-half of the property after the death of her husband. Subsequent to December 1, 1933, foreclosure proceedings were commenced on the property and the property purchased at chancery sale. Suit was filed in Michigan before the foreclosure suit was completed in Chicago. The cause was heard November 7, 1934, and on June 18, 1935, judgment was rendered in favor of plaintiff against George R. Dater in the amount of $15,536.32 and from which no appeal has been taken. On the same date judgment was entered in favor of Clara Price of no cause for action, from which judgment plaintiff appeals.[b]

WIEST, J.

The obligation in suit was executed in this State by defendant Clara A. Price, a married woman, and bore no relation to her separate estate and, without more, carried no personal liability when sued upon in this jurisdiction. But, it is claimed, that the obligation was accepted in the State of Illinois, and was there payable and, by the law of that State, Mrs. Price is not saved from liability by reason of want of capacity under the Michigan law of coverture.

As pointed out later in this opinion personal liability of Mrs. Price could not be enforced in Illinois under the theory of an Illinois contract.

In the case at bar negotiations for the loan, to be secured by mortgage, had reached the stage where the lender prepared the note and mortgage in Illinois and sent the same to an agent in Michigan, with direction as to execution by defendants in this State and, when executed, to be returned by such agent to the mortgagee in Illinois. Mrs. Price, at the request of the agent, executed the instruments and the agent mailed the same to the mortgagee.

The instant case does not involve conflict of laws relative to the construction, force and effect of the instruments, signed or executed in one State to be performed in another, but that of capacity of Mrs. Price to enter into such an obligation in this State.

---

[b] Statement of facts by Justice Sharpe, as part of the dissenting opinion.

. . .

It must be agreed that this case is governed by the law of Michigan or of Illinois. If by the law of Michigan, it is clear, and is not disputed, that defendant has no personal liability on the note, recoverable from her separate estate.

Assuming, however, that by the Michigan law of the forum the case is governed by the law of Illinois, it presents the unique situation in the realm of conflict of laws that by the law of Illinois, *Burr v. Beckler,* 264 Ill. 230 (106 N. E. 206) . . . the case is governed by the law of Michigan.

In *Burr v. Beckler,* the wife, a resident of Illinois, was sojourning temporarily in Florida. Her husband owed a concern in Illinois, of which he was treasurer, on an overdraft. He informed his wife that he could borrow the necessary money to pay the overdraft from an estate of which he was trustee. The wife executed a note and trust deed in Florida and mailed them to her husband, as trustee, at Chicago, Illinois, as he had directed her to do. The husband also signed the trust deed but the opinion does not state when. The court held that delivery of the note and trust deed by the wife was complete in Florida, the law of that State governed her capacity to contract and, because she was not competent to enter into a contract under the law of Florida, her note and trust deed were void.

The question is not whether the decision is in harmony with the law of Michigan but whether it governs this case. Here, manual delivery was as complete as in the *Burr Case* because it was made to a bank which had been designated by the mortgagee for that purpose.

In neither case had there been a binding engagement by the mortgagee to make the loan prior to the delivery. In neither case had the money been paid in advance of the delivery or contemporaneously therewith. There is nothing in the *Burr Case* to indicate that the mortgagee could not have refused to make the loan or that the mortgagors could not have refused to take the money or could not have abandoned the matter after the wife deposited the papers in the mail. The *Burr* opinion indicates no circumstance fixing the effect of the manual delivery which is not present here. The *Burr Case* is directly applicable and, consequently, under the law of Illinois it must be held that the capacity of defendant Clara A. Price is governed by the law of Michigan. Under the law of Michigan, a married woman cannot bind her separate estate through personal engagement for the benefit of others. Defendant Price is not liable. . . .

NORTH, C. J., and FEAD and TOY, JJ., concurred with WIEST, J.

SHARPE, J. (dissenting).

. . .

It is conceded that under the law of Illinois a married woman is as free to contract as a man, while in Michigan a married woman has not the legal capacity to bind herself or her separate estate by signing these notes.

. . .

In the case at bar all of the negotiations for the loan occurred in Chicago, the property upon which the mortgage was placed was located in Chicago, and no money was to be paid by plaintiff until such time as the defendants could show good title to the property. We think the mailing of the papers to Chicago was for the purpose of enabling the plaintiff to ascertain if the title to the real estate was satisfactory and was but a preliminary step in the whole transaction. The final act in the making of the loan was the payment of the money in Chicago. This concluded the negotiations and made it an Illinois contract.

The judgment of the trial court should be reversed and the case remanded to enter a judgment in favor of plaintiff for $15,536.32 with interest from June 18, 1935. Plaintiff should recover costs.

BUSHNELL, J., concurred with SHARPE, J.

BUTZEL, J. (dissenting). I concur in the result reached by Justice Sharpe. The place of contracting controls the question of the capacity of the parties to contract.

. . .

It is true that the physical act of signing the note in the instant case took place in Michigan and the notes were mailed to plaintiff in Chicago, but there was no absolute delivery until the plaintiff had satisfied itself of the status of the title to the mortgaged property and until an actual cloud had been removed. Until that time the transaction was conditional and the notes of no binding force and effect.

We do not believe that the case of *Burr v. Beckler* . . . should in any way be controlling on this court in determining the *lex loci contractus*. The problem in the instant case is termed by the authorities as one of "qualifications." The prevailing view in answer to the problem is that the law of the forum should control on the question of *lex loci contractus*. An excellent treatment of the entire subject may be found in an article entitled, *The Theory of Qualifications and the Conflict of Laws,* by Professor Lorenzen in 20 Columbia Law Review, p. 247 [1920].

Were we not to be controlled by our own law and obliged each time to ascertain what a foreign State would have held under similar circumstances, our decisions would be in hopeless confusion and it would be necessary each time to examine the decisions of other States in determining the *lex loci contractus*. The question, however, is foreclosed in this State . . . that the law of the place of contracting is to be determined in accordance with the law of the forum.

The judgment should be reversed, with costs to plaintiff.

BUSHNELL, J., concurred with BUTZEL, J.

POTTER, J., did not sit.

IN RE SCHNEIDER'S ESTATE

New York Surrogate's Court, New York County
198 Misc. 1017, 96 N.Y.S.2d 652 (1950)

FRANKENTHALER, S.

This case presents a novel question in this State in the realm of the conflict of laws. Deceased, a naturalized American citizen of Swiss origin died domiciled in New York County, leaving as an asset of his estate certain real property located in Switzerland. In his will he attempted to dispose of his property, including the parcel of Swiss realty, in a manner which is said to be contrary to the provisions of Swiss internal law. That law confers upon one's legitimate heirs, a so-called *legitime,* i.e., a right to specified fractions of a decedent's property, which right cannot be divested by testamentary act. The precise issue, therefore, is whether this deceased had the power to dispose of the realty in the manner here attempted.

Ordinarily, the courts of a country not the situs of an immovable are without jurisdiction to adjudicate questions pertaining to the ownership of that property. . . .

Actions concerning realty are properly litigable only before the courts of the situs. However, in this case the administratrix appointed prior to the probate of the will has liquidated the foreign realty and transmitted the proceeds to this State. She is now accounting for the assets of the estate including the fund representing that realty. As a consequence, this court is called upon to direct the administration and distribution of the substituted fund and to determine the property rights therein. . . .

In doing so, however, reference must be made to the law of the situs, as the question of whether the fund shall be distributed to the devisee of the realty under the terms of the will is dependent upon the validity of the original devise thereof . . . which must be determined under the law of the situs of the land itself.

The court is confronted at the outset with a preliminary question as to the meaning of the term "law of the situs"—whether it means only the internal or municipal law of the country in which the property is situated or whether it also includes the conflict of laws rules to which the courts of that jurisdiction would resort in making the same determination. If the latter is the proper construction to be placed upon that term, then this court must, in effect, place itself in the position of the foreign court and decide the matter as would that court in an identical case.

The meaning of the term "law of the situs" can be ascertained best from a consideration of the reasons underlying the existence of the rule which requires the application thereof. The primary reason for its existence lies in the fact that the lawmaking and law-enforcing agencies of the country in which land is situated have exclusive control over such land. . . .

As only the courts of that country are ultimately capable of rendering enforcible judgments affecting the land, the legislative authorities thereof have the exclusive power to promulgate the law which shall regulate its ownership and transfer. When the land itself formed the estate asset upon which the will was intended to operate, the power of sovereign to enforce such laws created rights therein between the parties in interest. If an instrument which was intended to transfer that land did not meet the standards set by that law or violated some provisions thereof regarding the land, the courts had the physical power to deny it effect and enforce instead the rights decreed by the law of that country or the law of any other country which the lawmaking agencies deemed appropriate in a particular case.

Hence, the rights which were created in that land are those which existed under the whole law of the situs and as would be enforced by those courts which normally would possess exclusive judicial jurisdiction (Griswold, *Renvoi Revisited,* 51 Harv. L. Rev. 1165, 1186; cf. Schreiber, *The Doctrine of Renvoi in Anglo-American Law,* 31 Harv. L. Rev. 523, 559). If another court, in this case our own, is thrust into a position where it is obliged to adjudicate the same questions concerning title to that land, or a substitute therefor, it should be guided by the methods which would be employed in the country of situs. The purely fortuitous transfer of the problem to the courts of another State by virtue of a post-mortuary conversion of the land, effected for the purpose of administering the entire estate in the country of domicile, ought not to alter the character of the legal relations which existed with respect to the land at the date of death and which continued to exist until its sale. Consequently, this court, in making a determination of ownership, must ascertain the body of local law to which the courts of the situs would refer if the matter were brought before them.

It has been urged, however, that a reference to the conflict of laws rules of the situs may involve an application of the principle of *renvoi,* and if so it would place the court in a perpetually-enclosed circle from which it could never emerge and that it would never find a suitable body of substantive rules to apply to the particular case (see Schreiber, *op. cit. supra;* *Matter of Chadwick,* 109 Misc. 696, and authorities cited). This objection is based upon the assumption that if the forum must look to the whole law of the situs, and that law refers the matter to the law of domicile, this latter reference must be considered to be the whole law of the latter country also, which would refer the matter back to the law of the situs, which process would continue without end. That reasoning is based upon a false premise, for as has been said by Dean Griswold (*Renvoi Revisited, op. cit. supra,* p. 1190): "Recognition of the foreign conflict of laws rule will not lead us into an endless chain of references if it is clear for any reason that the particular foreign conflicts rule (or any rule along the line of reference) is one which refers to the internal law alone. . . ."

The precise question here considered, namely whether there shall be a reference to the entire law of the situs to determine the ownership of the proceeds of foreign realty, is one of first impression in this State. Nevertheless, the above stated principles, together with the rule enunciated in the Restatement of the Conflict of Laws, in the English authorities on the subject and in analogous cases in courts of this State and others, require us to accept it as a part of our law and to hold that a reference to the law of the situs necessarily entails a reference to the whole law of that country, including its conflict of laws rules.

The rule as formulated in the Restatement is as follows: "§ 8. *Rule in questions of title to land or divorce.* (1) All questions of title to land are decided in accordance with the law of the state where the land is, including the Conflict of Laws rules of that state. (2) All questions concerning the validity of a decree of divorce are decided in accordance with the law of the domicile of the parties, including the Conflict of Laws rules of that state." In all other cases the Restatement rejects the *renvoi* principle and provides that where a reference is made to foreign law that law should be held to mean only the internal law of the foreign country (Restatement, § 7; cf. note, *A Distinction in the Renvoi Doctrine,* 35 Harv. L. Rev. 454).

The English rule as to *renvoi* in the field of immovables has been established and defined in two leading decisions (*Matter of Baines,* unreported, stated in Dicey on Conflict of Laws [5th ed.], p. 877 and *Matter of Ross* [1930], 1 Ch. 377; see, also, *Matter of Askew* [1930], 2 Ch. 259). In both cases the English courts were confronted with the precise question here involved. In the *Baines* case (*supra*) the decedent, an English national died leaving land in Egypt which was sold subsequent to his death and the proceeds transmitted to England. The will, although valid under English law, would have been invalid under the local law of Egypt. However, under the Egyptian conflict of law rules the succession to land is governed by the internal law of the country of which the decedent was a national. Accordingly, the will was upheld.

Similarly, in the *Ross* case (*supra*) a question arose concerning title to an Italian estate which the testatrix had owned at her death. A claim was made by her son, similar to that interposed in this case, that he was entitled to a "legitima portio" under local Italian law, which right, it was asserted, should attach to the proceeds of a sale of the land. In answer to this contention, the court declared (p. 405) that the "lex situs must . . . be construed in the way the Courts of the country where the immovables are situate would themselves determine. On this basis, the expert evidence is clear that the Italian Courts would decide the succession to the immovable property in the same manner as the English Court would determine it if the immovable property in question belonged to an Englishman and was situate in England." In both of these cases, the courts employed the law which would have been enforced in the courts of the situs. . . .

The decisions in this State also indicate the applicability of the doctrine of *renvoi* in this field.

. . .

Thus it is now necessary to ascertain the whole of the applicable Swiss law and apply it to this case. However, the court's attention has been first called to the Swiss-American Treaty of 1850 (proclaimed Nov. 9, 1855; 2 Malloy Treaties, p. 1763), and particularly to articles V and VI thereof.ᶜ From a reading of those articles, the court concludes that the said treaty does not require a different procedure or reference than that heretofore outlined, and does not itself provide a basis for determining the descent and distribution of the property here involved.

. . .

The treaty merely directs, as does the common law of this State, that initially a reference must be made to the laws of the situs. But the conflict of laws rules and the rules concerning the rights and privileges of foreign nationals and domiciliaries are as much a part of the "laws" of the situs as are its internal laws, as noted above.

Concerning the actual content of Swiss law, the expert witnesses summoned by the respective parties are in agreement that the Swiss internal law would apply to the real and personal estate of a Swiss citizen domiciled in Switzerland, and that the laws of the country of domicile would, under the Swiss theory of unity of succession, apply to all of the Swiss property belonging to a foreign national.

The experts disagreed, however, upon the ultimate question in this case, i.e., the Swiss rule applicable to the distribution of the Swiss realty of a person of *hybrid* nationality domiciled not in Switzerland but in the country of his second citizenship. Under Swiss law the decedent herein was vested with dual nationality. The law of that country provides that a citizen, in order to divest himself of the cloak of citizenship must formally renounce his allegiance in the manner prescribed by statute. Such formal act of renunciation was not performed by the decedent. The

---

ᶜ Articles V and VI read as follows:

ARTICLE V.

The citizens of each one of the contracting parties shall have power to dispose of their personal property within the jurisdiction of the other, by sale, testament, donation, or in any other manner; and their heirs, whether by testament or ab intestato, or their successors, being citizens of the other party, shall succeed to the said property, or inherit it, and they may take possession thereof, either by themselves or by others acting for them; they may dispose of the same as they may think proper, paying no other charges than those to which the inhabitants of the country wherein the said property is situated shall be liable to pay in a similar case. In the absence of such heir, heirs, or other successors, the same care shall be taken by the authorities for the preservation of the property that would be taken for the preservation of the property of a native of the same country, until the lawful proprietor shall have had time to take measures for posessing himself of the same.

The foregoing provisions shall be applicable to real estate situated within the States of the American Union, or within the Cantons of the Swiss Confederation, in which foreigners shall be entitled to hold or inherit real estate.

But in case real estate situated within the territories of one of the contracting parties should fall to a citizen of the other party, who, on account of his being an alien, could not be permitted to hold such property in the State or in the Canton in which it may be situated, there shall be accorded to the said heir, or other successor, such term as the laws of State or Canton will permit to sell such property; he shall be at liberty at all times to withdraw and export the proceeds thereof without difficulty, and without paying to the Government any other charges than those which in a similar case would be paid by an inhabitant of the country in which the real estate may be situated.

ARTICLE VI.

Any controversy that may arise among the claimants to the same succession, as to whom the property shall belong, shall be decided according to the laws and by the judges of the country in which the property is situated.

assumption of a new allegiance by naturalization in the United States did not of itself suffice to free him of fealty to Switzerland. In such event, he became a person of twin or dual citizenship, a status which is recognized under Swiss law. . . .

The court has carefully examined the authorities and materials submitted by the experts and has formed its conclusion upon the basis of those authorities. None of the cases submitted involved the precise facts here presented. They rather present guides, signs and close analogies. From these indicia, however, the court concludes that the Swiss law would refer a matter such as this to the New York internal law, under which law the will is a valid disposition of the testator's property. The testamentary power of this decedent would not be curtailed by the *legitime.*

The language in the Swiss cases, most of which pertain only to the question of the jurisdiction of courts, indicated that the place in which "property is situated," as referred to in the treaty, means, in the case of foreign domiciliaries, the country of domicile, upon the Swiss legal fiction that a decedent's entire estate follows his person and is located at his domicile. Such a rule amounts to a statement that the place of *actual* location of property (Switzerland) refers all questions to the law of the place of *presumed* location, i.e., the country of domicile. The Swiss courts treat the reference to its own law as a reference to its own conflict of law rules and policies concerning the devolution of estates of foreigners.

In the case of one who is of both Swiss and American nationality, but who is not a Swiss domiciliary, it appears that the same rule applies; domicile is controlling and its laws provide the substantive rules of decision.

. . .

Consequently, the court holds that the testamentary plan envisaged by the testator and set out in his will is valid, even in its application to the Swiss realty. The proceeds of that realty must therefore be distributed pursuant to the directions contained in the will.

. . .

[B] Characterization

HAUMSCHILD v. CONTINENTAL CASUALTY COMPANY

Wisconsin Supreme Court
7 Wisc. 2d 130, 95 N.W. 2d 814 (1959)

Action by the plaintiff Jacquelyn Haumschild against the defendants Le Roy Gleason, Continental Casualty Company, and others to recover damages for personal injuries sustained as a result of a motor vehicle accident.

The plaintiff and Gleason were married in Lincoln county, Wisconsin, on November 17, 1956, and lived together as wife and husband until some time in March, 1957. . . .

At all times material to the instant action for personal injuries both the plaintiff and Gleason have had their domicile in Wisconsin.

On December 19, 1956, the plaintiff was injured while riding in a motor truck being driven by Gleason. . . .

Such accident occurred in California, and the instant action is the outgrowth of such accident.

The defendants moved for summary judgment dismissing the action on the grounds that under California law one spouse is immune from suit in tort by the other spouse. . . . The circuit court granted defendants' motion and judgment was entered on August 26, 1958, dismissing the action. The plaintiff has appealed therefrom.

CURRIE, J. This appeal presents a conflict-of-laws problem with respect to interspousal liability for tort growing out of an automobile accident. Which law controls, that of the state of the forum, the state of the place of wrong, or the state of domicile? Wisconsin is both the state of the forum and of the domicile while California is the state where the alleged wrong was committed. Under Wisconsin law a wife may sue her husband in tort. Under California law she cannot.[d]

This court was first faced with this question in *Buckeye v. Buckeye* (1931), 203 Wis. 248, 234 N. W. 342. In that case Wisconsin was the state of the forum and domicile, while Illinois was the state of the place of wrong. It was there held that the law governing the creation and extent of tort liability is that of the place where the tort was committed, citing Goodrich, *Conflict of Laws* (1st ed.), p. 188, sec. 92. From this premise it was further held that interspousal immunity from tort liability necessarily is governed by the law of the place of injury. This principle of conflict of laws has been consistently applied in all subsequent interspousal actions in automobile accident cases. . . .

The principle enunciated in the *Buckeye Case* and followed in subsequent Wisconsin cases, that the law of the place of wrong controls as to whether one spouse is immune from suit in tort by the other, is the prevailing view in the majority of jurisdictions in this country. Anno. 22 A. L. R. (2d) 1248, 1251–1253, entitled, *Conflict of laws as to right of action between husband and wife or parent and child.* It is also the rule adopted in Restatement, Conflict of Laws, p. 457, sec. 378, and p. 470, sec. 384 (2). However, criticism of the rule of the *Buckeye Case,* by legal writers, some of them recognized authorities in the field of conflict of laws, and recent decisions by the courts of California, New Jersey, and Pennsylvania, have caused us to re-examine the question afresh.

In 1942, Prof. Walter Wheeler Cook of the Northwestern University Law School faculty published his book entitled, *The Logical and Legal Bases of the Conflict of Laws.* It was his conclusion that the law of the domicile, and not the place of wrong, should be applied in determining whether a wife had capacity to sue her husband in tort. Pages 248 to 250 and 345 to 346 of text. Also, in 1942, Max Rheinstein in an article in 41 Michigan Law Review, 83, 97, advocated that the law of domicile should be applied in conflict-of-laws situations to determine whether there is an immunity for tort grounded on family relationship. Ernst Rabel, in his *The Conflict of Laws: A Comparative Study* (1945), pp. 322, 323, pointed out that in the civil-law countries of western Europe prohibitions, which exclude lawsuits in tort between husband and wife, are considered part of family law and, therefore, the law of the domicile governs and not the law of the place of wrong.

The most-comprehensive treatment of the problem that we have discovered is the excellent 30-page article in 15 University of Pittsburgh Law Review, 397, entitled, *Interspousal Liability for Automobile Accidents in the Conflict of Laws: Law and Reason versus the Restatement,* by Alan W. Ford, published in 1954. The article contains a careful analysis of the American cases

---

[d] The reason was that under California law as it read at the time, recovery by the wife would have been community property (i.e., with an undivided half interest in the husband) and to permit recovery would have meant permitting the husband to benefit from his wrong.

on the subject commencing with our own *Buckeye Case*. The author's conclusion is stated as follows (p. 423):

> "The *lex fori* and the *lex loci delicti* rules have already been criticized as inadequate. Between them, these two rules encompass all of the American cases. To find a more-desirable alternative we must, therefore, go beyond those cases. The foreign experience, briefly discussed above, is a useful starting point. As that experience suggests, there is some logic in separating questions of status and tort, in determining the incidents of the marital relationship by the family law, and the problems of tort by the law of torts. If a conflicts problem is involved, there is no reason why both questions should be determined by the law of torts. Instead, the two questions should remain separate, and problems of status or capacity could be referred, by an appropriate conflicts rule, to the law of the place of the domicile."

Ford, in his article, cited four cases of interspousal immunity in which American courts have refused to apply the law of the place of wrong to an automobile accident situation but instead applied their own law of the forum. In all four cases one spouse sued the other in the state of domicile where there existed the immunity from suit in tort in a situation where the accident had occurred in a state which had abolished the immunity. The decisions were based on the ground that the public policy of the forum state forbade one spouse suing the other in tort.[2] The holdings in these four cases are highly significant because they are inconsistent in result with the theory that the injured spouse possessed a vested right in the cause of action which had accrued in the state where the alleged negligence occurred. Furthermore, these cases are authority for the principle that public policy may be a controlling factor to be considered by the court of the forum state in determining which law it will apply in resolving a conflict-of-laws problem. This factor of public policy is also acknowledged in Restatement, Conflict of Laws, pp. 9, 10, sec. 5, comment *b*.

The first case to break the ice and flatly hold that the law of domicile should be applied in determining whether there existed an immunity from suit for tort based upon family relationship is *Emery v. Emery* (1955), 45 Cal. (2d) 421, 289 Pac. (2d) 218.

. . .

[In that case two California children sued their brother and father in California for injuries arising out of an auto accident in Idaho. California law was held to apply, barring the action.]

Since the decision in *Emery v. Emery, supra,* two other courts have held that, when a court is confronted with a conflict-of-laws problem in order to resolve an issue of whether there is an immunity from suit for tort based upon a family relationship, the law to be applied is that of the domicile state.

. . .

The two reasons most often advanced for the common-law rule, that one spouse may not sue the other, are the ancient concept that husband and wife constitute in law but one person, and that to permit such suits will be to foment family discord and strife. The Married Women's Acts

---

[2] Conversely, after New York had abolished the immunity, it refused to hold that it offended the public policy of the forum state to apply the law of the state of wrong and deny recovery where the state in which the accident occurred still preserved the immunity. *Coster v. Coster* (1943), 289 N. Y. 438, 46 N. E. (2d) 509, 146 A. L. R. 702, rehearing denied, 290 N. Y. 662, 49 N. E. (2d) 621.

of the various states have effectively destroyed the "one person" concept thereby leaving as the other remaining reason for the immunity the objective of preventing family discord. . . .

Clearly this policy reason for denying the capacity to sue more properly lies within the sphere of family law, where domicile usually controls the law to be applied, than it does tort law, where the place of injury generally determines the substantive law which will govern. . . .

We are convinced that, from both the standpoint of public policy and logic, the proper solution of the conflict-of-laws problem, in cases similar to the instant action, is to hold that the law of the domicile is the one that ought to be applied in determining any issue of incapacity to sue based upon family relationship.

However, in order to adopt such a conflict-of-laws rule it will be necessary to overrule at least six prior decisions of this court, and to partially overrule two others. If it ever is proper for a court to depart from *stare decisis,* we scarcely can perceive of a more-justifiable situation in which to do so. In the first place, the rule being discarded is one lying in the field of conflict of laws as applied to torts so that there can hardly have been any action taken by the parties in reliance upon it. Secondly, strong reasons of public policy exist for supplanting such rule by a better one which does not unnecessarily discriminate against the citizens of our own state.

The most-compelling argument against taking such step is that it departs from the rule of the Restatement, and disturbs the sought-after ideal of establishing some uniformity in the conflict-of-laws field. However, as well appears from the cases hereinbefore cited, there is a clearly discernible trend away from the rule of the Restatement in so far as it requires that the law of the place of wrong is to be applied in determining questions of incapacity to sue based on family status. Furthermore, it must be recognized that, in the field of the conflict of laws, absolutes should not be made the goal at the sacrifice of progress in furtherance of sound public policy. The American Law Institute is now engaged in redrafting a revised Restatement of Conflict of Laws. In such work of revision the question of whether the law of the domicile, rather than the law of the place of wrong, should be applied, in resolving an issue of interfamily immunity from suit in tort, will undoubtedly receive consideration.[e]

After most careful deliberation, it is our considered judgment that this court should adopt the rule that, whenever the courts of this state are confronted with a conflict-of-laws problem as to which law governs the capacity of one spouse to sue the other in tort, the law to be applied is that of the state of domicile. We, therefore, expressly overrule the cases of *Buckeye v. Buckeye, supra;* [as well as five other decisions of the Supreme Court of Wisconsin] . . . .

It is interesting to note that, if the rule now adopted had been applied in the first six cited overruled automobile accident cases, the result in four of such cases would have been to hold that there was no interspousal immunity from suit, because the parties were domiciled in Wisconsin. Only in [two of the cases] would immunity from suit have been found to exist if the law of the domicile, as interpreted by this court, had been applied to such issue.

The *Forbes Case*[f] is the only one of the eight where the place of wrong was Wisconsin. The parties were nonresidents domiciled in Illinois. For the reasons hereinbefore set forth, it is apparent that Illinois rather than Wisconsin was the state most concerned with the policy

---

[e] In fact, the *Restatement (Second) of Conflict of Laws,* published in 1971, said that the law applicable to immunity from tort liability to another member of defendant's family "will usually be the local law of the state of the parties' domicile." § 169.

[f] *Forbes v. Forbes,* 226 Wis. 477, 277 N.W. 112 (1938).

considerations of whether the plaintiff wife had capacity to sue her husband. Furthermore, the plaintiff in the *Forbes Case* would not have fared worse in Wisconsin than she would have in the state of domicile.

. . .

Perhaps a word of caution should be sounded to the effect that the instant decision should not be interpreted as a rejection by this court of the general rule that ordinarily the substantive rights of parties to an action in tort are to be determined in the light of the law of the place of wrong. This decision merely holds that incapacity to sue because of marital status presents a question of family law rather than tort law.

. . .

The concurring opinion by Mr. Justice Fairchild protests that we should not adopt the conflict-of-laws rule, that interspousal immunity to suit in tort should be determined by the law of the domicile, because this was not urged in the briefs or arguments of counsel. . . .

While the appellant's counsel did not request that we overrule *Buckeye v. Buckeye, supra,* and the subsequent Wisconsin cases dealing with this particular conflict-of-laws problem, he did specifically seek to have this court apply California's conflict-of-laws principle, that the law of the domicile is determinative of interspousal capacity to sue, to this particular case. However, to do so would violate the well-recognized principle of conflict of laws that, where the substantive law of another state is applied, there necessarily must be excluded such foreign state's law of conflict of laws. Restatement, Conflict of Laws, p. 11, sec. 7 (b); 11 Am. Jur., *Conflict of Laws,* p. 296, sec. 3; 15 C. J. S., *Conflict of Laws,* p. 872, sec. 7; Griswold, *Renvoi Revisited,* 51 Harvard Law Review, 1165, 1170, 1173;[4] and note in 18 George Washington Law Review, 559.

The reason why the authorities on conflict of laws almost universally reject the renvoi doctrine (permitting a court of the forum state to apply the conflict-of-laws principle of a foreign state) is that it is likely to result in the court pursuing a course equivalent to a never-ending circle. For example, in the instant case, if the *Buckeye v. Buckeye* line of Wisconsin cases is to be followed, the Wisconsin court first looks to the law of California to see whether a wife can sue her husband in tort. California substantive law holds that she cannot. However, California has adopted a conflict-of-laws principle that holds that the law of the domicile determines such question. Applying such principle the court is referred back to Wisconsin law because Wisconsin is the state of domicile. Again the court applies Wisconsin law and, under the prior holdings of the *Buckeye v. Buckeye* line of authorities, would have to again refer to California law because such line of cases does not recognize that the law of domicile has anything to do with interspousal immunity, but holds that the law of the state of injury controls.

Wisconsin certainly should not adopt the much-criticized renvoi principle in order not to overrule the *Buckeye v. Buckeye* line of cases, and still permit the plaintiff to recover. Such a result we believe would contribute far more to produce chaos in the field of conflict of laws than to overrule the *Buckeye v. Buckeye* line of cases and adopt a principle the soundness of which has been commended by so many reputable authorities.

---

[4] While Griswold in such article written in 1938 himself advocates the application of the renvoi doctrine in a case like the instant one, he concedes that the overwhelming weight of authority is contra. Cook, in his *The Logical and Legal Bases of the Conflict of Laws,* pp. 248–250, expressly rejects Griswold's proposed solution and recommends instead the adoption of the conflict-of-laws principle that the law of the domicile should be applied in the first instance to a question of interspousal immunity to suit in tort.

By the Court.—Judgment reversed, and cause remanded for further proceedings not inconsistent with this opinion.

FAIRCHILD, J. (*concurring*). I concur in the reversal of the judgment, but do not find it necessary to reexamine settled Wisconsin law in order to do so. A fundamental change in the law of Wisconsin such as the one announced by the majority in this case, which will importantly affect many people, should be made, if at all, in a case where the question is necessarily presented. Both parties assumed that their case would be decided under the principle which is being overturned by the majority, and accordingly, we have not had the benefit of brief or argument upon the validity of the principle.

1. *Solution of this case without overruling previous decisions.* Plaintiff wife alleges a personal injury tort cause of action arising in California against defendant husband. Defendant husband pleads that she has no cause of action because she was his wife. It has been the rule in Wisconsin that the existence or nonexistence of immunity because of family relationship is substantive and not merely procedural, and is to be determined by the law of the locus state. The law of California is that the existence or nonexistence of immunity is a substantive matter, but that it is an element of the law of status, not of tort. The tort law of California is no more concerned with immunity than is Wisconsin's. Thus it makes no difference under the facts of this case whether we look directly to the law of Wisconsin to determine that immunity is not available as a defense or look to the law of Wisconsin only because California, having no general tort principle as to immunity, classifies immunity as a matter of status.

2. *Policy questions requiring full consideration.* Under the principle announced by the majority that the existence or nonexistence of immunity is a matter of status, our courts must henceforth recognize immunity as a defense where the alleged tort occurred in Wisconsin, but the parties are married and are domiciled in an immunity state. This would mean that such an act is or is not a remedial wrong depending upon the state where the parties happen to be domiciled.

The determination of domicile is not always easy, yet the courts will henceforth be required to determine it in many cases where it has heretofore been considered immaterial. A good many married couples who may have domicile in other states are in Wisconsin for extended periods. Some, for example, are students at colleges and universities, some stationed here for military duty, some temporarily assigned here by employers, and some vacationing. Under the rule abandoned by the majority, a tortious act done in Wisconsin by a nonresident and injuring his spouse gave rise to the same civil liability as if done by a permanent resident.

The problem involved apparently has its principal impact because of injuries sustained in automobile accidents where members of a family travel together across state lines. Under the new rule Wisconsin courts will not countenance the defense of immunity for a Wisconsin husband when sued by his wife for an injury occurring in an immunity state. I concede there is some merit to the logic relied upon and that there may be some practical benefit to Wisconsin people. It is to be remembered, however, that under the law of many states a wife will have no cause of action for simple negligence of her husband because she will be a gratuitous guest. The fact that she and her husband are domiciled in Wisconsin and that they are on a family trip which began in Wisconsin will not exempt her from that principle of tort law. Thus the purely practical benefit to Wisconsin people which might appear at first blush to arise from the new rule will be limited.

. . .

I would dispose of the present case upon the theory that California law governs the existence of the alleged cause of action and that in California the immunity question cannot be decided by resort to the law of torts but rather the law of status. I would leave to a later case the consideration of whether the Wisconsin rule of choice of law as to the defense of family immunity should remain as heretofore or, if it is to be changed, which rule will be best.

I am authorized to state that MR. JUSTICE BROWN concurs in this opinion.

MERTZ v. MERTZ

New York Court of Appeals
271 N.Y. 466, 3 N.E.2d 597 (1936)

LEHMAN, J. The plaintiff has brought an action in this State against her husband to recover damages for personal injuries which, she alleges, she sustained in the State of Connecticut through her husband's negligent operation of an automobile, owned and controlled by him. Under the law of New York the rule is well established that a husband is not liable to his wife for personal injuries caused by his negligence. (*Schultz v. Schultz,* 89 N. Y. 644; *Allen v. Allen,* 246 N. Y. 571.) The complaint alleges that under the law of the State of Connecticut a husband is liable for such injuries. The parties are residents of the State of New York. The problem presented upon this appeal is whether a wife residing here may resort to the courts of this State to enforce liability for a wrong committed outside of the State, though under the laws of this State a husband is immune from such liability.

"A trespass, negligent or willful, upon the person of a wife, does not cease to be an unlawful act though the law exempts the husband from liability for the damage." The immunity of the husband is based upon the common law doctrine of the merger of the beings of husband and wife in the unity of marriage. Each spouse is disabled under our law from maintaining an action against the other for personal injuries. (*Schubert v. Schubert Wagon Co.,* 249 N. Y. 253, 256.) We are told that the rule "exists merely as a product of judicial interpretation, is vestigial in character, and embodies no tenable policy of morals or social welfare." That is a strong indictment of the existing law, and if true calls for change in the law. In spite of such arguments, this court has held that the rule of law exists by tradition and authority, and change, if any, must be made by the Legislature. "We are not at liberty to extend it by dubious construction." (*Schubert v. Schubert Wagon Co., supra,* p. 258.) It is equally true that we are not at liberty to disregard it as long as it remains part of the law of the State.

The Legislature of Connecticut has chosen to remove the common law disability. There a wife may maintain an action against her husband for damages caused by his wrong and no exception has been engrafted there upon the general rule that "illegality established, liability ensues." The sovereign power of each State is coterminous with its territorial limits. Its law alone determines what acts may be performed there with impunity and from what acts liability enforceable in its courts shall flow. The law of one State has in other jurisdictions such force only as is lent to it by the law of such jurisdiction. A cause of action for personal injuries is transitory. Liability follows the person and may be enforced wherever the person may be found. None the less, a cause of action arising in one State may be enforced in another State only by the use of remedies afforded by the law of the forum where enforcement is sought. The courts of the State of New

York are not concerned with the wisdom of the law of Connecticut or of the internal policy back of that law. They must enforce a transitory cause of action arising elsewhere, unless enforcement is contrary to the law of this State. So we have said, "The courts are not free to refuse to enforce a foreign right at the pleasure of the judges, to suit the individual notion of expediency or fairness. They do not close their doors unless help would violate some fundamental principle of justice, some prevalent conception of good morals, some deep-rooted tradition of the common weal." (*Loucks v. Standard Oil Co.,* [p. 37, *supra.*]) (Cf. American Law Institute, Restatement of the Law of Conflict of Laws, § 612.)

In that case the administrator of a resident of this State who was killed in Massachusetts sued here to recover the damages caused by his death. In Massachusetts, as in New York, statutes have created a cause of action for death caused by wrongful act. The remedies are not in all respects alike. In Massachusetts there are limitations upon a recovery which are not contained in the New York statute. Nevertheless in each State the statute provides a remedy through suit by the administrator and no public policy to be found in the "Constitution, the statutes or judicial records" of this State, no "fundamental principle of justice," no "prevalent conception of good morals" or "deep-rooted tradition of the common weal" precluded the administrator from enforcing, in our courts, by the remedy available under our law, the cause of action arising in Massachusetts for wrong committed there. This court then held only that in such case the courts may not read into the law a limitation created by a supposed public policy, founded on its own notion of expediency and justice. It did not hold that the courts might disregard a limitation, contained in the law of the State, established by authority and tradition, because the court could not discern a sound public policy back of the law.

The law of the forum determines the jurisdiction of the courts, the capacity of parties to sue or to be sued, the remedies which are available to suitors and the procedure of the courts. Where a party seeks in this State enforcement of a cause of action created by foreign law, he can avail himself only of the remedies provided by our law, and is subject to the general limitations which are part of our law. So we pointed out in *Loucks v. Standard Oil Co.* (*supra*) and the same rule is generally applied in all other jurisdictions. "If no form of action is provided by the law of a State for the enforcement of a particular foreign right, no action to enforce that right can be maintained in the State." (Restatement of Law of Conflict of Laws, § 608.) Our courts are not concerned with the internal policy of the State which created the cause of action. They are concerned solely with the law of this State which determines the jurisdiction of its courts and the remedies that may be accorded here. The law of this State attaches to the marriage status a reciprocal disability which precludes a suit by one spouse against the other for personal injuries. It recognizes the wrong but denies remedy for such wrong by attaching to the person of the spouse a disability to sue. No other State can, outside of its own territorial limits, remove that disability or provide by its law a remedy available in our courts which our law denies to other suitors. So we said in *Herzog v. Stern* (264 N. Y. 379). A disability to sue which arises solely from the marital status and which has no relation to a definition of wrong or the quality of an act from which liability would otherwise spring, may perhaps be an anachronistic survival of a common law rule. Even then, the courts should not transform an anachrony into an anomaly, and a disability to sue attached by our law to the person of a wife becomes an anomaly if another State can confer upon a wife, even though residing here, capacity to sue in our courts upon a cause of action arising there.

The judgment should be affirmed, with costs.

CROUCH, J. (dissenting). The plaintiff and defendant, residents of New York, are wife and husband. The action is for personal injuries sustained, through the defendant's gross negligence, by the plaintiff in Connecticut while a passenger in defendant's automobile. The complaint alleges that by the law of Connecticut a wife, under such circumstances, may maintain an action against a husband. The Appellate Division affirmed a judgment dismissing the complaint for insufficiency and lack of jurisdiction. It was held that "the cause of action asserted offends our public policy to so great an extent that the court is without jurisdiction to entertain it."

Without pausing to inquire whether the word "jurisdiction" was accurately used, we accept it as a convenient symbol applying to a refusal to enforce a claim created by a foreign law. In approaching the question whether the refusal was justified, certain general principles may be dogmatically stated. The cause of action rests primarily upon the law of Connecticut. If we entertain it, whether we say we are enforcing the original foreign law or a copy of it incorporated in our own rule of conflicts, is immaterial as a practical matter. It is not penal; it is transitory; and our courts will enforce it according to the substantive law of Connecticut unless it "is contrary to the strong public policy" of our own State. (Restatement of Law of Conflict of Laws, § 612). We are left, then, to determine whether the law of Connecticut, which permits a wife to sue a husband for personal injuries, is contrary to some strong public policy of New York.

It may be freely conceded that back of the New York rule which withholds from the wife the right to sue the husband for personal injuries is a public policy of the kind which is back of every other rule of law. But neither in the history of the rule nor in its operation is there anything to indicate that that policy is founded upon a definite view—or even upon some vague feeling—that justice or the public welfare would be affected by a contrary rule. . . . [T]he rule exists merely as a product of judicial interpretation, is vestigial in character, and embodies no tenable policy of morals or of social welfare. To urge that it survives because it is an aid to conjugal peace disregards reality. Conjugal peace would be as seriously jarred by an action for breach of contract, or on a promissory note, or for an injury to property, real or personal, all of which the law permits, as by one for personal injury. In short, even though we assume that there is some shadowy element of policy back of the rule, it should give way to "the controlling public policy . . . that the courts of each State shall give effect to all valid causes of action created by the laws of another State except possibly in extreme cases." (Hubbs, J., in *Herzog v. Sern,* 264 N. Y. 379, 387; cf. Restatement of Law of Conflict of Laws, § 612, comment (c); 44 Yale Law Journal, 158.)

The judgment should be reversed, with costs in all courts.

Judgment affirmed

LEVY v. DANIELS' U-DRIVE AUTO RENTING CO.

Connecticut Supreme Court
108 Conn. 333, 143 A. 163 (1928)

WHEELER, C. J. The complaint alleged these facts: The defendant, the Daniels' U-Drive Auto Renting Company, Incorporated, rented in Hartford to Sack an automobile which he operated and in which Levy, the plaintiff, was a passenger. During the time the automobile was rented and operated, the defendant renting company was subject to § 21 of Chapter 195 of the Public Acts of Connecticut (1925) which provides: "Any person renting or leasing to another any motor vehicle owned by him shall be liable for any damage to any person or property caused by the operation of such motor vehicle while so rented or leased." While the plaintiff was a passenger Sack brought the car to a stop on the main highway at Longmeadow, Massachusetts, and negligently allowed it to stand directly in the path of automobiles proceeding southerly in the same direction his automobile was headed, without giving sufficient warning to automobiles approaching from his rear, and without having a tail light in operation, and when, due to inclement weather, the visibility was reduced to an exceedingly low degree. At this time the defendant Meginn negligently ran into and upon the rear end of the car Sack was operating and threw plaintiff forcibly forward causing him serious injuries. The specific acts of Meginn's negligence are set up at length in the complaint; it is not essential at this time to recite them. The plaintiff suffered his severe injuries in consequence of the concurrent negligence of both defendants.

The defendant demurred to the complaint upon several grounds, upon only one of which the trial court rested its decision, namely, that the liability of the defendant must be determined by the law of Massachusetts which did not impose upon persons renting automobiles any such obligation as the Connecticut Act did. . . .

It is the defendant's contention in support of this ground of demurrer that the action set forth in the complaint is one of tort and since Massachusetts has no statute like, or substantially like, the Connecticut Act it must be determined by the common law of that State, under which the plaintiff must prove, to prevail, the negligence of the defendant in renting a defective motor vehicle and in failing to disclose the defect. If this were the true theory of the complaint, the conclusion thus reached must have followed. "The *locus delicti* determined the existence of the cause of action. . . ."

Under the law of Massachusetts the plaintiff, concededly, would have a cause of action against Sack and Meginn for their tortious conduct in the operation of the cars they were driving. The plaintiff concedes the correctness of this. His counsel, however, construe the complaint as one in its nature contractual. The Act makes him who rents or leases any motor vehicle to another liable for any damage to any person or property caused by the operation of the motor vehicle while so rented or leased. Liability for "damage . . . caused by the operation of such motor vehicle" means caused by its tortious operation. This was undoubtedly the legislative intent, otherwise the Act would be invalid. The plaintiff concedes this to be the true construction of these words and the defendant acquiesces in this construction.

The complaint alleges a tortious operation of the automobile rented to Sack by the defendant causing the injuries to the plaintiff as alleged and constituting an action *ex delicto*. The statute gives, in terms, the injured person a right of action against the defendant which rented the automobile to Sack, though the injury occurred in Massachusetts. It was a right which the statute gave directly, not derivatively, to the injured person as a consequence of the contract of hiring.

The purpose of the statute was not primarily to give the injured person a right of recovery against the tortious operator of the car, but to protect the safety of traffic upon highways by providing an incentive to him who rented motor vehicles to rent them to competent and careful operators by making him liable for damage resulting from the tortious operation of the rented vehicles. The common law would not hold the defendant liable upon the facts recited in the complaint for the negligence of Sack in the operation of this automobile. Huddy on Automobiles (8th Ed.) § 200, and cases cited. The rental of motor vehicles to any but competent and careful operators, or to persons of unknown responsibility, would be liable to result in injury to the public upon or near highways, and this imminent danger justified, as a reasonable exercise of the police power, this statute, which requires all who engage in this business to become responsible for any injury inflicted upon the public by the tortious operation of the rented motor vehicle.

. . .

Statutes of this character are so clearly within the reasonable exercise of the police power that we do not deem it necessary to fortify his opinion, or the opinion we have already expressed, by detailed reference to the cases. The statute made the liability of the person renting motor vehicles a part of every contract of hiring of a motor vehicle in Connecticut. A liability *ex delicto* is created by the law of the place of the delict. . . . A liability arising out of a contract depends upon the law of the place of contract "unless the contract is to be performed or to have its beneficial operation and effect elsewhere, or it is made with reference to the law of another place. . . ."

We will enforce rights of action on contracts arising in other jurisdictions unless these contravene our own law, or our own fundamental and important public policy imperatively requires their non-enforcement. . . .

If the liability of this defendant under this statute is contractual, no question can arise as to the plaintiff's right to enforce this contract, provided the obligation imposed upon this defendant was for the "direct, sole and exclusive benefit" of the plaintiff. The contract was made in Connecticut; at the instant of its making the statute made a part of the contract of hiring the liability of the defendant which the plaintiff seeks to enforce. The law inserted in the contract this provision. The statute did not create the liability; it imposed it in case the defendant voluntarily rented the automobile. Whether the defendant entered into this contract of hiring was its own voluntary act; if it did it must accept the condition upon which the law permitted the making of the contract. The contract was for the "direct, sole and exclusive benefit" of the plaintiff, who is alleged to have been injured through the tortious operation of the automobile rented by the defendant to Sack. . . .

The contract was made for him and every other member of the public. That the beneficiary was undetermined because each of the public was a beneficiary is of no consequence. His injury determines his identity and right of action. . . .

The demurrer should have been overruled.

NOTES AND QUESTIONS

(1)(a) Renvoi tends at first view to look like a game—and analogies to tennis, or volleyball, are easily adduced. But in looking at *Annesley, Dater,* and *Schneider,* do you think any of the cases were incorrectly decided?

(b) *Dater* might be thought to yield an unfair result, but only if the married women's disability is thought to be unfair or obsolete. As compared to *Milliken v. Pratt,* the place of contracting is more clearly in the state without the impediment to contracting, yet the interest of the wife is protected, because Illinois would protect it. If the Michigan court looked only to the internal law of Illinois, then suit in Michigan would result in judgment for the Illinois plaintiff, while suit in Illinois would result in judgment for the Michigan defendant. Would that be the better outcome?g

(c) *Schneider* is in some ways like *Barrie,* in that in both cases real property in a state other than the decedent's domicile is at issue. While one cannot be sure what the just outcome in *Barrie* should have been, the actual outcome has to be wrong: either the testratrix revoked her will or the revocation was a forgery; she surely did not intend that the nephews receive some of her property, the church the remainder. In *Schneider,* in contrast, there is unity of succession, i.e., the testator's intent is completely complied with, as would not have been true had Swiss internal law been followed with regard to the property located at his death in Switzerland.

(2)(a) The difference between *Dater* and *Schneider* on the one hand and *Annesley* on the other is that in *Annesley* not only the forum but the first state of reference engaged in renvoi. Accordingly, what looked like a useful device for Miss Annesley to overcome the argument that her mother really was domiciled in France boomeranged. But that was only another way of saying that in these circumstances France would apply its own law. There is no reason why the reference back and forth should go on indefinitely.

(b) The cases here reproduced suggest the image of mirrors or tennis balls, because the first state of reference looks "back" to the law of the forum state ("remission renvoi"). The technique of renvoi is available also (indeed with less confusion) when the first state of reference looks to a third state's law. If, for example, Mr. Schneider had died domiciled in France but the proceeds of his real property in Switzerland had (as in the actual case) been brought to New York, the New York court would, it seems, have looked first to the law of the situs (Switzerland) and then been referred by Swiss law to the law of France ("transmission renvoi").

(3) In an important recent article, Professor Larry Kramer undertook to revive renvoi, which had been largely rejected by the Restatement (Second) of Conflict of Laws (1971) and by most writers and commentators.h Kramer argues that if a court of state *A* (the forum state) ignores the choice of law rules of state *B*, application of whose law it is contemplating, it risks misunderstanding the scope and purpose of the law of state *B*.

(a) Kramer gives the example (with several variations) of a bet recorded in a contract executed in Michigan between P, a resident of Michigan, and D, a resident of Illinois. Michigan enforces gambling contracts, Illinois prohibits such contracts as a matter of public policy. P wins the bet, D declines to pay, and P sues D in Michigan. Consider how this case should be decided by the Michigan court.

---

g Dean Griswold, in the article cited in *Schneider* as well as in several later cases, wrote:

It would seem that the majority of the court was correct. Moreover, the observation of a commentator that "having once got on the renvoi merry-go-round, there is no logical reason" why the Michigan court should have stopped at the reference back to Michigan law, seems unsound. The Michigan court never got on a renvoi merry-go-round. It referred to the whole law of Illinois, and having found how the Illinois court would dispose of the case, it did the same. Why should the court have looked only to the internal law of Illinois, and let an Illinois plaintiff succeed in Michigan when it would not have succeeded in Illinois where the contract was made?

Griswold, *Renvoi Revisited,* 51 Harv. L. Rev. 1165, 1208 (1938).

h 66 N.Y.U.L. Rev. 979 (1991).

(b) Kramer writes that in deciding whether to apply Michigan or Illinois law, the Michigan court will be helped by exploring the scope of the Illinois law: if the Illinois law applies only to contracts made in Illinois, there is no real conflict, and the Michigan court can comfortably apply the law of Michigan to enforce the contract. If, on the other hand, Illinois construes its anti-gambling law to apply to all residents of Illinois, there is a true conflict, which will call for further analysis.

(c) Kramer then adds another element: the parties specified in their contract that the law of Michigan would be applicable. Now the Michigan court has to decide whether parties' choice of the applicable law can trump restrictions imposed by law on particular contracts. Again, Kramer invites the reader to consider not only the law of Michigan but the law of Illinois. If the latter, for instance, favors so-called "party autonomy" (see chapter 4, § 4.02 *infra*), the Michigan court ought to feel comfortable in applying Michigan law to uphold the contract, even, it seems, if ordinarily Michigan does not uphold party autonomy in the face of a prohibition. In that case, Illinois law favors upholding the contract because the parties elected Michigan law, and Michigan law favors upholding the contract because gambling is not prohibited. Renvoi has aided the resolution of the problem, by removing the conflict between the two laws.

(4)(a) Renvoi cannot solve all the problems—as going through variations of Professor Kramer's examples will demonstrate. But it can offer (or reinforce) solutions in a number of variations, and can make the analysis more satisfying even in situations in which it does not offer a clear resolution.

(b) The important thing to understand about renvoi, as about the other devices illustrated in this chapter, is that it is not a doctrine, but a technique, designed to avoid the effects of inexorable rules. If there are no inexorable rules, renvoi is generally not necessary.

(c) *Haumschild* illustrates the preceding statement: If the court is prepared, as the majority is here, to discard the inexorable rule that all aspects of a tort action are governed by the law of the place of injury, renvoi is not needed; if like Judge Fairchild, the court is reluctant to overthrow both black letter law and a string of precedents, renvoi offers a useful way to avoid an undesirable result.

(d) In the actual case, the majority and the concurring judge reach the same result. Try to work out when this will be so, and when not. For example, (i) California couple, accident in Wisconsin; (ii) Wisconsin couple, accident in Ohio (a state that would not use California's approach based on status); etc. . . .

(e) Note Judge Fairchild's variation on renvoi: he does not ask about California's choice of law rule, but about how California would characterize its interspousal immunity rule.

(5)(a) In the following two chapters, the first focusing on torts, the second on intentional acts, the inexorable rules will give way, as you will see, to a variety of approaches looking to interests, contacts, and expectations. As you study the developments there illustrated, consider whether, or to what extent, renvoi has a place even in looser systems of choice of law.[j]

---

[j] The EEC Convention of 1980 on the Law Applicable to Contractual Obligations, discussed in §4.02 *infra*, expressly excludes renvoi. See Article 15, Documents Supplement p. 50. The official Report accompanying the Convention (the Giuliano-Lagarde Report) explains that when the parties have made an express choice of law, they must have meant that the substantive provisions of the chosen law should be applied; if the parties did not choose the applicable law, the law to be applied pursuant to the Convention (Article 4) is the law with which the transaction is most closely connected; applying the renvoi, the Report argues, would be inconsistent with the process of finding that law. See Giuliano and Lagarde, *Report on the Convention on the Law Applicable to Contractual Obligations*, 23 O.J. Eur. Comm. No. C 282/37 (31 October 1980).

§ 2.01   CHOICE OF LAW □ 65

(b) In Chapter 6, devoted to diversity of citizenship jurisdiction, renvoi will come back in a somewhat different guise, as federal courts are instructed by *Klaxon v. Stentor Mfg. Co.* to follow the whole law, including the choice of law, of the states in which they sit.

(6) *Mertz* is a mirror image case to *Haumschild,* in that the forum is the state with the immunity rule.

(a) What does the court mean by the statement (p. 59) that New York recognizes the wrong but denies remedy for such wrong? After the case is decided, can Mrs. Mertz bring an action in Connecticut based on the same action?

(b) The lower court, as appears from Judge Church's dissent, held that the cause of action by a wife against a husband "offends our public policy to so great an extent the court is without jurisdiction to entertain it." Judge Lehman is at pains to knock that view down, quoting at length from *Loucks.* But he says to apply the law of the other state would "transform an anachrony into an anomaly." What does that mean?

(c) Would renvoi have helped Mrs. Mertz?

(d) Shortly after the decision in *Mertz,* the New York state legislature adopted Domestic Relations Law § 57[k] (presently General Obligations Law § 3–313) reading in pertinent part as follows:

> A married woman has a right of action against her husband for his wrongful or tortious acts resulting to her in any personal injury, . . . or resulting in injury to her property, as if they were unmarried, and she is liable to her husband for her wrongful or tortious acts resulting in any such personal injury to her husband or to his property, as if they were unmarried.

So much for the notion of conjugal harmony creating immunity. The effect of the change, however, was largely counteracted by an amendment to the New York Insurance Law adopted at the same time:[l]

> No policy or contract of automobile liability insurance shall be deemed to insure against any liability of an insured because of death of or injuries to his or her spouse or because of injury to, or destruction of property of his or her spouse unless express provision relating specifically thereto is included in the policy.

(e) Suppose the events of *Mertz* recur, but the injured New York spouse brings suit in Connecticut. Must the car owner's insurer defend in Connecticut, and pay any judgment based on the driver's negligence? How should a Connecticut court treat this case? Is it a problem of choice of laws in torts? In contracts? Something else?[m]

(f) In *New Amsterdam Casualty Co. v. Stecker,* 3 N.Y.2d 1, 163 N.Y.S.2d 626, 143 N.E.2d 357 (1957), the facts were just as described in the preceding paragraph, except that the insurance

---

[k] New York L. 1937, c. 669, § 1.

[l] New York L. 1937, c. 669, § 2 adding new subd. 3–a to § 109 of the Insurance Law, later contained in § 167(3) and since 1984 in § 3420(g) of that law.

[m] In *Williamson v. Massachusetts Bonding & Insurance Co.,* 142 Conn. 573, 116 A.2d 169 (1955), a New York couple had an automobile accident while driving in Connecticut, and the wife sued the husband in Connecticut for negligence and secured a judgment in her favor. The insurance company declined to pay the judgment, relying on N.Y. Ins. Law § 167(3), and the wife brought suit against the company. The Supreme Court of Connecticut held for the wife, on the ground that § 167(3) was intended only for actions arising out of the New York amendment to its Domestic Relations law, and not for foreign causes of action.

company did not wait for the Connecticut courts to resolve the question, but instead sought a declaratory judgment from the New York courts that (i) it was not required to defend the action in Connecticut; and (ii) it would not be required to pay any judgment that might result from a determination that the wife (who was driving) had negligently caused injury to her husband (the passenger). Should such a declaratory judgment be granted?[n] Would it be binding in Connecticut?

---

§ 2.02 Substance and Procedure

LEVY v. STEIGER

Massachusetts Supreme Judicial Court
233 Mass. 600, 124 N.E. 477 (1919)

TORT for personal injuries received by the plaintiffs when they were riding as guests in a motor vehicle which came into collision with a motor vehicle driven by the defendant at the intersection of Pawtucket Avenue and Waterman Avenue in the town of East Providence in the State of Rhode Island.

In the Superior Court the actions were tried together before *Hammond*, J., who at the request of the plaintiffs ruled that St. 1914, c. 553, was applicable to the cases on trial although the injuries were received in the State of Rhode Island. [The Massachusetts statute, reversing the prior rule, provided that the burden of proof with regard to contributory negligence was on the defendant.]

The jury found for the plaintiff in the first action in the sum of $5,000 and for the plaintiff in the second action in the sum of $2,000; and the defendant alleged exceptions.

DE COURCY, J.

. . .

It is elementary that the law of the place where the injury was received determines whether a right of action exists; and that the law of the place where the action is brought regulates the remedy and its incidents, such as pleading, evidence and practice. . . .

While there may be cases where it is difficult to decide whether a particular enactment relates to procedure or to substantive rights, it was settled in *Duggan v. Bay State Street Railway,* 230 Mass. 370, where its construction and constitutionality were in question, that this "due care"

---

[n] The Court of Appeals said yes:

> To apply the law of Connecticut in determining what the contract of the parties was would be to give extraterritorial effect to the laws of that State, a result which is proscribed by established principles of law. . . .

3 N.Y.2d at 5, 163 N.Y.S.2d at *629,* 143 N.E.2d at *359.* As to the intent of the New York legislature,

> The manifest purpose of subdivision 3 of section 167 was to protect insurance carriers from collusive actions between spouses arising out of automobile accidents. Surely the Legislature recognized that the possibility of fraud and collusion is the same no matter where the accident occurs.
>
> It is that possibility which the statute was intended to guard against, and the language of subdivision 3 of section 167 if literally applied will accomplish that result. There is not the slightest difference in the fraud potential between accidents occurring in New York and those occurring elsewhere.

3 N.Y.2d at 7–8, 163 N.Y.S.2d at 631, 143 N.E.2d at 360.

statute, so called, is one of procedure. As the court expressly said, in construing the statute, with a view to determining its constitutionality (page 377): "These two parts of the statute do not undertake to change the substantive law of negligence in any respect. The tribunal hearing the case must still be satisfied on all the evidence that the plaintiff was in the exercise of due care and did not by his own acts of omission or commission help to produce his injury, and that the defendant was negligent." And again (page 380): "The present statute simply affects procedure and the burden of proof. It does not work any modification of fundamental rights."

Exceptions overruled.

GRANT v. McAULIFFE

California Supreme Court
41 Cal. 2d 859, 264 P.2d 944 (1953)

TRAYNOR, J.

On December 17, 1949, plaintiffs W. R. Grant and R. M. Manchester were riding west on United States Highway 66 in an automobile owned and driven by plaintiff D. O. Jensen. Defendant's decedent, W. W. Pullen, was driving his automobile east on the same highway. The two automobiles collided at a point approximately 15 miles east of Flagstaff, Arizona. Jensen's automobile was badly damaged, and Jensen, Grant, and Manchester suffered personal injuries. Nineteen days later, on January 5, 1950, Pullen died as a result of injuries received in the collision. Defendant McAuliffe was appointed administrator of his estate and letters testamentary were issued by the Superior Court of Plumas County [California]. All three plaintiffs, as well as Pullen, were residents of California at the time of the collision. After the appointment of defendant, each plaintiff presented his claim for damages. Defendant rejected all three claims, and on December 14, 1950, each plaintiff filed an action against the estate of Pullen to recover damages for the injuries caused by the alleged negligence of the decedent. Defendant filed a general demurrer and a motion to abate each of the complaints. The trial court entered an order granting the motion in each case. Each plaintiff has appealed. The appeals are based on the same ground and have therefore been consolidated.

The basic question is whether plaintiffs' causes of action against Pullen survived his death and are maintainable against his estate. The statutes of this state provide that causes of action for negligent torts survive the death of the tort feasor and can be maintained against the administrator or executor of his estate. (Civ. Code, § 956; Code Civ. Proc., § 385; Prob. Code, §§ 573, 574.) Defendant contends, however, that the survival of a cause of action is a matter of substantive law, and that the courts of this state must apply the law of Arizona governing survival of causes of action. There is no provision for survival of causes of action in the statutes of Arizona, although there is a provision that in the event of the death of a party to a pending proceeding his personal representative can be substituted as a party to the action (Arizona Code, 1939, § 21–534), if the cause of action survives. (Arizona Code, 1939, § 21–530.) The Supreme Court of Arizona has held that if a tort action has not been commenced before the death of the tort feasor a plea in abatement must be sustained. (*McClure v. Johnson,* 50 Ariz. 76, 82 [69 P.2d 573]. . . .)

Thus, the answer to the question whether the causes of action against Pullen survived and are maintainable against his estate depends on whether Arizona or California law applies. In actions on torts occurring abroad, the courts of this state determine the substantive matters inherent in the cause of action by adopting as their own the law of the place where the tortious acts occurred, unless it is contrary to the public policy of this state. . . . But the forum does not adopt as its own the procedural law of the place where the tortious acts occur. It must, therefore, be determined whether survival of causes of action is procedural or substantive for conflict of laws purposes.

This question is one of first impression in this state. The precedents in other jurisdictions are conflicting. In many cases it has been held that the survival of a cause of action is a matter of substance and that the law of the place where the tortious acts occurred must be applied to determine the question. . . .

The Restatement of the Conflict of Laws, section 390, is in accord. It should be noted, however, that the majority of the foregoing cases were decided after drafts of the Restatement were first circulated in 1929. Before that time, it appears that the weight of authority was that survival of causes of action is procedural and governed by the domestic law of the forum. . . . Many of the cases, decided both before and after the Restatement, holding that survival is substantive and must be determined by the law of the place where the tortious acts occurred, confused the problems involved in survival of causes of action with those involved in causes of action for wrongful death. . . . A cause of action for wrongful death is statutory. It is a new cause of action vested in the widow or next of kin, and arises on the death of the injured person. Before his death, the injured person himself has a separate and distinct cause of action and, if it survives, the same cause of action can be enforced by the personal representative of the deceased against the tort feasor. The survival statutes do not create a new cause of action, as do the wrongful death statutes. . . . They merely prevent the abatement of the cause of action of the injured person, and provide for its enforcement by or against the personal representative of the deceased. They are analogous to statutes of limitation, which are procedural for conflict of laws purposes and are governed by the domestic law of the forum. (*Biewend v. Biewend,* 17 Cal.2d 108, 114 [109 P. 2d 701, 132 A.L.R. 1264].) Thus, a cause of action arising in another state, by the laws of which an action cannot be maintained thereon because of lapse of time, can be enforced in California by a citizen of this state, if he has held the cause of action from the time it accrued. (Code Civ. Proc., § 361; *Stewart v. Spaulding,* 72 Cal. 264, 266 [13 P. 661].) . . .

Defendant contends, however, that the characterization of survival of causes of action as substantive or procedural is foreclosed by *Cort v. Steen,* 36 Cal.2d 437, 442 [224 P. 2d 723], where it was held that the California survival statutes were substantive and therefore did not apply retroactively. The problem in the present proceeding, however, is not whether the survival statutes apply retroactively, but whether they are substantive or procedural for purposes of conflict of laws. " 'Substance' and 'procedure' . . . are not legal concepts of invariable content" (*Black Diamond Steamship Corp. v. Stewart & Sons,* 336 U.S. 386, 397 [69 S.Ct. 622, 93 L.Ed. 754]. See, also, *Guaranty Trust Co. v. York,* [p. 455, *infra*]; *Sampson v. Channell,* [p. 444, *infra*]; *Estate of Caravas,* 40 Cal.2d 33, 41–42 [250 P. 2d 593]; W. W. Cook, *The Logical and Legal Bases of the Conflict of Laws* (1942), c. 6: "Substance and Procedure"), and a statute or other rule of law will be characterized as substantive or procedural according to the nature of the problem for which a characterization must be made.

Defendant also contends that a distinction must be drawn between survival of causes of action and revival of actions, and that the former are substantive but the latter procedural. On the basis of this distinction, defendant concludes that many of the cases cited above as holding that survival is procedural and is governed by the domestic law of the forum do not support this position, since they involved problems of "revival" rather than "survival." The distinction urged by defendant is not a valid one. Most of the statutes involved in the cases cited provided for the "revival" of a pending proceeding by or against the personal representative of a party thereto should he die while the action is still pending. But in most "revival" statutes, substitution of a personal representative in place of a deceased party is expressly conditioned on the survival of the cause of action itself.[1] If the cause of action dies with the tort feasor, a pending proceeding must be abated. A personal representative cannot be substituted in the place of a deceased party unless the cause of action is still subsisting. In cases where this substitution has occurred, the courts have looked to the domestic law of the forum to determine whether the cause of action survives as well as to determine whether the personal representative can be substituted as a party to the action. . . .

Defendant's contention would require the courts to look to their local statutes to determine "revival" and to the law of the place where the tort occurred to determine "survival," but we have found no case in which this procedure was followed.

Since we find no compelling weight of authority for either alternative, we are free to make a choice on the merits. We have concluded that survival of causes of action should be governed by the law of the forum. Survival is not an essential part of the cause of action itself but relates to the procedures available for the enforcement of the legal claim for damages. Basically the question is one of the administration of decedents' estates, which is a purely local proceeding. The problem here is whether the causes of action that these plaintiffs had against Pullen before his death survive as liabilities of his estate. Section 573 of the Probate Code provides that "all actions founded . . . upon any liability for physical injury, death or injury to property, may be maintained by or against executors and administrators in all cases in which the cause of action . . . is one which would not abate upon the death of their respective testators or intestates. . . ." Civil Code, section 956, provides that "A thing in action arising out of a wrong which results in physical injury to the person . . . shall not abate by reason of the death of the wrongdoer . . . " and causes of action for damage to property are maintainable against executors and administrators under section 574 of the Probate Code. (See *Hunt v. Authier,* 28 Cal.2d 288, 292–296 [169 P. 2d 913, 171 A.L.R. 1379]; *Cort v. Steen, supra,* 36 Cal.2d 437, 439–440.) Decedent's estate is located in this state, and letters of administration were issued to defendant by the courts of this state. The responsibilities of defendant, as administrator of Pullen's estate, for injuries inflicted by Pullen before his death are governed by the laws of this state. This approach has been followed in a number of well-reasoned cases. . . . It retains control of the administration of estates by the local Legislature, and avoids the problems involved in determining the administrator's amenability to suit under the laws of other states. The common law doctrine *actio personalis moritur cum persona* had its origin in a penal concept of tort liability. (See Prosser, *Law of Torts* 950–951; Pollock, *The Law of Torts* (10th ed.) 64, 68.) Today, tort liabilities of the sort involved in these actions are regarded as compensatory. When, as in the present case, all of the parties were residents of this state, and the estate of the deceased tort feasor is being

---

[1] For example, Code Civ. Proc., § 385: "An action or proceeding does not abate by the death, or any disability of a party . . . *if the cause of action survive or continue.*" (Italics added.) See also 28 U.S.C.A., Rule 25(a)(1) [leg. hist., U.S.Rev.Stat., § 955 (1874); Judiciary Act of 1789, § 31]: "If a party dies *and the claim is not thereby extinguished,* the court . . . may order substitution . . ." of the personal representative. (Italics added.) The exact language of Rule 25(a)(1) is repeated in Arizona Code, 1939, § 21–530.

administered in this state, plaintiffs' right to prosecute their causes of action is governed by the laws of this state relating to administration of estates.

The orders granting defendant's motions to abate are reversed, and the causes remanded for further proceedings.

GIBSON, C. J., SHENK, J., and CARTER, J., concurred.

SCHAUER, J.—I dissent. In *Cort v. Steen* (1950), 36 Cal.2d 437, 442 [224 P. 2d 723], this court held that under the doctrine of nonsurvivability the abatement of an action by the death of the injured person through the tort feasor's act or otherwise, or by the death of the tort feasor, abates the wrong as well; that the effect of a survival statute is to create a right or cause of action rather than to either continue an existing right or revive or extend a remedy theretofore accrued for the redress of an existing wrong; and that consequently a survival statute enacted after death of the tort feasor did not apply to the tort or cause of action involved. And more recently, in *Estate of Arbulich* (1953), *ante,* pp. 86, 88–89 [257 P. 2d 433], we recognized the rule that the burden of proof provisions of the Probate Code sections (259 *et seq.*) dealing with reciprocal inheritance rights are not merely procedural in nature, but, rather, are substantive statutes regulating succession, and that consequently such rights are to be determined by the law as it existed on the date of decedent's death. (See, also, *Estate of Giordano* (1948), 85 Cal.App. 2d 588, 592, 594 [193 P. 2d 771].)

Irreconcilably inconsistent with the cases cited in the preceding paragraph, the majority now hold that "Survival is not an essential part of the cause of action itself but relates to the procedures available for the enforcement of the legal claim for damages. Basically the question is one of the administration of decedents' estates, which is a purely local proceeding." If the above stated holding is to prevail, then for the sake of the law's integrity and clarity, and in fairness to lower courts and to counsel, the cited cases should be expressly overruled. But even more regrettable than the failure to either follow or unequivocally overrule the cited cases is the character of the "rule" which is now promulgated: the majority assert that henceforth "a statute or other rule of law will be characterized as substantive or procedural according to the nature of the problem for which a characterization must be made," thus suggesting that the court will no longer be bound to consistent enforcement or uniform application of "a statute or other rule of law" but will instead apply one "rule" or another as the untrammeled whimsy of the majority may from time to time dictate, "according to the nature of the problem" as they view it in a given case. This concept of the majority strikes deeply at what has been our proud boast that ours was a government of laws rather than of men.

Although any administration of an estate in the courts of this state is local in a procedural sense, the rights and claims both in favor of and against such an estate are substantive in nature, and vest irrevocably at the date of death. . . .

Since this court has clearly held that a right or cause of action created by a survival statute is likewise substantive, rather than procedural, we should hold, if we would follow the law, that the trial court properly granted defendant's motions to abate.

SPENCE, J., concurred.

EDMONDS, J.—I concur in the conclusion that the order granting the defendant's motion to abate should be affirmed.

IN RE COHN

United Kingdom Chancery Division
[1945] 1 Ch. 5 (1944)

Mrs. Hedwig Cohn, her late husband, Max Cohn, and their daughter, Mrs. Gerda Oppenheimer, were German nationals and at all material times were domiciled in Germany. By a joint will made on April 10, 1918, in the German language, in Germany, Mrs. Cohn and her husband (who predeceased her) appointed each other their heirs and declared that "after "the death of the survivor of us the entire estate shall pass "in equal shares to our children," Mrs. Oppenheimer, Mrs. Else Freudenthal and Siegfried Cohn. On October 14, 1940, Mrs. Cohn and Mrs. Oppenheimer were killed in London in an air raid as the result of the same explosion. On June 5, 1942, letters of administration with a translation of the will were granted to the Public Trustee. The Public Trustee took out a summons to ascertain (inter alia) whether the succession to the movable property of Mrs. Cohn was to be determined according to English or German law.

UTHWATT J. read a judgment, in which he said: On the evidence I find as a fact that the circumstances in which Mrs. Cohn and Mrs. Oppenheimer were killed were such that it is uncertain and cannot be proved which of them survived the other. The order of these deaths is, and always will be, uncertain. The question arises whether or not Mrs. Cohn's movable property is to be administered on the footing that Mrs. Oppenheimer survived Mrs. Cohn.

There is a difference between the law of England and the law of Germany regarding the presumption which is to be made about the order of the deaths in the circumstances stated. The law of England, by s. 184 of the Law of Property Act, 1925, prescribes that, where two or more persons have died in circumstances rendering it uncertain which of them survived the other or others "such deaths shall (subject to "any order of the court"), for all purposes affecting the title "to the property, be presumed to have occurred in order of "seniority, and accordingly the younger shall be deemed to "have survived the elder." The Civil Code of Germany makes different provision. In the first book of the German Civil Code, headed "General Principles," the first chapter of the first part deals with "Natural Persons." Article 20 contained in that chapter provides that, if several persons perish in a common danger, it is presumed that they have died simultaneously. On July 4, 1939, this was replaced by the following article:—"If it cannot be proved that of several deceased persons or persons declared dead one has survived the other, it is presumed that they have died simultaneously." It may be observed in passing that the date of the widening of the scope of art. 20 effected by the amendment is of interest to the general historian. Under German law Mrs. Oppenheimer can benefit under the will of Mrs. Cohn only if she (Mrs. Oppenheimer) was the survivor of the two.

It was argued by Mr. Danckwerts, on behalf of those interested in Mrs. Oppenheimer's estate, that the first question which the court was called on to ascertain was whether or not Mrs. Oppenheimer survived Mrs. Cohn; that, in ascertaining that fact, the method of proof was determined by the lex fori (the law of England)—a general proposition which cannot be disputed; and that, when once it was shown that it was uncertain which of them survived the other, s. 184 of the Law of Property Act, 1925, came into operation as part of the lex fori compelling the court to draw the inference or proceed on the footing that Mrs. Oppenheimer survived Mrs. Cohn. It was, according to his argument, only after reaching that point, that one turned to the law of the domicile.

In my opinion, this argument is not well founded. The law of the domicile, namely the law of Germany, is alone relevant in determining the effect of the testamentary dispositions of movables made by Mrs. Cohn, the basis on which the movables are to be administered, and the facts which it is necessary to ascertain to administer that estate. If, for instance, under the law of Germany, it was not necessary for the efficacy of the disposition in her favour that Mrs. Oppenheimer should survive Mrs. Cohn, but was only necessary that she should survive either Mr. or Mrs. Cohn, no inquiry as to survivorship such as is here being made would have been necessary. The question of survivorship is, in fact, opened up by the provisions of German law as to inheritance and is formally not: "Did or did not Mrs. Oppenheimer survive Mrs. Cohn?" but "Is the administration of Mrs. Cohn's estate to proceed on the footing that Mrs. Oppenheimer survived Mrs. Cohn or on the footing that she did not?" The purpose to which the inquiry as to survivorship is directed must be kept in mind. The mode of proving any fact bearing on survivorship is determined by the lex fori. The effect of any fact so proved is for the purpose in hand determined by the law of the domicile. The fact proved in this case is that it is impossible to say whether or not Mrs. Oppenheimer survived Mrs. Cohn. Proof stops there. Section 184 of the Law of Property Act, 1925, does not come into the picture at all. It is not part of the law of evidence of the lex fori, for the section is not directed to helping in the ascertainment of any fact but contains a rule of substantive law directing a certain presumption to be made in all cases affecting the title to property. As a rule of substantive law the section is relevant where title is governed by the law of England. It has no application where title is determined by the law of any other country.

I turn now to consider the law of Germany in relation to the facts proved, unhampered by s. 184 of the Law of Property Act, 1925. In my view, the provision contained in the article of July 4, 1939, is part of the general substantive law of Germany and not part of its law of evidence. Its terms and the place in which the repealed article dealing with the same general subject-matter was to be found make that clear. That rule of law has to be applied, inter alia, as part of the Law of Inheritances, contained in the German Civil Code. Predicating of Mrs. Oppenheimer that she is presumed to have died simultaneously with Mrs. Cohn, it is clear that Mrs. Oppenheimer was not a person living at the time when the succession to Mrs. Cohn's estate opened, and that, accordingly, having regard to arts. 1922 and 1923 of the German Civil Code, the defendants, Mrs. Freudenthal and Siegfried Cohn, take Mrs. Cohn's movable estate.

NOTES AND QUESTIONS

(1)(a) Perhaps no device of choice of law analysis is so delusive as the distinction between substance and procedure. With its characteristic simplicity, the first *Restatement of Conflict of Laws* said:

> § 585. **What Law Governs Procedure.**
>
> All matters of procedure are governed by the law of the forum.
>
> § 584. **Determination Of Whether Question Is One Of Procedure.**
>
> The court at the forum determines according to its own Conflict of Laws rule whether a given question is one of substance or procedure.

That formulation is not wrong, and has not really been overtaken by later developments. But while § 584 is correct in stating that the initial characterization is for the forum to make, § 585 is often a conclusion, not a tool for analysis.[a] In *Grant v. McAuliffe,* for example, it is hard to believe that it is the "procedural" character of the issue of whether a tort action survives the death of the tortfeasor that determines the result. At best, the characterization of that issue as procedural is an escape device to avoid result that the majority would regard as unfortunate.

(b) Judge Traynor, one of the judicial pioneers in choice of law (and a professor of conflict of laws after his retirement from the Supreme Court of California), defended the result in *Grant v. McAuliffe,* but seemed not satisfied by the analysis:

> It may not be amiss to add that although the opinion in the case is my own, I do not regard it as ideally articulated, developed as it had to be against the brooding background of a petrified forest. Yet I would make no more apology for it than that in reaching a rational result it was less deft than it might have been to quit itself of the familiar speech of choice of law.[b]

What methods can you suggest that would reach the same result, but with a more satisfying rationale?

(c) Note that characterization of a problem as procedural always leads to the use of the law of the forum; in *Grant,* for example, if the Arizona court also characterized the issue as procedural, suit in that state would result in judgment for the defendant. Some (though not all) of the other possible techniques lead to uniform results, regardless of the forum. More of this later.

(2)(a) Some matters involved in litigation are clearly procedural, and not really capable of choice of law at all. If a court hears motions on Tuesday afternoons, for instance, no one would suggest that the calendar should be varied for a case arising out of an accident in Arizona, because in that state motions are heard on Friday. Whether plaintiff opens and closes, or plaintiff opens and defendant closes, comes in that category; so do such matters as availability of a six-person or twelve-person jury; requirement that a jury verdict be unanimous or by a stated majority; the number of days within which to respond to a pleading; the availability of interlocutory appeals; the scope of discovery; and joinder of parties. There is no good reason for varying the practice of a court in these matters according to the type of action, where it arose, or what "substantive law" should govern its resolution.

(b) Another group of subjects, sometimes called "adjective law," may also be characterized as procedural, but not inevitably or for all purposes. For example, application of a statute of limitations, or a statute of frauds, might follow the law of the forum, or some other law. Presumptions, standing to sue, and burden of proof (for instance, with regard to contributory fault) may also fall in this category. Without, at this stage, attempting to develop a comprehensive definition, consider what it is about the subjects mentioned in this paragraph that is different from the subjects mentioned in paragraph (a).

(c) The suggestion emerges that for choice of law purposes, not all the subjects mentioned in paragraph (b) should in all cases be decided according to the law of the forum—i.e., characterized as procedural. In what other contexts would you think this characterization is

---

[a] The *Restatement (Second) of Conflict of Laws* is far less categorical, devoting 23 sections to the topic. The general principle is stated as follows:

> **§ 122. Issues Relating to Judicial Administration.**
>
> A court usually applies its own local law rules prescribing how litigation shall be conducted even when it applies the local law rules of another state to resolve other issues in the case.

[b] Traynor, *Is This Conflict Really Necessary?* 37 Tex. L. Rev. 657, 670, note 35.

important? See, e.g., *Levy v. Steiger* and *Duggan v. Bay State St. Ry,* cited in that case. Are the issues in the two cases the same? See also *Sampson v. Channel,* p. 444, *infra,* which cites *Levy v. Steiger* in still a different context.

(d) Is there yet another category, focusing on the remedy, as contrasted with liability? For example, where would availability of specific performance of a contract go?[c] What about measure of damages? Or availability of a counter-claim or set-off?[d]

(3)(a) *In re Cohn* is an example of rigid resort to characterization, and also depends on an assumption that the Cohn family was domiciled in Germany that seems improbable. But taking the court at its word, if the issue of proof of survival of persons killed in a common disaster is procedural (i.e., a matter of evidence), English law applies, Gerda, the daughter, is deemed to have survived Hedwig, her mother, and therefore Gerda's children share in Gerda's one third of the estate. If the issue is deemed to be substantive (e.g., a matter of succession law), there is no presumption in favor of Gerda, she fails to qualify as survivor of her mother, and the other two children, Siegfried and Else, divide the estate. If the issue is procedural under German law and substantive under English law, renvoi might be appropriate. In the actual case, the holding is that the issue is substantive under both English and German law, and so the law of the domicile of Hedwig and Gerda, i.e., German law, applies.

(b) Is the case wrongly decided? Outline an opinion coming out the other way.

(4)(a) A recurring question, addressed in the three following cases as well as in others scattered throughout the book, concerns the statute of limitations. A priori, how should the problem of prescription or time bar be handled in litigation involving more than one state?

(b) Consider the following possibilities, in each case on the assumption that the underlying cause of action will be governed by the law of state *B*, but the action is brought in state *A*.[e]

  (i) The court in *A* always applies *A*'s statute of limitations, regardless of the period of limitations that would be applied if the action were brought in *B;*

  (ii) The court in *A* first determines what law governs the transaction, and if that determination looks to *B*, applies *B*'s statute of limitations as well;

  (iii) The choice between (i) and (ii) depends on how *B* characterizes its statute of limitations;

  (iv) The court in *A* applies either *A*'s or *B*'s period of limitations, whichever is shorter;

  (v) The court in *A* applies either *A*'s or *B*'s period of limitations, whichever is longer;

  (vi) The choice between (iv) and (v) depends on whether plaintiff is or is not a resident of *A;*

  (vii) Other. . . .

(c) Various explanations, none wholly satisfactory or exclusive, have been given for barring actions by lapse of time. Some emphasize the prevention of claims where the proof is unreliable,

---

[c] See, e.g., *Silvestri v. Slatowski,* 423 Pa. 498, 224 A.2d 212 (1966), holding that the forum decides this issue according to its own law, even where the law of another state determines liability.

[d] The *Restatement (Second) of Conflict of Laws* says, in § 128, that forum law governs "unless . . . ." The "unless" clause is designed to prevent a situation under which plaintiff might recover in *A* on an action governed by *B*'s law without the possibility of considering a claim that under *B*'s law would reduce the recovery.

[e] The use of the word "state" for present purposes does not distinguish between a state in the United States and a nation-state, but simply refers to a place with a defined territory and a government which administers a body of law.

because witnesses move away, or die, or forget, and documents are lost; others emphasize the desirability of repose from exposure for potential defendants, permitting them to close their books—literally and figuratively—on events long past. In some instances—for example actions based on allegations of injury from use of a defective product—statutes of limitations and their interpretations reflect differing judgments by legislatures or courts as to the interests of society in protecting injured parties, or manufacturers, or insurance companies. Is your selection among the options in paragraph (b) dependent on your approach to the overall question of time-bar?

§ 2.03 The Special Problems of Statutes of Limitations

BOURNIAS v. ATLANTIC MARITIME CO.

United States Court of Appeals, Second Circuit
220 F.2d 152 (1955)

HARLAN, CIRCUIT JUDGE.

Libelant, a seaman, was employed on respondents' vessel at the time she was changed from Panamanian to Honduran registry. As originally filed the libel contained two causes of action. The first was based on several Articles of the Panama Labor Code, under which the libelant claimed an extra three-months' wages payable to seaman upon change of registry, and other amounts for vacation, overtime and holiday pay. The second was for penalties under 46 U.S.C.A. § 596 for failure to pay these amounts promptly.

The respondents filed exceptive allegations asserting, *inter alia,* that the action was barred by the one-year statute of limitations contained in Article 623 of the Panama Labor Code. . . . The question of whether the action was barred by lapse of time was set down for a separate hearing.

At this hearing the Court held that the defense of laches, which was treated by Court and counsel as going only to the claim for advances, had not been substantiated, but that the Panama statute of limitations did bar the claims under the Panama Labor Code, and that in consequence the claim for penalties must also fail *pro tanto.* . . .

Article 623 of the Labor Code of Panama, applicable to Articles 127, 154, 166 and 170 of the Code, upon which the libelant based his first cause of action, reads:

> Actions and rights arising from labor contracts not enumerated in Article 621 shall prescribe [i.e., shall be barred by the Statute of Limitations] in a year from the happening of the events from which arise or are derived the said actions and rights.

The libelant's employment terminated on December 27, 1950, and since his libel was not filed until December 29, 1952, his first cause of action would be barred by Article 623 if it is controlling in this action.

In actions where the rights of the parties are grounded upon the law of jurisdictions other than the forum, it is a well-settled conflict-of-laws rule that the forum will apply the foreign substantive law, but will follow its own rules of procedure. Restatement of Conflict of Laws § 585; Beale, *Conflict of Laws* § 584.1 (1935); Stumberg, *Conflict of Laws* 134 *et seq.* (2d Ed. 1951). While it might be desirable, in order to eliminate "forum-shopping," for the forum to apply the entire foreign law, substantive and procedural—or at least as much of the procedural law as might significantly affect the choice of forum, it has been recognized that to do so involves an unreasonable burden on the judicial machinery of the forum, see Restatement of Conflict of Laws, Introductory Note to Chapter 12, and perhaps more significantly, on the local lawyers involved, see Ailes, *Substance and Procedure in the Conflict of Laws,* 39 Mich.L.Rev. 392, 416 (1941). Consequently, for at least some questions the law applied is that of the forum, with which the lawyers and judges are more familiar, and which can be administered more conveniently. . . .

The general rule appears established that for the purpose of deciding whether to apply local law or foreign law, statutes of limitations are classified as "procedural." Stumberg, *Conflict of Laws* 147 (1951); Lorenzen, *Statutes of Limitation and the Conflict of Laws,* 28 Yale L.J. 492 (1919). Hence the law of the forum controls. . . .

This rule has been criticized as inconsistent with the rationale expressed above, since the foreign statute, unlike evidentiary and procedural details, is generally readily discovered and applied, and a difference in periods of limitation would often be expected to influence the choice of forum. Lorenzen, *supra;* Stumberg, *op. cit., supra.* The rule is in fact an accident of history. Lorenzen, *supra;* see also *Developments in the Law—Statutes of Limitations,* 63 Harv.L.Rev. 1177, 1187 (1950). And although it may perhaps be explained as a device for giving effect to strong local policies on limitations, this explanation would not satisfy the objections of its critics. *Lorenzen, supra.* Be all this as it may, this general rule is firmly embedded in our law.

But as might be expected, some legislatures and courts, perhaps recognizing that in light of the rationale of the underlying conflict-of-laws doctrine it is anomalous to classify across-the-board statutes of limitation as "procedural," have created exceptions to the rule so categorizing such statutes. A legislative example are the so-called "borrowing statutes" which require the courts of the forum to apply the statute of limitations of another jurisdiction, often that where the cause of action arose, when the forum's statute has been tolled. See Note, *Legislation Governing the Applicability of Foreign Statutes of Limitation,* 35 Col.L.Rev. 762 (1935). A court-made exception, and the one with which we are concerned here, is that where the foreign statute of limitations is regarded as barring the foreign right sued upon, and not merely the remedy, it will be treated as conditioning that right and will be enforced by our courts as part of the foreign "substantive" law. See Beale, *Conflict of Laws* §§ 604.3, 605.1 (1935). Such exceptions operate *pro tanto* to give the result which commentators have advocated.

It is not always easy to determine whether a foreign statute of limitations should be regarded as "substantive" or "procedural," for the tests applied by the courts are far from precise. In *The Harrisburg,* 119 U.S. 199, (1886), the Supreme Court held "substantive" a limitation period contained in a wrongful death statute, emphasizing that "the liability and the remedy are created by the same statutes, and the limitations of the remedy are therefore to be treated as limitations of the right," 119 U.S. at page 214. It now appears settled that limitation periods in wrongful death statutes will be regarded as "substantive." Restatement of Conflict of Laws § 397. And the rule of *The Harrisburg* has been stated to apply not merely to rights to sue for wrongful death, but to any statute-created right unknown to the common law. . . .

But the fact that the limitation is contained in the same section or the same statute is material only as bearing on construction. It is merely a ground for saying that the limitation goes to the right created, and accompanies the obligation everywhere. The same conclusion would be reached if the limitation was in a different statute, provided it was directed to the newly created liability so specifically as to warrant saying that it qualified the right. . . .

§ 2.03   CHOICE OF LAW   □   77

Two other approaches to the problem were suggested in our opinion in *Wood & Selick, Inc., v. Compagnie Generale Transatlantique,* 2 Cir., 1930, 43 F.2d 941. First, that the foreign law might be examined to see if the defense possessed the attributes which the forum would classify as "procedural" or "substantive;" that is, for example, whether the defense need be pleaded, as a "substantive" period of limitations need not be in this country. Second, the foreign law might be examined to see if the operation of limitation completely extinguished the right, in which case limitation would be regarded as "substantive." Still other tests are suggested by *Goodwin v. Townsend,* 3 Cir., 1952, 197 F.2d 970—namely, whether the foreign limitation is regarded as "procedural" or "substantive" by the courts of the foreign state concerned, and possibly whether the limitation is cast in language commonly regarded as "procedural."

Which, then, of these various tests should be applied here? It appears to us that it should be the one which *Davis v. Mills,* 194 U.S. 451, (1904), suggests for use where the right and its limitation period are contained in separate statutes, viz.: Was the limitation "directed to the newly created liability so *specifically* as to warrant saying that it qualified the right"? 194 U.S. at page 454, italics supplied. To be sure Davis was concerned with the statute of limitations of a sister state (Montana), but there is nothing in Mr. Justice Holmes' opinion to suggest that the application of the test there laid down is limited to that type of case. And where, as here, we are dealing with a statute of limitations of a foreign country, and it is not clear on the face of the statute that its purpose was to limit the enforceability, outside as well as within the foreign country concerned, of the substantive rights to which the statute pertains, we think that as a yardstick for determining whether that was the purpose this test is the most satisfactory one. It does not lead American courts into the necessity of examining into the unfamiliar peculiarities and refinements of different foreign legal systems, and where the question concerns the applicability of a code provision of a civil law country, this test seems more appropriate than any of the others.

Even though the limitation period here is contained in the same statute as enacts the right sought to be enforced, *The Harrisburg, supra,* still, as noted later, because of the breadth of the Panama Labor Code, as contrasted with the limited scope of the statute involved in *The Harrisburg,* the limitation period should not automatically be regarded as "substantive." Nor would it be appropriate to make this case turn on the fact that the right sued upon was unknown at common law . . . when we are dealing with the statutes of a country where the common law does not exist. And we do not think that it should matter whether the foreign court has interpreted its statute as being "procedural" or "substantive" for some other purpose, which may have happened in *Goodwin, supra,* or whether the foreign practice requires that limitation be pleaded, *Wood & Selick, supra.* "The tendency to assume that a word which appears in two or more legal rules, and so in connection with more than one purpose, has and should have precisely the same scope in all of them, runs all through legal discussions. It has all the tenacity of original sin and must constantly be guarded against." Cook, *Substance and Procedure in the Conflict of Laws,* 42 Yale L.J. 333, 337 (1933). No more should it matter whether the foreign right is extinguished altogether by the mere passage of time, or is instead only repressed into a dormant state, subject to "revival" if the defense of limitation is waived or renounced, *Wood & Selick, supra.* Such a distinction would generally be difficult to apply, and might also lead to results out of the pattern of the precedents; that is, if the defense could be waived under foreign law, a limitation period might be considered "procedural" even though it was contained in a specific statute giving a remedy for wrongful death. Such limitations, however, are almost invariably held "substantive." Restatement of Conflict of Laws § 397. And whether the wording of the limitation period seems more like "procedural" or "substantive" language, Goodwin, *supra,* does not appear to have been generally considered important.

It is true that the test we prefer leaves much to be desired. It permits the existence of a substantial gray area between the black and the white. But it at least furnishes a practical means of mitigating what is at best an artificial rule in the conflict of laws, without exposing us to the pitfalls inherent in prolonged excursions into foreign law; and it permits us to avoid the shortcomings discussed above. We conclude, therefore, that the "specificity" test is the proper one to be applied in a case of this type, without deciding, of course, whether the same test would also be controlling in cases involving domestic or other kinds of foreign statutes of limitations.

Applying that test here it appears to us that the libelant is entitled to succeed, for the respondents have failed to satisfy us that the Panamanian period of limitation in question was specifically aimed against the particular rights which the libelant seeks to enforce. The Panama Labor Code is a statute having broad objectives, viz.: "The present Code regulates the relations between capital and labor, placing them on a basis of social justice, so that, without injuring any of the parties, there may be guaranteed for labor the necessary conditions for a normal life and to capital an equitable return for its investment." In pursuance of these objectives the Code gives laborers various rights against their employers. Article 623 establishes the period of limitation for *all* such rights, except certain ones which are enumerated in Article 621. And there is nothing in the record to indicate that the Panamanian legislature gave special consideration to the impact of Article 623 upon the particular rights sought to be enforced here, as distinguished from the other rights to which that Article is also applicable. Were we confronted with the question of whether the limitation period of Article 621 (which carves out particular rights to be governed by a shorter limitation period) is to be regarded as "substantive" or "procedural" under the rule of "specificity" we might have a different case; but here on the surface of things we appear to be dealing with a "broad," and not a "specific," statute of limitations. And this being a case brought on the admiralty side of the federal court, we are of course limited to considering the foreign law material before us, and we may not take judicial notice of anything beyond that. *Black Diamond S. S. Corp. v. Robert Stewart & Sons,* 1949, 336 U.S. 386, 396–397, 69 S.Ct. 622, 93 L.Ed. 754.

We therefore conclude that under the proper test the respondents have not made out their defense. In so holding we reach the same result as we did in the similar situation involved in *Wood & Selick,* 1930, 43 F.2d 941.

For reasons already discussed, we think this conclusion is not affected, on the one hand, by the testimony of the respondents' expert to the effect that in his opinion Article 623 would be regarded under Panamanian law as a "substantive" limitation upon the libelant's rights under the Panama Labor Code, or, on the other hand, by the libelant's showing that under Panamanian law this statute of limitations has some of the same attributes as such statutes do under our law, and that the libelant's rights under the Panama Labor Code may not be altogether extinguished by the passage of the period of limitation. And we consider quite inconclusive the argument that the prescription period of Article 623 is addressed to both "Actions and rights." Nor in reaching our conclusion have we been influenced by the lower Court's statement that it felt justified in regarding Article 623 as "procedural." Even treating this as a finding, despite the Court's view, which we discuss in a moment, that the respondents should prevail whether Article 623 be regarded as "substantive" or as "procedural," we would not consider ourselves bound by it. For that conclusion seems to have been reached without the Court having addressed itself to the "specificity" rule, so that the finding would rest on a wrong legal premise and should therefore be disregarded.

In conclusion, the Trial Judge, in finding for the respondents, held that when an admiralty court enforces a foreign-created right, it must also enforce the foreign statute of limitations, whether that statute be denominated "substantive" or "procedural." . . . And *Guaranty Trust Co. v. York,* requiring federal courts in diversity cases to apply state limitation periods, has no application in cases such as this, which are not governed by the rule of *Erie R. R. v. Tompkins,* as the Supreme Court took pains to point out in *Levinson v. Deupree,* 345 U.S. 648, (1953), and we may therefore not safely assume that the *Guaranty Trust Co.* holding expresses a rule of federal policy which would be applicable here. . . .

Reversed.

WEST v. THEIS

Idaho Supreme Court
15 Idaho 167, 96 p. 932 (1908)

AILSHIE, C. J. . . .

On April 2, 1888, the defendant, Charles Theis, at Richfield, Kansas, executed and delivered to I. D. West his four promissory notes for the sum of $2,000 each, and therein promised and agreed to pay the same at the office of Ritter & Doubleday in the city of Columbus, state of Kansas. The plaintiff here is the widow of I. D. West, and executrix of his estate. The defendant, Theis, left Kansas after the maturity of two of these notes and before the maturity of the other two, and before the statute of limitations had run as against any of these obligations. He thereafter located in the state of Washington, where he resided continuously for a period of more than six years, which period is prescribed by the statutes of that state as the limit within which actions of this character must be commenced. He thereafter came into the state of Idaho, and this action was brought against him on May 10, 1906. The defendant answered, admitting the execution of the notes as alleged in the complaint, and pleaded the statute of limitations of the state of Washington as a bar to the action in this state under sec. 4079, Rev. Stat. of Idaho. The proper solution of this question must necessarily depend upon the construction to be placed on secs. 4069 and 4079 of the Rev. Stat. of this state. Those sections are as follows:

> Sec. 4069. If, when the cause of action accrues against a person, he is out of the state, the action may be commenced within the term herein limited, after his return to the state, and if, after the cause of action accrues, he departs from the state, the time of his absence is not part of the time limited for the commencement of the action.

> Sec. 4079. When a cause of action has arisen in another state or territory, or in a foreign country, and by the laws thereof an action thereon cannot be maintained against a person by reason of the lapse of time, an action thereon shall not be maintained against him in this state, except in favor of one who has been a citizen of this state, and who has held the cause of action from the time it accrued.

Statutes similar to the foregoing have been considered and construed by the courts of last resort of a number of the states and different conclusions have been reached by the different courts. . . .

We find from an examination of the decisions of courts of last resort, in considering and passing upon the meaning and intent of these statutes, that they hold: first, that section 4069 has reference to the time when a right of action arises or the right to commence an action has arrived, and that the period excluded from the computation of time applies both to residents and nonresidents of the state, and that the words "after his return to the state" refer as well to one who comes into the state who has never before been in the state, as to one who has departed from the state and returns to its jurisdiction; second, that sec. 4079, in referring to "a cause of action that has arisen in another state," has reference to the state or jurisdiction in which the contract or obligation was to be performed or discharged, and has no reference whatever to any intermediate state or jurisdiction through which the defendant may travel or in which he may reside between the time of executing the contract and the commencement of the action thereon.

We shall not attempt to review the authorities supporting the respondent's contention more than to say that the reasoning employed therein does not appeal to us as sound or logical, nor do they seem to us to portray or set forth the true meaning or intent of these statutory provisions. For example, in *Luce v. Clark*,[a] the court holds in substance that where a debt is made payable according to the terms of the contract in one state, and when it becomes due the debtor resides in another state, the "cause of action" cannot be said to have arisen in the state where the debt is payable, for the reason that the debtor is not personally within its jurisdiction. This is substantially the same position taken in *Osgood v. Artt*.[b] To our minds, there is a patent fallacy in this contention. Whenever a debt becomes due, and is not paid in accordance with the terms of the contract, a cause of action thereupon arises. This exists as an absolute and unqualified right independent of where the debtor may be. . . .

It seems to us a strange and novel doctrine to hold that a debtor may by his own acts without the knowledge or consent of his creditor, create for himself a defense that can defeat the creditor's right of recovery. When the debtor enters into a contract within a jurisdiction to pay a certain sum of money within that jurisdiction, a duty and obligation at once arises requiring him to discharge the act at the time and place contracted, and the creditor has a right to assume that he will be there at the time and place when and where the obligation matures ready to discharge it. The debtor, in the face of his contract, should not be allowed to select the jurisdiction in which he will establish his residence and thereby set the statute of limitations of a foreign jurisdiction to running against his creditor without the latter's consent, nor should the creditor be required to keep a detective force in order to keep track of his whereabouts and the various jurisdictions in which he locates, and a law firm to keep him posted as to the statutes of limitations of those several jurisdictions. If the debtor fails to discharge his obligation in accordance with his contract and to keep faith with his creditor he ought not to be heard to plead as a bar in one jurisdiction, that he had previously acquired the defense of the statute of limitations, by residing in another state for the period establishing the bar. It should be remembered that the statute of limitations is not a defense to the action, but is rather a plea to the remedy. . . . Another thing that is of vital importance in this and similar cases is that under the law of the state where the contract was made, it is still enforceable. As in this case, under the statute of Kansas, the bar of the statute of limitations ceased to run when Theis removed from the jurisdiction, and, at the time this action was commenced, it could have been maintained, under the laws of that state and a judgment *in rem* could have been entered against any property he might have had in that state; or, indeed,

---

[a] 49 Minn. 356, 51 N.W. 1162 (1892).

[b] 10 Fed. 365 (N.D. Ill. 1882).

a personal judgment might have been recovered against him had he been within the jurisdiction. Now, we do not think it was the purpose or intention of sec. 4079 of our statute to relieve a man from his liability on an obligation incurred in a foreign state by reason of the plea of the statute of limitations of another state or of any country except that particular state in which the contract was executed, and the state in which it is sued upon. The state to which that section refers is evidently the state in which the contract was to be performed. That is clearly the state referred to by the expression "has arisen in another state." In our opinion, it is the intention of our statute to avail a debtor who has entered into a contract to be performed in a foreign state of two, and only two, pleas of the bar of the statute of limitations;—first, he may show that he has resided in this state for a period exceeding that of the bar of the statute of limitations of this state; second, he may show that the cause of action is barred by the statute of limitations of the state in which it was to be performed. Beyond this he may not go.

. . .

The trial court erred in allowing the plea of the statute of limitations of the state of Washington, and for that reason the judgment must be reversed. . . .

MACK TRUCKS, INC. v. BENDIX-WESTINGHOUSE AUTOMOTIVE AIR BRAKE CO.

United States Court of Appeals, Third Circuit
372 F.2d 18 (1966)

HASTIE, CIRCUIT JUDGE.

This is an action for indemnity. It is of federal cognizance solely under diversity jurisdiction. The District Court for the Western District of Pennsylvania dismissed the action as barred by the statute of limitations. This appeal followed.

The claim for indemnity arose in this way. Bendix-Westinghouse Automotive Air Brake Co. sold brake pedal assemblies, manufactured for it by Latrobe Die Casting Co., to Mack Trucks, Inc., for incorporation in vehicles manufactured by Mack. A truck, incorporating such a brake assembly, was sold to a resident of Florida. While the vehicle was being operated in Florida, the brake assembly broke, causing an accident. A person injured in the accident sued Mack and the operator of the truck in a Florida court and recovered a judgment for $13,028.95, which Mack paid. A formal "Satisfaction of Judgment," duly executed by counsel, was filed and entered in the records of the Florida court on June 30, 1960.

Mack gave Bendix timely notice of the Florida suit, although Florida procedural rules prevented the joining of Bendix as an additional defendant. However, it was not until October 10, 1963, more than three years after the satisfaction of the Florida judgment, that Mack brought this suit for indemnity against Bendix in the Western District of Pennsylvania. Bendix joined Latrobe as a third-party defendant.

One defense was the statute of limitations. Since this was a diversity case, the district court, no different from a Pennsylvania state court, was obligated to apply Pennsylvania choice of law rules to determine what statute of limitations was applicable. *Guaranty Trust Co. of New York v. York,* 326 U.S. 99, (1945), In most situations, Pennsylvania courts apply the statute of limitations of the forum.

However, there is a statutory exception to this rule. Pennsylvania courts must respect and apply the following Pennsylvania "borrowing" statute:

> When a cause of action has been fully barred by the laws of the state or country in which it arose, such bar shall be a complete defense to an action thereon brought in any of the courts of this commonwealth.

12 p. S. § 39.

Thus, if this "cause of action . . . arose" in Florida, reference must be made to the appropriate Florida statute of limitations. *Mangene v. Diamond,* 3d Cir. 1956, 229 F.2d 554. The district court concluded that the cause of action arose in Florida. We agree.

The concept of "the arising of a cause of action" is used frequently to systematize and facilitate the application of statutes of limitations. Usually, the problem is to determine when the statute begins to run. In this context, the familiar rule is that the statute begins to run when the cause of action arises, as determined by the occurrence of the final significant event necessary to make the claim suable. With reference to claims for indemnification for loss, this means that the cause arises when the plaintiff sustains the loss for which he can claim indemnification.

In the present case, the cause of action for indemnity arose when Mack satisfied the judgment, an event evidenced by formal entry of record in the Florida court on June 30, 1960.

The Pennsylvania borrowing statute utilizes this concept of the arising of a cause of action in relation to place rather than time in order to specify the circumstances in which a Pennsylvania court shall apply another state's statute of limitations and to identify the appropriate state. We think the concept of when a cause arises and the concept of where a cause arises, both used to aid in the application of statutes of limitations, are *in pari materia*. In other words, the cause arises where as well as when the final significant event that is essential to a suable claim occurs.

In this case the cause of action arose when a judgment was entered against and later satisfied by Mack in Florida. By the same token, Florida is the state where the cause of action for indemnity arose.

In an effort to avoid this conclusion, the appellant cites *Griffith v. United Air Lines,* 1964, 416 Pa. 1, 203 A.2d 796. There it was held that the measure of damages in a tort case should be determined in accordance with the law of the place having the most significant contacts with the relevant transactions and with the parties rather than by the law of the place of the wrong. In so holding, the court announced a common law conflict of laws rule for the choice of law to be applied in deciding the merits of certain issues. No statute was controlling, and there was no question of when or where the cause of action arose, though apparently it arose at the place of wrong.

Here we have a very different situation. Under the Pennsylvania borrowing statute a court is required to apply the statute of limitations of the state where the cause of action arose without regard to any contacts of any other state with the parties and their prior dealings. And certainly neither the *Griffith* case nor any other of which we know suggests that the residence of the parties or the place of their earlier dealings before the claim became suable have any relevance to determining when or where the cause arose. Indeed, in *Foley v. Pittsburgh-Des Moines Co.,* Chief Justice Stern explicitly stated that the accrual of a cause of action occurs when suable harm is done the plaintiff, "not when the causes are set in motion which ultimately produce injury as a consequence." 363 Pa. at 38, 68 A.2d at 535.

Perhaps it would be arguable, on the merits of the present controversy, that in determining the existence or extent of an obligation to indemnify, the forum should be guided, as was the court in the *Griffith* case, by the substantive law of Pennsylvania because of cumulatively significant Pennsylvania "contacts." But we do not have that problem here. We have to answer only the narrow question of the meaning of the phrase "where the cause of action arose," as used in the Pennsylvania borrowing statute and applied to a situation in which the cause of action came into existence upon the happening of certain events in Florida.

It remains to determine what period of limitations Florida law specifies for such an action as this. Section 95.11(5) (e) of Florida Statutes Annotated stipulates that "an action upon a contract, obligation or liability not founded upon an instrument of writing" must be brought within three years after the action shall have accrued. While the relationship between Mack and Bendix-Westinghouse in this case resulted from a transaction of sale evidenced by a writing, no express promise to indemnify appears or is claimed. Rather, the plaintiff is suing on an imposed obligation which the seller must bear, even in the absence of such a promise. Thus, this is "an action upon a . . . liability not founded upon an instrument of writing. . . ." As one Florida court has expressed the controlling concept, an action or a liability is "founded upon a written instrument" for purposes of statute of limitations only if that instrument contains an undertaking "to do the thing for the nonperformance of which the action is brought."

We conclude, as did the trial court, that the three-year Florida statute of limitations is applicable to the claim in suit. There is no contention or evidence that the statute was tolled for any period. Accordingly, since this cause accrued not later than June 30, 1960, the date upon which Mack's satisfaction of the Florida judgment was entered in the records of the Florida court, the present action was barred at the time of its filing on October 10, 1963.

The judgment will be affirmed.

FREEDMAN, CIRCUIT JUDGE (dissenting).

The determination under the Pennsylvania Borrowing Statute (Act of June 26, 1895, p. L. 375, § 1) of where the present "cause of action" for indemnity "arose" involves two difficulties. There is first the generally elusive concept of a "cause of action." To this is added the nature of the present action for indemnity, originating in an implied warranty and founded on a quasi contractual right of restitution which matured after a recovery in tort.

The majority has wisely rejected a decision based on the predominance of the tort or contract elements which would lead to Florida as the *lex loci delictus* if the tort element prevailed and to Pennsylvania as the *lex loci contractus* if the contract element governed. I disagree, however, with the majority's conclusion that the place where the cause of action arose should be fixed where the event occurs which starts the running of the time for the statute of limitations.[3] This, it seems to me, has the attraction of simplicity but is just as inappropriate a test as are the labels of contract or tort in executing the policy of the Pennsylvania Borrowing Statute. It is not required by any Pennsylvania precedents old or new and is inconsistent with the modern trend of Pennsylvania law.

---

[3] My view makes it unnecessary to reach the question whether if the cause of action is held to have arisen in Florida, the Pennsylvania Borrowing Statute must be held to look not merely to the period of limitations of Florida, but also to Florida's tolling provision. The Pennsylvania Borrowing Statute provides that the bar is a defense in Pennsylvania "when a cause of action has been fully barred by the laws of the state . . . in which it arose." The Florida statute (Fla.Stat.Annot., § 95.07) provides in relevant part: "If, when the cause of action shall accrue against a person, he is out of the state, the action may be commenced within the term herein related after his return to the state . . ."

It is true that Mack's right to indemnity was against loss and not against liability and therefore arose only on Mack's payment to the injured party in satisfaction of the judgment. The use of this event as the time when the cause of action for indemnity arises is appropriate as the point of origin of the indemnitee's claim against the indemnitor. Even this rule, however, is often expressed without distinction between the time of payment and the time of satisfaction of the judgment. But at least for ordinary purposes, where the short interval between the payment and satisfaction of the judgment has no significance for the period of limitations involved, the rule is simple, easily applicable, and meets no countervailing elements.

A holding, however, that the place where a cause of action arose is to be conclusively equated with the location of the vagrant event which sets the time running, leads to serious problems. The place of the apparently simple element of payment is subject to fortuitous variations and may even be contrived. A corporation with a nationwide business may make or receive payment in any one of the states. If the place of payment is to be decisive, such a party can determine what statute of limitations shall bind it by a conscious choice of the office from which payment will be made, or conversely of the office to which payment ultimately will be made. When the payment is made in satisfaction of a judgment it may seem that the place of judgment should be the determinative factor. But there are many cases where indemnity arises on a payment which is made in settlement of a claim without the entry of a judgment. Even after a judgment, the possibility of appeal or the difficulty in obtaining satisfaction by execution may lead to a negotiated settlement effected in a place outside the state where the judgment was entered. It would be contrary to the law's deep-seated preference for settlement rather than litigation to make it an advantage for a party to have his liability determined by a judgment rather than by a settlement.

In the present case the cause of action is said to have arisen in Florida because it is there that Mack satisfied the judgment and thus started the time to run which marked when the cause of action arose. But suppose the judgment had not been satisfied, but a simple payment or even a settlement under the judgment had been made in Pennsylvania? Or suppose that a judgment had later been entered in Pennsylvania in a suit on the Florida judgment and the Pennsylvania judgment alone had been marked satisfied of record after a payment made in Pennsylvania? Would any of these circumstances alter the determination of where the cause of action arose?

It seems to me that the place where payment is made in settlement of a claim or in satisfaction of a recorded judgment does not contain the same undeviating element as does the time of payment, which is the inherent point of origin of the cause of action for indemnity. I therefore believe that the Pennsylvania courts would interpret the Borrowing Statute by the application of general choice of law principles rather than promulgate a general rule whose effect in many cases would be to vest one party with the power to choose the controlling statute of limitations by manipulation of the place of payment.

Pennsylvania is in the forefront of jurisdictions which have recently adopted a pragmatic standard of choice of law which eschews mechanical formulas. This standard reduces the possibility of manipulation to insignificance. It stresses the interests of the jurisdictions involved and emphasizes a principle of realism in preference to an automatic test applied by a rule of thumb. The Supreme Court of Pennsylvania adopted this modern standard in *Griffith v. United Air Lines, Inc.,* 416 Pa. 1, 203 A.2d 796 (1964). There the court refused to apply the Colorado limitation on damages against the estate of a Pennsylvania decedent even though he was killed in Colorado in the crash of an airplane. The court applied the law of Pennsylvania because the decedent and the transaction itself, in which decedent had purchased his ticket from defendant in Philadelphia for a flight from that city to Arizona, had such contacts with Pennsylvania that Pennsylvania's interest in the outcome was more significant than that of Colorado. This interest principle, which has moved rapidly into the foreground of acceptance in American states,[5] has been applied by the Supreme Court of Pennsylvania in an increasing number of recent cases and is now firmly established in Pennsylvania decisional law. A similar statutory rule for contract actions now prevails in Pennsylvania under the Uniform Commercial Code. I think Pennsylvania would take a similar approach in construing the Borrowing Statute.

Pennsylvania's interest in the period of limitations to be applied in this action far outweighs the interest of Florida.[8] Florida's real interest was in the negligence action for the accident which occurred in Florida. That action, in which Florida's interest dominated, terminated in a judgment, which was satisfied by payment. The present action for indemnity, on the other hand, is dominated by Pennsylvania's interest. Mack's right of indemnity is based upon a business transaction whose essential contacts all were in Pennsylvania. The brake pedal assembly was manufactured, purchased, delivered and installed in the truck in Pennsylvania where Mack was engaged in business. Pennsylvania therefore has a substantial interest in determining for itself when such a party's cause of action for indemnity should be barred. Otherwise the question would be left to the accident of the particular location where the events which effectuate the right to indemnity may have chanced to occur, and which the original parties would have had no means of foreseeing when they transacted their business. The rapid movement of motor vehicles across state lines should not result in a wayward choice of the place where a cause of action for indemnity arises, even though it is appropriate and just that a party injured by the negligence of the driver should be able to obtain redress for his injuries at the place where the accident occurred, if necessary by the use of a longarm statute.

Nor do I see any reason to restrict the modern Pennsylvania conflicts rule to so-called substantive law questions such as the existence or extent of the obligation to indemnify as distinguished from the present problem of the statute of limitations. Indeed, while limitations of action may fall under the heading of procedure, to the litigant a determination that his suit is completely barred by the statute of limitations is substantively far more drastic and important than a ruling on the extent of his right to indemnity. But I believe there is a deeper problem involved. Statutes of limitation seem simple on their face because the time period they fix can be measured by the clock. Experience has shown, however, that even here unexpected problems arise which present significant alternatives that can only be determined by a choice of policy. In some cases this policy has been settled by statute and where the courts have followed the letter of the statute they have made an unspoken choice not to alleviate its hardship. In Pennsylvania an early Colonial statute[9] provided for the tolling of the period of limitations in favor of persons under the disabilities of minority, coverture, mental incompetency, imprisonment, or absence beyond the sea. Much of this statute was later held to have been impliedly repealed by a subsequent statute. Among the statutory tolling provisions still in effect is one which exists

---

[5] *E.g., Babcock v. Jackson,* [§ 3.03, *infra*] (1963); *Auten v. Auten,* [§ 4.01[B], *infra*] (1984): see *Bernkrant v. Fowler,* [§ 4.01[A], *infra*] (1961); *Schmidt v. Driscoll Hotel, Inc.,* 249 Minn. 376, 82 N.W.2d 365 (1957). Many leading articles are cited in *Griffith v. United Air Lines, Inc.,* 416 Pa. 1, 203 A.2d 796 (1964).

[8] There may, of course, be cases where two or more states have significant interests in having their period of limitations applied. Cf. *George v. Douglas Aircraft Co., Inc.,* 332 F.2d 73, 79 n. 6 (2d Cir. 1964).

[9] Act of March 27, 1713, 1 Smith's Laws 76, § 5, 12 Purdon's Pa.Stat.Annot. § 35.

where a defendant makes service of process impossible by becoming a nonresident after the cause of action arose.

In those cases where the legislature has not provided relief the courts have had the choice of watching the clock or inquiring into the purpose of the statute. In recognizing the underlying purpose of the statute courts have early held that it would not be applied to bar a suit if the plaintiff was diverted from bringing it by the affirmative fraud of his adversary. In *Ayers v. Morgan,* 397 Pa. 282, 154 A.2d 788 (1959), the Supreme Court of Pennsylvania held that the statute of limitations was suspended in malpractice cases where the injury was unknown and undiscoverable by the plaintiff. In doing so it departed from the traditional rule, which the New York Court of Appeals followed a few years later, that the principle of repose requires the barring of suit in such cases in the absence of specific legislative relief. Similar problems arise where the cause of action results from the accumulation of injuries over a long period of time, as in silicosis, and where negligent industrial operations result in the poisoning of the atmosphere and cause injuries which take long to mature as recognizable illness. These statutes and decisions are a far cry from the view that the statute of limitations is capable of application as a simple chronological measure.

Borrowing statutes, like the statutes of limitations themselves, reflect an underlying policy. They have existed in various forms in many states,[16] and usually were intended to prevent a nonresident defendant from being subjected to an indefinite liability because the forum's period of limitations was suspended by tolling statutes during the defendant's absence from the jurisdiction.[17] Since in Pennsylvania the tolling provisions were inapplicable to defendants who were nonresidents at the time the cause of action arose and who had not entered the jurisdiction within the statutory period,[18] the Pennsylvania borrowing legislation must have had the broader purpose of assuring that the decision as to when the claim should be barred would be governed by the policy of the jurisdiction with the most significant interest in the claim,—the jurisdiction in which the "cause of action" "arose."[19] The Pennsylvania Borrowing Statute therefore early gave recognition to what is now the modern principle of the importance of the interest of the respective jurisdictions in the underlying transaction. This principle is recognized, at least impliedly, in two of the cases cited by the majority. In *Orschel v. Rothschild,* 238 Ill.App. 353 (1925), not only had the plaintiff made the payment giving rise to the right of indemnity in Illinois whose statute of limitations the court applied, but the court also pointed out that the Illinois Borrowing Statute was inapplicable because the plaintiff was a resident of the forum. This in turn resulted from the restricted nature of the tolling statute which was inapplicable if neither party was a resident of the state when the cause of action accrued. In *Runkle v. Pullin,* 49 Ind.App. 619, 97 N.E. 956 (1912), while the court adopted the view that the time when a cause of action arises determines also the place where it arises, both parties to the transaction had resided in Indiana, but the defendant had become a nonresident when plaintiff paid the balance due on the note and remained a nonresident although he was within the jurisdiction at the time he was served.

---

[16] See Ester, *Borrowing Statutes of Limitation and Conflict of Laws,* 15 U.Fla.L.R. 33, 79–84 (1962), collecting and classifying the statutes of the various states and territories, and listing 38 states as having borrowing statutes of general application.

[17] *George v. Douglas Aircraft Co., Inc.,* 332 F.2d 73, 77 (2 Cir.1964); *Developments in the Law—Statutes of Limitations,* 63 Harv.L.R. 1177, 1262–63 (1950); Ester, *supra,* at p. 42.

[18] Act of May 22, 1895, p. L. 112, § 1, 12 Purdon's Pa.Stat.Annot. § 40.

[19] See *George v. Douglas Aircraft Co., Inc.,* 332 F.2d 73, 77 (2 Cir.1964) discussing an analogous New York statute of 1902.

In the circumstances, therefore, Indiana had every possible contact with the transaction and almost every possible contact with the parties.

The Pennsylvania Borrowing Statute in speaking of a "cause of action" and where it "arose" has not undertaken to define these terms, but has left them to be given content by judicial refinement and clarification. This includes judicial developments in the future as well as those which have taken place in the past. While we may not alter the legislative command that the statutory period fixed by the foreign state shall prevail in the designated cases, nevertheless, what is a "cause of action" and when and where it "arose" are matters for judicial interpretation and should reflect current views of the relative significance of state interest as a determinant of decision.

I would hold, therefore, that the present cause of action for indemnity arose in Pennsylvania where there originated the contractual relationship between the parties out of which the right of indemnity arose, rather than in Florida where the accident occurred and satisfaction of the judgment was made which ripened the claim for indemnity and started the time of the running of the statute of limitations. Since it is agreed that the action was within the time fixed as the period of limitations in Pennsylvania. I dissent from the conclusion that the action was barred.

NOTES AND QUESTIONS

(1)(a) Judge Harlan (as he then was) is quite good at dismissing "traditional" substitutes for choice of law reasoning. Serious issues such as statutes of limitations or burden of proof or survival of actions cannot, he knows, just be called "substantive" or "procedural," unless one knows what follows from that characterization. These issues are not matters of judicial administration, such as the subjects listed in question (2)(a) on page 73, *supra*. On the other hand, provisions for consequences of the passage of time between cause and action are different from suits concerning the consequence of the fault of the injured party in a suit based on negligence, or limitations on damages for wrongful death, or the right of election of a surviving spouse against decedent's will. Unlike the first *Restatement* (p. 72, *supra*), Judge Harlan is looking for a particular rule focused on statutes of limitations.

(b) In singling out limitations of actions, Judge Harlan is in tune with legislatures. Though general conflict of laws statutes are rare—at least in the common law world[c]—many states have provided by statute for choice of law with respect to limitations of time, usually by "borrowing," as in *West v. Theis* and *Mack Trucks*. Generally borrowing results in the shorter of two periods being applied, i.e., option (iv) in question (4)(b), page 74, *supra*. Do the three cases here reproduced lead you to support that option?

(2)(a) While there is no general statute of limitations in federal courts, apart from those included in particular acts,[d] admiralty courts in the United States generally look to the statute

---

[c] Germany and Italy have long had Introductory Laws to their Civil Codes devoted to choice of law, but both states have recently adopted special conflict of laws statutes—Germany effective in 1986, Italy in 1995. Austria and Switzerland have also recently adopted conflict of laws (or "Private International Law") statutes—Austria effective 1979, Switzerland effective 1989.

[d] E.g., in the Carriage of Goods by Sea Act, 46 U.S.C. § 1303(b), and the Death on the High Seas Act, 46 U.S.C. § 763.

of limitations of the state where they are sitting in administering the looser doctrine of laches.[e] The district court in *Bournias* looked to the New York statute, including its borrowing statute, and accordingly dismissed the action. Judge Harlan rejected that approach without discussion, except for a reference at the close of the opinion to the fact that *Erie* and *Guaranty Trust Co. v. York*[f] are not applicable. The outcome of the case, however, seems to be that New York's statute of limitations—presumably the ordinary six-year period for actions on a contract—applies, but its borrowing statute does not. The opinion is not, in the words of Gilmore and Black, "a model of lucidity."[g]

(b) Having rejected the lower court's resort to borrowing, which avoids having to characterize statutes of limitations as procedural or substantive, and having rejected that system of classification, Judge Harlan searches for a reason not to apply Panama's one-year statute. Has he found such a reason?

(c) The law on which the case turns was a result of the volatility of "flags of convenience" shipping. In most major industrial countries, the combination of taxes and labor union pressure were perceived as making international shipping, particularly bulk (non-conference) vessels, prohibitively expensive.[h] A number of countries offered registry to foreign-owned shipping, with low taxes and availability of local seamen. The leading flag of convenience states in the 1950's and 1960's were the so-called Pan-Lib-Hon countries—Panama, Liberia, and Honduras—and there was much competition among them. As labor unions organized in one state and pressed for higher wages, or the tax rate seemed likely to increase, shipowners often shifted registry of their vessels, sometimes with little notice to the seamen who would be losing their jobs. The amendment to the Panamanian Labor Code on which Mr. Bournias based his claim was designed, evidently, to alleviate the lot of these crew members, as well as to provide a disincentive to shipowners to continue their nation-hopping. Putting aside the question of proof, which is likely to be almost impossible, try to imagine how the Panamanian legislature might have addressed the question of limitations applicable to the new action:

(i) No one considered the issue at all;

(ii) The matter was considered and no reason was advanced for departing from the general one-year period in the Labor Code; or

(iii) The union representatives sought a two-year period, the shipowners urged six months, and eventually a compromise of one year was agreed on, which did not require a special provision in the amendment.

Do any of these possibilities contribute to analysis of the distinction between "specific" and "general" statutes?

(d) Assuming that it is possible to distinguish between "specific" and "general" statutes of limitations, as seems improbable with respect to the Panama Labor Code but might be possible with respect, say, to the Alabama Employer's Liability Act, what is the argument for treating

---

[e] Put simply, this seems to mean that the state statute is usually applied, unless the delay in bringing the action is both excusable and harmless. See C. Gilmore and C. Black, *The Law of Admiralty* 774–76 (2d ed. 1975).

[f] See §§ 6.01, 6.03, *infra*.

[g] Gilmore and Black, N. e, *supra*, at 778.

[h] For the Supreme Court's description of flag of convenience shipping, in the context of the attempt of U.S. labor unions to organize the crew members, see *McCulloch v. Sociedad Nacional de Marineros de Honduras*, 372 U.S. 10 (1963), reproduced at p. 881, *infra*.

one differently from the other? Is Judge Harlan adopting option (iii) from question (4)(b) (p. 74, *supra*). Or is he doing the characterization himself?

(e) Consider, finally, the result of the decision. The cause of action sued on does not exist in the United States, and is time-barred in Panama; yet plaintiff prevails. Does this make sense? Render justice?

(3)(a) In *Bournias,* there was no question where the action arose. In *Mack Trucks,* however, it was that question which divided the majority and the dissent, though there was no uncertainty about the facts. Judge Freedman (writing after the watershed in American choice of law in the early 1960's)[i] urges that the words "the state where the action arose" be construed as if they read "the state whose law governs the relationship between the parties." Is that approach precluded, as the majority says, by the statute itself?

(b) Suppose that in addition to the limitations problem, there were a difference in the applicable substantive law. Suppose, for example, that under the law of Florida, indemnity actions were possible only under express warranties, whereas in Pennsylvania the implied warranty of merchantability gives rise to an indemnity by a purchaser who has paid a judgment to an injured third party. What law would the majority apply?

(c) Note that the Pennsylvania borrowing statute involved in *Mack Trucks* refers to the state or country "in which [the cause of action] *arose.*" The New York borrowing statute relied on by the lower court in *Bournias*[j] (but not mentioned by the Court of Appeals) speaks of the state "where the cause of action *accrued;*"[k] the Idaho statutes involved in *West v. Theis* use both terms. Is there a difference?

(d) Suppose—as we will see became largely true in the "conflicts revolution" that swept the United States in the 1960's—that in a tort action the place of the accident did not necessarily determine the governing law. *Alabama Great Southern R.R. v. Carroll,* in other words, might come out differently, applying Alabama rather than Mississippi law. But the implication from *Mack Trucks* is that if there were a question of time bar and Alabama had a borrowing statute, Mississippi law would still govern that question. Judge Freedman would regard that as foolishness; could you draft a borrowing statute (or some other kind of statute dealing with causes of action touching on more than one state) that would write his views into legislation? Note (for future reference) two problems: (i) questions of time bar are ordinarily decided at the commencement of an action, but once choice-of-law rules become more flexible, some inquiry into the facts may prove necessary; (ii) the question as put assumes that some body of law will govern all aspects of a given lawsuit: that may turn out not to be true.

(4)(a) In *West v. Theis,* a plaintiff sues on a debt eighteen years after it came due, and prevails. Is that fair? Would you come out the same way if instead of an action on a promissory note, Mrs. West's claim were for assault, based on a blow Mr. Theis, she says, had given to her late husband in Kansas in 1888?

(b) *West v. Theis* involves not only a borrowing statute (§ 4079), but also a tolling statute (§ 4069). Tolling statutes seem to have been designed to prevent claims from becoming time-barred while potential defendants were out of the state, and borrowing statutes ameliorated the effect of tolling when the defendant could have been sued in the first state. In these days of

---

[i] See Chapter 3, *infra.*

[j] *Bournias v. Atlantic Maritime Co.,* 117 F. Supp. 864 (S.D.N.Y. 1954).

[k] Former N.Y. Civil Practice Act § 13, presently C.P.L.R. § 202.

much greater opportunity for personal jurisdiction over absent defendants than was true at the time of the *West* case, do tolling statutes still make sense?[l]

(c) Note that the Idaho borrowing statute, § 4079, bars actions barred by a shorter foreign period of limitations only for non-residents of the state. Many states have similar provisions,[m] but Pennsylvania, for example, does not. Isn't there something unfair about saying "we will apply the shorter of two possible periods of limitation for non-resident plaintiffs, but for our own residents, we permit suit whenever our own statute has not run out"? Is it unconstitutional?

(d) In *Canadian Northern Ry. v. Eggen,* 252 U.S. 553 (1920), the plaintiff, a citizen of South Dakota, brought suit in federal district court in Minnesota against the railroad, a Canadian corporation, for injuries incurred in Saskatchewan. Minnesota had a six-year statute of limitations, but a borrowing statute substantially like Idaho's § 4079. The district court dismissed the action, because it was brought after the relevant one-year Canadian statute had expired. The Court of Appeals reversed on the ground that the borrowing statute was repugnant to Article IV, section 2 of the Constitution, the Privileges and Immunities Clause.[n] The Supreme Court disagreed:

> It is plain that the act assailed was not enacted for the purpose of creating an arbitrary or vexatious discrimination against non-residents of Minnesota. . . . It gives a non-resident the same rights in Minnesota courts as a resident citizen has, for a time equal to that of the statute of limitations where his cause of action arose. . . .
>
> The State of Minnesota . . . recognized (the) right of citizens of other States to institute and maintain suits in its courts as a fundamental right, protected by the Constitution, and for one year from the time his cause of action accrued, the respondent was given all of the rights which citizens of Minnesota had under it. . . .
>
> The principle on which this holding rests is that the constitutional requirement is satisfied if the non-resident is given access to the courts of the State upon terms which in themselves are reasonable and adequate for the enforcing of any rights he may have, even though they may not be technically and precisely the same in extent as those accorded to resident citizens . . . .[o]

Is this persuasive? Reconsider the question after reading *Hughes v. Fetter,* § 5.01, *infra.*[p]

(e) If a state may relieve its own people from the effects of its borrowing statute, should the benefit attach to the state's residents, or to its domiciliaries? In *Antone v. General Motors Corp.,* 64 N.Y.2d 20, 484 N.Y.S.2d 514, 473 N.E.2d 742 (1984), plaintiff brought suit against General Motors, alleging that he had been injured in an accident in Pennsylvania on September 12, 1977, attributable to a defect in a 1975 Buick automobile. After he purchased the car but before the accident, plaintiff moved from Olean, N.Y. to Rossiter, Pa., to live in a nursing home where he was employed. Because he had not purchased his car from an authorized Buick dealer, plaintiff

---

[l] Note that some tolling statutes provide that they do not apply while jurisdiction over the defendant can be obtained without service within the state. See, e.g., N.Y. C.P.L.R. § 207(3).

[m] See, e.g., N.Y. C.P. L.R. § 202.

[n] Documents Supplement, p. 4.

[o] 252 U.S. at 560–61, 561–62.

[p] For a lengthy discussion of the Privileges and Immunities clause and conflict of laws, which approves the result, but not the reasoning in *Eggen,* see Currie & Schreter, *Unconstitutional Discrimination in the Conflict of Laws: Privileges and Immunities,* 69 Yale L.J. 1323 (1960), repr. in B. Currie, *Selected Essays on the Conflict of Laws* 445 (1963).

did not learn until June 1980 that his 1975 Buick was subject to a recall campaign due to a problem that might have led to his accident. Plaintiff brought suit in August 1980, within New York's three-year tort statute of limitations, but beyond the two-year period applicable to tort actions in Pennsylvania. General Motors pleaded the Pennsylvania statute of limitations, applicable through the New York borrowing statute;[q] plaintiff contended that he was residing at the Pennsylvania nursing home as part of his job, but remained domiciled in New York, where he maintained a mailing address. Should the New York court entertain this action?[r]

§ 2.04 Time Bar a Generation Later: Of Discovery Rules and Statutes of Repose

(1)(a) In the wake of the massive increase in medical malpractice actions and product liability actions directed at substances whose deleterious effect is felt months or even years after the injured person's exposure, a recurring problem facing litigants and courts since the 1970's has been to determine when a limitations period begins to run. If the answer given is when the injury occurred—i.e., the time of the treatment or drug or industrial exposure (as with regard to use of asbestos in construction), the injury may not come to light until after the period of limitations has expired. If the statute begins to run when the injury is discovered, defendants may be vulnerable to suit indefinitely and insurers for years long past may find themselves charged with coverage long after their books for the year in question have been closed.[a]

(b) In some states, courts sympathetic to the injured parties adopted a "discovery rule," holding that the statute of limitations runs from the time the plaintiff discovered or by reasonable diligence should have discovered that he or she has been harmed.[b] Many states adopted so-called "statutes of repose," placing an outer limit of time on negligence or related claims—typically 8-10 years, i.e., longer than the typical statute of limitations but shorter than an unrestricted discovery rule. In some states, certain kinds of actions, for instance actions based on exposure to asbestos or breast implants were carved out of statutes of repose; in other states there is no such exclusion. Some state courts held, in construing statutes of repose, that the time begins to run when the injury is discovered, which may well be before the plaintiff associates the injury with a particular product or practice.

(2) None of the recent statutes amending or supplementing statutes of limitation seem to have focused on the issue of whether they are regulating procedure or substance, and whether they go to a right or a remedy. Thus little guidance is available from the legislatures to address the inevitable problems of choice of law.

(a) Suppose plaintiff is treated with a given drug in state A; four years later, plaintiff, now domiciled in state B, learns that she has an injury attributable to that drug. Both state A and

---

[q] Note m, *supra*.

[r] The Court of Appeals said "no." "We agree with the lower courts that 'residence' under CPLR § 202 is distinct from 'domicile,' and that the plaintiff was not a resident of New York on September 12, 1977." 64 N.Y.2d at 26, 484 N.Y.S.2d at 516, 473 N.E.2d at 744.

[a] This was one of the causes—though not the only one—for the troubles of Lloyd's of London in the 1990's. See, e.g., Adam Raphael, *Ultimate Risk: The Inside Story of the Lloyd's Catastrophe*, esp. ch. 6 "Asbestos" (1994). It also figured in the decision of the London Insurers that became the subject of the *Insurance Antitrust Case*, Ch. 10, § 10.04, *infra*.

[b] The New York courts long held out against a discovery rule; eventually, in 1986, the state legislature adopted an amendment, N.Y. C.P. L.R. §214-c, which provides that the three-year period within which to commence an action for personal injury caused by the latent effects of exposure to any substance or combination of substances shall be computed from the date of discovery of the injury by the plaintiff or from the date when such injury should have been discovered by the exercise of reasonable diligence.

state *B* have a three-year tort statute, but under the law of *A* plaintiff would be barred, while under the discovery rule applicable in *B* she would be free to bring the action. Plaintiff sues *D*, a nationwide pharmaceutical company, in *B*, and *D* moves to dismiss the action as time-barred. What result?

(b) Suppose the same facts as in (a), but with the laws reversed, so that state *A* would permit the action to go forward under some form of discovery rule but (if all contacts were within the state) *B* would not. Now what result?

(c) Must you be consistent, or could you develop a principled approach whereby plaintiff could maintain her action in both cases?ᶜ

BAXTER v. STURM, RUGER & CO., INC.

United States Court of Appeals
Second Circuit.
13 F.3d 40 (1993)

Before MESKILL, PRATT, and MAHONEY, CIRCUIT JUDGES.

ORDER

This appeal from the United States District Court, 827 F.Supp. 96, for the District of Connecticut, Cabranes, C.J., came on to be heard on the transcript of record from said district court and was argued by counsel. On consideration of the briefs, appendix, record and the oral argument in this appeal, it is hereby ORDERED that the Clerk of this Court transmit to the Clerk of the Connecticut Supreme Court a Certificate in the form attached, together with a complete set of the briefs, appendix and record filed with this Court by the parties. This panel retains jurisdiction so that, once we receive a response from the Connecticut Supreme Court, we may dispose of all of the issues raised in this appeal.

APPENDIX

Certificate to the Connecticut Supreme Court pursuant to Connecticut General Statutes s 51-199a (certification of unsettled question of state law).

In 1990, Andrew T. Baxter, the son of the plaintiff William L. Baxter (Baxter), was shot in the abdomen when a firearm accidentally discharged. The firearm had been designed and manufactured by the defendant, Sturm, Ruger & Co. Inc. (Sturm, Ruger), in Connecticut and had been shipped in 1968 to a distributor in Oregon. The firearm had then been purchased and given to Baxter, an Oregon resident.

ᶜ It is worth pointing out that Congress saw this problem in connection with legislation concerning environmental hazards covered by the Superfund Act, 42 U.S.C. §9658, which avoids the choice of law problem as well as the problem of bar prior to discovery by providing a federally mandated discovery rule for all state-based tort actions asserting exposure to hazardous substances, pollutants, or contaminants released into the environment. The relevant statute of limitations still applies, but only from the date that plaintiff knew (or reasonably should have known) that the damages on which the action is based were caused or contributed to by the hazardous substance concerned. No comparable federal statute would be applicable to the problem in the text, which does not arise from environmental contamination.

On August 30, 1991, Baxter brought this diversity action against Sturm, Ruger, a Delaware corporation with corporate offices in Connecticut, asserting three claims. First, Baxter alleged that Sturm, Ruger was liable for injuries arising from the accidental discharge of the firearm pursuant to the Connecticut Product Liability Act, Connecticut General Statutes § 52-572m to 52-572r. Second, Baxter alleged that Sturm, Ruger had negligently performed a retrofit program, through which certain models of Sturm, Ruger firearms, like that owned by Baxter, were modified to eliminate a design and manufacturing defect that caused those firearms to discharge accidentally. Third, Baxter asserted a claim for punitive damages pursuant to Connecticut General Statutes § 52-240b.

Sturm, Ruger raised several affirmative defenses, including the assertion that Baxter's claims were barred by the Oregon statute of repose for product liability actions, Oregon Revised Statutes § 30.905. That provision states:

Time limitation for commencement of action

(1) Notwithstanding ORS 12.115 or 12.140 and except as provided in subsection (2) of this section and ORS 30.907, a product liability civil action shall be commenced not later than eight years after the date on which the product was first purchased for use or consumption.

(2) Except as provided in ORS 30.907, a product liability civil action shall be commenced not later than two years after the date on which the death, injury or damage complained of occurs.

The Oregon Supreme Court has held that the time limit in subsection (2) is subordinate to that in subsection (1), making eight years the outside time limit within which to file a product liability claim. See Sealey v. Hicks, 309 Ore. 387, 392, 788 P. 2d 435, 437, cert. denied, 498 U.S. 819 (1990). Moreover, the Sealey Court characterized subsection (1) as a statute of repose because its prescribed time limit begins to run on the date of first purchase of the product, regardless of the date of injury. This provision may, therefore, bar an action before an injury is sustained. By contrast, subsection (2) is a statute of limitation because its prescribed time period begins to run on the date of injury.

Baxter moved for partial summary judgment on Sturm, Ruger's statute of repose defense, and Sturm, Ruger also moved for summary judgment on that ground. In deciding these motions, the district court first determined that, under Connecticut choice of law rules, Oregon substantive law would apply to Baxter's claims. The court then considered whether section 30.905 would be characterized as substantive or procedural under Connecticut choice of law rules. If section 30.905 were considered substantive, it would apply and would bar Baxter's product liability claims. If considered procedural, however, it would not apply. Rather, the district court would apply the statute of repose of Connecticut, the forum state. That statute, Connecticut General Statutes § 52-577a, provides in pertinent part:

Limitation of action based on product liability claim

(a) No product liability claim as defined in section 52-572m shall be brought but within three years from the date when the injury, death or property damage is first sustained or discovered or in the exercise of reasonable care should have been discovered except that, subject to subsections (c), (d) and (e), no such action may be brought against any party . . . later than ten years from the date that the party last parted with possession or control of the product.

. . .

(c) The ten-year limitation provided for in subsection (a) shall not apply to any product liability claim brought by a claimant who is not entitled to [workers'] compensation, . . . provided the claimant can prove that the harm occurred during the useful safe life of the product.

From Sturm, Ruger's posture on this appeal, we understand it to have conceded that Baxter "can prove that the harm occurred during the useful safe life of the product."

The district court held that Connecticut courts would consider the Oregon statute of repose to be substantive for choice of law purposes. Acknowledging the absence of a controlling decision from the Connecticut Supreme Court, the district court based its decision on "the weight of authority in other jurisdictions," . . .the Oregon Supreme Court's analysis of section 30.905 in *Sealey*, Chief Judge Cabranes' previous decision in a case involving Georgia's product liability statute, and a scholarly treatise, Russell J. Weintraub, *Commentary on the Conflict of Laws* 58 (3d ed. 1986). Accordingly, the district court granted Sturm, Ruger's motion for summary judgment on all of Baxter's claims.

Moreover, the district court decided several other motions, one of which was Sturm, Ruger's motion for certification of the statute of repose issue to the Connecticut Supreme Court. Baxter opposed the motion, and the district court denied it. Understandably, Baxter stated at oral argument before us that he no longer opposed certification.

On appeal, Baxter contends that the district court erred in concluding that Connecticut courts would characterize section 30.905 as substantive for choice of law purposes. Baxter also challenges the district court's dismissal of his negligence claim on the ground that section 30.905, even if applicable to his product liability claim, does not apply to claims of negligent acts or omissions that allegedly occurred after the sale of the product. Because Baxter's first contention raises an unsettled question of Connecticut law, we certify, sua sponte, the following question of law to the Connecticut Supreme Court:

> Is a statute of repose, such as Oregon Revised Statutes § 30.905(1), properly considered substantive for choice of law purposes under Connecticut law?

Although Connecticut courts have characterized statutes of repose as procedural in certain contexts,...those cases are not dispositive here. The Restatement (Second) of Conflict of Laws advises that, in determining the proper characterization of a legal concept for choice of law purposes, a court should not automatically import a characterization of that concept from a non-choice of law context. Restatement (Second) of Conflict of Laws § 7, cmt. d, illus. 2,3 (1971). Rather, courts should ascertain whether the policies underlying the substantive-procedural characterization in the non-choice of law context also support the use of that characterization in the choice of law context. See id. The certified issue thus involves policy choices that are best resolved by the Connecticut Supreme Court.

Moreover, decisions by courts in other jurisdictions about the proper characterization of statutes of repose in the choice of law context are not controlling here because district courts in diversity cases must apply the choice of law rules of the forum state. Klaxon Co. v. Stentor Elec. Mfg. Co., 313 U.S. 487, 496 (1941). . . . Accordingly, in this case, only Connecticut's characterization of statutes of repose is dispositive.

Finally, we note that, prior to the district court's decision in this case, several federal district courts in Connecticut had addressed the certified issue and had unanimously held that Connecticut courts would characterize statutes of repose as procedural. . . . Because those decisions have been called into question by the contrary decision of the district court in this case, resolution of the certified issue by the Connecticut Supreme Court will provide guidance to this Court and to the Connecticut district courts that may face the issue in the future.

The foregoing is hereby certified to the Supreme Court of Connecticut pursuant to Connecticut General Statutes § 51-199a as ordered by the United States Court of Appeals for the Second Circuit.

BAXTER v. STURM, RUGER & CO., INC.

Supreme Court of Connecticut.
230 Conn. 335, 644 A.2d 1297 (1994)

Before PETERS, C.J., and BORDEN, NORCOTT, KATZ and PALMER, JJ.

PETERS, Chief Justice.

The sole issue in this appeal, on certification from the United States Court of Appeals for the Second Circuit, is whether Connecticut law treats a foreign statute of repose as substantive or procedural for choice of law purposes.... We conclude that statutes of repose, such as Oregon Revised Statutes (ORS) § 30.905(1), are indistinguishable from statutes of limitation for purposes of choice of law characterization and, accordingly that, under the established rule in Connecticut for statutes of limitation, ORS § 30.905(1) should properly be characterized as procedural.

In the District Court, in the Second Circuit Court of Appeals, and in this court, the parties have acknowledged that the proper characterization of ORS § 30.905(1) is dispositive of the defendant's motion for summary judgment. If the statute is substantive, as the District Court held, it governs this litigation and bars the plaintiff's claims.[5] The absence of clearly controlling Connecticut precedents on this question of characterization persuaded the Second Circuit Court of Appeals to seek our guidance by way of certification.

Our analysis of the certified question can best be pursued by considering three underlying issues: (1) under Connecticut law, what are the criteria that determine whether a statute of limitation is procedural or substantive for choice of law purposes; (2) for what purposes does Connecticut law distinguish between statutes of limitation and statutes of repose; and (3) for choice of law purposes, does Connecticut law distinguish between statutes of limitation and statutes of repose? This analysis leads us to conclude that, under Connecticut law, ORS § 30.905(1) should be characterized as procedural and, therefore, that the plaintiff's claim is not time-barred.

---

[5] The Oregon Supreme Court has ruled that subsection (2) of ORS § 30.905 is subordinate to subsection (1). Since the action was filed in 1991, more than eight years after the firearm was purchased in 1968, the action would be time-barred by the eight year statute of repose contained in subsection (1). If ORS § 30.905(1) were to be treated as procedural, on the other hand, then General Statutes § 52-577a would apply and the plaintiff's complaint would be timely. The complaint was brought within the three year limitation period prescribed by § 52-577a(a), and the defendant concedes that the repose provision in subsection (c) of that statute does not apply in this case.

I

Connecticut law has well developed criteria that determine whether a statute of limitation is procedural or substantive for choice of law purposes. "[U]nder the general rule applicable in the usual case . . . statutes of limitation relate to the remedy as distinguished from the right." *Morris Plan Industrial Bank v. Richards*, 131 Conn. 671, 673, 42 A.2d 147 (1945). "It is undisputed that, as a principle of universal application, remedies and modes of procedure depend upon the lex fori." *Thomas Iron Co. v. Ensign-Bickford Co.*, 131 Conn. 665, 668, 42 A.2d 145 (1945). On the other hand, "if the limitation is so interwoven with . . . the cause of action as to become one of the congeries of elements necessary to establish the right, that limitation goes with the cause of action wherever brought." *Thomas Iron Co. v. Ensign-Bickford Co.*, supra, at 669, 42 A.2d 145.

Under our law, proper characterization of a statute of limitation, therefore, requires a determination of whether the limitation is directed at the cause of action " 'so specifically as to warrant saying that it qualifie[s] the right.' " *Thomas Iron Co. v. Ensign-Bickford Co.*, supra, 131 Conn. at 670, 42 A.2d 145, quoting *Davis v. Mills*, 194 U.S. 451, 454, (1903). If so, the limitation is characterized as substantive, and the lex loci applies. Otherwise, the limitation merely qualifies the remedy rather than the right, it is characterized as procedural, and the lex fori app

A limitation period is considered "one of the congeries of elements necessary to establish the right," and therefore characterized as substantive, only when it applies to a new right created by statute. In such circumstances, "[t]he time within which the suit must be brought operates as a limitation of the liability itself as created, and not of the remedy alone." (Emphasis added.) *The Harrisburg*, 119 U.S. 199, 214 (1886) (involving action for wrongful death, which did not exist at common law); *Morris Plan Industrial Bank v. Richards*, supra, at 674, 42 A.2d 147. Thus, for the limitation period of the lex loci to apply, the underlying right upon which the lawsuit is based must not have existed at common law. Otherwise, the limitation period established by the lex fori governs. *Morris Plan Industrial Bank* (common law fraud action); *Thomas Iron Co. v. Ensign-Bickford Co.*, (worker's compensation statute codifying negligence action).

The present case involves product liability claims. Oregon recognized product liability actions at common law. In oral argument before this court the defendant conceded that, if ORS § 30.905(1) were a statute of limitation, the *Thomas Iron Co.* rule would apply and ORS § 30.905(1) would properly be characterized as procedural.

II

Acknowledging that the Connecticut rule for statutes of limitation would not support its motion for summary judgment, the defendant claims that statutes of repose, such as ORS § 30.905(1), are always substantive. Undoubtedly, statutes of repose differ in some respects from statutes of limitation. "While statutes of limitation are sometimes called 'statutes of repose,' the former bars right of action unless it is filed within a specified period of time after injury occurs, while 'statute[s] of repose' [terminate] any right of action after a specific time has elapsed, regardless of whether there has as yet been an injury." We must therefore consider for what purposes Connecticut law has distinguished between statutes of limitation and statutes of repose.

In several cases in which Connecticut case law has characterized statutes of repose for domestic law purposes, this court has looked to the comparable law for statutes of limitations. A salient example is the case law under General Statutes § 52-577a, which is a statute of repose because the rights that it delimits can expire "before an individual has been injured and the cause of action has begun to accrue." . . . Analogizing to the law governing statutes of limitation, we have characterized § 52-577a as procedural for purposes of its retroactive application; and for purposes of article first, § 10, the open courts provision of the Connecticut constitution. As a matter of domestic law, therefore, the characterization of a statute of repose as procedural or as substantive is governed by the same test that applies to statutes of limitation.

III

We recognize that the Restatement (Second) of Conflict of Laws cautions against an automatic transfer of characterizations from domestic law into conflict of laws. In § 7, comment d, illustration 3, the Restatement advises that a court "should not hold [a statute] procedural merely because it has previously been so characterized in [a] local law context . . . unless it is convinced that the policy underlying the distinction between substance and procedure in choice-of-law dictates such result." We must decide, therefore, whether reasons of policy support characterizing a repose statute as procedural or substantive for choice of law purposes in accordance with the rules that we have developed for statutes of limitation.

Whether they take the form of statutes of limitation or of statutes of repose, time constraints on the initiation of product liability actions serve the important public policy of preventing the litigation of stale claims. This policy both promotes fairness to defendants and helps to ensure the reliability of the fact-finding process. "For example, some of the evidentiary problems that may arise in connection with trying cases involving older products include the fact that an older product is more likely to have undergone misuse or alteration since manufacture, the possibility that a jury may inappropriately apply a standard reflecting subsequent technological development when assessing liability, and the fact that witnesses and documents may be difficult to obtain. See Martin, 'Statute of Repose for Product Liability Claims,' 50 Fordham L.Rev. 745, 747-48 (1982)." *Daily v. New Britain Machine Co.*, [200 Conn. 562, at 583, 512 A.2d 893, at 904-905.

The defendant maintains, however, that the policies effectuated by statutes of repose differ fundamentally from those served by statutes of limitation. The defendant relies on decisions of courts in other jurisdictions that have held statutes of repose to be substantive because, in their view, unlike statutes of limitation, statutes of repose operate as a grant of immunity serving primarily to "relieve potential defendants from anxiety over liability for acts committed long ago" . . . We are unpersuaded that such a difference in policy exists.

This court has long held that "[i]t is consonant with the purpose of protecting defendants against stale claims that the legislature should enact a statute... which may on occasion bar an action even before the cause of action accrues." We have acknowledged that legislatures enact statutes of repose in furtherance of " 'the public policy of allowing people, after the lapse of a reasonable time, to plan their affairs with a degree of certainty, free from the disruptive burden of protracted and unknown potential liability' . . . It is clear, however, that this rationale applies to statutes of limitation as well. Whether seen as a sanction imposed on plaintiffs who sleep on their rights or as a benefit conferred upon defendants to reduce the risk and uncertainty of liability, statutes of limitation and statutes of repose serve the same public policy of avoiding the litigation of stale claims. . . ."

We are persuaded, therefore, that our conclusion that statutes of repose are to be analyzed, for choice of law purposes, by the same test that governs statutes of limitation, is consonant with the Restatement's admonition. Although domestic law precedents are a useful point of reference, we are not simply importing the characterization of domestic law cases into the choice of law context. Rather, recognizing the basic similarity in the policies served by statutes of limitation and statutes of repose, we are persuaded that it is appropriate to use the same analytic test to determine whether such statutes are procedural or substantive.

IV

We therefore hold that statutes of repose, like statutes of limitation, are neither substantive nor procedural *per se* for choice of law purposes. In any given case, the characterization of the applicable statute of repose depends on the nature of the underlying right that forms the basis of the lawsuit. If the right existed at common law, then the statute of repose is properly characterized as procedural because it functions only as a qualification on the remedy to enforce the preexisting right. If, however, the right is newly created by the statute, then the statute of repose is properly characterized as substantive because the period of repose is so integral a part of the cause of action "as to warrant saying that it qualifie[s] the right." Applying this test in the present circumstances, we conclude that, in light of the common law origin of the law of products liability, ORS § 30.905(1) is procedural and the plaintiff's cause of action is not time-barred.

The certified question asked: "Is a statute of repose, such as Oregon Revised Statutes § 30.905(1), properly considered substantive for choice of law purposes under Connecticut law?" Our answer is: No.

BAXTER v. STURM, RUGER & CO. INC.

*United States Court of Appeals
Second Circuit
32 F.3d 48 (1994)*

Before: MESKILL, PRATT and MAHONEY, CIRCUIT JUDGES.

PER CURIAM:

This case returns to us after our certification of a question of Connecticut law to the Connecticut Supreme Court. . . .

In August 1991, the plaintiff, William L. Baxter, asserting diversity jurisdiction, brought three Connecticut state law claims against Sturm, Ruger and Co., Inc. (Sturm, Ruger), a Delaware corporation with corporate offices in Connecticut. . . . In a ruling not contested on appeal, the district court held that Oregon substantive law would apply to Baxter's claims.

As an affirmative defense, Sturm, Ruger asserted that Baxter's claims were time barred pursuant to Oregon Revised Statutes § 30.905(1). . . . Because Baxter's action against Sturm, Ruger was brought more than eight years after the firearm had first been purchased, the district court concluded that the claims were time barred. Accordingly, the district court ordered judgment in favor of Sturm, Ruger on all of Baxter's claims.

Baxter appealed to this Court, primarily asserting that the district court had erred in determining that, under Connecticut law, statutes of repose were considered substantive. Because of the absence of Connecticut case law on this issue, we certified, sua sponte, the following question to Connecticut's highest court: "Is a statute of repose, such as Oregon Revised Statutes § 30.905(1), properly considered substantive for choice of law purposes under Connecticut law?" The Connecticut Supreme Court, after a thorough discussion of the issue, answered our question in the negative. In accordance with that decision, we reverse the district court's determination that Baxter's claims are time barred. . . .

FURTHER NOTES AND QUESTIONS

(3)(a) Are you satisfied with the outcome in the *Baxter* case? With the reasoning?

(b) Application by the Supreme Court of Connecticut of Connecticut law makes sense, if the court regards its legislation as properly applied to a Connecticut manufacturer. But that is not at all the reasoning reflected in the court's opinion, is it?

(c) Chief Justice Peters, it seems, approaches the question in the same way as Judge Harlan did in *Bournias*—with a specificity test. Here the Oregon statute of repose is not specific, as the Connecticut court sees it, because it qualified a pre-existing right, and was not part of the creation of a new right. Is that persuasive? Should the Connecticut court have explored how the Oregon Supreme Court (or the Oregon legislature) characterized the statute? Recall the difference on an analogous question between the majority and the concurrence in *Haumschild*, p. 52 *supra*.

(d) Suppose the laws remain the same, but the gun was made in Oregon, the accident occurred in Connecticut, and suit was brought in Oregon. Would the action be barred? Is the analysis the same as in questions (2)(a) and (b), pp. 91–92 *supra*, or are discovery rules different from statutes of repose in this context?

(4)(a) Just by way of preview, note that we have not questioned why the U.S. Court of Appeals certifies the question to the Connecticut Supreme Court. If the issue is characterization of the Oregon statute, and the answer is that that statute is procedural, why should the federal court not do its own characterization? More on this question in Chapter 6.[k]

(b) Note that the Court of Appeals states that it certified the question sua sponte. Since the defendant had prevailed in the District Court, it doubtless did not have certification in mind when the appeal was argued. But suppose the Court of Appeals had invited the parties to frame the question to be put to the Connecticut court. Try your hand at drafting a question that might have improved defendant's chances.

(c) How about the following:

When the law of another state governs an action brought before the courts of Connecticut, would that law include the other state's statute of repose?

Would such a question, omitting the suggestion that everything depends on the substantive/procedural distinction, be acceptable? Do you think it might have changed the outcome in *Baxter*?

(5)(a) In 1984 the English parliament, on recommendation of the Law Commission, adopted a Foreign Limitation Periods Act.[l] The thrust of this Act is that periods of limitations are

---

[k] See § 6.02 and in particular *Sampson v. Channell* and questions (3) and (4), pp. 451–52 *infra*.
[l] L. 1984 c. 16, Documents Supplement p. 59.

substantive, i.e., that the period of limitations of the jurisdiction whose law is applicable to the claim (the lex causae) will be applied to determine whether or not the action is time barred. Would you favor this approach? What problem would you see in applying such a rule?[m] How should the question of time bar be handled if there is controversy about the law to be applied?

(b) The European Economic Community Convention of 1980 on the Law Applicable to Contractual Obligations (the Rome Convention), discussed in more detail in Chapter 4, adopts, in Article 10(1)(d) the same approach as the English statute, but applicable only to contract claims. There is no specific exception to Article 10(1)(d), but presumably Article 16 on *ordre public* could be raised in the context of time bar as well.

(c) When the Restatement (Second) of Conflict of Laws (1971) was being updated in the 1980's, no provision caused more controversy than section 142, addressed to the statute of limitations.

The final version reads as follows:[n]

> Whether a claim will be maintained against the defense of the statute of limitations is determined under the principles stated in §6.
>
> In general, unless the exceptional circumstances of the case make such a result unreasonable:
>
> (1) The forum will apply its own statute of limitations barring the claim.
>
> (2) The forum will apply its own statute of limitations permitting the claim unless:
>
> > (a) maintenance of the claim would serve no substantial interest of the forum; and
> >
> > (b) the claim would be barred under the statute of limitations of a state having a more significant relationship to the parties and the occurrence.

Would you favor this approach? Is the approach a neutral one, or does it prefer preclusion to court access?

(d) What would be wrong with a statute or rule that read as follows:

> Whenever an action is regarded as timely brought by the law of the state or country where it arose or by the law of this state, it may be brought in this state.

(e) Another effort to address the problem of time-bar is the Uniform Conflict of Laws -Limitations Act, promulgated in 1982, and as of 1997 adopted by 6 states. Note that here, too, the drafters could not get away from providing an escape clause.

§2. Conflict of Laws; Limitation Periods.

> (a) Except as provided by Section 4, if a claim is substantively based:
>
> > (1) upon the law of one other state, the limitation period of that state applies; or
> >
> > (2) upon the law of more than one state, the limitation period of one of those states chosen by the law of conflict of laws of this State, applies.

---

[m] Note that there is a hardship exception, s. 2(2), applicable, for instance, if the plaintiff, while in hospital, had been led to believe her claim for injury would be met and when it was not and she filed suit, the short foreign limitation period was asserted to bar her suit. See Jones v. Trollope Colls Cementations Overseas Ltd., The Times Jan 26, 1990 (C.A.).

[n] American Law Institute, Restatement (Second) of Conflict of Laws, 1988 Supplement.

(b) The limitation period of this State applies to all other claims.

§ 3. Rules Applicable to Computation of Limitation Period.

If the statute of limitations of another state applies to the assertion of a claim in this State, the other state's relevant statutes and other rules of law governing tolling and accrual apply in computing the limitation period, but its statutes and other rules of law governing conflict of laws do not apply.

§4. Unfairness.

If the court determines that the limitation period of another state applicable under Sections 2 and 3 is substantially different from the limitation period of this State and has not afforded a fair opportunity to sue upon, or imposes an unfair burden in defending against, the claim, the limitation period of this State applies.

(f) Consider how the *Baxter* case would have come out (i) if brought in England; (ii) if brought in a state prepared to adopt § 142 of the revised Restatement; (iii) if brought in a state that has adopted the Uniform Act.

(6)(a) In many ways, the effort to characterize statutes of limitation as substantive or procedural is artificial, more so even than the effort to draw a substance/procedure distinction in other contexts. In Chapter 5, we explore the extent to which the U.S. Supreme Court does or should interfere with choice of law by the state courts. In brief, the answer is sometimes on issues of substance, virtually never on matters of procedure. In that context, how would you think statutes of limitations should be characterized?

(b) Could the Supreme Court, for instance, adopt the formulation of the revised Restatement, question (5)(c) *supra?* Or must the question be left up to each state, without intervention by higher authority?

(c) Would you think the preceding questions call for different answers depending on whether the forum state's limitations period is longer or shorter than that of state X? Whether the statute in question is a traditional statute of limitations, a statute of repose, or a "discovery rule"?

(d) These questions are addressed further, though not really resolved, in Chapter 5. See *Wells v. Simonds Abrasive Co.*, p. 374; *Home Insurance Co. v. Dick*, p. 382; *Sun Oil Co. v. Wortman*, p. 422, *infra.*

CHAPTER 3

MODERN AMERICAN CONFLICTS ANALYSIS: TORTS

§ 3.01 The Range of Modern Thinking

As we saw in Chapters 1 and 2, "black letter" law was never so rigid, nor so unwaveringly applied, as the defenders of stability and predictability contended. There were always some courts—and a good many commentators—who believed other values should be considered in choice of law situations, particularly in tort cases, in which a rule looking solely to the place of injury would lead to injured persons going without compensation. However, the traditional rule, as reflected, for instance, in *Alabama Great Southern R.R. v. Carroll,*[a] was literally embodied in black letters in the American Law Institute's *Restatement of Conflict of Laws,* published in final version in 1934, with Professor Joseph Henry Beale of the Harvard Law School as Reporter, followed a year later by publication of Beale's three-volume *Treatise on the Conflict of Laws* (1935). Section 378 of the original *Restatement,* characteristically concise and unambiguous, read:

> The law of the place of wrong determines whether a person has sustained legal injury.[b]

The *Restatement,* and Beale's writings and casebooks over the first third of the twentieth century were immensely influential, but always controversial. David Cavers, a young colleague (and former student) of Beale's at Harvard, wrote an article challenging the whole *Restatement* approach before that work even came out in final form,[c] and a generation of Beale's contemporaries, led by Walter Wheeler Cook and Ernest Lorenzen of Yale, among others, kept up a steady stream of protests against Beale's system.[d] On the other hand, Beale had many followers, not only among the courts, but also among scholars, led by Professor (later Judge) Herbert Goodrich.[e]

In the 1940's, a group of scholars who had come to the United States to escape from Hitler's Europe, and who had never been drawn into the Beale system—Rabel, Rheinstein, Nussbaum, Nadelmann, and Ehrenzweig, among others—began to publish books and articles bringing a quite different orientation to the field, and while they did not directly influence the courts, they contributed to a continuous reexamination of the basic premises on which the American system of conflict of laws had been built. In the 1950's and early 1960's, Professor Brainerd Currie

---

[a] Section 1.01, *supra.*

[b] Other sections spell out this rule: with respect to absolute liability vs. negligence, § 379; contributory negligence, § 385; the fellow-servant rule, § 386; vicarious liability, § 387; survival of tort claims, § 390; actions for wrongful death, § 391; the measure of damages, § 412; punitive damages, § 421,—but always with the same result—i.e., the law of the place of the wrong governs.

[c] D. Cavers, *A Critique of the Choice of Law Problem,* 47 Harv. L. Rev. 173 (1933), reprinted in D. Cavers, *The Choice of Law, Selected Essays,* 1933–1983 (1985).

[d] See W.W. Cook, *The Logical and Legal Bases of the Conflict of Laws,* (1942); E. Lorenzen, *Selected Articles on the Conflict of Laws,* (1943).

[e] See H. Goodrich, *Conflict of Laws,* (1st ed. 1928, 3d ed. 1949).

of the University of Chicago and of Duke University published a series of articles advocating (as we shall see) a quite different approach to choice of law from that reflected in the *Restatement*. For its part, the American Law Institute initiated a project for a new Restatement (Second) of Conflict of Laws, with Professor Willis Reese of Columbia as Reporter. While this project was underway, substantial changes—some called it a revolution—took place in the approach of American courts to choice of law problems, influenced partly by a general movement in the law in favor of plaintiffs and persons likely to become plaintiffs.[f] Succeeding drafts of the Restatement (Second) both influenced and were influenced by the decisions of courts experimenting with new approaches. When the *Restatement* (*Second*) appeared in final form in 1971, it certified the demise of the first *Restatement;* whether its own approach—midway between the conservatives and the revolutionaries—would stand up over time was far from clear.

In this context, Professor Cavers, 30 years after publication of his iconoclastic "Critique",[g] gave a series of lectures at the University of Michigan, entitled "Policy, Justice, and Principle in the Choice of Law Process." Chapter 2 of the published version of these lectures,[h] in which the author puts judicial robes on five of the most prominent participants in the debate (including himself) forms the first section of this chapter.

Cavers, *ADAMS v. KNICKERBOCKER*: FIVE IMAGINARY CASES

The Choice of Law Process, Ch. 2 (1965) [*]

Case 1

Adams v. Knickerbocker Nature Study Society, Inc. Adams is a dues-paying member of the Society (hereafter called "Knickerbocker"). Knickerbocker is a nonprofit corporation organized under the laws of the State of New York to promote nature study. Its principal office is in New York City, but it maintains a summer camp for adult nature lovers in New York's Adirondacks. In 1961 Andrew Adams, a New York domiciliary and botanist, enrolled for a two-week session. He was taken in a camp truck with fellow-campers to visit Mount Greylock, tallest peak in the Berkshires in Massachusetts. After lunch, at the foot of the mountain, the truck driver carelessly started up in reverse and in so doing ran over Adams who had stooped to observe an unusual species of toadstool.

Adams sustained serious injuries and was hospitalized for two months in Pittsfield, Massachusetts. In June 1962, the New York trial court in which Adams was suing for damages granted Knickerbocker summary judgment. Knickerbocker had shown that, under Massachusetts law, a charitable corporation is not liable for its servants' torts. Under New York law (as a consequence of a series of judicial decisions[1]), Knickerbocker would have no immunity; so if Adams had

---

[f] These developments are obviously beyond the scope of this volume, and, in any event, generalizations are hazardous. It seems not unreasonable, however, to suggest that the "conflicts revolution" as set forth in this chapter be considered in the context of greatly magnified concerns for the legal rights of consumers, minorities, women, employees, children, and others often in the past left behind by established rules of law.

[g] Note c, *supra*.

[h] The lectures were delivered in January, 1964; they were published in revised form in 1965, entitled simply "The Choice of Law Process."

[*] Reprinted with permission of the University of Michigan Press.

[1] The gradual erosion of the limited immunity granted by New York law to charitable institutions seems to have been completed by *Bing v. Thunig*, 2 N.Y.2d 656, 143 N.E.2d 3 (1957).

been allowed to show the driver's negligence, the corporation's charitable character would have been no defense to it. The Appellate Division affirmed the order below in a memorandum opinion, one judge dissenting without opinion. The case now comes to the Court of Appeals which, after hearing extensive argument developing a number of the current methodologies, renders its decision in a series of opinions from which I am quoting the following excerpts.

GRISWOLD, J.

". . .The object of our legal system, I suppose, is to provide "equal justice under law." This is something different from "justice," which is a very elusive concept, and surely as much of an unruly horse as "public policy." If we are to have "equal justice under law," there must be law, which means that there must be rules of law. Cases must be put into groups or categories, and cases which rightly fall within the same category should receive the same decision. This need not be a mechanical process. Indeed, it cannot be such a process, for the problems which arise in human relations have infinite variation. Nevertheless, we should not be deluded by the variation. We should recognize that our function is to develop rules of law so that, in so far as possible, similar cases will be similarly decided.

"This problem, which runs through the law, becomes especially acute in the field of conflict of laws. The conflict of laws is, I take it, 'the subject which determines the effect to be given to extra-state elements in any situation.' "(Griswold, *Renvoi Revisited,* 51 Harv. L. Rev. 1165, 1198 (1938).)

"Though a case has extra-state elements, it is still incumbent upon us to find or develop rules of law for its decision, if we are to meet our responsibility to establish, so far as possible, 'equal justice under law.' " Through long experience, American courts have developed the basic rule that many problems in the law of torts are to be decided by the law of the state where the tort occurred. For the time being, we can put aside difficult problems presented when the tort occurs in more than one state—when, for example, the force originates in one state and takes effect in another. Nothing like that happened here. All of the events directly connected with the injury in this case occurred in Massachusetts.

"The rule which has been developed in such cases was stated succinctly in Section 378 of the original *Restatement of the Conflict of Laws.* This Section reflects the great weight of authority in this country, both before and since its promulgation. Since, in this case, the place of the tort was clearly in the Commonwealth of Massachusetts, its law renders the charitable character of a defendant corporation a defense to all actions for personal injuries caused by its servants, whether these actions are brought by the beneficiaries of its activities or by strangers. Section 388 of the *Restatement* specifically provides, 'If there is a defense on the merits to the plaintiff's claim by the law of the place of wrong, no recovery can be had on the claim in another state."

"In reaching this conclusion, I am not unaware of criticisms of the 'place of tort' rule; nor have I overlooked recent ferment, both academic and judicial, in the field of conflict of laws. I do not think that the place of tort rule should be applied woodenly. For example, it may well be unwise to apply it to the question of survival of causes of action, either on the plaintiff's side or on the defendant's. This means that each problem must be considered carefully and thoughtfully. Nevertheless, in such considerations, we should never forget that what we are seeking is a rule of law. The rule that basic aspects of a tort are covered by the place of the tort is such a rule of law. I know of no other rule which shows any capacity of replacing it. The decision of each case on an *ad hoc* basis should be plainly recognized as the antithesis of a rule of law.

"Earlier in this opinion a definition of conflict of laws has been given. But what is the purpose or objective of the conflict of laws? It is not simply to provide a means of deciding cases, for that could be done by flipping a coin, or by always applying the domestic law of the forum. Is it not true that the conflict of laws 'can have as its only purpose the effort to make the result reached in a particular case independent of the forum in which it is brought'? (Griswold, *In Reply to Mr. Cowan's Views of Renvoi,* 86 U. of Pa. L. Rev. 257, 261 (1939).)

"This is especially true and important within the confines of a Federal system. If we were setting up the United States today, we would almost surely think it foolish to have different rules of law applicable every few hundred miles within its territory. But we have a Federal system, with more than fifty separate legal units. Quite apart from the function of conflict of laws in the international scene, its function within the United States is to bring order out of this chaos, and to provide some rules of law which will make it possible for states to decide cases having some external elements on a rational and reasonably consistent basis.

"Within the United States, there can very rarely be any legitimate basis for one state to apply its 'public policy' against the laws of another state. Nor should any state, in seeking 'justice,' fail to apprehend that there will be no justice unless cases are decided in accordance with law, that is, in the conflict-of-laws area, on a basis which will be accepted by other states, and will lead, in so far as humanly possible, to the same decision of a controversy no matter where the suit is brought.

"Thus, as it seems to me, to say that each state must seek the result which it regards as just under all the circumstances, including the extra-state elements and laws, is simply to deny the existence and purpose of the conflict of laws. It is as much a denial of the purpose of the conflict of laws as is the decision of each case by law of the forum, regardless of its extra-state elements. This should be apparent on its face. It is made apparent when the question of forum-shopping is considered. If each court simply decides what it regards as 'just,' or, on the other hand, if it applies only its own law, then diverse precedents will surely develop, and counsel for plaintiffs will be remiss in their duty if they do not study all the cases in all the states, and file their suit (as they often can) in a state which will give them a favorable result.

"Not only is this a denial of true justice, a denial of the purpose of the conflict of laws, but also it is a denial of law itself. It provides no opportunity for certainty in the law. It makes it difficult to plan transactions having interstate elements. Even after an injury of some sort has occurred, there is, under such a rule, no basis for advising a client as to his rights, or for settling or adjusting the dispute without litigation. All that the lawyer can say is, 'Well, it depends upon the state in which the suit is brought. We will have to see where we can serve the defendant, and then try to find the state where the prospects are best. Perhaps we should sue in three or four states, and then nurse the several cases along until we see how the precedents develop.'

"All of this is fun for lawyers, and provides much for the law professors to write about. But it is not law. It is not conflict of laws, if that term has any real and constructive meaning and objective. We will not have law in this area, we will not fulfill the objectives of the conflict of laws, unless we can provide rules for cases under which the same cases will be decided the same way no matter where the suit is brought, to the extent that this is possible within the limits of human frailty. We will not always be successful in achieving uniformity, but we will surely have more success if we constantly hold up uniformity of result as a major objective, and recognize that there can be no true justice without it.

"To this end, the rule that the law applicable in such a case as the one now before us is the law of the place of the tort seems to me to be well calculated to provide a rule of decision which is understandable by lawyers both before and after an injury has occurred. In order to achieve this rule of law, this measure of certainty and uniformity, we will no doubt have to give up a measure of flexibility. But if flexibility is carried to the point where each case must be decided on all its facts, we no longer have any rule of law. Between the two, I prefer some law to chaos which seems to the particular court dealing with it to be resolved in terms of justice.

"In the long run, therefore, it seems to me more in the interest of justice under law to persist in the position taken by the court below, unless and until a significantly better rule can be offered in place of the one we have. No alternative rule has been advanced having comparable virtues of simplicity and certainty, and therefore I would affirm.

"I should add, however, that the case before us illustrates the possibilities for flexibility, and the opportunity for refinement, which exist under the rule that such cases should be decided in accordance with the law of the place of tort. We still have to decide what that law is, and it may, in some cases, be different when there is an external element in the situation than it would be in a case where all of the facts are internal. Thus, if it had been shown that Massachusetts would, in a case exactly like the instant case, hold that its immunity laws did not apply to corporations mainly active in, and organized under the laws of, other states denying immunity, then adherence to the *Restatement* rules in this case would not advance the goal of uniformity. In such a situation New York should not be more royalist than the king. It should follow the Massachusetts law by applying its own law. (See Griswold, *Renvoi Revisited,* 51 Harv. L. Rev. 1165 (1938).) However, we have no showing here that a Massachusetts court would not apply its own rule to this case."

RHEINSTEIN, J.

". . . My brother Griswold has invoked the authority of the *Restatement* and adjures us not to depart from it. However, as experience throughout the world shows, efforts to secure adherence to mechanical rules for choice of law will not procure uniformity in the long run. The rule that the law of the place of wrong should apply involves circular reasoning to begin with, as Savigny noted long ago. Moreover, it is not firmly supported by authority where the place of injury is not the same as the place where the defendant acted. (See Rheinstein, *The Place of Wrong: A Study in the Method of Case Law,* 19 Tulane L. Rev. 4, 165 (1944).) Finally, though I recognize a place for the doctrine of renvoi in choice of law, Judge Griswold's own willingness to depart from the *Restatement* by recourse to renvoi, permitting reference to the Massachusetts conflict-of-laws rules, reinforces the validity of my observation. Use of sound choice-of-law method in the instant case would make renvoi here unnecessary.

"We should take advantage of this case to adopt the methodology developed on the Continent over the past half century, under the leadership of German scholars—particularly the late Dr. Ernst Rabel, whose monumental study of the conflict of laws on a comparative basis has been published under the auspices of the University of Michigan Law School. The approach there developed calls for avoidance of broad sweeping rules, such as the one Judge Griswold invoked, which purports to cover all civil wrongs. Instead, one would recognize that the court in choice-of-law cases must deal with much narrower, more specific problems. If our rules for choice of law are no broader than the problems, then we can find a specific jurisdiction-selecting choice-of-law rule for each problem, and these rules can embody specific policy judgments that make good sense. Courts will find it possible to adhere to them, and, in time, the uniformity of result that Judge Griswold rightly prizes can be attained.

"Applying this approach to the principal case, I find the specific problem confronting this court is what law should govern the question whether a charitable corporation is immune from liability for its servant's torts. Now this problem has arisen because states have sought to conserve the assets of such corporations for their charitable uses and not to allow persons injured by them, especially their beneficiaries, to jeopardize a charity's continuance by claiming what might be a large share of the corporate assets for such damages. Other states, taking account of insurance, have changed this rule and think it better to protect injured persons by subjecting their charitable corporations to all claims for liability—in practice imposing on them only the need to carry adequate liability insurance.

"The foregoing makes it clear that this problem is one which should be resolved by the law of the state of incorporation, at least where the corporate defendant's office and the bulk of its activities are in that state and where the plaintiff, a beneficiary of those activities, was domiciled there and also had entered into his relationship with the defendant there.

"By applying the law of New York in these circumstances, the court will be giving effect to the reasonable expectations of both parties and will subject neither to a surprise. The plaintiff would have every reason to suppose that disputes arising out of his relationship with the defendant would be resolved by reference to New York law. Certainly he could not be expected to have taken out accident insurance for risks due to his participation in Knickerbocker's activities outside New York State. And, needless to say, the defendant has not sought to allege that the insurance protection it required for its New York activities did not extend to out-of-state risks.

"The protection of reasonable expectations is one of the most important objectives of the conflict of laws. As the foregoing analysis makes plain, it can be attained here by holding the New York law denying immunity to charitable corporations applicable to this defendant. I would therefore order the judgment below reversed."[2]

REESE, J.

"My brothers Griswold and Rheinstein have divided on the question whether this case should be rested on the authority of the *Restatement of the Conflict of Laws*. But that 1934 work is being extensively revised, and, in the spring of 1963, the American Law Institute brought out Tentative Draft No. 8 of the *Restatement of Conflict of Laws Second* dealing with 'Wrongs." To be sure, Draft No. 8 has not yet been passed upon by the Institute's annual meeting, but the Tentative Draft has the approval not only of the advisers to the Reporter, but also the Institute's sixty-member Council.

"Section 379 of *Restatement Second,* which states 'The General Principle' for the 'Torts' topic of the 'Wrongs' chapter, has adopted a different approach to choice of law in the field of torts from that reported in its predecessor. Taking account of the diversity of questions that may arise in torts cases, the draftsmen have used a far more flexible concept than the place of wrong to identify the proper source of law. Instead of the place of wrong, the new provision would require the application of the law of the state which has 'the most significant relationship with the occurrence and with the parties.' The succeeding section adds, however, that where a personal

---

[2] This opinion has been revised along lines suggested by Professor Rheinstein to give greater emphasis in Judge Rheinstein's opinion to the prior relationship of the parties and their consequent expectations. This emphasis required some revision in my report of Judge Rheinstein's reasoning in Case 2.

injury and the defendant's conduct occur in the same state, its law will 'almost invariably' be applied (*Id.* § 379a (1).)

"In my opinion this court should lend its support to this reformulation of the principles of American case law. The language, to be sure, is unfamiliar, but it reflects the spirit of flexibility to be found in our case law dealing with choice of law.

"If we adopt this formulation, we must ask ourselves what state has the most significant relationship to this tort. The question cannot be answered easily. Here tortious conduct by the defendant's agent occurred in Massachusetts and the harm also occurred there. Yet the local law of Massachusetts to which we are referred would deny liability. Section 379 of the *Restatement Second,* presenting the rationale of the new criterion, recognizes that the significance of the relationship may vary with the issue raised, but this does not appear to be helpful here. We note that the comment on this point does not include charitable immunities among the several examples in which the separate treatment of issues leads to differentiated appraisals of significance. In dealing with the analogous question of intra-family immunity, *Restatement Second* in § 390 adopts a special rule referring that matter to the local law of the family domicil. Yet, in § 390a, *Restatement Second* deals specifically with the problem of charitable immunity and relegates it to its general formula. I can scarcely believe this would have been done if the draftsmen had intended the issue to be resolved by a reference to the place of incorporation. In that event, they would have done as they did in the case of the intra-family immunity and referred to that source of law specifically.

"The comment to § 390a recognizes that, if the immunity rule of the place having the most significant relationship is designed to protect only local charities from tort liability, it should not be applied to an out-of-state charity. But, as Judge Griswold observed, we have not been shown that such is the intent of the Massachusetts law.

"Somewhat reluctantly, in view of the cogent argument of my brother Rheinstein, with whose approach the new *Restatement* is in closer agreement than may have been recognized, I conclude that the state having the most significant relationship with the occurrence giving rise to this claim is the Commonwealth of Massachusetts, and so I agree with my brother Griswold that the judgment below should be affirmed."[3]

CURRIE, J.

"The authority on which Judge Griswold would have us rely is bankrupt and discredited. *Restatement Second,* in its efforts to conceal the fact with new verbalisms, only leads us deeper

---

[3] Professor Reese disapproves of Judge Reese's opinion. He views the state of the charity's incorporation and principal activities as having the "most significant relationship with the occurrence and with the parties," at least in this action by a New York plaintiff against a New York defendant. His opposition may foreshadow a change in the current Tentative Draft of *Restatement Second.* However, as recently as his comment on *Babcock v. Jackson,* Professor Reese wrote:

But what of issues that involve neither standards of conduct nor a special relationship? The measure of damages, charitable immunity, survival of actions, and the effect of a release given to one joint tortfeasor upon the liability of other tortfeasors are examples. The state of conduct and injury does not have as great an interest in the resolution of these issues as in issues involving standards of conduct. Yet conduct and injury are the most important elements of a tort. When these two elements are grouped in a single state, it is believed that for purposes of guidance and predictability the law of this state should control unless there is some countervailing reason for applying another law. It may be that, generally at least, a state where both parties are domiciled will have a demonstrably greater interest in these issues than the state of conduct and injury. Reese, *Comment on Babcock v. Jackson,* 63 Colum. L. Rev. 1251, 1255 (1963).

into the morass wherein our efforts to develop a body of international 'rules' for choice of law have left us floundering. Moreover, the appeal of Judge Rheinstein's proposal disappears when one realizes that, like the rules of the first *Restatement,* the specific problems to be identified by this method would have to be approached without regard to the particular policy underlying each of the conflicting laws. We should have to choose laws without knowing the interests of the respective states involved in the litigation. Our decision might, therefore, frustrate the policy of one state without advancing the policy of the other.

"In this case, as in every choice-of-law case involving a controversy in which this state may have an interest, it is our duty sitting as a court of New York State to ascertain the State's policies that may be engaged in the litigation. When, as to any issue, such a policy is identified, we should determine whether there is any reasonable basis for asserting a New York interest in applying that policy to the instant case. If New York has such an interest, then, as a New York court, we should advance that interest by applying New York law. To be sure, we may often have occasion to ask whether the other state has a conflicting policy which we should take into account in formulating New York policy or in the identifying of its interest. Plainly there is no need to exercise that precaution here.

"The case we have before us is a clear example of a false conflict. The policy of New York in seeking to assure compensation to New Yorkers injured by charitable corporations' negligent activities is to deprive such New York corporations of their common-law immunity. Obviously this New York policy is concerned with New York corporations, not with Massachusetts corporations. We should therefore apply the New York law and so give effect to New York's interest. In so doing, we shall not in any way frustrate or impair the Massachusetts policy to conserve the assets of its charitable corporations. That policy reflects the traditional, albeit dubious, trust-fund theory. No Massachusetts corporation will lose assets by our granting judgment to this plaintiff against this defendant. I would reverse the decision below."

CAVERS, J.

"I agree in substance with the criticisms which Judges Rheinstein and Currie have directed to the first *Restatement* and which Judge Currie directs to the alternative approach that Judge Rheinstein would have us adopt. Both would compel us to employ jurisdiction-selecting rules, and, in so doing, to use what I have elsewhere termed 'a blindfold test' which would oblige us to choose between two states without regard to the content of their respective laws. (See Cavers, *A Critique of the Choice of Law Problem,* 47 Harv. L. Rev. 173 (1933).)

"I regret that my brother Reese finds no support for reversal in the language of *Restatement Second.* Advantage might be taken of § 379(3) to give weight to the issue before the court in determining the 'most significant relationship.' Here we are dealing with the claim of a New York citizen who had been taken to Massachusetts and negligently injured there by the servant of a New York charitable corporation. Given these facts the relationship of the New York rule denying immunity with the 'occurrence' and 'the parties' is far more significant on the immunity issue than the relationship of the Massachusetts rule granting immunity. That state's only connection is the circumstance that the injury happened to occur there. Judge Reese's lawyerly argument based on §§ 390a and 390g, which deal with charitable and family immunities respectively, would be more impressive if *Restatement Second* were not in tentative draft. If we reverse this decision, the American Law Institute may bring its charitable immunity section into line with our position.

"I agree with Judge Currie's conclusion that what we have here is a false conflict. Properly viewed there is no real conflict between the laws of New York and Massachusetts. If we consider fairness to the parties as well as the purposes of the two states' laws, the case for reversal is reinforced. Knickerbocker's liability is one with which it must live in all its day-to-day activities in New York State. No doubt it has long since insured itself against the resulting risk, and its insurer could scarcely have reduced its premiums on the chance that Knickerbocker would do damage in a state with a law like Massachusetts'. The impact of variations in state tort laws on insurance premiums is easily exaggerated. Professor Peck could not even detect differences in premiums caused by the adoption of a comparative negligence rule in a neighboring state. (Peck, *Comparative Negligence and Automobile Liability Insurance,* 58 Mich L. Rev. 689, 718–25 (1960).) As for the plaintiff, he is one of those whom this state in doing away with immunity was seeking to protect.

"Judge Griswold fears uncertainty in the law if we depart from the *Restatement's* broad formula. But our decision in this case would provide a clear guide for any like case. If, in a like case, the plaintiff should seek a Massachusetts forum rather than our own, I should hope that Massachusetts would also apply the New York rule. However, our decision now should not depend on evidence that Massachusetts is prepared to take that step. Once we are satisfied that considerations of policy and fairness require New York law to be applied, we should not hestitate to invoke it simply because we cannot be sure that a Massachusetts court at some future time will do as we have done. I vote for reversal."

Voting to reverse the judgment for the defendant: RHEINSTEIN, CURRIE, and CAVERS, JJ.

Voting to affirm: GRISWOLD and REESE, JJ.

Case 2

In Case 2, the laws of the two states are the same and the facts differ from Case 1 only in that there is a new plaintiff, John Ball, a Massachusetts citizen residing in the neighborhood who had been struck and seriously injured when the truck backed up. He, too, had lost below on the immunity ground.

In this case, Judges Griswold and Reese[4] find no difficulty in reaching the same results as they had reached in the previous case and on essentially the same grounds. Accordingly, they voted to affirm. Judge Rheinstein, who in Case 1 had placed some emphasis on the relationship of the New York plaintiff to the New York defendant, could not find in Case 2 any basis for an expectation on the part of the Massachusetts plaintiff that New York law would be applied to his claim. However, since Judge Rheinstein considered the central choice-of-law problem posed by a case involving a charitable corporation's claim of immunity to involve the financial position of such corporations, he concluded that the New York law imposing liability should be applied. As a New York corporation, Knickerbocker's expectations would be shaped by the New York law, and presumably it would have protected itself by insurance. Accordingly, he voted to reverse. Judge Currie also found Case 2 a bit troublesome. To quote from his opinion:

"In abolishing common-law immunity for a charitable corporation, New York was legislating for the protection of New York citizens. If its law is to be extended to protect John Ball, a citizen

---

[4] Professor Reese, having disapproved of Judge Reese's opinion in Case 1, see note 3, *supra,* was not prepared to accept it in this case, though the Massachusetts domicil of the plaintiff would strengthen the grounds for applying that state's law if one were to follow the analysis the former uses in the passage quoted in note 3, *supra.*

of Massachusetts, it must be that New York recognizes another and different interest here, an altruistic interest to protect whoever may be injured by the negligence of a New York corporation, in whatever state he may be. Yet this seems a reasonable assumption; it avoids the possibility of inter-state retaliation and the resulting need to resort to reciprocity.

"I detect nothing in the adoption of the New York rule that would restrict its benefits to New York citizens. Moreover, if such a restriction were imposed here while New York citizens injured in Massachusetts were permitted to recover, the discrimination might be viewed as a violation of the Privileges and Immunities Clause of the Constitution. Such would not be the case, of course, if this extension of New York's financial protection to cover a Massachusetts citizen injured in that state were in any sense an intrusion into Massachusetts affairs. (See Currie & Schreter, *Unconstitutional Discrimination in the Conflict of Laws: Privileges and Immunities,* 69 Yale L.J. 1323, 1361, 1377–78 (1960).) The contrary is true; the compensation paid by way of damages to an injured Massachusetts citizen can only be a benefit to the Commonwealth. I would vote to reverse.

Judge Cavers agreed with Judge Currie's conclusion in the following passage: "When a few years ago this court finally did away with the last vestiges of its former policy to grant charitable immunity, it seems plain that it simply wished to put nonprofit corporations on the same footing as other corporations with respect to civil responsibility. I see no reason why Knickerbocker should have an immunity thrust upon it simply because its victim is a Massachusetts citizen. It has been argued that to allow Ball to recover is to grant him a windfall that he would not have recovered if he had been hit by the truck of a Massachusetts educational institution. I doubt the aptness of the term 'windfall' to describe the recovery of damages by anyone who had been in contact with the rear end of a reversing truck. The plaintiff obtained no more than compensation for the injury sustained. It would be fair to deny him that compensation only if this were the necessary consequence of furthering the purpose of a Massachusetts law. Such is not the case."

Since Judge Rheinstein had cast his vote for the plaintiff, this case also goes to the plaintiff by 3–2 vote.

Voting to reverse the judgment for the defendant: RHEINSTEIN, CURRIE, and CAVERS, JJ.

Voting to affirm: GRISWOLD and REESE, JJ.

Case 3

Case 3 is more complex. It differs from Case 1 in the way the accident comes about and in its date, 1958. On the trip to Mount Greylock, the Knickerbocker truck broke down in Massachusetts ten miles from the destination, and an accommodating farmer offered to rent the Knickerbocker representative an old truck of his for use while the Knickerbocker truck was being repaired. When the farmer explained that he had not registered his truck that year, the Knickerbocker representative said, "Oh, we'll chance it." As in the first case, the truck-driver backed into the plaintiff, Adams, the New York camper, on a highway, but this time under circumstances where neither party could be shown to have been negligent. Yet in 1958, under Massachusetts law, the driver of an unregistered motor vehicle was an "outlaw on the highways," liable for whatever injuries he caused.[5] New York had no such rule. The plaintiff, of course,

---

[5] The Massachusetts statute, which had been interpreted to render an unregistered motor vehicle on the highway a "nuisance" and the owner or operator liable for damage caused by it without proof of negligence, *Koonovsky v. Quellette,* 226 Mass. 474, 116 N.E. 243 (1917); *cf. Strogoff v. Motor Sales Co. Inc.,* 302 Mass. 345, 18 N.E.2d 1016

relied on the violation of the Massachusetts statute to establish liability. The defendant moved for a summary judgment, relying on the Massachusetts law granting charitable immunity, and the plaintiff's failure to allege negligence. The motion was granted on both grounds and the order sustained in the Appellate Division.

Judge Griswold, of course, voted to uphold the decision below on immunity ground but also expressed the opinion that, but for the defendant's immunity, the Massachusetts law governing unregistered vehicles would have been applicable. His belief that the same state's law should govern both issues led him to remark, "I cannot refrain from observing the paradox which would have been produced had a majority been ready to follow Judge Cavers in denying defendant the immunity which Massachusetts law would confer while giving plaintiff the benefit of the Massachusetts strict liability rule. If all the facts of this case had been in New York, plaintiff would have lost for failure to prove negligence. If all the facts of this case had been in Massachusetts, plaintiff would have lost because of the Massachusetts charitable immunity rule. Now, by reason of the division of the facts of the case between the two states, Judge Cavers would perform the miracle of creating a cause of action where none existed in either state. If this represents justice, then so does the principle: 'Heads I win: tails you lose.'"

Judge Rheinstein, having dealt with the charitable immunity issue in the manner indicated by his opinion in Case 1, calling for the application of the law of New York, then turned to the question whether the defendant should be subjected to absolute liability by an application of the Massachusetts law.

"For the reasons noted," Judge Rheinstein continued, "the relationship of plaintiff and defendant was centered in New York and their expectations framed with reference to New York law. New York law should therefore determine the extent to which its own immunity rule can be said to have been abandoned. It is one thing to expose our charities to vicarious liability when the harm done by their servants is the consequence of those servants' careless or intentionally wrongful conduct in another state and to invoke the law of the place of injury for the standards to govern that conduct. It is quite another thing, however, to expose our charities to a drastic sanction of strict civil liability for failure to register a motor vehicle pursuant to the law of another state, an omission unconnected with the actual infliction of plaintiff's injury. I would therefore reject the application of the Massachusetts 'outlaw-on-the-highways' rule to this defendant, at least in a case in which the defendant is sued by its New York beneficiary.

"The Massachusetts statute should be disregarded for the following additional reasons: The statute is meant to deter Massachusetts people from driving on Massachusetts highways automobiles for which no license fee has been paid to the state of Massachusetts. The statute is essentially a fiscal law, reinforced by the penal provision. The fact that the penalty goes, as a windfall, to a private individual rather than to the public treasury is irrelevant. Whether we like it or not, at present, states still adhere to the tradition that they will not mutually assist each other in the enforcement of their fiscal and penal laws."[6]

Judge Reese, though prepared to hold that Massachusetts' relationship to the occurrence was the most significant and that therefore its law should govern the issue of charitable immunity,

---

(1939) (out-of-state owner not liable for driver's unauthorized, unanticipated entry into Massachusetts), was amended in 1959 to remove such vehicles from the nuisance category and to render violation merely evidence of negligence. Mass. Ann. Laws ch. 90, § 9 (Supp. 1963).

[6] I prepared this opinion after Professor Rheinstein had intimated that the special relationship of the parties would have led Judge Rheinstein to apply New York law rather than Massachusetts law as I had originally supposed.

noted that he appeared to be in a minority position on this point. Observing that, on the issue as to the standard of liability to govern the defendant's conduct, the relationship of Massachusetts to the occurrence was even more clearly the most significant, Judge Reese nevertheless voted to reverse the order granting the defendant's motion for a summary judgment but to dismiss the plaintiff's case without prejudice. Judge Reese's explanation of his decision is contained in the following passage from his opinion.

> I do not rest my position on the ground that the Massachusetts "outlaw-on-the-highways" rule is a "penal law in the international sense" (see *Huntington v. Attrill,* 146 U.S. 657, 673 (1892); *Loucks v. Standard Oil Co. of New York,* 224 N.Y. 99, 103, 120 N.E. 198, 199 (1918)) though a strong argument could be made for such a characterization. Rather, I rest my vote for dismissal on the ground that the imposition of civil liability for personal injuries on this defendant in the circumstances of this case would be so outrageous an injustice that, as a matter of sound public policy, we should refuse to give effect to the Massachusetts rule. Although the implementation of such a decision calls for dismissal without prejudice rather than a summary judgment for the defendant on the merits, I take comfort in the realization that a Massachusetts forum can—and doubtless would—protect this defendant by applying its own rule of charitable immunity. I also note with satisfaction that, since the occurrence leading to this action took place, Massachusetts has abandoned its draconic rule. (See, in this connection, the observations of Holmes, J., in *Union Trust Co. v. Grosman,* 245 U.S. 412, 417 (1918).)[7]

Judge Currie, after having been led again by his governmental interest analysis to apply New York law to the immunity issue, addressed himself to the question whether it would be proper to give effect to what would appear to be the clear interest of Massachusetts in imposing a civil sanction on this violation of the control which it exercises over vehicles on its highways through its vehicle registration law. He decided that it would not be proper. His opinion on the point follows:

CURRIE, J. ". . . Agreeing as I must with Judge Griswold that the result reached by Judge Cavers in applying both the New York law denying charitable immunity and the Massachusetts law of strict liability for unregistered vehicles is paradoxical, I would affirm the judgment for the defendant.

"True it is that choice of law must proceed on an issue-by-issue basis; but modern conflict-of-laws analysis can make no more serious mistake than to indulge in an unprincipled eclecticism, picking and choosing from among the available laws in order to reach a result that cannot be squared with the interests of any of the related states. Issue-by-issue analysis should not result in the cumulation of negative policies to produce a result not contemplated by the law of either state.

"The problem has its counterpart in other choice-of-law situations. For example, I find unprincipled eclecticism in the case of *Lillegraven v. Tengs,* 375 P. 2d 139 (Alaska 1962), in which the Alaska court allowed an Alaskan injured in British Columbia to recover from the Alaskan owner of the automobile causing the injury under the British Columbia owner-liability law, despite the facts that the built-in one-year limitation period in that statute had expired before the suit was brought in Alaska and that Alaska had no owner-liability law. This strikes me as

---

[7] This opinion, which I prepared after ascertaining the view of Professor Reese, was substituted for the original opinion by Judge Reese, which applied Massachusetts law to both issues.

a perversion of the government-interest analysis, not to be avoided by the classification of limitations as procedural, and I am glad to endorse the convincing criticism of the decision which appears in 1963 Duke Law Journal at 762.

"Unlike Judge Cavers, I do not find distressingly paradoxical the results even of such cases as *Marie v. Garrison* and *Scheer v. Rockne Motors,* cited by him, where the courts reach results at variance with the identical laws of the states concerned. Their results might be reached, if with some difficulty, by a fair approximation of the governmental-interest analysis. A plaintiff's claim may fall between two stools and be governed by the common law rather than by the statute of either state.

"In our case, however, the problem is different. While Massachusetts has a policy of deterring the operation of unlicensed vehicles, it does not extend that policy to charities (here I follow Judge Cavers in his apparent assumption that Massachusetts would impose vicarious liability on the driver's employer, but not in the case of a charity). While New York has a policy of requiring compensation for its injured residents, it has no policy of imposing liability in the absence of negligence. To impose liability on this New York corporation, which has been free from fault, simply in order to carry out a nonexistent Massachusetts policy of deterrence, seems to me entirely unjustified. (I hope my brethren will note that I have not found it necessary to refer to the doctrine that no state enforces the penal laws of another.)

"It is one thing to fall between two stools; it is quite another to put together half a donkey and half a camel, and then ride to victory on the synthetic hybrid."[8]

Judge Cavers noted that there was no conflict between the Massachusetts outlaw-on-the-highways rule and the New York law which attaches no civil consequences to nonregistration since New York had no reason to assert the applicability of its law to conduct on the Massachusetts highways. Moreover, while admitting that the Massachusetts law was a "drastic" method of assuring more responsible ownership and use of automobiles on the state's highways, he rejected the view that the civil sanction was merely a fiscal measure and observed that a strict liability rule providing for compensation to injured persons could no longer be viewed as penal in the international sense. "Surely," he added, "the day has passed when we should resort to public policy to provide a haven in our state for a defendant who is being called upon to reimburse the plaintiff for damage that the defendant has caused in the state whose law he has violated. Nor do I find myself ready to join Judge Rheinstein in what appears to me to be a piecemeal restoration of New York's former charitable immunity doctrine. Are we prepared now to hold that New York would deny recovery to a beneficiary of a New York charity in a case of injury outside New York in which New York's domestic rule imposed strict liability?"

Judge Cavers next addressed himself to the characterization by Judges Griswold and Currie of the result he would reach as "paradoxical" in permitting the plaintiff to recover in a two-state case when he would fail if the accident had been localized in either state.

"I find nothing paradoxical in the differing results to which Judge Griswold points. That a paradox may seem to exist is due to our habituation to choice-of-law thinking that requires us to choose between legal systems rather than between specific conflicting rules. Otherwise, we should think it natural enough that a two-state case involving two distinct policy problems should

---

[8] This opinion represents a condensation of a draft opinion prepared by Professor Currie and substituted for Judge Currie's original opinion which applied Massachusetts law to the liability issue while applying New York law to the immunity issue.

not always have the same result as a one-state case involving the same problems. (*Cf.* Harper, *Policy Bases in the Conflict of Laws: Some Reflections on the Reading of Professor Lorenzen's Essays,* 56 Yale L.J. 1155, 1163 (1947).) Where both states have the same policies on the problem at issue then I agree it would be paradoxical, to put it mildly, for a two-state case to produce a different result than the same case in either state. Yet traditional conflicts thinking has permitted such results. (*Marie v. Garrison,* 13 Abb. N.C. 210 (N.Y. 1883); *cf. Scheer v. Rockne Motors Corp.,* 68 F.2d 942 (2d Cir. 1934), discussed in Cavers, *The Two "Local Law" Theories,* 63 Harv. L. Rev. 822 (1950).)

"Judge Currie's joinder in the charge of paradox cannot be laid to addiction to jurisdiction-selecting rules, and I agree with him that, when laws are chosen on an issue-by-issue basis, care must be taken not to combine rules in such fashion as to work injustice. I am prepared to accept his quarrel with the Alaska court's action in using its longer statute of limitations to permit an action to be brought against a party who could be held liable only by invoking a rule of liability in a jurisdiction whose 'built-in' period of limitation had expired. The case is rather suggestive of the case that *Kilberg* would have presented if New York had neither a survival nor a wrongful death statute. On the other hand, Judge Currie's acceptance of the results of *Marie* and *Scheer* leads me to distrust the process of interest analysis that can produce them. If pushed too far, it can yield unrealistic delimitations of state interests.

"What characterizes the case where it is improper to join rules drawn from two states to produce a cause of action that would be recognized as a domestic cause in neither state is the fact that the rules thus combined are closely related in purpose—the 'built-in' statute of limitations being an example. Another example is suggested by the law-fact pattern of *Brewster v. Boston Herald-Traveler Corp.,* 188 F. Supp. 565 (D.C. Mass. 1960), though the actual case did not pose the issue. Massachusetts denies truth as a defense to a malicious libel and also denies the recovery of punitive damages, whereas Maine allows truth as an absolute defense and also allows the recovery of punitive damages for malicious libel. I submit—and I am sure Judge Currie would agree—that a Maine court should not grant punitive damages for a true but defamatory statement maliciously published in Massachusetts concerning a Maine plaintiff. It is reasonable in that situation to assume that the Massachusetts rules are related, that in requiring publishers to compensate persons maliciously harmed by true statements, the Commonwealth's lawmakers did so with an awareness that the recovery would be limited to the actual harm sustained. For a Maine court to impose liability for malicious truth, which it could do only by reason of the Massachusetts law, without at the same time adopting the Massachusetts measure of damages, is for it to exploit the interstate situation unfairly. (Perhaps I should add that this hypothetical case would resemble *Kilberg* and that bulwark of the vested rights theory, *Slater v. Mexican National R.R.,* 194 U.S. 120 (1904), only if Maine also allowed recovery for the malicious publication of truth.)

"What Judge Currie has done in the principal case is to insist that two rules, unrelated in policy, be drawn from a single source. Massachusetts' policy of granting immunity to charitable corporations has no relation to its policy of imposing strict liability on drivers of unregistered vehicles. Massachusetts excepts its charities from that rule just as it excepts them from all its rules imposing liability for tort. The fact that the liability is strict introduces no distinguishing element. Must a New York court refuse to impose liability for tortious conduct in Massachusetts on a New York charitable corporation unless it can be shown that the defendant would have been liable under the New York law of torts? If so, then we are letting the Massachusetts immunity rule in by the back door. Yet I had supposed that most of us were agreed that the state of injury had no reasonable basis for injecting its immunity rule into a case in which the charity's state of incorporation and principal activities had done away with the immunity doctrine.

"As I see it, New York has given to its charities just the same status with respect to vicarious liability for their servants' conduct as it has given to any other legal entity of its creation. The policy embodied in that action is not delimited by New York views as to the basis of tort liability or by the views of other states as to the status of their charities. The New York charitable corporation in Massachusetts should be held answerable to Massachusetts law governing conduct there.

"I would reverse."[9]

Voting to affirm the summary judgment for defendant: GRISWOLD, RHEINSTEIN, CURRIE, JJ.

Voting to reverse the summary judgment for defendant but to dismiss the plaintiff's action: REESE, J.

Voting to reverse the summary judgment for defendant: CAVERS, J.

Case 4

Case 4 will be recognized by conflicts cognoscenti as the product of plagiarism rather than imagination. In it both the New York nature lover and a Massachusetts citizen are the victims of the truck-driver's negligence—a New York truck this time—but the accident is fatal to both. The relicts of the victims sue as personal representatives for the wrongful deaths of their spouses in the New York courts for $100,000 each. The defendant, in addition to pleading the Massachusetts law on charitable immunity, pleads the Massachusetts wrongful death act, which at that time restricted damages for wrongful death from a minimum of $2,000 to a maximum of $20,000, the amount between those limits being determined by the degree of the defendant's culpability. Again the defendant prevailed below on the immunity issue. Since on appeal the majority voted to apply New York law on the immunity issue on grounds we have already reported, the excerpts from the opinions presented below relate only to the damage issue.

On that issue Judge Griswold voted that Massachusetts law should be applied, quoting from Mr. Justice Holmes's opinion in the *Slater* case,[10] in which Holmes said, "It seems to us unjust to allow a plaintiff to come here absolutely depending on the foreign law for the foundation of his case, and yet to deny the defendant the benefit of whatever limitations on his liability that law would impose." Judge Griswold also invoked *Loucks v. Standard Oil Co. of N.Y.*,[11] an action by the widow of a New Yorker killed in Massachusetts, in which the New York Court of Appeals, *per* Cardozo, J., enforced the Massachusetts rule limiting damages for wrongful death against a New York corporate defendant.

In taking this position, Judge Griswold had to dispose of *Kilberg v. Northeast Airlines, Inc.*,[12] the case that inspired Case 4. In *Kilberg,* the New York Court of Appeals in an elaborated dictum—virtually a letter of advice to plaintiff's counsel—declared that New York's strong public

---

[9] All of this section of his opinion following the first paragraph was added by Judge Cavers after the revision of Judge Currie's opinion, reported in note 8, *supra.*

[10] *Slater v. Mexican National R.R.*, 194 U.S. 120, 126 (1904).

[11] p. 34, *supra*. The plaintiff did not contend in *Loucks* that the New York rule be applied.

[12] p. 129, *infra; (1961).*

policy, manifested by a constitutional provision forbidding limitations on recovery for wrongful death, justified a refusal to apply the Massachusetts limitation to a case arising out of the death of an airplane passenger, a New York domiciliary, in a Massachusetts crash which ended a flight that had begun in New York, even though the liability for wrongful death had to depend on Massachusetts law, the New York wrongful death act having long been held not to apply to out-of-state deaths. This rule was later sustained against constitutional attack when the full bench of the Second Circuit in *Pearson v. Northeast Airlines, Inc.,* reversed a 2–1 decision by a three-judge panel.[13] The Supreme Court denied *certiorari.*

To narrow *Kilberg,* Judge Griswold relied on the emphasis given in the *Kilberg* opinion to the fact that the place of injury in an airplane accident is highly fortuitous. In view of the considerations special to air travel, he insisted that the dictum should be confined to the type of situation that gave rise to the *Kilberg* case.

Judge Rheinstein saw the damage claims of the two plaintiffs as giving rise to separate problems. He voted to apply the Massachusetts limitation to the claim of the Massachusetts plaintiff, Mrs. Ball, but not to that of the New York plaintiff, Mrs. Adams. He explained his position as follows:

> The Massachusetts plaintiff has never entered into any special relationship with the defendant corporation. Neither he nor his survivors had any reason ever to expect that, in the case of his being injured or killed in Massachusetts, any law other than that of Massachusetts would determine the amount of recovery. If he regarded the Massachusetts law as insufficient for his needs or those of his family, he had the opportunity of supplementing a potential recovery by taking out accident insurance.
>
> In contrast, the New York decedent has a close relationship with the New York corporation of which he had become a member. He could reasonably expect that his relationship to that body would be determined by New York law in all respects, including the corporation's out-of-state activities. For him, no reason existed why he should take out accident insurance to supplement claims he or members of his family might have against Knickerbocker.[14]

Judge Reese, though voting with Judge Griswold to apply Massachusetts law on the issue of immunity, was obliged by reason of their minority position to consider whether the Massachusetts ceiling on damages should apply to the claims of either or both plaintiffs. He called attention to the fact that, while Tentative Draft No. 8 of *Restatement Second* applied the general test of "most significant relationship" to find the source of the measure of damages for torts generally (see § 390b), nevertheless, the Draft promised in a Reporter's Note (at 129) that there "will be a separate section dealing with damages for wrongful death." Judge Reese's opinion continues:

> Though it would be premature to assert what the American Law Institute's position will eventually be, I suspect it not unlikely that it will reflect the position taken in *Kilberg* which, as I read that opinion, certainly calls for the application of the higher measure of damages in the law of the state from which both parties come if that state has a strong public policy calling for its use.
>
> As *Kilberg* made plain, New York's public policy against a ceiling limitation on the damages recoverable for wrongful death is strong. I believe the plaintiff, Mrs. Adams, the

---

[13] 309 F.2d 553 (2d Cir. 1962), *reversing* 307 F.2d 131 (2d Cir. 1962) [p. 135, *infra*]. The court divided 6 to 3.

[14] This opinion represents a slightly condensed version of an opinion provided by Professor Rheinstein and substituted for the original opinion by Judge Rheinstein, which applied Massachusetts law to both plaintiffs' claims.

widow of a New York citizen, should have the benefit of this policy. On the other hand, I see no basis for projecting this policy to the claim of the plaintiff, Mrs. Ball, as the widow of a Massachusetts citizen, for the wrongful death in Massachusetts of her husband. I concur with Judge Rheinstein in holding that, if the defense of immunity is to be denied, the New York measure of damages is to be applied in the case of Mrs. Adams and the Massachusetts measure in the case of Mrs. Ball.[15]

Judge Currie saw a false problem in the claims of the New Yorker's representative and therefore had no difficulty in applying New York law. Unlike *Kilberg* where the defendant was a Massachusetts corporation, here there was no conflicting Massachusetts interest. Moreover, Judge Currie voted to apply the New York measure of damages in the case of the Massachusetts decedent's representative, expressing his views in an opinion from which the following excerpt is taken.

CURRIE, J.

". . . It would be possible, of course, for New York's courts to hold that the policy of compensation without arbitrary limitation is designed primarily for New York people, and to classify nonresidents on the basis of the laws of their home states in order to deny them the protection of New York law when it is withheld from them by their own law. I would not make such classifications arbitrarily, however. In some situations—for example in the case in which domestic law protects married women from liability for the debts of their husbands—I would be quick to classify and to deny the nonresident married woman a protection, or a disability, not bestowed or imposed by her home state. In other cases—concerning, for example, debtors' exemptions—I should much prefer the principle of equal treatment for all. (See Currie, *Selected Essays on the Conflict of Laws,* 545–57 (1963).)

"Here, since New York will apply its law to give full compensation to the survivors of the New York citizen killed in Massachusetts, I would apply the principle of equality and do the same for the survivors of the deceased citizen of Massachusetts. I find comfort in the fact that the New York defendant's liability insurance will cover it in both cases; in the arrangement of such insurance there is no way to predict whether the victim will be a citizen of New York or of Massachusetts.

"Of course I am here venturing to define the scope of New York's policy, which is essentially a task for the legislature. If I am wrong I invite the legislature to correct our decision should I lead my brethren into error as well. But if New York's policy is to be narrowly and selfishly defined in this situation, out of consideration for those local interests that would benefit from such a definition, the decision should be made by the legislature, which is the proper institution to respond to pressures from local private interests—not by this court, in which sensitivity to such pressures would be, to say the least, unbecoming."[16]

As to the New York plaintiff, Judge Cavers joined with Judges Rheinstein, Reese, and Currie in their conclusion, but his opinion manifested some misgivings. Why, he asked, in the New Yorker's case, should a New York court be free to disregard the ceiling that the Massachusetts

---

[15] This opinion, which I prepared after ascertaining the view of Professor Reese, was substituted for the original opinion by Judge Reese, which applied Massachusetts law to both plaintiffs' claims.

[16] This opinion represents a slightly condensed version of a draft opinion prepared by Professor Currie in substitution for Judge Currie's original opinion, which I had prepared and which applied the New York no-ceiling rule to the New York plaintiff's claim and the Massachusetts ceiling to the Massachusetts plaintiff's claim.

legislature had persisted in imposing on recoveries for wrongful death if, as he assumed, it would be ready to recognize a Massachusetts rule to determine whether strict liability or negligence was the basis of the plaintiff's case? On this point Judge Cavers said: "Here we find both states in agreement that wrongful death is actionable and differing only as to the measurement of compensation. On that latter issue, is not the New York law the preferable source of the measure not only because New York has expressed a strong policy against limitations on wrongful death recoveries but because the representative of a New Yorker is claiming compensation from the New York defendant corporation which had taken the plaintiff's decedent from New York into Massachusetts in carrying out a transaction imposing a duty of care on the defendant to the decedent? That relationship provides a ready basis for the application of New York law, and there are no countervailing considerations calling for the Massachusetts ceiling.

"In contrast, in the case of the Massachusetts decedent, there seems little reason in the fatal chance encounter with an out-of-state stranger to afford his survivors a far higher standard of recovery than is available to them under the laws of their home state. The cases of a Massachusetts patron of Knickerbocker and of a New Yorker, who without prior relationship to a New York defendant was killed in Massachusetts, would be more difficult. Fortunately, we need not decide them now.

"Though I sympathize with Judge Currie's desire to assure equality of treatment in our courts to the two widows whose bereavement occurred in the same accident, I believe the implications of his position should be carefully weighed before this court should accept it. I view the advantage which I would have us accord the New York plaintiff, Mrs. Adams, as exceptional, one that springs not merely from the fact that her husband was a New Yorker and the defendant, a New York corporation, but from the further fact that, as I pointed out above, they were in Massachusetts as a consequence of a prior special relationship which they had formed in New York. Suppose we were to hold now that Mrs. Ball can recover unlimited damages for the death of her husband, a stranger to that relationship. How then could we justly deny the claim to full recovery under New York law of the next Massachusetts plaintiff widowed by a New York corporation's Massachusetts operations, even though no New Yorker were hurt in the same accident? Surely the mere coincidence that a single negligent act claimed two victims is not a firm basis for distinguishing between those two cases.

"Yet ought we to take the position that a New York citizen or corporation always carries the New York rule against ceilings on wrongful death recoveries wherever that citizen or the corporation may go? Moreover, if we insist on our no-ceiling law as a rule always to be observed in the New York courts, regardless of the out-of-state decedents and the state laws involved, I see no reason why the courts of other states should not also apply it when their citizens sue New York defendants in their own forums. (Though I write of out-of-state decedents and New York defendants, I scarcely need remark how simplistic those labels are and how many and diverse the connections between the respective parties and states can be.)

"I submit that we are not required by considerations of policy or justice to impose as heavy a burden as Judge Currie's chivalrous response to Mrs. Ball's distressing plight would cast on New York defendants. I am not resigned to that prospect by the realization that their liability insurance carriers would absorb all or a considerable part of the cost and that this in turn would probably not bulk large when spread over the premiums paid by all New Yorkers. We are dealing with damages for wrongful death. In these days when six-figure verdicts in wrongful death actions are becoming a commonplace, the comfort Judge Currie takes in the defendant's liability insurance coverage in the instant case (if it in fact suffices) may easily be unjustified in cases involving individual defendants or accidents less commonly insured against.

"The remedy to prevent such hardships as the anachronistic damage ceiling of Massachusetts may impose on Mrs. Ball in this case lies, I submit, in the hands of the Massachusetts legislature.

"I would reverse as to Mrs. Adams and affirm as to Mrs. Ball."[17]

Voting to affirm as to Mrs. Adams: GRISWOLD, J.

Voting to reverse as to Mrs. Adams: RHEINSTEIN, REESE, CURRIE, and CAVERS, JJ.

Voting to affirm as to Mrs. Ball: GRISWOLD, RHEINSTEIN, REESE, and CAVERS, JJ.

Voting to reverse as to Mrs. Ball: CURRIE, J.

Case 5

Ball v. Berkshire Natural History Society, Inc. We have examined four cases, each of which has been patterned on the first: the charitable corporation of New York injuring the plaintiff or causing wrongful death in Massachusetts. Case 5 reverses the law-fact pattern by switching the facts, not the laws. The charitable corporation is now the Berkshire Natural History Society, Inc., a Massachusetts educational corporation (which I shall call "Berkshire") with activities centered in the Commonwealth, including a camp for nature lovers near Mount Greylock in the Berkshire Mountains of Massachusetts. The campers, who include John Ball of Boston, go on a trip in a camp truck to the Adirondack Mountains in New York State. There the negligence of the truck driver results in the serious injury of Ball. He is rushed to an Albany hospital where he spends two months before returning to his home in Boston for convalescence.

When sued in New York under the New York Non-Resident Motorist Statute,[18] Berkshire moves for summary judgment, setting forth the Massachusetts law on charitable immunity. The trial court grants defendant's motion, and the Appellate Division affirms 3 to 2. Once more we shall poll our judges sitting as the New York Court of Appeals.

Judge Griswold adheres to the place-of-injury rule and votes to reverse. However, he cannot refrain from observing wryly that, despite the critical attitude displayed by his brothers Currie and Cavers toward the *Restatement's* rules, they show no hesitancy to apply the law of the place of injury in this case. This leads him to speculate whether they find the place-of-injury rule acceptable in this case because it favors plaintiff. Judge Rheinstein would, as before, classify the problem of charitable immunity as one of special concern to the state of incorporation, which not only was the seat of the corporation's activities but also the home of the plaintiff. In the light of these facts and the parties' expectations resulting therefrom, he would apply Massachusetts law. He would therefore affirm. Judge Reese, having found the "most significant relationship" to have been with Massachusetts in Case 1, now is led by the coincidence of the place of the defendant's servant's conduct with the place of injury to conclude that that relationship is now with New York. Accordingly, he votes to reverse.[19]

---

[17] This opinion was substituted by Judge Cavers for his original opinion, after reading the new opinion by Judge Currie. The original opinion reached the same result as the substitute.

[18] N.Y. Vehicle & Traffic Law § 253.

[19] Professor Reese disapproves of Judge Reese's opinion and would apply the law of Massachusetts in this case. He views the state of the charity's incorporation and principal activities as having the "most significant relationship with the occurrence and with the parties," at least in this action by a Massachusetts plaintiff. *Cf.* note 3, *supra.*

Judge Currie is prepared to deny immunity in this case. Excerpts from his opinion follow:

CURRIE, J.

". . . It is plain that Massachusetts has an interest in the application of its immunity rule to protect the defendant Massachusetts charitable corporation. But does New York have a conflicting interest to assure the compensation of the plaintiff, a Massachusetts citizen temporarily in New York at the time of injury?

"Certainly this court could declare an interest on the part of New York in applying its policy of compensation to all persons injured in the state in order to compensate medical creditors, and to avoid a burden on our public institutions, merely on the ground that a real tendency to create such a burden exists. That such a construction of New York law would not unconstitutionally encroach on the interests of Massachusetts is the teaching of *Carroll v. Lanza*,[h] 349 U.S. 408 (1955). I would not rush to the conclusion, however, that so broad a construction should be given to New York's law. Our esteemed colleague in California, Justice Traynor, recently refrained deliberately from giving California policy a construction as broad as could constitutionally be sustained, preferring a moderate construction that would avoid conflict. (*Bernkrant v. Fowler,* 55 Cal. 2d 588, 360 P. 2d 906 (1961).)[i] A construction of the Jones Act that refrained from asserting an American interest in protecting local medical creditors when foreign seamen are injured aboard foreign vessels in our ports has met with approval. (See Currie, *Selected Essays on the Conflict of Laws,* ch. 7 (1963).)

"In one aspect at least, the question is whether the domestic gain achieved by the broader construction, judged in relation to the impairment of foreign interests, is such that the purpose to achieve it can reasonably be attributed to the legislature. In another aspect, the question is perhaps how particularistic the courts can afford to be. Would it be practical for us to assert New York's interest in foreigners injured here only when the apprehended burden on local people and institutions actually materializes? Doubt has been expressed as to the willingness of courts to particularize very much in matters of this kind. (See Currie, *Mutuality of Collateral Estoppel: Limits of the Bernhard Doctrine,* 9 Stan L. Rev. 281 (1957).) Happily this appears to have been too pessimistic. (See *Teitelbaum Furs, Inc. v. Dominion Ins. Co.,* 25 Cal. Rptr. 559, 375 P. 2d 439 (1962); *United States v. United Air Lines, Inc.,* 216 F. Supp. 709 (D. Nev. 1962).)

"I need not decide in this case whether to give New York's policy in that respect a broad or a narrow construction, however, for I construe New York's policy of full compensation as designed to discourage the negligent operation of motor vehicles within this state, irrespective of who the victim may be. I am satisfied that such laws as this are designed to have a deterrent effect, though we may all be skeptical as to how effectively they accomplish that purpose. (See Currie, *Selected Essays on the Conflict of Laws,* 210, 294, 323, 371, 488, 540, 701 (1963); Currie, *Comment on Babcock v. Jackson,* 63 Colum. L. Rev. 1212, 1237 (1963).)

"We need not speculate what a court in a disinterested third state would do if such a case were to come before it under circumstances that prevented dismissal on the ground of an inconvenient forum. (See Currie, *The Disinterested Third State,* 28 Law & Contemp. Prob. 754 (1963).)[20]

---

[h] Summarized at p. 400 *infra.*

[i] Reproduced at p. 239, *infra.*

[20] This opinion represents a slightly condensed version of a draft opinion prepared by Professor Currie in substitution for Judge Currie's original opinion which I had prepared and which had rested the New York interest in the application of New York law on New York's concern for the burden of medical care.

"I would apply New York law and therefore vote for reversal."

Judge Cavers reached the same conclusion as Judge Currie, but in doing so may have projected the position noted in the next-to-the-last paragraph of the latter's opinion beyond the point which Judge Currie would find acceptable. "I am not content," Judge Cavers said, "to rest my decision simply on the ground that it advances the domestic policy of this state to do so, if it is possible to justify our preference of the New York law on a principle that would seem persuasive to a court of a disinterested third state, or even to a Massachusetts court. I believe grounds for such a principle of preference exist.

"A basic function of this and, indeed, of any modern state is to provide a highway system and regulate its use, including the prescription of standards of safe motoring. Another mode of regulation is the imposition of civil liability for damages on the motorist who negligently injures another. Still another mode of regulation is to require the provision of financial protection to persons injured on its highways and so to the institutions that minister to them. This state has now determined that these needs are paramount to the protection of charitable institutions from liability, and, therefore, as a part of its scheme of highway regulation, subjects them to its civil liability laws.

"A principle preferring this policy determination by the state of the highway accident to the contrary policy of a state from which the plaintiff and defendant highway users have come preserves the integrity of the state system of regulation without intruding unfairly upon the responsibilities of the other state. To exclude from the New York policy either out-of-state residents who are injured here or out-of-state institutions whose agents have caused injuries here could be justified only if their inclusion were unreasonable or otherwise unfair. Certainly to impose New York law need cause no hardship to institutions operating under the laws of other states which afford them more protection. They have the option to conduct their activities elsewhere. If they enter New York State, they, like New York institutions, can seek such protection as insurance can provide against the financial risk they are assuming.

"I should hope that the reasonableness of this principle would be recognized by courts of other states, whatever their laws as to charitable immunities. I would include in this hope the Commonwealth of Massachusetts, if it continues to adhere to its ancient rule for injuries inflicted there by the servants of its charities.

"It does not follow from the foregoing that a New York charitable corporation whose servants negligently inflicted injury on a New York plaintiff on the Massachusetts highways should enjoy the protection of the Massachusetts immunity. There is no inconsistency in allowing the Massachusetts plaintiff to recover for his New York injury against a Massachusetts corporation while allowing a New York plaintiff to recover for his Massachusetts injury against a New York corporation. A principle is reasonable which would give preference to the law denying immunity when that law exists in the state of injury since that state in denying immunity is by the same token expressing concern that injured persons be compensated. The injury that takes place within the state plainly falls within reach of that concern. On the other hand, a principle is also reasonable which, in a case against a charitable corporation from a nonimmunity state, would deny preference to the law granting immunity when that law exists in the state of injury. The latter state in granting immunity is by the same token subordinating any concern that injured persons be compensated to its concern for the financial health of its charities. It is not the fact that an injury has taken place within that state which arouses the latter concern; it is whether the defendant is connected with the immunity-granting state.

"The imposition of liability in both cases would also be defensible against a charge of inconsistency if one were to apply the 'significant relationship" test of § 379 of *Restatement Second* with a view to the respective purposes of the competing rules, as § 379(3) permits. The fact that an injury takes place within a state which denies immunity for injuries is significant; the same fact in a state that grants immunity for injuries is not in itself significant. To find a significant relationship with the latter state's law, one should ask why it grants immunity. If it is due to the desire to protect the funds of charitable corporations, then the location of the charity, not the fact of injury, becomes significant, although not necessarily controlling.

"I vote to reverse."

Voting to affirm judgment for defendant: RHEINSTEIN, J.

Voting to reverse judgment for defendant: GRISWOLD, REESE, CURRIE, and CAVERS, JJ.[21]

The Five Cases in a Massachusetts Forum

I shall not attempt to report the cases that would parallel Cases 2 through 4 with the new law-fact pattern. I shall follow instead the law teacher's practice of leaving some cases for the class to worry about. Suppose, however, that the five cases had been litigated in Massachusetts. A Massachusetts court devoted to the first *Restatement's* analysis and ready to accept the *Restatement Second* variant would find no difficulty in applying its own law in the first four cases; if it were prepared to follow the *Restatement Second* variant, its decisions would depend on whether it adopted Judge Reese's reading of the black letter or Professor Reese's. However, in Case 5, a Massachusetts forum being asked to hold its charity liable to compensate the Massachusetts plaintiff for his New York injury by application of "the law of the place of the wrong" might take shelter in that ready refuge of a parochially-minded court, public policy, and refuse to allow the New York claim to be enforced. This position could, of course, be circumvented by means of a New York judgment against the charity which the Full Faith and Credit Clause would compel Massachusetts to enforce.[22]

A Massachusetts court, if converted to the approach in Case 1 of Rheinstein, Currie, or Cavers, JJ., should not find it hard to adopt that approach in holding the New York corporation liable, though in Case 3 it might be glad of a chance to restrict the application of its obsolete "outlaw on the highways' rule and though in Case 4 it would probably refuse to allow damages for a wrongful death in Massachusetts to exceed the limit set by the Massachusetts law, even in the case of the New York widow. However, in Case 5, all the New York judges save Judge Rheinstein had held the Massachusetts charity liable in New York by applying the New York law.[23] As Massachusetts judges, presumably, Judges Griswold and Reese would hold fast to the same position. However, Judge Currie would regard Massachusetts, a state having a clear interest in protecting its charities from liability, as being well nigh bound to stand by that policy rather than hold its charity liable. Judge Cavers can do no more than express the hope that Massachusetts would apply the New York rule.

. . . .

---

[21] But it should be recalled that Professor Reese would have Judge Reese join Judge Rheinstein. See note 19, *supra*.

[22] Massachusetts could not constitutionally refuse to enforce the New York judgment on the ground that the claim on which it was based was contrary to the public policy of Massachusetts. Fauntleroy v. Lum, 210 U.S. 230 (1908); [Reproduced at p. 639, *infra*.]

[23] As to Judge Reese, see note 21, *supra*.

NOTES AND QUESTIONS

1(a) Judge Griswold comes through the *Adams v. Knickerbocker* series as wooden and unimaginative. But is he perhaps the true idealist, searching for *equal justice,* not Platonic justice, and eliminating the element of the case that changes not only with the forum, as he says, but with the particular judge hearing the case?

(b) Griswold makes the point (controverted by some of his colleagues) that predictability is important, even in tort. Is he right? Even if primary activity is not affected by choice of law, he argues, advice and conduct of counsel depends on predictability. Is that not persuasive? Reconsider this question after reading the cases in the remainder of this chapter.

(c) Assuming Judge Griswold is persuasive about the need for a rule, rather than what he calls ad hoc decision-making, has he chosen (or followed) the right rule? Would any other rule—for example looking to the law of the place of registry of the vehicle—do just as well?

(d) Is Griswold's support of renvoi, p. 107, (and p. 63, note g) inconsistent with his plea for predictability?

(2)(a) Judge Rheinstein takes up Griswold's argument about uniformity, but says adherence to mechanical rules will not achieve it in the long run. Why not?

(b) Rheinstein also says, at p. 107, that looking to the place of the wrong is circular reasoning. Perhaps he means an act is wrongful only according to some system of law, and so determination of the wrong cannot precede the determination of the source of law. But if the rule is rephrased in terms of looking to the place of injury, is it still circular?

(c) Rheinstein rejects broad rules such as "choice of law in torts depends on . . ." in favor of looking for sources of law for particular issues, such as the relation between the driver and the owner, or the plaintiff and the membership corporation, or the corporation and the state of its incorporation. Are narrow rules easier to frame than broad ones?

(d) What if two rules may be related, but one cannot tell for sure? Suppose, for instance, that if state *A* provides for punitive damages for reckless conduct, but no res ipsa loquitur, state *B* excludes punitive damages in tort actions, but recognizes res ipsa loquitur as a basis for tort recovery.[j] Are the two rules related in each state? Could one choose punitive damages from *A,* and res ipsa from *B?* Or would that be "unprincipled eclecticism" ?

(e) Rheinstein seeks to explore each rule in terms of its purpose, and then to ask whether that purpose would be served by application of the rule to the case before him. Does that work here?

(f) Is Rheinstein focusing on the seat of the relationship? Or on the expectation of the parties? Or something else still? Note that in *Case 1,* all of the approaches come out the same. Later on, it becomes necessary to choose among the approaches.

(3)(a) Judge Reese (here portrayed as early drafts of the *Restatement (Second) of Conflict of Laws* were being issued) comes out in *Case 1* as not very different from Judge Griswold. True, the shot across the state boundary might separate conduct and injury; so might a product liability

---

[j] I.e., the plaintiff may recover on the basis of a showing of injury connected to defendant's activity, without proving the defendant's negligence.

case where the manufacturer is in one state and the consumer is in another. But for the typical case arising out of a motor vehicle accident, Judge Reese seems very close to the "good old rule" of Griswold and Beale.

(b) As can be seen from the footnotes to Judge Reese's opinions,[k] Professor Reese felt his views had been caricatured by Professor Cavers, and that the *Restatement* (*Second*) was in fact more flexible than suggested by Judge Reese's opinions in *Adams v. Knickerbocker*. But the change in the *Restatement* that Footnote 3 suggested might be forthcoming was not very momentous. In the final (1971) version, § 168 reads:

The law selected by application of § 145 determines issues of charitable immunity.

Section 145, the principal section devoted to choice of law in torts, reads as follows:

§ 145. The General Principle

(1) The rights and liabilities of the parties with respect to an issue in tort are determined by the local law of the state which, with respect to that issue, has the most significant relationship to the occurrence and the parties under the principles stated in § 6.

(2) Contacts to be taken into account in applying the principles of § 6 to determine the law applicable to an issue include:

(a) the place where the injury occurred,

(b) the place where the conduct causing the injury occurred,

(c) the domicile, residence, nationality, place of incorporation and place of business of the parties, and

(d) the place where the relationship, if any, between the parties is centered.

These contacts are to be evaluated according to their relative importance with respect to the particular issue.

Has Professor Cavers fairly reflected the *Restatement* (*Second*) in the *Adams* series?[l]

(c) Should § 145(2) be changed so that (a) and (b) are not counted twice?

(4)(a) Judge Currie introduces a concept that the other judges have not raised—the interest of the state concerned. If there is a New York interest in the case before him, he says, then as a New York judge his duty is to further that interest—if there is a reasonable basis for doing

---

[k] Notes 3, 4, 7, 15, and 19.

[l] Section 6 of the *Restatement* (*Second*), reads as follows:

§ 6. Choice-of-Law Principles

(1) A court, subject to constitutional restrictions, will follow a statutory directive of its own state on choice of law.

(2) When there is no such directive, the factors relevant to the choice of the applicable rule of law include:

(a) the needs of the interstate and international systems,

(b) the relevant policies of the forum,

(c) the relevant policies of other interested states and the relative interests of those states in the determination of the particular issue,

(d) the protection of justified expectations,

(e) the basic policies underlying the particular field of law,

(f) certainty, predictability and uniformity of result, and

(g) ease in the determination and application of the law to be applied.

so. Is that an attractive approach? Does it destroy the basic assumption of conflict of laws, as Judge Griswold suggests in his opinion in Case 1?

(b) Currie's approach clearly encourages forum shopping, but so do many other institutions and devices in the United States legal system, including diversity jurisdiction, removal, transfer, and "long-arm" (and related) bases for judicial jurisdiction. Is shopping for a forum whose interest coincides with that of the plaintiff—e.g., full compensation for personal injuries—a bad thing?

(c) Currie's great contribution to conflict of laws analysis is the concept of the *false conflict*. In *Case 1,* for example, it seems that New York has an interest, but Massachusetts has none. Thus, though there is a true difference between the laws of New York and Massachusetts, there is only a false conflict between their interests. Does *Case 2* also present a false conflict? What about *Case 3?* Or *Alabama Great Southern R.R. v. Carroll*?

(d) Note that "false conflict," as Currie uses the term, does not mean, as is sometimes mistakenly said, "no conflict" between the laws of the two states. Clearly Massachusetts and New York have come to a different evaluation of the relative importance of compensating injured persons and shielding charitable institutions. But at least in *Case 1,* Currie can further New York's interest (as he defines it) in compensating a New York injured person without impairing Massachusetts' interests in protecting a Massachusetts charity. How do you think Judge Currie would decide *Adams v. Berkshire Natural History Society* (not one of the cases presented by Cavers), in which (assuming states have interests in cases of this kind at all) there would be a true conflict?[m]

(e) Note that the concept of false conflict need not depend on accepting the proposition stated in paragraph (a) above. A court prepared to accept Currie's analysis of the interests involved could well decide *Case 1* in favor of Mr. Adams, even if it were sitting in Massachusetts or New Hampshire. Only in *Case 5* does Judge Currie bow to hometown justice, deciding a true conflict in favor of the interest of the forum—i.e., for plaintiff if he sits in New York, for defendant if he sits in Massachusetts. And it is in this case that Judge Cavers keeps going where Currie stops.

(f) One final point about Currie's approach, which, as we will see, recurs throughout the actual cases in this and the following chapter. Though he occasionally speculates about what the legislature would have said if it had considered a given problem—for instance, compensating Mr. Ball, the non-resident, in *Case 4*—Currie basically assumes he can discern a state's interest from reading the relevant statute or line of cases which establish a rule of law.

(i) Do states really have interests in private controversies, as contrasted with tax collection, prosecution for crime, enforcement of environmental controls, and so on?

(ii) Assuming the first part of the question is answered "yes," how can one tell what the interest is?

(5)(a) Judge Cavers, having gone along with Judge Currie up to a point, wants to solve true as well as false conflicts by seeking a way to accord fairness to the parties. Is this anything other than what Judge Griswold calls the "elusive concept of justice"?

(b) Can one be more fair to one party than to others without preferring, say, plaintiffs, or New Yorkers, or widows . . . ? Is it possible, as Cavers attempts, to talk about preference in terms of principle?

---

[m] See the excerpt from Currie quoted at p. 200, question (3)(a), *infra*.

(c) Cavers (see p. 123, *supra*) would grant preference to the law denying immunity if that is the law of the place of injury, but deny preference to the law of granting immunity when that law exists in the state of injury. He says "there is no inconsistency . . . ." Is that right? What assumptions does Cavers make about the interests of the respective states?

(d) Try putting Cavers' principles of preference in terms of "significant relationship," as he proposes at p. 124. The fact that an injury is caused by a charity in a non-immunity state (i.e., *Case 5*) is significant, Cavers says; the fact that an injury is caused by a charity in an immunity state (i.e., *Case 1*) "is not in itself significant." In the latter case, he says, the significant fact is the location of the charity. Are you persuaded?

(e) Principles of preferences, too, will recur throughout this and the next chapter, though not with the frequency of interest analysis à la Currie. If you are not persuaded by Cavers as discussed in paragraphs (c) and (d), does that lead you to reject all principles of preference, as contrasted with "neutral principles"? Or could you accept the idea of principles of preference generally—for example that a will or contract will be upheld if it would be valid under any of the possibly applicable laws—without subscribing to Cavers' particular preferences?

(f) Consider how, in the field of personal injury, the following issues might fit into a system of preferences:

charitable immunity	—	no immunity
compensatory damages only	—	punitive damages allowed
only economic loss compensated	—	recovery for pain and suffering permitted
liability only for negligence	—	strict liability
contributory fault bars all recovery	—	damages apportioned according to comparative fault
gratuitous passengers barred from recovery against host owner or drivers	—	no guest statute
workers' compensation bars all other recovery	—	tort recovery by employees from third parties permitted
limit on damages for wrongful death	—	no limit on wrongful death recoveries

(i) On what basis could a court, as contrasted with a legislature, develop such preferences?

(ii) Notice that in the catalogue of issues here set out, all the rules favoring plaintiffs appear on one side, all those favoring defendants on the other. It is much more probable that any given state will have some rules from one column, some from the other, and some not clear.[n]

---

[n] For example, New York never had a guest statute, and abolished limits on recovery for wrongful death in 1894. But it generally does not permit punitive damages in wrongful death, for years had an unfavorable rule on time-bar in cases involving undiscovered injury from harmful products such as asbestos or IUD's, and until the mid-1970's had a rule that not only barred all recovery in cases where the injured party was guilty of contributory negligence but placed the burden on plaintiff to prove freedom from contributory fault.

Could a system of preferences—i.e., a principled system—choose among these rules to enable, say, a plaintiff guilty of contributory negligence (not a bar under the law of *A*) to recover for pain and suffering (permitted in *B* but not *A*)? Look again at the exchange between Currie and Cavers in *Case 3* at pp. 114–17, *supra*.

---

§ 3.02 Lex Loci Discarded

KILBERG v. NORTHEAST AIRLINES

New York Court of Appeals
9 N.Y.2d 34, 211 N.Y.S.2d 133, 172 N.E.2d 526 (1961)

CHIEF JUDGE DESMOND.

Defendant is a common carrier of passengers by air. Plaintiff's intestate, a passenger on one of defendant's planes, was killed in August, 1958 when the airship crashed and burned at Nantucket, Massachusetts, in the course of a flight from a New York airport. The complaint pleads three causes of action but this appeal has to do, immediately, with the second count only. That part of the complaint has been dismissed for insufficiency by the Appellate Division. . . . Plaintiff appeals here from the dismissal. We shall have occasion farther on in this opinion to discuss the first cause of action in which plaintiff sues under the Massachusetts wrongful death statute.

The disputed second cause of action alleges that plaintiff's intestate before boarding the plane at La Guardia Airport bought from defendant a ticket for transportation to Nantucket, that defendant by causing his death in the crash breached its contract to carry him safely and that as a result the passenger's estate and his dependent suffered substantial damages (stated as $150,000) for which his administrator sues and which include "loss of accumulations of prospective earnings of the deceased." There was in effect at the time of this disaster section 2 of chapter 229 of the General Statutes of Massachusetts which gave a cause of action against a common carrier for negligently causing a passenger's death but limited to not less than $2,000 or more than $15,000 the damages to be awarded therefor.[a] Special Term, citing *Dyke v. Erie Ry. Co.* (45 N. Y. 113 [1871]) and other authorities, held that plaintiff could sue in contract and that the law of New York, the place of contract, governed such a cause of action and not the law of Massachusetts, the place of the wrong. The Appellate Division, considering the *Dyke* decision inapplicable, took the position that the second cause of action, however labeled or phrased, is in tort for negligently causing death and as such is subject to the damage limitation of the Massachusetts wrongful death statute.

Plaintiff's submission as to this second count is that it sounds in contract and so is governed for all purposes by the law of New York, the place of contract. If the alleged contract breach had caused injuries not resulting in death, a New York-governed contract suit would, we will

---

[a] The Massachusetts statute read as follows:

Damages for death by negligence of common carrier. If the proprietor of a common carrier of passengers . . . causes the death of a passenger, he or it shall be liable in damages in the sum of not less than two thousand nor more than fifteen thousand dollars, to be assessed with reference to the degree of culpability of the defendant or of his or its servants or agents, and recovered and distributed as provided in section one, and to the use of the persons and in the proportions, therein specified.

assume, be available (*Restatement, Conflict of Laws,* § 337). But it is law long settled that wrongful death actions, being unknown to the common law, derive from statutes only and that the statute which governs such an action is that of the place of the wrong. Language found in the old case of *Doedt v. Wiswall* (15 How. Prac. 128, 141, *affd.* 15 How. Prac. 145)[b] cannot be used to overrule so basic a rule. It follows, as the Appellate Division correctly held here, that plaintiff as administrator has no separate right to sue this carrier in contract for causing his intestate's death, . . . that the cause of action for injuries did not survive, . . . and that the second cause of action had to be dismissed.

That does not mean, however, that for this alleged wrong plaintiff cannot possibly recover more than the $15,000 maximum specified in the Massachusetts act. Modern conditions make it unjust and anomalous to subject the traveling citizen of this State to the varying laws of other States through and over which they move. The number of States limiting death case damages has become smaller over the years but there are still 14 of them (compare the list in Tiffany, *Death by Wrongful Act* [1st ed., 1893], p. xvii, with the data found in *Martindale-Hubbell Law Digests,* 1960 ed., Vol. IV). An air traveler from New York may in a flight of a few hours' duration pass through several of those commonwealths. His plane may meet with disaster in a State he never intended to cross but into which the plane has flown because of bad weather or other unexpected developments, or an airplane's catastrophic descent may begin in one State and end in another. The place of injury becomes entirely fortuitous. Our courts should if possible provide protection for our own State's people against unfair and anachronistic treatment of the lawsuits which result from these disasters. There is available, we find, a way of accomplishing this conformably to our State's public policy and without doing violence to the accepted pattern of conflict of law rules.

Since both Massachusetts . . . and New York . . . authorize wrongful death suits against common carriers, the only controversy is as to amount of damages recoverable. New York's public policy prohibiting the imposition of limits on such damages is strong, clear and old. Since the Constitution of 1894, our basic law has been (N. Y. Const., art. I, § 16; N. Y. Const. [1894], art. I, § 18) that "The right of action now existing to recover damages for injuries resulting in death shall never be abrogated; and the amount recoverable shall not be subject to any statutory limitation." Each later revision of the State Constitution has included this same prohibition against limitations of death action damages. The reasons for its adoption are set forth in the proceedings of the 1894 Constitutional Convention. . . . New York's original wrongful death law (L. 1847, ch. 450), passed very soon after Lord Campbell's Act became law in Great Britain, had like the latter no restriction as to damages. The Legislature later imposed such limits but the convention which drew the 1894 Constitution rejected and forbade them. "The argument which evidently controlled the convention in its action consisted of the claim that the arbitrary limitation was absurd and unjust in measuring the pecuniary values of all lives to the next of kin by the same arbitrary standard.' . . ." The absurdity and injustice have become increasingly apparent in the six decades that have followed. For our courts to be limited by this damage ceiling (at least as to our own domiciliaries) is so completely contrary to our public policy that we should refuse to apply that part of the Massachusetts law (see *Mertz v. Mertz* [p. 58, *supra*]; *Shannon*

---

[b] This was a case, decided by the state Supreme Court (not the Court of Appeals) in 1857, arising out of the death by drowning of a passenger on a ferry which was due to alleged negligence of the operator of the ferry. The ferry owner died before the action was brought, and under New York law as it then was, an action in tort did not survive the death of the tortfeasor. (Compare *Grant v. McAuliffe,* § 2.02, *supra.*) Plaintiff sought therefore to bring her action in contract, and the court sustained the action.

v. *Irving Trust Co.,* 275 N. Y. 95, 102, 103[1937]). The Massachusetts cases likewise say that Massachusetts will enforce the *lex loci delicti* in wrongful death suits unless Massachusetts public policy forbids. . . .

An illustration of our readiness to reject such arbitrary limitations, on public policy grounds, is *Conklin v. Canadian-Colonial Airways* (266 N. Y. 244 [1935]). In the *Conklin* suit plaintiff's intestate had purchased in Albany a plane ticket to Newark, New Jersey, which on its face limited to $5,000 defendant's liability for negligently causing a passenger's death. That limitation, just like the limitation here in question, was contrary to New York's public policy but valid in New Jersey which was the place of the plane disaster and of defendant's alleged wrongdoing. The public policy which allowed us to strike down the contractual limitation in Conklin's case has no less effect here. We will still require plaintiff to sue on the Massachusetts statute but we refuse on public policy grounds to enforce one of its provisions as to damages.

Actually, we have in *Wooden v. Western N. Y. & Pa. R. R. Co.* (126 N. Y. 10, 16–17 [1891]) a flat holding by our court that, in an action brought for causing a wrongful death in Pennsylvania, the New York courts would enforce our limitation of damages (as it then existed) although Pennsylvania had no such limitation. The reason, equally pertinent here, is that the "restriction pertains to the remedy rather than the right" (p. 16) and "does not strictly affect the rule of damages, but rather the extent of damages, and that extent, as limited or unlimited, does not enter into any definition of the right enforced or the cause of action permitted to be prosecuted." *Loucks v. Standard Oil Co.* [§ 1.04, *supra*] does not overrule *Wooden* (*supra*). Looking at the true holding of the *Loucks* case rather than picking out language from the opinion, we find that the court was merely deciding that the minimum set for recovery in the Massachusetts wrongful death statute did not make it a "penal statute" unenforcible [sic] here because contrary to our public policy. . . .

As to conflict of law rules it is of course settled that the law of the forum is usually in control as to procedures including remedies. . . . However, as Professor Leflar says (*Conflict of Laws,* § 60), remedial and substantive "shade into each other constantly" and "the law of the forum normally determines for itself" whether a given question is one of substance or procedure. . . . As to whether the measure of damages should be treated as a procedural or a substantive matter in wrongful death cases, there is authority both ways. . . . It is open to us, therefore, particularly in view of our own strong public policy as to death action damages, to treat the measure of damages in this case as being a procedural or remedial question controlled by our own State policies.

Some of the older Federal cases (see *Northern Pacific R. R. Co. v. Babcock,* 154 U.S. 190 [1894]; *Slater v. Mexican Nat. R. R. Co.,* 194 U. S. 120, 126 [1904]) gave defendants the benefits of limitations of damages found in the law of the place of wrong, regardless of where the actions were brought. Those cases, however, are not binding on us and do not bring into play the full faith and credit clause of the Constitution (see *Wells v. Simonds Abrasive Co.* [§ 5.01, *infra*]. We think that time has proven the wisdom and practicality of the *Slater* case dissent, which adopted the rule of *Wooden v. Western N. Y. & Pa. R. R. Co.* (*supra*).

From all of this it follows that while plaintiff's second or contract cause of action is demurrable, his first count declaring under the Massachusetts wrongful death action is not only sustainable but can be enforced, if the proof so justifies, without regard to the $15,000 limit. Plaintiff, therefore, may apply if he be so advised for leave to amend his first cause of action accordingly.

The judgment appealed from should be affirmed, with costs.

FULD, J. (concurring).

I, too, believe that the judgment dismissing the contract cause of action alleged in the second count of the complaint should be affirmed. However, having made that determination, I would go no further.

To expatiate on this, I would say that, while I agree that the second count—the only one before us—fails to state a cause of action, I find no warrant or justification for going beyond that single issue and considering, *sua sponte,* questions which underlie the complaint's first count alleging a cause of action for wrongful death under the Massachusetts statute. I do not mean to suggest that, in passing upon a case, a court is confined to the authorities furnished or the arguments advanced by counsel, for I deem it clear that, within certain limits, a court is free to reach a decision concerning the issue posed on any ground available. . . . But, as I have already indicated, this does not entitle a court to discuss or decide an issue which not only is not argued by the parties, but actually is not raised or presented by the record.

In this case, the court is called upon to decide only the sufficiency of the second cause of action, sounding in contract, and, quite obviously, whether the monetary limitation specified in the Massachusetts wrongful death statute may be disregarded has nothing whatsoever to do with that decision. Consequently, I feel constrained to limit my discussion to the validity of the contract cause of action. Decision on the question whether the maximum prescribed by the Massachusetts statute measures the amount which the plaintiff may recover on his first cause of action should await an appeal where that issue is presented and the parties have had an opportunity of briefing and arguing it.

As to the question before us, the sufficiency of the contract cause of action, one might well begin by noting that in *Baker v. Bolton* (1 Camp. 493), decided in 1808, Lord ELLENBOROUGH declared, by way of dictum, that, "In a civil court, the death of a human being could not be complained of as an injury." Learned authors attacked the rule thus announced as "obviously unjust"—it had as its consequence that "it was more profitable for the defendant to kill the plaintiff than to scratch him" (Prosser, *Torts* [2d ed., 1955], p. 710)—and as being "based upon a misreading of legal history." (3 Holdsworth, *History of English Law* [3d ed., 1923], p. 336; see, also, Salmond, *Torts* [12th ed., 1957], p. 625; Winfield, *Death as Affecting Liability in Tort,* 29 Colum. L. Rev. 239, 252–253.) Nevertheless, harsh and anomalous though it was, the rule prevailed in England and in this country until the enactment of wrongful death statutes. (See 2 Harper and James, *The Law of Torts* [1956], pp. 1284–1285; *Prosser, op. cit.,* pp. 709–710; Salmond, *op. cit.,* pp. 623–625.)

Although it appears that in England, even before enactment in 1846 of the wrongful death statute known as Lord Campbell's Act, it had been held that, "where death is caused by the breach of a carrier's implied contract for safe carriage, the executor or administrator, although he could not sue in tort, [could] sue in contract, and recover damages suffered by the decedent's estate," no such exception seems to have been recognized in the United States. In fact, in New York, this English exception for wrongful death arising out of a breach of contract of safe carriage was disavowed in this court as early as 1866 in the case of *Green v. Hudson Riv. R. R. Co.* (2 Keyes 294; 2 Abb. Ct. App. 277, *affg.* 28 Barb. 9), where the complaint alleged "that the deceased became a passenger on a train from Albany to New York, under the usual engagement to be safely carried, and that by the gross carelessness and unskillfulness of the defendant's agents, a collision occurred, by means of which the said [passenger] was then and there killed." Although the rule was acknowledged to be "harsh or narrow" the court, nevertheless, denied recovery and concluded that "It is sufficient that the rule is settled so firmly that courts would travel beyond their province into the boundaries of legislation by any attempt to alter it, or to create, by their decision, causes of action not before known."

Thus, whatever may have been the English rule as to recovery for death arising out of a breach of contract of safe carriage, in New York, at least, there was no recovery at common law. The question arises, then, whether, following enactment of a wrongful death statute in this State, an action could be brought on contract for damages for death resulting from the breach of a carrier's agreement. The answer seems to be in the affirmative where the wrongful act causing death, as well as the agreement, occurred in this State. . . . This, though, does not resolve the problem presented by the case before us, where, although the agreement of safe carriage was made in New York, the wrongful act causing death occurred elsewhere.

If this were a matter of first impression, it might be effectively argued that, where "two or more communities are touched or affected by a factual sequence," the "guide to the governing law" should be the jurisdiction having "the most significant contact or contacts' (Harper, *Policy Bases of the Conflict of Laws: Reflections on Rereading Professor Lorenzen's Essays,* 56 Yale L. J. 1155, 1161 [1947]). And, since the contract of safe carriage was undertaken in New York and since this fact provides a more "significant contact" than the adventitious occurrence of the crash in Massachusetts, it might well be further urged, this State's wrongful death statute and not that of Massachusetts should apply.

Impressed though I am by the theoretical soundness of such a position, I am forced to the conclusion that it is foreclosed by our decisions. . . . Since, as is apparent, plaintiff's intestate could not have maintained the cause of action alleged in the second count, there was no right of action to survive his death.

In sum, then, limiting consideration to the only matter before us, it is my conclusion that no action *ex contractu* is available to the plaintiff under either the common law of New York or its wrongful death statute and that, therefore, the Appellate Division properly granted the defendant's motion to dismiss the second cause of action.

FROESSEL, J. (concurring).

We concur for affirmance of the judgment appealed from, dismissing plaintiff's second cause of action. We should reach no other question. . . .

Moreover, the court is laying down a new rule of law whereby we disregard the Massachusetts limitation as to damages in a wrongful death action, thereby undermining the accepted pattern of conflict of law rules, in effect overruling numerous decisions of this court, and completely disregarding the overwhelming weight of authority in this country.

It has long been recognized as the law of this State that the right to maintain an action for wrongful death is dependent upon the existence of a statute creating such a right at the place where the injury resulting in death occurred. . . . Equally well settled is the proposition that our own statute creating such a cause of action (Decedent Estate Law, § 130) is not to be given extraterritorial effect in cases where the wrongful death occurred outside of this State. . . .

Plaintiff's right to maintain this action must therefore stem from the provisions of the Massachusetts statute (Mass. Gen. Stats., ch. 229, § 2). That statute, however, expressly limits the extent of the right given, and declares that the damages assessed thereunder shall not be more than $15,000. In effect, this is tantamount to providing that there shall be no cause of action for wrongful death beyond this amount. The majority, by giving extraterritorial effect to our prohibition against the limitation of recovery in such actions, would permit plaintiff to recover on the basis of the foreign law, and yet not be bound by its express limitation. Such action was vigorously condemned by the Supreme Court of the United States in *Slater v. Mexican Nat. R. R. Co.* (194 U. S. 120, 126) where Mr. Justice HOLMES, writing for the court, stated: "It seems to us unjust to allow a plaintiff to come here absolutely depending on the foreign law for the foundation of his case, and yet to deny the defendant the benefit of whatever limitations on his liability that law would impose."

No sound reason appears why our courts, in enforcing such a right at all, should not enforce it in its entirety. This court has no power to determine what the public policy of Massachusetts should be (*Coster v. Coster,* 289 N. Y. 438, 443 [1943]), and we may not ignore foreign law affecting the substantive rights of the parties merely because such law differs from our own (*id.,* at p. 442).

In *Loucks v. Standard Oil Co.,* although it was suggested that our courts might refuse to enforce a right based upon a foreign statute "that outrages the public policy of New York," this court held that a Massachusetts act, very similar to the one with which we are now confronted, must be enforced, despite the fact that we "cannot give them the same judgement that our law would give if the wrong had been done here.' . . ."

. . .

Furthermore, questions relating to such defenses as contributory (comparative) negligence (*Fitzpatrick v. International Ry. Co.,* 252 N. Y. 127 [1929]), charitable immunity (*Kaufman v. American Youth Hostels,* 5 N Y 2d 1016 [1959]), incapacity of wife to sue (*Coster v. Coster,* 289 N. Y. 438, *supra*) and the Statute of Limitations (*Lipton v. Lockheed Aircraft Corp.,* 307 N. Y. 775 [1954]) have all been regarded by this court as regulated by the law of the place of the injury rather than our own law, since they involve the substantial rights of the parties. In each of these cases we applied a foreign rule of law, although such rule was clearly contrary to the law of our own State, and we applied it whether it benefited the plaintiff or the defendant. In our opinion, the defense raised in the case at bar must be treated in the same manner—*viz.,* by applying the law of Massachusetts, the place of death.

The majority would apply our own law of damages because the place of injury is entirely fortuitous. The same argument may be made with respect to each of the cases just referred to. We should not overrule well-established principles, nor "refuse to enforce a foreign right" at our pleasure, to suit our "individual notion of expediency or fairness" (*Loucks v. Standard Oil Co.,* [p. 37] *supra*).

The position adopted by the majority may result in the situation where, in a single airplane crash in which numerous passengers from various States are killed, a different law will be applied in each action resulting therefrom. The courts of each State, if they followed the majority view, would then apply their own law of damages to the case. As Judge CARDOZO pointed out in the *Loucks* case (*supra*), "The theory of the statute personal, a body of national law which the citizen carries about with him . . . is a theory which has yielded generally in this country to the principles of the territorial system and the doctrine of vested rights' (224 N.Y. at 109). We should not attempt to revive it now.

The case of *Conklin v. Canadian-Colonial Airways* has no applicability to the question before us. That case involved the validity of a *contractual* limitation upon a carrier's common-law liability. In the instant case, not only is the limitation imposed by statute rather than by contract, but, as we have seen, there was no underlying common-law liability.

Finally, we have grave doubts as to the constitutionality of the majority view in light of the decision of the Supreme Court of the United States in *Hughes v. Fetter* [p. 367, *infra*] and section 1738 of title 28 of the United States Code, the implementing statute under the full faith and credit clause of the United States Constitution (art. IV, § 1),^c which provides that full faith and credit be accorded to the acts of the Legislature of any State.

Accordingly, the judgment appealed from dismissing plaintiff's second cause of action should be affirmed, with costs.

PEARSON v. NORTHEAST AIRLINES, INC.

United States Court of Appeals, Second Circuit
309 F.2d 553
cert. denied, 372 U.S. 363 (1962)

KAUFMAN, CIRCUIT JUDGE, with whom CLARK, WATERMAN, SMITH, HAYS and MARSHALL, CIRCUIT JUDGES, concur.

The principal question considered by this Court *en banc* is whether a federal court sitting in the state of New York may constitutionally "apply" a Massachusetts statute giving a cause of action for wrongful death and refuse, for reasons of state policy, to follow a provision of that statute which would limit the plaintiff's recovery to $15,000. The question arises in an action for wrongful death occasioned by a plane crash in Massachusetts. The action was brought in the United States District Court for the Southern District of New York, and was tried before Judge McGohey. The judge ruled that plaintiff's recovery was not bound by the arbitrary limit of $15,000 provided by Chapter 229, section 2, of the Massachusetts General Laws. In so doing he relied on the holding of the New York Court of Appeals, in *Kilberg v. Northeast Airlines, Inc.* The jury thereafter awarded damages well in excess of the statutory maximum and judgment was entered accordingly.[2] From this adverse judgment, the defendant airline appealed to this Court, claiming, *inter alia,* that the recovery should have been limited, as a matter of law, in accordance with the Massachusetts statute. The appeal was first heard by a panel of this Court consisting of Chief Judge Lumbard, Judge Swan and this writer. A majority of that panel held, over my dissent, that the Full Faith and Credit Clause of the United States Constitution barred New York courts, and a federal court hearing an action brought in New York by virtue of diversity jurisdiction, from awarding unlimited recovery in a lawsuit "based" upon the Massachusetts statute. The issue being one of great significance—the constitutional power of the states to develop conflict of laws doctrine—it was ordered, upon application by the plaintiff-appellee and the affirmative vote of a majority of the active judges of this circuit, that the appeal be reheard *en banc.*

As a consequence of this rehearing and extensive reconsideration of the issues and pertinent authorities, six active judges of this Court have reached a conclusion contrary to that of the majority of the original panel, and adopt this writer's dissent from the opinion of the panel. We hold that the ruling of the New York Court of Appeals in Kilberg was a proper exercise of the

---

^c Documents Supplement, p. 4.

[2] The jury brought in a verdict in the sum of $134,043.77. The court's judgment was later amended to include an additional $26,160.88 of interest.

state's power to develop conflict of laws doctrine; and the court's refusal to apply the limitation of recovery provision in the Massachusetts statute a constitutional exercise of such power. The judgment of the District Court is therefore affirmed, as modified in accordance with the panel's unanimous holding on the issue of prejudgment interest. This issue requires no further discussion.

Several additional considerations which we shall discuss, convince us that the conclusion we have reached is compelled.

The essential facts are not in dispute. Marilyn W. Pearson, widow and administratrix of the estate of John S. Pearson, and a citizen and domiciliary of New York, commenced the present action against Northeast Airlines, Inc. to recover damages for the death of her husband, allegedly caused by the defendant's negligence. Northeast Airlines is a Massachusetts corporation authorized to do business in New York. Pursuant to that authorization, it maintains ticket offices throughout the state, and actively promotes the use of its transportation facilities by New York citizens by means of widespread advertising. It operates a full schedule of flights from New York airports and earns a substantial amount of revenue from New York citizens. The decedent, a New York citizen and domiciliary, purchased his flight ticket at the New York offices of Northeast Airlines. He boarded the Northeast plane at La Guardia Airport, in the City of New York, bound for Nantucket Island, Massachusetts, and on the evening of August 15, 1958, the decedent's plane crashed in the vicinity of Nantucket.

Another action, having no connection with the Pearson family, had already been maintained in the courts of the State of New York by the administrator of Edward J. Kilberg, also a passenger on the same ill-fated flight to Nantucket. The highest court in New York ruled in that case that the action, by virtue of New York choice of law rules, was properly founded upon the liability created by the Massachusetts Wrongful Death Act. It stated, however, that New York courts should, if appropriate, award damages in excess of the statutory $15,000 maximum recovery required by the Massachusetts statute. . . . Judge McGohey, constrained by the edict of *Klaxon Co. v. Stentor Electric Mfg. Co.* [p. 449, *infra*], and *Erie R. R. Co. v. Tompkins* [p. 435, *infra*], properly applied the principles of New York conflict of laws enunciated in Kilberg and declined to recognize the Massachusetts limitation upon liability.

This writer has already criticized the argument apparently adopted by the panel opinion, that New York was constitutionally disabled from applying its own substantive rules of law to a cause of action arising out of a plane crash in Massachusetts. See dissent, 307 F.2d at 136. Although Judge Swan did not expressly approve this proposition of constitutional law, the inference seemed inescapable that, in effect, the panel majority had exalted the *lex loci delicti* to constitutional status with the consequence that New York was barred from applying the whole or any part of its own wrongful death policy to the events occurring in Nantucket. If this is indeed the rationale of the panel's opinion, then it is the first decision to "freeze" into constitutional mandate a choice-of-law rule derived from what may be described as the Ice Age of conflict of laws jurisprudence—at a time when that jurisprudence is in an advanced stage of thaw. A majority of this Court rejects this rationale for the same reasons which prompted this writer to reject it in his dissenting opinion.

It is suggested, however, that a different constitutional analysis supports the result reached by the panel. The proponents of this analysis are willing to assume that New York's "contacts" with the transaction are sufficient to support an application of New York's entire wrongful death statute to this accident although it occurred outside the territory of New York. In adopting this approach they would concede that the facts of this case—i.e., (a) Mr. Pearson's purchase of his airplane ticket at a New York office of a foreign corporation doing a large part of its business in New York; (b) his attempt to travel from New York, where he was domiciled, on a regularly scheduled flight most of which was conducted over New York; and (c) the New York domicile of his wife, administratrix and beneficiary under the Wrongful Death Act—are so closely related to the State of New York that it would have the constitutional power to apply its own wrongful death law to this litigation. However, the proponents of this constitutional analysis would deem it contrary to the mandate of the Full Faith and Credit Clause if New York were to entertain a claim for wrongful death "under" the Massachusetts act but apply New York principles governing the extent of permitted recovery. In summary, they urge that once a New York court recognizes a claim for wrongful death based on Massachusetts law, that law must control every incident of the claim. They argue that New York is not required to give *any* faith or credit to the Massachusetts act, but once it gives Massachusetts law *some* faith and credit it must also give it *full* faith and credit.

We find this construction of the constitutional mandate untenable. Despite the resourceful arguments put forth in its behalf, we are not persuaded that a statutory limitation upon the amount of money that may be recovered should merit any greater obeisance than statutory limitations addressed to the length of time during which the action may be brought, or to the parties who are empowered to bring that suit, or to the survival or abatement of the cause of action upon the death of the injured party. In each instance the statute qualifies the rights and obligations to which the statutory cause of action gives birth.

We are directed to no precedent, and are unaware of any compelling logic independent of precedent, which requires a state to enforce such statutory qualifications whenever it chooses to recognize a foreign-based cause of action. For example, the cases are numerous in which a forum state applies its own statute of limitations despite the fact that a limitations period of different duration is expressly incorporated in the statute of the foreign jurisdiction creating a cause of action. See, e.g., *Bournias v. Atlantic Maritime Co.* This is usually accomplished by referring to the statute of limitations as involving mere "procedure" and not "substance." The niceties of such legal legerdemain do not concern us; it is the result that speaks loudly. The Supreme Court has specifically held that a state does not violate the Full Faith and Credit Clause in applying its statute of limitations so as to bar a cause of action still viable in the *locus delicti.* See *Wells v. Simonds Abrasive Co.* [p. 374, *infra*]. The *Wells* case tells us that this is true even though the forum state is refusing to apply a statute of limitations "built into" a statutory cause of action for wrongful death as an "integral" or "substantive" provision.

Despite the effort in *Wells* to pierce to the core of the constitutional issue rather than be occupied by mere labels, we are told that the case is not controlling in the litigation before us, because statutes of limitations involve merely matters of "procedure," of judicial house-keeping. We are further told in buttress of this proposition that it is sheer verbiage to say that the difference between a right limited to $15,000 and one that may run to $160,000 is mere "procedure." But the verbiage is equally thin that would explain any constitutional distinction between time limitations and dollar limitations as one between "procedure" and "substance." It is true that one of the purposes of the statute of limitations is to relieve a court system from dealing with "stale" claims where the facts in dispute occurred long enough ago that evidence is either forgotten or manufactured. But the wide variety of statutory periods cannot be explained solely on the basis of stale evidence. There is no doubt another element, of a more "substantive" character, which might be described as a concern for the interests of the potential defendant.

We do not rest, however, on cases upholding the constitutional power of the forum to disregard the statute of limitations of the *locus delicti*. The Supreme Court has, within the past year, cited with approval two cases emanating from the highest courts of two of our states which applied a rule of local law to govern an incident of a cause of action based upon the law of a foreign state. See *Richards v. United States,* 369 U.S. 1, 12 n. 26 [citing *Grant v. McAuliffe*, p. 67, *supra*, and *Haumschild v. Continental Casualty Co.*, p. 52, *supra*.]

Our decision cannot, therefore, be interpreted to condone a forum's applying its own rules in a wanton manner by labeling matters "procedural" while arbitrarily choosing the parts of a foreign statute it wishes to enforce by labeling them "substantive." We do hold, however, that a state with substantial ties to a transaction in dispute has a legitimate constitutional interest in the application of its own rules of law.

[The Court discusses the cases reproduced in Chapter 5, § 5.02, from *Alaska Packers* to *Watson v. Employers Liability Assurance Corp.*]

We believe that in doing so New York is not bound to model *all* of the rules governing this litigation in which it is conceded it has a legitimate interest, on Massachusetts law. We are convinced that New York may examine each issue in the litigation—the conduct which creates liability, the parties who may bring an action, the extent of liability, the period during which the liability may be sued upon, and in appropriate cases, matters of immunity, insurance procedure, etc.—and by weighing the contacts of various states with the transaction, New York may, without interfering with the Constitution, shape its rules controlling the litigation.

. . . The adoption of such a principle would effect an incursion by Massachusetts upon the public policy of New York far more serious than the purported incursion upon Massachusetts policy which we have upheld today. If Massachusetts local rules must, by constitutional compulsion, govern every aspect of a transaction so intimately affecting the interests of New York, then the concept of full faith and credit is being utilized as an extraordinary example of oppressiveness to legitimate and lawful state interests.

. . . .

We therefore see no escape from the proposition we announce today, that a legitimately interested state may, under the circumstances of this case, apply a firmly fixed and long existing policy of its own, although this would remove a defense provided by an "integral" provision of the locus' statute creating the cause of action. . . .

. . .

The field of conflict of laws, the most underdeveloped in our jurisprudence from a practical standpoint, is just now breaking loose from the ritualistic thinking of the last century. Recent opinions of the Supreme Court and the great wave of academic writing reinforce this trend toward flexible and articulate selection of the laws governing multistate transactions. The development will be stillborn if we impose inflexible constitutional strictures in the name of national unity, restrictions which could not be repaired by state or federal legislation.[21]

---

[21] See Freund, *Chief Justice Stone & the Conflict of Laws,* 59 Harv. L. Rev. 1210, 1235–36 (1946):

If the task of Conflict of Laws is to understand, harmonize, and weigh competing interests in multistate events, and if the desideratum of uniformity will be approached most satisfactorily by evolving rules that deliberately seek these objectives, then we seem to be hardly ready for a set of precepts imposed in the process of Supreme Court decision as fixed canons of constitutional law.

FRIENDLY, CIRCUIT JUDGE, with whom LUMBARD, CHIEF JUDGE, and MOORE, CIRCUIT JUDGE, join (dissenting).

I find nothing in the Federal Constitution that would prevent the legislature of New York from amending its wrongful death act, Decedent Estate Law, § 130 *et seq.,* to include the death in a sister state of a New York resident travelling on a flight from New York on a ticket purchased in New York, or the courts of New York from now reading its wrongful death act to cover such a case. Whether any one of these "contacts' would alone warrant New York in thus applying its own wrongful death act and refusing any "faith and credit" to the "public acts' of the sister state, certainly the combination does. . . .

. . . I would agree also that New York is constitutionally free to overrule decisions that forbid or restrict the personal representatives of a party to a contract of carriage made in New York from suing, on the contract, for wrongful death wherever it may occur. Our brothers' fears as to the imposition of inflexible constitutional strictures on the development of choice of law rules are thus quite needless; the majority seems rather to be supporting itself with ghosts of its own conjuring.

It is common ground that New York has not followed any of the courses just outlined. All seven of the judges of the Court of Appeals in *Kilberg* repudiated an action *ex contractu.* The majority likewise disclaimed any idea that recovery might be had, in tort, under New York's wrongful death act. Chief Judge Desmond said, with entire clarity: "We will still require plaintiff to sue on the Massachusetts statute but we refuse on public policy grounds to enforce one of its provisions as to damages"—"We . . . refuse to apply that part of the Massachusetts law. . . ." New York under the *Kilberg* doctrine thus gives some faith and credit to the foreign wrongful death act. . . .

. . . Appellant contends that the Full Faith and Credit Clause, Art. IV, § 1, and the Due Process Clause of the 14th Amendment forbid this.

A superficially attractive answer is that if New York could validly arrive at the *Kilberg* result on a theory of contract or through amendment or construction of its own wrongful death act, the Constitution does not demand a different conclusion because New York attains the same goal through excising or altering a provision of the Massachusetts Act. I say "superficially attractive" since the two processes differ not only conceptually—which may not be altogether unimportant in a legal system designed to maintain a certain degree of order among fifty states— but practically as well. Although the primary interest of the framers of the Constitution in the area of intergovernmental relations was doubtless to set boundaries between the new Federal Government and the states, they were concerned also with preventing encroachments by one state upon another. See *Ogden v. Saunders,* 12 Wheat. 213, 369, 6 L.Ed. 606 (1827). Madison characterized the Full Faith and Credit Clause as among those "which provide for the harmony and proper intercourse among the States." *The Federalist No. 42.* Granted that whenever a New York court enters a judgment, it is enforcing New York "law," and that New York may often make the same rules that govern transactions within New York apply to events in a sister state, it does not follow that when New York looks to a statute of a sister state as the source of a claim enforceable in its courts, the Constitution allows it to decline, in the Supreme Court's words, "to give full faith and credit to all those substantial provisions of the statute which inhered in the cause of action or which name conditions on which the right to sue depend[s]."

An important reason why a forum state may not do this is that it thereby interferes with the proper freedom of action of the legislature of the sister state. The terms and conditions of a claim created by statute inevitably reflect the legislature's balancing of those considerations that favor and of those that oppose the imposition of liability. The legislature may be quite unwilling to create the claim on terms allowing it to be enforced without limit of amount as most common law rights can be, or for a period bounded only by statutes of limitations ordinarily applicable. The Full Faith and Credit Clause insures that, in making its choice, the legislature creating the claim need not have to weigh the risk that the courts of sister states looking to its "public acts" as a source of rights will disregard substantial conditions which it has imposed—a calculation that would involve variables so numerous and unpredictable as to preclude any intelligent choice. This consideration is inapplicable to instances where the forum, looking solely to its own substantive law, wholly disregards that of the sister state, as the Supreme Court held permissible in *Alaska Packers;* there nothing turns on whether or not the lawmakers of the sister state have acted or how they have acted. True, conduct in the enacting state has been given consequences different from what the legislators of that state desired; but that is the inevitable result of the duplicate law-making jurisdiction that can never be wholly avoided even in our federal system— not of action taken by the legislators of the enacting state in the absence of which the forum would not impose liability at all. The increasing scope of statutory liabilities makes it particularly vital that lawmakers of one state should know that once a transitory right has been created by them, it will receive the uniform enforcement from other states which the Full Faith and Credit Clause contemplated, see *Hughes v. Fetter,* [p. 367, *infra*], compar *id.,* fn. 10, and that they should not be obliged to speculate that other states may take what is liked and reject what is disliked—a prospect that might well discourage or prevent enactments otherwise deemed desirable.

. . . .

It is true that the Full Faith and Credit Clause does not demand that, in enforcing a right given by statute of a sister state, the forum must abandon its own procedural rules. Thus the forum may and ordinarily will apply its own rules as to such matters as discovery, evidence and mode of trial; it would be free to give a jury trial although the foreign statute provided for trial to a judge, or vice versa, just as it may disregard venue limitations in the statute giving rise to the claim. When the foreign state has not made a period of limitations a qualification on the right, the forum may apply its own longer statute, *Bournias v. Atlantic Maritime Co.* Likewise the forum may enforce a statute of limitations shorter than what the enacting state has "built in" to the right; no state can require another to keep its courts open for the enforcement of a claim given by the former's law which the latter would not enforce if created solely by its own. *Wells v. Simonds Abrasive Co.* [p. 374, *infra*]. However, merely labeling a difference from the foreign law as "procedural" or "remedial" rather than substantive will not defeat application of the Full Faith and Credit Clause. . . .

. . . .

. . . A limit on the amount of recovery on a statutory right bears no resemblance to those "limitations . . . imposed to promote practicality, convenience, and the integrity of local practice" which, as this Court has said, are properly denominated "procedure."

. . . In this field of law also, there may be a "twilight zone" where a determination by the forum state that a matter is procedural will be respected even though another court in its independent judgment would regard the issue as substantive. The survival of a claim against a deceased resident defendant, *Grant v. McAuliffe,* cited by the majority, may lie in this zone.

But the transformation of a penal and limited statutory liability into a compensatory and unlimited one goes far beyond the widest concept of "procedure" or "remedy. . . ."

We would reverse the judgment of the District Court, as was done in the decision of the panel written by JUDGE SWAN.

NOTES AND QUESTIONS

(1) Is *Kilberg*

(a) correctly decided;

(b) correct in result but not in reasoning;

(c) wrongly decided?

(2)(a) Note plaintiff's attempt to use characterization as a way out of the law of the place of injury rule. Like the plaintiff in *Horn v. North British Ry.* almost a century earlier, plaintiff in *Kilberg* seeks to frame the claim as one in contract. Judge Desmond rejects this effort, but then tells plaintiff's counsel what they should have argued and acts as if they had done so.

(b) Judge Fuld, who plays a major role in the [r]evolution shown throughout this chapter, is not prepared to join the majority's judicial excursion, but then indulges in a history lesson of his own, possibly preparing the way for subsequent developments.[d] Judge Froessel, too, is disturbed by the court's going beyond the argument of the parties, but also raises serious substantive arguments. Is he correct in accusing the majority of refusing to enforce a foreign right "at our pleasure" to suit our "individual notion of expediency or fairness"? Whose foreign right?

(c) Judge Desmond emphasizes that he is not just speculating about the public policy of New York, as one might suggest that Judge Reese was doing in *Case 3* of the *Adams v. Knickerbocker* series (p. 114, *supra*). As to wrongful death damages, there is the highest expression of public policy, a provision in the state's constitution. Would the rationale of *Kilberg* then not apply to cases involving charitable immunity, guest statutes, or contributory negligence?

(3) Before exploring the reasoning in *Kilberg* further, consider how the professors turned judges would approach *Kilberg*.

(a) Would *Judge Currie* regard *Kilberg* as a true conflict case? Suppose instead of Northeast, Mr. Kilberg's fatal flight had been performed by Eastern Air Lines, at the time a corporation with its headquarters in New York. Would that reduce (eliminate?) the interest of Massachusetts?

(b) *Judge Rheinstein,* one supposes, would stress the fact that the ticket was purchased, and the flight begun in New York. Suppose Mr. Kilberg had been traveling on the return flight on a ticket that had been bought in Massachusetts? Would that change anything?

(c) *Judge Reese* promised in *Case 4* that there would be a separate section on damages for wrongful death when the *Restatement (Second)* came out in final form. Whether in real life he was able to keep the second half of his promise (p. 118) is not clear. Section 178 of *Restatement (Second)* says:

---

[d] See, for instance, the suggestion, at p. 133, *supra,* that he might, "if this were a matter of first impression," be prepared to search out the most significant contact or contacts.

The law selected by application of the rule of § 175 determines the measure of damages in an action for wrongful death.

Section 175, in turn, reads:

In an action for wrongful death, the local law of the state where the injury occurred determines the rights and liabilities of the parties unless, with respect to the particular issue, some other state has a more significant relationship under the principles stated in § 6 to the occurrence and the parties, in which event the local law of the other state will be applied.

What do you think Judge Reese would regard as the most significant contacts in *Kilberg?* Would the outcome be different if the flight had been from Philadelphia to Nantucket?

(d) *Judge Cavers* in *Case 4* comes out for the New York plaintiff and against the Massachusetts plaintiff, where the defendant is a New York corporation. How do you think he would come out in the actual case, with a Massachusetts defendant?

In Chapter 5 of the book from which the *Adams* cases are taken, Cavers indicates that he would also come out for plaintiff in *Kilberg,* stressing that plaintiff was a New York domiciliary.[e] He would not place too much emphasis on that fact, however, but would stress also the carrier-passenger relationship. "But suppose," he writes, "the wrongful death had resulted, not from the crash in landing but from the negligent handling of the plane at the Nantucket airport where the plaintiff's decedent was not a passenger but one of several sightseers who were killed."[f] Assuming the sightseer were the same Mr. Kilberg, i.e., a domiciliary of New York, is the argument for full recovery weaker than in the actual case?

(e) Cavers puts another variation on *Kilberg,* and then a variation on the variation:[g]

(i) A Nantucket bank president, while bicycling to work one morning, carelessly runs down and kills a New York tourist. Some months later, the victim's executor sues the bank president in New York for $100,000, getting service upon the banker while he was attending a convention at the Waldorf.

(ii) The bicyclist who ran down and killed the New York tourist was not the local banker but another tourist, a lady who is also from New York. She is sued in New York and pleads the Massachusetts statute.

How, under the Cavers approach, should the two cases be decided?[h]

(4) Judge Desmond, of course, adopts none of the views of the professors. But what is his rationale?

(a) Is it just New York public policy to protect New York domiciliaries? Would the same public policy apply to non-New Yorkers?

(b) What about the argument at p. 131, *supra,* that he is only concerned with remedies, which are normally governed by the law of the forum, not with substantive rights. Does that make sense?[i]

---

[e] D. Cavers, *The Choice of Law Process,* 168–70 (1965).

[f] *Id.* at 170.

[g] *Id.* at 148–49.

[h] Cavers himself writes that he would decide case (i) by applying Massachusetts law, without much difficulty; case (ii) is much harder, but in the end, he writes, it presents a false conflict and so New York law should apply.

[i] This part of *Kilberg* was in fact abandoned by the New York Court of Appeals within a year. *Davenport v. Webb,* 11 N.Y.2d 892, 182 N.E.2d 902, 230 N.Y.S.2d 17 (1962).

§ 3.02   CHOICE OF LAW   □   143

(c) The critical sentence in the majority opinion of Judge Desmond says:

> We will still require plaintiff to sue on the Massachusetts statute but we refuse on public policy grounds to enforce one of its provisions as to damages.

Can the court do this? If Judge Desmond does not want to apply Massachusetts law, why doesn't he just apply New York law, instead of some from here, some from there? Apart from the constitutional question raised by Judge Froessel, which becomes the central focus of *Pearson*, is it rational to borrow a portion of a state's law but not the rest? Recall on this point the discussion in *Bournias* (the laid-off Panamanian seaman).[j] Is borrowing a cause of action but not the statute of limitations less disturbing than borrowing a cause of action but not the statute concerning damages?

(5)(a) The holding of *Kilberg* almost succumbed to a constitutional attack in *Pearson v. Northeast Airlines I*,[k] but as shown by the opinion here reproduced, that holding was reversed by the full Court of Appeals for the Second Circuit, sitting en banc, and the U.S. Supreme Court denied review. A full discussion of the issues raised in *Pearson* must await exploration of the role of the Constitution in choice of law cases in the United States (Chapter 5, *infra*), and of the impact of *Erie R. Co. v. Tompkins* on choice of law decisions by federal courts exercising diversity jurisdiction (Chapter 6, *infra*). Suffice it to say, for the moment, that by 1962 federal courts (i) believed themselves required to follow the decisions of the highest courts in the state where they sat on matters of substance, which they understood to include choice of law;[1] but (ii) that this obligation to follow state practice only applied to the extent the federal court viewed the state court precedents as constitutional.[m]

(b) Judge Kaufman, who was in the minority in the panel that heard *Pearson I* but whose views prevailed on rehearing, puts the question starkly. He says the inference seems inescapable that the panel's decision holding *Kilberg* unconstitutional "in effect . . . had exalted the *lex loci delicti* to constitutional status," and that if this decision would prevail, it would " 'freeze' into constitutional mandate a choice-of-law rule derived from what may be described as the Ice Age of conflict of laws jurisprudence—at a time when that jurisprudence is in an advanced stage of thaw." On that basis alone, isn't Judge Kaufman right? Consider the debates in the *Adams v. Knickerbocker* series; should any of those views be required by constitutional mandate?

(c) Judge Friendly and his fellow dissenters are anxious to demonstrate that they do not belong to the Ice Age. There may be a minimum contacts requirement for constitutionality of a choice of law;[n] but surely the minimum required link to New York is met in a case involving purchase of a ticket in New York by a New Yorker for a journey that began in New York. Thus, if the New York Court of Appeals had simply held that an action for the death of a New York domiciliary brought in a New York court is governed by New York's wrongful death statute, there would be no constitutional infirmity. But that, as the dissenters point out, is not what the

---

[j] Chapter 2, p. 75, and Question 2, p. 87, *supra*.

[k] 307 F.2d 131 (2d Cir. 1962) (first hearing).

[1] See *Klaxon Co. v. Stentor Electric Mfg. Co.*, reproduced in Chapter 6 at p. 449, *infra*, as well as the discussion throughout that chapter.

[m] Very few cases illustrate this pattern; several of those that do, led to reversals in the Supreme Court. See, e.g., *Watson v. Employers Liability Assurance Corp.*, p. 392, *infra*; *Clay v. Sun Insurance Office Ltd.*, p. 395, *infra*; and *Carroll v. Lanza*, p. 400, *infra*, in all of which the circuit court believed the state rule to be unconstitutional.

[n] See Chapter 5, especially the discussion of *Home Insurance Co. v. Dick*, p. 382, *infra*, and *Allstate Insurance Co. v. Hague*, p. 402, *infra*.

court in *Kilberg* did. It took some of the law of Massachusetts and some of the law of New York. That, says Judge Friendly is "half faith and credit," not what the Constitution calls for. Is Judge Kaufman's answer convincing?

(d) The dissent argues (see p. 140, *supra*) that not only Northeast Airlines, but the Commonwealth of Massachusetts itself is deprived of a constitutionally protected right. Judge Kaufman (p. 138 *supra*) rejects this argument:

> The adoption of such a principle would effect an incursion by Massachusetts upon the public policy of New York far more serious than the purported incursion upon Massachusetts policy which we have upheld today. If Massachusetts local rules must, by constitutional compulsion, govern every aspect of a transaction so intimately affecting the interests of New York, then the concept of full faith and credit is being utilized as an extraordinary example of oppressiveness to legitimate and lawful state interests.

(e) Judge Friendly is perhaps unfair in attributing to Judge Kaufman the unsound argument that all the New York court was doing was applying procedural rules of the forum. Judge Desmond said that, but not Judge Kaufman. Judge Kaufman does make the point that application of forum law in choice of law cases has long been sustained with regard to various issues—notably periods of limitation, but also standing, and survival or abatement of actions—but to argue rather the opposite, i.e., that splitting up the source of law has been permitted with respect to other significant issues.

Is the whole image persuasive of a block of law from which some amount can be chipped off, but not too much?

(6) One of the criticisms of *Kilberg*—and there were many[o] —was that it seemed to focus only on New York domiciliaries. This point was soon put to the test.

(a) One of the other passengers on the ill-fated Northeast Airlines plane was a Mr. Trauth, a resident of New Jersey. The case brought by his widow came before the same U.S. District Judge who heard *Pearson,* i.e., who believed that *Erie v. Tompkins* required him to follow the New York Court of Appeals decision in *Kilberg*.[p] But of course *Kilberg* (as well as *Pearson*) concerned residents of New York. New Jersey had no limitation on damages for wrongful death, but also had not, at the time, adopted any departure from lex loci delicti along the lines of *Kilberg*. How should *Trauth v. Northeast Airlines* be decided?

(b) The federal district court held for the airline. It looked first to the way the New York courts would decide, concluded that those courts would look to the New Jersey choice-of-law rule, and found that that rule pointed to application of the law of the place of injury, i.e., Massachusetts.

(c) Professor Cavers considered this outcome wrong, because granting Mr. Trauth's widow the right to unlimited recovery would advance the purposes of the New Jersey law just as much as it would advance the purposes of the New York law in the case of the New York widow.[q]

---

[o] Compare, e.g., Comment, *Selection of Law Governing Measure of Damages for Wrongful Death,* 61 Colum. L. Rev. 1497, 1512 (1961), with Comment, *Lex Loci Delicti or Lex Fori? Conflict of Laws in Wrongful Death Actions and the Kilberg Case,* 28 U. Chi. L. Rev. 733, 742 (1961), and 74 Harv. L. Rev. 1652 (1961). See also B. Currie, *Conflict, Crisis and Confusion in New York,* in *Selected Essays on the Conflict of Laws,* p. 690 (1963).

[p] *Trauth v. Northeast Airlines,* Civ. No. 149–256 (S.D.N.Y. 1961), not reported officially but described in Currie, *Selected Essays on the Conflict of Laws,* p. 719 (1963).

[q] D. Cavers, *The Choice of Law Process,* p. 171 (1965).

Professor Currie, interestingly enough, came out the other way, since New York, in his view, had no interest in applying its protective policy because the deceased and his dependents were non-residents.[r] Consider how the other members of the *Adams v. Knickerbocker* panel might address *Trauth*.

---

§ 3.03 The Search for a Theory

BABCOCK v. JACKSON

New York Court of Appeals
12 N.Y.2d 473, 240 N.Y.S.2d 743, 191 N.E.2d 279 (1963)

FULD, J.

On Friday, September 16, 1960, Miss Georgia Babcock and her friends, Mr. and Mrs. William Jackson, all residents of Rochester, left that city in Mr. Jackson's automobile, Miss Babcock as guest, for a week-end trip to Canada. Some hours later, as Mr. Jackson was driving in the Province of Ontario, he apparently lost control of the car; it went off the highway into an adjacent stone wall, and Miss Babcock was seriously injured. Upon her return to this State, she brought the present action against William Jackson, alleging negligence on his part in operating his automobile.

At the time of the accident, there was in force in Ontario a statute providing that "the owner or driver of a motor vehicle, other than a vehicle operated in the business of carrying passengers for compensation, is not liable for any loss or damage resulting from bodily injury to, or the death of any person being carried in . . . the motor vehicle" (Highway Traffic Act of Province of Ontario [Ontario Rev. Stat. (1960), ch. 172], § 105, subd. [2]). Even though no such bar is recognized under this State's substantive law of torts . . . the defendant moved to dismiss the complaint on the ground that the law of the place where the accident occurred governs and that Ontario's guest statute bars recovery. The court at Special Term, agreeing with the defendant, granted the motion and the Appellate Division, over a strong dissent by JUSTICE HALPERN, affirmed the judgment of dismissal without opinion.

The question presented is simply drawn. Shall the law of the place of the tort[2] *invariably* govern the availability of relief for the tort or shall the applicable choice of law rule also reflect a consideration of other factors which are relevant to the purposes served by the enforcement or denial of the remedy?

The traditional choice of law rule, embodied in the original *Restatement of Conflict of Laws* (§ 384), and until recently unquestioningly followed in this court . . . has been that the substantive rights and liabilities arising out of a tortious occurrence are determinable by the law of the place of the tort. It had its conceptual foundation in the vested rights doctrine, namely, that a right to recover for a foreign tort owes its creation to the law of the jurisdiction where

---

[r] B. Currie, *Conflict, Crisis, and Confusion in New York,* 1963 Duke L.J. 1, 31 reprinted in B. Currie, *Selected Essays on the Conflict of Laws,* pp. 690, 719 (1963).

[2] In this case, as in nearly all such cases, the conduct causing injury and the injury itself occurred in the same jurisdiction. The phrase "place of the tort," as distinguished from "place of wrong" and "place of injury," is used herein to designate the place where both the wrong and the injury took place.

the injury occurred and depends for its existence and extent solely on such law. . . . Although espoused by such great figures as Justice HOLMES (see *Slater v. Mexican Nat. R. R. Co.,* 194 U. S. 120) and Professor Beale (2 *Conflict of Laws* [1935], pp. 1286–1292), the vested rights doctrine has long since been discredited because it fails to take account of underlying policy considerations in evaluating the significance to be ascribed to the circumstance that an act had a foreign situs in determining the rights and liabilities which arise out of that act.[3] "The vice of the vested rights theory," it has been aptly stated, "is that it affects to decide concrete cases upon generalities which do not state the practical considerations involved." (Yntema, *The Hornbook Method and the Conflict of Laws,* 37 Yale L. J. 468, 482–483 [1928].) More particularly, as applied to torts, the theory ignores the interest which jurisdictions other than that where the tort occurred may have in the resolution of particular issues. It is for this very reason that, despite the advantages of certainty, ease of application and predictability which it affords (see Cheatham and Reese, *Choice of the Applicable Law,* 52 Colum. L. Rev. 959, 976 [1952]), there has in recent years been increasing criticism of the traditional rule by commentators and a judicial trend towards its abandonment or modification.

Significantly, it was dissatisfaction with "the mechanical formulae of the conflicts of law" (*Vanston Committee v. Green,* 329 U. S. 156, 162 [1946]) which led to judicial departure from similarly inflexible choice of law rules in the field of contracts, grounded, like the torts rule, on the vested rights doctrine. According to those traditional rules, matters bearing upon the execution, interpretation and validity of a contract were determinable by the internal law of the place where the contract was made, while matters connected with their performance were regulated by the internal law of the place where the contract was to be performed.

In *Auten v. Auten* [p. 246, *infra*], however, this court abandoned such rules and applied what has been termed the "center of gravity" or "grouping of contacts" theory of the conflict of laws. "Under this theory," we declared in the *Auten* case, "the courts, instead of regarding as conclusive the parties' intention or the place of making or performance, lay emphasis rather upon the law of the place 'which has the most significant contacts with the matter in dispute.'" The "center of gravity" rule of *Auten* has not only been applied in other cases in this State, as well as in other jurisdictions, but has supplanted the prior rigid and set contract rules in the most current draft of the *Restatement of Conflict of Laws.* (See *Restatement, Second, Conflict of Laws,* § 332b [Tentative Draft No. 6, 1960].)[a]

Realization of the unjust and anomalous results which may ensue from application of the traditional rule in tort cases has also prompted judicial search for a more satisfactory alternative in that area. In the much discussed case of *Kilberg v. Northeast Airlines* this court declined to apply the law of the place of the tort as respects the issue of the quantum of the recovery in a death action arising out of an airplane crash, where the decedent had been a New York resident and his relationship with the defendant airline had originated in this State. In his opinion for the court, Chief Judge DESMOND described, with force and logic, the shortcomings of the traditional rule:

---

[3] See Cavers, *A Critique of the Choice-of-Law Problem,* 47 Harv. L. Rev. 173, 178; Cheatham, *American Theories of Conflict of Laws: Their Role and Utility,* 58 Harv. L. Rev. 361, 379–385; Cook, *The Logical and Legal Bases of the Conflict of Laws,* 33 Yale L. J. 457, 479 *et seq.;* Hill, *Governmental Interest and the Conflict of Laws,* 27 U. Chi. L. Rev. 463; Lorenzen, *Territoriality, Public Policy and the Conflict of Laws,* 33 Yale L. J. 736, 746–749; Yntema, *The Hornbook Method and the Conflict of Laws,* 37 Yale L. J. 468, 474 *et seq.*

[a] Section 188 in the final version.

Modern conditions make it unjust and anomalous to subject the traveling citizen of this State to the varying laws of other States through and over which they move. . . . An air traveler from New York may in a flight of a few hours' duration pass through . . . commonwealths [limiting death damage awards]. His plane may meet with disaster in a State he never intended to cross but into which the plane has flown because of bad weather or other unexpected developments, or an airplane's catastrophic descent may begin in one State and end in another. The place of injury becomes entirely fortuitous. Our courts should if possible provide protection for our own State's people against unfair and anachronistic treatment of the lawsuits which result from these disasters.

The emphasis in *Kilberg* was plainly that the merely fortuitous circumstance that the wrong and injury occurred in Massachusetts did not give that State a controlling concern or interest in the amount of the tort recovery as against the competing interest of New York in providing its residents or users of transportation facilities there originating with full compensation for wrongful death. Although the *Kilberg* case did not expressly adopt the "center of gravity" theory, its weighing of the contacts or interests of the respective jurisdictions to determine their bearing on the issue of the extent of the recovery is consistent with that approach.

The same judicial disposition is also reflected in a variety of other decisions, some of recent date, others of earlier origin, relating to workmen's compensation, tortious occurrences arising out of a contract, issues affecting the survival of a tort right of action and intrafamilial immunity from tort and situations involving a form of statutory liability. These numerous cases differ in many ways but they are all similar in two important respects. First, by one rationale or another, they rejected the inexorable application of the law of the place of the tort where that place has no reasonable or relevant interest in the particular issue involved. And, second, in each of these cases the courts, after examining the particular circumstances presented, applied the law of some jurisdiction other than the place of the tort because it had a more compelling interest in the application of its law to the legal issue involved.

The "center of gravity" or "grouping of contacts" doctrine adopted by this court in conflicts cases involving contracts impresses us as likewise affording the appropriate approach for accommodating the competing interests in tort cases with multi-State contacts. Justice, fairness and "the best practical result" may best be achieved by giving controlling effect to the law of the jurisdiction which, because of its relationship or contact with the occurrence or the parties, has the greatest concern with the specific issue raised in the litigation. The merit of such a rule is that "it gives to the place 'having the most interest in the problem' paramount control over the legal issues arising out of a particular factual context" and thereby allows the forum to apply "the policy of the jurisdiction 'most intimately concerned with the outcome of [the] particular litigation.' " (*Auten v. Auten,* [p. 246, *infra*].

Such, indeed, is the approach adopted in the most recent revision of the *Conflict of Laws Restatement* in the field of torts. According to the principles there set out, "The local law of the state which has the most significant relationship with the occurrence and with the parties determines their rights and liabilities in tort" (*Restatement, Second, Conflict of Laws,* § 379[1]; also Introductory Note to Topic 1 of Chapter 9, p. 3 [Tentative Draft No. 8, 1963]),[b] and the relative importance of the relationships or contacts of the respective jurisdictions is to be evaluated

---

[b] Note that the final version reads "the local law which, with respect to that issue, has the most significant relationship. . . ."

in the light of "the issues, the character of the tort and the relevant purposes of the tort rules involved" (§ 379[2], [3]).

Comparison of the relative "contacts" and "interests" of New York and Ontario in this litigation, vis-à-vis the issue here presented, makes it clear that the concern of New York is unquestionably the greater and more direct and that the interest of Ontario is at best minimal. The present action involves injuries sustained by a New York guest as the result of the negligence of a New York host in the operation of an automobile, garaged, licensed and undoubtedly insured in New York, in the course of a week-end journey which began and was to end there. In sharp contrast, Ontario's sole relationship with the occurrence is the purely adventitious circumstance that the accident occurred there.

New York's policy of requiring a tort-feasor to compensate his guest for injuries caused by his negligence cannot be doubted—as attested by the fact that the Legislature of this State has repeatedly refused to enact a statute denying or limiting recovery in such cases . . .—and our courts have neither reason nor warrant for departing from that policy simply because the accident, solely affecting New York residents and arising out of the operation of a New York based automobile, happened beyond its borders. Per contra, Ontario has no conceivable interest in denying a remedy to a New York guest against his New York host for injuries suffered in Ontario by reason of conduct which was tortious under Ontario law. The object of Ontario's guest statute, it has been said, is "to prevent the fraudulent assertion of claims by passengers, in collusion with the drivers, against insurance companies' (*Survey of Canadian Legislation,* 1 U. Toronto L. J. 358, 366) and, quite obviously, the fraudulent claims intended to be prevented by the statute are those asserted against Ontario defendants and their insurance carriers, not New York defendants and their insurance carriers. Whether New York defendants are imposed upon or their insurers defrauded by a New York plaintiff is scarcely a valid legislative concern of Ontario simply because the accident occurred there, any more so than if the accident had happened in some other jurisdiction.

It is hardly necessary to say that Ontario's interest is quite different from what it would have been had the issue related to the manner in which the defendant had been driving his car at the time of the accident. Where the defendant's exercise of due care in the operation of his automobile is in issue, the jurisdiction in which the allegedly wrongful conduct occurred will usually have a predominant, if not exclusive, concern. In such a case, it is appropriate to look to the law of the place of the tort so as to give effect to that jurisdiction's interest in regulating conduct within its borders, and it would be almost unthinkable to seek the applicable rule in the law of some other place.

The issue here, however, is not whether the defendant offended against a rule of the road prescribed by Ontario for motorists generally or whether he violated some standard of conduct imposed by that jurisdiction, but rather whether the plaintiff, because she was a guest in the defendant's automobile, is barred from recovering damages for a wrong concededly committed. As to that issue, it is New York, the place where the parties resided, where their guest-host relationship arose and where the trip began and was to end, rather than Ontario, the place of the fortuitous occurrence of the accident, which has the dominant contacts and the superior claim for application of its law. Although the rightness or wrongness of defendant's conduct may depend upon the law of the particular jurisdiction through which the automobile passes, the rights and liabilities of the parties which stem from their guest-host relationship should remain constant and not vary and shift as the automobile proceeds from place to place. Indeed, such a result, we note, accords with "the interests of the host in procuring liability insurance adequate under the applicable law, and the interests of his insurer in reasonable calculability of the premium." (Ehrenzweig, *Guest Statutes in the Conflict of Laws,* 69 Yale L. J. 595, 603.)

Although the traditional rule has in the past been applied by this court in giving controlling effect to the guest statute of the foreign jurisdiction in which the accident occurred, it is not amiss to point out that the question here posed was neither raised nor considered in those cases and that the question has never been presented in so stark a manner as in the case before us with a statute so unique as Ontario's.[13] Be that as it may, however, reconsideration of the inflexible traditional rule persuades us, as already indicated, that, in failing to take into account essential policy considerations and objectives, its application may lead to unjust and anomalous results. This being so, the rule, formulated as it was by the courts, should be discarded.[14]

In conclusion, then, there is no reason why all issues arising out of a tort claim must be resolved by reference to the law of the same jurisdiction. Where the issue involves standards of conduct, it is more than likely that it is the law of the place of the tort which will be controlling but the disposition of other issues must turn, as does the issue of the standard of conduct itself, on the law of the jurisdiction which has the strongest interest in the resolution of the particular issue presented.

The judgment appealed from should be reversed, with costs, and the motion to dismiss the complaint denied.

VAN VOORHIS, J. (dissenting).

The decision about to be made of this appeal changes the established law of this State, one of the most recent decisions the other way being *Kaufman v. American Youth Hostels* (5 N.Y.2d 1016), where all of the "significant contacts" were with New York State except the mountain which plaintiff's intestate was climbing when she met her death. The defense of immunity of a charitable corporation under the Oregon law, where the accident occurred, was inapplicable under the law of New York where the defendant corporation was organized and staffed, and plaintiff and his intestate resided. Nevertheless the court declined to strike that defense from the answer, based upon Oregon law. Concerning, as it did, solely the status of the defendant corporation, *Kaufman v. American Youth Hostels* presented a stronger case for the application of New York law than does the present. The case of *Auten v. Auten,* involving a separation agreement between English people and providing for the support of a wife and children to continue to live in England, accomplished no such revolution in the law as the present appeal. *Auten v. Auten* dealt with contracts, the agreement was held to be governed by the law of the country where it was mainly to be performed, which had previously been the law, and the salient expressions "center of gravity," "grouping of contacts", and similar catchwords were employed as a shorthand reference to the reconciliation of such rigid concepts in the conflict of laws as

---

[13] We note that the Supreme Court of Canada has upheld the refusal of the Quebec courts to apply the Ontario guest statute to an accident affecting Quebec residents which occurred in Ontario. (See *McLean v. Pettigrew,* [1945] 2 D. L. R. 65.) This decision was dictated by the court's resort to the English choice of law rule, whereby the foreign tort is deemed actionable if actionable by the law of the forum and not justifiable by the law of the place of the tort. (See *Phillips v. Eyre,* [1870] L. R. 6 Q. B. 1, 28–29; see, also, Dicey, *Conflict of Laws* [7th ed., 1958], p. 940.) However that may be, it would seem incongruous for this court to apply Ontario's unique statute in circumstances under which its own sister Provinces would not.

[14] It of course follows from our decision herein that, given the facts of the present case, the result would be the same and the law of New York applied where the foreign guest statute requires a showing of gross negligence. [The rule was, in fact, changed to a gross negligence rule in 1973. See note i, p. 201, *infra.*]

the formulae making applicable the place where the contract was signed or where it was to be performed—rules which themselves were occasionally in conflict with one another. In the course of the opinion it was stated that "even if we were not to place our emphasis on the law of the place with the most significant contacts, but were instead simply to apply the rule that matters of performance and breach are governed by the law of the place of performance, the same result would follow" [p. 249, *infra*]. The decision in *Auten v. Auten* rationalized and rendered more workable the existing law of contracts. The name "grouping of contacts" was simply a label to identify the rationalization of existing decisions on the conflict of laws in contract cases which were technically inconsistent, in some instances. The difference between the present case and *Auten v. Auten* is that *Auten* did not materially change the law, but sought to formulate what had previously been decided. The present case makes substantial changes in the law of torts. The expressions "center of gravity," "grouping of contacts," and "significant contacts" are catchwords which were not employed to define and are inadequate to define a principle of law, and were neither applied to nor are they applicable in the realm of torts.

Attempts to make the law or public policy of New York State prevail over the laws and policies of other States where citizens of New York State are concerned are simply a form of extraterritoriality which can be turned against us wherever actions are brought in the courts of New York which involve citizens of other States. . . . Undoubtedly ease of travel and communication, and the increase in interstate business have rendered more awkward discrepancies between the laws of the States in many respects. But this is not a condition to be cured by introducing or extending principles of extraterritoriality, as though we were living in the days of the Roman or British Empire, when the concepts were formed that the rights of a Roman or an Englishman were so significant that they must be enforced throughout the world even where they were otherwise unlikely to be honored by "lesser breeds without the law." Importing the principles of extraterritoriality into the conflicts of laws between the States of the United States can only make confusion worse confounded. If extraterritoriality is to be the criterion, what would happen, for example, in case of an automobile accident where some of the passengers came from or were picked up in States or countries where causes of action against the driver were prohibited, others where gross negligence needed to be shown, some, perhaps, from States where contributory negligence and others where comparative negligence prevailed? . . .

In my view there is no overriding consideration of public policy which justifies or directs this change in the established rule or renders necessary or advisable the confusion which such a change will introduce.

The judgment dismissing the complaint should be affirmed.

CHIEF JUDGE DESMOND and JUDGES DYE, BURKE and FOSTER concur with JUDGE FULD; JUDGE VAN VOORHIS dissents in an opinion in which JUDGE SCILEPPI concurs.

NOTES AND QUESTIONS

(1)(a) Some observers, including the present author writing in 1967,[c] have regarded *Kilberg* as the watershed case on choice of law in torts, though Judge Desmond spoke of protection for our State's people ". . . without doing violence to the accepted pattern of conflict of law rules."[d]

---

[c] Lowenfeld & Mendelsohn, *The United States and the Warsaw Convention,* 80 Harv. L. Rev. 497, 528–31 (1967).

[d] P. 130, *supra*.

§ 3.03 CHOICE OF LAW □ 151

Other observers have looked on *Kilberg* as one more escape device case, and looked on *Babcock* as the watershed decision.[e] In some sense both views are right. *Babcock* set the pattern for later cases—in New York and elsewhere—but it might well not have come out as it did (or commanded a majority of the Court of Appeals) without *Kilberg*. Moreover, it was *Kilberg* that expressed most directly the New York court's feeling that the lex loci rule was "unjust and anomalous," a phrase quoted twice by Judge Fuld in *Babcock*. It is also probably true, as Professor Reese wrote eight years after the case came down, that *Babcock* was "almost certainly the most significant contribution to choice-of-law that has been made in this century."[f] *Kilberg* was perceived by the critics as too parochial, and "public policy" as an "unattractive analytical tool;"[g] *Babcock*, in contrast, was regarded as sophisticated—"the decision," as Professor Harold Korn has put it, "that at last moved the modern choice-of-law revolution out of the academic journals and into the courts."[h]

(b) Before going through the court's analysis, two distinctions between *Kilberg* and *Babcock* are worth mentioning: (i) *Babcock* is not a death case, and so no constitutional provision in the forum state is applicable; (ii) the place of accident is not another state in the United States, and so no issue can arise under the Full Faith and Credit clause.

(2)(a) While the affirmative aspects of *Babcock v. Jackson,* as we shall see, created a good deal of confusion in later cases, there was nothing confusing about the negative statement. "Shall the law of the place of the tort *invariably* govern . . .?," Judge Fuld asks after stating the facts, and the answer is "no": "[T]he vested rights doctrine has long since been discredited. . . ."

(b) Note Judge Fuld's explanation for burying the vested rights theory (pp. 145-46):

(i) it fails to take account of underlying policy considerations;

(ii) it focuses on generalities, and ignores particular issues; and

(iii) it ignores the interests of states other than those where the tort occurred.

Is that a fair judgment? How should Judge Griswold answer?

(3)(a) Speaking of the members of the panel in *Adams v. Knickerbocker,* which of the others has the right to be pleased with the opinion in *Babcock?* Is it possible that they all do?

(b) Professor Currie, writing in a symposium on *Babcock* in the Columbia Law Review, said the majority opinion contained "items of comfort for almost every critic of the traditional system."[i] Is that true? If so, is it analytically troubling, in that the various theories are mutually exclusive?

(4)(a) Taking the approaches one by one, look first at Judge Fuld's enumeration of contacts (p. 148, *supra*). Plaintiff is domiciled in New York, defendant is domiciled in New York, and

---

[e] See, e.g., Rosenberg, Hay and Weintraub, *Cases and Materials on Conflict of Laws* 520 (10th ed. 1996), and Cramton, Currie, Kay and Kramer, *Conflict of Laws* 165 (5th ed. 1993).

[f] Reese, *Chief Judge Fuld and Choice of Law,* 71 Colum. L. Rev. 548, 552 (1971).

[g] See, for a pre-*Kilberg* critique, Paulsen & Sovern, *"Public Policy" in the Conflict of Laws,* 56 Colum. L. Rev. 969 (1956).

[h] Korn, *The Choice of Law Revolution: A Critique,* 83 Colum. L. Rev. 772, 827 (1983).

[i] Currie, *Comment on Babcock v. Jackson,* 63 Colum. L. Rev. 1233, 1234 (1963). He added that while on the surface, the opinion gives the greatest encouragement to the philosophy of the *Restatement (Second)*, "[p]aradoxically, I believe that the decision, rightly understood, spells the doom of all attempts, such as that of the *Restatement,* to solve the problems of conflict of laws by a compendium of choice-of-law rules . . ." *Id.* at 1235.

the automobile is licensed, garaged, and and insured in New York. The only link to Ontario is the crash. Thus the count is 5–1 in favor of New York. Or is it 3–1?

(b) The next paragraph discusses New York's policy, inferred not from a constitutional provision, but from the repeated refusal of the legislature to enact a guest statute.[j] The talk of policy blends into a discussion of state interest—not of New York, but of Ontario. Postponing for the moment the question of how Judge Fuld can tell what Ontario's real interest is, economic, moral, or jurisprudential,[k] note the distinction drawn between issues concerning the way the car was operated—speed limits, "no passing" zones, etc.—and issues concerning legal relationships—husband-wife, host-guest, perhaps other immunities. As to the latter, Judge Fuld says, Ontario has "no conceivable interest," i.e., the case presents, in Currie's terms, a false conflict.

(c) Thus far, Judge Fuld seems to be focusing on things as they stand after the crash. In the next paragraph, however the focus shifts to "the place where the parties resided, where their guest-host relationship arose and where the trip began and was to end." If these are the decisive factors, as Rheinstein would argue, then the place of the accident is truly fortuitous, in that the rights and liabilities "should remain constant" anywhere the car might carry Miss Babcock and the Jacksons.

(d) Even Judge Cavers is not left out, for the opinion ends both in reiteration of the point about addressing a choice of law case issue-by-issue, and in an appreciation of a fair and just (not "unjust and anomalous") result.

(5) In *Babcock v. Jackson,* all the relevant factors—where the car is based, the domicile of both parties, and the beginning and scheduled end of the trip—pointed the same way. On the one hand, this made the revolution, whose time had probably come anyhow, relatively easy; on the other hand, it was hard to tell—hard for lower courts, for counsel, for professors, and for the Court of Appeals as well—what would happen if in the next case the factors were not overlapping. For the next decade, the New York Court of Appeals struggled with variations on *Babcock,* as illustrated in the remainder of this chapter. Quite apart from choice of law, consider these cases as an illustration, compressed into a relatively short time period, of the common law process, moving in half-steps, not always in a straight line, and sometimes with changing objectives.

§ 3.04 The New York Experience

DYM v. GORDON

New York Court of Appeals
16 N.Y.2d 120, 262 N.Y.S.2d 463, 209 N.E.2d 792 (1965)

BURKE, J.

The plaintiff, a guest in the defendant driver's automobile, seeks to recover damages against her host for injuries which concededly were the result of ordinary negligence in its operation.

---

[j] For an account of the rise and fall of guest statutes in the United States, including repeated refusals of the U.S. Supreme Court to entertain constitutional challenges to guest statutes, see Note, *The Present Status of Automobile Guest Statutes,* 59 Cornell L. Rev. 659 (1974).

[k] See p. 168, Question 1(e) and Note d.

§ 3.04   CHOICE OF LAW   □   153

Both the plaintiff and defendant are New York domiciliaries and if the accident had occurred here the defendant would doubtless be liable. However, the accident and negligent conduct took place in the State of Colorado, a jurisdiction which has enacted a "guest statute"[1] barring a guest's recovery against the host unless "willful and wanton disregard" of safety can be shown. The trial court, professedly invoking the conflict of laws rule recently defined in the case of *Babcock v. Jackson,* decided as a matter of law that New York law was applicable. The Appellate Division unanimously reversed the judgment and held that Colorado law must apply. I believe that the determination of the Appellate Division is in accord with the rationale in *Babcock.* . . .

This case was tried on an agreed set of facts. Both plaintiff and defendant, domiciled in New York, were temporarily residing in Colorado. Both parties were Summer students at the University of Colorado and had arrived at separate times in Boulder, Colorado, traveling by separate means of transportation. At the time of leaving New York there had been no arrangement between defendant and plaintiff to meet in Colorado and no plan or intention on the part of either that plaintiff would ride in the defendant's automobile at any time. On August 11, 1959, without any prior arrangement, plaintiff entered defendant's automobile with his consent for the purpose of being driven to a place of instruction in Longmont, Colorado. Both parties intended that plaintiff be driven only to that destination and no plans were made for any other trip. The plaintiff's injuries were received as a result of a collision with another car that occurred during the short ride to Longmont.

In deciding what law to apply I of course recognize that we no longer mechanically turn to the common-law rule of *lex loci delictus* in tort cases. The place of impact rule was a reasonable one at a time when travelers were few and when most persons had more contacts with the jurisdiction in which they found themselves than mere physical presence. Our courts now have adopted a rule of choice of law in a conflict situation which looks to reason and justice in its selection of which law should apply and which fits the needs of today's world where long and frequent travel is no longer reserved to a few. (See *Kilberg v. Northeast Airlines* [p. 129, *supra.*]; *Mertz v. Mertz* [p. 58, *supra.*], *Babcock v. Jackson* [p. 145, *supra.*].)

The plaintiff claims that the conflict of laws doctrine enunciated in *Babcock* (*supra*) mandates application of the New York negligence rule. Plaintiff refers to insurance written and delivered in New York, registration of the automobile here, the domicile of both parties in New York and also to the policy of the New York law. By the use of those references plaintiff attempts to use a quantitative rather than a qualitative test and tends to distort *Babcock* into a rule of domicile or one directed toward public policy. I think the *Babcock* rule compels a contrary result.

Following our approach in *Babcock,* it is necessary first to isolate the issue, next to identify the policies embraced in the laws in conflict, and finally to examine the contacts of the respective jurisdictions to ascertain which has a superior connection with the occurrence and thus would have a superior interest in having its policy or law applied. The issue here is simply whether in an automobile host-guest relationship a negligent driver should be liable to his injured passenger. The New York law finds nothing in the host-guest relationship which warrants a digression from the usual negligence rule of ordinary care. In Colorado, however, this relationship

---

[1] The Colorado statute (Col. Rev. Stats., § 13–9–1) provides, in pertinent part, that:

No person transported by the owner or operator of a motor vehicle as his guest, without payment for such transportation, shall have a cause of action for damages against such owner or operator for injury, death or loss in case of accident, unless such accident shall have been intentional on the part of such owner or operator or caused by his intoxication, or by negligence consisting of a willful and wanton disregard of the rights of others.

is treated specially and, while ordinary negligence is usually enough for recovery in that state, injuries arising out of this relationship are compensable only if they result from "willful and wanton" conduct. Contrary to the narrow view advanced by plaintiff, the policy underlying Colorado's law is threefold: the protection of Colorado drivers and their insurance carriers against fraudulent claims, the prevention of suits by "ungrateful guests," and the priority of injured parties in other cars in the assets of the negligent defendant. Examining Colorado's interest in light of its public policy we find that over and above the usual interest which Colorado may bring to bear on all conduct occurring within its boundaries, Colorado has an interest in seeing that the negligent defendant's assets are not dissipated in order that the persons in the car of the blameless driver will not have their right to recovery diminished by the present suit.

Finally we come to the question of which state has the more significant contacts with the case such that its interest should be upheld. In this regard, the factual distinctions between this case and *Babcock* do have considerable influence. *Babcock* did not involve a collision between two cars; thus only New Yorkers were involved and it was unnecessary for us to consider the interests of Ontario in the rights of those in a car of a nonnegligent driver. In *Babcock* we pointed out that the host-guest relationship was seated in New York and that the place of the accident was "entirely fortuitous." In this case the parties were dwelling in Colorado when the relationship was formed and the accident arose out of Colorado based activity; therefore, the fact that the accident occurred in Colorado could in no sense be termed fortuitous. Thus it is that in this case, where Colorado has such significant contacts with the *relationship itself* and the *basis of its formation*, the application of its law and underlying policy are clearly warranted.

Of compelling importance in this case is the fact that here the parties had come to rest in the State of Colorado and had thus chosen to live their daily lives under the protective arm of Colorado law. Having accepted the benefits of that law for such a prolonged period, it is spurious to maintain that Colorado has no interest in a relationship which was formed there. In *Babcock* the New Yorkers at all times were *in transitu* and we were impressed with the fundamental unfairness of subjecting them to a law which they in no sense had adopted.

To say that this relationship was formed in Colorado implies that the parties had acquired so sufficient a nexus with that jurisdiction that relationships formed there were in the real sense Colorado relationships. In other words, it is neither the physical situs where the relationship was created nor the time of its creation which is controlling but rather these factors in conjunction with the general intent of the parties as inferred from their actions. There is no doubt that had the accident in *Babcock* occurred while the parties were on their way to a restaurant after having stopped for the night at a motel that the same result would obtain. By the same token, it would make no difference here if the parties had planned, while still in New York, to go to Colorado for a year's study and, while there, engage in skiing at Aspen; the fact that they had planned the trip here would not justify the application of New York law if an accident occurred involving people in another car while traveling from Boulder to Aspen some months later.

Other cases in our court have given due consideration to the special relationships there involved when deciding conflict issues. In the case of *Mertz v. Mertz* we recognized that the matter of whether or not a wife may recover against her husband in tort is treated differently in some states because of special incidents in that relationship as recognized by the jurisdiction concerned. Since the relationship itself is the reason for the special treatment, we concluded that the jurisdiction where the relationship was seated had the primary interest in having its laws applied.

In workmen's compensation cases the rule that the law of the place of injury was solely controlling was abandoned and the interest of the state in which the employment relationship was created was given special consideration. . . .[a] In *Kilberg* the court emphasized the significant contacts which New York State had with the case. Not only was the plaintiff's intestate a resident of New York but the contract for the trip had been made in this State by the purchase of a ticket here and this contract had been partly performed in New York. The action was thereby one on a New York created relationship.

These decisions demonstrate that considerations of where and how a relationship was formed are significant in this class of cases. This analysis is much to be preferred over an approach which merely looks to the fortuitous place of the happening of the accident, or simply applies the law of the domicile or one which blithely applies the public policy of the forum under the denomination of "governmental interests."

The alleged contacts referred to by plaintiff may be classified under the heading of domicile. Certainly it is merely a long-handed method of reciting that the parties were domiciled in New York to state that the car was registered here and that the insurance was written here. These and many other factors may usually be presumed from the fact of domicile; they have no independent significance as regards the host-guest relationship apart from their inclusion as natural incidents of domicile.

Judicial hostility to "guest" statutes and a preoccupation with New York social welfare problems and the relative liability of insurers should not be treated as "contacts" which are found then to outweigh the factual contacts. These views also depend on the mores of the particular forum and its allied public policy. Such a tack is altogether too provincial.

Here, necessarily, the only valid competing consideration bearing on the host-guest relationship is that of domicile. However appealing it might seem to give effect to our own public policy on this issue, merely because the negligent driver of the car in the collision, and his guest, are domiciled here, to do so would be to totally neglect the interests of the jurisdiction where the accident occurred, where the relationship arose and where the parties were dwelling, and to give an overriding significance to a single factor reminiscent of the days when British citizens travelled to the four corners of the world secure in the belief that their conduct would be governed solely by the law of England. "The suggestion sounds like an echo of the theory of the statute personal, a body of national law which the citizen carries about with him (Beale, *Conflict of Laws*, §§ 54, 55; *Am. Banana Co. v. United Fruit Co.,* 213 U. S. 347, 356). That is a theory which has yielded generally in this country to the principles of the territorial system." (*Loucks v. Standard Oil Co.,* [p. 34, *supra*].) To give domicile or an alleged public policy such a preferred status is to substitute a conflicts rule every bit as inflexible and arbitrary as its *lex loci* predecessor. Such was not our intention in *Babcock*. It is suggested that New York has a dominant governmental interest in seeing that the plaintiff receives compensation because it is this State that she will look to for welfare payments should she become a public charge as a result of her injuries. Such an argument is hardly a legal one. Were we to give our attention to such considerations we might just as well speculate about the possibility that the New York defendant could become a public charge if the plaintiff were to be given recovery. There is no guarantee that the recovery will not far exceed the insurance coverage in this or in any other case. A reflection on the import of this argument gives one the feeling that a preference for whatever law will compensate the New York tort plaintiff lurks in the background. The suggestion that our courts should apply

---

[a] Citing, *inter alia, Alaska Packers,* p. 386, *infra.*

this State's policy of compensation for innocent tort victims to all cases of returning domiciliaries is tantamount to saying that different rules or interests of other jurisdictions should be denied application in a New York forum on the ground of their not suiting our public policy. The principles justifying our refusal to apply foreign law on the ground of public policy are well defined, and a mere difference between the foreign rule and our own will not warrant such refusal.

Public policy, per se, plays no part in a choice of law problem. (See *Intercontinental Hotels Corp. v. Golden,* 15 N.Y. 2d 9; *Haag v. Barnes,* [p. 249, *infra*].) Moreover, as stated in *Loucks v. Standard Oil Co.,*

> The courts are not free to refuse to enforce a foreign right at the pleasure of the judges, to suit the individual notion of expediency or fairness. They do not close their doors unless help would violate some fundamental principle of justice, some prevalent conception of good morals, some deep-rooted tradition of the common weal.

The present decision represents no departure from the rule announced in *Babcock;* merely an example of its application. Neither is it my intention to suggest that in all cases the rule depends on the existence of some relationship for its vitality, nor do I wish to imply that in all relationship cases the seat of the relationship should be paramount. Long ago it became apparent that due to improved methods of travel and communication, together with the increased mobility of the population in general, the old rule of *lex loci* no longer was a just rule in many cases. The rule announced in *Babcock* allows the courts the flexibility necessary to deal with those cases.

In our case there is no doubt that, because the parties were dwelling in Colorado and because the relationship was based there, the place of the occurrence of the accident with the other car was not "entirely fortuitous." Therefore, Colorado, concerned with the fate of all motorists on its highways, has the most significant contacts with the matter in controversy and a dominant interest in it. Here as in *Davenport v. Webb* [p. 142, n. i., *supra*] the sole connection of New York State is one of domicile. It is evident that in this case the law of the state in which the parties were living and in which the relationship was created must be held to be controlling. This conclusion does not subject "the traveling citizens of this State to the varying laws of other States through and over which they move" (*Kilberg v. Northeast Airlines*) and is fully consonant with the *Babcock* rule.

Accordingly, the order of the Appellate Division should be affirmed, without costs.

FULD, J. (dissenting).

In the light of this court's decision in *Babcock v. Jackson,* I cannot understand how an affirmance may here be justified. The view expressed by the majority is inconsistent not only with the rationale underlying *Babcock* but with the rule there explicitly stated, that the law to be applied to resolve a particular issue in a tort case with multi-jurisdictional contacts is "the law of the jurisdiction which, because of its relationship or contact with the occurrence or the parties, has the greatest concern" with the matter in issue and "the strongest interest" in its resolution.

. . . .

There is, indeed, no material distinction between the factual situation here presented and that in the *Babcock* case, and the very same considerations which there impelled us to select as controlling the law of New York, rather than that of the place of injury, are equally decisive here. In each case, suit was brought in this State by one New Yorker against another for injuries sustained in another jurisdiction while riding as a guest in a vehicle registered, regularly based

§ 3.04   CHOICE OF LAW □ 157

and insured in New York. And, in both cases, there was in effect in the foreign jurisdiction a statute which, unlike the law of New York, barred claims of this kind by the guest against the host based on ordinary negligence.[3] In *Babcock,* the plaintiff was injured when the defendant lost control of his automobile and it went off the highway and into an adjacent stone wall; in the case before us, the defendant, failing to observe a stop sign, collided with another car operated by a resident of Kansas and apparently registered in that state. The only other difference between the cases is that in *Babcock* the guest-host relationship originated in New York and the parties' trip began and was to end in this State, whereas in the present case that relationship arose in Colorado where the parties were temporarily residing—though they both returned to their homes in New York shortly after the accident.

It was our endeavor in *Babcock* to identify, in the first instance, the policies embodied in the particular laws in conflict, then to ascertain the interests of the jurisdictions involved in the application of their respective policies in view of their contacts with the case and, by such process, to determine which jurisdiction had "the superior claim for application of its law" (12 N.Y. 2d, at p. 483; see, also, Cavers, *Comments on Babcock v. Jackson,* 63 Colum. L. Rev. 1219, 1221). Ontario's contact there consisted solely of the occurrence of the accident within its territory, and we concluded that that contact was not a "significant" one, as respects the issue of liability of host to guest, since the policy reflected in its guest statute—the protection of Ontario defendants and their insurance carriers against fraudulent claims—had no relevant application to an accident involving New York parties and a New York-insured vehicle in which no Ontario defendant or insurer had any interest. In other words, the fact that the accident happened in Ontario was not a contact which gave that jurisdiction a legally cognizable interest in having its policy applied to the case. New York's contacts, on the other hand, gave it a vital interest in the application of its strong and long-standing policy "of requiring a tort-feasor to compensate his guest for injuries caused by his negligence."[4]

Nothing turns on the circumstance that in this case the guest-host relationship was formed in the foreign jurisdiction. It seems indisputably clear that a jurisdiction may be said to be "concerned" with a specific issue, if that term is to have any meaningful content, only when its governmental interests and policies enter into the making of a particular decision. Accordingly, the decisive consideration, in the present case, is that Colorado's guest statute, paralleling Ontario's, has as its prime objective the protection of Colorado driver-defendants and their insurance carriers against fraudulent claims and lawsuits. (See, e.g., *Vogts v. Guerrette,* 142 Col. 527, 534; *Bashor v. Bashor,* 103 Col. 232, 237–238; see, also, *Shea v. Olson,* 185 Wash. 143, 154–155, cited in the *Vogts* case, 142 Col., at p. 534.) Manifestly, that policy of Colorado can in no way be served by applying its statute to an action, such as the present, which is brought in New York and involves not residents of Colorado or their insurance carriers but only New

---

[3] The Ontario statute (in *Babcock*), which completely barred the claims of a guest-passenger, differs from that of Colorado, which permits recovery on a showing of "willful and wanton" conduct, but this distinction, as indicated in the *Babcock* case [p. 149, n. 14, *supra*] is of no consequence for present purposes.

[4] To the plaint that the concepts, "significant contacts," "center of gravity," and "interests of the respective states," are mere "catchwords' (opinion of DESMOND, Ch. J., [p. 159, *infra*]), I would but recall Professor Cheatham's telling observation (in discussing the use of such expressions) that they are "at least as adequate to define a principle of law as the terms 'due process of law,' 'property,' 'reasonableness,' and 'unjust enrichment,' which the courts constantly employ" (Cheatham, *Comments on Babcock v. Jackson,* 63 Colum. L. Rev. 1229, 1230–1231)—and, I would add, as adequate as "traditional notions of fair play" and "substantial justice" used by the Supreme Court in *International Shoe Co. v. Washington* and *McGee v. International Life Ins. Co.* [pp. 486, 491, *infra*].

Yorkers and a New York based and insured vehicle. The mere fact that the guest-host relationship between the New York parties originated in Colorado has, in truth, as little relevance to the policy underlying that state's guest statute and, by that token, as little bearing on that statute's applicability as did the fact, in *Babcock,* of the occurrence of the accident in Ontario in relation to the similar policy embodied in its guest statute. Under the circumstances of the present case, then, Colorado, to paraphrase what we wrote in *Babcock,* "has no conceivable interest in denying a remedy to a New York guest against his New York host for injuries suffered in [Colorado] by reason of conduct which was tortious under [Colorado] law."

Nor is the majority's position advanced by its further suggestion . . . that the Colorado statute also reflects (1) an antipathy on the part of Colorado to suits by "ungrateful" guests (see *Dobbs v. Sugioka,* 117 Col. 218, 220) and (2) a policy to assure "the priority of injured parties in other cars in the assets of the negligent defendant." Indeed, as regards the latter asserted policy, there does not appear to be any Colorado pronouncement even to intimate that the Colorado Legislature was motivated by any such objective. In any event, though, Colorado would be legitimately concerned with the application of these alleged policies only in relation to matters within its legislative competence, such as the burdens of the Colorado courts, the regulation of the affairs and relationships of Colorado citizens or the protection of Colorado claimants or insurers. . . . Whether such considerations might be of significance in particular circumstances not here present, they certainly have no relevance in the context of this suit between New York domiciliaries in a New York court, in which no burden is being imposed on the Colorado courts and no citizen of Colorado appears to be in any way interested. The majority's emphasis on the involvement of another vehicle in the accident . . . is thus misplaced since the other automobile was driven by a resident from Kansas and was apparently licensed in that state.

New York, on the other hand, just as in *Babcock,* as the permanent residence of the plaintiff and the defendant and the place to which they returned to live shortly after the accident, has a predominant interest in vindicating its own policy of requiring negligent driving hosts to compensate their injured guests. It is apparent that the consequences resulting from an uncompensated injury generally affect the community in which the injured party resides, in this case, New York. If a plaintiff who returns to live here after sustaining injuries in another state requires additional medical treatment, as is usually the case, or is unable to meet his normal economic commitments and becomes a public charge, it is the people of New York—whose services will go uncompensated and whose tax dollars will be charged in the form of welfare payments—who will feel the repercussions of such eventualities and not the distant and unconcerned residents of the state of injury, where a guest-host relationship between the New York parties may have been formed. . . . There is thus no question but that Colorado's "contacts," though quantitatively greater than those of Ontario in *Babcock,* are still not "significant" as respects the specific issue presented and that the "contacts" of New York in relation to that issue are decidedly superior.

No one of the cases cited in the court's opinion supports its view that conclusive effect must be given, in a case involving a special relationship, to the law of the place where the relationship arose. As examination of each of those cases readily discloses, this court applied the law of one jurisdiction rather than that of the other not per se because the relationship between the parties originated in that jurisdiction but because analysis of all the material facts demonstrated that the latter had the more compelling interest in the application of its law to the matter in issue. (See *Babcock v. Jackson,* [pp. 146-47, *supra.*)

Nor is my conclusion as to the superiority of New York's claim for the application of its law in this case in any way grounded—as suggested in the majority opinion—on a "quantitative" assessment of the contacts of the respective jurisdictions, or on the decisive effect of any *single* such factor as domicile or the public policy of this State. Rather, the essential inquiry is, and has been, to determine whether it is Colorado or New York which has "the greatest concern with the specific issue raised in the litigation." (*Babcock v. Jackson,* [p. 147] *supra.*) It is clear that in this case it is New York which has the predominant concern and, consequently, it is the law of this State, not Colorado, which should be applied.

In conclusion, then, I would say, as did the court in *Babcock* . . . that "New York's policy of requiring a tort-feasor to compensate his guest for injuries caused by his negligence cannot be doubted . . . and our courts have neither reason nor warrant for departing from that policy simply because the accident, solely affecting New York residents and arising out of the operation of a New York based automobile, happened beyond its borders."

The order of the Appellate Division should be reversed and the judgment of the Supreme Court reinstated.

Chief Judge Desmond (dissenting).

Concurring with Judge Fuld, I would reverse because of the rule stated and applied in *Babcock v. Jackson* . . . that is, that "New York's policy of requiring a tort-feasor to compensate his guest for injuries caused by his negligence" is not to be departed from "simply because the accident, solely affecting New York residents and arising out of the operation of a New York based automobile, happened beyond its borders." Similarly in *Kilberg v. Northeast Airlines* . . . we gave effect to a "strong, clear and old" public policy of New York in refusing, even though the particular wrongful death occurred in Massachusetts, to enforce as against the estate of a New York resident the Massachusetts statute limiting recovery in death actions. What we did in those decisions was to announce for New York a modern public policy which abandoned the old sweeping rule that the law to be applied in every tort case was the law of the place of the wrong. *Babcock* and *Kilberg* (*supra*) together should be the law of this present case.

I do not think that any fear of being accused of making or using "mechanical" rules should deter us from developing such new decisional formulae as the need for them appears in our society. "Mechanical" is a mere epithet in this connection. It is our duty as the highest court of our State to formulate and announce the law, otherwise how can the lower courts decide cases and how can lawyers advise their clients?

No guides satisfactory to me are found in the concepts currently favored by teachers and writers on conflict of laws, such as "significant contacts," "center of gravity," and "interests of the respective states." I voted with the majority in *Babcock v. Jackson* on my concept of New York State's public policy but I agree with so much of the dissenting opinion of Judge Van Voorhis therein as says that "contacts," "interests," "center of gravity," etc., are catchwords representing at best not methods or bases of decision but considerations to be employed in setting up the new rules of law required by changing times. Counting up "contacts" or locating the "center of gravity" or weighing the respective "interests" of two states can never be a satisfactory way of deciding actual lawsuits. As this case demonstrates, Judges will disagree as to where these balances and centers and interests lie. For instance, how can you isolate and compare the "interests" of Colorado and New York in this lawsuit? Colorado has no "interest" at all in the determination of the question whether plaintiff, a New York resident, should be denied recovery in a New York court against another New York resident. No more did Massachusetts have any "interest" in limiting the Kilberg estate's recovery, or Ontario an interest in having plaintiff Babcock turned out of a New York court. The jurisdiction where an accident occurs has, of course, a special "interest" and responsibility in enforcing its own "rules of the road" (see *Babcock*). The state where an injured plaintiff lives may have an "interest" in seeing to it that adequate compensation is provided, lest the injured person become a public charge. But no state can have any discoverable "interest" in the application of its own special public policies as to liability and compensation in tort litigations in another state between two persons, both resident of that other state.

New York's public policy in cases like this as to protecting its own residents from foreign state deprivations of reasonable protection and indemnity was settled for me by *Kilberg v. Northeast Airlines* and *Babcock v. Jackson,* and that public policy calls for a reversal.

JUDGES DYE, VAN VOORHIS and SCILEPPI concur with JUDGE BURKE; JUDGE FULD dissents and votes to reverse in an opinion in which CHIEF JUDGE DESMOND concurs in a separate opinion and in each of which JUDGE BERGAN concurs.

Order affirmed.

KELL v. HENDERSON

New York Supreme Court (St. Lawrence Cty.)
47 Misc.2d 992, 263 N.Y.S.2d 647 (1965)
aff"d. 26 A.D.2d 595, 270 N.Y.S.2d (1966)

HUGHES, JUDGE

. . . [A]t the time the accident took place, the infant was riding as a passenger in an automobile owned by the defendant Helen M. Henderson and operated by her son, the defendant Albert B. Henderson, when said automobile left the highway and struck a bridge. The case has been at issue on the trial calendar, Supreme Court, St. Lawrence County. The residence and domicile of all the parties to this action is in the Province of Ontario, Dominion of Canada. The vehicle in which the accident occurred was licensed and registered in the said Province. The trip involved in the accident originated in the Province of Ontario, Canada. The infant plaintiff here was invited as a passenger in said automobile in the City of Brockville, Province of Ontario, Dominion of Canada, for the purpose of a pleasure trip to the United States. All the above facts show that the parties were and are Ontario residents and that the vehicle was owned and registered there and that the guest-host relationship arose in Ontario and that the trip started there and was to end there.

It is the defendants' position that under the decision of *Babcock v. Jackson* . . . this action should be governed by Ontario law which would bar recovery by the infant plaintiff herein against the defendants. It is the defendants' position that as to the narrow ground of what law should govern, the guest-host relationship, the law of the place where the contacts are qualitatively greater or more importantly numerous, must govern and control the case. In the *Babcock* case, *supra,* the Court of Appeals in a reverse situation held that the Ontario statute would not bar a New York passenger from recovering from a New York driver in the New York Court where the accident happened in Canada.

§ 3.04   CHOICE OF LAW   □   161

The conflict of laws doctrine enunciated in *Babcock, supra,* recognizes that we no longer mechanically turn to the common law rule of *lex loci delicti* in tort cases. The Courts now have adopted a rule of choice of law in a conflict situation which looks to reason and justice in its selection of which law is to apply and which fits the needs of today's changing world where frequent travel is the rule, rather than the exception. See *Kilberg v. Northeast Airlines, Mertz v. Mertz, Babcock v. Jackson, supra.*

This case is one of first impression. Prior to the *Babcock* case, there is no question whatsoever but that the laws of the State of New York would apply in this instance. If we are to accept the position of the defendants, it would require our Courts to apply the Ontario law to accidents that occur in New York State involving Ontario residents that are in transit in this State.

. . . .

The most recent case is *Dym v. Gordon.* . . . That case involved two New York State domiciliaries that were residing in the State of Colorado where the accident occurred. The Court, in that case, held that the law of the place of the accident must govern. In that case, the Court made it clear that matters of insurance such as where the insurance policy is written, as well as whether someone may become a public charge, are not matters that are to be taken into consideration. The Court in *Dym v. Gordon* stated: "Public Policy, per se, plays no part in a choice of law problem." In refusing to apply the laws of the State of New York and requiring that the law of the State of Colorado which has a "guest statute" must be applied, the Court went on to say the following: "The present decision represents no departure from the rule announced in *Babcock;* merely an example of its application. . . ."

It must be borne in mind that a car upon the highways of the State of New York is subject to the laws of the State of New York, both in it operation, its degree of maintenance and its right to be upon the highway. This Court has no problem whatsoever in arriving at the conclusion that if this case merely involved a property damage claim, the laws of the State of New York would be applicable, and, further, that if it involved some violation of the Vehicle and Traffic Laws of the State of New York also, the laws of this State would apply. In addition thereto, the method of gaining jurisdiction of the parties and the methods and procedures involved in the bringing of a law suit are governed by the procedures set forth in the Civil Practice Law and Rules promulgated by the Legislature of the State of New York. It must also be borne in mind that in communities located close to State lines or other countries such as Canada, it is very common for people to travel in and out of both states or countries and that although the happening of an accident may be termed fortuitous, the place where the parties are when the accident happens may or may not be necessarily fortuitous.

The law is well established that in the State of New York the owner of a motor vehicle used on New York State highways with permission is liable for damages to a person injured as the result of any negligence by the operator. See Section 388, former Section 59, of the Vehicle and Traffic Law of the State of New York. That section provides substantially that every owner of a vehicle used or operated in this State shall be liable and responsible for death or injuries to the person or property resulting from negligence in the use or operation of such vehicle in the business of such owner or otherwise by any person using or operating the same with the permission, express or implied, of such owner. This section of the law is not limited to New York State residents, and, consequently, out of state owners and operators who elect to use the highways of our state subject themselves to this statute. The law makes no distinction between residents and non-residents, people in transit or otherwise. The law does not provide for any exceptions. It does not permit defendants in the type of case before the court to plead the defense of a foreign guest statute, which is in direct conflict with one of our statutes governing travel upon our highways in which we have a keen interest.

. . . .

The Court, accordingly, denies the motion of the defendant to serve an amended answer, [setting forth the Ontario guest statute as a complete defense.]

MACEY v. ROZBICKI

New York Court of Appeals
18 N.Y.2d 289, 274 N.Y.S.2d 591, 221 N.E.2d 380 (1966)

CHIEF JUDGE DESMOND.

. . . Plaintiff Macey is a sister of defendant-driver Rita Rozbicki and sister-in-law of defendant-owner Vincent Rozbicki. All three lived in Buffalo but the Rozbickis had a summer residence at Waverly Beach, Ontario, just across the Niagara River from Buffalo. In late June, 1962, plaintiff went from Buffalo to the summer place to stay with her relatives for about 10 days. A week later, riding as a passenger in the Rozbicki automobile, she was injured in a collision in a Canadian village near the Waverly Beach house. The parties had intended to drive on a Canadian highway to Niagara Falls, Ontario, and to return to Waverly Beach. Defendants' answer pleaded the Ontario guest statute as a complete defense, which plaintiff moved to dismiss for insufficiency. Defendants countered with a motion for summary judgment. Special Term, concluding that *Babcock* did not control, gave judgment for defendants. The Appellate Division affirmed. We agree with the dissenting Justices at the Appellate Division that New York law is to be applied in this case.

The *Babcock* rule is that in such conflict situations controlling effect is to be given "to the law of the jurisdiction which, because of its relationship or contact with the occurrence or the parties, has the greatest concern with the specific issue raised in the litigation. . . ." The *Babcock* facts which pursuant to this rule dictated that New York law be used were that the parties were New Yorkers, that the car was garaged, licensed and insured in this State and that the journey began and ended in New York. In the present case the relationship of two sisters living permanently in New York was not affected or changed by their temporary meeting together in Canada for a short visit there, especially since the arrangements for that visit had undoubtedly been made in New York State. Every fact in this case was New York related, save only the not particularly significant one that the particular trip on the day of the accident was between two points in Canada. The important "contacts" here were all with New York State, not Ontario.

The *Dym* decision, as the majority *Dym* opinion clearly states, "represents no departure from the rule announced in *Babcock;* merely an example of its application" [p. 156, *supra*]. The notable differences between the *Babcock* situation and that in *Dym* was that in the latter the parties had separately gone to Colorado for a comparatively long stay, that there had been no arrangement made in New York for their meeting in Colorado, but merely a chance encounter in Colorado and a casual invitation to Mrs. Dym to ride in Gordon's car to a place where they were both going. The principal situs of the relationship was in Colorado.

The order appealed from should be reversed, with costs in all courts, defendants' motion denied and plaintiff's motion to strike the defense granted.

Keating, J. (concurring).

I concur for reversal, but on entirely different grounds from those stated by the Chief Judge. . . .

The automobile was insured in New York and hence the defendant Rozbicki paid for and received coverage for *any* liability resulting from the negligent operation of his automobile.

The Legislature sometime ago enacted a compulsory insurance law. The purpose of that enactment is outlined in section 310 of the Vehicle and Traffic Law which states that:

> The legislature is concerned over the rising toll of motor vehicle accidents and the suffering and loss thereby inflicted. The legislature determines that it is a matter of grave concern that motorists shall be financially able to respond in damages for their negligent acts, so that innocent victims of motor vehicle accidents may be recompensed for the injury and financial loss inflicted upon them.

Neither this declaration of policy nor the standard required provisions for an auto liability insurance policy make any distinction between guests, pedestrians or other injured parties. Nor is there any provision indicating that the legislative concern extended only to those injured within the political lines that separate New York from her sister States and the Canadian Provinces. (Insurance Law, § 167, subd. 2.) Indeed, section 311 (subd. 4) of the Vehicle and Traffic Law provides that every automobile liability insurance policy issued under the compulsory insurance act shall provide insurance "against loss from the liability imposed by law for damages . . . arising out of the ownership, maintenance, use, or operation of [said] motor vehicle . . . within the state of New York, or elsewhere in the United States in North America or the Dominion of Canada."

Keeping in mind this strong and unequivocal declaration of public policy, we must decide whether any reason in law, logic or policy exists for denying this injured New York resident recovery against this negligent tort-feasor.

The defendants urge us, as they have successfully urged the two courts below, to disregard the mandate of our Legislature and deny recovery because the Province of Ontario where the accident occurred proscribes all tort actions by a guest-passenger against a host-driver. Although we specifically rejected this argument in *Babcock v. Jackson,* the defendant asserts that that case is not controlling here because "the relationship of guest and host was created in Canada . . . because the parties were remaining in Canada [for more than a week end] . . . [and] the accident with the other car was in Canada." These distinguishing factors are presumably of such import, the defendants tell us, that it is our duty to ignore New York law.

. . . .

[The Judge summarizes *Babcock v. Jackson.*]

In determining which law should govern cases involving the guest statute of a foreign jurisdiction and whether a particular State has an interest in the application of its law it seems to me to be of no more than minor significance where the guest-host relationship arose, where the trip was to begin and end, and how short the visit of the parties was in the place where the accident occurred. Neither of these factors has any relation whatever to the New York policy of affording recovery to injured residents of this State or for that matter to the policies of other jurisdictions in denying a remedy.

The only facts having any significant bearing on the applicable choice of law in guest statute cases are the residence of the parties and the place in which the automobile is insured and registered. As we noted in *Babcock,* only these facts have any relation to the policies sought to be vindicated by the *ostensibly* conflicting laws. And here as in *Babcock* neither the policies of New York nor Ontario will be furthered by denying recovery. . . .

Unfortunately the answer to the problem presented by this case does not seem to be as clear as it should be. Both lower courts that have passed on the question have held Ontario law to be applicable and the decision of this court is not unanimous. The reason for this confusion and dissent appears to be our recent decision in *Dym v. Gordon* . . . in which we refused to apply New York law in a guest statute case. The facts in that case closely parallel those in the case at bar.

. . . There are really only two facts which appear to distinguish this case from *Dym v. Gordon.*

In *Dym,* "At the time of leaving New York there had been no arrangement between defendant and plaintiff to meet in Colorado and no plan or intention on the part of either that the plaintiff would ride in the defendant's automobile at any time.' . . ." I frankly fail to see the effect this should have in determining what interest either New York or the foreign jurisdiction has in the outcome of the litigation. Indeed it appears that the court in *Dym* was of the same opinion because we wrote that the result would have been the same "if the parties had planned, while still in New York, to go to Colorado for a year's study and, while there, engage in skiing at Aspen; *the fact that they had planned the trip here would not justify the application of New York law if an accident occurred involving people in another car while traveling from Boulder to Aspen some months later."* (emphasis added.)

The second distinguishing fact appears to be that, in *Dym,* the parties were going to spend six weeks in Colorado taking courses at the University of Colorado. In the case at bar the defendants were going to spend at least three months in Ontario where they owned a summer home. At least as to the defendants then it may be said that their residential nexus with Ontario was greater than that of the defendant in *Dym.* On the other hand, the plaintiff in the case at bar was only going to spend 10 days in Ontario. Here the majority, contrary to its decision in *Dym,* holds New York law applicable. Is this difference of 32 days going to determine whether the laws and policies of this State will be given effect? If this is the meaning of the decision then I cannot agree. I am of the opinion that the interest a particular jurisdiction has in the application of its law should and can only be determined by an examination of the facts of the case in light of the relevant policy considerations. (See Currie, *Comments on Babcock v. Jackson,* 63 Colum. L. Rev. 1212, 1235.) In guest statute cases, where the parties are New York residents and the automobile is insured under the laws of this State, the length of the visit to the jurisdiction in which the accident occurred is of little relevance. Counting days and examining calendars has no relationship to the making of a choice of law. Even if a cut-off date were picked, the result would be no more than another version of the arbitrary rule of *lex loci delicti* with an equally unsupportable basis.

In *Dym v. Gordon* great emphasis appeared to be placed upon the intent of the parties as to which law would govern their rights. Thus it was written "it is neither the physical situs where the relationship was created nor the time of its creation which is controlling but rather these factors in conjunction with the general intent of the parties as inferred from their actions." If this is the thrust of the *Dym* decision, it seems to me that we are engaging in an absolute fiction for no apparent reason. The parties did not here, or in *Babcock* or *Dym,* have any intent as to what law would govern their rights in some future litigation arising out of an accident.

. . . .

Having said all this and being of the opinion that this case and *Dym v. Gordon* are indistinguishable and that *Dym v. Gordon* and *Babcock v. Jackson* are irreconcilable, I reach the inevitable conclusion that we should no longer follow the decision in *Dym v. Gordon*.

. . . .

JUDGES FULD, BURKE, SCILEPPI and BERGAN concur with CHIEF JUDGE DESMOND; JUDGE KEATING concurs in a separate opinion; JUDGE VAN VOORHIS dissents and votes to affirm.

FARBER v. SMOLACK

New York Court of Appeals
20 N.Y.2d 198, 282 N.Y.S.2d 248, 229 N.E.2d 36 (1967)

BERGAN, JUDGE.

Defendant Robert Smolack owned a 1960 Triumph station wagon which he suggested his brother Arthur Smolack drive with Arthur's family from New York to Florida in April, 1960. On the way back to New York from Florida an accident occurred in North Carolina while Arthur was driving in which Arthur's wife was killed and his two children were injured.

This is an action by the administrator of the wife and the guardian of the infant Kenneth S. Smolack and by Melvin M. Smolack, individually since he had reached the age of 21 by the time of trial, against Robert Smolack, as owner, based on Arthur's negligence. All of the parties to the action, as well as the decedent, were residents of New York. The action was dismissed by the court at Trial Term; the Appellate Division affirmed by a divided court.

The negligence of the driver Arthur Smolack is established prima facie. In driving the car on the return trip to New York the driver noticed the car lost compression and "was pulling to the right." A stop was made at Fayetteville, North Carolina, where an exhaust manifold gasket was replaced and the front end alignment checked.

The car continued to pull to the right between Fayetteville and Weldon and greater left-side pressure had to be maintained on the steering wheel to keep in a straight line. This condition was not further checked by the driver. North of Weldon there was a sharp pulling to the right and the car skidded when the driver pulled the wheel in the opposite direction. The road surface was wet. The driver did not stop after this skid or reduce speed which had been 35 to 40 miles an hour; and shortly thereafter the car again pulled sharply to the right, went into a skid and overturned.

It could be determined on these facts taken most favorably to the plaintiffs that, in continuing to drive at undiminished speed under these mechanical and road conditions, the operator was negligent. Had the accident occurred in New York his negligence would have been attributed to the defendant owner who had given express permission to operate the car under the statute as it then read (Vehicle and Traffic Law, Consol. Laws, c. 71, § 59, subd. 1; now in identical language § 388, subd. 1).

Under the law of North Carolina the operation of a motor vehicle involved in an accident is evidence prima facie that its use was with the consent of the owner; and that the operator was "a person for whose conduct the owner was legally responsible, for the owner's benefit" (General Statutes of North Carolina, § 20–71.1, subds. [a], [b]).

This statute differs from New York law in basic concept. The North Carolina enactment has been construed by the Supreme Court of that State as a rule of evidence. "Proof of registration or admission of ownership furnishes, by virtue of the statute, *prima facie* evidence that the driver is agent of the owner in the operation, and is sufficient to support, but not compel, a verdict on the agency issue. It takes the issue to the jury" (*Mitchell v. White,* 256 N.C. 437, 441, 124 S.E.2d 137, 140 [1962]).

The statute, as the court noted, "creates a rule of evidence. It has no other or further force or effect." Its construction has been developed in a series of decisions. . . .

It would, accordingly, be held in North Carolina that a plaintiff who shows the use of a motor vehicle by a driver not the owner makes out a case sufficient to go to the jury against the owner on both permission and use beneficial to the owner, even though the owner denies the use was beneficial to him; but the jury would be instructed that if it found the use were solely for the benefit of the user, it should return a verdict for the owner.

Thus, under North Carolina law, the defendant owner Robert Smolack would be responsible prima facie for Arthur Smolack's negligence, but the jury would be told that if it found the use had not been for Robert's benefit, its verdict would be for Robert. The defendant's showing of absence of benefit to him, however, would not be conclusive on the jury.

There is some slight evidence in this case that the taking of the car to Florida was, in some part at least, for the benefit of the owner Robert, who used it on two occasions in Florida on his business and this evidence would undoubtedly be competent in support of the prima facie case created by the statute on the question of the "owner's benefit."

The New York statute, on the other hand, imposes a responsibility on the owner for negligence by one having permissive use of the vehicle without regard to benefit to the owner, and liability under the New York statute would be much more certain than under the statute of North Carolina on the present record.

We should, accordingly, determine whether, as plaintiffs argue, it would be permissible to apply the New York statute to this case. If *Babcock v. Jackson,* applies to the facts shown by this record, the conflicts of law question should be resolved according to the New York rule of liability.

All of the people involved, as it has been noted, were citizens and domiciliaries of New York; the car was registered in New York; arrangements for its use had been made in New York; and it was on its way back to New York when the accident occurred.

Thus, the locality of the accident itself in North Carolina was the merest lateral chance. The basic juridical components suggest application of New York law. The essential conditions of forum jurisdiction laid down in *Babcock,* as elucidated and limited in *Dym v. Gordon,* and again strongly reaffirmed in *Macey v. Rozbicki,* accordingly have been met in the present case.

It is true that the New York statute which attributes liability to an owner who has given permission applies in literal terms to the use and operation of a vehicle "in this state" (former Vehicle and Traffic Law, § 59, subd. 1), but, of course, most statutes regulating motor vehicle operations in terms or by necessary implication are written to apply to the State which enacts them.[b] However, since the present litigation is concerned with New York residents, arising from New York relationships, the rule apportioning liability from these relationships ought to be governed by New York law.

In *Macey v. Rozbicki (supra)* the accident occurred in Ontario, and, although neither the briefs nor the opinions of the court deal with this aspect of the statute, the implications of the decision suggest that this court did not regard section 388 as a bar to recovery since the owner was deemed to be responsible under New York law for the operation of a vehicle in Ontario with his consent.

The transitory use of the car does not necessarily impose the law of the State of transit on this relationship and, in this respect, the local law of the State of transit as to permissive use of the motor vehicle by its owner is not essentially different in its New York consequence from the law of the State of transit relating to liability to a gratuitous guest considered in *Babcock*.

In addressing ourselves to the policy of treating this sort of transitory tort arising entirely from New York relationships as governed by New York law, there is no logical basis to distinguish the application to out-of-State accidents of the New York law of liability to gratuitous guests and the New York law of liability arising from permissive use of a vehicle.

Decisions such as *Cherwien v. Geiter,* 272 N.Y. 165, 5 N.E.2d 185 [1936], and *Miranda v. Lo Curto,* 249 N.Y. 191, 163 N.E. 557 [1928], which took a more restrictive view, must be deemed to have yielded to the rule of *Babcock,* as did those cases which took a more restrictive view of liability to gratuitous guests.

Nor should we place undue emphasis on the term to which reference has been made "in this state" in the statute. It is clear that in adding the words "in this state" to the predecessor of subdivision 1 of section 388 (§ 59) in 1958 (L.1958, ch. 577), the Legislature was not concerned with extraterritorial effect. It was substituting "in this state" for the former words "upon a public highway" in order to cover the situation of an accident on private roadways and parking lots (1958 Report of N.Y.Law Rev.Comm. [N.Y.Legis.Doc., 1958, No. 65], pp. 589–590).

We turn now to the applicability of the New York statute authorizing an action for wrongful death (Decedent Estate Law, Consol.Laws, c. 13, § 130)[c] to this out-of-State accident. Prior to our decision in *Babcock v. Jackson, supra,* we consistently followed the choice of law rule that the statute applied "only to actions brought for damages for a wrong committed here causing the death of a person. . . ."

But, as the court noted in *Long v. Pan Amer. World Airways, Inc.,* 16 N.Y.2d 337, 343, 266 N.Y.S.2d 513, 213 N.E.2d 796, it would be "highly incongruous and unreal to have the flexible principle of *Babcock* apply in a case where the victim of a tort is injured but not where he is killed."

Accordingly, when a fatal accident occurs out of State and New York is, as here, the jurisdiction having "the most significant relationship" with the issue presented, our wrongful death statute determines the rights of the victim's survivors. (See *Gore v. Northeast Airlines,* 2 Cir., 373 F.2d 717.) To the extent that earlier decisions declined to give extraterritorial effect to the statute, they are overruled.

---

[b] Section 59(1) read as follows: "Every owner of a vehicle used or operated in this state shall be liable and responsible for the death or injuries to person or property resulting from negligence in the use or operation of such vehicle. . . ."

[c] Now Estates Powers and Trusts Law § 5-4.1.

The order should be reversed and a new trial granted, with costs to abide the event.

FULD, C. J., and VAN VOORHIS, BURKE, KEATING and BREITEL, JJ., concur with BERGAN, J.

SCILEPPI, J., dissents and votes to affirm.

NOTES AND QUESTIONS

(1)(a) In *Dym v. Gordon,* all the judges say they are following *Babcock,* yet they split three ways. In part, the difficulty stems from the fact that the guest-host relationship did not begin in the same place as the domicile of the parties; in part it stems from a different evaluation of the interest of the (other) states concerned.

(b) Judge Burke, paraphrasing, as he thinks, the holding of the *Babcock* case, says:

> . . . it is necessary first to isolate the issue, next to identify the policies embraced in the laws in conflict, and finally to examine the contacts of the respective jurisdictions to ascertain which has a superior connection with the occurrence and thus would have a superior interest in having its policy or law applied (at p. 153).

Has he done the paraphrase correctly? Putting the question more sharply, is Judge Burke right to say that the examination of contacts is for the purpose of evaluating the relative interests?

(c) Look back at Question 4(a), p. 151, *supra,* following *Babcock,* in which the contacts were counted either 5–1 or 3–1 in favor of New York. What is the count here?

(d) Judge Burke, of course, rejects this question, so that we need not decide whether place of accident and of injury are counted twice, or how many points are attributable to the car. He looks for a qualitative, not a quantitative test. Here, he says, (at p. 154) the place of accident "could in no sense be termed fortuitous," because Colorado was where the relationship was formed, and the activity was centered. He gets worried, however, at putting too much emphasis on where the relationship was formed. What if Miss Dym and Mr. Gordon had planned their trip while still in New York? His answer is "it would make no difference," but possibly he would lose someone from his 4–3 majority.

(e) What, then, about the relative interests? New York's interest, Judge Burke says, is basically the domicile of the parties. As for Colorado's interests, they seem to be three times as great as Ontario's. Why? Is the argument about the second car persuasive? Is there any reason to suppose Colorado is more hostile to ungrateful guests than Ontario? And what if . . .?[d]

(2)(a) Judge Fuld, dissenting in *Dym,* says, I wrote *Babcock,* I know what it means, and "[t]here is . . . no material distinction between the factual situation here presented and that in the *Babcock* case." That is true if one comes down on the first leg of *Babcock,* i.e., the common domicile of host and guest. The difference between *Dym* and *Babcock* emerges only in the context of the second leg of *Babcock,* the focus on the place where the relationship was formed. Here, says Judge Fuld, (p. 157), nothing turns on that circumstance.

---

[d] In fact, the evidence seems to be the other way. Professor Trautman reports that the purpose of the Ontario guest statute was to protect owner and drivers against ungrateful guests, Trautman, *Two Views on Kell v. Henderson,* 67 Colum. L. Rev. 465, 468–69 (1967), and one of Canada's leading treatises reports an "unverified legend" that the reason for the law was that Premier Mitch Hepburn of Ontario had been personally sued by some hitch-hikers to whom he had kindly given a lift. Linden, *Canadian Tort Law,* 614 (3d ed. 1982).

(b) The majority and the dissent disagree about whether Colorado has an interest in the accident. Judge Burke says Colorado had "the most significant contacts" . . . and therefore "a dominant interest in [the accident]." Judge Fuld, paraphrasing *Babcock,* says Colorado "has no conceivable interest. . . ." How can one tell?

(c) Professor Cavers, in a comment on *Dym v. Gordon* that appears as a postscript to the book is which the *Adams v. Knickerbocker* series was published, wrote that Judge Burke's discussion of the various motives of the Colorado guest statute demonstrates "that we have accepted too easily the explanation of *Babcock* in terms of an Ontario guest law that pursued a single goal," i.e., the prevention of collusion between host and guest against the insurance company.[e] "Moreover," he writes,

> the idea that Colorado, in enacting a guest statute, is concerned with the protection of drivers and insurers only when they are Coloradan is an over-simplification. The Colorado legislature can, to be sure, protect Colorado drivers and insurers more effectively than drivers and their insurers from other states who injure guest passengers in Colorado, and its law will impinge chiefly upon Colorado people. However, if a conflicts scholar in the Colorado legislature had offered an amendment reading:
>
>> provided, however, that this statute shall not apply to persons domiciled in other states who operate motor vehicles in this state with respect to injuries inflicted in this state on guest passengers domiciled in other states,
>
> would this have truly reflected the legislative purpose?[f]

(d) If the Cavers amendment had been adopted, of course, Colorado's guest statute would not by its terms have applied to *Dym.* Absent the amendment, is *Dym* a true conflict case? Even so, assuming none of the judges is prepared to resolve all true conflicts in favor of applying forum law, a weighing of interests is required.

(e) "At this point," Professor Cavers writes, "I see the need for a principle of preference. . . ."[g] How, on the basis of Judge Cavers' opinions in *Adams v. Knickerbocker,* do you think he would fashion the relevant principle?[h]

(f) Finally, Judge Desmond. In *Kilberg,* in which Judge Desmond wrote for the majority, the court stressed public policy, and he asks here, what was wrong with that? Forget those "concepts currently favored by teachers and writers on conflict of laws," he says (p. 159). Is he right? Is interest analysis just intellectual snobbery, and public policy of the forum straight talk?

(3) Pity the poor lower court judge confronted with *Kell v. Henderson,* with *Babcock* and *Dym* as the operative precedents.

---

[e] D. Cavers, *The Choice of Law Process* 298 (1965).

[f] *Id.* at 298–99. Cavers adds a footnote:

If that bill were ever studied in committee, I should hope that someone would offer an amendment confining its effect to persons from states not having guest statutes.

[g] *Id.* at 300.

[h] In his book, at 300–01, Professor Cavers refers to the principle under which,

> [W]hen the matter at issue is the application of a standard of conduct or of financial protection incident to a relationship which is higher than that prevailing in the state of injury, the court should apply the higher standard when it exists in the state where the relationship has its seat.

In *Dym,* he thinks the relationship does not have its seat in New York, and he accordingly would hold for defendant.

(a) Is *Kell* the precise reverse of *Babcock?* Or does the mirror image mix up right and left? Remember that while the facts are reversed, a true mirror case would require the suit to be brought in Ontario.

(b) Reliance on the Vehicle and Traffic Law is, in a sense, a substitute for conflict of laws analysis. Why shouldn''t the statute be construed as if it, too, were modified by the Cavers amendment?

(c) Look back at Judge Cavers' opinion in Case 5, *Ball v. Berkshire Natural History Society,* the "mirror image" of *Adams I,* but as in *Kell,* in the same forum. Judge Cavers says (at p. 123, *supra*) that his two principles are both reasonable, stressing the concern for compensation for accident victims when the accident takes place in the forum state, the lack of concern for immunity for a forum state corporation when the accident takes place in an immunity state. Thus, it seems that he would decide *Kell v. Henderson* in favor of plaintiff. Professor Cavers, putting a hypothetical case just like *Kell,* thinks Judge Burke would decide it in favor of defendant.[i] We will never know.

(d) What if instead of reversing the law/fact pattern of *Babcock,* as in *Kell,* the law/fact pattern of *Dym* were reversed. Two students from Colorado, who did not know each other, come to New York University summer school, one gives the other a ride, and an accident occurs. Suit is brought in New York. Would Judge Burke come out for plaintiff? Judge Fuld for defendant?[j]

(4)(a) *Macey v. Rozbicki* exposes *Dym v. Gordon* to parody. Where was the relationship between the two sisters formed? Was it in their parents' home many years ago, wherever it was that they grew up? Or in New York, where they talked about their summer plans? Or when Ms. Macey entered the Rozbickis' automobile in Waverly Beach, Ontario? Defendants' link to Ontario was stronger in *Macey* than defendants' link to Colorado in *Dym,* but plaintiff's link to Ontario was weaker. Do any of these details matter?

(b) Judge Desmond, who was impatient with the law professors in *Dym,* here is willing to count contacts, a task made easier by his identification of the relevant relationship as that of the two sisters, both domiciled in New York. The place where the trip began may be a contact, but it is "not particularly significant." Thus, *Dym* is easily distinguished.

(c) For Judge Keating, new on the court after 16 years in Congress, the case is easy. New York has a strong policy concerning compensation for victims of motor vehicle accidents that does not distinguish between guests, pedestrians, and other injured parties, or between in– and out-of-state accidents. Never mind the attempt to distinguish *Macey* from *Dym* by reference to the origin of the relationship. *Dym* should be overruled, and New York's interest proclaimed. For the time being, however, Judge Keating carries none of his fellow judges with him, not even Judges Fuld or Desmond, who dissented in *Dym.*

(5) *Farber v. Smolack* is not generally thought of as an important case, but it makes two contributions worth noting.

(a) First, the court makes clear that the analysis in the guest statute cases can be applied to other issues, such as the rules of vicarious liability. In doing this, the court is prepared to read quite loosely the statute that favored plaintiff in *Kell* when read literally.

---

[i] Cavers, *The Choice of Law Process* at 307.

[j] For an amusing and instructive opinion for the Court of Appeals in *Kell v. Henderson,* see Rosenberg, *Two Views on Kell v. Henderson,* 67 Colum. L. Rev. 459 (1967).

§ 3.04   CHOICE OF LAW □ 171

(b) More important, the court articulates what must have been implicit in *Macey*: it is not necessary to apply half of the law of the place of injury, as in *Kilberg*. Here it simply applies New York's wrongful death statute, on the basis that New York is the state having the most significant relationship with the issue presented. Thus, the gap left in *Kilberg* and *Pearson* is filled, and whatever constitutional doubts existed about those cases is resolved. It would, after all, make little sense, as Judge Bergan points out, to have one choice of law rule for common law actions for injury and another rule for statutory actions for wrongful death.

(6) One more case in this annual trek to the New York Court of Appeals needs to be at least summarized, before coming to the denouement in the next section: *Miller v. Miller,* 22 N.Y.2d 12, 290 N.Y.S.2d 734, 237 N.E.2d 877 (1968).

(a) Two brothers, one domiciled in New York, the other domiciled in Maine, were riding in the latter's car in Maine when the car crashed into a bridge railing, killing the New York brother. Three months later, the Maine brother decided to take over the New York branch of the family business previously headed by his brother, and he and his wife (in whose name the car had been registered) moved to New York. Shortly thereafter, the deceased brother's wife brought suit in New York against the former Maine brother and his wife, now New York domiciliaries. The defendants pleaded the Maine statutory limitation on recovery for wrongful death, $20,000 per person, which was in effect when the accident happened, but was repealed before the case reached the Court of Appeals. How, in light of the New York cases from *Kilberg* through *Farber*, should this case be decided?

(b) Once again, the Court of Appeals divided 4–3. Judge Keating, this time speaking for the majority, said the question was easy:

> It is obvious, merely in outlining the New York prohibition against limitations on recovery, that this state is vitally concerned with the manner in which the wife and children of a New York decedent will be compensated for the economic loss they have suffered as a result of the wrongful killing of their "bread winner."[k]

(c) Judge Keating conceded that "[o]ur inquiry cannot . . . stop merely in defining a New York interest . . . ." It was important also to consider fairness to the parties, including "the nonresident . . . who has patterned his conduct upon the law of the jurisdiction where he was acting, . . . as well as the possible interest of a sister State. . . .":

> As we view the facts in this case, however, we perceive no substantial countervailing considerations . . . which would warrant rejection of our own law in favor of that of Maine. The Maine statute with which we are concerned here, dealing as it does with the nature of the remedy for concededly tortious conduct, is obviously not the kind of statute which regulates conduct, and, therefore, is not the kind of statute upon which a person would rely in governing his conduct. The only justifiable reliance which would be present here would involve the purchase of liability insurance in light of the remedies available to an injured person. No such reliance is claimed here.[l]

As to the possible interest of Maine in limiting the recovery awarded to its resident, that no longer applied, since the defendants were no longer residents of Maine.

---

[k] 22 N.Y.2d at 18, 290 N.Y.S.2d at 739, 237 N.E.2d at 880.

[l] 22 N.Y.2d at 19, 290 N.Y.S.2d at 740, 237 N.E.2d at 881. Insurance costs are not relevant, the court explains, because Maine law imposed no limit on recoveries for injuries not resulting in death, and automobile insurance policies sold in Maine did not distinguish between liability for death or injury.

(d) Judge Breitel, new to this controversy,[m] dissented in a long, vigorous opinion:

> Accepting as more or less valid the modern but only emerging analyses for choosing the applicable or proper rules of law to achieve a just result in this case and cases of like kind, the significant contacts, the interests of the concerned jurisdictions, the minimal requirements for uniformity of result, the relevance of what a neutral forum would select as the applicable rules of law, and the expectations of the parties to the accident suggest that the application of the Maine rule is the most reasonable choice.[n]

If *Babcock* was the leading case, he argued, the significant contacts—the car, the injury, and defendant's residence—were centered in Maine.

> Even on an interest analysis, leaving aside for the moment the post-accident events, it may be argued that the Maine limitation should be applied [citing Cavers' principle of preference looking, in the absence of a previously existing relationship, to the lower standard of conduct or of financial protection of the state where defendant acted].[o]

It is true, Judge Breitel said, that under "another choice-of-law technique based on interest analysis" according to Currie, New York law should be applied. But Judge Breitel rejects this approach, under which

> a rigid personal law would be substituted for the one-time just as rigid, territorial law which invariable applied the law of the place of the tort. . . . Such a conclusion is contrary to the facts of a society territorially organized as this one is. Overall, the greatest value of interest analysis is in resolving false conflicts. When true conflicts are involved, as in this case, excluding, of course, the post-accident events, the problem does not lend itself to such automatic solution or the facile evaluation of predominant interests.[p]

(e) Having gone through the many theories and approaches, Judge Breitel would come down with Rheinstein:

> Justice favors the fulfillment of expectations for two reasons. First, parties may have acted in reliance upon their assumption that courts would apply a certain rule of decision, and application of a different rule would then be unjust. . . .
>
> Justified expectations are also relevant in a second, more intangible, way: it is jurisprudentially significant that parties' rights be determined by the law or system of rules which they most probably believed would control their relationship. In this respect, the application of the proper law of the tort exercises an influence in "promoting an unconscious acceptance of legality and legal order."[q]

(f) What about the holding of *Kilberg* that limits on recovery for wrongful death are contrary to New York public policy, at least when applied to residents of New York? "[T]he case presents no problem," Judge Breitel wrote, "because the facts are so distinguishable."

(g) Finally, there were the two post-accident events—the repeal by Maine of its statutory damages ceiling, and defendants' move to New York. Judge Keating thought both were relevant;

---

[m] Judge Breitel, who joined the Court of Appeals in 1967, had concurred with the majority in *Farber*, but had not written.

[n] 22 N.Y.2d at 23, 290 N.Y.S.2d at 743, 237 N.E.2d at 883.

[o] 22 N.Y.2d at 25–26; 290 N.Y.S.2d at 745, 237 N.E.2d at 885.

[p] 22 N.Y.2d at 26, 27, 290 N.Y.S.2d at 746, 747, 237 N.E.2d at 885–86, 886.

[q] 22 N.Y.2d at 28, 290 N.Y.S.2d at 747, 237 N.E.2d at 886, quoting from Kegel, a leading German conflicts scholar, in *The Crisis of Conflict of Laws,* 112 Receuil des Cours 91, 184 (Hague Acad. Int'l L. 1964).

Judge Breitel thought neither one was a sound basis for determining the choice of the applicable law. Are the two events different from this perspective?

Reconsider the question of post-accident change of domicile when reading *Allstate Insurance Co. v. Hague*.[r]

---

§ 3.05 Denouement in New York

TOOKER v. LOPEZ

New York Court of Appeals
24 N.Y.2d 569, 301 N.Y.S.2d 519, 249 N.E.2d 394 (1969)

KEATING, J.

On October 16, 1964, Catharina Tooker, a 20-year-old coed at Michigan State University, was killed when the Japanese sports car in which she was a passenger overturned after the driver had lost control of the vehicle while attempting to pass another car. The accident also took the life of the driver of the vehicle, Marcia Lopez, and seriously injured another passenger, Susan Silk. The two girls were classmates of Catharina Tooker at Michigan State University and lived in the same dormitory. They were en route from the university to Detroit, Michigan, to spend the weekend.

Catharina Tooker and Marcia Lopez were both New York domiciliaries. The automobile which Miss Lopez was driving belonged to her father who resided in New York, where the sports car he had given his daughter was registered and insured.

This action for wrongful death was commenced by Oliver P. Tooker, Jr., the father of Catharina Tooker, as the administrator of her estate. The defendant asserted as an affirmative defense the Michigan "guest statute" which permits recovery by guests only by showing willful misconduct or gross negligence of the driver. The plaintiff moved to dismiss the affirmative defense on the ground that under the governing choice-of-law rules it was New York law rather than Michigan law which applied. The motion was granted by the Special Term Justice who concluded that: "New York State 'has the greatest concern with the specific issue raised in the litigation' and that New York law should apply." The Appellate Division (Third Department) agreed with "the cogent argument advanced by Special Term" but felt "constrained" by the holding in *Dym v. Gordon* to apply the Michigan guest statute.

We are presented here with a choice-of-law problem which we have had occasion to consider in several cases since our decision in *Babcock v. Jackson* rejected the traditional rule which looked invariably to the law of the place of the wrong. Unfortunately, as we recently had occasion to observe, our decisions subsequent to rejection of the *lex loci delictus* rule "have lacked a precise consistency." This case gives us the opportunity to resolve those inconsistencies in a class of cases which have been particularly troublesome.

In *Babcock v. Jackson*, . . . [t]his court rejected unequivocally the traditional *lex loci delictus* rule and refused to apply Ontario law. We noted that the traditional rule placed controlling reliance upon one fact which had absolutely no relation to the purpose of the ostensibly conflicting laws

---

[r] See § 5.03, *infra*.

and thus resulted in decisions which often frustrated the interests and policies of the State in which the accident had taken place as well as our own State.

. . . .

Babcock v. Jackson was followed by *Dym v. Gordon.*

. . . Since the case, in fact, involved another vehicle and injured third parties, we concluded that Colorado, unlike Ontario in *Babcock v. Jackson,* had an interest in the application of its law. Faced with a true conflict of laws, a closely divided court determined that Colorado law ought to govern since the parties had resided in that State for so prolonged a period of time and there, therefore, seemed no unfairness in subjecting them to the law of Colorado.

The decision in *Dym v. Gordon,* upon which the Appellate Division relied in the instant case, is clearly distinguishable from the facts here. There is here no third-party "non-guest" who was injured and there is no question of denying such a party priority in the assets of the negligent defendant. We cannot, however, in candor rest our decision on this basis in light of a subsequent decision which refused to apply the Ontario guest statute in a case indistinguishable from *Dym v. Gordon.* (See *Macey v. Rozbicki.*)

The primary point of division in *Dym v. Gordon* focused not upon the choice-of-law rule quoted earlier, but rather upon the construction placed on the Colorado guest statute which, upon reflection, we conclude was mistaken.

The teleological argument advanced by some (see Cavers, *Choice-of-Law Process,* p. 298) that the guest statute was intended to assure the priority of injured nonguests in the assets of a negligent host, in addition to the prevention of fraudulent claims, overlooks not only the statutory history but the fact that the statute permits recovery by guests who can establish that the accident was due to the gross negligence of the driver. If the purpose of the statute is to protect the rights of the injured "non-guest," as opposed to the owner or his insurance carrier, we fail to perceive any rational basis for predicating that protection on the degree of negligence which the guest is able to establish. . . .

This purpose can never be vindicated when the insurer is a New York carrier and the defendant is sued in the courts of this State. Under such circumstances, the jurisdiction enacting such a guest statute has absolutely no interest in the application of its law.

The failure to come to grips with this problem in *Macey v. Rozbicki* resulted in a decision which has confused and clouded the choice-of-law process in New York. . . .

The court correctly concluded that New York law governed, but in so doing ignored the rationale of *Babcock* and *Dym* in order to avoid a reconsideration of the construction placed on the guest statute. Thus the court wrote:

> In the present case the relationship of two sisters living permanently in New York was not affected or changed by their temporary meeting together in Canada for a short visit there, especially since the arrangements for that visit had undoubtedly been made in New York State. Every fact in this case was New York related, save only the not particularly significant one that the particular trip on the day of the accident was between two points in Canada.

Substituted for a rational choice-of-law rule was a method of decision based on contact counting—a method open to the same criticism of unreasonableness as the earlier *lex loci delictus* rule. . . .

Viewed in the light of the foregoing discussion, the instant case is one of the simplest in the choice-of-law area. If the facts are examined in light of the policy considerations which underlie the ostensibly conflicting laws it is clear that New York has the only real interest in whether recovery should be granted and that the application of Michigan law "would defeat a legitimate interest of the forum State without serving a legitimate interest of any other State."

The policy of this State with respect to all those injured in automobile accidents is reflected in the legislative declaration which prefaces New York's compulsory insurance law:

[Judge Keating repeats the quotation set out in his concurring opinion in *Macey v. Rozbicki*, p. 163, *supra*.]

New York's "grave concern" in affording recovery for the injuries suffered by Catharina Tooker, a New York domiciliary, and the loss suffered by her family as a result of her wrongful death, is evident merely in stating the policy which our law reflects. On the other hand, Michigan has no interest in whether a New York plaintiff is denied recovery against a New York defendant where the car is insured here. The fact that the deceased guest and driver were in Michigan for an extended period of time is plainly irrelevant. Indeed, the Legislature, in requiring that insurance policies cover liability for injuries regardless of where the accident takes place has evinced commendable concern not only for residents of this State, but residents of other States who may be injured as a result of the activities of New York residents. Under these circumstances we cannot be concerned with whether Miss Tooker or Miss Lopez were in Michigan for a summer session or for a full college education.

The argument that the choice of law in tort cases should be governed by the fictional expectation of the parties has been rejected unequivocally by this court. In *Miller v. Miller* we wrote:

> We reject the argument . . . that the choice of applicable law in this tort action should be determined on the basis of the expectations of the parties as derived from their contact with the State of the place of the accident. Such a determination of the applicable laws is based upon an obvious fiction having little to do with the laws in conflict.
>
> . . . .

. . . .

The dissenting opinion makes much of the fact that it was purely "adventitious" that Miss Tooker, a temporary resident in Michigan, chose to ride in Miss Lopez's automobile rather than an automobile owned by a Michigan domiciliary. This factor we are told requires the application of Michigan law. Choice-of-law decisions in guest statute cases, the dissent suggests, ought to turn on whether or not it was "adventitious" that the passenger was in a car registered and insured in New York as opposed to the jurisdiction in which the relationship is seated and has its purpose.

The dissent is, of course, correct that it was "adventitious" that Miss Tooker was a guest in an automobile registered and insured in New York. For all we know, her decision to go to Michigan State University as opposed to New York University may have been "adventitious." Indeed, her decision to go to Detroit on the weekend in question instead of staying on campus and studying may equally have been "adventitious." The fact is, however, that Miss Tooker went to Michigan State University; that she decided to go to Detroit on October 16, 1964; that she was a passenger in a vehicle registered and insured in New York; and that as a result of all these "adventitious" occurrences, she is dead and we have a case to decide. Why we should be concerned with what might have been is unclear.

Certainly we cannot make believe that the car was registered and insured in Michigan any more than we can make believe that Miss Tooker is not dead. Moreover, it is difficult to comprehend why we should adopt such "a rule of make believe." The only reason suggested by the dissent is that such a rule is "a simple rule easy to apply with a high degree of certainty. . . ." We cannot agree that this is so. But even if we did, we would reject the rule for the same reason we rejected the *lex loci delictus* rule which this description more aptly fits. To state the matter simply, we are concerned with rational and just rules and not merely simple rules.

We rejected the *lex loci delictus* rule because it placed controlling reliance upon one factor totally unrelated to the policies reflected by the ostensibly conflicting laws. The only fact less relevant to those policies in guest statute cases is whether the presence of the guest in the particular automobile was "adventitious."[2]

The dissent concedes that

> there is no total escape from considering the policies of other States. But this necessity should not be extended to produce anomalies of results out of the same accident, with unpredictability, and lack of consistency in determinations. Thus, it is hard to accept the implicit consequence that Miss Silk, the Michigan resident injured in the accident, should not be able to recover in Michigan (and presumably in New York) but a recovery can be had for her deceased fellow-passenger in the very same accident.

Applying the choice-of-law rule which we have adopted, it is not an "implicit consequence" that the Michigan passenger injured along with Miss Lopez should be denied recovery. Under the reasoning adopted here, it is not at all clear that Michigan law would govern. We do not, however, find it necessary or desirable to conclusively resolve a question which is not now before us. It suffices to note that any anomaly resulting from the application of Michigan law to bar an action brought by Miss Silk is "the implicit consequence" of a Federal system which, at a time when we have truly become one nation, permits a citizen of one State to recover for injuries sustained in an automobile accident and denies a citizen of another State the right to recover for injuries sustained in a similar accident. The anomaly does not arise from any choice-of-law rule.

Indeed, the rule advanced by the dissent, unlike the rule we have adopted, will only foster rather than alleviate such anomalies. Thus, suppose in *Babcock v. Jackson* the driver of the vehicle had picked up a hitchhiker in Ontario who was injured along with his guest, Miss Babcock. And suppose in *Macey v. Rozbicki* Mrs. Rozbicki had invited her next-door neighbor to go with her and her sister to church and both the Ontario guest and Miss Macey were injured. Under the rule advanced by the dissent, Ontario law would clearly apply to govern the right of the "Ontario" guests since it was purely "adventitious' that they were in a New York car rather than an Ontario car. On the other hand, the same rule would permit recovery by the "New York" guests since it was not "adventitious' that they should have been in a New York vehicle at the time. We agree with the dissent that a rule which fosters such "lack of consistency" and "unpredictability" without any compensating features is hardly worthy of adoption or consideration.

---

[2] Similar reasons compel the rejection of the rule suggested by the *Restatement, 2d, Conflict of Laws*, p. O. D., pt. II, § 159, upon which the dissent relies. Where the guest-host relationship "arose" or is "centered" is wholly irrelevant to policies reflected by the laws in conflict. Any language in our earlier opinions lending support to a contrary view has, as Judge Burke notes in his concurring opinion, been overruled. We would note that there is some question as to whether the portion of the *Restatement*, relied upon by the dissent, is applicable to the precise facts present here.

Before concluding this opinion we cannot fail to take note of one additional argument raised in the dissenting opinion to the effect that the choice-of-law rule articulated in our recent decisions merely amounts to a rule which will always result in the application of New York law—"a domiciliary conceptualism that rested on a vested right accruing from the fact of domicile" (*Miller v. Miller* [dissenting opinion]). This argument ignores the fact that our decisions since *Babcock v. Jackson* have not always resulted in the application of the law of New York and have, indeed, indicated proper recognition and respect for the legitimate concerns of other jurisdictions and the real expectations of the parties....

. . . .

[The court summarizes three cases in which the Court of Appeals applied law other than that of New York. In the first case, *Intercontinental Hotels Corp. v. Golden,* 15 N.Y.2d 9, 254 N.Y.S.2d 527, 203 N.E.2d 210 (1964), the court enforced a gambling debt incurred by the New York defendant at a legal casino in Puerto Rico, though enforcement of such debts would be illegal if they were incurred in New York; in the second case, *Oltarsh v. Aetna Casualty Ins. Co.,* 15 N.Y.2d 111, 256 N.Y.S.2d 577, 204 N.E.2d 622 (1965), the court upheld a direct action by a New York plaintiff against a liability insurer arising out of an accident in Puerto Rico, as was permitted by the law of Puerto Rico, though New York did not permit suit against insurers until after judgment against the insured. In the third case, (*Estate of Clark,* p. 346, *infra,* the court applied Virginia rather than New York law to determine the widow's share of an estate.]

These decisions, rendered in various stages of the development of the choice-of-law rule recently articulated, are nevertheless consistent with that rule. (B. Currie, *The Disinterested Third State,* 28 Law & Contemporary Problems, 754, 757.) They refute completely the implication in the dissenting opinion that we have adopted a rule which will always result in the application of New York law. Rather we have adopted a rule founded in reason and justice which affords easy application in most if not all situations.

The order of the Appellate Division should be reversed, with costs, and the order of Special Term reinstated.

CHIEF JUDGE FULD (concurring).

I join in the court's opinion but, in doing so, I would add these few brief comments.

Our court has, consistently with the approach adopted in *Babcock v. Jackson,* emphasized the need for analyzing and measuring the relevant interests of the states involved as to the particular issue presented in order to determine the decisional rule which is to govern. We departed from the traditional choice-of-law rule in personal injury cases, because it "fails to take account of underlying policy considerations," and adopted a principle designed to afford an "appropriate approach for accommodating the competing interests in tort cases with multi-State contacts." We were willing to sacrifice the absolute certainty assured by the old rule for the more just, fair and practical result that may best be achieved by giving controlling effect to the law of the state which has the greatest concern with, or interest in, the specific issue raised in the litigation.

In consequence of the change—and this was, of course, to be anticipated—our decisions in multi-state highway accident cases have not featured consistency. Indeed, guest-host suits have proved to be, as Judge KEATING notes "a class of cases which have been particularly troublesome." The time has come, it seems to me, for us to endeavor to minimize what some have characterized as an *ad hoc* case-by-case approach by laying down guidelines, as well as we can, for the solution of guest-host conflicts problems. We have had sufficient experience with enough variations of the patterns of fact and law in this type of case to permit us to acknowledge that several choice-of-law rules governing different types of fact patterns have been forged by our recent decisions.

Babcock and the decisions it heralded place in our hands an instrument not confined to the rare and unusual situation. Rather, they comprise a sound foundation for a set of basic principles which the practicing lawyer, as well as the conflicts scholar, may be able to wield with good results. They have helped us uncover the underlying values and policies which are operative in this area of the law. Now that these values and policies have been revealed, we may proceed to the next stage in the evolution of the law—the formulation of a few rules of general applicability, promising a fair level of predictability. Although no rule may be found or framed to guarantee a satisfying result in every case, we cannot hope to deal justly with the legion of multi-state highway accident cases by regarding each case as one of a kind and unique. We should attempt, as has been suggested, to avoid "both unreasonable rules and an unruly reasonableness that is destructive of many of the values of law and that loses sight of the need for coordinating a multi-state system." (Rosenberg, *Two Views on Kell v. Henderson,* 67 Colum. L. Rev. 459, 464.)

Without attempting too much, I believe that we may accept the following principles as sound for situations involving guest statutes in conflicts settings:

 1. When the guest-passenger and the host-driver are domiciled in the same state, and the car is there registered, the law of that state should control and determine the standard of care which the host owes to his guest.

 2. When the driver's conduct occurred in the state of his domicile and that state does not cast him in liability for that conduct, he should not be held liable by reason of the fact that liability would be imposed upon him under the tort law of the state of the victim's domicile. Conversely, when the guest was injured in the state of his own domicile and its law permits recovery, the driver who has come into that state should not—in the absence of special circumstances—be permitted to interpose the law of his state as a defense.

 3. In other situations, when the passenger and the driver are domiciled in different states, the rule is necessarily less categorical. Normally, the applicable rule of decision will be that of the state where the accident occurred but not if it can be shown that displacing that normally applicable rule will advance the relevant substantive law purposes without impairing the smooth working of the multi-state system or producing great uncertainty for litigants. (Cf. *Restatement, 2d, Conflict of Laws,* p. O.D., pt. II, §§ 146, 159.)

Guidelines of the sort suggested will not always be easy of application, nor will they furnish guidance to litigants and lower courts in all cases. They are proffered as a beginning, not as an end, to the problems of sound and fair adjudication in the troubled world of the automobile guest statute.

Since, in the case before us, the guest-passenger and the host-driver were both domiciled in this State and the automobile was here registered, we look to New York law to determine the standard of care to be applied between those parties.

BURKE, J. (concurring).

From all that has been written, it is apparent that our decision in *Dym* is overruled. I mark the passing of *Dym* with regret as I viewed that case as an expression of a policy of this court that we would not always hold a foreign guest statute inapplicable where the defendant was from

New York. It is evident that the philosophy of the court has changed since *Dym* and, as a result of this transformation, we have firmly embarked upon an interest analysis approach to a conflicts problem. For that reason, I join in the majority opinion and concur in its adoption of the views first expressed by Judge KEATING in *Macey v. Rozbicki*. While this approach may indeed provide certainty for guest statute cases, it does not, I feel, remove all future problems from the area. Reference to the status of Miss Silk illustrates this point.

It is not at all clear whether the majority would conclude that she too, although not a New York resident, could recover should she bring an action against this defendant. Logically, the majority might declare, as they have in this case, that "the Legislature, in requiring that insurance policies cover liability for injuries regardless of where the accident takes place . . . has evidenced commendable concern not only for residents of this State, but residents of other States who may be injured as a result of the activities of New York residents." The dissenters, however, intimate that since Miss Silk could not recover in Michigan, she would presumably be barred from a recovery in this court.

I am not now prepared to decide that question nor am I ready to suggest what this State's interest would be in the present situation if the car were not insured in New York. I merely refer to these situations to illustrate the difficulty which we shall encounter in future guest statute cases even under the standard adopted by the majority today. . . . I view the entire matter as one of national concern which cannot be settled by any rule this court might proffer. As the matter is of Federal dimension, only Federal legislation will ultimately succeed in resolving these continuing controversies in a rational and equitable manner.

Until such needed legislation is forthcoming, it will remain incumbent upon us to resolve these guest statute controversies as they arise. Since the onus is presently with us, I would reverse the order of the Appellate Division in this case and reinstate the order of Special Term.

. . . .

BREITEL, J. (dissenting) . . ..

Except for the facts that plaintiff and the deceased were New York residents, that defendant's deceased daughter had a New York operator's license, that the registered owner of the car was a New York resident, and that the car was registered and insured in New York, every other facet of the accident was based in Michigan and was as localized as it could be in that State. The students were in residence at the university, were not in sojourn for short courses or interim sessions, or on tour. The trip was intrinsically and exclusively a Michigan trip, concerned only with Michigan places, roads, and conditions.

The registration and ownership of the car and the residence of its driver, as well as that of plaintiff's deceased daughter, were adventitious so far as this trip was concerned. The same trip with the same purposes with some automobile would have or could have taken place among a similar group of students from other States or Michigan, or by the same students, even if the States of residence and automobile ownership and insurance were changed. Indeed, defendant might have chosen to have the automobile registered and insured in either Michigan or New York, and in his daughter's name, since the car, as a matter of family arrangements, was really hers rather than his.

In this highly mobile and automotive Nation the slight admixture of multi-state contacts as occurred here is now very frequent, and is becoming increasingly so. Unless conflicts rules move over to substitute a completely personal law for the territorial system that infuses Anglo-American jurisprudence and underlies the understanding and expectations of Americans, it is still true that the law of a territory governs the conduct and qualifiedly the status of persons, resident and nonresident, within it, except in the extraordinary situation where the localization of persons and conduct is adventitious. At least this has been true until quite recently. No doubt, in *Miller v. Miller,* in a context sufficiently different from this case and involving a death action statute rather than a guest-host statute, and, therefore, not controlling here, the majority took a different view.

What the rules, exemplified by *Babcock v. Jackson* and *Farber v. Smolack* established, and very rightly so, was that when the territory in which the accident occurs is wholly adventitious to the relationship or status among the parties, that factor should not determine the applicable law. In each of these cases the seat and purpose of the relationship was established to be elsewhere than where the accident occurred. It was the place of the accident that could be changed without changing or affecting the other relationships. In short, except in a rather minimal way, the conduct of the parties was not affected by the place where the accident occurred. It was, therefore, adventitious.

The converse occurred in this case. The incidental registration and ownership of the car, and the domicile of these Michigan students, did not influence their conduct or the establishment or nature of the relationship among them. Regardless of these facts they would undoubtedly have entered into the same relationship, made the same trip, and behaved the same way. These facts were, therefore, extrinsic or adventitious.

On this view, *Dym v. Gordon* was soundly decided, and this case, which is even stronger on its intrinsic facts because of the young women's being students in residence, as that term is used in the academic world, should be decided the same way. What that means concretely is that when plaintiff's deceased daughter as a Michigan student in residence became a guest of a fellow student in her car (however registered or owned), or even in a borrowed or rented car, for a Michigan automobile trip, she formed the relationship and accepted the consequence of that relationship under Michigan law, just as much as she did, on a different issue, in determining the standard of care to be applied to the automobile operator's conduct. This is not only a simple rule easy to apply with a high degree of certainty but offends no sense of justice except perhaps of those who look either to personal law or have a conscious or unconscious predilection for law of the forum as reflecting a higher degree of justice.

The fact is that the law to be applied should not itself be the paramount influence in weighing the circumstances of a case in which a choice of law must be made; rather the choice of law should be the conclusion of a selective process which looks initially to the circumstances or factors. To be sure, in considering the significance of the factors or circumstances of a case one must be influenced by the purposes of the relevant rules of law, since there can be no naked selection of facts without purpose anymore than there can be an application of a whole jurisprudence to a complex of multi-state facts. It is in this sense that the process of isolating the issues together with the significant policies is relevant . . . . This still does not mean that a preference for the policy of a relevant rule should in actual practice as so often happens, to the exclusion of everything else, determine its selection. . . .

. . .

There are truly difficult cases where the division between the significant and adventitious facts is elusive. This case is hardly such a one. The trouble with overextending the successive and changing rationales from *Auten v. Auten* [p. 246 *infra*] in the contract field, through the *Babcock* case and its progeny, is to introduce the very uncertainty and chaotic unpredictability that the extremist critics of any change from the *lex loci* rules predicted. It is not necessary to fulfill the worst of those predictions if one significant factor is recalled.

In modern theories in the field of conflicts, the analysts have generally posited, or in fact assumed, as a significant factor the place where the transaction occurred (*Restatement, 2d, Conflict of Laws,* Comment d, and Reporter's Note to Comment d). What has happened of course, is that lip service is paid to the factor of place, and promptly ignored thereafter, if the forum prefers its own policy preconceptions and especially if it requires denial of recovery to a plaintiff in a tort case. Of course, the contrary is likely to occur, where the new rules might otherwise displace the factor of locus, as in *Kell v. Henderson.* . . .

If the trend continues uninterruptedly, the shift to a personal law approach in conflicts law, especially in the torts field, will continue apace. Apart from the fact that such a development is not logically consistent with Anglo-American jurisprudence, it would create a sharp division between intra-national conflicts rules and extra-national conflicts rules. It is most unlikely that such a development would be recognized elsewhere. Inevitably, the goals of uniformity, let alone predictability, in conflict rules would be frustrated, and the arbitrary results produced by forum-selection would be proliferated beyond tolerable limits.

For all of these reasons, I dissent and vote to affirm, and would deny the motion to dismiss the affirmative defense.

Opinion by Judge KEATING in which Chief Judge FULD and Judges BURKE and BERGAN concur; Chief Judge FULD and Judge BURKE also concur in separate opinions; Judge BREITEL dissents and votes to affirm in a separate opinion in which Judges SCILEPPI and JASEN concur.

NEUMEIER v. KUEHNER

New York Court of Appeals
31 N.Y.2d 121, 335 N.Y.S.2d 64, 286 N.E.2d 454 (1972)

CHIEF JUDGE FULD.

A domiciliary of Ontario, Canada, was killed when the automobile in which he was riding, owned and driven by a New York resident, collided with a train in Ontario. That jurisdiction has a guest statute, and the primary question posed by this appeal is whether in this action brought by the Ontario passenger's estate, Ontario law should be applied and the New York defendant permitted to rely on its guest statute as a defense.

The facts are quickly told. On May 7, 1969, Arthur Kuehner, the defendant's intestate, a resident of Buffalo, drove his automobile from that city to Fort Erie in the Province of Ontario, Canada, where he picked up Amie Neumeier, who lived in that town with his wife and their children. Their trip was to take them to Long Beach, also in Ontario, and back again to Neumeier's home in Fort Erie. However, at a railroad crossing in the Town of Sherkston—on the way to Long Beach—the auto was struck by a train of the defendant Canadian National Railway Company. Both Kuehner and his guest-passenger were instantly killed.

Neumeier's wife and administratrix, a citizen of Canada and a domiciliary of Ontario, thereupon commenced this wrongful death action in New York against both Kuehner's estate and the Canadian National Railway Company. The defendant estate pleaded, as an affirmative defense, the Ontario guest statute and the defendant railway also interposed defenses in reliance upon it. In substance, the statute provides that the owner or driver of a motor vehicle is not liable for damages resulting from injury to, or the death of, a guest-passenger unless he was guilty of gross negligence. It is worth noting, at this point, that, although our court originally considered that the sole purpose of the Ontario statute was to protect Ontario defendants and their insurers against collusive claims (see *Babcock v. Jackson*), "Further research . . . has revealed the distinct possibility that one purpose, and perhaps the only purpose, of the statute was to protect owners and drivers against ungrateful guests." (Reese, *Chief Judge Fuld and Choice of Law,* 71 Colum. L. Rev. 548, 558; see Trautman, *Two Views on Kell v. Henderson: A Comment,* 67 Colum. L. Rev. 465, 469.)

The plaintiff, asserting that the Ontario statute "is not available . . . in the present action", moved, to dismiss the affirmative defenses pleaded. The court at Special Term, holding the guest statute applicable, denied the motions (63 Misc. 2d 766) but, on appeal, a closely divided Appellate Division reversed and directed dismissal of the defenses. It was the court's belief that such a result was dictated by *Tooker v. Lopez.*

In reaching that conclusion, the Appellate Division misread our decision in the *Tooker* case—a not unnatural result in light of the variant views expressed in the three separate opinions written on behalf of the majority. It is important to bear in mind that in *Tooker,* the guest-passenger and the host-driver were both domiciled in New York, and our decision—that New York law was controlling—was based upon, and limited to, that fact situation. Indeed, two of the three judges who wrote for reversal—Judge KEATING and Judge BURKE—expressly noted that the determination then being made left open the question whether New York law would be applicable if the plaintiff passenger happened to be a domiciliary of the very jurisdiction which had a guest statute.[1] Thus, *Tooker v. Lopez* did no more than hold that, when the passenger and driver are residents of the same jurisdiction and the car is there registered and insured, its law, and not the law of the place of accident, controls and determines the standard of care which the host owes to his guest.

What significantly and effectively differentiates the present case is the fact that, although the host was a domiciliary of New York, the guest, for whose death recovery is sought, was domiciled in Ontario, the place of accident and the very jurisdiction which had enacted the statute designed to protect the host from liability for ordinary negligence. It is clear that, although New York has a deep interest in protecting its own residents, injured in a foreign state, against unfair or anachronistic statutes of that state, it has no legitimate interest in ignoring the public policy of a foreign jurisdiction—such as Ontario—and in protecting the plaintiff guest domiciled and injured there from legislation obviously addressed, at the very least, to a resident riding in a vehicle traveling within its borders.

To distinguish *Tooker* on such a basis is not improperly discriminatory. It is quite true that, in applying the Ontario guest statute to the Ontario-domiciled passenger, we, in a sense, extend a right less generous than New York extends to a New York passenger in a New York vehicle with New York insurance. That, though, is not a consequence of invidious discrimination; it is, rather, the result of the existence of disparate rules of law in jurisdictions that have diverse and important connections with the litigants and the litigated issue.

---

[1] In the other concurring opinion [at p. 178, *supra*], I wrote that in such a case—where the passenger is a resident of the state having a guest statute—"the applicable rule of decision will [normally] be that of the state where the accident occurred."

The fact that insurance policies issued in this State on New York-based vehicles cover liability, regardless of the place of the accident, certainly does not call for the application of internal New York law in this case. The compulsory insurance requirement is designed to *cover* a car-owner's liability, not *create* it; in other words, the applicable statute was not intended to impose liability where none would otherwise exist. This being so, we may not properly look to the New York insurance requirement to dictate a choice-of-law rule which would invariably impose liability. As Justice MOULE wrote in the course of his dissenting opinion below.

> The statute does not purport to impose liability where none would otherwise exist. We must observe that Judge KEATING's statement that the Legislature "has evinced commendable concern not only for the residents of this State, but residents of other States who may be injured as a result of the activities of New York residents" was in the context, not of proving that New York had a governmental interest in overriding foreign rules of liability, but of demonstrating that it was immaterial in that case that the driver and passenger, while domiciliaries of New York, were attending college in Michigan. While New York may be a proper forum for actions involving its own domiciliaries, regardless of where the accident happened, it does not follow that we should apply New York law simply because some may think it is a better rule, where doing so does not advance any New York State interest, nor the interest of any New York State domiciliary.

When, in *Babcock v. Jackson,* we rejected the inexorable choice-of-law rule in personal injury cases because it failed to take account of underlying policy considerations, we were willing to sacrifice the certainty provided by the old rule for the more just, fair and practical result that may best be achieved by giving controlling effect to the law of the jurisdiction which has the greatest concern with, or interest in, the specific issue raised in the litigation. In consequence of the change effected—and this was to be anticipated—our decisions in multi-state highway accident cases, particularly in those involving guest-host controversies, have, it must be acknowledged, lacked consistency. This stemmed, in part, from the circumstance that it is frequently difficult to discover the purposes or policies underlying the relevant local law rules of the respective jurisdictions involved. It is even more difficult, assuming that these purposes or policies are found to conflict, to determine on some principle basis which should be given effect at the expense of the others.

The single all-encompassing rule which called, invariably, for selection of the law of the place of injury was discarded, and wisely, because it was too broad to prove satisfactory in application. There is, however, no reason why choice-of-law rules, more narrow than those previously devised, should not be successfully developed, in order to assure a greater degree of predictability and uniformity, on the basis of our present knowledge and experience. (See, e.g., Cavers, *The Choice of Law Process,* 121–122; Reese, *Chief Judge Fuld and Choice of Law,* 71 Colum. L. Rev. 548, 555, 561–562; Reese, *Choice of Law: Rules or Approach,* 57 Cornell L. Rev. 315, 321 *et seq.;* Rosenberg, *Comments on Reich v. Purcell,* 15 UCLA L. Rev. 641, 642, 646–647.) "The time has come," I wrote in *Tooker,* "to endeavor to minimize what some have characterized as an *ad hoc* case-by-case approach by laying down guidelines, as well as we can, for the solution of guest-host conflicts problems." *Babcock* and its progeny enable us to formulate a set of basic principles that may be profitably utilized, for they have helped us uncover the underlying values and policies which are operative in this area of the law. To quote again from the concurring opinion in *Tooker,* "Now that these values and policies have been revealed, we may proceed to the next stage in the evolution of the law—the formulation of a few rules of general applicability, promising a fair level of predictability." Although it was recognized that no rule may be formulated to guarantee a satisfactory result in every case, the following principles were proposed as sound for situations involving guest statutes in conflicts settings:

> 1. When the guest-passenger and the host-driver are domiciled in the same state, and the car is there registered, the law of that state should control and determine the standard of care which the host owes to his guest.
>
> 2. When the driver's conduct occurred in the state of his domicile and that state does not cast him in liability for that conduct, he should not be held liable by reason of the fact that liability would be imposed upon him under the tort law of the state of the victim's domicile. Conversely, when the guest was injured in the state of his own domicile and its law permits recovery, the driver who has come into that state should not—in the absence of special circumstances—be permitted to interpose the law of his state as a defense.
>
> 3. In other situations, when the passenger and the driver are domiciled in different states, the rule is necessarily less categorical. Normally, the applicable rule of decision will be that of the state where the accident occurred but not if it can be shown that displacing that normally applicable rule will advance the relevant substantive law purposes without impairing the smooth working of the multistate system or producing great uncertainty for litigants.

The variant views expressed not only in *Tooker* but by Special Term and the divided Appellate Division in this litigation underscore and confirm the need for these rules. Since the passenger was domiciled in Ontario and the driver in New York, the present case is covered by the third stated principle. The law to be applied is that of the jurisdiction where the accident happened unless it appears that "displacing [that] normally applicable rule will advance the relevant substantive law purposes" of the jurisdictions involved. Certainly, ignoring Ontario's policy requiring proof of gross negligence in a case which involves an Ontario-domiciled guest at the expense of a New Yorker does not further the substantive law purposes of New York. In point of fact, application of New York law would result in the exposure of this State's domiciliaries to a greater liability than that imposed upon resident users of Ontario's highways. Conversely, the failure to apply Ontario's law would "impair"—to cull from the rule set out above—"the smooth working of the multi-state system [and] produce great uncertainty for litigants" by sanctioning forum shopping and thereby allowing a party to select a forum which could give him a larger recovery than the court of his own domicile. In short, the plaintiff has failed to show that this State's connection with the controversy was sufficient to justify displacing the rule of *lex loci delictus*.

Professor Willis Reese, the Reporter for the current *Conflict of Laws Restatement,* expressed approval of rules such as those suggested above; they are, he wrote, "the sort of rules at which the courts should aim" (Reese, *Chief Judge Fuld and Choice of Law,* 71 Colum. L. Rev. 548, 562; see, also, Reese, *Choice of Law: Rules or Approach,* 57 Cornell L. Rev. 315, 321, 323, 328). Indeed, in discussing the present case following the determination at Special Term that Ontario law should govern, he expressed the opinion that any other result would have been highly unreasonable (71 Colum. L. Rev., at p. 563):

> So far as the New York law was concerned, Judge Keating had argued in *Tooker v. Lopez* that New York's motor vehicle compulsory insurance law revealed a "commendable concern" not only for New York residents but also for non-residents injured by New Yorkers. On this basis, it could perhaps be argued that New York policy would be furthered by

application of the New York rule imposing upon the driver the duty of exercising ordinary care for the protection of his guest. But could this argument really be made with a straight face in support of an Ontario guest picked up in Ontario and who enjoyed no similar protection under Ontario Law? Was the New York rule really intended to be manna for the entire world? One can well understand the relief with which the trial judge seized upon Judge Fuld's third rule and followed it by holding the Ontario statute applicable.

In each action, the Appellate Division's order should be reversed, that of Special Term reinstated, without costs, and the questions certified answered in the negative.

BREITEL, J. (concurring).

I agree that there should be a reversal, but would place the reversal on quite narrow grounds. It is undesirable to lay down prematurely major premises based on shifting ideologies in the choice of law. True, Chief Judge FULD in his concurring opinion in the *Tooker* case took the view that there had already occurred sufficient experience to lay down some rules of law which would reduce the instability and uncertainty created by the recent departures from traditional *lex loci delictus*. This case, arising so soon after, shows that the permutations in accident cases, especially automobile accident cases, is disproof that the time has come.

Problems engendered by the new departures have not gone unnoticed and they are not confined to the courts of this State (Juenger, *Choice of Law in Interstate Torts,* 118 U. Pa. L. Rev. 202, 214–220). They arise not merely because any new departure of necessity creates problems, but much more because the departures have been accompanied by an unprecedented competition of ideologies, largely of academic origin, to explain and reconstruct a whole field of law, each purporting or aspiring to achieve a single universal principle.

Babcock v. Jackson, an eminently correctly and justly decided case, applied the then current new doctrine of grouping of contacts. Troubles arose only when the universality of a single doctrine was assumed (*Macey v. Rozbicki; Dym v. Gordon*). By the time of *Miller v. Miller* and the *Tooker* case, the new doctrine had been displaced by a still newer one, that of governmental interests developed most extensively by the late Brainerd Currie, and the court was deeply engaged in probing the psychological motivation of legislatures of other States in enacting statutes restricting recoveries in tort cases. Now, evidently, it is suggested that this State and other States may have less parochial concerns in enacting legislation restricting tort recoveries than had been believed only a short time ago. The trouble this case has given the courts below and now this court stems, it is suggested, more from a concern in sorting out ideologies than in applying narrow rules of law in the traditional common-law process.

What the *Babcock* case taught and what modern day commentators largely agree is that *lex loci delictus* is unsoundly applied if it is done indiscriminately and without exception. It is still true, however, that the *lex loci delictus* is the normal rule, as indeed Chief Judge FULD noted in the *Tooker* case, to be rejected only when it is evident that the situs of the accident is the least of the several factors or influences to which the accident may be attributed. Certain it is that States are not concerned only with their own citizens or residents. They are concerned with events that occur within their territory, and are also concerned with the "stranger within the gates."

In this case, none would have ever assumed that New York law should be applied just because one of the two defendants was a New York resident and his automobile was New York insured, except for the overbroad statements of the Currie doctrine in the *Tooker* case, stemming from one particular school of academic thinking in the field of conflicts law.

Consequently, I agree that there should be a reversal and the defenses allowed to stand. The conclusion, however, rests simply on the proposition that plaintiff has failed by her allegations to establish that the relationship to this State was sufficient to displace the normal rule that the *lex loci delictus* should be applied, the accident being associated with Ontario, from inception to tragic termination, except for adventitious facts and where the lawsuit was brought.

BERGAN, J. (dissenting).

The doctrine of *lex loci delictus,* whatever its other shortcomings may be, including a somewhat abrasive effect on inconsistent law of the forum, had at least the virtues of certainty and reckonability.

But the operation of the guest statutes of other jurisdictions worked out so differently—unjustly by New York standards—that in a series of highly debatable and debated decisions from *Babcock v. Jackson* to *Tooker v. Lopez* this court refused to follow the rule of *lex loci delictus* in special situations and applied New York law in New York litigation to motor vehicle torts occurring in other jurisdictions.

The rationale of departure from the settled rule was that New York had a greater "concern" or "interest" in the controversy or the parties; or had closer "contacts" than the jurisdiction of the situs of the accident. The direction taken and justified by the rationale of "interest" or "contact," however, necessarily started with the court's preference for the local rule and a belief in its greater justice.

There is a difference of fundamental character between justifying a departure from *lex loci delictus* because the court will not, as a matter of policy, permit a New York owner of a car licensed and insured in New York to escape a liability that would be imposed on him here; and a departure based on the fact a New York resident makes the claim for injury. The first ground of departure is justifiable as sound policy; the second is justifiable only if one is willing to treat the rights of a stranger permitted to sue in New York differently from the way a resident is treated. Neither because of "interest" nor "contact" nor any other defensible ground is it proper to say in a court of law that the rights of one man whose suit is accepted shall be adjudged differently on the merits on the basis of where he happens to live.

This crunch in the rule announced in *Babcock* was inevitable as it worked its way into the practice. And the difficulty was recognized in *Tooker.* Although *Tooker,* unlike the present case, involved a New York plaintiff and thus was similar to *Babcock* and the cases which had followed *Babcock,* the opinion of the court laid it down that the New York owner of a car insured in New York would not be permitted to escape liability through the guest statute of Michigan and that this was the main ground of decision. The court in *Tooker* said [p. 174]:

> This purpose [of a statute of another jurisdiction establishing higher standards for the recovery of guests in vehicles] can never be vindicated when the insurer is a New York carrier and the defendant is sued in the courts of this State. Under such circumstances, the jurisdiction enacting such a guest statute has absolutely no interest in the application of its law.

The decision was 4-to-3; but a majority of the Judges expressly subscribed to the opinion by Judge Keating even though Chief Judge Fuld and Judge Burke stated additional grounds of concurrence. The quoted statement of policy in the *Tooker* opinion, which was the court's statement and not the view of an individual Judge has the normal binding effect of such an opinion.

Reading these words of the opinion of the court the Bar would reasonably anticipate that the more basic and justifiable ground for refusing a New York vehicle the differential benefit of a foreign statute would be applied in future. Such a rule would offer more in the way of reckonability and predictability than the elusive grouping of "contacts" or "interests."

Hence the Appellate Division was justified in reading *Tooker* to dismiss the asserted defense in this action. What the court is deciding today is that although it will prevent a New York car owner from asserting the defense of a protective foreign statute when a New York resident in whose rights it has an "interest" sues; it has no such "interest" when it accepts the suit in New York of a nonresident. This is an inadmissible distinction.

The order should be affirmed.

JUDGES BURKE, SCILEPPI and GIBSON concur with CHIEF JUDGE FULD; JUDGE BREITEL concurs in a separate opinion in which JUDGE JASEN concurs; JUDGE BERGAN dissents and votes to affirm in an opinion.

NOTES AND QUESTIONS

(1)(a) The facts of *Tooker v. Lopez* seem to be just like those in *Dym v. Gordon,* except that the parties' connections with the state of accident were stronger—they were full-time college students, not just attending summer school. It is true that their accident did not involve a second car, but that circumstance in *Dym* can never have supported more than a make-weight argument. Does *Tooker* then signal the triumph of interest analysis, and the demise, at least in New York, of emphasis on contacts or the most significant relationship?

(b) The answer to the preceding question would seem to be yes, except that the decision was again 4–3, and given Judge Fuld's expressed restlessness, seems to bear the seeds of its own destruction.

(c) Several of the opinions seem concerned about Ms. Silk, the third young woman in the car, who was domiciled in Michigan. Should she be able to recover in an action in New York? Recall Case 4 in the *Adams v. Knickerbocker* series, in which both Adams, the citizen of New York, and Ball, the citizen of Massachusetts, were killed, and Judges Currie and Cavers parted company as to Mr. Ball. Is Susan Silk's case (which is not, of course, before the court) just like Neumeier?

(d) Judge Breitel says (at p. 180) that "the law to be applied should not itself be the paramount influence in weighing the circumstances of a case in which a choice of law must be made." He then goes on to say, as Cavers might, that the substance of the law in question is relevant, and he seems to pull back from the suggestion that he is choosing among jurisdictions rather than rules. Judge Breitel in *Tooker* seems to be embracing *Restatement* (*Second*), though perhaps with even greater emphasis on territoriality than emerges from § 145.[a] What do you make of his discussion of adventitiousness?[b]

(2)(a) Judge Fuld's rules, proposed in *Tooker* and accepted by the court (again by a bare majority) in *Neumeier,* are stated in terms of guest-passenger and host-driver only. Are they

---

[a] See p. 126, *supra*.

[b] Adventitious [from Latin *advenire* meaning "to come to"}: Coming from without; foreign; extraneous; extrinsic; accidentally or casually present. (The New Century Dictionary).

adaptable to wrongful death limits, vicarious liability, comparative negligence, and other conflicts with respect to torts—true and false?

(b) Are they principles of preference, in the sense in which Cavers uses the term?

(c) Assuming the *Neumeier* rules are applicable to the other issues of tort law we have seen in this chapter, consider which of the cases in this chapter would come out differently if the rules were to be applied.[c]

(d) What if, as in *Kilberg, Pearson,* and many other tort actions, the defendant is a corporation? Does it make sense to look to the defendant's domicile in such a case?

(e) Are there actually three rules? Or is it fair to say that there is only one *Neumeier* rule? "When plaintiff and defendant have a common domicile, the law of that state will be applied; otherwise the law of the place of accident governs."

(3)(a) Apart from the rules, which may be regarded as an elaborate dictum, Judge Fuld makes some important observations on governmental interests. Is he right in denying, in the last full paragraph of his opinion in *Neumeier,* that New York has any interest in compensating the family of a resident of Ontario killed as a result of the negligence of a New York driver?

(b) Would he (should he?) say the same thing if the accident happened in Ontario, as in the actual case, but the passenger was domiciled in, say, Pennsylvania? Or in Ohio (which had a guest statute)?

(c) Judge Bergan not only accuses Judge Fuld of discrimination between two parties properly before the court. He also suggests that the *Neumeier* rules sacrifice justice without promoting predictability. He is right, isn't he, if the answer to the preceding question is unclear.

(d) A word may be in order in connection with *Tooker* and *Neumeier* about the concept of domicile, so readily accepted as a "contact," or support for "state interest," or as the basis for distinction under Judge Fuld's rules. Remember that determining domicile may itself not be so easy. For instance, for some purposes (including tuition at the state university), Miss Tooker and Miss Lopez, though not Miss Lopez's father, might be considered to have been domiciled in Michigan. Could the role of domicile be modified so that borderline domicile has less force in choice of law than unequivocal domicile?

(4) After the extraordinary run of choice-of-law in tort cases in the New York Court of Appeals in the period 1961–72, that court essentially withdrew from the field.[d] However, in a series of cases arising from diversity jurisdiction, federal courts in New York were required to interpret the law prevailing in New York.

---

[c] The author's tentative answers are as follows:

Same Outcome	Different Outcome	Not Clear
Babcock	*Dym* (Plaintiff wins)	*Miller* (depends on whether domicile is fixed at time of accident or suit)
Macey	Kell (Defendant wins)	
Farber		
Tooker		

[d] Two minor decisions were rendered by the court in the 1970's. *Towley v. King Arthur Rings,* 40 N.Y.2d 129, 351 N.E.2d 728, 386 N.Y.S.2d 80 (1976) (*Neumeier* rules applied to bar recovery by an Iowa guest from a New York host for an accident in Colorado); *Cousins v. Instrument Flyers, Inc.,* 44 N.Y.2d 698, 376 N.E.2d 914, 405 N.Y.S.2d 441 (1978) (Airplane accident in Pennsylvania, plaintiff's counsel failed to invoke Pennsylvania's comparative negligence rule and thus New York law applied, but general rule in tort cases remains *lex loci delicti.*)

(a) In *Chila v. Owens,*[e] a domiciliary of New Jersey attending college in Ohio was injured in an accident in Ohio while she was a passenger in a car driven by a student at the same college who was a domiciliary of New York. The car was owned by another New York domiciliary and was registered and insured in New York. Ohio, but not New Jersey or New York, had a guest statute. Judge Weinfeld, shortly after *Neumeier v. Kuehner,* applied that case to find for plaintiff, holding that plaintiff from New Jersey and defendant from New York came under the first of Judge Fuld's rules. Do you agree?

(b) In *Rosenthal v. Warren*[f] the widow of a New York resident brought suit in New York against a Massachusetts surgeon and a Boston hospital for the death of her husband arising out of an operation performed at the hospital. Defendants pleaded the Massachusetts limitation on damages for wrongful death, which by then had reached $50,000. The Court of Appeals for the Second Circuit rejected the defense (2–1). "In no way," Judge Oakes wrote for the majority, "did the [New York Court of Appeals] retreat [in *Neumeier*] from the position it had staked out in *Kilberg* and *Miller,* refusing to apply other states' wrongful death limitations in the case of a *New York* domiciliary."[g] So much for the second *Neumeier* rule, when a New York plaintiff was involved. Judge Lumbard, dissenting, thought the court's holding "flies in the face of the interest-analysis approach to conflict of laws issues . . . embraced by the New York Court of Appeals in *Babcock v. Jackson.*"[h]

(c) In *O'Connor v. Lee-Hy Paving Corp.,*[i] a New York resident employed by a consultant on shopping centers was killed on a construction site in Virginia by a motor-grader operated by the defendant grading and paving company. The widow brought suit in New York, by attachment of an insurance policy maintained by the paving company.[j] Under Virginia law, apparently, the sole remedy lay in Workmen's Compensation against the actual employer, and the action for wrongful death against the third party would be precluded.[k] The Court of Appeals for the Second Circuit, however, affirming the lower court, applied New York law to uphold the action:

> Although we do not pretend to full understanding of *Babcock v. Jackson,* the many decisions of the [New York] Court of Appeals in its wake and might think that, in the light of fifteen years of experience under *Babcock,* the departure from the certainty of the *lex loci delictus* rule was not such a famous victory as it first appeared to be, . . . we see no indication that the highest court of New York has wavered in its determination to afford New York tort plaintiffs the benefit of New York law more favorable than the law of the *lex loci delictus* whenever there is a fair basis for doing so.
>
> . . . .
>
> Here the basis for applying the more favorable New York law . . . is at least as great as in the cases cited . . . . Appellants have failed to furnish us with persuasive reasons to believe that, if confronted with the problem here presented, the New York Court of Appeals

---

[e] 348 F. Supp. 1207 (S.D.N.Y. 1972).

[f] 475 F.2d 438 (2d Cir. 1973).

[g] 475 F.2d at 442.

[h] 475 F.2d at 447–9.

[i] 579 F.2d 194 (2d Cir. 1978), *cert. denied* 439 U.S. 1034 (1978).

[j] The jurisdictional aspect of this case and of *Rosenthal v. Warren, supra* is discussed in Chapter 7, p. 606, *infra.*

[k] For a brief description of workers' compensation law, see p. 216, *infra.*

would turn away from the position it had consistently followed since *Kilberg* and subject a New York resident, employed in New York, to Virginia law which prevents him or his estate from suing for negligence a non-employer alleged to have negligently injured or killed him at the worksite.[l]

(d) The federal court was, at least theoretically, not making a choice-of-law decision but judging how the state's highest court would decide on the basis of the precedents reproduced in this chapter.[m] Do you think the federal court reads the state precedents correctly?

(e) If the answer to the preceding cases is "yes," should the rule be reformulated as follows

> When the plaintiff in an out-of-state accident is domiciled in New York and there is reasonable basis for exercising jurisdiction over the defendant,[n] the law of New York will be applied.

---

§ 3.06 Traveling Around the Country: Still More on Guest Statutes

While no state in the United States had as intensive an experience with guest statutes and similar impediments to recovery for negligent acts causing injury as New York did, state after state was faced with the basic problem, both in the variations seen in New York, and in variations such as those suggested by the second of the *Neumeier* rules, where the parties were domiciled in different states but the accident happened in the state of the driver's domicile.[a] This section presents excerpts from three well-known cases, followed by a Minnesota case reproduced at length because it introduces another approach, not yet discussed in this chapter.

1. *Cipolla v. Shaposka,* 439 Pa. 563, 267 A.2d 854 (1970). Two friends, one domiciled in Pennsylvania, the other in Delaware, were driving home from school in Delaware in the Delaware resident's car, when an accident occurred causing injury to plaintiff, the resident of Pennsylvania. Delaware had a guest statute, Pennsylvania did not, and suit was brought in Pennsylvania. That state, shortly after *Kilberg* and *Babcock,* had abandoned the lex loci theory in favor of an approach evaluating which state has the greater interest in the application of its law.[b]

> As it is Pennsylvania's policy that its guests should be permitted to recover for injuries caused by their hosts' negligence and as appellants are Pennsylvania residents, Pennsylvania is a concerned jurisdiction and has a contact relevant to the issue before us. This is the only relevant contact with Pennsylvania, however. As it is Delaware's policy that its hosts should not be required to compensate their guests for their (the hosts') negligence and as [defendant] is a Delaware resident, Delaware is a concerned jurisdiction and has a contact relevant to the issue before us. The fact that the automobile involved in the accident is registered and housed in Delaware gives that state another contact for it appears that

---

[l] 579 F.2d at 205–206. The court added a footnote expressing its belief that the New York Court of Appeals would regard Virginia's restriction on the right to sue third parties "as being quite as unreasonable" as a guest statute or a wrongful damage ceiling.

[m] For more on this issue, discussed briefly in *Pearson v. Northeast Airlines,* p. 135, *supra,* see Chapter 6, § 6.02, *infra.*

[n] But see Note j, *supra.*

[a] Of course, if *Miller v. Miller* is seen without attention to the post-accident change of domicile, it is a *Neumeier* -2 case.

[b] *Griffith v. United Air Lines, Inc.,* 416 Pa. 1, 203 A.2d 796 (1964).

§ 3.06   CHOICE OF LAW □ 191

A Tentative Scorecard on the N.Y. Court of Appeals
Choice of Law in Interstate Transportation Accidents - 1961-72

	P's Domicile	D's Domicile	Relationship Began	Place of Accident	True/False Conflict	Outcome P or D	Gov. Law	Theory of Decision
Kilberg								
Babcock								
Kell								
Dym								
Macey								
Farber								
Miller								
Tooker								
Neumeier								

insurance rates will depend on the state in which the automobile is housed rather than the domicile of the owner or driver. Morris, *Enterprise Liability and the Actuarial Process—The Insignificance of Foresight*, 70 Yale L.J. 554, 574 (1961). Thus, it appears that Delaware's contacts are qualitatively greater than Pennsylvania's and that it has the greater interest in having its law applied to the issue before us.[2]

Also, it seems only fair to permit a defendant to rely on his home state law when he is acting within that state.[3] . . . Inhabitants of a state should not be put in jeopardy of liability exceeding that created by their state's laws just because a visitor from a state offering higher protection decides to visit there. This is, of course, a highly territorial approach, but "departures from the territorial view of torts ought not to be lightly undertaken." *Gordon v. Parker,* 83 F. Supp. 40, 42 (D.Mass.1949). "To withdraw . . . actions and affairs from the reach of domestic law because the persons (or at least one of the persons) participating in them are not domestic to the state causes a wrench away from customary attitudes towards law that may lead the disadvantaged party to 'regard the distinction as involving a personal discrimination against him rather than as a step toward comity between states.'" Cavers, *supra* at 135. The very use of the term true conflict implies that there is no one correct answer, but as a general approach a territorial view seems preferable to a personal view.

These approaches to the solution of this true conflict lead to the conclusion that Delaware has an interest both qualitatively and quantitatively greater than Pennsylvania's.

Thus, in *Cipolla,* the Pennsylvania Supreme Court decided what it regarded as a true conflict case, contrary to the law of the forum and contrary to the interests of its domiciliary. The dissenting judge said:

In my view, each State has but one relevant contact with respect to host-guest liability—the domicile of the party who will benefit from their respective State's policy.

After examining the views of the authorities around the country, judicial and academic, the construction that states place on their own guest statutes, and the construction which Delaware itself has adopted, I am led to the conclusion that allowing recovery by the guest for his host's negligence represents the better rule of law in the circumstances of the instant case. It must be remembered, however, that it is only because I believe that Delaware and Pennsylvania, on the basis of relevant contacts, are equally concerned that I feel free to choose either jurisdiction's law. I have in the end concluded that Pennsylvania's rule is the better rule of law, not out of "State chauvinism," but because I am firmly convinced that it represents "emerging" policy and the "sounder view of the law."

2. *Foster v. Leggett,* 484 S.W.2d 827 (Ky. 1972). Again, two friends were driving together in a state with a guest statute, Ohio, when a (fatal) accident took place. The driver was domiciled in Ohio, and his passenger was domiciled in Kentucky, which had no guest statute. Suit was brought by the the passenger's administratrix in Kentucky. The Court of Appeals of Kentucky, having previously abandoned lex loci in a case where both parties were domiciled in Kentucky,[c] thought the basic rule should be to apply the law of the forum, unless there was good reason to depart from that law.

---

[2] In this analysis the fact that the accident occurred in Delaware is not a relevant contact because the Delaware statute does not set out a rule of the road.

[3] See Cavers' Principle Two, *The Choice of Law Process,* at 146.

[c] *Wessling v. Paris,* 417 S.W.2d 259 (Ky. 1967).

When the court has jurisdiction of the parties, its primary responsibility is to follow its own substantive law. The basic law is the law of the forum, which should not be displaced without valid reasons. We have not, therefore, tried to adopt a rule, or rules, for all cases of this kind which may come before us.

In the case at bar, contacts with Kentucky were numerous and significant. Decedent was a lifelong resident of Kentucky. While [defendant] was a resident of Ohio, he kept a rented room near his work in Kentucky, stayed in it on the average of two nights per week and all of his employment and most of his social relationships were in Kentucky. The fatal journey began in Kentucky and was to have been concluded in Kentucky.

So we conclude that the reasons [defendant] here advances, that the accident occurred in the State of Ohio and that [defendant] was domiciled and had a residence in that state, are not sufficient in view of the contacts the State of Kentucky had with the parties to justify the displacement of the law of this forum with the law of the State of Ohio. We are now reaffirming our position that if there are significant contacts—not necessarily the most significant contacts—with Kentucky, the Kentucky law should be applied.

One judge dissented because he favored the law of the place of injury. A second dissent was prepared to reject that doctrine, but would have applied *Restatement (Second) of Conflict of Laws*, which he interpreted as pointing to the local law of the state where the injury occurred unless with respect to a particular issue some other state has a more significant relationship.

3. *Labree v. Major,* 111 R.I. 657, 306 A.2d 808 (1973). Once more, the accident occurred in a state with a guest statute, and suit was brought in a state with no guest statute. This time, however, plaintiff passenger was domiciled in the guest statute state, Massachusetts, and defendant driver was domiciled in the forum state, Rhode Island. Thus, the law/fact pattern was the same as in *Neumeier v. Kuehner.* The outcome, however, was different:

We are required in deciding this case to weigh the interests of Massachusetts and Rhode Island in this litigation. . . . Interest analysis, however, is not merely a determination of how a state may best protect its citizens as litigants. Rather, where the laws of two states with contacts in a case point to opposite results, interest analysis requires an assessment of the policy underlying each state's law. From such an assessment, a court can determine which result will advance the policy of one state without frustrating the result of the other. . . . As applied to this case, Massachusetts has no real interest in protecting a Rhode Island driver against ungrateful guests.

Rhode Island's policy of allowing recovery by passengers for the ordinary negligence of their hosts is not limited to the protection of Rhode Island guests. The state has an interest in enforcing the standard of care of an automobile operator no matter where his guest resides. Thus, had the accident in the instant case occurred in Rhode Island, the defendant would have been liable for his negligence towards his guest. Should, then, a duty imposed by Rhode Island law upon Rhode Island drivers driving in Rhode Island be imposed upon Rhode Island drivers when they are outside the state? [Our precedents make clear that we] would provide recovery to a Rhode Island guest from a Rhode Island driver for an accident in Massachusetts as well as to a Massachusetts guest injured by a Rhode Island driver in Rhode Island. We feel that Rhode Island's interest in imposing upon its drivers a duty of ordinary care towards their passengers transcends consideration of the guest's residence and of the state in which the vehicle is operated. Therefore, a Rhode Island driver has the same duty of care towards a Massachusetts passenger whether he is driving in Rhode Island or Massachusetts.

Accordingly, the court upheld judgment for plaintiff.

The Rhode Island Supreme Court, like many courts around the country, felt obliged to comment on the New York cases, and it was particularly anxious to explain its difference with Judge Fuld:

> Before turning to the other issues of this case, we intend to explain why we reach a different conclusion on a similar fact pattern from that of the New York Court of Appeals in *Neumeier v. Kuehner*. . . .
>
> [W]e must take issue with his third rule, the rule on which the *Neumeier* decision was based.
>
> The third rule provides that when a passenger and driver are from different states, ordinarily the law of the state where the accident occurred will apply. We feel this principle represents a retreat to the doctrine of *lex loci delicti*. If the accident occurs in a state which is the domicile of neither the host nor guest, little reason exists to apply the law of that state. Therefore, one must resort to interest analysis to determine whether the law of the domicile of the plaintiff or of the defendant should apply. Moreover, Judge Fuld provides an exception to his third rule, which may in practice require a case-by-case analysis of governmental interests.
>
> We agree with Judge Fuld that, if possible, a set of guidelines is preferable to an *ad hoc* approach. See Reese, *Choice of Law: Rules or Approach,* 57 Cornell L.Rev. 315 (1972). However, his third rule neither avoids case-by-case analysis nor produces the most desired result. We prefer a rule that looks to the residence of the parties rather than to the place of the accident in resolving conflicts problems arising out of automobile accidents. Thus, where a driver is from a state which allows a passenger to recover for ordinary negligence, the plaintiff should recover, no matter what the law of his residence or the place of the accident. We adopt this rule because the only state with an interest in protecting the driver and his insurer does not do so. We are conscious that our conclusion will not be unanimously accepted. See Cavers, *Cipolla and Conflicts Justice,* 9 Duquesne L.Rev. 360, 369–70 (1971). However, certain authorities do support our conclusion, and we feel it is sound. We find nothing wrong in a state holding its citizens to a higher standard of care than that of the states to which they may travel, no matter who may be injured by their misconduct.

MILKOVICH v. SAARI

Minnesota Supreme Court
295 Minn. 155, 203 N.W.2d 408 (1973)

Todd, Justice

Plaintiff and both defendants are residents of Thunder Bay (formerly Port Arthur), Ontario, Canada. On November 8, 1968, they left Thunder Bay for Duluth, Minnesota, to shop and attend a play. The car belonged to defendant Erma Saari, who drove the first part of the trip. At the United States Customs House at Pigeon River, Minnesota, defendant Judith Rudd took over the driving, and about 40 miles south of the border the car left the road and crashed into rock formations adjacent to the road, causing the injuries to plaintiff. Plaintiff was hospitalized at Duluth for approximately 12 months and thereafter returned to her home in Thunder Bay.

Defendant Saari's automobile was garaged, registered, and insured in the Province of Ontario, Canada. Ontario has a guest statute, and if the law of Ontario is to be applied to this case, plaintiff would have to establish gross negligence in order to recover. Minnesota does not have a guest statute, and the rulings of the court would be correct if Minnesota law is to apply.

1. The field of "conflict of laws" in tort matters has undergone dramatic change in the last decade. Prior to that time, most courts were willing to accept the doctrine of "lex loci," which proved to be easy to administer since the happening of an accident in any particular forum established that the law of the place of the accident would apply. Criticism of this entrenched doctrine mounted from all sides. The issue was met head on in *Babcock v. Jackson*. There the New York Court of Appeals, in an opinion by MR. JUSTICE (now CHIEF JUSTICE) FULD, held that where plaintiff was a New York resident and commenced a trip in the State of New York with the defendant, a New York resident, and was involved in an accident in Ontario, Canada, plaintiff was entitled to have her claim decided under the law of the State of New York. The legislature of New York had rejected the guest statute, which was the law of Ontario and the law of the place of the accident. The decision was premised on the doctrine that New York had the most significant contacts with the litigants and that consequently New York law should apply. The court further held that the law of Ontario, the place of the accident, should not apply, since Ontario had no significant contact with the litigants.

Application of *Babcock* to different fact situations has been confusing.

[The court summarizes *Dym, Macey* and *Kell*.]

While New York was experiencing its difficulties in the changing field of conflict of laws, a fact situation arose in a case appealed to the Supreme Court of New Hampshire, which allowed its learned MR. CHIEF JUSTICE KENISON to enunciate a doctrine which has been followed by many courts throughout the country, including our own Minnesota court. In *Clark v. Clark,* 107 N.H. 351, 222 A.2d 205 (1966), a husband and wife had left their home in New Hampshire to proceed to another part of New Hampshire for a visit and were to return that evening. Part of their trip took them through Vermont, where the accident occurred. The plaintiff wife brought action in New Hampshire against her husband and sought an order of the court that the substantive law of New Hampshire governed the rights of the parties. New Hampshire had no guest statute and Vermont did. In a carefully reasoned opinion, MR. CHIEF JUSTICE KENISON traced the history and difficulty of the *lex loci* rule. He then proceeded to adopt five basic "choice-influencing considerations' to be applied to these cases. The basic premises for the considerations adopted by the court were first proposed by Professor Robert Leflar in his article, *Choice-Influencing Considerations in Conflicts Law,* 41 N.Y.U. L. Rev. 267, 279 [1966], and briefly stated, the tests selected by the New Hampshire court are: (a) Predictability of results; (b) maintenance of interstate and international order; (c) simplification of the judicial task; (d) advancement of the forum's governmental interests; and (e) application of the better rule of law.

The court pointed out that the first three tests caused very few problems. Predictability of results can be overlooked since basically this test relates to consensual transactions where people should know in advance what law will govern their act. Obviously, no one plans to have an accident, and, except for the remote possibility of forum shopping, this test is of little import in an automobile accident case. As to the second consideration, the court found little trouble since under this heading no more is called for than that the court apply the law of no state which does not have substantial connection with the total facts and the particular issue being litigated.

The third point, simplification of the judicial task, poses no problem since the courts are fully capable of administering the law of another forum if called upon to do so.

The court observed that in selecting the law of a particular case the last two considerations carry most weight. In the case before it, the court found adequate governmental interest in applying its state's law and concluded that the New Hampshire law was unquestionably the better law and should be applied.

2. During this same period, the law of the State of Minnesota has undergone a change. Minnesota had followed the doctrine of *lex loci* as recently as . . . 1958. . . .

On April 1, 1966, our court handed down two decisions which indicated our determination to replace *lex loci* with a more rational choice-of-law methodology: *Balts v. Balts,* 273 Minn. 419, 142 N.W.2d 66; and *Kopp v. Rechtzigel,* 273 Minn. 441, 141 N.W.2d 526. In these cases, we cited with approval *Babcock v. Jackson, supra,* and, in *Balts,* we quoted with approval language from *McSwain v. McSwain,* 420 Pa. 86, 93, 215 A.2d 677, 681 (1966):

> . . . Time found the rule [of *lex loci delicti*] increasingly criticized as a mechanical methodology, predicated on the out-moded "vested right" theory, and emphasizing certainty and predictability at the expense of other, frequently more relevant considerations.

273 Minn. 425; 142 N.W.2d 70. In *Balts,* we applied a newly adopted doctrine which allowed an action by a parent against a child for tort and applied this Minnesota rule of law to Minnesota residents who were injured in an accident in Wisconsin, whose law did not permit such a recovery.

In the *Kopp* case, despite the existence of a guest statute in South Dakota, we applied Minnesota common-law rules of negligence and allowed recovery by a Minnesota plaintiff against a Minnesota defendant who was injured in a South Dakota accident where the trip originated in Minnesota and the parties intended to return to Minnesota.

[The court summarizes several additional cases in which it applied Minnesota rather than North or South Dakota law to accidents occurring in those states—in one instance where plaintiff passenger was domiciled in Minnesota, in the other where defendant was domiciled in Minnesota.]

3. The facts of this case now complete the cycle. The choice-influencing considerations proposed by Professor Leflar and set forth by Mr. Chief Justice Kenison in *Clark v. Clark, supra,* were adopted by our court in *Schneider v. Nichols, supra,* indicating our preference for the better-law approach and our rejection of the guest statute concept of various jurisdictions. We have come to the conclusion in this case that plaintiff should be allowed to proceed with her action under our common-law rules of negligence and should not be bound by the guest statute requirements of the Province of Ontario.

4. As we indicated earlier in this opinion, the New York case of *Kell v. Henderson, supra,* is on "all fours' with the facts of this case. Professor Leflar, whose original article provided the groundwork for the opinion of Mr. Chief Justice Kenison in *Clark v. Clark, supra,* which is the foundation of the approach our court has taken in these matters, had occasion to comment on the effect of *Kell v. Henderson, supra,* in an article entitled, *Conflicts Law: More on Choice-Influencing Considerations,* 54 Calif.L.Rev. 1584. Professor Leflar set forth the fact situation of the *Kell* case. He then proceeded to analyze the decision in the light of these choice-influencing considerations. He pointed out that predictability was irrelevant since automobile accidents are seldom planned, and that, since the accident occurred in New York, that state was an appropriate jurisdiction in which to try the lawsuit. He further pointed out that neither international order or ease of judicial administration had much bearing on the case.

5. On the consideration of governmental interest, Professor Leflar found adequate support for the decision rendered by the New York court. In so doing, he rejected the concept of the practical interest of the state in the supervision and safety of its state highways since the rule in question, unlike rules of the road and definitions of negligence, does not bear upon vehicle operation as such. Instead, he pointed out that the factor to be considered is the relevant effect the New York rule has on the duty of host to guest and the danger of collusion between them to defraud the host's insurer. New York's interest in applying its own law rather than Ontario law on these issues, he found to be based primarily on its status as a justice-administering state. In that status, it is strongly concerned with seeing that persons who come into the New York courts to litigate controversies with substantial New York connections have these cases determined according to rules consistent with New York concepts of justice, or at least not inconsistent with them. That will be as true for nondomiciliary litigants as for domiciliaries. This interest will not manifest itself clearly if the out-of-state rule does not run contrary to some strong socio-legal policy of the forum, but it will become a major consideration if there is such a strong opposing local policy.

Professor Leflar then pointed out that this consideration leads to preference for what is regarded as the better rule of law, that New York has such a preference, and that it is a vigorous one. He concluded that the combination of the last two items, governmental interest and better rule of law, called for the application of New York law. His statements and reasoning apply equally to the facts of this case and lead to the conclusion that Minnesota should apply its better rule of law and should allow plaintiff to proceed with her action.

6. Strong support for the better-rule-of-law concept appears in an article by Professor Albert A. Ehrenzweig, *"False Conflicts" and the "Better Rule": Threat and Promise in Multistate Tort Law,* 53 Va.L.Rev. 847, 853 [1967], in which he wrote:

> Express recognition of the forum's right and duty to apply its own better rule as such is an ancient tradition which apparently succumbed to the 19th century's internationalist conceptualism. We need only remember the priority given by early statutists to the *statuta favorabilia* of the forum against foreign *statuta odiosa,* or Master Aldricus' choice of the custom *"potior et utilior,"* or Byzantium's *philanthropoteron.* The wide-spread disregard of foreign Sunday laws, fellow-servant rules, and married women's incapacities, as well as statutes of frauds, and limitations on wrongful death damages, may serve as modern examples.
>
> Now, we shall, of course, not "ask the judge simply to express a preference between two rules." This would, indeed, "abolish our centuries-old subject." But we should face the "fact of life" that judges, our best judges, often take advantage of the "looseness in the joints of the [choice-of-law] apparatus," or employ "manipulative techniques such as characterization and renvoi," and all-purpose tools such as the "most significant relationship," in order to substitute a better foreign rule for much "that is archiac and foolish" in their own law.

. . ..

7. We have already noted the relative unimportance of predictability of results to tort actions. Similarly, the simplification of the judicial task need not concern us to any great extent since we have no doubt our judicial system could in the appropriate case apply the guest statute rule of gross negligence as readily as our common-law rule. Interstate and international relations are maintained without harm where, as here, the forum state has a substantial connection with the facts and issues involved. This requirement is amply met by the fact that the accident occurred

in Minnesota, as well as by the fact that plaintiff was hospitalized for well over a month in the state.

The compelling factors in this case are the advancement of the forum's governmental interests and the application of the better law. While there may be more deterrent effect in our common-law rule of liability as opposed to the guest statute requirement of gross negligence, the main governmental interest involved is that of any "justice-administering state." Leflar, *Conflicts Law: More on Choice-Influencing Considerations,* 54 Calif.L.Rev. 1584, 1594. In that posture, we are concerned that our courts not be called upon to determine issues under rules which, however, accepted they may be in other states, are inconsistent with our own concept of fairness and equity. We might also note that persons injured in automobile accidents occurring within our borders can reasonably be expected to require treatment in our medical facilities, both public and private. In the instant case, plaintiff incurred medical bills in a Duluth hospital which have already been paid, but we are loath to place weight on the individual case for fear it might offer even minor incentives to "hospital shop" or to create litigation-directed pressures on the payment of debts to medical facilities. Suffice it to say that we recognize that medical costs are likely to be incurred with a consequent governmental interest that injured persons not be denied recovery on the basis of doctrines foreign to Minnesota.

In our search for the better rule, we are firmly convinced of the superiority of the common-law rule of liability to that of the Ontario guest statute. We can find little reason for the strict limitation of a host's liability to his guest beyond the fear of collusive suits and the vague disapproval of a guest "biting the hand that feeds him." Neither rationale is persuasive. We are convinced the judicial system can uncover collusive suits without such overinclusive rules, and we do not find any discomfort in the prospect of a guest suing his host for injuries suffered through the host's simple negligence.

Accordingly, we hold that Minnesota law should be applied to this lawsuit.

Affirmed.

PETERSON, Justice (dissenting).

The "center-of-gravity-of-the contacts' theory of conflict of laws has been adopted in this state, and we have applied it in situations where an automobile trip started and was intended to terminate in this state, where the host-guest relationship was formed in this state, or where the place of registration or garaging of the automobile was in this state. Until today, however, we have not considered the mere happening of an automobile accident in this state a sufficient contact with the forum to establish the center of gravity here. In my view, the center of gravity is in Ontario, not Minnesota.

The "choice-influencing factor" in the majority opinion is simply that Minnesota law is "better law" because, unlike Ontario law, this state has no guest statute. Notwithstanding our undoubted preference for this forum's standard of liability, I am not persuaded that decision should turn on that factor alone. We may assume that these Canadian citizens have concurred in the rule of law of their own government as just, so the law of this American forum is not for them the "better" standard of justice. The litigation, indeed, was first initiated by plaintiff in the courts of Ontario and was later commenced in Minnesota as an act of forum shopping.

Our own cases, of course, do not compel such a decision. Two cases from other jurisdictions that are "on all fours' are not persuasive. The New York case of *Kell v. Henderson,* is not the decision of that state's highest court and, in addition, is at odds with the later case of *Arbuthnot v. Allbright,* 35 A.D.2d 315, 316 N.Y.S.2d 391 (1970). The Wisconsin case of *Conklin v. Horner,* 38 Wis.2d 468, 157 N.W.2d 579 (1968), is a final expression of its highest court, based upon a well-written majority opinion of Mr. Justice Heffernan. I nevertheless am more persuaded by the dissenting opinion of two justices. Mr. Chief Justice Hallows, in dissent, appropriately observed that the so-called "methodology of analysis" is really little more than a mechanical application of the law of the forum. As he wrote (38 Wis.2d 491, 157 N.W.2d 590): "If we are going to be consistent only in applying the law of the forum, then we are merely giving lip service to the new 'significant contacts' rule."

NOTES AND QUESTIONS

(1) It is sometimes believed that interest analysis inevitably results in choice of the law of the forum, at least if that choice favors a party domiciled in the forum state. Some of the New York cases would support that belief. Both the Pennsylvania and the Rhode Island cases here excerpted contradict that belief. In *Cipolla,* the Pennsylvania Supreme Court concludes that Delaware has the greater interest, leading to no recovery for the plaintiff domiciled in Pennsylvania. Very likely, if the case had been litigated in Delaware, the same result would have been reached. In *Labree,* the Rhode Island Supreme Court applies Rhode Island law, though it leads to liability on the part of the Rhode Island defendant in favor of a Massachusetts plaintiff. If that case had been heard in Massachusetts, plaintiff might well have lost.

(a) Do these cases, then, present a more attractive form of interest analysis than, say, the version espoused by Judge Keating in New York?

(b) Are they more attractive than Judge Fuld's version of interest analysis in *Tooker* and *Neumeier?* Or is that not interest analysis at all?

(2)(a) What interest of Delaware is served in *Cipolla?*

(b) Note that the Pennsylvania Supreme Court, in Footnote 2, p. 192, *supra,* is careful to state that nothing turns on the fact that the accident occurred in Delaware. What matters, it seems, are the domicile of the driver, and the place of registration and garage of the car. Is that believable? If all the facts had been the same except that the accident had taken place a few miles down the road in Pennsylvania, do you suppose the Pennsylvania court would still apply Delaware law?

(c) Note that *Cipolla* presents the first of the two situations set out in Rule 2 of the *Neumeier* rules, and comes out as Judge Fuld would come out. The variation set out in the preceding question—same parties, accident in Pennsylvania—would come out for Plaintiff under Judge Fuld's rules, but perhaps not with the court that decided *Cipolla.*

(d) How would you expect Cavers to react to *Cipolla?* Is it analogous to any of the cases in *Adams v. Knickerbocker?*

(e) In fact, in a symposium on the case, Professor Cavers celebrated the method and result adopted by the Pennsylvania Supreme Court:

> . . . [T]he majority opinion in *Cipolla v. Shaposka* is noteworthy in its refusal to transmute interest analysis into insurer's liability or to identify the better choice of law with the better rule of law, even though the better rule it rejected was its own. It had also recognized that

the mere presence in a state of a visitor from another state should not be the occasion for application of the latter state's law to discriminate in the visitor's favor—or, I think one may infer, against him. In so doing, it has displayed a proper concern for territoriality in the choice-of-law process. It has advanced the search for "conflicts justice."[d]

Is it wrong to identify the better rule of law with the better choice of law? More of this in connection with *Milkovich,* Question 5, *infra.*

(3)(a) In one of his early essays, Professor Currie wrote:

1. Normally, even in cases involving foreign elements, the court should be expected, as a matter of course, to apply the rule of decision found in the law of the forum.

2. When it is suggested that the law of a foreign state should furnish the rule of decision, the court should, first of all, determine the governmental policy expressed in the law of the forum. It should then inquire whether the relation of the forum to the case is such as to provide a legitimate basis for the assertion of an interest in the application of that policy. . . .

. . . .

5. If the court finds that the forum has an interest in the application of its policy, it should apply the law of the forum, even though the foreign state also has an interest in the application of its contrary policy. . . .[e]

Is this what the Kentucky Court of Appeals is doing in *Foster v. Leggett*? Is it persuasive?

(b) The Kentucky court, like Professor Currie, was not prepared to write off all choice of law rules, and was prepared to apply another State's law if there were valid reasons. The place of the accident plus the domicile of the defendant are not enough, however, to divert the court from applying the law of the forum. What combination of circumstances might have been enough? Suppose, for example, that the trip had not originated in Kentucky, or that plaintiff's decedent had not been domiciled in Kentucky. Would the court come out the other way? What if both these differences from the actual case were true?

(c) The Kentucky court says it is not counting contacts. One might point to the fact that the trip originated and was supposed to end in Kentucky, to the fact that defendant kept a room in Kentucky and to the fact that he worked in Kentucky and had most of his social relationships there as outweighing the contacts with Ohio. But the court says that is not the point. As long as there are *some* significant contacts—"not necessarily the most significant contacts"—with Kentucky, it will apply the law of the forum.

(d) As paragraph (b) above indicates, it is hard to imagine a case heard in Kentucky with no contacts in that state, but not impossible. Suppose a plaintiff from Indiana brought suit in Kentucky against a defendant from Ohio arising from an auto accident in Ohio; the fateful trip did not originate in Kentucky, but defendant worked in Kentucky and, as in the actual case, he was served at his place of employment. Currie wrote:

---

[d] Cavers, *Cipolla and Conflicts Justice,* 9 Duquesne L. Rev. 360; reprinted in Cavers, *The Choice of Law, Selected Essays,* 191–92 (1985).

[e] B. Currie, *Notes on Methods and Objectives in the Conflict of Laws,* 1959 Duke L. J. 171, 178, reprinted in B. Currie, *Selected Essays on the Conflict of Laws,* 177, 183–84 (1963). For a somewhat modified version of this excerpt, see Rosenberg, Hay and Weintraub, *Cases and Materials on Conflict of Laws,* 513 (10th ed. 1996).

§ 3.06   CHOICE OF LAW □ 201

4. If the court finds that the forum state has no interest in the application of its policy, but that the foreign state has, it should apply the foreign law.[f]

Do you think the Kentucky court would apply that rule to the case put?

(e) In the actual case, the Kentucky Court of Appeals applies Kentucky law to recovery on behalf of a Kentucky plaintiff. Consider how the other cases in this section would have come out had the Kentucky judges been sitting on the Supreme Court of Pennsylvania, Rhode Island and Minnesota. *Cipolla*, prettly clearly, would have come out the other way, *Milkovich* the same way; what about *Labree* ? Would the Kentucky judges have decided *Neumeier* in favor of plaintiff?

(4)(a) *Labree v. Major,* as noted earlier, is like *Neumeier* in that the injured party brings suit in defendant's domicile, which would have granted recovery in a case involving only local elements. Is the Rhode Island court's definition of state interest persuasive—not altruism, as suggested in *Adams v. Knickerbocker,*[g] but deterrence and punishment of its drivers when they are careless, whenever injury results?

(b) The Rhode Island Supreme Court agrees with Judge Fuld's longing for rules, but does not like the rules (or at least the third rule) proposed by Fuld. Do you favor the rule proposed by the Rhode Island court? Would it follow that if the driver were from a state that did not allow a passenger to recover for ordinary negligence—as in *Cipolla, Foster,* and *Milkovich*—there would be no recovery? Or do you suppose the Rhode Island court would propose another rule to cover those cases? Try drafting such a rule, to accompany the one put forth in *Labree*.

(5)(a) In *Milkovich v. Saari,* the Minnesota Supreme Court expresses impatience with *Babcock* and all that followed. It says let us be candid and select among laws the one that seems to us most just. It finds support in an article by Professor Robert Leflar, and in a decision by the Supreme Court of New Hampshire. But Leflar proposes the better law as one of five equal considerations; the Minnesota court is quick to dismiss the first three considerations, and it blends governmental interests with better law. Does the "better law" approach, as used by the Supreme Court of Minnesota, go beyond the domain of judges? Can it be fitted into democratic theory?

(b) Professor Leflar wrote that attention to "better law" tends to serve the ends of justice by putting the litigation in a more impersonal, less subjective framework, rather than by choosing between one or the other party.[h] Is that convincing? Could it serve the ends of law reform, so that, say, the Delaware court in *Cipolla* or the Ontario court in *Babcock* or *Milkovich,* could decide in favor of plaintiff and against the law of its own state?[i]

(c) Leflar also says, Let's call a spade a spade, instead of playing around with escape devices (see Chapter 2) or inventing theories tailored to the occasion. That may be good advice for a judge. Advocates, on the other hand, rarely feel comfortable making such an argument directly,

---

[f] See Note e, *supra.*

[g] See Judge Currie's opinion in *Case 2,* p. 112, *supra.*

[h] Leflar, *Choice Influencing Considerations in Conflicts Law,* 41 N.Y.U. L. Rev. 267 at 296–97 (1966). See also Professor Leflar's treatise, *American Conflicts Law,* 212 (3d ed. 1977).

[i] In fact, Ontario reconsidered its guest statute twice in the period of the conflict of laws revolution in neighboring states from New York to Minnesota. In 1966, the statute was changed from an absolute ban on recovery by guests to a provision making the host-driver liable only for gross negligence. Stats. Ont. 1966, c. 64, s. 20(2). The limitation on suits by passengers against owners or drivers was finally abolished in Ontario in 1977, c. 55, s. 26, repealing s. 132(3) of the Highway Traffic Act, R.S.O. 1970 c. 202.

though of course they always try to put their client's cause in its most sympathetic light. For advocates, a theory that purports to be neutral, yet favors their client in the particular case, is usually more attractive.

(d) In a society accustomed on the one hand to compensation for victims of accidents and on the other hand to almost universal use of insurance (except, as Cavers points out, for bicyclists and horseback riders[j]), it is fairly easy to demonstrate that good law (or rather "better law") leads to recovery without barriers such as charitable or spousal immunity, guest statutes, wrongful death limits, and the like. Making workers' compensation a truly exclusive remedy for industrial accidents is perhaps a bit harder, though as we saw, Judge Friendly in *Lee-Hy Paving* did not think the New York Court of Appeals would think so.[k] But as the pendulum swings back from ever rising damage awards to concern for the cost of insurance, and as legislatures address, for instance, the so-called medical malpractice crisis by imposing conditions on recovery for injuries alleged to have been caused by doctors and hospitals, the search for the better law may not always be so easy. Suppose, for example, that instead of the $50,000 wrongful death limit invoked in *Rosenthal v. Warren*,[l] Massachusetts adopted a limit on recovery in actions for medical malpractice of $250,000, plus a requirement of investigation into the medical procedure by a panel of physicians prior to institution of suit.[m] Rosenthal's widow brings an action for $1 million in New York; she says the peer review requirement is really a local evidence rule not transferable to New York, and in any event is "bad law" pushed through the legislature by the medical lobby in Massachusetts. In New York, in contrast, attempts to restrain medical malpractice suits have failed (let us suppose), because the lawyers' lobby proved to be more powerful than the doctors' lobby. Is it clear, then, that New York's law would be the "better law"?[n]

(6)(a) *Paul v. National Life*, 352 S.E.2d 550, 63 A.L.R.4th 155 (W.Va. 1986), arose out of a one-car accident in Indiana in which the driver as well as the passenger, both domiciled in West Virginia, were killed. The administrator of the passenger's estate brought a wrongful death action against the driver's estate, and the defendant pleaded the Indiana guest statute. The lower court granted summary judgment for the defendant, on the basis that West Virginia applies *lex loci delicti* in tort cases.

 The Supreme Court of West Virginia rejected the approaches of *Babcock* and the Restatement (Second), saying it preferred a rule, not a method of analysis. 352 S.E.2d at 554. The court also rejected the "newfangled five-factor costume" proposed by Professor Leflar. Id. at 555.

---

[j] D. Cavers, *The Choice of Law: Selected Essays*, 1938–83, at 197.

[k] See Question (4)(c), p. 189, *supra*.

[l] See question (4)(b), p. 189, *supra*.

[m] In fact Massachusetts adopted a statute in 1975 requiring every action for medical malpractice to be submitted to a panel consisting of a physician, a Justice of the Superior Court, and an attorney selected from a list prepared by the state medical society and bar association. Mass. Gen. L. Ch. 631 § 60B. In 1986, Massachusetts adopted another statute, imposing a ceiling of $500,000 for pain and suffering and other "general damages" in medical malpractice actions, except for severe injuries as defined. Id. §60H. For the wide variety of recent legislative efforts to address the medical malpractice problem, see e.g., 2 D. Louisell & H. Williams, *Medical Malpractice*, ¶¶ 18.02, 20.07 and sources there cited, (1990 and Supp.).

[n] The example is drawn from Hancock, *Policy Controlled State Interest Analysis in Choice of Law, Measure of Damages, Torts Cases,* 26 Int'l & Comp. Q. 799, 810 (1977), reprinted in M. Hancock, *Studies in Modern Choice-of-Law: Torts, Insurance, Land Titles,* 117 at 128, (1984). However, Hancock, who is in many respects an advocate of the better law approach, does not answer the question posed in the text. For a discussion of Hancock's views, see the present author's review of the book cited, 38 Stanford L. Rev. 1411 (1986).

[W]e remain convinced [Justice Neely wrote for the court] that the traditional rule, for all of its faults, remains superior to any of its modern competitors. Moreover, if we are going to manipulate conflicts doctrine in order to achieve substantive results, we might as well manipulate something we understand. . . .We therefore reaffirm our adherence to the doctrine of lex loci delicti today.

However, . . . [t]oday we declare that automobile guest passenger statutes violate the strong public policy of this State in favor of compensating persons injured by the negligence of others. Accordingly, we will no longer enforce the automobile guest statutes of foreign jurisdictions in our courts.

Id. at 556.

(b) Putting aside the anti-intellectual tone of the opinion, of which only a hint appears in this excerpt, is Justice Neely more candid than the other cases we have seen? Would Chief Judge Desmond be pleased?º

(7)(a) The American "conflicts revolution" provoked enormous interest among conflicts scholars in Europe.ᵖ On the one hand, the European scholars seemed delighted that much of the debate was going on among the professors, almost as in Europe; on the other hand, most were dismayed at the lack of order, organization, and predictability that seemed to have overcome choice of law in the United States. A good many authors frankly worried that the "American disease" might spread across the ocean and undermine a system based on rules.

These rules themselves were not as firm as might be thought.ᑫ Recent efforts to codify choice of law in Western Europe and in the European Community show some of the same tendencies to be flexible and to permit justice to prevail in individual cases as is apparent, for instance, in the *Restatement (Second) of Conflict of Laws* in the United States.ʳ Moreover, the fact that nearly all choice of law questions in Europe are international, while most such questions in the United States involve choice among the laws of member states of the same nation, suggests that the considerations applicable to American and European choice of law problems are not precisely parallel. Still, it is worth listening to a thoughtful criticism from abroad.

º Justice Neely, in a footnote, adds that "we do not intend [the rule] as an invitation to flagrant forum shopping." He would not, for instance, permit a resident of a guest statute state to sue another resident of a guest statute state over an accident occurring in a guest statute jurisdiction. Some connection of West Virginia with the controversy would be required before the new rule would be applied.

ᵖ For a selected bibliography up to 1972, see Cavers, *Review of A. Shapira, The Interest Approach to Choice of Law,* 85 Harv. L. Rev. 1499 (1972). See also Vitta, note t, *infra,* at Notes 6–8. From 1964 on, nearly every year a course at the Hague Academy on International Law was devoted either to exposition or to criticism of the American approach to choice-of-law, usually focusing on torts and particularly on *Babcock* and the succeeding cases reproduced in this chapter, plus the accompanying doctrinal debates.

ᑫ See, e.g., the case of José and Hilda, in which the Constitutional Court of the Federal Republic of Germany struck down an important section of the Introductory Law (on choice of law) of the German Civil Code of 1900, in favor of the constitutionally guaranteed right to marry. The case is discussed in Juenger, *The German Constitutional Court and Conflict of Laws,* 20 Am. J. Comp. L, 290 (1972).

ʳ For summaries of some of the legislative revisions of conflict of laws rules, see 28 Am. J. Comp. L. 197–285 (1980); see also Lowenfeld, *Renvoi Among the Law Professors: An American's View of the European View of American Conflict of Laws,* 30 Am. J. Comp. L. 99 (1982), focusing primarily on the proposed EEC Convention on the Law Applicable to Contractual Obligations, reproduced in the Documents Supplement at pp. 44–54.

(b) Professor Edoardo Vitta of the University of Florence, in opening a symposium in Bologna on the American Conflicts Revolution in 1981,[s] wrote:

> Europeans tend to criticize all the new theories for granting judges a measure of freedom that goes beyond the limits of appropriate judicial discretion. Accordingly prospective litigants are left in doubt as to how their case is going to be decided, which impairs the fundamental principle of certainty of the law.
>
> . . . [M]odern American conflict theories, advocating completely new approaches and sudden changes, deviate from the traditional manner of creating new law. It therefore appears that behind the widespread criticism of the new theories' break with the principle of legal certainty, there looms an even larger issue. That is to say, the new approaches may have abandoned generally accepted notions about the value of legal rules and judicial law-making.[t]

How should this point be answered on behalf of participants, or domestic observers, of this "American Revolution"?

(c) Professor Vitta contended that none of the American theories—"the most significant relationship," "governmental interest analysis," and especially "better law" can escape the criticism reflected in the preceding excerpt. All, he writes, require a high degree of subjectivity on the part of the judge, and also tend to rely in practice on the law of the forum, which in turn puts too much importance on the law of judicial jurisdiction.[u] Is this a valid criticism?

(d) Consider whether the *Schultz* case in the next section, and *Cooney* in the last section of this chapter, both of which came down after the Bologna symposium, should make the outsiders temper their criticism, or intensify it.

---

§ 3.07 Do the Neumeier Rules Fit All Sizes? Another Look at the New York Court of Appeals

After the intense preoccupation with choice of law case in the decade ending with *Neumeier*—nine tort cases in just over ten years, plus four succession cases[a] and several cases involving contract or insurance issues,[b] a pause set in. No important choice of law case came before New York's highest court for thirteen years.[c] When one such case did come before the Court, it involved neither a guest statute nor a wrongful death ceiling but the issue with which the five "judges' had wrestled in the *Adams v. Knickerbocker* series, §3.01 *supra*—immunity for charitable organizations.

---

[s] The year and place of the symposium were designed to commemorate what might be regarded as the birth of conflict of laws, when the "Four Doctors" lectured in Bologna in 1281. For a brief historical summary by one of the participants in the symposium, see Juenger, *American and European Conflicts Law,* 30 Am. J. Comp. L. 117 (1982).

[t] Vitta, *The Impact in Europe of the American Conflicts Revolution,* 30 Am. J. Comp. L. 1 at 3 (1982).

[u] *Id.* at 4–6.

[a] See Chapter 4, §4.03, *infra*.

[b] See *Golden* and *Oltarsh* summarized in *Tooker v. Lopez* at p. 177 *supra*, plus *Intercontinental Planning Ltd. v. Daystrom*, p. 254 *infra*.

[c] For a searching discussion of the New York experience by a former law clerk to Judge Fuld, see Harold L. Korn, "The Choice of Law Revolution: A Critique," 83 Colum. L. Rev. 773 (1983).

SCHULTZ v. BOY SCOUTS OF AMERICA, INC.

New York Court of Appeals
65 N.Y.2d 189, 491 N.Y.S.2d 90, 480 N.E.2d 679 (1985)

SIMONS, J. Plaintiffs, Richard E. and Margaret Schultz, instituted this action to recover damages for personal injuries they and their sons, Richard and Christopher, suffered because the boys were sexually abused by defendant Edmund Coakeley and for damages sustained as a result of Christopher's wrongful death after he committed suicide. Coakeley, a brother in the Franciscan order, was the boys' school teacher and leader of their scout troop. Plaintiffs allege that the sexual abuse occurred while Coakeley was acting in those capacities and the causes of action before us on this appeal charge defendants Boy Scouts of America, Inc., and the Brothers of the Poor of St. Francis, Inc. (sued as Franciscan Brothers of the Poor, Inc.), with negligently hiring and supervising him.

Plaintiffs are domiciled in New Jersey and some of the injuries were sustained there. Thus, a choice-of-law issue is presented because New Jersey recognizes the doctrine of charitable immunity and New York does not. Defendants contend New Jersey law governs this litigation and that its courts have already determined that plaintiffs' claims are barred in a separate action against the Roman Catholic Archdiocese of Newark (*see, Schultz v. Roman Catholic Archdiocese,* 95 N.J. 530, 472 A.2d 531). Following the rationale of *Babcock v. Jackson* and similar cases, we hold that New Jersey law applies and that plaintiffs are precluded from relitigating its effect on the claims they assert.

I

In 1978 plaintiffs were residents of Emerson, New Jersey, where their two sons, Richard, age 13, and Christopher, age 11, attended Assumption School, an institution owned and operated by the Roman Catholic Archdiocese of Newark. By an agreement with the Archdiocese, defendant Brothers of the Poor of St. Francis, Inc., supplied teachers for the school. One of those assigned was Brother Edmund Coakeley, who also served as the scoutmaster of Boy Scout Troop 337, a locally chartered Boy Scout troop sponsored and approved by defendant Boy Scouts of America. Richard and Christopher attended Coakeley's class and were members of his scout troop.

In July 1978 Coakeley took Christopher Schultz to Pine Creek Reservation, a Boy Scout camp located in upstate New York near the Oneida County community of Foresport. The camp was located on land owned by Peter Grandy, who was also a resident of Emerson, New Jersey. The complaint alleges that while at the camp, Coakeley sexually abused Christopher, that he continued to do so when Christopher returned to Assumption School in New Jersey that fall and that he threatened Christopher with harm if he revealed what had occurred. The complaint also alleges that Coakeley sexually abused Richard Schultz and made similar threats to him during a scout trip to Pine Creek Reservation on Memorial Day weekend in 1978. Plaintiffs claim that as a result of Coakeley's acts both boys suffered severe psychological, emotional and mental pain and suffering and that as a result of the distress Coakeley's acts caused, Christopher Schultz committed suicide by ingesting drugs on May 29, 1979. They charge both defendants with negligence in assigning Coakeley to positions of trust where he could molest young boys and in failing to dismiss him despite actual or constructive notice that Coakeley had previously been dismissed from another Boy Scout camp for similar improper conduct.

The complaint contains four causes of action. In the first two, plaintiff Richard E. Schultz, as administrator of Christopher's estate, seeks damages for Christopher's wrongful death and for his psychological, emotional and physical injuries prior to death. In the third cause of action, plaintiff Richard E. Schultz, suing as father and natural guardian, seeks damages for similar personal injuries on behalf of his son Richard. In the fourth cause of action, plaintiffs seek damages for their own injuries, including destruction of their family life, expenditures for medical and psychological care and treatment, mental anguish and psychological injuries.

After answering, defendants moved for summary judgment, urging that plaintiffs' claims were barred by New Jersey's charitable immunity statute (N.J. Stat. Ann. § 2A:53A-7) and that plaintiffs were collaterally estopped from relitigating the application of the statute because of the prior New Jersey judgment. In opposition, plaintiffs contended that under applicable choice-of-law principles, New York should apply its law, not that of New Jersey, and, alternatively, that even if the New Jersey charitable immunity statute applies under choice-of-law rules, the New York courts should refuse to enforce it on public policy grounds. Special Term granted defendants' motions, severing plaintiffs' causes of action and dismissing the complaint against them on collateral estoppel grounds, implicitly finding New Jersey law applicable. A divided Appellate Division affirmed.

II

A

The choice-of-law question presented in the action against defendant Boy Scouts of America is whether New York should apply its law in an action involving codomiciliaries of New Jersey when tortious acts were committed in New York. This is the posture of the appeal although defendant is a Federally chartered corporation created exclusively for educational and charitable purposes pursuant to an act of Congress (see, 36 USC § 21) that originally maintained its national headquarters in New Brunswick, New Jersey, but moved to Dallas, Texas, in 1979. New Jersey is considered defendant's domicile because its national headquarters was in that State. Its change of domicile after the commission of the wrongs from New Jersey to Texas, which no longer recognizes the doctrine of charitable immunity, provides New York with no greater interest in this action than it would have without the change. Our decision recognizing a postaccident change in domicile in *Miller v. Miller* [p. 171 supra] is distinguishable because in that case the defendant's domicile was changed to New York, which was the forum and also the plaintiff's domicile.

The question presented in the action against defendant Franciscan Brothers is what law should apply when the parties' different domiciles have conflicting charitable immunity rules. The Franciscan order is incorporated in Ohio and it is a domiciliary of that State.

At the time these causes of action arose Ohio, like New Jersey, recognized charitable immunity. . . . The Ohio rule denied immunity in actions based on negligent hiring and supervision, however, whereas New Jersey does not (*see, Schultz v. Roman Catholic Archdiocese, supra*). For this reason, no doubt, defendant Franciscan Brothers does not claim Ohio law governs and the choice is between the law of New York and the law of New Jersey.

As for the locus of the tort, both parties and the dissent implicitly assume it is New York because most of Coakeley's acts were committed here. Under traditional rules, the law of the place of the wrong governs all substantive issues in the action (see, Kaufman v. American Youth Hostels, 5 N.Y.2d 1016), but when the defendant's negligent conduct occurs in one jurisdiction and the plaintiff's injuries are suffered in another, the place of the wrong is considered to be the place where the last event necessary to make the actor liable occurred. Thus, the locus in this case is determined by where the plaintiffs' injuries occurred.

The first and fourth causes of action, the wrongful death of Christopher and plaintiffs' own psychological and other injuries respectively, allege injuries inflicted in New Jersey. New York's only interests in these claims are as the forum State and as the jurisdiction where the tortious conduct underlying plaintiffs' claims against defendants, *i.e.*, the negligent assignment and failure to dismiss Coakeley, occurred. Standing alone, these interests are insufficient to warrant application of New York law, at least when the relevant issue is a loss-distribution rule, like charitable immunity, rather than one regulating conduct. The second and third causes of action seek damages for the psychological, emotional and physical injuries suffered by Christopher and Richard Schultz, injuries which occurred in both New York and New Jersey, because a fair reading of the complaint indicates that both boys suffered injuries when Coakeley molested them and also after they returned home. These two causes of action sufficiently implicate New York's interests to require a resolution of the choice-of-law problem in the case.

B

Historically, choice-of-law conflicts in tort actions have been resolved by applying the law of the place of the wrong. In *Babcock v. Jackson* we departed from traditional doctrine, however, and refused to invariably apply the rule of *lex loci delicti* to determine the availability of relief for commission of a tort. In doing so, we applied New York law to an action involving New York parties in which recovery was sought for injuries received in an automobile accident in Ontario, Canada. Ontario's guest statute barred recovery by the plaintiff passenger but we refused to apply Ontario law in the New York action, holding that "controlling effect" must be given "to the law of the jurisdiction which, because of its relationship or contact with the occurrence or the parties, has the greatest concern with the specific issue raised in the litigation." Employing this "grouping of contacts" and "interest analysis", we noted that New York was where the parties were domiciled, where the automobile involved was garaged, licensed and insured, where the guest-host relationship arose and where the trip began and was to end, whereas Ontario's only contact with the case was the "purely adventitious" occurrence of the accident there.

Key, however, was New York's interest in requiring a tort-feasor to compensate his guest for injuries caused by his negligence. That concern would have been completely thwarted if Ontario's laws were applied to the action, whereas the application of New York's law would not threaten the policy underlying Ontario's statute, its interest in preventing fraudulent claims against its defendants and their insurer.

The analysis was flexible and to the extent that it may have placed too much emphasis on contact-counting without specifying the relative significance of those contacts, the necessary refinements were added in later decisions of this court. In four of the five subsequent tort cases presenting the same *Babcock*-style fact pattern of common New York domiciliaries and a foreign locus having loss-distribution rules in conflict with those of New York we reached results consistent with *Babcock* and applied New York law (see, *Tooker v. Lopez,* [Michigan guest statute]; *Miller v. Miller,* [Maine damage limitation in wrongful death action]; *Farber v. Smolack,* [North Carolina statute on vicarious liability of automobile owner for negligence of driver]; *Macey v. Rozbicki,* [Ontario guest statute]). In the fifth case, the first decided after *Babcock,* we applied the law of the foreign locus, including its restrictive guest statute (see, *Dym v. Gordon*). Although our opinion in *Dym* attempted to distinguish *Babcock,* we subsequently concluded that our reading of the Colorado guest statute in *Dym* was "mistaken" (*see, Tooker v. Lopez*). In each of the five cases, however, the court rejected the indiscriminate grouping of contacts, which in *Babcock* had been a consideration coequal to interest analysis, because it bore no reasonable relation to the underlying policies of conflicting rules of recovery in tort actions. Interest analysis became the relevant analytical approach to choice of law in tort actions in New York. "[T]he law of the jurisdiction having the greatest interest in the litigation will be applied and . . . the [only] facts or contacts which obtain significance in defining State interests are those which relate to the purpose of the particular law in conflict." Under this formulation, the significant contacts are, almost exclusively, the parties' domiciles and the locus of the tort (it;see, *Tooker v. Lopez*; *Neumeier v. Kuehner,* [adopting the three governing rules proposed in Tooker, the first and third of which are pertinent to the facts of this appeal]).

Thus, under present rules, most of the nondomicile and nonlocus contacts relied on in *Babcock v. Jackson (supra),* such as where the guest-host relationship arose and where the journey was to begin and end, are no longer controlling in tort actions involving guest statutes.

Both *Tooker* and *Neumeier* continued to place some importance on where the automobile involved was insured, but this is not inconsistent with the present rule because usually a defendant host's automobile will be insured in the State of his domicile and also because it reflects a recognition that the insurer, rather than the individually named defendant, is often "the real party in interest." Insofar as issues of liability insurance might also be relevant in a case such as the one before us involving charitable immunity, the record provides no relevant information on the subject.

These decisions also establish that the relative interests of the domicile and locus jurisdictions in having their laws apply will depend on the particular tort issue in conflict in the case. Thus, when the conflicting rules involve the appropriate standards of conduct, rules of the road, for example, the law of the place of the tort "will usually have a predominant, if not exclusive, concern" (*Babcock v Jackson, supra,* at [p. 148]; *see,* Restatement [Second] of Conflicts of Law § 145 comment d, at 418) because the locus jurisdiction's interests in protecting the reasonable expectations of the parties who relied on it to govern their primary conduct and in the admonitory effect that applying its law will have on similar conduct in the future assume critical importance and outweigh any interests of the common-domicile jurisdiction.

Conversely, when the jurisdictions' conflicting rules relate to allocating losses that result from admittedly tortious conduct, as they do here, rules such as those limiting damages in wrongful death actions, vicarious liability rules, or immunities from suit, considerations of the State's admonitory interest and party reliance are less important. Under those circumstances, the locus jurisdiction has at best a minimal interest in determining the right of recovery or the extent of the remedy in an action by a foreign domiciliary for injuries resulting from the conduct of a codomiciliary that was tortious under the laws of both jurisdictions (*see, Tooker v Lopez,* [*supra* at p. 175]; *Miller v. Miller,* [*supra* at p. 171–72]; *Babcock v. Jackson,* [*supra* at p. 148]. Analysis then favors the jurisdiction of common domicile because of its interest in enforcing the decisions of both parties to accept both the benefits and the burdens of identifying with that jurisdiction and to submit themselves to its authority.[2]

---

[2] New York's rule holding charities liable for their tortious acts, or its rule of nonimmunity as the dissent characterizes it, is also a loss-allocating rule, just as New Jersey's charitable immunity statute is.

These considerations made the need for change in the *lex loci delicti* rule obvious in *Babcock*, but the validity of this interest analysis is more clearly demonstrated in the split domicile case of *Neumeier v Kuehner*. In *Neumeier* we applied Ontario's guest statute in an action on behalf of an Ontario decedent against a New York defendant at least in part because the Ontario statute, which contained reciprocal benefits and burdens depending on one's status as either host or guest, was "obviously addressed" to Ontario domiciliaries such as plaintiff's decedent. In *Babcock* New York had an important interest in protecting its own residents injured in a foreign State against unfair or anachronistic statutes of that State but it had no similar interest in *Neumeier* in protecting a guest domiciled in Ontario and injured there.

C

As to defendant Boy Scouts, this case is but a slight variation of our *Babcock* line of decisions and differs from them on only two grounds: (1) the issue involved is charitable immunity rather than a guest statute, and (2) it presents a fact pattern which one commentator has characterized as a "reverse" *Babcock* case because New York is the place of the tort rather than the jurisdiction of the parties' common domicile (see, Korn, *The Choice-of-Law Revolution: A Critique*, 83 Colum. L. Rev. 772, 789).

Although most of our major choice-of-law decisions after Babcock involved foreign guest statutes in actions for personal injuries, we have not so limited them, but have applied the Babcock reasoning to other tort issues as well.

Nor is there any logical basis for distinguishing guest statutes from other loss-distributing rules because they all share the characteristic of being postevent remedial rules designed to allocate the burden of losses resulting from tortious conduct in which the jurisdiction of the parties' common domicile has a paramount interest. There is even less reason for distinguishing *Babcock* here where the conflicting rules involve the defense of charitable immunity. Both plaintiffs and defendant Boy Scouts in this case have chosen to identify themselves in the most concrete form possible, domicile, with a jurisdiction that has weighed the interests of charitable tort-feasors and their victims and decided to retain the defense of charitable immunity. Significantly, the New Jersey statute excepts from its protection actions by nonbeneficiaries of the charity who suffer injuries as a result of the negligence of its employees or agents (see, NJ Stat. Ann. § 2A:53A-7). Plaintiffs and their sons, however, were beneficiaries of the Boy Scouts' charitable activities in New Jersey and should be bound by the benefits and burdens of that choice. Additionally, the State of New Jersey is intimately interested in seeing that the parties' associational interests are respected and its own loss-distributing rules are enforced so that the underlying policy, which is undoubtedly to encourage the growth of charitable work within its borders, is effectuated.

Thus, if this were a straight Babcock fact pattern, rather than the reverse, we would have no reason to depart from the first *Neumeier* rule and would apply the law of the parties' common domicile. Because this case presents the first case for our review in which New York is the forum-locus rather than the parties' common domicile, however, we consider the reasons most often advanced for applying the law of the forum-locus and those supporting application of the law of the common domicile.

The three reasons most often urged in support of applying the law of the forum-locus in cases such as this are: (1) to protect medical creditors who provided services to injured parties in the locus State, (2) to prevent injured tort victims from becoming public wards in the locus State and (3) the deterrent effect application of locus law has on future tort-feasors in the locus State (see, Comments on *Babcock v. Jackson, A Recent Development in Conflict of Laws*, 63 Colum. L. Rev. 1212, 1222-1226, 1237-1238; Korn, *supra*, at 841, 962). The first two reasons share common weaknesses. First, in the abstract, neither reason necessarily requires application of the locus jurisdiction's law, but rather invariably mandates application of the law of the jurisdiction that would either allow recovery or allow the greater recovery. They are subject to criticism, therefore, as being biased in favor of recovery. Second, on the facts of this case neither reason is relevant since the record contains no evidence that there are New York medical creditors or that plaintiffs are or will likely become wards of this State. Finally, although it is conceivable that application of New York's law in this case would have some deterrent effect on future tortious conduct in this State, New York's deterrent interest is considerably less because none of the parties is a resident and the rule in conflict is loss-allocating rather than conduct-regulating.

Conversely, there are persuasive reasons for consistently applying the law of the parties' common domicile. First, it significantly reduces forum-shopping opportunities, because the same law will be applied by the common-domicile and locus jurisdictions, the two most likely forums. Second, it rebuts charges that the forum-locus is biased in favor of its own laws and in favor of rules permitting recovery. Third, the concepts of mutuality and reciprocity support consistent application of the common-domicile law. In any given case, one person could be either plaintiff or defendant and one State could be either the parties' common domicile or the locus, and yet the applicable law would not change depending on their status. Finally, it produces a rule that is easy to apply and brings a modicum of predictability and certainty to an area of the law needing both.

As to defendant Franciscan Brothers, this action requires an application of the third of the rules set forth in *Neumeier* because the parties are domiciled in different jurisdictions with conflicting loss-distribution rules and the locus of the tort is New York, a separate jurisdiction. In that situation the law of the place of the tort will normally apply, unless displacing it "will advance" the relevant substantive law purposes without impairing the smooth working of the multi-state system or producing great uncertainty for litigants (*Neumeier v. Kuehner*, [at p. 184, *supra*]). For the same reasons stated in our analysis of the action against defendant Boy Scouts, application of the law of New Jersey in plaintiffs' action against defendant Franciscan Brothers would further that State's interest in enforcing the decision of its domiciliaries to accept the burdens as well as the benefits of that State's loss-distribution tort rules and its interest in promoting the continuation and expansion of defendant's charitable activities in that State. Conversely, although application of New Jersey's law may not affirmatively advance the substantive law purposes of New York, it will not frustrate those interests because New York has no significant interest in applying its own law to this dispute. Finally, application of New Jersey law will enhance "the smooth working of the multi-state system" by actually reducing the incentive for forum shopping and it will provide certainty for the litigants whose only reasonable expectation[3] surely would have been that the law of the jurisdiction where plaintiffs are domiciled and defendant sends its teachers would apply, not the law of New York where the parties had only isolated and infrequent contacts as a result of Coakeley's position as Boy Scout leader. Thus, we conclude that defendant Franciscan Brothers has met its burden of

---

[3] As the dissent notes, we rejected the notion that the parties' reasonable expectations of the applicable law was determinative in *Miller v. Miller* and *Tooker v. Lopez*. Our discussion here is limited to application of the "uncertainty" standard of the third of the Neumeier rules to defendant Franciscan Brothers.

demonstrating that the law of New Jersey, rather than the law of New York, should govern plaintiffs' action against it.

III

Plaintiffs contend that even if the New Jersey charitable immunity statute is applicable to this action, it should not be enforced because it is contrary to the public policy of New York.

The public policy doctrine is an exception to implementing an otherwise applicable choice of law in which the forum refuses to apply a portion of foreign law because it is contrary or repugnant to its State's own public policy (see, Paulsen & Sovern, *"Public Policy" in the Conflict of Laws*, 56 Colum. L. Rev. 969). The doctrine is considered only after the court has determined that the applicable substantive law under relevant choice-of-law principles is not the forum's law. Having found that, the court must enforce the foreign law "unless some sound reason of public policy makes it unwise for us to lend our aid" (*Loucks v. Standard Oil Co.*, [p. 37 *supra*.] [Cardozo, J.]).

The party seeking to invoke the doctrine has the burden of proving that the foreign law is contrary to New York public policy. It is a heavy burden for public policy is not measured by individual notions of expediency and fairness or by a showing that the foreign law is unreasonable or unwise (*Loucks v Standard Oil Co*). Public policy is found in the State's Constitution, statutes and judicial decisions and the proponent of the exception must establish that to enforce the foreign law "would violate some fundamental principle of justice, some prevalent conception of good morals, some deep-rooted tradition of the common weal" expressed in them. In addition, the proponent must establish that there are enough important contacts between the parties, the occurrence and the New York forum to implicate our public policy and thus preclude enforcement of the foreign law (*see, Paulsen & Sovern, supra*, at 981).

When we have employed the exception in the past and refused to enforce otherwise applicable foreign law, the contacts between the New York forum, the parties and the transaction involved were substantial enough to threaten our public policy.

[The court reviews *Kilberg* and *Mertz*.]

Thus, although New York discarded the doctrine of charitable immunity long ago (*see, Bing v. Thunig*, 2 N.Y.2d 656, 667 [1957]) and enforcement of New Jersey's statute might well run counter to our fundamental public policy, we need not decide that issue because there are not sufficient contacts between New York, the parties and the transactions involved to implicate our public policy and call for its enforcement.

IV

Finally, defendants contend that inasmuch as New Jersey law governs this action, plaintiffs are estopped under the doctrine of third-party issue preclusion from relitigating the effect of the New Jersey charitable immunity statute by their earlier New Jersey court action . . ..

The issue presented to us, whether plaintiffs' claims against these defendants are barred by the New Jersey charitable immunity statute, was actually litigated and determined by a final judgment of its courts. . . . Plaintiffs are correct that collateral estoppel would not apply if we applied New York law or refused to enforce the New Jersey statute on public policy grounds. We have resolved those issues against them, however.

Accordingly, the order of the Appellate Division should be affirmed, with costs.

JASEN, J. (dissenting). I respectfully dissent. In my view, the majority overstates the significance of New Jersey's interests in having its law apply in this case and understates the interests of New York. A more balanced approach, which recognizes that the conflict in this case involves not only New Jersey's law of charitable immunity but also New York's law of charitable nonimmunity, and which accords a proper analysis and fairer significance to the policies underlying the latter, would dictate a different result. Because New Jersey's interests in having its law of charitable immunity apply are rather attenuated in this case and, by sharp contrast, New York's interests as the "locus-forum" in applying its rule of charitable nonimmunity are overriding—especially in light of the heinous nature of the alleged tortious conduct involved and the repugnancy of immunizing those responsible from liability—it is my view that New York law should govern this case. A brief highlighting of those factors which I believe to be most pertinent illustrates what, in my view, the majority has either understated or overlooked.

New Jersey's interests, denominated by the majority as loss-distribution, are hardly pressing under the circumstances. While it is true that laws providing for charitable immunity typically are intended to serve the purpose of protecting and promoting the charities incorporated within a state's jurisdiction, that function is virtually irrelevant in this case. Presently, neither corporate defendant is a resident of New Jersey. The Brothers of the Poor of St. Francis (the Franciscan Brothers) has at all relevant times been a resident of the State of Ohio, a jurisdiction which recognizes only a limited charitable immunity that does not extend to negligence in the selection and retention of personnel. The Boy Scouts of America, although originally incorporated in New Jersey at the time of its alleged tortious conduct, has since relocated in Texas, a State which has wholly rejected charitable immunity. While ordinarily a change in residence subsequent to the events upon which a lawsuit is predicated ought not to affect the rights and liabilities of the parties in order to avoid forum-shopping, there is no such reason to deny giving effect to the change in residence here. Rather, a defendant's post-tort change in residence—as opposed to that of a plaintiff—is often critical insofar as it affects state interest analysis. (see, Weintraub, Commentary on the Conflict of Laws § 6.28, at 331, 334 [2d. ed]; Sedler, *The Governmental Interest Approach to Choice of Law: An Analysis and a Reformulation*, 25 U.C.L.A. L. Rev. 181, 241-242; Note, *Post Transaction or Occurrence Events in Conflicts of Laws*, 69 Colum. L. Rev. 843, 865.) Indeed, as this court stated in *Miller v. Miller* [p. 171, *supra*]: "To the extent that the [foreign State's] limitation evinced a desire to protect its residents in wrongful death actions, that purpose cannot be defeated here since no judgment in this action will be entered against a . . . resident [of that State. It] would have no concern with the nature of the recovery awarded against defendants who are no longer residents of that State and who are, therefore, no longer proper objects of its legislative concern . . ." [22 N.Y. 2d at 21-22].

Consequently, because the majority cannot in actuality rely upon New Jersey's interest in protecting resident charities—into which category neither corporate defendant now falls—the decision today is, in effect, predicated almost exclusively upon the plaintiffs' New Jersey domicile. What emerges from the majority's holding is an entirely untoward rule that nonresident plaintiffs are somehow less entitled to the protections of this State's law while they are within our borders . . ..

There can be no question that this State has a paramount interest in preventing and protecting against injurious misconduct within its borders. This interest is particularly vital and compelling where, as here, the tortious misconduct involves sexual abuse and exploitation of children, regardless of the residency of the victims and the tort-feasors. Despite the majority's denial, New York's law in question is intimately connected to this overriding interest.

As the majority stresses, a charitable immunity law such as New Jersey's typically serves a loss-distribution purpose reflecting a legislative paternalism toward resident charities. But that is obviously not true with regard to a rule, such as New York's, which denies charitable immunity. Consequently, it is mistaken to adjudge the propriety of applying the latter law by giving weight only to the interests served by the former. A closer attention to the specific policy purposes of New York's charitable nonimmunity rule is essential to a more appropriate resolution of the conflict.

These purposes, to which the majority refuses to accord any significance, are preventive, protective and compensatory. Indeed, in *Bing v. Thunig* (2 N.Y.2d 656), where New York's prior rule of charitable immunity was abolished, this court held that "[i]t is not alone good morals but sound law that individuals and organizations should be just before they are generous, and there is no reason why that should not apply to charitable [institutions] . . . Insistence upon . . . damages for negligent injury serves a two-fold purpose, for it both assures *payment of an obligation to the person injured and gives warning that justice and the law demand exercise of care.*" [emphasis added].)

As previously discussed, there can be little doubt that New York has an interest in insuring that justice be done to nonresidents who have come to this State and suffered serious injuries herein. There is no cogent reason to deem that interest any weaker whether such guests are here for the purpose of conducting business or personal affairs, or, as in this case, have chosen to spend their vacation in New York. Likewise, it cannot be denied that this State has a strong legitimate interest in deterring serious tortious misconduct, including the kind of reprehensible malfeasance that has victimized the nonresident infant plaintiffs in this case. . . .

Moreover, New York's strong interest in deterring injurious misconduct, as well as in providing compensatory justice and protection to persons victimized by wrongdoing within this State, is reflected in the traditional principle of lex loci which, despite the majority's sub silentio disavowal, remains in this State "the general rule in tort cases to be displaced only in extraordinary circumstances." (*Cousins v Instrument Flyers*, 44 N.Y.2d 698, 699; *see also, Neumeier v Kuehner, Tooker v Lopez*). Indeed, despite the so-called "choice of law revolution" *lex loci* is still acknowledged almost universally as a central factor in determining the state, or states, in which the significant interests lie. (see, Restatement [Second] of Conflict of Laws § 145 [2][a],[b]; § 146.) This rule ought not to be applied mechanically or rigidly to reach absurd results. But, neither ought it to be disregarded indiscriminately, without giving due consideration to the nature or extent of the relationship which accrues between the tort in question and a particular jurisdiction because that jurisdiction is the locus state. (see, Reese, *The Second Restatement of Laws Revisited*, 34 Mercer L. Rev. 501, 513–515.)

Here, there are no extraordinary circumstances justifying displacement of the usual rule of lex loci and the consequent disregard of New York's interest as the jurisdiction in which the infant plaintiffs were victimized . . . ..

This is clearly not a case in which the locus can be discounted as purely fortuitous or adventitious. . . . The infant plaintiffs and the defendants' tort-feasor were not merely in transitu in New York. Rather, they were here for a stay, albeit a short one, and as such they deliberately submitted themselves to the protections and responsibilities of this State's laws which should now govern the consequences of the tortious conduct committed while within New York's borders.

Additionally, apart from the foregoing, I believe that this court ought not to apply New Jersey's law of charitable immunity by reason of its incompatibility with this State's settled public policy. Almost 30 years ago, when this court abolished charitable immunity for this State, we explained that the rule was inherently incongruous, contrary to both good morals and sound law, out of tune with modern day needs, unfair and confused. Surely, a rule deemed so archaic and anachronistic by this court ought not now to be given effect and, thereby, insulate defendants from whatever responsibility they should bear for the heinous acts of misconduct performed in this State.

. . .

Finally, I find no merit to defendants' arguments for the application of collateral estoppel. . . . Inasmuch as New York law should be applied in this case by reason of this State's significant interests and because application of New Jersey's law would contravene this State's public policy, collateral estoppel is inapplicable.

. . .

For all these reasons, I would reverse the order of the Appellate Division, apply the law of New York denying immunity to defendant charities, and permit plaintiffs to proceed on their complaint.

Chief Judge WACHTLER and Judges MEYER, KAYE and ALEXANDER concur with Judge SIMONS Judge JASEN dissents and votes to reverse in a separate opinion.

NOTES AND QUESTIONS

1. Only one member of the court that had decided *Neumeier* still sat on the court that decided *Schultz*, and that judge, Matthew Jasen, was not with the majority in either case. Yet there was clearly an institutional pressure to carry on the teaching of the prior decisions of the Court of Appeals. Does the court do that persuasively?

2.(a) The suggestion was made in Chapter 1 that while domicile may be a strong connecting factor when it is firmly established, the power of domicile as a dispositive factor should be diminished, if not disregarded entirely, when the facts used to establish domicile are doubtful, as, for instance in *White v. Tennant* and *Estate of Jones*, §1.03[B] *supra*. By that criterion, how do you judge the court's treatment of *Schultz* as a common domicile case à la *Babcock* and *Neumeier* rule 1?

(b) The court itself seems not wholly persuaded by its analysis focused on domicile, since it also inquires in depth about the place of the tort. Where is the locus delicti? Is there really one locus for some counts, another for others?

(c) The court says that *Schultz* is the first case since the conflicts revolution in which New York is the forum/locus. But unlike *Kell v. Henderson*, [p. 160], which did not reach the Court of Appeals, here the court rejects both of these connecting factors, and dismisses the complaint. Why?

3. The Court distinguishes—more explicitly than in prior cases—between conduct-regulating and loss-allocating rules. Aren't all the rules we have seen thus far loss-allocating rules? Of course New Jersey does not encourage camp counselors to molest young Boy Scouts, any more than

Ontario encourages drivers to try beat an oncoming train across a grade crossing. What is gained by this distinction?

4. This may be as good a place as any to come back to the *Adams v. Knickerbocker* series, which as noted, focused on the same defense, charitable immunity, but in the context of an automobile accident, not child molestation with tragic end. Consider how each of the "judges' would have decided *Schultz*.

(i) would Judge Griswold have applied New York law in favor of plaintiffs?

(ii) Would Judge Rheinstein have focused on the relationship formed in New Jersey?

(iii) What about Judge Reese? Did the conduct and the injury occur in the same state, or not? Which of the contacts are the most significant?

(iv) Judge Currie, it seems, would apply the law of the forum unless. . . . Would he find a reason here not to apply New York law?

(v) Finally, Judge Cavers. Is this a case in which it is reasonable to deny immunity to a charitable corporation from an immunity state coming into a non-immunity state? (see p. 123 *supra*).

§ 3.08 Variations on the Law of Torts

In the 1970's and 1980's, guest statutes and low limits of liability for wrongful death largely disappeared from the American scene. In significant part the demise of these limitations on compensation for victims of accidents was influenced by developments in choice of law cases—bridges, one can fairly say, to tort reform. But reforms in the tort system took several other paths as well, as study after study showed that some accident victims received no relief at all, others were overcompensated, and the professionals in the system—lawyers, insurance adjusters, experts—took surprisingly large shares of the costs of the system. Each of these reforms, making the "common law" less common, presented problems when situations arose with connections (not to say "contacts") with more than one state. A recurring question was whether the lessons learned, and the precedents created, in the "choice of law revolution" focused on guest statutes and damage limits could be applied to these other reforms adopted in some states but not others, or adopted in different versions, with distinct criteria and different dollar amounts.

1. *Uninsured Motorist Insurance*

In part in response to the drive for no-fault compensation plans as discussed below, many states adopted laws requiring liability insurers to provide coverage designed for persons injured through the negligence of other motorists from whom no recovery could be had because they carried no insurance. In states that adopted uninsured motorist statutes, all automobile insurance policies were required to provide coverage in such situations for injuries to the insured, to passengers in his vehicle, and usually also to members of his immediate family, up to a specified amount. The amount of coverage varied from state to state, but still required the injured person to establish his or her entitlement to recover in tort, i.e., to establish that the accident was caused by the negligence of the uninsured motorist and that the beneficiary was not at fault (or less at fault than the uninsured motorist). Thus uninsured motorist programs contained elements of contract—the insurance policy, and elements of tort—the basis for recovery under the policy. How one state's uninsured motorist statute would be applied in litigation in another state, and in particular what would happen when the injured person owned several vehicles each covered by an uninsured motorist policy, became the focus of *Allstate Ins. Co. v. Hague*, the leading recent case on constitutional control of choice of law, reproduced in Chapter 5.[a]

2. *Workers' Compensation*

This form of protection, focused on industrial accidents, had been widely adopted throughout the United States—as in other industrial states—since the first quarter of the twentieth century.[b] The essence of workers' compensation is that an employee injured in the course of his employment will be compensated for his injury according to a specified formula—different in different states but invariably less than what one might expect from a jury verdict—but without regard to the defenses that might be available in a tort action, such as the fault of the employee or the fault of a fellow servant,[c] and without the need to establish fault on the part of the employer. In return for the right to be compensated from a fund to which all employers are required to contribute, workers under most workers' compensation plans are precluded from bringing suit in tort against their employer arising out of an accident. A significant difference among different state workers' compensation plans concerns the admissibility of suits in tort by the injured worker against third parties—for instance against the manufacturer of a machine that injured the employee or against the prime contractor in a construction project where the injured worker is the employee of a subcontractor. How these problems were handled in a multistate context gave rise to many of the cases concerning the Constitution and choice of law in the 1930's and 1940's.[d]

A new twist on workers compensation cases was introduced by the New York Court of Appeals in the *Dole* case decided in 1972, which permitted a third party held liable in a tort suit by an injured worker to seek contribution from the employer on the basis of comparative fault, even though the employer could not have been sued by the employee directly.[e] The effect of this innovation, in the context where the employment relation is centered in a state that does not permit contribution in these circumstances, is the issue in the *Cooney* case, the last case reproduced in this chapter and the most recent decision on choice of law by the New York Court of Appeals as this book went to press.

3. *No-Fault Compensation*

A. *No-Fault Compensation in a Nutshell*

The most radical aspect of tort reform, adopted in about half the states of the United States, was *no-fault* or *first party* automobile insurance. The proponents of no-fault compensation plans, as a substitute for the system based on negligence litigation and liability insurance, argued that the deterrent feature of the tort system was largely a myth, and that the compensation feature was too uncertain: slightly injured persons were often overcompensated (because defendants found it cheaper to settle than to litigate), severely injured persons were often undercompensated,

---

[a] See §5.03 infra.

[b] See generally Arthur Larson, The Law of Workmen's Compensation (1952), kept up by Matthew Bender as *Larson's Workers' Compensation Law* (Loose-leaf 12 vols.) esp. Vol. 1. Ch. 1-2.

[c] Recall *Alabama Great Southern Railroad Co. v. Carroll*, p. 1, *supra*.

[d] See, e.g., the *Alaska Packers* and *Pacific Employers* cases in Chapter 5, §5.02[B] *infra;* and also *Carroll v. Lanza*, summarized at p. 400, and the *Magnolia* and *McCartin* cases in Chapter 8, §8.01 [B].

[e] *Dole v. Dow Chemical Co.*, 30 N.Y. 2d 143, 331 N.Y.S. 2d 382, 282 N.E. 2d 288 (1972) subsequently adopted by the legislature as N.Y. C.P. L.R. §§ 1401-04. These provisions, in turn, were modified in 1996. See p. 229, *Note*.

sometimes not compensated at all, and some plaintiffs "won the lottery" with the high jury awards that made newspaper headlines.[f]

The proponents of no-fault automobile insurance would have favored a comprehensive system in which first party insurance replaced the tort system completely in respect of vehicle accidents, so that automobile accident insurance would resemble life insurance, in which fault or cause of death (suicide apart) is never an issue. To make such a system work, however, it would be necessary to eliminate the indeterminate elements in tort damages generally referred to as "pain and suffering," and also related items of tort damages such as loss of consortium, loss of society, grief, and the like, as well as punitive damages.

No state of the United States adopted a comprehensive no-fault plan such as prevails, for example, in New Zealand.[g] Many states, however, adopted a form of no-fault compensation in which injured parties would be compensated by their own insurer for "basic economic loss," but could bring an action in tort only if they were seriously injured, or their medical expenses exceeded a threshold defined by the legislature. In some states, basic economic loss is subjected to a ceiling—for instance $50,000 in New York; in others, medical expenses are covered by the first party insurer without limit. Where loss of earnings is included in basic economic loss, many states provide for a deductible, or, say, for 80 percent of wages up to $1,500 per month. If two or more persons each covered by no-fault insurance are involved in a traffic accident, each is supposed to collect from his or her own insurer, and the issue of fault is not addressed.[h] Within a given state, the tensions are typically raised by persons who seek to break through the threshold in order to claim damages for "pain and suffering." When an accident touches upon more than one state—for instance persons domiciled in a no-fault state involved in an accident in a tort state or vice versa, the tensions may run in several directions. Some persons may seek to take advantage of no-fault when their prospects in a tort action do not seem bright; others will seek to escape from the system's ban on tort actions.

B. *No-Fault Accident Compensation and the Conflict of Laws*

1. With few exceptions, the effort to secure passage of no-fault compensation plans by state legislatures was too controversial—overall and with respect to particular definitions and thresholds—to give the opportunity to think through with care the choice of law aspects of accident compensation plans. The most that legislatures did was to focus either on territoriality— i.e., "all persons injured in this state are subject to the plan regardless of their residence" or on domicile/residence, i.e., "all persons resident in this state or who own vehicles registered in this state are subject to the plan, regardless of where the injury occurs." *A priori*, which of these two approaches do you find more attractive? Which more accurately reflects the interest of a state enacting no-fault legislation? Does one approach interfere more than the other with the interests of another state?

2.(a) Suppose P, a resident of a no-fault state A, is injured in a tort state B, through the fault of D, a resident of B and therefore not covered by a no-fault plan. Should P be required to be

---

[f] The most influential book, by two law professors was Robert E. Keeton and Jeffrey O'Connell, *Basic Protection for the Traffic Victim* (1965). Another influential study was known as the Rockefeller Report, actually a Report to Governor Rockefeller of New York by the New York Department of Insurance, entitled *Automobile Insurance . . . For Whose Benefit* (1970).

[g] A brief summary of the New Zealand system appears in Marc A. Franklin and Robert L. Rabin, *Tort Law and Alternatives* (5th ed. 1992).

[h] We omit here discussion of claims between insurers which some but not all plans provided for, in which fault may reappear, but generally subject to arbitration.

content with her first party insurance? Could she recover first party insurance from her insurer in state *A*, and also bring a tort action against *D* in state *B*?

(b) Suppose the same facts as in (a) except that state *B* is also a no-fault state but with greater benefits (for instance a smaller deductible for lost earnings). Should *P*'s compensation be provided pursuant to the laws of *A*, her state of residence? Or should the law of state *B* apply as the place of accident?

c) Would formulations such as the *Neumeier* rules help in sorting out the preceding questions? For example, suppose *P* and *D*, both resident in a tort state *B* are involved in an accident in *A*, a no-fault state whose law is based on territoriality. If *P* sues *D* in state *B*, the tort state, should the common domicile rule of *Babcock* and *Neumeier* supply the solution, so that the law of *B* governs?

3(a) More generally, is the appropriate analogy to choice of law in tort, or to choice of law in contract?

(b) Alternatively, should courts in no-fault states adopt a principle of preference, such as that in §1-105 of the Uniform Commercial Code,[i] to the effect that the forum state's no-fault plan will be applied unless there is no rational basis for doing so? Conversely, should courts in tort states take the position that the common law will not be derogated from unless the mandate for doing so is unambiguous?

(c) How about a different type of principle of preference, for instance along the lines advocated by Cavers, J. in Case 5 of the *Adams v. Knickerbocker* series, p. 123, *supra*?

4. As of year-end 1997, many of these questions, and others like them, had found their way into the courts, but no "leading case," such as *Babcock* or *Neumeier* had emerged. Courts tended to rely on those cases, on the Restatement, or on writings by Currie, Leflar, and others, without exploring whether the sources developed in different contexts were persuasive in the new setting.

The two cases that follow illustrate the different approaches of courts in Illinois and Ohio—both tort states—to the law of Michigan, a no-fault state. The second case, *Kurent v. Farmers Insurance,* also shows an ingenious attempt to link no-fault and uninsured motorist insurance, which persuades three of the judges of the Ohio Supreme Court, but not the majority.

Finally, *Cooney v. Osgood Machinery* shows the New York Court of Appeals once more engaged in choice of law analysis, not about no-fault insurance, but about a claim for contribution from an out-of-state employer covered by a workers compensation system.

SCHULZE v. ILLINOIS HIGHWAY TRANSPORTATION COMPANY

Appellate Court of Illinois, Third District.
97 Ill.App. 3d 508, 423 N.E.2d 278, 53 Ill.Dec. 86 (1981)

MILLS, Justice:

The North Pekin 4-H Club contracted with defendant Illinois Highway Transportation Company (IHT), an Illinois corporation with its principal place of business in Illinois, to transport a group by bus round trip between North Pekin, Illinois, and Ft. Dearborn, Michigan. The bus,

---
[i] Documents Supplement p. 55.

driven by defendant Doreen Foster, an Illinois resident, left the highway and overturned near Paw Paw, Michigan. Plaintiffs in this case, all Illinois residents, are various passengers and spouses of passengers allegedly injured in that mishap. At the pleading stage, the trial judge decided that Illinois law should be applied to this case but certified that decision for immediate appeal. . . .

Plaintiffs allege that IHT was negligent in failing to provide a bus that was in proper mechanical condition, failing properly to inspect the bus to determine its mechanical and roadway worthiness, failing to provide seat belts, and employing an incompetent driver. IHT was covered by an insurance policy complying with a Michigan statute which adopted what defendants describe as "a modified no-fault plan." It is unnecessary to discuss the various provisions of the Michigan law. We need only observe that if it were applied to this case, plaintiffs would be assured a certain amount of recovery without showing defendants' negligence; but they would be precluded from seeking certain kinds of damages, and a limit would be placed upon the damages recoverable.

(1) The parties agree that the choice of law issue in this case is governed by Ingersoll v. Klein (1970), 46 Ill.2d 42, 262 N.E.2d 593, wherein the court said: "In our opinion, the local law of the State where the injury occurred should determine the rights and liabilities of the parties, unless Illinois has a more significant relationship with the occurrence and with the parties, in which case, the law of Illinois should apply." The Ingersoll court relied upon Tentative Draft No. 9 of Restatement (Second) of Conflicts, § 379 (subsequently adopted, with minor changes, as Restatement (Second) of Conflicts, § 145), which stated that four contacts are of primary importance in determining which of two states has the more significant relationship with the occurrence and the parties: (1) place of injury, (2) place of conduct causing injury, (3) domicile and place of business of parties, and (4) place where parties' relationship is centered.

(2) In this case contact 1 lies with Michigan, and contacts 3 and 4 lie with Illinois. As to contact 2, Foster's alleged negligent conduct occurred in Michigan, but IHT's acts or omissions occurred in Illinois. This tally, however, is not itself determinative, for *Ingersoll* adopted a "more significant relationship" test, not a "greater number of contacts" test. Thus, rather than merely count contacts, a court is also to consider the relative importance of the various contacts.

The Ingersoll court embraced the more significant relationship approach in order to avoid the "unjust and anomalous results" which often had occurred under the doctrine of *lex loci delicti*. In that case, it was mere happenstance that the fatal crash occurred on the Iowa, not the Illinois, side of the Mississippi River. We are compelled to say that here, too, the place of injury was fortuitous. The same type of accident and the same injuries could just as easily have occurred on an Illinois or Indiana highway. The fact that Michigan was the parties' destination is of no particular significance. Thus, we can give little weight to the "place of injury" contact in deciding which state has the more significant relationship to this case.

The place where the negligent conduct occurred also is of little importance here. If the conflicting laws of Michigan and Illinois dealt with whether a defendant's conduct constituted negligence, then the place where the conduct occurred would be an important contact. Here, however, the dissimilarity between Michigan and Illinois law concerns the right of a party to recover and the amount of recovery allowable. Under these circumstances, the place of the parties' domicile is of primary importance, for that is the state which presumably will feel the social and economic impact of recovery or nonrecovery.

In many tort cases, the fourth contact place of the parties' relationship is inapplicable. However, when, as here, that factor is present and the injury was caused by an act done in the course of the relationship, then the place where the relationship is centered has an important contact with the parties and the occurrence.

Considering the relative importance of the contacts with regard to the issues at hand that Michigan and Illinois have with this case, we must conclude that Illinois has a more significant relationship with the occurrence and the parties and that Illinois law should apply. Our decision is in conformity with every post-Ingersoll case in which the parties have all been Illinois residents. . . .

Defendants contend that Michigan, having adopted a comprehensive statute governing recovery for personal injuries and property damage in traffic accidents, has a strong interest in seeing that law applied to this case. By this argument, defendants seemed to advocate weighing the interests of Illinois and Michigan, and seeing which would be more directly affected by a decision as to the applicable law. Some jurisdictions decide choice of law questions under this "state interest" analysis. And, of course, even courts using the more significant relationship approach often become concerned with which state is more "interested" in the outcome of the litigation. This is not surprising, for a state's interest in the litigation would likely increase in proportion to the number of its contacts with the parties and the occurrence. However, the more significant relationship test is the rule in Illinois, and defendants' assertion that Michigan has an "interest" in having its law applied does not directly address the issue before us.

But even were we to look to the respective interests of Illinois and Michigan in this case, we would disagree with defendants' assertion that the comprehensive nature of the Michigan statute and the policies behind it demonstrate Michigan's overriding interest in the case at bar. In *Shavers v. Kelley (1978), 402 Mich. 554, 267 N.W.2d 72,* the court said that the Michigan no-fault statute was designed to remedy five evils characteristic of the common law tort system: (1) failure of many injured people to receive any compensation because of the complete bar of contributory negligence, (2) frequent over-or under-compensation of injuries, (3) lengthy delays in compensation, (4) the heavy burden of the tort system upon the judiciary, and (5) the discrimination against the poor and uneducated. Nothing in Shavers, however, would suggest that the statute was designed to attack these evils outside of Michigan. Thus, the policies and interests of the State of Michigan will be unaffected by the application of Illinois law to this case.

Illinois, on the other hand, has a vital interest in determining the extent to which its citizens will be allowed to recover damages from one another. We have, then, what some courts and commentators have termed a "false conflict," i. e., only one of the two states involved has any interest in having its law applied. Under such circumstances, the law of the only interested state will apply.

Because Illinois has the more significant relationship with the parties and occurrence involved in this case, the trial court was correct in determining that Illinois law should apply.

Affirmed.

KURENT v. FARMERS INSURANCE OF COLUMBUS, INC.

Supreme Court of Ohio.
62 Ohio St.3d 242, 581 N.E.2d 533 (1991)

Plaintiffs-appellants, Thomas E. and Kathleen Kurent, are residents of Ohio and have an automobile insurance policy with defendant-appellee, Farmers Insurance of Columbus, Inc. ("Farmers"), a corporation organized under the laws of Ohio.

The Kurents were traveling in Michigan on July 11, 1987, when they became involved in an automobile accident proximately caused by Michael Karczewski, a Michigan resident. Karczewski was insured by AAA Michigan ("AAA"). The Kurents claim bodily and emotional injuries as a result of the accident.

The Kurents filed a claim against Karczewski and AAA to recover damages for their injuries. AAA denied the Kurents' claim based on AAA's position that the Kurents' injuries did not meet the threshold limit under Michigan no-fault law.

Michigan's no-fault insurance laws abolish tort liability for ordinary injuries arising from automobile accidents. In Michigan an insured person injured by an insured driver may recover specified benefits, based on costs actually incurred, from his own insurer regardless of fault. . . . The insured tortfeasor driver is subject to tort liability for non-economic damages caused by the use of his automobile only if the injured person suffers damages beyond the threshold limit. The threshold limit in Michigan is defined as death, serious impairment of a bodily function, or permanent serious disfigurement.

After AAA refused their claim, the Kurents sought uninsured coverage and medical payments coverage from Farmers. Claiming that Michigan law applies, Farmers denied the uninsured motorist claim because Karczewski was insured as required by Michigan law.

The Kurents filed suit against Farmers in the Common Pleas Court of Summit County, seeking a declaration of their rights and benefits under their insurance policy. On cross-motions for summary judgment, the trial court granted the Kurents' motion for summary judgment, holding that they were entitled to collect under the uninsured portion of their policy because (1) Ohio law controls under a conflict of laws "interest analysis" and (2) AAA's denial of coverage was sufficient to meet the uninsured motorist criteria in their policy.

On appeal the court of appeals reversed and held that under the terms of the insurance agreement the Kurents were not entitled to uninsured motorist coverage.

HERBERT R. BROWN, Justice.

. . .

The basis of Farmers' obligation to the Kurents lies in the insurance contract and our analysis begins with an examination of the policy as it applied when the Kurents entered Michigan and became involved in the accident with Karczewski.

Under Part I—Liability, the Kurents' insurance policy provides:

> An insured person may become subject to the financial responsibility law, compulsory insurance law or similar law of another state or in Canada. This can happen because of

ownership, maintenance or use of your insured car when you travel outside of Ohio. We will interpret this policy to provide any broader coverage required by those laws, except to the extent that other liability insurance applies. No person may collect more than once for the same elements of loss.

The effect of this contractual provision was to provide the Kurents with adequate insurance coverage when they left Ohio and became subject to the laws of a different jurisdiction. The contract's out-of-state provision required Farmers to provide no-fault liability coverage as required by Michigan law while the Kurents were traveling in Michigan. Accordingly, the Kurents received no-fault coverage from Farmers for the Michigan accident. The no-fault benefits consisted of economic damages, which included lifetime medical expenses for their injuries and wage loss during the first three years after the date of the accident, subject to certain restrictions.

Central to the dispute is the Kurents' claim for non-economic damages. Under Michigan no-fault laws the Kurents are not entitled to recover non-economic damages unless their claim reaches the threshold level. Accordingly, they seek non-economic damages under the uninsured motorist coverage of their policy.

The uninsured motorist provision of the Kurents' policy provides in relevant part:

> We will pay all sums which an insured person is legally entitled to recover as damages from the owner or operator of an uninsured motor vehicle because of bodily injury sustained by the insured person. The bodily injury must be caused by accident and arise out of the ownership, maintenance or use of the uninsured motor vehicle.
>
> Determination as to whether an insured person is legally entitled to recover damages or the amount of damages shall be made by agreement between the insured person and us.

The uninsured motorist provision is subject to the following definition and limitation:

> 3. Uninsured motor vehicle means a motor vehicle which is:
>
> a. Not insured by a bodily injury liability bond or policy at the time of the accident.
>
> * * *
>
> d. Insured by a bodily injury liability bond or policy at the time of the accident but the Company denies coverage or is or becomes insolvent. (Emphasis added.)

The policy's language complies with [the Ohio statute] which requires insurance companies to offer uninsured motorist coverage to Ohio residents. The General Assembly enacted [the statute] to protect Ohio residents from financially irresponsible drivers. . . . The basic purpose of [the statute] is to protect persons injured in automobile accidents from uncompensated losses because a tortfeasor lacked liability coverage. It is a protection against injury at the hands of irresponsible or impecunious drivers. It was not intended to provide coverage in every uncompensated situation. . . .

The Kurents' claim for uninsured motorist coverage is determined by their contractual relationship with Farmers. Under the contract the Kurents must show (1) Karczewski's vehicle was uninsured and (2) they are legally entitled to recover from him.

The Kurents claim they satisfied the policy and statutory definition of an uninsured vehicle in that AAA 'denied coverage'based on the fact that the Kurents' injuries did not rise to Michigan's threshold level. Farmers, on the other hand, maintains that AAA did not deny coverage to the Kurents because they were not "legally entitled to recover" non-economic damages.

We agree with Farmers. According to Ohio law, the phrase "legally entitled to recover" means the insured must be able to prove the elements of his or her claim. . . . [T]he Kurents are only entitled to recover damages which Karczewski is legally liable to pay.

Michigan law determines Karczewski's legal liability to the Kurents. He is a Michigan resident and the accident occurred in Michigan. A motorist traveling in Michigan accepts Michigan law as it pertains to accidents occurring in Michigan. That motorist does not have the option, for example, of claiming that Ohio's speed limit or traffic laws govern simply because the motorist resides in Ohio. The notion that Ohio law somehow controls the amount of damages flowing from torts committed on Michigan highways is akin to a contention that a Michigan resident who commits murder in Ohio is exempt from the death penalty because Michigan does not recognize capital punishment.

Under Michigan law, the Kurents have not proved all the elements of their claim against Karczewski because they have not shown non-economic damages beyond the threshold level. Therefore, the Kurents are not "legally entitled to recover" from Karczewski and may not collect uninsured motorist coverage for their claim against him.

Our decision to apply Michigan tort law to the underlying accident is consistent with the Restatement [Second] of the Law of Conflicts approach. Specifically, Section 146 creates a presumption that the law of the place of the injury controls unless another jurisdiction has a more significant relationship to the lawsuit. Comment d to Section 146 emphasizes that the state in which both the conduct and the injury occur has the dominant interest in regulating that conduct, determining whether it is tortious in character, and determining whether the interest is entitled to legal protection.

Section 145 of the Restatement sets forth factors to determine whether one state has a more significant relationship to the lawsuit. These include the place of injury, the place where the conduct causing the injury occurred, the residence or place of incorporation and/or business of the parties, and the place where the relationship between the parties is centered.

The Kurents argue that these factors weigh more heavily in favor of Ohio's interest. They urge that Ohio's policy to fully compensate injured drivers for non-economic damages, regardless of amount, must apply to an Ohio contract between two Ohio parties. Essentially their argument is that even though Michigan tort law applies to the actual accident, Ohio tort law should be applied to the accident for purposes of determining uninsured motorist coverage. They argue that Michigan's interests are unaffected by any decision we reach today because Michigan law will still protect its resident, Karczewski, from liability. Their position is that if they are not allowed to recover for non-economic damages under their uninsured motorist provision, they will have been deprived of the uninsured motorist protection for which they paid and which Ohio law requires.

We are not persuaded that Ohio's interests are sufficient to override the presumption that the place where the injury occurred determines the rights and liabilities of the parties. The Kurents are only entitled to uninsured motorist coverage when they are injured by an uninsured motorist. Since Karczewski is not an uninsured motorist, they have not been denied their uninsured motorist benefits and [the Ohio uninsured motorist statute] has not been violated.

. . .

Accordingly, we hold that when an Ohio resident is injured in an automobile accident in a no-fault insurance state, by a resident of that state who is insured under that state's no-fault insurance laws, the Ohio resident's legal right to recover from the tortfeasor-motorist must be determined with reference to the no-fault state's laws. Where the no-fault state does not recognize a claim against the tortfeasor-motorist, the Ohio insured is not entitled to collect uninsured motorist benefits from his own insurer.

For the above-stated reasons, the judgment of the court of appeals is affirmed.

MOYER, C.J., and HOLMES and WRIGHT, JJ., concur.

ALICE ROBIE RESNICK J. dissenting.

I respectfully dissent from both the analysis employed by the majority and the result reached in this case. First, a majority of this court once again permits an insurance company to use the immunity granted to a tortfeasor in order to avoid liability to its insured on an insurance contract for which premiums have been paid. This is egregiously unfair. . . .

. . .

Furthermore, the majority opinion is confusing as to whether this case presents a conflict-of-laws issue. The trial court applied an interest analysis and resolved the issue by holding that Ohio law should be applied. The court of appeals ruled that the trial court erred in employing a conflict-of-laws analysis because there was no conflict, but then went on to employ the Michigan no-fault laws. The majority opinion purports to decide the case on grounds unrelated to a conflict-of-laws analysis, but refers to such an analysis by stating that "[o]ur decision to apply Michigan tort law to the underlying accident is consistent with the Restatement of the Law of Conflicts approach. . . ." The question becomes whether this case involves a conflict-of-laws issue. Examination of [the Ohio statute requiring uninsured motorist coverage] presents a negative answer.

[The dissent quotes the statute.]

The clear effect of the above language is that every automobile insurance contract issued in the state of Ohio must provide uninsured motorist coverage. There is no conflict-of-laws issue because an insurance company must comply with Ohio law when issuing a policy of insurance in Ohio on an Ohio vehicle. In other words, an insurance company violates the requirement of Ohio law that it provide uninsured motorist coverage whenever it issues a policy that lacks or attempts to exclude such coverage on an automobile registered or principally garaged in Ohio. The holding of the majority allows an insurance company to completely circumvent the clear mandates of [the statute] simply because an Ohio resident travels out of state. Given the amount of interstate travel today, such a ruling can have calamitous ramifications for Ohio residents.

. . .

In effect, the majority holds that when an Ohio resident enters another state, his or her automobile insurance contract changes and is governed by the law of that state. This conclusion is undeniable given the majority's ruling that the out-of-state provision in the Kurents' policy requires Farmers to become a no-fault insurer. This is troublesome because we are dealing with an Ohio resident purchasing a policy issued in Ohio which must conform to Ohio law. An Ohio resident is held to know Ohio law when entering into an insurance contract in this state. However, the majority essentially requires the insured to know the insurance and tort laws of every state through which the insured might travel. More important, I seriously question whether an automobile insurance policy may circumvent the mandatory uninsured motorist provisions of [Ohio law.] For all of the above reasons, I dissent.

SWEENEY and DOUGLAS, JJ., concur in the foregoing dissenting opinion.

COONEY v. OSGOOD MACHINERY, INC.

New York Court of Appeals
81 N.Y.2d 66, 612 N.E.2d 277, 595 N.Y.S.2d 919 (1993)

CHIEF JUDGE KAYE.

The issue on this appeal is whether a Missouri statute barring contribution claims against an employer—which conflicts with New York law permitting such claims—should be given effect in a third-party action pending here. Applying relevant choice of law principles, we conclude that the Missouri workers' compensation statute should be given effect, and therefore affirm the dismissal of the third-party complaint seeking contribution against a employer.

I.

The facts relevant to this appeal are essentially undisputed. In 1957 or 1958, Kling Brothers, Inc. (succeeded in interest by third-party defendant Hill Acme Co.) manufactured a 16-foot wide "Pyramid Form Bending Roll," a machine to shape large pieces of metal. The device was sold in 1958 to a Buffalo company, American Standard Inc., through a New York sales agent, defendant Osgood Machinery, Inc., which assisted American in the setup and initial operation of the machine. American closed its Buffalo plant around 1961, and the history of the bending roll is obscured until 1969, when Crouse Company—which obtained the equipment in some unknown manner—sold the machine to Paul Mueller Co., a Missouri domiciliary.

Mueller installed the bending roll in its Springfield, Missouri, plant and subsequently modified it by adding a foot switch. In October 1978, plaintiff Dennis J. Cooney, a Missouri resident working at the Missouri plant, was injured while cleaning the machine. The machine was running at the time—a piece of wood having been wedged in the foot switch—and Cooney was unable to reach the switch to stop the machine and avoid injury.

In Missouri, Cooney filed for and received workers' compensation benefits. Because under Missouri law an employer providing such benefits "shall be released from all other liability . . . whatsoever, whether to the employee or any other person," he could not additionally sue his employer, Mueller, in tort. Cooney did, however, bring a products liability action against Osgood—the machine's initial sales agent—in Supreme Court, Erie County. (Missouri apparently would not have had personal jurisdiction over Osgood.) Seeking contribution from parties it deems more culpable in the event it is found liable to Cooney, Osgood brought a third-party action against Mueller, American Standard, and Hill Acme. Mueller invoked the Missouri statute shielding employers from both direct claims by employees and contribution claims by others, and moved for summary judgment dismissing Osgood's third-party complaint. In light of the conflict between the Missouri statute and New York law permitting contribution claims against employers, Supreme Court undertook a choice of law analysis and concluded that New York law should apply. The Appellate Division unanimously reversed and dismissed the third-party complaint as well as all cross claims against Mueller. We now affirm.

II.

An inevitable consequence of a mobile society, where people and goods routinely cross State and national borders, is that disputes may implicate the interests of several jurisdictions having conflicting laws. Choice of law principles become relevant, however, only when a State can, consistent with the Full Faith and Credit and Due Process Clauses of the Constitution, choose between the conflicting laws. A State may lack sufficient nexus with a case so that choice of its law is arbitrary or fundamentally unfair. Mueller argues that New York's connection with the case is so tenuous that a decision to apply New York contribution law would be unconstitutional.

. . . New York's contacts with the present case are, in the aggregate, sufficient to satisfy the constitutional threshold. Osgood has alleged that Mueller has a substantial presence in this State, and there is indication in the record that Mueller does business in New York. Additionally, Osgood, which seeks contribution under New York law, is a domiciliary of this State. Finally, Osgood's alleged tortious conduct with respect to the machine arose in New York, where the machine was ordered, operated for several years, and eventually shipped out of State.

We conclude, therefore, that this State has sufficient interest in the litigation so that if we chose to apply New York law on the contribution issue, that decision would not run afoul of the Federal Constitution. Accordingly, we turn to a choice of law analysis.

III.

The traditional approach to choice of law problems arising in tort was simply to apply lex loci delicti, the law of the place of the tort, to all substantive issues in the case. The theoretical underpinning of that rule was the vested rights doctrine: the right to recover in tort is created by, and exists solely to the extent of, the law of the jurisdiction where the injury occurred.

Although the vested rights doctrine did have the salutary characteristics of predictability and ease of application, it failed to accord any significance to the policies underlying the conflicting laws of other jurisdictions (see, *Babcock, Miller v Miller*). Thus in *Babcock* the Court adopted a more flexible approach intended to give "controlling effect to the law of the jurisdiction which, because of its relationship or contact with the occurrence or the parties, has the greatest concern with the specific issue raised in the litigation." (Babcock, [p. 147 *supra*]. [The court summarizes the development from *Babcock* to *Neumeier* and summarizes the *Neumeier* rules.] Although drafted in terms of guest statutes—drivers and passengers—these rules could, in appropriate cases, apply as well to other loss allocation conflicts (see, *Schultz* [applying first and third *Neumeier* rules to conflicting charitable immunity laws]).

Assuming that the interest of each State in enforcement of its law is roughly equal—a judgment that, insofar as guest statutes are concerned, is implicit in the second and third *Neumeier* rules—the situs of the tort is appropriate as a "tie breaker" because that is the only State with which both parties have purposefully associated themselves in a significant way (see, Korn, The Choice-of-Law Revolution: A Critique, 83 Colum. L. Rev. 772, 801 [1983]). Moreover, locus is a neutral factor, rebutting an inference that the forum State is merely protecting its own domiciliary or favoring its own law (see, *Schultz,* 65 N.Y.2d, at 201). Additionally, the place of injury was the traditional choice of law crucible.

. . .

Contribution rules—as involved in the present case—are loss allocating, not conduct regulating. Had conduct regulating been at issue here, our analysis would be greatly simplified, for the traditional rule of *lex loci delicti* almost invariably obtains. Similarly, if the parties shared the same domicile, we would generally apply that jurisdiction's loss distribution law. Instead, our analysis is necessarily more complicated, calling upon us to evaluate the relative interests of jurisdictions with conflicting laws and, if neither can be accommodated without substantially impairing the other, finding some other sound basis for resolving the impasse.

Interest Analysis

The general scheme of workers' compensation acts is that an employer regardless of culpability is required to make specified payments to an injured employee and in exchange, the law immunizes the employer from further liability. Immunity "is part of the quid pro quo in which the sacrifices and gains of employees and employers are to some extent put in balance, for, while the employer assumes a new liability without fault, [it] is relieved of the prospect of large damage verdicts" (2A Larsen, Workmen's Compensation Law § 65.11 [1993]).

Some States immunize employers only from direct actions by injured workers; others extend protection from third-party contribution actions as well. The Missouri Supreme Court, in rejecting State and Federal constitutional challenges to the Missouri statute at issue here, noted that immunity " 'is the heart and soul of this legislation which has, over the years been of highly significant social and economic benefit to the working [person], the employer and the State.' " (*State ex rel. Maryland Hgts. Concrete Contrs. v. Ferriss*, 588 S.W.2d 489, 491 [Mo.], quoting *Seaboard Coast Line R.R. Co. v. Smith*, 359 So. 2d 427, 429 [Fla.].) The court, quoting further from the Florida case, also observed that "the right to contribution is not a vested right on which legislation may not impinge" (588 S.W.2d, at 491).

Missouri's decision to shield employers from contribution claims is thus a policy choice implicating significant State interests: "to deny a person the immunity granted . . . by a work[er]'s compensation statute of a given state would frustrate the efforts of that state to restrict the cost of industrial accidents and to afford a fair basis for predicting what these costs will be." (Restatement [Second] of Conflict of Laws § 184, comment *b*) Indeed, as the Restatement concluded in a related context, for another State "to subject a person who has been held liable in work[er]'s compensation to further unlimited liability in tort or wrongful death would frustrate the work[er]'s compensation policy of the State in which the award was rendered." (Restatement [Second] of Conflict of Laws § 183, comment c, at 544.)

Arrayed against Missouri's interest in maintaining the integrity of its workers' compensation scheme is New York's interest in basic fairness to litigants. Under traditional joint and several liability rules, when more than one tortfeasor was responsible for plaintiff's injury, each was potentially liable for the entire judgment, irrespective of relative culpability. Indeed, plaintiff was not even required to sue all the wrongdoers, but could recover the entire judgment from the "deep pocket," who then had no recourse (*Sommer v. Federal Signal Corp.*, 79 N.Y.2d 540, 556).

In *Dole v. Dow Chem. Co.* (30 N.Y.2d 143, 148-149 [1972]), this Court mitigated the inequity by allowing a defendant that pays more than its fair share of a judgment, as apportioned by the fact finder in terms of relative fault, to recover the difference from a codefendant. The Legislature, also recognizing the desirability of contribution, subsequently codified the Dole principles in CPLR article 14 (L. 1974, ch. 742). Stated simply, the "goal of contribution, as announced in Dole and applied since, is fairness to tortfeasors who are jointly liable." (*Sommer v. Federal Signal Corp.*, 79 N.Y.2d, at 556-557.)

Manifestly, the interests of Missouri and New York are irreconcilable in this case. To the extent we allow contribution against Mueller, the policy underlying the Missouri workers' compensation scheme will be offended. Conversely, to the extent Osgood is required to pay more than its equitable share of a judgment, the policy underlying New York's contribution law is affronted. It is evident that one State's interest cannot be accommodated without sacrificing the other's, and thus an appropriate method for choosing between the two must be found.

This is a true conflict in the mold of *Neumeier*'s second rule, where the local law of each litigant's domicile favors that party, and the action is pending in one of those jurisdictions. Under that rule, the place of injury governs, which in this case means that contribution is barred. This holding is consistent with the result reached historically, and reflects application of a neutral factor that favors neither the forum's law nor its domiciliaries. Moreover, forum shopping by defendants—who might attempt to invoke CPLR 1403 and bring a separate action for contribution in New York if sued elsewhere—is eliminated.[2]

A primary reason that locus tips the balance, of course, is that ordinarily it is the place with which both parties have voluntarily associated themselves. In this case, there is some validity to Osgood's argument that it did nothing to affiliate itself with Missouri. Indeed, a decade after Osgood's last contact with the bending roll, the machine wound up in Missouri through no effort, or even knowledge, of Osgood. Moreover, the record establishes that Osgood was not in the business of distributing goods nationwide, but limited its activities to New York and parts of Pennsylvania, and thus Osgood may not have reasonably anticipated becoming embroiled in litigation with a Missouri employer.

For this reason, our decision to apply Missouri law rests as well on another factor that should, at times, play a role in choice of law: the protection of reasonable expectations (see, Restatement [Second] of Conflict of Laws § 6 [2] [d]; *Allstate Ins. Co. v. Hague*, [p. 402, *infra*] [Stevens, J., concurring]; *Schultz*, [p. 205, *supra*] ["protecting the reasonable expectations of the parties' is one reason locus law is generally preferred when there are conflicting conduct-regulating rules"]).[3] In sum, we conclude that Missouri law should apply because, although the interests of the respective jurisdictions are irreconcilable, the accident occurred in Missouri, and unavailability of contribution would more closely comport with the reasonable expectations of both parties in conducting their business affairs.

IV.

Finally, we turn to Osgood's contention that New York's public policy precludes application of the Missouri statute in this case. Under the public policy exception, when otherwise applicable foreign law would "violate some fundamental principle of justice, some prevalent conception

---

[2] New York law permitting contribution against an employer is clearly a minority view (see generally, Annotation . . . 100 ALR3d 350). A result that might impose New York law on the carefully structured workers' compensation schemes of other States—especially when the accident occurred there—is undesirable.

[3] In view of the unambiguous statutory language barring third-party liability and the Missouri Supreme Court's holding in Ferriss, Mueller could hardly have expected to be haled before a New York court to respond in damages for an accident to a Missouri employee at the Missouri plant. By contrast, in ordering its business affairs Osgood could have had no reasonable expectation that contribution would be available in a products liability action arising out of the sale of industrial equipment. Indeed, Osgood's activity in connection with the bending roll occurred in 1958, some 14 years before Dole was decided and the principles of full contribution were introduced into our law. . . .

We have eschewed reliance on the fictional expectation of the parties based on mere contact with the locus of an accident (*Miller v. Miller*, [p. 171, *supra*]), but reasonable, justifiable expectations are another matter.

of good morals, some deep-rooted tradition of the common weal" (*Loucks v. Standard Oil Co.*, [p. 34, *supra*] [Cardozo, J.]), the court may refuse to enforce it.

. . .

Although we have noted that public policy may be found in the State Constitution, statutes and judicial decisions, plainly not every difference between foreign and New York law threatens our public policy. Indeed, if New York statutes or court opinions were routinely read to express fundamental policy, choice of law principles would be meaningless. Courts invariably would be forced to prefer New York law over conflicting foreign law on public policy grounds.

The refusal of courts to enforce foreign law as repugnant to public policy reached its zenith prior to the advent of modern choice of law doctrine. In fact, commentators have opined that in earlier times the public policy rationale really substituted as a choice of law mechanism when the prevailing rigid choice of law rules permitted no flexibility (see, Paulsen and Sovern, "Public Policy" in the Conflict of Laws, 56 Colum. L. Rev. 969, 981 [1956]. That theory is supported by some of our cases.

. . .

The thrust of Osgood's argument is that New York's law permitting contribution is so strong that any encroachment upon the right violates fundamental public policy. . . . We disagree.

Accordingly, the order of the Appellate Division should be affirmed, with costs.

Judges Simons, Titone, Hancock, Jr., Bellacosa and Smith concur.

Note: In 1996 the New York legislature acted to limit the effect of the breach in the workers' compensation system introduced by *Dole v. Dow Chemical Co.* p. 216, *supra*, which, as the court pointed out in *Cooney,* p. 228, note 2, was "clearly a minority view." The legislature amended the Workers' Compensation statute to restrict claims by covered employees against third parties, as well as claims for contribution by third parties against employers, to cases of "grave injury" as (narrowly) defined.[j] Thus the situation that gave rise to the Cooney case could still arise, but only in cases of death, loss of limb, permanent paralysis, permanent brain injury, blindness or deafness. The report of the *Cooney* case does not describe the extent of the worker's injury.

---

[j] 1996 N.Y. Laws Ch. 635, amending Workers Compensation Law §11.

CHAPTER 4

MODERN CONFLICTS THINKING AND INTENTIONAL ACTS

§ 4.01 Choice of Law With Regard to Contracts

Choice of law with regard to claims arising out of contracts, as we saw in Chapter 1, was never so rigid as it was with respect to torts. The very fact that there were two obvious connecting factors—place of contracting and place of performance—made the "black letter" law more flexible; the fact that the place of contracting was often not self-evident—for instance when the parties communicated by mail, telegraph, or telephone—and the fact that different obligations of performance undertaken by the parties to a contract might be centered in different states, gave room for maneuvering. Thus, the fortress not being so impregnable, the revolution in choice of law in contracts was not so striking. Still, courts in the United States could not help but be impressed by theories concerning the center of gravity, the most significant relationship, justified expectations, governmental interests, and principles of preference—perhaps even "better law"—in the context of disputes concerning contracts.[a]

Over and above considerations that might well be common to disputes about controversies caused by intentional as well as by accidental acts, the law of contracts reflects two pressures, whose different assessments in different states inevitably affected the choice of law process. On the one hand, the law of contracts tends to honor the principle of validation—*ut magis valeat quam pereat:* if a contract would be valid under the law of State *A* but not under the law of State *B,* and both states had some connection with the transaction, the parties would be presumed to have intended to perform a valid juridical act, leading to the conclusion that the law of *A* should be applied. A fortiori, if the parties had selected a law of a state to govern their contractual relationship, and that state had some connection with the transaction or the parties (and perhaps even without such connection), the law so chosen would normally be given effect. On the other hand, as the law moved from a protective attitude—e.g., for married women, wards of the court, minors, etc.—to a preference for freedom of contract, and back to a protective concern for consumers vis-à-vis manufacturers, borrowers vis-à-vis finance companies, insureds vis-à-vis insurance companies, and so on—the law became concerned that protective legislation not be too easily avoided by artificial contacts, choice of law clauses not really bargained for, and choice of forum clauses.

[a] See, for example, the following statement by the Supreme Court of Texas, in a case involving a dispute about a contract (a release) relied on as a defense to a product liability action:

> Most of the numerous inadequacies inherent in *lex loci delicti* also exist in the other traditional lex loci rules, including the *lex loci contractus.* Each of these traditional rules sacrifices just and reasoned results for the ease and predictability of mechanistic decision-making.

Duncan v. Cessna Aircraft Co., 665 S.W.2d 414, 421 (Tex. 1984).

All these points are illustrated in the cases that follow. It is worth remarking, however, that while there are more than enough contract choice-of-law cases to fill a chapter in a casebook, such cases are relatively rare in the last third of the twentieth century compared with tort cases, both within the United States and internationally.[b] In part this is because of the common usage in contracts of choice-of-law clauses; in greater part it is due to the similarity of the basic principles of contract law concerning sales of goods, employment, licensing, and similar commercial transactions. While every interstate and international contractual transaction has the potential for creating a choice of law problem, in fact most transactions, even when disputes arise and litigation takes place, do not involve a choice between the law of *A* and the law of *B*. It is no accident that the cases in the first part of this chapter concern odd rules, such as declaration of a person as a spendthrift, oral promises to make a will, and promises to support an illegitimate child, not the normal stuff of contract disputes such as whether goods sold were delivered on time, whether they conformed to specifications in the contract, whether an offer was accepted or rejected in time, and so on. In the United States, of course, most contract disputes are governed by the Uniform Commercial Code, effective in every state;[c] even internationally, the differences in law from state to state tend to be at the margin, not at the heart of contractual disputes.[d]

[A] Interstate Contracts and Governmental Interests

LILIENTHAL v. KAUFMAN

Oregon Supreme Court
239 Or. 1, 395 P.2d 543 (1964)

DENECKE, J.

This is an action to collect two promissory notes. The defense is that the defendant maker has previously been declared a spendthrift by an Oregon court and placed under a guardianship and that the guardian has declared the obligations void. The plaintiff's counter is that the notes were executed and delivered in California, that the law of California does not recognize the disability of a spendthrift, and that the Oregon court is bound to apply the law of the place of the making of the contract. The trial court rejected plaintiff's argument and held for the defendant.

This same defendant spendthrift was the prevailing party in our recent decision in *Olshen v. Kaufman*, 235 Or. 423, 385 P.2d 161 (1963). In that case the spendthrift and the plaintiff, an Oregon resident, had gone into a joint venture to purchase binoculars for resale. For this purpose plaintiff had advanced moneys to the spendthrift. The spendthrift had repaid plaintiff by his personal check for the amount advanced and for plaintiff's share of the profits of such venture. The check had not been paid because the spendthrift had had insufficient funds in his account. The action was for the unpaid balance of the check.

The evidence in that case showed that the plaintiff had been unaware that Kaufman was under a spendthrift guardianship. The guardian testified that he knew Kaufman was engaging in some business and had bank accounts and that he had admonished him to cease these practices; but he could not control the spendthrift.

---

[b] See Reese, *American Choice of Law*, 30 Am. J. Comp. L. 135, 139 (1982).

[c] But note that the drafters of the Code made provision for the situation in which one, but not all concerned states, had adopted the Code. See U.C.C. § 1–105, Documents Supplement, p. 55.

[d] See, generally, A. Lowenfeld, *International Private Trade* (3d ed. 1996).

The statute applicable in that case and in this one is ORS 126.335:

> After the appointment of a guardian for the spendthrift, all contracts, except for necessaries, and all gifts, sales and transfers of real or personal estate made by such spendthrift thereafter and before the termination of the guardianship are voidable.

(Repealed 1961, ch 344, § 109, now ORS 126.280) We held in that case that the voiding of the contract by the guardian precluded recovery by the plaintiff and that the spendthrift and the guardian were not estopped to deny the validity of plaintiff's claim. Plaintiff does not seek to overturn the principle of that decision but contends it has no application because the law of California governs, and under California law the plaintiff's claim is valid.

The facts here are identical to those in *Olshen v. Kaufman, supra,* except for the California locale for portions of the transaction. The notes were for the repayment of advances to finance another joint venture to sell binoculars. The plaintiff was unaware that defendant had been declared a spendthrift and placed under guardianship. The guardian, upon demand for payment by the plaintiff, declared the notes void. The issue is solely one involving the principles of conflict of laws.

We could quickly dispose of some of the conflict problems involved by applying principles previously stated some years ago by this court and other courts and writers. We are restrained from following this easy course for two reasons: First, "Contracts is by common consent the most complex and also the most confused part of Conflict of Laws." *Restatement (Second), Conflict of Laws,* Tentative Draft No. 6, p 1.[e] "Conflict of laws was in a far more unexplored state than it is now when Professor Beale began work on the original Restatement of the nineteen-twenties." Reese, *Contracts and the Restatement of Conflict of Laws, Second,* 9 Int. & Comp. L. Q. 531, 532 (1960). Second, the field of conflict of laws is today filled with judicial and pedagogical groping; the blazes of the future trail still remain faint and far apart. "In certain fields, as currently in Conflict of Laws, the wilderness grows wilder, faster than the axes of discriminating men can keep it under control." Traynor, *Law and Social Change in a Democratic Society,* 1956 Ill.L.For. 230, 234.

Under these circumstances our duty is threefold,—to decide this case correctly, to indicate generally our views on the course to be taken in this particular part of the conflict of laws, but at the same time to refrain from making any pronouncements which might in the future restrain this court from taking a course which by that time has proved to be the most desirable.

Before entering the choice-of-law area of the general field of conflict of laws, we must determine whether the laws of the states having a connection with the controversy are in conflict. Defendant did not expressly concede that under the law of California the defendant's obligation would be enforceable, but his counsel did state that if this proceeding were in the courts of California, the plaintiff probably would recover. We agree.

At common law a spendthrift was not considered incapable of contracting. *Taylor v. Koenigstein,* 128 Neb. 809, 260 N.W. 544, 546 (1935). Incapacity of a spendthrift to contract is a disability created by the legislature. California has no such legislation. In addition, the Civil Code of California provides that all persons are capable of contracting except minors, persons judicially determined to be of unsound mind, and persons deprived of civil rights. § 1556. Furthermore, § 1913 of the California Code of Civil Procedure provides: ". . . that the authority

---

[e] The sentence remains in the final version of the *Restatement,* in the Introductory Note to the chapter on contracts, p. 557.

of a guardian . . . does not extend beyond the jurisdiction of the Government under which he was invested with his authority."

Defendant contends that the law of California should not be applied in this case by the Oregon court because the invalidity of the contract is a matter of remedy, rather than one of substance. Matters of remedy, procedure, are governed by the law of the forum. What is a matter of substance and what is a matter of procedure are sometimes difficult questions to decide. Stumberg states the distinction as follows: ". . . procedural rules should be classified as those which concern methods of presenting to a court the operative facts upon which legal relations depend; substantive rules, those which concern the legal effect of those facts after they have been established." Stumberg, *Principles of Conflict of Laws* (3d ed), 133. Based upon this conventional statement of the distinction, it is obvious that we are not concerned with a procedural issue, but with a matter of substantive law.

Plaintiff contends that the substantive issue of whether or not an obligation is valid and binding is governed by the law of the place of making, California. This court has repeatedly stated that the law of the place of contract "must govern as to the validity, interpretation, and construction of the contract." *Jamieson v. Potts,* 55 Or. 292, 300, 105 P. 93, (1910). *Restatement 408, Conflict of Laws,* § 332, so announced and specifically stated that "capacity to make the contract" was to be determined by the law of the place of contract.

This principle, that *lex loci contractus* must govern, however, has been under heavy attack for years. For example, see Lorenzen, *Validity and Effects of Contracts in the Conflict of Laws,* 30 Yale L.J. 565, 655 (1921), 31 Yale L.J. 53 (1921). The strongest criticism has been that the place of making frequently is completely fortuitous and that on occasion the state of making has no interest in the parties to the contract or in the performance of the contract. *Stumberg, supra,* at 231. The principle is undermined when it is observed that in many of the decisions, the state of the place of making had other associations with the contract, e.g., it was also the place of performance and the domicile of one of the parties. In our decisions stating this principle, the state whose law was applied had connections with the contract in addition to being the place of making. *Jamieson v. Potts, supra* (55 Or. 292); *McGirl v. Brewer,* 132 Or. 422, 443, 280 P. 508, 285 P. 208 (1930). As a result of this long and powerful assault, the principle is no longer a cornerstone of the law of conflicts. Tentative Draft No. 6, p 3, *Restatement (Second), Conflict of Laws,* comments on the new contracts chapter: "First, it no longer says dogmatically that the validity of a contract is governed by the law of the place of contracting."[f]

There is no need to decide that our previous statements that the law of the place of contract governs were in error. Our purpose is to state that this portion of our decision is not founded upon that principle because of our doubt that it is correct if the *only* connection of the state whose law would govern is that it was the place of making.

In this case California had more connection with the transaction than being merely the place where the contract was executed. The defendant went to San Francisco to ask the plaintiff, a California resident, for money for the defendant's venture. The money was loaned to defendant in San Francisco, and by the terms of the note, it was to be repaid to plaintiff in San Francisco.

On these facts, apart from *lex loci contractus,* other accepted principles of conflict of laws lead to the conclusion that the law of California should be applied. *Sterrett v. Stoddard Lbr. Co.,* 150 Or. 491, 504, 46 P.2d 1023 (1935), rests, at least in part, on the proposition that the

---

[f] This statement remains in the final version of the *Second Restatement,* in the Introductory Note to Chapter 8 (1971).

validity of a note is determined by the law of the place of payment. Tentative Draft No. 6, p 30, *Restatement (Second), Conflict of Laws*, § 332b(a) states: "if the place of contracting and the place of performance are in the same state, the local law of this state determines the validity of the contract, ..."[g]

The place of payment, unlike the place of making, is usually not determined fortuitously. The place is usually selected by the payee and the payee normally selects his place of business or the location of his bank. The parties at the time of contract normally do not have in mind the problem of what law should govern. If they did, it is our belief that the payee would intend the law of the place of payment to be governing.

There is another conflict principle calling for the application of California law. Stumberg terms it the application of the law which upholds the contract. *Stumberg, supra*, at 237. Ehrenzweig calls it the "Rule of Validation." Ehrenzweig, *Conflict of Laws*, 353 (1962). Mr. Justice Harlan, speaking for the majority in *Kossick v. United Fruit Co.*, 365 US 731, 741 (1961),[h] stated such a rule and cited Ehrenzweig. *Accord*, Leflar, *The Validity of Contracts and the Conflict of Laws*, 2 Ark. L. Bull. 3 (1930). The "rule" is that, if the contract is valid under the law of any jurisdiction having significant connection with the contract, i.e., place of making, place of performance, etc., the law of that jurisdiction validating the contract will be applied. This would also agree with the intention of the parties, if they had had any intentions in this regard. They must have intended their agreement to be valid.

Stumberg, supra, at 237, observes that this principle has been most frequently applied in cases in which the claim of invalidity has been based upon the contention that the contract is usurious. The same principle, however, has been applied to other types of cases. The "rule of validation" is appealing because it is founded upon the same reasoning that is followed in other aspects of the law of contracts. This court and all other courts reiterate that contracts are "sacred and shall be enforced by the courts of justice unless some other over-powering rule of public policy intervenes which renders such agreement illegal or unenforceable. . . . Without such a rule the commerce of the world would soon lapse into a chaotic state." *Bliss v. Southern Pacific Co.*, 212 Or. 634, 646, 321 P.2d 324 (1958). . . .

Thus far all signs have pointed to applying the law of California and holding the contract enforceable. There is, however, an obstacle to cross before this end can be logically reached. In *Olshen v. Kaufman, supra*, we decided that the law of Oregon, at least as applied to persons domiciled in Oregon contracting in Oregon for performance in Oregon, is that spendthrifts' contracts are voidable. Are the choice-of-law principles of conflict of laws so superior that they overcome this principle of Oregon law?

To answer this question we must determine, upon some basis, whether the interests of Oregon are so basic and important that we should not apply California law despite its several intimate connections with the transaction. The traditional method used by this court and most others is framed in the terminology of "public policy." The court decides whether or not the public policy

---

[g] The final version of this section reads:

"If the place of negotiating the contract and the place of performance are in the same state, the local law of this state will usually be applied. . . ." *Restatement (Second), Conflict of Laws*, § 188 (3).

[h] In this case a seaman alleged that his employer had made an oral promise to assume responsibility for any injury resulting from improper treatment for an injury that the seaman might receive in a Public Health Service Hospital. The statement by Justice Harlan supported the application of general maritime law, rather than the statute of frauds under New York law.

of the forum is so strong that the law of the forum must prevail although another jurisdiction, with different laws, has more and closer contacts with the transaction. Included in "public policy" we must consider the economic and social interests of Oregon. When these factors are included in a consideration of whether the law of the forum should be applied this traditional approach is very similar to that advocated by many legal scholars. This latter theory is "that choice-of-law rules should rationally advance the policies or interests of the several states (or of the nations in the world community)." Hill, *Governmental Interest and the Conflict of Laws—A Reply to Professor Currie,* 27 Chi. L. Rev. 463, 474 (1960); Currie, *Selected Essays on the Conflict of Laws,* 64–72 (1963), reprint from 58 Col.L.Rev. 964 (1958).

The traditional test this court and many others have used in determining whether the public policy of the forum prevents the application of otherwise applicable conflict of laws principles is stated in the oft-quoted opinion of Mr. Justice Cardozo in *Loucks v. Standard Oil Co. of N.Y.* [p. 37, *supra*]. Foreign law will not be applied if it "* * * would violate some fundamental principle of justice, some prevalent conception of good morals, some deep-rooted tradition of the common weal."

. . .

How "deep rooted [the] tradition of the common weal," particularly regarding spendthrifts, is illustrated by our decisions on foreign marriages. This court has decided that Oregon's policy voiding spendthrifts' contracts is not so strong as to void an Oregon spendthrift's marriage contract made in Washington. *Sturgis v. Sturgis,* 51 Or. 10, 93 P. 696, (1908), was a suit for divorce and alimony. Defendant had been declared a spendthrift by an Oregon court. The guardian refused to consent to the spendthrift's marriage. The spendthrift got married in Washington. The marriage was held valid. Although the case involved a spendthrift's contract and, therefore, is persuasive in this case, it should not be considered determinative since marriage contracts are unique and the law applicable to marriage contracts does not necessarily apply to other types of contracts.

On the other hand, we have held a foreign marriage, made before the expiration of six months from the rendition of an Oregon divorce decree, is absolutely void in the courts of Oregon. . . .

The difficulty in deciding what is the fundamental law forming a cornerstone of the forum's jurisprudence and what is not such fundamental law, thus allowing it to give way to foreign law, is caused by the lack of any even remotely objective standards. . . .

However, as previously stated, if we include in our search for the public policy of the forum a consideration of the various interests that the forum has in this litigation, we are guided by more definite criteria. In addition to the interests of the forum, we should consider the interests of the other jurisdictions which have some connection with the transaction.

Some of the interests of Oregon in this litigation are set forth in *Olshen v. Kaufman, supra.* The spendthrift's family which is to be protected by the establishment of the guardianship is presumably an Oregon family. The public authority which may be charged with the expense of supporting the spendthrift or his family, if he is permitted to go unrestrained upon his wasteful way, will probably be an Oregon public authority. These, obviously, are interests of some substance.

Oregon has other interests and policies regarding this matter which were not necessary to discuss in *Olshen.* As previously stated, Oregon, as well as all other states, has a strong policy favoring the validity and enforceability of contracts. This policy applies whether the contract is made and to be performed in Oregon or elsewhere.

The defendant's conduct,—borrowing money with the belief that the repayment of such loan could be avoided—is a species of fraud. Oregon and all other states have a strong policy of protecting innocent persons from fraud. "The law . . . is intended as a protection to even the foolishly credulous, as against the machinations of the designedly wicked." *Johnson v. Cofer,* 204 Or. 142, 150, 281 P.2d 981 (1955).

It is in Oregon's commercial interest to encourage citizens of other states to conduct business with Oregonians. If Oregonians acquire a reputation for not honoring their agreements, commercial intercourse with Oregonians will be discouraged. If there are Oregon laws, somewhat unique to Oregon, which permit an Oregonian to escape his otherwise binding obligations, persons may well avoid commercial dealings with Oregonians.

The substance of these commercial considerations, however, is deflated by the recollection that the Oregon Legislature has determined, despite the weight of these considerations, that a spendthrift's contracts are voidable.

California's most direct interest in this transaction is having its citizen creditor paid. As previously noted, California's policy is that any creditor, in California or otherwise, should be paid even though the debtor is a spendthrift. California probably has another, although more intangible, interest involved. It is presumably to every state's benefit to have the reputation of being a jurisdiction in which contracts can be made and performance be promised with the certain knowledge that such contracts will be enforced. Both of these interests, particularly the former, are also of substance.

We have, then, two jurisdictions, each with several close connections with the transaction, and each with a substantial interest, which will be served or thwarted, depending upon which law is applied. The interests of neither jurisdiction are clearly more important than those of the other. We are of the opinion that in such a case the public policy of Oregon should prevail and the law of Oregon should be applied; we should apply that choice-of-law rule which will "advance the policies or interests of" Oregon.

Courts are instruments of state policy. The Oregon Legislature has adopted a policy to avoid possible hardship to an Oregon family of a spendthrift and to avoid possible expenditure of Oregon public funds which might occur if the spendthrift is required to pay his obligations. In litigation Oregon courts are the appropriate instrument to enforce this policy. The mechanical application of choice-of-law rules would be the only apparent reason for an Oregon court advancing the interests of California over the equally valid interests of Oregon. The present principles of conflict of laws are not favorable to such mechanical application.

We hold that the spendthrift law of Oregon is applicable and the plaintiff cannot recover.

Judgment affirmed.

O'CONNELL, J., specially concurring.

In my dissent in *Olshen v. Kaufman,* I expressed the view that ORS 126.335 should be construed to permit a creditor to recover from a spendthrift under the circumstances of that case. A majority of the court felt otherwise.

Although I disagree with the rationale in that case, I must now accept it to the extent that it is applicable. I believe that it is applicable in the case before us and that its application forces us to choose the law of Oregon in preference to the law of California.

In the *Olshen* case we had to choose between two competing policies; on one hand the policy of protecting the interest of persons dealing with spendthrifts which, broadly, may be described as the interest in the security of transactions, and on the other hand the policy of protecting the interests of the spendthrift, his family and the county. It was decided that the Oregon Legislature adopted the latter policy in preference to the former.

The case at bar involves the same choice even though the contract was made in California and it was to be performed there. The fact that California was the setting for the making and performance of the contract is of no significance except that [t]it requires us to consider California's interest in protecting its own citizens. That interest is an interest in the security of commercial transactions and was before this court in the *Olshen* case. To distinguish the *Olshen* case it would be necessary to assume that although the legislature intended to protect the interest of the spendthrift, his family and the county when local creditors were harmed, the same protection was not intended where the transaction adversely affected foreign creditors. I see no basis for making that assumption. There is no reason to believe that our legislature intended to protect California creditors to a greater extent than our own.

GOODWIN, J., dissenting.

I am unable to agree with the conclusion of the majority.

"Public policy" as a basis for decision has an overtone of predestination which sometimes tends to limit analysis. See Paulsen and Sovern, *"Public Policy" in the Conflict of Laws,* 56 Colum. L. Rev. 969, 988 (1956). In a situation in which the law of the forum differs from the law of the jurisdiction having the majority of contacts with the transaction, the invocation of "public policy" may also produce a result that is contrary to generally accepted principles. 56 Colum. L. Rev. at 988.

In *Loucks v. Standard Oil Co.,* Mr. Justice Cardozo discussed the situation in which an action's contacts with the forum state are so important that foreign law should not be applied. He pointed out that foreign law would not be applied if it "would violate some fundamental principle of justice, some prevalent conception of good morals, some deep-rooted tradition of the common weal."

In the instant case, the majority finds in effect that to apply the law of California would be to violate some deep-rooted tradition of our common weal. On the facts of this case, I believe the mere assertion of such a proposition suffices to refute it.

As a general rule the power conferred by a statute providing for the guardianship of a spendthrift's property is an extraordinary one, and should be exercised with great caution. I am aware of no compelling public reason for saving spendthrifts from the result of their folly at the expense of innocent merchants.

. . .

The majority opinion acknowledges that at common law a spendthrift was not considered incapable of contracting. The majority also points out that "[t]his court has decided that Oregon's policy voiding spendthrift's contracts is not so strong as to void an Oregon spendthrift's marriage contract made in Washington." These two statements suggest that the protection of Oregon spendthrifts is not "some deep-rooted tradition of the common weal." Furthermore, in the instant case, no "fundamental principle of justice" or "prevalent conception of good morals" would be violated if the law of California were applied.

The plaintiff was a merchant in California who was approached in the ordinary course of business by a seemingly competent person and asked to enter into a business arrangement. The notes were executed, delivered, and made payable in California. If the parties gave any thought to law at all, which is unlikely, they would have assumed that California law would apply to their business. Consequently, if California law were to be applied, it would neither surprise the parties nor shock the conscience of the court. It would hardly violate any "fundamental principle of justice" or "prevalent conception of good morals."

. . .

The transaction in the case at bar has adequate contacts with the state of California to make California law appropriate, and the law of California would uphold the validity of the contract. The presumed intentions of the parties would be carried out if the contract were enforced.

. . .

In the case before us, I believe that the policy of both states, Oregon and California, in favor of enforcing contracts, has been lost sight of in favor of a questionable policy in Oregon which gives special privileges to the rare spendthrift for whom a guardian has been appointed.

The majority view in the case at bar strikes me as a step backward toward the balkanization of the law of contracts. *Olshen v. Kaufman* held that there was a policy in this state to help keep spendthrifts out of the almshouse. I can see nothing, however, in Oregon's policy toward spendthrifts that warrants its extension to permit the taking of captives from other states down the road to insolvency.

I would enforce the contract.

SLOAN, J., joins in this dissent.

BERNKRANT v. FOWLER

California Supreme Court
55 Cal. 2d 588, 12 Cal. Rptr. 266, 360 P.2d 906 (1961)

TRAYNOR, Justice.

Plaintiffs appeal on the clerk's transcript from a judgment for defendant as executrix of the estate of John Granrud. They contend that the findings of fact do not support the judgment.

Some time before 1954 plaintiffs purchased the Granrud Garden Apartments in Las Vegas, Nevada. In 1954 the property was encumbered by a first deed of trust given to secure an installment note payable to third parties and a second deed of trust given to secure an installment note payable to Granrud at $200 per month plus interest. Granrud's note and deed of trust provided for subordination to a deed of trust plaintiffs might execute to secure a construction loan. In July 1954, there remained unpaid approximately $11,000 on the note secured by the first deed of trust and approximately $24,000 on the note payable to Granrud. At that time Granrud wished to buy a trailer park and asked plaintiffs to refinance their obligations and pay a substantial part of their indebtedness to him. At a meeting in Las Vegas he stated that if plaintiffs would do so, he would provide by will that any debt that remained on the purchase price at the time of his death would be cancelled and forgiven. Plaintiffs then arranged for a new loan of $25,000, the most they could obtain on the property, secured by a new first deed of trust. They used the proceeds to pay the balance of the loan secured by the existing first deed of trust and $13,114.20 of their indebtedness to Granrud. They executed a new note for the balance of $9,227 owing Granrud, payable in installments of $175 per month secured by a new second deed of trust. This deed of trust contained no subordination provision. The $13,114.20 was deposited in Granrud's bank account in Covina, California and subsequently used by him to buy a trailer park. Plaintiffs incurred expenses of $800.90 in refinancing their obligations.

Granrud died testate on March 4, 1956, a resident of Los Angeles County. His will, dated January 23, 1956, was admitted to probate, and defendant was appointed executrix of his estate. His will made no provision for cancelling the balance of $6,425 due on the note at the time of his death. Plaintiffs have continued to make regular payments of principal and interest to defendant under protest.

Plaintiffs brought this action to have the note cancelled and discharged and the property reconveyed to them and to recover the amounts paid defendant after Granrud's death. The trial court concluded that the action was barred by both the Nevada and the California statute of frauds; that to remove the bar of the statutes, the action must be one for quasi-specific performance in which an heir or beneficiary under the will would be an indispensable party; and that defendant was not estopped to rely on the statutes of frauds.

. . .

Subdivision 6 of section 1624 of the Civil Code provides that "An agreement which by its terms is not to be performed during the lifetime of the promisor, or an agreement to devise or bequeath any property, or to make any provision for any person by will" is "invalid, unless the same, or some note or memorandum thereof, is in writing, and subscribed by the party to be charged or by his agent." See also Code Civ.Proc. § 1973, subd. 6. Plaintiffs concede that in the absence of an estoppel, the contract in this case would be invalid under this provision if it is subject thereto. They contend, however, that only the Nevada statute of frauds is applicable and point out that the Nevada statute has no counterpart to subdivision 6. Defendant contends that the California statute of frauds is applicable, and that if it is not, the Nevada statute of frauds covering real property transactions invalidates the contract.[2]

We have found no Nevada case in point. We believe, however, that Nevada would follow the general rule in other jurisdictions, that an oral agreement providing for the discharge of an obligation to pay money secured by an interest in real property is not within the real property

---

[2] Nevada Revised Statutes, section 111.205, subdivision 1, provides:

No estate or interest in lands, other than for leases for a term not exceeding 1 year, nor any trust or power over or concerning lands, or in any manner relating thereto, shall be created, granted, assigned, surrendered or declared after December 2, 1861, unless by act or operation of law, or by deed or conveyance, in writing, subscribed by the party creating, granting, assigning, surrendering, or declaring the same, or by his lawful agent thereunto authorized in writing.

Section 111.210, subdivision 1, provides:

Every contract for the leasing for a longer period than one year, or for the sale of any lands, or any interest in lands, shall be void unless the contract, or some note or memorandum thereof, expressing the consideration, be in writing, and be subscribed by the party by whom the lease or sale is to be made.

provision of the statute of frauds, on the ground that the termination of the security interest is merely incidental to and follows by operation of law from the discharge of the principal obligation. . . .

We are therefore confronted with a contract that is valid under the law of Nevada but invalid under the California statute of frauds if that statute is applicable. We have no doubt that California's interest in protecting estates being probated here from false claims based on alleged oral contracts to make wills is constitutionally sufficient to justify the Legislature's making our statute of frauds applicable to all such contracts sought to be enforced against such estates. See *Rubin v. Irving Trust Co.*, 305 N.Y. 288, 298, 113 N.E.2d 424; *Emery v. Burbank*, 163 Mass. 326–329, 39 N.E. 1026, 28 L.R.A. 57. The Legislature, however, is ordinarily concerned with enacting laws to govern purely local transactions, and it has not spelled out the extent to which the statute of frauds is to apply to a contract having substantial contacts with another state. Accordingly, we must determine its scope in the light of applicable principles of the law of conflict of laws.

In the present case plaintiffs were residents of Nevada, the contract was made in Nevada, and plaintiffs performed it there. If Granrud was a resident of Nevada at the time the contract was made, the California statute of frauds, in the absence of a plain legislative direction to the contrary, could not reasonably be interpreted as applying to the contract even though Granrud subsequently moved to California and died here. . . . The basic policy of upholding the expectations of the parties by enforcing contracts valid under the only law apparently applicable would preclude an interpretation of our statute of frauds that would make it apply to and thus invalidate the contract because Granrud moved to California and died here. Such a case would be analogous to *People v. One 1953 Ford Victoria,* 48 Cal.2d 595, 311 P.2d 480, where we held that a Texas mortgagee of an automobile mortgaged in Texas did not forfeit his interest when the automobile was subsequently used to transport narcotics in California although he had failed to make the character investigation of the mortgagor required by California law. A mortgagee entering into a purely local transaction in another state could not reasonably be expected to take cognizance of the law of all the other jurisdictions where the property might possibly be taken, and accordingly, the California statute requiring an investigation to protect his interest could not reasonably be interpreted to apply to such out of state mortgagees. Another analogy is found in the holding that the statute of frauds did not apply to contracts to make wills entered into before the statute was enacted (*Rogers v. Schlotterback,* 167 Cal. 35, 45, 138 P. 728). Just as parties to local transactions cannot be expected to take cognizance of the law of other jurisdictions, they cannot be expected to anticipate a change in the local statute of frauds. Protection of rights growing out of valid contracts precludes interpreting the general language of the statute of frauds to destroy such rights whether the possible applicability of the statute arises from the movement of one or more of the parties across state lines or subsequent enactment of the statute. See Currie and Schreter, *Unconstitutional Discrimination in the Conflict of Laws: Privileges and Immunities,* 69 Yale L.J. 1323, 1334.

In the present case, however, there is no finding as to where Granrud was domiciled at the time the contract was made. Since he had a bank account in California at that time and died a resident here less than two years later it may be that he was domiciled here when the contract was made. Even if he was, the result should be the same. The contract was made in Nevada and performed by plaintiffs there, and it involved the refinancing of obligations arising from the sale of Nevada land and secured by interests therein. Nevada has a substantial interest in the contract and in protecting the rights of its residents who are parties thereto, and its policy is that the contract is valid and enforcible. California's policy is also to enforce lawful contracts. That policy, however, must be subordinated in the case of any contract that does not meet the requirements of an applicable statute of frauds. In determining whether the contract herein is subject to the California statute of frauds, we must consider both the policy to protect the reasonable expectations of the parties and the policy of the statute of frauds. See Cheatham and Reese, *Choice of the Applicable Law,* 52 Colum. L. Rev. 959, 978–980. It is true that if Granrud was domiciled here at the time the contract was made, plaintiffs may have been alerted to the possibility that the California statute of frauds might apply. Since California, however, would have no interest in applying its own statute of frauds unless Granrud remained here until his death, plaintiffs were not bound to know that California's statute might ultimately be invoked against them. Unless they could rely on their own law, they would have to look to the laws of all of the jurisdictions to which Granrud might move regardless of where he was domiciled when the contract was made. We conclude, therefore, that the contract herein does not fall within our statute of frauds. Since there is thus no conflict between the law of California and the law of Nevada, we can give effect to the common policy of both states to enforce lawful contracts and sustain Nevada's interest in protecting its residents and their reasonable expectations growing out of a transaction substantially related to that state without subordinating any legitimate interest of this state.

The judgment is reversed.

NOTES AND QUESTIONS

(1)(a) *Lilienthal v. Kaufman* illustrates the tension mentioned in the introductory note between the principle of validation and the concern of the state to protect certain persons even from their own actions. In *Lilienthal,* the statute, it seems, was designed to protect the spendthrift (something like an uncontrollable gambler) from himself, for his benefit and for that of his family. The law says, in effect, that Mr. Kaufman should buy bread and shoes for his children before he buys binoculars for commercial purposes. Is this the kind of "state interest" that courts should respect and further?

(b) An attempt by defendant's counsel to assert that the spendthrift law is remedial rather than substantive is met with the contempt it deserves. But plaintiff's assertion that the place of contracting governs the issue of capacity to contract[i] —is equally rebuffed by an essentially modern court, not prepared to accept the views of Beale and the first *Restatement* as to contracts, any more than it would be with respect to torts. The *Restatement (Second) of Conflict of Laws,* cited several times by the Oregon Supreme Court, says, in its final version:

§ 188. Law governing in Absence of Effective Choice by the Parties.

(1)—The rights and duties of the parties with respect to an issue in contract are determined by the local law of the state which, as to that issue, has the most significant relationship to the transaction and the parties under the principles states in § 6.[j]

---

[i] *Restatement of the Law of Conflict of Laws* § 332(a) (1934).

[j] For the principles stated in § 6, see p. 126, note 1, *supra;* Subsection (2) of § 188 lists among the contacts to be taken into account:

(a) the place of contracting;

By that standard, what law should be applied to *Lilienthal*?

(c) The court seems to decide the case on the basis of governmental interest, which it calls public policy, though it is prepared, unlike Currie, at least in his earlier writings,[k] to weigh Oregon's interests against those of the other state. Does the court have its thumb on the scale?

(d) The court cites two of its prior decisions, one upholding a marriage celebrated outside of Oregon despite violation of the groom's spendthrift regime; the other striking down an out-of-state marriage in violation of the required waiting period following an Oregon divorce. Public policy, it seems, is not an absolute, but marriage weighs more than a binoculars venture, and a restraint in a divorce decree weighs more than a spendthrift regime. Is all this, in Judge Griswold's question, law?[l]

(2)(a) Judge O'Connell says this case is governed by the prior case against the same defendant, when his partner in the binoculars venture was a citizen of Oregon. Surely, he says, the legislature would not have wanted to protect the spendthrift against fellow Oregonians, but not against Californians. Is that persuasive? Or would you be more persuaded by the following comment by Professor Cavers:

> . . . I submit that there is a marked difference in the fairness of exposing Oregonians to the risk that the Oregonians with whom they deal are under guardianship from that of exposing a Californian to the same risk in California.
>
> . . . The court was not compelled to attribute to the Oregon legislature such indifference to the consequences of providing a haven for its spendthrifts who have chosen to find victims outside their home state.[m]

(b) Nothing much is said in this case about expectations of the parties. Would you want to know whether some kind of recording statute was applicable to spendthrift guardianships, so that a prudent person thinking about dealing with an Oregonian could easily find out about such status at the same time that he checks about his credit rating and general reputation?

(c) Consider the following variations:

(i) The spendthrift guardianship was recorded, and Mr. Lilienthal could easily have found out about it;

(ii) Mr. Lilienthal made a thorough record check of Mr. Kaufman and nothing showed up about his guardianship, because there was no applicable recording statute;

(iii) There was no applicable recording statute, but it didn't matter, because in fact Mr. Lilienthal did not conduct any check.

(b) the place of negotiation of the contract;

(c) the place of performance;

(d) the location of the subject matter of the contract; and

(e) the domicil, residence, nationality, place of incorporation and place of business of the parties.

[k] See Chapter 3, Question 3(a), p. 200, *supra*. For a somewhat later version, in which Currie proposes a "substitute for all that part of the Restatement dealing with choice of law," and advocates, in case of a true conflict between the interests of the two states "[a] more moderate and restrained interpretation of the policy or interest of one state or the other . . ." see Currie, in *Symposium:* "Comments on Babcock v. Jackson," 63 Colum. L. Rev. 1212, 1233 at 1242 (1963).

[l] See Chapter 3, p. 105–107, *supra*.

[m] D. Cavers, *The Choice of Law Process*, 191–92 (1965).

Would any of these facts change your view of the case? On what theory compatible with the law of contracts?

(d) Would you like to know other facts about the case? For instance, whether the interest rate was unusually high? Whether the parties had had previous dealings? Or are all such questions directed too much at justice in the individual case, when the search ought to be for legal norms?

(e) Putting the preceding question in less philosophical and more operational terms, should the Supreme Court of Oregon have remanded the case to the lower court, with instructions to make findings concerning the points raised in paragraphs (c) and (d)?[n]

(3)(a) *Bernkrant v. Fowler* is often cited as an example of enlightened, rather than chauvinistic or "hometown" interest analysis. Justice Traynor looks for a California interest, doesn't find any, and therefore applies Nevada law. Thus the case looks like *Adams v. Knickerbocker I* in a Massachusetts court, as to which Professor Cavers, in the postscript to the cases wrote (at p. 124) that he could "only hope" that the court apply the law of New York.

(b) Is *Bernkrant* correctly decided? Suppose all there is to support the claim is the rather improbable story (even for Las Vegas) told by the Bernkrants about the "sporting offer" of Mr. Granrud, who is now dead.[o] Isn't the California rule, whether called substantive or procedural, designed precisely to prevent imposition on the court in cases of this kind?

(c) Justice Traynor, along with Judge Fuld of New York, was among the most influential judicial participants in the "conflicts revolution." Is this case more impressive than *Grant v. McAuliffe,* the case about the survival of tort claims reproduced in Chapter 2, *supra*?[p]

(4)(a) Justice Traynor cites the well-known case of *Emery v. Burbank,*[q] decided by Oliver Wendell Holmes when he was a member of the Supreme Judicial Court of Massachusetts.

> A Massachusetts domiciliary, Mrs. Rumery, made an oral promise in Maine to bequeath her entire estate to the plaintiff, Miss Emery, if Miss Emery would leave her domicile in Maine and come to Massachusetts to take care of Mrs. Rumery until she died.
>
> Miss Emery did so, but of course when Mrs. Rumery's will was opened, Miss Emery was not mentioned, and she brought suit against Mrs. Rumery's executor. The court, on the basis of a Massachusetts statute saying that no agreement to make a will shall be binding unless in writing, found against the plaintiff, saying:
>
>> If the policy of Massachusetts makes void an oral contract of this sort made within the State, the same policy forbids that Massachusetts testators should be sued here upon such contracts without written evidence, wherever they are made.[r]

---

[n] Cramton, D. Currie, & Kay report in their casebook that an interview with Mr. Lilienthal indicated that inquiry had been made on his behalf through two Portland banks; that the resulting report concluded that Kaufman's credit appeared to be good; and that there was no mention whatever of a spendthrift declaration. Cramton, Currie, & Kay, *Conflict of Laws* 273 (3d ed. 1981).

[o] According to the lower court, the refinancing cost the Bernkrants about $800, for which their debt, if they won the lawsuit, would be reduced by about $11,000. See *Bernkrant v. Fowler,* 8 Cal. Rptr. 326, 328 (Dist. Ct. App. 1960).

[p] Page 67, *supra.* Among Traynor's other famous decisions in conflict of laws was *Reich v. Purcell,* 67 Cal. 2d 551, 63 Cal. Rptr. 31, 432 P.2d 727 (1967), involving a head-on collision in Missouri, which had a limit on wrongful death recoveries, by two Ohio residents who were in the process of moving to California, and a resident of California. The court rejected the *lex loci delicti* and applied the law of Ohio, which (like California) had no limit on recovery for wrongful death, on the basis that Ohio was the relevant domicile, and the only state with a real interest.

[q] 163 Mass. 326, 326 N.E. 1026 (1895).

[r] 163 Mass. at 328, 39 N.E. at 1027.

Is *Emery v. Burbank* a sounder decision than *Bernkrant v. Fowler*?[s]

(b) Two distinctions can be drawn between *Emery* and *Bernkrant*. The property in *Emery* was in Massachusetts, the forum state, and the testatrix was unquestionably domiciled there. In *Bernkrant* the property was in Nevada, and the domicile of Mr. Ganrud at the time of the alleged promise is not clear. Possibly he changed his domicile from Nevada to California before he died, possibly he was domiciled in California all the time. Do these distinctions make any difference?

(c) If Mr. Granrud was domiciled in California, at least at the time of his death, is it correct to say, as Justice Traynor does, that California had no interest in the outcome of the case?

(5)(a) The California Supreme Court found that the Nevada statute of frauds did not apply to the transaction, because it applied only to a transaction concerning real property, not to a discharge of an obligation secured by an interest in real property. But, as Professors Cavers points out, Nevada had another statute, a so-called Dead Man's Act, which provided ". . . No person shall be allowed to testify: (a) When the other party to the transaction is dead . . ."[t] Thus if the action had been brought in Nevada, plaintiffs would probably have lost; if all the events had taken place in California, plaintiffs would certainly have lost. It is not clear, at least to Cavers, that this proves the decision is wrong. From the point of view of advocacy, however, it suggests that counsel for the estate did not work as hard as they should have.

(b) Professor Currie loved *Bernkrant v. Fowler*, which he said proved that his method was not equivalent to hometown justice. In a footnote at the end of an article on Justice Traynor, completed before *Bernkrant* was decided, he wrote:

> . . . so revolutionary an opinion cannot go unremarked. It is probably the only judicial opinion concerning the Statute of Frauds that does not so much as mention the substance procedure dichotomy. The analysis is explicitly in terms of governmental policies and interests . . . The restraint and moderation with which domestic interests are defined raise a standard to which the wise and honest can repair, and should be a reproach to those who feel that the method of governmental-interest analysis must necessarily produce egocentric or provincial results . . .[u]

(c) Professor Cavers also approved the decision in *Bernkrant*, but with some doubts. He makes an interesting point that we have not encountered previously. Currie, it seems, would have called the *Bernkrant* case a true conflicts case, which is why he is so pleased at the demonstration of the California court's broad-mindedness. Justice Traynor, however, finds that California has no interest in the transaction, and therefore concludes that he has a false conflict before him. Since the finding is not self-evident, Cavers points out, "the concept of the false conflict becomes for such a case the conclusion rather than the premise of the decision."[v]

---

[s] The other case referred to by Justice Traynor, *Rubin v. Irving Trust Co.*, 305 N.Y. 288, 113 N.E.2d 424 (1953), involved an oral promise made in Florida by the decedent to his brother not to change his will. Both brothers were domiciled in New York, which had a statute invalidating oral promises regarding wills; Florida had no comparable statute. The New York Court of Appeals applied New York law to render the promise ineffective.

[t] Nev. Rev. Stat. § 48.010 (1957), quoted in Cavers, *Oral Contracts to Provide by Will and the Choice-of-Law Process: Some Notes on Bernkrant*, in Perspectives of Law: Essays in Honor of Austin W. Scott, 38, 67, (1964) repr. in D. Cavers, *The Choice of Law, Selected Essays 1933–1983*, p. 91, 117 (1985).

[u] Currie, *Justice Traynor and the Conflict of Laws*, 13 Stan. L. Rev. 719, 778 (1961), repr. in D. Currie, *Selected Essays on the Conflict of Laws*, 629, 688 (1963).

[v] Cavers, *Some Notes on Bernkrant*, in Essays for A. W. Scott, note t, *supra*, at 65, Selected Essays at 115.

(6) The preceding questions have been critical both of *Lilienthal* and of *Bernkrant.* If both cases are wrongly decided, could you come up with a principle under which both cases would be decided correctly, assuming, for example, that they are brought before the same court, which seeks in the second case (whichever comes first) not to reverse the doctrine of the first case?

[B] The Most Significant Relationship

In *Babcock v. Jackson,* Judge Fuld spoke of the dissatisfaction with the mechanical formulae of the conflicts of law, and pointed to the decision of the Court of Appeals almost a decade earlier in *Auten v. Auten,* which had led the way in abandoning such rules, and searching for the "center of gravity."[w] In a sense, then, *Auten,* rather than *Kilberg* or *Babcock,* may be seen as the pathbreaking decision. No doubt it was *Auten* that gave support and impetus to the project for a *Restatement (Second) of Conflict of Laws,* which was just then getting started.[x] Drafts of the *Restatement,* in turn, are cited for support in *Babcock.*[y] Neither *Auten* nor its counterpart, *Haag v. Barnes,* is a typical contracts case. Consider, as you read these cases, whether the discussion can be transferred to more typical contracts controversies—over sales, loans, leases, employment contracts, and the like.

AUTEN v. AUTEN

New York Court of Appeals
308 N.Y. 155, 124 N.E.2d 99 (1954)

FULD, J.

In this action to recover installments allegedly due for support and maintenance under a separation agreement executed in this state in 1933, the wife's complaint has been dismissed, on motion for summary judgment, upon the ground that her institution of an action for separation in England constituted a repudiation and a rescission of the agreement under New York law. Determination of the appeal, involving as it does a question of conflict of laws, requires examination of the facts disclosed by the papers before us.

Married in England in 1917, Mr. and Mrs. Auten continued to live there with their two children until 1931. In that year, according to plaintiff, defendant deserted her, came to this country and, in the following year, obtained a Mexican divorce and proceeded to "marry" another woman. Unable to come to terms with the ocean between them, plaintiff made a trip to New York City to see and talk to defendant about adjustment of their differences. The outcome was the separation agreement of June, 1933, upon which the present action is predicated. It obligated the husband to pay to a trustee, for the "account of" the wife, who was to return to England, the sum of £50 a month for the support of herself and the children. In addition, the agreement provided that the parties were to continue to live separate and apart, that neither should sue "in any action relating to their separation" and that the wife should not "cause any complaint to be lodged against . . . [the husband], in any jurisdiction, by reason of the said alleged divorce or remarriage."

---

[w] *Babcock v. Jackson,* Chapter 3, at p. 146, *supra.*

[x] See Reese, *Chief Judge Fuld and Choice of Law,* 71 Colum. L. Rev. 548, (1971).

[y] See pp. 146–47, *supra.*

Immediately after the agreement was signed, plaintiff returned to England, where she has since lived with her children, and it is alleged by her—but disputed by defendant—that the latter is also domiciled in that country. Be that as it may, defendant failed to live up to his agreement, making but a few payments under it, with the result that plaintiff was left more or less destitute in England with the children. About a year after the agreement had been executed, in August of 1934, plaintiff filed a petition for separation in an English court, charging defendant with adultery. Defendant was served in New York with process in that suit on December 4, 1936, and, in July, 1938, an order was entered requiring defendant to pay alimony *pendente lite*. This English action—which, we are told, never proceeded to trial—was instituted upon advice of English counsel that it "was the only method" by which she "could collect money" from defendant; it was done, plaintiff expressly declares, to "enable" her "to enforce" the separation agreement, and not with any thought or intention of repudiating it.

The years passed, and in 1947, having realized nothing as a result of the English action and little by reason of the New York separation agreement, plaintiff brought the present suit to recover the sum of $26,564, which represents the amount allegedly due her, under the agreement, from January 1, 1935 to September 1, 1947.

In his answer, defendant admitted making the agreement, but, by way of a separate defense—one of several—claimed that plaintiff's institution of the separation suit in England operated as a repudiation of the agreement and effected a forfeiture of her right to any payments under it. . . .

Both of the courts below, concluding that New York law was to be applied, held that under such law plaintiff's commencement of the English action and the award of temporary alimony constituted a rescission and repudiation of the separation agreement, requiring dismissal of the complaint. Whether that is the law of this state, or whether something more must be shown to effect a repudiation of the agreement, need not detain us, since in our view it is the law of England, not that of New York, which is here controlling.

Choosing the law to be applied to a contractual transaction with elements in different jurisdictions is a matter not free from difficulty. The New York decisions evidence a number of different approaches to the question. . . .

Most of the cases rely upon the generally accepted rules that "All matters bearing upon the execution, the interpretation and the validity of contracts . . . are determined by the law of the place where the contract is made," while "All matters connected with its performance . . . are regulated by the law of the place where the contract, by its terms, is to be performed." . . . What constitutes a breach of the contract and what circumstances excuse a breach are considered matters of performance, governable, within this rule, by the law of the place of performance. . . .

Many cases appear to treat these rules as conclusive. Others consider controlling the intention of the parties and treat the general rules merely as presumptions or guideposts, to be considered along with all the other circumstances. . . . And still other decisions, including the most recent one in this court, have resorted to a method—first employed to rationalize the results achieved by the courts in decided cases . . .—which has come to be called the "center of gravity" or the "grouping of contacts" theory of the conflict of laws. Under this theory, the courts, instead of regarding as conclusive the parties' intention or the place of making or performance, lay emphasis rather upon the law of the place "which has the most significant contacts with the matter in dispute." (*Rubin v. Irving Trust Co.,* 305 N.Y. 288, 305. . . .)[z]

---

[z] See p. 245, note s, *supra.*

Although this "grouping of contacts" theory may, perhaps, afford less certainty and predictability than the rigid general rules, . . . the merit of its approach is that it gives to the place "having the most interest in the problem" paramount control over the legal issues arising out of a particular factual context, thus allowing the forum to apply the policy of the jurisdiction "most intimately concerned with the outcome of [the] particular litigation" (3 Utah L. Rev., pp. 498–499). Moreover, by stressing the significant contacts, it enables the court, not only to reflect the relative interests of the several jurisdictions involved (see *Vanston Committee v. Green,* 329 U. S. 156, 161–162), but also to give effect to the probable intention of the parties and consideration to "whether one rule or the other produces the best practical result." . . .

Turning to the case before us, examination of the respective contacts with New York and England compels the conclusion that it is English law which must be applied to determine the impact and effect to be given the wife's institution of the separation suit. It hardly needs stating that it is England which has all the truly significant contacts, while this state's sole nexus with the matter in dispute—entirely fortuitous, at that—is that it is the place where the agreement was made and where the trustee, to whom the moneys were in the first instance to be paid, had his office. The agreement effected a separation between British subjects, who had been married in England, had children there and lived there as a family for fourteen years. It involved a husband who, according to the papers before us, had willfully deserted and abandoned his wife and children in England and was in the United States, when the agreement was signed, merely on a temporary visa. And it concerned an English wife who came to this country at that time because it was the only way she could see her husband to discuss their differences. The sole purpose of her trip to New York was to get defendant to agree to the support of his family, and she returned to England immediately after the agreement was executed. While the moneys were to be paid through the medium of a New York trustee, such payments were "for account of" the wife and children, who, it was thoroughly understood, were to live in England. The agreement is instinct with that understanding; not only does it speak in terms of English currency in providing for payments to the wife, not only does it recite that the first payment be made to her "immediately before sailing for England," but it specifies that the husband may visit the children "if he should go to England."

In short, then, the agreement determined and fixed the marital responsibilities of an English husband and father and provided for the support and maintenance of the allegedly abandoned wife and children who were to remain in England. It merely substituted the arrangements arrived at by voluntary agreement of the parties for the duties and responsibilities of support that would otherwise attach by English law. There is no question that England has the greatest concern in prescribing and governing those obligations, and in securing to the wife and children essential support and maintenance. And the paramount interest of that country is not affected by the fact that the parties separate and provide for such support by a voluntary agreement. It is still England, as the jurisdiction of marital domicile and the place where the wife and children were to be, that has the greatest concern in defining and regulating the rights and duties existing under that agreement, and, specifically, in determining the circumstances that effect a termination or repudiation of the agreement.

Nor could the parties have expected or believed that any law other than England's would govern the effect of the wife's institution of a separation action. It is most unlikely that the wife could have intended to subject her rights under English law to the law of a jurisdiction several thousand miles distant, with which she had not the slightest familiarity. On the contrary, since it was known that she was returning to England to live, both parties necessarily realized that any action which she took, whether in accordance with the agreement or in violation of it, would have to occur in England. If any thought was given to the matter at all, it was that the law of the place where she and the children would be should determine the effect of acts performed by her.

It is, perhaps, not inappropriate to note that, even if we were not to place our emphasis on the law of the place with the most significant contacts, but were instead simply to apply the rule that matters of performance and breach are governed by the law of the place of performance, the same result would follow. Whether or not there was a repudiation, essentially a form of breach (see *Restatement, Contracts,* § 318; 4 *Corbin on Contracts* [1951], § 954, pp. 829–834), is also to be determined by the law of the place of performance (cf. *Wester v. Casein Co. of America,* 206 N. Y. 506; *Restatement, Conflict of Laws,* § 370, *Caveat*), and that place, so far as the wife's performance is concerned, is England. Whatever she had to do under the agreement—"live separate and apart from" her husband, "maintain, educate and support" the children and refrain from bringing "any action relating to [the] separation"—was to be done in England. True, the husband's payments were to be made to a New York trustee for forwarding to plaintiff in England, but that is of no consequence in this case. It might be, if the question before us involved the manner or effect of payment to the trustee, but that is not the problem; we are here concerned only with the effect of the wife's performance. . . .

Since, then, the law of England must be applied, and since, at the very least, an issue exists as to whether the courts of that country treat the commencement of a separation action as a repudiation of an earlier-made separation agreement, summary judgment should not have been granted.[2]

As to defendant's further contention that, in any event, plaintiff's commencement of the English action amounted to a material breach of her covenant not to sue, barring recovery upon the agreement, we need but say that this question, too, must be governed by English law, and for the same reasons already set forth.

The judgment of the Appellate Division and that of Special Term insofar as they dismiss the complaint should be reversed, with costs in all courts, and the matter remitted for further proceedings in accordance with this opinion.

HAAG v. BARNES

New York Court of Appeals
9 N.Y.2d 554, 216 N.Y.S.2d 65, 175 N.E.2d 441 (1961)

FULD, J.

This appeal is concerned with the effect in New York of an agreement made in another State for the support of a child born out of wedlock.

The complainant Dorothy Haag alleges that in 1947 she moved from Minnesota and took up residence in New York City and that since then she has been a resident of this State. The defendant

---

[2] In point of fact, the English lawyers, whose affidavits have been submitted by plaintiff, unequivocally opine that the institution of a separation suit and the award of alimony *pendente lite* did not, under the law of England, constitute a repudiation of the separation agreement or bar the present action to recover amounts due under it.

Norman Barnes, on the other hand, is now and was, during the period involved in this litigation, a resident of Illinois.

According to the statements contained in the complainant's affidavits, she met the defendant in the spring of 1954 in New York. She was a law secretary and had been hired by the defendant through an agency to do work for him while he was in New York on one of his business trips. The relationship between the man and the girl soon "ripened into friendship" and, on the basis of representations that he loved her and planned to divorce his wife and marry her, she was "importuned" into having sexual relations with him.

The complainant further alleges that she became pregnant as a result of having sexual relations with the defendant and that, upon being informed of this, he asked her to move to Illinois to be near him. She refused and, instead, went to live in California with her sister to await the birth of her child. Fearing that the defendant was losing interest in her, however, she returned to Chicago before the child was born and, upon attempting to communicate with the defendant, was referred to his attorney. The latter told Dorothy to choose a hospital in Chicago, which she did, and the baby was born there in December, 1955, the defendant paying the expenses.

Shortly after the birth of the child, her attempts to see the defendant in New York failed and she was advised by his attorney to return to Chicago in order that an agreement might be made for the support of her and her child. Returning to that city, she procured an attorney, recommended by a friend in New York, and signed an agreement on January 12, 1956. The agreement provides, in pertinent part, as follows:

    1. It recites payment to the complainant by the defendant of $2,000 between September, 1955 and January, 1956 and a willingness on his part to support her child in the future, on condition that such payments "shall not constitute an admission" that he is the child's father;

    2. The defendant promises to pay $50 a week and $75 a month, i.e., a total of $275 a month, "continuing while [the child] is alive and until she attains the age of sixteen years;"

    3. The complainant agrees "to properly support, maintain, educate, and care for [the child];"

    4. The complainant agrees to keep the child in Illinois for at least two years, except if she marries within that period;

    5. The complainant "remise[s], release[s] and forever discharge[s] NORMAN BARNES . . . from all manner of actions . . . which [she] now has against [him] or ever had or which she . . . hereafter can, shall or may have, for, upon or by reason of any matter, cause or thing whatsoever . . . including . . . the support of [the child];" and

    6. The parties agree that their agreement "shall in all respects be interpreted, construed and governed by the laws of the State of Illinois."

Shortly after the agreement was signed, the complainant received permission, pursuant to one of its provisions, to live in California where she remained for two years. She then returned to New York where she and her child have ever since been supported by the defendant in full compliance with the terms of his agreement. In fact, he has provided sums far in excess of his agreement; all told, we were informed on oral argument, the defendant has paid the complainant some $30,000.

The present proceeding was instituted in 1959 by the service of a complaint and the defendant was thereafter arrested pursuant to section 64 of the New York City Criminal Courts Act. A

§ 4.01 CHOICE OF LAW 251

motion, made by the defendant, to dismiss the proceeding was granted by the Court of Special Sessions and the resulting order was affirmed by the Appellate Division.

The ground urged for dismissal was that the parties had entered into an agreement providing for the support of the child which has been fully performed; that in this agreement the complainant relinquished the right to bring any action for the support of the child; and that, in any event, the action is precluded by the laws of the State of Illinois which, the parties expressly agreed, would govern their rights under the agreement. In opposition, the complainant contended that New York, not Illinois, law applies; that the agreement in question is not a sufficient basis for a motion to dismiss under either section 63 of the New York City Criminal Courts Act or section 121 of the Domestic Relations Law, since both of these provisions provide that "An agreement or compromise made by the mother . . . shall be binding only when the court shall have determined that adequate provision has been made;" and that, even were the Illinois law to apply, it does not bar the present proceeding.

The motion to dismiss was properly granted; the complainant may not upset a support agreement which is itself perfectly consistent with the public policy of this State, which was entered into in Illinois with the understanding that it would be governed by the laws of that State and which constitutes a bar to a suit for further support under Illinois law.

The complainant is correct in her position that, since the agreement was not court approved, it may not be held to be a bar to her suit under New York internal law. (See N. Y. City Crim. Cts. Act, § 63; Domestic Relations Law, § 121.) On the other hand, it is clear that the agreement is a bar under the internal law of Illinois since it provides, in the language of that State's statute, for a "sum not less than eight hundred dollars." (See Ill. Rev. Stat., former ch. 17, § 18, amd. by former ch. 17, § 52 [now ch. 106, § 65].) The simple question before us, therefore, is whether the law of New York or of Illinois applies.

The traditional view was that the law governing a contract is to be determined by the intention of the parties. . . . The more modern view is that "the courts, instead of regarding as conclusive the parties' intention or the place of making or performance, lay emphasis rather upon the law of the place 'which has the most significant contacts with the matter in dispute.' " (See *Auten v. Auten;* see, also, *Rubin v. Irving Trust Co.*) Whichever of these views one applies in this case, however, the answer is the same, namely, that Illinois law applies.

The agreement, in so many words, recites that it "shall in all respects be interpreted, construed and governed by the laws of the State of Illinois" and, since it was also drawn and signed by the complainant in Illinois, the traditional conflicts rule would, without doubt, treat these factors as conclusive and result in applying Illinois law. But, even if the parties' intention and the place of the making of the contract are not given decisive effect, they are nevertheless to be given heavy weight in determining which jurisdiction " 'has the most significant contacts with the matter in dispute.' " (*Auten v. Auten,* 308 N. Y. 155, 160, *supra.*) And, when these important factors are taken together with other of the "significant contacts" in the case, they likewise point to Illinois law. Among these other Illinois contacts are the following: (1) both parties are designated in the agreement as being "of Chicago, Illinois," and the defendant's place of business is and always has been in Illinois; (2) the child was born in Illinois; (3) the persons designated to act as agents for the principals (except for a third alternate) are Illinois residents, as are the attorneys for both parties who drew the agreement; and (4) all contributions for support always have been, and still are being, made from Chicago.

Contrasted with these Illinois contacts, the New York contacts are of far less weight and significance. Chief among these is the fact that child and mother presently live in New York and that part of the "liaison" took place in New York. When these contacts are measured against the parties' clearly expressed intention to have their agreement governed by Illinois law and the more numerous and more substantial Illinois contacts, it may not be gainsaid that the "center of gravity" of this agreement is Illinois and that, absent compelling public policy to the contrary, . . . Illinois law should apply.

As to the question of public policy, we would emphasize that the issue is *not* whether the New York statute reflects a different public policy from that of the Illinois statute, but rather whether enforcement of the particular agreement before us under Illinois law represents an affront to our public policy. (Cf. *Loucks v. Standard Oil Co.* [p. 34, *supra*]; *Mertz v. Mertz* [p. 58, *supra*]; *Restatement 2d, Conflict of Laws,* Tentative Draft No. 6, § 332a, comment g.) It is settled that the New York Paternity Law requires something more than the provision of "the bare necessities otherwise required to be supplied by the community," that, "although providing for indemnification of the community, [it] is chiefly concerned with the welfare of the child." (See *Schaschlo v. Taishoff,* 2 N.Y.2d 408, 411.) In our judgment, enforcement of the support agreement in this case under Illinois law and the refusal to allow its provisions to be reopened in the present proceeding does not do violence to this policy.

As matter of fact, the agreement before us clearly goes beyond "indemnification of the community" and the provision of "bare necessities." Whether we read it as a whole, or look only to the financial provisions concerned ($275 a month until the child reaches the age of 16), we must conclude that "the welfare of the child" is fully protected. (See *Rhyne v. Katleman,* 285 App. Div. 1140, *affg.* 206 Misc. 202 [$10,000 lump sum held sufficient].) The public policy of this State having been satisfied, there is no reason why we should not enforce the provisions of the parties' support agreement under Illinois law and treat the agreement as a bar to the present action for support.

The order of the Appellate Division should be *affirmed*.

NOTES AND QUESTIONS

(1)(a) The suggestion in Question (6), p. 246, *supra,* that both *Lilienthal* and *Bernkrant* (may) have been wrongly decided invites (though it does not compel) the thought that losing counsel may have been inadequate—not a surprising phenomenon at a time when counsel schooled in the past encounter courts anxious to break out from unsatisfactory traditions. Does the same thought come to mind in connection with *Auten*? With *Haag*?

(b) Consider *Auten* from the point of view of Mrs. Auten's lawyer, confronted with a decision of the lower court that his client loses because her attempt to vindicate her rights under the agreement between her and her husband resulted, under New York law, in forfeiture of those rights. Should counsel

    (i) challenge the interpretation of New York law; or

    (ii) propose that some other law be applied?

Can he do both? Would each argument help, or hurt, the other?[a]

---

[a] Note Judge Fuld, at p. 247, *supra,* saying we need not reach the question of interpreting New York law.

(c) Judge Fuld, at p. 247, *supra,* states the black letter law concerning contracts in two halves—one for validity, the other for performance. Which is involved in *Auten*?

(d) Judge Fuld goes on to reject these rules, in favor of "grouping of contacts," "center of gravity," "the place which has the most significant contacts with the matter in dispute," "the place having the most interest in the problem," etc. Are these all synonyms?

(e) Is the principle announced by Judge Fuld in *Auten*—for a unanimous Court of Appeals such as never occurred in the *Kilberg/Babcock/Neumeier* series—a neutral principle? Suppose research revealed that under English law a covenant not to sue would be upheld, and an action such as initiated by Mrs. Auten would result in abandonment of rights under the agreement. Do you think Judge Fuld would have strained to apply New York law, and construed that law to strike down covenants not to sue in the circumstances of this case?[b] Or is that an unfair question, proved unfair by the result in *Haag v. Barnes*?

(2)(a) If one counts contacts, in *Auten,* almost all the contacts were in New York, except for plaintiff's domicile; while the wife's obligation—to maintain, educate and support the children—may have been centered in England, the husband's obligation was to pay money to the wife, and payment was to be made in New York. Yet the wife prevailed. On the strength of *Auten,* should plaintiff have prevailed in *Haag* as well?

(b) Judge Fuld says, at p. 252, *supra,* that as contrasted with the Illinois contacts, the New York contacts were of far less weight and significance. Plaintiff says, well, yes, there were not so many *contacts* with New York, but what about New York's public policy? After all, we are talking about support for a child growing up in New York. Does Judge Fuld answer this point persuasively?

(c) Suppose that instead of performing—indeed over-performing—his obligation under the contract, Mr. Barnes had defaulted on his $275 per month commitment to Miss Haag and the child. Miss Haag brings her suit in New York, (i) for support under New York law; (ii) for arrearages under the Illinois contract. Barnes moves to strike the first count entirely because his obligation is defined by the law of Illinois. Should that motion be granted?

(d) Judge Fuld in *Haag v. Barnes* is faced with the contention that the Illinois contract should not be recognized because it is against the public policy of the forum. His reply, going back to Cardozo's famous statement in *Loucks,*[c] is that the contract, though different from a New York contract for these circumstances in that it was not submitted for approval to a court, is not contrary to the fundamental policy of New York. Indeed a New York court might well have approved the terms of the contract. Had the contract called for an $800 lump sum settlement, or for payments of $50 per month, one suspects, the result might be different.

(e) What about the choice of law clause in *Haag*? Judge Fuld mentions it, but it does not seem to be decisive. One feels the case would have come out just as it did without that clause. On the other hand, if Mr. Auten's counsel had included a choice of New York law provision in the contract between Mr. and Mrs. Auten, would that have tipped the scales in favor of applying New York law? Or would such a provision be just another factor (contact?) to be weighed with all the others? More on choice of law clauses in the next section.

---

[b] Note Judge Fuld's doubts on the New York internal law. The *Restatement* (*Second*) *of Contracts* approves, in § 285(2), of covenants not to sue, but does not address the question in the context of family law.

[c] Chapter 1, p. 37, *supra.*

(3) Consider whether the *Auten/Haag* analysis, which as we saw, was adapted to tort cases, can usefully be applied to other types of contract disputes. For example, in an age when the purchase and sale of businesses has become commonplace, a recurring claim is by "finders" who bring a buyer and seller together, and assert they are entitled to a commission. Some states—notably New York—amended their statutes of frauds to provide that an agreement to pay compensation for services rendered by an intermediary in negotiating a loan, or negotiating the purchase or sale of a business or a business opportunity, is not enforceable unless it (or a memorandum thereof) is in writing subscribed by the party to be charged.[d] Other states, including New Jersey and Massachusetts, did not see fit to amend their statutes of frauds to include such contracts. If the broker or finder was in one state, the client in another and the acquired business still elsewhere, where was the center of gravity of the arrangement between finder and client? Should it follow the principal transaction? Or the place of business of the finder? A comparison of two decisions involving the same New York statute, New York finders, and out-of-state clients, is instructive.

(a) In *Intercontinental Planning, Ltd. v. Daystrom, Inc.*, 24 N.Y.2d 372, 300 N.Y.S.2d 817, 248 N.E.2d 576 (1969), a New York finder introduced *D*, a New Jersey company, to *R*, a French company, and made a written arrangement that if *D* acquired *R*, the finder would receive a stated commission. It turned out, however, that *R* was acquired by *S*, and later *S* acquired *D*. The original finder claimed to be entitled to a commission, asserting that *D* had orally promised to extend the earlier arrangement to its negotiations with *S*.

The New York Court of Appeals, drawing on the mandate in *Auten* to apply the law of the jurisdiction most intimately concerned with the outcome of the litigation, applied New York law and upheld summary judgment for the defendants, *D* and *S*:

> It is clear that New York has the paramount interest in the application of its law when the contacts which New Jersey and this State have with the instant controversy are examined in relation to the policies and purposes to be vindicated by the conflicting laws.
>
> . . .
>
> [O]ne of the policies embraced by [the statute] is to protect the principals in the sale of a business interest from the type of claim being asserted here—a claim for a $2,780,000 finder's fee not supported by the written evidence.
>
> This policy would include foreign principals who utilize New York brokers or finders because of the nature of the brokerage business as it is conducted here. It is common knowledge that New York is a national and international center for the purchase and sale of business and interests therein. We conclude therefore that the Legislature . . . intended to protect not only its own interests, but also those who come to New York and take advantage of our position as an international clearing house and market place . . . .[e]

(b) In *Bushkin Associates, Inc. v. Raytheon Company*, 393 Mass. 622, 473 N.E.2d 662 (1985), a New York finder *B* had suggested to Raytheon, a Massachusetts-based company, that the widow of the founder of the Beech Aircraft Corporation might be willing, under certain conditions, to sell that company. According to *B*, he and officials of Raytheon subsequently agreed by telephone that if Raytheon acquired Beech, he would be paid a commission of 1 percent of the value of

---

[d] See, e.g., N.Y. Gen'l Obligations Law § 5–701 (a)(10), formerly Personal Property Law § 31 (10), adopted in 1949.

[e] 24 N.Y.2d at 382–84, 300 N.Y.S.2d at 826–27, 248 N.E.2d at 582–83.

§ 4.01　　　　　　　　　　　　　　　　　　　CHOICE OF LAW　　☐　255

the transaction. After some discussion, Raytheon notified *B* that it was not interested in acquiring Beech. All this took place in 1974–75.

Five years later, having used other intermediaries, Raytheon in fact acquired Beech for $800 million, paying nothing to *B*. *B* filed suit in federal court in Massachusetts. On appeal, the Circuit Court certified the question to the Supreme Judicial Court of Massachusetts for a ruling on the Massachusetts conflict of laws rule.

B, the New York finder, argued for application of Massachusetts law, pointing out that Raytheon had its principal place of business in Massachusetts, that its corporate officers who worked on the acquisition lived and worked in Massachusetts, and that his offer of a fee arrangement had been orally accepted in Massachusetts. Raytheon, the Massachusetts-based corporation, argued for New York law, pointing out that the finder was a New York corporation with its sole place of business in New York, that the proprietor of the corporation was a New Yorker, that he had initiated the contacts with Raytheon from New York, and that *B*'s services, if any, were performed in New York.

The Supreme Judicial Court said it would follow the *Second Restatement* and Leflar's choice-influencing considerations.[f]

> We do not view the process intended under § 188 [of the Restatement Second][g] for determining the State with the most significant relationship to the issue as simply adding up various contacts . . . In any event, the contacts analyzed by themselves (without regard to § 6 principles) lead us neither to Massachusetts nor to New York as the state with the more significant relationship to the transaction or the parties. No simple and objective test can provide an acceptable choice-of-law answer in this case, nor should it.
>
> [Moreover], [w]e find . . . that the "relative interests of New York and Massachusetts in the determination of the particular issue in this case" . . . point clearly to neither state . . .
>
> Where relevant contacts and considerations are balanced, or nearly so, we are inclined to resolve the choice by choosing that law "which would carry out and validate the transaction in accordance with intention, in preference to a law that would tend to defeat it" . . . In this case, the law that will validate the agreement, if indeed there was an agreement, is that of Massachusetts.[h]

(c) Clearly neither *Daystrom* nor *Bushkin* is a pure interest analysis, or significant relationship, or parties' expectations case, though all of these figure in the decisions. What they do demonstrate, as do the principal cases reproduced thus far in this chapter, is the room for advocacy, including theory, in resolving choice-of-law cases where the parties have not indicated a choice themselves. The following section takes up the consequences of choice of law expressed by the parties.

---

[f] Recall *Milkovich v. Saari,* Chapter 3, p. 194 and Question 5, p. 201–202, *supra.*

[g] Page 242, *supra.*

[h] 473 N.E.2d at 669–71.

§ 4.02 Party Autonomy and Conflict of Laws

[A] Express Choice of Law

May parties to a contract select the law applicable to their relationship? Professor Beale thought not,[a] and so, among others, did Learned Hand, essentially because the law gives effect to the acts of private parties, and not vice versa.[b] The first *Restatement of Conflict of Laws* contained no provision concerning choice of law by the parties.

In England, in contrast, it was understood at least since the end of the eighteenth century that the parties may expressly select the law by which their contract is to be governed, even, apparently, if that law had no connection with the parties. or the transaction.[c] This view was consistent with the cast of English law generally, governed predominantly by considerations of commerce, and less by considerations designed to effect social goals.[d]

The leading English (and therefore international commercial) case on choice of law by parties is *Vita Food Products, Inc. v. Unus Shipping Co. Ltd.*, [1939] A.C. 277 (P.C.). The case involved a contract to carry 1876 barrels of herring by ship from Newfoundland to New York on a Canadian-flag vessel. The ship ran aground in Nova Scotia due to the negligence of the captain. Eventually the herrings reached New York, but in a damaged condition, and the consignees sued the ship owner in Nova Scotia for damage to the herring and related expenses.

The bill of lading (i.e., the contract between the shipper or consignee and the carrier) contained a clause exempting the shipowner from liability for negligence in navigation, but under the law of Newfoundland (then an independent member of the British Commonwealth) the exemption clause would probably have been ineffective, because the proper notice (the "clause paramount") did not appear on the bill of lading. However, the bill of lading contained a clause providing that it was to be governed by English law, and that law would uphold the exemption from liability. The herring company brought suit in Nova Scotia, and when the courts of that province sustained the exemption clause, it appealed to the Judicial Committee of the Privy Council.[e]

---

[a] See J. H. Beale, *The Conflict of Laws,* Vol. II § 332.2, p. 1079–80 (1935).

[b] See, e.g., L. Hand, *J. & E. Gerli & Co. v. Cunard S.S. Co.,* 48 F.2d 115, 117 (2d Cir. 1931):

People cannot by agreement substitute the law of another place; they may of course incorporate any provisions they wish into these agreements—a statute like anything else—and when they do, courts will try to make sense out of the whole, so far as they can. But an agreement is not a contract, except as the law says it shall be, and to try to make it one is to pull on one's bootstraps. Some law must impose the obligation, and the parties have nothing whatever to do with that; no more than with whether their acts are torts or crimes.

[c] See G. C. Cheshire and P.M. North, *Private International Law,* 476–(12th ed. North and Fawcett 1992); *Dicey and Morris on The Conflict of Laws,* 1212-13 (12th ed. Collins 1993). The first case to establish the rule expressly was *Gienar v. Meyer,* (1796) 2 H. Bl. 603, 126 Eng. Rep. 728, remitting Dutch seamen to the courts of the Netherlands on a claim for their wages.

[d] Compare the reluctance of the British with respect to the European Convention on Jurisdiction and Judgments, p. 622, n. k, *infra*.

[e] The Judicial Committee of the Privy Council is the highest court of the British Commonwealth. It consists essentially of the judicial members of the House of Lords, in some instances augmented by a jurist from the jurisdiction where the case arose. Though technically the Privy Council is deciding the law applicable in the jurisdiction from which appeal is taken, in fact its decisions are accorded the same weight in the British legal system as decisions of the House of Lords. Appeals from Canadian courts to the Privy Council were ended in 1949, at the same time as the word "dominion" was dropped from governmental usage in Canada.

The herring company argued in the Privy Council that the choice of law clause should not be given effect because the contract to carry cargo between Newfoundland and New York on a Canadian flag ship had no connection with England. Lord Wright, writing for the Privy Council, rejected that argument:

> . . . In their Lordships' opinion the express words of the bill of lading must receive effect, with the result that the contract is governed by English law. It is now well settled that by English law (and the law of Nova Scotia is the same) the proper law of the contract "is the law which the parties intended to apply." That intention is objectively ascertained, and, if not expressed, will be presumed from the terms of the contract and the relevant surrounding circumstances. . . . [W]here the English rule that intention is the test applies, and where there is an express statement by the parties of their intention to select the law of the contract, it is difficult to see what qualifications are possible, provided the intention expressed is bona fide and legal, and provided there is no reason for avoiding the choice on the ground of public policy. In the present case, however, it might be said that the choice of English law is not valid. . . . It might be said that the transaction, which is one relating to the carriage on a Nova Scotian ship of goods from Newfoundland to New York between residents in these countries, contains nothing to connect it in any way with English law, and therefore that choice could not be seriously taken. Their Lordships reject this argument both on grounds of principle and on the facts. Connection with English law is not as a matter of principle essential. . . . In any case parties may reasonably desire that the familiar principles of English commercial law should apply. . . .[f]

In the civil law tradition, the choice of the parties was usually respected, but only if the law chosen had some internal connection with the parties or the transaction.[g] Whether "internal connection" included only the parties' domicile or nationality plus the place of contracting and the place of performance, or whether, as under English law, it would include also a reference contained in a standard commercial form to, say, the law of England, the law of New York, or the law applicable at the place of arbitration, was much debated. Typically German writers and courts were receptive to "party autonomy,"[h] French authorities less so, but gradually moving toward a common position in favor of limited party autonomy.[i] In Latin America, several countries followed the lead of Chile in providing that a contract to be performed in their country is subject to their law, regardless of where it was made or what it provides about the applicable law.[j]

---

[f] [1939] A.C. at 289-91.

[g] See E. Rabel, *The Conflict of Laws, A Comparative Study*, Vol. II, pp. 359–431 (2d ed. 1960); M. Wolff, *Private International Law*, pp. 417–21 (2d ed. 1950).

[h] For a discussion of German and other European authorities, see, e.g., C. Reithmann, *Internationales Vertragsrecht*, 2–17 (3d ed. 1980); F. Vischer, *Internationales Vertragsrecht*, 39–53 (1962); G. Kegel, *Internationales Privatrecht*, 483 (7th ed. 1995); *Int'l Encyclopedia of Comp. Law* Vol. III, Ch. 24, pp. 13–53 (1976).

[i] In 1927, J-P Niboyet, then the leading French scholar on conflict of laws, wrote "The law is no longer entitled to its name if it is subject to being excluded without restraint by those whom it must govern." Niboyet, *La Théorie de L'Autonomie de la Volonté*, 16 Recueil des Cours 1, 55, 57 (Hague Academy Int'l L. 1927). In his treatise, published two decades later, Niboyet accepted party autonomy, but warned of its excesses. Niboyet, *Traité de Droit International Privé*, Vol. V, pp. 51–60 (1948). Recent French writers are unreservedly in favor of party autonomy for contracts. See e.g., H. Batiffol and P. Lagarde, *Droit International Privé*, Vol. II, pp. 224–41; P. Mayer, *Droit International Privé* pp. 454-70 (5th ed. 1994); B. Audit, *Droit International Privé* pp. 136-48 (1991).

[j] See Chile, Codigo de Comercio, Art. 113, referring to Codigo Civil, Art. 16, Para 3.

The *Restatement (Second) of Conflict of Laws* accepts party autonomy in choice of law in contracts, on the ground that the "[p]rime objectives of contract law are to protect the justified expectations of the parties and to make it possible for them to foretell with accuracy what will be their rights and liabilities under the contract."[k] But the Restatement is significantly more restrictive than, for example, the formulation by Lord Wright in *Vita Food Products*:

§ 187. Law of the State Chosen by the Parties

(1) The law of the state chosen by the parties to govern their contractual rights and duties will be applied if the particular issue is one which the parties could have resolved by an explicit provision in their agreement directed to that issue.

(2) The law of the state chosen by the parties to govern their contractual rights and duties will be applied, even if the particular issue is one which the parties could not have resolved by an explicit provision in their agreement directed to that issue, unless either

   (a) the chosen state has no substantial relationship to the parties or the transaction and there is no other reasonable basis for the parties' choice, or

   (b) application of the law of the chosen state would be contrary to a fundamental policy of a state which has a materially greater interest than the chosen state in the determination of the particular issue and which, under the rule of § 188, would be the state of the applicable law in the absence of an effective choice of law by the parties.

(3) In the absence of a contrary indication of intention, the reference is to the local law of the state of the chosen law.

Note that § 187 of the *Restatement* distinguishes between two kinds of issues. Subsection (1) is addressed to the kinds of issues as to which the parties could have spelled out their relationship in the contract itself. Just as one might say "the words in this agreement shall have the meaning given to them by the *Oxford English Dictionary,* or better, by Pamphlet No. 350 of the International Chamber of Commerce,[l] so one might say (1) the agreement shall be interpreted according to the law of California, or Illinois, or France. The *Restatement* places no restrictions or qualifications on choice of law under this heading. Subsection (2) is addressed to the more problematical issues—as to capacity to contract, or to engage in a transaction that may be lawful in *A*, forbidden in *B*. Party autonomy is still permitted, but subject to two limitations—there must be a reasonable relationship between the parties or the transaction and the law chosen, and that law must not be contrary to a fundamental policy of a state which has a materially greater interest in the issue and whose law would be applied absent a choice of law by the parties (note not the policy of the forum). Consider, as you read the cases in this section, whether the *Restatement's* formulation is too liberal, too restrictive, or just about right.

---

[k] *Restatement (Second) of Conflict of Laws,* § 187, Comment *e*.

[l] This happens to be the brochure containing the so-called INCOTERMS, definitions of standard trade terms such as "c.i.f.," "f.o.b.," etc. (1980).

§ 4.02   CHOICE OF LAW □ 259

SIEGELMAN v. CUNARD WHITE STAR

United States Court of Appeals, Second Circuit
221 F.2d 189 (1955)

Before CLARK, CHIEF JUDGE, and FRANK and HARLAN, CIRCUIT JUDGES.

HARLAN, CIRCUIT JUDGE.

Plaintiff, in his own right and as administrator of his wife's estate, brings this action to recover for injuries suffered by his wife on the defendant's vessel, the R.M.S. Queen Elizabeth. The action was begun in a New York state court on December 14, 1951, and removed on diversity grounds to the federal district court for the Southern District of New York on January 3, 1952, the requisite jurisdictional amount being present.

On September 9, 1949, the Compass Travel Bureau, Inc., Cunard's New York agent, issued to Mr. and Mrs. Elias Siegel-man a document describing itself as a "Contract Ticket." It was a large sheet of light green paper, about 13 inches long and 11 inches wide. On the back were certain notices to passengers, relating to baggage, time of collection of ticket, location of the company's piers and offices, etc. On the front was printed in black Cunard's promise to provide specified transportation, in this case from New York to Cherbourg, subject to certain exceptions, and to 22 "terms and conditions," also printed in black. Printed in red in heavier type was a notice directing the attention of passengers to these "terms and conditions." Also printed in red, and in capital letters, was a statement that "it is mutually agreed that this contract ticket is issued by the Company and accepted by the passenger on the following terms and conditions." The paper also contained a space where the departure time, the names of the passengers and of the ship, and other data were typed in. The paper was stated to be non-transferable. In a space provided for the signature of the company, the name of the Compass Travel Bureau was typed. The paper was not signed by either of the passengers.

On September 24, 1949, when the Queen Elizabeth had been at sea four days, Mrs. Siegelman was injured. While she was seated in a dining room chair, she and the chair were overthrown. Her chair was alleged to be the only one in the dining room which was not bolted to the floor. Upon returning to New York, the Siegelmans retained an attorney to prosecute their claim against Cunard. On August 31, 1950, after Cunard's doctor had examined Mrs. Siegelman, Cunard offered $800, the approximate amount of medical expenses stated to have been incurred by the plaintiff and his wife, in settlement of the claim. This offer was made to the Siegelmans' lawyer over the telephone by Swaine, a claim agent of Cunard. Noticing that the ticket required suits for bodily injury to be brought within a year of the injury, and that the injury had occurred barely less than a year ago, the lawyer asked Swaine whether it would be necessary to begin suit in order to protect his clients' rights. Swaine is said to have stated that no suit was necessary, that the filing of an action would be futile in view of the prospect of early settlement, and that Cunard's offer would stand open.

Subsequently Mrs. Siegelman died. Then, on January 4, 1951, Cunard withdrew its offer, which had not yet been accepted, stating that it could not be tendered to any one other than the injured party.

On December 14, 1951, this suit was begun, claiming on behalf of the deceased damages for pain and medical expenses, and on behalf of her husband, damages for other medical expenses and for loss of consort. Cunard denied legal responsibility for the accident, and set up as a further defense the plaintiff's failure to bring the action within a year of the date the injury was suffered.

In January, 1953, the defendant moved to dismiss the action on the latter ground. Treating the motion as one for summary judgment, and having received affidavits from the attorneys and from the plaintiff, the court found the issues for the defendant, and dismissed the complaint.

On this appeal appellant asserts that Cunard is barred from using the period of limitation as a defense, because of Swaine's statement that suit was unnecessary. The provisions of the "Contract Ticket" relevant to the appeal are as follows:

> 10. . . . No suit, action or proceeding against the Company or the ship, or the Agents of either, shall be maintainable for loss of life of or bodily injury to any passenger unless . . .(b) . . . the suit, action or proceeding is commenced within one year from the day when the death or injury occurred.
>
> 11. The price of passage hereunder has been fixed partly with reference to the liability assumed by the Company as defined by this contract, and no agreement, alteration or amendment creating any other or different liability shall be valid unless made in writing and signed for the Company by its Chief Agent at the port of embarkation.
>
> 20. All questions arising on this contract ticket shall be decided according to English Law with reference to which this contract is made.

Before reaching the merits of the plaintiff's claim, we must deal with a number of preliminary questions: (1) Are federal or state choice-of-law rules to be applied here? (2) What is the applicable choice-of-law rule of the proper authority? (3) If the applicable choice-of-law rule points to the use of English law, what difference is made by the facts that English law was not pleaded or proved below, and that the plaintiff made no attempt to supply affidavits of experts on English law, after the trial Judge had offered him an opportunity to do so?

I.

[The court holds that because this claim is for a tort committed on the high seas, it is not subject to the rules stemming from *Erie R. Co. v. Tompkins*. Accordingly, the federal choice of law rule will be applied.]

II.

Our next question is: under the federal choice-of-law rule, what law governs the issues here? We are not concerned with the law applicable to the accident. Instead we must decide what law applies to the validity and interpretation of certain provisions of the "Contract Ticket," and to the effect of Swaine's conduct upon Cunard's right to resort to the one-year limitation period in the contract.

The ticket stipulated that "All questions arising on this contract ticket shall be decided according to English Law with reference to which this contract is made." Considering, as we do, the ticket to be a contract—see *Foster v. Cunard White Star,* 2 Cir., 1941, 121 F.2d 12—the provision that English law should govern must be taken to represent the intention of both parties. Therefore, this provision, if effective under the federal choice-of-law rule, renders English law applicable here, even though, absent the provision, some other law would govern under the applicable federal conflicts rule. . . .

[S]ince we cannot assume that the parties' choice of law will always foreclose the court from applying another law, our question is whether the contract provision here should have the effect, under federal conflicts rules, of making the English law applicable to the particular questions posed by this case. While this question may appear on the surface to be purely one of conflict of laws, we think it also involves interpretation of the contract.

[The court holds that the reference is to internal English law, not to what an English court might decide under its choice of law rules. Further, the choice of law clause covers validity as well as interpretation, and includes the question of what conduct may amount to waiver.]

We now come to the inquiry as to the extent to which this provision, so construed, is to be given effect in deciding the particular issues before us. Those issues are: (1) Is the one-year limitation period provided in the contract for the bringing of suits valid? (2) Does Swaine's conduct prevent Cunard from using the period as a defense? and (3) How is this matter affected by the clause requiring alterations of the contract to be in writing? It appears not to be contested that the ticket should be treated as a contract and that failure to bring the action within the contract limitation period would be a defense under English law—see *Jones v. Oceanic Steam Navigation Co.,* [1924] 2 K.B. 730, but since the same result would follow under American law—see 46 U.S.C.A. § 183(b); *Scheibel v. Agwilines, Inc.,* 2 Cir., 1946, 156 F.2d 636—we need not decide whether English law is applicable to the first of these issues. As to the second and third issues— where English and American law may differ—in the view which we take of the case, we need really only deal with applicability of English law to the second issue—*viz.,* whether Swaine's conduct prevents Cunard from using the one-year limitations provision as a defense—although in light of what we say below we think that English law would clearly control the third issue—*viz.,* the effect of the "alterations" clause.

As we have said, we construe the contract as establishing the intention of the parties that English law should govern both the interpretation and validity of its terms. And we think it clear that the federal conflicts rule will give effect to the parties' intention that English law is to be applied to the *interpretation* of the contract. Stipulating the governing law for this purpose is much like stipulating that words of the contract have the meanings given in a particular dictionary. See Cheatham, Goodrich, Griswold, & Reese, *Cases on Conflict of Laws* 461 (1951). On the other hand, there is much doubt that parties can stipulate the law by which the *validity* of their contract is to be judged. Beale, *Conflict of Laws* § 332.2 (1935). To permit parties to stipulate the law which should govern the validity of their agreement would afford them an artificial device for avoiding the policies of the state which would otherwise regulate the permissibility of their agreement. It may also be said that to give effect to the parties' stipulation would permit them to do a legislative act, for they rather than the governing law would be making their agreement into an enforceable obligation. And it may be further argued that since courts have not always been ready to give effect to the parties' stipulation, no real uniformity is achieved by following their wishes. See Beale, *op. cit. supra,* at page 1085.

Here, of course, the question is neither one of interpretation nor one of validity, but instead involves the circumstances under which parties may be said to have partially rescinded their agreements or to be barred from enforcing them. The question is, however, more closely akin to a question of validity. Nevertheless, we see no harm in letting the parties' intention control. Instead of viewing the parties as usurping the legislative function, it seems more realistic to regard them as relieving the courts of the problem of resolving a question of conflict of laws. Their course might be expected to reduce litigation, and is to be commended as much as good draftsmanship which relieves courts of problems of resolving ambiguities. To say that there may be no reduction in litigation because courts may not honor the provision is to reason backwards. A tendency toward certainty in commercial transactions should be encouraged by the courts. Furthermore, in England, where much of the litigation on these contracts might be expected to arise, the parties' stipulation would probably be respected. *Vita Food Products, Inc. v. Unus Shipping Co., Ltd.,* [1939] A.C. 277 (P.C.) (similar provision in bill of lading given effect; construed, however, as referring to England's whole law, including its conflicts rules).

Where the law of the parties' intention has been permitted to govern the validity of contracts, it has often been said (1) that the choice of law must be *bona fide,* and (2) that the law chosen must be that of a jurisdiction having some relation to the agreement, generally either the place of making or the place of performance. The second of these conditions is obviously satisfied here. The fact that a conflicts question is presented in the absence of a stipulation is some indication that the first condition is also satisfied. Furthermore, there does not appear to be an attempt here to evade American policy. We have no statute indicating a policy contrary to England's on this subject. And there is no suggestion that English law is oppressive to passengers. We regard the primary purpose of making English law govern here as being not to substitute English for American policies, but rather on the one hand, to achieve uniformity of result, which is often hailed as the chief objective of the conflict of laws, and on the other hand, to simplify administration of the contracts in question. Cunard's employees need be trained in only one set of legal rules.

This is not to suggest that English and American policies on this subject are identical. Any difference in law reflects some difference in policy. Consequently, to the extent English and American policies may differ on this question, we would consider that the parties may choose to have the English policies apply. But we express no opinion on what result would follow if we had stronger policies at stake, or if the parties had attempted a feigned rather than a genuine solution of the conflicts problem.

III.

We must next decide whether it is within our competence to apply English law, which was neither pleaded nor proved below.

. . .

[The court holds that it is, and that it is open to plaintiff to demonstrate, if he can, that English law is not as the district judge understood it.]

IV.

Finally we come to the substantive question whether Swaine's conduct prevents Cunard from successfully invoking the contractual limitation period as a defense.

Upon argument of the motion to dismiss the complaint as untimely, the plaintiff submitted affidavits opposing the motion. One of these was an affidavit of the lawyer retained by the Siegelmans to press their claim against Cunard. The lawyer described the circumstances of Cunard's offer of settlement:

> I had made a demand for $5,000 to settle these claims and Mr. Swaine advised me that he would have to take the matter up with his committee. Thereafter on August 31, 1950,

three weeks before the limitation on the commencement of action expired, Mr. Swaine countered with an offer of $800.00.

In that conversation Mr. Swaine told me that such offer was predicated to cover plaintiffs' special damages but from the tenor of the conversation, it appeared to me that such offer might be somewhat increased.

I told Mr. Swaine that I would communicate this offer to my clients and that I would thereafter call him to advise him of their wishes in the matter. However, I told him that it might take sometime for my clients to consider such offer in view of the fact that at this time my clients were living apart. Mr. Swaine replied that there was no rush on the offer because it would stand open on the file and that the defendant believed our special damages should be paid as a matter of good will.

Since the time to commence this action was going to expire three weeks later, on September 24, 1950, I told Mr. Swaine it appeared that I would have to commence my action in order to protect my clients' interests. Mr. Swaine answered that said suit was not necessary and that there was no point to commencing an action at this time since it appeared to both of us that there was an excellent chance of settling the matter.

On the basis of these assertions, which were uncontroverted, the plaintiff sought to establish either waiver of the limitation or that the defendants were estopped from relying upon it. The trial Judge appears to have held that the plaintiff was not entitled to assume that Swaine was authorized to waive the limitation, and held for the defendant.

At this state of the proceedings, though, we think that the Judge should have assumed that Swaine's acts bound the defendant. If Swaine had actually or impliedly been authorized to waive periods of limitation, and had done so, then the defendant could hardly rely on the contractual limitation. The scope of Swaine's authority was a fact which the plaintiff might have established on trial. It was material, and could not properly have been presumed to be undisputed. Therefore, this question should not have been resolved against the losing party on summary judgment.

If we assume, however, that Swaine was authorized to speak as he did, it does not follow that the plaintiff should prevail. For taking the facts as he has stated them, he has not established waiver or estoppel under English law.

It appears true that in England a promise, supported by consideration, not to plead the statute of limitations is a sufficient answer to a defense based on the statute. 20 *Halsbury's Laws of England, Limitation of Actions* § 803 (2d Ed. 1936). And if there were a promise here, the plaintiff's forbearance from suit within the limitations period might be good consideration. But it is not possible to treat the statements said to have been made by Swaine as a promise. The most reasonable interpretation of his remarks is that because of the excellent chances of settlement, filing suit would turn out to be wasted effort. Under this view of the matter, Swaine's statement cannot be regarded as even a statement that Cunard intended not to plead the limitations period as a defense in the event that efforts at settlement proved unfruitful. But even if his statements could be regarded as a statement of what Cunard's intention was at that time, and if it could be shown that Cunard's intention then was otherwise, still there would seem to be no right to recovery. For in *Yorkshire Insurance Co. v. Craine,* [1922] 2 A.C. 541 (P.C.), the Judicial Committee of the Privy Council stated that in order to raise an estoppel by representation, the authorities required a misrepresentation of *fact,* and a misrepresentation of intention would not suffice, in spite of the frequently-quoted statement that the state of a man's mind is as much a fact as the state of his digestion.

Furthermore, even if Swaine's conduct were held to suspend the running of the limitations period, we do not think that under English law, the running of the period would never resume. At the time of the statements in issue, about three weeks remained in the one-year period. After the withdrawal of Cunard's offer on January 4, 1951, it could no longer be thought that Cunard would not use the defense of untimeliness to any action thereafter brought. Even if the limitations period was tolled, therefore, while the offer was outstanding, this lawsuit should have been commenced within three weeks of the receipt of the January 4 letter. The situation is analogous to that obtaining in fraud cases, where the English rule is that the period of limitations is neither suspended altogether nor begins at the time the fraudulent acts were committed, but begins instead at the time fraud is discovered or could be discovered with reasonable diligence. § 26, Limitation Act, 1939, 2 & 3 Geo. 6, c. 21.

The plaintiff states that he was delayed for six months in obtaining letters of administration. But this delay apparently would not toll the statute of limitations under English law. 20 *Halsbury's Laws of England, Limitation of Actions* §§ 782, 821 (2d Ed. 1936, and Supp. 1953). Again, though, even if the running of the period were suspended, this lawsuit was begun too late, for letters of administration appear to have been granted on June 7, 1951, and this action was not commenced until December 14, 1951.

On this view of the case it is not necessary to decide the effect English law would give to the provision requiring all alterations to the contract to be in writing and over the signature of Cunard's chief agent at the port of embarkation.

Affirmed.

FRANK, CIRCUIT JUDGE (dissenting).

This case presents an important question relative to the rights of American passengers travelling from American ports on English vessels. Here a ticket, covering a voyage from New York to Cherbourg, was purchased by an American in New York. (As I think its very form and appearance important, I have attached a facsimile of the ticket as an Appendix to this opinion.) The injury to the passenger occurred on the high seas on September 24, 1949. This suit was brought on December 14, 1951. The statute of limitations had not then run. But the district court granted a summary judgment, dismissing the suit, on the ground that clause 10 of the passenger's ticket provided that no suit should be commenced except within one year. The plaintiff's undisputed affidavit showed that, in New York, on August 31, 1949, about three weeks before the year expired, defendant's claim agent, in connection with an offer of settlement made by him to the passenger, told the latter's lawyer that it would not be necessary to file suit within the year. On January 4, 1951, after the year had elapsed, defendant withdrew the settlement offer.

1. The first question is as to the legal effect of the claim agent's conduct as a waiver or estoppel with reference to the one-year period of limitations contained in clause 10. As the ticket was a contract made in New York, it may be that this question is to be solved by reference to New York "law."[2] On the other hand, as it was to be primarily performed on the high seas, it may be that "maritime law" governs. Since, however, there appear to be no decisions concerning "maritime law" on this subject, I think we may assume that pertinent federal decisions, dealing with cases of intra-mural waiver or estoppel, will tell us the "maritime law." (It is to be noted

---

[2] There is also the fact that the transportation began in New York. Cf. *Conklin v. Canadian-Colonial Airways, Inc.*, 266 N.Y. 244, 248–249, 194 N.E. 692.

that my colleagues, who apply "English law" do not cite English decisions relative to "maritime law.")

Disregarding for the moment clause 20 of the ticket (referring to "English law"), I think it clear that, under federal and New York decisions, the defendant waived (or is estopped to assert) the one-year provision (clause 10) and thereby completely abandoned it.

. . .

[The judge reviews several cases concerning claims against insurance companies, holding that once the insurance company is notified of the claim and begins negotiating, it may not enforce a contractual period of limitation shorter than that of the general state statute.]

In citing insurance-contract cases, I follow the lead of my colleagues who, in discussing "English law" concerning waiver, cite and rely on *Yorkshire Ins. Co. v. Craine* [1922] A.C. 541.

2. My colleagues, in holding that there was no waiver or estoppel, rely principally on that English decision and on clause 20 which reads: "All questions arising on this contract ticket shall be decided according to English Law with reference to which this contract is made."

I think this clause does not import "English law" concerning a waiver after the injury occurred. For, at best, as my colleagues apparently concede, the words "*on* this contract" are ambiguous, i. e., do not (to say the least) unambiguously cover the post-injury conduct, in New York, of defendant's claim agent.

Because the contract was made in New York, for a journey beginning in New York, the usual rule [3b] is that its provisions must be interpreted according to New York "law," or by the "maritime law" which, as previously noted, must (absent decisions on the subject) be learned from federal "law" as to internal transactions. What, then, of a provision, clause 20, which ambiguously refers to "English law?" Surely, in interpreting that ambiguous provision, we should not look to English decisions. Thus to consult "English law," in interpreting an American contract ambiguously referring to "English law," would indeed be a pulling-yourself-up-by-your-own-bootstraps device. Especially is this true here, since the interpretation of a clause in a contract like this involves an important internal public policy. For, since the document was a fixed printed form prepared by defendant and tendered to the passenger, clause 20, under New York and federal decisions, must be construed most strongly against defendant. . . .

This rule is given special emphasis when, as here, the contract contains a multitude of complicated provisions relative to a subject matter with which the tendering party is peculiarly familiar and the other party is not. There is an added fact, not here controlling but surely not to be ignored: The provisions of the ticket are printed in small type and in a crowded way. While they are not wholly illegible, they are difficult to read, as any one will discover who tries reading them. (One can be sure that the steamship company does not thus print its advertisements addressed to prospective passengers.)

3. Although I think the foregoing sufficient to render "English law" inapplicable to the issue before us, the following factors are also pertinent:

(a) The New York and federal courts, in holding that there is a waiver in circumstances like those here, rest their decisions on the ground that "it would be contrary to justice" (or the like) to rule otherwise. Accordingly, we have here an important public policy of the forum which,

---

[3b] Of course, dogmatism on the subject of conflict rules is out of place. No clearcut, certain and uniform rules exist. See further, *infra,* point 7 of this opinion and note 22.

I think, precludes the application of contrary English decisions. In short, I do not agree with my colleagues' statement that, if the English "law" concerning waiver is as they report it, it is not "oppressive to passengers."

(b) Consider a suit brought in this country on a contract made in England to be performed in England, and where a breach of the contract happened in England. Under the usual "conflict" rule, English "law" would be ordinarily decisive as to the interpretation of the contract. That "law" would not govern, I think, with reference to acts, in New York, asserted to be a discharge—by way of release, rescission, accord and satisfaction, or an account stated; see *Restatement of Conflict of Laws,* Section 373, Comments a and b. Accordingly, I think "American law" governs the legal effect, as a waiver, of the New York conduct of defendant after the injury occurred.

. . .

5. [The judge argues that Clause 11 of the ticket, stating that no waiver of liability shall be valid unless in writing signed by the Chief Agent, does not apply to Clause 10, the time limitation, because that is not a clause covering liability.]

Moreover, the federal and New York cases hold that, when such a contract provides that no change of liability shall be valid unless in writing and signed by a designated official, such a provision may be waived by acts, similar to those of the claim agent here, of agents of the obligor other than the official designated in the provision. . . .

6. I call attention to another factor which, while unnecessary to my conclusion, I think supports it: The ticket is what has been called a "contract of adhesion" or a "take-it-or-leave-it" contract. In such a standardized or mass-production agreement, with one-sided control of its terms, when the one party has no real bargaining power, the usual contract rules, based on the idea of "freedom of contract," cannot be applied rationally. For such a contract is "sold not bought." The one party dictates its provisions; the other has no more choice in fixing those terms than he has about the weather. The insurance policy cases are outstanding examples, but there are many others. Our courts, in particular contexts, have, in effect, nullified many provisions of such agreements, if unfair to the weaker party who must take-or-leave. Often our courts have done so by rather strained constructions of seemingly unambiguous language or by other indirect or "back-door" methods. Referring to such decisions, several brilliant commentators have suggested that the courts forthrightly adopt a general doctrine which calls for refusal to enforce directly—i. e., without recourse to such indirect devices—highly unfair provisions of all so-called "contracts of adhesion" where there was no possibility of real bargaining. These writers urge that some decisions, in cases where this point of view was not presented to, or considered by, the courts should not now be deemed controlling. Their position is that of Holmes and Corbin, i. e., that the courts will do justice better by forth-rightly, not obliquely, articulating important doctrines of public policy. The commentators on "adhesion" contracts do not at all suggest that all standardized contracts be stricken down, for they recognize that such contracts often serve a highly useful purpose where the parties are not markedly unequal in bargaining power (as in many "commercial" contracts). . . .

An ordinary contract has been called a sort of private statute, mutually made by the parties and governing their relations. But in a take-it-or-leave-it contract, absent actual freedom to contract, the parties do not "legislate" by mutual agreement; the dominant party "legislates" for both. Salleilles, who in France in 1901, coined the phrase "contract of adhesion," used it to describe contracts "in which one predominant unilateral will dictates its law to an undetermined multiple rather than to an individual, . . .as in all contracts which, as the Romans said, resemble a law more than the meeting of the minds."

All this has special pertinence here: A party, like the passenger here, having no real choice about the matter, cannot in fairness be said to have joined in a "choice of law" merely because the carrier has inserted a provision that some particular foreign "law" shall govern; therefore it would seem that that party should not be bound by such a provision. I shall not elaborate this point, since it is amply discussed in a recent excellent article, Ehrenzweig, *Adhesion Contracts in The Conflict of Laws,* 53 Col.L.Rev. (1953) 1072, where most of the authorities are cited and considered.

7. I grant that, in this context, I am stressing the need to do justice in particular instances. I do so unashamedly. For it is generally agreed that the decisions of conflict-of-laws cases by mechanized rules, without regard to particularized justice, cannot be defended on the ground that they have promoted certainty and uniformity, since such results have not been thus achieved.[22] Several wise commentators have urged that the element of justice should have a dominating influence.[23]

8. Finally, I am by no means sure that, even if English intramural "law" applied to the waiver, the result would be that which my colleagues report.

My colleagues take, as an analogy, the English cases on the tolling or suspension of statutes of limitation. They cite no English cases using that analogy. The American cases, cited and discussed in point 1 of this opinion, have expressly rejected that analogy in situations involving a waiver, through settlement negotiations, of a contractual, as distinguished from a statutory, time limitation; they hold that the waiver operates to eliminate, not merely to suspend, the contractual provision. Absent English decisions, contra, I think we should assume that the English courts will so hold.

Appendix.

The following is a facsimile of the ticket:

---

[22] See, e. g., Cavers, *A Critique of The Choice of Law [Problem],* 47 Harv.L.Rev. (1933) 173, 177; Rheinstein, *Book Review,* 28 Ind.L.Rev. (1953) 443; Rheinstein, *Conflict of Laws in the Uniform Commercial Code,* 16 L. & Contemp. Problems (1951) 114; cf. Goodrich, *Directive or Dialectic,* 6 Vand.L.Rev. (1953) 442; Goodrich, *Yielding Place to New: Rest and Motion in The Conflict of Laws,* 50 Col.L.Rev. (1950) 881.

[23] See, e. g., Cavers, *A Critique of The Choice of Law [Problem],* 47 Harv.L.Rev. (1933) 173, 178, 186 et seq.; Kronstein, *Crisis of Conflict of Laws,* 37 Georgetown L.Rev. (1949) 483, 484; Morris, *The Proper Law of A Tort,* 64 Harv.L.Rev. (1951) 881; *Shaw, Savill, Albion & Co. v. The Fredericksburg,* 2 Cir., 189 F.2d 952, 956; cf. Green, *Judge and Jury* (1930), 76–77, 97, 151.

Cunard White Star Ltd
EXAMINED
Cabin Class

CUNARD WHITE STAR LIMITED

NOTICE TO PASSENGERS

Passengers must identify and claim their baggage from the Baggage Master on the pier before it will be put on board the ship. Baggage required during the voyage must be distinctly labeled to this effect before embarking.

This ticket will be collected immediately after sailing.

The Purser will collect the difference on any children not specified in the ticket or where misrepresentation has been made as to age.

Passengers should arrange to be at the Pier at least two hours before time appointed for sailing in order to have sufficient time to check their baggage, have their tickets examined, etc. Unless this is done passage will not be guaranteed as the ships sail promptly at the appointed time.

LOCATION OF COMPANY'S PIERS

NEW YORK	Piers 54-56, North River, foot of West 14th Street and Pier 90, North River, foot of West 50th Street
BOSTON	Cunard White Star Pier, East Boston
SAINT JOHN	
HALIFAX	Piers 20, 21, 22, Southern Terminals
MONTREAL	Sheds 2, 3 and 5, Foot of St. Francois Xavier Street
QUEBEC	Pier No. 29
	Ships dock in West Saint John

U. S. OFFICES

NEW YORK, N. Y. (Main Office)	Cunard Building, 25 Broadway or 441 Park Ave. corner 56th St.
BALTIMORE, MD.	1015 American Building
BOSTON, MASS.	393 Boylston Street
CHICAGO, ILL.	41 So. La Salle Street
CLEVELAND, OHIO	1414 Euclid Avenue
DETROIT 26, MICH.	512 Book Building
LOS ANGELES, CAL.	606 South Hill Street
MINNEAPOLIS, MINN.	Suite 2220, Foshay Tower
PHILADELPHIA, PA.	1616 Walnut Street
PITTSBURGH, PA.	444 Oliver Avenue
PORTLAND, ME.	112 High Street
ST. LOUIS, MO.	311 North 11th Street
SAN FRANCISCO, CAL.	210 Post Street
SEATTLE, WASH.	Exchange Building
WASHINGTON, D. C.	1304 K Street, N. W.

CANADIAN OFFICES
OF CUNARD DONALDSON, LTD.

HALIFAX, N. S.	Granville and George Streets
MONTREAL, QUE.	230 Hospital Street, P. O. Box 2550
QUEBEC, QUE.	67 St. Peter's Street
ST. JOHN, N. B.	162 Prince William Street
TORONTO, ONT.	Bay and Wellington Streets
VANCOUVER, B. C.	626 W. Pender Street
WINNIPEG, MAN.	224 Portage Avenue

PISACANE v. ITALIA SOCIETA PER AZIONI DI NAVIGAZIONE

United States District Court, Southern District of New York
219 F. Supp. 424 (1963)

FREDERICK VAN PELT BRYAN, District Judge.

Plaintiff Pisacane sues for personal injuries sustained while a passenger aboard defendant's vessel M/V Vulcania on the high seas. Defendant Italian Line moves for summary judgment under Rule 56, F.R.Civ.P., upon the ground that the action is time-barred by a passage ticket contract between the parties which bars institution of suit more than one year after the happening of an injury.

Plaintiff is an American citizen residing in Florida and defendant is an Italian corporation. Jurisdiction is based on diversity of citizenship.

Plaintiff was injured on September 28, 1958, while the Vulcania, an Italian flag vessel was en route from Naples, Italy, to New York. He had apparently purchased a round trip ticket on May 9, 1958 from a travel agency in New York which he exchanged in Genoa, Italy, on July 25, 1958, for the passage ticket under which he was traveling at the time of the accident. The Vulcania sailed from Naples on September 20, 1958 and arrived in New York some time thereafter. Suit was instituted on October 27, 1959, some thirteen months after the injury.

The condition of the passage ticket upon which defendant relies provided that,

> No action or proceeding against the company for death or injury of any kind to the passenger shall be instituted unless . . . the action or suit arising therefrom is commenced within one year from the date when the death or injury occurred.

This was one of thirty-five conditions incorporated by reference into the passage ticket by an italicized proviso on its face, reading "This passage ticket is subject to the terms and conditions printed on coupons B) and C) and on the inside of the ticket cover." The conditions were printed on the coupons in Italian and on the ticket cover in English and plaintiff reads both languages.

The law governing the contract relationship of the parties rather than that which governs the accident itself determines the validity and effect of the contractual time-bar provision.

The complaint in this diversity action states a claim sounding in maritime tort. It is clear therefore that federal maritime choice of law rules must be used to determine the applicable law. *Siegelman v. Cunard White Star, Ltd.*

If such choice of law rules required that American law be applied to the contract, the contract would be valid, the statute of limitations binding, and plaintiff would be barred by the contract from suing after the limitation of one year had expired. But under federal choice of law rules American law does not govern this contract.

Condition thirty-five of the passage ticket provided that it was to be "subject to the Italian Law." While such a provision is not conclusive for choice of law purposes, where, as here, the contract was made in the forum specified, the voyage commenced there, and the vessel sailed under the flag of the forum, the center of gravity of the contract lies there and the law of that country should be applied to the contract. See *Siegelman v. Cunard White Star, Ltd.* . . . Italian law therefore governs the contractual relationship of the parties here.

To establish the applicable Italian law, defendant has submitted an affidavit by an expert on that subject. The affidavit states that "the passage ticket is adequate evidence" of the existence of a contract of transportation and its terms under Article 396 of the Italian Code of Navigation. Speaking next to the validity of the contractual period of limitations, it states that Article 418 of the Code of Navigation is applicable, providing,

> The rights arising under contacts of transportation of persons . . . are barred by the statute of limitations [one year] after the arrival of the passenger at his destination. . . .

Finally, Article 2936 of the Italian Civil Code is stated to be relevant, as well. It provides that,

> Any agreement conceived for the purpose of changing the terms of the law with regard to the statute of limitations is null and void.

The affidavit of defendant's expert is based on a hypothetical state of facts different in material respects from the facts in the case at bar. But disregarding this and assuming that Article 418 is applicable to a case where plaintiff asserts rights under general maritime law rather than under the contract of transportation itself, the affidavit poses a problem which requires denial of defendant's motion. Under Italian law, as it is stated in the affidavit, it is at least a question as to whether Article 2936 does not render void the contractual limitation of one year *from the date of the injury* upon the ground that it was "conceived for the purpose of changing the terms of the law" since the limitation period provided by Article 418 is one year *from the date of arrival at destination.*

Since the statutory and contractual limitation periods are different on their faces, it would appear that the contract provision is, in fact, void under Italian law and I would be compelled so to hold on the record before me were I required to do so in order to dispose of this motion. However, since the question is one of fact, and the presence of such a question requires denial of defendant's motion under Rule 56, it is unnecessary and perhaps unwise to do more on the basis of a single affidavit at this point in the litigation.

It may be noted, moreover, that if the contractual limitation in the passage ticket is in fact void, it is not unlikely that defendant will be unable to avail himself of the statutory limitation provided by Article 418 of the Italian Code of Navigation in its stead. See *Bournias v. Atlantic Maritime Co., Ltd.* [§ 2.03 *supra*]. However, because this question involves different factors it plainly should not be resolved on the papers now before me.

Defendant's motion is denied.

SOUTHERN INTERNATIONAL SALES v. POTTER & BRUMFIELD DIV.

United States District Court, Southern District of New York
410 F. Supp. 1339 (1976)

Edward Weinfeld, District Judge.

This motion for summary judgment requires the court to pass upon the binding effect of a stipulation of the parties as to the law governing the interpretation of their contract.

Defendant Potter & Brumfield is an Indiana-based manufacturer of electrical products. Plaintiff Southern International is a Puerto Rican corporation. By agreement dated April 2, 1969, plaintiff became defendant's exclusive sales representative for Puerto Rico and adjacent United States islands. The agreement provided, among other things, that either party could terminate it "for any reason whatsoever" upon thirty days' notice, and that it "shall be interpreted in accordance with the laws of the State of Indiana." On December 21, 1971, Potter & Brumfield notified Southern International that the contract would be terminated as of February 20, 1972. Southern claims that it had performed "outstandingly" and that the termination was motivated by defendant's purpose to capitalize on the contacts Southern had developed by dealing directly with them.

In September 1972, Southern brought this diversity action, claiming that the termination violated the Puerto Rican Dealers' Contracts Act, which provides in pertinent part:

> Notwithstanding the existence in a dealer's contract of a clause reserving to the parties the unilateral right to terminate the existing relationship, no principal or grantor may directly or indirectly perform any act detrimental to the established relationship or refuse to renew said contract on its normal expiration, except for just cause.

Defendant does not dispute that its agreement with plaintiff was a "dealer's contract" as defined in the Act. Although it contends it did have "just cause" for the cancellation, its position on this motion for summary judgment is that the Dealers' Contracts Act does not apply because the parties agreed that Indiana law would govern their contract's interpretation, and Indiana would give effect to the clause allowing unilateral termination. Plaintiff argues that, upon all the circumstances surrounding the execution and performance of the contract, Puerto Rican law applies despite the provision that Indiana law governs its interpretation. The court agrees with plaintiff and denies the motion for summary judgment.

Since this is a diversity case, New York state choice of law principles apply on the issue of whether the law of Indiana or Puerto Rico governs.[2] There are, as defendant notes, a number of New York cases that hold the parties' choice of law to control where their contract has a reasonable relation to the jurisdiction whose law they choose. It cannot seriously be challenged that the contract at issue bore a reasonable relation to Indiana. Defendant has its headquarters and facilities there, and it shipped, processed, and did the paperwork in Indiana on Southern's orders for merchandise. But this begins rather than ends inquiry. There is also authority from the New York Court of Appeals suggesting that the parties' intention and stipulation as to the law governing their contract is but one factor, albeit a weighty one, in deciding the ultimate question—namely, which jurisdiction has the most significant contacts with the matter at issue.[4] Under this analysis the significance of the parties' choice of Indiana law would pale when viewed against the facts that almost all of the equipment sold by Southern on defendant's behalf was sold in Puerto Rico, for Puerto Rican accounts and for use in Puerto Rico; the solicitation of customers occurred in Puerto Rico; and plaintiff signed the contract there. More to the point, the application of Indiana law would frustrate the fundamental policy expressed in the Puerto Rican Dealers' Contracts Act. According to the Statement of Motives that accompanied the Act:

> The Commonwealth of Puerto Rico can not remain indifferent to the growing number of cases in which domestic and foreign enterprises, without just cause, eliminate their dealers, or without fully eliminating them, such enterprises gradually reduce and impair the extent of their previously established relationships, as soon as these dealers, concessionaires or agents have created a favorable market and without taking into account their legitimate interests.

---

[2] *Klaxon Co. v. Stentor Elec. Mfg. Co.* [§ 6.02, *infra*].

[4] *Haag v. Barnes* [p. 249, *supra*].

The Legislative Assembly of Puerto Rico declares that the reasonable stability in the dealer's relationship in Puerto Rico is vital to the general economy of the country, to the public interest and to the general welfare, and in the exercise of its police power, it deems it necessary to regulate, insofar as pertinent, the field of said relationship, so as to avoid the abuse caused by certain practices.

This strong legislative policy could easily be circumvented were the court to announce a rule that would allow a manufacturer, by wielding its economic might against a distributor, to exact a stipulation as to governing law compelling the distributor to forsake the protection afforded him by the Puerto Rican legislature. The facts presented here fit squarely within the rule of section 187 of the *Second Restatement of Conflict of Laws*. . . .

Section 188 of the *Second Restatement* applies in the absence of an effective choice of law by the parties, and calls for the application of the law of the state that "has the most significant relationship to the transaction and the parties" in light of the policy factors that shape choice of law.

Whether one applies the "most significant relation" test expressed in section 188 and in *Auten v. Auten* or the more recent "governmental interest" analysis of *Intercontinental Planning, Ltd. v. Daystrom, Inc.*,[7] Puerto Rican law would plainly govern the validity of the contract in the absence of the parties' stipulation. As noted above, plaintiff is a Puerto Rican company and the contract's essential purpose was to create a means by which defendant could distribute its products to the Puerto Rican market. Puerto Rico's contacts with the parties and the transaction, and its substantial interest in seeing that its local distributors are not exploited by foreign manufacturers, far outweigh the contacts with Indiana or Indiana's interest, if any, in the validity of the unilateral termination clause of the contract at issue.

Under the circumstances, the general rule giving effect to the parties' choice of law must bow to the exception stated in section 187 of the *Second Restatement*. While the New York courts have yet to rule on the exact issue here presented, there is every reason to believe that they would follow the *Restatement* approach. It has found support in other courts, and in a case decided in this district and applying New York law. Moreover, the New York courts have cited section 187 of the *Second Restatement* with approval. . . .

While the failure to enforce the parties' choice of law does invalidate their contract to some extent, "[f]ulfillment of the parties' expectations is not the only value in contract law; regard must also be had for state interests and for state regulation. The chosen law should not be applied without regard for the interests of the state which would be the state of the applicable law with respect to the particular issue involved in the absence of an effective choice by the parties."[12]

Since Puerto Rican law governs this controversy, the factual question whether Potter & Brumfield had "just cause" as defined in the Dealers' Contracts Act for the termination of its contract with Southern presents an issue of fact which is in dispute. Thus, defendant's motion for summary judgment is *denied*.

NOTES AND QUESTIONS

(1)(a) Are you troubled by the argument of Beale, L. Hand, Niboyet, and others, that party autonomy in choice of law is a legislative act not performed by legislators? Has commercial expediency overwhelmed political theory?

---

[7] [See Question (3)(a), p. 254, *supra*.]

[12] *Second Restatement of Conflict of Laws*, § 187, Comment g.

(b) In a comment to § 187, the *Restatement* (*Second*) replies:

This view is now obsolete and, in any event, falls wide of the mark. The forum in each case selects the applicable law by application of its own choice of law rules. There is nothing to prevent the forum from employing a choice of law rule which provides that, subject to stated exceptions, the law chosen by the parties shall be applied to determine the validity of a contract and the rights created thereby. The law of the state chosen by the parties is applied, not because the parties themselves are legislators, but simply because this is the result demanded by the choice of law rule of the forum.[a]

End of question?

(c) What if the law chosen by the parties would invalidate a transaction but, say, it would be valid under the law of the forum?[b]

(d) Look again at § 1–105 of the Uniform Commercial Code.[c] Is its effect the same as that of § 187 of the *Restatement*?

(e) Is § 187 in effect a principle of preference in favor of validation of contracts? Against regulation?

(f) The general view is that party autonomy works to avoid regulation of a private law character,—statutes of limitation, registration, formalities, and the like—but not of a public law character. One could not, for example, avoid a prohibition on abortion by a choice of law contract, or, say, an embargo on trade with Cuba.[d] Looking at the cases in this section, does any of them meet the definition suggested by this distinction?

(2) Though choice of law clauses are very common, particularly in commercial contracts, not many reported cases discuss the problems raised by such clauses. *Siegelman* is in some ways a disappointing case, because one cannot escape the impression that it is not really a contract case at all, a ticket on a steamship being a contract only in a technical sense, not in the sense of reflecting a bargain made between parties after negotiation. Also, the controversy is not really about performance or breach of a contract, but about how the contract affects some inept behavior (not to say malpractice) in connection with a tort claim. Still, *Siegelman* is a "leading case," the judges are among the most eminent in the nation's history, and the debate between Judge (later Justice) Harlan and Judge (formerly Professor) Frank is instructive.

(a) For Judge Harlan the road is straight. Plaintiff has a cause of action that would be valid under New York law, but is barred by clause 10 of the ticket, a one-year limitation. That clause would be upheld under English law, and that law is chosen by Clause 20. Any suggestion of waiver is negated by Clause 11, which would also be upheld by English law. But . . .

> we express no opinion on what result would follow if we had stronger policies at stake.

What kind of policies might be strong enough? For example, a contractual limitation on wrongful death recovery, linked to choice of English law? . . . A two-month period within which to bring suit?

---

[a] *Restatement* (*Second*) *of Conflict of Laws,* § 187, Comment e.

[b] The *Restatement,* in the same Comment, says in that case the choice will be regarded as a mistake, and the rule of § 188 will be applied either to validate or invalidate the transaction.

[c] Documents Supplement, p. 55.

[d] See, in this connection, *Regazzoni v. K.C. Sethia* (*1944*) *Ltd.,* Chapter 10, p. 899, *infra.*

(b) Judge Harlan distinguishes (at p. 261, *supra*) between interpretation of a contract and validity of the contract. The case before him is not quite either one, but he says it is closer to validity, which makes it harder to sustain choice of law by the parties. Is this the same distinction, using different words, made between Subsections (1) and (2) of § 187 of the *Restatement?*

(c) Judge Frank says (at p. 265, *supra*) that the majority is pulling itself up by its bootstraps, in interpreting the phrase "arising on this contract" in Clause 20 to include the issue of waiver. "Surely," he says, "we should not look to English decisions [on that point.]" Is he right? How should Judge Harlan reply?

(d) What about Judge Frank's argument that the ticket is a contract of adhesion? He would not say that therefore the ticket is not valid; is he arguing that choice of law clauses on all such contracts should be disregarded? Construed against the drafters?

(e) Writing nearly a decade before the "conflicts revolution," Judge Frank concludes, "unashamedly," as he says, by stressing the need to do justice in particular instances.[e] Does this strengthen or weaken his argument?

(f) The *Pisacane* case presents an ironic echo to *Siegelman*. Here the carrier says the contractual period of limitations is valid, and the passenger seeks to invoke the choice of law clause to strike down the time-bar. Italian law also has a one-year statute of limitations, but it runs from the arrival of the passenger at his destination, not from the date of injury. Although suit here was commenced more than a year after the ship arrived (assuming 10–12 days maximum for the voyage from Naples to New York), the court holds for plaintiff. The contractual period of limitation is invalidated by the Italian Civil Code, and the period of limitation in the Code of Navigation falls under the famous "specificity rule" of *Bournias*.[f] Does this make sense? Why isn't the choice of law clause applied so as to make the Italian Code of Navigation applicable?

(3)(a) Very few American cases invalidate choice of law clauses among merchants. Judge Weinfeld, sitting in *Southern International Sales* as a disinterested forum expressly applies § 187 of the *Restatement*. He has no trouble with Subsection (2)(a); clearly the law of the seller's principal place of business has a "substantial relationship" to the transaction.[g] But why does he get to Subsection (2) at all? Why isn't the problem governed by Subsection (1)?

(b) In order to apply Subsection (2), the court has to determine that, absent the choice of law clause, the law of Puerto Rico would be applicable, and Judge Weinfeld makes that determination. Is it right?

(c) Does the Puerto Rico Dealers' Contracts Act, then, (i) express a *fundamental* policy of Puerto Rico, as Judge Weinfeld sees it? (ii) Does Puerto Rico have a *materially greater interest* than Indiana in determination of the controversy?

(d) Is *Southern International Sales* consistent, or inconsistent, with *Siegelman?*

(4)(a) Shortly after entry into effect of the Brussels Convention on Jurisdiction and the Enforcement of Judgments discussed in Chapters 7 and 8,[h] the European Economic Community appointed a group of experts to consider a proposal for one or more conventions among the

---

[e] Recall Griswold, J. in *Adams v. Knickerbocker I* at p. 106.

[f] See Chapter 2, § 2.03, *supra*.

[g] Note, incidentally, that the Uniform Commercial Code, § 1–105, Documents Supplement, p. 55, uses the term "reasonable relation."

[h] See Chapter 7, § 7.06, and Chapter 8, § 8.03[A], *infra*.

members of the Community concerning private international law. Their first draft proposed a convention applicable to contractual and non-contractual obligations (i.e. including torts).[i] The final draft of 1980, which became known as the Rome Convention, was limited to the Law Applicable to Contractual Obligations. Unlike the Brussels Convention, which is mandatory for all members of the European Common Market,[j] the Rome Convention is not mandatory, but by the early 1990's it had entered into effect in nearly all member states of the expanding European Union, either by legislative enactment or ratification, or as a guide applied by the courts of those states.[k] It is instructive to compare the Convention with modern thinking in the United States.

(b) The Rome Convention[l] firmly adopts party autonomy (Article 3(1)), without any requirement, such as in § 187 of the *Restatement,* that the issue in question be one that the parties could have resolved by an explicit provision or that the state whose law is chosen have a relationship with the parties or the transaction. But the commitment to freedom of choice, as the Convention calls it, is far from absolute. The Convention does not preclude the court from applying what it calls a "mandatory rule" of a state other than that of the law chosen, provided "all the other elements relevant to the situation" are connected with that other state. (Article 3(3) and 7(1)).[m] This retreat from party autonomy seems to be less than under *Restatement* § 187(2), since under the *Restatement* only the net balance under § 188, not "all the elements" have to point to the law of the state not chosen for the choice to be ineffective. For example, if *Southern International Sales* had been decided under the Rome Convention, substituting, say, Germany for Indiana and Belgium for Puerto Rico, the choice of law might well have been upheld.[n] Note that the definition of "mandatory" is a rule of state *X* (i.e., not of the forum state and not of the state of the law chosen) that cannot be displaced by a choice of law rule.

(c) The Rome Convention, reflecting the tension between freedom and protection seen throughout this chapter, takes back Article (3)(1) in other respects as well. A choice of law clause cannot deprive a consumer of the protection of the mandatory rules of the country in which he has his principal residence, if the sale, or the solicitation, occurred in that country or if the consumer was induced by the seller to travel to the latter's country or to another country to make his purchase (Article 5). Similarly choice of law will not apply to contracts of employment outside the country of habitual residence of the employee, even if the employment is to be in another

---

[i] The draft was published in English in 21 Am. J. Comp. L. 584 (1973).

[j] See Chapter 8, § 8.03[A].

[k] The Rome Convention formally entered into effect on April 1, 1991. After some hesitation, the parties also signed a Brussels Protocol, providing for jurisdiction of the European Court of Justice to interpret controversies under the Rome Convention, comparable to its jurisdiction to give rulings on disputes under the Brussels Convention on Jurisdiction and Judgments See Chapter 8, pp. 718–34, *infra.* The history and background of the Convention are presented in Giuliano & Lagarde, *Report on the Convention on the Law Applicable to Contractual Obligations,* 23 O.J. Eur. Comm. No. C 282, (31 October 1980). See also, e.g., P. North, ed. *Contract Conflicts* (1982); P. Kaye, *The New Private International Law of Contract of the European Community* (1993).

[l] The Rome Convention appears in the Documents Supplement at, pp. 44–54.

[m] Note that Articles 3(3) and 7 do not require the forum court in *A* to apply mandatory rules of *B,* but only to consider whether to give effect to those rules notwithstanding the parties' choice of law, and taking into account the rather general factors listed in Article 7(1). Note also that Article 7(1) does not refer to mandatory rules of the forum, which may be applied under Article 7(2).

[n] For a similar case in Belgium, arising not under the Rome Convention but under the New York Convention for enforcing a foreign arbitral award, see *Audi Union v. Adelin Petit,* Chapter 8, p. 742, *infra.*

country—say an Italian workman employed by a British oil company in drilling operations in the North Sea (Article 6).

(d) Article 4 of the Rome Convention addresses the law applicable to a contract if no effective choice of law has been made.º The provisions sounds rather like the *Second Restatement*—"the law of the country with which [the contract] is most closely connected" is roughly the same as "the law of the state which . . . has the most significant relationship to the transaction" in *Restatement (Second)* § 188(1), and the reference in the *Restatement* to determination by issue is paralleled in Article 4 of the Rome Convention by reference to a "severable part of the contract." Indeed, one of Europe's leading conflicts scholars has suggested, perhaps only half in jest, an American-European Restatement on Conflict of Laws—one day.ᴾ But there are a number of differences. Perhaps the most interesting is a concept much discussed in European literature but not generally familiar in the United States, the performance that is characteristic of the contract (Article 4(2)). The idea is that if A is to construct a building or give a concert, and B is to make payment, then A's performance is the characteristic one, B's the more general one, and the place of A's performance will be presumed to determine the governing law. Generally in a sales contract, the place of characteristic performance would be the place of delivery. Paragraph 5 of Article 4 acknowledges that this technique will not always work.

(e) Assuming the Rome Convention were in effect in all the relevant states and substituting those states for the jurisdictions relevant to the cases thus far reproduced or discussed in this chapter, consider how they would be decided under the Convention:

> *Bernkrant, Auten,* and *Haag* would not be covered (see Article 1(2)(b)).
>
> *Lilienthal*—see Article 11
>
> *Vita Food Products*—see Articles 3(1), 3(3), 7(1)
>
> *Daystrom* and *Bushkin*—see Articles 4, 9
>
> *Siegelman* and *Pisacane*—see Articles 3, 5(2), 5(4)(a)
>
> *Southern International Sales*—see Articles 3(1), 3(3), 7(1)

[B] Choice of Forum Clauses

1. As Implying A Choice of Law

Must a choice of law by the parties to a contract be express to be effective? The European Convention speaks of choice "expressed or demonstrated with reasonable certainty . . ." The *Restatement* makes no mention of the question in the black letter, but suggests in a comment that even if the contract does not refer to the law of any given state, the court may nevertheless be able to conclude that the parties did wish a particular state's law to apply, if for example the contract contains reference to a legal doctrine peculiar to the law of a particular state.ᵃ Nothing

---

º For the question of whether an effective choice has been made, see first Article 8(1), and then Article 8(2). For criticism of this and other provisions of the Rome Convention, see Weintraub, *Functional Developments in Choice of Law for Contracts,* 187 Recueil des Cours 239, 278–89 (Hague Academy Int'l Law 1984).

ᴾ O. Lando, *New American Choice-of-Law Principles and the European Conflict of Laws of Contracts,* 30 Am. J. Comp. L. 19, 35 (1982).

ᵃ *Restatement (Second) of Conflict of Laws,* § 187, Comment a.

is stated about a choice of law derived from a choice of forum. The English view, in contrast, ties jurisdiction of courts and applicable law together in several ways. Order 11 of the Rules of the Supreme Court, the English basis for jurisdiction over non-residents, discussed in detail in Chapter 7, p. 495, Question 5, *infra,* provides for jurisdiction of an English court (in the discretion of the judge) on the basis (inter alia) of a contract which "is by its terms, or by implication, governed by English law,"[b] and it seems to provide the reverse as well, i.e. that if a contract provides for adjudication or arbitration in England, there will be a strong inference of intention to have the contract governed by English law. How far this inference can be stretched is the subject of the two cases in this subsection.

TZORTZIS AND SYKIAS v. MONARK LINE A/B

Court of Appeal (U.K.)
[1968] 1 W.L.R. 406, [1968] 1 Lloyd's L. Rep. 337

LORD DENNING, M.R.:

On Nov. 7, 1963, there was a contract between Swedish sellers (Monark Line A/B, of Stockholm) and Greek buyers (Mr. Tzortzis and Mr. Sykias, of the Piraeus) whereby the sellers sold the steamship *Montrose,* to the buyers at a price of £38,000 in freely transferable pounds sterling. A deposit was to be made with a Stockholm bank and the cash amount was to be paid in pounds sterling transferable into Swedish kronor. The vessel was to be delivered and taken over at a Swedish west coast port. The memorandum of agreement was in the standard form in use in Scandinavia which had been approved by the Norwegian Shipowners' Association and adopted by the Baltic and International Maritime Conference. Later on disputes arose which were submitted to arbitration. The question now arises: What is the proper law of the contract? Is it Swedish law or English law?

[It was reasonably clear that the buyers' rights in relation to damages were ampler under Swedish law than under English law. Swedish law appeared to enable an innocent party to recover pre-contract expenses which had become wasted due to the contract going off because of the other party's breach, whereas in English law one could only recover damages which flowed from the breach.]

If you read the contract apart from the arbitration clause, it is clear that it has its closest and most real connection with Sweden. Sweden was the place of the contract. It was the place where the contract was to be performed both as to payment and delivery. But then we come to the arbitration clause which reads:

> If any dispute should arise in connection with the interpretation and fulfilment of this contract, same shall be decided by arbitration in the city of London and shall be referred to a single Arbitrator to be appointed by the parties hereto. If the parties cannot agree upon the appointment of the single Arbitrator, the dispute shall be settled by three Arbitrators, each party appointing one Arbitrator, the third being appointed by the High Court or the corresponding court at the place where the arbitration is to be held. . . .

When the dispute arose, each side appointed an arbitrator. The third one was appointed by the High Court in England. There is apparently no provision in the Arbitration Act, 1950, for

---

[b] Order 11, r.1(1)(d)(iii), Documents Supplement, p. 79.

the Court here appointing such a third arbitrator: but it was done by the High Court by consent. The High Court appointed Mr. MacCrindle as the third arbitrator. Then the question arose as to which was the proper law they were to apply. Was it English law or Swedish law? The arbitrators held that, in view of the arbitration clause, they were to apply English law. It was taken to the Commercial Judge, Mr. Justice Donaldson, who affirmed their decision.

Now the buyers bring the case to this Court. The amount in dispute is comparatively small; but the matter, they say, is of considerable importance. This standard form of agreement is widely used. The buyers contend that, as this contract had its closest and most real connection with Sweden, Swedish law should be applied, even in a London arbitration. They say that there is no difficulty in London in obtaining evidence as to Swedish law, and that London arbitrators have often to apply foreign law. The sellers answer that, by providing for arbitration in London, the parties have impliedly agreed that English law should be applied.

It is clear that, if there is an express clause in a contract providing what the proper law is to be, that is conclusive in the absence of some public policy to the contrary. But where there is no express clause, it is a matter of inference from the circumstances of the case. Now there is no express clause here, but only a clause that arbitration is to be in London. What is the proper inference in such a case?

. . .

An express choice of a tribunal is an implied choice of the proper law.

Both on the cases and the textbooks, I am satisfied in this case that, by choosing the City of London as the place of arbitration, the parties have impliedly chosen English law as the proper law of the contract.

I would dismiss this appeal.

Lord Justice SALMON:

I entirely agree with my Lord that the learned Judge and the arbitrator correctly decided that the proper law of this contract is English law.

The law by which the contract is to be governed depends on the intention of the parties. When that intention is expressed in the contract, rarely does any difficulty arise. When it is not expressed, difficulties often do arise. In circumstances such as those, the intention has to be inferred. There are many factors which then have to be taken into account—*lex loci contractus, lex loci solutionis,* and many others. Sometimes it is said that you have to ask yourself the question: What is the system of law with which the transaction has its closest and most real connection? In this case, if you leave out of account the language in which the arbitration clause is framed, there can be no question but that the system of law to be applied would be Swedish law. That clearly is the system with which the transaction has its closest and most real connection. All the other factors which usually point, perhaps strongly, perhaps feebly, to one system of law or another, here point to the Swedish system of law.

It seems to me, however, that you cannot leave out of account the terms in which the arbitration clause is framed. I agree with Mr. Eckersley[c] that in this case a choice of English law is to be inferred from the parties' express choice of an English arbitration. This in any view is here an irresistible inference which overrides all the other factors. . . . It is almost incredible that in the circumstances of this case these parties should have hit upon London with English

---

[c] Counsel for sellers.

arbitrators if they did not intend English law to be applied. I say "English arbitrators," although that is not spelt out in the contract. It is, however, quite obvious that these businessmen must have known that the overwhelming probabilities were that, if a dispute arose, they would first of all try to agree an arbitrator who was resident in or around London. If they could not agree, they would each appoint an arbitrator who lived in or around London. If the arbitrators did not agree, then the High Court would appoint by consent, as they did in this case, an arbitrator who was a member of the English Bar and who knew a good deal about English law and probably very little about Swedish law. This third arbitrator would in fact decide the case. It is of course theoretically possible that the parties might have appointed an arbitrator from Holland, Spain or Timbuctoo. I suppose it is also theoretically possible that the Judge who was asked to appoint the arbitrator might have appointed the leader of the Swedish Bar. But looking at the realities of the situation, I have no doubt at all that they intended that to happen which in fact did happen in the present case.

We know, of course, that often in the Commercial Court and in other Courts it is necessary to apply foreign law to a contract, and that this is certainly not beyond the capacity of English lawyers; but to the ordinary commercial man, entering into a contract of this sort, who goes out of his way to say arbitration in London before English arbitrators, the sensible inference, as was pointed out by Lord Maugham, L.C., and Lord Wright, is that the law of the seat of the arbitration is intended to be the law to be applied to the contract. If the intention had been otherwise, one would have expected the parties to state expressly which system of foreign law they intended to apply.

Mr. Kerr,[d] in the course of his very attractive argument, said it would be insular to hold that English law should be applied. I am afraid I do not agree with him. If this contract instead of inserting "London" had inserted "Paris," although the case would not have come before me for decision, had I been asked, I should have said that since the parties stipulated arbitration in Paris by French arbitrators, they intended French law to apply. I say the same about an English arbitration in London—English law. After all, English law has certainly not yet been devalued, and there is no reason to suppose that these gentlemen did not desire this contract to be governed by the law of the land where they wished it to be held.

Mr. Kerr has admitted (as he had to in the face of the authorities) that if the choice was between two systems of law, namely the system of one of the contracting parties living in country A, or the system of the other contracting party living in country B, the fact that the arbitration clause provided that the arbitration should take place in country A would be the strongest possible indication that the parties intended the contract to be governed by the system of law of country A. He says it is different where the parties living respectively in countries A and B provide for an English arbitration. As my brother, Lord Justice Edmund Davies pointed out during the course of the argument, I should have thought this is almost an *a fortiori* case. I think it is not at all unnatural, in circumstances such as these, that the parties agree for the contract to be arbitrated on neutral territory by neutral arbitrators in accordance with the system of law which very often does govern commercial contracts. Indeed, it is not uncommon in the shipping world to find foreign shipowners in their contracts agreeing that any dispute between them shall be decided by the English Commercial Court according to English law.

---

[d] Counsel for buyers, and later a Justice of the High Court and the Court of Appeal, as well as one of the drafters of the 1979 Arbitration Act.

I agree that this appeal must be dismissed.

Lord Justice EDMUND DAVIES:

Despite the attractive and valiant submissions by Mr. Michael Kerr, the view expressed by my Lords appears to me to be so clearly right, with respect, that I desire to say nothing more than that I entirely agree that this appeal must be dismissed.

CIE. TUNISIENNE DE NAVIGATION S.A. v. CIE. D'ARMEMENT MARITIME S.A.

House of Lords (1970)
[1971] A.C. 572

Lord REID:

My Lords, in 1967 the respondents, a Tunisian company, wished to have a quantity of oil shipped from La Skhirra to Bizerta—both ports in Tunisia. They approached a firm of brokers in Paris who put them in touch with the appellants who are French shipowners. The parties negotiated a contract in Paris and it was left to the brokers to prepare the written contract. They selected an English printed form which appears to be often used abroad. This form was for a tanker voyage charter-party which required considerable adaptation because under the contract there were to be a number of shipments spread over nine months in vessels supplied as required by the appellants.

After six shipments a dispute arose and the respondents claimed damages. The contract provides that any dispute shall be settled in London, each party appointing a merchant or broker as arbitrator. Arbitrators were duly appointed and the first question which arose was as to the proper law of the contract. On this the arbitrators made an interim award adjudging that the proper law of the contract is French law and stating as a question of law for the decision of the Court the question whether the proper law is French law or English law.

One of the printed clauses in the form deals with the proper law. Clause 13 reads:

> This Contract shall be governed by the laws of the Flag of the Vessel carrying the goods, except in cases of average or general average, when same to be settled according to the York-Antwerp Rules, 1950.

This clause remains unaltered in the signed contract. The printed form, being for a charter-party, had blanks at the beginning for the insertion of the name of the shipowner's tanker and its flag. These were left blank. Clause 28 provides:

> Shipments to be effected in tonnage owned, controlled or chartered by the Compagnie d'Armement Maritime S.A. of 16.000/25.000 tons 10% more or less at Owners' option.

The first question is whether it is possible to give any meaning to clause 13. The printed form, including clause 13, obviously contemplates that there is to be one vessel and one flag and that the law of that flag shall be the proper law. But under clause 28 there could be a variety of vessels with a variety of flags. Which is to be selected as determining the proper law? Even if one could hold that with regard to a dispute concerning a particular voyage the law of the flag of the vessel making that voyage should prevail, that would not provide for the dispute in this case which does not relate to any particular voyage.

We do not know and cannot inquire as to why clause 13 was left unaltered. We have to construe it as we find it. Normally where a clause was drafted by the parties or their agents we can assume that they must have intended it to mean something. But we cannot make that assumption here. The broker, relying on the form having proved useful in the past, may never even have read clause 13 and the strong probability is that the parties, being faced with a form in a foreign language which they assumed or were assured by the broker embodied their previous agreement, would not scrutinize the printed matter. Indeed one can say with some confidence that if any of them had scrutinized clause 13 he would have seen that it required adaptation. But whether they read clause 13 or not the parties are bound by what they signed.

Even if it were relevant it would be useless to ask in this case what the parties in fact intended as to the proper law, because it is found as a fact in the interim award that there was no discussion at any time of the law by which the transaction was to be governed. But clause 13, like any other provision in a contract, must be construed in light of the facts known to both parties at the time when it was agreed. They knew that the appellants owned a number of tankers flying the French flag and it is found in the interim award that it was contemplated by both parties that vessels owned by the appellants would be used at least primarily to perform the contract.

If the parties had contemplated that the appellants' vessels would always be used except in some unforeseen circumstances I would have held that clause 13 could be held to mean that the contract was to be governed by the law of the flag of those vessels, i.e., the law of France. But in my opinion this finding is too indefinite to justify such a gloss. "Primarily" might mean in the first instance or it might mean in the majority of cases. The parties must have known that many other tankers not owned by the appellants would be available on this route, and that, as the dates of shipment were to be determined by the respondents, vessels other than those belonging to the appellants might well have to be used. In my judgment clause 13 must in the circumstances be regarded as having failed in its purpose to determine the proper law of the contract.

If that is so then we are no longer concerned with the parties' intention. In the absence of any positive indication of intention in the contract the law will determine the proper law by deciding with what country or system of law the contract has the closest connection. Here three countries are involved. The contract was negotiated and signed in France and the freight was payable in Paris in French francs. The contract was to be performed in Tunisia. The only connection with England was that any dispute was to be settled by arbitration in London. The contract is in the English language and in English form but it was not argued, in my view rightly, that any great importance should be given to this.

Until this case reached this House it appears to have been assumed that France and Tunisia could be treated as one country or as having the same system of law. It is stated in the interim award that:

> . . . The civil law of Tunisia (which until 1956 was a French colony) is based on the Code Napoleon.

and that *"Neither side contended for any other system of law"* than French or English law. On that basis when one comes to weigh the various factors which tell in favour of French or of English law being regarded as the proper law, the fact that Tunisia was to be the place of performance of the contract would be put in the scale for French law. Then it is clear that the balance comes down heavily in favour of French law. On the one hand, there are the place where the contract was negotiated and signed, the place of performance, the place where and the currency in which the freight was to be paid, and the place where the parties resided and carried on business: on the other hand, there is only the place where disputes were to be settled by arbitration. But I wish to reserve my opinion as to how far in a case of this kind it is proper to disregard the fact that two countries are separate and independent countries, each with its own system of law, on the ground that those countries are or have recently been closely associated, or that their systems of law are very similar but both very different from English law.

The respondents do not deny that if we are free to apply the general rule, that the proper law is the law of the place with which the contract is most closely associated, then the proper law would be French law. Their case is that that general rule does not apply where there is an arbitration clause requiring disputes to be settled by arbitration in England. They admit that such a clause does not prevent the parties from agreeing that some other law shall be the proper law, but they maintain that, if such an agreement cannot be deduced from the terms of the contract, then the arbitration clause is decisive as to the proper law and requires an English Court to hold that the proper law is the law of England.

Of course the fact that the parties have agreed that arbitration shall take place in England is an important factor and in many cases it may be the decisive factor. But it would in my view be highly anomalous if our law required the mere fact that arbitration is to take place in England to be decisive as to the proper law of the contract. For the reasons given by others of your Lordships I agree that this is not the law of England.

I would therefore allow this appeal.

Lord Morris of Borth-Y-Gest

. . .

In *Vita Food Products Inc. v. Unus Shipping Company Ltd.,* there was an express clause which provided that the contracts should be governed by English law. Lord Wright pointed out that it was well settled that by English law the proper law of the contract is the law which the parties intended to apply. He said:

> . . . But where the English rule that intention is the test applies, and where there is an express statement by the parties of their intention to select the law of the contract, it is difficult to see what qualifications are possible, provided the intention expressed is bona fide and legal, and provided there is no reason for avoiding the choice on the ground of public policy. . . .

He then examined the reasons why it might have been said that in that case the choice of English law was not valid. He considered whether it could be said that the transaction in issue in that case contained nothing to connect it with English law. In pointing out that connection with English law is not, as a matter of principle, essential he said:

> . . . The provision in a contract (e.g., of sale) for English arbitration imports English law as the law governing the transaction, and those familiar with international business are aware how frequent such a provision is even where the parties are not English and the transactions are carried on completely outside England. . . .

When read in their context and in their place in the reasoning which Lord Wright was developing I do not consider that the words "English arbitration imports English law" should be taken as laying down that from an agreement for an English arbitration there arises a conclusive presumption that English law is to apply.

The case of *Tzortzis and Sykias v. Monark Line A/B* arose out of a contract which was made in Stockholm for the sale of a ship. The sellers were Swedish. The buyers were Greek. Delivery was to be in Sweden. There was to be a deposit at a Stockholm bank—where payment (in sterling transferable to Swedish kroner) was to be made. The contract provided that any dispute in connection with its interpretation and fulfil-ment should be decided by arbitration in the City of London.

There being no express clause providing what the proper law was to be that question fell to be decided as a matter of inference from all the circumstances of the case. The conclusion that English law was the proper law of the contract may well have been a reasonable one (though no occasion now arises to form any opinion as to this) but some of the statements concerning the inferences to be drawn from an arbitration provision are, in my view, expressed much too positively. The circumstance that parties agree that any differences are to be settled by arbitration in a certain country may and very likely will lead to an inference that they intend the law of that country to apply. But it is not a necessary inference or an inevitable one though it will often be the reasonable and sensible one. Before drawing it, all the relevant circumstances are to be considered.

My conclusion, therefore, is that clause 13 should be interpreted as containing an agreement that French law is to govern. If the clause has failed to be positive its existence at least negatives any inference that might otherwise have arisen from the terms of the arbitration clause. On that basis and upon a consideration of all the relevant circumstances it should be held that French law is the governing law. The transaction had a much closer and more real connection with French law than with English law. The contract was negotiated in France in the French language through a French firm of brokers and was made in France. There was to be payment in France and in French currency. One party was a company incorporated in Tunisia. The other party was a company incorporated under French law which at the time was registered as a French company.

If I had been of the view that clause 13 ought to be regarded as non-existent then it would have been a matter for decision as to whether these and the other considerations already noted were not so weighty as to negative and supersede any inference that might be drawn from the terms of the arbitration clause if considered alone.

I would allow the appeal.

Lord WILBERFORCE:

My Lords, two alternatives are put forward for the proper law of this contract, French law and English. I have no doubt that the decision should be in favour of the former.

Briefly to recapitulate the facts: the contract is between a shipowning company incorporated under French law with a registered office, at the relevant time, in French Somaliland, whose ships carry the French flag; and a company incorporated in Tunis, until 1956 a French Protectorate, whose civil law is based on the Code Napoléon. It was for the carriage of a specified tonnage of oil between two Tunisian ports by ships to be provided by the appellants. Negotiations for the contract were conducted in Paris, in the French language, through Paris-Maritime S.A., a French firm of brokers. Payment under it was to be made in France, in French currency. The contract was made on an English standard form, but one which, it was found, is frequently used for tanker fixtures in chartering centres outside London. It contained an arbitration clause providing for arbitration in London.

Disputes arose and the matter went to arbitration: each side appointed a very experienced London arbitrator. These arbitrators, without resorting to the appointment of an umpire, decided that the proper law was French law. The matter went to the High Court on a special case and was heard by Mr. Justice Megaw, a Judge of great experience in these matters. He upheld the arbitrators' decision. One would think that this would be the end of the matter—all the more when it is appreciated what the nature of the dispute was. This was whether the respondents are entitled to damages for breach of contract according to the English law of anticipatory breach, or whether their right to damages is conditioned by certain requirements of French law as to matters to be done before damages in such a case can be claimed, and also whether any damages are to be limited as provided in sect. 1150 of the French Civil Code.[e] To suppose that contracting parties, in the position of these companies, intended that their rights in this matter should be governed by English law seems a surprising proposition: yet this was so decided by the Court of Appeal. The Appeal Committee of this House thought that this House ought to review the matter.

How, then, was a decision reached in favour of English law? Some reliance was placed on the use in the contract of English expressions, but this can be of little weight since in general they relate to maritime situations well known under all systems and, indeed, referred to in the Hague Rules. The main argument was based on clause 18 of the contract which, as stated, provides for arbitration in London. The existence of such a clause, failing an express choice of any other law, is said to give rise to a conclusive presumption that the parties intended English law to govern, however strongly other factors may point away from it. In so holding, the Court of Appeal was following its earlier decision in *Tzortzis and Sykias v. Monark Line A/B,* where, though the contract was closely connected with Swedish law, the presumption in favour of English law arising from the arbitration clause was described by Lord Justice Salmon as "irresistible." There is no doubt that the strength of this so-called presumption has increased both in recent decisions at first instance and in certain, but not all, text-books. Thus Professor Cheshire in his *Private International Law,* 7th ed. (1965), at p. 193, says that

> . . . for better or for worse English law is committed to the view that *qui elegit judicem elegit jus.* An express choice of a tribunal is an implied choice of the proper law.

The editors of Dicey's *Conflict of Laws* are more circumspect: ("usually permits the inference"— 8th ed. (1967), at p. 705). So, too, Professor Wolff in *Private International Law,* 2nd ed. (1950), at p. 421.

I shall examine this doctrine in the light of authority, but before I do so there is a special argument to be considered, on the terms of the contract. This is based upon clause 13 of the contract (cited by my noble and learned friend, Lord Reid) and takes two alternative forms: (1) that the clause should be interpreted so as to amount to an express choice of law sc. French law; (2) that even if it is inept to do so, it has sufficient force to negative any implied choice of law through the arbitration clause. I do not deal at any length with either of these arguments. The first must command respect from its acceptance by Mr. Justice Megaw. But I find the required process of adaptation, with the aid of a qualified finding of fact that it was contemplated that the appellants' vessels would be primarily used, to pass beyond legitimate interpretation to a process of rewriting. With the exception of the reliance placed on subsequent actings, which

---

[e] Article 1150 reads:

The obligor is liable only for damages that were or could have been foreseen at the time of the contract, provided the non-performance of the obligation is not due to his fraud [*dol*].

I think inadmissible, I adopt the reasoning of the Court of Appeal, particularly of Lord Justice Salmon, on this point. The second argument seems to me much more dubious. It rests on the fact that this clause, on this hypothesis meaningless and incapable of adaptation, was not struck out of the contract. This shows, it is said, an intention to displace the law of the place of arbitration by some other law of the parties' choice and this neutralizing effect remains even though the choice is abortive. This is certainly an ingenious and subtle argument, too subtle and ingenious for me. To attribute a legal effect to a clause which is, on this hypothesis, meaningless, seems to me a remarkable acrobatic. To deny its normal effect to a clause (18) because of the presence of some printed words of no effect—a corpse which the undertakers have not removed—is a stranger adventure than I can embark on. I cannot find in clause 13, either way, the solution to the case: this must be found in a proper evaluation of the arbitration clause.

My Lords, I am still of opinion that it is not necessary to embark on citation of authorities in order to establish how the proper law of a contract is to be arrived at. The law has been more than once in recent times stated in this House and if one desires a summary of the main principles the rules in Dicey-Morris' Digest are convenient. For myself I prefer the formulation in the 7th ed. (1958), at p. 73, which I find clearer and simpler. In the absence of an express choice of law, rule 148 (2) applies, as follows:

> When the intention of the parties to a contract with regard to the law governing the contract is not expressed in words, their intention is to be inferred from the terms and nature of the contract, and from the general circumstances of the case, and such inferred intention determines the proper law of the contract.

Whether the result is a matter of "inferred intention" or not may be open to jurisprudential discussion; but the advantage of this formulation is that (correctly in my opinion) it requires consideration together of the terms and nature of the contract and the general circumstances of the case. In certain recent judgments, particularly in relation to arbitration clauses, there is a tendency to split this into two stages: first, see if there is an arbitration clause; if so, that is conclusive, and the general circumstances (place of performance, money of payment, etc.) are irrelevant. I think that this is wrong; all should be considered together as elements relevant to intention, inferred or presumed. I see no justification for giving a prerogative effect to one of these elements, to the extent of refusing even to consider others, whether within or outside the contract, which are just as relevant (though not necessarily as weighty) to the parties' intention.

How strong, then, is the inference to be drawn from a (London) arbitration clause? That the selection of a certain place for arbitration and, by inference, of nationals or residents of that place, as arbitrators is an indication that the parties intended the law of that place to govern is a sound general rule. But it should not be treated as giving rise to a conclusive or irresistible inference, as recent pronouncements appear to suggest. One of the reasons commonly given for attributing overwhelming force to the clause is that arbitrators in London are only to be supposed to be conversant with English law but I venture to think that in commercial matters, at the present time, this may give insufficient recognition to the international character of the City of London as a commercial centre—the reason, rather than any preference for English rules, for which arbitration in London is selected. In this case the arbitrators had no difficulty in finding for French law and I do not suppose they would find ascertainment of the French law as to damages any more difficult than the English law of anticipatory breach. So, unless otherwise constrained, I would regard the clause as a weighty indication, but one which may yield to others.

I do not find that the leading cases, when properly understood, suggest a different approach.

[There follows a discussion of four cases from 1894 to 1938.] I fully accept that, especially where the parties are of different nationality and there is no other relevant factor, a clause providing for arbitration in a third country is a strong indication which, because there is no other, may be called conclusive, in favour of the proper law of that country.

Lastly, I must refer to the well-known and important dictum of Lord Wright in the Privy Council case of *Vita Food Products Inc. v. Unus Shipping Company Ltd.* This is (among other things) a leading authority on the question to what extent parties to a contract are free to select for themselves the law which is to govern it. Lord Wright discusses this in an illuminating manner, and the passage contains these words:

> . . . The provision in a contract (e.g., of sale) for English arbitration imports English law as the law governing the transaction . . .

The respondents in the present case are not the first to pick out these words as stating a definite rule. It would be surprising if it did, in view of Lord Wright's observations that

> . . . questions relating to the conflict of laws rules cannot generally be stated in absolute terms but rather as prima facie presumptions. . . .

(see also Wright's *Legal Essays and Addresses,* (1939), at p. 164). If this was his view in relation to a case where parties have expressly chosen the governing law, it would seem unlikely that he regarded an implied choice through an arbitration clause as having stronger effect. But it is clear enough what he is arguing. He is concerned to show that connection of the contract with English law is not essential, and the proposition is designed to illustrate this. The illustration is precisely as effective whether an arbitration clause is regarded as conclusive or strongly presumptive or weakly presumptive: there was no need for Lord Wright to commit himself to any one of these.

So I come, in conclusion, to the *Tzortzis case* and the present appeal; cases virtually identical in principle. In each case there were substantial foreign elements. In *Tzortzis* Lord Denning, M.R., said

> If you read the contract apart from the arbitration clause, it is clear that it has its closest and most real connection with Sweden. Sweden was the place of the contract. It was the place where the contract was to be performed both as to payment and delivery. But then we come to the arbitration clause . . .

Lord Justice Salmon uses even stronger language. . . . In the present case, too, Lord Denning, M.R., accepts that the system of law with which the contract has the closest and most real connection is French law [1969] 2 Lloyd's Rep., at p. 73; [1969] 1 W.L.R., at p. 1344). Similarly Lord Justice Salmon, though he states this as a matter of concession. But in both cases the Court held that this was overridden, not outweighed, by the arbitration clause. In *Tzortzis* Lord Denning, M.R., seems to have regarded the arbitration clause as a "very strong indication," though he later quotes Professor Cheshire who puts the matter more strongly still. Lord Justice Salmon says firmly that the choice of an English arbitration

> . . . is . . . an irresistible inference which overrides all the other factors. . . .

and this is the approach followed in the present case.

My Lords, for the reasons given I am of opinion that this language is too strong, too absolute. Neither authority, nor commercial reality support the necessity for so rigid a rule. An arbitration clause must be treated as an indication, to be considered together with the rest of the contract and relevant surrounding facts. Always it will be a strong indication; often, especially where there are parties of different nationality or a variety of transactions which may arise under the contract, it will be the only clear indication. But in some cases it must give way where other indications are clear. It is not necessary to express an opinion as to the correctness of the result in the *Tzortzis case;* it is the process with which it is necessary to disagree. The right result was to be arrived at by weighing the important indications in favour of Swedish law against the indication from the arbitration clause and the different nationality of the parties. It is necessary to disagree with the result in the present case, where every indication points so strongly to French law that this law must govern unless the inference from London arbitration is irresistible or conclusive.

One further observation. It is surely regrettable that, after a choice of English arbitrators, these foreign parties should have been subjected to litigation in three Courts on top of the arbitration and that on a preliminary point. I venture to think that a question of the proper law of a commercial contract ought to be regarded as primarily a matter to be found by arbitrators: for, after all, the question is one of estimating competing factors in the light of commercial intention. As was said long ago

> . . . the only certain guide is to be found in applying sound ideas of business, convenience, and sense to the language of the contract . . . [*Jacobs, Marcus & Co. v. Crédit Lyonnais,* (1884) 12 Q.B.D. 589, at p. 601.]

The expertise of City of London arbitrators (which motivates the use of London arbitration clauses) suggests that these considerations are best left to them and the proposition that this being a "matter of law" is something better left to the Courts is one the correctness of which is open on the record. If, for uniformity or otherwise, supervision by the Courts is sometimes required, I cannot but think that, otherwise than in exceptional cases by leave, decision by the commercial Judge should end the matter.

I would allow the appeal.

Lord DIPLOCK: . . .

As I have already said for the purposes of this transaction France and Tunisia may be regarded as sharing a common system of law. That was the system of law of the place where each party resided, of the place where the contract was negotiated and made, of the ports of shipment and of discharge, of the place of payment and was the law of the flag of the vessels which the parties contemplated would be used at least primarily for the carriage. The only connection of the transaction with English law was provided by an arbitration clause which was intended to operate only as a choice of curial law. Clearly French law was the system of law with which the contract had its closest and most real connection.

My Lords, in the instant case any implication that the arbitration clause was intended to operate as a choice of proper law as distinct from curial law was negatived by the retention in the contract of clause 13. I do not wish to throw any doubt upon the proposition that an arbitration clause is generally intended by the parties to operate as a choice of the proper law of the contract as well as the curial law and should be so construed unless there are compelling indications to the contrary in the other terms of the contract or the surrounding circumstances of the transaction. The mere fact that there are other systems of law with which the transaction has a closer connection is not sufficient to rebut the implication. In international transactions, particularly on commodity markets where the same shipment of goods may be bought and sold many times before delivery of the actual goods to the last buyer, it is of great commercial convenience that all the contracts relating to such sales should be subject to the same proper law irrespective of the place of shipment or discharge, the residence or nationality of the parties, or the place where the contract was made. This is the basis on which commodity markets operate and the choice of arbitral form is understood as being intended as a choice of proper law.

But strong as the implication may be, it can be rebutted as other implications of intention can be rebutted. It is not a positive rule of law which is independent of the intentions of the parties. In the instant case I am satisfied that it has been rebutted, and I would allow the appeal.

As Conferring and Ousting Jurisdiction of Courts

A choice of forum clause—i.e., a clause in a contract providing that all disputes arising out of or related to this agreement shall be resolved in the High Court of Justice in London, or in the Supreme Court of New York County,—may be viewed from two sides. (i) Does such a clause require, or entitle, the court selected by the parties to hear the case, assuming that no other connective factors link the transaction or the parties to the forum; and (ii) does such a clause preclude another court from hearing the action, when that court would, absent the clause, have jurisdiction over the parties and the controversy? The first two cases illustrate both of these questions, arising in different phases of the same controversy. The third case illustrates when a choice of forum clause may fail.

UNTERWESER REEDEREI G.m.b.H. v. ZAPATA OFF-SHORE COMPANY

Court of Appeal (U.K.)
[1968] 2 Lloyd's L. Rep. 158

Lord Justice WILLMER:

This is an application for leave to appeal from an order made by Mr. Justice Karminski on July 4, 1968, whereby he dismissed the defendants' application to set aside an order of the learned Registrar giving leave to serve a writ out of the jurisdiction. In order to deal with the application, it has been necessary to go into all the circumstances of the case, and in substance to hear the appeal. The question at issue between the parties arises out of a marine casualty which took place in January, 1968. The plaintiffs are well-known towage contractors and owners of a tug called the *Bremen*. The defendants are a company incorporated in the United States of America who carry on business *inter alia* in the operation of oil rigs.

In November, 1967, the plaintiffs and the defendants entered into a contract in writing for the towage of an oil rig called the *Chaparral* belonging to the defendants from a place called Venice in Louisiana to Ravenna in Italy by the tug *Bremen*. We have been referred to a number of the clauses in the contract, only one of which need be mentioned now. The concluding provision of the contract was:

> Any dispute arising must be treated before the London Court of Justice.

The towage from Venice began on Jan. 4, 1968. By Jan. 9, when the tow was still within the Gulf of Mexico, disaster overtook it, and it was necessary to take refuge in the port of Tampa in Florida. Each party blamed the other for the disaster which occurred, and each has asserted a claim for damages. The plaintiff tug-owners say that the defendants were at fault in that the oil rig being towed was not in a seaworthy condition. The defendants on their part say that the tug was not seaworthy to undertake the voyage, and also that it was negligently operated. There are all the elements present for an interesting battle to ascertain whose fault it was. The defendants got their blow in first, because immediately upon arrival of the tug and tow at Tampa they instituted proceedings in Admiralty in the United States District Court at Tampa, and in the course of those proceedings the tug was arrested. The release of the tug was eventually obtained upon security being furnished satisfactory to the defendants in the sum of U.S. $3,500,000.

On Feb. 21, 1968, the plaintiffs issued the writ in the present action and sought leave to serve that writ out of the jurisdiction on the American owners of the oil rig. Leave to serve the writ out of the jurisdiction was obtained from the learned Registrar, and it was that matter which came before the learned Judge. The grounds upon which the plaintiffs sought leave to serve the writ out of the jurisdiction were, first, that the contract was one which "by its terms, or by implication, was governed by English law," and secondly, that the contract contained an express term to the effect that the High Court should have jurisdiction.[f]

In the meantime, however, the present plaintiffs had taken steps to defend themselves in the proceedings which were being carried on in Tampa. Those proceedings involved taking depositions from a number of witnesses, and in that operation both the present plaintiffs and the present defendants took part. Depositions appear to have been taken from a considerable number of witnesses. But from an early date the plaintiffs took exception to the jurisdiction of the Court at Tampa, and instituted proceedings to set aside or stay the American action. Those proceedings came before the United States District Court in Tampa on Apr. 29, 1968, when judgment was reserved. Up to date, so far as we have been informed, no judgment has yet been delivered, and it is not, therefore, known whether the action instituted by the defendants in America will be set aside or stayed. At present, however, assuming that leave to serve this writ out of the jurisdiction stands, there is a situation when proceedings are on foot in both countries. The position is further complicated by the fact that, just before the matter came before Mr. Justice Karminski at the beginning of this month, the plaintiffs launched proceedings for exoneration or limitation of their liability in the United States of America. It is to be pointed out that that is a course which they had to take, if the American proceedings were allowed to continue, within six months of the institution of those proceedings. Time was running out against them, and they were, therefore, forced to institute those proceedings at the beginning of this month in order to preserve their rights.

The learned Judge knew of the institution of those proceedings but he did not actually know (although I have no doubt that he had good reason to suspect) that, immediately following the institution of those proceedings, an order would be made by the American Court which, among other things, enjoined the defendants against prosecuting any claim of theirs against the plaintiffs pending the determination of the plaintiffs' limitation proceedings. That, it has been said, would effectively prevent the defendants, if they were so minded, from putting forward a counterclaim in any proceedings in this country. That is a matter much relied upon by the defendants as showing

---

[f] The reference is to Order 11 of the Rules of the Supreme Court, reproduced in the Documents Supplement at p. 79. The provision concerning jurisdiction on the basis of application of English law is Order 11, r.1 (1) (d) (iii); former rule 2, concerning selection of an English forum by contract, discussed by Justice Diplock, is now r.1 (1) (d) (iv).

that, as a matter of convenience, and in order to avoid duplication of proceedings, leave ought not to be granted to serve this writ out of the jurisdiction.

Reliance is also placed upon the fact that, under American procedure, it appears that a party sued as a defendant there (as are the present plaintiffs) who has a counterclaim against the plaintiff in that country, is compelled to assert that counterclaim within a certain limit of time, or he will be for all time barred. That is another reason why it is suggested on behalf of the defendants that, as a matter of convenience, proceedings ought not to be allowed to continue in this country, since it is said that it will be necessary for the present plaintiffs to assert their claim by way of counterclaim in the United States.

The law on the subject, I think, is not open to doubt, and I do not think that it is really necessary to cite the authorities to which we have been referred. It is always open to parties to stipulate (as they did in this case) that a particular Court shall have jurisdiction over any dispute arising out of their contract. Here the parties chose to stipulate that disputes were to be referred to the "London Court," which I take as meaning the High Court in this country. *Prima facie* it is the policy of the Court to hold parties to the bargain into which they have entered. *Prima facie* it is to be presumed, therefore, that the plaintiffs should have leave to prosecute their proceedings in this country, and in pursuance of that to serve their writ out of the jurisdiction. But that is not an inflexible rule, as was shown, for instance, by the case of *The Fehmarn,* [1957] 1 Lloyd's Rep. 511; (C.A.) [1957] 2 Lloyd's Rep. 551, in which I was myself concerned, and which came to this Court. That was a case in which the Court in its discretion declined to give effect to a stipulation made by the parties in their contract conferring jurisdiction on a foreign Court.

I approach the matter, therefore, in this way, that the Court has a discretion, but it is a discretion which, in the ordinary way and in the absence of strong reason to the contrary, will be exercised in favour of holding parties to their bargain. The question is whether sufficient circumstances have been shown to exist in this case to make it desirable, on the grounds of balance of convenience, that proceedings should not take place in this country, the stipulated forum, but that the parties should be left to fight out their battles in the United States of America.

The learned Judge in his discretion came to the conclusion that it was proper to grant leave to serve the writ out of the jurisdiction so that the action might proceed in this country. We in this Court should not interfere with the Judge's exercise of his discretion unless it is shown that he acted on some wrong principle, or misapprehended the facts, or unless it is shown that his exercise of his discretion was plainly wrong.

It is said that the situation has to some extent altered since the time when the learned Judge had the matter before him, by reason particularly of the plaintiffs' institution of exoneration and limitation proceedings in the United States to which I have referred. That is the only new factor which has arisen since the time when the learned Judge delivered his judgment.

I am unable to see that the Judge acted on any wrong principle. I do not think that the new facts said to have been brought to light really alter the complexion of the case to any material extent, nor am I prepared to say that the learned Judge's exercise of his discretion is shown to have been plainly wrong.

I should record the fact that in an affidavit put in on behalf of the plaintiffs today, the offer is made (and Mr. Lloyd on behalf of the plaintiffs has renewed it in the course of the argument) to waive the provisions of the restraining order which has been obtained by the plaintiffs in the United States so as to relieve the defendants of any difficulty which they might otherwise have in putting forward a counterclaim in this country if they want to. I should also record the fact that an offer has been made on behalf of the plaintiffs (which still holds good) to hold the security which has been furnished in America as available to cover any counterclaim which may be brought in this country. I refer to those two circumstances because I think that they are in their turn relevant to the question whether it is right to allow these plaintiffs to pursue their action in this country in accordance with their contractual bargain. I think that it is, and that the learned Judge reached the right conclusion.

In the circumstances I think that the appropriate order for us to make is that the defendants be granted leave to appeal, but that the appeal be dismissed.

Lord Justice DIPLOCK:

I agree, and add very little.

It has long been recognized that the jurisdiction of the High Court to give leave for service of a writ, or notice of a writ, out of the jurisdiction under Order 11, r. 1, is one which should be exercised with caution, because there are circumstances set out in that rule in which service outside the jurisdiction is authorized which are in conflict with the ordinary rules of comity, that is to say, the Courts in this country assert a jurisdiction in themselves wider than that which they recognize in the Courts of other countries. . . .

Those observations should be read in relation to an application for service out of the jurisdiction under r. 1. Rule 2, which is a separate rule and applies to this case, authorizes service out of the jurisdiction where the contract contains a term to the effect that the High Court has jurisdiction to hear and determine any action in respect to the contract.ᵘ This does not raise any question of conflict with ordinary comity because, so far as I know, it is the policy of the Courts of most countries, if it be reasonable at any rate to do so, to see that parties keep their word; and having had the privilege of reading a memorandum brief which has been accepted in the Federal District Court at Tampa on behalf of the plaintiffs in this action, it looks to me as if there is some ground at any rate for saying that the Federal Courts and State Courts in the United States take the same view.

When it comes to a case under Order 11, r. 2, as distinct from a case under Order 11, r. 1, I say again in this case, as I said in *Mackender*:

> . . . Where parties have agreed to submit all their disputes under a contract to the exclusive jurisdiction of a foreign court, I myself should require very strong reasons to induce me to permit one of them to go back on his word. . . .ᵛ

We should, I think, apply the same principle whether the forum of contractual choice is England or of some other country. The question arises more frequently before us where the forum of contractual choice is some other country, as in *Mackender's case, sup.*, where the choice was Belgium. In the present case the choice of the parties was the English Court, and as I say I should myself require strong grounds for saying that one of the parties should not keep his word.

There is, of course, undoubtedly a discretion on the part of the Court in this case to refuse to allow service of the writ outside the jurisdiction, despite the contractual term in the contract. The learned Judge from whom this appeal is brought recognized that he had a discretion. So

---

ᵘ As pointed out in the preceding note, the text of Rule 2 remains unchanged, but it has been integrated into Rule 1(1)(d), so that the point about different criteria would seem to be no longer valid.

ᵛ See p. 496 note y *infra*.

far as I can see he applied his mind to all the relevant matters; and, even if I myself might have come to some other conclusion, I do not think that any ground has been put forward which would justify the Court in interfering with his discretion. Having said that, let me say, as must have been apparent during the course of this hearing, I agree entirely with his decision. I should have done the same myself.

THE BREMEN et al. v. ZAPATA OFF-SHORE CO.

United States Supreme Court
407 U.S. 1 (1972)

MR. CHIEF JUSTICE BURGER delivered the opinion of the Court.

We granted certiorari to review a judgment of the United States Court of Appeals for the Fifth Circuit declining to enforce a forum-selection clause governing disputes arising under an international towage contract between petitioners and respondent. The circuits have differed in their approach to such clauses. For the reasons stated hereafter, we vacate the judgment of the Court of Appeals.

In November 1967, respondent Zapata, a Houston-based American corporation, contracted with petitioner Unterweser, a German corporation, to tow Zapata's ocean-going, self-elevating drilling rig *Chaparral* from Louisiana to a point off Ravenna, Italy, in the Adriatic Sea, where Zapata had agreed to drill certain wells.

Zapata had solicited bids for the towage, and several companies including Unterweser had responded. Unterweser was the low bidder and Zapata requested it to submit a contract, which it did. The contract submitted by Unterweser contained the following provision, which is at issue in this case:

> Any dispute arising must be treated before the London Court of Justice.

In addition the contract contained two clauses purporting to exculpate Unterweser from liability for damages to the towed barge.[2]

After reviewing the contract and making several changes, but without any alteration in the forum-selection or exculpatory clauses, a Zapata vice president executed the contract and forwarded it to Unterweser in Germany, where Unterweser accepted the changes, and the contract became effective.

On January 5, 1968, Unterweser's deep sea tug *Bremen* departed Venice, Louisiana, with the *Chaparral* in tow bound for Italy. On January 9, while the flotilla was in international waters in the middle of the Gulf of Mexico, a severe storm arose. The sharp roll of the *Chaparral* in

---

[2] The General Towage Conditions of the contract included the following:

    1. . . . [Unterweser and its] masters and crews are not responsible for defaults and/or errors in the navigation of the tow.

    2. . . .

    b) Damages suffered by the towed object are in any case for account of its Owners.

In addition, the contract provided that any insurance of the *Chaparral* was to be "for account of" Zapata. Unterweser's initial telegraphic bid had also offered to "arrange insurance covering towage risk for rig if desired." As Zapata had chosen to be self-insured on all its rigs, the loss in this case was not compensated by insurance.

Gulf waters caused its elevator legs, which had been raised for the voyage, to break off and fall into the sea, seriously damaging the *Chaparral*. In this emergency situation Zapata instructed the *Bremen* to tow its damaged rig to Tampa, Florida, the nearest port of refuge.

On January 12, Zapata, ignoring its contract promise to litigate "any dispute arising" in the English courts, commenced a suit in admiralty in the United States District Court at Tampa, seeking $3,500,000 damages against Unterweser *in personam* and the *Bremen in rem,* alleging negligent towage and breach of contract.[3] Unterweser responded by invoking the forum clause of the towage contract, and moved to dismiss for lack of jurisdiction or on *forum non conveniens* grounds, or in the alternative to stay the action pending submission of the dispute to the "London Court of Justice." Shortly thereafter, in February, before the District Court had ruled on its motion to stay or dismiss the United States action, Unterweser commenced an action against Zapata seeking damages for breach of the towage contract in the High Court of Justice in London, as the contract provided. Zapata appeared in that court to contest jurisdiction, but its challenge was rejected, the English courts holding that the contractual forum provision conferred jurisdiction.[4]

In the meantime, Unterweser was faced with a dilemma in the pending action in the United States court at Tampa. The six-month period for filing action to limit its liability to Zapata and other potential claimants was about to expire,[5] but the United States District Court in Tampa had not yet ruled on Unterweser's motion to dismiss or stay Zapata's action. On July 2, 1968, confronted with difficult alternatives, Unterweser filed an action to limit its liability in the District Court in Tampa. That court entered the customary injunction against proceedings outside the limitation court, and Zapata refiled its initial claim in the limitation action.

It was only at this juncture, on July 29, after the six-month period for filing the limitation action had run, that the District Court denied Unterweser's January motion to dismiss or stay Zapata's initial action. In denying the motion, that court relied on the prior decision of the Court of Appeals in *Carbon Black Export, Inc. v. The Monrosa,* 254 F. 2d 297 (CA5 1958), cert. dismissed, 359 U. S. 180 (1959). In that case the Court of Appeals had held a forum-selection clause unenforceable, reiterating the traditional view of many American courts that "agreements in advance of controversy whose object is to oust the jurisdiction of the courts are contrary to public policy and will not be enforced." 254 F. 2d, at 300–301.[7] Apparently concluding that it was bound by the *Carbon Black* case, the District Court gave the forum-selection clause little, if any, weight. Instead, the court treated the motion to dismiss under normal *forum non conveniens* doctrine applicable in the absence of such a clause, citing *Gulf Oil Corp. v. Gilbert,* 330 U. S. 501 (1947). Under that doctrine "unless the balance is strongly in favor of the defendant, the

---

[3] The *Bremen* was arrested by a United States marshal acting pursuant to Zapata's complaint immediately upon her arrival in Tampa. The tug was subsequently released when Unterweser furnished security in the amount of $3,500,000.

[4] Zapata appeared specially and moved to set aside service of process outside the country. Justice Karminski of the High Court of Justice denied the motion on the ground the contractual choice-of-forum provision conferred jurisdiction and would be enforced absent a factual showing it would not be "fair and right" to do so. He did not believe Zapata had made such a showing, and held that it should be required to "stick to [its] bargain." The Court of Appeal dismissed an appeal on the ground that Justice Karminski had properly applied the English rule.

[The court quotes from Lord Justice Willmer's opinion, p. 290, *supra.*]

[5] 546 U. S. C. §§ 183, 185. See generally G. Gilmore & C. Black, *Admiralty* § 10–15 (1957).

[7] The *Carbon Black* court went on to say that it was, in any event, unnecessary for it to reject the more liberal position taken in *Wm. H. Muller & Co. v. Swedish American Line Ltd.,* 224 F. 2d 806 (CA2), *cert. denied,* 350 U. S. 903 (1955), because the case before it had a greater nexus with the United States than that in *Muller.*

plaintiff's choice of forum should rarely be disturbed." *Id.,* at 508. The District Court concluded "[t]he balance of conveniences here is not strongly in favor of [Unterweser] and [Zapata's] choice of forum should not be disturbed."

Thereafter, on January 21, 1969, the District Court denied another motion by Unterweser to stay the limitation action pending determination of the controversy in the High Court of Justice in London and granted Zapata's motion to restrain Unterweser from litigating further in the London court. The District Judge ruled that, having taken jurisdiction in the limitation proceeding, he had jurisdiction to determine all matters relating to the controversy. He ruled that Unterweser should be required to "do equity" by refraining from also litigating the controversy in the London court, not only for the reasons he had previously stated for denying Unterweser's first motion to stay Zapata's action, but also because Unterweser had invoked the United States court's jurisdiction to obtain the benefit of the Limitation Act.

On appeal, a divided panel of the Court of Appeals affirmed, and on rehearing *en banc* the panel opinion was adopted, with six of the 14 *en banc* judges dissenting. As had the District Court, the majority holding rested on the *Carbon Black* decision, concluding that "at the very least" that case stood for the proposition that a forum-selection clause "will not be enforced unless the selected state would provide a more convenient forum than the state in which suit is brought." From that premise the Court of Appeals proceeded to conclude that, apart from the forum-selection clause, the District Court did not abuse its discretion in refusing to decline jurisdiction on the basis of *forum non conveniens.* It noted that (1) the flotilla never "escaped the Fifth Circuit's mare nostrum, and the casualty occurred in close proximity to the district court;" (2) a considerable number of potential witnesses, including Zapata crewmen, resided in the Gulf Coast area; (3) preparation for the voyage and inspection and repair work had been performed in the Gulf area; (4) the testimony of the *Bremen* crew was available by way of deposition; (5) England had no interest in or contact with the controversy other than the forum-selection clause. The Court of Appeals majority further noted that Zapata was a United States citizen and "[t]he discretion of the district court to remand the case to a foreign forum was consequently limited"— especially since it appeared likely that the English courts would enforce the exculpatory clauses.[8] In the Court of Appeals' view, enforcement of such clauses would be contrary to public policy in American courts under *Bisso v. Inland Waterways Corp.,* 349 U. S. 85 (1955), and *Dixilyn Drilling Corp. v. Crescent Towing & Salvage Co.,* 372 U. S. 697 (1963). Therefore, "[t]he district court was entitled to consider that remanding Zapata to a foreign forum, with no practical contact with the controversy, could raise a bar to recovery by a United States citizen which its own convenient courts would not countenance."[9]

We hold, with the six dissenting members of the Court of Appeals, that far too little weight and effect were given to the forum clause in resolving this controversy. For at least two decades we have witnessed an expansion of overseas commercial activities by business enterprises based

---

[8] The record contains an undisputed affidavit of a British solicitor stating an opinion that the exculpatory clauses of the contract would be held "prima facie valid and enforceable" against Zapata in any action maintained in England in which Zapata alleged that defaults or errors in Unterweser's tow caused the casualty and damage to the *Chaparral.* In addition, it is not disputed that while the limitation fund in the District Court in Tampa amounts to $1,390,000, the limitation fund in England would be only slightly in excess of $80,000 under English law.

[9] The Court of Appeals also indicated in passing that even if it took the view that choice-of-forum clauses were enforceable unless "unreasonable" it was "doubtful" that enforcement would be proper here because the exculpatory clauses would deny Zapata relief to which it was "entitled" and because England was "seriously inconvenient" for trial of the action.

§ 4.02   CHOICE OF LAW □ 297

in the United States. The barrier of distance that once tended to confine a business concern to a modest territory no longer does so. Here we see an American company with special expertise contracting with a foreign company to tow a complex machine thousands of miles across seas and oceans. The expansion of American business and industry will hardly be encouraged if, notwithstanding solemn contracts, we insist on a parochial concept that all disputes must be resolved under our laws and in our courts. Absent a contract forum, the considerations relied on by the Court of Appeals would be persuasive reasons for holding an American forum convenient in the traditional sense, but in an era of expanding world trade and commerce, the absolute aspects of the doctrine of the *Carbon Black* case have little place and would be a heavy hand indeed on the future development of international commercial dealings by Americans. We cannot have trade and commerce in world markets and international waters exclusively on our terms, governed by our laws, and resolved in our courts.

Forum-selection clauses have historically not been favored by American courts. Many courts, federal and state, have declined to enforce such clauses on the ground that they were "contrary to public policy," or that their effect was to "oust the jurisdiction" of the court. Although this view apparently still has considerable acceptance, other courts are tending to adopt a more hospitable attitude toward forum-selection clauses. This view, advanced in the well-reasoned dissenting opinion in the instant case, is that such clauses are prima facie valid and should be enforced unless enforcement is shown by the resisting party to be "unreasonable" under the circumstances. We believe this is the correct doctrine to be followed by federal district courts sitting in admiralty. It is merely the other side of the proposition recognized by this Court in *National Equipment Rental, Ltd. v. Szukhent*, 375 U. S. 311 (1964), holding that in federal courts a party may validly consent to be sued in a jurisdiction where he cannot be found for service of process through contractual designation of an "agent" for receipt of process in that jurisdiction. In so holding, the Court stated:

> [I]t is settled . . . that parties to a contract may agree in advance to submit to the jurisdiction of a given court, to permit notice to be served by the opposing party, or even to waive notice altogether.

Id., at 315–316. This approach is substantially that followed in other common-law countries including England. It is the view advanced by noted scholars and that adopted by the *Restatement of the Conflict of Laws*.[13] It accords with ancient concepts of freedom of contract and reflects an appreciation of the expanding horizons of American contractors who seek business in all parts of the world. Not surprisingly, foreign businessmen prefer, as do we, to have disputes resolved in their own courts, but if that choice is not available, then in a neutral forum with expertise in the subject matter. Plainly, the courts of England meet the standards of neutrality and long experience in admiralty litigation. The choice of that forum was made in an arm's-length negotiation by experienced and sophisticated businessmen, and absent some compelling and countervailing reason it should be honored by the parties and enforced by the courts.

The argument that such clauses are improper because they tend to "oust" a court of jurisdiction is hardly more than a vestigial legal fiction. It appears to rest at core on historical judicial resistance to any attempt to reduce the power and business of a particular court and has little place in an era when all courts are overloaded and when businesses once essentially local now

---

[13] *Restatement (Second) of the Conflict of Laws* § 80 (1971); Reese, *The Contractual Forum: Situation in the United States,* 13 Am. J. Comp. Law 187 (1964); A. Ehrenzweig, *Conflict of Laws* § 41 (1962). See also Model Choice of Forum Act (National Conference of Commissioners on Uniform State Laws 1968).

operate in world markets. It reflects something of a provincial attitude regarding the fairness of other tribunals. No one seriously contends in this case that the forum-selection clause "ousted" the District Court of jurisdiction over Zapata's action. The threshold question is whether that court should have exercised its jurisdiction to do more than give effect to the legitimate expectations of the parties, manifested in their freely negotiated agreement, by specifically enforcing the forum clause.

There are compelling reasons why a freely negotiated private international agreement, unaffected by fraud, undue influence, or overweening bargaining power,[14] such as that involved here, should be given full effect. In this case, for example, we are concerned with a far from routine transaction between companies of two different nations contemplating the tow of an extremely costly piece of equipment from Louisiana across the Gulf of Mexico and the Atlantic Ocean, through the Mediterranean Sea to its final destination in the Adriatic Sea. In the course of its voyage, it was to traverse the waters of many jurisdictions. The *Chaparral* could have been damaged at any point along the route, and there were countless possible ports of refuge. That the accident occurred in the Gulf of Mexico and the barge was towed to Tampa in an emergency were mere fortuities. It cannot be doubted for a moment that the parties sought to provide for a neutral forum for the resolution of any disputes arising during the tow. Manifestly much uncertainty and possibly great inconvenience to both parties could arise if a suit could be maintained in any jurisdiction in which an accident might occur or if jurisdiction were left to any place where the *Bremen* or Unterweser might happen to be found.[15] The elimination of

---

[14] The record here refutes any notion of overweening bargaining power. Judge Wisdom in the Court of Appeals noted:

> Zapata has neither presented evidence of nor alleged fraud or undue bargaining power in the agreement. Unterweser was only one of several companies bidding on the project. No evidence contradicts its Managing Director's affidavit that it specified English courts "in an effort to meet Zapata Off-Shore Company half way." Zapata's Vice President has declared by affidavit that no specific negotiations concerning the forum clause took place. But this was not simply a form contract with boilerplate language that Zapata had no power to alter. The towing of an oil rig across the Atlantic was a new business. Zapata did make alterations to the contract submitted by Unterweser. The forum clause could hardly be ignored. It is the final sentence of the agreement, immediately preceding the date and the parties' signatures. . . .

428 F. 2d 888, 907.

[15] At the very least, the clause was an effort to eliminate all uncertainty as to the nature, location, and outlook of the forum in which these companies of differing nationalities might find themselves. Moreover, while the contract here did not specifically provide that the substantive law of England should be applied, it is the general rule in English courts that the parties are assumed, absent contrary indication, to have designated the forum with the view that it should apply its own law. See, *e. g., Tzortzis v. Monark Line A/B,* [p. 279, *supra.*]; see generally 1 T. Carver, *Carriage by Sea* 496–497 (12th ed. 1971); G. Cheshire, *Private International Law* 193 (7th ed. 1965); A. Dicey & J. Morris, *The Conflict of Laws* 705, 1046 (8th ed. 1967); Collins, *Arbitration Clauses and Forum Selecting Clauses in the Conflict of Laws: Some Recent Developments in England,* 2 J. Mar. L. & Comm. 363, 365–370 and n. 7 (1971). It is therefore reasonable to conclude that the forum clause was also an effort to obtain certainty as to the applicable substantive law.

The record contains an affidavit of a Managing Director of Unterweser stating that Unterweser considered the choice-of-forum provision to be of "overriding importance" to the transaction. He stated that Unterweser towage contracts ordinarily provide for exclusive German jurisdiction and application of German law, but that "[i]n this instance, in an effort to meet [Zapata] half way, [Unterweser] proposed the London Court of Justice. Had this provision not been accepted by [Zapata], [Unterweser] would not have entered into the towage contract . . ." He also stated that the parties intended, by designating the London forum, that English law would be applied. A responsive affidavit by Hoyt Taylor, a vice president of Zapata, denied that there were any discussions between Zapata and Unterweser concerning the forum clause or the question of the applicable law.

all such uncertainties by agreeing in advance on a forum acceptable to both parties is an indispensable element in international trade, commerce, and contracting. There is strong evidence that the forum clause was a vital part of the agreement,[16] and it would be unrealistic to think that the parties did not conduct their negotiations, including fixing the monetary terms, with the consequences of the forum clause figuring prominently in their calculations. Under these circumstances, as Justice Karminski reasoned in sustaining jurisdiction over Zapata in the High Court of Justice, "[t]he force of an agreement for litigation in this country, freely entered into between two competent parties, seems to me to be very powerful."

Thus, in the light of present-day commercial realities and expanding international trade we conclude that the forum clause should control absent a strong showing that it should be set aside. Although their opinions are not altogether explicit, it seems reasonably clear that the District Court and the Court of Appeals placed the burden on Unterweser to show that London would be a more convenient forum than Tampa, although the contract expressly resolved that issue. The correct approach would have been to enforce the forum clause specifically unless Zapata could clearly show that enforcement would be unreasonable and unjust, or that the clause was invalid for such reasons as fraud or overreaching. Accordingly, the case must be remanded for reconsideration.

We note, however, that there is nothing in the record presently before us that would support a refusal to enforce the forum clause. The Court of Appeals suggested that enforcement would be contrary to the public policy of the forum under *Bisso v. Inland Waterways Corp.,* 349 U. S. 85 (1955), because of the prospect that the English courts would enforce the clauses of the towage contract purporting to exculpate Unterweser from liability for damages to the *Chaparral.* A contractual choice-of-forum clause should be held unenforceable if enforcement would contravene a strong public policy of the forum in which suit is brought, whether declared by statute or by judicial decision. See, *e. g., Boyd v. Grand Trunk W. R. Co.,* 338 U. S. 263 (1949). It is clear, however, that whatever the proper scope of the policy expressed in *Bisso,* it does not reach this case. *Bisso* rested on considerations with respect to the towage business strictly in American waters, and those considerations are not controlling in an international commercial agreement. Speaking for the dissenting judges in the Court of Appeals, Judge Wisdom pointed out:

> [W]e should be careful not to over-emphasize the strength of the [*Bisso*] policy. . . . [T]wo concerns underlie the rejection of exculpatory agreements: that they may be produced by overweening bargaining power; and that they do not sufficiently discourage negligence. . . . Here the conduct in question is that of a foreign party occurring in international waters outside our jurisdiction. The evidence disputes any notion of overreaching in the contractual agreement. And for all we know, the uncertainties and dangers in the new field of transoceanic towage of oil rigs were so great that the tower was unwilling to take financial responsibility for the risks, and the parties thus allocated responsibility for the voyage to the tow. It is equally possible that the contract price took this factor into account. I conclude that we should not invalidate the forum selection clause here unless we are firmly convinced

---

[16] See nn. 14–15, *supra.* Zapata has denied specifically discussing the forum clause with Unterweser, but, as Judge Wisdom pointed out, Zapata made numerous changes in the contract without altering the forum clause, which could hardly have escaped its attention. Zapata is clearly not unsophisticated in such matters. The contract of its wholly owned subsidiary with an Italian corporation covering the contemplated drilling operations in the Adriatic Sea provided that all disputes were to be settled by arbitration in London under English law, and contained broad exculpatory clauses. App. 306–311.

that we would thereby significantly encourage negligent conduct within the boundaries of the United States. 428 F. 2d, at 907–908. (Footnotes omitted.)

Courts have also suggested that a forum clause, even though it is freely bargained for and contravenes no important public policy of the forum, may nevertheless be "unreasonable" and unenforceable if the chosen forum is *seriously* inconvenient for the trial of the action. Of course, where it can be said with reasonable assurance that at the time they entered the contract, the parties to a freely negotiated private international commercial agreement contemplated the claimed inconvenience, it is difficult to see why any such claim of inconvenience should be heard to render the forum clause unenforceable. We are not here dealing with an agreement between two Americans to resolve their essentially local disputes in a remote alien forum. In such a case, the serious inconvenience of the contractual forum to one or both of the parties might carry greater weight in determining the reasonableness of the forum clause. The remoteness of the forum might suggest that the agreement was an adhesive one, or that the parties did not have the particular controversy in mind when they made their agreement, yet even there the party claiming should bear a heavy burden of proof. Similarly, selection of a remote forum to apply differing foreign law to an essentially American controversy might contravene an important public policy of the forum. For example, so long as *Bisso* governs American courts with respect to the towage business in American waters, it would quite arguably be improper to permit an American tower to avoid that policy by providing a foreign forum for resolution of his disputes with an American towee.

This case, however, involves a freely negotiated international commercial transaction between a German and an American corporation for towage of a vessel from the Gulf of Mexico to the Adriatic Sea. As noted, selection of a London forum was clearly a reasonable effort to bring vital certainty to this international transaction and to provide a neutral forum experienced and capable in the resolution of admiralty litigation. Whatever "inconvenience" Zapata would suffer by being forced to litigate in the contractual forum as it agreed to do was clearly foreseeable at the time of contracting. In such circumstances it should be incumbent on the party seeking to escape his contract to show that trial in the contractual forum will be so gravely difficult and inconvenient that he will for all practical purposes be deprived of his day in court. Absent that there is no basis for concluding that it would be unfair, unjust, or unreasonable to hold that party to his bargain.

In the course of its ruling on Unterweser's second motion to stay the proceedings in Tampa, the District Court did make a conclusory finding that the balance of convenience was "strongly" in favor of litigation in Tampa. However, as previously noted, in making that finding the court erroneously placed the burden of proof on Unterweser to show that the balance of convenience was strongly in its favor.[19] Moreover, the finding falls far short of a conclusion that Zapata would

---

[19] Applying the proper burden of proof, Justice Karminski in the High Court of Justice at London made the following findings, which appear to have substantial support in the record:

[Zapata] pointed out that in this case the balance of convenience so far as witnesses were concerned pointed in the direction of having the case heard and tried in the United States District Court at Tampa in Florida because the probability is that most, but not necessarily all, of the witnesses will be American. The answer, as it seems to me, is that a substantial minority at least of witnesses are likely to be German. The tug was a German vessel and was, as far as I know, manned by a German crew . . . .. Where they all are now or are likely to be when this matter is litigated I do not know, because the experience of the Admiralty Court here strongly points out that maritime witnesses in the course of their duties move about freely. The homes of the German crew presumably are in Germany. There is probably a balance of numbers in favour of the Americans, but not, as I am inclined to think, a very heavy balance.

It should also be noted that if the exculpatory clause is enforced in the English courts, many of Zapata's witnesses on the questions of negligence and damage may be completely unnecessary.

be effectively deprived of its day in court should it be forced to litigate in London. Indeed, it cannot even be assumed that it would be placed to the expense of transporting its witnesses to London. It is not unusual for important issues in international admiralty cases to be dealt with by deposition. Both the District Court and the Court of Appeals majority appeared satisfied that Unterweser could receive a fair hearing in Tampa by using deposition testimony of its witnesses from distant places, and there is no reason to conclude that Zapata could not use deposition testimony to equal advantage if forced to litigate in London as it bound itself to do. Nevertheless, to allow Zapata opportunity to carry its heavy burden of showing not only that the balance of convenience is strongly in favor of trial in Tampa (that is, that it will be far more inconvenient for Zapata to litigate in London than it will be for Unterweser to litigate in Tampa), but also that a London trial will be so manifestly and gravely inconvenient to Zapata that it will be effectively deprived of a meaningful day in court, we remand for further proceedings.

. . .

The judgment of the Court of Appeals is vacated and the case is remanded for further proceedings consistent with this opinion.

MR. JUSTICE DOUGLAS, dissenting.

. . .

Respondent is a citizen of this country. Moreover, if it were remitted to the English court, its substantive rights would be adversely affected. Exculpatory provisions in the towage control provide (1) that petitioners, the masters and the crews "are not responsible for defaults and/or errors in the navigation of the tow" and (2) that "[d]amages suffered by the towed object are in any case for account of its Owners."

Under our decision in *Dixilyn Drilling Corp v. Crescent Towing & Salvage Co.,* 372 U. S. 697, 698 [1963], "a contract which exempts the tower from liability for its own negligence" is not enforceable, though there is evidence in the present record that it is enforceable in England. That policy was first announced in *Bisso v. Inland Waterways Corp.,* 349 U. S. 85; . . . Although the casualty occurred on the high seas the *Bisso* doctrine is nonetheless applicable. . . .

Moreover, the casualty occurred close to the District Court, a number of potential witnesses, including respondent's crewmen, reside in that area, and the inspection and repair work were done there. The testimony of the tower's crewmen, residing in Germany, is already available by way of depositions taken in the proceedings.

All in all, the District Court judge exercised his discretion wisely in enjoining petitioners from pursuing the litigation in England.*

---

* It is said that because these parties specifically agreed to litigate their disputes before the London Court of Justice, the District Court, absent "unreasonable" circumstances, should have honored that choice by declining to exercise its jurisdiction. The forum-selection clause, however, is part and parcel of the exculpatory provision in the towing agreement which, as mentioned in the text, is not enforceable in American courts. For only by avoiding litigation in the United States could petitioners hope to evade the *Bisso* doctrine.

Judges in this country have traditionally been hostile to attempts to circumvent the public policy against exculpatory agreements. For example, clauses specifying that the law of a foreign place (which favors such releases) should control have regularly been ignored. Thus, in *The Kensington,* 183 U. S. 263, 276, the Court held void an exemption from liability despite the fact that the contract provided that it should be construed under Belgian law which was more tolerant. And see *E. Gerli & Co. v. Cunard S. S. Co.,* 48 F. 2d 115, 117 (CA2); *Oceanic Steam Nav. Co. v. Corcoran,* 9 F. 2d 724, 731 (CA2); *In re Lea Fabrics, Inc.,* 226 F. Supp. 232, 237 (NJ); *F. A. Straus & Co. v. Canadian P.*

I would affirm the judgment below.

CARVALHO v. HULL, BLYTH (ANGOLA) LTD.

Court of Appeal (U.K.)
[1979] 1 W.L.R. 1228

Interlocutory appeal from DONALDSON J.

On April 29, 1977, the plaintiff, Joaquim Carvalho, resident in Portugal, issued a specially indorsed writ in the High Court in London claiming against Hull, Blyth (Angola) Ltd., a company registered in England, but carrying on business in independent Angola, the balance of moneys (20,000,000 escudos) due under a contract made between the parties on December 5, 1973, in Luanda, Angola, then a province of metropolitan Portugal. . . .

On July 22, 1977, a summons was issued on behalf of the defendants asking that the writ be set aside on the ground that the High Court had no jurisdiction in the matter, or alternatively that the proceedings be stayed on the ground that the parties had agreed to submit the dispute to the exclusive jurisdiction of the courts of Angola. Clause 14 of the contract on which the plaintiff's claim was based, provided (as translated in the documents exhibited to the defendants' affidavit evidence):

> In the case of litigation arising, the District Court of Luanda shall be considered the sole competent court to adjudicate to the exclusion of all others.

DONALDSON J., in chambers . . . said that he found strong grounds for refusing a stay of the proceedings in England "either as a matter of construction of [clause 14], or because it would be just and proper to allow the plaintiff to continue."

BROWNE L.J.

This is an appeal by the defendants from a decision of Donaldson J. given on February 19, 1979, when he refused the defendants' application to stay the plaintiff's action, but gave leave to appeal.

. . .

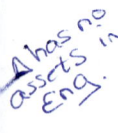

The plaintiff formerly lived in Angola, but left in August 1975 and now lives in Portugal. The defendants are an English registered company, so there is no doubt that the English courts have jurisdiction, but we are told that the defendants have no assets here. They have carried

---

R. Co., 254 N. Y. 407, 173 N. E. 564; *Siegelman v. Cunard White Star,* 221 F. 2d 189, 199 (CA2) (Frank, J., dissenting). 6A A. Corbin on Contracts § 1446 (1962).

> The instant stratagem of specifying a foreign forum is essentially the same as invoking a foreign law of construction except that the present circumvention also requires the American party to travel across an ocean to seek relief. Unless we are prepared to overrule *Bisso* we should not countenance devices designed solely for the purpose of evading its prohibition.

> It is argued, however, that one of the rationales of the *Bisso* doctrine, "to protect those in need of goods or services from being overreached by others who have power to drive hard bargains" (349 U. S., at 91), does not apply here because these parties may have been of equal bargaining stature. Yet we have often adopted prophylactic rules rather than attempt to sort the core cases from the marginal ones. In any event, the other objective of the *Bisso* doctrine, to "discourage negligence by making wrongdoers pay damages" (*ibid.*) applies here and in every case regardless of the relative bargaining strengths of the parties.

on and still carry on business entirely in Angola. They have carried on business there for 100 years. Their present business is that of ships' agents, and they also carry on business as motor traders through subsidiary companies.

In 1970 their motor trading business was reorganised in such a way that there were five subsidiary companies known as the U.N.A.I.O. Group: in each of these companies the defendants owned 51 per cent. of the shares and the plaintiff owned 49 per cent. By a contract dated December 5, 1973, the plaintiff agreed to sell and the defendants agreed to buy all his shares in the five subsidiary companies for a total price of 76 million escudos. Clause 6 of the contract provided for the payment of the price by four instalments. The first three instalments were paid. The fourth instalment of 20 million escudos (of which the sterling equivalent is about £300,000) should have been paid in January 1976 but has not been paid. On April 29, 1977, the plaintiff issued his writ in this action claiming that sum or its sterling equivalent. I have already quoted clause 14 of the contract.

Mr. Wood, for the defendants, submits that the proper law of the contract is Angolan law and tells us that the defence to the plaintiff's claim will be: (1) that, under Angolan law, the "economic hardship" suffered by the U.N.A.I.O. Group as a result of events in Angola from 1975 onwards would entitle them to a reduction or postponement of the payment claimed in the action; (2) that, under the Angolan Exchange Control Regulations, the defendants are precluded from making any payments otherwise than in Angola in the new currency, known as kwangas, which has superseded the escudo. . . .

Until 1951 Angola was a colony of Portugal. In 1951 it became a province of Portugal. In January 1975, after a coup d'etat in Portugal in 1974 the new Portuguese government announced that Angola would become independent in November 1975. In 1975 civil war broke out in Angola, but on November 11 Angola did become independent and, in due course, a new constitution was promulgated to which I will refer in a moment. A party or group known as M.P.L.A. assumed power—that being the Popular Movement for the Liberation of Angola—and Dr. Neto became President. Since then Angola has been recognised by Her Majesty's Government, among a number of other states, and ambassadors have been exchanged between Angola and this country.

The plaintiff, as I have said, left Angola in August 1975. There was before DONALDSON J. an affidavit by Mr. Englefield, the plaintiff's solicitor, in these terms:

> 1. I have the carriage of this action on behalf of the plaintiff and have spoken to him on a number of occasions both in this country and in Portugal. The plaintiff has informed me that in August 1975 he was forced to leave Angola with his family and received threats against his life and the lives of his family. The plaintiff left behind in Angola his house, furniture, balance in his bank account and four farms belonging to him. The plaintiff's property and farms have now been taken over by officers of the Marxists's government.
> 2. The plaintiff is unwilling to return to Angola and believes that if he does so he will be liquidated.

Since the hearing before DONALDSON J. an affidavit has been sworn by the plaintiff himself, verifying that affidavit and including a list of the property which he says he left behind in Angola and which has been confiscated. That affidavit was put before us without objection from Mr. Wood.

I should now refer to the Constitution, which is exhibited to Dr. de Almeida's affidavit of October 28, 1977. Article 1 provides:

The People's Republic of Angola is a sovereign, independent and democratic state, the foremost objective of which is the total liberation of the Angolan people from the vestiges of colonialism and from domination and aggression by Imperialism and the construction of a prosperous and democratic country, completely free from any form of exploitation of man by man, materialising the inspirations of the popular masses.

Article 2:

All sovereignty is vested in the Angolan people. The political, economic and social guidance of the nation are vested in the M.P.L.A., its lawful representative, consisting of a wide front which includes all the patriotic forces engaged in the anti-Imperialist struggle.

Article 7:

The People's Republic of Angola is a lay state, there being complete separation between the state and religious institutions. All religions will be respected and the state will grant protection for churches, places and objects of worship, provided that they comply with state laws.

Article 10:

The People's Republic of Angola recognises, protects and guarantees private property and activities, even those of foreigners, provided that they are useful to the economy of the country and the interests of the Angolan people.

Article 44:

The exercise of the jurisdictional function aimed at the realisation of democratic justice is exclusively incumbent on the courts. The organisation, composition and competence of the courts will be fixed by law.

Article 45:

The judges will be independent in the exercise of their duties.

Article 58:

The laws and regulations currently in force will be applicable where not revoked or altered and provided that they do not conflict with the spirit of this Law and the Angolan Revolutionary Process.

In *The Eleftheria* [1970] P. 94, 99–100 BRANDON J. said—and this is the passage, as I understand it, quoted by DONALDSON J.:

The principles established by the authorities can, I think, be summarised as follows: (1) Where plaintiffs sue in England in breach of an agreement to refer disputes to a foreign court, and the defendants apply for a stay, the English court, assuming the claim to be otherwise within its jurisdiction, is not bound to grant a stay but has a discretion whether to do so or not. (2) The discretion should be exercised by granting a stay unless strong cause for not doing so is shown. (3) The burden of proving such strong cause is on the plaintiffs. (4) In exercising its discretion the court should take into account all the circumstances of the particular case. (5) In particular, but without prejudice to (4), the following matters, where they arise, may properly be regarded:—(a) In what country the evidence on the issues of fact is situated, or more readily available, and the effect of that on the relative convenience and expense of trial as between the English and foreign courts. (b) Whether the law of the foreign court applies and, if so, whether it differs from English law in any material respects. (c) With what country either party is connected, and how closely. (d) Whether the defendants genuinely desire trial in the foreign country, or are only seeking procedural advantages. (e) Whether the plaintiffs would be prejudiced by having to sue in the foreign court because they would: (i) be deprived of security for their claim; (ii) be unable to enforce any judgment obtained; (iii) be faced with a time-bar not applicable in England; or (iv) for political, racial, religious or other reasons be unlikely to get a fair trial.

Rule 30 in *Dicey and Morris, The Conflict of Laws,* 9th ed. (1973), p. 222, on which the judge also relied, is in these terms:

Where a contract provides that all disputes between the parties are to be referred to the exclusive jurisdiction of a foreign tribunal, the court will stay proceedings instituted in England in breach of such agreement, unless the plaintiff proves that it is just and proper to allow them to continue.^g

It is clear from the affidavits filed on behalf of the plaintiff, and it is not disputed by the defendants, that, when the contract was made in December 1973, Angola was a province of Portugal. The law applied was Portuguese law and the legal system then in force was procedurally and substantively Portuguese. The judicial organisation of Portuguese Angola was part of the judicial system of Portuguese Europe and was in every respect identical with it. The qualification of judges was the same as in Portugal: see the affidavits of Dr. de Almeida, and Dr. Carvalho, for the plaintiffs; and Dr. Oliveira for the defendants. Angola clearly then had no separate legal system and there was no such thing as Angolan law except, perhaps, in some native customary courts. Now Angola is an independent sovereign state with a new constitution. It is true that it seems, from the affidavits filed on behalf of the defendants, that in general Portuguese law is still applied and that the previous structure of the courts still exists, except for the abolition of the right of appeal to the Supreme Court in Lisbon. But it seems to me plain from the Constitution that this situation can be changed at any moment: see especially articles 44 and 58. It seems, from the proviso to article 58, that, without any formal change, the previous law will not be applied if it does "conflict with the spirit of this law and the Angolan revolutionary process."

It is also clear from the defendants' evidence that the system for the appointment of judges has completely changed. According to the evidence filed on behalf of the defendants, the District Court of Luanda still exists under the same name but, in my judgment, the judge was right in holding that it is a different court from the court in contemplation when the contract was made. It was then a Portuguese court in all the respects to which I have already referred. It is now an Angolan court operating within the framework of the Angolan constitution and legal system and applying Angolan law.

One can perhaps test it in this way. If the parties had known in December 1973 what the situation would be in Angola now, would they have agreed to include clause 14 in the contract? I think it is impossible to say that the answer must be "Yes." There is a complete conflict in the affidavit evidence about the present situation as to the administration of justice in Angola. This court cannot resolve this conflict but, in my view, it is unnecessary to do so to arrive at the conclusion that the present District Court of Luanda is a different court from that contemplated by the contract. If my conclusion on the construction point is right, it is unnecessary to decide the discretion point. . . .

---

^g Rule 32 in the 12th edition (1993).

Mr. Wood's criticism of *Dicey*, as I understood it, was that it put the burden on the plaintiff too low and that it did not sufficiently emphasise the importance of holding people to their contracts. But, as I have already quoted from p. 223, *Dicey* does refer specifically to the importance of making people abide by their contracts and, in my judgment, there is no real difference between the two tests of "just and proper" and "strong cause."

GEOFFREY LANE L.J.:

I agree.

It seems to me that [Articles 2, 10, 44, and 58 of the Angolan Constitution] make it plain that the existing application of Portuguese law may be very short-lived, and it is impossible to predict what effect those articles, when applied, may have upon the present system of law in Angola and on the contents of the Portuguese laws which are presently administered there.

Accordingly, for those short reasons, it seems to me that the judge was right in deciding the first point, namely what he called the construction point, in favour of the plaintiff. Put perhaps more accurately, there was ample ground on which he could come to the conclusion which he did.

So far as the second point is concerned, namely, the discretion point, there it is plain that the same reasoning can be applied. . . .

. . .

I wish to add only this. One of the matters which the judge did mention was the fact that the plaintiff was reluctant to return to Angola and, indeed, has declared his intention of not returning to Angola on the basis that he feared for his life if he were to go back there. On all the evidence it seems to me that, plainly, the plaintiff was the sort of person who would be anathema to the present government in Angola. That can scarcely be disputed, and it seems to me there was a ground for the plaintiff's fear. However, that is not a matter on which I would desire to base my decision.

Appeal dismissed with costs.

NOTES AND QUESTIONS

(1)(a) It is often assumed that parties—and certainly lawyers—prefer when possible to have the law of their own state applied. *Tzortzis* shows the reverse, with the Swedish seller seeking to have English law applied to the contract it seems to have breached, and the Greek buyers seeking to have Swedish law applied to measure their damages. Whether either party thought of the question before the deal broke down is, of course, highly doubtful.

(b) The *Tzortzis* case is reproduced here not to make the preceding point, but to illustrate that agreement on a forum may lead to a choice of law—and indeed is very likely to do so if the forum chosen is in England. Lord Denning—like Justice Holmes fond of one-liners—says "An express choice of a tribunal is an implied choice of the law," even though the choice was made by use of a standard printed forum, and even though the forum referred not to a court, but only to arbitration. Justice Salmon concedes that it is Sweden's system of law with which the transaction has its "closest and most real connection."[a] But the inference that English law was

---

[a] Recall Rule 145 of *Dicey,* Chapter 1 at p. 17, *supra.*

chosen by the parties, he says, is "an almost irresistible inference, which overrides all the other factors." It follows that if a party wants arbitration in London but not English law, it had better say so expressly, as in the Statement, "The law of France shall govern the validity and interpretation of this agreement."

(c) Notice that Justice Salmon cites Lord Wright for the proposition that the seat of the arbitration is the source of the law to be applied. But that statement, in the *Vita Food Products* case, was made in a rather different context, as both Lord Morris and Lord Wilberforce point out in *Cie. Tunisienne*—i.e., to show that application of English law did not require a link between England and the underlying transaction. Moreover, Lord Wright ended up with English conflicts law, which is clearly not the case in *Tzortzis*.

(d) *Tzortzis* was not appealed to the House of Lords, and when the next case came along, the Court of Appeal, overruling the arbitrators and the judge, took the same position. For the House of Lords, that position—irresistible inferences and inevitable conclusions—was too strong. As Lord Morris put it, before one draws such an inference, all the relevant circumstances are to be considered. What are the relevant circumstances in *Cie. Tunisienne*?

(e) The several Law Lords answer the preceding question quite differently. Lord Reid points to a choice–of–law clause in the contract (Cl.13) calling for the law of the flag of the vessel carrying the goods; even if that clause is ineffective because shipments were made on different vessels flying different flags, it showed that the parties (as well as the drafters of the clause) did not want or accept the automatic inference from the choice of forum clause that the Court of Appeal spoke of in *Tzortzis*. Lord Wilberforce, however, thinks this is breathing life into a corpse which the undertakers have not yet removed.

Lord Wilberforce, for many years the leading judicial member of the House of Lords, disregards Clause 13, but focuses on the citizenship and place of business of the parties, the object of the contract, the place of negotiation, place of payment and currency, and the use of French brokers—in short all the circumstances of the contract. Lord Morris agrees with Lord Reid but hints that he could agree with Lord Wilberforce as well. Lord Diplock, for many years a commercial judge, agrees with his colleagues in this case: The Court of Appeal in *Tzortzis* and *Cie. Tunisienne* had overstated the inference, in calling it irresistible. "I do not wish," he adds, however, "to throw any doubt upon the proposition that an arbitration clause is *generally* intended by the parties to operate as a choice of the proper law of the contract . . . and should be so construed unless there are compelling indications to the contrary. . . ."

(f) The speech of Lord Wilberforce in *Cie. Tunisienne* is a convenient occasion to take brief note of the traditional English method to search for the proper law of the contract. English style.[b] It seems there is a three-step process: (1) See if there is an express choice of law; if not, then (2) see if the intention can be inferred from the circumstances; if still not, only then (3) look for the system of law with which the transaction has its clearest and most real connection. Where Wilberforce differs from (and overrules) Lord Denning is that Denning would regard the presence of a choice of forum clause as sufficient to lead to the required inference under step (2), while Wilberforce and his colleagues in *Cie. Tunisienne* say that we must look at all the circumstances

---

[b] Lord Wilberforce says he prefers the Seventh to the Eighth edition of Dicey on this point. The Tenth and Eleventh editions of Dicey (1980, 1987) went back to the formulation approved by Wilberforce. The Twelfth edition (1993) paraphrases Articles 3(1) and 4(1) of the Rome Convention (Documents Supplement p. 45), which seems to make inference of intent somewhat more difficult, and in default of choice by the parties looks to the law of the country with which it is most closely connected, which in turn is subject to the presumptions set out in Article 4(2).

before deciding whether the choice of forum clause does lead to the inference, without, as he says "giving a prerogative effect to one these elements."

In the American approach (using for this purpose §§ 187 and 188 of the Restatement) the technique is quite different: (1) If there is an express choice of law, it is necessary to inquire whether it meets the criteria for autonomy, which, as we saw, may well include examination into the system of law with which the transaction has its most significant relationship; and (2) if there is no express choice of law, inferred intent is one of the factors considered, along with the other criteria set forth in § 188 and § 6. Choice of forum, without more, seems to play little or no role.

(2)(a) Turning now to the efficacy of choice of forum clauses themselves, the two versions of *Zapata* show the different points of departure. The English court says parties should be held to their bargain, and has no trouble with the question of why it should spend English taxpayers' money resolving a dispute between an American and a German company. The American courts at three levels wrestle with the reverse problem, how private parties can oust them of jurisdiction in a controversy with both parties before them.

    (i) Is the English case correctly decided?[c]

    (ii) Is the American case correctly decided?

(b) One point that English and American cases—as well as decisions from other states—are agreed on is that a choice of forum clause fairly bargained about constitutes consent by the defendant to in personam jurisdiction in the forum chosen with respect to controversies arising out of or related to the contract. The defendant may assert that another action is pending, that the forum chosen is inconvenient, or that discretion ought not to be exercised in favor of permitting service out of the forum state (as in the English *Zapata* case), but arguments that defendant is not present or doing business in the chosen forum are not relevant, because the basis of jurisdiction is consent.[d]

(c) The most serious question raised in *Zapata* in the United States is whether a choice forum clause may be exclusive, i.e., whether, if a clause in a contract reads "Any dispute . . ." or "all disputes ,. . ." a court other than the one chosen in the contract may or must decline to assert jurisdiction which would be available absent the contractual provision. Until *Zapata,* many courts in the United States had held that clauses purporting to "oust the jurisdiction" of courts were void as against public policy.[e] Putting aside the question of adhesion contracts or

---

[c] It is not clear that American courts would decide the English *Zapata* case the same way that the English court did. See, for example, N.Y. Business Corp. Law § 1314, Documents Supplement p. 56, providing for jurisdiction over actions against a foreign corporation by another foreign corporation only on the basis of one of five stated links with New York, either of the cause of action or the parties.

The effect of BCL § 1314 was diminished in 1984 by passage of two amendments to the General Obligations Law, Documents Supplement p. 56, one permitting the choice of New York law, regardless of any link to the state, in any transaction valued at $250,000 or more; the other permitting choice of a New York forum if there is a choice of New York law, consent to jurisdiction, and a transaction valued at $1,000,000 or more. The motivation for these amendments came largely from the New York banking community, in contemplation of large transnational loan agreements in which not all the lenders were New York banks. Note also that for actions brought under this section, the doctrine of forum non conveniens was declared not applicable.

[d] For affirmation of this point by the U.S. Supreme Court, see *National Equipment Rental, Ltd. v. Szukhent*, 375 U.S. 311 (1964), cited in *Zapata*/U.S.

[e] For a list of such cases, see Gruson, *Forum-Selection Clauses in International and Interstate Commercial Agree-*

overweening bargaining power by one side what public policy would be violated by a forum selection clause? To reverse the question, what public policy would be vindicated by disregarding such a clause?[f]

(d) The rule prior to *Zapata* had evolved from absolute opposition to forum selection clauses, as suggested by the quotation from Judge Frank,[g] to one of weighing the reasonableness of a forum selection provision, along the lines of forum non conveniens or choice of law balancing, as the Court of Appeals did in *Zapata*. A heavy weight in such balancing, in *Zapata* and prior cases, was the inference (or expectation or likelihood) that the forum chosen by contract would apply some substantive law that would not or might not pass muster in the court doing the balancing. Chief Justice Burger, in effect, says a contract is a contract, and plaintiff should have thought of that before (i) it agreed to the forum clause; and (ii) it agreed to an exculpatory clause that it now hopes to strike down. In fact, he suggests, plaintiff probably did think about these points; at least he finds the statements to the contrary on behalf of Zapata not convincing. Is the Chief Justice's approach persuasive? For international trade only, or for all contracts between persons of roughly equal bargaining power?

(3)(a) The brief excursion into maritime law in the discussion of *Vita Food Products* may have led to the conclusion that contracting out of liability for negligence in navigation is acceptable, so long as the appropriate notice is given. That case, however, and the U.S. legislation discussed, involved carriage of goods under a bill of lading; towing is different.[h] As to towing, the U.S. Supreme Court had held in 1955 in *Bisso*[i] that a clause in a contract releasing the tug from all liability for negligence[j] is contrary to public policy.

The Court in *Zapata* does not overrule *Bisso,* but quotes with approval the dissenting opinion of Judge Wisdom in *Zapata,* saying that one should not overemphasize the strength of the *Bisso* policy. In effect, *Bisso* is confined to inland waters. The inference, contrary to Justice Douglas' dissent, is that if he had to decide the merits of *Zapata,* the Chief Justice would not strike down the exculpatory clause. Even if that inference is wrong (or if the Chief Justice could not carry a majority of the Court on the point), he is prepared in an international context to honor a forum selection clause regardless of the effect on the underlying controversy, so long as the chosen court is a fair one.[k] In the context of *Zapata,* which type of clause in a contract is entitled to

---

ments, 1982 U. Ill. L. Rev. 133, 138–47. The landmark case in the United States signalling a shift was *Wm. H. Muller & Co. v. Swedish American Line Ltd.,* 224 F.2d 806 (2d Cir), *cert. denied,* 350 U.S. 903 (1955); however, the Second Circuit retreated from its position in *Indussa Corp. v. S. S. Ranborg,* 377 F.2d 200 (2d Cir. 1967). Both of these cases involved the Carriage of Goods by Sea Act, 46 U.S.C. § 1300 et seq. See also the *Carbon Black* case discussed by the Supreme Court in *Zapata,* pp. 295–97, *supra.*

[f] Judge Jerome Frank, who as we saw in *Siegelman,* was no friend of choice of law clauses (at least where one party was a consumer), explained the decisions to refuse to recognize forum selection clauses as follows:

Perhaps the true explanation is the power of the hypnotic phrase "oust the jurisdiction." Give a bad dogma a good name and its bite may become as bad as its bark.

Kulukundis Shipping Co. v. Amtorg Trading Corp. 126 F.2d 978, 984 (2d Cir. 1942). The quotation refers to an agreement to arbitrate, a special type of forum selection clause, as discussed in the next section.

[g] Note f, *supra.*

[h] See G. Gilmore & C. Black, *The Law of Admiralty,* 515–20 (2d ed. 1975).

[i] *Bisso v. Inland Waterways Corp.,* 349 U.S. 85 (1955).

[j] I.e., immunizing the tug from liability to the tow and placing all liability for injury to third parties from the towing operation on the tow.

[k] Note that in Footnote 15, the court cites *Tzortzis,* but not *Cie. Tunisienne.*

greater weight—choice of law or choice of forum? Suppose, for example, the towing contract had contained no choice of forum clause but had provided that "this contract and all controversies arising out of or in relation to this contract shall be governed by the law of England." The action goes forward in Tampa, Unterweser pleads the exculpatory clause, and *Zapata* says such a clause is contrary to U.S. public policy. Unterweser replies (i) this contract is subject to English law and policy; and anyway (ii) the *Bisso* policy only applies to inland transport. What result would you predict? . . . favor?

(b) Some other aspects of *Zapata,* which appear to sound in procedure or admiralty, but in a real sense present conflict of laws questions, are worth pondering:

(i) Chief Justice Burger has little difficulty with the argument that by filing a limitation petition, Unterweser waived its right to object to the jurisdiction of the Tampa court. One should not be forced into that type of choice between substantive and jurisdictional challenges.[1] But then the District Court enjoins all the parties from litigating anywhere else in the world about the *Chaparral.* Can it do this? Should the English court respect the injunction?

(ii) Zapata says that it too is covered by the injunction, and therefore cannot put in its counterclaim in the English action. Unterweser offers to waive that restraint, and the English court thanks the company for doing so. Is it for a private party to waive an injunction issued by a court pursuant to statute?

(iii) Finally, Zapata says, "If we have to litigate in England, we won't have the benefits of the $3.5 million security bond on file in Tampa." Unterweser says "Be our guest." Can it do that?

(4)(a) The Supreme Court in *Zapata* concedes that there may be situations when jurisdiction of a court should be sustained notwithstanding a forum selection clause, if the party seeking to avoid the effect of the clause could show that "trial in the contractual forum will be so gravely difficult and inconvenient that he will for all practical purposes be deprived of his day in court." (p. 300 *supra.*) The lower court erred (i) in placing the burden on the party seeking to invoke, rather than the one seeking to avoid, the choice of forum clause; and (ii) in considering the standard one of "balance of convenience" rather than deprivation of a meaningful day in court. Do you think the *Zapata* standard is the right one? Or is the burden too heavy?

(b) Not many American cases have been reported in which the burden set by the Court in *Zapata* has been met. Most are cases of extreme change in circumstances, for instance contracts by U.S. firms with Iranian entities calling for adjudication in Iran, entered into at the time of the pro-American regime of the Shah, but being invoked at the time of the anti-American regime of Ayatollah Khomeini during and after the Hostage Crisis of 1979–81.[m] The *Carvalho* case decided by the English Court of Appeal also grew out of a revolutionary change, but in a context where the forum state maintained diplomatic relations with the revolutionary state and was a disinterested state as between the plaintiff and the defendant as well as the chosen forum. Is the English standard for disregarding a forum selection clause, as stated in *The Eleftheria* and in Dicey, and applied in *Carvalho,* the same as that formulated by Chief Justice Burger in *Zapata*?

---

[1] Compare the *Etablissements Rohr* case, Chapter 8, p. 726.

[m] See e.g., *Rockwell International Systems v. Citibank,* 719 F.2d 583 (2d Cir. 1983); *McDonnell Douglas Corp. v. Islamic Republic of Iran,* 758 F.2d 341 (8th Cir. 1985).

(c) By those standards, is *Carvalho* correctly decided? What is the rationale for the decision?

(d) Justice Browne says the parties would not have made the agreement as they did had they known then what they know now. That is true of a great many contracts, including all those in which there is a sharp rise or fall in price. What distinguishes this case from other cases in which parties are held to their bargain?

(e) Both justices distinguish between what they call the construction point and the discretion point. Is there anything to this distinction other than the relation between the upper and the lower court? How can Clause 14 be "construed" not to be applicable, as contrasted with saying Dr. Carvalho couldn't get a fair hearing in Luanda today?

(5)(a) Coming back to the United States, *Zapata* was an admiralty case, and thus, it seems, not technically binding on state courts, on federal courts sitting in diversity cases, and probably not even on federal courts sitting in non-admiralty federal question cases. But is it persuasive in regard to:

(i) international commercial cases, not involving admiralty;

(ii) commercial cases with no international elements;

(iii) other contractual relationships, such as contracts of employment, insurance for individuals, leases and rentals?

(b) Breaking down the classification in a different way, suppose Alabama refuses even after *Zapata* to accept forum-selection clauses to oust the jurisdiction of its courts. An action for breach of contract is brought in (or removed to) the federal district court in Birmingham and defendant pleads a provision in the contract calling for all disputes to be resolved in the state or federal courts of New York. Is the issue one of contract law, so that the federal court must follow the Alabama rule, or one of procedure, related to forum non conveniens, so that federal courts would follow *Zapata*?[n]

(c) In fact, most state as well as courts in the United States that have considered the issue have accepted *Zapata* as persuasive.[o] The *Restatement (Second) of Conflict of Laws,* published shortly before the decision in *Zapata,* (and indeed cited at n. 13)—provided:

§ 80. The parties' agreement as to the place of the action *cannot oust a state of judicial jurisdiction, but such an agreement* will be given effect unless it is unfair or unreasonable. [italics added]

In a pocket supplement published in 1986, the words placed in italics above are eliminated.[p]

(d) One more point, relevant both to choice of judicial forum clauses, as discussed in this section, and to agreements to arbitrate, discussed in the next section. Suppose A and B have a contract calling for adjudication of all disputes under or related to the contract in the courts

---

[n] This issue came to the Supreme Court 15 years after *Zapata,* and the Court split three ways. *Stewart Organization, Inc. v. Ricoh,* 487 U.S. 22 (1988). The majority held that the forum selection clause was a factor, but not necessarily dispositive, in considering a motion for transfer within the federal court system under 28 U.S.C. §1404(a); Justice Kennedy would have held the forum selection clause controlling; and Justice Scalia would have regarded the issue one of state law and therefore governed by the law of Alabama. For discussion of the *Erie* doctrine in the context of conflict of laws generally, see Chapter 6, *infra.*

[o] See, e.g., *Smith, Valentine & Smith, Inc. v. Superior Court,* 17 Cal. 3d 491, 131 Cal. Rptr. 374, 551 P.2d 1206 (1976). For a comprehensive survey, see the articles by Walter Heiser cited at p. 337, note p, *infra.*

[p] *Restatement (Second) of Conflict of Laws,* 1986 Supplement, § 80.

of state *X*. A brings an action in *Y* to rescind the contract, alleging that the contract was procured by fraud. B moves to dismiss on the basis that all disputes related to the contract should be brought in *X*. What result?[q]

[C] Agreements to Arbitrate

A provision in a contract that all (or specified) disputes will be submitted to arbitration is, of course, a particular type of forum selection clause, much in use both in national and in transnational commerce. A well-drafted arbitration clause will provide at a minimum for the subjects covered, the place of arbitration, and the manner of selecting arbitrators. Arbitration clauses often contain, in addition, reference to an administering institution, such as the American Arbitration Association, the International Chamber of Commerce, or a great number of trade associations; to the law applicable to the contract and the arbitration; and to entry of judgment on the award rendered.

Some persons regard arbitration—domestic as well as international—as more convenient, and less expensive than litigation; usually confidential; and less encumbered with rules of procedure, evidence, motion practice, etc. Others, including much of the bar, view arbitration uncertainly, since it tends to operate with less rigid rules; largely free from precedent and appeal; almost never with the kind of discovery known and loved by American lawyers in civil litigation; and with decisionmakers who may or may not be lawyers but are not professional judges.[r] In the international context, arbitration fulfills an additional highly important function, in that it avoids the issue of jurisdiction. When neither party wants to litigate in the other state's courts—whether by consent, doing business, or long-arm jurisdiction—an agreement to arbitrate in Paris, London, Geneva or New York is a common practice.

To explore in detail the law and practice of arbitration would go well beyond the scope of this volume.[s] Following up the discussion of *Zapata,* however, a look at international agreements to arbitrate is necessary to round out the discussion of forum selection clauses and of party autonomy in contracts generally.[t]

---

[q] See *Scherk v. Alberto–Culver,* at note 14, p. 319, *infra.* Though *Scherk* and *Prima Paint,* there cited, both involved agreements to arbitrate, it seems the answer there given applies to selection of a judicial forum as well.

[r] We here speak of commercial arbitration, not arbitration concerning labor relations or arbitration pursuant to statute, as for no-fault auto accidents, insurance claims, medical malpractice, etc.

[s] For a useful treatise, dealing both with domestic and with international commercial arbitration, see M. Domke, *Commercial Arbitration* (Rev. ed. Wilner 1984). See also A. Lowenfeld, *International Litigation and Arbitration,* ch. IV (2d ed. 2002); Gary W. Born, *International Commercial Arbitration in the United States* (1994).

[t] The other side of the process of international arbitration—enforcement of arbitral awards—is taken up in Chapter 8, § 8.03[B], *infra.*

GILBERT v. BURNSTINE

New York Court of Appeals
255 N.Y. 348, 174 N.E. 706 (1931)

O'BRIEN, J.

The following facts are alleged in the complaint and admitted in the reply: In the year 1925, at New York, defendants, who are citizens and residents of this State, contracted in writing for the sale and delivery to plaintiff within the United States of a quantity of zinc concentrates. By a clause in the contract the parties agreed that all differences arising thereunder should be "arbitrated at London pursuant to the Arbitration Law of Great Britain." Differences arose concerning an alleged failure to deliver in accordance with the terms of the contract and plaintiff served notice upon defendants at New York requesting them to concur in the nomination of a certain named individual or of some other resident of London as sole arbitrator. The notice also stated that in the event of defendants' failure to concur in the nomination of an arbitrator, plaintiff would apply to the High Court of Justice of England for such an appointment pursuant to the provisions of the Arbitration Act of 1889 (52 and 53 Vict., ch. 49). On defendants' failure to comply with this notice, plaintiff obtained from the King's Bench Division an order permitting him to issue a form of process which is described in the complaint as an originating summons. This process was served upon defendants at New York and it directed them to appear at a certain time and place in London before a master in chambers so that an arbitrator might be appointed. Defendants again failed to comply and thereupon the master appointed an arbitrator. He issued a notice which was served upon defendants at New York requiring them to furnish him at a specified time and place in London with all documents relevant to the matters in dispute. This notice, like the others, was ignored by defendants. The arbitrator, after causing a peremptory notice to be served upon them, also at New York, proceeded with the arbitration at London and made an award for & 46,000 against them. The complaint alleges that all these proceedings were duly had in accordance with the English Arbitration Act of 1889 and demands judgment for the amount of the award. Defendants admit their execution of the arbitration clause in the contract but deny that they ever made submission to arbitration and deny also that the proceedings were had in accordance with the English law. They defend this action on the ground that their agreement is contrary to public policy, that the service of the notices and the originating summons is void, that no court of England ever acquired jurisdiction of their persons or property, that the award was obtained without due process of law and that its enforcement would deprive them of property without due process of law. They argue that the sole question in the case is whether the British court acquired personal jurisdiction in the absence of personal service upon them within British territory.

Settlements of disputes by arbitration are no longer deemed contrary to our public policy. Indeed, our statute encourages them. Contracts directed to that end are now declared valid, enforceable and irrevocable save upon such grounds as exist at law or in equity for the revocation of any contract. . . . Defendants' agreement without reservation to arbitrate in London according to the English statute necessarily implied a submission to the procedure whereby that law is there enforced. Otherwise the inference must be drawn that they never intended to abide by their pledge. They contracted that the machinery by which their arbitration might proceed would be foreign machinery operating from the foreign court. No other fair conclusion can be drawn from their language. Their contract constitutes something more than a simple executory one subject to breach. Not only under the foreign statute but also under our own arbitration law, it has become irrevocable in the sense that one of the parties without the consent of the other cannot deprive it of its enforcibility. . . . In order, therefore, to determine the issue asserted by defendants that jurisdiction never was acquired, the question must be decided whether their agreement to submit to that jurisdiction is contrary to our public policy.

Generally, extraterritorial jurisdiction of alien tribunals, however vigorously asserted, is denied by us. Of its own force, process issued from the court of a foreign state against our citizen and served upon him here is void. Without his consent he cannot be made subject to it, but whenever he agrees to be bound by its service, his conduct presents a problem. Contracts made by mature men who are not wards of the court should, in the absence of potent objection, be enforced. Pretexts to evade them should not be sought. Few arguments can exist based on reason or justice or common morality which can be invoked for the interference with the compulsory performance of agreements which have been freely made. Courts should endeavor to keep the law at a grade at least as high as the standards of ordinary ethics. Unless individuals run foul of constitutions, statutes, decisions or the rules of public morality, why should they not be allowed to contract as they please? Our government is not so paternalistic as to prevent them. Unless their stipulations have a tendency to entangle national or state affairs, their contracts in advance to submit to the process of foreign tribunals partake of their strictly private business. Our courts are not interested except to the extent of preserving the right to prevent repudiation. In many instances problems not dissimilar from the one presented by this case have been solved. Vigor has been infused into process otherwise impotent. Consent is the factor which imparts power. . . .

Public policy, therefore, would not forbid defendants to appoint an agent to accept service or to confess judgment in their behalf, nor does it after service forbid them in person to acknowledge receipt of it. If the fact be clear that in advance of any form of litigation or arbitration they actually intended to contract that in the event of such a proceeding they would render themselves subject to foreign process, the same policy ought to prevail. That such was their clear intent has been assumed at Special Term and the Appellate Division and the same conclusion now reached by us is plainly supported by the language of the agreement. We will not entertain the theory that, when they agreed to arbitrate at London according to the English Arbitration Act, they contracted with a reservation to refuse to place themselves on English soil and to resist the English law outside that territory. . . .

We do not say that the defendants in subjecting themselves to arbitration in accordance with the British Arbitration Act became bound to submit, not only to the requirements of that act, but to the entire *corpus juris* as developed by the British courts. We do say that there was an implied submission to the terms of the act itself, and to any rules or procedural machinery adopted by competent authority in aid of its provisions. If the arbitration contract had provided that an arbitrator might be named by the London Chamber of Commerce upon notice to the parties, there would be little doubt that notice would be adequate though the defendants were not in Great Britain at the time of its transmission. We cannot say upon this record that any different conclusion ought to follow from notice and nomination at the instance of a judge. The case does not involve the question whether the defendants, staying out of the arbitration, may still challenge in this State the existence of a contract to arbitrate, or the breach of such a contract, unaffected by any adjudication pronounced by the British courts. The case involves no more than this, whether staying out of the arbitration, they are bound by an award, made after due compliance with the requirements of the procedural machinery established by the British statute, unless they are able to show that no contract has been made or broken.

The judgment of the Appellate Division and that of the Special Term should be reversed and defendant's motion for judgment on the pleadings denied, with costs in all courts.

SCHERK v. ALBERTO-CULVER CO.

United States Supreme Court
417 U.S. 506 (1974)

MR. JUSTICE STEWART delivered the opinion of the Court.

Alberto-Culver Co., the respondent, is an American company incorporated in Delaware with its principal office in Illinois. It manufactures and distributes toiletries and hair products in this country and abroad. During the 1960's Alberto-Culver decided to expand its overseas operations, and as part of this program it approached the petitioner Fritz Scherk, a German citizen residing at the time of trial in Switzerland. Scherk was the owner of three interrelated business entities, organized under the laws of Germany and Liechtenstein, that were engaged in the manufacture of toiletries and the licensing of trademarks for such toiletries. An initial contact with Scherk was made by a representative of Alberto-Culver in Germany in June 1967, and negotiations followed at further meetings in both Europe and the United States during 1967 and 1968. In February 1969 a contract was signed in Vienna, Austria, which provided for the transfer of the ownership of Scherk's enterprises to Alberto-Culver, along with all rights held by these enterprises to trademarks in cosmetic goods. The contract contained a number of express warranties whereby Scherk guaranteed the sole and unencumbered ownership of these trademarks. In addition, the contract contained an arbitration clause providing that "any controversy or claim [that] shall arise out of this agreement or the breach thereof" would be referred to arbitration before the International Chamber of Commerce in Paris, France, and that "[t]he laws of the State of Illinois, U. S. A. shall apply to and govern this agreement, its interpretation and performance."

The closing of the transaction took place in Geneva, Switzerland, in June 1969. Nearly one year later Alberto-Culver allegedly discovered that the trademark rights purchased under the contract were subject to substantial encumbrances that threatened to give others superior rights to the trademarks and to restrict or preclude Alberto-Culver's use of them. Alberto-Culver thereupon tendered back to Scherk the property that had been transferred to it and offered to rescind the contract. Upon Scherk's refusal, Alberto-Culver commenced this action for damages and other relief in a Federal District Court in Illinois, contending that Scherk's fraudulent representations concerning the status of the trademark rights constituted violations of § 10 (b) of the Securities Exchange Act of 1934, 48 Stat. 891, 15 U. S. C. § 78j (b), and Rule 10b–5 promulgated thereunder, 17 CFR § 240.10b–5.

In response, Scherk filed a motion to dismiss the action for want of personal and subject-matter jurisdiction as well as on the basis of *forum non conveniens,* or, alternatively, to stay the action pending arbitration in Paris pursuant to the agreement of the parties. Alberto-Culver, in turn, opposed this motion and sought a preliminary injunction restraining the prosecution of arbitration proceedings.[2] On December 2, 1971, the District Court denied Scherk's motion to dismiss, and,

---

[2] Scherk had taken steps to initiate arbitration in Paris in early 1971. He did not, however, file a formal request for arbitration with the International Chamber of Commerce until November 9, 1971, almost five months after the filing of Alberto-Culver's complaint in the Illinois federal court.

on January 14, 1972, it granted a preliminary order enjoining Scherk from proceeding with arbitration. In taking these actions the court relied entirely on this Court's decision in *Wilko v. Swan,* 346 U. S. 427, which held that an agreement to arbitrate could not preclude a buyer of a security from seeking a judicial remedy under the Securities Act of 1933, in view of the language of § 14 of that Act, barring "[a]ny condition, stipulation, or provision binding any person acquiring any security to waive compliance with any provision of this subchapter. . . ." 48 Stat. 84, 15 U. S. C. § 77n. The Court of Appeals for the Seventh Circuit, with one judge dissenting, affirmed, upon what it considered the controlling authority of the *Wilko* decision. Because of the importance of the question presented we granted Scherk's petition for a writ of certiorari.

I

The United States Arbitration Act, now 9 U. S. C. § 1 *et seq.,* reversing centuries of judicial hostility to arbitration agreements,[4] was designed to allow parties to avoid "the costliness and delays of litigation," and to place arbitration agreements "upon the same footing as other contracts . . ." H. R. Rep. No. 96, 68th Cong., 1st Sess., 1, 2 (1924); see also S. Rep. No. 536, 68th Cong., 1st Sess. (1924). Accordingly, the Act provides that an arbitration agreement such as is here involved "shall be valid, irrevocable, and enforceable, save upon such grounds as exist at law or in equity for the revocation of any contract." 9 U. S. C. § 2. The Act also provides in § 3 for a stay of proceedings in a case where a court is satisfied that the issue before it is arbitrable under the agreement, and § 4 of the Act directs a federal court to order parties to proceed to arbitration if there has been a "failure, neglect, or refusal" of any party to honor an agreement to arbitrate.

In *Wilko v. Swan, supra,* this Court acknowledged that the Act reflects a legislative recognition of the "desirability of arbitration as an alternative to the complications of litigation," but nonetheless declined to apply the Act's provisions. That case involved an agreement between Anthony Wilko and Hayden, Stone & Co., a large brokerage firm, under which Wilko agreed to purchase on margin a number of shares of a corporation's common stock. Wilko alleged that his purchase of the stock was induced by false representations on the part of the defendant concerning the value of the shares, and he brought suit for damages under § 12 (2) of the Securities Act of 1933, 15 U. S. C. § 77l. The defendant responded that Wilko had agreed to submit all controversies arising out of the purchase to arbitration, and that this agreement, contained in a written margin contract between the parties, should be given full effect under the Arbitration Act.

The Court found that "[t]wo policies, not easily reconcilable, are involved in this case." On the one hand, the Arbitration Act stressed "the need for avoiding the delay and expense of litigation," and directed that such agreements be "valid, irrevocable, and enforceable" in federal courts. On the other hand, the Securities Act of 1933 was "[d]esigned to protect investors" and to require "issuers, underwriters, and dealers to make full and fair disclosure of the character of securities sold in interstate and foreign commerce and to prevent fraud in their sale," by creating "a special right to recover for misrepresentation. . . ." In particular, the Court noted that § 14 of the Securities Act, 15 U. S. C. § 77n, provides:

---

[4] English courts traditionally considered irrevocable arbitration agreements as "ousting" the courts of jurisdiction, and refused to enforce such agreements for this reason. This view was adopted by American courts as part of the common law up to the time of the adoption of the Arbitration Act. See H. R. Rep. No. 96, 68th Cong., 1st Sess., 1, 2 (1924); Sturges & Murphy, *Some Confusing Matters Relating to Arbitration under the United States Arbitration Act,* 17 Law & Contemp. Prob. 580.

§ 4.02   CHOICE OF LAW   □   317

Any condition, stipulation, or provision binding any person acquiring any security to waive compliance with any provision of this subchapter or of the rules and regulations of the Commission shall be void.

The Court ruled that an agreement to arbitrate "is a 'stipulation,' and [that] the right to select the judicial forum is the kind of 'provision' that cannot be waived under § 14 of the Securities Act."[6] Thus, Wilko's advance agreement to arbitrate any disputes subsequently arising out of his contract to purchase the securities was unenforceable under the terms of § 14 of the Securities Act of 1933.

Alberto-Culver, relying on this precedent, contends that the District Court and Court of Appeals were correct in holding that its agreement to arbitrate disputes arising under the contract with Scherk is similarly unenforceable in view of its contentions that Scherk's conduct constituted violations of the Securities Exchange Act of 1934 and rules promulgated thereunder. For the reasons that follow, we reject this contention and hold that the provisions of the Arbitration Act cannot be ignored in this case.

[The Court discusses, without deciding, whether provisions of the 1933 Act, concerning original issues, apply with respect to the 1934 Act, concerning trading in securities already issued.]

Accepting the premise, however, that the operative portions of the language of the 1933 Act relied upon in *Wilko* are contained in the Securities Exchange Act of 1934, the respondent's reliance on *Wilko* in this case ignores the significant and, we find, crucial differences between the agreement involved in *Wilko* and the one signed by the parties here. Alberto-Culver's contract to purchase the business entities belonging to Scherk was a truly international agreement. Alberto-Culver is an American corporation with its principal place of business and the vast bulk of its activity in this country, while Scherk is a citizen of Germany whose companies were organized under the laws of Germany and Liechtenstein. The negotiations leading to the signing of the contract in Austria and to the closing in Switzerland took place in the United States, England, and Germany, and involved consultations with legal and trademark experts from each of those countries and from Liechtenstein. Finally, and most significantly, the subject matter of the contract concerned the sale of business enterprises organized under the laws of and primarily situated in European countries, whose activities were largely, if not entirely, directed to European markets.

Such a contract involves considerations and policies significantly different from those found controlling in *Wilko*. In *Wilko,* quite apart from the arbitration provision, there was no question but that the laws of the United States generally, and the federal securities laws in particular, would govern disputes arising out of the stock-purchase agreement. The parties, the negotiations, and the subject matter of the contract were all situated in this country, and no credible claim could have been entertained that any international conflict-of-laws problems would arise. In this case, by contrast, in the absence of the arbitration provision considerable uncertainty existed at

---

[6] The arbitration agreement involved in *Wilko* was contained in a standard form margin contract. But see the dissenting opinion of Mr. Justice Frankfurter, 346 U. S. 427, 439, 440, concluding that the record did not show that "the plaintiff [Wilko] in opening an account had no choice but to accept the arbitration stipulation . . ." The petitioner here would limit the decision in *Wilko* to situations where the parties exhibit a disparity of bargaining power, and contends that, since the negotiations leading to the present contract took place over a number of years and involved the participation on both sides of knowledgeable and sophisticated business and legal experts, the *Wilko* decision should not apply. See also the dissenting opinion of Judge Stevens of the Court of Appeals in this case, 484 F. 2d 611, 615. Because of our disposition of this case on other grounds, we need not consider this contention.

the time of the agreement, and still exists, concerning the law applicable to the resolution of disputes arising out of the contract.[9]

Such uncertainty will almost inevitably exist with respect to any contract touching two or more countries, each with its own substantive laws and conflict-of-laws rules. A contractual provision specifying in advance the forum in which disputes shall be litigated and the law to be applied is, therefore, an almost indispensable precondition to achievement of the orderliness and predictability essential to any international business transaction. Furthermore, such a provision obviates the danger that a dispute under the agreement might be submitted to a forum hostile to the interests of one of the parties or unfamiliar with the problem area involved.[10]

A parochial refusal by the courts of one country to enforce an international arbitration agreement would not only frustrate these purposes, but would invite unseemly and mutually destructive jockeying by the parties to secure tactical litigation advantages. In the present case, for example, it is not inconceivable that if Scherk had anticipated that Alberto-Culver would be able in this country to enjoin resort to arbitration he might have sought an order in France or some other country enjoining Alberto-Culver from proceeding with its litigation in the United States. Whatever recognition the courts of this country might ultimately have granted to the order of the foreign court, the dicey atmosphere of such a legal no-man's-land would surely damage the fabric of international commerce and trade, and imperil the willingness and ability of businessmen to enter into international commercial agreements.[11]

The exception to the clear provisions of the Arbitration Act carved out by *Wilko* is simply inapposite to a case such as the one before us. In *Wilko* the Court reasoned that "[w]hen the security buyer, prior to any violation of the Securities Act, waives his right to sue in courts, he gives up more than would a participant in other business transactions. The security buyer has a wider choice of courts and venue. He thus surrenders one of the advantages the Act gives him . . ." 346 U. S., at 435. In the context of an international contract, however, these advantages

---

[9] Together with his motion for a stay pending arbitration, Scherk moved that the complaint be dismissed because the federal securities laws do not apply to this international transaction, cf. *Leasco Data Processing Equipment Corp. v. Maxwell* [Ch. 10, p. 930, *infra*]. Since only the order granting the injunction was appealed, this contention was not considered by the Court of Appeals and is not before this Court.

[10] See Quigley, *Accession by the United States to the United Nations Convention on the Recognition and Enforcement of Foreign Arbitral Awards,* 70 Yale L. J. 1049, 1051 (1961). For example, while the arbitration agreement involved here provided that the controversies arising out of the agreement be resolved under "[t]he laws of the State of Illinois," *supra,* n. 1, a determination of the existence and extent of fraud concerning the trademarks would necessarily involve an understanding of foreign law on that subject.

[11] The dissenting opinion argues that our conclusion that *Wilko* is inapplicable to the situation presented in this case will vitiate the force of that decision because parties to transactions with many more direct contacts with this country than in the present case will nonetheless be able to invoke the "talisman" of having an "international contract." *Post,* at 529. Concededly, situations may arise where the contacts with foreign countries are so insignificant or attenuated that the holding in *Wilko* would meaningfully apply. Judicial response to such situations can and should await future litigation in concrete cases. This case, however, provides no basis for a judgment that only United States laws and United States courts should determine this controversy in the face of a solemn agreement between the parties that such controversies be resolved elsewhere. The only contact between the United States and the transaction involved here is the fact that Alberto-Culver is an American corporation and the occurrence of some—but by no means the greater part—of the pre-contract negotiations in this country. To determine that "American standards of fairness," *post,* at 528, must nonetheless govern the controversy demeans the standards of justice elsewhere in the world, and unnecessarily exalts the primacy of United States law over the laws of other countries.

become chimerical since, as indicated above, an opposing party may by speedy resort to a foreign court block or hinder access to the American court of the purchaser's choice.[12]

Two Terms ago in *The Bremen v. Zapata Off-Shore Co.,* 407 U. S. 1, we rejected the doctrine that a forum-selection clause of a contract, although voluntarily adopted by the parties, will not be respected in a suit brought in the United States " 'unless the selected state would provide a more convenient forum than the state in which suit is brought.' " *Id.,* at 7. Rather, we concluded that a "forum clause should control absent a strong showing that it should be set aside." *Id.,* at 15. We noted that "much uncertainty and possibly great inconvenience to both parties could arise if a suit could be maintained in any jurisdiction in which an accident might occur or if jurisdiction were left to any place [where personal or *in rem* jurisdiction might be established]. The elimination of all such uncertainties by agreeing in advance on a forum acceptable to both parties is an indispensable element in international trade, commerce, and contracting." *Id.,* at 13—

An agreement to arbitrate before a specified tribunal is, in effect, a specialized kind of forum-selection clause that posits not only the situs of suit but also the procedure to be used in resolving the dispute.[13] The invalidation of such an agreement in the case before us would not only allow the respondent to repudiate its solemn promise but would, as well, reflect a "parochial concept that all disputes must be resolved under our laws and in our courts. . . . We cannot have trade and commerce in world markets and international waters exclusively on our terms, governed by our laws, and resolved in our courts." *Id.,* at 9.[14]

For all these reasons we hold that the agreement of the parties in this case to arbitrate any dispute arising out of their international commercial transaction is to be respected and enforced by the federal courts in accord with the explicit provisions of the Arbitration Act.[15]

---

[12] The dissenting opinion raises the specter that our holding today will leave American investors at the mercy of multinational corporations with "vast operations around the world . . . ." *Post,* at 533. Our decision, of course, has no bearing on the scope of the substantive provisions of the federal securities laws for the simple reason that the question is not presented in this case. See n. 8, *supra.*

[13] Under some circumstances, the designation of arbitration in a certain place might also be viewed as implicitly selecting the law of that place to apply to that transaction. In this case, however, "[t]he laws of the State of Illinois" were explicitly made applicable by the arbitration agreement. See n. 1, *supra.*

[14] In *The Bremen* we noted that forum-selection clauses "should be given full effect" when "a freely negotiated private international agreement [is] unaffected by fraud. . . ." 407 U. S., at 13, 12. This qualification does not mean that any time a dispute arising out of a transaction is based upon an allegation of fraud, as in this case, the clause is unenforceable. Rather, it means that an arbitration or forum-selection clause in a contract is not enforceable if the *inclusion of that clause in the contract* was the product of fraud or coercion. Cf. *Prima Paint Corp. v. Flood & Conklin Mfg. Co.,* 388 U. S. 395.

Although we do not decide the question, presumably the type of fraud alleged here could be raised, under Art. V of the Convention on the Recognition and Enforcement of Foreign Arbitral Awards, see n. 15, *infra,* in challenging the enforcement of whatever arbitral award is produced through arbitration. Article V (2)(*b*) of the Convention provides that a country may refuse recognition and enforcement of an award if "recognition or enforcement of the award would be contrary to the public policy of that country."

[15] Our conclusion today is confirmed by international developments and domestic legislation in the area of commercial arbitration subsequent to the *Wilko* decision. On June 10, 1958, a special conference of the United Nations Economic and Social Council adopted the Convention on the Recognition and Enforcement of Foreign Arbitral Awards. In 1970 the United States acceded to the treaty, [1970] 3 U. S. T. 2517, T. I. A. S. No. 6997, and Congress passed Chapter 2 of the United States Arbitration Act, 9 U. S. C. § 201 *et seq.,* in order to implement the Convention. Section 1 of the new chapter, 9 U. S. C. § 201, provides unequivocally that the Convention "shall be enforced in United States courts in accordance with this chapter."

Accordingly, the judgment of the Court of Appeals is reversed and the case is remanded to that court with directions to remand to the District Court for further proceedings consistent with this opinion.

Mr. Justice Douglas, with whom Mr. Justice Brennan, Mr. Justice White, and Mr. Justice Marshall concur, dissenting.

. . .

The basic dispute between the parties concerned allegations that the trademarks which were basic assets in the transaction were encumbered and that their purchase was induced through serious instances of fraudulent representations and omissions by Scherk and his agents within the jurisdiction of the United States. If a question of trademarks were the only one involved, the principle of *The Bremen v. Zapata Off-Shore Co.,* 407 U. S. 1, would be controlling.

We have here, however, questions under the Securities Exchange Act of 1934, which in § 3 (a)(10) defines "security" as including any "note, stock, treasury stock, bond, debenture, certificate of interest or participation in any profit-sharing agreement. . . ." 15 U. S. C. § 78c (a)(10). . . .

Section 10 (b) of the 1934 Act makes it unlawful for any person by use of agencies of interstate commerce or the mails "[t]o use or employ, in connection with the purchase or sale of any security," whether or not registered on a national securities exchange, "any manipulative or deceptive device or contrivance in contravention of such rules and regulations as the Commission may prescribe." 15 U. S. C. § 78j (b).

. . .

There has been much support for arbitration of disputes; and it may be the superior way of settling some disagreements. If A and B were quarreling over a trademark and there was an arbitration clause in the contract, the policy of Congress in implementing the United Nations Convention on the Recognition and Enforcement of Foreign Arbitral Awards, as it did in 9 U. S. C. § 201 *et seq.,* would prevail. But the Act does not substitute an arbiter for the settlement of disputes under the 1933 and 1934 Acts. Art. II (3) of the Convention says:

> The court of a Contracting State, when seized of an action in a matter in respect of which the parties have made an agreement within the meaning of this article, shall, at the request

---

The goal of the Convention, and the principal purpose underlying American adoption and implementation of it, was to encourage the recognition and enforcement of commercial arbitration agreements in international contracts and to unify the standards by which agreements to arbitrate are observed and arbitral awards are enforced in the signatory countries. See Convention on the Recognition and Enforcement of Foreign Arbitral Awards, S. Exec. Doc. E, 90th Cong., 2d Sess. (1968); Quigley, *Accession by the United States to the United Nations Convention on the Recognition and Enforcement of Foreign Arbitral Awards,* 70 Yale L. J. 1049 (1961). Article II (1) of the Convention provides:

> Each Contracting State shall recognize an agreement in writing under which the parties undertake to submit to arbitration all or any differences which have arisen or which may arise between them in respect of a defined legal relationship, whether contractual or not, concerning a subject matter capable of settlement by arbitration.

In their discussion of this Article, the delegates to the Convention voiced frequent concern that courts of signatory countries in which an agreement to arbitrate is sought to be enforced should not be permitted to decline enforcement of such agreements on the basis of parochial views of their desirability or in a manner that would diminish the mutually binding nature of the agreements. See G. Haight, Convention on the Recognition and Enforcement of Foreign Arbitral Awards: Summary Analysis of Record of United Nations Conference, May/June 1958, pp. 24–28 (1958).

Without reaching the issue of whether the Convention, apart from the considerations expressed in this opinion, would require of its own force that the agreement to arbitrate be enforced in the present case, we think that this country's adoption and ratification of the Convention and the passage of Chapter 2 of the United States Arbitration Act provide strongly persuasive evidence of congressional policy consistent with the decision we reach today.

of one of the parties, refer the parties to arbitration, unless it finds that the said agreement is null and void, inoperative or incapable of being performed.

[1970] 3 U. S. T. 2517, 2519, T. I. A. S. No. 6997.

But § 29 (a) of the 1934 Act makes agreements to arbitrate liabilities under § 10 of the Act "void" and "inoperative." Congress has specified a precise way whereby big and small investors will be protected and the rules under which the Alberto-Culvers of this Nation shall operate. They or their lawyers cannot waive those statutory conditions, for our corporate giants are not principalities of power but guardians of a host of wards unable to care for themselves. It is these wards that the 1934 Act tries to protect. Not a word in the Convention governing awards adopts the standards which Congress has passed to protect the investors under the 1934 Act. It is peculiarly appropriate that we adhere to *Wilko*—more so even than when *Wilko* was decided. Huge foreign investments are being made in our companies. It is important that American standards of fairness in security dealings govern the destinies of American investors until Congress changes these standards.

The Court finds it unnecessary to consider Scherk's argument that this case is distinguishable from *Wilko* in that *Wilko* involved parties of unequal bargaining strength. Instead, the Court rests its conclusion on the fact that this was an "international" agreement, with an American corporation investing in the stock and property of foreign businesses, and speaks favorably of the certainty which inheres when parties specify an arbitral forum for resolution of differences in "any contract touching two or more countries."

This invocation of the "international contract" talisman might be applied to a situation where, for example, an interest in a foreign company or mutual fund was sold to an utterly unsophisticated American citizen, with material fraudulent misrepresentations made in this country. The arbitration clause could appear in the fine print of a form contract, and still be sufficient to preclude recourse to our courts, forcing the defrauded citizen to arbitration in Paris to vindicate his rights.

It has been recognized that the 1934 Act, including the protections of Rule 10b–5, applies when foreign defendants have defrauded American investors, particularly when, as alleged here, they have profited by virtue of proscribed conduct within our boundaries. This is true even when the defendant is organized under the laws of a foreign country, is conducting much of its activity outside the United States, and is therefore governed largely by foreign law. The language of § 29 of the 1934 Act does not immunize such international transactions, and the United Nations Convention provides that a forum court in which a suit is brought need not enforce an agreement to arbitrate which is "void" and "inoperative" as contrary to its public policy. When a foreign corporation undertakes fraudulent action which subjects it to the jurisdiction of our federal securities laws, nothing justifies the conclusion that only a diluted version of those laws protects American investors.

. . . Here, as in *Wilko,* the allegations of fraudulent misrepresentation will involve "subjective findings on the purpose and knowledge" of the defendant, questions ill-determined by arbitrators without judicial instruction on the law. An arbitral award can be made without explication of reasons and without development of a record, so that the arbitrator's conception of our statutory requirement may be absolutely incorrect yet functionally unreviewable, even when the arbitrator seeks to apply our law. We recognized in *Wilko* that there is no judicial review corresponding to review of court decisions. The extensive pretrial discovery provided by the Federal Rules of Civil Procedure for actions in district court would not be available. And the wide choice of venue provided by the 1934 Act, would be forfeited. The loss of the proper judicial forum carries with it the loss of substantial rights.[11]

When a defendant, as alleged here, has, through proscribed acts within our territory, brought itself within the ken of federal securities regulation, a fact not disputed here, those laws—including the controlling principles of *Wilko*—apply whether the defendant is foreign or American, and whether or not there are transnational elements in the dealings. Those laws are rendered a chimera when foreign corporations or funds—unlike domestic defendants—can nullify them by virtue of arbitration clauses which send defrauded American investors to the uncertainty of arbitration on foreign soil, or, if those investors cannot afford to arbitrate their claims in a far-off forum, to no remedy at all.

Moreover, the international aura which the Court gives this case is ominous. We now have many multinational corporations in vast operations around the world—Europe, Latin America, the Middle East, and Asia. The investments of many American investors turn on dealings by these companies. Up to this day, it has been assumed by reason of *Wilko* that they were all protected by our various federal securities Acts. If these guarantees are to be removed, it should take a legislative enactment. I would enforce our laws as they stand, unless Congress makes an exception.

The virtue of certainty in international agreements may be important, but Congress has dictated that when there are sufficient contacts for our securities laws to apply, the policies expressed in those laws take precedence. Section 29 of the 1934 Act, which renders arbitration clauses void and inoperative, recognizes no exception for fraudulent dealings which incidentally have some international factors. The Convention makes provision for such national public policy in Art. II (3). Federal jurisdiction under the 1934 Act will attach only to some international transactions, but when it does, the protections afforded investors such as Alberto-Culver can only be full-fledged.

MITSUBISHI MOTORS CORPORATION v. SOLER CHRYSLER-PLYMOUTH, INC.

United States Supreme Court
473 U.S. 614 (1985)

Justice BLACKMUN delivered the opinion of the Court.

The principal question presented by these cases is the arbitrability, pursuant to the Federal Arbitration Act and the Convention on the Recognition and Enforcement of Foreign Arbitral Awards, of claims arising under the Sherman Act and encompassed within a valid arbitration clause in an agreement embodying an international commercial transaction.

---

[11] The agreements in this case provided that the "laws of the State of Illinois" are applicable. Even if the arbitration court should read this clause to require application of Rule 10b–5's standards, Alberto-Culver's victory would be Pyrrhic. The arbitral court may improperly interpret the substantive protections of the Rule, and if it does its error will not be reviewable as would the error of a federal court. And the ability of Alberto-Culver to prosecute its claim would be eviscerated by lack of discovery. These are the policy considerations which underlay *Wilko* and which apply to the instant case as well.

I

Petitioner-cross-respondent Mitsubishi Motors Corporation (Mitsubishi) is a Japanese corporation which manufactures automobiles and has its principal place of business in Tokyo, Japan. Mitsubishi is the product of a joint venture between, on the one hand, Chrysler International, S.A. (CISA), a Swiss corporation registered in Geneva and wholly owned by Chrysler Corporation, and, on the other, Mitsubishi Heavy Industries, Inc., a Japanese corporation. The aim of the joint venture was the distribution through Chrysler dealers outside the continental United States of vehicles manufactured by Mitsubishi and bearing Chrysler and Mitsubishi trademarks. Respondent-cross-petitioner Soler Chrysler-Plymouth, Inc. (Soler), is a Puerto Rico corporation with its principal place of business in Pueblo Viejo, Guaynabo, Puerto Rico.

On October 31, 1979, Soler entered into a Distributor Agreement with CISA which provided for the sale by Soler of Mitsubishi-manufactured vehicles within a designated area, including metropolitan San Juan. On the same date, CISA, Soler, and Mitsubishi entered into a Sales Procedure Agreement which, referring to the Distributor Agreement, provided for the direct sale of Mitsubishi products to Soler and governed the terms and conditions of such sales. Paragraph VI of the Sales Agreement, labeled "Arbitration of Certain Matters," provides:

> "All disputes, controversies or differences which may arise between [Mitsubishi] and [Soler] out of or in relation to Articles I-B through V of this Agreement or for the breach thereof, shall be finally settled by arbitration in Japan in accordance with the rules and regulations of the Japan Commercial Arbitration Association."

Initially, Soler did a brisk business in Mitsubishi-manufactured vehicles. As a result of its strong performance, its minimum sales volume, specified by Mitsubishi and CISA, and agreed to by Soler, for the 1981 model year was substantially increased. In early 1981, however, the new-car market slackened. Soler ran into serious difficulties in meeting the expected sales volume, and by the spring of 1981 it felt itself compelled to request that Mitsubishi delay or cancel shipment of several orders. About the same time, Soler attempted to arrange for the transshipment of a quantity of its vehicles for sale in the continental United States and Latin America. Mitsubishi and CISA, however, refused permission for any such diversion, citing a variety of reasons,[11] and no vehicles were transshipped. Attempts to work out these difficulties failed. Mitsubishi eventually withheld shipment of 966 vehicles, apparently representing orders placed for May, June, and July 1981 production, responsibility for which Soler disclaimed in February 1982.

The following month, Mitsubishi brought an action against Soler in the United States District Court for the District of Puerto Rico under the Federal Arbitration Act and the Convention.[22]

---

[11] The reasons advanced included concerns that such diversion would interfere with the Japanese trade policy of voluntarily limiting imports to the United States; that the Soler-ordered vehicles would be unsuitable for use in certain proposed destinations because of their manufacture, with use in Puerto Rico in mind, without heaters and defoggers; that the vehicles would be unsuitable for use in Latin America because of the unavailability there of the unleaded, high-octane fuel they required; that adequate warranty service could not be ensured; and that diversion to the mainland would violate contractual obligations between CISA and Mitsubishi.

[22] The complaint alleged that Soler had failed to pay for 966 ordered vehicles; that it had failed to pay contractual "distress unit penalties," intended to reimburse Mitsubishi for storage costs and interest charges incurred because of Soler's failure to take shipment of ordered vehicles; that Soler's failure to fulfill warranty obligations threatened Mitsubishi's reputation and goodwill; that Soler had failed to obtain required financing; and that the Distributor and Sales Agreements had expired by their terms or, alternatively, that Soler had surrendered its rights under the Sales Agreement.

Mitsubishi sought an order, pursuant to [the Federal Arbitration Act] to compel arbitration in accord with ¶ VI of the Sales Agreement. Shortly after filing the complaint, Mitsubishi filed a request for arbitration before the Japan Commercial Arbitration Association.

Soler denied the allegations and counterclaimed against both Mitsubishi and CISA. It alleged numerous breaches by Mitsubishi of the Sales Agreement, raised a pair of defamation claims, and asserted causes of action under the Sherman Act; the federal Automobile Dealers' Day in Court Act, 15 U.S.C. § 1221 et seq.; the Puerto Rico competition statute, P.R.Laws Ann., Tit. 10, § 257 et seq. (1976); and the Puerto Rico Dealers' Contracts Act, P.R.Laws Ann., Tit. 10, § 278 et seq. (1978 and Supp.1983). In the counterclaim premised on the Sherman Act, Soler alleged that Mitsubishi and CISA had conspired to divide markets in restraint of trade. To effectuate the plan, according to Soler, Mitsubishi had refused to permit Soler to resell to buyers in North, Central, or South America vehicles it had obligated itself to purchase from Mitsubishi; had refused to ship ordered vehicles or the parts, such as heaters and defog-gers, that would be necessary to permit Soler to make its vehicles suitable for resale outside Puerto Rico; and had coercively attempted to replace Soler and its other Puerto Rico distributors with a wholly owned subsidiary which would serve as the exclusive Mitsubishi distributor in Puerto Rico.

After a hearing, the District Court ordered Mitsubishi and Soler to arbitrate each of the issues raised in the complaint and in all the counterclaims save two and a portion of a third. With regard to the federal antitrust issues, it recognized that the Courts of Appeals, following *American Safety Equipment Corp. v. J.P. Maguire & Co.*, 391 F.2d 821 (CA2 1968), uniformly had held that the rights conferred by the antitrust laws were "of a character inappropriate for enforcement by arbitration." The District Court held, however, that the international character of the Mitsubishi-Soler undertaking required enforcement of the agreement to arbitrate even as to the antitrust claims. It relied on *Scherk v. Alberto-Culver Co.*, in which this Court ordered arbitration, pursuant to a provision embodied in an international agreement, of a claim arising under the Securities Exchange Act of 1934 notwithstanding its assumption, *arguendo*, that *Wilko v. Swan* [346 U.S. 427 (1953)], which held nonarbitrable claims arising under the Securities Act of 1933, also would bar arbitration of a 1934 Act claim arising in a domestic context.

The United States Court of Appeals for the First Circuit affirmed in part and reversed in part. 723 F.2d 155 (1983). It first rejected Soler's argument that Puerto Rico law precluded enforcement of an agreement obligating a local dealer to arbitrate controversies outside Puerto Rico. It also rejected Soler's suggestion that it could not have intended to arbitrate statutory claims not mentioned in the arbitration agreement. Assessing arbitrability "on an allegation-by-allegation basis," the court then read the arbitration clause to encompass virtually all the claims arising under the various statutes, including all those arising under the Sherman Act.

Finally, after endorsing the doctrine of American Safety, precluding arbitration of antitrust claims, the Court of Appeals concluded that neither this Court's decision in Scherk nor the Convention required abandonment of that doctrine in the face of an international transaction. Accordingly, it reversed the judgment of the District Court insofar as it had ordered submission of "Soler's antitrust claims" to arbitration. . . .

We granted certiorari primarily to consider whether an American court should enforce an agreement to resolve antitrust claims by arbitration when that agreement arises from an international transaction.

II

At the outset, we address the contention raised in Soler's cross-petition that the arbitration clause at issue may not be read to encompass the statutory counterclaims stated in its answer to the complaint. . . .Soler reasons that, because it falls within the class for whose benefit the federal and local antitrust laws and dealers' Acts were passed, but the arbitration clause at issue does not mention these statutes or statutes in general, the clause cannot be read to contemplate arbitration of these statutory claims.

We do not agree, for we find no warrant in the Arbitration Act for implying in every contract within its ken a presumption against arbitration of statutory claims. . . . [A]s with any other contract, the parties' intentions control, but those intentions are generously construed as to issues of arbitrability.

There is no reason to depart from these guidelines where a party bound by an arbitration agreement raises claims founded on statutory rights. . . . Of course, courts should remain attuned to well-supported claims that the agreement to arbitrate resulted from the sort of fraud or overwhelming economic power that would provide grounds "for the revocation of any contract." But, absent such compelling considerations, the Act itself provides no basis for disfavoring agreements to arbitrate statutory claims by skewing the otherwise hospitable inquiry into arbitrability.

. . .

III

We now turn to consider whether Soler's antitrust claims are nonarbitrable even though it has agreed to arbitrate them. In holding that they are not [arbitrable], the Court of Appeals followed the decision of the Second Circuit in *American Safety Equipment Corp. v. J.P. Maguire & Co.* Notwithstanding the absence of any explicit support for such an exception in either the Sherman Act or the Federal Arbitration Act, the Second Circuit there reasoned that "the pervasive public interest in enforcement of the antitrust laws, and the nature of the claims that arise in such cases, combine to make . . . antitrust claims . . . inappropriate for arbitration." We find it unnecessary to assess the legitimacy of the American Safety doctrine as applied to agreements to arbitrate arising from domestic transactions. As in *Scherk v. Alberto-Culver Co.*, we conclude that concerns of international comity, respect for the capacities of foreign and transnational tribunals, and sensitivity to the need of the international commercial system for predictability in the resolution of disputes require that we enforce the parties' agreement, even assuming that a contrary result would be forthcoming in a domestic context.

Even before Scherk, this Court had recognized the utility of forum-selection clauses in international transactions. [The Court summarizes and quotes from *The Bremen v. Zapata* and *Scherk*.]

The *Bremen* and *Scherk* establish a strong presumption in favor of enforcement of freely negotiated contractual choice-of-forum provisions. Here, as in *Scherk*, that presumption is reinforced by the emphatic federal policy in favor of arbitral dispute resolution. And at least since this Nation's accession in 1970 to the [UN Arbitration] Convention, and the implementation of the Convention in the same year by amendment of the Federal Arbitration Act, that federal policy applies with special force in the field of international commerce. Thus, we must weigh the concerns of *American Safety* against a strong belief in the efficacy of arbitral procedures for the resolution of international commercial disputes and an equal commitment to the enforcement of freely negotiated choice-of-forum clauses.

At the outset, we confess to some skepticism of certain aspects of the *American Safety* doctrine. As distilled by the First Circuit, the doctrine comprises four ingredients. First, private parties play a pivotal role in aiding governmental enforcement of the antitrust laws by means of the private action for treble damages. Second, "the strong possibility that contracts which generate antitrust disputes may be contracts of adhesion militates against automatic forum determination by contract." Third, antitrust issues, prone to complication, require sophisticated legal and economic analysis, and thus are "ill-adapted to strengths of the arbitral process, i.e., expedition, minimal requirements of written rationale, simplicity, resort to basic concepts of common sense and simple equity." Finally, just as "issues of war and peace are too important to be vested in the generals, . . . decisions as to antitrust regulation of business are too important to be lodged in arbitrators chosen from the business community— particularly those from a foreign community that has had no experience with or exposure to our law and values." See *American Safety*, 391 F.2d, at 826-827.

Initially, we find the second concern unjustified. The mere appearance of an antitrust dispute does not alone warrant invalidation of the selected forum on the undemonstrated assumption that the arbitration clause is tainted. A party resisting arbitration of course may attack directly the validity of the agreement to arbitrate. See *Prima Paint Corp. v. Flood & Conklin Mfg. Co.*, 388 U.S. 395 (1967). Moreover, the party may attempt to make a showing that would warrant setting aside the forum-selection clause—that the agreement was "[a]ffected by fraud, undue influence, or overweening bargaining power;" that "enforcement would be unreasonable and unjust;" or that proceedings "in the contractual forum will be so gravely difficult and inconvenient that [the resisting party] will for all practical purposes be deprived of his day in court." The Bremen. But absent such a showing—and none was attempted here—there is no basis for assuming the forum inadequate or its selection unfair.

Next, potential complexity should not suffice to ward off arbitration. . . . [A]daptability and access to expertise are hallmarks of arbitration. The anticipated subject matter of the dispute may be taken into account when the arbitrators are appointed, and arbitral rules typically provide for the participation of experts either employed by the parties or appointed by the tribunal. Moreover, it is often a judgment that streamlined proceedings and expeditious results will best serve their needs that causes parties to agree to arbitrate their disputes; it is typically a desire to keep the effort and expense required to resolve a dispute within manageable bounds that prompts them mutually to forgo access to judicial remedies. In sum, the factor of potential complexity alone does not persuade us that an arbitral tribunal could not properly handle an antitrust matter.

For similar reasons, we also reject the proposition that an arbitration panel will pose too great a danger of innate hostility to the constraints on business conduct that antitrust law imposes. International arbitrators frequently are drawn from the legal as well as the business community; where the dispute has an important legal component, the parties and the arbitral body with whose assistance they have agreed to settle their dispute can be expected to select arbitrators accordingly.[18]

---

[18] See Craig, Park, & Paulsson, *supra*, § 12.03, p. 28; Sanders, Commentary on UNCITRAL Arbitration Rules § 15.1, in 2 Yearbook Commercial Arbitration at 203 (1977).

We are advised by Mitsubishi and amicus International Chamber of Commerce, without contradiction by Soler,

We decline to indulge the presumption that the parties and arbitral body conducting a proceeding will be unable or unwilling to retain competent, conscientious, and impartial arbitrators.

We are left, then, with the core of the American Safety doctrine—the fundamental importance to American democratic capitalism of the regime of the antitrust laws. Without doubt, the private cause of action plays a central role in enforcing this regime. The treble-damages provision wielded by the private litigant is a chief tool in the antitrust enforcement scheme, posing a crucial deterrent to potential violators.

The importance of the private damages remedy, however, does not compel the conclusion that it may not be sought outside an American court. . . .

There is no reason to assume at the outset of the dispute that international arbitration will not provide an adequate mechanism. To be sure, the international arbitral tribunal owes no prior allegiance to the legal norms of particular states; hence, it has no direct obligation to vindicate their statutory dictates. The tribunal, however, is bound to effectuate the intentions of the parties. Where the parties have agreed that the arbitral body is to decide a defined set of claims which includes, as in these cases, those arising from the application of American antitrust law, the tribunal therefore should be bound to decide that dispute in accord with the national law giving rise to the claim. Cf. *Wilko v. Swan*, 346 U.S., at 433–434.[19] And so long as the prospective litigant effectively may vindicate its statutory cause of action in the arbitral forum, the statute will continue to serve both its remedial and deterrent function.

Having permitted the arbitration to go forward, the national courts of the United States will have the opportunity at the award-enforcement stage to ensure that the legitimate interest in the

---

that the arbitration panel selected to hear the parties' claims here is composed of three Japanese lawyers, one a former law school dean, another a former judge, and the third a practicing attorney with American legal training who has written on Japanese antitrust law.

The Court of Appeals was concerned that international arbitrators would lack "experience with or exposure to our law and values." The obstacles confronted by the arbitration panel in this case, however, should be no greater than those confronted by any judicial or arbitral tribunal required to determine foreign law. See, e.g., Fed. Rule Civ.Proc. 44.1. Moreover, while our attachment to the antitrust laws may be stronger than most, many other countries, including Japan, have similar bodies of competition law.

[19] In addition to the clause providing for arbitration before the Japan Commercial Arbitration Association, the Sales Agreement includes a choice-of-law clause which reads: "This Agreement is made in, and will be governed by and construed in all respects according to the laws of the Swiss Confederation as if entirely performed therein." The United States raises the possibility that the arbitral panel will read this provision not simply to govern interpretation of the contract terms, but wholly to displace American law even where it otherwise would apply. Brief for United States as Amicus Curiae 20. The International Chamber of Commerce opines that it is "[c]onceivabl[e], although we believe it unlikely, [that] the arbitrators could consider Soler's affirmative claim of anticompetitive conduct by CISA and Mitsubishi to fall within the purview of this choice-of-law provision, with the result that it would be decided under Swiss law rather than the U.S. Sherman Act." Brief for International Chamber of Commerce as Amicus Curiae 25. At oral argument, however, counsel for Mitsubishi conceded that American law applied to the antitrust claims and represented that the claims had been submitted to the arbitration panel in Japan on that basis. Tr. of Oral Arg. 18. The record confirms that before the decision of the Court of Appeals the arbitral panel had taken these claims under submission. See District Court Order of May 25, 1984, pp. 2-3. We therefore have no occasion to speculate on this matter at this stage in the proceedings, when Mitsubishi seeks to enforce the agreement to arbitrate, not to enforce an award. Nor need we consider now the effect of an arbitral tribunal's failure to take cognizance of the statutory cause of action on the claimant's capacity to reinitiate suit in federal court. We merely note that in the event the choice-of-forum and choice-of-law clauses operated in tandem as a prospective waiver of a party's right to pursue statutory remedies for antitrust violations, we would have little hesitation in condemning the agreement as against public policy.

enforcement of the antitrust laws has been addressed. The Convention reserves to each signatory country the right to refuse enforcement of an award where the "recognition or enforcement of the award would be contrary to the public policy of that country." Art. V(2)(b); see *Scherk*, [p. 319 *supra*] n. 14. While the efficacy of the arbitral process requires that substantive review at the award-enforcement stage remain minimal, it would not require intrusive inquiry to ascertain that the tribunal took cognizance of the antitrust claims and actually decided them.[20]

As international trade has expanded in recent decades, so too has the use of international arbitration to resolve disputes arising in the course of that trade. The controversies that international arbitral institutions are called upon to resolve have increased in diversity as well as in complexity. Yet the potential of these tribunals for efficient disposition of legal disagreements arising from commercial relations has not yet been tested. If they are to take a central place in the international legal order, national courts will need to "shake off the old judicial hostility to arbitration," *Kulukundis Shipping Co. v. Amtorg Trading Corp.*, 126 F.2d 978, 985 (CA2 1942), and also their customary and understandable unwillingness to cede jurisdiction of a claim arising under domestic law to a foreign or transnational tribunal. To this extent, at least, it will be necessary for national courts to subordinate domestic notions of arbitrability to the international policy favoring commercial arbitration. See *Scherk, supra*.[21]

Accordingly, we "require this representative of the American business community to honor its bargain," *Alberto-Culver Co. v. Scherk*, 484 F.2d 611, 620 (CA7 1973) (Stevens, J., dissenting), by holding this agreement to arbitrate "enforce[able] . . . in accord with the explicit provisions of the Arbitration Act." *Scherk*.

The judgment of the Court of Appeals is affirmed in part and reversed in part, and the cases are remanded for further proceedings consistent with this opinion.

It is so ordered.

Justice POWELL took no part in the decision of these cases.

Justice STEVENS, with whom Justice BRENNAN joins, and with whom Justice MARSHALL joins except as to Part II, dissenting.

. . . This Court's holding rests almost exclusively on the federal policy favoring arbitration of commercial disputes and vague notions of international comity arising from the fact that the automobiles involved here were manufactured in Japan. Because I am convinced that the Court of Appeals' construction of the arbitration clause is erroneous, and because I strongly disagree with this Court's interpretation of the relevant federal statutes, I respectfully dissent. In my

---

[20] See n. 19, *supra*. We note, for example, that the rules of the Japan Commercial Arbitration Association provide for the taking of a "summary record" of each hearing, Rule 28.1; for the stenographic recording of the proceedings where the tribunal so orders or a party requests one, Rule 28.2; and for a statement of reasons for the award unless the parties agree otherwise, Rule 36.1(4). Needless to say, we intimate no views on the merits of Soler's antitrust claims.

[21] We do not quarrel with the Court of Appeals' conclusion that Art. II(1) of the Convention, which requires the recognition of agreements to arbitrate that involve "subject matter capable of settlement by arbitration," contemplates exceptions to arbitrability grounded in domestic law. . . .

The utility of the Convention in promoting the process of international commercial arbitration depends upon the willingness of national courts to let go of matters they normally would think of as their own. Doubtless, Congress may specify categories of claims it wishes to reserve for decision by our own courts without contravening this Nation's obligations under the Convention. But we decline to subvert the spirit of the United States' accession to the Convention by recognizing subject-matter exceptions where Congress has not expressly directed the courts to do so.

opinion, (1) a fair construction of the language in the arbitration clause in the parties' contract does not encompass a claim that auto manufacturers entered into a conspiracy in violation of the antitrust laws; (2) an arbitration clause should not normally be construed to cover a statutory remedy that it does not expressly identify; (3) Congress did not intend § 2 of the Federal Arbitration Act to apply to antitrust claims; and (4) Congress did not intend the Convention on the Recognition and Enforcement of Foreign Arbitral Awards to apply to disputes that are not covered by the Federal Arbitration Act.

I

. . .

The federal policy favoring arbitration cannot sustain the weight that the Court assigns to it. A clause requiring arbitration of all claims "relating to" a contract surely could not encompass a claim that the arbitration clause was itself part of a contract in restraint of trade. Nor in my judgment should it be read to encompass a claim that relies, not on a failure to perform the contract, but on an independent violation of federal law. The matters asserted by way of defense do not control the character, or the source, of the claim that Soler has asserted. Accordingly, simply as a matter of ordinary contract interpretation, I would hold that Soler's antitrust claim is not arbitrable.

II

. . .

Until today all of our cases enforcing agreements to arbitrate under the Arbitration Act have involved contract claims. In one, the party claiming a breach of contractual warranties also claimed that the breach amounted to fraud actionable under § 10(b) of the Securities Exchange Act of 1934. *Scherk v. Alberto-Culver Co.* But this is the first time the Court has considered the question whether a standard arbitration clause referring to claims arising out of or relating to a contract should be construed to cover statutory claims that have only an indirect relationship to the contract. In my opinion, neither the Congress that enacted the Arbitration Act in 1925, nor the many parties who have agreed to such standard clauses, could have anticipated the Court's answer to that question.

On several occasions we have drawn a distinction between statutory rights and contractual rights and refused to hold that an arbitration barred the assertion of a statutory right. . . .

III

. . .

The Sherman and Clayton Acts reflect Congress' appraisal of the value of economic freedom; they guarantee the vitality of the entrepreneurial spirit. Questions arising under these Acts are among the most important in public law.

The unique public interest in the enforcement of the antitrust laws is repeatedly reflected in the special remedial scheme enacted by Congress. Since its enactment in 1890, the Sherman Act has provided for public enforcement through criminal as well as civil sanctions. . . .

The special interest in encouraging private enforcement of the Sherman Act has been reflected in the statutory scheme ever since 1890. Section 7 of the original Act used the broadest possible language to describe the class of litigants who may invoke its protection. . . .

The provision for mandatory treble damages—unique in federal law when the statute was enacted—provides a special incentive to the private enforcement of the statute, as well as an especially powerful deterrent to violators. . . . The interest in wide and effective enforcement has thus, for almost a century, been vindicated by enlisting the assistance of "private Attorneys General;" we have always attached special importance to their role because "[e]very violation of the antitrust laws is a blow to the free-enterprise system envisaged by Congress."

There are, in addition, several unusual features of the antitrust enforcement scheme that unequivocally require rejection of any thought that Congress would tolerate private arbitration of antitrust claims in lieu of the statutory remedies that it fashioned. . . . An antitrust treble-damages case "can only be brought in a District Court of the United States." The determination that these cases are "too important to be decided otherwise than by competent tribunals" surely cannot allow private arbitrators to assume a jurisdiction that is denied to courts of the sovereign States.

. . .

IV

The Court assumes for the purposes of its decision that the antitrust issues would not be arbitrable if this were a purely domestic dispute, but holds that the international character of the controversy makes it arbitrable. The holding rests on vague concerns for the international implications of its decision and a misguided application of Scherk v. Alberto-Culver, Co.

. . . As the Court acknowledges, the only treaty relevant here is the Convention on the Recognition and Enforcement of Foreign Arbitral Awards. [The dissent concludes that the Convention does not require the result reached by the majority.]. . .

Lacking any support for the proposition that the enforcement of our domestic laws in this context will result in international recriminations, the Court seeks refuge in an obtuse application of its own precedent, *Scherk v. Alberto-Culver Co.*, in order to defend the contrary result. The *Scherk* case was an action for damages brought by an American purchaser of three European businesses in which it was claimed that the seller's fraudulent representations concerning the status of certain European trademarks constituted a violation of § 10(b) of the Securities Exchange Act of 1934. The Court [distinguished *Scherk* from *Wilko* on the basis] that the outcome in *Wilko* was governed entirely by American law whereas in *Scherk* foreign rules of law would control and, if the arbitration clause were not enforced, a host of international conflict of laws problems would arise. . . . [In contrast], I consider it perfectly clear that the rules of American antitrust law must govern the claim of an American automobile dealer that he has been injured by an international conspiracy to restrain trade in the American automobile market. . . .

. . .The merits of [Soler's claims against Chrysler and Mitsubishi] are controlled entirely by American law. It is true that the automobiles are manufactured in Japan and that Mitsubishi is a Japanese corporation, but the same antitrust questions would be presented if Mitsubishi were owned by two American companies instead of by one American and one Japanese partner. When Mitsubishi enters the American market and plans to engage in business in that market over a period of years, it must recognize its obligation to comply with American law and to be subject to the remedial provisions of American statutes.

V

The Court's repeated incantation of the high ideals of "international arbitration" creates the impression that this case involves the fate of an institution designed to implement a formula for world peace.[41] But just as it is improper to subordinate the public interest in enforcement of antitrust policy to the private interest in resolving commercial disputes, so is it equally unwise to allow a vision of world unity to distort the importance of the selection of the proper forum for resolving this dispute. Like any other mechanism for resolving controversies, international arbitration will only succeed if it is realistically limited to tasks it is capable of performing well— the prompt and inexpensive resolution of essentially contractual disputes between commercial partners. As for matters involving the political passions and the fundamental interests of nations, even the multilateral convention adopted under the auspices of the United Nations recognizes that private international arbitration is incapable of achieving satisfactory results.

In my opinion, the elected representatives of the American people would not have us dispatch an American citizen to a foreign land in search of an uncertain remedy for the violation of a public right that is protected by the Sherman Act. This is especially so when there has been no genuine bargaining over the terms of the submission, and the arbitration remedy provided has not even the most elementary guarantees of fair process. Consideration of a fully developed record by a jury, instructed in the law by a federal judge, and subject to appellate review, is a surer guide to the competitive character of a commercial practice than the practically unreviewable judgment of a private arbitrator.

Unlike the Congress that enacted the Sherman Act in 1890, the Court today does not seem to appreciate the value of economic freedom. I respectfully dissent.

NOTES AND QUESTIONS

(1)(a) In *Zapata,* it was possible to demonstrate both aspects of a forum selection clause in the context of a single controversy. The three cases in this section demonstrate *first*, jurisdiction conferred by an arbitration agreement (*Gilbert*), *second*, jurisdiction of courts defeated by an arbitration agreement; and *third*, jurisdiction of arbitral tribunals defined, and (at least in comparison with prior practice) expanded. Though hostility to arbitration remains, it is clearly declining, as arbitration agreements become the preferred form of forum selection for international transactions.

(b) *Gilbert v. Burnstine,* in a real sense, is a case about the law of contracts. When a party makes a promise, the court says, it is held to the consequences. Here, it agreed to dispute resolution in London, and it cannot avoid that agreement by arguments (though they succeeded in the lower courts) about extraterritorial jurisdiction.

(c) Of course, an arbitration cannot go forward without jurisdiction, but as the court holds, that jurisdiction depends on agreement, not on territory or activity. What startled many observers at the time, but seems routine today, is that the consent extended not just to jurisdiction of the

---

[41] E.g., Charter of the United Nations and Statute of the International Court of Justice, 59 Stat. 1031, T.S. No. 993 (1945); Constitution of the International Labor Organisation, 49 Stat. 2712, T.S. No. 874 (1934); Treaty of Versailles, S.Doc. 49, 66th Cong., 1st Sess., pt. 1, pp. 8-17 (1919) (Covenant of the League of Nations); Kant, Perpetual Peace, A Philosophical Sketch, in Kant's Political Writings 93 (H. Reiss, ed. 1971).

arbitration tribunal, but also to supporting jurisdiction by the court and master in London, to appoint an arbitrator, to order service of process in a stated fashion, and (though it seems not to have been done in the actual case) to issue a judgment upon the award.

(d) Did the parties select English law to govern their contract? That, as we saw, would have been the inference in *Tzortzis* and many other cases. The New York Court of Appeals is more cautious. It says only that they adopted the procedural law of the chosen forum, including the English Arbitration Act. It is not inevitable that the arbitrator would have applied English law to the controversy between Gilbert and Burnstine, which seemed to concern a contract of sale made in New York calling for delivery of the goods in New York. He might well have said that under English conflict of laws, the proper law of the contract was the law of New York. In any event, whatever law the arbitrator applied (if indeed there was a legal issue) would not affect the attitude of the New York court toward the arbitration carried out in accordance with the agreement of the parties. Similarly, if arbitration were held in New York, the scope of review by the courts would be very narrow, essentially limited to due process concerns such as lack of proper notice, misconduct or conflict of interest of the arbitrators, and an award exceeding the terms of the agreement to arbitrate. Choice of law, interpretation of the law, determination of facts, inclusion or exclusion of evidence, would all be up to the arbitrators. If the parties had wanted decision by judicial authorities, they would not have selected arbitration.[a]

(e) In the full last paragraph of its opinion in *Gilbert v. Burnstine,* the court suggests that defendants might still be able to show (i) that there was no contract at all; or (ii) that there was no breach. The suggestion, half a century later, is probably wrong on both counts. If the defendants, admitting that they had signed the document in question, wanted to challenge its validity—for instance by claiming it had been induced by fraud—they would be expected to make that argument to the arbitral tribunal, and not to bring a judicial action to rescind the contract or to sit back and wait for an action to enforce an award rendered in an arbitration that they did not participate in.[b] A determination by the arbitrator that the contract was valid and had been breached would, as discussed above, be entitled to recognition and enforcement, except in a state that did not recognize arbitral awards—or foreign arbitral awards—at all. While that description would have fit a good many states in the 1930's, it does not fit many states outside Latin America in the last years of the century twentieth century.[c]

---

[a] This very general and necessarily superficial discussion is applicable not just to New York, but to most arbitration laws in the United States, the federal arbitration act, 9 U.S.C. § 1 *et seq.,* and (with some variations) in most major commercial states. Until recently, the law was different in the United Kingdom, as shown in the *Tzortzis* and *Cie. Tunisienne* cases, both of which reached the courts on appeal from arbitral awards via the so-called "case stated" procedure. That procedure was severely limited for international cases in the Arbitration Act of 1979, 1979 Laws. c. 42, and essentially abolished in the Arbitration Act of 1996, 1996 Laws c. 33, which also expressly provides (in s. 46) that the arbitral tribunal shall decide the dispute in accordance with the law chosen by the parties, and if there is no such choice, then according to the conflict of laws rules which it considers applicable. Thus the difference between international arbitration in London and in other leading commercial centers is now slight.

[b] The leading American case on this point is *Prima Paint Corporation v. Flood & Conklin Mfg. Co.,* 388 U.S. 395 (1967). Most other commercial states' law is the same, either by statute or by judicial decision. Until recently, the prevailing view under English law was the reverse, that is if either party asserted that the contract containing the agreement to arbitrate was void *ab intitio,* the validity of the contract had to be submitted for determination by the court. That approach was changed in *Harbour Assurance Co. (UK) Ltd. v. Kansa General International Assurance Co. Ltd.*, [1993] 3 W.L.R. 42, [1993] 3 All E.R. 897 (C.A.), holding that the validity of the contract, like other issues between the parties, were for the arbitrators to decide.

[c] Even in Latin America, which was traditionally hostile to international arbitration, the receptivity to arbitration is increasing; as of year-end 1997, the Inter-American Convention on Commercial Arbitration, similar to the UN Convention discussed in Note (4)(a), *infra,* had more than twelve adherents.

§ 4.02   CHOICE OF LAW □ 333

(2)(a) *Scherk v. Alberto-Culver* shows the other side of the agreement to arbitrate, avoiding litigation in courts. Putting aside the question of whether the particular dispute is arbitrable, the general rule, in the United States and in most commercial states, is that the existence of an arbitration clause in a contract is a ground for stay or dismissal of an action in court. Under § 3 of the U.S. Arbitration Act,[d]

> If any suit or proceeding be brought in any of the courts of the United States upon any issue referable to arbitration under an agreement in writing for such arbitration, the court in which such suit is pending, upon being satisfied that the issue involved in such suit or proceeding is referable to arbitration under such an agreement, shall on application of one of the parties stay the trial of the action until such arbitration has been had . . .

Ousting the jurisdiction of the courts was evidently not an overriding concern of Congress when it adopted the federal Arbitration Act as far back as 1925.[e] Why would the concern with preserving the jurisdiction of courts against agreements selecting a judicial forum that we saw in *Zapata* not be equally applicable to agreements selecting an arbitral forum?

(b) In *Zapata*, the forum selection clause ran up against the argument that honoring the clause would lead to recognition of an exculpatory provision in the contract that might not be recognized in the United States, but that argument persuaded only Justice Douglas. In *Scherk*, two years later, the same argument is made, and this time Justice Douglas persuades three other justices, still not enough to change the result. On the one hand the argument is much more specific in *Zapata;* there is no particular clause in *Scherk* that will be upheld in one forum and rejected another. There is, however, a presumption, reflected in the securities acts and in the *Wilko* case, that arbitration would not adequately protect victims of securities fraud. What is the Court's answer?

(3) In *Scherk,* the parties made the kind of compromise quite common in international transactions: "You choose the law, I'll choose the forum." The chosen forum is arbitration in Paris under the rules of the International Chamber of Commerce, but the law to be applied is the law of Illinois, which evidently embraces the law of the United States, including the Securities Exchange Act of 1934.

(a) Do you think a typical arbitration tribunal—say a German professor designated by Scherk, an American lawyer designated by Alberto-Culver, and a retired French judge designated by the ICC—could handle such a case? Justice Douglas argues that while such a panel could deal with a breach of warranty of merchantability under the American Uniform Commercial Code, or a trademark question under the law of Switzerland, U.S. securities legislation is different. Is he right?

(b) Suppose the agreement between Scherk and Alberto-Culver had contained no choice–of–law clause, or had said the law of Switzerland governs. Would (should?) the Supreme Court have come out differently?

(4)(a) In 1958, after many years of negotiations, a Convention was signed at the United Nations in New York on the Recognition and Enforcement of Foreign Arbitral Awards. The United States took until 1970 to become party to the New York Convention, the United Kingdom until 1975, but by the 1990's, more than a hundred states were parties, including all the states traditionally chosen as places for international arbitration (Switzerland, France, United Kingdom, the

---

[d] 9 U.S.C. § 3.

[e] New York's arbitration act, presently N.Y. CPLR § 7501–14 was adopted in 1920.

Netherlands, Sweden); China, the Soviet Union and its successor states, as well as all the states of Eastern Europe; all the members of the European Community, as well as Japan, Mexico, and the United States. Canada, which had refrained from adhering to the convention because of concern about disturbing the delicate balance between the federal government and the provinces, did so in 1986, after its own constitutional problems had settled down.

Despite its title focused only on awards, the New York Convention has two functions: Article II deals with enforcement of agreements to arbitrate; Article V with enforcement of arbitral awards.[f] Article II obligates contracting states to recognize agreements in writing to submit differences in respect to a defined legal relationship to arbitration, but only "concerning a subject matter capable of settlement by arbitration." What kinds of subjects might not be capable of settlement by arbitration?

(b) Until *Scherk v. Alberto-Culver,* it was thought that controversies concerning securities legislation, antitrust and other competition law, patents, and similar "public" law issues were not capable of arbitration. It seems, therefore, that if the Supreme Court had held that the dispute in *Scherk* was not capable of settlement by arbitration, that would not have been a violation of the Convention, because the decision on arbitrability is for each state to make in good faith on its own. This is why, apparently, the Court uses the New York Convention as support for its holding (see p. 319, note 15), rather than resting its decision on the Convention. Nevertheless the case was understood as a major boost for the New York Convention and for international arbitration altogether.

(c) Faced with its own prior decisions in *Wilko,* holding securities disputes not arbitrable, and in *Zapata,* holding forum selection clauses in international transactions enforceable, the Court decides (5–4) that *Scherk* was more akin to *Zapata* than to *Wilko.* Do you agree?

(d) In saying that in international commerce forum selection clauses, including arbitration clauses, are favored even when they might not be acceptable in wholly domestic cases, both Chief Justice Burger and Justice Stewart emphasize the conflict of laws problems that might otherwise be created. What kinds of cases would you think should not be accorded this preference?

(e) Think back to *Siegelman v. Cunard White Star.*[g] If the ticket had read "All claims arising out of this voyage not settled by negotiation shall be submitted to binding arbitration in London," would a suit in tort in New York have been dismissed? Suppose the ticket said "All claims arising out of this voyage . . . shall be submitted to arbitration, at the passenger's option, in London, New York, Chicago, Los Angeles, or Paris"?

(5)(a) A particular concern of those who feared the spread of arbitration has been the field of antitrust and competition law. The perception was that arbitrators (whether or not lawyers) may be competent to determine quality of merchandise and to interpret provisions of a commercial contract, but are not likely to be sensitive to issues of public interest. If, for instance, a manufacturer and a distributor made a contract covering a given area, arbitrators could decide whether the rights granted were intended to be exclusive and whether either party broke its promise, but they might not understand or be sympathetic to defenses based on a contention that a prohibition against resale outside the territory, or a requirement that in order to buy product

---

[f] The United Nations Convention on the Recognition and Enforcement of Foreign Arbitral Awards is reproduced in the Documents Supplement, p. 128. Article V concerning awards is dealt with in the chapter on judgments, Chapter 8, § 8.03[B], *infra.*

[g] Page 259, *supra.*

A, distributor must also buy product B, were unlawful. For many years, both in the United States and in some European states, agreements to submit future disputes to arbitration were deemed not enforceable with respect to antitrust claims.[h] Is the Supreme Court in Mitsubishi persuasive in rejecting this attitude, at least in international transactions?

(b) Soler had two principal arguments in opposing arbitration of his antitrust claim. (i) Antitrust issues, reflecting the public interest, ought not to be submitted to arbitrators at all; and (ii) the choice of law clause in the contract selected Swiss law, and thus excluded Soler's opportunity to establish before the arbitrators a claim based on U.S. antitrust law. The Court is quite straightforward in rejecting the first argument. Justice Blackmun sees no reason to suppose that arbitrators cannot do a good a job as judges, and finds no overwhelming handicap in the fact that all three arbitrators are Japanese. (p. 326, note 18). But what about the second question? Does the choice of Swiss law exclude application of U.S. law? Or is this a good place for the application of renvoi, i.e., the arbitrators in Tokyo looking to the whole law of Switzerland, which for purposes of antitrust law would (or should?) look to the law of the market, i.e., U.S. law?

(c) Giving an affirmative answer to the preceding answer assumes that Swiss law (i) would not reject U.S. antitrust law as "foreign public law"[i] or contrary to public policy; and (ii) view the proper law applicable to the antitrust claim to be United States law, notwithstanding the parties' election of Swiss law. Alternatively, could the Japanese arbitrators simply disregard the choice of law clause in respect of the antitrust issues and look directly to U.S. law?

(d) The present author, writing shortly after the *Mitsubishi* case came down, urged the second alternative, on the ground, essentially, that antitrust law, like export controls, tax laws, or criminal law, could not be avoided by choice of law clauses, and is thus different from statutes of limitations, extent of implied warranties, and similar "private law."[j] But the article conceded that the point made was "in the nature of prediction or advice, rather than generalisation from reported judicial decision or arbitral awards."[k]

(e) In December 1987, the Swiss parliament adopted for the first time a comprehensive Federal Statute on Private International Law.[l] Article 187 reads as follows:

> 1. Claims of restraint of competition are governed by the law of the country in whose market the restraint directly affects the damaged or injured party.
>
> 2. If claims of restraint of competition are governed by foreign law, no damages can be awarded in Switzerland beyond those that would be awarded under Swiss law in case of an unlawful restraint of competition.

Consider how that statute, had it been in effect at the time the *Mitsubishi* case came up, might have influenced the thinking of both the majority and the dissent in the Supreme Court.

(f) When *Mitsubishi* was decided by the U.S. Supreme Court, it was regarded everywhere (not just in the United States) as a landmark case. A few years later, an arbitral tribunal sitting

---

[h] See e.g., the German Law against Restrictive Business Practices (GWB) Art. 91(1). For a debate and citation of the principal U.S. cases, see, Pitofsky, Loevinger, and Aksen, *Symposium on Arbitration and Antitrust,* 44 N.Y.U. L. Rev. 1069 (1969).

[i] See chapter 10, § 10.02. *infra.*

[j] A. Lowenfeld, *The Mitsubishi case: another view,* 2 Arbitration Int'l 178 at 185-88 (July 1986), replying to T. Carbonneau, *Mitsubishi: the Folly of Quixotic Internationalism,* 2 Arbitration Int'l 116 (April 1986).

[k] Id. at 187.

[l] *Systematische Sammlung des Bundesrechts* (SR) 291, English annotated version in Karrer, Arnold, and Patocchi, *Switzerland's Private International Law* (2d ed. 1994).

in Geneva in a contract dispute between a Belgian and an Italian firm, declined to consider a defense that the contract was invalid because it contravened the competition articles of the Treaty Establishing the European Community (the Treaty of Rome). The Federal (Supreme) Court of Switzerland set aside the resulting arbitral award and sent the case back to the arbitrators, directing them to pass on the competition law defense, and rejecting the view that the arbitrators' jurisdiction did not extend to these public law provisions. The court pointed out that the arbitrators could not fairly award damages for breach of a contract that might be unlawful.[m]

(6)(a) Coming back to *Mitsubishi*, Justice Blackmun writes, in Footnote 19, that

> in the event the choice-of-forum and choice-of-law clauses operated in tandem as a prospective waiver of a party's right to pursue statutory remedies for antitrust violations, we would have little hesitation in condemning the agreement as against public policy.

How could the court put this position into effect?

(b) Is the Court's answer, in the paragraph following note 19, persuasive? Suppose the arbitration goes ahead, Mitsubishi establishes to the satisfaction of the arbitrators that Soler did not meet its purchase quota or did not pay all its bills, and the tribunal rejects Soler's antitrust counterclaim. Could a U.S. court decline to give effect to the award? Would you expect different answers to this question if the arbitrators' decision was based on

   (i) a conclusion after hearing that the territorial restraint imposed by Mitsubishi was not illegal under U.S. law;

   (ii) a refusal to apply U.S. antitrust law as against the public policy of Japan;

   (iii) the arbitrators' conclusion that Swiss law excluded application of U.S. law; or

   (iv) rejection by the arbitrators of renvoi, and therefore application of Swiss internal law only?

(c) Suppose Mitsubishi prevails on the contract claim, and the arbitrators find Soler liable for $1.2 million. Soler prevails on the counterclaim, in the amount of $500,000. Soler contends that he is entitled to treble damages on his antitrust claim, so that he is owed $300,000. The arbitral tribunal, however, holds that punitive damages, including treble damages in antitrust actions, are contrary to Japanese public policy, or more simply that arbitrators lack jurisdiction to award punitive damages. Accordingly, the tribunal issues an award in favor of Mitsubishi for $700,000 ($1,200,000 -$500,000), and this award comes to be enforced in a United States court pursuant to the UN Convention. What would Justice Blackmun say? What should he say?

(d) If you are uneasy about Justice Blackmun's fallback position, does that lead you to the view that Justice Stevens' dissent is the better view? Or are you persuaded by the broader lesson from the trilogy of *Zapata, Scherk,* and *Mitsubishi,* that the United States is now firmly committed to upholding forum selection clauses in international commercial transactions, and that is as it should be.

(*P.S.* 1)

1) The arbitration between Mitsubishi and Soler never took place, as Soler went into bankruptcy. Thus many of the questions raised above remain untested.

---

[m] *G S.A. v. V. SpA*, 118 BGE (ATF) II 193 (April 28, 1992), excerpted in English in 18 Yb. Commercial Arbitration 143 (1993). The case is discussed in Daniel Hochstrasser, *Choice of Law and "Foreign" Mandatory Rules in International Arbitration,* 11 J. Int'l Arbitration 57 (1994), and more briefly in A. Lowenfeld, *International Litigation and the Quest for Reasonableness,* 223-25 (1996).

2) The distinction drawn by the Supreme Court in *Scherk*, suggesting that international controversies involving the securities laws were arbitrable but domestic securities controversies were not, broke down in the 1980's,[n] and contracts between securities firms and their customers now routinely provide for arbitration of all disputes.

3) As of year-end 1997, the Supreme Court had not ruled on the arbitrability of domestic antitrust controversies. Several Courts of Appeals, but not all, have applied the lesson of *Mitsubishi* to domestic antitrust cases, and have enforced agreements to arbitrate. Attempts to secure review by the Supreme Court of these holdings have not succeeded.[o]

4) Apart from arbitration, the teaching of *Zapata* in favor of upholding forum selection clauses has been broadly, but not universally, accepted by both federal and state courts in the United States, including a Supreme Court decision in a consumer contract with a ticket that resembles the one in *Siegelman*.[p] 5) In a case bringing together the teaching of Zapata and Mitsubishi, the Supreme Court upheld a clause in a bill of lading calling for arbitration in Tokyo and application of Japanese law, rejecting the argument that the clause lessened the carrier's liability in violation of §3(8) of the Carriage of Goods by Sea Act (COGSA), 46 U.S.C. App. §1303(8).[q]

§ 4.03 Donative Transfers and Conflict of Laws

Throughout this chapter we have seen the tension between giving effect to the intentions of parties and frustrating those intentions in the interests of protecting those deemed in need of protection and thereby vindicating public interests. This tension is even more apparent in connection with disposition of property at death. On the one hand, people ought to be able to do with their property what they like. On the other hand, most societies believe that widows (or surviving spouses) are entitled to some protection against disinheritance; states in the French tradition tend to restrain testamentary freedom further, for protection of children of the deceased. Because the intentions of the deceased cannot be proved by testimony, most states have formal requirements with respect to wills, revocation of wills, and contracts to make wills.[a] Also, certain kinds of dispositions are subject to particular restraints, for example gifts to religious institutions or to all charities made within *x* months of death.[b] Finally, some kinds of gifts with strings

---

[n] See *Shearson/American Express, Inc. v. McMahon*, 482 U.S. 220 (1987); *Rodriguez de Quijas v. Shearson/American Express, Inc.*, 490 U.S. 477 (1989).

[o] See, e.g., *Nghiem v. NEC Electronics, Inc.*, 25 F.3d 1437 (9th Cir. 1994), cert. denied, 512 U.S. 1046 (1994); *Kotam Electronics, Inc. v. JBL Consumer Products, Inc.*, 93 F.3d 724 (1996), cert. denied, 117 S. Ct. 946 (1997).

[p] *Carnival Cruise Lines, Inc. v. Shute*, 499 U.S. 585 (1991). See also *Stewart Organization Inc. v. Ricoh Corporation*, 487 U.S. 22 (1988). For a comprehensive survey, see Walter W. Heiser, "Forum Selection Clauses in State Courts: Limitations on Enforcement after *Stewart* and *Carnival Cruise*," 45 Fla. L. Rev 361 (July 1993); "Forum Selection Clauses in Federal Courts: Limitations on Enforcement after *Stewart* and *Carnival Cruise*," 45 Fla. L. Rev. 553 (Sept. 1993). For an earlier, historical survey, see Michael Gruson, "Forum Selection Clauses in International and Interstate Commercial Agreements," [1982] Univ. Illinois L. Rev. 133.

[q] *Vimar Seguros y Reaseguros, S.A. v. M/V Sky Reefer*, 515 U.S. 528 (1995).

[a] Recall *Estate of Barrie*, Chapter 1, p. 20, *supra*; also *Bernkrant v. Fowler*, p. 239, *supra*.

[b] For an interesting conflict of laws case growing out of such a restraint, see *Toledo Society for Crippled Children v. Hickock*, 152 Tex. 578, 261 S.W.2d 692 (1953) criticized in Hancock, *In the Parish of St. Mary le Bow, in the Ward of Cheap*, 16 Stan. L. Rev. 561 (1964). See also Lowenfeld, *Book Review of Hancock's Collected Essays*, 38 Stan. L. Rev. 1411, 1417–24 (1986).

attached are subject to the rule against perpetuities, which (in different versions in different jurisdictions) prevents the suspension of alienation for more than a given period, in order not to keep property indefinitely out of the market place.[c] Responses to these issues have been different in different states. Whenever a person dies domiciled in one state with assets in another, or changes domicile after having created a trust, drawn (or revoked) a will, or otherwise acted in respect of assets that may survive him or her, a potential conflict of laws problem arises. A recurring question is whether different conflict of laws rules should apply to dispositions inter vivos and dispositions at death.

We focus here again on New York state, whose highest court went through a period of activity in this area almost as intense, and roughly at the same time, as its activity in the field of choice of law in torts (Chapter 3, *supra*). To some extent, the considerations and uncertainties that we saw with respect to automobile and airplane accidents are apparent here as well. All but the first case, however, involve construction of a statute, and in fact as the cases here reproduced made their way through the courts, a major legislative reform was under way, which, among other things, produced for the first time in the United States an effort to codify the choice of law rules concerning wills.

[A] Inter Vivos vs. Testamentary Transfers

WYATT v. FULRATH

New York Court of Appeals
16 N.Y.2d 169, 264 N.Y.S.2d 233, 211 N.E.2d 637 (1965)

BERGAN, J.

The Duke and Duchess of Arion were nationals and domiciliaries of Spain. Neither of them had ever been in New York, but through a long period of political uncertainty in Spain, from 1919 to the end of the Civil War, they sent cash and securities to New York for safekeeping and investment.

Under the law of Spain this was the community property of the spouses. Substantial parts of it were placed with the New York custodians in joint accounts. In establishing or in continuing these accounts, the husband and wife either expressly agreed in writing that the New York law of survivorship would apply or agreed to a written form of survivorship account conformable to New York law.

The husband died in November, 1957; the wife in March, 1959. After the husband's death the wife took control of the property in New York and undertook to dispose of it by a will executed according to New York law and affecting property in New York (Decedent Estate Law, § 47). Some additional property in joint account in England was transferred by the wife to New York after the husband's death which had not been placed by either spouse in New York during the husband's life.

---

[c] This is, of course, a very simplified statement. Even Professor Leach's famous attempt to put the subject in a "nutshell" took over 30 pages. Leach, *Perpetuities in a Nutshell*, 51 Harv. L. Rev. 638 (1938). The statement of the rule by John Chipman Gray was "No interest is good unless it must vest, if at all, not later than twenty-one years after some life in being at the creation of the interest."

§ 4.03 CHOICE OF LAW □ 339

This action is by plaintiff as an ancillary administrator in New York of the husband against defendant as executor of the wife's will to establish a claim of title to one half of the property which at the time of the husband's death was held in custody accounts under sole or joint names of the spouses by banks in New York and London.

The total value of the property in New York is about $2,275,000, of which about $370,000 was transferred by the wife after the husband's death from the London accounts to New York. Plaintiff also seeks an accounting and damages for conversion.

The main issue in the case is whether the law of Spain should be applied to the property placed in New York during the lives of the spouses, in which event only half of the property would have gone to the wife at her husband's death, or the law of New York, in which event all of such jointly held property would have gone to her as survivor. (Banking Law, § 134, former subd. 3.)

The banks which were custodians of the property are protected from liability, of course, by the form of survivorship agreement in making the transfer of the jointly held property in their custody to the wife (Banking Law, § 134, former subd. 3). The controversy here is not with the custodians, but between the representatives of the owners of the property, and is to be governed by the legal capacity of the husband and wife, as citizens and domiciliaries of Spain, to make an agreement as to their community property inconsistent with Spanish law.

The agreements giving full title to the survivor in the joint accounts were executed either in Spain, or if not there at least not in New York, and were, in any event, executed by persons who were domiciliaries and citizens of Spain. Usually rights flowing from this kind of legal act are governed by the law of the domiciliary jurisdiction. . . .

It is abundantly established in the record that the law of Spain would have prevented either spouse in the circumstances shown here from agreeing that community property go entirely to the survivor on the death of either; but half would go to the survivor and at least two thirds of the remaining half would pass to the heirs of the deceased spouse.

Dispositions of property in violation of this prohibition are shown to be void according to Spanish law. It is provided that all the assets of a marriage shall be deemed to be community property until it is proved they belong privately to either (Spanish Civ. Code, art. 1407). A gift from one to the other, except minor personal gifts, is void and the spouses are without capacity to renounce by contract or otherwise their rights and obligations concerning community property (arts. 1334, 1394).

But New York has the right to say as a matter of public policy whether it will apply its own rules to property in New York of foreigners who choose to place it here for custody or investment, and to honor or not the formal agreements or suggestions of such owners by which New York law would apply to the property they place here. (Cf. Decedent Estate Law, § 47; Personal Property Law, § 12–a.)

It seems preferable that as to property which foreign owners are able to get here physically, and concerning which they request New York law to apply to their respective rights, when it actually gets here, that we should recognize their physical and legal submission of the property to our laws, even though under the laws of their own country a different method of fixing such rights would be pursued.

Thus we would at once honor their intentional resort to the protection of our laws and their recognition of the general stability of our Government which may well be deemed inter-related things.

Such a law conflicts choice seems to be suggested by *Hutchison v. Ross* (262 N. Y. 381, 187 N.E. 65 [1933].) although there are some differences between that case and this. There a husband who, with his wife, was domiciled in Quebec, established a trust of personal property for the benefit of the wife in New York with a New York trustee and with the expressed intention the trust should be governed by New York law.

Its validity was determined according to New York law even though by the law of Quebec it would have been decided differently. Of course, the New York trustee had there acquired legal title of the property and here the banks were mere bailees in relation to the property in their possession.

Still the case suggests a direction to our present public policy and, in the course of an examination of great depth into the conflicts problem, Judge Lehman noted: "Physical presence in one jurisdiction is a fact, the maxim [*mobilia sequuntur personam*] is only a juristic formula which cannot destroy the fact. . . . When the owner of personal property authorizes its removal from his domicile or acquires property elsewhere, he must be deemed to know that his property comes under the protection of, and subject to the laws of the jurisdiction to which it has been removed, and that appeal may be made to the courts of that jurisdiction for the determination of conflicting rights in such property."

The Special Term in the case before us found for the defendant [i.e., the wife's executor] largely on the basis of *Ross* and the Appellate Division affirmed without opinion. We agree that this disposition is the correct one as to property placed in New York during the husband's lifetime.

. . .

But the property in the value of about $370,000 transferred from London to New York by the wife after the husband's death raises a somewhat different question. Adjudication of its title requires further factual exploration. At the time of the husband's death this property and other property were held in three-name custody accounts by London depositories. The accounts were in the names of the husband, the wife and their daughter Hilda, who had no proprietary interest.

One of the accounts, it is asserted, was a "safe custody account" opened under simple letters of instruction. The other accounts seem not to have been governed by any formal documents.

The reasons grounded on New York policy and affected by the physical transfer of the property to New York during the lifetime of the spouses and by their directions relating to it do not necessarily apply to property of Spanish nationals placed in a third country during their lifetime.

If the local law of the third country would deem title to have passed to the wife on the death of the husband, we would treat this property as we now treat that placed in New York during their lives.

But if the third country would have applied the Spanish community property law or, if it is not demonstrated what rule would be applied by the third country and the subject is open or equivocal, we would, under general principles, feel bound to apply the law of Spain to the title of property owned by these Spanish nationals.

The facts necessary to decide this question were not resolved at Special Term, largely because this was not an issue on which attention was focused at trial. One question for resolution would be the precise form of instruction or agreement pursuant to which the property was placed in custody accounts in London; the other question would be how, on those facts as found, the title would be regarded in English law. If upon such further inquiry it be found the wife did not succeed

§ 4.03   CHOICE OF LAW   □   341

to full title to the property in London an accounting for the portion not belonging to her would be indicated.

The order should be modified to direct the remission to Special Term to determine the rights of parties in respect of the property transferred by the wife from London to New York after the husband's death in accordance with this opinion and, as modified, affirmed, without costs.

Chief Judge DESMOND (dissenting).

Resolution of the dispute as to this property (or any part of it) by any law other than that of Spain, the matrimonial domicile, is utterly incompatible with historic and settled conflict of laws principles and is not justifiable on any ground. No policy ground exists for upsetting the uniform rules and no precedent commands such a result.

"Conflict of Laws" (or, more aptly, "Private International Law") rules involve no actual conflict or collision between the laws of separate jurisdictions but are the accepted methods of accommodation and comity between sovereign States, worked out consensually over the centuries, not arbitrarily or from mere politeness but as expressing reason and justice. Thus, as to real property the applicable law is always that of the State wherein the land is situated since it is an attribute of every sovereign to control his own actual territory. Movables, on the other hand, are considered to be incidental to their owner's person and so to be governed as to title by the laws of his domicile. These are not *ad hoc* holdings subject to the moment or the mode or to the conveniences of a particular case but are part of the generally acknowledged fundamentals of international comity. The twentieth century with its shrinking distances and enlarging wars is a poor time to make sudden and uncalled for changes particularly when the changes are urged on us not because the old rules are outdated or proven to be unjust but, apparently, because in this particular case there appears in the record a small and unconvincing indication that this husband and his wife may have intended a result inconsistent with that which would result from application of the law of their domicile, Spain.

The majority of this court is throwing overboard not one but three of the oldest and strongest conflict rules: first, that with exceptions not pertinent here the law of the domicile of the owner governs as to the devolution of personal property; second, that the law of the matrimonial domicile controls as to the property and contract rights of husband and wife *inter sese;* and, third, that whether such personalty is separate or community property is determined by the law of the matrimonial domicile.

For no reason of law that we know of but on the authority of one decision of slight or no relevance (*Hutchison v. Ross*) the majority chooses to turn its back on these rules and to destroy the community status, fixed as such by the laws of Spain, of personalty owned during marriage by Spanish nationals always domiciled in Spain and neither of whom was ever in New York State.

Completely applicable here is the Spanish Civil Code which subjects to the statutory regime of community property all marriages of Spanish nationals in Spain, which applies to property outside as well as within Spain and which makes all property acquired by the married couple or either of them during marriage community property, and forbids the alteration of such community property either unilaterally or by mutual consent, to the extent even of voiding a gift from one party to another or renunciation by either spouse of any right or obligation in respect to the community property (Spanish Civ. Code, arts. 9, 1315, 1334, 1394, 1401). The only exception to all this arises when an antenuptial contract has been made. There is no proof or claim of any such contract here. The Spanish statutes are clear and no one disputes their meaning. The Duke and Duchess of Arion were Spanish nationals, were married in Spain and always had their domicile there as had their ancestors for generations or centuries. Neither was ever in New York. New York State's only contact with this property was that for purposes of convenience or safety the husband and wife left valuable property in the custody of New York banks for safekeeping only. The banks were mere bailees without other title or interest. To say that setting up of joint accounts of personalty in New York subjected that personalty to New York law rather than to the law of the matrimonial domicile is to refuse to follow one of the most basic of Conflict of Laws rules.

. . .

Research has not turned up any other decision similar to the one now being made. For the proposition that New York law applies because joint accounts were created or attempted to be created in this State, the trial court and respondent put their whole reliance on *Hutchison v. Ross* and the conclusion there stated that "The validity of a trust of personal property must be determined by the law of this State, when the property is situated here and the parties intended that it should be administered here in accordance with the laws of this State." The differences between our case and *Hutchison* are of substance and not detail.

. . .

Among other differences, the *Hutchison* case dealt with the validity of a conveyance whereas here there was the merest deposit of property for safekeeping in New York—that is, a bailment without change of title. As respondent in his answer in this cause admits, the New York banks acted in a "solely . . . ministerial capacity as custodian and depositary." *Hutchison v. Ross* involved a situation where not only title had passed to a trustee but application of the foreign law would have destroyed rights of third parties created and acquired in good faith and which merited protection. Not only did *Hutchison v. Ross* not overrule the *Mesa* decision[d] but it stands apart and on its own facts.

If the intent of the parties to apply New York law is to control, there was undisputed proof in the *Hutchison* case (*supra*) of such intent, whereas in ours there is no real proof at all. The signing by the Duke and Duchess in Spain of routine joint-account-for-custody agreements on forms supplied by the New York banks is not substantial proof that these people (who had no apparent reason for so doing) were attempting to abrogate as to these items of property the ancient community laws of their country. There is no other proof of such an intent to substitute New York law and a much more reasonable explanation of the documents exacted by the banks is that they operated and were intended merely to release the banks on payment to one spouse or the other. It is to be emphasized that here, unlike the *Hutchison* case, no rights of third persons are involved or in need of protection. The court below mentioned the difficulties which New York banks would encounter if they had to comply with the laws of other jurisdictions. Such inconvenience there may be, but surely it does not justify repeal of the basic rules without any felt necessity for such abrogation and with no real proof that even the parties themselves ever intended such a result. Most extraordinary would be the results of a holding that any temporary deposit for emergency safekeeping of personal property in New York vaults puts the property

---

[d] In *Matter of Mesa y Hernandez,* 172 App. Div. 467, 159 N.Y.S. 59, *aff'd,* 219 N.Y. 566, 114 N.E. 1069 (1916), it was held that the widow of a decedent domiciled in Cuba was entitled under the community property law of Cuba to one half of the decedent's assets acquired during the marriage, and that this amount was not subject to New York's transfer tax.

under New York law for all purposes regardless of the ancient maxims, regardless of the law of the domicile and regardless of the intent of the parties.

We would reverse and grant judgment as demanded in the complaint, with costs in all courts.

JUDGES DYE, FULD, and BURKE concur with Judge BERGAN; CHIEF JUDGE DESMOND dissents in an opinion in which Judges VAN VOORHIS and SCILEPPI concur.

NOTES AND QUESTIONS

(1)(a) Consider, *a priori,* how one should create a set of principles for choice of law in the area of donative transfers. Would you favor:

(i) preference for restraints;

(ii) preference for party autonomy—i.e., validation of the donor's intent whenever possible;

(iii) neutral principles—e.g., a strict rule in favor of domicile, or of situs, whichever way it cuts;

(iv) preference for the law of the forum?

(b) Is the preceding question too general? Should the answers be different for different kinds of restraints—for instance, for those designed to protect the interests of family members; those controlling gifts to charity; and those directed to the property itself, such as rules against perpetuities?

(2)(a) The traditional conflict of laws rule (putting aside land) has been that a will is governed as to substance according to the law of the domicile of the testator at death. The rule with respect to trusts is not quite so clear, but in general an inter vivos trust is governed by the situs of the trust, which normally means the domicile or place of business of the trustee. Many other devices, including, as in *Wyatt v. Fulrath,* a joint bank account with survivorship, and a Totten trust (i.e., a savings account opened by A in trust for B[e]) are treated as if they were inter vivos trusts. Are these distinctions reasonable?

(b) For example, in *National Shawmut Bank v. Cumming,*[f] a settlor domiciled in Vermont conveyed his property in trust to a Massachusetts trust company, with income to himself for his life, remainder to his nieces and nephews. At his death the widow claimed the principal of the trust, on the ground that the trust was invalid under Vermont law because it was made for the purpose of depriving her of her succession. Had Mr. Cumming attempted to create the trust by will, the widow would probably have prevailed; since the trust had been created inter vivos (though without depriving himself of the income from the property), the rules above stated would say Massachusetts law governs, the trust is valid, and the widow is effectively cut out. Do you agree with such a result?[g]

---

[e] Named after *In re Totten,* 179 N.Y. 112, 71 N.E. 748 (1904). Such an arrangement is not a real trust, since A can withdraw funds at any time; after A's death, however, it passes to B without going through A's estate.

[f] 325 Mass. 457, 91 N.E.2d 337 (1950).

[g] That was indeed the holding of the Massachusetts court. For a criticism of the result, and of the *Restatement (Second)* for essentially accepting it, though suggesting that "it may be held that the local law of [the settlor's] domicil is applicable," see Lowenfeld, *Tempora Mutantur . . .—Wills and Trusts in the Conflicts Restatement,* 72 Colum. L. Rev. 382, 387–90 (1972). The relevant section of the *Restatement* is § 270, and the "may be" language appears in Comment *b.*

Reconsider this question after reading the *Clark* case in the next section.

(3)(a) Turning to *Wyatt v. Fulrath,* the first point is that the case does not involve a trust, and probably not even an estate plan, but rather an account designed to preserve assets in a safe place while Spain went through years of turmoil and civil war. Should the case nevertheless be treated as a party autonomy case, as if the operative document had read as follows?

> Notwithstanding any law that may be applicable at our domicile, we hereby direct that the law of New York govern both the relations between us and the bank and the disposition of the assets here deposited in the event of the death of either or both of us.

(b) Numerous bank and custody accounts were involved, some without any statement about the applicable law. The signature card on the account with Guaranty Trust Co. read:

> All rights arising hereunder shall be determined according to the laws of the State of New York, and the provisions hereof shall be binding upon our several heirs, next of kin and legal representatives.
>
> Signature DUCHESS OF ARION
Signature ARION

Is that an estate plan? An effective choice of law? Or simply a statement that the account holders' relations with the bank are subject to New York law?

(c) If the quoted provision does evidence an intent to make an estate plan, by whose law should the capacity of the Duke and Duchess to make such a plan be judged?

(4)(a) *Wyatt v. Fulrath* reached the New York Court of Appeals in the middle of the period of activity concerning choice of law in torts; the opinion, in fact, appears in the same volume of the New York reports as *Dym v. Gordon.*[h] Is it decided under governmental interest analysis? What is New York's interest? Is it a worthy one?

(b) Note that Chief Judge Desmond, the proponent of public policy of the forum in *Kilberg* and *Dym,* is outraged by the majority's view in *Wyatt.* Knowing Judge Desmond from his other opinions on conflict of laws, it seems improbable that his dismay stems from devotion to black letter law. What is his underlying concern here?

(c) Is the court's disposition of the property deposited in England consistent with the rest of the opinion? Note the resemblance between this phase of the case and *Schneider's Estate.*[i]

(d) Note a quite different but important feature of accounts such as those in *Wyatt v. Fulrath.* As currencies in nearly all developing and many developed countries are unstable if not valueless, it is common for persons of wealth from such countries to keep their assets in safe, stable financial centers such as New York, London or Zurich. The almost universal practice is that banks in these places accept the money, securities or other valuables for investment or safe keeping, without inquiring about exchange controls or tax laws of the states of their clients' domicile or nationality. Often (as in the case of the Duke and Duchess of Arion) arrangements are made that statements are not to be rendered at all, or are to be sent to some place other than the home address of the depositor.[j] The tradition is that "public law" is not recognized outside the state

---

[h] Chapter 3, p. 152, *supra.*

[i] Chapter 2, p. 48, *supra.*

[j] For much of the time, the Duke and Duchess got their information and gave their instructions through a contact in Paris.

imposing the tax or control.ᵏ The question is whether, having decided not to honor Spain's exchange controls or tax laws, the state should similarly disregard "private law," such as provisions in a civil code concerning community property or inheritance.

(5) As noted in the introduction to this section, New York adopted a completely revised Estates, Powers and Trusts Law in 1966, including one part dedicated entirely to choice of law with respect to wills. Assuming that in this area, more than, say, with respect to torts or even contracts, express rules are desirable, look at New York's E.P.T.L. § 3–5.1 (Documents Supplement, p. 28) to see if the right decisions were made.

(a) Note first the distinction between "formal" and "intrinsic" validity (Para. (a)(3) and (4)). For real property, both formal and intrinsic validity are governed by the law of the jurisdiction where the land is situated. For personal property, or real property in New York, there is a principle of validation as to formalities; if the formalities required at one of four possible places are complied with, and the will is in writing signed by the testator, the will is valid (Para. (c)). As to intrinsic validity of wills of personal property, the statute points to the law of the domicile of the decedent at death.

Should the drafters have stopped right there? What more needs to be said?

(b) Suppose T makes a will, intrinsically valid where made, and thereafter changes his domicile. Suppose, for example, T lives in Greenwich, Connecticut with his wife and children, but works in New York. When the children grow up, T sells the house in the suburbs, moves to New York with his wife, and then dies. Should New York or Connecticut law govern?ˡ

Paragraph (b)(2) would say New York, but Paragraph (d) would point to the law of Connecticut. Is that the right answer?

Should a New York court ask what Connecticut courts would do in these circumstances? Paragraph (e) says no with respect to interpretation, but is silent about intrinsic validity.

(c) Recall the problem about whether Miss Barrie, the Illinois lady with property in Iowa, did or did not mean to revoke her will, which surfaced with the word "void" written on it.ᵐ Paragraph (f) of the New York statute seems to solve that problem (though not for real property), but like the statute in *Barrie,* it doesn't do anything about revocation by operation of law. Suppose, to repeat the question posed in Chapter 1, T makes a will, while single and domiciled in Illinois, in favor of his mother. He then marries, moves to New York, and dies, leaving personal property both in New York and in Illinois. If under Illinois law a marriage revokes a prior will and under New York law it does not,ⁿ would the mother take the New York property and the wife the Illinois property? Or should Illinois follow New York's rule as to T's domicile at death?ᵒ

ᵏ See Chapter 10, § 10.02, *infra.*

ˡ The law of wills as such is not likely to be significantly different. But, for example, under New York law, various "testamentary substitutes," E.P.T.L. § 5–1.1(b)(1), Documents Supplement, pp. 31–32, 36–39, would be included in a spouse's estate for purposes of election by the other spouse. In Connecticut, assets conveyed during a donor's lifetime, regardless of retained powers or motive, would not be included in his estate. See, e.g., *Cherniack v. Home Nat'l Bank & Trust Co.,* 151 Conn. 367, 198 A.2d 58 (1964).

ᵐ See *Estate of Barrie,* Chapter 1, p. 20, *supra.*

ⁿ Strangely enough, a marriage revokes a prior will under E.P.T.L. § 5–1.3 if the will was executed prior to September 1, 1930, but not otherwise. Evidently the legislature thought that the right of election of a surviving spouse, which went into effect on that date, served the purpose.

ᵒ Look also at § 5–1.4, Documents Supplement, p. 42, providing for revocation of a will by a divorce. Again, unity of succession for personal property would be undermined if this section, rather than **paragraph (b)(2)**, were applied to non-New York domiciliaries leaving property in New York.

(d) We shall return to paragraph (g) concerning powers of appointment in connection with the *Bauer* case in the next section.P But paragraph (h) is perhaps the most interesting provision of all. What do you think is the rationale for such a provision? Is it, like the holding in *Wyatt*, a decision in favor of New York banks? In favor of party autonomy? Do you think a New York court would accept the reverse of paragraph (h)—i.e., a New York domiciliary putting his assets in the Wilmington Trust Company and making a will stating that he elects to have the disposition of his property governed by the laws of Delaware? Reconsider this question after reading the *Clark* case in the next section.

(e) Note, finally, the provisions in § 5–1.1(a) and (c), concerning the right by a surviving spouse to elect against a will leaving her (or him) less than the share prescribed by the statute. Paragraph (b) provides that certain inter vivos transactions effected by the decedent after the marriage and after August 31, 1966 may be treated as part of the estate against which the elective right is measured; and paragraph (d)(7) relates the right of election under § 5–1.1 to the choice of law provision of § 3–5.1(h). These provisions, too, are relevant to the *Clark* case, though the case arose before they took effect.q

[B] Party Autonomy and State Interests

ESTATE OF CLARK

New York Court of Appeals
21 N.Y.2d 478, 288 N.Y.S.2d 993, 236 N.E.2d 152, (1968)

CHIEF JUDGE FULD.

This appeal poses an interesting and important question concerning a widow's right of election to take against her husband's will. More particularly, may her husband, domiciled in a foreign state, by selecting New York law to regulate his testamentary dispositions, cut off or otherwise affect the more favorable right given his widow to elect by the law of their domicile?

In the case before us, Robert V. Clark, Jr., died in October of 1964, domiciled in Virginia, and there his widow continues to reside. His estate, consisting of property in Virginia and in New York, had an aggregate value of more than $23,000,000—the bulk of which consisted of securities on deposit with a New York bank. His will, made in 1962, contained a provision that "this Will and the testamentary dispositions in it and the trusts set up shall be construed, regulated and determined by the laws of the State of New York." It devised the Clark residence in Virginia, together with its contents, to the widow and created for her benefit a preresiduary marital

---

P See question (6)(c), p. 364, *infra*.

q The concept of the testamentary substitute had been introduced in New York two decades earlier in the famous case of *Newman v. Dore*, 275 N.Y. 371, 9 N.E.2d 966 (1937), in which a trust of all his assets created three days before his death by a man of 80 years who retained the right to the income, a power of revocation, and substantial management control, was declared illusory in a suit by his 30-year-old wife. As to Totten trusts, see *Krause v. Krause*, 285 N.Y. 27, 32 N.E.2d 799 (1941). For a convenient, brief discussion not directed to choice of law issues, see Clark, *The Recapture of Testamentary Substitutes to Preserve the Spouse's Elective Share: An Appraisal of Recent Statutory Reforms*, 2 Conn. L. Rev. 513 (1970). For legislation similar to New York's provisions concerning testamentary substitutes, see Uniform Probate Code, § 2–201–2–207, 8 U.L.A. 73 et. seq. 1983. As of 1998, the Code was in force in 16 states.

deduction trust—under which she would receive the income for life, with a general testamentary power of appointment over the principal of the trust. The residue of the estate, after payment of estate taxes, was placed in trust for the testator's mother. There has been a bi-state administration of the estate. The New York executors are administering the major portion of the estate—consisting, as noted, of securities held in New York during Mr. Clark's lifetime—and the Virginia executors are administering the balance, including the real and tangible personal property located in Virginia.

The testamentary trust for the widow's benefit would satisfy the requirements of section 18 of our Decedent Estate Law. However, it is conceded that, under the statutes of Virginia, the widow has an absolute and unconditional right to renounce her husband's will and take her intestate share (in the absence of issue, one half) of his estate outright (Virginia Code, § 64–16).[1] Timely notice of the widow's election having been given, the New York executors initiated this special proceeding in the Surrogate's Court, pursuant to section 145–a of the New York Surrogate's Court Act. The petition requests a determination denying the widow any right of election on the grounds that the terms of the will barred her from recourse to Virginia law and that, under New York law, the testamentary provisions in her favor were sufficient. The executors contend that, by declaring that his testamentary dispositions should be construed by the laws of New York, the testator meant to bar his widow from exercising her Virginia right of election and that section 47 of the Decedent Estate Law requires that we give effect to his purpose. That section—replaced, since the testator's death, by a very similar provision (EPTL 3–5.1, subd. [h])[r] —provided, in essence, that, when a nondomiciliary testator recites in his will that he elects that his *"testamentary dispositions"* shall be construed and regulated by the laws of New York, "the validity and effect of *such dispositions* shall be determined by such laws."[2]

The Surrogate upheld the executors' position. On appeal, the Appellate Division reversed, deciding that the widow's right to take in opposition to the will must be determined by the law of the domicile of the parties. Section 47—which relates solely to the decedent's "testamentary dispositions" and their validity and effect—was inapplicable, the court concluded, because "the right of a widow to inherit despite the will is not a 'testamentary disposition' in any sense" but is, on the contrary, "a restriction on the right to make a testamentary disposition."

We thoroughly agree with the Appellate Division's construction of the statute and with the conclusion it reached.

As already appears, section 47 permits a foreign domiciliary to have the validity and effect of his "testamentary dispositions" construed and regulated by the laws of this State. A regard for the language of the statute, as well as its legislative history and the policy to be served by

---

[1] In contrast, the New York right of election statute, in effect at the time of this testator's death (Decedent Estate Law, § 18), permits a decedent to defeat his spouse's right by creating a trust of the requisite size for her benefit and giving her the net income therefrom for life.

[r] Documents Supplement, p. 29.

[2] Section 47 read, in somewhat greater detail, as follows: "The validity and effect of a testamentary disposition of real property, situated within the state . . . are regulated by laws of the state, without regard to the residence of the decedent. Except where special provision is otherwise made by law, the validity and effect of a testamentary disposition of any other property situated within the state, and the ownership and disposition of such property . . . are regulated by the laws of the state or country, of which the decedent was a resident, at the time of his death. *Whenever a decedent, being a citizen of the United States or a citizen or subject of a foreign country, wherever resident, shall have declared in his will that he elects that such testamentary dispositions shall be construed and regulated by the laws of this state, the validity and effect of such dispositions shall be determined by such laws.*" (Emphasis supplied.)

it, clearly demonstrates that the words "testamentary dispositions" and "the validity and effect of such dispositions" do not encompass the right accorded a spouse to elect to take in opposition to the will.

Indeed, our statutes, in terms, draw a distinction between the two concepts, between the decedent's "testamentary disposition" and the spouse's right to elect. Section 145 of the Surrogate's Court Act (now SCPA 1420)—a statute procedurally related to section 47—gave the surrogate jurisdiction to determine "the validity, construction or effect of any *disposition* of property contained in a will." And, in contrast, section 145-a of the Surrogate's Court Act (now SCPA 1421) gave the court jurisdiction of proceedings for the "determination as to the validity or effect of any *election* to take an intestate share against the provisions of a will." This latter provision appeared in our law for the first time in 1929 (eff. Sept. 1, 1930) as part of the same legislative package which included the first statute creating a right to elect against a will (L. 1929, ch. 229, §§ 4, 9). It is apparent—and highly significant—that the Legislature deemed it necessary to adopt this new procedural section (§ 145-a), despite the long-time presence on the statute books of the above-mentioned provisions empowering the surrogate to determine "the validity [and] effect of a *testamentary disposition.*" It is also significant that the proceeding now before us was brought, and properly so, under section 145-a, dealing with the "validity or effect of any election" rather than under section 145 which deals with testamentary dispositions.

The difference between the wording of section 145 and the much more recent section 145-a merely reflects the profound differences, in history and design, between the law of testamentary dispositions, of which section 47 of the Decedent Estate Law is a part, and the law of election to take in opposition to testamentary dispositions, embodied in section 18.

Unlike the expressions of intent which constitute testamentary dispositions, the right of election, both in Virginia and New York, is statutory in nature and exists wholly outside of, and in direct contravention to, the provisions of a will. Section 18 of the Decedent Estate Law, when enacted in 1929, introduced into this State a "new public policy which no longer permit[ted] a testator to dispose of his property, as he please[d]." This being so, it necessarily follows that the widow's right of election—or, more precisely, its availability or nonavailability—is not a "testamentary disposition" whose validity and effect may be controlled by the provisions of a will under section 47. In the words of the Appellate Division, the spouse's right of election, far from being a testamentary disposition, is a "restriction on the right [of the decedent] to make [such] a . . . disposition."

A moment's reflection is all that is necessary to establish the difference between statutes which have to do with restrictions placed on the decedent's testamentary power—for instance, to disinherit his spouse or other members of his family—and those which bear on discerning and carrying out the testator's wishes and desires. Section 47 is an example of the latter sort of legislation. Its earliest version (Code Civ. Pro., § 2694 [L. 1880, ch. 178]) simply reflected the traditional choice of law rules, referring dispositions of personal property to the law of the decedent's domicile. It provided that the "validity and effect . . . of a testamentary disposition" of real property were to be regulated by the law of the situs and those of personalty by the law of the domicile; no exception was made for a case in which the testator might express a contrary intent.

Despite this statute, cases decided before.. as well as after . . . its adoption, held that, when personalty had been placed outside the domiciliary jurisdiction, a testamentary disposition of the property which violated (for example) the domicile's rule against perpetuities or its mortmain statute—the cases dealt almost invariably with charitable bequests—would be given effect if valid under the law where the property was situated. The declared purpose of the courts was, if possible, to give effect to, and not frustrate, the testamentary dispositions; the reasoning underlying these determinations was that perpetuities and mortmain affected only the administration of the property in the hands of the recipient and that, therefore, these questions were of concern only to the situs jurisdiction and not to that of the domicile.

Some years later, in 1911, in apparent recognition of this practice of the courts, section 47 was amended, expressly to permit a nondomiciliary to choose to have his testamentary disposition of his property regulated by New York law (L. 1911, ch. 244). The distinction between the decedent's "testamentary disposition" and the spouse's right of election, as well as the inapplicability of section 47 to the present case, is pointed up by the fact that, when this amendment to section 47 was adopted, New York's first right of election statute was still some 18 years in the future (Decedent Estate Law, § 18 [L. 1929, ch. 229, § 4]).

Moreover, consideration of general principles of choice of law serve to confirm the conclusion, at which we have arrived, that it is the law of Virginia as to the widow's right of election, not that of New York, which here controls. As between two states, the law of that one which has the predominant, if not the sole, interest in the protection and regulation of the rights of the person or persons involved should, of course, be invoked. *Matter of Crichton* (20 N.Y.2d 124 [1967]) is illustrative. A domiciliary of New York had placed his personal property in a state (Louisiana) which had a very different method of protecting a surviving spouse. In deciding that the law of the domicile ought to be applied, our court noted that Louisiana had no "interest in protecting and regulating the rights of married persons residing and domiciled in New York." On the contrary, we declared, "New York, as the domicile of Martha and Powell Crichton, has not only the dominant interest in the application of its law and policy but the only interest."

Although a declaration contained in a will that its law was to control might give a foreign state an interest in the application of its law that it would otherwise lack, this interest would not extend to a matter, such as the right of election, which is completely unrelated to, and indeed in contravention of, the decedent's intent. Thus, in the *Crichton* case, the court made it exceeding plain that such a declaration would not be given any effect, if to do so would be to "avoid the New York statutory provision for the protection of the surviving spouse." But, urge the appellants before us, even if a testator domiciled in *New York* could not avoid his spouse's right of election in that way, this State's interest in encouraging nonresidents to invest their funds here ought to be given effect, even at the expense of the rights given to a surviving spouse by the law of the domicile of the decedent and his widow. The authorities upon which they rely, however, fail to support such a proposition.

In *Wyatt v. Fulrath* and *Hutchison v. Ross* we permitted nondomiciliaries to make dispositions of property located here which would have violated the public policy of their domicile, and it is asserted that a similar result should be reached in this case. *Hutchison* and *Wyatt,* however, are inapposite; both involved *inter vivos* transactions between husband and wife. Such *inter vivos* dispositions, unlike the unilateral provisions of a will, have traditionally been upheld if permitted under the law of place where the property was located.

Indeed, in the *Hutchison* case, this court specifically referred to the distinction drawn between *inter vivos* and testamentary dispositions. After noting that "The rules that both the capacity to make a valid conveyance of tangible chattels and securities and the essential validity of such conveyance are determined by the law of the state where chattel is situated . . . have been generally applied to conveyances *inter vivos,"* the court went on to say that "[t]hey are not generally applied to passage of title by will or the intestacy of a decedent owner. With possible limitations, not relevant to the question here presented [cases cited], the rule is well established that the essential validity of a testamentary trust must be determined by the law of the decedent's domicile."

In point of fact, recent legislative changes serve to confirm our conclusion that a widow of a nondomiciliary cannot be deprived of the right of election given to her by the law of the jurisdiction in which she and her husband were domiciled. In 1965, the Legislature undertook a thorough re-evaluation of the law governing rights of election in this State and, as a result, adopted section 18–b of the Decedent Estate Law, to take effect September 1, 1966. The new section explicitly provided (subd. 4) that the New York provisions "shall *not be available* to the spouse of a decedent who at the time of his death was not domiciled in this state." In 1966, that same rule was restated as subdivision 6 of section 18–c and, again, as section 5–1.1 of the new Estates Powers and Trusts Law which was to go into effect the following year. Thus, three successive legislative enactments had specifically provided that, regardless of any expression of intent, the spouse of a nondomiciliary was not entitled to exercise a right of election under New York law. The purpose of the provision was undoubtedly to insure that the spouse's rights were to be determined by the law of the domicile (Fourth Report of Temporary State Commission on Estates, N. Y. Legis. Doc., 1965, No. 19, pp. 150–151). This was considered necessary to achieve uniformity between the law which had been applied to real property and the existing law as to personal property which the commission found, "under established rules, is governed by the law of the decedent's domicile."

However, effective September 1, 1967, the spouse of a nondomiciliary was given an additional right; section 5–1.1 (subd. [d], par. [6]) of the new Estates Powers and Trusts Law[s] was amended (L. 1967, ch. 686, § 39) to give to the surviving spouse the opportunity to elect against the will under New York law where the testator made an election to have his testamentary dispositions governed by New York law. "The right of election granted by this section," the amended provision reads, "is not available to the spouse of a decedent who was not domiciled in this state at the time of death, unless such decedent elects, under paragraph (h) of 3–5.1 [formerly Decedent Estate Law, § 47], to have the disposition of his property governed by the laws of this state."

The effect of this provision, quite obviously, was to render the New York right of election *"available"*—that is, afford an opportunity—to a nondomiciliary to elect the New York right of election where, under prior law, she would have been limited to her rights under the law of the domicile. It was consistent with the policy of uniformity since, where a testator had declared that his will should be governed by the law of a foreign jurisdiction, no interest of the domicile would be prejudiced by extending to the surviving spouse the greater protections which New York law might provide. (See Scoles, *Conflict of Laws and Elections in Administration of Decedents' Estates,* 30 Ind. L. J. 293, 307.) Be that as it may, though, the statute was certainly not intended to *deprive* her of any rights afforded by the domicile in a case such as this, where it would provide her with a greater protection than the law of New York. On the contrary, as we have already observed, the amended statute extends an *additional* protection which she would not otherwise have had. In short, the statute manifests a strong legislative policy to limit the testator's power to deprive his spouse of support; it is designed to complement, not to frustrate, the policies of sister states directed toward the same end.

---

[s] Present Para. (d)(7), Documents Supplement p. 35.

While Virginia, as well as New York, has demonstrated concern for surviving spouses, the two states have done so in substantially different ways. A right to the income of a trust, sufficient under our law (Decedent Estate Law, § 18), is by no means the equivalent of taking the principal outright as would be the widow's right upon her election under Virginia law. Whether the widow in the case before us would be adequately provided for under the will or our own law is irrelevant, for the same principles must apply to an estate of $23,000 as to one of $23,000,000, and we reject the notion that New York ought to impose upon its sister states its own views as to the adequacy of a surviving spouse's share.

In sum, Virginia's overwhelming interest in the protection of surviving spouses domiciled there demands that we apply its law to give the widow in this case the right of election provided for her under that law. We find nothing in section 47 of the Decedent Estate Law or in the public policy of New York which would permit a decedent, by a mere expression of intent, to change this result.

The order appealed from should be affirmed, with costs to all parties appearing separately and filing separate briefs payable out of the estate.

THE LANARI ESTATE

Aristide Lanari was an Italian citizen domiciled in France, with assets in many parts of the world. He had a daughter by a first marriage, and a second wife. Through a series of inter vivos gifts, joint accounts with right of survivorship, and a holographic will, he sought to leave virtually all of his property to his wife Roberta. When he died, his daughter sought a declaration from the French court that the will and the inter vivos dispositions were invalid, except as to one fourth of his property, since she was entitled to the rest as the sole child. Meanwhile the widow sought to take possession of the joint bank account in New York, and when the bank declined to turn over the funds, the widow (later replaced by her brother-in-law, Mr. Watts), brought suit. The daughter contested the New York action, and the widow (and later the widow's sisters) contested the French action.

MACCOUN/WATTS v. LANARI/MEYER

Court of Appeal, Aix-en-Provence
October 22, 1964

Whereas . . . Aristide Lanari, of Italian nationality, died at La Turbie, France, leaving on the one hand, Maria Lanari, wife of Mr. Meyer, his daughter born of his first marriage, on the other hand Roberta Maccoun, his second wife; whereas in a holographic will he named the latter his universal legatee, declaring that he was bequeathing to her in addition, as a specific legacy, the full ownership of Villa Casa at La Turbie, together with the furniture and furnishings contained therein, while he expressed the desire that his daughter's share in his estate be taken out of the assets which he possessed in Egypt.

Whereas the action instituted by Mrs. Meyer against Mrs. Roberta Maccoun, wife of Mr. Lanari, and continued after the death of the latter against her sisters, her sole heirs, sought to obtain a declaration that Mrs. Maccoun had been guilty of concealment of estate assets; that other assets located in foreign countries represented the proceeds of disguised gifts between spouses in violation of the provisions of articles 1098 and 1099 of the Civil Code and, consequently, should be returned to the estate; that the joint accounts opened in foreign banks in the names of the deceased and of his wife, and fed with the husband's personal funds, did not confer any personal right on Mrs. Lanari Maccoun in the assets contained in said accounts; that Mrs. Lanari Maccoun was entitled only to one-fourth of the estate, in accordance with article 1098 of the Civil Code; and finally that a settlement and partition of the estate as well as a determination of the rights of each spouse should be made. . . .

Whereas the judgment appealed from allowed the demands [of Mrs. Meyer, the daughter] . . .

Whereas, the appellants contend, [i] that Article 1098 of the Civil Code, which limits the gifts that may be made by one spouse to the other spouse who had children by a prior marriage to one fourth of the estate, is inapplicable in this case, because the deceased was an Italian national, his wife was an American national, and his daughter was a Swiss national, and determination of the reserved share and disposable portion of the estate must be made in accordance with the law of the deceased's nationality; [ii] that even if the reserved share falls under the law governing the estate; i.e., French law, it should be computed differently for personal and for real properties, because the latter are governed by different laws according to their situs; and that [in taking this difference of applicable law into account], the reserved share of Mrs. Meyer, the daughter, had been fulfilled by the gifts made to her by her father; [iii] that the court below rendered a decision regarding property located in foreign countries, which it did not have jurisdiction to render, in that it ordered the notary in charge of the liquidation and partition of the estate to take into account the value and devolution of the real properties located abroad; [iv] that since the assets located abroad and here claimed by Mrs. Meyer represented gifts made by Mr. Lanari to his wife during his lifetime, the law governing such gifts should be the law of the place of the transaction, especially when the donor and the donee had intended to be subject to said law; that in the present case, more particularly regarding the opening of the joint accounts in his and his wife's names, said acts had been carried out in accordance with the law of the country in which they were performed; that, therefore, the Tribunal of Nice had no jurisdiction in respect of said acts; that, in any event, even if it had jurisdiction, it could not declare that they constituted disguised gifts in the sense of French law or declare them void pursuant to said law without violating the "locus regit actum" rule and disregarding the intention of the parties to be subject to the law of the place of the gift; [W]hereas, finally, they claim that the Tribunal, in ordering the return of the foreign assets to the estate, allowed to Mrs. Meyer, a non-French heir, a right from which she is excluded by the provisions of the law of July 14, 1819.

Whereas, the respondent answers that [i] that the Civil Tribunal of Nice rightly declared that it had jurisdiction over the estate regarding the real property situated in France and the personal property wherever located, Mr. Lanari having died in France; [ii] that the law of the place where the estate was opened is the only applicable law regarding the devolution of the estate, particularly for determining the reserved share and disposable portion of the estate; [iii] that the disguised gifts represented by transfers of funds or securities belonging to Mr. Lanari into joint accounts in the names of both spouses, into safes rented in both names, or into accounts or safes in the name of the wife, were rightly declared void by the court below in application of French law; and [iv] that in fact, the application of the "locus regit actum" rule to these gifts, as proposed by Mesdames Maccoun, would lead to disregarding the family bond between the donor and the donee, which bond is at the basis of the special status of gifts between spouses;

Whereas . . . under French law testamentary estates are governed by the same law which governs intestacy, with the sole exception of matters left to the discretion of the testator by the succession law; Whereas said exception does not include the rules concerning the reserved share and disposable portion between spouses, which are rules of public policy for the purpose of protecting the immediate family, particularly the children of the donor, against excessive generosity of the latter . . . whether by gifts or legacies;

Whereas Aristide Lanari died at La Turbie (France) where it is not contested that he was domiciled [and accordingly] his estate is subject to French law as regards, on the one hand, the real property situated in France, and, on the other hand, the personal property wherever actually located on the date of death, the personal estate being considered to be situated at the domicile of the deceased; Whereas the court below did not exceed the limits of its jurisdiction and did not render any decision on the devolution of real property situated abroad; . . .

Whereas the "locus regit actum" rule is inapplicable to this case since the question is not whether the gift was valid as to its form but whether it may be used to reduce the interests of the heir pursuant to the succession law which, as already stated, is the only applicable law regarding the protection of the reserved share and the disposable portion between spouses; Whereas, for the same reason, the intent of the donor, expressed by a choice of the place where the gift is effected, is powerless to avoid the succesion law and to subject the gift to the law of that place;

Whereas, in fact, it appears from the documents submitted in the case that during the months which preceded his death Mr. Lanari placed a very important part of his personal assets either in joint accounts, in his wife's names (at the Swiss Bank Corporation in New York and Banca Svizzera in Chiasso, Switzerland), or in rented safes or accounts opened in his wife's name only (Credit Comercial, Milan; Banca Svizzera, Chiasso); Whereas in thus scattering his assets in various foreign countries, in such a way as to enable Mrs. Maccoun to collect the funds and securities herself, Mr. Lanari intended to facilitate for his wife the withdrawal upon his death of the larger portion of his estate, as indicated in the letter which he addressed to his wife on February 15, 1961 and which is reproduced in the judgment appealed from.

Whereas, far from denying that it really was a matter of gifts, the appellants expressly admit the fact that these actions had the character of disguised gifts, whose character was rightly recognized by the court below, though they had been made under the appearance of simple deposits; Whereas, through these gifts, Lanari was frustrating the normal devolution of his property, particularly the rule which protects the children of the first marriage; Whereas the judgment appealed from, by application of article 1099 of the Civil Code, has rightly declared said gifts void with respect to Mrs. Meyer and whereas such nullity exists without any necessity to ascertain whether the disposable portion—in this case representing one-fourth of the estate—was actually exceeded; . . .

For These Reasons . . .

THE COURT: at a public hearing, all parties being represented, admits *as to form* the appeal of Mrs. Maccoun, wife of Mr. Watts, Mrs. Maccoun, wife of Mr. Parsons, and Mrs. Maccoun, wife of Mr. Crocker; *on the merits:* dismisses the appeal, denies all new or contrary demands of the parties, and confirms the judgment appealed from.

WATTS v. SWISS BANK CORPORATION

New York Court of Appeals
27 N.Y.2d 270, 317 N.Y.S.2d 315, 265 N.E.2d 739 (1970)

BREITEL, J. . . .

. . .

Aristide Lanari, an Italian citizen, and his second wife, Roberta, an American citizen, both domiciled in France, opened in a New York City office of the Swiss bank a purportedly joint bank account with right of survivorship. The documents dated in November, 1960 and signed by Aristide and Roberta provided that *inter se* they occupied the status of "true" joint tenants, and, further, that the account should be governed by the laws of the State of New York (see *Wyatt v. Fulrath*).

Upon Aristide's death in September, 1961, the widow requested the bank to turn over the balance of the account to her as surviving joint tenant. Before the bank could comply, it received notice from Mrs. Maria Elena Meyer, the decedent's only child, a daughter by his first wife, that she claimed the fund.

Before any action was taken in New York, the daughter sought a declaratory judgment against the widow in an appropriate French court that the funds in New York were part of Aristide's estate and that the widow had no rights to them. Under the forced heirship law of France, it was not possible for Aristide to donate to his wife more than one fourth of his assets. Any attempted transfer in violation of this statute is void in its entirety upon the challenge of a child of a first marriage. One month later, on April 5, 1962, the widow instituted this action in New York against the bank to compel a turnover of the funds. The daughter and an ancillary administrator of Aristide Lanari's estate were interpleaded by the bank. Shortly after the appearances in both actions, the widow died, leaving as legatees three sisters to whom she bequeathed her entire estate, except for two legacies to others of $10,000 each. In the French action the sisters were substituted as defendants and continued its defense. The French action proceeded to a determination in favor of the daughter. In the New York action the executors of the widow's estate were substituted as plaintiffs. The widow's executors are respectively husbands of two of her legatee sisters.

Plaintiffs and appellants, the executors of the widow, argue that they should not be precluded by the French judgment. They contend that there was no substantial identity of parties or issues in the two actions, and, assuming *arguendo* that there was an identity of parties and issues, public policy forbids recognition of the foreign judgment.

Preliminarily, the law of the rendering jurisdiction, insofar as it limits the effect of its own judgments, would also limit elsewhere the preclusive effect of the judgment and the definition of the parties bound. At least this is true as to recognition of judgments between States of the Union. . . . *A fortiori*, the limitation should apply to extranational judgments. . . . The burden of proof in establishing the conclusive effect in the rendering jurisdiction of a prior judgment is upon the party asserting it . . .

. . .

Generally speaking, the doctrine of *res judicata* gives "binding effect to the judgment of a court of competent jurisdiction and prevents the parties to an action, and those in privity with them, from subsequently relitigating any questions that were necessarily decided therein." It has been said that the term privity does not have a technical and well-defined meaning. It denominates a rule, however, to the effect that under the circumstances, and for the purposes of the case at hand, a person may be bound by a prior judgment to which he was not a party of record (Restatement, Judgments, § 83, Comment *a*). It includes those who are successors to a property interest, those who control an action although not formal parties to it, those whose interests are represented by a party to the action, and possibly coparties to a prior action (Restatement, Judgments, §§ 81–90).

Authorities are in accord that a person may so involve himself with litigation in which he is interested that the result is *res judicata* against him . . . The character and extent of the participation in litigation which will in legal effect make one a party is most often an issue of fact. As a consequence, no single fact is determinative but all the circumstances must be considered from which one may infer whether or not there was participation amounting to a sharing in control of the litigation . . .

The record justifies the conclusion that the relationship of Sewell Watts, one of the executors of the widow and husband of her sister, with Coudert Brothers, the law firm representing the widow and her substituted sisters, was such that he had practical control of all proceedings. Watts was responsible for retaining Coudert Brothers to represent the widow in the French action. Contact that the involved members of the family had with Coudert Brothers was through Watts. Watts testified before trial that "[e]verybody sends everything to me and I send everything to Coudert Bros." After the widow's death a multiple power of attorney was executed by both executors, in their representative capacities, and the sisters of Roberta, authorizing Coudert Brothers to "continue all actions or proceedings commenced by [Roberta and] to commence proceedings or procedural acts for effecting the execution or collection of all rights of the said ROBERTA MACCOUN LANARI." It is of no little importance in appraising the relationship between Watts and Coudert Brothers, that he signed the power several days before the others. Coudert Brothers thereafter retained counsel to appear in the French action in behalf of the parties of record, the three sisters.

It is of singular significance that the two actions were prosecuted simultaneously by the same law firm. This alone supports a strong probability that the executors, who concededly controlled the New York action, were inextricably involved in the progress of the foreign action. It is difficult to conceive that the managers of the New York action would not see to it, if it were in their power (as it was), that the French defense was managed as they thought it should be.

The undisputed facts of the relationship between Coudert Brothers and Watts, as well as the reliance placed on Watts by other members of the family, suggests, if it does not compel, the conclusion that Watts exercised practical control of the French proceeding on behalf of the estate as well as the sisters. Such control should and does conclude the executors from relitigating the issue of the ownership of the funds. Consequently, the Appellate Division findings rather than those of the trial court should be affirmed.

The argument that there was no identity of issues before the two courts is unsubstantiated. . . . The determination of the interests of the respective parties to the assets in the joint account was common to both actions.

In the alternative, plaintiffs argue that recognition of the French judgment should be refused on the ground that such recognition is repugnant to the public policy of New York. Under principles of comity the courts should give full effect to a judgment rendered by a French court of competent jurisdiction (*Johnston v. Compagnie Generale Transatlantique* [p. 694, *infra*]. Recognition will not be withheld merely because the choice of law process in the rendering jurisdiction applies a law at variance with that which would be applied under New York choice of law principles. It is concluded that no contravention of public policy sufficient to justify nonrecognition has been demonstrated by appellants.*

MATTER OF BAUER

New York Court of Appeals
14 N.Y.2d 272, 251 N.Y.S.2d 23, 200 N.E.2d 207 (1964)

CHIEF JUDGE DESMOND.

In 1917 Dagmar Bauer, then a resident of New York, executed in New York City an irrevocable trust indenture which stipulated that she should receive the life income and that the remainder should go to her husband. In the event her husband predeceased her, the principal was to be distributed to such person or persons as she appointed by her will and, failing a valid disposition in her will, to the settlor's next of kin pursuant to the statutes of the State of New York. Settlor's husband predeceased her. She died a resident of London, England, in 1956. Her will, probated in England, contained a clause whereby she gave her property including any property over which she had a power of appointment "except the property otherwise disposed of by this my Will or any Codicil hereto" to Midland Bank Executor and Trust Company Limited in trust for Dr. Barnardo's Homes: National Incorporated Association of Stepney Causeway, London. A codicil revoked the prior bequest and left the trust fund to Midland Bank for the benefit of two nieces for life with the remainder to Dr. Barnardo's Homes, etc., a charitable corporation of the United Kingdom and Northern Ireland.

Special Term held: that the law of England, where the owner of the power resided at the time of her death, governed; that under English law suspension of alienation dated from the date of exercise of power of appointment and not from the date of its creation; that the power was validly exercised in the codicil and the suspension of interests thereunder was valid but that even under New York law the exercise of the power should be upheld; and that the trust corpus should be turned over to Midland Bank to be held in trust under the terms of the codicil.

The Appellate Division, modifying, decided as follows: that it was the intention of the settlor to have New York law apply to all questions of distribution or construction of the instrument; that the settlor had created a remainder interest in the trust and that the permissible period of suspension must be computed from the time the trust was created; that the codicil, suspending alienation for three lives (the settlor's and those of two nieces), was not an effective exercise of the power of appointment; and that the power was effectively exercised in the residuary clause.

. . .

---

* Of course, if the sisters were not barred from relitigating the issue they could rely, as they do, on cases like *Wyatt v. Fulrath* and *Hutchison v. Ross* which allow the application of New York law to assets in this State, otherwise subject to the forced heirship rules of a civil law jurisdiction. In that event the daughter would rely on *Matter of Crichton* (20 N.Y.2d 124) and *Matter of Clark*. On the view taken, the issue may not be reached.

We agree with the dissenting opinion at the Appellate Division and summarize our holdings as follows:

(1) The law to be applied here is the law of New York which was the donor's domicile and where there was executed the trust agreement containing the power of appointment. This rule applies where the same person is donor and donee.

(2) The trust was irrevocable and created a remainder interest but no reversionary interest in Mrs. Bauer. She retained no more than a testamentary power of appointment and hers was, therefore, one of the "measuring lives."

(3) The original trust plus the codicil trust thus involved three lives in being, resulting in unenforcibility under the applicable former New York law (Personal Property Law, former § 11; Real Property Law, former § 42) and thus the attempt in the will and codicil to exercise the power of appointment was ineffective.

(4) Since the residuary clause specifically excludes "property otherwise disposed of by this . . . will or any codicil," it cannot be construed to refer to the appointive property as to which the will contained an invalid dispositive clause.

(5) Since, therefore, there has been no valid testamentary disposition of the trust principal it must, as directed by the indenture itself, be distributed to the settlor's next of kin pursuant to the statutes of New York.

The order appealed from should be modified accordingly, with costs to parties filing separate briefs.

DYE, J. (dissenting).

The validity of the power of appointment and the future interest herein should be governed by the law of England where the sole owner of the beneficial power resided at the time of her demise. Under English law, the future interest and suspension of the power of alienation date from the exercise of the power of appointment and not from the date of its creation.

The order of the Appellate Division should be modified by reinstating the order of Special Term and, as so modified, should be affirmed.

FULD, J. (dissenting).

I agree with JUDGE DYE.

We deal here with a testatrix (Dagmar Bauer) who died in England, where she had long been domiciled, after there executing a will in which she exercised a general power of appointment, of which she was donor as well as donee, pursuant to a trust indenture executed in New York almost 40 years earlier. The court's decision to apply New York law to test the validity of Mrs. Bauer's exercise in England (in 1954) of the power of appointment which she had reserved to herself (in 1917) strikes me as an unfortunate example of adherence to mechanical and arbitrary formulae. The same considerations which prompted a departure from the inflexible and traditional choice-of-law rules in other cases (see, e.g., *Auten v. Auten; Babcock v. Jackson*), it seems to me, should move the court to re-examine the wisdom and justice of continuing to apply similarly inflexible rules, without regard to significant underlying factors, in disposing of cases such as the present one.

The traditional rule which identifies the instrument exercising the power with the instrument creating it, for the purpose of testing the validity of the exercise of the power, assumes that ownership of the appointive property remains at all times in the donor of the power and that the donee of the power serves merely as a conduit or agency through which the donor's intention with respect to the appointive property is realized. (See, e.g., 3 Powell, *Law of Real Property* [1952], p. 287.) Such an assumption is, perhaps, justified where the power created is "special" and confines the donee's exercise of the power within the limits proscribed by the instrument creating the power. However, the assumption is certainly not justified when the power created is "general" or "beneficial," whether exercisable by deed or will or by will alone, and no restrictions of any other kind are imposed on its exercise by the donee. In the latter case—and in the one before us upon the death of Mrs. Bauer's husband—it is evident that the donee is vested with the equivalence of ownership as to the appointive property. (See, e.g., Cheshire, *Private International Law* [6th ed., 1961], p. 578.)[1] And this is particularly true where the donor and donee of the general power are the same person.[2] This being so, it runs counter to reason to assume that the donor in such a case becomes his own agent to preserve an attachment to the place where the original trust agreement was executed, even though he has abandoned that place as his residence and acquired a new domicile in another jurisdiction, to the laws of which he voluntarily subjected himself.

In exercising the general power of appointment in England 37 years after she had conferred such power upon herself, Mrs. Bauer was justified in treating the appointive property as her own, and it is reasonable to suppose that, in disposing of such property under a will executed in England by an English solicitor, designating an English institutional executor and trustee to administer the trust and conferring benefits, at least in part, upon an English charity, Mrs. Bauer (through her English solicitor) had exercised the power in the light of English, rather than New York, law. The inference is inescapable that she intended the disposition of the appointive property to be governed by the same law which would govern the disposition of her personal estate, namely, the law of her last domicile. Since no discernible New York policy or interest dictates the application of its law to invalidate the disposition by the English testatrix valid under her personal law—and, indeed, now valid under present New York law—such intention should be given effect.

I do not, of course, mean to suggest that New York law would not govern the validity and effect of the provisions of the *trust indenture.* That instrument was executed in 1917 against the background of New York law, which Mrs. Bauer at that time undoubtedly intended would control. However, I reject as insupportable any suggestion . . . that the law governing the trust conclusively governs the exercise of the power of appointment in every case, even to the extent of overriding the manifest intent of the donor-donee to have the law of his last domicile apply so as to effect a valid exercise of the general power.

. . . I would disavow the rule requiring the inexorable application of the law governing the instrument creating the power and I would apply the law of the jurisdiction intended by the donor-donee to control—in the case before us, England which, quite obviously, has the principal, if not the sole, interest and concern with " 'the outcome of . . . [this] litigation.' " (*Auten v. Auten*)

---

[1] It should be noted that, under section 2041 of the Internal Revenue Code (U. S. Code, tit. 26, § 2041), the right to exercise the power is made taxable, for estate tax purposes, to the donee of the power.

[2] In support of this position, it is highly significant that, by virtue of section 141 of new article 5 of the Real Property Law (L. 1964, ch. 864, eff. June 1, 1965), property covered by a general power of appointment, "not presently exercisable" (for instance, by will alone), can be subjected to the claims of the donee's creditors where the donee was also the donor of the power.

The order of the Appellate Division should be reversed and that of Special Term reinstated.

JUDGES VAN VOORHIS, BURKE and SCILEPPI concur with Chief JUDGE DESMOND; JUDGES DYE and FULD dissent in separate opinions in each of which the other concurs and JUDGE BERGAN concurs in both.

NOTES AND QUESTIONS

(1)(a) Is *Clark* justly decided? Correctly decided?

(b) It seems that Judge Fuld has effectively abrogated D.E.L. § 47, recently reenacted as E.P.T.L. § 3–5.1(h), without ruling it unconstitutional. How did he do it?

Are you persuaded, after a moment's reflection or longer, by the distinction between a testamentary disposition and election against a testamentary disposition, one subject to designation by the donor, the other not?

(c) The argument was made on behalf of Mr. Clark's executors that *Wyatt v. Fulrath* established either that the donor's intent, or that the situs of the assets, determined the governing law; here, as in *Wyatt,* both pointed to New York. Does Judge Fuld adequately distinguish *Wyatt*? Does he in effect overrule it?

(d) Judge Fuld spends a good deal of time on legislative history. The history is confusing, not least because the legislature reenacted D.E.L. § 47 (with slight modification) while *Clark* was pending on appeal; thus the old statute received a new interpretation, while the history of the new statute contains no mention of the leading case concerning the old. This issue comes back in the *Renard* case, discussed in question (4) below. Judge Fuld, however, seeks to draw support from the history of the statute entitling the surviving spouse to elect against a will. He points out that the choice of law provision, D.E.L. § 47, was adopted in 1911, while the election provision did not come into force until 1930. That suggests, he says, that D.E.L. § 47 was not concerned with the share of surviving spouses, but with such things as perpetuities and restraints on gifts to charities. Is that persuasive?

Next, he points out, in 1966 the legislature said that a spouse of a non-domiciliary could not elect against a will under New York law. That, says Judge Fuld, shows that the legislature assumed that the surviving spouse could elect under the law of the testator's domicile. Isn't the opposite inference at least as likely?

Finally, the judge points out that the legislature amended the election statute to permit a surviving spouse to elect under New York law if the non-domiciliary chose to have his will governed by New York law. Judge Fuld says that shows that the legislature wanted to give the surviving spouse an option. Again, isn't the opposite inference at least equally likely, i.e., that it wanted to correct an injustice that might result if the widow or widower were not able to elect at all?

(2)(a) In *Estate of Crichton,*[a] cited by the court in *Clark,* the decedent, a native of Louisiana but domiciled in New York for many years up to his death, died leaving substantial assets in Louisiana. His will left his entire estate to his children from two marriages, and nothing to his second wife, from whom he had been separated (but not divorced) for 27 years. The wife appeared in the New York probate proceeding, not in the first instance to claim her elective share under New York law, but to claim one-half of the estate under the community property law of Louisiana,

---

[a] 20 N.Y.2d 124, 281 N.Y.S.2d 811, 228 N.E.2d 799 (1967).

arguing that *Wyatt v. Fulrath* and *Hutchison v. Ross* had shown that the New York rule looked to situs, not domicile. Speaking for a unanimous court, Judge Keating, the firm advocate of interest analysis,[b] rejected the wife's contention:

> For reasons which become obvious merely in stating the purpose of [Louisiana's community property] rule, Louisiana has no . . . interest in protecting and regulating the rights of married persons residing and domiciled in New York.
>
> . . .
>
> New York, as the domicile of Martha and Powell Crichton, has not only the dominant interest in the application of its law and policy but the only interest. . . .[c]

(b) *Crichton,* it seems, was different from *Wyatt* because there was nothing except the situs of the assets to connect the estate to Louisiana; in *Wyatt* and *Hutchison,* in contrast, there was express (or implied) intent of the donor. But if *Crichton* can be distinguished from *Wyatt* on this basis, how does *Clark* fit in? If, on the contrary, *Clark* and *Crichton* together point to domicile, is *Wyatt* out of line?[d] *Watts v. Swiss Bank Corporation* might have provided an answer, as Judge Breitel indicates in the footnote at the close of his opinion, but since that case was decided on the ground of res judicata, it does not do so.

(c) After *Wyatt* and *Watts,* do you think an inter vivos disposition still stands a better chance of surviving interest analysis à la *Clark* than a testamentary disposition? Suppose, for instance, that after August 31, 1966 Mr. Clark had created a revocable New York trust, with the Irving Trust Company of New York as trustee, to pay the income to himself for life, thereafter to pay the income from one half of the trust property to his wife for her life, and from the other half to his mother for her life, remainder to the Clark museum.[e] The widow seeks not only to elect against Mr. Clark's will, but to include the trust property as part of the estate. Under which law should such a claim be decided?[f] Could she make a combined election, taking the definition of testamentary substitute (i.e., the denominator) from New York, and the elective share (i.e., the numerator) from Virginia?

(3)(a) Turning to the *Lanari* estate, note how many of the same issues that might arise in an American case come up in the French case, except that the interest of the state is directed more to protecting descendants than surviving spouses. The widow's attempt to get around the law of domicile (France) by looking to nationality (decedent Italian, daughter Swiss, wife American) fails; so does looking to the place of contracting—i.e., the opening of the bank accounts. So also does the effort by the widow to turn a choice of law into a jurisdiction question. It is not extraterritorial jurisdiction, the Court of Appeal at Aix says, to pass on the succession to personal property of a French domiciliary, wherever situated, even if that means setting aside gifts made during his lifetime and valid where made.

---

[b] Recall *Macey v. Rozbicki; Miller v. Miller; Tooker v. Lopez,* Chapter 3, pp. 162, 171, 173, *supra,* respectively.

[c] 20 N.Y.2d at 134, 281 N.Y.S.2d at 820. 228 N.E.2d at 806. For a discussion of *Crichton* in its historical context, see Juenger, *Marital Property and the Conflict of Laws: A Tale of Two Countries,* 81 Colum. L. Rev. 1061, 1076–77 (1981).

[d] For an article making this and other points about the New York cases and concluding with a quotation from Lewis Carroll, see Donovan and Farr, *Conflicts "Through the Looking Glass," or the Present State of the Choice of Law Rules in New York Involving Rights of Election,* 26 N.Y. L. Sch. L. Rev. 1007 (1981).

[e] See N.Y. E.P.T.L. § 5–1.1(b)(1)(E), § 7–1.10. In fact, the Clark Museum in Williamstown, Mass. was endowed by the same family, heirs of the Singer Sewing Machine fortune.

[f] Recall *Cumming,* question (2)(b), p. 343, *supra.*

(b) Is the French decision really res judicata in New York? Putting aside the question of privity of the parties, did the French court decide title to the account in New York, so that a decision for the widow (or her executor) would have led to inconsistent judgments? Or did the French court decide only that the law of domicile governs the inventory of the decedent's assets?

(c) If one compares *Wyatt* with *Watts,* the type of account appears to be essentially the same, but the intent to benefit the survivor is much clearer in *Watts.* Suppose Mr. Lanari had created an irrevocable inter vivos trust, "to Swiss Bank (New York) in trust for myself for life, remainder to my beloved wife Roberta." Do you think:

(i) the French court would have come out the same way;

(ii) if so, would the New York court have also come out the same way?

(4)(a) The puzzle of the *Clark* case received one more twist in *Estate of Renard,* 108 Misc. 2d 31, 437 N.Y.S.2d 860 (1981), decided by the Surrogate (i.e., probate judge) of New York County:

> Jane Renard was born in France in 1899. For 30 years, from 1941 to 1971, she was domiciled in New York, where she served for several years as secretary to William Nelson Cromwell, founder of the New York law firm of Sullivan and Cromwell, who also became her lawyers. In 1965 she became a U.S. citizen. In 1971 she retired and moved to Paris, leaving the bulk of her estate—some $320,000 in cash and securities—in New York. She executed a will at the Paris offices of Sullivan and Cromwell, designating New York law as controlling and naming a senior partner of S & C as well as the Bank of New York as executors.
>
> Ms. Renard had an adopted son, Philip, who was a dual citizen of France and the United States, domiciled in California. Ms. Renard made a French will leaving her Paris apartment to Philip. In her New York will, however, she left only $6,000 to Philip, with the remainder divided between a French friend and a French charitable Society for Assistance to Members of the Legion of Honor.
>
> When the will was offered for probate in New York, Philip objected, asserting that under *Clark,* French law should be applied, so that he would succeed to one half of her estate. The French charity responded, arguing for application of New York law in accordance with the testatrix's intent and E.P.T.L. § 3–5.1(h).

How should this case be decided?

(b) The Surrogate decided to uphold the will, and rejected the claims of the son, basically on two grounds. *First,* he held that § 3–5.1(h) called for application of New York law. Not only did the *Clark* case involve different statutory language; Surrogate Midonick construed the legislative history, question (1)(d), *supra,* as showing that the legislature, and the Commission that had proposed the revision of the whole body of New York estates law, had in mind D.E.L. § 47 as it was understood prior to *Clark,* i.e., as permitting non-domiciliaries to elect New York law to avoid foreign forced heirship.[g]

Second, as Judge Fuld had done in *Clark,* the Surrogate examined *Renard* under what he understood to be the prevailing choice of law approach of the New York Court of Appeals.

---

[g] In *In re Cook,* 204 Misc. 704, 123 N.Y.S.2d 568 (N.Y. Cty. Surr. Ct. 1953), cited in an appendix to the Report of the Commission that drafted § 3–5.1(h), the Surrogate sustained a will designating New York law, thus depriving the daughter of a Cuban testator of her forced share under Cuban law. For the antecedent to *Cook* and citation to the legislative report, see *Lowenfeld,* 72 Colum. L. Rev. at 390, n.58.

362 ☐ MODERN CONFLICTS THINKING: INTENTIONAL ACTS § 4.03

"Choice of law rules," he wrote, "entail the balancing of diverse policy considerations," and it was not clear that the considerations bearing on elective shares of spouses applied to forced heirship claims of descendants. Moreover, in *Renard,* New York had had a "long standing and substantial relationship with the decedent," and the son had no particular relationship with France:

> The conflicting policies here are New York's interest in the freedom of testamentary disposition, under which a child's claim is protected only in very limited situations not relevant here, and France's policy of narrowly circumscribing testamentary freedom in favor of descendants. Nor does the law of California, where the son resides, support forced heirship by children . . .. In any event, France's interest in having its policy implemented, if any, is attenuated by the fact that the decedent's son was a resident of California when she died, and has remained such. Cf. *Neumeier v. Kuehner, Matter of Crichton.*[h]

How the case would have come out if Philip had been a French domiciliary, or Ms. Renard had never been domiciled in New York, was not stated.

(c) The son, of course, appealed. The Court of Appeals, in a one-paragraph opinion, joined by four members of the court, affirmed on the basis of the Surrogate's first ground, i.e., the interpretation of § 3–5.1(h); it said nothing about (and by inference was not satisfied with) the second ground advanced by the Surrogate, concerning choice of law principles and comparative interest or contacts analysis.[i]

(d) Chief Judge Cooke wrote a lengthy dissent, essentially based on *Clark.* Judge Cooke pointed to the observation of Judge Fuld in *Clark* that D.E.L. § 47 had been replaced by a very similar provision.

> Unlike the majority, I am unwilling to avoid the impact of this observation by characterizing it as a mere dictum and am unable to discern any critical distinction between the current statute and its predecessor. The language and legislative history of EPTL 3–5.1 (subd [h]) make clear that the statutes are indistinguishable on the question presented here.
>
> The majority's apparent dissatisfaction with the *Clark* holding does not justify the decision here. The *Clark* decision, with its implications for EPTL 3–5.1, has been left undisturbed since 1968 by the Legislature, despite the ready means available to that body to correct any perceived misinterpretation of its intent.
>
> Effectively overruling *Matter of Clark,* the majority today drastically alters the law relating to a nondomiciliary's testamentary disposition of property located in New York. Not only may a forced heirship be avoided by a choice-of-law clause, but so may any right accorded by the law of the domicile protective of persons surviving the decedent, including any spousal right of election more favorable than that accorded by New York. No sound jurisprudential or other policy reason has been articulated for such a result. I would adhere to *Matter of Clark* and hold EPTL 3–5.1 inapplicable to a forced heirship claim.[j]

Whether Judge Cooke is correct that *Clark* is overruled with respect to spousal shares as well as with respect to forced heirship is, of course not clear.[k]

---

[h] 108 Misc. 2d at 40, 437 N.Y.S.2d at 866.

[i] 56 N.Y.2d 973, 453 N.Y.S.2d 625, 439 N.E.2d 341 (1982).

[j] 56 N.Y.2d at 977–80, 453 N.Y.S.2d at 627–29, 439 N.E.2d at 343–45 (Cooke, C.J. dissenting).

[k] Surrogate Midonick stepped down from the bench shortly after his opinion in *Renard;* when the Court of Appeals passed on the case, he wrote an article in the New York Law Journal about the case. He pointed out that the majority

§ 4.03   CHOICE OF LAW   □ 363

(e) Even if *Clark* was wrong, and even if Judge Cooke is mistaken as to the extent to which *Clark* has been overruled, is he not right in criticizing the Court of Appeals in *Renard* for adopting half of the opinion of a lower court judge without any explanation of its own?[l]

(5) (a) Between 1930 and 1986, New York's law on election by the surviving spouse, stated:

> The decedent's estate, against which a right of election granted by this section may be asserted, shall not include any real property of the decedent situated outside of this state.[m]

In 1986, the legislature changed this rule, and provided:

> The decedent's estate shall include all property of the decedent, wherever situated.[n]

(b) From the point of view of the surviving spouse, the change is clearly advantageous provided it can be given effect, since it removes one more device by which the testator can limit the inheritance of his (or her) spouse. Is it sound legislative policy from the point of view of conflict of laws?

(c) If T, the decedent, dies domiciled in New York with $300,000 in his net estate in New York and $60,000 worth of real property in New Jersey, the surviving spouse, entitled to elect against T's will and to take one third of T's estate,[o] can take $120,000 from T's New York assets, with the inheritance of the legatees under the will reduced proportionately. Suppose, however, T leaves a mansion in Florida worth $3,000,000, and a will leaving all his property to his children by a prior marriage. In a suit in Florida between the children (the legatees) and the widow, should Florida apply its own law, which would not permit election by a spouse not domiciled in Florida, or should it apply New York law, borrowing from the thinking of Clark, and award the widow $1,100,000, less what she received from the New York assets?

(d) *Matter of the Estate of Rhodes*[p] presented a variation of the hypothetical in the preceding question. The decedent husband died domiciled in Florida, leaving real property in New York state and personal property in Florida. His will left the New York property to his former wife Frances (apparently pursuant to a divorce settlement), and the remainder to his children. The will made no provision for his surviving spouse Myrna. Myrna exercised her right of election under Florida law, but that law did not take account of out-of-state real property. Accordingly, Myrna filed a petition with the New York court to elect against the New York property. Frances, the first wife and legatee under the will, opposed the petition. How should this case be decided?[q] Is the solution provided by the statute unfair?[r]

---

of the Court of Appeals did not contradict Chief Judge Cooke's statement that it had effectively overruled *Clark*. He continued

> A profound respect for the adversary process compels us to conclude that the application of *Renard* to the surviving spouse's right of election is still an open issue, while we await a holding precisely in point . . .
>
> We have serious doubt, however, as to *Clark*'s continued viability . . .

Midonick and Ordover, Choice of Law after Renard, N.Y.L.J. Nov. 22, 1982, p.1, col. 1.

[l] As of year-end 1997, E.P.T.L. § 3–5.1(h) had not again come before appellate courts in a reported case.

[m] N.Y. E.P.T.L. § 5-1.1(d)(8) (1966-86).

[n] N.Y. E.P.T.L. § 5-1.1(d)(8) (1986-); E.P.T.L. § 5-1.1-A(c)(7) [governing succession to property of persons dying after September 1, 1992] (1992-).

[o] This is the elective share provided for under §5-1.1-A(a) (1992), without reference to the survival of children or other family members.

[p] 160 Misc. 2d 262, 607 N.Y.S.2d 893 (Sup. Ct. Rensselaer Cty. 1994).

[q] See E.P.T.L. § 5-1.1(d)(7), Documents Supplement p. 35, replicated in the 1992 version, § 5-1.1-A(c)(6), Documents Supplement p. 40.

[r] For further discussion of this type of problem, see Scoles and Hay, *Conflict of Laws*, §§ 20.15-.16 (2d ed. 1992).

(6)(a) *Matter of Bauer* is different from the other cases in this series, in that the case turns on a rather technical (and archaic) rule—the New York rule against perpetuities as it read until 1959. Under that rule, any disposition that suspended the power of alienation by more than two designated lives was void in its creation.[s] The majority took a traditional view, whereby exercise of a power of appointment is considered to be analogous to filling in a line left blank in an instrument previously created, and has to be construed as of the date of the instrument. Thus the majority acts as if Mrs. Bauer, domiciled in New York, had in 1917 created a trust for herself for life, then to the nieces for their lives, with the remainder to vest only at the death of the last niece to die—a total of three lives, and therefore void.

(b) Judge Fuld says this "runs counter to reason." Mrs. Bauer properly treated the property as her own, was clearly domiciled in England, had an English lawyer, and sought to benefit an English charity. No interest of New York could possibly be frustrated by her disposition. Is Judge Fuld right in framing the question in terms of the policy or interest of New York?

(c) Unlike *Clark*, *Bauer* came before the Court of Appeals in time for the commission and legislature revising New York's law in this field to take account of the decision. Look at E.P.T.L. § 3–5.1(g):[t]

(i) Why is this paragraph so complicated?

(ii) Why the distinction between Subparagraphs (2)(A) and (2)(B)?

(iii) Why the distinction between Subparagraphs (2)(B) and (2)(C)?

(iv) For the facts of *Bauer*, does the legislature come out for Judge Desmond or Judge Fuld?[u]

(7) Putting the New York experience as shown in the cases in this section to one side and deciding on a clean slate, how do you now think a state in the United States ought to resolve

(i) the distinction, if any, between wills and inter vivos dispositions of a testamentary character;

(ii) the freedom to dispose of one's assets as against restraints designed for protection of family;

(iii) the impact of conflict of laws on either or both of the preceding questions?

---

[s] Since 1958, New York's rule against perpetuities reads like that of a majority of states in the common law world, the measuring time being "lives in being," plus (since 1960) 21 years. N.Y. E.P.T.L. § 9–1.1.

[t] Documents Supplement, p. 29. A general power of appointment is one that can be exercised without restriction as to beneficiaries; a special power of appointment is one limited as to beneficiaries—e.g., "to the children of A," or to "worthy graduates of the Horace Mann School." A presently exercisable power is one that can be exercised by deed during the donee's lifetime.

[u] The *Restatement (Second) of Conflict of Laws* seems to favor the majority view in *Bauer*, though it quotes Judge Fuld's dissent at length. See § 270, Comment *e*, § 274 Reporter's Note.

PART II

THE CONSTITUTION AND CONFLICT OF LAWS

CHAPTER 5

THE CONSTITUTION AND CHOICE OF LAW

Most of the cases we have seen thus far have in some sense grown out of the federal structure that is the United States, with its unrestricted movement of persons and goods but independent courts and legislatures. One might have supposed, therefore, that as umpire of the federal system, the U.S. Supreme Court would have been heavily engaged in resolving conflicts between states, and between states and the federal union. In fact in the areas we deal with here—choice of law in private civil litigation—the role of the U.S. Constitution, and of the Supreme Court has been quite modest.

In the first section we see a brief and controversial intervention by the Supreme Court in the area of access to courts, opening up the question of how much the Full Faith and Credit Clause of the Constitution applies to laws, as contrasted to judgments; in the second section a longer series of cases traces the occasional intervention but gradual withdrawal of the Supreme Court from the field of choice of law by state (and lower federal) courts; the third section looks in detail at the most recent reconsideration by the Supreme Court of its involvment in the choice of law process in the United States.[a]

§ 5.01 The Transitory Action and the Obligation to Provide a Forum

HUGHES v. FETTER

United States Supreme Court
341 U.S. 609 (1951)

Mr. Justice Black delivered the opinion of the Court.

Basing his complaint on the Illinois wrongful death statute, appellant administrator brought this action in the Wisconsin state court to recover damages for the death of Harold Hughes, who was fatally injured in an automobile accident in Illinois. The allegedly negligent driver and an insurance company were named as defendants. On their motion the trial court entered summary judgment "dismissing the complaint on the merits." It held that a Wisconsin statute, which creates a right of action only for deaths caused in that state, establishes a local public policy against Wisconsin's entertaining suits brought under the wrongful death acts of other states.[2] The

---

[a] The relevant excerpts of the U.S. Constitution are reproduced in the Documents Supplement at pp. 1–8.

[2] Wis. Stat., 1949, § 331.03. This section contains language typically found in wrongful death acts but concludes as follows: "provided, that such action shall be brought for a death caused in this state."

Wisconsin Supreme Court affirmed, notwithstanding the contention that the local statute so construed violated the Full Faith and Credit Clause of Art. IV, § 1 of the Constitution. The case is properly here on appeal under 28 U. S. C. § 1257.

We are called upon to decide the narrow question whether Wisconsin, over the objection raised, can close the doors of its courts to the cause of action created by the Illinois wrongful death act.[4] Prior decisions have established that the Illinois statute is a "public act" within the provision of Art. IV, § 1 that "Full Faith and Credit shall be given in each State to the public Acts . . . of every other State." It is also settled that Wisconsin cannot escape this constitutional obligation to enforce the rights and duties validly created under the laws of other states by the simple device of removing jurisdiction from courts otherwise competent. We have recognized, however, that full faith and credit does not automatically compel a forum state to subordinate its own statutory policy to a conflicting public act of another state; rather, it is for this Court to choose in each case between the competing public policies involved. The clash of interests in cases of this type has usually been described as a conflict between the public policies of two or more states. The more basic conflict involved in the present appeal, however, is as follows: On the one hand is the strong unifying principle embodied in the Full Faith and Credit Clause looking toward maximum enforcement in each state of the obligations or rights created or recognized by the statutes of sister states; on the other hand is the policy of Wisconsin, as interpreted by its highest court, against permitting Wisconsin courts to entertain this wrongful death action.[10]

We hold that Wisconsin's policy must give way. That state has no real feeling of antagonism against wrongful death suits in general.[11] To the contrary, a forum is regularly provided for cases of this nature, the exclusionary rule extending only so far as to bar actions for death not caused locally. The Wisconsin policy, moreover, cannot be considered as an application of the *forum non conveniens* doctrine, whatever effect that doctrine might be given if its use resulted in denying enforcement to public acts of other states. Even if we assume that Wisconsin could refuse, by reason of particular circumstances, to hear foreign controversies to which nonresidents were parties, the present case is not one lacking a close relationship with the state. For not only were appellant, the decedent and the individual defendant all residents of Wisconsin, but also appellant was appointed administrator and the corporate defendant was created under Wisconsin laws. We also think it relevant, although not crucial here, that Wisconsin may well be the only jurisdiction in which service could be had as an original matter on the insurance company defendant. And while in the present case jurisdiction over the individual defendant apparently could be had in Illinois by substituted service, in other cases Wisconsin's exclusionary statute might amount to a deprivation of all opportunity to enforce valid death claims created by another state.

Under these circumstances, we conclude that Wisconsin's statutory policy which excludes this Illinois cause of action is forbidden by the national policy of the Full Faith and Credit Clause.

---

[4] The parties concede, as they must, that if the same cause of action had previously been reduced to judgment, the Full Faith and Credit Clause would compel the courts of Wisconsin to entertain an action to enforce it. *Kenney v. Supreme Lodge,* 252 U. S. 411.

[10] The present case is not one where Wisconsin, having entertained appellant's lawsuit, chose to apply its own instead of Illinois' statute to measure the substantive rights involved. This distinguishes the present case from those where we have said that *"Prima facie* every state is entitled to enforce in its own courts its own statutes, lawfully enacted." *Alaska Packers Assn. v. Commission,* [p. 386 *infra*] see also, *Williams v. North Carolina,* [p. 749, *infra*].

[11] It may well be that the wrongful death acts of Wisconsin and Illinois contain different provisions in regard to such matters as maximum recovery and disposition of the proceeds of suit. Such differences, however, are generally considered unimportant. See cases collected 77 A. L. R. 1311, 1317–1324.

The judgment is reversed and the cause is remanded to the Supreme Court of Wisconsin for proceedings not inconsistent with this opinion.

Reversed and remanded.

MR. JUSTICE FRANKFURTER, whom MR. JUSTICE REED, MR. JUSTICE JACKSON, and MR. JUSTICE MINTON join, dissenting.

This is an action brought in the Wisconsin State courts to recover for the wrongful death of Harold G. Hughes. Hughes was killed in an automobile accident in Illinois. An Illinois statute provides that an action may be brought to recover damages for a wrongful death occurring in that State. Smith-Hurd's Ill. Ann. Stat., 1936, c. 70, §§ 1, 2. A Wisconsin statute provides that an action may not be brought in the courts of that State for a wrongful death occurring outside Wisconsin. Wis. Stat., 1949, § 331.03. The Wisconsin courts, obeying the command of the Wisconsin statute, dismissed the action. I cannot agree that the Wisconsin statute, so applied, is contrary to Art. IV, § 1 of the United States Constitution: "Full Faith and Credit shall be given in each State to the public Acts, Records, and judicial Proceedings of every other State."

The Full Faith and Credit Clause was derived from a similar provision in the Articles of Confederation. Art. 4, § 3. The only clue to its meaning in the available records of the Constitutional Convention is a notation in Madison's Debates that "Mr. Wilson & Docr. Johnson [who became members of the committee to which the provision was referred] supposed the meaning to be that Judgments in one State should be the ground of actions in other States, & that acts of the Legislatures should be included, for the sake of Acts of insolvency &c.—." II Farrand, *The Records of the Federal Convention,* 447.[a] This Court has, with good reason, gone far in requiring that the courts of a State respect judgments entered by courts of other States. *Fauntleroy v. Lum,* [p. 639, infra]; *Kenney v. Supreme Lodge,* 252 U. S. 411; *Milwaukee County v. M. E. White Co.,* 296 U. S. 268; cf. *Magnolia Petroleum Co. v. Hunt,* [p. 655, infra]. But the extent to which a State must recognize and enforce the rights of action created by other States is not so clear.

    1. In the field of commercial law—where certainty is of high importance—we have often imposed a rather rigid rule that a State must defer to the law of the State of incorporation, or to the law of the place of contract.

. . .

    2. In cases involving workmen's compensation, there is also a pre-existing relationship between the employer and employee that makes certainty of result desirable. The possible interest of the forum in protecting the workman, however, has made this Court reluctant to impose rigid rules.

. . .

    3. In the tort action before us, there is little reason to impose a "state of vassalage" on the forum. The liability here imposed does not rest on a pre-existing relationship between the plaintiff and defendant. There is consequently no need for fixed rules which would enable parties, at the time they enter into a transaction, to predict its consequences.

. . .

---

[a] For more on the origins of the Full Faith and Credit Clause, see Chapter 8, p. 644, question 3, *infra*.

This Court should certainly not require that the forum deny its own law and follow the tort law of another State where there is a reasonable basis for the forum to close its courts to the foreign cause of action. The decision of Wisconsin to open its courts to actions for wrongful deaths within the State but close them to actions for deaths outside the State may not satisfy everyone's notion of wise policy. See *Loucks v. Standard Oil Co.,* [p. 34, *supra*]. But it is neither novel nor without reason. Compare the similar Illinois statute which was before this Court in *Kenney v. Supreme Lodge, supra.* Wisconsin may be willing to grant a right of action where witnesses will be available in Wisconsin and the courts are acquainted with a detailed local statute and cases construing it. It may not wish to subject residents to suit where out-of-state witnesses will be difficult to bring before the court, and where the court will be faced with the alternative of applying a complex foreign statute—perhaps inconsistent with that of Wisconsin on important issues—or fitting the statute to the Wisconsin pattern. The legislature may well feel that it is better to allow the courts of the State where the accident occurred to construe and apply its own statute, and that the exceptional case where the defendant cannot be served in the State where the accident occurred does not warrant a general statute allowing suit in the Wisconsin courts. The various wrongful death statutes are inconsistent on such issues as beneficiaries, the party who may bring suit, limitations on liability, comparative negligence, and the measure of damages. . . . The measure of damages and the relation of wrongful death actions to actions for injury surviving death have raised extremely complicated problems, even for a court applying the familiar statute of its own State. . . . These diversities reasonably suggest application by local judges versed in them. . . .

No claim is made that Wisconsin has discriminated against the citizens of other States and thus violated Art. IV, § 2 of the Constitution. . . . Nor is a claim made that the lack of a forum in Wisconsin deprives the plaintiff of due process. . . . Nor is it argued that Wisconsin is flouting a federal statute. . . . The only question before us is how far the Full Faith and Credit Clause undercuts the purpose of the Constitution, made explicit by the Tenth Amendment, to leave the conduct of domestic affairs to the States. Few interests are of more dominant local concern than matters governing the administration of law. This vital interest of the States should not be sacrificed in the interest of a merely literal reading of the Full Faith and Credit Clause.

There is no support, either in reason or in the cases, for holding that this Court is to make a *de novo* choice between the policies underlying the laws of Wisconsin and Illinois. I cannot believe that the Full Faith and Credit Clause provided a "writer's inkhorn" so that this Court might separate right from wrong.

> *Prima facie* every state is entitled to enforce in its own courts its own statutes, lawfully enacted. One who challenges that right, because of the force given to a conflicting statute of another state by the full faith and credit clause, assumes the burden of showing, upon some rational basis, that of the conflicting interests involved those of the foreign state are superior to those of the forum.

Mr. Justice Stone, in *Alaska Packers Assn. v. Commission,* [p. 389, *infra*].

In the present case, the decedent, the plaintiff, and the individual defendant were residents of Wisconsin. The corporate defendant was created under Wisconsin law. The suit was brought in the Wisconsin courts. No reason is apparent—and none is vouchsafed in the opinion of the Court—why the interest of Illinois is so great that it can force the courts of Wisconsin to grant relief in defiance of their own law.

§ 5.01   THE CONSTITUTION AND CONFLICT OF LAWS   □   371

Finally, it may be noted that there is no conflict here in the policies underlying the statute of Wisconsin and that of Illinois. The Illinois wrongful death statute has a proviso that

> no action shall be brought or prosecuted in this State to recover damages for a death occurring outside of this State where a right of action for such death exists under the laws of the place where such death occurred and service of process in such suit may be had upon the defendant in such place.

Smith-Hurd's Ill. Ann. Stat., 1936, c. 70, § 2. The opinion of the Court concedes that "jurisdiction over the individual defendant apparently could be had in Illinois by substituted service." Smith-Hurd's Ill. Ann. Stat., 1950, c. 95, § 23. Thus, in the converse of the case at bar—if Hughes had been killed in Wisconsin and suit had been brought in Illinois—the Illinois courts would apparently have dismissed the suit. There is no need to be "more Roman than the Romans."*

FIRST NATIONAL BANK OF CHICAGO v. UNITED AIR LINES

United States Supreme Court
342 U.S. 396 (1952)

Mr. Justice Black delivered the opinion of the Court.

John Louis Nelson was killed when one of respondent's airliners crashed in Utah. Claiming $200,000 under the Utah wrongful death statute, petitioner brought this action in a United States district court in Illinois. Decedent prior to his death was a resident and citizen of Illinois; petitioner, his executor, is an Illinois bank; and respondent, United Air Lines, Inc., is a Delaware corporation doing business in Illinois. Since the jurisdictional amount and diversity of citizenship requirements have been met, the case is properly triable under 28 U. S. C. § 1332 unless ch. 70, § 2 of the Illinois Revised Statutes bars the action. This Illinois law provides:

> no action shall be brought or prosecuted in this State to recover damages for a death occurring outside of this State where a right of action for such death exists under the laws of the place where such death occurred and service of process in such suit may be had upon the defendant in such place.

The District Court and Court of Appeals, relying on the doctrine declared in *Erie R. Co. v. Tompkins,* [p. 435, *infra*] as discussed and applied in later cases, held that in a diversity case such as this the state statute was binding on the federal as well as state courts in Illinois and constituted a bar to maintenance of this action. In so doing, they rejected two constitutional contentions made by petitioner: (1) Congress having granted diversity jurisdiction to federal district courts pursuant to power granted by Article III of the Constitution, that jurisdiction cannot be abridged or destroyed by the Illinois statute; (2) the Illinois statute violates the Full Faith and Credit Clause of the United States Constitution (Art. IV, § 1) in providing that claims for Utah deaths shall not be enforced in Illinois state courts where service on defendants could be had in Utah. We need not discuss this first constitutional contention or the *Erie R. Co. v. Tompkins* problems presented by it, for we recently held in *Hughes v. Fetter* that a Wisconsin statute, much like that of Illinois, did violate the Full Faith and Credit Clause. It was to consider this full faith and credit question with reference to the Illinois statute that we granted certiorari.

---

* Compare Freund, *Chief Justice Stone and the Conflict of Laws,* 59 Harv. L. Rev. 1210, 1220 (1946).

The Wisconsin statute invalidated in *Hughes v. Fetter, supra,* barred suit in the Wisconsin courts for any wrongful death caused outside the state. The Illinois statute before us today is the exact duplicate of the Wisconsin statute with the single exception that suit is permitted in Illinois under another state's wrongful death statute if service of process cannot be had on the defendant in the state where the death was brought about. That Illinois is willing for its courts to try some out-of-state death actions is no reason for its refusal to grant full faith and credit as to others. The reasons supporting our invalidation of Wisconsin's statute apply with equal force to that of Illinois. This is true although Illinois agrees to try cases where service cannot be obtained in another state. While we said in *Hughes v. Fetter* that it was relevant that Wisconsin might be the only state in which service could be had on one of the defendants, we were careful to point out that this fact was not crucial. Nor is it crucial here that Illinois only excludes cases that can be tried in other states. We hold again that the Full Faith and Credit Clause forbids such exclusion. The District Court should not have dismissed this case.

Reversed.

Mr. Justice Jackson, whom Mr. Justice Minton joins, concurring in the result.

I part company with the Court as to the road we will travel to reach a destination where all agree we will stop, at least for the night. But sometimes the path that we are beating out by our travel is more important to the future wayfarer than the place in which we choose to lodge.

There are two possible routes to the agreed destination. One requires that a state statute prescribing jurisdictional limitations on its own courts be declared unconstitutional—a path which a century and a half of precedent constrains us to avoid if another way is available. This, together with adherence to the views expressed in dissent in *Hughes v. Fetter,* persuades me to resolve the issue of jurisdiction of federal courts by reference to the Act of Congress which confers that jurisdiction.

Whether or not Illinois may validly close her own courts to litigation of this kind, Illinois most assuredly cannot prescribe the subject matter jurisdiction of federal courts even when they sit in that State. Congress already has done this, 28 U. S. C. § 1332 (a) (1), and state law is powerless to enlarge, vary, or limit this requirement. The parties to this case have showed the diversity of citizenship and amount in controversy required by Congress, and therefore the federal court, by virtue of the law of its own being, has jurisdiction of their action.

The suggestion that *Erie R. Co. v. Tompkins,* and its progeny diminish the jurisdiction of a federal court sitting in a diversity case by assimilating any limitation that the state may impose on her own courts seems to confuse the law of jurisdiction with substantive law. In *Erie* and the cases which have followed, this Court has gone far in requiring that a federal court exercising diversity jurisdiction apply the same law as would be applied if the action were brought in the state courts. But in so doing the Court has been interpreting the Rules of Decision Act, 28 U. S. C. § 1652, which reads as follows:

> The laws of the several states, except where the Constitution or treaties of the United States or Acts of Congress otherwise require or provide, shall be regarded as rules of decision in civil actions in the courts of the United States, in cases where they apply.

It is indeed fanciful to suggest that a state statute relating to the power of its own courts is an applicable "rule of decision" under this statute, when Congress in passing the federal jurisdictional grant has specifically "otherwise required and provided." 28 U. S. C. § 1332 (a)

(1). The petitioner enters the federal court not by the grace of the laws of Illinois but by the grace of the laws of the United States.

The establishment of jurisdiction is, however, the beginning and not the end of the decision of the case in the trial court. What law must be applied in adjudicating the substantive rights of these parties? The opinion of the Court is silent on this point, but its line of reasoning seems to imply that the federal trial court must look to Illinois law for a conflicts rule which would govern this kind of case if brought in Illinois courts. Since Illinois has, pursuant to statute, refused to entertain such actions as this, it might be supposed that such law would be hard to find.

In my view, the federal court no more derives substantive law for this case from Illinois than it does its jurisdiction. For regardless of what Illinois might say on this subject, the Constitution has "otherwise provided." I believe, as expressed in *Hughes v. Fetter,* that the State was free to refuse this case a forum, but, if it undertook to adjudicate the rights of the parties, the Constitution would require it to apply the law of Utah, because all elements of the wrong alleged here occurred in Utah. For the essence of the Full Faith and Credit Clause is that certain transactions, wherever in the United States they may be litigated, shall have the same legal consequences as they would have in the place where they occurred. *Order of United Commercial Travelers v. Wolfe,* 331 U. S. 586; *Hancock Mutual Life Ins. Co. v. Yates,* 299 U. S. 178.

There is undoubtedly some area of freedom for state conflicts law outside the requirements of the Full Faith and Credit Clause. In such matters, unreached by constitutional law, the state rule would prevail in a diversity court. *Klaxon Co. v. Stentor Co.* [p. 449, *infra*]. But if a transaction is so associated with one jurisdiction that the Constitution compels any forum in which the transaction is litigated to apply the law of that jurisdiction, is it not the Constitution instead of state conflicts law which determines what law the federal court shall apply?

The Court's detour follows this itinerary: the federal court is bound by the law of Illinois; Illinois law is wrong; we will remake the law of Illinois to provide the exact opposite to that which the state has provided; then the federal court can apply the law we have remade and pretend it is applying Illinois law. This is too tortuous an excursion for me. Since as a matter of constitutional provision liability for this alleged tort must be adjudged under Utah law and, the case being within the statutory jurisdiction of the District Court, it may ascertain and apply the law of Utah without straining it through the Illinois sieve.

MR. JUSTICE REED, dissenting.

I dissent on the ground that *Hughes v. Fetter,* should not be extended to compel a state to entertain an action for wrongful death if the claim could be effectively litigated in the courts of the state where the cause of action arose.

The reasoning for this conclusion is stated in the dissent in *Hughes v. Fetter, supra.*

MR. JUSTICE FRANKFURTER, dissenting.

As to any question based on diversity jurisdiction, the series of cases culminating in *Woods v. Interstate Realty Co.,* 337 U. S. 535, disposes of it.[b] As to the constitutional claim under the Full Faith and Credit Clause, I adhere to the views expressed in *Hughes v. Fetter.*

---

[b] In this case the Supreme Court held that a diversity action brought by an out-of-state corporation that had failed to designate an agent in the state to receive service of process must be dismissed, since the corporation would have been barred from suing in the courts of the state where the federal district court sat. See Chapter 6, p. 454, note f *infra*.

WELLS v. SIMONDS ABRASIVE CO.

United States Supreme Court
345 U.S. 514 (1953)

Mr. Chief Justice Vinson delivered the opinion of the Court.

Cheek Wells was killed in Alabama when a grinding wheel with which he was working burst. The wheel had been manufactured by the respondent, a corporation with its principal place of business in Pennsylvania. The administratrix of the estate of Cheek Wells brought an action for damages in the federal court for the Eastern District of Pennsylvania after one year, but within two years, after the death. Jurisdiction was based upon diversity of citizenship.

The section of the Alabama Code upon which petitioner predicated her action for wrongful death provided that action ". . . must be brought within two years from and after the death . . ." The respondent moved for summary judgment on the ground the Pennsylvania wrongful death statute required suit to be commenced within one year. In an opinion on that motion, the district judge found that the Pennsylvania statute, which was analogous to the Alabama statute, had a one-year limitation. He further found that the Pennsylvania conflict of laws rule called for the application of its own limitation rather than that of the place of the accident. Deeming himself bound by the Pennsylvania conflicts rule, he ordered summary judgment for the respondent. The Court of Appeals for the Third Circuit affirmed.

We granted certiorari limited to the question whether this Pennsylvania conflicts rule violates the Full Faith and Credit Clause of the Federal Constitution.

The states are free to adopt such rules of conflict of laws as they choose, *Kryger v. Wilson,* 242 U. S. 171 (1916), subject to the Full Faith and Credit Clause and other constitutional restrictions. The Full Faith and Credit Clause does not compel a state to adopt any particular set of rules of conflict of laws; it merely sets certain minimum requirements which each state must observe when asked to apply the law of a sister state.

Long ago, we held that applying the statute of limitations of the forum to a foreign substantive right did not deny full faith and credit, *McElmoyle v. Cohen,* 13 Pet. 312 (1839); *Townsend v. Jemison,* 9 How. 407 (1850); *Bacon v. Howard,* 20 How. 22 (1857). Recently we referred to ". . . the well-established principle of conflict of laws that 'If action is barred by the statute of limitations of the forum, no action can be maintained though action is not barred in the state where the cause of action arose.' *Restatement, Conflict of Laws* § 603 (1934)." *Order of United Commercial Travelers v. Wolfe,* 331 U. S. 586, 607 (1947).

The rule that the limitations of the forum apply (which this Court has said meets the requirements of full faith and credit) is the usual conflicts rule of the states. However, there have been divergent views when a foreign statutory right unknown to the common law has a period of limitation included in the section creating the right. The Alabama statute here involved creates such a right and contains a built-in limitation. The view is held in some jurisdictions that such a limitation is so intimately connected with the right that it must be enforced in the forum state along with the substantive right.

We are not concerned with the reasons which have led some states for their own purposes to adopt the foreign limitation, instead of their own, in such a situation. The question here is whether the Full Faith and Credit Clause compels them to do so. Our prevailing rule is that the Full Faith and Credit Clause does not compel the forum state to use the period of limitation of a foreign state. We see no reason in the present situation to graft an exception onto it. Differences based upon whether the foreign right was known to the common law or upon the arrangement of the code of the foreign state are too unsubstantial to form the basis for constitutional distinctions under the Full Faith and Credit Clause.

. . .

Our decisions in *Hughes v. Fetter,* 341 U. S. 609 (1951), and *First National Bank v. United Air Lines,* 342 U. S. 396 (1952), do not call for a change in the well-established rule that the forum state is permitted to apply its own period of limitation. The crucial factor in those two cases was that the forum laid an uneven hand on causes of action arising within and without the forum state. Causes of action arising in sister states were discriminated against. Here Pennsylvania applies her one-year limitation to all wrongful death actions wherever they may arise. The judgment is

Affirmed.

MR. JUSTICE JACKSON, with whom MR. JUSTICE BLACK and MR. JUSTICE MINTON join, dissenting.

We are unable to accept the results or follow the reasoning of the Court. Petitioner's decedent, a resident of Alabama, was killed in that State by a bursting emery wheel alleged to have been defective. It was manufactured by respondent, a Pennsylvania corporation. Finding it impossible to serve process on the defendant in Alabama, petitioner brought an action in the United States Court for the Eastern District of Pennsylvania. Her action was based on a statute of Alabama which conferred a right of action for wrongfully causing death and required that the action be brought within two years from the death. This she did, but her complaint was dismissed on the ground that, since the federal court was sitting in Pennsylvania, it was bound by the Pennsylvania statute of limitations of one year and, hence, that her action was barred. I believe the United States District Court, though sitting in Pennsylvania, should apply the law of Alabama, both as to liability and as to limitation.

The respondent relies upon the line of cases that began with *Erie R. Co. v. Tompkins.* A careful reading of the *Erie* decision will show that, so far as it applies at all, it is authority for the plaintiff's and not the defendant's position. The *Erie* injury occurred in Pennsylvania, but the action was brought in a United States District Court in New York. Although the trial court sat in New York, this Court held that it must decide liability by Pennsylvania law, that is, by the law of the state of injury, not that of the forum state, which holding, if applied here, would require that this case be adjudged by the law of Alabama even though it is brought in a federal court sitting in another state. That opinion, by Mr. Justice Brandeis, will be searched in vain for any hint that this result depended on the New York law of conflicts, which is not even paid the respect of mention. *Erie R. Co. v. Tompkins* held that there is no federal common law of torts and that federal courts must not improvise one of their own but must follow that state's law *which is applicable to the case.*

That the applicable state law was that of Pennsylvania, instead of that of the forum, was assumed without discussion of the reason because it was pursuant to what is probably the best-settled rule of conflicts in tort cases. It was stated by Mr. Justice Holmes, as follows: ". . . [I]t is established as the law of this court that when a person recovers in one jurisdiction for a tort committed in another he does so on the ground of an obligation incurred at the place of the tort that accompanies the person of the defendant elsewhere, and that is not only the ground but the measure of the maximum recovery." *Western Union Telegraph Co. v. Brown,* 234 U. S. 542, 547. See also *Slater v. Mexican National R. Co.,* 194 U. S. 120, 126; Cardozo, J. in *Loucks v. Standard Oil Co.,* [p. 34, *supra*]. The existence and justice of this principle is recognized by its adoption as the policy of federal law. The Federal Tort Claims Act makes the basic test of the Government's liability whether a private person "would be liable to the claimant . . . in accordance with the law of the place where the act or omission occurred." 60 Stat. 812, 843.[c]

Klaxon Co. v. Stentor Co., [p. 449, *infra*] also cited by respondent, contains language that would seem to make all conflict questions depend on the law of the forum. But that was an action on contract in which conflict considerations prevail that are not present in tort cases. It is but *dictum* so far as it touches this statutory tort case.

Most of these decisions are actuated by a laudable but undiscriminating yen for uniformity within the forum state. Thus, "Otherwise, the accident of diversity of citizenship would constantly disturb equal administration of justice in coordinate state and federal courts sitting side by side." *Klaxon Co. v. Stentor Co.,* [at p. 450, *infra*] citing the *Erie* case; and the Court's opinion here refers to it as a "crucial factor" that "the forum laid an uneven hand on causes of action arising within and without the forum state."

But the essence of the Full Faith and Credit Clause of the Constitution is that uniformities other than just those within the state are to be observed in a federal system. The whole purpose and the only need for requiring full faith and credit to foreign law is that it does differ from that of the forum. But that disparity does not cause the type of evil aimed at in *Erie R. Co. v. Tompkins,* namely, that the same event may be judged by two different laws, depending upon whether a state court or a federal forum within that state is available. Application of the Full Faith and Credit Clause prevents this disparity by requiring that the law where the cause of action arose will follow the cause of action in whatever forum it is pursued.

The Court's decision, in contrast with our position, would enable shopping for favorable forums. Suppose this plaintiff might have obtained service of process in several different states—an assumption not extravagant in the case of many national corporations. Under the Court's holding, she could choose from as many varieties of law as of forums. Under our theory, wherever she elected to sue (if she had a choice), she would take Alabama law with her. Suppose even now she can get service in a state with no statute of limitations or a long one; can she thereby revive a cause of action that has expired under Alabama law? The Court's logic would so indicate. The life of her cause of action is then determined by the fortuitous circumstances that enable her to make service of process in a certain state or states.

. . .

This case is in United States Court, not by grace of Pennsylvania, but by authority of Congress, and what I said in *First National Bank of Chicago v. United Air Lines,* seems to me applicable here. I had supposed, before *Hughes v. Fetter,* that the Commonwealth of Pennsylvania could close its courts to trial of this case. But no one would have questioned, I should think, that if the cause were entertained it must be tried in accordance with the law of the place of the wrong. . . .

---

[c] In fact, in *Richards v. United States,* 369 U.S. 1 (1962), the Supreme Court interpreted this phrase to refer to the whole law of the state where the act or omission occurred, including that state's conflict of laws rules. Accordingly, though the wrongful act was committed in Oklahoma, Oklahoma's choice of law rule required the Court of Claims to apply Missouri law.

. . .

. . . Even as to general statutes of limitations recent decisions have bound the right and the limitation into a single bundle to be taken by the federal court as a whole. . . .

But whatever may be the argument concerning general statutes of limitations as applied to common-law causes, this Court long ago recognized a distinction as to limitations on the action created by statutes in the pattern of the Lord Campbell Act. . . .

. . .

The Supreme Court of Alabama has held the same doctrine applicable to the very statute in question, saying, "This is not a statute of limitations, but of the essence of the cause of action, to be disclosed by averment and proof." *Parker v. Fies & Sons,* 243 Ala. 348, 350, 10 So. 2d 13, 15. The doctrine is well recognized in the literature of the law of conflicts.

. . .

We think that the better view of the case before us would be that it is Alabama law which giveth and only Alabama law that taketh away.

NOTES AND QUESTIONS

(1) In a famous letter to George Washington shortly before the opening of the Constitutional Convention in Philadelphia, James Madison spoke of various positive powers with which he would endow the national government, and then added:

> Over the above this positive power, a negative in all cases whatsoever on the legislative acts of the States . . . appears to me to be absolutely necessary, and to be the least possible encroachment of the State jurisdictions . . . The great desideratum which has not yet been found for Republican Governments seems to be some disinterested and dispassionate umpire in disputes between different passions and interests in the State . . . In Monarchies the sovereign is more neutral to the interests and views of different parties; but unfortunately he too often forms interests of his own repugnant to those of the whole. Might not the national prerogative here suggested be found sufficiently disinterested for the decision of local questions of policy, whilst it would be sufficiently restrained from the pursuit of interests adverse to those of the whole Society? . . .
>
> The national supremacy ought also to be extended as I conceive to the Judiciary departments.[d]

Consider what tools the Supreme Court could have available to it to play the role of umpire suggested by Madison. Would you look to the Full Faith and Credit clause, or the Due Process clause, the Commerce clause, the Diversity Jurisdiction, the Supremacy clause, the Privileges and Immunities clause? All of these? And more?[e]

(2)(a) *Hughes v. Fetter* seems to illustrate the Supreme Court's role as umpire. But between what interests? Is it Wisconsin vs. the national interest, as stated by Justice Black for the majority? Or between Wisconsin and Illinois, as stated by Justice Frankfurter for the dissenters?

---

[d] Letter from James Madison to George Washington, April 16, 1787, 2 *Writings of James Madison* 344, 346–47 (Hunt, ed. 1901), repr. in James Madison, *The Forging of American Federalism* 184, 185–86 (S. Padover ed. 1953).

[e] Remember that Equal Protection entered the Constitution only in the XIV Amendment, adopted after the Civil War.

(b) Does the outcome of the case depend on the difference in perception suggested in the preceding question, or could you decide Wisconsin vs. Illinois in favor of Illinois?

(c) Note that these questions, as well as others in this chapter, seem to have turned on state or governmental interests well before interest analysis became the currency of state choice-of-law cases in the 1960's under the influence of Professor Currie.

(3)(a) A transitory action is an action that (at least in theory[f]) can be brought wherever jurisdiction can be obtained over the defendant. It is different from local actions, typically involving land or property tied to the land, which may only be brought where the land is situated.[g] Has the Supreme Court, in *Hughes v. Fetter,* raised the concept of a transitory action to a constitutional level?

(b) Whose rights are protected by permitting the Illinois cause to be litigated in Wisconsin?

(c) Note that Wisconsin is one of the few states in the Union that has for many years permitted direct actions against insurance companies, rather than only against the insured.[h] Illinois would not have permitted this, yet the Supreme Court mentions the fact that the insurance company (the "corporate defendant") was created under Wisconsin laws. Isn't this half faith and credit, as discussed in *Pearson v. Northeast Airlines*?[i]

(4)(a) Footnote 10 on page 368, *supra,* suggests that Wisconsin could have heard the case and applied its own law, including (i) no limit on wrongful death damages, at a time when such a limit was applicable in Illinois; (ii) no guest statute, at a time when Illinois had one; (iii) no interspousal immunity, which would have applied in Illinois (although not relevant to the *Hughes* case); and (iv) direct action against the insurance company. If on all these issues, and perhaps others, Wisconsin's courts are unfettered (no pun intended), why is the requirement to hear the action constitutionally mandated?

(b) The text at footnote 11 (p. 368, *supra,*) suggests that Wisconsin could have eliminated wrongful death actions altogether, for instance by adopting a comprehensive no-fault system. The Supreme Court apparently would not compel Wisconsin to keep the doors of its courts open only to plaintiffs suffering injury from out-of-state accidents. Here, however, it seems that Wisconsin is discriminating improperly, an impression confirmed by the reference to *Hughes v. Fetter* in the last paragraph of *Wells* at p. 375, *supra.* Against whom does the Wisconsin statute discriminate?

(c) Justice Frankfurter answers the preceding question by saying there is no discrimination, because Wisconsin is dealing only with its own citizens. Does that dispose of the question?

(5)(a) Justice Frankfurter tries to put forward a rational explanation why Wisconsin might have passed § 331.03. It may not want to apply foreign law, he suggests, or to adjudicate disputes where witnesses are far away. Do these hypothetical explanations support his position?

---

[f] I.e., putting aside questions of forum non conveniens, venue, and statutes of limitations.

[g] For the famous case confirming the local action rule in the United States, decided by Chief Justice Marshall, sitting as circuit justice, in favor of the former president, see *Livingston v. Jefferson,* Fed. Cas. No. 8411, 1 Brock. 203 (C.C. Va. 1811). For a decision departing from the ancient doctrine, see *Reasor-Hill Corp. v. Harrison,* 220 Ark. 521, 249 S.W.2d 994 (1952).

[h] This is why the *Haumschild* case, Chapter 2, p. 52, *supra,* is titled *Haumschild v. Continental Casualty Co.,* though the issue before the court is claims between spouses. For more on direct action statutes, see *Watson v. Employers Liability Assurance Co.,* p. 392, *infra.*

[i] Chapter 3, p. 135, *supra.* See especially Judge Friendly's dissent at pp. 139–41.

§ 5.01 THE CONSTITUTION AND CONFLICT OF LAWS □ 379

(b) Suppose the explanation is different: Suppose when the Wisconsin legislature came to write its direct action statute, the insurance industry, which opposed that legislation, argued that its adoption would draw the whole world to Wisconsin courts. The proponents then said "All right, we will make sure that doesn't happen. After all, it is only our accidents that we care about."[j] Would such an explanation strengthen support for the dissenters' position in *Hughes*?

(c) The Supreme Court decides this case under the Full Faith and Credit clause, which of course applies only between the states of the Union. Suppose all the facts were the same except that the accident took place in Ontario. Would the result be different?

(d) Professor Currie, in a long article on *Hughes* and *First National Bank*, concluded that they were "distinctly aberrational as an application of the Full Faith and Credit Clause."[k] However, he believed that the cases were justified by the Equal Protection clause.[l] Is that more persuasive than the explanation given by the Court?

(e) In the next to last paragraph of the majority's opinion, the Court also refers to the fact that plaintiff might not be able to sue anywhere, though as Justice Black says, that is not crucial in the actual case. Is this now a matter of due process?

(6)(a) The last question seems to be answered in the negative in *First National Bank*, because the Illinois statute has the safety valve lacking in the Wisconsin statute, but the two cases come out the same way. Was *First National Bank* worth hearing at all?

(b) One feature that makes *First National Bank* of interest is that the Court had before it two issues—resolution of either of which would make it unnecessary to decide the other—but both were Constitutional issues, one under Article III, the other under Article IV. Did the court choose the wrong issue, as Justice Jackson argues?

(c) Discussion of *Erie* and its impact on conflict of laws is reserved for the next chapter, but it goes without saying that the *Erie* doctrine cannot compel the federal courts to follow an unconstitutional state rule, whether written or judge-made. But is Justice Jackson not correct that the jurisdiction of the federal courts is determined by Congress in accordance with Article III of the Constitution, and cannot be abridged by state laws? Would it upset the parity between state and federal courts if the *First National Bank* case were permitted to go forward as a diversity action in federal court, though barred in the courts of Illinois?

(d) If Justice Jackson is right and the doors of the federal court remain open, is the objection to state door-closing statutes of the Wisconsin/Illinois type eliminated? Substantially reduced? Would this outcome be a justification for the existence of diversity jurisdiction?

(e) Justice Jackson scores a nice debater's point in taunting the majority for requiring the district court to look to Illinois' choice of law in a situation that until now Illinois will not have encountered. He would require the federal district court to apply Utah law in this case, because that is where the airplane went down, and he says this is not contrary to *Klaxon*, because here the Constitution compels application of Utah law. The implication is that the courts of Illinois would also have to apply Illinois law. Isn't this contrary to footnote 10 in *Hughes v. Fetter?* Or would Jackson distinguish the two cases for choice-of-law purposes?[m]

---

[j] In fact this scenario is not what happened. The Wisconsin wrongful death statute was adopted in 1857, 74 years before the direct action statute was adopted.

[k] Currie, *The Constitution and the "Transitory" Cause of Action*, 73 Harv. L. Rev., 36, 268, at 271 (1959), repr. in B. Currie, *Selected Essays on the Conflict of Laws*, 283 at 329 (1963).

[l] 73 Harv. L. Rev. at 293, *Selected Essays* at 350.

[m] Of course it is fair to point out that Justice Jackson dissented in *Hughes*.

(f) Suppose Justice Jackson is correct that *Erie* does not apply to the issue of access to federal courts, but wrong about a constitutional requirement to apply Utah law. Could the federal court nevertheless do its own choice-of-law analysis, or would *Klaxon* still apply? More of this question in the next chapter.

(7)(a) In *Wells v. Simonds Abrasive Co.,* the forum state once again closes its doors to an action based on an out-of-state accident, but this time the Supreme Court approves. What is the difference between *Wells* on one side, and *Hughes* and *First National Bank* on the other?

(b) Chief Justice Vinson answers this question by saying that in *Hughes* and *First National Bank* the forum laid an uneven hand on causes of action arising within and without the state. Granted that most kinds of discrimination are disfavored in modern American constitutional law, what is the element of discrimination against which the Supreme Court is guarding in these cases?

(c) Perhaps *Wells* is not the product of discrimination as the Court defines it. But it is the product of jurisdictional rules in a federal system (a few years before long-arm statutes gain acceptance), with much worse effects on the plaintiff than in *Hughes* and *First National Bank.* For one thing, in the first two cases, plaintiff could have brought suit in Illinois and Utah; in *Wells,* as we learn from the dissent, the widow tried and failed to get jurisdiction over the manufacturer of the defective product in Alabama. For another, in the first two cases, plaintiffs were citizens of the forum state, whereas in *Wells* plaintiff was a non-resident. Is the Court simply saying that statutes of limitations are for the forum to determine, and federal courts are not available to provide relief from whatever the state determines?

(d) The Chief Justice dismisses the difference between common law and statutory causes of action for purposes of selecting the applicable period of limitations. The specificity rule did not make much sense when addressed to a peculiar cause of action, such as the right of a seaman for severance pay when the ship changed registry, involved in *Bournias;*[n] to apply it in the context of an ordinary negligence action depending on whether the injured person died or survived is no more persuasive than the common law's refusal to recognize actions for wrongful death in the first place.[o] Nonetheless Justice Jackson, in dissent, lays great stress on the point.

(8)(a) According to Justice Jackson, as noted above, the reason plaintiff brought suit in Pennsylvania was that she could not obtain jurisdiction over the manufacturer in her home state. Suppose she had a different motive:

> (i) In Alabama, the recovery under the workers' compensation law would have barred all other recovery; or

> (ii) Pennsylvania had a more favorable product liability law than Alabama.

Would either of these motives affect your preference between the views of Justices Vinson and Jackson in this case?

(b) Suppose Pennsylvania had a three-year statute of limitations and no borrowing provision, and the action was commenced more than two but less than three years after the accident: it seems that the majority in *Wells* would say the action could be brought, and Jackson would argue that it should be barred. Would there then be a due process problem, i.e., Simonds Abrasive being deprived of the the protection of Alabama law?

---

[n] Chapter 2, p. 75 and p. 87, question (2), *supra.*

[o] See *Baker v. Bolton,* (Campb. 493, 170 Eng. Rep. (1808); Malone, *The Genesis of Wrongful Death,* 17 Stan. L. Rev. 1043 (1965). For a review of the origins of the common law rule in connection with a maritime claim, see *Moragne v. States Marine Lines, Inc.,* 398 U.S. 375 (1970).

(c) Suppose the same facts, but Pennsylvania's three-year statute comes with a borrowing provision.[p] Is that not an uneven hand? What if the borrowing statute is inapplicable when the plaintiff is a citizen or resident of the home state?[q]

9(a) Finally, note the insistence of Justice Jackson, concurring in *First National Bank* and dissenting in *Wells,* on a constitutional requirement to apply the law of the place where the accident occurred. He accepts the majority's reliance on *Erie* and *Klaxon* as promoting, indeed requiring, uniformity with the law of the state where the action is heard.

> But the essence of the Full Faith and Credit Clause of the Constitution [he writes] is that uniformities other than just those within the state are to be observed in a federal system . . . [Thus] the law where the cause of action arose will follow the cause of action wherever it is pursued.

Justice Jackson spelled out this argument in a famous article, published in 1945,[r] and reiterated in 1955 in a book on the Supreme Court.[s]

Consider, as you trace the development of the Supreme Court's approach to choice of law and constitutional challenge in the next section, to what extent Justice Jackson's argument (i) was accurate in 1952 and 1953; and (ii) remains persuasive in the wake of the "conflicts revolution" of the 1960's.[t]

---

§ 5.02 The Rise and Fall of Supreme Court Supervision over Choice of Law

Surprisingly few cases concerning choice of law have come before the U.S. Supreme Court in the exercise of its constitutional review function, virtually none in the nineteenth century.[a] From time to time a state regulation designed to protect local consumers from out-of-state insurance companies was challenged,[b] and now and then the losing party in a choice of law case succeeded in persuading the Supreme Court to review (but usually not to overturn) his case.[c] The first major case in which the Supreme Court reversed a state court decision on choice of law was not rendered until the close of the third decade of the twentieth century.

---

[p] Recall *Mack Trucks, Inc. v. Bendix-Westinghouse Auto. Co.,* Chapter 2, p. 81, *supra.*

[q] Recall *Canadian No. Ry. v. Eggen,* discussed in question (4)(d), p. 90, *supra.*

[r] Jackson, *Full Faith and Credit—The Lawyer's Clause of the Constitution,* 45 Colum. L. Rev. 1 (1945).

[s] R. Jackson, *The Supreme Court in the American System of Government* (1955):

It seems to me that disagreement as to which of conflicting or competing state laws applies raises a federal question under the Full Faith and Credit Clause and that our hope for a better general legal system would be well served by wider application of that clause.

[t] Recall that Judge Kaufman, in *Pearson v. Northeast Airlines,* Chapter 3, p. 135, at 137, cites the majority's opinion in *Wells* in support of his contention that the Constitution does not command application of the law of the place of injury.

[a] See generally Dodd, *The Power of the Supreme Court to Review State Decisions in the Field of Conflict of Laws,* 39 Harv. L. Rev. 533, 550–60 (1926). Of course, during the reign of *Swift v. Tyson,* § 6.01, *infra,* the Court occasionally heard choice-of-law cases on appeal from lower federal courts, in exercise of its supervisory power over those courts, as contrasted with its function as umpire of the federal system. See, e.g., *Pritchard v. Norton,* 106 U.S. 124 (1882), reversing the decision of the Circuit Court for the District of Louisana on a question of whether the place of making, or the place of performance, should govern a contract of indemnity.

[b] See, e.g., the cases discussed in question (1), pp. 397–98, *infra.*

[c] See, e.g., *Kryger v. Wilson,* question (1)(a), p. 397, *infra.*

[A] Home Town Justice Struck Down

HOME INSURANCE COMPANY v. DICK

United States Supreme Court
281 U.S. 397 (1930)

MR. JUSTICE BRANDEIS delivered the opinion of the Court.

Dick, a citizen of Texas, brought this action in a court of that State against Compañia General Anglo-Mexicana de Seguros S. A., a Mexican corporation, to recover on a policy of fire insurance for the total loss of a tug. Jurisdiction was asserted *in rem* through garnishment, by ancillary writs issued against The Home Insurance Company and Franklin Fire Insurance Company, which reinsured, by contracts with the Mexican corporation, parts of the risk which it had assumed. The garnishees are New York corporations. Upon them, service was effected by serving their local agents in Texas appointed pursuant to Texas statutes, which require the appointment of local agents by foreign corporations seeking permits to do business within the State.

The controversy here is wholly between Dick and the garnishees. The defendant has never been admitted to do business in Texas; has not done any business there; and has not authorized anyone to receive service of process or enter an appearance for it in this cause. It was cited by publication, in accordance with a Texas statute; attorneys were appointed for it by the trial court; and they filed on its behalf an answer which denied liability. But there is no contention that thereby jurisdiction *in personam* over it was acquired. Dick's claim is that, since the obligation of a reinsurer to pay the original insurer arises upon the happening of the loss and is not conditional upon prior payment of the loss by the insurer, the New York companies are indebted to the Mexican company and these debts are subject to garnishment in a proceeding against the latter *quasi in rem,* even though it is not suable *in personam*. The garnishees concede that inability to sue the Mexican corporation in Texas, *in personam,* is not material, if a cause of action against it existed at the time of garnishment and there was within the State a *res* belonging to it. But they deny the existence of the cause of action or of the *res*.

Their defense rests upon the following facts. This suit was not commenced till more than one year after the date of the loss. The policy provided: "It is understood and agreed that no judicial suit or demand shall be entered before any tribunal for the collection of any claim under this policy, unless such suits or demands are filed within one year counted as from the date on which such damage occurs." This provision was in accord with the Mexican law to which the policy was expressly made subject.[1] It was issued by the Mexican company in Mexico to one Bonner, of Tampico, Mexico, and was there duly assigned to Dick prior to the loss. It covered the vessel only in certain Mexican waters. The premium was paid in Mexico; and the loss was "payable in the City of Mexico in current funds of the United States of Mexico, or their equivalent elsewhere." At the time the policy was issued, when it was assigned to him, and until after the

---

[1] The policy contained also the provision: "The present policy is subjected to the disposition of the Commercial Code, in that it does not alter or modify the stipulations which that same contains." The dispositions of the Commercial Code thus incorporated are: "Article 1038. The rights of action derived from commercial acts shall be subject to prescription in accordance with the provisions of this Code. Article 1039. The periods fixed for the enforcement of rights of action arising out of commercial acts shall be fatal except restitution against same is given. Article 1043. One year shall prescribe actions derived from contracts of life insurance, sea and land."

loss, Dick actually resided in Mexico, although his permanent residence was in Texas. The contracts of reinsurance were effected by correspondence between the Mexican company in Mexico and the New York companies in New York. Nothing thereunder was to be done, or was in fact done, in Texas.

In the trial court, the garnishees contended that since the insurance contract was made and was to be performed in Mexico, and the one year provision was valid by its laws, Dick's failure to sue within one year after accrual of the alleged cause of action was a complete defense to the suit on the policy; that this failure also relieved the garnishees of any obligation as reinsurers, the same defense being open to them, *New York State Marine Ins. Co. v. Protection Ins. Co.*, 1 Story 458, 460; and that they, consequently, owed no debt to the Mexican company subject to garnishment.[3] To this defense, Dick demurred, on the ground that Article 5545 of the Texas Revised Civil Statutes (1925) provides: "No person, firm, corporation, association or combination of whatsoever kind shall enter into any stipulation, contract, or agreement, by reason whereof the time in which to sue thereon is limited to a shorter period than two years. And no stipulation, contract, or agreement for any such shorter limitation in which to sue shall ever be valid in this State."

The trial court sustained Dick's contention and entered judgment against the garnishees. On appeal, both in the Court of Civil Appeals (8 S.W. (2d) 354) and in the Supreme Court of the State (15 S.W. (2d) 1028), the garnishees asserted that, as construed and applied, the Texas statute violated the due process clause of the Fourteenth Amendment and the contract clause. Both courts treated the policy provision as equivalent to a foreign statute of limitation; held that Article 5545 related to the remedy available in Texas courts; concluded that it was validly applicable to the case at bar; and affirmed the judgment of the trial court. The garnishees appealed to this Court on the ground that the statute, as construed and applied, violated their rights under the Federal Constitution. . . .

First. Dick contends that this Court lacks jurisdiction of the action, because the errors assigned involve only questions of local law and of conflict of laws. The argument is that while a provision requiring notice of loss within a fixed period, is substantive because it is a condition precedent to the existence of the cause of action, the provision for liability only in case suit is brought within the year is not substantive because it relates only to the remedy after accrual of the cause of action; that while the validity, interpretation and performance of the substantive provisions of a contract are determined by the law of the place where it is made and is to be performed, matters which relate only to the remedy are unquestionably governed by the *lex fori;* and that even if the Texas court erred in holding the statute applicable to this contract, the error is one of state law or of the interpretation of the contract, and is not reviewable here.

The contention is unsound. There is no dispute as to the meaning of the provision in the policy. It is that the insurer shall not be liable unless suit is brought within one year of the loss. Whether the provision be interpreted as making the commencement of a suit within the year a condition precedent to the existence of a cause of action, or as making failure to sue within the year a breach of a condition subsequent which extinguishes the cause of action, is not of legal

---

[3] Besides the defense here discussed the answers both of the Mexican corporation and of the garnishees alleged: (2) that the suit was not brought within the period provided by the Commercial Code of Mexico, and that thereby the right of action was completely barred upon the expiration of one year; (3) that the policy was void because of plaintiff's misrepresentations as to the value of the vessel; (4) that the vessel was not a total loss and was abandoned in violation of the terms of the policy. None of these defenses needs to be considered.

significance here. Nor are we concerned with the question whether the provision is properly described as relating to remedy or to substance. However characterized, it is an express term in the contract of the parties by which the right of the insured and the correlative obligation of the insurer are defined. If effect is given to the clause, Dick cannot recover from the Mexican corporation and the garnishees cannot be compelled to pay. If, on the other hand, the statute is applied to the contract, it admittedly abrogates a contractual right and imposes liability, although the parties have agreed that there should be none.

The statute is not simply one of limitation. It does not merely fix the time in which the aid of the Texas courts may be invoked. Nor does it govern only the remedies available in the Texas courts. It deals with the powers and capacities of persons and corporations. It expressly prohibits the making of certain contracts. As construed, it also directs the disregard in Texas of contractual rights and obligations wherever created and assumed; and it commands the enforcement of obligations in excess of those contracted for. Therefore, the objection that, as applied to contracts made and to be performed outside of Texas, the statute violates the Federal Constitution, raises federal questions of substance; and the existence of the federal claim is not disproved by saying that the statute, or the one year provision in the policy, relates to the remedy and not to the substance.

That the federal questions were not raised in the trial court is immaterial. For, the Court of Civil Appeals and the Supreme Court of the State considered the questions as properly raised in the appellate proceedings and passed on them adversely to the federal claim. . . . The case is properly here on appeal. The motion to dismiss the appeal is overruled; and the petition for certiorari is, therefore, denied.

Second. The Texas statute as here construed and applied deprives the garnishees of property without due process of law. A State may, of course, prohibit and declare invalid the making of certain contracts within its borders. Ordinarily, it may prohibit performance within its borders, even of contracts validly made elsewhere, if they are required to be performed within the State and their performance would violate its laws. But, in the case at bar, nothing in any way relating to the policy sued on, or to the contracts of reinsurance, was ever done or required to be done in Texas. All acts relating to the making of the policy were done in Mexico. All in relation to the making of the contracts of re-insurance were done there or in New York. And, likewise, all things in regard to performance were to be done outside of Texas. Neither the Texas laws nor the Texas courts were invoked for any purpose, except by Dick in the bringing of this suit. The fact that Dick's permanent residence was in Texas is without significance. At all times here material, he was physically present and acting in Mexico. Texas was, therefore, without power to affect the terms of contracts so made. Its attempt to impose a greater obligation than that agreed upon and to seize property in payment of the imposed obligation violates the guaranty against deprivation of property without due process of law.

. . .

It is true . . . that a State is not bound to provide remedies and procedure to suit the wishes of individual litigants. It may prescribe the kind of remedies to be available in its courts and dictate the practice and procedure to be followed in pursuing those remedies. Contractual provisions relating to these matters, even if valid where made, are often disregarded by the court of the forum, pursuant to statute or otherwise. But the Texas statute deals neither with the kind of remedy available nor with the mode in which it is to be pursued. It purports to create rights and obligations. It may not validly affect contracts which are neither made nor are to be performed in Texas.

Third. Dick urges that Article 5545 of the Texas law is a declaration of its public policy; and that a State may properly refuse to recognize foreign rights which violate its declared policy. Doubtless, a State may prohibit the enjoyment by persons within its borders of rights acquired elsewhere which violate its laws or public policy; and, under some circumstances, it may refuse to aid in the enforcement of such rights. . . .

But the Mexican corporation never was in Texas; and neither it nor the garnishees invoked the aid of the Texas courts or the Texas laws. The Mexican corporation was not before the court. The garnishees were brought in by compulsory process. Neither has asked favors. They ask only to be let alone. We need not consider how far the State may go in imposing restrictions on the conduct of its own residents, and of foreign corporations which have received permission to do business within its borders; or how far it may go in refusing to lend the aid of its courts to the enforcement of rights acquired outside its borders. It may not abrogate the rights of parties beyond its borders having no relation to anything done or to be done within them.

Fourth. Finally, it is urged that the Federal Constitution does not require the States to recognize and protect rights derived from the laws of foreign countries—that as to them the full faith and credit clause has no application. See *Aetna Life Ins. Co. v. Tremblay,* 223 U. S. 185. The claims here asserted are not based upon the full faith and credit clause. Compare *Royal Arcanum v. Green,* 237 U. S. 531; *Modern Woodmen of America v. Mixer,* 267 U. S. 544. They rest upon the Fourteenth Amendment. Its protection extends to aliens. Moreover, the parties in interest here are American companies. The defense asserted is based on the provision of the policy and on their contracts of reinsurance. The courts of the State confused this defense with that based on the Mexican Code. They held that even if the effect of the foreign statute was to extinguish the right, Dick's removal to Texas prior to the bar of the foreign statute, removed the cause of action from Mexico and subjected it to the Texas statute of limitation. And they applied the same rule to the provision in the policy. Whether or not that is a sufficient answer to the defense based on the foreign law, we may not consider; for, no issue under the full faith and credit clause was raised. But in Texas, as elsewhere, the contract was subject to its own limitations.

Reversed.

[B] The Intersection of Full Faith and Credit and Due Process

Two years after *Home Insurance Co. v. Dick,* another choice of law case came before the Supreme Court, and again the Supreme Court imposed its view of the proper choice of law—this time under the Full Faith and Credit Clause.

In *Bradford Electric Light Co. v. Clapper,* 286 U.S. 145 (1932), the Vermont employee of a Vermont electric company was killed in the course of repairing a substation located in New Hampshire. His widow brought a tort suit against the electric company in New Hampshire, which was permissible under New Hampshire law; under Vermont law, such a suit would not be permitted, because (absent contrary agreement) workmen's compensation was the exclusive remedy, regardless of the place of an employee's injury. The suit was removed to federal district court, and that court, as well as the Court of Appeals, upheld a jury verdict in favor of plaintiff. The Supreme Court, again in an opinion by Justice Brandeis, reversed.

There was, of course, no due process problem, since the accident had occurred in New Hampshire and there were clearly sufficient contacts with that state to support application of New Hampshire's law. But though New Hampshire might refuse to enforce the Vermont law as obnoxious to its public policy, it could not, under the Full Faith and Credit clause, refuse to give effect to a substantive defense: "That a statute is a 'public act' within the meaning of the Full Faith and Credit Clause," the Court said, "is settled."[d]

Justice Stone concurred, because he assumed that the state courts of New Hampshire would apply Vermont law to these facts, and (six years before *Erie*) that "what they would do we should do."[e] But he doubted that "the legal consequences of acts of the employer or employee [in New Hampshire] which grow out of/or affect the status in New Hampshire, must, by mandate of the Constitution, be either defined or controlled, in the New Hampshire courts, by the laws of Vermont, rather than of New Hampshire."[f]

Justice Stone's doubts were soon translated into opinions of the Supreme Court, in two complementary decisions, both written by Stone.

ALASKA PACKERS ASSOCIATION v. INDUSTRIAL ACCIDENT COMMISSION OF CALIFORNIA

United States Supreme Court
294 U.S. 532 (1935)

MR. JUSTICE STONE delivered the opinion of the Court.

This is an appeal from a judgment of the Supreme Court of California upholding an award of compensation, by the state Industrial Accident Commission, to appellee Palma, against appellant, his employer, and holding that the award does not infringe prohibitions of the Federal Constitution. The award was made in conformity to the statutes of California, where the contract of employment was entered into, rather than those of Alaska, where the injury occurred.

On May 13, 1932, Palma, a non-resident alien, and appellant, doing business in California, executed at San Francisco a written contract of employment. Palma agreed to work for appellant in Alaska during the salmon canning season; the appellant agreed to transport him to Alaska and, at the end of the season, to return him to San Francisco where he was to be paid his stipulated wages, less advances. The contract recited that appellant had elected to be bound by the Alaska Workmen's Compensation Law and stipulated that the parties should be subject to and bound by the provisions of that statute. Section 58 of the California Workmen's Compensation Act was then in force, which provides:

"The commission shall have jurisdiction over all controversies arising out of injuries suffered without the territorial limits of this state in those cases where the injured employee is a resident of this state at the time of the injury and the contract of hire was made in this State, . . ." At that time the California Supreme Court had held that this section was applicable to non-residents of California, since the privileges and immunities clause of the Federal Constitution prevented

---

[d] 286 U.S. at 154–55.

[e] 286 U.S. at 163 (Stone, J. concurring).

[f] *Id.* at 164.

§ 5.02   THE CONSTITUTION AND CONFLICT OF LAWS   □   387

giving any effect to the requirement that the employee be a resident. The California Workmen's Compensation Act also provides, § 27 (a):

> No contract, rule or regulation shall exempt the employer from liability for the compensation fixed by this act, . . .

In August, 1932, after his return from Alaska to California, the employee applied for and later received an award by the California Commission in compensation for injuries received by him in the course of his employment in Alaska. On petition for review by the state supreme court, appellant assailed the California statute, as he does here, as invalid under the due process and the full faith and credit clauses of the Federal Constitution. Insofar as the California statute denies validity to the agreement that the parties should be bound by the Alaska Workmen's Compensation Act, and attempts to give a remedy for injuries suffered by a non-resident employee without the state, it is challenged as a denial of due process. Petitioner also insists that as the Alaska statute affords, in Alaska, an exclusive remedy for the injury which occurred there, the California courts denied full faith and credit to the Alaska statute by refusing to recognize it as a defense to the application for an award under the California statute.

In refusing to set aside the award of the state commission, the Supreme Court of California ruled. . . . that § 58 of the California Compensation Act was applicable to Palma, although a non-resident alien; that, as the contract of employment was entered into within the state, the stipulation that the Alaska Act should govern was invalid under § 27 (a). It concluded that the Alaska statute afforded a remedy to the employee in Alaska and held that by setting up the defense of the Alaska statute in California the two statutes were brought into conflict, and that in the circumstances neither the due process clause nor the full faith and credit clause denied to the state the power to apply its own law, to the exclusion of the Alaska Act, in fixing and awarding compensation for the injury.

1. The question first to be considered is whether a state, which may constitutionally impose on employer and employee a system of compensation for injuries to the employee in the course of his employment within the state, . . . is precluded by the due process clause, in the special circumstances of this case, from imposing liability for injuries to the employee occurring in Alaska.

. . .

Obviously the power of a state to effect legal consequences is not limited to occurrences within the state if it has control over the status which gives rise to those consequences. That it has power, through its own tribunals, to grant compensation to local employees, locally employed, for injuries received outside its borders, and likewise has power to forbid its own courts to give any other form of relief for such injury, was fully recognized by this Court in *Bradford Electric Light Co. v. Clapper*. Objections which are founded upon the Fourteenth Amendment must, therefore, be directed, not to the existence of the power to impose liability for an injury outside state borders, but to the manner of its exercise as being so arbitrary or unreasonable as to amount to a denial of due process.

We cannot say that the statutory requirement of California, that the provisions for compensation shall extend to injuries without the state when the contract for employment was entered into within it, is given such an unreasonable application in the present case as to transcend constitutional limitations. The employee, an alien more than 2,000 miles from his home in Mexico, was, with fifty-three others, employed by petitioner in California. The contract called for their transportation to Alaska, some 3,000 miles distant, for seasonal employment of between two and three months, at the conclusion of which they were to be returned to California, and were there to receive their wages.

The meagre facts disclosed by the record suggest a practice of employing workers in California for seasonal occupation in Alaska, under such conditions as to make it improbable that the employees injured in the course of their employment in Alaska would be able to apply for compensation there. It was necessary for them to return to California in order to receive their full wages. They would be accompanied by their fellow workers, who would normally be the witnesses required to establish the fact of the injury and its nature. The probability is slight that injured workmen, once returned to California, would be able to retrace their steps to Alaska, and there successfully prosecute their claims for compensation. Without a remedy in California, they would be remediless, and there was the danger that they might become public charges, both matters of grave public concern to the state.

California, therefore, had a legitimate public interest in controlling and regulating this employer-employee relationship in such fashion as to impose a liability upon the employer for an injury suffered by the employee, and in providing a remedy available to him in California. In the special circumstances disclosed, the state had as great an interest in affording adequate protection to this class of its population as to employees injured within the state. Indulging the presumption of constitutionality which attaches to every state statute, we cannot say that this one, as applied, lacks a rational basis or involved any arbitrary or unreasonable exercise of state power.

. . .

2. Even though the compensation acts of either jurisdiction may, consistently with due process, be applied in either, the question remains whether the California court has failed to accord full faith and credit to the Alaska statute in refusing to allow it as a defense to the award of the California Commission. Appellant contends that as the provisions of the Alaska statute conflict with those of the California statutes, the full faith and credit clause and [the implementing act], requiring that full faith and credit be accorded to territorial statutes, . . . compel recognition of the Alaska statute as a defense to the proceedings before the California Commission; that the award of the Commission should accordingly be set aside, leaving the employee to his remedy under the Alaska statute in California, if California provides the remedy, or remitting the parties to their proceeding in Alaska under the territorial statute.

Both statutes are compensation acts, substituting for the common law recovery for negligence a right to recover compensation at specified rates for injuries to employees in the course of their employment. . . .

To the extent that California is required to give full faith and credit to the conflicting Alaska statute, it must be denied the right to apply in its own courts a statute of the state, lawfully enacted in pursuance of its domestic policy. . . .

The subject of our inquiry is therefore whether the full faith and credit clause requires the state of California to give effect to the Alaska statute rather than its own.

It has often been recognized by this Court that there are some limitations upon the extent to which a state will be required by the full faith and credit clause to enforce even the judgment of another state, in contravention of its own statutes or policy. . . .

In the case of statutes, the extra-state effect of which Congress has not prescribed, where the policy of one state statute comes into conflict with that of another, the necessity of some accommodation of the conflicting interests of the two states is still more apparent. A rigid and literal enforcement of the full faith and credit clause, without regard to the statute of the forum, would lead to the absurd result that, wherever the conflict arises, the statute of each state must be enforced in the courts of the other, but cannot be in its own. Unless by force of that clause a greater effect is thus to be given to a state statute abroad than the clause permits it to have at home, it is unavoidable that this Court determine for itself the extent to which the statute of one state may qualify or deny rights asserted under the statute of another. . . .

The necessity is not any the less whether the statute and policy of the forum is set up as a defense to a suit brought under the foreign statute or the foreign statute is set up as a defense to a suit or proceedings under the local statute. In either case, the conflict is the same. In each, rights claimed under one statute prevail only by denying effect to the other. In both the conflict is to be resolved, not by giving automatic effect to the full faith and credit clause, compelling the courts of each state to subordinate its own statutes to those of the other, but by appraising the governmental interests of each jurisdiction, and turning the scale of decision according to their weight.

The enactment of the present statute of California was within state power and infringes no constitutional provision. *Prima facie* every state is entitled to enforce in its own courts its own statutes, lawfully enacted. One who challenges that right, because of the force given to a conflicting statute of another state by the full faith and credit clause, assumes the burden of showing, upon some rational basis, that of the conflicting interests involved those of the foreign state are superior to those of the forum. It follows that not every statute of another state will override a conflicting statute of the forum by virtue of the full faith and credit clause; that the statute of a state may sometimes override the conflicting statute of another, both at home and abroad; and, again, that the two conflicting statutes may each prevail over the other at home, although given no extraterritorial effect in the state of the other.

. . .

The interest of Alaska is not shown to be superior to that of California. No persuasive reason is shown for denying to California the right to enforce its own laws in its own courts, and in the circumstances the full faith and credit clause does not require that the statutes of Alaska be given that effect.

Affirmed.

PACIFIC EMPLOYERS INSURANCE CO. v. INDUSTRIAL ACCIDENT COMMISSION

United States Supreme Court
306 U.S. 493 (1939)

Mr. Justice Stone delivered the opinion of the Court.

The question is whether the full faith and credit which the Constitution requires to be given to a Massachusetts workmen's compensation statute precludes California from applying its own workmen's compensation act in the case of an injury suffered by a Massachusetts employee of a Massachusetts employer while in California in the course of his employment.

Petitioner, an insurance carrier, under the California Workmen's Compensation, Insurance and Safety Act, for the Pacific Coast branch of the employer, Dewey & Almy Chemical Company, a Massachusetts corporation, filed its petition in the California District Court of Appeal to set aside an award of compensation to an employee by the California Industrial Accident Commission. The grounds of the petition were, among others, that the employee, because he was regularly employed at the head office of the corporation in Massachusetts and was temporarily in California on the business of the employer when injured there, was subject to the workmen's compensation law of Massachusetts, and that the California Commission, in applying the California Act and in refusing to recognize the Massachusetts statute as a defense, had denied to the latter the full faith and credit to which it was entitled under Article IV, § 1 of the Constitution. The order of the District Court of Appeal denying the petition was affirmed by the Supreme Court of California. We granted certiorari, 305 U. S. 563, the question presented being of public importance.

The injured employee, a resident of Massachusetts, was regularly employed there under written contract in the laboratories of the Dewey & Almy Chemical Company as a chemical engineer and research chemist. In September, 1935, in the usual course of his employment he was sent by his employer to its branch factory in California, to act temporarily as technical adviser in the effort to improve the quality of one of the employer's products manufactured there. Upon completion of the assignment he expected to return to the employer's Massachusetts place of business, and while in California he remained subject to the general direction and control of the employer's Massachusetts office, from which his compensation was paid.

He instituted the present proceeding before the California Commission for the award of compensation under the California Act for injuries received in the course of his employment in that state, naming petitioner as insurance carrier under that Act; the Hartford Accident & Indemnity Company, as insurer under the Massachusetts Act, was made a party. The California Commission directed petitioner to pay the compensation prescribed by the California Act, including the amounts of lien claims filed in the proceeding for medical, hospital and nursing services and certain further amounts necessary for such services in the future.

. . .

While in the circumstances now presented, either state, if its system for administering workmen's compensation permitted, would be free to adopt and enforce the remedy provided by the statute of the other, here each has provided for itself an exclusive remedy for a liability which it was constitutionally authorized to impose. But neither is bound, apart from the compulsion of the full faith and credit clause, to enforce the laws of the other, *Milwaukee County v. White Co.,* 296 U. S. 268, 272; and the law of neither can by its own force determine the choice of law to be applied in the other. . . .

To the extent that California is required to give full faith and credit to the conflicting Massachusetts statute it must be denied the right to apply in its own courts its own statute, constitutionally enacted in pursuance of its policy to provide compensation for employees injured in their employment within the state. It must withhold the remedy given by its own statute to its residents by way of compensation for medical, hospital and nursing services rendered to the injured employee, and it must remit him to Massachusetts to secure the administrative remedy which that state has provided. We cannot say that the full faith and credit clause goes so far.

While the purpose of that provision was to preserve rights acquired or confirmed under the public acts and judicial proceedings of one state by requiring recognition of their validity in other states, the very nature of the federal union of states, to which are reserved some of the attributes of sovereignty, precludes resort to the full faith and credit clause as the means for compelling a state to substitute the statutes of other states for its own statutes dealing with a subject matter concerning which it is competent to legislate. As was pointed out in *Alaska Packers Assn. v. Industrial Accident Comm'n:* "A rigid and literal enforcement of the full faith and credit clause, without regard to the statute of the forum, would lead to the absurd result that, wherever the conflict arises, the statute of each state must be enforced in the courts of the other, but cannot be in its own." And in cases like the present it would create an impasse which would often leave the employee remediless. Full faith and credit would deny to California the right to apply its own remedy, and its administrative machinery may well not be adapted to giving the remedy afforded by Massachusetts. Similarly, the full faith and credit demanded for the California Act would deny to Massachusetts the right to apply its own remedy, and its Department of Industrial Accidents may well be without statutory authority to afford the remedy provided by the California statute.

. . .

This Court must determine for itself how far the full faith and credit clause compels the qualification or denial of rights asserted under the laws of one state, that of the forum, by the statute of another state. See *Alaska Packers Assn. v. Industrial Accident Comm'n.* But there would seem to be little room for the exercise of that function when the statute of the forum is the expression of domestic policy, in terms declared to be exclusive in its application to persons and events within the state. Although Massachusetts has an interest in safeguarding the compensation of Massachusetts employees while temporarily abroad in the course of their employment, and may adopt that policy for itself, that could hardly be thought to support an application of the full faith and credit clause which would override the constitutional authority of another state to legislate for the bodily safety and economic protection of employees injured within it. Few matters could be deemed more appropriately the concern of the state in which the injury occurs or more completely within its power. . . .

[T]he full faith and credit exacted for the statute of one state does not necessarily preclude another state from enforcing in its own courts its own conflicting statute having no extra-territorial operation forbidden by the Fourteenth Amendment. . . .

. . .

Here, California legislation not only conflicts with that of Massachusetts providing compensation for the Massachusetts employee if injured within the state of California, but it expressly provides, for the guidance of its own commission and courts, that "No contract, rule or regulation shall exempt the employer from liability for the compensation fixed by this Act." The Supreme Court of California has declared in its opinion in this case that it is the policy of the state, as expressed in its Constitution and Compensation Act, to apply its own provisions for compensation, to the exclusion of all others, and that "It would be obnoxious to that policy to deny persons who have been injured in this state the right to apply for compensation when to do so might require physicians and hospitals to go to another state to collect charges for medical care and treatment given to such persons."

Full faith and credit does not here enable one state to legislate for the other or to project its laws across state lines so as to preclude the other from prescribing for itself the legal consequences of acts within it.

Affirmed.

[C] Forum Law and Out-of-State Contracts

As we saw in Chapter 4, *supra,* choice of law clauses in contracts were generally honored in the United States, but not if they offended against some fundamental policy of a state that had a materially greater interest in a given issue than the state whose law was chosen.[g] If a state believed that its materially greater interest in an issue would be frustrated by a contract choosing another state's law, could it invalidate the choice of law as well as a provision in a contract that would be sustained under the law chosen in the contract, but not by the law of the forum? Two cases raising this question, both involving insurance contracts, came before the Supreme Court ten years apart.

WATSON v. EMPLOYERS LIABILITY ASSURANCE CORPORATION

United States Supreme Court
348 U.S. 66 (1954)

Mr. Justice Black delivered the opinion of the Court.

Louisiana has an insurance code which comprehensively regulates the business of insurance in all its phases.[1] This case brings to us challenges to the constitutionality of certain provisions of that code allowing injured persons to bring direct actions against liability insurance companies that have issued policies contracting to pay liabilities imposed on persons who inflict injury. . . .

This is such a direct action brought by the appellants, Mr. and Mrs. Watson, in a Louisiana state court claiming damages against the appellee, Employers Liability Assurance Corporation, Ltd., on account of alleged personal injuries suffered by Mrs. Watson. The complaint charged that the injuries occurred in Louisiana when Mrs. Watson bought and used in that State "Toni Home Permanent" a hair-waving product alleged to have contained a highly dangerous latent ingredient put there by its manufacturer. The manufacturer is the Toni Company of Illinois, a subsidiary of the Gillette Safety Razor Company which has its headquarters in Massachusetts.

The particular problem presented with reference to enforcing the Louisiana statute in this case arises because the insurance policy sued on was negotiated and issued in Massachusetts and delivered in Massachusetts and Illinois.[2] This Massachusetts-negotiated contract contains a clause, recognized as binding and enforceable under Massachusetts and Illinois law, which prohibits direct actions against the insurance company until *after* final determination of the Toni Company's obligation to pay personal injury damages either by judgment or agreement.[3] Contrary

---

[g] See *Restatement of Conflict of Laws (Second)* § 187, reproduced at p. 258, *supra.*

[1] Title 22, La. Rev. Stat., 1950.

[2] The insurance policy was issued to "The Toni Company, a Division of the Gillette Safety Razor Company . . ." Gillette is a Delaware Corporation with headquarters in Boston where the contract was negotiated with the Boston office of Employers. The Toni Company manufactures the hair-waving product in Chicago, Illinois.

[3] "12. Action Against Company. No action shall lie against the company unless, as a condition precedent thereto, the insured shall have fully complied with all the terms of this policy, nor until the amount of the insured's obligation

§ 5.02   THE CONSTITUTION AND CONFLICT OF LAWS   □   393

to this contractual "no action" clause, the challenged statutory provisions permit injured persons to sue an insurance company *before* such final determination. As to injuries occurring in Louisiana, one provision of the State's direct action statute makes it applicable, even though, as here, an insurance contract is made in another state and contains a clause forbidding such direct actions.[4] Another Louisiana statutory provision, with which Employers long ago complied, compels foreign insurance companies to consent to such direct suits in order to get a certificate to do business in the State.[5] The basic issue raised by the attack on both these provisions is whether the Federal Constitution forbids Louisiana to apply its own law and compels it to apply the law of Massachusetts or Illinois.

After the case was removed to the United States District Court because of diversity Employers moved to dismiss, contending that the two Louisiana statutory provisions contravened the Equal Protection, Contract, Due Process and Full Faith and Credit Clauses of the Federal Constitution. With emphasis on the due process contention, the District Court dismissed the case, holding both statutory provisions unconstitutional as to policies written and delivered outside the State of Louisiana. 107 F. Supp. 494. The Court of Appeals agreed with the District Court and affirmed the dismissal. 202 F. 2d 407. Provisions of Louisiana's statutes having been held invalid as repugnant to the Federal Constitution, the case is properly here on appeal.

The denial of equal protection and impairment of contract contentions are wholly void of merit. The State's direct action provisions fall with equal force upon all liability insurance companies, foreign and domestic. Employers points to no other provisions of the Louisiana law or to facts of any nature which give the slightest support to any charge of discriminatory application of the direct action statute. And since the direct action provisions became effective before this

---

to pay shall have been finally determined either by judgment against the insured after actual trial or by written agreement of the insured, the claimant and the company.

"Any person or organization or the legal representative thereof who has secured such judgment or written agreement shall thereafter be entitled to recover under this policy to the extent of the insurance afforded by this policy. Nothing contained in this policy shall give any person or organization any right to join the company as a co-defendant in any action against the insured to determine the insured's liability.

"Bankruptcy or insolvency of the insured or of the insured's estate shall not relieve the company of any of its obligations hereunder."

[4] "The injured person or his or her heirs, at their option, shall have a right of direct action against the insurer within the terms and limits of the policy in the parish where the accident or injury occurred or in the parish where the insured has his domicile, and said action may be brought against the insurer alone or against both the insured and the insurer, jointly and in solido. This right of direct action shall exist whether the policy of insurance sued upon was written or delivered in the State of Louisiana or not and whether or not such policy contains a provision forbidding such direct action, provided the accident or injury occurred within the State of Louisiana. . . . It is the intent of this section that any action brought hereunder shall be subject to all of the lawful conditions of the policy or contract and the defenses which could be urged by the insurer to a direct action brought by the insured, provided the terms and conditions of such policy or contract are not in violation of the laws of this state." La. Rev. Stat., 1950, § 22:655, as amended by Act 541 of the Louisiana Legislature of 1950. As to the scope of this provision according to Louisiana courts, see *Rome v. London & Lancashire Indemnity Co. of America,* La. App., 169 So. 132.

[5] "No certificate of authority to do business in Louisiana shall be issued to a foreign or alien liability insurer until such insurer shall consent to being sued by the injured person or his or her heirs in a direct action as provided in Section 655 of this title, whether the policy of insurance sued upon was written or delivered in the State of Louisiana or not, and whether or not such policy contains a provision forbidding such direct action, provided that the accident or injury occurred within the State of Louisiana. The said foreign or alien insurer shall deliver to the Secretary of State as a condition precedent to the issuance of such authority, an instrument evidencing such consent." La. Rev. Stat., 1950, § 22:983, as amended by Act 542 of the Louisiana Legislature of 1950.

insurance contract was made, there is a similar lack of substantiality in the suggestion that Louisiana has violated Art. I, § 10, of the United States Constitution which forbids states to impair the obligation of contracts. *Munday v. Wisconsin Trust Co.,* 252 U. S. 499, 503.

Had the policy sued on been issued in Louisiana there would be no arguable due process question. See *Merchants Mutual Auto. Liability Ins. Co. v. Smart,* 267 U. S. 126, 129–130. But because the policy was bought, issued and delivered outside of Louisiana, Employers invokes the due process principle that a state is without power to exercise "extraterritorial jurisdiction," that is, to regulate and control activities wholly beyond its boundaries. Such a principle was recognized and applied in *Home Ins. Co. v. Dick,* 281 U. S. 397, a case strongly relied on by Employers. There Texas was denied power to alter the terms of an insurance contract made in Mexico between persons then in that country, covering a vessel only while in Mexican waters, and containing a provision that the contract was to be governed by the laws of Mexico. Thus, the subject matter of the contract related in no manner to anything that had been done or was to be done in Texas. For this reason, Texas was denied power to alter the obligations of the Mexican contract. But this Court carefully pointed out that its decision might have been different had activities relating to the contract taken place in Texas upon which the State could properly lay hold as a basis for regulation. . . .

Some contracts made locally, affecting nothing but local affairs, may well justify a denial to other states of power to alter those contracts. But, as this case illustrates, a vast part of the business affairs of this Nation does not present such simple local situations. Although this insurance contract was issued in Massachusetts, it was to protect Gillette and its Illinois subsidiary against damages on account of personal injuries that might be suffered by users of Toni Home Permanents anywhere in the United States, its territories, or in Canada. As a consequence of the modern practice of conducting widespread business activities throughout the entire United States, this Court has in a series of cases held that more states than one may seize hold of local activities which are part of multistate transactions and may regulate to protect interests of its own people, even though other phases of the same transactions might justify regulatory legislation in other states. . . .

Louisiana's direct action statute is not a mere intermeddling in affairs beyond her boundaries which are no concern of hers. Persons injured or killed in Louisiana are most likely to be Louisiana residents, and even if not, Louisiana may have to care for them. Serious injuries may require treatment in Louisiana homes or hospitals by Louisiana doctors. The injured may be destitute. They may be compelled to call upon friends, relatives, or the public for help. Louisiana has manifested its natural interest in the injured by providing remedies for recovery of damages. It has a similar interest in policies of insurance which are designed to assure ultimate payment of such damages. Moreover, Louisiana courts in most instances provide the most convenient forum for trial of these cases. But modern transportation and business methods have made it more difficult to serve process on wrongdoers who live or do business in other states. In this case efforts to serve the Gillette Company were answered by a motion to dismiss on the ground that Gillette had no Louisiana agent on whom process could be served. If this motion is granted, Mrs. Watson, but for the direct action law, could not get her case tried without going to Massachusetts or Illinois although she lives in Louisiana and her claim is for injuries from a product bought and used there. What has been said is enough to show Louisiana's legitimate interest in safeguarding the rights of persons injured there. In view of that interest, the direct action provisions here challenged do not violate due process.

What we have said above goes far toward answering the Full Faith and Credit Clause contention. That clause does not automatically compel a state to subordinate its own contract laws to the laws of another state in which a contract happens to have been formally executed. Where, as here, a contract affects the people of several states, each may have interests that leave it free to enforce its own contract policies. . . . We have already pointed to the vital interests of Louisiana in liability insurance that covers injuries to people in that State. Of course Massachusetts also has some interest in the policy sued on in this case. The insurance contract was formally executed in that State and Gillette has an office there. But plainly these interests cannot outweigh the interest of Louisiana in taking care of those injured in Louisiana. Since this is true, the Full Faith and Credit Clause does not compel Louisiana to subordinate its direct action provisions to Massachusetts contract rules. *Pacific Employers Ins. Co. v. Commission*. But cf. *John Hancock Mut. Life Ins. Co. v. Yates*, 299 U. S. 178; *Hughes v. Fetter*.

What we have already said disposes of the contention that Louisiana's law compelling foreign insurance companies to consent to direct actions is unconstitutional. That contention is that the Due Process Clause of the Fourteenth Amendment forbids a state to compel a foreign corporation to surrender constitutional rights as a condition of being permitted to do business in the state. . . . That principle is inapplicable to this case because, as we have just decided, Louisiana has a constitutional right to subject foreign liability insurance companies to the direct action provisions of its laws whether they consent or not.

Reversed.

[MR. JUSTICE FRANKFURTER had doubts about the lawfulness of Louisiana's rewriting an out-of-state contract. He concurred in the result, however, on the basis that Louisiana could condition the out-of-state insurance company's entry on an undertaking to observe a public policy binding on all local insurance companies and strictly related to the protection of serious interests. Here, Employers had given its consent to direct action and was bound by that consent.]

CLAY v. SUN INSURANCE OFFICE, LTD.

United States Supreme Court
377 U.S. 179 (1964)

MR. JUSTICE DOUGLAS delivered the opinion of the Court.

This case, which invoked the diversity jurisdiction of the Federal District Court in a suit to recover damages under a [property] insurance policy, was here before. 363 U. S. 207. The initial question then as now is whether the 12-month-suit clause in the policy governs, in which event the claim is barred, or whether Florida's statutes nullifying such clauses if they require suit to be filed in less than five years are applicable and valid, in which event the suit is timely. The policy was purchased by petitioner in Illinois while he was a citizen and resident of that State. Respondent, a British company, is licensed to do business in Illinois, Florida, and several other States.

A few months after purchasing the policy, petitioner moved to Florida and became a citizen and resident of that State; and it was in Florida that the loss occurred two years later. When the case reached here, the majority view was that the underlying constitutional question—whether consistently with due process, Florida could apply its five-year statute to this Illinois contract—should not be reached until the Florida Supreme Court, through its certificate procedure, had construed that statute and resolved another local law question. On remand the Court of Appeals certified the two questions to the Florida Supreme Court, which answered both questions in petitioner's favor. 133 So. 2d 735. Thereafter the Court of Appeals held that it was not compatible with due process for Florida to apply its five-year statute to this contract and that judgment should be entered for respondent. 319 F. 2d 505. We again granted certiorari. . . .

While there are Illinois cases indicating that parties may contract—as here—for a shorter period of limitations than is provided by the Illinois statute, we are referred to no Illinois decision extending that rule into other States whenever claims on Illinois contracts are sought to be enforced there. We see no difficulty whatever under either the Full Faith and Credit Clause or the Due Process Clause. We deal with an ambulatory contract on which suit might be brought in any one of several States. Normally, as the Court held in *Pacific Employers Ins. Co. v. Industrial Accident Comm'n,* a State having jurisdiction over a claim deriving from an out-of-state employment contract need not substitute the conflicting statute of the other State (workmen's compensation) for its own statute (workmen's compensation)—where the employee was injured in the course of his employment while temporarily in the latter State. We followed the same route in *Watson v. Employers Liability Assurance Corp.,* where we upheld a state statute allowing direct actions against liability insurance companies in the State of the forum, even though a clause in the contract, binding in the State where it was made, prohibited direct action against the insurer until final determination of the obligation of the insured.

The Court of Appeals relied in the main on *Hartford Accident & Indemnity Co. v. Delta & Pine Land Co.,* and *Home Ins. Co. v. Dick.* Those were cases where the activities in the State of the forum were thought to be too slight and too casual, as in the *Delta & Pine Land Co.* case (292 U. S., at 150), to make the application of local law consistent with due process, or wholly lacking, as in the *Dick* case. No deficiency of that order is present here. As MR. JUSTICE BLACK, dissenting, said when this case was here before:

> Insurance companies, like other contractors, do not confine their contractual activities and obligations within state boundaries. They sell to customers who are promised protection in States far away from the place where the contract is made. In this very case the policy was sold to Clay with knowledge that he could take his property anywhere in the world he saw fit without losing the protection of his insurance. In fact, his contract was described on its face as a "Personal Property Floater Policy (World Wide)." The contract did not even attempt to provide that the law of Illinois would govern when suits were filed anywhere else in the country. Shortly after the contract was made, Clay moved to Florida and there he lived for several years. His insured property was there all that time. The company knew this fact. Particularly since the company was licensed to do business in Florida, it must have known it might be sued there. . . .

363 U.S. at 221.

. . . Florida has ample contacts with the present transaction and the parties to satisfy any conceivable requirement of full faith and credit or of due process.

Reversed.

NOTES AND QUESTIONS

(1) *Home Insurance Co. v. Dick* was not the first case in which the Supreme Court passed on a claim that a state court had erred—constitutionally—in a choice of law decision.

(a) In *Kryger v. Wilson,* 242 U.S. 171 (1916), *A* agreed by a contract "made and to be performed in Minnesota" to sell land located in North Dakota to *B*. *B* defaulted, and *A*, having served notice of cancellation in accordance with North Dakota law, brought suit in North Dakota to quiet title to the land. *B* appeared in the action and contended that the contract remained in effect, because *A* had not cancelled it in accordance with the requirements of Minnesota law. The North Dakota court found for *A,* and *B* appealed to the Supreme Court, alleging that he had been deprived of his property without due process of law. The Court, in an opinion by Justice Brandeis, found no lack of due process:

> the most that [*B*] can say is that the state court made a mistaken application of doctrines of the conflict of laws in deciding that the cancellation of a land contract is governed by the law of the situs instead of the place of making and performance. But that, being purely a question of local common law, is a matter with which this court is not concerned.[h]

(b) In *New York Life Insurance Co. v. Dodge,* 246 U.S. 357 (1918), a Missouri resident had applied in Missouri for a life insurance policy issued by the defendant. Subsequently he borrowed against the policy to pay the premiums, and then stopped paying premiums altogether. The company used the reserve value of the policy to pay off the loan, and then advised the insured that his policy had lapsed.

All this was consistent with the law of New York. Under Missouri's anti-lapse law, however, the company would have been required to (i) take three fourths of the policy's reserve value; (ii) use this sum to pay off the loan; and (iii) convert the remainder into term life insurance in the face amount of the policy for as long a period as the remainder would purchase according to the insurance tables in effect. The insured had died within this period, and his widow accordingly claimed under the policy. The company defended on the ground that New York law governed the policy, as well as the loans made against the policy. The Missouri courts found in favor of the widow, but the Supreme Court (5–4) reversed, on the ground that the Missouri legislature could not under the XIV Amendment destroy a New York contract, or prohibit its citizens from making it. The dissenters, in an opinion by Justice Brandeis, thought the contract to borrow against the policy had been made in Missouri; that a provision that it was ". . . deemed to have been made in New York" was ineffective to avoid the mandatory law of Missouri; and that in any event the contract was within the reasonable scope of Missouri's exercise of its police powers.

(c) Four years later, the Supreme Court, in effect took back its holding in *Dodge*. In *Mutual Life Insurance Co. of New York v. Liebing,* 259 U.S. 209 (1922), the facts were essentially the same, but this time the Court ruled for the plaintiff. *Dodge* was not formally overruled, but distinguished. Justice Holmes, writing for a unanimous court, said, that in *Dodge* the contract had said that "cash loans can be obtained," while here the contract read "the company will . . . loan amounts within the limits of the cash surrender value." What difference did that make?

---

[h] Note the citation to *Kryger* in *Wells v. Simonds Abrasive Co.,* at p. 374, *supra* for the proposition that states are free (within limits) to adopt such rules of conflict of laws as they choose.

Since the company had no discretion whether to make or refuse the loan, nothing of importance was to be done in New York, and the Missouri court was justified in treating the contract as a Missouri contract.

Clearly, no constitutional doctrine could be built on such distinctions, or indeed on the issue of where a contract was deemed to be made. The insurance cases[i] were different from *Kryger* in that they involved consumer protection regulation by the state, rather like that in *Watson* a generation later. But what was said in *Kryger* could well have been said in *Dodge* and *Liebing*. As long as there were sufficient links with either state, the decision on whether a contract "was made" in one state or the other does not rise to the level of a constitutional question.[j]

(2) Turning to *Home Insurance Co. v. Dick,* that case has continuing validity, though its sweep has been much reduced by later cases.

(a) Is *Dick* like the hypothetical variation on *Wells,* question (8)(b), p. 380, *supra,* where the forum has a longer statute of limitations than the place where the cause of action arose? Justice Brandeis (at pp. 383–84) says no. Why not?

(b) Jurisdiction over the insurer in *Dick* was by attachment of the obligation from the reinsurer, Home, to the real defendant, Anglo-Mexicana, said to be located wherever the reinsurer did business, including Texas. Thus jurisdiction is quasi-in-rem, on the model of *Seider v. Roth,* and drawing on *Harris v. Balk.*[k] Justice Brandeis says (at p. 385) "We need not consider how far the State may go in imposing restrictions on the conduct of its own residents, and of foreign corporations which have received permission to do business within its borders . . ." Do you think this may be the key to the case? Would it have come out the same way if

   (i) Anglo-Mexicana were licensed to do business in Texas; or

   (ii) If Dick had been the original insured rather than an assignee?

Or would the contract to insure a boat in Mexican waters, made in Mexico, still be beyond the legislative jurisdiction of Texas?

(c) Suppose the policy had insured the tug wherever in the world it might sail, rather than only in designated Mexican internal waters. Do you think the case would have come out differently? Notice that Justice Black makes this suggestion in *Watson* at p. 394, and again in *Clay* at p. 396, as quoted by Justice Douglas. Keep these questions in mind in comparing *Home Insurance v. Dick* to *Allstate v. Hague* in the next section.

(3)(a) *Alaska Packers* and *Pacific Employers* together seem to mark the demise of the Full Faith and Credit clause as a constitutional device for control of choice of law decisions. Workmen's compensation, the movement that swept the United States in the second decade of the twentieth century in response to the scandal of uncompensated industrial accidents, typically calls for compensation out of insurance required to be maintained by employers, with claims

---

[i] See also *New York Life Ins. Co. v. Head.* 234 U.S. 148 (1914); *Hoopeston Canning Co. v. Cullen,* 318 U.S. 313 (1943).

[j] For a much criticized case that does in fact turn on the place of making of a contract, see *Hartford Accident & Indem. Co. v. Delta & Pine Land Co.,* 292 U.S. 143 (1943), holding that Mississippi courts could not consistently with due process enforce a Mississippi law invalidating a short contractual limitation period in a policy insuring against embezzlement by employees, even though the employee had worked (and apparently embezzled) in Mississippi and the employer was a Mississippi corporation, because the contract had been entered into in Tennessee, whose law would uphold the contract provision.

[k] See Chapter 7, p. 602, question (2); p. 605, question (4)(b), *infra.*

passed on by an industrial accident commission established by the state. The commission interprets and applies the state's workmen's compensation law, but only that law; it does not, in other words, apply the law of any other state. Since workmen's compensation is usually compulsory both on the basis of contracts of employment entered into in a state and on the basis of work performed in a state, there is frequent opportunity for overlap, when employees engaged in one state work in another. If the Full Faith in Credit clause were taken literally, as Justice Stone points out (pp. 390–91), each state would be precluded from applying its own workmen's compensation scheme, but probably unable to apply the statute of the other state. Accordingly, Justice Stone says, in *Alaska Packers*:

> the conflict is to be resolved, not by giving automatic effect to the full faith and credit clause, compelling the courts of each state to subordinate its own statutes to those of the other, but by appraising the governmental interests of each jurisdiction, and turning the rule of decision according to their weight.

Does he mean the second part of the quoted sentence suggesting a balancing of interests?

(b) Note that while much of the opinion in *Pacific Employers* tracks, or indeed quotes, *Alaska Packers,* the suggestion that the interests of the two states be compared is at least partly taken back in the later case, "[T]here would seem to be little room for the exercise of that function, when the statute of the forum is the expression of domestic policy, in terms declared to be exclusive in its application to persons and events within the state." (p. 391).

(c) The result seems to be a link between the Due Process and Full Faith and Credit clauses. If California, in both cases, did not have a legitimate interest in the application of its own law, then Full Faith and Credit might compel its courts to apply (or at least to recognize) the law of another concerned state; but so long as California's interest in application of its own law is consistent with due process, that interest may not be defeated by full faith and credit to another state's law. Consider this relationship between the two clauses again in connection with the recognition of judgments in Chapter 8, § 8.01, *infra.*[l]

(d) In the two decisions by Justice Stone in the 1930's, the conflict was only between two workers' compensation statutes, California's evidently having the more liberal payments schedule. The advantage of workers' compensation, of course, is that it eliminated what Prosser called "the three wicked sisters of the common law—contributory negligence, assumption of risk and the fellow servant rule."[m] It also obviated the necessity of establishing that the employer was negligent, and in many cases the need to retain a lawyer. However, the schedule for compensation awards tends to be lower than tort recoveries, in some instances substantially so. Thus many persons, in circumstances where they believe they can establish negligence, have sought to resort to common law actions, notwithstanding statutory provisions that the compensation remedy is exclusive. Some of these efforts have involved suits in states other than where the employment contract was centered, as in *Bradford Electric Co. v. Clapper,* some have involved actions against persons other than the employer, for instance actions against a prime contractor brought by an

---

[l] See particularly *Fauntleroy v. Lum,* p. 639, and Justice Stone's dissent in *Yarborough,* p. 650, *infra.*

[m] See Prosser & Keeton, *The Law of Torts,* 573 (5th ed. 1984).

David Lloyd George, campaigning for workers compensation (and for his own election) popularized the slogan "The cost of the product should bear the blood of the workman." Quoted in *Prosser & Keeton* at 573, but without precise location.

employee of a subcontractor,[n] or actions against a manufacturer of a machine causing a workplace injury, as in *Wells v. Simonds Abrasive Co.*[o]

(e) Both a second state and a different defendant were involved in *Carroll v. Lanza,* 349 U.S. 408 (1955).[p] A construction employee engaged in Missouri by a subcontractor and injured on the job in Arkansas collected workmen's compensation in Missouri, and then brought suit in Arkansas against the prime contractor. Under the law of Missouri, apparently, no actions in tort arising out of the accident would have been possible against anyone; in Arkansas, the ban on tort actions arising from industrial accidents applied only to claims against the employer, not to claims against third parties. The contractor removed the action to the federal district court in Arkansas, which rejected a motion to dismiss, and after trial, entered judgment for the employee. The Court of Appeals, though agreeing with the district court in its interpretation of Arkansas law (i.e., on whether a prime contractor was a third party for this purpose), reversed, on the basis that the full Faith and Credit clause required application of the Missouri statute and therefore dismissal of the action in tort.

The Supreme Court reinstated the decision of the district court. In an opinion by Justice Douglas, the Court said that *Bradford Electric Co. v. Clapper* was no longer valid after *Pacific Employers;* the fact that the action in F–2 was a common law rather than a compensation claim was not a material difference.

> [T]he *Pacific Employers Insurance Co.* case teaches that in these personal injury cases the State where the injury occurs need not be a vassal to the home State and allow only that remedy which the home State has marked as the exclusive one. The State of the forum also has interests to serve and to protect. . . .[q]

The Court rejected the suggestion that *Carroll v. Lanza* was like *Hughes v. Fetter*:

> The present case is a much weaker one for application of the Full Faith and Credit Clause. Arkansas, the State of the forum, is not adopting any policy of hostility to the public Acts of Missouri. It is choosing to apply its own rule of law to give affirmative relief for an action arising within its borders.[r]

(4)(a) *Watson v. Employers Liability Assurance Corp.* addresses the question left open in *Home Insurance Co. v. Dick*—whether the outcome would be different if the insurance company did business in the state seeking to apply its law to an out-of-state contract. Is there something unfair about the outcome?

(b) Justice Black has no trouble with the equal protection and contract clause claims, because in-and out-of-state parties are treated the same, and because the statute was in place before the policy was issued. The claim under the due process clause is harder, because the policy was issued in Massachusetts, and thus, the insurance company argues, the case is governed by *Home Insurance Co. v. Dick*. The injury, however, is in the state of the forum, and there is no need to resort to quasi-in-rem jurisdiction to bring the claim against the insurance company. Are these distinctions convincing? Or is the Court simply saying it doesn't want to be involved? Note that

---

[n] See, e.g., *Byrd v. Blue Ridge Rural Elec. Cooperative,* Chapter 6, p. 455, *infra.*

[o] For another variation, see *O'Connor v. Lee-Hy Paving Co.,* Chapter 3, p. 189, question (4)(c) *supra.*

[p] For more workers' compensation cases before the Supreme Court, distringuished because they involved *awards,* i.e., were arguably analogous to final judgments, see Chapter 8, § 8.01[B], *infra.*

[q] 349 U.S. at 412.

[r] 349 U.S. at 413.

Watson, like *Clay* and *Carroll v. Lanza,* was a case where the lower (federal) court had thought the constitution commanded application of another state's law, and the Supreme Court said there is no such command.

(c) Justice Black explains in detail (at p. 394, *supra*) that Louisiana's direct action statute "is not a mere intermeddling in affairs . . . which are no concern of hers." He goes on to say "What we have said [about Louisiana's legitimate interest] goes far toward answering the Full Faith and Credit Clause contention." Is it true after *Watson* (as well as the workmen's compensation cases) that Full Faith and Credit no longer plays a role in constitutional supervision of choice of law? Or would that be an exaggeration? Can you think of a situation in which it would not be a violation of due process for F–2 to apply its own law but nevertheless the Full Faith and Credit clause would require application of the law of F–1?

(d) The law, including Constitutional law, often moves in half steps. In *Watson,* the product was bought in Louisiana, the injury occurred there, and suit was brought there, all as provided in the statute. Suppose now a visitor to Louisiana buys a Toni shampoo in a hotel drug store, uses it in Louisiana, but the injury is not felt until she returns to her home in New York. (i) Could she still bring suit (as a matter of constitutional law) in Louisiana, naming the insurance company as a defendant? (ii) Could she bring suit against the insurance company in New York in reliance on the Louisiana direct action statute.?[s] (iii) What if she had purchased the shampoo in Louisiana but not used it until her return to New York? If the New York court were permitted to entertain the action in either case (ii) or case (iii), could it be *required* to do so?

(e) A clue to the last question is presented by *Clay,* and in particular by the technique of certification to the Supreme Court of Florida adopted by the Supreme Court in *Clay I.*[t] When the Florida Supreme Court answered the question put to it by saying that it would apply Florida law to the contract made in Illinois, the constitutional question could not be avoided. Had the Florida court held that Illinois law should be applied *as a choice of law matter,* there would have been no constitutional question. When the Fifth Circuit held that Illinois law should be applied *by command of the Constitution,* however, the U.S. Supreme Court stepped in a second time and reversed.

(5) Summarizing the development from *New York Life* and *Home Insurance* through *Watson* and *Clay,* has the Supreme Court bowed out of the choice of law business? Or is there some residual control reserved by the Supreme Court, that might be revived if (or as) the "conflicts revolution" got out of hand?

§ 5.03 The Supreme Court Reconsiders Its Role in Choice of Law

For close to two decades following the decision in *Clay,* the Supreme Court did not take another choice of law case. The 1960's, as we saw in Chapters 3 and 4, were the years of the "conflicts revolution," when *Restatement I* was almost everywhere discarded, and various alternatives, from

---

[s] See *Oltarsh v. Aetna Ins. Co.,* 15 N.Y.2d 111, 256 N.Y.S.2d 577, 204 N.E.2d 622 (1965), permitting a New York woman to bring suit in New York against an insurance company for an injury sustained in Puerto Rico, in reliance on Puerto Rico's direct action statute.

[t] Under the certification procedure pioneered in Florida and now available in about half the states, a federal court may put to the highest state court a question of state law on which it is not clear and which is necessary to the decision of the federal case. See C. Wright, *Federal Courts* 333–35 and sources there cited (5th ed. 1994).

governmental interest analysis to the most significant relationship to principles of preference caught on, alone or together. That decade also saw the spread of plaintiff-centered judicial jurisdiction, as long-arm statutes were adopted in every state in the United States following passage of the first such statute in Illinois in 1955.[a] In the late 1970's the Supreme Court seemed to be taking renewed interest in judicial jurisdiction, as it granted review and wrote important opinions in four cases in four years.[b] Numerous writers suggested that the time had come for the Court to take similar interest in developments in choice of law.[c] When the Court did finally grant review from the decision of the Supreme Court of Minnesota in *Hague v. Allstate Insurance Co.*,[d] many Supreme Court watchers and conflict of law connoisseurs looked forward with anticipation to a renewed effort by the Court to bring the Constitution back into the field of conflict of laws.[e]

ALLSTATE INSURANCE CO. v. HAGUE

United States Supreme Court
449 U.S. 302 (1981)

JUSTICE BRENNAN announced the judgment of the Court and an opinion in which JUSTICE WHITE, JUSTICE MARSHALL, and JUSTICE BLACKMUN join.

This Court granted certiorari to determine whether the Due Process Clause of the Fourteenth Amendment or the Full Faith and Credit Clause of Art. 4, § 1, of the United States Constitution bars the Minnesota Supreme Court's choice of substantive Minnesota law to govern the effect of a provision in an insurance policy issued to respondent's decedent.

I

Respondent's late husband, Ralph Hague, died of injuries suffered when a motorcycle on which he was a passenger was struck from behind by an automobile. The accident occurred in Pierce County, Wis., which is immediately across the Minnesota border from Red Wing, Minn. The operators of both vehicles were Wisconsin residents, as was the decedent who, at the time of the accident, resided with respondent in Hager City, Wis., which is one and one-half miles from Red Wing. Mr. Hague had been employed in Red Wing for the 15 years immediately preceding his death and had commuted daily from Wisconsin to his place of employment.

Neither the operator of the motorcycle nor the operator of the automobile carried valid insurance. However, the decedent held a policy issued by petitioner Allstate Insurance Company covering three automobiles owned by him and containing an uninsured motorist clause insuring

---

[a] See Chapter 7 for a detailed discussion of these developments.

[b] *Shaffer v. Heitner* (1977), *Kulko v. Superior Court* (1978) *World-Wide Volkswagen* and *Rush v. Savchuk* (1980). All these cases are reproduced or summarized in Chapter 7, *infra*.

[c] See, e.g., Silberman, *Shaffer v. Heitner: The End of an Era*, 53 N.Y.U. L. Rev. 33 (1978).

[d] 289 N.W.2d 43 (Minn. 1979).

[e] Professor Martin, for instance, writing after certiorari had been granted but before the decision came down, expressed the hope that *Hague* would provide a coherent constitutional choice of law test to replace the "confused theory of the past." Martin, *Personal Jurisdiction and Choice of Law*, 78 Mich. L. Rev. 872 at 888 (1980).

him against loss incurred from accidents with uninsured motorists. The uninsured motorist coverage was limited to $15,000 for each automobile.[3]

After the accident, but prior to the initiation of this lawsuit, respondent moved to Red Wing. Subsequently, she married a Minnesota resident and established residence with her new husband in Savage, Minn. At approximately the same time, a Minnesota Registrar of Probate appointed respondent personal representative of her deceased husband's estate. Following her appointment, she brought this action in Minnesota District Court seeking a declaration under Minnesota law that the $15,000 uninsured motorist coverage on each of her late husband's three automobiles could be "stacked" to provide total coverage of $45,000. Petitioner defended on the ground that whether the three uninsured motorist coverages could be stacked should be determined by Wisconsin law, since the insurance policy was delivered in Wisconsin, the accident occurred in Wisconsin, and all persons involved were Wisconsin residents at the time of the accident.

The Minnesota District Court disagreed. Interpreting Wisconsin law to disallow stacking, the court concluded that Minnesota's choice-of-law rules required the application of Minnesota law permitting stacking. The court refused to apply Wisconsin law as "inimical to the public policy of Minnesota" and granted summary judgment for respondent.

The Minnesota Supreme Court, sitting en banc, affirmed the District Court. The court, also interpreting Wisconsin law to prohibit stacking, applied Minnesota law after analyzing the relevant Minnesota contacts and interests within the analytical framework developed by Professor Leflar.[7] See Leflar, *Choice-Influencing Considerations in Conflicts Law,* 41 N. Y. U. L. Rev. 267 (1966). The state court, therefore, examined the conflict-of-laws issue in terms of (1) predictability of result, (2) maintenance of interstate order, (3) simplification of the judicial task, (4) advancement of the forum's governmental interests, and (5) application of the better rule of law. Although stating that the Minnesota contacts might not be, "in themselves, sufficient to mandate application of [Minnesota] law,"[8] 289 N. W. 2d 43, 49 (1978), under the first four factors, the court concluded that the fifth factor—application of the better rule of law—favored selection of Minnesota law. The court emphasized that a majority of States allow stacking and that legal decisions allowing stacking "are fairly recent and well considered in light of current uses of automobiles." *Id.,* at 49. In addition, the court found the Minnesota rule superior to Wisconsin's "because it requires the cost of accidents with uninsured motorists to be spread more broadly through insurance premiums than does the Wisconsin rule." *Ibid.* Finally, after rehearing en banc, the court buttressed its initial opinion by indicating "that contracts of insurance on motor vehicles are in a class by themselves" since an insurance company "knows the automobile is a movable item which will be driven from state to state." 289 N. W. 2d 50, 50 (1979). From this premise the court concluded that application of Minnesota law was "not so arbitrary and unreasonable as to violate due process." *Ibid.*

---

[3] Ralph Hague paid a separate premium for each automobile including an additional separate premium for each uninsured motorist coverage.

[7] Minnesota had previously adopted the conceptual model developed by Professor Leflar in *Milkovich v. Saari* [p. 194 at 197-98, *supra*].

[8] The court apparently was referring to sufficiency as a matter of choice-of-law and not as a matter of constitutional limitation on its choice-of-law decision.

II

It is not for this Court to say whether the choice-of-law analysis suggested by Professor Leflar is to be preferred or whether we would make the same choice-of-law decision if sitting as the Minnesota Supreme Court. Our sole function is to determine whether the Minnesota Supreme Court's choice of its own substantive law in this case exceeded federal constitutional limitations. Implicit in this inquiry is the recognition, long accepted by this Court, that a set of facts giving rise to a lawsuit, or a particular issue within a lawsuit, may justify, in constitutional terms, application of the law of more than one jurisdiction. See, *e.g., Watson v. Employers Liability Assurance Corp.,* n. [13], *infra.* See generally *Clay v. Sun Insurance Office, Ltd.* (hereinafter cited as *Clay II*). As a result, the forum State may have to select one law from among the laws of several jurisdictions having some contact with the controversy.

In deciding constitutional choice-of-law questions, whether under the Due Process Clause or the Full Faith and Credit Clause,[10] this Court has traditionally examined the contacts of the State, whose law was applied, with the parties and with the occurrence or transaction giving rise to the litigation. See *Clay II*. In order to ensure that the choice of law is neither arbitrary nor fundamentally unfair, see *Alaska Packers Assn. v. Industrial Accident Commission,* the Court has invalidated the choice of law of a State which has had no significant contact or significant aggregation of contacts, creating state interests, with the parties and the occurrence or transaction.[11]

---

[10] This Court has taken a similar approach in deciding choice-of-law cases under both the Due Process Clause and the Full Faith and Credit Clause. In each instance, the Court has examined the relevant contacts and resulting interests of the State whose law was applied. See, *e.g., Nevada v. Hall,* 440 U. S. 410, 424 (1979). Although at one time the Court required a more exacting standard under the Full Faith and Credit Clause than under the Due Process Clause for evaluating the constitutionality of choice-of-law decisions, see *Alaska Packers Assn. v. Industrial Accident Comm'n,* (interest of State whose law was applied was no less than interest of State whose law was rejected), the Court has since abandoned the weighing of interests requirement. *Carroll v. Lanza;* see *Nevada v. Hall, supra;* Weintraub, *Due Process and Full Faith and Credit Limitations on a State's Choice of Law,* 44 Iowa L. Rev. 449 (1959). Different considerations are of course at issue when full faith and credit is to be accorded to acts, records and proceedings outside the choice-of-law area, such as in the case of sister state court judgments.

[11] Prior to the advent of interest analysis in the state courts as the "dominant mode of analysis in modern choice of law theory," Silberman, *Shaffer v. Heitner: The End of an Era,* 53 N.Y.U. L. Rev. 33, 80, n. 259 (1978); cf. *Richards v. United States,* 369 U. S. 1, 11–13, and nn. 26–27 (1962) (discussing trend toward interest analysis in state courts), the prevailing choice of law methodology focused on the jurisdiction where a particular event occurred. See, *e. g., Restatement of the Law, Conflict of Laws* (1934) (hereinafter cited as *Restatement First*). For example, in cases characterized as contract cases, the law of the place of contracting controlled the determination of such issues as capacity, fraud, consideration, duty, performance, and the like. *Id.,* § 332; see Beale, *What Law Governs the Validity of a Contract,* 23 Harv. L. Rev. 260, 270–271 (1910). In the tort context, the law of the place of the wrong usually governed traditional choice-of-law analysis. *Restatement First, supra,* § 378; see *Richards v. United States, supra,* 369 U. S., at 11–12.

Hartford Accident and Indemnity Co. v. Delta & Pine Land Co., 292 U. S. 143 (1934), can, perhaps, best be explained as an example of that period. In that case, the Court struck down application by the Mississippi courts of Mississippi law which voided the limitations provision in a fidelity bond written in Tennessee between a Connecticut insurer and Delta, both of which were doing business in Tennessee and Mississippi. By its terms, the bond covered misapplication of funds "by any employee 'in any position, anywhere. . . .'" *Id.,* at 145. After Delta discovered defalcations by one of its Mississippi-based employees, a lawsuit was commenced in Mississippi.

That case, however, has scant relevance for today. It implied a choice-of-law analysis which, for all intents and purposes, gave an isolated event—the writing of the bond in Tennessee—controlling constitutional significance, even though there might have been contacts with another State (there Mississippi) which would make application of its law neither unfair nor unexpected. See Martin, *Personal Jurisdiction and Choice of Law,* 78 Mich. L. Rev. 872, 874, and n. 11 (1980).

§ 5.03   THE CONSTITUTION AND CONFLICT OF LAWS   □   405

Two instructive examples of such invalidation are *Home Insurance Company v. Dick,* and *John Hancock Mutual Life Insurance Co. v. Yates.* In both cases, the selection of forum law rested exclusively on the presence of one nonsignificant forum contact.

Home Insurance Company v. Dick involved interpretation of an insurance policy which had been issued in Mexico, by a Mexican insurer, to a Mexican citizen, covering a Mexican risk. The policy was subsequently assigned to Mr. Dick, who was domiciled in Mexico and "physically present and acting in Mexico," although he remained a nominal, permanent resident of Texas. The policy restricted coverage to losses occurring in certain Mexican waters and, indeed, the loss occurred in those waters. Dick brought suit in Texas against a New York reinsurer. Neither the Mexican insurer nor the New York reinsurer had any connection to Texas.[12] The Court held that application of Texas law to void the insurance contract's limitation-of-actions clause violated due process.[13]

The relationship of the forum State to the parties and the transaction was similarly attenuated in *John Hancock Mutual Life Insurance Company v. Yates.* There, the insurer, a Massachusetts corporation, issued a contract of insurance on the life of a New York resident. The contract was applied for, issued and delivered in New York where the insured and his spouse resided. After the insured died in New York, his spouse moved to Georgia and brought suit on the policy in Georgia. Under Georgia law, the jury was permitted to take into account oral modifications when deciding whether an insurance policy application contained material misrepresentations. Under New York law, however, such misrepresentations were to be evaluated solely on the basis of the written application. The Georgia court applied Georgia law. This Court reversed, finding application of Georgia law to be unconstitutional.

Dick and *Yates* stand for the proposition that if a State has only an insignificant contact with the parties and the occurrence or transaction, application of its law is unconstitutional.[14] *Dick* concluded that nominal residence—standing alone—was inadequate; *Yates* held that a postoccurrence change of residence to the forum State—standing alone—was insufficient to justify application of forum law. Although instructive as extreme examples of selection of forum law, neither *Dick* nor *Yates* governs this case. For in contrast to those decisions, here the Minnesota contacts with the parties and the occurrence are obviously significant. Thus, this case is like *Alaska Packers, Cardillo v. Liberty Mutual Insurance Co.,* 330 U. S. 469 (1947), and *Clay II*— cases where this Court sustained choice-of-law decisions based on the contacts of the State, whose law was applied, with the parties and occurrence.

In *Alaska Packers,* the Court upheld California's application of its Workmen's Compensation Act, where the most significant contact of the worker with California was his execution of an employment contract in California. The worker, a nonresident alien from Mexico, was hired in California for seasonal work in a salmon canning factory in Alaska. As part of the employment contract, the employer, who was doing business in California, agreed to transport the worker

---

[12] Dick sought to obtain *quasi-in-rem* jurisdiction by garnishing the reinsurance obligation of the New York reinsurer. The reinsurer had never transacted business in Texas, but it "was cited by publication, in accordance with a Texas statute; attorneys were appointed for it by the trial court; and they filed on its behalf an answer which denied liability." There would be no jurisdiction in the Texas Courts to entertain such a lawsuit today. See *Rush v. Savchuk,* 444 U. S. 320 (1980); *Shaffer v. Heitner,* 433 U. S. 186 (1977); Silberman, *supra,* 53 N.Y.U. L. Rev., at 62–65.

[13] The Court noted that the result might have been different if there had been some connection to Texas upon "which the State could properly lay hold as the basis of the regulations there imposed." *Home Insurance Co. v. Dick, supra,* n. 5; see *Watson v. Employers Liability Corp., supra,* 348 U. S., 66 at 71.

[14] See generally, Weintraub, *supra,* 44 Iowa L. Rev., at 455–457.

to Alaska and to return him to California when the work was completed. Even though the employee contracted to be bound by the Alaska Workmen's Compensation Law and was injured in Alaska, he sought an award under the California Workmen's Compensation Act. The Court held that the choice of California law was not "so arbitrary or unreasonable as to amount to a denial of due process," 294 U. S., at 542, because "without a remedy in California, [he] would be remediless," *ibid.*, and because of California's interest that the worker not become a public charge, *ibid.*

In *Cardillo v. Liberty Mutual Co., supra,* a District of Columbia resident, employed by a District of Columbia employer and assigned by the employer for the three years prior to his death to work in Virginia, was killed in an automobile crash in Virginia in the course of his daily commute home from work. The Court found the District's contacts with the parties and the occurrence sufficient to satisfy constitutional requirements, based on the employee's residence in the District, his commute between home and the Virginia workplace, and his status as an employee of a company "engaged in electrical construction work in the District of Columbia and surrounding areas." *Id.,* at 571.[16]

Similarly, *Clay II* upheld the constitutionality of the application of forum law. There a policy of insurance had issued in Illinois to an Illinois resident. Subsequently the insured moved to Florida and suffered a property loss in Florida. Relying explicitly on the nationwide coverage of the policy and the presence of the insurance company in Florida and implicitly on the plaintiff's Florida residence and the occurrence of the property loss in Florida, the Court sustained the Florida court's choice of Florida law.

The lesson from *Dick* and *Yates,* which found insufficient forum contacts to apply forum law, and from *Alaska Packers, Cardillo,* and *Clay II,* which found adequate contacts to sustain the choice of forum law,[17] is that for a State's substantive law to be selected in a constitutionally permissible manner, that State must have a significant contact or significant aggregation of contacts, creating state interests, such that choice of its law is neither arbitrary nor fundamentally unfair. Application of this principle to the facts of this case persuades us that the Minnesota Supreme Court's choice of its own law did not offend the Federal Constitution.

III

Minnesota has three contacts with the parties and the occurrence giving rise to the litigation. In the aggregate, these contacts permit selection by the Minnesota Supreme Court of Minnesota law allowing the stacking of Mr. Hague's uninsured motorist coverages.

---

[16] The precise question raised was whether the Virginia Compensation Commission "had sole jurisdiction over the claim." *Cardillo v. Liberty Mutual Ins. Co.,* 330 U. S. 469, 472–473 (1947). In finding that application of the District's law did not violate either due process or full faith and credit requirements, the Court in effect treated the question as a constitutional choice-of-law issue.

[17] The Court has upheld choice-of-law decisions challenged on constitutional grounds in numerous other decisions. See *Nevada v. Hall, supra* (upholding California's application of California law to automobile accident in California between two California residents and a Nevada official driving car owned by State of Nevada while engaged in official business in California); *Carroll v. Lanza; Watson v. Employers Liability Corp., supra; Pacific Employers Insurance Co. v. Industrial Accident Comm'n,* . . . . Thus, *Nevada v. Hall, supra,* and *Watson v. Employers Liability Corp., supra,* upheld application of forum law where the relevant contacts consisted of plaintiff's residence and the place of the injury. *Pacific Employers Insurance Co. v. Industrial Accident Comm'n,* and *Carroll v. Lanza,* relied on the place of the injury arising from the respective employee's temporary presence in the forum State in connection with his employment.

First, and for our purposes a very important contact, Mr. Hague was a member of Minnesota's workforce, having been employed by a Red Wing, Minn., enterprise for the 15 years preceding his death. While employment status may implicate a state interest less substantial than does resident status, that interest is nevertheless important. The State of employment has police power responsibilities towards the nonresident employee that are analogous, if somewhat less profound, than towards residents. Thus, such employees use state services and amenities and may call upon state facilities in appropriate circumstances.

In addition, Mr. Hague commuted to work in Minnesota, a contact which was important in *Cardillo v. Liberty Mutual Co., supra,* 330 U. S., at 475–476 (daily commute between residence in District of Columbia and workplace in Virginia), and was presumably covered by his uninsured motorist coverage during the commute.[18] The State's interest in its commuting nonresident employees reflects a state concern for the safety and well-being of its workforce and the concomitant effect on Minnesota employers.

That Mr. Hague was not killed while commuting to work or while in Minnesota does not dictate a different result. To hold that the Minnesota Supreme Court's choice of Minnesota law violated the Constitution for that reason would require too narrow a view of Minnesota's relationship with the parties and the occurrence giving rise to the litigation. An automobile accident need not occur within a particular jurisdiction for that jurisdiction to be connected to the occurrence.[19] Similarly, the occurrence of a crash fatal to a Minnesota employee in another State is a Minnesota contact.[20] If Mr. Hague had only been injured and missed work for a few weeks, the effect on the Minnesota employer would have been palpable and Minnesota's interest in having its employee made whole would be evident. Mr. Hague's death affects Minnesota's interest still more acutely, even though Mr. Hague will not return to the Minnesota workforce. Minnesota's workforce is surely affected by the level of protection the State extends to it, either directly or indirectly. Vindication of the rights of the estate of a Minnesota employee, therefore, is an important state concern.

Mr. Hague's residence in Wisconsin does not—as Allstate seems to argue—constitutionally mandate application of Wisconsin law to the exclusion of forum law.[21] If, in the instant case,

---

[18] The policy issued to Mr. Hague provided that Allstate would pay to the insured, or his legal representative, damages "sustained by the insured, caused by accident and arising out of the ownership, maintenance or use of [an] uninsured automobile. . . ." No suggestion has been made that Mr. Hague's uninsured motorist protection is unavailable because he was not killed while driving one of his insured automobiles.

[19] Numerous cases have applied the law of a jurisdiction other than the situs of the injury where there existed some other link between that jurisdiction and the occurrence. See, *e. g., Cardillo v. Liberty Mutual Ins. Co., supra; Alaska Packers Assn. v. Industrial Accident Comm'n, supra; Rosenthal v. Warren,* 475 F.2d 438 (CA2), cert. denied, 414 U. S. 856 (1973); *Clark v. Clark,* 107 N.H. 351, 222 A.2d 205 (1966); *Tooker v. Lopez,* 24 N.Y.2d 569, 301 N.Y.S.2d 519, 249 N.E.2d 394 (1969); *Babcock v. Jackson,* 12 N. Y.2d 473, 240 N. Y. S.2d 743, 191 N.E.2d 279 (1963).

[20] The injury or death of a resident of State A in State B is a contact of State A with the occurrence in State B. See cases cited in n. 19, *supra.*

[21] Petitioner's statement that the instant dispute involves the interpretation of insurance contracts which were "underwritten, applied for, and paid for by Wisconsin residents and issued covering cars garaged in Wisconsin," Brief for Petitioner, at 6, is simply another way of stating that Mr. Hague was a Wisconsin resident. Respondent could have replied that the insurance contract was underwritten, applied for and paid for by a Minnesota worker and issued covering cars that were driven to work in Minnesota and garaged there for a substantial portion of the day. The former statement is hardly more significant than the latter since the accident in any event did not involve any of the automobiles which were covered under Mr. Hague's policy. Recovery is sought pursuant to the uninsured motorist coverage.

the accident had occurred in Minnesota between Mr. Hague and an uninsured Minnesota motorist, if the insurance contract had been executed in Minnesota covering a Minnesota registered company automobile which Mr. Hague was permitted to drive, and if a Wisconsin court sought to apply Wisconsin law, certainly Mr. Hague's residence in Wisconsin, his commute between Wisconsin and Minnesota, and the insurer's presence in Wisconsin should be adequate to apply Wisconsin's law.[22] See generally *Cardillo v. Liberty Mutual Co., supra; Alaska Packers Assn. v. Industrial Accident Commission, supra; Home Insurance Company v. Dick.* Employment status is not a sufficiently less important status than residence, see generally *Carroll v. Lanza; Alaska Packers Assn. v. Industrial Accident Commission,* when combined with Mr. Hague's daily commute across state lines and the other Minnesota contacts present, to prohibit the choice-of-law result in this case on constitutional grounds.

Second, Allstate was at all times present and doing business in Minnesota.[23] By virtue of its presence, Allstate can hardly claim unfamiliarity with the laws of the host jurisdiction and

---

In addition, petitioner's statement that the contracts were "underwritten . . . by Wisconsin residents" is not supported by the stipulated facts if petitioner means to include Allstate within that phrase. Indeed, the policy, which is part of the record, recites that Allstate signed the policy in Northbrook, Ill. Under some versions of the hoary rule of *lex loci contractus,* and depending on the precise sequence of events, a sequence which is unclear from the record before us, the law of Illinois arguably might apply to govern contract construction, even though Illinois would have less contact with the parties and the occurrence than either Wisconsin or Minnesota. No party sought application of Illinois law on that basis in the court below.

[22] Of course Allstate could not be certain that Wisconsin law would necessarily govern any accident which occurred in Wisconsin, whether brought in the Wisconsin courts or elsewhere. Such an expectation would give controlling significance to the wooden *lex loci delicti* doctrine. While the place of the accident is a factor to be considered in choice-of-law analysis, to apply blindly the traditional, but now largely abandoned, doctrine, Silberman, *supra,* 53 N.Y.U. L. Rev., at 80, n. 259; see n. 11, *supra,* would fail to distinguish between the relative importance of various legal issues involved in a lawsuit as well as the relationship of other jurisdictions to the parties and the occurrence or transaction. If, for example, Mr. Hague had been a Wisconsin resident and employee who was injured in Wisconsin and was then taken by ambulance to a hospital in Red Wing, Minn., where he languished for several weeks before dying, Minnesota's interest in ensuring that its medical creditors were paid would be obvious. Moreover, under such circumstances, the accident itself might be reasonably characterized as a bi-state occurrence beginning in Wisconsin and ending in Minnesota. Thus, reliance by the insurer that Wisconsin law would necessarily govern any accident that occurred in Wisconsin, or that the law of another jurisdiction would necessarily govern any accident that did not occur in Wisconsin, would be unwarranted. See n. 11, *supra;* cf. *Rosenthal v. Warren,* 475 F. 2d 438 (CA2), cert. denied, 414 U. S. 856 (1973) (Massachusetts hospital could not have purchased insurance with expectation that Massachusetts law would govern damage recovery as to New York patient who died in hospital and whose widow brought suit in New York).

If the law of a jurisdiction other than Wisconsin did govern, there was a substantial likelihood, with respect to uninsured motorist coverage, that stacking would be allowed. Stacking was the rule in most States at the time the policy was issued. Indeed, the Wisconsin Supreme Court, in *Nelson v. Employers Mutual Casualty Co.,* 63 Wis. 2d 558, 563–566, and nn. 2–3, 217 N.W.2d 670, 672–674, and nn. 2–3 (1974), identified 29 States, including Minnesota, whose law it interpreted to allow stacking, and only 9 States whose law it interpreted to prohibit stacking. Clearly then, Allstate could not have expected that an anti-stacking rule would govern any particular accident in which the insured might be involved and thus cannot claim unfair surprise from the Minnesota Supreme Court's choice of forum law.

[23] The Court has recognized that examination of a State's contacts may result in divergent conclusions for jurisdiction and choice-of-law purposes. See *Kulko v. Superior Court,* 436 U.S. 84, 98 (1978) (no jurisdiction in California but California law "arguably might" apply); *Shaffer v. Heitner, supra,* 433 U.S., at 215 (no jurisdiction in Delaware, although Delaware interest "may support the application of Delaware law"); cf. *Hanson v. Denckla,* 357 U.S. 235, 254, and n. 27 (1958) (no jurisdiction in Florida; the "issue is personal jurisdiction, not choice of law," an issue which the Court found no need to decide). Nevertheless, "both inquiries 'are often closely related and to a substantial degree depend upon similar considerations.' " 433 U.S., at 224–225 (BRENNAN, J., concurring in part and dissenting in part).

surprise that the state courts might apply forum law to litigation in which the company is involved. "Particularly since the company was licensed to do business in [the forum], it must have known it might be sued there, and that [the forum] courts would feel bound by [forum] law."[24] *Clay v. Sun Insurance Office Limited, [I]* (Black, J., dissenting).[25] Moreover, Allstate's presence in Minnesota gave Minnesota an interest in regulating the company's insurance obligations insofar as they affected both a Minnesota resident and court appointed representative—respondent—and a longstanding member of Minnesota's workforce—Mr. Hague. See *Hoopeston Canning Co. v. Cullen*, 318 U. S. 313, 316 (1943).

Third, respondent became a Minnesota resident prior to institution of this litigation. The stipulated facts reveal that she first settled in Red Wing, Minn., the town in which her late husband had worked.[26] She subsequently moved to Savage, Minn., after marrying a Minnesota resident who operated an automobile service station in Bloomington, Minn. Her move to Savage occurred "almost concurrently," 289 N. W. 2d, at 45, with the initiation of the instant case.[27] There is no suggestion that Mrs. Hague moved to Minnesota in anticipation of this litigation or for the purpose of finding a legal climate especially hospitable to her claim.[28] The stipulated facts, sparse as they are, negate any such inference.

While *John Hancock Mutual Life Insurance Company v. Yates, supra,* held that a postoccurrence change of residence to the forum State was insufficient in and of itself to confer power on the forum State to choose its law, that case did not hold that such a change of residence was irrelevant. Here, of course, respondent's bona fide residence in Minnesota was not the sole contact Minnesota had with this litigation. And in connection with her residence in Minnesota, respondent was appointed personal representative of Mr. Hague's estate by the Registrar of Probate for the County of Goodhue, Minn. Respondent's residence and subsequent appointment in Minnesota as personal representative of her late husband's estate constitute a Minnesota contact which gives Minnesota an interest in respondent's recovery, an interest which the court below

---

Here, of course, jurisdiction in the Minnesota courts is unquestioned, a factor not without significance in assessing the constitutionality of Minnesota's choice of its own substantive law. Cf. *id.,* at 225 ("the decision that it is fair to bind a defendant by a State's laws and rules should prove to be highly relevant to the fairness of permitting that same State to accept jurisdiction for adjudicating the controversy").

[24] There is no element of unfair surprise or frustration of legitimate expectations as a result of Minnesota's choice of its law. Because Allstate was doing business in Minnesota and was undoubtedly aware that Mr. Hague was a Minnesota employee, it had to have anticipated that Minnesota law might apply to an accident in which Mr. Hague was involved. See *Clay II; Watson v. Employers Liability Assurance Corp.; Alaska Packers Assn. v. Industrial Accident Commission;* cf. *Home Insurance Co. v. Dick,* (neither insurer nor reinsurer present in forum State). Indeed, Allstate specifically anticipated that Mr. Hague might suffer an accident either in Minnesota or elsewhere in the United States, outside of Wisconsin, since the policy it issued offered continental coverage. Cf. *id.,* at 403 (coverage limited to losses occurring in certain Mexican waters which were outside of jurisdiction whose law was applied). At the same time, Allstate did not seek to control construction of the contract since the policy contained no choice-of-law clause dictating application of Wisconsin law. See *Clay II* (nationwide coverage of policy and lack of choice-of-law clause).

[25] Mr. Justice Black's dissent in the first *Clay* decision, a decision which vacated and remanded a lower court determination to obtain an authoritative construction of state law that might moot the constitutional question, subsequently commanded majority support in the second *Clay* decision. *Clay II.*

[26] The stipulated facts do not reveal the date on which Mrs. Hague first moved to Red Wing.

[27] These proceedings began on May 28, 1976. Mrs. Hague was remarried on June 19, 1976.

[28] The dissent suggests that considering respondent's postoccurrence change of residence as one of the Minnesota contacts will encourage forum shopping. *Post,* at [416]. This overlooks the fact that her change of residence was bona fide and not motivated by litigation considerations.

identified as full compensation for "resident accident victims" to keep them "off welfare rolls" and able "to meet financial obligations," 289 N. W. 2d., at 49.

In sum, Minnesota had a significant aggregation[29] of contacts with the parties and the occurrence, creating state interests, such that application of its law was neither arbitrary not fundamentally unfair. Accordingly, the choice of Minnesota law by the Minnesota Supreme Court did not violate the Due Process Clause or the Full Faith and Credit Clause.

Affirmed.

JUSTICE STEWART took no part in the consideration or decision of this case.

JUSTICE STEVENS, concurring in the judgment.

As I view this unusual case—in which neither precedent nor constitutional language provides sure guidance—two separate questions must be answered. First, does the Full Faith and Credit Clause *require* Minnesota, the forum State, to apply Wisconsin law? Second, does the Due Process Clause of the Fourteenth Amendment *prevent* Minnesota from applying its own law? The first inquiry implicates the federal interest in ensuring that Minnesota respect the sovereignty of the State of Wisconsin; the second implicates the litigants' interest in a fair adjudication of their rights.

I realize that both this Court's analysis of choice-of-law questions[4] and scholarly criticism of those decisions have treated these two inquiries as though they were indistinguishable. Nevertheless, I am persuaded that the two constitutional provisions protect different interests and that proper analysis requires separate consideration of each.

I

The Full Faith and Credit Clause is one of several provisions in the Federal Constitution designed to transform the several States from independent sovereignties into a single, unified Nation. The Full Faith and Credit Clause implements this design by directing that a State, when acting as the forum for litigation having multistate aspects or implications, respect the legitimate interests of other States and avoid infringement upon their sovereignty. The Clause does not, however, rigidly require the forum State to apply foreign law whenever another State has a valid interest in the litigation. See *Nevada v. Hall; Alaska Packers Assn. v. Industrial Accident Comm'n; Pacific Employers Insurance Co. v. Industrial Accident Comm'n.*[8] On the contrary, in view of

---

[29] We express no view whether the first two contacts, either together or separately, would have sufficed to sustain the choice of Minnesota law made by the Minnesota Supreme Court.

[4] Although the Court has struck down a state court's choice of forum law on both due process, see, *e. g., Home Insurance Co. v. Dick,* and full faith and credit grounds, see, *e. g., John Hancock Insurance Co. v. Yates,* no clear analytical distinction between the two constitutional provisions has emerged. The Full Faith and Credit Clause, of course, was inapplicable in *Home Insurance* because the law of a foreign nation, rather than of a sister State, was at issue; a similarly clear explanation for the Court's reliance upon the Full Faith and Credit Clause in *John Hancock Insurance* cannot be found. Indeed, *John Hancock Insurance* is probably best understood as a due process case. See Reese, *supra,* 78 Colum. L. Rev., at 1589, and n. 17; Weintraub, *Due Process and Full Faith and Credit Limitations on a State's Choice of Law,* 44 Iowa L. Rev. 449, 457–458 (1959).

[8] As the Court observed in *Alaska Packers, supra,* an overly rigid application of the Full Faith and Credit Clause would produce anomalous results:

A rigid and literal enforcement of the full faith and credit clause, without regard to the statute of the forum, would lead to the absurd result that, wherever the conflict arises, the statute of each state must be enforced in the courts of the other, but cannot be in its own.

294 U. S., at 547.

the fact that the forum State is also a sovereign in its own right, in appropriate cases it may attach paramount importance to its own legitimate interests.[9] Accordingly, the fact that a choice-of-law decision may be unsound as a matter of conflicts law does not necessarily implicate the federal concerns embodied in the Full Faith and Credit Clause. Rather, in my opinion, the Clause should not invalidate a state court's choice of forum law unless that choice threatens the federal interest in national unity by unjustifiably infringing upon the legitimate interests of another State.

In this case, I think the Minnesota courts' decision to apply Minnesota law was plainly unsound as a matter of normal conflicts law. Both the execution of the insurance contract and the accident giving rise to the litigation took place in Wisconsin. Moreover, when both of those events occurred, the plaintiff, the decedent, and the operators of both vehicles were all residents of Wisconsin. Nevertheless, I do not believe that any threat to national unity or Wisconsin's sovereignty ensues from allowing the substantive question presented by this case to be determined by the law of another State.

The question on the merits is one of interpreting the meaning of the insurance contract. Neither the contract itself, nor anything else in the record, reflects any express understanding of the parties with respect to what law would be applied or with respect to whether the separate uninsured motorist coverage for each of the decedent's three cars could be "stacked." Since the policy provided coverage for accidents that might occur in other States, it was obvious to the parties at the time of contracting that it might give rise to the application of the law of States other than Wisconsin. Therefore, while Wisconsin may have an interest in ensuring that contracts formed in Wisconsin in reliance upon Wisconsin law are interpreted in accordance with that law, that interest is not implicated in this case.

Petitioner has failed to establish that Minnesota's refusal to apply Wisconsin law poses any direct or indirect threat to Wisconsin's sovereignty. In the absence of any such threat, I find it unnecessary to evaluate the forum State's interest in the litigation in order to reach the conclusion that the Full Faith and Credit Clause does not require the Minnesota courts to apply Wisconsin law to the question of contract interpretation presented in this case.

II

It may be assumed that a choice-of-law decision would violate the Due Process Clause if it were totally arbitrary or if it were fundamentally unfair to either litigant. I question whether a judge's decision to apply the law of his own State could ever be described as wholly irrational. For judges are presumably familiar with their own state law and may find it difficult and time consuming to discover and apply correctly the law of another State. The forum State's interest in the fair and efficient administration of justice is therefore sufficient, in my judgment, to attach a presumption of validity to a forum State's decision to apply its own law to a dispute over which it has jurisdiction.

The forum State's interest in the efficient operation of its judicial system is clearly not sufficient, however, to justify the application of a rule of law that is fundamentally unfair to one of the litigants. Arguably, a litigant could demonstrate such unfairness in a variety of ways. Concern about the fairness of the forum's choice of its own rule might arise if that rule favored

---

[9] For example, it is well established that "the Full Faith and Credit Clause does not require a State to apply another State's law in violation of its own legitimate public policy." *Nevada v. Hall,* 440 U. S. 410, 422 (1979) (footnote omitted).

residents over nonresidents, if it represented a dramatic departure from the rule that obtains in most American jurisdictions, or if the rule itself was unfair on its face or as applied.[15]

The application of an otherwise acceptable rule of law may result in unfairness to the litigants if, in engaging in the activity which is the subject of the litigation, they could not reasonably have anticipated that their actions would later be judged by this rule of law. A choice-of-law decision that frustrates the justifiable expectations of the parties can be fundamentally unfair. This desire to prevent unfair surprise to a litigant has been the central concern in this Court's review of choice-of-law decisions under the Due Process Clause.[16]

Neither the "stacking" rule itself, nor Minnesota's application of that rule to these litigants, raises any serious question of fairness. As the plurality observes, "[s]tacking was the rule in most States at the time the policy was issued." Moreover, the rule is consistent with the economics of a contractual relationship in which the policyholder paid three separate premiums for insurance coverage for three automobiles, including a separate premium for each uninsured motorist coverage.[18] Nor am I persuaded that the decision of the Minnesota courts to apply the "stacking" rule in this case can be said to violate due process because that decision frustrates the reasonable expectations of the contracting parties.

Contracting parties can, of course, make their expectations explicit by providing in their contract either that the law of a particular jurisdiction shall govern questions of contract interpretation,[19] or that a particular substantive rule, for instance "stacking," shall or shall not apply.[20] In the absence of such express provisions, the contract nonetheless may implicitly reveal

---

[15] Discrimination against nonresidents would be constitutionally suspect even if the Due Process Clause were not a check upon a State's choice-of-law decisions. See Currie & Schreter, *Unconstitutional Discrimination in the Conflict of Laws: Equal Protection,* 28 U. Chi. L. Rev. 1 (1960); Currie & Schreter, *Unconstitutional Discrimination in the Conflict of Laws: Privileges and Immunities,* 69 Yale L. J. 1323 (1960); Note, *Unconstitutional Discrimination in Choice of Law,* 77 Colum. L. Rev. 272 (1977). Moreover, both discriminatory and substantively unfair rules of law may be detected and remedied without any special choice-of-law analysis; familiar constitutional principles are available to deal with both varieties of unfairness. See *e. g.,* Martin, *Constitutional Limitations on Choice of Law,* 61 Corn. L. Rev. 185, 199 (1976).

[16] Upon careful analysis, most of the decisions of this Court that struck down on due process grounds a state court's choice of forum law can be explained as attempts to prevent a State with a minimal contact with the litigation from materially enlarging the contractual obligations of one of the parties where that party had no reason to anticipate the possibility of such enlargement. See, *e. g., Home Insurance Co. v. Dick; Hartford Accident & Indemnity Co. v. Delta & Pine Land Co.;* cf. *John Hancock Insurance Co. v. Yates* (similar concern under Full Faith and Credit Clause, see n. 11, *supra*). See generally Weintraub, *supra,* 44 Iowa L. Rev., at 457–460.

[18] The "stacking" rule provides that all of the uninsured motorist coverage purchased by an insured party may be aggregated, or "stacked," to create a fund available to provide a recovery for a single accident.

[19] For example, in *Home Insurance Co. v. Dick,* 281 U. S. 397, 403, and n. 1 (1930), the insurance policy was subject, by its express terms, to Mexican law.

[20] *Home Insurance Co., supra,* again provides a useful example. In that case, the insurance policy expressly provided a one-year limitations period for claims arising thereunder. 281 U. S., at 403. Similarly, the insurance policy at issue in *Hartford Accident & Indemnity Co. v. Delta & Pine Land Co.,* 292 U. S. 143, 146 (1934), also prescribed a specific limitations period.

While such express provisions are obviously relevant, they are not always dispositive. In *Clay v. Sun Insurance Office, Ltd.,* the Court allowed the lower court's choice of forum law to override an express contractual limitations period. The Court emphasized the fact that the insurer had issued the insurance policy with the knowledge that it would cover the insured property wherever it was taken. The Court also noted that the insurer had not attempted to provide in the policy that the law of another State would control.

In *Watson v. Employers Liability Corp.,* 348 U. S. 66, 68 (1954), the insurance policy expressly provided that an

the expectations of the parties. For example, if a liability insurance policy issued by a resident of a particular State provides coverage only with respect to accidents within that State, it is reasonable to infer that the contracting parties expected that their obligations under the policy would be governed by that State's law.[21]

In this case, no express indication of the parties' expectations is available. The insurance policy provided coverage for accidents throughout the United States; thus, at the time of contracting, the parties certainly could have anticipated that the law of States other than Wisconsin would govern particular claims arising under the policy. By virtue of doing business in Minnesota, Allstate was aware that it could be sued in the Minnesota courts; Allstate also presumably was aware that Minnesota law, as well as the law of most States, permitted "stacking." Nothing in the record requires that a different inference be drawn. Therefore, the decision of the Minnesota courts to apply the law of the forum in this case does not frustrate the reasonable expectations of the contracting parties, and I can find no fundamental unfairness in that decision requiring the attention of this Court.[23]

In terms of fundamental fairness, it seems to me that two factors relied upon by the plurality—the plaintiff's post-accident move to Minnesota and the decedent's Minnesota employment—are either irrelevant to or possibly even tend to undermine the plurality's conclusion. When the expectations of the parties at the time of contracting are the central due process concern, as they are in this case, an unanticipated post-accident occurrence is clearly irrelevant for due process purposes. The fact that the plaintiff became a resident of the forum State after the accident surely cannot justify a ruling in her favor that would not be made if the plaintiff were a nonresident. Similarly, while the fact that the decedent regularly drove into Minnesota might be relevant to the expectations of the contracting parties,[24] the fact that he did so because he was employed

---

injured party could not maintain a direct action against the insurer until after the insured's liability had been determined. The Court found that neither the Due Process Clause nor the Full Faith and Credit Clause prevented the Louisiana courts from applying forum law to permit a direct action against the insurer prior to determination of the insured's liability. As in *Clay,* the Court noted that the policy provided coverage for injuries anywhere in the United States. 348 U. S., at 71–72. An additional, although unarticulated, factor in *Watson* was the fact that the litigant urging that forum law be applied was not a party to the insurance contract. While contracting parties may be able to provide in advance that a particular rule of law will govern disputes between them, their expectations are clearly entitled to less weight when the rights of third party litigants are at issue.

[21] In *Home Insurance Co., supra,* the insurance policy was issued in Mexico by a Mexican corporation and covered the insured vessel only in certain Mexican waters.

[23] Comparison of this case with *Home Insurance Co. v. Dick,* 281 U. S. 397 (1930), confirms my conclusion that the application of Minnesota law in this case does not offend the Due Process Clause. In *Home Insurance Co.,* the contract expressly provided that a particular limitations period would govern claims arising under the insurance contract and that Mexican law was to be applied in interpreting the contract; in addition, the contract was limited in effect to certain Mexican waters. The parties could hardly have made their expectations with respect to the applicable law more plain. In this case, by way of contrast, nothing in the contract suggests that Wisconsin law should be applied or that Minnesota's "stacking" rule should not be applied. In this case, unlike *Home Insurance Co.,* the court's choice of forum law results in no unfair surprise to the insurer.

[24] Even this factor may not be of substantial significance. At the time of contracting, the parties were aware that the insurance policy was effective throughout the United States and that the law of any State, including Minnesota, might be applicable to particular claims. The fact that the decedent regularly drove to Minnesota, for whatever purpose, is relevant only to the extent that it affected the parties' evaluation, at the time of contracting, of the likelihood that Minnesota law would actually be applied at some point in the future. However, because the applicability of Minnesota law was perceived as possible at the time of contracting, it does not seem especially significant for due process purposes that the parties may also have considered it likely that Minnesota law would be applied. This factor merely reinforces the expectation revealed by the policy's national coverage.

in Minnesota adds nothing to the due process analysis. The choice-of-law decision of the Minnesota courts is consistent with due process because it does not result in unfairness to either litigant, not because Minnesota now has an interest in the plaintiff as resident or formerly had an interest in the decedent as employee.

III

Although I regard the Minnesota courts' decision to apply forum law as unsound as a matter of conflicts law, and there is little in this record other than the presumption in favor of the forum's own law to support that decision, I concur in the plurality's judgment. It is not this Court's function to establish and impose upon state courts a federal choice-of-law rule, nor is it our function to ensure that state courts correctly apply whatever choice-of-law rules they have themselves adopted. Our authority may be exercised in the choice-of-law area only to prevent a violation of the Full Faith and Credit or the Due Process Clause. For the reasons stated above, I find no such violation in this case.

JUSTICE POWELL, with whom THE CHIEF JUSTICE and JUSTICE REHNQUIST join, dissenting.

My disagreement with the majority is narrow. I accept with few reservations Part II of the majority opinion, which sets forth the basic principles that guide us in reviewing state choice-of-law decisions under the Constitution. The Court should invalidate a forum State's decision to apply its own law only when there are no significant contacts between the State and the litigation. This modest check on state power is mandated by the Due Process Clause of the Fourteenth Amendment and the Full Faith and Credit Clause of Art. 4, § 1. I do not believe, however, that the Court adequately analyzes the policies such review must serve. In consequence, it has found significant what appear to me to be trivial contacts between the forum State and the litigation.

I

At least since *Carroll v. Lanza,* 349 U. S. 408 (1955), the Court has recognized that both the Due Process and the Full Faith and Credit Clauses are satisfied if the forum has such significant contacts with the litigation that it has a legitimate state interest in applying its own law. The significance of asserted contacts must be evaluated in light of the constitutional policies that oversight by this Court should serve. Two enduring policies emerge from our cases.

First, the contacts between the forum State and the litigation should not be so "slight and casual" that it would be fundamentally unfair to a litigant for the forum to apply its own State's law. . . .

Second, the forum State must have a legitimate interest in the outcome of the litigation before it. . . . [F]or a forum State to further its legitimate public policy by applying its own law to a controversy, there must be some connection between the facts giving rise to the litigation and the scope of the State's lawmaking jurisdiction.

Both the Due Process and Full Faith and Credit Clauses ensure that the States do not "reach out beyond the limits imposed on them by their status as coequal sovereigns in a federal system." *World-Wide Volkswagen Corp. v. Woodson* [p. 531, *infra*] (addressing Fourteenth Amendment limitations on state court jurisdiction). As the Court stated in *Pacific Ins. Co., supra:* "[T]he full faith and credit clause does not require one state to substitute for its own statute, *applicable to persons and events within it,* the conflicting statute of another state." *Id.,* at 502 (emphasis added). The State has a legitimate interest in applying a rule of decision to the litigation only if the facts to which the rule will be applied have created effects within the State, toward which the State's public policy is directed. To assess the sufficiency of asserted contacts between the forum and the litigation, the Court must determine if the contacts form a reasonable link between the litigation and a state policy. In short, examination of contacts addresses whether "the state has an interest in the application of its policy in this instance." Currie, *The Constitution and Choice of Law; Governmental Interests and the Judicial Function,* in B. Currie, *Selected Essays on the Conflict of Laws* 188, 189 (1963). If it does, the Constitution is satisfied.

John Hancock Mut. Life Ins. Co. v. Yates, 299 U. S. 178 (1936), illustrates this principle. A life insurance policy was executed in New York, on a New York insured with a New York beneficiary. The insured died in New York; his beneficiary moved to Georgia and sued to recover on the policy. The insurance company defended on the ground that the insured, in the application for the policy, had made materially false statements that rendered it void under New York law. This Court reversed the Georgia court's application of its contrary rule that all questions of the policy's validity must be determined by the jury. The Court found a violation of the Full Faith and Credit Clause, because "[i]n respect to the accrual of the right asserted under the contract . . . there was no occurrence, nothing done, to which the law of Georgia could apply." In other words, the Court determined that Georgia had no legitimate interest in applying its own law to the legal issue of liability. Georgia's contacts with the contract of insurance were nonexistent. See *Home Ins. Co. v. Dick.*

In summary, the significance of the contacts between a forum State and the litigation must be assessed in light of these two important constitutional policies.[3] A contact, or a pattern of contacts, satisfies the Constitution when it protects the litigants from being unfairly surprised if the forum State applies its own law, and when the application of the forum's law reasonably can be understood to further a legitimate public policy of the forum State.

II

Recognition of the complexity of the constitutional inquiry requires that this Court apply these principles with restraint. Applying these principles to the facts of this case, I do not believe, however, that Minnesota had sufficient contacts with the "persons and events" in this litigation to apply its rule permitting stacking. I would agree that no reasonable expectations of the parties were frustrated. The risk insured by petitioner was not geographically limited. See *Clay v. Sun Ins. Office, Ltd., supra,* 377 U. S., at 182. The close proximity of Hager City, Wis. to Minnesota, and the fact that Hague commuted daily to Red Wing, Minn., for many years should have led the insurer to realize that there was a reasonable probability that the risk would materialize in Minnesota. Under our precedents, it is plain that Minnesota could have applied its own law to an accident occurring within its borders. The fact that the accident did not, in fact, occur in Minnesota is not controlling because the expectations of the litigants *before* the cause of action accrues provide the pertinent perspective.

The more doubtful question in this case is whether application of Minnesota's substantive law reasonably furthers a legitimate state interest. The Court attempts to give substance to the tenuous

---

[3] The Court today apparently recognizes that the significance of the contacts must be evaluated in light of the policies our review serves. It acknowledges that the sufficiency of the same contacts sometimes will differ in jurisdiction and choice-of-law questions. The Court, however, pursues the rationale for the requirement of sufficient contacts in choice-of-law cases no further than to observe that the forum's application of its own law must be "neither arbitrary nor fundamentally unfair." But this general prohibition does not distinguish questions of choice of law from those of jurisdiction, or from much of the jurisprudence of the Fourteenth Amendment.

contacts between Minnesota and this litigation. Upon examination, however, these contacts are either trivial or irrelevant to the furthering of any public policy of Minnesota.

First, the post-accident residence of the plaintiff-beneficiary is constitutionally irrelevant to the choice-of-law question. *John Hancock Mut. Life Ins. Co. v. Yates, supra.* The Court today insists that *Yates* only held that a post-occurrence move to the forum State could not "in and of itself" confer power on the forum to apply its own law, but did not establish that such a change of residence was irrelevant. What the *Yates* Court held, however, was that "there was no occurrence, *nothing* done, to which the law of Georgia could apply." 229 U. S., at 182 (emphasis added). Any possible ambiguity in the Court's view of the significance of a post-occurrence change of residence is dispelled by *Home Ins. Co. v. Dick,* cited by the *Yates* Court, where it was held squarely that Dick's post-accident move to the forum State was "without significance."

This rule is sound. If a plaintiff could choose the substantive rules to be applied to an action by moving to a hospitable forum, the invitation to forum shopping would be irresistable. Moreover, it would permit the defendant's reasonable expectations at the time the cause of action accrues to be frustrated, because it would permit the choice-of-law question to turn on a post-accrual circumstance. Finally, post-accrual residence has nothing to do with facts to which the forum State proposes to apply its rule; it is unrelated to the substantive legal issues presented by the litigation.

Second, the Court finds it significant that the insurer does business in the forum State. The State does have a legitimate interest in regulating the practices of such an insurer. But this argument proves too much. The insurer here does business in all 50 States. The forum State has no interest in regulating that conduct of the insurer unrelated to property, persons or contracts executed within the forum State.[4] The Court recognizes this flaw and attempts to bolster the significance of the local presence of the insurer by combining it with the other factors deemed significant: the presence of the plaintiff and the fact that the deceased worked in the forum State. This merely restates the basic question in the case.

Third, the Court emphasizes particularly that the insured worked in the forum State.[5] The fact that the insured was a nonresident employee in the forum State provides a significant contact for the furtherance of some local policies. See, *e. g., Pacific Ins. Co. v. Industrial Accident Comm'n; Alaska Packers Assn. v. Industrial Accident Comm'n.* The insured's place of employment is not, however, significant in this case. Neither the nature of the insurance policy, the events related to the accident, nor the immediate question of stacking coverage are in any way

---

[4] The petitioner in *John Hancock Mut. Life Ins. Co. v. Yates, supra,* did business in Georgia, the forum State, at the time of that case. See *The Insurance Almanac,* 715 (1935). Also, Georgia extensively regulated insurance practices within the State at that time. See Georgia Code § 56–101 *et seq.* (1933). This Court did not hint in *Yates* that this fact was of the slightest significance to the choice-of-law question, although it would have been crucial for the exercise of *in personam* jurisdiction.

[5] The Court exacts double service from this fact, by finding a separate contact in that the insured commuted daily to his job. This is merely a repetition of the facts that the insured lived in Wisconsin and worked in Minnesota. The State does have an interest in the safety of motorists who use its roads. This interest is not limited to employees, but extends to all nonresident motorists on its highways. This safety interest, however, cannot encompass, either in logic or in any practical sense, the determination whether a nonresident's estate can stack benefit coverage in a policy written in another State regarding an accident that occurred on another State's roads.

Cardillo v. Liberty Mutual Co., 330 U. S. 469 (1947), hardly establishes commutation as an independent contact; the case merely approved the application of a forum State's law to an industrial accident occurring in a neighboring State when the employer and the employee both resided in the forum State.

affected or implicated by the insured's employment status. The Court's opinion is understandably vague in explaining how trebling the benefits to be paid to the estate of a nonresident employee furthers any substantial state interest relating to employment. Minnesota does not wish its workers to die in automobile accidents, but permitting stacking will not further this interest. The substantive issue here is solely one of compensation, and whether the compensation provided by this policy is increased or not will have no relation to the State's employment policies or police power. See n. 5, *supra.*

Neither taken separately nor in the aggregate do the contacts asserted by the Court today indicate that Minnesota's application of its substantive rule in this case will further any legitimate state interest.[6] The Court focuses only on physical contacts *vel non,* and in doing so pays scant attention to the more fundamental reasons why our precedents require reasonably policy-related contacts in choice-of-law cases. Therefore, I dissent.

NOTES AND QUESTIONS[f]

(1)(a) Do you think *Hague* was correctly decided, or are you disappointed?

(b) If you are satisfied with the result, are you persuaded by Justice Brennan's plurality opinion? by Justice Stevens' concurrence? or would you have written a still different opinion? How do you think Justice Black would have come out? How about Justice Stone?

(c) If you are dissatisfied with the result, do you believe Justice Powell's dissent, with two more votes, would have made a satisfactory majority opinion? Could you have done better?

(2)(a) Note that Justice Brennan and Justice Powell agree that for a Minnesota court to apply Minnesota law there must be some level of contacts, or affiliating circumstances, between the parties or the event and the forum state. They both say that they approve of *Home Insurance v. Dick,* but Justice Powell says *Hague* is like *Dick,* while Justice Brennan says it is different. What are the differences?

(b) Both Justice Brennan and Justice Powell discuss at some length a case not so far mentioned in the Chapter, *John Hancock Mut. Life Ins. Co. v. Yates,* 299 U.S. 178 (1936). In that case a New York resident had bought life insurance in New York and had answered "no" to a question on the application whether he had recently been under a doctor's care. In fact he was under treatment for cancer, of which he died within a month of taking out the policy. Justice Brennan calls the case an extreme example of selection of forum law, quite different from *Hague.* Justice Powell implies that *Yates* is not so different from *Hague*—i.e., in both cases the forum state "has no legitimate interest in applying its own law to the issue of legal liability." (p. 415). Granting that *Yates* was correctly decided, is *Hague* similar, or decisively different?

---

[6] The opinion of JUSTICE STEVENS, concurring, supports my view that the forum State's application of its own law to this case cannot be justified by the existence of relevant minimum contacts. As JUSTICE STEVENS observes, the principal factors relied on by the Court are "either irrelevant or possibly even tend to undermine the [Court's] conclusion." The interesting analysis he proposes to uphold the State's judgment is, however, difficult to reconcile with our prior decisions and may create more problems than it solves. For example, it seems questionable to measure the interest of a State in a controversy by the degree of conscious reliance on that State's law by private parties to a contract. *Ante* at [413]. Moreover, scrutinizing the strength of the interests of a nonforum State may draw this Court back into the discredited practice of weighing the relative interests of various States in a particular controversy.

[f] The present author acted as counsel for Mrs. Hague in the Supreme Court, and his own articles cited in these notes reflect that position. The effort here, however, is to present all sides of the question as impartially as possible.

(c) One of the points stressed in the Supreme Court on behalf of Mrs. Hague was that Allstate not only was suable in Minnesota, but in fact had sold some 100,000 insurance policies in that state. Justice White asked whether the contention was being made that there could never be a choice of law problem rising to the level of constitutional infirmity when judicial jurisdiction was as clear as in this case. How should counsel for Mrs. Hague reply?[g]

(d) One of the major criticisms of the decision in *Hague,* both by Justice Powell and in the law reviews,[h] is that events after the accident were counted by the Court in its aggregation of contacts. Thus *Hague* is in some sense like *Miller v. Miller,*[i] the case in which the two brothers were driving together in the Maine brother's car, and the Maine brother moves to New York after the accident but before the New York brother's widow brings suit. Absent fraudulent or spurious change of domicile, what constitutional principle is involved in this question?

(3)(a) Justice Stevens agrees with Justice Powell that the contacts between plaintiff's claim and the forum state were trivial or irrelevant. He also thinks that the Minnesota courts' decision to apply Minnesota law was "plainly unsound" as a matter of normal conflicts law. Why then does he vote to affirm? Is he saying that the issue is unimportant because Wisconsin had no real interest? Or because the national interest was not engaged? What kind of a case do you suppose would lead Justice Stevens to overturn a state court choice-of-law decision?

(b) Suppose Mr. and Mrs. Hague lived on the other side of Minnesota, in Fargo, North Dakota. Mr. Hague was riding as a passenger in a car driven and owned by his friend Mr. Brussels, also a resident of Fargo. Both Mr. Hague and Mr. Brussels worked across the river in Moorehead, Minnesota, but on the day of the fatal accident, Brussels and Hague were driving in North Dakota when Brussels, apparently through carelessness, lost control of his vehicle, resulting in the death of Mr. Hague. Mrs. Hague thereafter moved to Minnesota to live with her son, and also was appointed administratrix of her late husband's estate. When she brought suit in a Minnesota court, serving Mr. Brussels at his place of work, Brussels defended on the basis of the North Dakota guest statute.[j] The Minnesota court rejected the defense, on the ground that guest statutes are unjust and antiquated, and that Mrs. Hague's Minnesota domicile plus her role as administratrix of a Minnesota estate justified application of Minnesota's purer and more progressive law. The case, in other words, is very much like the actual case, except that no contract is involved and the insurance company is in the background. Would Justice Stevens view *Hague v. Brussels* just like *Hague v. Allstate*—no real interest of North Dakota and no national interest engaged? Or do you think the hypothetical case surpasses Justice Stevens' threshold of unfairness?

(c) In the course of the oral argument, counsel for Allstate was asked whether his arguments would be the same if the accident had happened a few miles away in Minnesota. How should

---

[g] Note that Justice Brennan says, in footnote 23, that the fact that Minnesota's jurisdiction was here unquestioned is "a factor that is not without significance."

[h] The law professors had a field day. Not since *Babcock v. Jackson* had there been so many articles and symposia in the law reviews, but unlike the reviews of *Babcock,* the reviews of *Hague* were more unfavorable than favorable. See, e.g., Symposium: *Choice of Law,* 14 U.C. Davis L. Rev. 837 (1981); Symposium: *Choice-of-Law Theory after Allstate Insurance Co. v. Hague,* 10 Hofstra L. Rev. 1 (1981); *A Response to the Hague Symposium,* 10 Hofstra L. Rev. 973 (1982); Hill, *Choice of Law and Jurisdiction in the Supreme Court,* 81 Colum. L. Rev. 960 (1981); Brilmayer, *Legitimate Interests in Multistate Problems: As Between State and Federal Law,* 79 Mich. L. Rev. 1315 (1981).

[i] Chapter 3, page 171, question (6).

[j] The hypothetical case is anachronistic by a few months. The accident in *Hague* occurred on July 1, 1974. On March 29, 1974, the Supreme Court of North Dakota declared that state's guest statute, N.D. Cent. Code § 39–15–§01 to–§03 invalid under the state constitution. *Johnson v. Hassett,* 217 N.W.2d 771 (N.D. 1974).

he answer? Is Allstate's case hopeless with that additional contact? Or is the issue still the same—construing a contract made in Wisconsin by a Wisconsin domiciliary in contemplation of Wisconsin law?

(d) Counsel for Mrs. Hague was asked, what if the contract had contained an express choice-of-Wisconsin law clause, and the Minnesota court had disregarded it? Would that be more arbitrary than the actual case?

(e) One more point about Justice Stevens' opinion: Whereas both Justice Brennan and Justice Powell think there is one constitutional question, Justice Stevens thinks there are two—one under the Full Faith and Credit clause, the other under the Due Process clause. Recall Justice Stone's statements in *Alaska Packers* and *Pacific Employers* that if F–2 has an interest that meets due process standards, full faith and credit to F–1's statutes cannot trump it. In what circumstances could due process be satisfied, yet F–2's choice of law fall as in violation of the Full Faith and Credit clause?[k]

Incidentally, we have seen that the few cases, primarily in the workers' compensation area, that have discussed the Full Faith and Credit clause in the choice of law context refer to the provision in Article IV about "Public Acts," which, the argument was, includes statutes. Could there be full faith and credit to a common law decision of other states, such as was involved here?

(4)(a) Coming back to the plurality opinion, Justice Brennan concludes that while taken one at a time none of the contacts he cites might be sufficient to support application of Minnesota law, the relevant question is whether *together* the contacts are sufficient. Isn't that the way other—non-constitutional—contact-counting is done for choice-of-law (as well as for judicial jurisdiction) purposes? Why should the method be different here?

(b) Commenting on the plurality opinion in *Hague,* Professor Hill writes:

> Uncritical aggregation is especially dangerous in the context of choice of law. If an individual contact is concededly inadequate, standing alone, it may be that, on grounds of sheer irrelevance, the contact has a value of zero. Such contacts add nothing to the aggregate, and there is even a danger that the aggregate will consist exclusively of such zero sum contacts.[l]

Is that a fair criticism of the opinion? Which (if any) of the contacts enumerated by Justice Brennan might be classed as of sheer irrelevance?

(c) Is playing the contact game—whether in terms of aggregation, or making small changes, as for instance in questions 3(b) and (c),—just beyond the capacity of the Supreme Court? Is it correct to say to the Court that once it starts down this path, it will have to hear as many choice-of-law cases as the New York Court of Appeals heard in the 1960's?[m]

(d) Perhaps the most interesting question in the oral argument of *Allstate v. Hague* was put to counsel for Mrs. Hague, who was suggesting that the Supreme Court ought not to become involved in this type of case, short of massive arbitrariness or discrimination. The Chief Justice asked, "Which do you think will be advanced by the approach you suggest . . . federalism or parochialism?" How should this question be answered—by an advocate, and by the Court itself?

---

[k] Recall that this question was asked once before, in discussing *Watson,* Question 4(c), p. 401, *supra.*

[l] Hill, *Choice of Law and Jurisdiction in the Supreme Court,* 81 Colum. L. Rev. 960 at 970 (1981).

[m] See, generally, Juenger, *Supreme Court Intervention in Jurisdiction and Choice of Law: A Dismal Prospect,* 14 U.C. Davis L. Rev. 907 (1981).

(5)(a) In a dialogue about the *Hague* case begun before and published shortly after the decision came down, Professors Lowenfeld and Silberman debated the appropriate role for the Supreme Court in the choice of law area, with Lowenfeld defending and Silberman regretting the outcome of the case. Silberman summed up:

> Perhaps our difference, then, does come down to a definition of fairness. . . . The plurality and dissent in *Hague* agree that a given choice of law is "fair" when it furthers a state interest; they disagree about which contacts are sufficient to support particular state interests. You say a case may be rightly or wrongly decided, but still may not be so unfair as to amount to arbitrary governmental action, which is the standard you require. I say that fairness includes in the present context a set of guidelines for choice of law decision-making, which will produce the kind of "substantial justice" that *International Shoe* taught us was demanded by the due process clause.[n]

Who has the better of this argument?

(b) Professor Reese regarded the *Hague* case as an "opportunity lost":

> Taken literally, the plurality and concurring opinions would indicate that the Supreme Court has withdrawn almost entirely from the choice-of-law field. This is to be regretted. . . . The *Hague* case offered the Court an occasion to adopt guidelines for determining what necessary federal limitations to impose upon the power of a state to apply its law to foreign facts. This was an opportunity lost. This was a backward step in the development of constitutional control of choice of law.[o]

Professor Lowenfeld responded:

> . . . I do not see the opportunity that [Reese] says was lost. Even Justice Story, who loved conflict of laws as he did the United States Constitution, never . . . cited the latter in support of his views of the former. We are not ready to constitutionalize choice of law in this country as we have done with so much of the rest of our law, and I doubt that we ever will be.[p]

Again, is Reese reading more into the Constitution than is there? Or is Lowenfeld underrating the power and duty to perform the umpiring function proposed by Mr. Madison in 1787?[q]

(c) The Court—both plurality and dissent—did not, of course, say that it was abandoning all supervision over choice of law by state courts. The lament of Reese and others stemmed only from the fact that what seemed to them like a strong case for reversal had not been reversed. Four years later, the Court did show that there was at least some room left for argument that a state court's choice of law was beyond the pale, in a context in which the principal controversy was about jurisdiction to adjudicate.

---

[n] Lowenfeld & Silberman, *Choice of Law and the Supreme Court,* 14 U.C. Davis L. Rev. 841, 868 (1981).

[o] Reese, *The Hague Case: An Opportunity Lost,* 10 Hofstra L. Rev. 195 at 201–02 (1981).

[p] Lowenfeld, *Three Might-Have-Beens: A Reaction to the Symposium on Allstate Insurance Co. v. Hague,* 10 Hofstra L. Rev. 1045 at 1048–49 (1981).

[q] See Question (1), p. 377, *supra.*

§ 5.04 The Supreme Court and Choice of Law after *Allstate v. Hague*

1. *Phillips Petroleum Co. v. Shutts,* 472 U.S. 797 (1985).

(a) The *Shutts* case was a complicated class action brought in Kansas on behalf some 33,000 "royalty owners" possessing rights to leases from which Phillips produced natural gas. Natural gas prices were controlled by the Federal Power Commission, but because proceedings before the Commission often took years to complete, gas producers were permitted to charge higher, unapproved rates during pendency of the proceedings, subject to an undertaking to make refunds to purchasers if the rate increases were disallowed. Phillips segregated the funds representing the unapproved rates, and did not pay royalties to the royalty owners on these sums until the rates were formally approved. The complaint was that during the interval, Phillips had use of the funds, but paid no interest thereon to the royalty owners. The 33,000 royalty owners in question were domiciled in all 50 states but predominantly in Texas and Oklahoma. Only 3 percent were domiciled in Kansas. Phillips moved to dismiss the action, arguing (i) that the Kansas court did not have jurisdiction over the absent class members, and (ii) that Kansas law should not be used to determine whether interest was due to the royalty owners and at what rate.

(b) The Kansas Supreme Court decided both issues in favor of plaintiffs, saying that in a nationwide class action where procedural due process guarantees of notice and adequate representation were met, "the laws of the forum should be applied unless compelling reasons exist for applying a different law."[a] Does that result seem sound in the light of *Hague*? Or does it take flexibility in choice of law one step too far?

(c) The U.S. Supreme Court upheld the jurisdiction of the Kansas court, on the ground that the members of the plaintiff class had been provided with adequate notice, opportunity to appear or to opt out, and legal representation. On choice of law, however, the Supreme Court reversed, with instructions to the Kansas court to reconsider the choice of law question in light of "constitutional limitations laid down in cases such as *Allstate* and *Home Insurance Co. v. Dick*."[b] Speaking for the Court, Justice Rehnquist wrote:

> . . . [W]hile a state may . . . assume jurisdiction over the claims of plaintiffs whose principal contacts are with other States, it may not use this assumption of jurisdiction as an added weight in the scale when considering the permissible constitutional limits on choice of substantive law. . . . Kansas must have a "significant contact or aggregation of contacts" to the claims asserted by each member of the plaintiff class, contacts "creating state interests" in order to ensure that the choice of Kansas law is not arbitrary or unfair. *Allstate* at [406]. Given Kansas' lack of "interest" in claims unrelated to that State, and the substantive conflict with jurisdictions such as Texas, we conclude that application of Kansas law to every claim in this case is sufficiently arbitrary and unfair as to exceed constitutional limits.[c]

(d) Justice Stevens dissented, finding no direct or substantive conflict between the relevant law of Kansas and that of any other jurisdiction:

> There is simply no demonstration here that the Kansas Supreme Court's decision has impaired the legitimate interest of any other States or infringed on their sovereignty in the slightest.

---

[a] 235 Kan. 195, 679 P.2d 1159 (1984).

[b] 472 U.S. at 823.

[c] Id. at 821-22.

... Arguments that a State court has merely applied general common law principles in a novel manner, or reconciled arguably conflicting laws erroneously in the face of unprecedented factual circumstances should not suffice to make out a constitutional issue.[d]

(e) Do you think *Shutts* represents a change mind after *Hague?* Or is the Court saying merely that when the claim to judicial jurisdiction is thin and the expectations of being subjected to a given forum's law are slight, the forum must be extra careful in its choice of law? Recall question (2)(c), page 418, *supra*.

(f) Following the decision of the U.S. Supreme Court, the Kansas Supreme Court remanded the case to the district court with instructions to carry out the mandate of the U.S. Supreme Court. Phillips argued that the law of each state where a leasehold was located should be applied to claims regarding that leasehold; plaintiffs argued that all the relevant laws were essentially alike, and that there was no real conflict. The District Court for Seward County held that the law of Texas, Oklahoma, and other relevant states was essentially like that of Kansas; accordingly, the judgment issued prior to review by the U.S. Supreme Court was reaffirmed. The Supreme Court of Kansas upheld the decision of the trial court.[e] This time, the U.S. Supreme Court denied review.[f]

2. *Sun Oil Co. v. Wortman,* 486 U.S. 717 (1988).

(a) A related question, not raised in *Shutts* but in a parallel class action also brought in Kansas against another major producer of natural gas, concerned the statute of limitations applicable to claims for interest on suspended royalty payments. Again, the Kansas trial court held that nothing in the U.S. Supreme Court's decision precluded application of the Kansas 5-year statute of limitations, and that therefore claims filed in 1979 for interest on suspended royalty payments made in 1976 were timely. The Supreme Court of Kansas affirmed this decision,[g] holding that the U.S. Supreme Court's decision in *Shutts* applied only to substantive law, not to procedural matters such as the appropriate statute of limitations.

(b) The U.S. Supreme Court granted certiorari to reexamine a question first decided in 1839 in *McElmoyle v. Cohen,*[h] (see *infra* p. 643), and reaffirmed most recently in *Wells v. Simonds Abrasive Co.* (p. 374, *supra*). The Court, in an opinion by Justice Scalia, reaffirmed its view that "the Constitution does not bar application of the forum State's statute of limitations to claims that in their substance are and must be governed by the law of a different State":[i]

... Petitioner initially argues that *McElmoyle v. Cohen,* supra, was wrongly decided when handed down. The holding of *McElmoyle,* that a statute of limitations may be treated as procedural and thus may be governed by forum law even when the substance of the claim must be governed by another State's law, rested on two premises, one express and one implicit. The express premise was that this reflected the rule in international law at the time the Constitution was adopted. This is indisputably correct, see *Le Roy v. Crowninshield,* 15 F.Cas. 362, 365, 371 (No. 8,269) (Mass.1820) (Story, J.) (collecting authorities), and is not challenged by petitioner. The implicit premise, which petitioner does challenge, was

---

[d] 472 U.S. at 836, 842.

[e] *Shutts v. Phillips Petroleum Co.*, 240 Kan. 764, 732 P.2d 1286 (1987).

[f] 487 U.S. 1223 (1988).

[g] Wortman v. Sun Oil Co., 241 Kan. 226, 755 P.2d 488 (1987).

[h] 38 U.S. (13 Pet.) 312, 327-28 (1839).

[i] 486 U.S. at 722.

that this rule from international law could properly have been applied in the interstate context consistently with the Full Faith and Credit Clause.

The first sentence of the Full Faith and Credit Clause was not much discussed at either the Constitutional Convention or the state ratifying conventions. However, the most pertinent comment at the Constitutional Convention, made by James Wilson of Pennsylvania, displays an expectation that it would be interpreted against the background of principles developed in international conflicts law. See 2 M. Farrand, The Records of the Federal Convention of 1787, p. 488 (rev. ed. 1966). Moreover, this expectation was practically inevitable, since there was no other developed body of conflicts law to which courts in our new Union could turn for guidance.

. . . The reported state cases in the decades immediately following ratification of the Constitution show that courts looked without hesitation to international law for guidance in resolving the issue underlying this case: which State's law governs the statute of limitations. The state of international law on that subject being as we have described, these early decisions uniformly concluded that the forum's statute of limitations governed even when it was longer than the limitations period of the State whose substantive law governed the merits of the claim. By 1820, the use of the forum statute of limitations in the interstate context was acknowledged to be "well settled." Obviously, judges writing in the era when the Constitution was framed and ratified thought the use of the forum statute of limitations to be proper in the interstate context. Their implicit understanding that the Full Faith and Credit Clause did not preclude reliance on the international law rule carries great weight.

. . .

The historical record shows conclusively, we think, that the society which adopted the Constitution did not regard statutes of limitations as substantive provisions, akin to the rules governing the validity and effect of contracts, but rather as procedural restrictions fashioned by each jurisdiction for its own courts. As Chancellor Kent explained in his landmark work, 2 J. Kent, Commentaries on American Law 462-463 (2d ed. 1832): "The period sufficient to constitute a bar to the litigation of sta[l]e demands, is a question of municipal policy and regulation, and one which belongs to the discretion of every government, consulting its own interest and convenience."

. . .

Unable to sustain the contention that under the original understanding of the Full Faith and Credit Clause statutes of limitations would have been considered substantive, petitioner argues that we should apply the modern understanding that they are so. It is now agreed, petitioner argues, that the primary function of a statute of limitations is to balance the competing substantive values of repose and vindication of the underlying right; and we should apply that understanding here, as we have applied it in the area of choice of law for purposes of federal diversity jurisdiction, where we have held that statutes of limitations are substantive, see *Guaranty Trust Co. v. York,* [p. 455 *infra*].

To address the last point first: *Guaranty Trust* itself rejects the notion that there is an equivalence between what is substantive under the *Erie* doctrine and what is substantive for purposes of conflict of laws. Except at the extremes, the terms "substance" and "procedure" precisely describe very little except a dichotomy, and what they mean in a particular context is largely determined by the purposes for which the dichotomy is drawn.

In the context of our *Erie* jurisprudence, that purpose is to establish (within the limits of applicable federal law, including the prescribed Rules of Federal Procedure) substantial uniformity of predictable outcome between cases tried in a federal court and cases tried in the courts of the State in which the federal court sits. See *Guaranty Trust, Hanna v. Plumer,* [p. 456 *infra*]. The purpose of the substance-procedure dichotomy in the context of the Full Faith and Credit Clause, by contrast, is not to establish uniformity but to delimit spheres of state legislative competence. How different the two purposes (and hence the appropriate meanings) are is suggested by this: It is never the case under Erie that either federal or state law—if the two differ—can properly be applied to a particular issue; but since the legislative jurisdictions of the States overlap, it is frequently the case under the Full Faith and Credit Clause that a court can lawfully apply either the law of one State or the contrary law of another . . . Today, for example, we do not hold that Kansas must apply its own statute of limitations to a claim governed in its substance by another State's law, but only that it may.

But to address petitioner's broader point of which the *Erie* argument is only a part—that we should update our notion of what is sufficiently "substantive" to require full faith and credit: We cannot imagine what would be the basis for such an updating. As we have just observed, the words "substantive" and "procedural" themselves (besides not appearing in the Full Faith and Credit Clause) do not have a precise content, even (indeed especially) as their usage has evolved. And if one consults the purpose of their usage in the full-faith-and-credit context, that purpose is quite simply to give both the forum State and other interested States the legislative jurisdiction to which they are entitled. If we abandon the currently applied, traditional notions of such entitlement we would embark upon the enterprise of constitutionalizing choice-of-law rules, with no compass to guide us beyond our own perceptions of what seems desirable. There is no more reason to consider recharacterizing statutes of limitation as substantive under the Full Faith and Credit Clause than there is to consider recharacterizing a host of other matters generally treated as procedural under conflicts law, and hence generally regarded as within the forum State's legislative jurisdiction. See, e.g., Restatement (Second) of Conflict of Laws § 131 (remedies available), § 133 (placement of burden of proof), § 134 (burden of production), § 135 (sufficiency of the evidence), § 139 (privileges) (1971).

In sum, long established and still subsisting choice-of-law practices that come to be thought, by modern scholars, unwise, do not thereby become unconstitutional. If current conditions render it desirable that forum States no longer treat a particular issue as procedural for conflict of laws purposes, those States can themselves adopt a rule to that effect, . . . or it can be proposed that Congress legislate to that effect under the second sentence of the Full Faith and Credit Clause. It is not the function of this Court, however, to make departures from established choice-of-law precedent and practice constitutionally mandatory. We hold, therefore, that Kansas did not violate the Full Faith and Credit Clause when it applied its own statute of limitations.

Petitioner also makes a due process attack upon the Kansas court's application of its own statute of limitations. Here again neither the tradition in place when the constitutional provision was adopted nor subsequent practice supports the contention. At the time the Fourteenth Amendment was adopted, this Court had not only explicitly approved (under the Full Faith and Credit Clause) forum-state application of its own statute of limitations, but the practice had gone essentially unchallenged. And it has gone essentially unchallenged since. "If a thing has been practised for two hundred years by common consent, it will need a strong case for the Fourteenth Amendment to affect it." *Jackman v. Rosenbaum Co.,* 260 U.S. 22 (1922).

A State's interest in regulating the work load of its courts and determining when a claim is too stale to be adjudicated certainly suffices to give it legislative jurisdiction to control the remedies available in its courts by imposing statutes of limitations. Moreover, petitioner could in no way have been unfairly surprised by the application to it of a rule that is as old as the Republic. There is, in short, nothing in Kansas' action here that is "arbitrary or unfair," Shutts III, 472 U.S., at 821-822 [p. 421, *supra*], and the due process challenge is entirely without substance.j

(c) Justice Brennan, who had written the plurality opinion in *Allstate v. Hague*, concurred in the judgment, but not in the reasoning of the majority, in an opinion concurred in by Justices Marshall and Blackmun (but not by Justice White, the fourth member of the plurality in *Hague*). As in other instances where he has declined to accept Justice Scalia's emphasis on the historical record (see e.g., *Burnham v. Superior Court*, p. 610 *infra*), Justice Brennan argued that the issue could not be addressed without inquiry into the interests of the two states involved—the claim state and the forum state:

> Were statutes of limitations purely substantive, the issue would be an easy one, for where, as here, a forum State has no contacts with the underlying dispute, it has no substantive interests and cannot apply its own law on a purely substantive matter. Nor would the issue be difficult if statutes of limitations were purely procedural, for the contacts a State has with a dispute by virtue of being the forum always create state procedural interests that make application of the forum's law on purely procedural questions "neither arbitrary nor fundamentally unfair." Phillips Petroleum, supra. Statutes of limitations, however, defy characterization as either purely procedural or purely substantive. The statute of limitations a State enacts represents a balance between, on the one hand, its substantive interest in vindicating substantive claims and, on the other hand, a combination of its procedural interest in freeing its courts from adjudicating stale claims and its substantive interest in giving individuals repose from ancient breaches of law. A State that has enacted a particular limitations period has simply determined that after that period the interest in vindicating claims becomes outweighed by the combination of the interests in repose and avoiding stale claims. One cannot neatly categorize this complicated temporal balance as either procedural or substantive.

> Given the complex of interests underlying statutes of limitations, I conclude that the contact a State has with a claim simply by virtue of being the forum creates a sufficient procedural interest to make the application of its limitations period to wholly out-of-state claims consistent with the Full Faith and Credit Clause. This is clearest when the forum State's limitations period is shorter than that of the claim State. A forum State's procedural interest in avoiding the adjudication of stale claims is equally applicable to in-state and out-of-state claims. That the State out of which the claim arose may have concluded that at that shorter period its substantive interests outweigh its procedural interest in avoiding stale claims would not make any difference; it would be " 'neither arbitrary nor fundamentally unfair,' " Phillips Petroleum, for the forum State to conclude that its procedural interest

---

j 486 U.S. 723-30.

is more weighty than that of the claim State and requires an earlier time bar, as long as the time bar applied in a nondiscriminatory manner to in-state and out-of-state claims alike.

The constitutional question is somewhat less clear where, as here, the forum State's limitations period is longer than that of the claim State. In this situation, the claim State's statute of limitations reflects its policy judgment that at the time the suit was filed the combination of the claim State's procedural interest in avoiding stale claims and its substantive interest in repose outweighs its substantive interest in vindicating the plaintiff's substantive rights. Assuming, for the moment, that each State has an equal substantive interest in the repose of defendants, then a forum State that has concluded that its procedural interest is less weighty than that of the claim State does not act unfairly or arbitrarily in applying its longer limitations period. The claim State does not, after all, have any substantive interest in not vindicating rights it has created. Nor will it do to argue that the forum State has no interest in vindicating the substantive rights of nonresidents: the forum State cannot discriminate against nonresidents, and if it has concluded that the substantive rights of its citizens outweigh its procedural interests at that period then it cannot be faulted for applying that determination evenhandedly.

If the different limitations periods also reflect differing assessments of the substantive interests in the repose of defendants, however, the issue is more complicated. It is, to begin with, not entirely clear whether the interest in the repose of defendants is an interest the State has as a forum or wholly as the creator of the claim at issue. Even if one assumes the latter, determining whether application of the forum State's longer limitations period would thwart the claim State's substantive interest in repose requires a complex assessment of the relative weights of both States' procedural and substantive interests. For example, a claim State may have a substantive interest in vindicating claims that, at a particular period, outweighs its substantive interest in repose standing alone but not the combination of its interests in repose and avoiding the adjudication of stale claims. Such a State would not have its substantive interest in repose thwarted by the claim's adjudication in a State that professed no procedural interest in avoiding stale claims, even if the forum State had less substantive interest in repose than the claim State, because the forum State would be according the claim State's substantive interests all the weight the claim State gives them. Such efforts to break down and weigh the procedural and substantive components and interests served by the various States' limitations periods would, however, involve a difficult, unwieldy and somewhat artificial inquiry that itself implicates the strong procedural interest any forum State has in having administrable choice-of-law rules.

In light of the forum State's procedural interests and the inherent ambiguity of any more refined inquiry in this context, there is some force to the conclusion that the forum State's contacts give it sufficient procedural interests to make it " 'neither arbitrary nor fundamentally unfair,' " *Phillips Petroleum,* for the State to have a per se rule of applying its own limitations period to out-of-state claims—particularly where, as here, the States out of which the claims arise view their statutes of limitations as procedural. The issue, after all, is not whether the decision to apply forum limitations law is wise as a matter of choice-of-law doctrine but whether the decision is within the range of constitutionally permissible choices, and we have already held that distinctions similar to those offered above "are too unsubstantial to form the basis for constitutional distinctions," [citing *Wells* at p. 375, *supra*]. This conclusion may not be compelled, but the arguments to the contrary are at best arguable,

§ 5.04   THE CONSTITUTION AND CONFLICT OF LAWS   □   427

and any merely arguable inconsistency with our current full-faith-and-credit jurisprudence surely does not merit deviating from 150 years of precedent holding that choosing the forum State's limitations period over that of the claim State is constitutionally permissible. . . .[k]

3(a) In addition to the debate about the statute of limitations, the defendant in *Wortman v. Sun Oil Co.* argued that the Kansas courts had not been faithful to the mandate in *Shutts* to apply the laws of the states concerned with the underlying claims. Justice Scalia, for the Court, replied as follows:

> To constitute a violation of the Full Faith and Credit Clause or the Due Process Clause, it is not enough that a state court misconstrue the law of another State. Rather, our cases make plain that the misconstruction must contradict law of the other State that is clearly established and that has been brought to the court's attention. . . . We cannot conclude that any of the interpretations at issue here runs afoul of this standard.[l]

Under this view, it seems that if a state court insists on applying its own law to a claim with which its own connections are slight, there is at least a chance that the Supreme Court will scrutinize, and possibly reverse the decision. If the state court announces that it is applying the law of another state, the chances of Supreme Court review are very slight, even if its conclusion that the law of the other state is like its own is doubtful.

(b) Justice O'Connor, who like Justice Scalia had not been on the Court when *Hague* was decided, dissented on this issue. "In my view," she wrote for herself and the Chief Justice, "the Supreme Court of Kansas violated the Full Faith and Credit Clause when it concluded that the three states in question would apply the interest rates set forth in the regulations of the Federal Power Commission . . .":[m]

> At bottom, the Kansas court's insistence on its equitable theory seems based on nothing more than its conviction that it would have been "fair" for the parties to agree that the oil and gas company should pay the same interest rates for suspended royalty payments arising from approved price increases that the company would have had to pay its customers for refunds arising from disapproved price increases. That is a wholly inadequate basis for concluding that three other states would conclude that the parties did make such an agreement. Even assuming that the result imposed on the parties by the Kansas court was "fair," which is not at all obvious, neither that court nor this Court has given any reason for concluding that the parties to the case before us agreed either to adopt the FPC interest rates or to be bound by the Kansas judiciary's notions of equity.

. . .

> Today's decision discards the important parts of our decision in *Shutts* and of the Full Faith and Credit Clause. Faced with the constitutional obligation to apply the substantive law of another state, a court that does not like that law apparently need only take two steps in order to avoid applying it. First, invent a legal theory so novel or strange that the other State has never had an opportunity to reject it; then, on the basis of nothing but unsupported speculation, "predict" that the other State would adopt that theory if it had the chance. To call this giving full faith and credit to the law of another State ignores the language of the

---

[k] 486 U.S. at 736-39.

[l] 486 U.S. at 730-31.

[m] 486 U.S. at 743-44.

Constitution and leaves it without the capacity to fulfill its purpose. Rather than take such a step, I would remand this case to the Supreme Court of Kansas with instructions to give effect to the interest rates established by law in Texas, Oklahoma, and Louisiana. I therefore respectfully dissent.[n]

(4) Notice Justice Scalia's statement that "if we abandon the . . . traditional notions of . . . entitlement [to apply the forum state's limitations period] we would embark upon the enterprise of constitutionalizing choice-of-law rules, with no compass to guide us beyond our own perceptions of what is desirable." Is that not just the argument that prevailed in *Allstate v. Hague* and was at least drawn into question in *Shutts*? Is Justice Scalia, for the Court, reinforcing *Hague* in the guise of a stress on procedure and tradition? Where, would you guess, would Justice Scalia have come out in *Hague* had he been on the Court when that case came up?

5. Recall the discussion in Chapter 2 of recent thinking about the problem of statutes of limitation and repose, and in particular the 1988 revision to § 142 of the Restatement (Second) of Conflict of Laws. (p. 100 *supra*).

(a) Assume the Kansas Supreme Court had adopted the Restatement formula. Would the result in *Sun Oil* be different?

(b) Putting aside Justice Scalia's reliance on the historical record, could the Supreme Court adopt the Restatement formula as a constitutional standard, holding, for example, that Kansas had no significant interest in hearing the claim (subsection (2)(a)), that Texas and Oklahoma in Sun Oil had a more significant relationship to the parties and the occurrence (subsection(2)(b)), and therefore that Kansas could not apply its own statute? Or is the formula suitable only for state courts (and federal courts applying state law) apart from constitutional restraints?

* * * * *

6. In the Virginia Convention of 1788 on the adoption of the Federal Constitution, opponents of the Constitution, concerned about excessive power granted to the national government, objected among other things to the creation of a federal judiciary. Patrick Henry, one of the leaders of the opposition, rising after James Madison had spoken at length in support of the Judiciary Article, said he was again driven to the "mournful recollection" at the surrender of our great rights, in this case because of the system of concurrent state and federal jurisdiction that he believed would destroy the judiciary of Virginia—"one of the best barriers against strides of power." In the course of his speech he said:

> [The federal courts'] jurisdiction, in disputes between citizens of different states, will be productive of the most serious inconveniences. The citizens of bordering states have frequent intercourse with one another. From proximity of the states to each other, a multiplicity of these suits will be instituted. I beg gentlemen to inform me of this—in what courts are they to go and by what law are they to be tried? Is it by a law of Pennsylvania or Virginia? Those judges must be acquainted with all the laws of the different states. I see arising out of that paper [the Constitution] a tribunal that is to be recurred to in all cases, when the destruction of the state judiciaries shall happen; and from the extensive jurisdiction of these paramount courts, the state courts must soon be annihilated.[o]

---

[n] *Id.* at 748-49.

[o] *Elliot's Debates on the Federal Constitution* 539, at 542 (1836).

John Marshall replied:

> The honorable member objects to suits being instituted in the federal courts, by citizens of one state, against the citizens of another state. Were I to contend that this was necessary in all cases, and that the government without it would be defective, I should not use my own judgment. But are not the objections carried too far? . . . [A] case may happen . . . in which a citizen of one state ought to be able to recur to this [federal] tribunal, to recover a claim from the citizen of another state. What is the evil which this can produce . . . What has he to get? Justice.
>
> . . . In the court of which state will it be instituted? said the honorable gentleman. It will be instituted in the court of the state where the defendant resides, where the law can come at him, and nowhere else. By the laws of which state will it be determined? said he. By the laws of the state where the contract was made. According to these laws, and those only can it be decided. Is this a novelty? No: it is a principle in the jurisprudence of this commonwealth. . . .[p]

Is Marshall spinning in his grave?

(b) The next chapter of this book, devoted to the *Erie* problem, has as its principal theme whether the Supreme Court was correct in giving up not only general federal common law, but also federal choice of law, leaving the Constitution as the only source of control over state (or lower federal) courts' choice of law. Consider as you read (or reread) the developments from *Swift v. Tyson* to *Erie* to *Klaxon Co. v. Stentor Electric Mfg. Co.* and beyond, whether in the light of *Hague* a federal common law of choice of law (i) would have been desirable; (ii) could have been imposed on the state courts in cases not importing the due process or full faith and credit clauses of the Constitution.[q]

---

[p] Id. at 556. The quotation continues:

> If a man contracted a debt in the East Indies, and it was sued for here, the decision must be consonant to the laws of that country. Suppose a contract made in Maryland, where the annual interest is at six per centum, and a suit instituted for it in Virginia; what interest would be given now, without any federal aid? The interest of Maryland most certainly; and if the contract had been made in Virginia, and suit brought in Maryland, the interest of Virginia must be given, without doubt. Would not the refusal of Justice to our citizens, from the courts of North Carolina, produce disputes between the states? Would the federal judiciary swerve from their duty in order to give partial and unjust decisions?

Id. at 556-57.

[q] For the suggestion that there may be a reservoir of non-constitutional choice of law that the Supreme Court could tap, see Silberman, *Can the State of Minnesota Bind the Nation? Federal Choice-of-Law Constraints After Allstate Insurance Co. v. Hague*, 10 Hofstra L. Rev. 103 (1981), and the reply thereto by the present author, Lowenfeld, *Three Might Have-Beens, A Reaction to the Symposium on Allstate Insurance Co. v. Hague*, 10 Hofstra L. Rev. 1045, 1049–57 (1981).

CHAPTER 6

FEDERAL COURTS AND CONFLICT OF LAWS—DIVERSITY JURISDICTION AND THE ERIE QUESTION

§ 6.01 Diversity Jurisdiction and the Applicable Law

Federal courts have existed in the United States since the Judiciary Act of 1789[a] While the scope of their jurisdiction has varied from time to time, it has always included controversies between citizens of different states (as well as suits between a citizen of a state and an alien) subject to a minimum amount in controversy.[b]

The records of the Constitutional Convention contain no explanation of the purposes of the diversity jurisdiction—the "greatest mystery," as Professor Wright called it.[c] Though it was clear to the framers of the Constitution that a proper government should have three branches (in contrast to the regime of the Articles of Confederation), they seem not to have given much thought to what law should be applied by the federal courts. Apart from the obvious (if not wholly convincing) argument that federal courts were needed to protect out-of-state litigants against local prejudice,[d] could federal jurisdiction be used to create a uniform body of judge-made law in areas in which Congress had not legislated or could not legislate? That, in essence, is the problem of *Swift v. Tyson* and *Erie R. Co. v. Tompkins*, reproduced below. Could federal courts be used to provide for impartial and uniform resolution of conflict of laws problems in controversies between citizens of different states? That, in essence, is the problem of *Klaxon Co. v. Stentor Electric Mfg. Co.*, reproduced in § 6.02. Some special problems for conflict of laws resulting from the contemporary solution of the first two questions are presented in § 6.03, *infra*.

---

[a] The Constitutional Convention, which was unanimous that there should be a National Judiciary, was sharply divided over the proposal that there be both a supreme court and inferior tribunals. The compromise, put forward by Madison and James Wilson, was to establish the Supreme Court in the Constitution, and to authorize "such inferior Courts as the Congress may from time to time ordain and establish." Constitution Article III, § 1. Congress did establish both district and circuit courts in the Judiciary Act of 1789, 1 Stat. 73. See, generally John P. Frank, *Historical Bases of the Federal Judicial System,* 13 Law & Contemp. Prob. 3 (1948).

[b] The amount was originally fixed at $500. It was raised to $2000 in 1887, $3000 in 1911, $10,000 in 1958, $50,000 in 1988, and $75,000 in 1996.

[c] C.A. Wright, *Federal Courts,* p. 3, also pp. 141-152-38 (5th ed. 1994), and the many sources there cited. See also H. Hart & H. Wechsler, *The Federal Courts and the Federal System* pp. 1522-24 (4th ed. R. Fallon Jr., D. Meltzer, D. Shapiro, 1996).

[d] The most famous statement of this argument appears in Chief Justice Marshall's opinion in *Bank of the United States v. Deveaux,* 9 U.S. (5 Cranch) 61, 87 (1809), to the effect that either "the Constitution itself contains apprehensions on this subject" or "views with indulgence" the apprehensions of others. Judge Friendly disputed this motivation. Friendly, *The Historic Basis of Diversity Jurisdiction,* 41 Harv. L. Rev. 483 (1928), and others have disputed Friendly and supported this explanation. See, e.g., Frank, Note a, *supra,* and the many sources cited in Wright and Hart & Wechsler, Note c, *supra*.

The overall problem presented by *Erie*—what is the source of law in a common law system and what are the respective roles of legislatures and courts—is, of course, central to an exploration of conflict of laws, not limited to the federal/state question presented by the diversity jurisdiction. Many of the technical problems raised in application of *Erie,* as well as the continuing debate over the desirability of diversity jurisdiction itself, are beyond the scope of the present volume.

SWIFT v. TYSON

United States Supreme Court
41 U.S. (16 Pet.) 1 (1842)

STORY, Justice, delivered the opinion of the court.

This cause comes before us from the circuit court of the southern district of New York, upon a certificate of division of the judges of that court. The action was brought by the plaintiff, Swift, as indorsee, against the defendant, Tyson, as acceptor, upon a bill of exchange dated at Portland, Maine, on the first day of May 1836, for the sum of $1540.30, payable six months after date, and grace, drawn by one Nathaniel Norton and one Jairus S. Keith upon and accepted by Tyson, at the city of New York, in favor of the order of Nathaniel Norton, and by Norton indorsed to the plaintiff. The bill was dishonored at maturity.

At the trial, the acceptance and indorsement of the bill were admitted, and the plaintiff there rested his case. The defendant then introduced in evidence the answer of Swift to a bill of discovery, by which it appeared, that Swift took the bill, before it became due, in payment of a promissory note due to him by Norton & Keith; that he understood, that the bill was accepted in part payment of some lands sold by Norton to a company in New York; that Swift was a *bonâ fide* holder of the bill, not having any notice of anything in the sale or title to the lands, or otherwise impeaching the transaction, and with the full belief that the bill was justly due. The particular circumstances are fully set forth in the answer in the record; but it does not seem necessary further to state them. The defendant then offered to prove, that the bill was accepted by the defendant, as part consideration for the purchase of certain lands in the state of Maine, which Norton & Keith represented themselves to be the owners of, and also represented to be of great value, and contracted to convey a good title thereto; and that the representations were in every respect fraudulent and false, and Norton & Keith had no title to the lands, and that the same were of little or no value. The plaintiff objected to the admission of such testimony, or of any testimony, as against him, impeaching or showing a failure of the consideration, on which the bill was accepted, under the facts admitted by the defendant, and those proved by him, by reading the answer of plaintiff to the bill of discovery. The judges of the circuit court thereupon divided in opinion upon the following point or question of law—whether, under the facts last mentioned, the defendant was entitled to the same defence to the action, as if the suit was between the original parties to the bill, that is to say, Norton, or Norton & Keith, and the defendant; and whether the evidence so offered was admissible as against the plaintiff in the action. And this is the question certified to us for our decision.

There is no doubt, that a *bonâ fide* holder of a negotiable instrument, for a valuable consideration, without any notice of facts which impeach its validity, as between the antecedent parties, if he takes it under an indorsement made before the same becomes due, holds the title

§ 6.01   THE CONSTITUTION AND CONFLICT OF LAWS   □   433

unaffected by these acts, and may recover thereon, although, as between the antecedent parties, the transaction may be without any legal validity. This is a doctrine so long and so well established, and so essential to the security of negotiable paper, that it is laid up among the fundamentals of the law, and requires no authority or reasoning to be now brought in its support. As little doubt is there, that the holder of any negotiable paper, before it is due, is not bound to prove that he is a *bonâ fide* holder for a valuable consideration, without notice; for the law will presume that, in the absence of all rebutting proofs, and therefore, it is incumbent upon the defendant to establish by way of defence, satisfactory proofs of the contrary, and thus to overcome the *primâ facie* title of the plaintiff.

In the present case, the plaintiff is a *bonâ fide* holder, without notice, for what the law deems a good and valid consideration, that is, for a pre-existing debt; and the only real question in the cause is, whether, under the circumstances of the present case, such a pre-existing debt constitutes a valuable consideration, in the sense of the general rule applicable to negotiable instruments. We say, under the circumstances of the present case, for the acceptance having been made in New York, the argument on behalf of the defendant is, that the contract is to be treated as a New York contract, and therefore to be governed by the laws of New York, as expounded by its courts, as well upon general principles, as by the express provisions of the 34th section of the judiciary act of 1789, ch. 20. And then it is further contended, that by the law of New York, as thus expounded by its courts, a pre-existing debt does not constitute, in the sense of the general rule, a valuable consideration applicable to negotiable instruments.

In the first place, then, let us examine into the decisions of the courts of New York upon this subject. . . .

[The court reviews the New York cases, which seem to confirm defendant's statement of New York law, but not to firmly settle the question.]

But, admitting the doctrine to be fully settled in New York, it remains to be considered, whether it is obligatory upon this court, if it differs from the principles established in the general commercial law. It is observable, that the courts of New York do not found their decisions upon this point, upon any local statute, or positive, fixed or ancient local usage; but they deduce the doctrine from the general principles of commercial law. It is, however, contended, that the 34th section of the judiciary act of 1789, ch. 20, furnishes a rule obligatory upon this court to follow the decisions of the state tribunals in all cases to which they apply. That section provides "that the laws of the several states, except where the constitution, treaties or statutes of the United States shall otherwise require or provide, shall be regarded as rules of decision, in trials at common law, in the courts of the United States, in cases where they apply." In order to maintain the argument, it is essential, therefore, to hold, that the word "laws," in this section, includes within the scope of its meaning, the decisions of the local tribunals. In the ordinary use of language, it will hardly be contended, that the decisions of courts constitute laws. They are, at most, only evidence of what the laws are, and are not, of themselves, laws. They are often re-examined, reversed and qualified by the courts themselves, whenever they are found to be either defective, or ill-founded, or otherwise incorrect. The laws of a state are more usually understood to mean the rules and enactments promulgated by the legislative authority thereof, or long-established local customs having the force of laws. In all the various cases, which have hitherto come before us for decision, this court have uniformly supposed, that the true interpretation of the 34th section limited its application to state laws, strictly local, that is to say, to the positive statutes of the state, and the construction thereof adopted by the local tribunals, and to rights and titles to things having a permanent locality, such as the rights and titles to real estate, and other matters immovable and intra-territorial in their nature and character. It never has been supposed by us, that the section did apply, or was designed to apply, to questions of a more general nature, not at all dependent upon local statutes or local usages of a fixed and permanent operation, as, for example, to the construction of ordinary contracts or other written instruments, and especially to questions of general commercial law, where the state tribunals are called upon to perform the like functions as ourselves, that is, to ascertain, upon general reasoning and legal analogies, what is the true exposition of the contract or instrument, or what is the just rule furnished by the principles of commercial law to govern the case. And we have not now the slightest difficulty in holding, that this section, upon its true intendment and construction, is strictly limited to local statutes and local usages of the character before stated, and does not extend to contracts and other instruments of a commercial nature, the true interpretation and effect whereof are to be sought, not in the decisions of the local tribunals, but in the general principles and doctrines of commercial jurisprudence. Undoubtedly, the decisions of the local tribunals upon such subjects are entitled to, and will receive, the most deliberate attention and respect of this court; but they cannot furnish positive rules, or conclusive authority, by which our own judgments are to be bound up and governed. The law respecting negotiable instruments may be truly declared in the language of Cicero, adopted by Lord MANSFIELD in *Luke v. Lyde,* 2 Burr. 883, 887, to be in a great measure, not the law of a single country only, but of the commercial world. *Non erit alia lex Romae, alia Athenis; alia nunc, alia posthac; sed et apud omnes gentes, et omni tempore alia eademque lex obtinebit.*[e]

It becomes necessary for us, therefore, upon the present occasion, to express our own opinion of the true result of the commercial law upon the question now before us. And we have no hesitation in saying, that a pre-existing debt does constitute a valuable consideration, in the sense of the general rule already stated, as applicable to negotiable instruments. Assuming it to be true (which, however, may well admit of some doubt from the generality of the language), that the holder of a negotiable instrument is unaffected with the equities between the antecedent parties, of which he has no notice, only where he receives it in the usual course of trade and business, for a valuable consideration, before it becomes due; we are prepared to say, that receiving it in payment of, or as security for, a pre-existing debt, is according to the known usual course of trade and business. And why, upon principle, should not a pre-existing debt be deemed such a valuable consideration? It is for the benefit and convenience of the commercial world, to give as wide an extent as practicable to the credit and circulation of negotiable paper, that it may pass not only as security for new purchases and advances, made upon the transfer thereof, but also in payment of, and as security for, pre-existing debts. The creditor is thereby enabled to realize or to secure his debt, and thus may safely give a prolonged credit, or forbear from taking any legal steps to enforce his rights. The debtor also has the advantage of making his negotiable securities of equivalent value to cash. But establish the opposite conclusion, that negotiable paper cannot be applied in payment of, or as security for, pre-existing debts, without letting in all the equities between the original and antecedent parties, and the value and circulation of such securities must be essentially diminished, and the debtor driven to the embarrassment of making a sale thereof, often at a ruinous discount, to some third person, and then, by circuity, to apply the proceeds to the payment of his debts. What, indeed, upon such a doctrine, would become of that large class of cases, where new notes are given by the same or by other parties,

---

[e] The same quotation appears as the last lines of Story's famous *Commentaries on the Conflict of Laws* § 645 (1st ed. 1834).

by way of renewal or security to banks, in lieu of old securities discounted by them, which have arrived at maturity? Probably, more than one-half of all bank transactions in our country, as well as those of other countries, are of this nature. The doctrine would strike a fatal blow at all discounts of negotiable securities for pre-existing debts.

. . .

[The court reviews decisions of the U.S. Supreme Court, English decisions of Lord Mansfield, Lord Eldon, and Lord Ellenborough among others, as well as decisions of the Supreme Court of Connecticut.]

[W]e entertain no doubt, that a *bonâ fide* holder, for a pre-existing debt, of a negotiable instrument, is not affected by any equities between the antecedent parties, where he has received the same, before it became due, without notice of any such equities. We are all, therefore, of opinion, that the question on this point, propounded by the Circuit Court for our consideration, ought to be answered in the negative; and we shall, accordingly, direct it so to be certified to the Circuit Court.

. . .

ERIE RAILROAD CO. v. TOMPKINS

United States Supreme Court
304 U.S. 64 (1938)

MR. JUSTICE BRANDEIS delivered the opinion of the Court.

The question for decision is whether the oft-challenged doctrine of *Swift v. Tyson* shall now be disapproved.

Tompkins, a citizen of Pennsylvania, was injured on a dark night by a passing freight train of the Erie Railroad Company while walking along its right of way at Hughestown in that State. He claimed that the accident occurred through negligence in the operation, or maintenance, of the train; that he was rightfully on the premises as licensee because on a commonly used beaten footpath which ran for a short distance alongside the tracks; and that he was struck by something which looked like a door projecting from one of the moving cars. To enforce that claim he brought an action in the federal court for southern New York, which had jurisdiction because the company is a corporation of that State. It denied liability; and the case was tried by a jury.

The Erie insisted that its duty to Tompkins was no greater than that owed to a trespasser. It contended, among other things, that its duty to Tompkins, and hence its liability, should be determined in accordance with the Pennsylvania law; that under the law of Pennsylvania, as declared by its highest court, persons who use pathways along the railroad right of way—that is a longitudinal pathway as distinguished from a crossing—are to be deemed trespassers; and that the railroad is not liable for injuries to undiscovered trespassers resulting from its negligence, unless it be wanton or wilful. Tompkins denied that any such rule had been established by the decisions of the Pennsylvania courts; and contended that, since there was no statute of the State on the subject, the railroad's duty and liability is to be determined in federal courts as a matter of general law.

The trial judge refused to rule that the applicable law precluded recovery. The jury brought in a verdict of $30,000; and the judgment entered thereon was affirmed by the Circuit Court of Appeals, which held, 90 F.2d 603, 604, that it was unnecessary to consider whether the law of Pennsylvania was as contended, because the question was one not of local, but of general, law and that

> upon questions of general law the federal courts are free, in the absence of a local statute, to exercise their independent judgment as to what the law is; and it is well settled that the question of the responsibility of a railroad for injuries caused by its servants is one of general law. . . . Where the public has made open and notorious use of a railroad right of way for a long period of time and without objection, the company owes to persons on such permissive pathway a duty of care in the operation of its trains. . . . It is likewise generally recognized law that a jury may find that negligence exists toward a pedestrian using a permissive path on the railroad right of way if he is hit by some object projecting from the side of the train.

The Erie had contended that application of the Pennsylvania rule was required, among other things, by § 34 of the Federal Judiciary Act of September 24, 1789. . . .

Because of the importance of the question whether the federal court was free to disregard the alleged rule of the Pennsylvania common law, we granted certiorari.

First. Swift v. Tyson, 16 Pet. 1, 18, held that federal courts exercising jurisdiction on the ground of diversity of citizenship need not, in matters of general jurisprudence, apply the unwritten law of the State as declared by its highest court; that they are free to exercise an independent judgment as to what the common law of the State is—or should be; and that, as there stated by Mr. Justice Story:

> the true interpretation of the thirty-fourth section limited its application to state laws strictly local, that is to say, to the positive statutes of the state, and the construction thereof adopted by the local tribunals, and to rights and titles to things having a permanent locality, such as the rights and titles to real estate, and other matters immovable and intraterritorial in their nature and character. It never has been supposed by us, that the section did apply, or was intended to apply, to questions of a more general nature, not at all dependent upon local statutes or local usages of a fixed and permanent operation, as, for example, to the construction of ordinary contracts or other written instruments, and especially to questions of general commercial law, where the state tribunals are called upon to perform the like functions as ourselves, that is, to ascertain upon general reasoning and legal analogies, what is the true exposition of the contract or instrument, or what is the just rule furnished by the principles of commercial law to govern the case.

. . . The federal courts assumed, in the broad field of "general law," the power to declare rules of decision which Congress was confessedly without power to enact as statutes. Doubt was repeatedly expressed as to the correctness of the construction given § 34, and as to the soundness of the rule which it introduced. But it was the more recent research of a competent scholar, who examined the original document, which established that the construction given to it by the Court was erroneous; and that the purpose of the section was merely to make certain that, in all matters except those in which some federal law is controlling, the federal courts exercising jurisdiction in diversity of citizenship cases would apply as their rules of decision the law of the State, unwritten as well as written.[5]

---

[5] Charles Warren, *New Light on the History of the Federal Judiciary Act of 1789* (1923) 37 Harv. L. Rev. 49, 51–52, 81–88, 108.

Criticism of the doctrine became widespread after the decision of *Black & White Taxicab Co. v. Brown & Yellow Taxicab Co.,* 276 U. S. 518 [1928]. There, Brown and Yellow, a Kentucky corporation owned by Kentuckians, and the Louisville and Nashville Railroad, also a Kentucky corporation, wished that the former should have the exclusive privilege of soliciting passenger and baggage transportation at the Bowling Green, Kentucky, railroad station; and that the Black and White, a competing Kentucky corporation, should be prevented from interfering with that privilege. Knowing that such a contract would be void under the common law of Kentucky, it was arranged that the Brown and Yellow reincorporate under the law of Tennessee, and that the contract with the railroad should be executed there. The suit was then brought by the Tennessee corporation in the federal court for western Kentucky to enjoin competition by the Black and White; an injunction issued by the District Court was sustained by the Court of Appeals; and this Court, citing many decisions in which the doctrine of *Swift v. Tyson* had been applied, affirmed the decree.

Second. Experience in applying the doctrine of *Swift v. Tyson,* had revealed its defects, political and social; and the benefits expected to flow from the rule did not accrue. Persistence of state courts in their own opinions on questions of common law prevented uniformity; and the impossibility of discovering a satisfactory line of demarcation between the province of general law and that of local law developed a new well of uncertainties.[8]

On the other hand, the mischievous results of the doctrine had become apparent. Diversity of citizenship jurisdiction was conferred in order to prevent apprehended discrimination in state courts against those not citizens of the State. *Swift v. Tyson* introduced grave discrimination by non-citizens against citizens. It made rights enjoyed under the unwritten "general law" vary according to whether enforcement was sought in the state or in the federal court; and the privilege of selecting the court in which the right should be determined was conferred upon the non-citizen. Thus, the doctrine rendered impossible equal protection of the law. In attempting to promote uniformity of law throughout the United States, the doctrine had prevented uniformity in the administration of the law of the State.

The discrimination resulting became in practice far-reaching. This resulted in part from the broad province accorded to the so-called "general law" as to which federal courts exercised an independent judgment. In addition to questions of purely commercial law, "general law" was held to include the obligations under contracts entered into and to be performed within the State, the extent to which a carrier operating within a State may stipulate for exemption from liability for his own negligence or that of his employee; the liability for torts committed within the State upon persons resident or property located there, even where the question of liability depended upon the scope of a property right conferred by the State; and the right to exemplary or punitive damages. Furthermore, state decisions construing local deeds, mineral conveyances, and even devises of real estate were disregarded.

In part the discrimination resulted from the wide range of persons held entitled to avail themselves of the federal rule by resort to the diversity of citizenship jurisdiction. Through this jurisdiction individual citizens willing to remove from their own State and become citizens of

---

[8] Compare 2 Warren, *The Supreme Court in United States History* (rev. ed. 1935) 89: "Probably no decision of the Court has ever given rise to more uncertainty as to legal rights; and though doubtless intended to promote uniformity in the operation of business transactions, its chief effect has been to render it difficult for business men to know in advance to what particular topic the Court would apply the doctrine. . . ." The Federal Digest, through the 1937 volume, lists nearly 1000 decisions involving the distinction between questions of general and of local law.

another might avail themselves of the federal rule. And, without even change of residence, a corporate citizen of the State could avail itself of the federal rule by re-incorporating under the laws of another State, as was done in the *Taxicab* case.

The injustice and confusion incident to the doctrine of *Swift v. Tyson* have been repeatedly urged as reasons for abolishing or limiting diversity of citizenship jurisdiction. Other legislative relief has been proposed. If only a question of statutory construction were involved, we should not be prepared to abandon a doctrine so widely applied throughout nearly a century. But the unconstitutionality of the course pursued has now been made clear and compels us to do so.

Third. Except in matters governed by the Federal Constitution or by Acts of Congress, the law to be applied in any case is the law of the State. And whether the law of the State shall be declared by its Legislature in a statute or by its highest court in a decision is not a matter of federal concern. There is no federal general common law. Congress has no power to declare substantive rules of common law applicable in a State whether they be local in their nature or "general," be they commercial law or a part of the law of torts. And no clause in the Constitution purports to confer such a power upon the federal courts. As stated by Mr. Justice Field when protesting in *Baltimore & Ohio R. Co. v. Baugh,* 149 U. S. 368, 401, against ignoring the Ohio common law of fellow servant liability:

> I am aware that what has been termed the general law of the country—which is often little less than what the judge advancing the doctrine thinks at the time should be the general law on a particular subject—has been often advanced in judicial opinions of this court to control a conflicting law of a State. I admit that learned judges have fallen into the habit of repeating this doctrine as a convenient mode of brushing aside the law of a State in conflict with their views. And I confess that, moved and governed by the authority of the great names of those judges, I have, myself, in many instances, unhesitatingly and confidently, but I think now erroneously, repeated the same doctrine. But, notwithstanding the great names which may be cited in favor of the doctrine, and notwithstanding the frequency with which the doctrine has been reiterated, there stands, as a perpetual protest against its repetition, the Constitution of the United States, which recognizes and preserves the autonomy and independence of the States—independence in their legislative and independence in their judicial departments. Supervision over either the legislative or the judicial action of the States is in no case permissible except as to matters by the Constitution specifically authorized or delegated to the United States. Any interference with either, except as thus permitted, is an invasion of the authority of the State and, to that extent, a denial of its independence.

The fallacy underlying the rule declared in *Swift v. Tyson* is made clear by Mr. Justice Holmes.[23] The doctrine rests upon the assumption that there is "a transcendental body of law outside of any particular State but obligatory within it unless and until changed by statute," that federal courts have the power to use their judgment as to what the rules of common law are; and that in the federal courts "the parties are entitled to an independent judgment on matters of general law":

> but law in the sense in which courts speak of it today does not exist without some definite authority behind it. The common law so far as it is enforced in a State, whether called common law or not, is not the common law generally but the law of that State existing

---

[23] *Kuhn v. Fairmont Coal Co.,* 215 U. S. 349, 370–372; *Black & White Taxicab Co. v. Brown & Yellow Taxicab Co.,* 276 U. S. 518, 532–36.

by the authority of that State without regard to what it may have been in England or anywhere else. . . .

the authority and only authority is the State, and if that be so, the voice adopted by the State as its own [whether it be of its Legislature or of its Supreme Court] should utter the last word.

Thus the doctrine of *Swift v. Tyson* is, as Mr. Justice Holmes said, "an unconstitutional assumption of powers by courts of the United States which no lapse of time or respectable array of opinion should make us hesitate to correct." In disapproving that doctrine we do not hold unconstitutional § 34 of the Federal Judiciary Act of 1789 or any other Act of Congress. We merely declare that in applying the doctrine this Court and the lower courts have invaded rights which in our opinion are reserved by the Constitution to the several States.

Fourth. The defendant contended that by the common law of Pennsylvania as declared by its highest court in *Falchetti v. Pennsylvania R. Co.,* 307 Pa. 203; 160 A. 859, the only duty owed to the plaintiff was to refrain from wilful or wanton injury. The plaintiff denied that such is the Pennsylvania law. In support of their respective contentions the parties discussed and cited many decisions of the Supreme Court of the State. The Circuit Court of Appeals ruled that the question of liability is one of general law; and on that ground declined to decide the issue of state law. As we hold this was error, the judgment is reversed and the case remanded to it for further proceedings in conformity with our opinion.

Reversed.

NOTES AND QUESTIONS

(1)(a) Looking first at *Swift v. Tyson,* Justice Story says there is "no doubt" that a bona fide holder of a negotiable instrument for value (i.e., an endorsee) takes the instrument free of any defenses that may be applicable between the original parties. How does he know this?

(b) Story was, of course, an extraordinarily learned scholar, and in fact wrote two treatises relevant to the question before him.[a] Thus when he says he speaks of "a doctrine so long and so well established," one may well believe him. Moreover, he adduces not only the great Lord Mansfield, but even Cicero, and then tells us the law was not otherwise in Athens, as well as Rome. Is this good enough?

(c) In addition to citing history and authority, Story makes an extended argument on the merits, directed to the utility of negotiable instruments, and to the disastrous effects of accepting the alleged New York variation, which in effect deprives a person who takes a negotiable instrument in payment for a prior obligation of the status of a bona fide holder.[b] Whom is Story trying to persuade?

(2)(a) Justice Story is compelled to face the argument that, right or wrong, New York is entitled to make its own rules for negotiable instruments, however commercially unsound and out of

[a] J. Story, *Commentaries on the Law of Promissory Notes* (1845); J. Story, *Commentaries on the Law of Bills of Exchange, Foreign and Inland* (1843).

[b] In fact Swift was a bank cashier in Portland, who had received the bill accepted by Tyson as part of routine banking business.

step with development of the law since Antiquity. Is there some suggestion that as applied to interstate transactions, New York's law is unconstitutional, in that it interferes with interstate commerce, or is applied extraterritorially?

(b) If that is not what Story means, how does he avoid the requirement of section 34 of the Judiciary Act that federal courts must regard state laws as rules of decision in trials at common law?

(3) Story gives essentially two answers to the preceeding question, and courts and scholars over the years have wondered for years whether both are essential or whether one is holding, the other dictum.

(a) *First,* he says, that the decisions of courts do not constitute laws, but are "at most, only evidence of what the laws are." He says courts make mistakes, and often correct or reverse themselves. Is he suggesting something like the civil law view of the role of courts as only explaining but not making law, which is a function only for the legislature?

If this is indeed Story's message, isn't it contrary to his view of his own role as finding and enunciating a rule of commercial law about which Congress has not legislated?

(b) *Second,* Story draws a distinction between general law, such as law affecting commercial contracts, and local "intra-territorial" law, such as the law of land titles, and presumably inheritance and family law. Under this view, even if New York's past consideration rule were embodied in a statute, the federal courts sitting in diversity cases would not be obliged to follow it, because New York could not trespass (at least in cases affecting citizens of different states) on questions of general—interstate and international—law.[c] Putting aside the difficulty of distinguishing at the margin between local and general law, is this not an attractive vision for a new nation, gradually settling a continent and governed by a dual system of courts, legislatures and executives? Can it be reconciled with the Rules of Decision Act?

(c) Do you suppose that Story expected that state courts and legislatures would follow the guidance of federal courts, and particularly the Supreme Court, on matters of general law such as the rights of holders in due course of negotiable instruments? Could Congress have authorized the Supreme Court to review decisions of state courts on questions of general law?

(4)(a) Some recent commentators have argued that *Swift v. Tyson* was misunderstood by later courts, and that it was the expansion created by later courts that created the mischief of which Brandeis and others complained.[d] For instance, in *Baltimore & Ohio R.R. v. Baugh*[e] (the dissent to which is cited in *Erie* at p. 438), plaintiff, a railroad worker, was injured on the job, as a result of the negligence of the engineer. Under Ohio law, the fellow servant rule[f] would not have applied, because the negligent person was a superior of the injured person, and the lower federal court found for plaintiff. The Supreme Court reversed, holding that the issue was one of general law, including the fellow servant rule without the local modification. Story would not have agreed with this decision, the argument goes, because it went beyond his view of general

---

[c] For a decision to this effect, in which a Mississippi statute concerning bills of exchange was denied effect upon an interstate transaction, see *Watson v. Tarpley,* 59 U.S. (18 How.) 517 (1856).

[d] See, e.g., T. Freyer, *Harmony & Dissonance: The Swift & Erie Cases in American Federalism* (1981); Hovenkamp, *Book Review of Freyer,* 34 Hastings L. J. 201 (1982); Conant, *The Commerce Clause, the Supremacy Clause and the Law Merchant: Swift v. Tyson and the Unity of Commercial Law,* 15 J. Mar. L. & Com. 153 (1984).

[e] 149 U.S. 368 (1893).

[f] Recall *Alabama Great Southern R.R. v. Carroll,* Chapter 1, p. 1, *supra.*

§ 6.01   THE CONSTITUTION AND CONFLICT OF LAWS   □   441

law. This interpretation may not explain Story's dictum (if that is what it was) about the meaning of the word "laws," but it could explain why the decision in Swift was concurred in by Chief Justice Taney and the other appointees of President Jackson who would not have shared the federalist views of Justice Story, but might have shared Story's distinction between law merchant and common law in a narrow sense.[g]

(b) Turning, then, to *Erie,* note that the argument before the Court of Appeals, and indeed the argument made by the parties before the Supreme Court, was about whether the railroad's duty to a person walking alongside its tracks was one of general or local law. What view do you think Story would have taken of that question?

(c) Note that this question is not only one of historical interest. If, contrary to the view of the commentators cited in paragraph (a), Story would have regarded the question presented in *Erie,* like the question presented in *Baugh,* as one of general law, that would go far toward confirming the view that he did indeed believe in a general common law, and that if the Supreme Court now rejected that belief, *Swift v. Tyson* should be overturned in its entirety. If, on the other hand, Story would have regarded this tort question as not coming under the general commercial/international rubric, the revolution achieved by *Erie* could have been more limited, for instance permitting some federal court input on conflict of laws. Note that while Justice Brandeis (at p. 436, *supra*) quotes both parts of Justice Story's interpretation of the Rules of Decision Act, when he comes to criticizing, he cites only the first part, and attributes to *Swift* all the evils that followed.

(d) Justice Brandeis cites the majority decision in *Black & White Taxicab Co.* as showing the unsoundness of *Swift v. Tyson,* and the dissent of Justice Holmes as exposing *Swift's* fundamental fallacy. Holmes, however, wrote in *Black & White*: "I should leave *Swift v. Tyson* undisturbed . . . , but I would not allow it to spread the assumed dominion into new fields."[h] Moreover, *Black & White* could easily have been disposed of as a case of a manipulative device to create diversity jurisdiction, akin to fraud.[i] Are you persuaded by a decision (*Erie*) that places so much weight on criticizing the prior doctrine by reference to cases of abuse of that doctrine?

(5)(a) Justice Brandeis founds much of his argument on Charles Warren's discovery of an earlier draft of what became section 34 of the Judiciary Act of 1789. That draft, by Senator Oliver Ellsworth, spoke of "the Statute law of the several States . . . and their unwritten or common law now in use. . . ."[j] Warren argued that the final version reflected no change in meaning, so that "[t]he laws of the several States" meant both statute and judge-made law. Isn't it equally possible that the Senate modified the draft to effect a change? Or at least to leave the point open?[k]

---

[g] See Conant. note d, *supra,* at 165 for elaboration of this point. By 1842 seven of the nine Justices had been appointed either by Jackson or by his successors. Justice Catron, appointed by President Van Buren, concurred in the result in a brief opinion suggesting that Story's statement of the law of what constitutes a holder in due course was too broad. Catron said nothing about the Rules of Decision Act or the more basic issues raised by Justice Story's opinion.

[h] 276 U.S. 518, 532 at 535 (1928) (Holmes, J. dissenting).

[i] Compare C. Wright, *Federal Courts* 373 (5th ed. 1994) and sources there cited. Since 1958 the problem of *Black & White Taxicab* has been eliminated by statute. See 28 U.S.C. 1332(c), Documents Supplement, p. 9.

[j] See Warren, *New Light on the History of the Federal Judiciary Act of 1789,* 37 Harv. L. Rev. 49 at 86–87 (1923).

[k] Among those who have made this point was Robert Jackson, at the time Solicitor General, in *The Rise and Fall of Swift v. Tyson,* 24 A.B.A.J. 609, 644 n.12. (1938). Among the uncertainties in the change of text was whether Congress wanted to limit the common law to be applied by federal courts to law in effect in 1789.

(b) Do you make anything of the fact, stressed by Judge Friendly in a famous article,[l] as well as by Justice Butler in his separate opinion in *Erie*,[m] that Congress continuously repassed section 34 of the Judiciary Act, without change, in the century between *Swift* and *Erie*?

(c) Whatever was the correct interpretation of the Judiciary Act, or of *Swift v. Tyson,* Justice Brandeis was surely correct that the benefits that might have been expected from *Swift* did not come. The unification of common law, however defined, did not occur, and discrimination in favor of out-of-state persons—typically railroads, insurance companies, and other professional defendants—seems to have grown. With interstate uniformity not preserved, and intrastate uniformity distorted, Brandeis' case against *Swift* as applied (whether or not that accurately reflected Story's vision) was strong. But, says Brandeis (p. 438), "[i]f only a question of statutory construction were involved, we should not be prepared to abandon a doctrine so widely applied throughout nearly a century." What is the constitutional infirmity that compels the court to do so in *Erie*?

(d) Justice Brandeis, in the most famous sentence of his most famous opinion, writes: "There is no federal general common law." Is that a statement of constitutional law? Of legal philosophy?

(6) It is sometimes forgotten that *Erie* was a 5–3 decision (with Justice Cardozo not participating); both Justice Butler and Justice Reed wrote substantial opinions—not dissents because they would both have come out for the railroad, but disagreements with the holding that *Swift v. Tyson* was unconstitutional.

(a) Justice Butler wrote that the majority's opinion

> strikes down as unconstitutional § 34 as construed by our decisions; it divests the Congress of power to prescribe rules to be followed by federal courts when deciding questions of general law. In that broad field it compels this and the lower federal courts to follow decisions of the courts of a particular State.[n]

Is that correct? Could Congress then not amend § 34 (or its successor[o]) to

(i) restore the rule of *Swift v. Tyson;*

(ii) carve out particular areas, such as negotiable instruments, or railroad accidents, in which the federal courts were free to apply their own view of the common law, subject to review by the Supreme Court?

(b) Justice Reed also questioned Brandeis' characterization of the issue as a constitutional one. He concurred in the disapproval of the doctrine of *Swift v. Tyson*. But he thought that action would require "only that we say that the words 'the laws' include in their meaning the decisions of the local tribunals," in other words accepting the argument of Charles Warren, and declaring the course pursued by *Swift* and its successor decisions merely erroneous, rather than unconstitutional. Presumably, if Justice Reed's view had prevailed, the questions put in the preceding paragraph would have been answered the other way. Would that have been a preferable solution, leaving the last word to Congress?[p]

---

[l] See Friendly, *In Praise of Erie—And of the New Federal Common Law,* 39 N.Y.U. L. Rev. 383, 390–91 (1964).

[m] See 304 U.S. at 86 (Butler J.).

[n] 304 U.S. at 90 (Butler J.)

[o] 28 U.S.C. § 1652. Documents Supplement, p. 61.

[p] It is interesting that Justice Frankfurter, as a professor, wrote in 1928 that "[*Swift*] is now too strongly imbedded in our law for judicial self-correction. Legislation should remove this doctrine. . . ." Frankfurter, *Distribution of*

(c) Justice Reed wrote, further:

> I am not at all sure whether, in the absence of federal statutory direction, federal courts would be compelled to follow state decisions. There was sufficient doubt about the matter to induce the first Congress to legislate. . . . If the opinion commits this Court to the position that the Congress is without power to declare what rules of substantive law shall govern the federal courts, that conclusion also seems questionable. The line between procedural and substantive law is hazy but no one doubts federal power over procedure. . . . The Judiciary Article and the necessary and proper clause of Article One may fully authorize legislation, such as this section of the Judiciary Act.^q

Is Justice Reed right in suggesting that the opinion of Justice Brandeis makes the Judiciary Act irrelevant?

(d) It is striking that Brandeis, nearly always a careful technician and craftsman, here declares a major federal doctrine unconstitutional without ever stating what section of the Constitution is violated. The popular view is that Brandeis must have meant the Tenth Amendment, but that refers to powers delegated (or not) to the United States. Surely Brandeis was not suggesting that Congress could not, in legislating about railroads, adopt rules of liability to strangers, as it had done with respect to liability to employees as early as 1908 in the Federal Employers' Liability Act.^r Is the logic of the *Erie* decision then that even where Congress could act, the courts cannot? Have we come full circle, back to a distinction between "law" and "laws"?

(e) The discussion of *Swift* and *Erie,* of courts and statutes, could easily fill this whole volume, and indeed the legal literature is vast.^s For present purposes, consider only how this discussion affects the question of choice of law in federal courts. Suppose, for example, when Mrs. Hague had sued Allstate Insurance Co. in state court in Minnesota, Allstate had removed to federal court. If *Erie* holds that the federal district court could not fashion its own rule about stacking of uninsured motorist liability policies, could it have decided on its own between Wisconsin and Minnesota law? This topic is explored in the next section.

Judicial Power Between United States and State Courts, 13 Cornell L.Q. 499, 529–30 (1928). Bills providing "[t]hat the decisions of the highest court of a State shall govern the courts of the United States in the ascertainment of the common law or general jurisprudence of such State," apparently drafted by Frankfurter at the suggestion of Justice Brandeis, were twice introduced into the Senate in the late 1920's, but died in committee. See Burbank, *The Rules Enabling Act of 1934,* 130 U. Pa. L. Rev. 1015, 1109, n. 433 (1982).

[q] 304 U.S. at 91–92. (Reed, J. concurring).

[r] 45 U.S.C. § 51 et seq.

[s] A notable recent exchange was Ely, *The Irrepressible Myth of Erie,* 87 Harv. L. Rev. 693 (1974); Chayes, *The Bead Game, Id.* 741; Ely, *The Necklace, Id.* 753. Mishkin, *The Thread,* 87 Harv. L. Rev. 1682 (1974). See Wright, *Federal Courts,* Ch. 9, pp. 374–421 (5th ed. 1994) for a summary of the continuing discussion and a representative (though not exhaustive) citation to sources.

§ 6.02 *Erie* and Choice of Law

SAMPSON v. CHANNELL

United States Court of Appeals, First Circuit
110 F.2d 754
cert. denied 310 U.S. 690 (1940)

MAGRUDER, CIRCUIT JUDGE.

On this appeal the question presented may be stated simply, but the answer is not free from difficulty. A car driven by defendant's testator collided in Maine with a car driven by the plaintiff, injuring both the plaintiff and his wife, who was a passenger. The wife sued and recovered judgment. We affirmed that judgment in *Channell v. Sampson,* Dec. 29, 1939, 1 Cir., 108 F.2d 315. In this, the husband's action, the jury found specially that the plaintiff's injury was caused by the negligence of defendant's testator, but brought in a general verdict for the defendant on the issue of contributory negligence. Judgment was entered for the defendant.

The action was brought in the federal district court for Massachusetts, there being the requisite diversity of citizenship. On the issue of contributory negligence the plaintiff requested the court to charge the jury, in accordance with the local Massachusetts rule, that "the burden of proving lack of care on the part of the plaintiff is on the defendant." This the court declined to do, but upon the contrary charged, in accordance with the Maine law, that the burden was upon the plaintiff to show affirmatively that no want of ordinary care on his part contributed to cause his injuries. The sole question raised is as to the correctness of this charge, and refusal to charge as requested.

Inquiry must first be directed to whether a federal court, in diversity of citizenship cases, must follow the applicable state rule as to incidence of burden of proof. If the answer is in the affirmative, the further point to be considered is whether the applicable state rule here is that of Massachusetts, where the action was brought, or Maine, where the accident occurred.

It would be an over-simplification to say that the case turns on whether burden of proof is a matter of substance or procedure. These are not clean-cut categories. During the reign of *Swift v. Tyson,* the federal courts in diversity of citizenship cases consistently held that the defendant had the burden of proving the plaintiff's contributory negligence, even though the suit arose in a state whose local rule was the contrary. . . .

They avoided having to apply the local rule under the Conformity Act, R.S. § 914, 28 U.S.C.A. § 724, by saying that burden of proof was not a mere matter of procedure but concerned substantive rights, as to which the federal courts on a matter of "general law" were free to take their own view. See *Herron v. Southern Pacific Co.,* 283 U.S. 91, 93, 94. The question of classification also arose where suit was brought in one state on an alleged tort committed in another state. But here it was generally held, in the state courts at least, that burden of proof as to contributory negligence was a matter of procedure; hence the rule of the forum would be applied despite a contrary rule of the locus delicti. *Levy v. Steiger* [p. 66, *supra*.]. . . .

In these two groups of cases the courts were talking about the same thing and labelling it differently, but in each instance the result was the same; the court was choosing the appropriate classification to enable it to apply its own familiar rule.

In another and quite different setting the question of classification has frequently arisen, namely, in cases involving the constitutionality of statutes shifting from the plaintiff to the defendant the burden of proof on the issue of contributory negligence, as applied retroactively to alleged torts committed before the date of the enactment. Here the courts, federal as well as state, have upheld the statutes as so applied. . . .

The courts say that such statutes introduce no change of the substantive law rule that contributory negligence is a complete bar to liability, but pertain only to the procedure by which the fact as to contributory negligence is to be established. . . .

It is apparent, then, that burden of proof does not fall within either category of "substance" or "procedure" by virtue of any intrinsic compulsion, but the matter has been made to turn upon the purpose at hand to be served by the classification. Therefore, inasmuch as the older decisions in the federal courts, applying in diversity cases the federal rule as to burden of proof as a matter of "general law," are founded upon an assumption no longer valid since *Erie Railroad Co. v. Tompkins,* . . . their classification of burden of proof as a matter of substance should be re-examined in the light of the objective and policy disclosed in the *Tompkins* case.

The opinion in that case sets forth as a moving consideration of policy that it is unfair and unseemly to have the outcome of litigation substantially affected by the fortuitous existence of diversity of citizenship. Hence, the greater likelihood there is that litigation would come out one way in the federal court and another way in the state court if the federal court failed to apply a particular local rule, the stronger the urge would be to classify the rule as not a mere matter of procedure but one of substantive law falling within the mandate of the *Tompkins* case. There will be, inescapably, a twilight zone between the two categories where a rational classification could be made either way, and where Congress directly,[4] or the Supreme Court under authority of the [Rules Enabling Act], 28 U.S.C.A. §§ 723b, 723c, would have power to prescribe a so-called rule of procedure for the federal courts. Thus, if Rule 8(c) of the Federal Rules of Civil Procedure could be construed as imposing upon the defendant the burden of proof of contributory negligence, it seems that this would be valid and conclusive of the case at bar, despite the contrary intimation in *Francis v. Humphrey,* D.C., 25 F.Supp. 1, 4, 5 [1938].[7] Rule 8(c) speaks of contributory negligence as an "affirmative defense," a phrase implying that the burden of proof is on the defendant.[8] Yet the only rule laid down is one of *pleading;* the defendant must

---

[4] A dictum in the majority opinion in the *Tompkins* case may be taken to assert that Congress could not constitutionally prescribe the substantive rules of law applicable in the federal courts in diversity of citizenship cases. It is not quite clear that this intimation was meant to be conveyed. See 52 Harv.L.Rev. 1002–1004. Certainly the court was not required to decide the point in the *Tompkins* case, because Congress has not asserted any such power, and indeed the only statute involved, the Rule of Decisions Act, so far as it commands anything, commands the federal courts to follow the state law. However this may be, it is not doubted that Congress has power to prescribe the "procedure" for the federal courts, and this would certainly include a power to include within the domain of "procedure" subject-matter falling within the borderland between substance and procedure, and rationally capable of classification within either category.

[7] Congress in the [Rules Enabling Act] uses "practice and procedure" in contrast with "substantive rights" but does not define these terms. Where statutory language is ambiguous, the courts properly are inclined to adopt the construction put upon the language by the agency charged with carrying out the statute. This would a fortiori be true when, as here, the agency happens to be the Supreme Court of the United States. Cf. *Sibbach v. Wilson & Co.,* 7 Cir., 1939, 108 F.2d 415 [aff'd. 312 U.S. 1 (1941)]. In the analogous situation where suit is brought in one state for an alleged tort committed in another, the courts generally classify burden of proof on the issue of contributory negligence as a matter of procedure and apply the lex fori. *Levy v. Steiger,* 233 Mass. 600, 124 N.E. 477; *Chicago Terminal R.R. v. Vandenberg,* 164 Ind. 470, 73 N.E. 990; and cases cited *supra,* in the text. Certainly the Supreme Court in construing the [Rules Enabling Act] could consider its power over procedure as embracing a subject-matter commonly though not universally classified as "procedure."

[8] The explanation probably is that the rules were drafted before *Swift v. Tyson, supra,* was overruled, and the Advisory

affirmatively plead contributory negligence. It is not inconsistent to require the defendant to plead contributory negligence if he wants to raise the issue, and yet to put the burden of proof on the plaintiff if the issue is raised. Since Rule 8(c) contains no prescription as to burden of proof, we must look elsewhere for the answer.

It seems to be said in *Francis v. Humphrey,* D.C., 25 F.Supp. 1, 4, and was suggested by counsel in the case at bar, that the question whether in diversity of citizenship cases burden of proof is to be classified as a matter of procedure or substantive law is to be determined by following the classification made by the courts of the state. No doubt we should look to those courts to tell us what their rule is and how it operates in local litigation. But once that is determined, the rule is the same whether it is labeled substantive law or procedure. Furthermore, as already pointed out, such a classification by the state court for one purpose does not mean that the classification is valid for another purpose. Surely the question whether a particular subject-matter falls within the power of the Supreme Court to prescribe rules of procedure under the [Rules Enabling Act], or is a matter of substantive law governed by the doctrine of the *Tompkins* case, cannot be foreclosed by the label given to the subject-matter by the state courts.

The inquiry then must be: considering the policy underlying *Erie Railroad Co. v. Tompkins, supra,* would that policy best be served by classifying burden of proof as to contributory negligence as a matter of procedure or substantive law? The incidence of burden of proof may determine the outcome of the case. This is true where the evidence is conflicting and the jury is not convinced either way. It is more pointedly true where, as sometimes happens, the injured person dies and no evidence is available on the issue of contributory negligence. If, in such a case, the burden of proof is on the defendant, the plaintiff wins, assuming the other elements of the cause of action are established. . . . If the burden is on the plaintiff, however, the defendant wins. . . .

Assuming the state rule to be one way and the federal rule the other, then the accident of citizenship becomes decisive of the litigation. The situation seems to call for the application of the rule in the *Tompkins* case. There is no important counter-consideration here, for the state rule can be easily ascertained and applied by the federal court without any administrative inconvenience. In thus concluding that for this purpose the incidence of the burden of proof as to contributory negligence is to be classified as a matter of substantive law, we are in harmony with the spirit of the *Tompkins* case, and at the same time are adhering to the classification maintained in an unbroken line of federal court decisions under *Swift v. Tyson, supra.*

. . .

Thus far, the case has been discussed as though suit had been brought in the federal court sitting in the state where the alleged tort occurred. But there is the complicating factor that the accident occurred in Maine and suit was brought in Massachusetts. This makes it necessary to consider three further points:

First, if the plaintiff had sued in a Massachusetts state court, would the Massachusetts Supreme Judicial Court have allowed the application of the Maine rule as to burden of proof? The answer is, no. The Court would have said that burden of proof is a matter of procedure only, and would

Committee assumed that the burden of proof was on the defendant because that had been the uniform federal rule under *Swift v. Tyson, supra.* We do not know, of course, whether the Supreme Court was aware that *Swift v. Tyson, supra,* was doomed to be overruled, but it may be pointed out that the Rules were transmitted by the Chief Justice to the Attorney General on December 20, 1937, and the *Tompkins* case was not argued in the Supreme Court until January 31, 1938.

have applied the Massachusetts rule that the burden is on the defendant to establish the plaintiff's contributory negligence. Such was the holding in *Levy v. Steiger,* 233 Mass. 600, 124 N.E. 477, and *Smith v. Brown,* Mass., 19 N.E.2d 732.

Second, would such a decision by the Supreme Judicial Court of Massachusetts be subject to reversal by the Supreme Court of the United States? Presumably we are permitted under the *Tompkins* case thus to attack the decision of a state court collaterally, so to speak, for the Supreme Court would hardly require the federal courts to follow a local decision which, had it been appealed, would have been reversed by the Supreme Court on constitutional grounds.

No question is involved of sovereign jurisdiction of the state over person or property, a segment of conflict of laws where the Supreme Court of the United States has long had the last word, under the due process clause.

[The court reviews the control by the Supreme Court of the choice of law by the state courts.]

Whatever the eventual development of this line of cases may be, we know of no decision indicating that the Supreme Court at the present time would reverse a decision of a state court in a case like *Levy v. Steiger, supra,* applying the lex fori rather than the lex loci delicti in the matter of burden of proof. Numerous decisions to this effect have been rendered by state courts, and it has never seemed to occur to anyone that a federal question was involved. . . .

It follows, therefore, that the unimpeachable law of Massachusetts in the case at bar is, that in a suit brought in Massachusetts the burden of proof as to contributory negligence is on the defendant, despite the contrary rule applicable in Maine where the accident occurred.

Third, this being the Massachusetts law, there remains the inquiry, what law must be applied in the federal court in Massachusetts when jurisdiction is invoked on the ground of diversity of citizenship? Under *Erie Railroad v. Tompkins, supra,* is it the Massachusetts or the Maine rule? We know of no considered decision by the Supreme Court on this point. In the *Tompkins* case, suit was brought in the federal court in New York on a tort alleged to have been committed in Pennsylvania. The question was whether the railroad owed a duty of care to an undiscovered pedestrian walking on a much-used path along the right of way near the tracks. The Supreme Court held that the lower court was in error in treating this question as a matter of "general law," and sent the case back for determination in accordance with the common law of Pennsylvania as declared by its highest court. There is no doubt that in this situation the state courts of New York would have applied the same rule of conflict of laws, and would have looked to the lex loci delicti. *Fitzpatrick v. International Ry. Co.,* 252 N.Y. 127, 169 N.E. 112, 68 A.L.R. 801. The decision in the *Tompkins* case manifestly tended to produce a uniformity in result in that particular situation, whether action on the Pennsylvania tort were brought in a New York state court or New York federal court. In *Mutual Benefit Ass'n v. Bowman,* 304 U.S. 549, 58 S.Ct. 1056, 1057, 82 L.Ed. 1521, suit was brought in the federal court in Nebraska on a contract of insurance made in New Mexico. The lower court decided a question of interpretation as a matter of "general law." In a brief per curiam opinion the Supreme Court reversed the judgment on the authority of *Erie Railroad v. Tompkins, supra,* and remanded the case to determine "the right of respondent to recover under the law of New Mexico." For all that appears, the Nebraska state courts would also have looked to the law of New Mexico to determine the interpretation of the contract. The case does not indicate what the decision would have been had it appeared that the Nebraska state courts would have applied a rule differing from that of the New Mexico courts. . . .

Until the point is finally ruled upon by the Supreme Court, lower courts must piece out as best they can the implications of the *Tompkins* case. The theory is that the federal court in Massachusetts sits as a court coordinate with the Massachusetts state courts to apply the Massachusetts law in diversity of citizenship cases. Under *Swift v. Tyson, supra,* the federal courts were free to disregard state court decisions on matters of "general law," and this included state court decisions on the common law relating to conflict of laws. . . . But under the *Tompkins* case the Massachusetts law must be determined by the state statutes and the common law as interpreted by the state courts, not by the federal court's notion of "general law." The powerful argument by Holmes, J., dissenting, in *Black & White Taxi Co. v. Brown & Yellow Taxi Co.,* . . . cited with approval by the majority opinion in the *Tompkins* case . . . seems to be applicable to that portion of the Massachusetts common law relating to conflict of laws quite as much as to the common law of contracts or torts. Except in the limited range of cases, already alluded to above, where state court decisions on points of conflict of laws are subject to reversal by the United States Supreme Court under the federal constitution, the rules applicable to conflict of laws are not "a transcendental body of law outside of any particular state but obligatory within it." If the federal court in Massachusetts on points of conflict of laws may disregard the law of Massachusetts as formulated by the Supreme Judicial Court and take its own view as a matter of "general law," then the ghost of *Swift v. Tyson, supra,* still walks abroad, somewhat shrunken in size, yet capable of much mischief. In the case at bar, it is difficult to see that any gain in the direction of uniformity would be achieved by creating a discrepancy between the rules of law applicable in the Massachusetts state and federal courts, respectively, in order to bring the law of the Massachusetts federal court in harmony with the law that would be applied in the state courts of Maine.

Our conclusion is that the court below was bound to apply the law as to burden of proof as it would have been applied by the state courts in Massachusetts.

This result may seem to present a surface incongruity, viz., the deference owing to the substantive law of Massachusetts as pronounced by its courts requires the federal court in that state to apply a Massachusetts rule as to burden of proof which the highest state court insists is procedural only. The explanation is that reasons of policy, set forth in the *Tompkins* case, make it desirable for the federal court in diversity of citizenship cases to apply the state rule, because the incidence of burden of proof is likely to have a decisive influence on the outcome of litigation; and this is true regardless of whether the state court characterizes the rule as one of procedure or substantive law. Certainly the federal court in Massachusetts cannot treat burden of proof as a matter of procedure in order to disregard the Massachusetts rule, and then treat it as substantive law in order to apply the Maine rule. Under the conclusion we have reached, if suit were brought in Massachusetts, the state and federal courts there would be in harmony as to burden of proof; and if suit were brought in Maine, the state and federal courts there would likewise be in harmony on this important matter. It is true that the rule applied in the Maine courts would not be the same as the rule applied in the Massachusetts courts. But this is a disparity that existed prior to *Erie Railroad v. Tompkins, supra,* and cannot be corrected by the doctrine of that case. It is a disparity that exists because Massachusetts may constitutionally maintain a rule of conflict of laws to the effect that the incidence of burden of proof is a matter of "procedure" to be governed by the law of the forum. *Levy v. Steiger, supra.*

For error in the instructions given to the jury on the burden of proof, the judgment must be reversed and the cause remanded for further proceedings not inconsistent with this opinion.

WILSON, CIRCUIT JUDGE, concurs in the result.

PETERS, DISTRICT JUDGE, dissents.

KLAXON COMPANY v. STENTOR ELECTRIC MANUFACTURING CO.

United States Supreme Court
313 U.S. 487 (1941)

MR. JUSTICE REED delivered the opinion of the Court.

The principal question in this case is whether in diversity cases the federal courts must follow conflict of laws rules prevailing in the states in which they sit. The frequent recurrence of the problem, as well as the conflict of approach to the problem between the Third Circuit's opinion here and that of the First Circuit in *Sampson v. Channell,* led us to grant certiorari.

In 1918, respondent, a New York corporation, transferred its entire business to petitioner, a Delaware corporation. Petitioner contracted to use its best efforts to further the manufacture and sale of certain patented devices covered by the agreement, and respondent was to have a share of petitioner's profits. The agreement was executed in New York, the assets were transferred there, and petitioner began performance there although later it moved its operations to other states. Respondent was voluntarily dissolved under New York law in 1919. Ten years later it instituted this action in the United States District Court for the District of Delaware, alleging that petitioner had failed to perform its agreement to use its best efforts. Jurisdiction rested on diversity of citizenship. In 1939 respondent recovered a jury verdict of $100,000, upon which judgment was entered. Respondent then moved to correct the judgment by adding interest at the rate of six percent from June 1, 1929, the date the action had been brought. The basis of the motion was the provision in § 480 of the New York Civil Practice Act directing that in contract actions interest be added to the principal sum "whether theretofore liquidated or unliquidated." The District Court granted the motion, taking the view that the rights of the parties were governed by New York law and that under New York law the addition to such interest was mandatory. 30 F. Supp. 425, 431. The Circuit Court of Appeals affirmed, 115 F.2d 268, and we granted certiorari, limited to the question whether § 480 of the New York Civil Practice Act is applicable to an action in the federal court in Delaware. . . .

The Circuit Court of Appeals was of the view that under New York law the right to interest before verdict under § 480 went to the substance of the obligation, and that proper construction of the contract in suit fixed New York as the place of performance. It then concluded that § 480 was applicable to the case because "it is clear by what we think is undoubtedly the better view of the law that the rules for ascertaining the measure of damages are not a matter of procedure at all, but are matters of substance which should be settled by reference to the law of the appropriate state according to the type of case being tried in the forum. The measure of damages for breach of a contract is determined by the law of the place of performance; *Restatement, Conflict of Laws* § 413." The court referred also to § 418 of the *Restatement,* which makes interest part of the damages to be determined by the law of the place of performance. Application of the New York statute apparently followed from the court's independent determination of the "better view" without regard to Delaware law, for no Delaware decision or statute was cited or discussed.

We are of opinion that the prohibition declared in *Erie R. Co. v. Tompkins,* against such independent determinations by the federal courts, extends to the field of conflict of laws. The conflict of laws rules to be applied by the federal court in Delaware must conform to those prevailing in Delaware's state courts. Otherwise, the accident of diversity of citizenship would constantly disturb equal administration of justice in coordinate state and federal courts sitting side by side. . . . Any other ruling would do violence to the principle of uniformity within a state, upon which the *Tompkins* decision is based. Whatever lack of uniformity this may produce between federal courts in different states is attributable to our federal system, which leaves to a state, within the limits permitted by the Constitution, the right to pursue local policies diverging from those of its neighbors. It is not for the federal courts to thwart such local policies by enforcing an independent "general law" of conflict of laws. Subject only to review by this Court on any federal question that may arise, Delaware is free to determine whether a given matter is to be governed by the law of the forum or some other law. . . . This Court's views are not the decisive factor in determining the applicable conflicts rule. . . . And the proper function of the Delaware federal court is to ascertain what the state law is, not what it ought to be.

. . .

Looking then to the Delaware cases, petitioner relies on one group to support his contention that the Delaware state courts would refuse to apply § 480 of the New York Civil Practice Act, and respondent on another to prove the contrary. We make no analysis of these Delaware decisions, but leave this for the Circuit Court of Appeals when the case is remanded.

Respondent makes the further argument that the judgment must be affirmed because, under the full faith and credit clause of the Constitution, the state courts of Delaware would be obliged to give effect to the New York statute. The argument rests mainly on the decision of this Court in *John Hancock Mutual Life Ins. Co. v. Yates,* 299 U. S. 178, where a New York statute was held such an integral part of a contract of insurance, that Georgia was compelled to sustain the contract under the full faith and credit clause. Here, however, § 480 of the New York Civil Practice Act is in no way related to the validity of the contract in suit, but merely to an incidental item of damages, interest, with respect to which courts at the forum have commonly been free to apply their own or some other law as they see fit. Nothing in the Constitution ensures unlimited extraterritorial recognition of all statutes or of any statute under all circumstances. *Pacific Employers Insurance Co. v. Industrial Accident Comm'n,* 306 U. S. 493; *Kryger v. Wilson,* 242 U. S. 171. The full faith and credit clause does not go so far as to compel Delaware to apply § 480 if such application would interfere with its local policy.

Accordingly, the judgment is reversed and the case remanded to the Circuit Court of Appeals for decision in conformity with the law of Delaware.

NOTES AND QUESTIONS

(1)(a) Not every choice of law case is a case of diversity of citizenship jurisdiction; indeed many of the cases we have seen, from *Alabama Great Southern R.R. v. Carroll* to *Babcock v. Jackson* and *Tooker v. Lopez* were common domicile (citizenship) cases. But every diversity of jurisdiction case is at least potentially a choice of law case, if domicile (citizenship) of the

§ 6.02   THE CONSTITUTION AND CONFLICT OF LAWS   □   451

parties is a relevant contact or interest.^a Which way does this point cut in looking at the *Klaxon* problem?

(b) We have seen that the conflicts revolution has placed increased emphasis on the domicile of the parties and on "governmental interests;" at the same time, it has, in general, become easier for plaintiffs to litigate in their own home state, rather than following defendants to their home states.^b Does it follow that the oft-disparaged reason for diversity jurisdiction, the alleged need to guard against "home town justice" has gained new justification?

(c) Consider governmental interest analysis in the context of *Klaxon* and the supposed rationale of diversity jurisdiction. Does *Klaxon* mean that a federal court can no longer serve as a neutral arbitrator, but (if the state where it sits adheres to the governmental interests approach) must also act to further that state's interest?

(2)(a) Assuming, as it seems one must, that *Erie* is constitutionally determined, are the cases in this section likewise constitutionally determined? Judge Magruder said (p. 448, *supra*) that "reasons of policy, set forth in the *Tompkins* case, make it *desirable* for the federal court . . . to apply the state rule," which suggests he was not convinced that there was a constitutional command. Does Justice Reed in *Klaxon* go further?

(b) One way to test the preceding question is to ask whether Congress, perhaps convinced by the argument in question (1), could constitutionally enact a statute providing that federal courts shall exercise their independent judgment on matters, of choice of law in diversity cases. Would such a statute be constitutional? If not, what provision of the Constitution would it violate?

(c) In *Erie,* the Supreme Court told the lower federal court, sitting in New York, to apply Pennsylvania law, and said nothing about New York's choice of law. In *Klaxon,* the Court of Appeals for the Third Circuit likewise applied the law of the state to which its conflict of laws rule pointed, but was reversed.[c] By the standards of *Klaxon,* was *Erie* wrongly decided? Or vice versa?

(d) Why *do* you suppose Justice Brandeis paid no attention to the state/state choice of law problem? For that matter, note that Justice Story, the great conflicts scholar, treated *Swift v. Tyson* as a federal/general vs. New York law case, without any attention to the law of Maine, where the bill of exchange had been drawn and where it was negotiated.

(3) *Klaxon,* being a Supreme Court case, is of course ultimately more important than *Sampson v. Channell*. But the opinion in *Klaxon* is thin, and the issue in controversy—prejudgment interest on a contract claim—not very interesting. *Sampson,* in contrast, raises at least two intertwined issues of federalism and choice of law, and Judge Magruder's opinion, just in terms of technique, is fascinating.[d] The controversy, of course, is about burden of proof of contributory negligence.

---

[a] Citizenship and domicile are here used interchangeably, which seems correct so long as all parties are citizens of the United States. Until 1988 an alien was deemed to be diverse to a citizen of the United States, even if he was domiciled in the United States. In 1988 § 1332(a) was amended so that an alien admitted to the United States for permanent residence is deemed for purposes of diversity jurisdiction to be a citizen of the State in which the alien is domiciled.

[b] See Chapter 7, *infra,* for exploration of developments in judicial jurisdiction.

[c] In fact the author of the opinion in the Court of Appeals was Judge Goodrich, who had been Beale's assistant in the first *Restatement of Conflict of Laws* and was himself the author of a hornbook on Conflict of Laws.

[d] Professor Freund reports that one member of the Supreme Court remarked that he had voted to deny certiorari in *Sampson* because he felt that the Court could not produce an opinion as excellent as Judge Magruder's. Freund, *Federal-State Relations in the Opinions of Judge Magruder,* 72 Harv. L. Rev. 1204, 1206 (1959).

Defendant is dead, and so his estate will probably be unable to meet a burden of proving that plaintiff was negligent; plaintiff, on the other hand, may not be able to establish his due care just before the collision. Whoever has the burden will lose the case.

(a) Is burden of proof an *Erie* issue at all?

(b) Could the federal courts make their own rule on the subject, derived, for example, from Rule 8(c) of the Federal Rules of Civil Procedure?[e] Or would that be going beyond the Rules Enabling Act provision that the rules "shall not abridge, enlarge or modify any substantive right?"[f]

(c) Even if the answer is that the Rules Enabling Act would not support a rule on burden of proof, does it follow that Congress could not adopt a rule concerning burden of proof in negligence cases? Assuming that such a rule, designed to achieve uniformity within the federal judicial system, would be constitutional if enacted by Congress, would it nevertheless be contrary to the teaching of *Erie*?[g]

(d) As between burden of proof and choice of law in diversity cases, which has the greater claim to an independent federal role?

(4)(a) If burden of proof, as Judge Magruder concludes, is "substantive" for *Erie* purposes, why should it not be governed as are the other aspects of choice of law, for instance on a limit on damages, or an applicable guest statute, or, say, a law requiring the wearing of seatbelts?

(b) Judge Magruder says (p. 448 *supra*) that if the preceding suggestion were adopted, the ghost of *Swift v. Tyson* would still walk abroad, albeit shrunken in size. Is that right?

(c) Magruder concedes a surface incongruity, but says he overcomes it. How?

(d) Is he saying the characterization for *Erie* purposes is to be made by the federal court, but for choice of law purposes not? Has renvoi made an unexpected return engagement?

(5)(a) Try drafting an opinion in *Sampson* that begins:

> For purposes of *Erie v. Tompkins,* we regard the question of burden of proof as procedural. . . .

(b) Now try drafting an opinion that begins:

> We believe the issue of burden of proof in this serious accident case goes to the allocation of loss, and is therefore governed by the law that governs the accident. . . .[h]

(6)(a) One of the important reasons given in *Erie* for overruling a century of precedent was the goal of reducing forum-shopping. Is this accomplished by *Klaxon*?

(b) Professor Cavers, a defender of *Klaxon,* says yes to the preceding question, because lawyers are unlikely to give up cases to out-of-state counsel, which *Klaxon* perhaps encourages, but would

---

[e] Documents Supplement, p. 23.

[f] 28 U.S.C. § 2072, Documents Supplement p. 62.

[g] See generally Freund, note d, *supra*, at 1207–08.

[h] For the hint of such an opinion, a few months before *Klaxon,* see *Sibbach v. Wilson,* 312 U.S. 1, 10–11 (1941). In *Sibbach,* the issue was whether Federal Rule 35, authorizing the federal court to order a party to submit to a physical examination, was "procedural," hence within the Rules Enabling Act, or substantive. The accident that gave rise to the suit had taken place in Indiana, but the litigation was in federal court in Illinois. In the course of its opinion upholding the federal rule, the Court said:

> . . . if the right to be exempt from such an order is one of substantive law, the Rules of Decision Act required the District Court, though sitting in Illinois, to apply the law of Indiana, the state where the cause of action arose, and to order the examination.

be quite prepared to go across courthouse square or even to the next major city where they would find a federal district court but could keep control of the case.[i]

(c) Further, Cavers writes, it is a mistake to think of the federal courts as a true judicial system, though of course they use a common set of rules of procedure. "For a large number of courts really to constitute a judicial system," he writes, "it is necessary that they be subject to the surveillance of a single supreme court which by its decisions can give direction to, and impose uniformity upon, the courts subordinate to it. This is a function which clearly the Supreme Court of the United States has not been discharging with respect to diversity cases involving choice of law problems for many decades. . . . It is plain, moreover, that the Court is confronted by demands upon its limited time and attention that are far too important to be set aside for the perplexing choice-of-law problems that arise in private litigation."[j] The implication is that while there might be uniformity between federal courts sitting in Massachusetts and Maine, there would be no assurance of conformity between federal courts, say in New York and Pennsylvania, belonging to different circuits.

(d) Writing in 1963, near the beginning of the conflicts revolution, Cavers had an even more serious concern: If the Supreme Court were to become involved, for instance, in a conflict of conflict of laws decisions among the circuits, he thinks it would be under great pressure to come up with what he calls that lowest common denominator—broad general jurisdiction-selecting rules that might be easy to follow, but would be antithetical to what he and his colleagues, as well as forward-looking judges had been trying to accomplish in the revolt against the tyranny of the first *Restatement.* Do you agree with that fear? Is it borne out by the performance of the Supreme Court in the (constitutional) cases in the preceding chapter?

(7)(a) Consider, finally, whether *Klaxon* imposes restraints on federal courts in experimenting on questions of state law generally, and choice of law questions in particular. In theory, that might well seem to be a danger, if federal courts in diversity cases were really, in Judge Frank's phrase, "to play the role of ventriloquist's dummy to the courts of some particular state."[k] For example, recall the *Kilberg* and *Pearson* cases[l] both arising out of the same accident, and both involving New York plaintiffs suing a corporate citizen of Massachusetts. If *Pearson,* the federal case, had been decided before *Kilberg,* the state case, it seems highly unlikely that it would have departed from lex loci delicti, thereby launching the conflicts revolution.

(b) Cavers takes a different view, arguing that federal courts, by not being bound by nation-wide precedents, have a "very important opportunity . . . to join with the state courts in developing the new approach [to choice of law]."[m]

Consider how the *Erie/Klaxon* rule has affected the choice of law process in the United States, on the basis of the federal diversity cases we have seen thus far—*Mack Trucks, Inc. v. Bendix-Westinghouse Automotive Co.* (Ch. 2); *Pearson v. Northeast Airlines, Chila v. Owens, Rosenthal v. Warren, O'Connor v. Lee-Hy Paving Co.,* (Ch. 3); *Southern International Sales Co. v. Potter*

---

[i] See Cavers, *The Changing Choice-of-Law Process and the Federal Courts,* 28 Law & Contemp. Prob. 732, 740–43 (1963), reprinted in D. Cavers, *The Choice of Law, Selected Essays 1933–1983,* 119, 130–33 (1985).

[j] *Id.* at 738–39, *Selected Essays* at 128.

[k] See *Richardson v. Commissioner of Internal Revenue,* 126 F.2d 562, 567 (2d Cir. 1942)

[l] Chapter 3, pp. 129, 135, *supra.*

[m] Cavers, note i, *supra,* at 739, *Selected Essays* at 129.

& *Brumfield* (Ch. 4); *First National Bank of Chicago v. United Airlines, Wells v. Simonds Abrasive Co.* (Ch. 5).[n]

§ 6.03 *Erie* and the Federal Judicial System

[A] Interest Analysis Again?

Erie R. Co. v. Tompkins, as has often been pointed out, was decided in the same year, 1938, that the Federal Rules of Civil Proceedure became effective. Thus the "Copernican Revolution" in the relation between the federal courts and the states was accomplished at both ends.

It is interesting to note that Justice Brandeis dissented from the order of the Supreme Court adopting the Rules, though without without opinion. 308 U.S. 649 (1937). It is not clear why he dissented—whether because he had not carefully studied the rules, or did not believe they should emanate from the Court, or believed they would lead to excessive centralization at the expense of experimentation and local interests.[a] Professor Freund noted that "Quite of a piece with his opposition to the [Rules] was his opinion for the Court in *Erie*. . . ."[b]

Judge Weinstein, looking back, had a different view:

> In a sense, the 1938 Supreme Court was clearing the decks for the important action that would take place in a few years. From this perspective, *Erie* and the Federal Rules were not at cross-purposes. Although they did turn federal practice upside-down, they were, in concert, reorienting the federal courts from a local role towards an increasingly national role. Both the Rules and *Erie* had the effect of freeing the federal courts from local tasks, and preparing them for the important role they were to play in the new national scheme.[c]

Inevitably, the twilight zone (in Judge Magruder's phrase) between substance and procedure remained indistinct. Often, as pointed out particularly by Professor Ely, courts, counsel, and commentators forgot that though the essence of the controversy remained constant—did federal or state law govern?—the sources of the controversy were distinct, depending on whether the asserted federal authority was drawn from the Rules Enabling Act, from the Rules of Decision Act, or perhaps from constitutional emanations from *Erie* itself.[d]

In fact, the Supreme Court's attitude toward these issues has shifted from time to time, reflecting changing views of federalism (as well as some rather technical issues). Some dozen cases of this kind have been decided by the Supreme Court, dealing with such subjects as the time when an action commences for purposes of the statute of limitations;[e] access to courts in the face of state door-closing rules;[f] security for costs in derivative shareholder suits;[g] the

---

[n] For a recent reaffirmation by the Supreme Court of the proposition that federal courts may not substitute their own view of the relevant state interests for the conflict of laws rules of the states where they sit, see *Day & Zimmerman, Inc. v. Challoner,* 423 U.S. 3 (1975).

[a] For some inconclusive but intriguing speculation, see Jack Weinstein, *The Ghost of Process Past: The Fiftieth Anniversary of the Federal Rules of Civil Procedure and Erie,* 54 Brooklyn L. Rev. 1, 21-23 (1988).

[b] Freund, *Mr. Justice Brandeis,* in *Mr. Justice,* 177, 191 (Dunham & Kurland eds. 2d ed. (1964).

[c] Weinstein, note a *supra,* at 20-21.

[d] See Ely, *The Irrepressible Myth of Erie,* 87 Harv. L. Rev. 693 (1974).

[e] *Ragan v. Merchants Transfer & Warehouse Co.,* 337 U.S. 530 (1949); *Walker v. Armco Steel Corporation,* 446 U.S. 740 (1980), both upholding the state rule.

[f] *Angel v. Bullington,* 330 U.S. 183 (1947); *Woods v. Interstate Realty Co.,* 337 U. S. 535 (1949), both holding

§ 6.03   THE CONSTITUTION AND CONFLICT OF LAWS   □   455

permissible scope of discovery alleged to interfere with state-protected rights of privacy;[h] and the issue raised in *Sampson v. Channell,* burden of proof of contributory negligence.[i] The three most important cases—*Guaranty Trust, Byrd,* and *Hanna*—are summarized very briefly below, not with sufficient detail to bring out the discussion which each case is capable of stimulating, but just enough, it is hoped, to refresh the reader's recollection of discussions elsewhere.

1. In *Guaranty Trust v. York,* 326 U.S. 99 (1945), a holder of notes issued by a corporation that became insolvent brought a diversity action in federal court in New York against the trustee of the noteholders, alleging that the trustee had failed to protect her interests (and those of similarly situated persons) and had failed to disclose its self-interest in sponsoring an offer to convert the notes into cash and stock. Under New York law the action would apparently have been barred by the statute of limitations, but the Court of Appeals held that in an action in equity the federal court need not apply the state limitations statute. The Supreme Court, in an opinion by Justice Frankfurter, reversed:

> [T]he question is not whether a statute of limitations is deemed a matter of "procedure" in some sense. The question is whether such a statute concerns merely the manner and the means by which a right to recover, as recognized by the State, is enforced, or whether such a limitation is a matter of substance in the aspect that alone is relevant to our problem, namely does it significantly affect the result of a litigation. . . .
>
> . . .
>
> Plainly enough, a statute that would completely bar recovery in a suit if brought in a State court bears on a State-created right vitally and not merely formally or negligibly. As to consequences that so intimately affect recovery or non-recovery a federal court in a diversity case should follow State law.
>
> . . .
>
> Whenever that law is authoritatively declared by a State, whether its voice be the legislature or its highest court, such law ought to govern in litigation founded on that law, whether the forum of application is a State or a federal court and whether the remedies be sought at law or may be had in equity.[j]

2. *Guaranty Trust* was the high-water mark of the deference to state rules. In *Byrd v. Blue Ridge Rural Electric Cooperative, Inc.,* 356 U.S. 525 (1958), the Court began to balance state against federal interests.

Byrd involved the familiar pattern of an employee injured in an industrial accident subject to workers' compensation seeking to bring an action in tort against a third party. In this case the plaintiff, a citizen of North Carolina, was employed by a contractor in building an electric power substation for Blue Ridge, a South Carolina corporation. Blue Ridge asserted that the claim was barred because plaintiff was its "statutory employee" and thus covered by the South Carolina

---

that if state courts could not hear a claim, neither could federal courts sitting in the state, even if the cause of action arose in another state. See also *First Nat'l Bank of Chicago v. United Air Lines,* and (respectively) *Wells v. Simonds Abrasive Co.,* Ch. 5, pp. 371, 374, *supra.*

[g] *Cohen v. Beneficial Industrial Loan Corp.,* 337 U.S. 541 (1949), also upholding the state rule.

[h] *Sibbach v. Wilson & Co.,* 312 U.S. 1 (1941) upholding Federal Rule 35.

[i] *Palmer v. Hoffman,* 318 U.S. 109 (1943) confirming Judge Magruder's view that while Federal Rule 8(c) controlled the obligation to plead, the burden of proof was subject to state law.

[j] 326 U.S. at 109, 110, 112.

Workmen's Compensation Act. This issue depended on whether the employees of the contractor did the same work as Blue Ridge's own employees. To simplify a complicated litigation history, the question was whether that issue should be decided by the judge or a jury. The defendant pointed to a recent decision of the Supreme Court of South Carolina holding that the issue was for the judge, and argued that under *Erie* and *Guaranty Trust,* the federal court must follow that ruling. The U.S. Supreme Court, in an opinion by Justice Brennan, disagreed:

> It may well be that in the instant personal-injury case the outcome would be substantially affected by whether the issue of immunity is decided by a judge or a jury. Therefore, were "outcome" the only consideration, a strong case might appear for saying that the federal court should follow the state practice.
>
> But there are affirmative countervailing considerations at work here. The federal system is an independent system for administering justice to litigants who properly invoke its jurisdiction. An essential characteristic of that system is the manner in which, in civil common-law actions, it distributes trial functions between judge and jury and, under the influence—if not the command—of the Seventh Amendment, assigns the decisions of disputed facts to the jury.[k]

Furthermore, it was by no means certain that committing the issue to the jury was "outcome determinative":

> We do not think the likelihood of a different result is so strong as to require the federal practice of jury determination of disputed factual issues to yield to the state rule in the interest of uniformity of outcome.[l]

3. Eight years after the decision in *Byrd,* the Supreme Court returned to the balancing theme, this time with the focus on a particular Federal Rule. *Hanna v. Plumer,* 380 U.S. 460 (1965), was a diversity action arising out of an automobile accident in South Carolina, in which an Ohio plaintiff alleged injury caused by the negligence of a Massachusetts citizen, now deceased. Plaintiff served the summons and complaint in Massachusetts in conformity with Federal Rule 4(d)(1),[m] by leaving a copy with the wife of the executor of the estate. The executor moved to dismiss, on the ground that service had not been made in conformity with a Massachusetts statute that required service on an executor to be in hand or by notice to the probate court. The U.S. District Court dismissed on the strength of *Guaranty Trust* and *Ragan,*[n] and the Court of Appeals affirmed. The Supreme Court, in an opinion by Chief Justice Warren, reversed. True, in a literal sense if service of process is ineffective, defendant wins. But that kind of " 'outcome-determination' analysis was never intended to serve as a talisman. . . . [C]hoices between state and federal law are to be made not by application of any automatic 'litmus paper' criterion, but rather by reference to the policies underlying the *Erie* rule."[o]

> There is, however, a more fundamental flaw in respondent's syllogism: the incorrect assumption that the rule of *Erie R. Co. v. Tompkins* constitutes the appropriate test of the validity and therefore the applicability of a Federal Rule of Civil Procedure.

---

[k] 356 U.S. at 537.

[l] *Id.* at 540.

[m] Documents Supplement, p. 15.

[n] Note e, *supra.*

[o] 380 U.S. at 466–67.

> When a situation is covered by one of the Federal Rules, the question facing the court is a far cry from the typical, relatively unguided *Erie* choice: the court has been instructed to apply the Federal Rule, and can refuse to do so only if the Advisory Committee, this Court, and Congress erred in their prima facie judgment that the Rule in question transgresses neither the terms of the Enabling Act nor constitutional restrictions.[p]

Justice Harlan, in a concurring opinion that many observers have found persuasive, would have approached the issue differently:

> To my mind the proper line of approach in determining whether to apply a state or a federal rule, whether "substantive" or "procedural," is to stay close to basic principles by inquiring if the choice of rule would substantially affect those primary decisions respecting human conduct which our constitutional system leaves to state regulation.
>
> . . .
>
> Whereas the unadulterated outcome and forum-shopping tests may err too far toward honoring state rules, I submit that the Court's "arguably procedural, *ergo* constitutional" test moves too fast and far in the other direction.[q]

[B] The Effect of Transfer on Choice of Law

VAN DUSEN v. BARRACK

*United States Supreme Court
376 U.S. 612 (1964)*

Mr. Justice Goldberg delivered the opinion of the Court.

This case involves the construction and application of § 1404 (a) of the Judicial Code of 1948. Section 1404 (a), which allows a "change of venue" within the federal judicial system, provides that: "For the convenience of parties and witnesses, in the interest of justice, a district court may transfer any civil action to any other district or division where it might have been brought." 28 U. S. C. § 1404 (a).

The facts, which need but brief statement here, reveal that the disputed change of venue is set against the background of an alleged mass tort. On October 4, 1960, shortly after departing from a Boston airport, a commercial airliner, scheduled to fly from Boston to Philadelphia, plunged into Boston Harbor. As a result of the crash, over 150 actions for personal injury and wrongful death have been instituted against the airline, various manufacturers, the United States, and, in some cases, the Massachusetts Port Authority. In most of these actions the plaintiffs have alleged that the crash resulted from the defendants' negligence in permitting the aircraft's engines to ingest some birds. More than 100 actions were brought in the United States District Court for the District of Massachusetts, and more than 45 actions in the United States District Court for the Eastern District of Pennsylvania.

---

[p] *Id.* at 469–71.

[q] 380 U.S. at 475–76 (Harlan, J. concurring).

The present case concerns 40 of the wrongful death actions brought in the Eastern District of Pennsylvania by personal representatives of victims of the crash.[1] The defendants, petitioners in this Court, moved under § 1404 (a) to transfer these actions to the District of Massachusetts, where it was alleged that most of the witnesses resided and where over 100 other actions are pending. The District Court granted the motion, holding that the transfer was justified regardless of whether the transferred actions would be governed by the laws and choice-of-law rules of Pennsylvania or of Massachusetts. 204 F. Supp. 426. The District Court also specifically held that transfer was not precluded by the fact that the plaintiffs had not qualified under Massachusetts law to sue as representatives of the decedents. The plaintiffs, respondents in this Court, sought a writ of mandamus from the Court of Appeals and successfully contended that the District Court erred and should vacate its order of transfer. 309 F. 2d 953. The Court of Appeals held that a § 1404 (a) transfer could be granted only if at the time the suits were brought, the plaintiffs had qualified to sue in Massachusetts, the State of the transferee District Court.

We granted certiorari to review important questions concerning the construction and operation of § 1404 (a). For reasons to be stated below, we hold that the judgment of the Court of Appeals must be reversed, that both the Court of Appeals and the District Court erred in their fundamental assumptions regarding the state law to be applied to an action transferred under § 1404 (a), and that accordingly the case must be remanded to the District Court.

I. Where the Action "Might Have Been Brought."

. . .

[The court holds that "there is no valid reason" for reading the quoted words to narrow the range of possible forums beyond those permitted by federal venue statutes. Since ancillary administrators could have been appointed for the Pennsylvania decedents in Massachusetts, the fact that the particular plaintiffs have not been appointed under Massachusetts law cannot defeat transfer.]

II. "The Interest of Justice": Effect of a Change of Venue Upon Applicable State Law.

A. The plaintiffs contend that the change of venue ordered by the District Court was necessarily precluded by the likelihood that it would be accompanied by a highly prejudicial change in the applicable state law. . . .

It is argued that Pennsylvania choice-of-law rules would result in the application of laws substantially different from those that would be applied by courts sitting in Massachusetts. The District Court held, however, that transfer could be ordered regardless of the state laws and choice-of-law rules to be applied in the transferee forum and regardless of the possibility that the laws applicable in the transferor State would significantly differ from those applicable in the transferee State. This ruling assumed that transfer to a more convenient forum may be granted on a defendant's motion even though that transfer would seriously prejudice the plaintiff's legal claim. If this assumption is valid, the plaintiffs argue, transfer is necessarily precluded—regardless of convenience and other considerations—as against the "interest of justice" in dealing with plaintiffs who have either exercised the venue privilege conferred by federal statutes, or had their cases removed from state into federal court.

---

[1] The plaintiffs are "Pennsylvania fiduciaries representing the estates of Pennsylvania decedents."

If conflict of laws rules are laid aside, it is clear that Massachusetts (the State of the transferee court) and Pennsylvania (the State of the transferor court) have significantly different laws concerning recovery for wrongful death. The Massachusetts Death Act provides that one who negligently causes the death of another "shall be liable in damages in the sum of not less than two thousand nor more than twenty thousand dollars, to be assessed with reference to the degree of his culpability. . . ." Mass. Ann. Laws, c. 229, § 2 (Supp. 1961). By contrast, under Pennsylvania law the recovery of damages (1) is based upon the more common principle of compensation for losses rather than upon the degree of the tortfeasor's culpability and (2) is not limited to $20,000. Some of the defendants urge, however, that these differences are irrelevant to the present case because Pennsylvania state courts, applying their own choice of law rules, would require that the Massachusetts Death Act be applied in its entirety, including its culpability principle and damage limitation. It follows that a federal district court sitting in Pennsylvania, and referring, as is required by *Klaxon Co. v. Stentor Elec. Mfg. Co., Inc.,* to Pennsylvania choice-of-law rules, would therefore be applying the same substantive rules as would a state or federal court in Massachusetts if the actions had been commenced there. This argument highlights the fact that the most convenient forum is frequently the place where the cause of action arose and that the conflict-of-laws rules of other States may often refer to the substantive rules of the more convenient forum. The plaintiffs, however, point to the decision of the New York Court of Appeals in *Kilberg v. Northeast Airlines, Inc.,* [p. 129, *supra*], and the decision of the Court of Appeals for the Second Circuit in *Pearson v. Northeast Airlines, Inc.,* [p. 135, *supra*], as indicating that Pennsylvania, in light of its laws and policies, might not apply the culpability and damage limitation aspects of the Massachusetts statute. The District Court, in ordering that the actions be transferred, found it both undesirable and unnecessary to rule on the question of whether Pennsylvania courts would accept the right of action provided by the Massachusetts statute while at the same time denying enforcement of the Massachusetts measure of recovery.[24] The District Court found it undesirable to resolve this question because the Pennsylvania courts had not yet considered it and because they would, in view of similar pending cases, soon have an opportunity to do so. The District Court, being of the opinion that the District of Massachusetts was in any event a more convenient place for trial, reasoned that the transfer should be granted forthwith and that the transferee court could proceed to the trial of the actions and postpone consideration of the Pennsylvania choice-of-law rule as to damages until a later time at which the Pennsylvania decisions might well have supplied useful guidance. Fundamentally, however, the transferring District Court assumed that the Pennsylvania choice of law rule was irrelevant because the transfer would be permissible and justified even if accompanied by a significant change of law.

The possibilities suggested by the plaintiffs' argument illustrate the difficulties that would arise if a change of venue, granted at the motion of a defendant, were to result in a change of law. Although in the present case the contentions concern rules relating to capacity to sue and damages, in other cases the transferee forum might have a shorter statute of limitations or might refuse to adjudicate a claim which would have been actionable in the transferor State. In such cases a defendant's motion to transfer could be tantamount to a motion to dismiss. In light, therefore, of this background and the facts of the present case, we need not and do not consider the merits of the contentions concerning the meaning and proper application of Pennsylvania's laws and

---

[24] The defendants, rejecting the view adopted by the Second Circuit in *Pearson v. Northeast Airlines, Inc.,* 309 F. 2d 553, contend that the Full Faith and Credit Clause requires Pennsylvania courts to follow all the terms of the Massachusetts Death Act. We intimate no view concerning this contention.

choice of law rules. For present purposes it is enough that the potential prejudice to the plaintiffs is so substantial as to require review of the assumption that a change of state law would be a permissible result of transfer under § 1404 (a).

The decisions of the lower federal courts, taken as a whole, reveal that courts construing § 1404 (a) have been strongly inclined to protect plaintiffs against the risk that transfer might be accompanied by a prejudicial change in applicable state laws. . . .

The legislative history of § 1404 (a) certainly does not justify the rather startling conclusion that one might "get a change of law as a bonus for a change of venue." Indeed, an interpretation accepting such a rule would go far to frustrate the remedial purposes of § 1404 (a). If a change of law were in the offing, the parties might well regard the section primarily as a forum-shopping instrument. And, more importantly, courts would at least be reluctant to grant transfers, despite considerations of convenience, if to do so might conceivably prejudice the claim of a plaintiff who had initially selected a permissible forum. We believe, therefore, that both the history and purposes of § 1404 (a) indicate that it should be regarded as a federal judicial housekeeping measure, dealing with the placement of litigation in the federal courts and generally intended, on the basis of convenience and fairness, simply to authorize a change of courtrooms.

Although we deal here with a congressional statute apportioning the business of the federal courts, our interpretation of that statute fully accords with and is supported by the policy underlying *Erie R. Co. v. Tompkins*. This Court has often formulated the *Erie* doctrine by stating that it establishes "the principle of uniformity within a state," *Klaxon Co. v. Stentor Elec. Mfg. Co., Inc.,* and declaring that federal courts in diversity of citizenship cases are to apply the laws "of the states in which they sit," *Griffin v. McCoach* [313 U.S. 498 (1941)]. A superficial reading of these formulations might suggest that a transferee federal court should apply the law of the State in which it sits rather than the law of the transferor State. Such a reading, however, directly contradicts the fundamental *Erie* doctrine which the quoted formulations were designed to express. As this Court said in *Guaranty Trust Co. v. York,* 326 U. S. 99, 109:

> *Erie R. Co. v. Tompkins* was not an endeavor to formulate scientific legal terminology. It expressed a policy that touches vitally the proper distribution of judicial power between State and federal courts. . . . The nub of the policy that underlies *Erie R. Co. v. Tompkins* is that for the same transaction the accident of a suit by a non-resident litigant in a federal court instead of in a State court a block away should not lead to a substantially different result.

Applying this analysis to § 1404 (a), we should ensure that the "accident" of federal diversity jurisdiction does not enable a party to utilize a transfer to achieve a result in federal court which could not have been achieved in the courts of the State where the action was filed. This purpose would be defeated in cases such as the present if nonresident defendants, properly subjected to suit in the transferor State (Pennsylvania), could invoke § 1404 (a) to gain the benefits of the laws of another jurisdiction (Massachusetts). What *Erie* and the cases following it have sought was an identity or uniformity between federal and state courts; and the fact that in most instances this could be achieved by directing federal courts to apply the laws of the States "in which they sit" should not obscure that, in applying the same reasoning to § 1404 (a), the critical identity to be maintained is between the federal district court which decides the case and the courts of the State in which the action was filed.

We conclude, therefore, that in cases such as the present, where the defendants seek transfer, the transferee district court must be obligated to apply the state law that would have been applied if there had been no change of venue. A change of venue under § 1404 (a) generally should be, with respect to state law, but a change of courtrooms.

We, therefore, reject the plaintiffs' contention that the transfer was necessarily precluded by the likelihood that a prejudicial change of law would result. In so ruling, however, we do not and need not consider whether in all cases § 1404 (a) would require the application of the law of the transferor, as opposed to the transferee, State. We do not attempt to determine whether, for example, the same considerations would govern if a plaintiff sought transfer under § 1404 (a) or if it was contended that the transferor State would simply have dismissed the action on the ground of *forum non conveniens*.

. . .

III. APPLICABLE LAW: EFFECT ON THE CONVENIENCE OF PARTIES AND WITNESSES.

. . .

In the present case the District Court held that the requested transfer could and should be granted regardless of whether the laws of the transferor State or of the transferee State were to be applied. . . .

. . . Since, however, Pennsylvania laws would govern the trial of the transferred cases, insofar as those laws may be significantly different from the laws governing the cases already pending in Massachusetts, the feasibility of consolidation and the benefits therefrom may be substantially altered. . . .

[I]t has long been recognized that: "There is an appropriateness . . . in having the trial of a diversity case in a forum that is at home with the state law that must govern the case, rather than having a court in some other forum untangle problems in conflict of laws, and in law foreign to itself." *Gulf Oil Corp. v. Gilbert*, 330 U. S. 501, 509. Thus, to the extent that Pennsylvania laws are difficult or unclear and might not defer to Massachusetts laws, it may be advantageous to retain the actions in Pennsylvania where the judges possess a more ready familiarity with the local laws.

If, on the other hand, Pennsylvania courts would apply the Massachusetts Death Act in its entirety, these same factors might well weigh quite differently.

. . .

It is appropriate, therefore, to reverse the judgment of the Court of Appeals and to remand to the District Court to reconsider the motion to transfer.

Accordingly, the judgment of the Court of Appeals for the Third Circuit is reversed and the cause remanded to the District Court for further proceedings in conformity with this opinion.

MR. JUSTICE BLACK concurs in the reversal substantially for the reasons set forth in the opinion of the Court, but he believes that, under the circumstances shown in the opinion, this Court should now hold it was error to order these actions transferred to the District of Massachusetts.

NOTES AND QUESTIONS

(1) As indicated in the introduction to this chapter, this is not the proper forum for exploring all the ramifications of *Erie*. Many of the questions raised by the series of cases from *Guaranty*

Trust through *Byrd* and *Hanna* are, however, at bottom choice of law issues, and it is pertinent to ask whether the techniques relevant to conflicts between the laws of New York and Massachusetts, or Kentucky and Ohio, are applicable to conflicts between state and federal law.

(a) Would it be fair to suggest that if there is a true conflict—i.e., if a state rule reflects a genuine state interest—the federal court in a diversity action must apply that rule, but if the state rule does not reflect an underlying judgment allocating risks and burdens, the federal court may disregard it?

(b) Would you want to amend the preceding formulation, leaving the first part intact, but conditioning the authority of the federal court to disregard the state rule on the existence of a genuine federal interest on the other side?

(c) Would the suggestion made in either paragraph (a) or paragraph (b) explain *Guaranty Trust, Byrd,* and *Hanna*?

(d) What about the cases cited in notes e–i, pp. 454–55, *supra*?[a]

(2)(a) In a portion of *Guaranty Trust* not quoted in the text, the Court said:

> . . . Congress afforded out-of-State litigants another tribunal, not another body of law. The operation of a double system of conflicting laws in the same State is plainly hostile to the reign of law.[b]

In *Byrd,* as we saw, the Court spoke of the federal system as "an independent system for administering justice."[c] In *Hanna,* the Court spoke of the "twin aims of the *Erie* rule: discouragement of forum shopping and an avoidence of inequitable administration of laws."[d] Of course these three statements were made over a twenty-year period by three different justices, and represent at least a shift in emphasis, if not in doctrine. Is there a way to reconcile the three statements?

(b) Does Justice Harlan's distinction between primary activity and litigation activity do it? Or is this another attempt, such as the general/local law distinction, or the substance/procedure distinction, that proposes rules of thumb when careful surveys are called for?

(3)(a) Returning to the mainstream of this volume, is *Van Dusen v. Barrack* correctly decided?

(b) If the decision troubles you, either as a theoretical or as a practical matter, does it suggest rethinking *Klaxon*? Or the transfer rules?

(c) Note that transfer in the federal system only became possible in 1948, when Congress adopted § 1404(a) in response to the Supreme Court's decision in *Gulf Oil Corp. v. Gilbert,*[e] which for the first time authorized a federal court with personal and subject matter jurisdiction to dismiss a case on the basis of forum non conveniens. If a case were dismissed on that ground, plaintiff would not obtain the advantage that he gets under *Barrack;* on the other hand, if neither

---

[a] Using an analysis something like that suggested in the text, Professor Ely concluded that *Sibbach v. Wilson* was wrongly decided in favor of the federal rule, *Ragan* was correctly decided in favor of the state rule, and *Hanna* was correctly decided in favor of the federal rule. Professor Chayes, generally agreeing with Ely's analysis, thinks just the opposite, i.e., that *Sibbach* was right, *Ragan* and *Hanna* wrong. See Ely, *The Irrepressible Myth of Erie,* 87 Harv. L. Rev. 693; Chayes, *The Bead Game,* 87 Harv. L. Rev. 74; Ely, *The Necklace,* 87 Harv. L. Rev. 753 (1974).

[b] 326 U.S. at 112.

[c] 356 U.S. at 537.

[d] 380 U.S. at 468.

[e] 330 U.S. 501 (1947).

dismissal nor transfer were possible when choice of law was likely to be critical, plaintiff's forum shopping would be rewarded. Of course, in a case like *Barrack,* it is hard to accuse the plaintiffs of shopping for a forum, in suing the airline at their domicile and the scheduled destination of the flight.

(d) Section 1404(a) applies not only to diversity actions, but also to federal question cases. If there is a conflict among circuits on interpretation of federal law, would you think the rule of *Van Dusen v. Barrack* should apply as well?[f]

(4) An interesting twist on *Van Dusen v. Barrack* concerned transfers under §1404 on motion of the plaintiff.[g]

(a) A Pennsylvania farmer who got his hand caught in a combine manufactured by the John Deere Company sought to bring suit against Deere more than three but less than four years after the accident. He was able to bring a breach of warranty suit in federal court in Pennsylvania against Deere, governed by Pennsylvania's four-year statute of limitations applicable to suits for breach of warranty, but he and his wife could not bring a companion tort suit, because such a suit would have been barred by Pennsylvania's two-year tort statute. Accordingly, plaintiffs brought suit against Deere in federal court in Mississippi, which has a six-year tort statute and a borrowing statute interpreted by the Mississippi Supreme Court not to apply to defendants that could at all times have been sued in the state. Since Deere did business in Mississippi, it appeared that under *Klaxon* a federal court would be required to entertain the action. After Deere answered but before the U.S. District Court for the Southern District of Mississippi could rule on the question of the time bar, plaintiffs moved in that court for transfer pursuant to § 1404 to the Western District of Pennsylvania, where the breach of warranty action was pending. The District Court granted the motion.

(b) Deere moved in the federal district court in Pennsylvania for summary judgment on the basis of the Pennsylvania statute of limitations, and the court granted the motion. The Court of Appeals for the Third Circuit affirmed, holding 2-1 that for *Klaxon* and then *Van Dusen v. Barrack* to operate, the choice of law of the state court being followed must be constitutional.[h] Since plaintiffs had never set foot in Mississippi and the defendant was neither a Mississippi corporation nor had manufactured or sold the machine in that state, application of Mississippi law would be "arbitrary, fundamentally unfair, and therefore unconstitutional." Consequently, because a Mississippi court could not apply its own law if plaintiffs' action were pending in state court, "neither *Klaxon* nor *Barrack* require that a federal diversity forum do so either." *Ferens v. Deere & Co. I*, 819 F.2d 423 (3d Cir. 1987). The dissenting judge wrote, "Depending on one's perspective, this case involves either skillful lawyering within established rules to obtain favorable law or unfair forum shopping." Either way, he concluded, it did not raise a constitutional problem. Id. at 427.

(c) Plaintiffs applied for certiorari, but before the Supreme Court could pass on the petition, it had decided *Sun Oil Co. v. Wortman*, p. 422 *supra*, which held that a state may apply its own statute of limitations to claims governed by the substantive law of another state without violating either the Full Faith and Credit or Due Process clauses of the Constitution. Accordingly, the

---

[f] For a forceful argument that the answer is no, see Marcus, *Conflicts among Circuits and Transfers Within the Federal System*, 93 Yale L. J. 677 (1984).

[g] Note that this question was expressly reserved in *Barrack*, p. 461 *supra,* just before part III.

[h] Recall in this connection *Pearson v. Northeast Airlines, Inc.*, p. 135, *supra.*

Court remanded *Ferens* to the Third Circuit for reconsideration in light of that case.[i] The inference was that since *Sun Oil* had held that there were no consitutional restrictions on application by a state court of the forum state's statute of limitations, regardless of what law governed the underlying claim, the Court of Appeals decision in *Ferens I* could not stand.

(d) On remand, the Court of Appeals stuck by its original ruling, again by 2-1, but on different grounds. The court now focused on the point that here plaintiffs, not defendants as in *Barrack* and most other cases involving §1404, had sought the transfer. The court held that plaintiffs' attempt to use the federal courts of Pennsylvania, (with a brief stop in Mississippi) to do what they could not achieve in the state courts of Pennsylvania would be contrary to the principles set forth in *Barrack* and *Erie*. Thus the Court of Appeals concluded that "the better construction of §1404(a) is that the state law of the transferee forum applies to plaintiff-initiated transfers." *Ferens v. Deere & Co. II*, 862 F.2d 31 (3d Cir. 1988).

(e) The Supreme Court again granted certiorari, and reversed. *Ferens v. John Deere Co.*, 494 U.S. 516 (1990). In a 5-4 decision, with Justice Kennedy writing for the majority, the Court held that policies underlying *Barrack* require the transferee forum to apply the law of the transferor court, whether it was plaintiff or defendant who applied for transfer. Justice Kennedy wrote: "[W]e believe that applying the law of the transferor forum effects the appropriate balance between fairness and simplicity."[j] The dissenters would have limited the rule of *Barrack* to transfers initiated by defendant. "The significant federal judicial policy expressed in *Erie* and *Klaxon*," Justice Scalia wrote, "is reduced to a laughingstock if it can too readily be evaded through filing-and-transfer."[k] Justice Scalia pointed out also that the "file-and-transfer ploy," as he called it, is available "not only to achieve the benefit of a longer statute of limitations, but also to bring home to the desired state of litigation all sorts of favorable choice-of-law rules regarding substantive liability—in an era when the diversity among the States in choice-of-law principles has become kaleidoscopic."

(5) In *Van Dusen v. Barrack,* involving a flight from Boston to Philadelphia, all the plaintiffs who had not brought suit in Boston appear to have sued in Philadelphia; thus as the result of the decision of the Supreme Court, the district court in Massachusetts had to apply the law of only two states, differing essentially in two related aspects—(i) Massachusetts would apply lex loci while Pennsylvania would apply a kind of interest analysis,[l] and (ii) Massachusetts had a limitation on recovery for wrongful death while Pennsylvania had none. In 1964, however, Congress adopted another provision for transfer, 28 U.S.C. § 1407, directed specifically to cases pending in different judicial districts involving common questions of fact.[m] According to the statute, consolidation is for pretrial purposes only; in practice once the cases are consolidated before a single judge, they tend to remain there for all purposes.[n] If actions filed in (or removed

---

[i] Ferens v. Deere & Co., 487 U.S. 1212 (1988).

[j] 494 U.S. at 532.

[k] 494 U.S. at 536.

[l] See *Griffith v. United Air Lines, Inc.,* 416 Pa. 1, 203 A.2d 796 (1964), which had been decided in the intermediate courts while *Barrack* was being litigated, and which came down as a decision of the Supreme Court of Pennsylvania six months after the decision in *Barrack.*

[m] Documents Supplement, p. 11; Note: *The Judicial Panel and the Conduct of Multi-district Litigation,* 87 Harv. L. Rev. 1001 (1974).

[n] See 87 Harv. L. Rev. at 1001–02, 1017, 1028–36; Weigel, *The Judicial Panel on Multi-district Litigation, Transferor Courts and Transferee Courts,* 78 F.R.D. 575, 583 (1978).

§ 6.03   THE CONSTITUTION AND CONFLICT OF LAWS   □   465

to) ten or twenty different federal district courts—for example in actions arising out of an airline disaster—are consolidated before a single judge, would you think the *Klaxon/Barrack* rule should apply, so that the transferee court would be required to apply the choice of law rule of every state from which an action was transferred, and which the transferor court would have been required to apply? Or would you favor some other solution, on the ground that no state court would or could have heard all the cases consolidated pursuant to § 1407?

Consider your answer in the light of the three airline accident cases summarized below, which may serve also as a last look back at the state of choice of law in torts in the United States, before moving on to jurisdiction and judgments in the following two chapters.º

(5)(a) *In re Air Crash Disaster at Boston, Massachusetts on July 31, 1973,* 399 F. Supp. 1106, (D. Mass. 1975) grew out of the crash of a Delta DC–9 aircraft while landing at Boston on a flight from Burlington, Vt. via Manchester, N.H. All but one of the 90 persons on board were killed, and wrongful death actions were filed against the airline in New Hampshire, Vermont, Massachusetts, Florida, and New York, in each case based on diversity of citizenship, Delta being a Delaware Corporation with its principal place of business in Georgia. All the cases were transferred to Chief Judge Caffrey of the U.S. District Court for Massachusetts pursuant to § 1407, except the cases filed in New York, which were transferred under § 1404 in lieu of dismissal for forum non conveniens. Delta moved for a declaration that the Massachusetts wrongful death limit, by then up to $200,000ᵖ be applied to all claims.

Judge Caffrey took the claims one by one, starting with the claims brought in Vermont. Delta said the Vermont choice of law rule in tort actions was lex loci delicti; the judge found, however, that the last decision of the Supreme Court of Vermont to take that approach was in 1961, based on decisions of New Hampshire, New York, and Pennsylvania courts. Since all these states had abandoned the doctrine of the first *Restatement,* and since the Vermont court had followed the second *Restatement* in a recent contracts case, Judge Caffrey concluded that the Vermont Supreme Court would so do also in a choice-of-law-in-tort case. Accordingly, for the plaintiffs who had filed suit in Vermont, the law of the state with the most significant contacts would be applied. Here all the Vermont plaintiffs were domiciled in that state, and had purchased their tickets and begun their journey there. Accordingly Vermont law—without a damage ceiling—would be applied, thereby furthering Vermont's interests without impairing those of Massachusetts.

Actions filed in New Hampshire were easier, because (as we saw in *Milkovich v. Saari*)ᵠ that state had abandoned lex loci in favor of Professor Leflar's choice-influencing considerations.ʳ The judge went through each of Leflar's criteria, and concluded that New Hampshire courts would apply New Hampshire law, also without a damage ceiling in suits by stated relatives or dependents.

The actions filed in Massachusetts involved residents of Virginia, Kentucky, and New Hampshire. Delta said that Massachusetts adhered to lex loci, and the judge agreed. The assertion

---

º For a somewhat different treatment of the same three cases, see D. Cavers, *Colliding Interests of Individuals and Enterprises in Conflict of Laws in the United States,* in *The Choice of Law, Selected Essays 1933–1983,* 385 at 390–94 (1985).

ᵖ In contrast to the $15,000 ceiling at the time of *Kilberg* and $20,000 at the time of *Barrack.* The statute was repealed effective Jan. 1, 1974, i.e., after the accident but prior to the decision in this case.

ᵠ Chapter 3, pp. 195–96, *supra.*

ʳ *Clark v. Clark,* 107 N.H. 351, 222 A.2d 205 (1966).

that Massachusetts had no interest in the case since Delta was not a Massachusetts corporation did not persuade the judge.

The actions filed in Florida required the judge to determine what Florida courts would do. After an elaborate analysis of Florida decisions and legislative developments, he concluded that they would regard the Massachusetts damage ceiling as contrary to Florida's public policy.

Finally, the New York cases presented a difficult problem, because it appeared that neither state nor federal courts in New York would have heard the cases, brought by domiciliaries of Connecticut, Maryland, and Vermont. Did it make sense to apply the law of a court that would not have heard the case?[s] Judge Caffrey said it did in this case, and found that the New York choice of law rule would point to the domicile of the decedents.

Thus five theories—*Restatement Second,* Leflar, Lex Loci, Public Policy, and law of decedent's domicile—were applied in a single case, involving only a single issue, and no persons domiciled in foreign countries.

(b) *In re Paris Air Crash of March 3, 1974,* 399 F. Supp. 732 (C.D. Cal. 1975) was a case with numerous issues, and claimants from 24 countries and at least 12 states of the United States.[t] A Turkish Airlines DC–10, bound from Paris to London, had gone down in a forest just outside of Paris, with the loss of all 346 passengers and crew. The accident investigation quickly indicated that the cause of the disaster was a faulty rear cargo door, which had been blown out of the aircraft, causing loss of cabin pressure, severing of electrical connections, and ultimately loss of control of the aircraft. After some skirmishing, 203 product liability claims on behalf of 337 decedents (and on behalf of the airline itself) were brought against the Douglas Aircraft division of the McDonnell Douglas Corporation, a Missouri corporation. Most were filed in the Central District of California, but 10 were transferred from other districts pursuant to § 1407. All actions were assigned to Judge Pierson Hall. After more than a year of furious litigation, particularly concerning discovery,[u] the defendants agreed not to contest liability and to apportion the damages between them.[v] The question was how, and under what law, to determine damages. Counsel for a group of 50 Japanese passengers, mostly unmarried young men, sought the law of their domicile, which would have been measured, apparently, by the loss to the estate, regardless of dependents, plus damages for grief by the parents; for the largest group, domiciled in Britain, the law of domicile was unattractive, because from the damages calculated roughly as in the United States, there would be a series of deductions for amounts the survivors had received or would receive by way of inheritance, life insurance, pension benefits, etc.; these plaintiffs contended for French law as the place of the accident, because French law would award "moral damages" and did not call for deductions for collateral benefits. Still other plaintiffs urged that California law should apply, particularly in view of indications by the judge that he regarded California's rule precluding punitive damages in wrongful death actions as unconstitutional.[w] . . . And so on. Judge Hall wrote:

---

[s] Note that this question was also left open in *Van Dusen v. Barrack,* at p. 461, *supra.*

[t] The citation is to the choice of law phase only. At least eleven other decisions in this case appear in the federal reports. For more on this litigation, see A. Lowenfeld, *Aviation Law,* Ch. 7, §§ 7.21, 7.3 (2d ed 1981); for still more, see S. Speiser, *Lawsuit,* pp. 420–69 (1980).

[u] See Lowenfeld, note t, *supra,* at pp. 7–189-194

[v] Besides McDonnell Douglas, the defendants included General Dynamics, which had built the door, and the Federal Aviation Administration, which according to plaintiffs, had carelessly inspected and certified the plans and had not required a design change after a similar accident almost led to disaster a year earlier.

[w] Judge Hall eventually so held, 427 F. Supp 701 (C.D. Cal. 1977), but that ruling was reversed three years later, 622 F.2d 1315 (9th Cir. 1980).

§ 6.03   THE CONSTITUTION AND CONFLICT OF LAWS   □   467

> The law on "choice of law" in the various states and in the federal courts is a veritable jungle, which, if the law can be found out, leads not to a "rule of action" but a reign of chaos dominated in each case by the Judge's "informed guess" as to what some *other* state than the one in which he sits *would* hold *its* law to be. . . . Here, if the rule laid down in some cases . . . were followed, this Court would have to "guess" what the courts in 24 foreign and 12 domestic jurisdictions would hold on the facts in this case, including their "choice-of-law" rules, and who knows what laws of what country or state that would lead to.[x]

Eventually Judge Hall decided that California law should apply, on the basis of its interest in (1) deterring misconduct of its defendants, (2) avoiding the imposition of excessive financial burdens on its resident defendants, and, he added, (3) providing a uniform rule of liability and damages "so that those who come under the ambit of California's strict product liability law . . . may know what risks they are subject to when they make and sell their products."[y] But, said some plaintiffs, what about loss of consortium, grief, and similar non-pecuniary loss, which seemed to be available under federal common law, according to a recent Supreme Court case in admiralty?[z] Yes, said Judge Hall: "The Court is this case must consider more than the *California* governmental interest. It must include the *United States interest* in this multi-nation situation, . . ." citing the federal interest in regulating various phases of civil aviation, including design, manufacture, and navigation, and so California's law would be liberalized for this case by adoption of the phrase "pecuniary loss" as construed in the *Gaudet* case.[a]

One case that gave the judge trouble was a case brought in Kansas, which had a $50,000 limitation of liability. Notwithstanding *Van Dusen v. Barrack,* however, "the interest of California and the Federal Government override the interest of Kansas," and the decision on choice of law would apply to that case as well.[b]

> The Court, in conclusion . . . holds that the "governmental interest" of both California and the United States, or either of them, outweighs any and all other interest of any State or Nation in determining the measure of damages in these cases; that California law applies because of California's "governmental interest;" and that the California law governs damages under the Rules of Decision Act, 28 U.S.C. § 1652, because of the overriding interest of the United States in the design and manufacture of aircraft.[c]

Does all this make sense? Is it consistent with *Erie* and *Klaxon*?

(c) In *DC–10 Paris,* the thrust of the claims was clearly against the manufacturer, and those who had collaborated in manufacture or inspection of the plane. *In re Air Crash Disaster Near Chicago, Illinois on May 24, 1979,*[d] also involved a DC–10, which lost an engine and crashed near Chicago's O'Hare International Airport on a flight to Los Angeles, with the loss of life of all 271 persons on board plus two persons on the ground. But this time it was not clear whether the disaster was caused by a defect for which the manufacturer was responsible or by faulty

---

[x] 399 F. Supp. at 739.

[y] 399 F. Supp. at 743.

[z] *Sea-Land Services, Inc. v. Gaudet,* 414 U.S. 573 (1974).

[a] 399 F. Supp. at 745, 747.

[b] 399 F. Supp. at 749. Note that Judge Hall did not inquire about the Kansas choice of law rule.

[c] 399 F. Supp. at 749.

[d] 644 F.2d 594 (7th Cir.), *cert. denied,* 454 U.S. 878 (1981).

maintenance, for which the carrier, American Airlines, would be liable. The disaster brought forth 118 actions filed in six jurisdictions but consolidated in the Northern District of Illinois under § 1407. The decedents were residents of 10 states, plus Puerto Rico, Japan, the Netherlands and Saudi Arabia. All the plaintiffs sought punitive damages from both McDonnell Douglas and American Airlines. Unlike Judge Hall, the Seventh Circuit took *Van Dusen v. Barrack* literally, exploring the choice of law rules of each of the states in which a claim had been filed. That turned out to be difficult, because McDonnell Douglas was a Maryland corporation with its principal place of business in Missouri, but the aircraft was manufactured (and the alleged defects occurred) in California. American Airlines was a Delaware corporation which had its principal place of business in New York until 1979, then moved to Texas, but its maintenance base, where its alleged misconduct occurred, was in Oklahoma. With respect to McDonnell Douglas, Missouri, but not California, as the court found, allowed punitive damages in death cases; with respect to American Airlines, Oklahoma and Texas, but not New York, allowed punitive damages in death cases. But to which states' law would the transferor courts have looked in these circumstances? In an opinion that fills more than fifty pages of the federal reporter, the court did what Judge Caffrey did, i.e., go through the choice of law rules of the transferor states, one by one; but many of its inquiries ended in deadlock. Illinois, for example, seemed to look to the "most significant relationship;" but for the manufacturer, was that Missouri or California? The court said it could not tell, and wound up with Illinois, as the place of injury. "Although either California or Missouri, taken separately, would have a greater interest than Illinois, the fact that the laws of these states are in absolute conflict indicates that neither state has an interest greater than the other's. Thus, in terms of a principled basis upon which a choice can be made, neither state has a "more significant interest' than Illinois."[e] As for claims against the airline, the same equipoise appeared between Oklahoma and New York, and so Illinois was chosen.

California, the court found, would use the "comparative impairment" approach to weigh true conflicts. Here Missouri would wish to punish McDonnell Douglas and California would wish to shield it. Again, equipoise, resolved by a demonstration of Illinois' strong interest, in theory as they would appear to a California court.[f]

On the basis of the cases reproduced in Chapter III from *Babcock* to *Neumeier,* the court concluded that "the New York test is the functional equivalent of the *Restatement Second* test," and so the result would be the same as the analysis made for the actions filed in Illinois.

And so on. Michigan might still apply lex loci, which fortunately for the court (but not the plaintiffs) was also Illinois. Likewise Puerto Rico.

In the end, none of the plaintiffs was permitted to seek punitive damages. But at the end of his 54-page opinion, Judge Sprecher concludes with a call for a federal statute governing airplane accident litigation.

> [I]t is clearly in the interests of passengers, airline corporations, airplane manufacturers, and state and federal governments, that airline tort liability be regulated by federal law. Of course, we are well aware of the fact that it is up to Congress, and not the courts, to create the needed uniform law.[g]

---

[e] 644 F.2d at 616.

[f] The same outcome resulted from the analysis of how California would compare the impairment of the interests of New York and Oklahoma with respect to American Airlines.

[g] 644 F.2d at 632–33.

(6) Taking the three mass disaster cases together, it is hard to quarrel with the assertion that a federal aviation accident act would be the desirable solution. But such legislation, raising all the problems of accident compensation in the United States generally—fault or no-fault, compensation vs. punitive damages, collateral benefits, pain and suffering, contingent fees and their regulation, etc., etc.—has proved impossible to adopt. A bill providing for federal choice of law rules, say limited to multi-party and multidistrict cases, might have a better chance.

(a) Would you favor such a bill?

(b) Should such a bill establish choice of law rules by statute? Or simply authorize the court to decide, free from the tyranny of *Barrack* and *Klaxon*?

(c) At what point, if at all, would such a bill run up against the constraints of *Erie* itself?

(7)(a) In 1988, the House of Representatives, but not the Senate, adopted H.R. 4807, a bill based on the proposition that a transferee judge in a mass disaster case involving at least 25 parties killed or seriously injured, should apply the substantive law of a single state, rather than the laws of the several states where the actions had been intitiated. The choice of that state need not depend on the choice of law rule of any state, but would be based on evaluation of a series of factors—no less than eleven.[h] Neither *Klaxon* nor *Van Dusen v. Barrack* would stand in the way. Over time, the drafters seem to have expected that a federal common law of conflict of laws would have developed, at least for cases arising from a single event, such as an airplane crash, in contrast to prolonged disasters such as cases involving asbestos, the Dalkon Shield, or Agent Orange.

(b) The present author doubted that uniformity or anything resembling uniformity could be achieved either through a statute with so many factors to choose from or from authorization by the Congress to the Courts to develop a common law of choice of law without specified criteria:

> Having thought about this question for close to three decades, I give up. The notion of a federal *common* choice-of-law in airplane crashes—common in the sense that it must be applied by all judges hearing cases of this kind—seems to me quite hopeless. I could no more draft a law to tell judges how to undertake this task than I could choose with confidence among the criteria put forward in H.R. 4807 for judges to apply without benefit of a statute.[i]

The next step, then would be to adopt a federal substantive law on recovery for death or injury arising out of commercial air travel—in other words a national solution where the choice among state laws proved unmanageable. Of course such a statute would require agreement on a number of highly controversial issues—from pain and suffering to contingent fees to fault-based or no-fault recoveries to punitive damages, third party claims—indeed a good part of the law of torts, not to speak of Congress' reluctance to legislate on matters traditionally left to the states.

(c) A decade later, neither a choice of law statute nor a substantive law statute had made its way through Congress. But the American Law Institute, addressing multiparty, multiforum, litigation in general, has proposed a scheme of liberal consolidation of actions, and a federal statute designed, as stated in the preamble "to foster consolidated treatment of similar cases that are dispersed in federal and state courts and whose individual adjudication would result in

---

[h] Court Reform and Access to Justice Act, H.R. 4807, tit. III, 100th Cong,, 2d Sess. 134, 134 Cong.Rec. H 7443, H 7455 (daily ed. Sept. 13, 1988).

[i] A. Lowenfeld, *Mass Torts and the Conflict of Laws: The Airline Disaster*, 1989 U. Ill. Law. Rev. 157 at 170.

duplicative and costly litigation."[j] Like H.R. 4807, the ALI draft would direct the transferee court to apply, to the extent feasible, a single State's law to all similar claims, preserving *Erie*, but for these purposes departing from the requirements of *Klaxon* and *Barrack*.

As to how to make the required choice of law, the ALI draft would establish a hierarchy of options, somewhat like the Neumeier rules.[k] Moreover, in tort claims the court would be directed to apply the options in the way Judge Weinfeld approached *Chila v. Owens* p. 189 question (4)(a) *supra,* that is to treat plaintiffs as sharing a common habitual residence or primary place of business if they are located in states whose laws are not in material conflict. Consider how the three airline crash cases described above would have come out under such a statute.

(d) Though much of the discussion of mass civil actions is focused on tort claims—transport accidents, toxic substances, pollution—mass actions may also be brought in other contexts, for instance against franchisors by franchisees operating under a standard contract. Subsections (d) and (e) of the ALI draft set out a different hierarchy of options for contract claims, designed to separate true from false conflicts by requiring the court to determine whether a given state "has a policy that would be furthered by the application of its law." Consider how this direction would work in an action by distributors in states with dealer protection laws against a manufacturer or franchisor whose primary place of business is in a state that would enforce termination clauses as written.[l]

(e) Note the special provisions concerning time bar (subsection (f)) and punitive damages (subsection (h)). Are they satisfactory (i) from the point of view of guiding the court and parties; (ii) from the point of view of justice?

(f) Did the present author (paragraph (b)) throw up his hands too soon?

---

§ 6.04 One More Look at the Substance/Procedure Puzzle

In the most recent *Erie* case as this volume went to press, the Supreme Court confronted the problem of how the command—the constitutional command—of *Erie* could be accommodated with the Seventh Amendment provision prohibiting reexamination by a court of a fact found by a jury. Again, this was a vertical, not a horizontal choice of law problem. The problem arose because the New York legislature, in an effort to control the rising levels of recoveries in personal injury actions, particularly in medical malpractice cases, decided that rather than imposing a monetary ceiling on such recoveries, it would give greater power to review jury verdicts to the Appellate Division, New York's intermediate appellate court. *A priori*, before reading the Supreme Court's decision in the *Gasperini* case that follows, how do you think that a federal court exercising diversity jurisdiction in New York should respond to this reform to the state judicial system?

---

[j] American Law Institute, *Complex Litigation: Statutory Recommendations and Analysis* (1994). The proposed Complex Litigation Act appears at Appendix A of the ALI volume, and in the Documents Supplement to this volume at p. 65.

[k] See ALI Draft, § 7, Documents Supplement p. 73.

[l] Recall, e.g., *Southern International Sales v. Potter & Brumfield Div.*, p. 272 *supra*.

(a) Should the reform contained in an amendment to New York's Civil Practice Law and Rules, simply be treated as a change in the rules for New York courts, inapplicable in federal court?[a] Alternatively,

(b) should the Court of Appeals for the Second Circuit, in cases tried in a federal court in New York, undertake the same review of jury verdicts as the Appellate Division exercises over jury verdicts in state courts?

(c) Can you think of a still different solution?

GASPERINI v. CENTER FOR HUMANITIES, INC.

United States Supreme Court
518 U.S. 415 (1996)

Justice GINSBURG delivered the opinion of the Court.

Under the law of New York, appellate courts are empowered to review the size of jury verdicts and to order new trials when the jury's award "deviates materially from what would be reasonable compensation." N.Y. Civ. Prac. Law and Rules (CPLR) § 5501(c) (McKinney 1995). Under the Seventh Amendment, which governs proceedings in federal court, but not in state court, "the right of trial by jury shall be preserved, and no fact tried by a jury, shall be otherwise re-examined in any Court of the United States, than according to the rules of the common law." U.S. Const., Amdt. 7. The compatibility of these provisions, in an action based on New York law but tried in federal court by reason of the parties' diverse citizenship, is the issue we confront in this case. We hold that New York's law controlling compensation awards for excessiveness or inadequacy can be given effect, without detriment to the Seventh Amendment, if the review standard set out in CPLR § 5501(c) is applied by the federal trial court judge, with appellate control of the trial court's ruling limited to review for "abuse of discretion."

I

Petitioner William Gasperini, a journalist for CBS News and the Christian Science Monitor, began reporting on events in Central America in 1984. He earned his living primarily in radio and print media and only occasionally sold his photographic work. During the course of his seven-year stint in Central America, Gasperini took over 5,000 slide transparencies, depicting active war zones, political leaders, and scenes from daily life. In 1990, Gasperini agreed to supply his original color transparencies to The Center for Humanities, Inc. (Center) for use in an educational videotape, *Conflict in Central America.* Gasperini selected 300 of his slides for the Center; its videotape included 110 of them. The Center agreed to return the original transparencies, but upon the completion of the project, it could not find them.

Gasperini commenced suit in the United States District Court for the Southern District of New York, invoking the court's diversity jurisdiction pursuant to 28 U.S.C. § 1332.[1] He alleged several

---

[a] Note, for example that most civil juries in New York consist of six persons, NY CPLR §4104, and that a five/sixth majority is sufficient to reach a verdict, NY CPLR §4113(a). In federal courts the general rule (though apparently not constitutionally required) remains that a jury consists of twelve persons and that a verdict must be unanimous.

[1] Plaintiff Gasperini, petitioner here, is a citizen of California; defendant Center, respondent here, is incorporated, and has its principal place of business, New York.

state-law claims for relief, including breach of contract, conversion, and negligence. The Center conceded liability for the lost transparencies and the issue of damages was tried before a jury.

At trial, Gasperini's expert witness testified that the "industry standard" within the photographic publishing community valued a lost transparency at $1,500. This industry standard, the expert explained, represented the average license fee a commercial photograph could earn over the full course of the photographer's copyright, i.e., in Gasperini's case, his lifetime plus 50 years. Gasperini estimated that his earnings from photography totaled just over $10,000 for the period from 1984 through 1993. He also testified that he intended to produce a book containing his best photographs from Central America.

After a three-day trial, the jury awarded Gasperini $450,000 in compensatory damages. This sum, the jury foreperson announced, "is [$]1500 each, for 300 slides." Moving for a new trial under Federal Rule of Civil Procedure 59, the Center attacked the verdict on various grounds, including excessiveness. Without comment, the District Court denied the motion.

The Court of Appeals for the Second Circuit vacated the judgment entered on the jury's verdict. Mindful that New York law governed the controversy, the Court of Appeals endeavored to apply CPLR § 5501(c), which instructs that, when a jury returns an itemized verdict, as the jury did in this case, the New York Appellate Division "shall determine that an award is excessive or inadequate if it deviates materially from what would be reasonable compensation." Surveying Appellate Division decisions that reviewed damage awards for lost transparencies, the Second Circuit concluded that testimony on industry standard alone was insufficient to justify a verdict; prime among other factors warranting consideration were the uniqueness of the slides' subject matter and the photographer's earning level.[2]

Guided by Appellate Division rulings, the Second Circuit held that the $450,000 verdict "materially deviates from what is reasonable compensation." Some of Gasperini's transparencies, the Second Circuit recognized, were unique, notably those capturing combat situations in which Gasperini was the only photographer present. But others "depicted either generic scenes or events at which other professional photojournalists were present." No more than 50 slides merited a $1,500 award, the court concluded, after "[g]iving Gasperini every benefit of the doubt." Absent evidence showing significant earnings from photographic endeavors or concrete plans to publish a book, the court further determined, any damage award above $100 each for the remaining slides would be excessive. Remittiturs "presen[t] difficult problems for appellate courts," the Second Circuit acknowledged, for court of appeals judges review the evidence from "a cold paper record." Nevertheless, the Second Circuit set aside the $450,000 verdict and ordered a new trial, unless Gasperini agreed to an award of $100,000.

This case presents an important question regarding the standard a federal court uses to measure the alleged excessiveness of a jury's verdict in an action for damages based on state law. We therefore granted certiorari.

II

Before 1986, state and federal courts in New York generally invoked the same judge-made formulation in responding to excessiveness attacks on jury verdicts: courts would not disturb

---

[2] [The Court cites three recent decisions in which claims for lost or damaged transparencies were reduced by New York's intermediate appellate court from $1,000 to $400, from $1,500 to $500, and from $1500 to $159 per transparency.]

an award unless the amount was so exorbitant that it "shocked the conscience of the court." As described by the Second Circuit: "The standard for determining excessiveness and the appropriateness of remittitur in New York is somewhat ambiguous. Prior to 1986, New York law employed the same standard as the federal courts, which authorized remittitur only if the jury's verdict was so excessive that it 'shocked the conscience of the court.'"

In both state and federal courts, trial judges made the excessiveness assessment in the first instance, and appellate judges ordinarily deferred to the trial court's judgment. . . .

In 1986, as part of a series of tort reform measures,[3] New York codified a standard for judicial review of the size of jury awards. Placed in CPLR § 5501(c), the prescription reads:

> "In reviewing a money judgment . . . in which it is contended that the award is excessive or inadequate and that a new trial should have been granted unless a stipulation is entered to a different award, the appellate division shall determine that an award is excessive or inadequate if it deviates materially from what would be reasonable compensation."

As stated in Legislative Findings and Declarations accompanying New York's adoption of the "deviates materially" formulation, the lawmakers found the "shock the conscience" test an insufficient check on damage awards; the legislature therefore installed a standard "invit[ing] more careful appellate scrutiny." At the same time, the legislature instructed the Appellate Division, in amended § 5522, to state the reasons for the court's rulings on the size of verdicts, and the factors the court considered in complying with § 5501(c). In his signing statement, then-Governor Mario Cuomo emphasized that the CPLR amendments were meant to rachet up the review standard: "This will assure greater scrutiny of the amount of verdicts and promote greater stability in the tort system and greater fairness for similarly situated defendants throughout the State. . . ."

New York state-court opinions confirm that § 5501(c)'s "deviates materially" standard calls for closer surveillance than "shock the conscience" oversight.

Although phrased as a direction to New York's intermediate appellate courts, § 5501(c)'s "deviates materially" standard, as construed by New York's courts, instructs state trial judges as well. . . . Application of § 5501(c) at the trial level is key to this case.

To determine whether an award "deviates materially from what would be reasonable compensation," New York state courts look to awards approved in similar cases. . . . The "deviates materially" standard, however, in design and operation, influences outcomes by tightening the range of tolerable awards.

III

In cases like Gasperini's, in which New York law governs the claims for relief, does New York law also supply the test for federal court review of the size of the verdict? The Center answers yes. The "deviates materially" standard, it argues, is a substantive standard that must be applied by federal appellate courts in diversity cases. The Second Circuit agreed. Gasperini, emphasizing that § 5501(c) trains on the New York Appellate Division, characterizes the provision as procedural, an allocation of decisionmaking authority regarding damages, not a hard cap on the amount recoverable. Correctly comprehended, Gasperini urges, § 5501(c)'s direction to the

---

[3] The legislature sought, particularly, to curtail medical and dental malpractice, and to contain "already high malpractice premiums." Legislative Findings and Declaration, Ch. 266, 1986 N.Y. Laws 470 (McKinney).

Appellate Division cannot be given effect by federal appellate courts without violating the Seventh Amendment's re-examination clause.

As the parties' arguments suggest, CPLR § 5501(c), appraised under *Erie R. Co. v. Tompkins*, and decisions in *Erie*'s path, is both "substantive" and "procedural": "substantive" in that § 5501(c)'s "deviates materially" standard controls how much a plaintiff can be awarded; "procedural" in that § 5501(c) assigns decisionmaking authority to New York's Appellate Division. Parallel application of § 5501(c) at the federal appellate level would be out of sync with the federal system's division of trial and appellate court functions, an allocation weighted by the Seventh Amendment. The dispositive question, therefore, is whether federal courts can give effect to the substantive thrust of § 5501(c) without untoward alteration of the federal scheme for the trial and decision of civil cases.

A

Federal diversity jurisdiction provides an alternative forum for the adjudication of state-created rights, but it does not carry with it generation of rules of substantive law. As *Erie* read the Rules of Decision Act: "Except in matters governed by the Federal Constitution or by Acts of Congress, the law to be applied in any case is the law of the State." [p. 438 *supra*]. Under the *Erie* doctrine, federal courts sitting in diversity apply state substantive law and federal procedural law.

Classification of a law as "substantive" or "procedural" for *Erie* purposes is sometimes a challenging endeavor. [The Court summarizes its decisions from *Guaranty Trust Co. v. York* through *Hanna v. Plumer*.]

Informed by these decisions, we address the question whether New York's "deviates materially" standard, codified in CPLR § 5501(c), is outcome-affective in this sense: Would "application of the [standard] . . . have so important an effect upon the fortunes of one or both of the litigants that failure to [apply] it would [unfairly discriminate against citizens of the forum State, or] be likely to cause a plaintiff to choose the federal court?" [*Hanna v. Plumer*], 380 U.S. at 468, n. 9].

We start from a point the parties do not debate. Gasperini acknowledges that a statutory cap on damages would supply substantive law for *Erie* purposes. See Reply Brief for Petitioner 2 ("[T]he state as a matter of its substantive law may, among other things, eliminate the availability of damages for a particular claim entirely, limit the factors a jury may consider in determining damages, or place an absolute cap on the amount of damages available, and such substantive law would be applicable in a federal court sitting in diversity").[9] Although CPLR § 5501(c) is less readily classified, it was designed to provide an analogous control.

New York's Legislature codified in § 5501(c) a new standard, one that requires closer court review than the common law "shock the conscience" test. More rigorous comparative evaluations attend application of § 5501(c)'s "deviates materially" standard. To foster predictability, the legislature required the reviewing court, when overturning a verdict under § 5501(c), to state its reasons, including the factors it considered relevant. We think it a fair conclusion that CPLR § 5501(c) differs from a statutory cap principally "in that the maximum amount recoverable is not set by statute, but rather is determined by case law." Brief for City of New York as *Amicus*

---

[9] While we have not specifically addressed the issue, courts of appeals have held that district court application of state statutory caps in diversity cases, post verdict, does not violate the Seventh Amendment. See *Davis v. Omitowoju*, 883 F.2d 1155, 1161-1165 (C.A.3 1989); *Boyd v. Bulala*, 877 F.2d 1191, 1196 (C.A.4 1989).

Curiae 11. In sum, § 5501(c) contains a procedural instruction, but the State's objective is manifestly substantive.

It thus appears that if federal courts ignore the change in the New York standard and persist in applying the "shock the conscience" test to damage awards on claims governed by New York law, " 'substantial' variations between state and federal [money judgments]" may be expected. We therefore agree with the Second Circuit that New York's check on excessive damages implicates what we have called Erie's "twin aims." Just as the *Erie* principle precludes a federal court from giving a state-created claim "longer life . . . than [the claim] would have had in the state court," *Ragan,* 337 U.S., at 533-534, so *Erie* precludes a recovery in federal court significantly larger than the recovery that would have been tolerated in state court.

B

CPLR § 5501(c), as earlier noted, see *supra,* at [p. 473], is phrased as a direction to the New York Appellate Division. Acting essentially as a surrogate for a New York appellate forum, the Court of Appeals reviewed Gasperini's award to determine if it "deviate[d] materially" from damage awards the Appellate Division permitted in similar circumstances. The Court of Appeals performed this task without benefit of an opinion from the District Court, which had denied "without comment" the Center's Rule 59 motion. Concentrating on the authority § 5501(c) gives to the Appellate Division, Gasperini urges that the provision shifts fact-finding responsibility from the jury and the trial judge to the appellate court. Assigning such responsibility to an appellate court, he maintains, is incompatible with the Seventh Amendment's re-examination clause, and therefore, Gasperini concludes, § 5501(c) cannot be given effect in federal court. Although we reach a different conclusion than Gasperini, we agree that the Second Circuit did not attend to "[a]n essential characteristic of [the federal-court] system," *Byrd v. Blue Ridge Rural Elec. Cooperative, Inc.,* when it used § 5501(c) as "the standard for [federal] appellate review,"

That "essential characteristic" was described in *Byrd,* a diversity suit for negligence in which a pivotal issue of fact would have been tried by a judge were the case in state court. The *Byrd* Court held that, despite the state practice, the plaintiff was entitled to a jury trial in federal court. In so ruling, the Court said that the *Guaranty Trust* "outcome–determination" test was an insufficient guide in cases presenting countervailing federal interests. The Court described the countervailing federal interests present in *Byrd* this way:

> The federal system is an independent system for administering justice to litigants who properly invoke its jurisdiction. An essential characteristic of that system is the manner in which, in civil common-law actions, it distributes trial functions between judge and jury and, under the influence—if not the command—of the Seventh Amendment, assigns the decisions of disputed questions of fact to the jury.

The Seventh Amendment, which governs proceedings in federal court, but not in state court,[14] bears not only on the allocation of trial functions between judge and jury, the issue in *Byrd;* it also controls the allocation of authority to review verdicts, the issue of concern here. The Amendment reads:

> In suits at common law, where the value in controversy shall exceed twenty dollars, the right of trial by jury shall be preserved, and no fact tried by a jury, shall be otherwise

---

[14] See *Walker v. Sauvinet,* 92 U.S. 90, 92, 23 L.Ed. 678 (1876).

re-examined in any Court of the United States, than according to the rules of the common law.

Byrd involved the first clause of the Amendment, the "trial by jury" clause. This case involves the second, the "re-examination" clause. In keeping with the historic understanding, the re-examination clause does not inhibit the authority of trial judges to grant new trials "for any of the reasons for which new trials have heretofore been granted in actions at law in the courts of the United States." Fed. Rule Civ. Proc. 59(a). That authority is large. . . . "The trial judge in the federal system," we have reaffirmed, "has . . . discretion to grant a new trial if the verdict appears to [the judge] to be against the weight of the evidence." *Byrd,* 356 U.S., at 540. This discretion includes overturning verdicts for excessiveness and ordering a new trial without qualification, or conditioned on the verdict winner's refusal to agree to a reduction (remittitur). See *Dimick v. Schiedt,* 293 U.S. 474, 486-487 (1935) (recognizing that remittitur withstands Seventh Amendment attack, but rejecting additur as unconstitutional).

In contrast, appellate review of a federal trial court's denial of a motion to set aside a jury's verdict as excessive is a relatively late, and less secure, development. Such review was once deemed inconsonant with the Seventh Amendment's re-examination clause. We subsequently recognized that, even in cases in which the Erie doctrine was not in play—cases arising wholly under federal law—the question was not settled; we twice granted certiorari to decide the unsettled issue, but ultimately resolved the cases on other grounds. See *Grunenthal v. Long Island R. Co.,* 393 U.S. 156, 158 (1968).

As the Second Circuit explained, appellate review for abuse of discretion is reconcilable with the Seventh Amendment as a control necessary and proper to the fair administration of justice: "We must give the benefit of every doubt to the judgment of the trial judge; but surely there must be an upper limit, and whether that has been surpassed is not a question of fact with respect to which reasonable men may differ, but a question of law." *Dagnello v. Long Island R. Co.,* 289 F.2d 797, 806 (C.A.2 1961). All other Circuits agree. We now approve this line of decisions, and thus make explicit what Justice Stewart thought implicit in our *Grunenthal* disposition: "[N]othing in the Seventh Amendment . . . precludes appellate review of the trial judge's denial of a motion to set aside [a jury verdict] as excessive." 393 U.S., at 164, (Stewart, J., dissenting).

C

In *Byrd,* the Court faced a one-or-the-other choice: trial by judge as in state court, or trial by jury according to the federal practice. In the case before us, a choice of that order is not required, for the principal state and federal interests can be accommodated. . . .

New York's dominant interest can be respected, without disrupting the federal system, once it is recognized that the federal district court is capable of performing the checking function, i.e., that court can apply the State's "deviates materially" standard in line with New York case law evolving under CPLR § 5501(c). We recall, in this regard, that the "deviates materially" standard serves as the guide to be applied in trial as well as appellate courts in New York.

Within the federal system, practical reasons combine with Seventh Amendment constraints to lodge in the district court, not the court of appeals, primary responsibility for application of § 5501(c)'s "deviates materially" check. Trial judges have the "unique opportunity to consider the evidence in the living courtroom context," while appellate judges see only the "cold paper record."

District court applications of the "deviates materially" standard would be subject to appellate review under the standard the Circuits now employ when inadequacy or excessiveness is asserted on appeal: abuse of discretion. In light of *Erie's* doctrine, the federal appeals court must be guided by the damage-control standard state law supplies, but as the Second Circuit itself has said: "If we reverse, it must be because of an abuse of discretion. . . . The very nature of the problem counsels restraint. . . . We must give the benefit of every doubt to the judgment of the trial judge." *Dagnello,* 289 F.2d, at 806.

IV

It does not appear that the District Court checked the jury's verdict against the relevant New York decisions demanding more than "industry standard" testimony to support an award of the size the jury returned in this case. As the Court of Appeals recognized, the uniqueness of the photographs and the plaintiff's earnings as photographer—past and reasonably projected—are factors relevant to appraisal of the award. Accordingly, we vacate the judgment of the Court of Appeals and instruct that court to remand the case to the District Court so that the trial judge, revisiting his ruling on the new trial motion, may test the jury's verdict against CPLR § 5501(c)'s "deviates materially" standard.

It is so ordered.

Justice STEVENS, dissenting.

While I agree with most of the reasoning in the Court's opinion, I disagree with its disposition of the case. I would affirm the judgment of the Court of Appeals. I would also reject the suggestion that the Seventh Amendment limits the power of a federal appellate court sitting in diversity to decide whether a jury's award of damages exceeds a limit established by state law.

. . .

The District Court had its opportunity to consider the propriety of the jury's award, and it erred. The Court of Appeals has now corrected that error after "drawing all reasonable inferences in favor of" petitioner. As there is no reason to suppose that the Court of Appeals has reached a conclusion with which the District Court could permissibly disagree on remand, I would not require the District Court to repeat a task that has already been well-performed by the reviewing court. I therefore would affirm the judgment of the Court of Appeals.

. . .

My disagreement is tempered, however, because the majority carefully avoids defining too strictly the abuse of discretion standard it announces. To the extent that the majority relies only on "practical reasons" for its conclusion that the Court of Appeals should give some weight to the District Court's assessment in determining whether state substantive law has been properly applied, I do not disagree with its analysis.

. . .

In the end, therefore, my disagreement with the label that the majority attaches to the standard of appellate review should not obscure the far more fundamental point on which we agree. Whatever influence the Seventh Amendment may be said to exert, *Erie* requires federal appellate courts sitting in diversity to apply "the damage control standard state law supplies."

Justice SCALIA, with whom the CHIEF JUSTICE and Justice THOMAS join, dissenting.

. . .

Granting appellate courts authority to decide whether an award is "excessive or inadequate" in the manner of CPLR § 5501(c) may reflect a sound understanding of the capacities of modern juries and trial judges. That is to say, the people of the State of New York may well be correct that such a rule contributes to a more just legal system. But the practice of federal appellate reexamination of facts found by a jury is precisely what the People of the several States considered not to be good legal policy in 1791. Indeed, so fearful were they of such a practice that they constitutionally prohibited it by means of the Seventh Amendment.

That Amendment was Congress's response to one of the principal objections to the proposed Constitution raised by the Anti-Federalists during the ratification debates: its failure to ensure the right to trial by jury in civil actions in federal court. The desire for an explicit constitutional guarantee against reexamination of jury findings was explained by Justice Story, sitting as Circuit Justice in 1812, as having been specifically prompted by Article III's conferral of "appellate Jurisdiction, both as to Law and Fact" upon the Supreme Court. "[O]ne of the most powerful objections urged against [the Constitution]," he recounted, was that this authority "would enable that court, with or without a new jury, to re-examine the whole facts, which had been settled by a previous jury." *United States v. Wonson*, 28 F.Cas. 745, 750 (No. 16,750) (C.C.Mass).

The second clause of the Amendment responded to that concern by providing that "[i]n [s]uits at common law . . . no fact tried by a jury, shall be otherwise re-examined in any Court of the United States, than according to the rules of the common law." U.S. Const., Amdt. 7. The Reexamination Clause put to rest "apprehensions" of "new trials by the appellate courts," *Wonson*, 28 F.Cas., at 750, by adopting, in broad fashion, "the rules of the common law" to govern federal-court interference with jury determinations. . . .

. . .

The Court, as is its wont of late, all but ignores the relevant history. It acknowledges that federal appellate review of district-court refusals to set aside jury awards as against the weight of the evidence was "once deemed inconsonant with the Seventh Amendment's re-examination clause," but gives no indication of why ever we held that view; and its citation of only one of our cases subscribing to that proposition fails to convey how long and how clearly it was a fixture of federal practice. . . . That our earlier cases are so poorly recounted is not surprising, however, given the scant analysis devoted to the conclusion that "appellate review for abuse of discretion is reconcilable with the Seventh Amendment."

No precedent of this Court affirmatively supports that proposition.

. . .

In the last analysis, the Court frankly abandons any pretense at faithfulness to the common law, suggesting that "the meaning" of the Reexamination Clause was not "fixed at 1791," contrary to the view that all our prior discussions of the Reexamination Clause have adopted. The Court believes we can ignore the very explicit command that "no fact tried by a jury shall be otherwise reexamined in any Court of the United States, than according to the rules of the common law" because, after all, we have not insisted that juries be all male, or consist of 12 jurors, as they were at common law. This is a desperate analogy, since there is of course no comparison between the specificity of the command of the Reexamination Clause and the specificity of the command that there be a "jury."

II

. . .The Court acknowledges that state procedural rules cannot, as a general matter, be permitted to interfere with the allocation of functions in the federal court system. Indeed, it is at least partly for this reason that the Court rejects direct application of § 5501(c) at the appellate level as inconsistent with an "essential characteristic" of the federal court system—by which the Court presumably means abuse-of-discretion review of denials of motions for new trials. But the scope of the Court's concern is oddly circumscribed. The "essential characteristic" of the federal jury, and, more specifically, the role of the federal trial court in reviewing jury judgments, apparently counts for little. The Court approves the "accommodat[ion]" achieved by having district courts review jury verdicts under the "deviates materially" standard, because it regards that as a means of giving effect to the State's purposes "without disrupting the federal system." But changing the standard by which trial judges review jury verdicts does disrupt the federal system, and is plainly inconsistent with "the strong federal policy against allowing state rules to disrupt the judge-jury relationship in federal court." *Byrd v. Blue Ridge Rural Elec. Cooperative, Inc.* The Court's opinion does not even acknowledge, let alone address, this dislocation.. . .

The Court commits the classic *Erie* mistake of regarding whatever changes the outcome as substantive, see ante. That is not the only factor to be considered. See *Byrd,* ("[W]ere 'outcome' the only consideration, a strong case might appear for saying that the federal court should follow the state practice. But there are affirmative countervailing considerations at work here"). Outcome-determination "was never intended to serve as a talisman," *Hanna v. Plumer,* and does not have the power to convert the most classic elements of the process of assuring that the law is observed into the substantive law itself. The right to have a jury make the findings of fact, for example, is generally thought to favor plaintiffs, and that advantage is often thought significant enough to be the basis for forum selection. But no one would argue that *Erie* confers a right to a jury in federal court wherever state courts would provide it; or that, were it not for the Seventh Amendment, *Erie* would require federal courts to dispense with the jury whenever state courts do so.

In any event, the Court exaggerates the difference that the state standard will make. It concludes that different outcomes are likely to ensue depending on whether the law being applied is the state "deviates materially" standard of § 5501(c) or the "shocks the conscience" standard. Of course it is not the federal appellate standard but the federal district-court standard for granting new trials that must be compared with the New York standard to determine whether substantially different results will obtain—and it is far from clear that the district-court standard ought to be "shocks the conscience." Indeed, it is not even clear (as the Court asserts) that "shocks the conscience" is the standard (erroneous or not) actually applied by the district courts of the Second Circuit. . . . In sum, it is at least highly questionable whether the consistent outcome differential claimed by the Court even exists. What seems to me far more likely to produce forum-shopping is the consistent difference between the state and federal appellate standards, which the Court leaves untouched. Under the Court's disposition, the Second Circuit reviews only for abuse of discretion, whereas New York's appellate courts engage in a de novo review for material deviation, giving the defendant a double shot at getting the damages award set aside. The only result that would produce the conformity the Court erroneously believes *Erie* requires is the one adopted by the Second Circuit and rejected by the Court: de novo federal appellate review under the § 5501(c) standard.

. . .

To say that application of § 5501(c) in place of the federal standard will not consistently produce disparate results is not to suggest that the decision the Court has made today is not a momentous one. The principle that the state standard governs is of great importance, since it bears the potential to destroy the uniformity of federal practice and the integrity of the federal court system. Under the Court's view, a state rule that directed courts "to determine that an award is excessive or inadequate if it deviates in any degree from the proper measure of compensation" would have to be applied in federal courts, effectively requiring federal judges to determine the amount of damages de novo, and effectively taking the matter away from the jury entirely.

* * *

There is no small irony in the Court's declaration today that appellate review of refusals to grant new trials for error of fact is "a control necessary and proper to the fair administration of justice." It is objection to precisely that sort of "control" by federal appellate judges that gave birth to the Reexamination Clause of the Seventh Amendment. Alas, those who drew the Amendment, and the citizens who approved it, did not envision an age in which the Constitution means whatever this Court thinks it ought to mean—or indeed, whatever the courts of appeals have recently thought it ought to mean.

When there is added to the revision of the Seventh Amendment the Court's precedent-setting disregard of Congress's instructions in Rule 59, one must conclude that this is a bad day for the Constitution's distinctive Article III courts in general, and for the role of the jury in those courts in particular. I respectfully dissent.

NOTES AND QUESTIONS

(1) (a) Note the irony that the case that reaches the Supreme Court is not a personal injury case at all, but a case about lost property. Does that make any difference?

(b) Given her overall striving for conformity in the spirit of *Erie*, is Justice Ginsburg persuasive in assigning the review of jury verdicts prescribed by the New York statute to the district courts, rather than to the Court of Appeals? Note that in New York's state court system, the decision to alter the jury's verdict is committed to a collegial body, normally made up of five justices; under *Gasperini*, the task is assigned to a single judge.

(2)(a) Justice Scalia, whose opinion is here much abridged, goes back, as he often does, to the original intent of the drafters of the Constitution and the Bill of Rights. Recall, in this connection, the emphasis in *Erie*—not wholly convincing—on the intent of the drafters of the Judiciary Act of 1789.[b] If the Founders had foreseen the *Erie* doctrine or something like it, do you think that they would have written the Seventh Amendment as they did?

Does this speculation suggest (i) that the Brandeis/Warren assumptions are wrong? (ii) That the problem arose when the Supreme Court decided, shortly after the Civil War, that the Seventh Amendment did not apply to trials in state courts?[c] Or (iii) that history — even if there could

---

[b] See *Erie* at p. 436 and question (5)(a) p. 441, *supra*.

[c] See, e.g. *Edwards v. Elliott*, 88 U.S. (21 Wall.) 532 at 557 (1874) *Walker v. Sauvinet*, 92 U.S. 90 at 92 (1875); cited by Justice Ginsburg in *Gasperini*; See also, *Minneapolis & St. Louis Railroad Co. v. Bombolis*, 246 U.S. 211 (1916) holding that even when a state court is hearing a claim under federal law—here the Federal Employers' Liability Act—it is not subject to the constraints of the Seventh Amendment;.

be agreement on the facts (which was not true in *Gasperini*) — is a poor guide to issues of judicial administration at the close of the Twentieth Century?

(3) *Gasperini* was a case (i) begun in New York and (ii) clearly governed by the law of New York. What if one or both of these conditions are not present?

(a) Suppose the action had been begun in, say Florida, which has no statute comparable to NY CPLR §5501(c), and then the case was transferred to federal court in New York pursuant to 28 U.S.C. §1404(a). Does *Gasperini* require the federal district court to review the verdict under New York's "deviates materially" standard? Or should the teaching of *Van Dusen v. Barrack* prevail to preserve whatever advantage plaintiff gained from his choice of forum?

(b) What about a cause of action tried in New York federal court but governed by the law of some other state? Suppose, for example, an accident happens in a hospital in Philadelphia, but the plaintiff brings an action in federal court in New York. If the court determines that the substantive law of Pennsylvania governs, must it nevertheless follow New York's standards on control of jury verdicts? Should it inquire about the "reasonable compensation" prevailing in Pennsylvania?

(c) While question (a) is unique to the federal system, question (b) could arise as well in state as in federal court. Is the answer for the federal court, then, determined by *Klaxon* — i.e., deal with the case as the New York courts would deal with it?

(4)(a) Finally, after working your way through these questions, do you conclude that *Gasperini* comes out right? Could Congress change it by statute? Should it?

(b) If you conclude that Congress should change the scheme set out in *Gasperini,* could the rule makers do so? See Fed. R. Civ. P. Rule 59.

PART III

JURISDICTION AND JUDGMENTS

CHAPTER 7

JURISDICTION OF COURTS AND CHOICE OF LAW

Jurisdiction to adjudicate within the American federal system is, of course, the stuff of first year procedure courses, and need not be repeated here in detail. But both the vocabulary of choice of law—contacts and interests, for example, and also expectations—and the results of the conflicts [r]evolution shed a new light on the issues underlying the struggle to sue someone in a place other than his home or principal place of business.

As the rules of judicial jurisdiction developed—part common law, part common sense (non-resident motorist laws, for example), and part constitutional law—the issues seemed to reflect considerations of the burdens of travel, of sovereignty, and sometimes nothing more than the convenience of the lawyers. So long as the substantive rules of law were stable throughout the land—the "common" law in Story's vision[a]—the reasons for preferring one forum over another were not very clear; even after Story's vision crumbled—long before *Erie v. Tompkins*—so long as choice of law rules were (or were perceived to be) uniform—the Beale vision—the consequences of suing or being sued in one forum rather than another were often marginal. As choice of law rules, too, began to loosen, and as the tendency of courts to apply the law of the forum or the law of plaintiff's domicile (often the same) became widespread, the selection of a forum took on a new dimension, rarely articulated to or by courts but well appreciated by counsel. The decline of federal common law, while reducing the consequence of one kind of forum shopping, further contributed to the importance of the other kind, the tug-of-war between suing where plaintiff chose to sue and where defendant was firmly established.

The cases and notes in this chapter are, to some extent, a review of the American law of judicial jurisdiction, informed by the perspective of developments in choice of law. In addition, the chapter focuses, in § 7.03, on transnational sales, and in § 7.06 on recent developments within the European Economic Community, which knows many of the challenges of building a federal system, while maintaining a system of independent sovereign nation-states.

There is no effort in this chapter to trace the developments in the law of jurisdiction in the United States from arrest to personal service to constructive service, implied consent, and doing business; nor to trace the gradual constitutionalization of the law of jurisdiction under the due process clause; nor even to ask why it happened that federal courts (with some exceptions) follow the boundary lines of the states where they sit in determining their jurisdiction to adjudicate.[b] The basic proposition that a person may be sued on any cause of action (except possibly for certain local actions linked to real property) at his domicile or where he or it is doing

---

[a] See *Swift v. Tyson* and the discussion thereof, Chapter 6, § 6.01, *supra*.

[b] See Fed. R. Civ. P. Rule 4(f), Documents Supplement, p. 16, which permits service of process outside the state within 100 miles of the place where the action is commenced or to be tried, but only in the context of third-party practice. See also *Arrowsmith v. United Press International*, 320 F.2d 219 (2d Cir. 1963).

business—Actor sequitur forum rei, in the Roman law phrase[c] —is here assumed.[d] The presentation begins with *International Shoe Co. v. Washington,* in which the Supreme Court undertakes, apparently for the first time, to set out a theoretical foundation for jurisdiction over non-residents on a more limited basis—linked, that is, to particular activity giving rise to the action.

§ 7.01 Modern Notions of "Fair Play"

INTERNATIONAL SHOE CO. v. WASHINGTON

United States Supreme Court
326 U.S. 310 (1945)

MR. CHIEF JUSTICE STONE delivered the opinion of the Court.

The questions for decision are (1) whether, within the limitations of the due process clause of the Fourteenth Amendment, appellant, a Delaware corporation, has by its activities in the State of Washington rendered itself amenable to proceedings in the courts of that state to recover unpaid contributions to the state unemployment compensation fund exacted by state statutes, Washington Unemployment Compensation Act, Washington Revised Statutes, § 9998–103a through § 9998–123a, 1941 Supp., and (2) whether the state can exact those contributions consistently with the due process clause of the Fourteenth Amendment.

The statutes in question set up a comprehensive scheme of unemployment compensation, the costs of which are defrayed by contributions required to be made by employers to a state unemployment compensation fund. The contributions are a specified percentage of the wages payable annually by each employer for his employees' services in the state. The assessment and collection of the contributions and the fund are administered by appellees. Section 14 (c) of the Act (Wash. Rev. Stat., 1941 Supp., § 9998–114c) authorizes appellee Commissioner to issue an order and notice of assessment of delinquent contributions upon prescribed personal service of the notice upon the employer if found within the state, or, if not so found, by mailing the notice to the employer by registered mail at his last known address. That section also authorizes the Commissioner to collect the assessment by distraint if it is not paid within ten days after service of the notice. By §§ 14e and 6b the order of assessment may be administratively reviewed by an appeal tribunal within the office of unemployment upon petition of the employer, and this determination is by § 6i made subject to judicial review on questions of law by the state Superior Court, with further right of appeal in the state Supreme Court as in other civil cases.

In this case notice of assessment for the years in question was personally served upon a sales solicitor employed by appellant in the State of Washington, and a copy of the notice was mailed by registered mail to appellant at its address in St. Louis, Missouri. Appellant appeared specially

---

[c] The plaintiff follows the forum of the defendant.

[d] Compare the charmingly drafted statement in New York CPLR § 301, Documents Supplement, p. 77. For well-known articles tracing the developments in the law of jurisdiction in the United States, see, e.g., *Developments in the Law: State-Court Jurisdiction,* 73 Harv. L. Rev. 909 (1960); Kurland, *The Supreme Court, the Due Process Clause and the In Personam Jurisdiction of State Courts—From Pennoyer to Denckla: A Review,* 25 U. Chi. L. Rev. 569 (1958); Hazard, *A General Theory of State-Court Jurisdiction,* 1965 Sup. Ct. Rev. 241.

§ 7.01 JURISDICTION AND JUDGMENTS □ 487

before the office of unemployment and moved to set aside the order and notice of assessment on the ground that the service upon appellant's salesman was not proper service upon appellant; that appellant was not a corporation of the State of Washington and was not doing business within the state; that it had no agent within the state upon whom service could be made; and that appellant is not an employer and does not furnish employment within the meaning of the statute.

The motion was heard on evidence and a stipulation of facts by the appeal tribunal which denied the motion and ruled that appellee Commissioner was entitled to recover the unpaid contributions. That action was affirmed by the Commissioner; both the Superior Court and the Supreme Court affirmed. 22 Wash. 2d 146, 154 P. 2d 801. Appellant in each of these courts assailed the statute as applied, as a violation of the due process clause of the Fourteenth Amendment, and as imposing a constitutionally prohibited burden on interstate commerce. The cause comes here on appeal under § 237 (a) of the Judicial Code, 28 U. S. C. § 344 (a), appellant assigning as error that the challenged statutes as applied infringe the due process clause of the Fourteenth Amendment and the commerce clause.

The facts as found by the appeal tribunal and accepted by the state Superior Court and Supreme Court, are not in dispute. Appellant is a Delaware corporation, having its principal place of business in St. Louis, Missouri, and is engaged in the manufacture and sale of shoes and other footwear. It maintains places of business in several states, other than Washington, at which its manufacturing is carried on and from which its merchandise is distributed interstate through several sales units or branches located outside the State of Washington.

Appellant has no office in Washington and makes no contracts either for sale or purchase of merchandise there. It maintains no stock of merchandise in that state and makes there no deliveries of goods in intrastate commerce. During the years from 1937 to 1940, now in question, appellant employed eleven to thirteen salesmen under direct supervision and control of sales managers located in St. Louis. These salesmen resided in Washington; their principal activities were confined to that state; and they were compensated by commissions based upon the amount of their sales. The commissions for each year totaled more than $31,000. Appellant supplies its salesmen with a line of samples, each consisting of one shoe of a pair, which they display to prospective purchasers. On occasion they rent permanent sample rooms, for exhibiting samples, in business buildings, or rent rooms in hotels or business buildings temporarily for that purpose. The cost of such rentals is reimbursed by appellant.

The authority of the salesmen is limited to exhibiting their samples and soliciting orders from prospective buyers, at prices and on terms fixed by appellant. The salesmen transmit the orders to appellant's office in St. Louis for acceptance or rejection, and when accepted the merchandise for filling the orders is shipped f.o.b. from points outside Washington to the purchasers within the state. All the merchandise shipped into Washington is invoiced at the place of shipment from which collections are made. No salesman has authority to enter into contracts or to make collections.

The Supreme Court of Washington was of opinion that the regular and systematic solicitation of orders in the state by appellant's salesmen, resulting in a continuous flow of appellant's product into the state, was sufficient to constitute doing business in the state so as to make appellant amenable to suit in its courts. But it was also of opinion that there were sufficient additional activities shown to bring the case within the rule frequently stated, that solicitation within a state by the agents of a foreign corporation plus some additional activities there are sufficient to render the corporation amenable to suit brought in the courts of the state to enforce an obligation arising out of its activities there. . . .

The court found such additional activities in the salesmen's display of samples sometimes in permanent display rooms, and the salesmen's residence within the state, continued over a period of years, all resulting in a substantial volume of merchandise regularly shipped by appellant to purchasers within the state. The court also held that the statute as applied did not invade the constitutional power of Congress to regulate interstate commerce and did not impose a prohibited burden on such commerce.

Appellant's argument, renewed here, that the statute imposes an unconstitutional burden on interstate commerce need not detain us. For 53 Stat. 1391, 26 U. S. C. § 1606 (a) provides that "No person required under a State law to make payments to an unemployment fund shall be relieved from compliance therewith on the ground that he is engaged in interstate or foreign commerce, or that the State law does not distinguish between employees engaged in interstate or foreign commerce and those engaged in intrastate commerce." It is no longer debatable that Congress, in the exercise of the commerce power, may authorize the states, in specified ways, to regulate interstate commerce or impose burdens upon it. . . .

Appellant also insists that its activities within the state were not sufficient to manifest its "presence" there and that in its absence the state courts were without jurisdiction, that consequently it was a denial of due process for the state to subject appellant to suit. It refers to those cases in which it was said that the mere solicitation of orders for the purchase of goods within a state, to be accepted without the state and filled by shipment of the purchased goods interstate, does not render the corporation seller amenable to suit within the state. . . . And appellant further argues that since it was not present within the state, it is a denial of due process to subject it to taxation or other money exaction. It thus denies the power of the state to lay the tax or to subject appellant to a suit for its collection.

Historically the jurisdiction of courts to render judgment *in personam* is grounded on their de facto power over the defendant's person. Hence his presence within the territorial jurisdiction of a court was prerequisite to its rendition of a judgment personally binding him. *Pennoyer v. Neff,* 95 U. S. 714, 733. But now that the *capias ad respondendum* has given way to personal service of summons or other form of notice, due process requires only that in order to subject a defendant to a judgment *in personam,* if he be not present within the territory of the forum, he have certain minimum contacts with it such that the maintenance of the suit does not offend "traditional notions of fair play and substantial justice." *Milliken v. Meyer,* 311 U. S. 457, 463. See Holmes, J., in *McDonald v. Mabee,* 243 U. S. 90, 91. Compare *Hoopeston Canning Co. v. Cullen,* 318 U. S. 313, 316, 319. See *Blackmer v. United States,* 284 U. S. 421; *Hess v. Pawloski,* 274 U. S. 352; *Young v. Masci,* 289 U. S. 253.

Since the corporate personality is a fiction, . . . it is clear that unlike an individual its "presence" without, as well as within, the state of its origin can be manifested only by activities carried on in its behalf by those who are authorized to act for it. To say that the corporation is so far "present" there as to satisfy due process requirements, for purposes of taxation or the maintenance of suits against it in the courts of the state, is to beg the question to be decided. For the terms "present" or "presence" are used merely to symbolize those activities of the corporation's agent within the state which courts will deem to be sufficient to satisfy the demands of due process. L. Hand, J., in *Hutchinson v. Chase & Gilbert,* 45 F. 2d 139, 141. Those demands may be met by such contacts of the corporation with the state of the forum as make it reasonable, in the context of our federal system of government, to require the corporation to defend the particular suit which is brought there. An "estimate of the inconveniences" which would result to the corporation from a trial away from its "home" or principal place of business is relevant in this connection. *Hutchinson v. Chase & Gilbert, supra,* 141.

"Presence" in the state in this sense has never been doubted when the activities of the corporation there have not only been continuous and systematic, but also give rise to the liabilities sued on, even though no consent to be sued or authorization to an agent to accept service of process has been given. . . . Conversely it has been generally recognized that the casual presence of the corporate agent or even his conduct of single or isolated items of activities in a state in the corporation's behalf are not enough to subject it to suit on causes of action unconnected with the activities there. To require the corporation in such circumstances to defend the suit away from its home or other jurisdiction where it carries on more substantial activities has been thought to lay too great and unreasonable a burden on the corporation to comport with due process. . . .

. . . [A]lthough the commission of some single or occasional acts of the corporate agent in a state sufficient to impose an obligation or liability on the corporation has not been thought to confer upon the state authority to enforce it, *Rosenberg Bros. & Co. v. Curtis Brown Co.,* 260 U. S. 516, other such acts, because of their nature and quality and the circumstances of their commission, may be deemed sufficient to render the corporation liable to suit. Cf. *Kane v. New Jersey,* 242 U. S. 160; *Hess v. Pawloski, supra; Young v. Masci, supra.* True, some of the decisions holding the corporation amenable to suit have been supported by resort to the legal fiction that it has given its consent to service and suit, consent being implied from its presence in the state through the acts of its authorized agents. . . . But more realistically it may be said that those authorized acts were of such a nature as to justify the fiction. . . .

It is evident that the criteria by which we mark the boundary line between those activities which justify the subjection of a corporation to suit, and those which do not, cannot be simply mechanical or quantitative. The test is not merely, as has sometimes been suggested, whether the activity, which the corporation has seen fit to procure through its agents in another state, is a little more or a little less. . . . Whether due process is satisfied must depend rather upon the quality and nature of the activity in relation to the fair and orderly administration of the laws which it was the purpose of the due process clause to insure. That clause does not contemplate that a state may make binding a judgment *in personam* against an individual or corporate defendant with which the state has no contacts, ties, or relations.

But to the extent that a corporation exercises the privilege of conducting activities within a state, it enjoys the benefits and protection of the laws of that state. The exercise of that privilege may give rise to obligations, and, so far as those obligations arise out of or are connected with the activities within the state, a procedure which requires the corporation to respond to a suit brought to enforce them, can, in most instances, hardly be said to be undue. . . .

Applying these standards, the activities carried on in behalf of appellant in the State of Washington were neither irregular nor casual. They were systematic and continuous throughout the years in question. They resulted in a large volume of interstate business, in the course of which appellant received the benefits and protection of the laws of the state, including the right to resort to the courts for the enforcement of its rights. The obligation which is here sued upon arose out of those very activities. It is evident that these operations establish sufficient contacts or ties with the state of the forum to make it reasonable and just, according to our traditional conception of fair play and substantial justice, to permit the state to enforce the obligations which appellant has incurred there. Hence we cannot say that the maintenance of the present suit in the State of Washington involves an unreasonable or undue procedure.

We are likewise unable to conclude that the service of the process within the state upon an agent whose activities establish appellant's "presence" there was not sufficient notice of the suit, or that the suit was so unrelated to those activities as to make the agent an inappropriate vehicle for communicating the notice. It is enough that appellant has established such contacts with the state that the particular form of substituted service adopted there gives reasonable assurance that the notice will be actual. . . . Nor can we say that the mailing of the notice of suit to appellant by registered mail at its home office was not reasonably calculated to apprise appellant of the suit.

. . .

Appellant having rendered itself amenable to suit upon obligations arising out of the activities of its salesmen in Washington, the state may maintain the present suit *in personam* to collect the tax laid upon the exercise of the privilege of employing appellant's salesmen within the state. For Washington has made one of those activities, which taken together establish appellant's "presence" there for purposes of suit, the taxable event by which the state brings appellant within the reach of its taxing power. The state thus has constitutional power to lay the tax and to subject appellant to a suit to recover it. The activities which establish its "presence" subject it alike to taxation by the state and to suit to recover the tax. . . .

Affirmed.

Mr. Justice Black delivered the following opinion.

. . .

It is my view . . . that we should dismiss the appeal as unsubstantial, . . . and decline the invitation to formulate broad rules as to the meaning of due process, which here would amount to deciding a constitutional question "in advance of the necessity for its decision." . . .

Certainly appellant cannot in the light of our past decisions meritoriously claim that notice by registered mail and by personal service on its sales solicitors in Washington did not meet the requirements of procedural due process. And the due process clause is not brought in issue any more by appellant's further conceptualistic contention that Washington could not levy a tax or bring suit against the corporation because it did not honor that State with its mystical "presence." For it is unthinkable that the vague due process clause was ever intended to prohibit a State from regulating or taxing a business carried on within its boundaries simply because this is done by agents of a corporation organized and having its headquarters elsewhere. To read this into the due process clause would in fact result in depriving a State's citizens of due process by taking from the State the power to protect them in their business dealings within its boundaries with representatives of a foreign corporation. Nothing could be more irrational or more designed to defeat the function of our federative system of government. Certainly a State, at the very least, has power to tax and sue those dealing with its citizens within its boundaries, as we have held before. *Hoopeston Canning Co. v. Cullen,* 318 U. S. 313. Were the Court to follow this principle, it would provide a workable standard for cases where, as here, no other questions are involved. The Court has not chosen to do so, but instead has engaged in an unnecessary discussion in the course of which it has announced vague Constitutional criteria applied for the first time to the issue before us. It has thus introduced uncertain elements confusing the simple pattern and tending to curtail the exercise of State powers to an extent not justified by the Constitution.

The criteria adopted insofar as they can be identified read as follows: Due Process does permit State courts to "enforce the obligations which appellant has incurred" if it be found "reasonable and just according to our traditional conception of fair play and substantial justice." And this in turn means that we will "permit" the State to act if upon "an 'estimate of the inconveniences' which would result to the corporation from a trial away from its 'home' or principal place of business," we conclude that it is "reasonable" to subject it to suit in a State where it is doing business.

. . .

I believe that the Federal Constitution leaves to each State, without any "ifs" or "buts," a power to tax and to open the doors of its courts for its citizens to sue corporations whose agents do business in those States. Believing that the Constitution gave the States that power, I think it a judicial deprivation to condition its exercise upon this Court's notion of "fair play," however appealing that term may be. Nor can I stretch the meaning of due process so far as to authorize this Court to deprive a State of the right to afford judicial protection to its citizens on the ground that it would be more "convenient" for the corporation to be sued somewhere else.

There is a strong emotional appeal in the words "fair play," "justice," and "reasonableness." But they were not chosen by those who wrote the original Constitution or the Fourteenth Amendment as a measuring rod for this Court to use in invalidating State or Federal laws passed by elected legislative representatives. No one, not even those who most feared a democratic government, ever formally proposed that courts should be given power to invalidate legislation under any such elastic standards.

. . .

True, the State's power is here upheld. But the rule announced means that tomorrow's judgment may strike down a State or Federal enactment on the ground that it does not conform to this Court's idea of natural justice.

. . .

McGEE v. INTERNATIONAL LIFE INSURANCE CO.

United States Supreme Court
355 U.S. 220 (1957)

Opinion of the Court by Mr. Justice Black, announced by Mr. Justice Douglas.

Petitioner, Lulu B. McGee, recovered a judgment in a California state court against respondent, International Life Insurance Company, on a contract of insurance. Respondent was not served with process in California but by registered mail at its principal place of business in Texas. The California court based its jurisdiction on a state statute which subjects foreign corporations to suit in California on insurance contracts with residents of that State even though such corporations cannot be served with process within its borders.[1]

Unable to collect the judgment in California petitioner went to Texas where she filed suit on the judgment in a Texas court. But the Texas courts refused to enforce her judgment holding

---

[1] Cal. Insurance Code, 1953, §§ 1610–1620.

it was void under the Fourteenth Amendment because service of process outside California could not give the courts of that State jurisdiction over respondent. 288 S. W. 2d 579. Since the case raised important questions, not only to California but to other States which have similar laws, we granted certiorari. 352 U.S. 924. It is not controverted that if the California court properly exercised jurisdiction over respondent the Texas courts erred in refusing to give its judgment full faith and credit. 28 U. S. C. § 1738.

The material facts are relatively simple. In 1944, Lowell Franklin, a resident of California, purchased a life insurance policy from the Empire Mutual Insurance Company, an Arizona corporation. In 1948 the respondent agreed with Empire Mutual to assume its insurance obligations. Respondent then mailed a reinsurance certificate to Franklin in California offering to insure him in accordance with the terms of the policy he held with Empire Mutual. He accepted this offer and from that time until his death in 1950 paid premiums by mail from his California home to respondent's Texas office. Petitioner, Franklin's mother, was the beneficiary under the policy. She sent proofs of his death to the respondent but it refused to pay claiming that he had committed suicide. It appears that neither Empire Mutual nor respondent has ever had any office or agent in California. And so far as the record before us shows, respondent has never solicited or done any insurance business in California apart from the policy involved here.

Since *Pennoyer v. Neff,* 95 U. S. 714, this Court has held that the Due Process Clause of the Fourteenth Amendment places some limit on the power of state courts to enter binding judgments against persons not served with process within their boundaries. But just where this line of limitation falls has been the subject of prolific controversy, particularly with respect to foreign corporations. In a continuing process of evolution this Court accepted and then abandoned "consent," "doing business," and "presence" as the standard for measuring the extent of state judicial power over such corporations. See Henderson, *The Position of Foreign Corporations in American Constitutional Law,* ch. V. More recently in *International Shoe Co. v. Washington,* 326 U. S. 310, the Court decided that "due process requires only that in order to subject a defendant to a judgment *in personam,* if he be not present within the territory of the forum, he have certain minimum contacts with it such that the maintenance of the suit does not offend 'traditional notions of fair play and substantial justice.' " *Id.,* at 316.

Looking back over this long history of litigation a trend is clearly discernible toward expanding the permissible scope of state jurisdiction over foreign corporations and other nonresidents. In part this is attributable to the fundamental transformation of our national economy over the years. Today many commercial transactions touch two or more States and may involve parties separated by the full continent. With this increasing nationalization of commerce has come a great increase in the amount of business conducted by mail across state lines. At the same time modern transportation and communication have made it much less burdensome for a party sued to defend himself in a State where he engages in economic activity.

Turning to this case we think it apparent that the Due Process Clause did not preclude the California court from entering a judgment binding on respondent. It is sufficient for purposes of due process that the suit was based on a contract which had substantial connection with that State. Cf. *Hess v. Pawloski,* 274 U. S. 352; *Henry L. Doherty & Co. v. Goodman,* 294 U. S. 623; *Pennoyer v. Neff,* 95 U. S. 714, 735. The contract was delivered in California, the premiums were mailed from there and the insured was a resident of that State when he died. It cannot be denied that California has a manifest interest in providing effective means of redress for its residents when their insurers refuse to pay claims. These residents would be at a severe disadvantage if they were forced to follow the insurance company to a distant State in order to hold it legally accountable. When claims were small or moderate individual claimants frequently could not afford the cost of bringing an action in a foreign forum—thus in effect making the company judgment proof. Often the crucial witnesses—as here on the company's defense of suicide—will be found in the insured's locality. Of course there may be inconvenience to the insurer if it is held amenable to suit in California where it had this contract but certainly nothing which amounts to a denial of due process. Cf. *Travelers Health Assn. v. Virginia ex rel. State Corporation Comm'n*, 339 U. S. 643. There is no contention that respondent did not have adequate notice of the suit or sufficient time to prepare its defenses and appear.

The California statute became law in 1949, after respondent had entered into the agreement with Franklin to assume Empire Mutual's obligation to him. Respondent contends that application of the statute to this existing contract improperly impairs the obligation of the contract. We believe that contention is devoid of merit. The statute was remedial, in the purest sense of that term, and neither enlarged nor impaired respondent's substantive rights or obligations under the contract. It did nothing more than to provide petitioner with a California forum to enforce whatever substantive rights she might have against respondent. At the same time respondent was given a reasonable time to appear and defend on the merits after being notified of the suit. Under such circumstances it had no vested right not to be sued in California. . . .

The judgment is reversed and the cause is remanded to the Court of Civil Appeals of the State of Texas, First Supreme Judicial District, for further proceedings not inconsistent with this opinion.

NOTES AND QUESTIONS

(1)(a) On its facts, *International Shoe* is an easy case. If one of the 11 to 13 salesmen working in Washington had been laid off by the company, there is no doubt that he could have applied for unemployment compensation in Washington. If the state was obligated to pay unemployment benefits to the laid-off employee, it could surely require the employer to contribute to the state unemployment insurance fund. And if the employer was obligated to contribute to that fund, there ought to be no impediment to enforcement of that obligation by the state in its courts.[e]

(b) Seen in this way, *International Shoe* is not only about judicial jurisdiction, but in the first instance about legislative jurisdiction—the right of a state to make its law applicable to a transaction with foreign as well as domestic elements.[f] Here, as a matter of choice of law, there is no possible challenge to application of Washington law to measure the contribution due in respect of persons employed in Washington.

(2)(a) *International Shoe* could have been decided as a "doing business" case. Hundreds of decisions in every state had passed on the question of how much activity within a state constituted doing business, and probably employing 13 salesmen over a period of years would have been enough to constitute "continuous and systematic" corporate activity in the state so as to sustain general jurisdiction over the company.[g] Chief Justice Stone, however, had something else in mind.

---

[e] Note that in 1945 it was unclear whether Washington could have enforced its claim for contribution to the insurance fund—a kind of tax—in other states. See Chapter 8, p. 673, question (9)(d), *infra*.

[f] More of this, in the international context, in Chapter 10, §§ 10.03–04, *infra*.

[g] That indeed is what the Supreme Court of Washington found (7–2 with the Chief Justice writing a long dissent).

Theories of jurisdiction over out-of-state corporations based on *consent,* or implied consent, had broken down in circumstances where the state exercising jurisdiction could not have excluded the corporation from doing a purely interstate business; and theories based on *presence* depended on a fiction that usually ended up asking the question it was supposed to answer—is there sufficient activity to make it reasonable to subject the corporation to jurisdiction in the forum?[h] Notions of *power,* for example, focused on whether F–1 could enforce a judgment rendered against a foreign corporation, also (i) got the question backwards;[i] and (ii) were really out of place in a federal union with a Full Faith and Credit clause. Definitions of doing business often turned on such unphilosophic questions as "if 13 salesmen were sufficient, what about 6, or 9, or 11?" As Professor Kurland put it:

> With doctrine in so bad a state of disrepair, the time had long since passed for the Supreme Court to acknowledge the truth of Holmes' dictum that "[t]he Constitution is not to be satisfied with a fiction." *International Shoe Co. v. Washington* afforded the Court an opportunity to begin to set its house in order in this field.[j]

(b) What then is the theory of *International Shoe?* Is it reasonableness? Fair play? Foreseeability? Something else?

(3) Though the opinion in *International Shoe* is not precise on the point, the thrust of the decision is that even if the defendant's activity in Washington did not rise to the level needed to support jurisdiction in respect of *all* kinds of claims, it was sufficient to support jurisdiction in respect to the claim in suit, because that claim grew out of the activity.

In addition to suit to collect unemployment insurance contributions, which of the following actions against International Shoe Company could, under the Supreme Court's decision, be brought in the courts of Washington?

(i) a suit by one of the salesmen for failure to pay his commission;

(ii) a suit by a retailer in Seattle for misdelivery of an order booked through one of the salesmen;

(iii) a suit by a retailer in Seattle for misdelivery of an order given by the retailer on a trip to St. Louis;

(iv) a suit by a retailer in San Francisco for misdelivery of an order;

(v) a suit by a retailer in Seattle for assault, alleging that one of the 13 salesmen had punched him in the nose during a shoe show in Seattle because he had said something disparaging about International's selection of shoes;

(vi) a suit by a shareholder of International Shoe Co. residing in Seattle, complaining that the company had paid excessive bonuses to its executives while reducing its dividend.

(4)(a) The message of *International Shoe* seemed to be that, within the constraints of fair play and substantial justice, any activity within a state—or even outside the state but with effect within

---

International Shoe Co. v. State, 22 Wash. 2d 146, 154 P.2d 801 (1945). For confirmation that continuous and substantial activities in a state by a corporation subjects it to general jurisdiction including claims unrelated to the activity, see *Perkins v. Benguet Consolidated Mining Co.,* 342 U.S. 437 (1952).

[h] Compare L. Hand, J. in *Hutchinson v. Chase & Gilbert,* 45 F.2d 139, at 141 (2d Cir. 1930).

[i] Thus, the right way to put the question, as developed in the next chapter, says F–2 will enforce the judgment of F–1 if F–1 had jurisdiction, and then inquire whether it did.

[j] Kurland, p. 486, note d, *supra,* at 586.

§ 7.01　　　　　　　　JURISDICTION AND JUDGMENTS　　□　495

it—might support jurisdiction over the person carrying out the activity in an action arising out of that activity. It took ten years for Illinois, the pioneer state in this field, to get the message and enact what became known as a "long-arm statute."[k] Wisconsin enacted a similar (but more comprehensive) statute in 1959, and New York adopted a statute modeled on the Illinois act as part of its comprehensive Civil Practice Law and Rules in 1963.[l] In the same year, the Commissioners on Uniform State Laws adopted a model long-arm statute similar to the Illinois and New York statutes, but providing expressly for jurisdiction in cases of "split torts," i.e., an act or omission outside the state causing an injury within it.[m] By the end of the 1960's, every state in the United States had adopted some form of long-arm statute, many following the model of Illinois or New York, others, such as California and Rhode Island, simply providing that "a court of this state may exercise jurisdiction on any basis not inconsistent with the Constitution of this state or of the United States."[n]

(b) More and more, actions against non-residents, and particulary non-resident corporations, have been brought under long-arm statutes rather than, as before, on the basis of "presence" or "doing business." This means, of course, that every such action is in a sense a choice of law case: While success in obtaining jurisdiction does not guarantee that the law of the forum would be applied, it does mean at least a preliminary determination that the cause of action arose in the forum state. It is only in cases where that was not so—e.g., a U.S. plaintiff buys a German car in Germany, transports it to the United States, and then is injured by a defect in that car—that other bases of jurisdiction, such as doing business or presence ("as heretofore," in the New York version)[o]—are still necessary.[p]

(5)(a) The development of long-arm jurisdiction came as a considerable shock to many members of the American legal community, particularly to those trained prior to World War II who had grown up on *Pennoyer v. Neff*,[q] which seemed to require the physical presence of the defendant in the forum state, and only rarely distinguished between general jurisdiction and jurisdiction in respect of particular causes of action linked to particular activity.[r] The use of activity-based jurisdiction was not a new phenomenon in the common law, however.

---

[k] Ill. Laws 1955, p. 2238, adopting Ill. Rev. Stat. c. 110, § 117, recodified as Sec. 2–209 of Ill. Code of Civil Practice (1982).

[l] N.Y.C.P.L.R. § 302. For the amended version as of 1998, see Documents Supplement, p. 77.

[m] Documents Supplement p. 87. Note that the comparable provision in the New York long-arm statute, § 302(a)(3) was not adopted until 1966, after several decisions by the New York Court of Appeals had declined to sustain jurisdiction in such circumstances.

[n] Calif. Code of Civil Procedure § 410.10. For the text of every state's long-arm provisions—whether statute or rule of court, see R. Casad and W. Richman, *Jurisdiction in Civil Actions*, (3d ed. 1998 plus Supp.).

[o] See N.Y.C.P.L.R. § 301, Documents Supplement, p. 77.

[p] Compare, e.g., *Delagi v. Volkswagen A.G. of Wolfsburg*, 29 N.Y.2d 426, 328 N.Y.S.2d 653, 278 N.W.2d 895 (1972) (held, no jurisdiction over manufacturer in tort action resulting from accident in car purchased in Germany, because manufacturer was not doing business in New York), with *Roorda v. Volkswagenwerk, A.G.*, 481 F. Supp. 868 (D. S.C. 1979) (jurisdiction against manufacturer upheld on basis that it was "present" in South Carolina through its agent, though car in question had not been purchased in state and accident had not occurred in state).

[q] 95 U.S. 714 (1878).

[r] ". . . Process from the tribunals of one State cannot run into another State, and summon parties there domiciled to leave its territory and respond to proceedings against them. Publication of process or notice within the State where the tribunal sits cannot create any greater obligation upon the non-resident to appear. Process sent to him out of the State, and process published within it, are equally unavailing in proceedings to establish his personal liability." 95 U.S. at 727.

As early as 1852, so-called "assumed jurisdiction" was conferred by statute on English courts, giving them discretionary power to summon absent defendants in stated circumstances, including both tort and contract claims.[s] The Rules of the Supreme Court promulgated in 1883, following the unification and reorganization of the English judicial system, contained Order 11, which, with some revisions, remains the basis for exercise by English courts of jurisdiction over absent defendants.[t] In contrast to the American technique, which lists the situations in which the court of a given state has jurisdiction and separately makes provision for service of process, Order 11 focuses on service itself: Service of the writ initiating the action may be made outside of England with leave of the court upon a showing that the claim fits within one of the categories set forth in Order 11. Moreover, in contrast to the American approach, which (at least in theory) views jurisdiction as either existing or not, leave under Order 11 is always discretionary.[u] If leave is granted (usually in the first instance by order of a Master upon *ex parte* application), defendant can apply to set the order aside,[v] and either side can appeal from the decision on that application.[w]

We saw an instance where discretion was exercised in favor of jurisdiction of the English court (technically upholding the order granting leave to serve the defendant outside of England) in *Unterweser Rederei v. Zapata Off-Shore Co.,* the English phase of the *Bremen* litigation;[x] another instance appears in the *Coast Lines* case in the next section. In other cases, though the terms of Order 11 are met, for instance a contract made within England but with a choice of forum clause designating another state, the courts will decline to exercise jurisdiction—i.e., will overrule the decision of the master granting leave.[y]

(b) Look at the bases of jurisdiction set out in Order 11, rule 1(1), especially (a), (c), (d)(i), (d)(iii), (d)(iv), (e) and (f). Which of these bases of jurisdiction seem fair to you?

(i) Should any of these bases be made mandatory, i.e., without discretion in the court?

(ii) Should any of the bases be excluded as essentially unfair or exorbitant?

(iii) As to the bases that do not normally support jurisdiction in the United States—e.g., (c), joinder of necessary or proper parties, or (d)(iii), a contract governed by the law of

---

[s] Common Law Procedure Act, 15 & 16 Vict. c. 76 s.18.

[t] The current text of Order 11 appears in the Documents Supplement at p. 79. Many jurisdictions in the British Commonwealth, including most of the provinces of Canada and Australia, have rules or statutes modeled on Order 11, though not always with the latest amendments.

[u] See Order 11, r.4(2), Documents Supplement, p. 82.

[v] R.S.C. Order 12, r. 8.

[w] Alternatively, the defendant may choose not to challenge the court's jurisdiction, but to apply for a stay of the proceedings on the ground that England is not a convenient forum or that the parties have agreed on a forum in another state.

[x] Chapter 4, p. 290, *supra*.

[y] For an interesting example of such a case, see *Mackender v. Feldia A.G.,* [1967] 2 Q.B. 590 (C.A.) In that case, a Lloyd's insurance syndicate had issued a policy in London to European diamond dealers. The policy contained a choice of forum clause designating the courts of Belgium, as well as a clause stating that the contract was governed by Belgian law. Following a claim of loss, the underwriters asserted that the whole contract was void because the dealers had not disclosed that they were engaged in smuggling. The underwriters sought a declaration of non-liability from the English court, upon a determination that the contract (including the choice of forum clause) was void for illegality. The Court of Appeal, reversing two High Court judges, held that leave had been improperly granted, the choice of forum clause being "strong ground why discretion should be exercised against leave to serve out of the jurisdiction."

the forum—would you favor amending American long-arm statutes to provide for jurisdiction where English law now does? Or would such amendment be unconstitutional?

(c) Is there any basis of jurisdiction on the list that you would regard as acceptable from the point of view of F–1 (i.e., England), but would reject as the basis of a judgment to be enforced in another country (e.g., the United States)?[z]

(6)(a) Turning briefly to *McGee v. International Life Insurance Co.,* that case has been regarded as the high-water mark of jurisdiction over non-residents in the United States, to be cut back in *Hanson v. Denckla* in the following year (see next section) and in several later cases as well. Does it go beyond *International Shoe*?

(b) Note that *McGee* seems to emphasise the interest—indeed "manifest interest" (pp. 492-93)—of California, the forum state, in providing for persons domiciled in the state who have difficulty collecting on insurance policies; in contrast, Chief Justice Stone's opinion in *International Shoe* seems (at pp. 488–89) to talk more in terms of contacts, though it concludes on a criterion of reasonableness, justice and fairness. In which case was there greater interest in the forum state?

In *International Shoe,* as we saw, the question of choice of law did not arise; if the courts of Washington had judicial jurisdiction, they would apply that state's law; in any other state, the cause of action would either not be entertained at all,[a] or Washington law would be applied as well. In *McGee,* however, choice of law may well have been at the heart of the decision to sue in California rather than in Texas. Suppose the following additional factors, not stated in Justice Black's opinion, were applicable:

> Under California law, an insurance company seeking to resist payment under a life insurance policy on the grounds of suicide has the burden of proof that the death was self-inflicted. Under Texas law, once it is established that death was not due to natural causes—say by a fall, a gunshot, or poison—the burden is on the beneficiary of the insurance policy to establish that the cause of death was an accident, and not the result of the deceased's intentional act.[b]

Would knowledge of this difference in the law affect the concept of fairness underlying the *McGee* case? Or are choice of law and jurisdiction so distinct that none of this should make any difference? This question is pursued in the next section and throughout the chapter.

---

[z] This question is explored in depth in the next chapter, particularly § 8.02[B].

[a] See note e, p. 493, *supra.*

[b] In fact, the Texas rule appears to be that there is a presumption against suicide, so that the party against whom the presumption operates (i.e., the insurance company) has the burden of producing evidence that the deceased took his own life. However, once the insurer has produced evidence, even though circumstantial, from which a jury could reasonably find that deceased committed suicide, the presumption is rebutted and is not to be treated as evidence. See R. Ray, *Texas Law of Evidence* § 105 and sources there cited (3d ed. 1980).

California law also has a presumption against suicide, but when that presumption shifts is less clear. See B. Witkin, *California Evidence* p. 184 (2d ed. 1966); *Cal. Civil Code Annotated,* § 3546. Thus, the distinction between the laws of the two states is not as sharp as suggested in the hypothetical in the text, but the outcome of a given case of accident/suicide may well turn on where it is litigated.

§ 7.02 The Interplay Between Jurisdiction and Choice of Law

HANSON v. DENCKLA

United States Supreme Court
357 U.S. 235 (1958)

MR. CHIEF JUSTICE WARREN delivered the opinion of the Court.

This controversy concerns the right to $400,000, part of the corpus of a trust established in Delaware by a settlor who later became domiciled in Florida. One group of claimants, "legatees," urge that this property passed under the residuary clause of the settlor's will, which was admitted to probate in Florida. The Florida courts have sustained this position. 100 So. 2d 378. Other claimants, "appointees" and "beneficiaries," contend that the property passed pursuant to the settlor's exercise of the *inter vivos* power of appointment created in the deed of trust. The Delaware courts adopted this position and refused to accord full faith and credit to the Florida determination because the Florida court had not acquired jurisdiction over an indispensable party, the Delaware trustee. [36 Del. Ch. 235], 128 A. 2d 819. We postponed the question of jurisdiction in the Florida appeal, No. 107, 354 U. S. 919,[a] and granted certiorari to the Delaware Supreme Court, No. 117, 354 U.S. 920.[b]

The trust whose validity is contested here was created in 1935. Dora Browning Donner, then a domiciliary of Pennsylvania, executed a trust instrument in Delaware naming the Wilmington Trust Co., of Wilmington, Delaware, as trustee. The corpus was composed of securities. Mrs. Donner reserved the income for life, and stated that the remainder should be paid to such persons or upon such trusts as she should appoint by *inter vivos* or testamentary instrument. The trust agreement provided that Mrs. Donner could change the trustee, and that she could amend, alter or revoke the agreement at any time. A measure of control over trust administration was assured by the provision that only with the consent of a trust "advisor" appointed by the settlor could the trustee (1) sell trust assets, (2) make investments, and (3) participate in any plan, proceeding, reorganization or merger involving securities held in the trust. A few days after the trust was established Mrs. Donner exercised her power of appointment. That appointment was replaced by another in 1939. Thereafter she left Pennsylvania, and in 1944 became domiciled in Florida, where she remained until her death in 1952. Mrs. Donner's will was executed Dec. 3, 1949. On that same day she executed the *inter vivos* power of appointment whose terms are at issue here. After making modest appointments in favor of a hospital and certain family retainers (the "appointees"), she appointed the sum of $200,000 to each of two trusts previously established with another Delaware trustee, the Delaware Trust Co. The balance of the trust corpus, over $1,000,000 at the date of her death, was appointed to her executrix. That amount passed under the residuary clause of her will and is not at issue here.

The two trusts with the Delaware Trust Co. were created in 1948 by Mrs. Donner's daughter, Elizabeth Donner Hanson, for the benefit of Elizabeth's children, Donner Hanson and Joseph Donner Winsor. In identical terms they provide that the income not required for the beneficiary's support should be accumulated to age 25, when the beneficiary should be paid of the corpus

---

[a] *Hanson v. Denckla.*

[b] *Lewis v. Hanson.*

§ 7.02   JURISDICTION AND JUDGMENTS   □   499

and receive the income from the balance for life. Upon the death of the beneficiary the remainder was to go to such of the beneficiary's issue or Elizabeth Donner Hanson's issue as the beneficiary should appoint by *inter vivos* or testamentary instrument; in default of appointment to the beneficiary's issue alive at the time of his death, and if none to the issue of Elizabeth Donner Hanson.

Mrs. Donner died Nov. 20, 1952. Her will, which was admitted to probate in Florida, named Elizabeth Donner Hanson as executrix. She was instructed to pay all debts and taxes, including any which might be payable by reason of the property appointed under the power of appointment in the trust agreement with the Wilmington Trust Co. After disposing of personal and household effects, Mrs. Donner's will directed that the balance of her property (the $1,000,000 appointed from the Delaware trust) be paid in equal parts to two trusts for the benefit of her daughters Katherine N. R. Denckla and Dorothy B. R. Stewart.

This controversy grows out of the residuary clause that created the last-mentioned trusts. It begins:

> All the rest, residue and remainder of my estate, real, personal and mixed, whatsoever and wheresoever the same may be at the time of my death, including any and all property, rights and interest over which I may have power of appointment which prior to my death has not been effectively exercised by me or has been exercised by me in favor of my Executrix, I direct my Executrix to deal with as follows. . . .

Residuary legatees Denckla and Stewart, already the recipients of over $500,000 each, urge that the power of appointment over the $400,000 appointed to sister Elizabeth's children was not "effectively exercised" and that the property should accordingly pass to them. Fourteen months after Mrs. Donner's death these parties petitioned a Florida chancery court for a declaratory judgment "concerning what property passes under the residuary clause" of the will. Personal service was had upon the following defendants: (1) executrix Elizabeth Donner Hanson, (2) beneficiaries Donner Hanson and Joseph Donner Winsor, and (3) potential beneficiary William Donner Roosevelt, also one of Elizabeth's children. Curtin Winsor, Jr., another of Elizabeth's children and also a potential beneficiary of the Delaware trusts, was not named as a party and was not served. About a dozen other defendants were nonresidents and could not be personally served. These included the Wilmington Trust Co. ("trustee"), the Delaware Trust Co. (to whom the $400,000 had been paid shortly after Mrs. Donner's death), certain individuals who were potential successors in interest to complainants Denckla and Stewart, and most of the named appointees in Mrs. Donner's 1949 appointment. A copy of the pleadings and a "Notice to Appear and Defend" were sent to each of these defendants by ordinary mail, and notice was published locally as required by the Florida statutes dealing with constructive service.[3] With the exception

---

[3] Fla. Stat., 1957, c. 48, § 48.01: "Service of process by publication may be had, in any of the several courts of this state, and upon any of the parties mentioned in § 48.02 in any suit or proceeding:

"(1) To enforce any legal or equitable lien upon or claim to any title or interest in real or personal property within the jurisdiction of the court or any fund held or debt owing by any party upon whom process can be served within this state.

. . .

"(5) For the construction of any will, deed, contract or other written instrument and for a judicial declaration or enforcement of any legal or equitable right, title, claim, lien or interest thereunder."

§ 48.02: "Where personal service of process cannot be had, service of process by publication may be had upon any party, natural or corporate, known or unknown, including: (1) Any known or unknown natural person . . . (2) Any corporation or other legal entity, whether its domicile be foreign, domestic or unknown . . ."

of two individuals whose interests coincided with complainants Denckla and Stewart, none of the nonresident defendants made any appearance.

The appearing defendants (Elizabeth Donner Hanson and her children) moved to dismiss the suit because the exercise of jurisdiction over indispensable parties, the Delaware trustees, would offend Section 1 of the Fourteenth Amendment. The Chancellor ruled that he lacked jurisdiction over these nonresident defendants because no personal service was had and because the trust corpus was outside the territorial jurisdiction of the court. The cause was dismissed as to them. As far as parties before the court were concerned, however, he ruled that the power of appointment was testamentary and void under the applicable Florida law. In a decree dated Jan. 14, 1955, he ruled that the $400,000 passed under the residuary clause of the will.

After the Florida litigation began, but before entry of the decree, the executrix instituted a declaratory judgment action in Delaware to determine who was entitled to participate in the trust assets held in that State. Except for the addition of beneficiary Winsor and several appointees, the parties were substantially the same as in the Florida litigation. Nonresident defendants were notified by registered mail. All of the trust companies, beneficiaries, and legatees except Katherine N. R. Denckla, appeared and participated in the litigation. After the Florida court enjoined executrix Hanson from further participation, her children pursued their own interests. When the Florida decree was entered the legatees unsuccessfully urged it as *res judicata* of the Delaware dispute. In a decree dated Jan. 13, 1956, the Delaware Chancellor ruled that the trust and power of appointment were valid under the applicable Delaware law, and that the trust corpus had properly been paid to the Delaware Trust Co. and the other appointees. [35] Del. Ch. [411], 119 A. 2d 901.

Alleging that she would be bound by the Delaware decree, the executrix moved the Florida Supreme Court to remand with instructions to dismiss the Florida suit then pending on appeal. No full faith and credit question was raised. The motion was denied. The Florida Supreme Court affirmed its Chancellor's conclusion that Florida law applied to determine the validity of the trust and power of appointment. Under that law the trust was invalid because the settlor had reserved too much power over the trustee and trust corpus, and the power of appointment was not independently effective to pass the property because it was a testamentary act not accompanied by the requisite formalities. The Chancellor's conclusion that there was no jurisdiction over the trust companies and other absent defendants was reversed. The court ruled that jurisdiction to construe the will carried with it "substantive" jurisdiction "over the persons of the absent defendants" even though the trust assets were not "physically in this state." Whether this meant jurisdiction over the person of the defendants or jurisdiction over the trust assets is open to doubt. In a motion for rehearing the beneficiaries and appointees urged for the first time that Florida should have given full faith and credit to the decision of the Delaware Chancellor. The motion was denied without opinion, Nov. 28, 1956.

The full faith and credit question was first raised in the Delaware litigation by an unsuccessful motion for new trial filed with the Chancellor Jan. 20, 1956. After the Florida Supreme Court decision the matter was renewed by a motion to remand filed with the Delaware Supreme Court. In a decision of Jan. 14, 1957, that court denied the motion and affirmed its Chancellor in all respects. The Florida decree was held not binding for purposes of full faith and credit because the Florida court had no personal jurisdiction over the trust companies and no jurisdiction over the trust *res.*

The issues for our decision are, *first,* whether Florida erred in holding that it had jurisdiction over the nonresident defendants, and *second,* whether Delaware erred in refusing full faith and

§ 7.02   JURISDICTION AND JUDGMENTS   □   501

credit to the Florida decree. We need not determine whether Florida was bound to give full faith and credit to the decree of the Delaware Chancellor since the question was not seasonably presented to the Florida court. *Radio Station WOW v. Johnson,* 326 U.S. 120, 128.

No. 107, The Florida Appeal. The question of our jurisdiction was postponed until the hearing of the merits. The appeal is predicated upon the contention that as applied to the facts of this case the Florida statute providing for constructive service is contrary to the Federal Constitution. 28 U. S. C. § 1257 (2). But in the state court appellants (the "beneficiaries") did not object that the statute was invalid as applied, but rather that the effect of the state court's exercise of jurisdiction in the circumstances of this case deprived them of a right under the Federal Constitution. Accordingly, we are without jurisdiction of the appeal and it must be dismissed. . . . Treating the papers whereon appeal was taken as a petition for certiorari, 28 U. S. C. § 2103, certiorari is granted.

Relying upon the principle that a person cannot invoke the jurisdiction of this Court to vindicate the right of a third party, appellees urge that appellants lack standing to complain of a defect in jurisdiction over the nonresident trust companies, who have made no appearance in this action. Florida adheres to the general rule that a trustee is an indispensable party to litigation involving the validity of the trust. In the absence of such a party a Florida court may not proceed to adjudicate the controversy. Since state law required the acquisition of jurisdiction over the nonresident trust company[8] before the court was empowered to proceed with the action, any defendant affected by the court's judgment has that "direct and substantial personal interest in the outcome" that is necessary to challenge whether that jurisdiction was in fact acquired. . . .

Appellants charge that this judgment is offensive to the Due Process Clause of the Fourteenth Amendment because the Florida court was without jurisdiction. There is no suggestion that the court failed to employ a means of notice reasonably calculated to inform nonresident defendants of the pending proceedings, or denied them an opportunity to be heard in defense of their interests. The alleged defect is the absence of those "affiliating circumstances" without which the courts of a State may not enter a judgment imposing obligations on persons (jurisdiction *in personam*) or affecting interests in property (jurisdiction *in rem* or *quasi in rem*).[12] While the *in rem* and *in personam* classifications do not exhaust all the situations that give rise to jurisdiction, they are adequate to describe the affiliating circumstances suggested here, and accordingly serve as a useful means of approach to this case.

In rem jurisdiction. Founded on physical power, *McDonald v. Mabee,* 243 U. S. 90, 91, the *in rem* jurisdiction of a state court is limited by the extent of its power and by the coordinate authority of sister States. The basis of the jurisdiction is the presence of the subject property within the territorial jurisdiction of the forum State. . . . Tangible property poses no problem

---

[8] Hereafter the terms "trust," "trust company" and "trustee" have reference to the trust established in 1935 with the Wilmington Trust Co., the validity of which is at issue here. It is unnecessary to determine whether the Delaware Trust Co., to which the $400,000 remainder interest was appointed and was paid after Mrs. Donner's death, is also an indispensable party to this proceeding.

[12] A judgment *in personam* imposes a personal liability or obligation on one person in favor of another. A judgment *in rem* affects the interests of all persons in designated property. A judgment *quasi in rem* affects the interests of particular persons in designated property. The latter is of two types. In one the plaintiff is seeking to secure a pre-existing claim in the subject property and to extinguish or establish the nonexistence of similar interests of particular persons. In the other the plaintiff seeks to apply what he concedes to be the property of the defendant to the satisfaction of a claim against him. Restatement, Judgments, 5–9. For convenience of terminology this opinion will use *"in rem"* in lieu of *"in rem* and *quasi in rem."*

for the application of this rule, but the situs of intangibles is often a matter of controversy.[15] In considering restrictions on the power to tax, this Court has concluded that "jurisdiction" over intangible property is not limited to a single State. *Tax Commission v. Aldrich,* 316 U. S. 174; *Curry v. McCanless,* 307 U. S. 357. Whether the type of "jurisdiction" with which this opinion deals may be exercised by more than one State we need not decide. The parties seem to assume that the trust assets that form the subject matter of this action[16] were located in Delaware and not in Florida. We can see nothing in the record contrary to that assumption, or sufficient to establish a situs in Florida.[17]

The Florida court held that the presence of the subject property was not essential to its jurisdiction. Authority over the probate and construction of its domiciliary's will, under which the assets might pass, was thought sufficient to confer the requisite jurisdiction. But jurisdiction cannot be predicated upon the contingent role of this Florida will. Whatever the efficacy of a so-called *"in rem"* jurisdiction over assets admittedly passing under a local will, a State acquires no *in rem* jurisdiction to adjudicate the validity of *inter vivos* dispositions simply because its decision might augment an estate passing under a will probated in its courts. If such a basis of jurisdiction were sustained, probate courts would enjoy nationwide service of process to adjudicate interests in property with which neither the State nor the decedent could claim any affiliation. The settlor-decedent's Florida domicile is equally unavailing as a basis for jurisdiction over the trust assets. For the purpose of jurisdiction *in rem* the maxim that personalty has its situs at the domicile of its owner[19] is a fiction of limited utility. *Green v. Van Buskirk,* 7 Wall. 139, 150. The maxim is no less suspect when the domicile is that of a decedent. In analogous cases, this Court has rejected the suggestion that the probate decree of the State where decedent was domiciled has an *in rem* effect on personalty outside the forum State that could render it conclusive on the interests of nonresidents over whom there was no personal jurisdiction. *Riley v. New York Trust Co.,* 315 U. S. 343, 353; *Baker v. Baker, Eccles & Co.,* 242 U. S. 394, 401; *Overby v. Gordon,* 177 U. S. 214.[20] The fact that the owner is or was domiciled within the forum State is not a sufficient affiliation with the property upon which to base jurisdiction *in rem*. Having concluded that Florida had no *in rem* jurisdiction, we proceed to consider whether a judgment purporting to rest on that basis is invalid in Florida and must therefore be reversed.

---

[15] See Andrews, *Situs of Intangibles in Suits against Non-Resident Claimants,* 49 Yale L. J. 241. [See also Lowenfeld, *In Search of the Intangible,* 53 N.Y.U. L. Rev. 102 (1978).]

[16] This case does not concern the situs of a beneficial interest in trust property. These appellees were contesting the validity of the trust. Their concern was with the legal interest of the trustee or, if the trust was invalid, the settlor. Therefore, the relevant factor here is the situs of the stocks, bonds, and notes that make up the corpus of the trust. Properly speaking such assets are intangibles that have no "physical" location. But their embodiment in documents treated for most purposes as the assets themselves makes them partake of the nature of tangibles. Cf. *Wheeler v. Sohmer,* 233 U. S. 434, 439.

[17] The documents evidencing ownership of the trust property were held in Delaware, cf. *Bank of Jasper v. First Nat. Bank,* 258 U. S. 112, 119, by a Delaware trustee who was the obligee of the credit instruments and the record owner of the stock. The location of the obligors and the domicile of the corporations do not appear. The trust instrument was executed in Delaware by a settlor then domiciled in Pennsylvania. Without expressing any opinion on the significance of these or other factors unnamed, we note that none relates to Florida.

[19] We assume *arguendo* for the purpose of this discussion that the trust was invalid so that Mrs. Donner was the "owner" of the subject property.

[20] Though analogous, these cases are not squarely in point. They concerned the efficacy of such judgments in the courts of another sovereign, while the issue here is the validity of such an exercise of jurisdiction within the forum State.

Prior to the Fourteenth Amendment an exercise of jurisdiction over persons or property outside the forum State was thought to be an absolute nullity,[21] but the matter remained a question of state law over which this Court exercised no authority.[22] With the adoption of that Amendment, any judgment purporting to bind the person of a defendant over whom the court had not acquired *in personam* jurisdiction was void within the State as well as without. *Pennoyer v. Neff*, 95 U. S. 714. Nearly a century has passed without this Court being called upon to apply that principle to an *in rem* judgment dealing with property outside the forum State. The invalidity of such a judgment within the forum State seems to have been assumed—and with good reason. Since a State is forbidden to enter a judgment attempting to bind a person over whom it has no jurisdiction, it has even less right to enter a judgment purporting to extinguish the interest of such a person in property over which the court has no jurisdiction.[23] Therefore, so far as it purports to rest upon jurisdiction over the trust assets, the judgment of the Florida court cannot be sustained. *Sadler v. Industrial Trust Co.*, 327 Mass. 10, 97 N. E. 2d 169.

In personam jurisdiction. Appellees' stronger argument is for *in personam* jurisdiction over the Delaware trustee. They urge that the circumstances of this case amount to sufficient affiliation with the State of Florida to empower its courts to exercise personal jurisdiction over this nonresident defendant. Principal reliance is placed upon *McGee v. International Life Ins. Co.*, 355 U. S. 220. In *McGee* the Court noted the trend of expanding personal jurisdiction over nonresidents. As technological progress has increased the flow of commerce between States, the need for jurisdiction over nonresidents has undergone a similar increase. At the same time, progress in communications and transportation has made the defense of a suit in a foreign tribunal less burdensome. In response to these changes, the requirements for personal jurisdiction over nonresidents have evolved from the rigid rule of *Pennoyer v. Neff*, 95 U. S. 714, to the flexible standard of *International Shoe Co. v. Washington*, 326 U. S. 310. But it is a mistake to assume that this trend heralds the eventual demise of all restrictions on the personal jurisdiction of state courts. See *Vanderbilt v. Vanderbilt*, 354 U. S. 416, 418. Those restrictions are more than a guarantee of immunity from inconvenient or distant litigation. They are a consequence of territorial limitations on the power of the respective States. However minimal the burden of defending in a foreign tribunal, a defendant may not be called upon to do so unless he has had the "minimal contacts" with that State that are a prerequisite to its exercise of power over him. See *International Shoe Co. v. Washington*, 326 U. S. 310, 319.

We fail to find such contacts in the circumstances of this case. The defendant trust company has no office in Florida, and transacts no business there. None of the trust assets has ever been held or administered in Florida, and the record discloses no solicitation of business in that State either in person or by mail. . . .

The cause of action in this case is not one that arises out of an act done or transaction consummated in the forum State. In that respect, it differs from *McGee v. International Life Ins. Co.*, 355 U. S. 220, and the cases there cited. In *McGee,* the nonresident defendant solicited

---

[21] See *Pennoyer v. Neff*, 95 U. S. 714, 720–728, 732; Story, *Commentaries on the Conflict of Laws* (6th ed. 1865), §§ 539, 550–551; Cooley, *Constitutional Limitations* (1st ed. 1868), 404–405; Rheinstein, *The Constitutional Bases of Jurisdiction*, 22 U. of Chi. L. Rev. 775, 792–793.

[22] See *Baker v. Baker, Eccles & Co.*, 242 U. S. 394, 403.

[23] This holding was forecast in *Pennoyer v. Neff, supra.* When considering the effect of the Fourteenth Amendment, this Court declared that in actions against nonresidents substituted service was permissible only where *"property in the State* is brought under the control of the court, and subjected to its disposition by process adapted to that purpose . . . ." (Emphasis supplied.) 95 U. S., at 733.

a reinsurance agreement with a resident of California. The offer was accepted in that State, and the insurance premiums were mailed from there until the insured's death. Noting the interest California has in providing effective redress for its residents when nonresident insurers refuse to pay claims on insurance they have solicited in that State, the Court upheld jurisdiction because the suit "was based on a contract which had substantial connection with that State." In contrast, this action involves the validity of an agreement that was entered without any connection with the forum State. The agreement was executed in Delaware by a trust company incorporated in that State and a settlor domiciled in Pennsylvania. The first relationship Florida had to the agreement was years later when the settlor became domiciled there, and the trustee remitted the trust income to her in that State. From Florida Mrs. Donner carried on several bits of trust administration that may be compared to the mailing of premiums in *McGee*.[24] But the record discloses no instance in which the *trustee* performed any acts in Florida that bear the same relationship to the agreement as the solicitation in *McGee*. Consequently, this suit cannot be said to be one to enforce an obligation that arose from a privilege the defendant exercised in Florida. Cf. *International Shoe Co. v. Washington,* 326 U. S. 310, 319. This case is also different from *McGee* in that there the State had enacted special legislation (Unauthorized Insurers Process Act) to exercise what *McGee* called its "manifest interest" in providing effective redress for citizens who had been injured by nonresidents engaged in an activity that the State treats as exceptional and subjects to special regulation. Cf. *Travelers Health Assn. v. Virginia,* 339 U. S. 643, 647–649; *Doherty & Co. v. Goodman,* 294 U. S. 623, 627; *Hess v. Pawloski,* 274 U. S. 352.

The execution in Florida of the powers of appointment under which the beneficiaries and appointees claim does not give Florida a substantial connection with the contract on which this suit is based. It is the validity of the trust agreement, not the appointment, that is at issue here.[25] For the purpose of applying its rule that the validity of a trust is determined by the law of the State of its creation, Florida ruled that the appointment amounted to a "republication" of the original trust instrument in Florida. For choice-of-law purposes such a ruling may be justified, but we think it an insubstantial connection with the trust agreement for purposes of determining the question of personal jurisdiction over a nonresident defendant. The unilateral activity of those who claim some relationship with a nonresident defendant cannot satisfy the requirement of contact with the forum State. The application of that rule will vary with the quality and nature of the defendant's activity, but it is essential in each case that there be some act by which the defendant purposefully avails itself of the privilege of conducting activities within the forum State, thus invoking the benefits and protections of its laws. *International Shoe Co. v. Washington,* 326 U. S. 310, 319. The settlor's execution in Florida of her power of appointment cannot remedy the absence of such an act in this case.

It is urged that because the settlor and most of the appointees and beneficiaries were domiciled in Florida the courts of that State should be able to exercise personal jurisdiction over the

---

[24] By a letter dated Feb. 5, 1946, Mrs. Donner changed the compensation to be paid the trust advisor. April 2, 1947, she revoked the trust as to $75,000, returning that amount to the trustee December 22, 1947. To these acts may be added the execution of the two powers of appointment mentioned earlier.

[25] The Florida Supreme Court's opinion makes repeated references to the "invalidity" of the trust, and uses other language of like import. See 100 So. 2d, at 381, 382, 383, 384, 385. Its ruling that the 1949 and 1950 "appointments" were ineffective to pass title to the property (because lacking the requisite testamentary formalities) proceeded from this initial ruling that the trust agreement was "invalid," 100 So. 2d, at 383, or "illusory," 100 So. 2d, at 384, and therefore created no power of appointment. There was no suggestion that the appointment was ineffective as an exercise of whatever power was created by the trust agreement.

nonresident trustees. This is a non sequitur. With personal jurisdiction over the executor, legatees, and appointees, there is nothing in federal law to prevent Florida from adjudicating concerning the respective rights and liabilities of those parties. But Florida has not chosen to do so. As we understand its law, the trustee is an indispensable party over whom the court must acquire jurisdiction before it is empowered to enter judgment in a proceeding affecting the validity of a trust. It does not acquire that jurisdiction by being the "center of gravity" of the controversy, or the most convenient location for litigation. The issue is personal jurisdiction, not choice of law. It is resolved in this case by considering the acts of the trustee. As we have indicated, they are insufficient to sustain the jurisdiction.[27]

Because it sustained jurisdiction over the nonresident trustees, the Florida Supreme Court found it unnecessary to determine whether Florida law made those defendants indispensable parties in the circumstances of this case. Our conclusion that Florida was without jurisdiction over the Delaware trustee, or over the trust corpus held in that State, requires that we make that determination in the first instance. As we have noted earlier, the Florida Supreme Court has repeatedly held that a trustee is an indispensable party without whom a Florida court has no power to adjudicate controversies affecting the validity of a trust. For that reason the Florida judgment must be reversed not only as to the nonresident trustees but also as to appellants, over whom the Florida court admittedly had jurisdiction.

No. 117, The Delaware Certiorari. The same reasons that compel reversal of the Florida judgment require affirmance of the Delaware one. Delaware is under no obligation to give full faith and credit to a Florida judgment invalid in Florida because offensive to the Due Process Clause of the Fourteenth Amendment. 28 U. S. C. § 1738. Even before passage of the Fourteenth Amendment this Court sustained state courts in refusing full faith and credit to judgments entered by courts that were without jurisdiction over nonresident defendants. *D'Arcy v. Ketchum,* 11 How. 165; *Hall v. Lanning,* 91 U. S. 160. See *Baker v. Baker, Eccles & Co.,* 242 U. S. 394; *Riley v. New York Trust Co.,* 315 U. S. 343. Since Delaware was entitled to conclude that Florida law made the trust company an indispensable party, it was under no obligation to give the Florida judgment any faith and credit—even against parties over whom Florida's jurisdiction was unquestioned.

It is suggested that this disposition is improper—that the Delaware case should be held while the Florida cause is remanded to give that court an opportunity to determine whether the trustee is an indispensable party in the circumstances of this case. But this is not a case like *Herb v. Pitcairn,* 324 U. S. 117, where it is appropriate to remand for the state court to clarify an ambiguity in its opinion that may reveal an adequate state ground that would deprive us of power to affect the result of the controversy. Nor is this a circumstance where the state court has never ruled on the question of state law that we are deciding. Although the question was left open in this case, there is ample Florida authority from which we may determine the appropriate answer.

The rule of primacy to the first final judgment is a necessary incident to the requirement of full faith and credit. Our only function is to determine whether judgments are consistent with the Federal Constitution. In determining the correctness of Delaware's judgment we look to what Delaware was entitled to conclude from the Florida authorities at the time the Delaware court's judgment was entered. To withhold affirmance of a correct Delaware judgment until Florida has

---

[27] This conclusion makes unnecessary any consideration of appellants' contention that the contacts the trust agreement had with Florida were so slight that it was a denial of due process of law to determine its validity by Florida law. See *Home Insurance Co. v. Dick,* 281 U. S. 397.

had time to rule on another question would be participating in the litigation instead of adjudicating its outcome.

The judgment of the Delaware Supreme Court is affirmed, and the judgment of the Florida Supreme Court is reversed and the cause is remanded for proceedings not inconsistent with this opinion.

Mr. Justice Black, whom Mr. Justice Burton and Mr. Justice Brennan join, dissenting.

I believe the courts of Florida had power to adjudicate the effectiveness of the appointment made in Florida by Mrs. Donner with respect to all those who were notified of the proceedings and given an opportunity to be heard without violating the Due Process Clause of the Fourteenth Amendment.[1] If this is correct, it follows that the Delaware courts erred in refusing to give the prior Florida judgment full faith and credit. U. S. Const., Art. IV, § 1; 28 U. S. C. § 1738.

Mrs. Donner was domiciled in Florida from 1944 until her death in 1952. The controversial appointment was made there in 1949. It provided that certain persons were to receive a share of the property held by the Delaware "trustee" under the so-called trust agreement upon her death. Until she died Mrs. Donner received the entire income from this property, and at all times possessed absolute power to revoke or alter the appointment and to dispose of the property as she pleased. As a practical matter she also retained control over the management of the property, the "trustee" in Delaware being little more than a custodian.[2] A number of the beneficiaries of the appointment, including those who were to receive more than 95% of the assets involved, were residents of Florida at the time the appointment was made as well as when the present suit was filed. The appointed property consisted of intangibles which had no real situs in any particular State although Mrs. Donner paid taxes on the property in Florida.

The same day the 1949 appointment was made Mrs. Donner executed a will, which after her death was duly probated in a Florida court. The will contained a residuary clause providing for the distribution of all of her property not previously bequeathed, including "any and all property, rights and interest over which I may have power of appointment which prior to my death has not been effectively exercised by me . . . ." Thus if the 1949 appointment was ineffective the property involved came back into Mrs. Donner's estate to be distributed under the residuary clause of her will. As might be anticipated the present litigation arose when legatees brought an action in the Florida courts seeking a determination whether the appointment was valid. The beneficiaries of the appointment, some of whom live outside Florida, and the Delaware trustee were defendants. They had timely notice of the suit and an adequate opportunity to obtain counsel and appear.

In light of the foregoing circumstances it seems quite clear to me that there is nothing in the Due Process Clause which denies Florida the right to determine whether Mrs. Donner's appointment was valid as against its statute of wills. This disposition, which was designed to

---

[1] In my judgment it is a mistake to decide this case on the assumption that the Florida courts invalidated the trust established in 1935 by Mrs. Donner while she was living in Pennsylvania. It seems quite clear to me that those courts had no such purpose. As I understand it, all they held was that an appointment made in Florida providing for the disposition of part of the trust property after Mrs. Donner's death was (1) testamentary since she retained complete control over the appointed property until she died, and (2) ineffective because not executed in accordance with the Florida statute of wills.

[2] Among other things Mrs. Donner reserved the right to appoint "advisers" serving at her sufferance who controlled all purchases, sales and investments by the "trustee." Evidence before the Delaware courts indicated that these advisers, not the Delaware "trustee," actually made all decisions with respect to transactions affecting the "trust" property and that the "trustee" mechanically acted as they directed.

take effect after her death, had very close and substantial connections with that State. Not only was the appointment made in Florida by a domiciliary of Florida, but the primary beneficiaries also lived in that State. In my view it could hardly be denied that Florida had sufficient interest so that a court with jurisdiction might properly apply Florida law, if it chose, to determine whether the appointment was effectual. *Watson v. Employers Liability Assurance Corp.,* 348 U. S. 66; *Osborn v. Ozlin,* 310 U. S. 53. True, the question whether the law of a State can be applied to a transaction is different from the question whether the courts of that State have jurisdiction to enter a judgment, but the two are often closely related and to a substantial degree depend upon similar considerations. It seems to me that where a transaction has as much relationship to a State as Mrs. Donner's appointment had to Florida its courts ought to have power to adjudicate controversies arising out of that transaction, unless litigation there would impose such a heavy and disproportionate burden on a nonresident defendant that it would offend what this Court has referred to as "traditional notions of fair play and substantial justice." *Milliken v. Meyer,* 311 U. S. 457, 463; *International Shoe Co. v. Washington,* 326 U. S. 310, 316. So far as the nonresident defendants here are concerned I can see nothing which approaches that degree of unfairness. Florida, the home of the principal contenders for Mrs. Donner's largess, was a reasonably convenient forum for all.[3] Certainly there is nothing fundamentally unfair in subjecting the corporate trustee to the jurisdiction of the Florida courts. It chose to maintain business relations with Mrs. Donner in that State for eight years, regularly communicating with her with respect to the business of the trust including the very appointment in question.

Florida's interest in the validity of Mrs. Donner's appointment is made more emphatic by the fact that her will is being administered in that State. It has traditionally been the rule that the State where a person is domiciled at the time of his death is the proper place to determine the validity of his will, to construe its provisions and to marshal and distribute his personal property. Here Florida was seriously concerned with winding up Mrs. Donner's estate and with finally determining what property was to be distributed under her will. In fact this suit was brought for that very purpose.

The Court's decision that Florida did not have jurisdiction over the trustee (and inferentially the nonresident beneficiaries) stems from principles stated the better part of a century ago in *Pennoyer v. Neff,* 95 U. S. 714. That landmark case was decided in 1878, at a time when business affairs were predominantly local in nature and travel between States was difficult, costly and sometimes even dangerous. There the Court laid down the broad principle that a State could not subject nonresidents to the jurisdiction of its courts unless they were served with process within its boundaries or voluntarily appeared, except to the extent they had property in the State. But as the years have passed the constantly increasing ease and rapidity of communication and the tremendous growth of interstate business activity have led to a steady and inevitable relaxation of the strict limits on state jurisdiction announced in that case. In the course of this evolution the old jurisdictional landmarks have been left far behind so that in many instances States may now properly exercise jurisdiction over nonresidents not amenable to service within their borders.[4] Yet further relaxation seems certain. Of course we have not reached the point where

---

[3] The suggestion is made that Delaware was a more suitable forum, but the plain fact is that none of the beneficiaries or legatees has ever resided in that State.

[4] See, *e. g., McGee v. International Life Ins. Co.,* 355 U. S. 220; *Travelers Health Assn. v. Virginia ex rel. State Corporation Comm'n,* 339 U. S. 643; *International Shoe Co. v. Washington,* 326 U. S. 310; *Milliken v. Meyer,* 311 U. S. 457; *Henry L. Doherty & Co. v. Goodman,* 294 U. S. 623; *Hess v. Pawloski,* 274 U. S. 352.

state boundaries are without significance, and I do not mean to suggest such a view here. There is no need to do so. For we are dealing with litigation arising from a transaction that had an abundance of close and substantial connections with the State of Florida.

Perhaps the decision most nearly in point is *Mullane v. Central Hanover Bank & Trust Co.,* 339 U. S. 306. In that case the Court held that a State could enter a personal judgment in favor of a trustee against nonresident beneficiaries of a trust even though they were not served with process in that State. So far as appeared, their only connection with the State was the fact that the trust was being administered there.[5] In upholding the State's jurisdiction the Court emphasized its great interest in trusts administered within its boundaries and governed by its laws. *Id.,* at 313. Also implicit in the result was a desire to avoid the necessity for multiple litigation with its accompanying waste and possibility of inconsistent results. It seems to me that the same kind of considerations are present here supporting Florida's jurisdiction over the nonresident defendants.

Even if it be assumed that the Court is right in its jurisdictional holding, I think its disposition of the two cases is unjustified. It reverses the judgment of the Florida Supreme Court on the ground that the trustee may be, but need not be, an indispensable party to the Florida litigation under Florida law. At the same time it affirms the subsequent Delaware judgment. Although in form the Florida case is remanded for further proceedings not inconsistent with the Court's opinion, the effect is that the Florida courts will be obliged to give full faith and credit to the Delaware judgment. This means the Florida courts will never have an opportunity to determine whether the trustee is an indispensable party. The Florida judgment is thus completely wiped out even as to those parties who make their homes in that State, and even though the Court acknowledges there is nothing in the Constitution which precludes Florida from entering a binding judgment for or against them. It may be argued that the Delaware judgment is the first to become final and therefore is entitled to prevail. But it only comes first because the Court makes it so. In my judgment the proper thing to do would be to hold the Delaware case until the Florida courts had an opportunity to decide whether the trustee is an indispensable party. Under the circumstances of this case I think it is quite probable that they would say he is not. See *Trueman Fertilizer Co. v. Allison,* 81 So. 2d 734. I can see no reason why this Court should deprive Florida plaintiffs of their judgment against Florida defendants on the basis of speculation about Florida law which might well turn out to be unwarranted.

MR. JUSTICE DOUGLAS, dissenting.

The testatrix died domiciled in Florida. Her will, made after she had acquired a domicile in Florida, was probated there. Prior to the time she established a domicile in Florida she executed a trust instrument in Delaware. By its terms she was to receive the income during her life. On her death the principal and undistributed income were to go as provided in any power of appointment or, failing that, in her last will and testament.

After she had become domiciled in Florida she executed a power of appointment; and she also provided in her will that if the power of appointment had not been effectively exercised, the property under the trust, consisting of intangibles, should pass to certain designated trusts.

The Florida court held that the power of appointment was testamentary in character and not being a valid testamentary disposition for lack of the requisite witnesses, failed as a will under Florida law. Therefore the property passed under the will. 100 So. 2d 378.

---

[5] There was no basis for *in rem* jurisdiction since the litigation concerned the personal liability of the trustee and did not involve the trust property.

Distribution of the assets of the estate could not be made without determining the validity of the power of appointment. The power of appointment, being integrated with the will, was as much subject to construction and interpretation by the Florida court as the will itself. Of course one not a party or privy to the Florida proceedings is not bound by it and can separately litigate the right to assets in other States. See *Riley v. New York Trust Co.,* 315 U. S. 343; *Baker v. Baker, Eccles & Co.,* 242 U. S. 394. But we have no such situation here. The trustee of the trust was in privity with the deceased. She was the settlor; and under the trust, the trustee was to do her bidding. That is to say, the trustee, though managing the *res* during the life of the settlor, was on her death to transfer the property to such persons as the settlor designated by her power of appointment or by her last will and testament, or, failing that, to designated classes of persons. So far as the present controversy is concerned the trustee was purely and simply a stakeholder or an agent holding assets of the settlor to dispose of as she designated. It had a community of interest with the deceased. I see no reason therefore why Florida could not say that the deceased and her executrix may stand in judgment for the trustee so far as the disposition of the property under the power of appointment and the will is concerned. The question in cases of this kind is whether the procedure is fair and just considering the interests of the parties. Cf. *Hansberry v. Lee,* 311 U. S. 32; *Mullane v. Central Hanover Trust Co.,* 339 U. S. 306, 312–317. Florida has such a plain and compelling relation to these out-of-state intangibles (cf. *Curry v. McCanless,* 307 U. S. 357), and the nexus between the settlor and trustee is so close, as to give Florida the right to make the controlling determination even without personal service over the trustee and those who claim under it. We must remember this is not a suit to impose liability on the Delaware trustee or on any other absent person. It is merely a suit to determine interests in those intangibles. Cf. *Mullane v. Central Hanover Trust Co., supra,* at 313. Under closely analogous facts the California Supreme Court held in *Atkinson v. Superior Court,* 49 Cal. 2d 338, 316 P. 2d 960, that California had jurisdiction over an absent trustee. I would hold the same here. The decedent was domiciled in Florida; most of the legatees are there; and the absent trustee through whom the others claim was an agency so close to the decedent as to be held to be privy with her—in other words so identified in interest with her as to represent the same legal right.

COAST LINES LTD. v. HUDIG & VEDER CHARTERING N.V.

Court of Appeal (U.K.)
[1972] 2 Q.B. 34 (C.A.)

LORD DENNING M.R.

In December 1967, an English company, Coast Lines Ltd., who are the owners of the motor-vessel *Grangefield,* let her on a voyage charter to a Dutch company—Hudig and Veder Chartering N.V. Under the charter, the vessel was to proceed to Rotterdam and there load a cargo and carry it to Drogheda, a port in the Republic of Ireland. The cargo was loaded at Rotterdam, but the vessel ran into very bad weather conditions. When she arrived at Drogheda it was found that some 65 tons of water had been taken inboard. The cargo was badly damaged. The water had got in by a broken bilge pipe. The pipe was found to be extremely rusted, corroded and wasted. The vessel cannot have been in a seaworthy condition when she started on the voyage. The cargo owners claimed damages from the shipowners. The shipowners admitted liability to the cargo owners, but then the shipowners claimed to be indemnified by the charterers.

On May 28, 1970, the shipowners—Coast Lines Ltd.—issued a writ against the charterers, Hudig and Veder Chartering N.V. . . . The plaintiffs applied ex parte to the master for leave to serve the writ on the proposed defendants out of the jurisdiction. The master gave leave. The defendants entered a conditional appearance and applied to set aside the service. Roskill J. refused to set it aside. The defendants appeal to this court.

1. *The Charterparty*

The charterparty is dated "Rotterdam, December 13, 1967." It was for carriage of cargo from Rotterdam in the Netherlands to Drogheda in Ireland. The negotiations leading to the fixture of the *Grangefield* were conducted over the telephone and on the telex between Hudig and Veder in Rotterdam and J. F. Thomas & Co. Ltd. (brokers for the owners) in Cardiff. It is customary in the Netherlands for the charterers' brokers to draw up and sign the charterparty. This charterparty was drawn up in Rotterdam and signed there on behalf of both parties by Hudig and Veder. Copies were subsequently sent to J. F. Thomas & Co. Ltd. The charterparty was made on the Gencon form. This is the form of charterparty which is the most widely used by all those in Rotterdam who are engaged in the European shipping trade. The Gencon form is used, irrespective of whether or not the charterparty has any connection with England or whether or not either party is English.

The charterparty is dated "Rotterdam, December 13, 1967." It was for carriage of cargo from Rotterdam in the Netherlands to Drogheda in Ireland. It contained an exemption for the shipowners in the terms usual in the Gencon form, [relieving the shipowners]—so far as the charterers were concerned—of any liability for the damage done to these goods: for, although the damage was due to the vessel being unseaworthy, nevertheless this was no fault of the owners or manager *personally.* It was quite permissible in English law for the shipowners to stipulate in the charterparty for that exemption: because the Carriage of Goods by Sea Act 1924 does not apply to charterparties.

2. *The Bill of Lading*

The bill of lading was issued in Rotterdam. It was for the carriage of 4,000 paper bags of bleaching earth (made in Germany) from Rotterdam to Drogheda. It was signed by agents on behalf of the master. It was in English and contained on the back a clause paramount which incorporated the Hague Rules. It bound the shipowner to exercise due diligence to make the ship seaworthy and made him liable for want of due diligence. It made the shipowner liable, therefore, in this case to the cargo owner.

It is apparent that, under that bill of lading, the shipowners were subject to a greater liability than that provided by the charterparty. The charterers must take responsibility for the presentation of that bill of lading. By that conduct the charterers imposed on the owners a greater liability than was stipulated for in the charterparty. On this account it has been held that the charterers were under a duty to indemnify the shipowners. This duty may be said to arise from the request of the charterers to the master to sign the bills of lading. But I would prefer to put it on an implied term in the charterparty to the effect that, in case the charterers should present—or cause to be presented—bills of lading imposing a greater liability on the shipowners than that contained in the charterparty, the charterers would indemnify the shipowners in respect of that greater liability.

3. *English Law and Netherlands Law*

If the charterparty is governed by English law, the shipowners will be able to rely on the indemnity of which I have just spoken. They will be entitled to call on the charterers to indemnify them against the liability to the cargo owners. The Hague Rules will not apply.

But, if the charterparty is governed by Netherlands law, the position will be quite different. The Netherlands Commercial Code (as it existed at the time of this shipment—it has been altered since) contained an article 517d which applied the Hague Rules to the carriage of goods by sea from Netherlands ports: and this has been held by the courts of the Netherlands to apply, not only to bills of lading, but also to charterparties: and to override any stipulation, express or implied, to the contrary. Even if a charterparty expressly says that it is to be governed by some other law, e.g., English law, nevertheless article 517d is regarded as mandatory to the Netherlands courts. They must apply the Netherlands Code to every shipment from a Netherlands port. If the shipowners should, therefore, sue the charterers in the Netherlands courts, or the charterers sue the shipowners, those courts must ignore English law altogether—they must ignore the exemption clause in the charterparty and the implications from it; they must hold that the shipowners are liable to the full extent set out in the Hague Rules, and cannot claim indemnity from the charterers.

In making this mandatory provision binding on their courts, the Netherlands are out on a limb by themselves. In an ideal world it would be different. If a contract is properly held to be governed by English law, then the courts of every country should apply English law to it. The Netherlands Code goes against this ideal. It says that every cargo of goods from a Netherlands port is to be governed by Netherlands law, no matter that the contract has nothing else to do with the Netherlands.

We are told that since 1969 the Netherlands have withdrawn this mandatory provision. They have come into line with the other maritime countries. So the point may not in future arise. But we have to deal with the position as it was in 1967.

In view of this difference, we have to consider these points:

1. What is the proper law of the contract? If it is Netherlands law, then the Netherlands Commercial Code will apply. The shipowners will not be entitled to an indemnity. If it is English law, and the case is allowed to proceed in the English courts, then the English courts will apply English law, and will give the shipowners an indemnity. But, if the shipowners are forced to sue in the Netherlands courts, those courts will (despite the contract being governed by English law) apply the Netherlands Code to it, and will refuse an indemnity.

2. If the proper law is English law, ought these courts to allow service out of the jurisdiction so that the case can proceed in the English courts? Or should they refuse and force the shipowners to go to the Netherlands courts?

4. *The Proper Law of the Contract*

In order to determine the proper law of the contract, the courts at one time used to have a number of presumptions to help them. Now we have to ask ourselves: What is the system of law with which the transaction has the closest and most real connection? This is not dependent on the intentions of the parties. They never thought about it. They had no intentions upon it. We have to study every circumstance connected with the contract and come to a conclusion. This new test is all very well. It is often easy to apply. But, there are sometimes cases where it is quite indecisive. The circumstances do not point to one country only. They point equally to two countries, or even to three. . . .

Apply the test here. One important circumstance is that the contract was made in Rotterdam by Dutch charterers for shipment at Rotterdam. That points to Netherlands law. Another important circumstance is that contract was for carriage in an English ship owned by English owners for carriage on the high seas. That points to English law. Put those two into the scales, one on one side, the other on the other. You find they are equal. Other circumstances point one way, then another. There is nothing to choose. So, as a last resort, you take the law of the flag, which is English law.

But then there is a further consideration. The contract contained an exemption clause which was valid under English law, but invalid under Netherlands law. That, I think, is important. In the maritime law of this country—and I believe of all other maritime countries—it is an accepted principle that a contract is, if possible, to be construed so as to make it valid rather than invalid. The Latin maxim is well-known. A stipulation must be construed *ut res magis valeat quam pereat*. Applying it here, the exemption clause in the charterparty is valid by English law, but invalid by Netherlands law. That is a pointer to English law as the proper law of the contract. . . .

I would add another consideration also. The commercial judge (Roskill J.) has held that the proper law is English law. We should be slow to differ from him on such a point. As Lord Wilberforce said recently: ". . . decision by the commercial judge should end the matter": see *Compagnie Tunisienne De Navigation S.A. v. Compagnie D'Armement Maritime S.A.* [1971] A.C. 572, 600.

I am of opinion, therefore, that the proper law of this contract is English law, and not Netherlands law.

5. *The Exercise of their Discretion*

Once it is held that the charterparty is by implication governed by English law, the next question is whether leave should be given to serve the writ out of the jurisdiction? This is a very serious question. The charterers are a Netherlands company. They owe no allegiance here. They have no place of business here. They have, as yet, no assets here. It is a strong thing to force them to come to England to contest a case against them. So we must be exceedingly careful before doing so. That was pointed out long ago: *The Hagen* [1908] P. 189. If the Netherlands courts were free to apply the proper law of the contract (i.e., English law), I would not be disposed to grant leave to serve out of the jurisdiction. But the Netherlands courts are not free. They are compelled by the Netherlands law to allow to apply a special law of the Netherlands, i.e., article 517d, which is not the proper law of the contract and which is out of line with the maritime law of all other countries. The Netherlands courts are compelled to apply a law which is contrary to the general understanding of commercial men.

In these circumstances, I do not think we should send the English owners to the Netherlands courts. We should retain the case in these courts where we can and will apply English law, which is the proper law of the contract.

I know that the charterers can avoid our English law by refusing to submit to the jurisdiction of the English courts. In that case any judgment of the English courts will not be enforceable in the Netherlands under the arrangements for the reciprocal enforcement of judgment: see The Reciprocal Enforcement of Foreign Judgments (the Netherlands) Order 1969 (S.I. 1969 No. 1063), Sch., art. III (2) (*a*) and IV (1). The English owners would then be forced to sue in the Netherlands, and the courts there would, no doubt, apply the Netherlands Commercial code. So, in a sense, the matter rests with the charterers. But, so far as these courts are concerned, I think that leave should be given to serve out of the jurisdiction.

I agree with the judgment of Roskill J., and I would dismiss the appeal.

MEGAW L.J.

[After concluding that "viewed as a whole and weighing all the relevant factors" the transaction has a "closer and more real connection with English law than with the law of the Netherlands," and that therefore "English law is the proper law of the charterparty contract."]

It is necessary now to consider the second issue: should the discretion which exists under R.S.C., Ord. 11, r. 1, be exercised so as to found jurisdiction in England against the Netherlands' charterers.

The principal argument of counsel for the charterers is that in all the circumstances it would be contrary to comity to permit the writ to be served out of the jurisdiction. There is, however, one factor here, to be found in the uncontradicted evidence of an expert in Netherlands law, which has led me to the conclusion that that argument ought not to prevail.

The Hague Rules, accepted as a result of international agreement, were expressly and deliberately restricted to bill of lading contracts. Charterparties were not included, for it was the general consensus that freedom of contract should remain in respect of them. The Netherlands Commercial Code, as it stood at the time which is relevant for this case, restricted freedom of contract by applying the Hague Rules restrictions in respect of all contracts for the carriage of goods by sea from Netherlands ports, irrespective whether the relevant contract was, or was evidenced by, a charterparty or a bill of lading. . . .

If this requirement (a requirement founded, no doubt, on what was at the time regarded as a matter of public policy in the Netherlands, which involved the ignoring or overriding of that which would otherwise have been the proper law of the contract) had related to ensuring the enforcement of the spirit or the letter of an accepted international convention (for example, the Hague Rules in relation solely to bills of lading) or had related to the prevention of an avoidance of such generally accepted rules by the device of making the contract subject to the law of another state, I should have been disposed to say that the English courts should, in their discretion, have refused leave to serve out of the jurisdiction. That would have been a proper instance of giving effect to the requirements of comity. But that is not the case here. Netherlands law at the relevant time was based upon a refusal to allow freedom of contract in respect of a charterparty, provided that there was involved any carriage of goods from any Netherlands port, whether or not it was the first port of loading under the relevant charterparty and whether or not there was any other element connecting the transaction with the Netherlands. On the other hand, the relevant international convention had, at least by implication, indicated that this was not a sphere in which the consensus of opinion internationally favoured such a restriction. If English law is the proper law of the contract, and the contract does not offend against the public policy of this country or what may be called the general public policy of maritime nations, to be implied from the terms of the international convention, comity, in my view, does not demand that a party who desires to have his dispute decided in accordance with the proper law of the contract should be precluded from having it so decided. That, on the evidence, would be the consequence of a refusal of leave to serve notice of the writ out of the jurisdiction in this case.

Accordingly, in agreement with Roskill J., and, I believe, for substantially the same reasons, I would hold that this is a proper case in which the discretion should be exercised under R.S.C., Ord. 11, r. 1. I would dismiss the appeal.

STEPHENSON L.J.

I have found difficulty in answering both the questions raised by this appeal.

What is the proper law of this contract? English or Dutch? This question cannot be answered by ascertaining the actual intention of the parties. If they had applied their minds to it the English shipowners would probably have answered "English" and the Dutch charterers "Dutch." If they had been asked to agree on the application of the other's law to the charterparty each would probably have refused and there would have been no contract; but there is a contract. . . .

I find the scales evenly balanced, but the court cannot leave them in everlasting equipoise because there would then be no proper law of the contract. But there is a proper law and that the court must impose on the contract, or extract from it, even if the operation is more like an adjustment than a reading of the scales.

Into the English scale the judge put the English nationality of the ship and of the shipowners, the place of business in Cardiff of their agents who negotiated the charterparty by telephone and telex, the provision for payment of freight and for calculating demurrage and dispatch in sterling and the English form and language of the charterparty. But he rightly gave little weight to the last two and disregarded the bill of lading.

Into the Dutch scale he put the place where the charterparty was signed, the nationality of the charterers, and the place of shipment. He rightly disregarded the earlier charterparty and its Dutch ship for which this charterparty was substituted, but apparently treated the fact that everything after shipment up to port of discharge was to take place outside the Netherlands as more significant than the fact that it was to take place outside England also.

Into the English scale Lord Denning M.R. has put the consideration that the parties would not have put their signatures—or rather allowed one of them to put a signature on behalf of both of them—to a contract which was partly invalid. . . .

I appreciate that this is a consideration which only has weight if intention, however artificially, comes into the ascertainment of the proper law. But if it does, there must go into the Dutch scale a counterbalancing consideration that the Dutch charterers are not lightly to have imputed to them, abetted by the other party, an intention to transgress the Commercial Code of their country, which their country's law forbids them to do by choosing the law of another country.

Bearing in mind all these matters, I confess that if I had to read the balance without assistance I should have been inclined to decide, by perhaps underestimating the power which the flag of the ship still has, that it tipped, if at all, in favour of Dutch law. But I am not willing to differ on such a nice and difficult point from the contrary view of Roskill J., reached without the help from commercial arbitrators which the judge had in the *Compagnie Tunisienne* case [1971] A.C. 572 but endorsed by the other members of this court, particularly in a branch of the law where their experience so far exceeds my own.

If the proper law of this contract is English and this court therefore has jurisdiction under R.S.C., Ord. 11, r. 1 (1) (*f*) (iii), to make the order under appeal, why should it not be made?

It is tempting to ask the question in that form when the contract by its terms makes English law its proper law but to reverse the approach where the contract does so by implication only and to ask: why *should* the order be made? Again it is tempting to say, as Farwell L.J. indicated in *The Hagen* [1908] P. 189, 201, that the court's discretion ought to be exercised only in plain cases to which the rule clearly applies but not in doubtful or borderline cases like the present.

However, I am satisfied that these temptations ought to be resisted; that the discretion given by the rule is unfettered except by comity, convenience and the justice of the case; and that the arguments elaborated by [counsel for the charterers] for reversing the judge's exercise of his discretion in favour of the owners must be rejected for the reasons given by the judge and by my Lords.

I agree therefore that this appeal fails.

Appeal dismissed with costs.
Leave to appeal refused.

NOTES AND QUESTIONS

(1)(a) By any criteria, *Hanson v. Denckla* is a hard case. The facts are confusing, the substantive law is unclear, the rationale of the majority in the Supreme Court is murky, and—the dispute being among sisters from Palm Beach each of whom seems to have had enough money anyway—this is one of the few constitutional cases in which one's personal sympathy or general outlook does not really help. This explains, perhaps, why Justices Warren, Black and Douglas, who have generally been together in cases arising under the Fourteenth Amendment, here go three different ways. Is this really a case about jurisdiction? About choice of law? Or about full faith and credit?

(b) Consider first the actions of Dora Browning Donner. In 1935, she creates an inter vivos trust of securities with the Wilmington Trust Company as trustee, to pay the income to herself for life, with the remainder as she may appoint by will or deed. The disposition is thus similar to the trust in *Matter of Bauer*,[c] and indeed, like Mrs. Bauer, Mrs. Donner changes her domicile some years after creating the trust. However, the problem here is not about the rule against perpetuities, but about the powers reserved by the grantor. She can change the trustee, she can amend, alter, or revoke the trust agreement, and if the trustee seeks to sell trust assets, make investments, or participate in a merger or reorganization involving the securities held in trust, it can do so only with the consent of an adviser appointed by her.

If this were a New York disposition, as we saw, it would probably be regarded as a testamentary substitute under E.P.T.L. § 5–1.1(b)(1)(E).[d] Under New York law, this would not matter here, because only the surviving spouse has a right of election,[e] and Mrs. Donner was a widow when she died. Some states regard such a disposition as illusory and altogether ineffective to transfer title. The transaction is not void, but is treated as if it created an agency or custody account, and the donor is regarded as if he or she retained full title.[f]

---

[c] Chapter 4 p. 356, *supra.*

[d] Documents Supplement, p. 32. See discussion in Chapter 4, p. 346, question (5)(e), *supra.*

[e] E.P.T.L. § 5–1.1(a).

[f] See *Restatement of the Law of Trusts,* § 57(2) (1935):

Where the settlor transfers property in trust and reserves not only a beneficial life estate and a power to revoke and modify the trust but also such power to control the trustee as to the administration of the trust that the trustee

(c) The Supreme Court of Florida said the question of a trust with so many reserved powers was one of first impression, but decided (i) that the disposition had not been effective to transfer title to the property in question prior to Mrs. Donner's death, and (ii) that in any event, her deed of appointment designed to be effective on her death could not transfer the property because it did not comply with the required formalities for testamentary dispositions.[g] Accordingly, (iii) the $400,000 held by the Wilmington Trust Company under the 1935 trust should not be transferred to the Delaware Trust Company to be part of Elizabeth's trusts, but should pass under the residual clause in the will, i.e., to Katherine and Dorothy.

The Florida courts applied Florida law to all three points. Postponing the question of judicial jurisdiction, is the choice of Florida law sound as to (i) the validity of the original trust?; as to (ii) the effectiveness of the deed of appointment?; as to (iii) the interpretation of the will?

(2)(a) Chief Justice Warren, writing after many of the choice of law cases reproduced in Chapter 5, *supra,* takes a relaxed view of the choice of law questions. Though he clearly disagrees with the choice of law by the Florida courts, he seems to have thought there was nothing the Supreme Court could or should do about it.[h] His view is that even if the Florida courts were wrong in looking to the domicile of the donor at her death, that decision is not so arbitrary as to justify intervention by the Supreme Court. But, by taking this position, is he doing indirectly what he would not do directly?

(b) Justice Black says the case is about exercise by Mrs. Donner of her power of appointment, an issue clearly governed by Florida law, and one for which the trust companies are not necessary (p. 506 and footnote 1). The Chief Justice says (p. 504 and footnote 25) that the issue is the validity of the 1935 trust agreement, and that for resolution of this issue the trust companies—at least Wilmington Trust—had to be before the court. Justice Douglas takes still another view: he says the case is about distribution of assets under the Florida will of a Florida domiciliary and that Florida has "a plain and compelling relation" to the out-of-state intangibles, including the assets held in the trusts. Is this case then a dispute about characterization?

(c) Professor Scott, not wholly persuaded by the Chief Justice's characterization but content with the result, says never mind: Even if the validity of the exercise of the power was at issue and Mrs. Donner was at the time domiciled in Florida, the law of Delaware should apply, on the same theory as that applied by the majority in *Bauer*—that exercise of a power of appointment is like filling in the blanks in an instrument created long ago.[i] But right or wrong—recall Justice Fuld's dissent in *Bauer*[j] —Scott concedes that "the choice of its own law by the Florida court

---

is the agent of the settlor, the disposition so far as it is intended to take effect after his death is testamentary and is invalid unless the requirements of the statutes relating to the validity of wills are complied with.

The Restatement (Second) of Trusts (1959) adopts, in § 57 Comment *b,* a more favorable attitude toward such dispositions. Professor Austin Scott, the Reporter for both the first and the second *Restatement of Trusts* and author of the leading multi-volume treatise on trusts, would favor sustaining both the creation of the trust and the exercise of the power of appointment, though he recognizes disagreement among courts of various states on the question. Scott, *Hanson v. Denckla,* 72 Harv. L. Rev. 695, 697–98 (1959).

[g] See *Hanson v. Denckla,* 100 So.2d 378 (Fla. 1956).

[h] See the text at p. 504, following Footnote 25, *supra.*

[i] But note that under New York E.P.T.L. § 3–5.1(g)(1) Documents Supplement, p. 29, the law of the donee's domicile at death would govern, not only as to intrinsic validity of the exercise of the power of appointment but also as to the question of whether such power had been exercised at all.

[j] Chapter 4, p. 357, *supra.*

§ 7.02　　　　　　　　　　JURISDICTION AND JUDGMENTS　　□　517

was certainly not so clearly unjustified as to amount to a violation of the Fourteenth Amendment, provided that the Florida court had jurisdiction."[k]

(3)(a) Coming then to the question of jurisdiction, notice what the Florida court did. The Circuit Court for Palm Beach County held (i) that there was no jurisdiction over the trust companies, but (ii) they were not indispensable parties and the litigation could proceed without them, on the basis of jurisdiction over Elizabeth and her children. The Supreme Court of Florida held (i) that there was jurisdiction over the trust companies, and therefore (ii) there was no need to decide whether they were indispensable parties. Thus Chief Justice Warren's conclusion that Florida adheres to the rule that a trustee is an indispensable party to litigation involving the validity of a trust (p. 505) is not based on findings of either the lower or the upper Florida court in this case. The Chief Justice says "as we understand it . . ." and rejects the suggestion of Justice Black (p. 508) that the case be remanded for a determination by the Florida courts whether the trust company is an indispensable party.[l] Is the implication of the majority's decision that it would be unconstitutional for Florida's courts to adjudicate the controversy without the full participation of the trust companies?

(b) The majority opinion in the Supreme Court examines the issue of jurisdiction under two headings—*in rem* and *in personam;* the suggestion in the preceding question is that the indispensable party point is a third way of looking at the issue. Aren't they really all the same question—i.e., whether within the limits of fair play and substantial justice (everyone having notice and an opportunity to be heard) the Florida courts are entitled to resolve this controversy? Or does posing the question in this way take unjustified liberties with *International Shoe*?

(c) If the question of overall fairness is the issue (or even a permissible way to look at the issue), is there really something unfair about telling Wilmington Trust Co. "here is a copy of the complaint in the action; you may appear and be heard, but if you do not appear the case will go on without you"?

(d) Incidentally, is the court concerned about the rights of Wilmington Trust, or about the rights of Elizabeth and her children? It was she, after all, who raised the lack of jurisdiction over a third party, and who sought to avoid the effects of the Florida litigation by going to the courts of Delaware.[m]

(e) Continuing our inquiry into overall fairness,

　　(i) Suppose it came out that when Wilmington Trust received notice of the action brought by Katherine and Dorothy, Wilmington's lawyer had a meeting with Elizabeth's lawyer, and together they decided on the strategy that the trust company should make no appearance—not even to challenge jurisdiction—but that Elizabeth should challenge the jurisdiction of the Florida court and commence an action in Delaware.

　　(ii) Alternatively, suppose there were no evidence of a coordinated strategy, but simply a decision made by the managers and legal advisers of Wilmington Trust not to appear in

---

[k] Scott, *Hanson v. Denckla,* 72 Harv. L. Rev. at 700.

[l] Professor Scott, note f, *supra,* at pp. 705–07 rejects this suggestion on practical grounds, since the assets themselves would remain in Delaware. He seems not to consider the possibility that, if Florida held the trust companies not to be indispensable parties, a resulting judgment might be entitled to full faith and credit in Delaware.

[m] For a discussion of the Supreme Court's disposition of the issue of standing to raise lack of jurisdiction over third parties, see Kurland, p. 486, note d, *supra,* at 615–17. See also *Phillips Petroleum Co. v. Shutts,* 472 U.S. 797 (1985), discussed in Chapter 5, § 5.04, *supra,* in which the court upheld the defendant's standing in a state class action to raise objections to jurisdiction over non-resident plaintiffs, and then dismissed the objection.

the Florida actions, because they thought this course of conduct would be most likely to lead to carrying out the wishes of the late Mrs. Donner—nothing, in other words, about the inconvenience or difficulty in defending in a far-off place, just calculation of where the best litigating prospects were.

How would either of these hypotheticals—neither farfetched—affect your view of the fairness of litigating this controversy in Florida? Notice, as Justice Douglas points out, that there is no possibility of liability for either trust company here. Wilmington Trust has to pay over either to Katherine and Dorothy, or to Delaware Trust for benefit of Elizabeth's children. While Delaware Trust stands to lose some management or trustee's fees, it too, has no real exposure.

(4)(a) *Hanson v. Denckla* is often understood as a signal by the Supreme Court that it is not moving to nationwide jurisdiction, and that *McGee* did not signal the end of all restraints on jurisdiction of state courts. Indeed, Chief Justice Warren so states at p. 503. But if *International Shoe* can be read both as a minimum contacts and as a fairness case, is the Court here saying that it chooses the former and not the latter interpretation?

(b) Even on the theory of minimum contacts, it is difficult to follow the Court's attempt (pp. 503–504) to distinguish the quantum of affiliating circumstances in *Hanson* from those in *McGee*. Is the Court suggesting, just before the "cf" reference to *International Shoe* on p. 504, that *McGee* involved specific jurisdiction related to the liability-creating activity, whereas the jurisdiction sought to be involved in *Hanson* was general?

(c) The "holding" of *Hanson v. Denckla,* the maxim for which the case stands, is of course the following (p. 504):

> . . . it is essential in each case [in order for the court to have jurisdiction] that there be some act by which the defendant purposefully avails itself of the privilege of conducting activities within the forum State, thus invoking the benefits and protection of its laws.

Does Justice Black reject this formulation, or does he simply disagree about its application to the trust companies in this case?

(5)(a) As we saw, *Hanson v. Denckla* involves issues of (i) jurisdiction, (ii) choice of law, and (iii) full faith and credit to judgments. Issue (i) is raised by the Florida case, issue (iii) by the Delaware case, and issue (ii), though relevant to both cases, seems not to concern the Supreme Court here. Why the distinction? Is it consistent with the developments traced in Chapter 5? Does it make you want to reconsider those developments?

(b) Work your way through possible variations on *Hanson v. Denckla,* in which the Florida court decides differently on (i) jurisdiction, (ii) choice of law, (iii) interpretation of the law chosen, and in each case the losing party seeks Supreme Court review. When will, and when won't the Supreme Court grant review? Do the answers come out differently if review is sought after decision in F–2 (Delaware)?

(6)(a) After the excitement and confusion of *Hanson v. Denckla,* the *Coast Lines* case is inevitably an anticlimax. But in a context where there are no constitutional constraints, and where exercise of jurisdiction depends on the discretion of the court, it is of interest to see how—much more openly than in the American cases—the decision on choice of law affects the decision on jurisdiction. *Coastal States* is not a case where Order 11 jurisdiction can be based on express choice of law; even an implied choice of law under Order 11, r.1(f)(iii)[n] is hard to make out

---

[n] Presently O.11, r.1(d)(iii), Documents Supplement, p. 79.

here. Does it come down to "If UK courts would apply English law and the foreign forum would apply foreign law, we will grant leave to bring the action in England"?

(b) Even saying yes to the preceding question does not solve the case here, because it is not at all clear what law English courts would apply. Lord Denning, with a trace, perhaps, of regret for the good old days, recites the new test he is required to follow—a search for the system of law with which the transaction has the closest and most real connection—rather like the teaching of *Restatement (Second) of Conflict of Laws*.° In conducting his search, Lord Denning puts the law of the flag of the vessel and the nationality of the owners on one side, the place of signature of the contract and the port of embarkation of the voyage on the other. The deciding element, he says, is that the clause exempting the shipowners from liability would be valid under English, but not under Dutch law. The principle of validation, he says, leads to English law, and that law in turn leads to an English forum. Is this persuasive? Isn't that principle, expressed in the Latin maxim *ut res magis valeat quam pereat,* intended to operate when deciding whether or not a contract was formed, and not whether a particular clause in a contract—particularly an exoneration clause—will be honored?

(c) Lord Justice Stephenson is not happy with the factor used by Lord Denning to tip the scales. The presumption that the parties would not have intended to violate the law of their own country is at least as persuasive as the presumption relied on by Lord Denning. If he had to choose, he would opt for Netherlands law; but he would not wish to overturn the discretion of the lower court judge.

(d) Lord Justice Megaw, also reaching for a principled way to decide the case, says that if the Dutch courts were free to apply the law they saw fit to apply, he might defer to them in the interests of comity; the mandatory character of Netherlands law, however, leads him to join Lord Denning. Is that sound? Why should an English court have more respect for a foreign court than for a foreign statute?

(e) Is the whole idea that the choice of law by the court determines the jurisdiction of the court perverse? Is it so different from the performance of the Florida and Delaware courts in *Hanson v. Denckla*?

In the two decades following the decision in *Hanson v. Denckla*, the Supreme Court did not revisit the issue of judicial jurisdiction, but hundreds of such cases—litigation about litigation—were heard throughout the United States in state and federal courts. Many of these cases turned on the drafting or interpretation of the recently adopted long-arm statutes, that is on statutes focused not on the location or permanent establishment of the defendant, but on the character of the claim as related to defendant's activity either in the forum state or causing effects in that state.

---

§ 7.03 Activity as the Basis of Judicial Jurisdiction

In theory, almost any kind of activity by a non-resident defendant in the forum state could support jurisdiction of a court in that state in a claim arising out of that activity, provided that

---

° See Dicey & Morris, *The Conflict of Laws (10th ed. 1980),* Rule 145, discussed in Chapter 1 at p. 17 *supra.*

the forum state's statutes authorized jurisdiction, and made provision for service of process out of state, or on an in-state official who would formally notify the defendant of the pending claim. A statute authorizing jurisdiction of a state court against a non-resident operator of a motor vehicle in the state had been approved by the Supreme Court as early as 1927,[a] and the Court had upheld other state statutes focused on other types of liability-creating activity as well, for instance selling securities.[b] Following *International Shoe* and the rise of the long-arm statutes,[c] litigation concerning jurisdiction of claims against non-residents focused largely on two types of actions, where the plaintiff claimed injury or loss in the forum state but the non-resident defendant had acted outside that state.

[A] *The Split Tort*

Suppose a manufacturer had negligently made a product in State *A* and sold it to someone who used the product in State *B*. As states in the United States (and elsewhere) developed various forms of product liability actions, and gradually—but at different times—eliminated the requirement of "privity" between the injured party and the manufacturer, it became evident that in order for injured parties to gain full benefit of the reform in tort or warranty law, the states would have to find a way to overcome two obstacles. They would have to find a way (i) to make their law applicable in the forum state, even if the manufacturer acted in a state where its actions would not give rise to liability (or would require greater proof than in the forum state); and (ii) to make it possible to bring manufacturers (including component makers) before their courts.

The first task was relatively easy. If a case arising out of manufacture of a defective product could be labeled a tort, as contrasted with liability arising from contract (warranty),—a trend that became a deluge in the United States in the 1960's[d] —no "conflicts revolution" was required to apply the law of the place of injury, typically the plaintiff's residence or domicile and the forum state. The second task, establishing jurisdiction over the out-of-town manufacturer in the forum state required something more. The jurisdictional statute would have to provide—or be construed to provide—that the defendant had acted in the forum state by causing injury in the state.

The original Illinois long-arm statute[e] provided (and still does) that Illinois courts have jurisdiction over a nonresident "who in person or through an agent does any of the [following] acts . . . : (b) The commission of a tortious act within this state."[f] In *Gray v. American Radiator & Standard Sanitary Corp.*, 22 Ill.2d 432, 176 N.E.2d 761 (1961), the Supreme Court of Illinois held that this formulation included the Ohio manufacturer of a safety valve inserted in Pennsylvania into a water heater used in Illinois, where it failed. Citing the 1934 *Restatement of Conflict of Laws*, the Illinois Supreme Court said that "[i]t is well established . . . that in law the place of a wrong is where the last event takes place which is necessary to render the actor liable."[g] Accordingly, the tort was committed in Illinois, and the long-arm statute applied.

---

[a] *Hess v. Pawloski*, 274 U.S. 352 (1927).

[b] *Henry L. Doherty & Co. v. Goodman*, 294 U.S. 623 (1935).

[c] See pp. 494–96 *supra*

[d] Compare William L. Prosser, "The Assault upon the Citadel," 69 Yale L.J. 1099 (1960) with Prosser, "The Fall of the Citadel," 50 Minn. L. Rev. 791 (1966).

[e] Ill. Rev. Stat. c. 110, § 17(1), recodified in 1982 as Ill. Code of Civil Procedure §2-209.

[f] Present Code of Civil Procedure §2-209(2).

[g] 22 Ill.2d at 435, 176 N.E.2d at 762-63. The reference is to § 377 of the First Restatement. The Restatement (Second) of Conflict of Laws contains no comparable black letter rule, but discusses the problem—as a choice of law matter—in §§ 145 and 146 in the context of determining the most significant relationship.

As to the argument that as so construed, the statute violated the Due Process clause, the court said that jurisdiction in Illinois was fair under *International Shoe*, and that the "purposeful activity" test of *Hanson v. Denckla* was satisfied, since the maker of the valve had not shown that the use of its product in Illinois was an isolated instance.

In New York, the Court of Appeals took a different view. In *Feathers v. McLucas*, 15 N.Y.2d 443, 261 N.Y.S.2d 8, 209 N.E.2d 68, cert. denied, 382 U.S. 905 (1965), plaintiffs were injured in New York by the explosion of a liquid propane gas tank manufactured in Kansas by the defendant. The tank was sold to a Missouri corporation, which mounted it on a wheel base and in turn sold it to a Pennsylvania trucking firm. The New York statute at the time read just like the Illinois statute,[h] and the Court of Appeals held that this did not cover a tort committed out of state. Speaking of the conclusion by the Illinois Court in *Gray* that a tort had been committed in that state, Judge Fuld wrote:

> It certainly does not follow that, if the "place of wrong" for purposes of conflict of laws is a particular state, the "place of the commission of a tortious act" is also that same state for purposes of interpreting a statute conferring jurisdiction, on that basis, over nonresidents. (See, e.g., *Hanson v. Denckla*. . .). Not only are these separate and distinct problems but rules formulated to govern their resolution embody different concepts expressed in different language.[i]

Shortly thereafter, the New York legislature added present subsection (a)(3) to §302, clearly providing for jurisdiction in cases of split torts, but subject to two major qualifications. Jurisdiction under §302 (a)(3) could be asserted if the defendant (i) regularly does or solicits business, engages in other persistent course of conduct, or derives substantial revenue from goods used or services rendered in the state; or (ii) expects or should reasonably expect the act in question to have consequences in the state and derives substantial revenue from interstate or international commerce.[j] Illinois did not amend its long-arm statute, which had proved adequate in *Gray*. Whether the qualifications set out in the New York statute, based on the Uniform Interstate and International Procedure Act (1963), reflect a requirement of the Due Process clause is not clear. Reconsider this question after reading (or re-reading) *World-Wide Volkswagen* in the next section.

[B] *Split Torts and Claims for Indemnity*

As the law of product liability developed to improve responsibility for defective products not only on the manufacturer but also on others in the chain of distribution, the situation often arose in which the injured party P brought suit against D-1, the nearest person available—often a retailer or dealer—and that person sought to implead or separately sue its vendor D-2 or others upstream from D-1, including the manufacturer, D-3, or the maker of a component part that had failed, D-4.[k] Whether claims against D-2, D-3 or D-4 were truly tort claims might depend on whether P amended his or her complaint to assert a claim against D-2, D-3, or D-4. But given the development of product liability that came more and more to be accepted in the United States

---

[h] N.Y. C.P.L.R. § 302(a)(2) but not (3), Documents Supplement p. 77.

[i] 15 N.Y.2d at 463, 261 N.Y.S.2d at 23, 209 N.E.2d at 79.

[j] Note also that §302(a)(3) does not apply to actions for defamation.

[k] This was, for instance, the situation in *Asahi Metal Industries v. Superior Court*, § 7.05[B], *infra*.

along with the demise of privity,[1] a manufacturer clearly came within the definition of one who sells any product and physical harm is caused by the product to the ultimate user or consumer,[m] and thus at least arguably within the definition of one who commits a tortious act within the state where the injury occurred. Not everyone, of course, saw it that way.

The West Coast Machinery Case

(1) The case arose out of a claim by an employee of the Boeing Company, who severly injured his hand while operating a large mechanical metal press at the Boeing plant near Seattle Washington. Mr. Deutsch, the employee, could not bring suit against Boeing because his relation with the employer was governed by the Washington worker's compensation statute. But he was not barred from bringing suit against West Coast Machinery Co., a Washington company that had sold the metal press to Boeing, and against Marubeni America, the American subsidiary of a Japanese trading company, which had purchased the machine from its parent company Marubeni Japan and had imported it to the United States. Marubeni Japan had purchased the machine from the manufacturer, Kansai Iron Works Ltd. of Osaka, Japan, and the machine had been delivered to Marubeni Japan in Kobe, Japan.

The case that came before the Supreme Court of Washington involved a claim for indemnification brought by Marubeni america against Kansai. Kansai, having been served in Osaka through judicial assistance by the Osaka District Court, moved in the Washington Superior Court to dismiss the claim against it for lack of jurisdiction.

(2)(a) How should Kansai's motion be decided?

(b) Should it matter that Mr. Deutsch was not himself a party to the claim against Kansai?

(3) The Washington long-arm statute read in pertinent part like the Illinois long-arm statute, and like the New York statute prior to its amendment, i.e., it asserted jurisdiction over any person as to any action arising from

(a) "the transaction of any business within this state," or

(b) ". . . the commission of a tortious act within this state."

Without more, would you think such a statute supports jurisdiction over Kansai? What additional information would you regard as relevant? Would you, for instance, want to know whether Kansai had sold other machines for use by Boeing? Or whether Kansai knew that the machine was ordered (through the three intermediaries) on behalf of Boeing? Or should these facts make no difference?

(4) The Superior Court rejected Kansai's motion to dismiss, and the decision was upheld by the state Supreme Court. *Deutsch v. West Coast Machinery Co.*, 80 Wash. 2d 707, 497 P.2d 1311 (1972), cert. denied, sub nom. *Kansai Iron Works Ltd. v. Marubeni-Iida, Inc.* 409 U.S. 1009 (1972). The court wrote:

> It is well established in this state that under the long-arm statute, RCW 4.28.185, our courts may assert jurisdiction over nonresident individuals and foreign corporations to the extent

---

[1] See, generally, Prosser and Keaton on the Law of Torts, Chapter 17, esp. pp 690-94 (5th ed.1984); American Law Institute, *Restatement (Third) of the Law of Torts: Products Liability* §§ 1 and 2 and Reporters' Notes thereto (P.O.D. 1997).

[m] The text is a slight paraphrase of the operative part of the immensely influential § 402A of the *Restatement (Second) of Torts* (1965).

permitted by the due process clause of the United States Constitution, except as limited by the terms of the statute. . . .In order to subject nonresident defendants and foreign corporations to the in personam jurisdiction of this state as the forum under RCW 4.28.185(1)(a) and (b), the following factors must coincide: (1) the nonresident defendant or foreign corporation must purposefully do some act or consummate some transaction in the forum state; (2) the cause of action must arise from, or be connected with, such act or transactions; and (3) the assumption of jurisdiction by the forum state must not offend traditional notions of fair play and substantial justice, consideration being given to the quality, nature, and extent of the activity in the forum state, the relative convenience of the parties, the benefits and protection of the laws of the forum state afforded the respective parties, and the basic equities of the situation.

In the instant case, the record shows numerous uncontroverted contacts between Kansai and the state of Washington. Kansai manufactured, packaged and shipped the press according to Boeing Company specifications. . .In June 1966, at the request of Kansai, Boeing personnel were present for a test operation of the press at its plant in Japan. And, as heretofore stated, in January 1967, Kansai sent its engineers to the Boeing Company in Washington to test the operation of the press; Kansai sent a replacement selector switch to Washington for installation on the press; in June 1967, Kansai sent its engineer to the Boeing Company with parts and to check the operation of the press; and, in July 1967, Kansai's engineer, Mr. Obatake, visited the Boeing Company with respect to the press.

From these facts, we are convinced that the first two essential factors for the Washington court to take jurisdiction under the long-arm statute have been fulfilled in that the activities of the petitioner, Kansai, incidental to its manufacture, testing, sale and subsequent inspections of the press at the Boeing Company, and the replacement of the selector switch and of other parts thereon, constituted the transaction of business within the state; that Kansai purposefully manufactured the press knowing that the Boeing Company was the ultimate buyer; and that the press was used as intended, which resulted in injury to the plaintiff in the state of Washington, due to the claimed defective manufacture.[n]

(5) In support of its holding, the court also argued that the sale of the fateful machine was not an isolated transaction, and that Kansai had sold machines throughout the United States. Should these sales court in the weighing of "fair play and substantial justice," even if the other sales were not made to companies in the state of Washington?[o]

(6) After the Washington Supreme Court upheld jurisdiction over Kansai, Kansai took no further part in the case. Instead Kansai brought an action in the Osaka District Court against Marubeni America, seeking a declaration of non-liability.[p] Shortly after the Washington trial court on remand issued a judgment ordering Kansai to pay $86,000, the Osaka district court

---

[n] 80 Wash. 2d at 711-13, 497 P.2d at 1314-15.

[o] The court cited with approval a case in which a Swedish manufacturer had sold a crane to a purchaser in Connecticut, which was later used in Pennsylvania where it caused injury. *Benn v. Linden Co.*, 326 F. Supp. 995 (E.D. Pa. 1971). In that case the federal court in Pennsylvania upheld jurisdiction over the manufacturer, on the basis that the knowledge that the crane was to be used somewhere in the United States was "sufficient to constitute the foreign manufacturer doing business within the state of Pennsylvania under that state's long-term statute."

[p] For a similar strategy employed by a Japanese company even before the American court has determined its jurisdiction, see A. Lowenfeld, "Forum Shopping, Antisuit Injunctions, Negative Declarations and Related Tools of International Litigation," 91 Am. J. Int'l L. 314 at 315 (1997).

upheld Kansai's claim and issued a judgment that Kansai was under no obligation to indemnify Marubeni America.[q]

(7) Next, Marubeni America brought an action in the Osaka District Court against Kansai to enforce the judgment of the Washington court. The Osaka court rejected the suit, holding that,

> since it disturbs the order of a whole legal system to recognize the co-existence of judgments that are inconsistent with each other within the same judicial system, it is appropriate to construe that it violates the order of Japan's judicial law to recognize, in a case where a final judgment of a Japanese court has already been issued, a foreign judgment that is inconsistent with the Japanese judgment, with regard to the same parties and same subject matter, irrespective of the time of the institution of lawsuit, the time of the issuance of judgment, and the time when a judgment becomes final and conclusive, and that the judgment of the foreign court is incompatible with public order or good morals in Japan. In the light of the foregoing, since the United States judgment in this request lacks a requisite as prescribed under subparagraph 3 of Article 200 of the Code of Civil Procedure,[r] it cannot be recognized as effective in our country. Therefore, it is not necessary to pass on the other issues, and this court is of the opinion that the request of the plaintiff is without foundation.

Thus the Washington judgment remained unsatisfied, and the American distributors were left to pay the damages to the injured worker.

(8)(a) Does this outcome suggest that the Washington court was too forum-oriented

(i) in adding up Kansai's contacts with Washington;

(ii) in counting, at least as supporting argument, Kansai's shipments to other parts of the United States?

Or is the way jurisdiction of courts in the United States is received abroad of no concern to an American court passing on a state statute in light of the Federal Constitution?

(b) Turning the question around, did the Osaka court commit error, *first*, in agreeing to hear the suit for a declaration of non-liability filed after the action for indemnity had been filed in Washington; *second*, in issuing a declaration of non-liability after the Washington court had issued a judgment holding Kansai liable; and *third*, in declining to enforce the Washington judgment?

[C] *Sales Contracts*

Apart from claims sounding in tort or (as in the indemnity actions) related to torts, expanded concepts of jurisdiction might well make it easier for parties on opposite sides of sales transactions to sue one another in plaintiff's, rather than in defendant's forum. Of course, in some instances the parties to such transactions provided for resolution of disputes between them by forum selection or arbitration clauses in their contracts.[s] If no such provision was made, it would be necessary to interpret the long-arm statutes in the forum where plaintiff elected to sue.

---

[q] The account of the proceedings in Japan is taken from Sawaki, "Battle of Lawsuits: Lis Pendens in International Relations," 23 Japanese Annual Int'l Law 17 (1979-80).

[r] Article 200 of the Code of Civil Procedure provides

An irrevocable judgment of a foreign court is valid only upon the fulfillment of the following conditions, namely:

. . .

(3) that the judgment is not incompatible with public order or good morals in Japan.

[s] Recall Ch. 4, §§ 4.02 [B] and [C].

§ 7.03   JURISDICTION AND JUDGMENTS   □   525

1) Assuming that the seller of a product from state *B* is amenable to suit in state *A* in an action brought by a person claiming to have been injured by the product, as shown in *Gray v. American Standard* and many other cases, is there any reason not to subject the same seller to suit in state *A* in a commercial dispute, say if plaintiff claims that it was overcharged, or that delivery was late, or that the product did not meet the specifications in the contract?

2) Suppose it is the seller who seeks to sue the buyer from *A* in state *B*, say because the buyer failed to make a timely payment, or because the buyer purported to cancel a contract that the seller asserts was binding. Is there a reason to make it easier for buyer to sue seller than for seller to sue buyer on its home grounds?

Most American courts as well as legislatures, were more sympathetic to the tort plaintiff in suits against sellers, at least when the claimed tort involved a genuine injury to plaintiff with no prior dealings with the defendant seller. They were leary of attempts by plaintiffs to convert commercial disputes into tort claims by allegations that the defendant never intended to keep its promise and hence was liable in tort for fraud.[t] Thus jurisdiction of claims by buyers against out-of-state sellers was generally not upheld, unless some additional element fitting the concept of "transaction of business" by defendant in the forum state could be shown—for instance that the contract in suit had been negotiated or signed in the forum state, that the parties had engaged in prior dealings in that state, or that the seller had come to the forum state to solicit the business that resulted in the contract, even if it was concluded elsewhere. In contrast to the English rule, which as shown in the *Coast Lines* case, p. 509 *supra,* makes express or even implied choice of English law a basis for (discretionary) exercise of judicial jurisdiction of the English court,[u] in United States practice, choice of forum law in a contract, while it might be a factor in determining jurisdiction,[v] would not without additional links to the forum, be a basis for upholding jurisdiction of the court whose law was chosen.[w]

Several states, including New York, amended their long-arm statutes to include jurisdiction over "any non-domiciliary. . .who contracts anywhere to supply goods or services in the state," even if defendant could be said neither to have been "doing business" or to have "transacted business" in the forum state.[x]

Fewer cases reflected the pattern posed by the second question—suits by sellers against nonresident buyers. The *White Lumber* case reproduced below does reflect this pattern, as well as the continuing uncertainty among American lawyers and judges about the proper way to adress issues of judicial jurisdiction in an age so very different from the time when the rules were developed.

---

[t] See, e.g., *Kramer v. Vogl*, 17 N.Y.2d 27, 267 N.Y.S. 2d 900, 215 N.E.2d 159 (1966); *Stanat Mfg. Co. v. Imperial Metals Finishing Co.*, 325 F. Supp 794, 795-96 (E.D.N.Y. 1971).

[u] See Order 11, r.l.(1)(d)(iii), Documents Supplement p. 79.

[v] See *Burger King Corporation v. Rudzewicz*, p. 557 question 8, *infra.*

[w] For a clear statement of this point, see, e.g., *Galgay v. Bulletin Co.*, 509 F. 2d 1062 at 1066 (2d Cir. 1974).

[x] See, e.g., N.Y. C.P.L.R. §302(a)(1), italicized phrase, adopted 1979, Documents Supplement p. 77, drawn from the Uniform International and Interstate Procedure Act §1.03.

STATE ex rel. WHITE LUMBER SALES, INC. v. SULMONETTI

Oregon Supreme Court
252 Or. 121, 448 P.2d 571 (1968)

GOODWIN, J.

White Lumber Sales, Inc., a Florida corporation, brings an original proceeding in mandamus to compel the trial court to quash the return of service made pursuant to O.R.S. 14.035(1)(a)[1] in an action by an unpaid seller of plywood. . . .

The sole question is whether the relator, herein referred to as White, constitutionally can be said to have transacted business within this state so as to bring itself within the long-arm jurisdiction of our courts in the action pending below.

The facts of the case at bar, insofar as they are material to the jurisdictional question, are as follows: Continental Forest Products, Inc., an Oregon corporation engaging in the wholesale lumber and plywood business, has its offices and principal place of business in Lake Oswego, Oregon. White is a lumber and plywood wholesaler with offices and principal place of business in Fort Lauderdale, Florida. White had purchased plywood from Continental in the past, and by telephone requested a quotation on an order of twenty cars of plywood to be manufactured to specifications furnished by White. After consulting its suppliers, Continental quoted White prices and terms for delivery to a site in Gainesville, Georgia. Continental thereafter received a telephoned purchase order from White and instructed a mill in Grants Pass to begin work toward filling the order. In due course of mail, the telephoned order was confirmed in writing. The first three cars of plywood were shipped pursuant to the purchase orders.

After receiving and paying for one car of plywood, White notified Continental of a complaint with reference to the conformity of the plywood to the order. A dispute between buyer and seller over the suitability of the plywood eventually resulted in an action being filed for the purchase price together with damages for the losses incurred in manufacturing plywood not shipped, and further damages for the alleged breach of the contract to buy the remainder of the twenty carloads.

Commendable advocacy on both sides has been expended in an attempt to define the place where and the time when title passed, who paid the freight, who had the risk of loss, and which end of the transcontinental telephone conversation marked the point where the contract was made. While these and similar inquiries may be relevant in solving certain problems in the substantive law of sales, we do not believe such definitions to be determinative of the question involved in this case.

Here, the state's jurisdiction to try a case has been challenged on grounds of fairness and justice. The meaningful inquiry, therefore, is whether a foreign purchaser has produced effects in the forum state of such significance that it is not manifestly unfair to require him to resolve a resulting legal dispute in this state.

---

[1] O.R.S. 14.035 "(1) Any person, firm or corporation whether or not a citizen or a resident of this state, who, in person or through an agent, does any of the actions enumerated in this subsection, thereby submits such person and, if an individual, his personal representative to the jurisdiction of the courts of this state, as to any cause of action or suit or proceeding arising from any of the following:

"(a) The transaction of any business within this state . . . ."

We have already settled the question of legislative intent. In *State ex rel Western Seed v. Campbell,* 250 Or. 262, 442 P.2d 215 (1968), we held that the Legislative Assembly intended the long-arm statute to reach to the outer limits of federal constitutional due process.

When jurisdiction over an out-of-state defendant is challenged, the due-process question is whether the alleged facts are such that the forum may exercise jurisdiction without offending traditional notions of fair play and substantial justice. *Internat. Shoe Co. v. Washington.* If we can answer that question in favor of jurisdiction, there is no constitutional impediment to holding that the alleged facts constitute, within the meaning of ORS 14.035(1)(a), the transaction of business within this state.

The pending litigation clearly lies in the wake of the order which White placed with Continental. Whether or not "title passed," the telephone order produced substantial business consequences in Oregon. Written confirmation merely reinforced the order. Physical presence within the forum state is not necessary to the existence of a tort within the state. . . . On the score of physical presence there is no substantial reason for distinguishing business transactions from personal injuries. . . .

The difficulty in applying subjective standards like fair play and substantial justice has not kept courts from attacking the due-process problem. The pattern that seems to be developing allows statutes similar to ORS 14.035 to confer jurisdiction. See *Buckley v. New York Post Corporation,* 373 F.2d 175 (2d Cir. 1967). While the *Buckley* case involved tort (libel) rather than contract, and the long-arm statute of Connecticut differs in some respects from our own, Judge Friendly's analysis of the due-process issue seems persuasive:

> . . . Once we free our minds from traditional thinking that the plaintiff must inevitably seek out the defendant, such a doctrine would not seem to violate basic notions of fair play; any view that it does must rest on an inarticulate premise, which a legislature is free to question, that plaintiffs are much more given to making unjust claims than defendants are to not paying just ones. Indeed, when the operative facts have occurred where the plaintiff sues, the convenience of both parties would often be served by a trial there, and the chief benefit to the defendant of a rule requiring the plaintiff to seek him out is the impediment this creates to the bringing of any suit at all . . . [citation omitted]. Unfairness inconsistent with notions of fair play occurs only when a defendant is "compelled to defend himself in a court of a State with which he has no relevant connection." D. Currie, . . . [*The Growth of the Long Arm: Eight Years of Extended Jurisdiction in Illinois,* 1963 U. Ill. L. F. 533] at 534. . . . 373 F.2d at 181.

. . .

In the case at bar, both parties are lumber merchants engaged in interstate commerce. Both parties used conventional and well-understood methods of communicating offers and acceptances. On the strength of a telephoned offer and acceptance, mills in Oregon were told to fabricate a special order of plywood, railroad cars were ordered, crews were assembled in Oregon to load the cars and in Georgia to unload them.

It is clear that the placing of the telephoned order had effects, or "significant contacts," in Oregon. In *McGee v. International Life Ins. Co., in personam* jurisdiction did not offend due process when a California beneficiary sued in his own state to enforce a mail-order contract made by a Texas insurance company. In *Hanson v. Denckla,* however, it was held that the interest of the local plaintiff would be insufficient to justify a state in asserting jurisdiction beyond its borders. The court held that the defendant must purposefully avail himself of the privilege of conducting activities within the forum state, thus invoking the benefits and protection of its laws.

From the *McGee* and *Hanson* cases, three criteria can be said to define the present outer limits of *in personam* jurisdiction based on a single act: First, the defendant must purposefully avail himself of the privilege of acting in the forum state or of causing important consequences in that state. Second, the cause of action must arise from the consequences in the forum state of the defendant's activities. Finally, the activities of the defendant or the consequences of those activities must have a substantial enough connection with the forum state to make the exercise of jurisdiction over the defendant reasonable. . . .

Obviously, the convenience of both parties could not be equally served by giving each a wholly free choice of the forum in which to conduct litigation of the type involved here. On the other hand, a defendant has no greater claim to preferred treatment than has a plaintiff. So long as the defendant is not compelled to defend himself in a distant state with which he has had no relevant connection, he cannot be said to have been denied either fair treatment or substantial justice. We are entitled to assume that buyers are as likely to receive justice in the courts of the states in which they choose to do business as in the courts of the states in which they choose to maintain their principal offices.

Accordingly, the demurrer to the alternative writ is sustained and the writ is dismissed.

. . .

O'CONNELL, J., dissenting.

. . .

The problem should not be stated in terms of whether it is "fair play" to require defendant to defend in plaintiff's forum; the problem is one of properly allocating the jurisdiction of the state courts which, if not subjected to common controls, could entertain claims inimical to the other states and their domiciliaries. Chief Justice Warren recognized that there are fundamental reasons in addition to fairness to the parties which dictate limitations on the jurisdictional reach of sister states when he said:

> Those restrictions are more than a guarantee of immunity from inconvenient or distant litigation. *They are a consequence of territorial limitations on the power of the respective states.* However minimal the burden of defending in a foreign tribunal, a defendant may not be called upon to do so unless he has had the "minimal contacts" with that State that are a prerequisite to its exercise of power over him. *Hanson v. Denckla,* at [p. 503, *supra*]. (Emphasis added.)

One form of jurisdictional allocation is found in the full faith and credit clause; each state is required to recognize the judgments of its sister states. But recognition is required only if the sister state had jurisdiction in rendering the judgment. Thus a state called upon to adjudicate a claim involving a non-domiciliary cannot act as a sovereign state (as it would if it were in an international community of states), but must put those limits on its sovereignty which are necessary to coordinate its assertion of power with those of its sister states. Stated in another way, a state must test its jurisdiction in each case by putting itself in the position of a sister state called upon to enforce a judgment sought by the plaintiff. The interests involved are bilateral: on one hand are the interests of plaintiff and his state, and on the other the interests of defendant and his state. Each state may wish to maximize its own interest but the constitutional compact into which the states entered requires each to exercise restraint in respect for the other's interests.

§ 7.03   JURISDICTION AND JUDGMENTS   □   529

How that conflict can be resolved will be examined more fully below. It is enough to note at this point that the doctrine of due process and an inquiry into what is "fair play" does not advance us toward a solution. The necessity of adjusting these conflicting interests between the states existed in the United States long before the adoption of the due process clause of the Fourteenth Amendment in 1868. And although due process notions in another form may have been used in resolving problems of jurisdiction prior to 1868, the more common rationale employed in deciding jurisdictional questions is a rather vaguely defined principle that sovereign states in passing upon the question of the scope of their jurisdiction must consider the sovereignty of other states.

Professor Philip Kurland has explained the evolution of our law respecting jurisdiction as follows:

> The real difficulty underlying these [earlier] attempts to work out a rationale for personal jurisdiction lay in the fact that the doctrines were borrowed from laws relating to wholly independent sovereignties which were not relevant to jurisdictions joined in a federation. The basic premise for such decisions was "that a judgment . . . is necessarily something to be enforced and that a state which is physically impotent to enforce its judgments should be treated as legally incompetent to adjudicate . . . ." But with the Full Faith and Credit Clause as an overriding principle, such a premise only puts the question; it does not answer it. The real question becomes not whether a state could itself enforce a judgment, but rather under what circumstances the national power should be used to assist the extraterritorial enforcement of a state's judicial decrees.

Kurland, *The Supreme Court, The Due Process Clause and The In Personam Jurisdiction of State Courts,* 25 U. Chi. L. Rev. 569, 585 (1958).

Max Rheinstein sees the problem of adjusting the jurisdictional reach of the states in our union as analogous to that which is involved in adjusting the claims of sovereignty in the international community. Thus he states the principle to be:

> ". . . If one state oversteps the limits of its sovereignty, it necessarily infringes upon that of another, and thus violates the Law of Nations by which respect is demanded of each state for the sovereignty of every other." Rheinstein, *The Constitutional Bases of Jurisdiction,* 22 U. Chi. L. Rev. 775, 795–96 (1955).

He then goes on to say:

> We thus reach the conclusion that, insofar as jurisdictional limitations are not based upon notions of fairness and due process, they are founded upon certain principles of the Law of Nations. By virtue of the Law of Nations, the territorial jurisdiction of each state is limited and these limitations of the Law of Nations must be regarded as being implied in the full faith and credit clause of the Constitution of the United States. *Id.* at 796.

It is not suggested that we are presently bound by the jurisdictional rules existing prior to 1868 and it is conceded that "we would, indeed, be hard put even to state what in detail these rules were." But the point that Rheinstein wishes to make is that in the main the limits of jurisdiction are to be set not by the application of the principle of due process but by other principles relating to the need for reciprocal restraints on sovereignty in order to effect a harmony in the administration of justice among the several states.

I believe the approaches suggested by Rheinstein and Kurland are sound. Even without them, I am firmly convinced that the determination of the scope of a state's jurisdiction is not to be found by an application of the principle of due process. I agree with Philip Kurland that "[t]he language of 'reasonableness' and 'fair play' to which the Court has resorted is rather a statement of a conclusion than a reason." The majority opinion in the present case illustrates the same decisional process. The court makes a few observations concerning "contacts" and, without explaining how these contacts are relevant to "fairness" to anyone, concludes that Oregon has jurisdiction.

Courts which purport to employ the so-called "interest analysis" do no better. Generally this amounts to little more than an identification of one or more ways in which the state asserting jurisdiction is affected by the transaction being litigated. Frequently in that process the side of the scale representing the interest of the defendant or the interest of any other state is given little or no attention.

. . .

I believe that the preference for defendant's domicile in setting the initial place of trial can be rested upon firmer grounds than those suggested. The preference can be justified on the simple ground that it is conducive to the most efficient method of administering justice in those situations where conflicting assertions of jurisdiction might be made. If plaintiff is permitted to choose his domicile as the place of trial as a matter of course, a number of complications may arise. A default judgment rendered in plaintiff's forum would not necessarily prevent defendant from obtaining a conflicting judgment in his own forum. Out of such a circumstance complex legal problems may be generated. Problems as complex may arise where the two actions have not ripened into judgment and efforts to abate are made. Add to this the various maneuvers that can be made by both parties to invoke the jurisdiction of the federal courts and the maze becomes more intricate. A glance at von Mehren and Trautman, *The Law of Multistate Problems* (1965) will demonstrate the chaos which can flow from jurisdictional conflict.[19]

The allocation of jurisdiction to defendant's domicile can be justified on still another ground. If plaintiff were permitted to obtain a valid judgment in his own forum and the judgment was not satisfied, he would ordinarily find it necessary to enforce the judgment by a proceeding brought in defendant's domicile. Conceding that an action to enforce a judgment is normally less complicated than an action to recover an initial judgment, nevertheless it seems reasonable to require the plaintiff to seek his relief in one proceeding. It not only makes for a more economical use of judicial machinery but it may avoid difficult legal questions as to the duty or power of the court to carry out the mandate of the sister-state judgment.

Finally, not the least of the reasons which can be advanced for the choice of defendant's domicile as the place of trial is that of adding an element of certainty to the rules of jurisdiction, thus providing the parties as well as the courts a greater measure of predictability. If we do not establish workable rules with some definiteness, the courts will be burdened with a great volume of threshold litigation on the question of jurisdiction and the parties must suffer the delay in the adjudication of the substantive issues in the case.

The recognition of a defendant's domicile as the prime place of trial would not preclude the application of the doctrine of forum non conveniens, nor would it preclude the forging of rules permitting certain classes of cases to be litigated in plaintiff's forum.[20]

---

[19] Notice that these conflicts are not nearly so likely to arise in a system which places jurisdiction at the defendant's domicile in the absence of some special showing that jurisdiction should be allowed elsewhere.

[20] Thus, for example, as suggested by von Mehren and Trautman, *supra*, note 8 at 1167:

It is not necessary to decide whether the principle of allocation of jurisdiction which I have suggested is a part of constitutional doctrine limiting the power of the Legislative Assembly in its assertion of jurisdiction.[21] We can read our long-arm statute as expressing a legislative purpose to reserve to this state only that jurisdiction which any state under a federation of states could legitimately claim. Since the statute does not purport to lay down any principles by which these conflicting interests are to be correlated we may assume that the Assembly delegated to us the task of establishing workable rules for the delineation of jurisdiction of our courts over non-domiciliaries.[22]

---

§ 7.04 The Supreme Court Rethinks Judicial Jurisdiction

WORLD-WIDE VOLKSWAGEN CORP. v. WOODSON, DISTRICT JUDGE OF CREEK COUNTY, OKLAHOMA

United States Supreme Court
444 U.S. 286 (1980)

Mr. Justice White delivered the opinion of the Court.

The issue before us is whether, consistently with the Due Process Clause of the Fourteenth Amendment, an Oklahoma court may exercise *in personam* jurisdiction over a nonresident automobile retailer and its wholesale distributor in a products-liability action, when the defendants' only connection with Oklahoma is the fact that an automobile sold in New York to New York residents became involved in an accident in Oklahoma.

I

Respondents Harry and Kay Robinson purchased a new Audi automobile from petitioner Seaway Volkswagen, Inc. (Seaway), in Massena, N. Y., in 1976. The following year the Robinson family, who resided in New York, left that State for a new home in Arizona. As they passed

---

. . . [I]n any class of cases in which the controversy arises out of conduct that is essentially multistate on the part of the defendant, and essentially local on the part of the plaintiff, an argument exists for reversing the jurisdictional preference traditionally accorded defendants.

These authors are of the opinion, however, that when the plaintiff and the defendant are both engaged in interstate commercial activities "the traditional bias in favor of the defendant should not be reversed unless the litigational considerations present are most compelling." *Id.* at 1169.

[21] Allocation of jurisdiction by this court could be regarded as the application of constitutional principle on the theory that, by implication, the Full Faith and Credit Clause requires the fixing of the limits of jurisdiction necessary in the adjustment of the conflicting sovereign interests of the states. It has been said that "[t]he great importance of *Pennoyer v. Neff* is that it identified the test under the Full Faith and Credit Clause with the test under the Due Process Clause . . . ." Kurland, *supra,* at 585. It may be suggested that *Pennoyer v. Neff* would have been of greater importance and would have caused less confusion in the development of the law if it had identified the test under the Full Faith and Credit Clause with a test *other* than the Due Process Clause—a test having some relevance to the need for reconciling the interests of the states in their assertion of jurisdiction.

[22] ". . . Since the broad statutory language is open to diverse interpretations, the courts themselves should undertake such a balancing process in determining the scope of jurisdictional statutes." *Developments in the Law—State-Court Jurisdiction,* 73 Harv. L. Rev. 909, 1002 (1960).

through the State of Oklahoma, another car struck their Audi in the rear, causing a fire which severely burned Kay Robinson and her two children.[1]

The Robinsons subsequently brought a products-liability action in the District Court for Creek County, Okla., claiming that their injuries resulted from defective design and placement of the Audi's gas tank and fuel system. They joined as defendants the automobile's manufacturer, Audi NSU Auto Union Aktiengesellschaft (Audi); its importer, Volkswagen of America, Inc. (Volkswagen); its regional distributor, petitioner World-Wide Volkswagen Corp. (World-Wide); and its retail dealer, petitioner Seaway. Seaway and World-Wide entered special appearances,[3] claiming that Oklahoma's exercise of jurisdiction over them would offend the limitations on the State's jurisdiction imposed by the Due Process Clause of the Fourteenth Amendment.

The facts presented to the District Court showed that World-Wide is incorporated and has its business office in New York. It distributes vehicles, parts, and accessories, under contract with Volkswagen, to retail dealers in New York, New Jersey, and Connecticut. Seaway, one of these retail dealers, is incorporated and has its place of business in New York. Insofar as the record reveals, Seaway and World-Wide are fully independent corporations whose relations with each other and with Volkswagen and Audi are contractual only. Respondents adduced no evidence that either World-Wide or Seaway does any business in Oklahoma, ships or sells any products to or in that State, has an agent to receive process there, or purchases advertisements in any media calculated to reach Oklahoma. In fact, as respondents' counsel conceded at oral argument, there was no showing that any automobile sold by World-Wide or Seaway has ever entered Oklahoma with the single exception of the vehicle involved in the present case.

Despite the apparent paucity of contacts between petitioners and Oklahoma, the District Court rejected their constitutional claim and reaffirmed that ruling in denying petitioners' motion for reconsideration.[5] Petitioners then sought a writ of prohibition in the Supreme Court of Oklahoma to restrain the District Judge, respondent Charles S. Woodson, from exercising *in personam* jurisdiction over them. They renewed their contention that, because they had no "minimal contacts," with the State of Oklahoma, the actions of the District Judge were in violation of their rights under the Due Process Clause.

The Supreme Court of Oklahoma denied the writ, 585 P. 2d 351 (1978),[6] holding that personal jurisdiction over petitioners was authorized by Oklahoma's "long-arm" statute, Okla. Stat., Tit. 12, § 1701.03 (a)(4) (1971).[7] Although the court noted that the proper approach was to test

---

[1] The driver of the other automobile does not figure in the present litigation.

[3] Volkswagen also entered a special appearance in the District Court, but unlike World-Wide and Seaway did not seek review in the Supreme Court of Oklahoma and is not a petitioner here. Both Volkswagen and Audi remain as defendants in the litigation pending before the District Court in Oklahoma.

[5] The District Court's rulings are unreported, and appear at App. 13 and 20.

[6] Five judges joined in the opinion. Two concurred in the result, without opinion, and one concurred in part and dissented in part, also without opinion.

[7] This subsection provides:

A court may exercise personal jurisdiction over a person, who acts directly or by an agent, as to a cause of action or claim for relief arising from the person's . . . causing tortious injury in this state by an act or omission outside this state if he regularly does or solicits business or engages in any other persistent course of conduct, or derives substantial revenue from goods used or consumed or services rendered, in this state. . . .

The State Supreme Court rejected jurisdiction based on § 1701.03 (a)(3), which authorizes jurisdiction over any person "causing tortious injury in this state by an act or omission in this state." Something in addition to the infliction of tortious injury was required.

jurisdiction against both statutory and constitutional standards, its analysis did not distinguish these questions, probably because § 1701.03 (a)(4) has been interpreted as conferring jurisdiction to the limits permitted by the United States Constitution.[8] The court's rationale was contained in the following paragraph, 585 P. 2d, at 354:

> In the case before us, the product being sold and distributed by the petitioners is by its very design and purpose so mobile that petitioners can foresee its possible use in Oklahoma. This is especially true of the distributor, who has the exclusive right to distribute such automobile [sic] in New York, New Jersey and Connecticut. The evidence presented below demonstrated that goods sold and distributed by the petitioners were used in the State of Oklahoma, and under the facts we believe it reasonable to infer, given the retail value of the automobile, that the petitioners derive substantial income from automobiles which from time to time are used in the State of Oklahoma. This being the case, we hold that under the facts presented, the trial court was justified in concluding that the petitioners derive substantial revenue from goods used or consumed in this State.

We granted certiorari, to consider an important constitutional question with respect to state-court jurisdiction and to resolve a conflict between the Supreme Court of Oklahoma and the highest courts of at least four other States.[9] We reverse.

II

The Due Process Clause of the Fourteenth Amendment limits the power of a state court to render a valid personal judgment against a nonresident defendant. *Kulko v. California Superior Court,* 436 U. S. 84, 91 (1978). A judgment rendered in violation of due process is void in the rendering State and is not entitled to full faith and credit elsewhere. *Pennoyer v. Neff,* 95 U. S. 714, 732–733 (1878). Due process requires that the defendant be given adequate notice of the suit, *Mullane v. Central Hanover Trust Co.,* 339 U. S. 306, 313–314 (1950), and be subject to the personal jurisdiction of the court, *International Shoe Co. v. Washington,* 326 U. S. 310 (1945). In the present case, it is not contended that notice was inadequate; the only question is whether these particular petitioners were subject to the jurisdiction of the Oklahoma courts.

As has long been settled, and as we reaffirm today, a state court may exercise personal jurisdiction over a nonresident defendant only so long as there exist "minimum contacts" between the defendant and the forum State. *International Shoe Co. v. Washington, supra,* at [p. 488]. The concept of minimum contacts, in turn, can be seen to perform two related, but distinguishable, functions. It protects the defendant against the burdens of litigating in a distant or inconvenient forum. And it acts to ensure that the States, through their courts, do not reach out beyond the limits imposed on them by their status as coequal sovereigns in a federal system.

The protection against inconvenient litigation is typically described in terms of "reasonableness" or "fairness." We have said that the defendant's contacts with the forum State must be such that maintenance of the suit "does not offend 'traditional notions of fair play and substantial justice.'" *International Shoe Co. v. Washington, supra,* quoting *Milliken v. Meyer,* 311 U. S. 457, 463 (1940). The relationship between the defendant and the forum must be such that it

---

[8] *Fields v. Volkswagen of America, Inc.,* 555 P. 2d 48 (Okla. 1976); *Carmack v. Chemical Bank New York Trust Co.,* 536 P. 2d 897 (Okla. 1975); *Hines v. Clendenning,* 465 P. 2d 460 (Okla. 1970).

[9] Cf. *Tilley v. Keller Truck & Implement Corp.,* 200 Kan. 641, 438 P. 2d 128 (1968); *Granite States Volkswagen, Inc. v. District Court,* 177 Colo. 42, 492 P. 2d 624 (1972); *Pellegrini v. Sachs & Sons,* 522 P. 2d 704 (Utah 1974); *Oliver v. American Motors Corp.,* 70 Wash. 2d 875, 425 P. 2d 647 (1967).

is "reasonable . . . to require the corporation to defend the particular suit which is brought there." Implicit in this emphasis on reasonableness is the understanding that the burden on the defendant, while always a primary concern, will in an appropriate case be considered in light of other relevant factors, including the forum State's interest in adjudicating the dispute, see *McGee v. International Life Ins. Co.,* the plaintiff's interest in obtaining convenient and effective relief, see *Kulko v. California Superior Court, supra,* at 92, at least when that interest is not adequately protected by the plaintiff's power to choose the forum, cf. *Shaffer v. Heitner,* [p. 580, *infra*] n. 37 (1977); the interstate judicial system's interest in obtaining the most efficient resolution of controversies; and the shared interest of the several States in furthering fundamental substantive social policies, see *Kulko v. California Superior Court, supra,* at 93, 98.

The limits imposed on state jurisdiction by the Due Process Clause, in its role as a guarantor against inconvenient litigation, have been substantially relaxed over the years. As we noted in *McGee v. International Life Ins. Co.,* this trend is largely attributable to a fundamental transformation in the American economy:

> Today many commercial transactions touch two or more States and may involve parties separated by the full continent. With this increasing nationalization of commerce has come a great increase in the amount of business conducted by mail across state lines. At the same time modern transportation and communication have made it much less burdensome for a party sued to defend himself in a State where he engages in economic activity.

The historical developments noted in *McGee,* of course, have only accelerated in the generation since that case was decided.

Nevertheless, we have never accepted the proposition that state lines are irrelevant for jurisdictional purposes, nor could we, and remain faithful to the principles of interstate federalism embodied in the Constitution. The economic interdependence of the State was foreseen and desired by the Framers. In the Commerce Clause, they provided that the Nation was to be a common market, a "free trade unit" in which the States are debarred from acting as separable economic entities. *H. P. Hood & Sons, Inc. v. Du Mond,* 336 U. S. 525, 538 (1949). But the Framers also intended that the States retain many essential attributes of sovereignty, including, in particular, the sovereign power to try causes in their courts. The sovereignty of each State, in turn, implied a limitation on the sovereignty of all of its sister States—a limitation express or implicit in both the original scheme of the Constitution and the Fourteenth Amendment.

Hence, even while abandoning the shibboleth that "[t]he authority of every tribunal is necessarily restricted by the territorial limits of the State in which it is established," *Pennoyer v. Neff, supra,* at 720, we emphasized that the reasonableness of asserting jurisdiction over the defendant must be assessed "in the context of our federal system of government," *International Shoe Co. v. Washington, supra,* and stressed that the Due Process Clause ensures not only fairness, but also the "orderly administration of the laws." As we noted in *Hanson v. Denckla,* 357 U. S. 235, 250–251 (1958):

> As technological progress has increased the flow of commerce between the States, the need for jurisdiction over nonresidents has undergone a similar increase. At the same time, progress in communications and transportation has made the defense of a suit in a foreign tribunal less burdensome. In response to these changes, the requirements for personal jurisdiction over nonresidents have evolved from the rigid rule of *Pennoyer v. Neff,* to the flexible standard of *International Shoe Co. v. Washington.* But it is a mistake to assume that this trend heralds the eventual demise of all restrictions on the personal jurisdiction

of state courts. Those restrictions are more than a guarantee of immunity from inconvenient or distant litigation. They are a consequence of territorial limitations on the power of the respective States.

Thus, the Due Process Clause "does not contemplate that a state may make binding a judgment *in personam* against an individual or corporate defendant with which the state has no contacts, ties, or relations." *International Shoe Co. v. Washington,* [at p. 489]. Even if the defendant would suffer minimal or no inconvenience from being forced to litigate before the tribunals of another State; even if the forum State has a strong interest in applying its law to the controversy; even if the forum State is the most convenient location for litigation, the Due Process Clause, acting as an instrument of interstate federalism, may sometimes act to divest the State of its power to render a valid judgment. *Hanson v. Denckla, supra.*

III

Applying these principles to the case at hand, we find in the record before us a total absence of those affiliating circumstances that are a necessary predicate to any exercise of state-court jurisdiction. Petitioners carry on no activity whatsoever in Oklahoma. They close no sales and perform no services there. They avail themselves of none of the privileges and benefits of Oklahoma law. They solicit no business there either through salespersons or through advertising reasonably calculated to reach the State. Nor does the record show that they regularly sell cars at wholesale or retail to Oklahoma customers or residents or that they indirectly, through others, serve or seek to serve the Oklahoma market. In short, respondents seek to base jurisdiction on one, isolated occurrence and whatever inferences can be drawn therefrom: the fortuitous circumstance that a single Audi automobile, sold in New York to New York residents, happened to suffer an accident while passing through Oklahoma.

It is argued, however, that because an automobile is mobile by its very design and purpose it was "foreseeable" that the Robinsons' Audi would cause injury in Oklahoma. Yet "foreseeability" alone has never been a sufficient benchmark for personal jurisdiction under the Due Process Clause. In *Hanson v. Denckla,* it was no doubt foreseeable that the settlor of a Delaware trust would subsequently move to Florida and seek to exercise a power of appointment there; yet we held that Florida courts could not constitutionally exercise jurisdiction over a Delaware trustee that had no other contacts with the forum State. In *Kulko v. California Superior Court,* 436 U. S. 84 (1978), it was surely "foreseeable" that a divorced wife would move to California from New York, the domicile of the marriage, and that a minor daughter would live with the mother. Yet we held that California could not exercise jurisdiction in a child-support action over the former husband who had remained in New York.

If foreseeability were the criterion, a local California tire retailer could be forced to defend in Pennsylvania when a blowout occurs there, see *Erlanger Mills, Inc. v. Cohoes Fibre Mills, Inc.,* 239 F. 2d 502, 507 (CA4 1956); a Wisconsin seller of a defective automobile jack could be haled before a distant court from damage caused in New Jersey, *Reilly v. Phil Tolkan Pontiac, Inc.,* 372 F. Supp. 1205 (NJ 1974); or a Florida soft-drink concessionaire could be summoned to Alaska to account for injuries happening there, see *Uppgren v. Executive Aviation Services, Inc.,* 304 F. Supp. 165, 170–171 (Minn. 1969). Every seller of chattels would in effect appoint the chattel his agent for service of process. His amenability to suit would travel with the chattel. We recently abandoned the outworn rule of *Harris v. Balk,* 198 U. S. 215 (1905), that the interest of a creditor in a debt could be extinguished or otherwise affected by any State having transitory jurisdiction over the debtor. *Shaffer v. Heitner,* 433 U. S. 186 (1977). Having interred the mechanical rule that a creditor's amenability to a *quasi in rem* action travels with his debtor, we are unwilling to endorse an analogous principle in the present case.[11]

This is not to say, of course, that foreseeability is wholly irrelevant. But the foreseeability that is critical to due process analysis is not the mere likelihood that a product will find its way into the forum State. Rather, it is that the defendant's conduct and connection with the forum State are such that he should reasonably anticipate being haled into court there. See *Kulko v. California Superior Court, supra; Shaffer v. Heitner* [p. 580]; and see *id.,* at [pp. 592–93, *infra*] (STEVENS, J., concurring in judgment). The Due Process Clause, by ensuring the "orderly administration of the laws," *International Shoe Co. v. Washington,* gives a degree of predictability to the legal system that allows potential defendants to structure their primary conduct with some minimum assurance as to where that conduct will and will not render them liable to suit.

When a corporation "purposefully avails itself of the privilege of conducting activities within the forum State," *Hanson v. Denckla,* it has clear notice that it is subject to suit there, and can act to alleviate the risk of burdensome litigation by procuring insurance, passing the expected costs on to customers, or, if the risks are too great, severing its connection with the State. Hence if the sale of a product of a manufacturer or distributor such as Audi or Volkswagen is not simply an isolated occurrence, but arises from the efforts of the manufacturer or distributor to serve, directly or indirectly, the market for its product in other States, it is not unreasonable to subject it to suit in one of those States if its allegedly defective merchandise has there been the source of injury to its owner or to others. The forum State does not exceed its powers under the Due Process Clause if it asserts personal jurisdiction over a corporation that delivers its products into the stream of commerce with the expectation that they will be purchased by consumers in the forum State. Compare *Gray v. American Radiator & Standard Sanitary Corp.,* [p. 520, *supra*].

But there is no such or similar basis for Oklahoma jurisdiction over World-Wide or Seaway in this case. Seaway's sales are made in Massena, N. Y. World-Wide's market, although substantially larger, is limited to dealers in New York, New Jersey, and Connecticut. There is no evidence of record that any automobiles distributed by World-Wide are sold to retail customers outside this tristate area. It is foreseeable that the purchasers of automobiles sold by World-Wide and Seaway may take them to Oklahoma. But the mere "unilateral activity of those who claim some relationship with a nonresident defendant cannot satisfy the requirement of contact with the forum State." *Hanson v. Denckla, supra,* at [p. 504].

In a variant on the previous argument, it is contended that jurisdiction can be supported by the fact that petitioners earn substantial revenue from goods used in Oklahoma. The Oklahoma Supreme Court so found, drawing the inference that because one automobile sold by petitioners had been used in Oklahoma, others might have been used there also. While this inference seems

---

[11] Respondents' counsel, at oral argument, sought to limit the reach of the foreseeability standard by suggesting that there is something unique about automobiles. It is true that automobiles are uniquely mobile, see *Tyson v. Whitaker & Son, Inc.,* 407 A. 2d 1, 6, and n. 11 (Me. 1979) (McKusick, C. J.), that they did play a crucial role in the expansion of personal jurisdiction through the fiction of implied consent, e.g., *Hess v. Pawloski,* 274 U. S. 352 (1927), and that some of the cases have treated the automobile as a "dangerous instrumentality." But today, under the regime of *International Shoe,* we see no difference for jurisdictional purposes between an automobile and any other chattel. The "dangerous instrumentality" concept apparently was never used to support personal jurisdiction; and to the extent it has relevance today it bears not on jurisdiction but on the possible desirability of imposing substantive principles of tort law such as strict liability.

less than compelling on the facts of the instant case, we need not question the court's factual findings in order to reject its reasoning.

This argument seems to make the point that the purchase of automobiles in New York, from which the petitioners earn substantial revenue, would not occur *but for* the fact that the automobiles are capable of use in distant States like Oklahoma. Respondents observe that the very purpose of an automobile is to travel, and that travel of automobiles sold by petitioners is facilitated by an extensive chain of Volkswagen service centers throughout the country, including some in Oklahoma.[12] However, financial benefits accruing to the defendant from a collateral relation to the forum State will not support jurisdiction if they do not stem from a constitutionally cognizable contact with that State. See *Kulko v. California Superior Court,* 436 U. S., at 94–95. In our view, whatever marginal revenues petitioners may receive by virtue of the fact that their products are capable of use in Oklahoma is far too attenuated a contact to justify that State's exercise of *in personam* jurisdiction over them.

Because we find that petitioners have no "contacts, ties, or relations" with the State of Oklahoma, *International Shoe Co. v. Washington, supra,* at 319, the judgment of the Supreme Court of Oklahoma is

Reversed.

Mr. Justice Brennan, dissenting.*

The Court holds that the Due Process Clause of the Fourteenth Amendment bars the States from asserting jurisdiction over the defendants in these two cases. In each case the Court so decides because it fails to find the "minimum contacts" that have been required since *International Shoe Co. v. Washington.* Because I believe that the Court reads *International Shoe* and its progeny too narrowly, and because I believe that the standards enunciated by those cases may already be obsolete as constitutional boundaries, I dissent.

I

The Court's opinions focus tightly on the existence of contacts between the forum and the defendant. In so doing, they accord too little weight to the strength of the forum State's interest in the case and fail to explore whether there would be any actual inconvenience to the defendant. The essential inquiry in locating the constitutional limits on state-court jurisdiction over absent defendants is whether the particular exercise of jurisdiction offends ""traditional notions of fair play and substantial justice.' " *International Shoe,* quoting *Milliken v. Meyer,* 311 U. S. 457, 463 (1940). The clear focus in *International Shoe* was on fairness and reasonableness. *Kulko v. California Superior Court,* 436 U. S. 84, 92 (1978). The Court specifically declined to establish a mechanical test based on the quantum of contacts between a State and the defendant:

> "Whether due process is satisfied must depend rather upon the quality and nature of the activity *in relation to the fair and orderly administration of the laws which it was the purpose of the due process clause to insure.* That clause does not contemplate that a state may make binding a judgment *in personam* against an individual or corporate defendant with which the state has *no* contacts, ties, or relations." [p. 489, *supra*] (emphasis added).

---

[12] As we have noted, petitioners earn no direct revenues from these service centers. See *supra,* at [532].

* This opinion applies also to *Rush et al. v. Savchuk,* [p. 607, question (4)(e) *infra*].

The existence of contacts, so long as there were some, was merely one way of giving content to the determination of fairness and reasonableness.

Surely *International Shoe* contemplated that the significance of the contacts necessary to support jurisdiction would diminish if some other consideration helped establish that jurisdiction would be fair and reasonable. The interests of the State and other parties in proceeding with the case in a particular forum are such considerations. *McGee v. International Life Ins. Co.,* for instance, accorded great importance to a State's "manifest interest in providing effective means of redress" for its citizens. See also *Kulko v. California Superior Court, supra,* at 92; *Shaffer v. Heitner,* [p. 580, *infra*]; *Mullane v. Central Hanover Trust Co.,* 339 U. S. 306, 313 (1950).

Another consideration is the actual burden a defendant must bear in defending the suit in the forum. *McGee, supra.* Because lesser burdens reduce the unfairness to the defendant, jurisdiction may be justified despite less significant contacts. The burden, of course, must be of constitutional dimension. Due process limits on jurisdiction do not protect a defendant from all inconvenience of travel, *McGee, supra,* at [493], and it would not be sensible to make the constitutional rule turn solely on the number of miles the defendant must travel to the courtroom.[1] Instead, the constitutionally significant "burden" to be analyzed relates to the mobility of the defendant's defense. For instance, if having to travel to a foreign forum would hamper the defense because witnesses or evidence or the defendant himself were immobile, or if there were a disproportionately large number of witnesses or amount of evidence that would have to be transported at the defendant's expense, or if being away from home for the duration of the trial would work some special hardship on the defendant, then the Constitution would require special consideration for the defendant's interests.

That considerations other than contacts between the forum and the defendant are relevant necessarily means that the Constitution does not require that trial be held in the State which has the "best contacts" with the defendant. See *Shaffer v. Heitner,* at [p. 596, *infra*] (BRENNAN, J., dissenting). The defendant has no constitutional entitlement to the best forum or, for that matter, to any particular forum. Under even the most restrictive view of *International Shoe,* several States could have jurisdiction over a particular cause of action. We need only determine whether the forum States in these cases satisfy the constitutional minimum.[2]

II

In each of these cases, I would find that the forum State has an interest in permitting the litigation to go forward, the litigation is connected to the forum, the defendant is linked to the forum, and the burden of defending is not unreasonable. Accordingly, I would hold that it is neither unfair nor unreasonable to require these defendants to defend in the forum State.

. . .

B

In [*World-Wide Volkswagen*] the interest of the forum State and its connection to the litigation is strong. The automobile accident underlying the litigation occurred in Oklahoma. The plaintiffs

---

[1] In fact, a courtroom just across the state line from a defendant may often be far more convenient for the defendant than a courtroom in a distant corner of his own State.

[2] The States themselves, of course, remain free to choose whether to extend their jurisdiction to embrace all defendants over whom the Constitution would permit exercise of jurisdiction.

were hospitalized in Oklahoma when they brought suit. Essential witnesses and evidence were in Oklahoma. The State has a legitimate interest in enforcing its laws designed to keep its highway system safe, and the trial can proceed at least as efficiently in Oklahoma as anywhere else.

The petitioners are not unconnected with the forum. Although both sell automobiles within limited sales territories, each sold the automobile which in fact was driven to Oklahoma where it was involved in an accident.[8] It may be true, as the Court suggests, that each sincerely intended to limit its commercial impact to the limited territory, and that each intended to accept the benefits and protection of the laws only of those States within the territory. But obviously these were unrealistic hopes that cannot be treated as an automatic constitutional shield.[9]

An automobile simply is not a stationary item or one designed to be used in one place. An automobile is *intended* to be moved around. Someone in the business of selling large numbers of automobiles can hardly plead ignorance of their mobility or pretend that the automobiles stay put after they are sold. It is not merely that a dealer in automobiles foresees that they will move. . . . The dealer actually intends that the purchasers will use the automobiles to travel to distant States where the dealer does not directly "do business." The sale of an automobile does *purposefully* inject the vehicle into the stream of interstate commerce so that it can travel to distant States. See *Kulko,* 436 U. S., at 94; *Hanson v. Denckla,* 357 U.S. 235, 253 (1958).

This case is similar to *Ohio v. Wyandotte Chemicals Corp.,* 401 U. S. 493 (1971). There we indicated, in the course of denying leave to file an original-jurisdiction case, that corporations having no direct contact with Ohio could constitutionally be brought to trial in Ohio because they dumped pollutants into streams outside Ohio's limits which ultimately, through the action of the water, reached Lake Erie and affected Ohio. No corporate acts, only their consequences, occurred in Ohio. The stream of commerce is just as natural a force as a stream of water, and it was equally predictable that the cars petitioners released would reach distant States.[10]

The Court accepts that a State may exercise jurisdiction over a distributor which "serves" that State "indirectly" by "deliver[ing] its products into the stream of commerce with the expectation that they will be purchased by consumers in the forum State. . . ." It is difficult to see why the Constitution should distinguish between a case involving goods which reach a distant State through a chain of distribution and a case involving goods which reach the same State because a consumer, using them as the dealer knew the customer would, took them there.[11] In each case the seller purposefully injects the goods into the stream of commerce and those goods predictably are used in the forum State.[12]

---

[8] On the basis of this fact the state court inferred that the petitioners derived substantial revenue from goods used in Oklahoma. The inference is not without support. Certainly, were use of goods accepted as a relevant contact, a plaintiff would not need to have an exact count of the number of petitioners' cars that are used in Oklahoma.

[9] Moreover, imposing liability in this case would not so undermine certainty as to destroy an automobile dealer's ability to do business. According jurisdiction does not expand liability except in the marginal case where a plaintiff cannot afford to bring an action except in the plaintiff's own State. In addition, these petitioners are represented by insurance companies. They not only could, but did, purchase insurance to protect them should they stand trial and lose the case. The costs of the insurance no doubt are passed on to customers.

[10] One might argue that it was more predictable that the pollutants would reach Ohio than that one of petitioners' cars would reach Oklahoma. The Court's analysis, however, excludes jurisdiction in a contiguous State such as Pennsylvania as surely as in more distant States such as Oklahoma.

[11] For example, I cannot understand the constitutional distinction between selling an item in New Jersey and selling an item in New York expecting it to be used in New Jersey.

[12] The manufacturer in the case cited by the Court, *Gray v. American Radiator & Standard Sanitary Corp.,* had no more control over which States its goods would reach than did the petitioners in this case.

Furthermore, an automobile seller derives substantial benefits from States other than its own. A large part of the value of automobiles is the extensive, nationwide network of highways. Significant portions of that network have been constructed by and are maintained by the individual States, including Oklahoma. The States, through their highway programs, contribute in a very direct and important way to the value of petitioners' businesses. Additionally, a network of other related dealerships with their service departments operate throughout the country under the protection of the laws of the various States, including Oklahoma, and enhance the value of petitioners' businesses by facilitating their customers' traveling.

Thus, the Court errs in its conclusion, . . . that "petitioners have *no* "contacts, ties, or relations' " with Oklahoma. There obviously are contacts, and, given Oklahoma's connection to the litigation, the contacts are sufficiently significant to make it fair and reasonable for the petitioners to submit to Oklahoma's jurisdiction.

III

It may be that affirmance of the judgments in these cases would approach the outer limits of *International Shoe's* jurisdictional principle. But that principle, with its almost exclusive focus on the rights of defendants, may be outdated. As MR. JUSTICE MARSHALL wrote in *Shaffer v. Heitner,* [p. 590, *infra*]: ""[T]raditional notions of fair play and substantial justice' can be as readily offended by the perpetuation of ancient forms that are no longer justified as by the adoption of new procedures. . . ."

International Shoe inherited its defendant focus from *Pennoyer v. Neff,* and represented the last major step this Court has taken in the long process of liberalizing the doctrine of personal jurisdiction. Though its flexible approach represented a major advance, the structure of our society has changed in many significant ways since *International Shoe* was decided in 1945. Mr. Justice Black, writing for the Court in *McGee v. International Life Ins. Co.,* recognized that "a trend is clearly discernible toward expanding the permissible scope of state jurisdiction over foreign corporations and other nonresidents."

. . .

As the Court acknowledges, . . . both the nationalization of commerce and the ease of transportation and communication [to which Justice Black referred] have accelerated in the generation since 1957.[13] The model of society on which the *International Shoe* Court based its opinion is no longer accurate. Business people, no matter how local their businesses, cannot assume that goods remain in the business' locality. Customers and goods can be anywhere else in the country usually in a matter of hours and always in a matter of a very few days.

In answering the question whether or not it is fair and reasonable to allow a particular forum to hold a trial binding on a particular defendant, the interests of the forum State and other parties loom large in today's world and surely are entitled to as much weight as are the interests of the defendant. The "orderly administration of the laws" provides a firm basis for according some

---

[13] Statistics help illustrate the amazing expansion in mobility since *International Shoe.* The number of revenue passenger-miles flown on domestic and international flights increased by nearly three orders of magnitude between 1945 (450 million) and 1976 (179 billion). U. S. Department of Commerce, Historical Statistics of the United States, pt. 2, p. 770 (1975); U. S. Department of Commerce, Statistical Abstract of the United States 670 (1978). Automobile vehicle-miles (including passenger cars, buses, and trucks) driven in the United States increased by a relatively modest 500% during the same period, growing from 250 billion in 1945 to 1,409 billion in 1976. Historical Statistics, *supra,* at 718; Statistical Abstract, *supra,* at 647.

protection to the interests of plaintiffs and States as well as of defendants.[14] Certainly, I cannot see how a defendant's right to due process is violated if the defendant suffers no inconvenience. . . .

The conclusion I draw is that constitutional concepts of fairness no longer require the extreme concern for defendants that was once necessary. Rather, as I wrote in dissent from *Shaffer v. Heitner,* . . . minimum contacts must exist "among the *parties,* the contested transaction, and the forum State."[15] The contacts between any two of these should not be determinative.

> [W]hen a suitor seeks to lodge a suit in a State with a substantial interest in seeing its own law applied to the transaction in question, we could wisely act to minimize conflicts, confusion, and uncertainty by adopting a liberal view of jurisdiction, unless considerations of fairness or efficiency strongly point in the opposite direction.[16]

Mr. Justice Black, dissenting in *Hanson v. Denckla,* expressed similar concerns by suggesting that a State should have jurisdiction over a case growing out of a transaction significantly related to that State "unless litigation there would impose such a heavy and disproportionate burden on a nonresident defendant that it would offend what this Court has referred to as 'traditional notions of fair play and substantial justice.' "[17] Assuming that a State gives a nonresident defendant adequate notice and opportunity to defend, I do not think the Due Process Clause is offended merely because the defendant has to board a plane to get to the site of the trial.

The Court opinion . . . suggests that the defendant ought to be subject to a State's jurisdiction only if he has contacts with the State "such that he should reasonably anticipate being haled into court there."[18] . . . There is nothing unreasonable or unfair, however, about recognizing commercial reality. Given the tremendous mobility of goods and people, and the inability of businessmen to control where goods are taken by customers (or retailers), I do not think that the defendant should be in complete control of the geographical stretch of his amenability to suit. Jurisdiction is no longer premised on the notion that nonresident defendants have somehow

---

[14] The Court has recognized that there are cases where the interests of justice can turn the focus of the jurisdictional inquiry away from the contacts between a defendant and the forum State. For instance, the Court indicated that the requirement of contacts may be greatly relaxed (if indeed any personal contacts would be required) where a plaintiff is suing a nonresident defendant to enforce a judgment procured in another State. *Shaffer v. Heitner,* [p. 589, *infra*], nn. 36, 37.

[15] In some cases, the inquiry will resemble the inquiry commonly undertaken in determining which State's law to apply. That it is fair to apply a State's law to a nonresident defendant is clearly relevant in determining whether it is fair to subject the defendant to jurisdiction in that State. *Shaffer v. Heitner,* [*infra* at p. 594] (Brennan, J., dissenting); *Hanson v. Denckla,* [p. 507 *supra*] (Black, J., dissenting). See n. 19, *infra*.

[16] Such a standard need be no more uncertain than the Court's test "in which few answers will be written 'in black and white. The greys are dominant and even among them the shades are innumerable.' *Estin v. Estin,* 334 U. S. 541, 545 (1948)." *Kulko v. California Superior Court,* 436 U. S. 84, 92 (1978).

[17] This strong emphasis on the State's interest is nothing new. This Court, permitting the forum to exercise jurisdiction over nonresident claimants to a trust largely on the basis of the forum's interest in closing the trust, stated:

> [T]he interest of each state in providing means to close trusts that exist by the grace of its laws and are administered under the supervision of its courts is so insistent and rooted in custom as to establish beyond doubt the right of its courts to determine the interests of all claimants, resident or nonresident, provided its procedure accords full opportunity to appear and be heard.

Mullane v. Central Hanover Trust Co., 339 U. S. 306, 313 (1950).

[18] The Court suggests that this is the critical foreseeability rather than the likelihood that the product will go to the forum State. But the reasoning begs the question. A defendant cannot know if his actions will subject him to jurisdiction in another State until we have declared what the law of jurisdiction is.

impliedly consented to suit. People should understand that they are held responsible for the consequences of their actions and that in our society most actions have consequences affecting many States. When an action in fact causes injury in another State, the actor should be prepared to answer for it there unless defending in that State would be unfair for some reason other than that a state boundary must be crossed.[19]

In effect the Court is allowing defendants to assert the sovereign rights of their home States. The expressed fear is that otherwise all limits on personal jurisdiction would disappear. But the argument's premise is wrong. I would not abolish limits on jurisdiction or strip state boundaries of all significance, see *Hanson, supra,* at [507-08] (Black, J., dissenting); I would still require the plaintiff to demonstrate sufficient contacts among the parties, the forum, and the litigation to make the forum a reasonable State in which to hold the trial.[20]

I would also, however, strip the defendant of an unjustified veto power over certain very appropriate fora—a power the defendant justifiably enjoyed long ago when communication and travel over long distances was slow and unpredictable and when notions of state sovereignty were impractical and exaggerated. But I repeat that that is not today's world. If a plaintiff can show that his chosen forum State has a sufficient interest in the litigation (or sufficient contacts with the defendant), then the defendant who cannot show some real injury to a constitutionally protected interest, see *O'Connor v. Lee-Hy Paving Corp.,* [p. 606, *infra*], should have no constitutional excuse not to appear.[21]

The plaintiffs in each of these cases brought suit in a forum with which they had significant contacts and which had significant contacts with the litigation. I am not convinced that the defendants would suffer any "heavy and disproportionate burden" in defending the suits. Accordingly, I would hold that the Constitution should not shield the defendants from appearing and defending in the plaintiffs' chosen fora.

MR. JUSTICE MARSHALL, with whom MR. JUSTICE BLACKMUN joins, dissenting.

For over 30 years the standard by which to measure the constitutionally permissible reach of state-court jurisdiction has been well established:

> [D]ue process requires only that in order to subject a defendant to a judgment *in personam,* if he be not present within the territory of the forum, he have certain minimum contacts with it such that the maintenance of the suit does not offend 'traditional notions of fair play and substantial justice.'

International Shoe Co. v. Washington, quoting *Milliken v. Meyer,* 311 U. S. 457, 463 (1940). The corollary, that the Due Process Clause forbids the assertion of jurisdiction over a defendant "with which the state has no contacts, ties, or relations," is equally clear. The concepts of fairness and substantial justice as applied to an evaluation of "the quality and nature of the [defendant's] activity," *ibid.,* are not readily susceptible of further definition, however, and it is not surprising that the constitutional standard is easier to state than to apply.

---

[19] One consideration that might create some unfairness would be if the choice of forum also imposed on the defendant an unfavorable substantive law which the defendant could justly have assumed would not apply. See n. 15, *supra*.

[20] For instance, in [*Rush*], if the plaintiff were not a bona fide resident of Minnesota when the suit was filed or if the defendant were subject to financial liability, I might well reach a different result. In [*Volkswagen*], I might reach a different result if the accident had not occurred in Oklahoma.

[21] Frequently, of course, the defendant will be able to influence the choice of forum through traditional doctrines, such as venue or *forum non conveniens,* permitting the transfer of litigation.

This is a difficult case, and reasonable minds may differ as to whether respondents have alleged a sufficient "relationship among the defendant[s], the forum, and the litigation," *Shaffer v. Heitner,* to satisfy the requirements of *International Shoe.* I am concerned, however, that the majority has reached its result by taking an unnecessarily narrow view of petitioners' forum-related conduct. The majority asserts that "respondents seek to base jurisdiction on one, isolated occurrence and whatever inferences can be drawn therefrom: the fortuitous circumstance that a single Audi automobile, sold in New York to New York residents, happened to suffer an accident while passing through Oklahoma." If that were the case, I would readily agree that the minimum contacts necessary to sustain jurisdiction are not present. But the basis for the assertion of jurisdiction is not the happenstance that an individual over whom petitioners had no control made a unilateral decision to take a chattel with him to a distant State. Rather, jurisdiction is premised on the deliberate and purposeful actions of the defendants themselves in choosing to become part of a nationwide, indeed a global, network for marketing and servicing automobiles.

Petitioners are sellers of a product whose utility derives from its mobility. The unique importance of the automobile in today's society, which is discussed in MR. JUSTICE BLACKMUN'S dissenting opinion, . . . needs no further elaboration. Petitioners know that their customers buy cars not only to make short trips, but also to travel long distances. In fact, the nationwide service network with which they are affiliated was designed to facilitate and encourage such travel. Seaway would be unlikely to sell many cars if authorized service were available only in Massena, N. Y. Moreover, local dealers normally derive a substantial portion of their revenues from their service operations and thereby obtain a further economic benefit from the opportunity to service cars which were sold in other States. It is apparent that petitioners have not attempted to minimize the chance that their activities will have effects in other States; on the contrary, they have chosen to do business in a way that increases that chance, because it is to their economic advantage to do so.

To be sure, petitioners could not know in advance that this particular automobile would be driven to Oklahoma. They must have anticipated, however, that a substantial portion of the cars they sold would travel out of New York. Seaway, a local dealer in the second most populous State, and World-Wide, one of only seven regional Audi distributors in the entire country, . . . would scarcely have been surprised to learn that a car sold by them had been driven in Oklahoma on Interstate 44, a heavily traveled transcontinental highway. In the case of the distributor, in particular, the probability that some of the cars it sells will be driven in every one of the contiguous States must amount to a virtual certainty. This knowledge should alert a reasonable businessman to the likelihood that a defect in the product might manifest itself in the forum State—not because of some unpredictable, aberrant, unilateral action by a single buyer, but in the normal course of the operation of the vehicles for their intended purpose.

It is misleading for the majority to characterize the argument in favor of jurisdiction as one of "'foreseeability' alone. . . ." As economic entities petitioners reach out from New York, knowingly causing effects in other States and receiving economic advantage both from the ability to cause such effects themselves and from the activities of dealers and distributors in other States. While they did not receive revenue from making direct sales in Oklahoma, they intentionally became part of an interstate economic network, which included dealerships in Oklahoma, for pecuniary gain. In light of this purposeful conduct I do not believe it can be said that petitioners "had no reason to expect to be haled before a[n Oklahoma] court." *Shaffer v. Heitner,* [p. 591, *infra*] and *Kulko v. California Superior Court,* 436 U. S. 84, 97–98 (1978).

The majority apparently acknowledges that if a product is purchased in the forum State by a consumer, that State may assert jurisdiction over everyone in the chain of distribution. . . . [p. 536] With this I agree. But I cannot agree that jurisdiction is necessarily lacking if the product enters the State not through the channels of distribution but in the course of its intended use by the consumer. We have recognized the role played by the automobile in the expansion of our notions of personal jurisdiction. See *Shaffer v. Heitner*, [p. 585, *infra*]; *Hess v. Pawloski*, 274 U. S. 352 (1927). Unlike most other chattels, which may find their way into States far from where they were purchased because their owner takes them there, the intended use of the automobile is precisely as a means of traveling from one place to another. In such a case, it is highly artificial to restrict the concept of the "stream of commerce" to the chain of distribution from the manufacturer to the ultimate consumer.

I sympathize with the majority's concern that persons ought to be able to structure their conduct so as not to be subject to suit in distant forums. But that may not always be possible. Some activities by their very nature may foreclose the option of conducting them in such a way as to avoid subjecting oneself to jurisdiction in multiple forums. This is by no means to say that all sellers of automobiles should be subject to suit everywhere; but a distributor of automobiles to a multistate market and a local automobile dealer who makes himself part of a nationwide network of dealerships can fairly expect that the cars they sell may cause injury in distant States and that they may be called on to defend a resulting lawsuit there.

In light of the quality and nature of petitioners' activity, the majority's reliance on *Kulko v. California Superior Court, supra*, is misplaced. *Kulko* involved the assertion of state-court jurisdiction over a nonresident individual in connection with an action to modify his child custody rights and support obligations. His only contact with the forum State was that he gave his minor child permission to live there with her mother. In holding that the exercise of jurisdiction violated the Due Process Clause, we emphasized that the cause of action as well as the defendant's actions in relation to the forum State arose *"not from the defendant's commercial transactions in interstate commerce,* but rather from his personal, domestic relations," 436 U. S., at 97 (emphasis supplied), contrasting Kulko's actions with those of the insurance company in *McGee v. International Life Ins. Co.*, 355 U. S. 220 (1957), which were undertaken for commercial benefit.*

Manifestly, the "quality and nature" of commercial activity is different, for purposes of the *International Shoe* test, from actions from which a defendant obtains no economic advantage. Commercial activity is more likely to cause effects in a larger sphere, and the actor derives an economic benefit from the activity that makes it fair to require him to answer for his conduct where its effects are felt. The profits may be used to pay the costs of suit, and knowing that the activity is likely to have effects in other States the defendant can readily insure against the costs of those effects, thereby sparing himself much of the inconvenience of defending in a distant forum.

Of course, the Constitution forbids the exercise of jurisdiction if the defendant had no judicially cognizable contacts with the forum. But as the majority acknowledges, if such contacts are present the jurisdictional inquiry requires a balancing of various interests and policies. I believe such contacts are to be found here and that, considering all of the interests and policies at stake, requiring petitioners to defend this action in Oklahoma is not beyond the bounds of the Constitution. Accordingly, I dissent.

---

* Similarly, I believe the Court in *Hanson v. Denckla,* was influenced by the fact that trust administration has traditionally been considered a peculiarly local activity.

MR. JUSTICE BLACKMUN, dissenting.

I confess that I am somewhat puzzled why the plaintiffs in this litigation are so insistent that the regional distributor and the retail dealer, the petitioners here, who handled the ill-fated Audi automobile involved in this litigation, be named defendants. It would appear that the manufacturer and the importer, whose subjectability to Oklahoma jurisdiction is not challenged before this Court, ought not to be judgment-proof. It may, of course, ultimately amount to a contest between insurance companies that, once begun, is not easily brought to a termination. Having made this much of an observation, I pursue it no further.

For me, a critical factor in the disposition of the litigation is the nature of the instrumentality under consideration. It has been said that we are a Nation on wheels. What we are concerned with here is the automobile and its peripatetic character. One need only examine our national network of interstate highways, or make an appearance on one of them, or observe the variety of license plates present not only on those highways but in any metropolitan area, to realize that any automobile is likely to wander far from its place of licensure or from its place of distribution and retail sale. Miles per gallon on the highway (as well as in the city) and mileage per tankful are familiar allegations in manufacturers' advertisements today. To expect that any new automobile will remain in the vicinity of its retail sale—like the 1914 electric car driven by the proverbial "little old lady"—is to blink at reality. The automobile is intended for distance as well as for transportation within a limited area.

It therefore seems to me not unreasonable—and certainly not unconstitutional and beyond the reach of the principles laid down in *International Shoe Co. v. Washington,* and its progeny—to uphold Oklahoma jurisdiction over this New York distributor and this New York dealer when the accident happened in Oklahoma. I see nothing more unfair for them than for the manufacturer and the importer. All are in the business of providing vehicles that spread out over the highways of our several States. It is not too much to anticipate at the time of distribution and at the time of retail sale that this Audi would be in Oklahoma. Moreover, in assessing "minimum contacts," foreseeable use in another State seems to me to be little different from foreseeable resale in another State. Yet the Court declares this distinction determinative. . . .

MR. JUSTICE BRENNAN points out in his dissent, . . . that an automobile dealer derives substantial benefits from States other than its own. The same is true of the regional distributor. Oklahoma does its best to provide safe roads. Its police investigate accidents. It regulates driving within the State. It provides aid to the victim and thereby, it is hoped, lessens damages. Accident reports are prepared and made available. All this contributes to and enhances the business of those engaged professionally in the distribution and sale of automobiles. All this also may benefit defendants in the very lawsuits over which the State asserts jurisdiction.

My position need not now take me beyond the automobile and the professional who does business by way of distributing and retailing automobiles. Cases concerning other instrumentalities will be dealt with as they arise and in their own contexts.

I would affirm the judgment of the Supreme Court of Oklahoma. Because the Court reverses that judgment, it will now be about parsing every variant in the myriad of motor vehicle fact situations that present themselves. Some will justify jurisdiction and others will not. All will depend on the "contact" that the Court sees fit to perceive in the individual case.

KEETON v. HUSTLER MAGAZINE, INC.

United States Supreme Court
465 U.S. 770 (1984)

JUSTICE REHNQUIST delivered the opinion of the Court.

Petitioner Kathy Keeton sued respondent Hustler Magazine, Inc., and other defendants in the United States District Court for the District of New Hampshire, alleging jurisdiction over her libel complaint by reason of diversity of citizenship. The district court dismissed her suit because it believed that the Due Process Clause of the Fourteenth Amendment to the United States Constitution forbade the application of New Hampshire's long-arm statute in order to acquire personal jurisdiction over respondent. The Court of Appeals for the First Circuit affirmed, 682 F.2d 33 (CA1 1982), summarizing its concerns with the statement that "the New Hampshire tail is too small to wag so large an out-of-state dog." *Id.,* at 36. We granted certiorari, and we now reverse.

Petitioner Keeton is a resident of New York. Her only connection with New Hampshire is the circulation there of copies of a magazine that she assists in producing. The magazine bears petitioner's name in several places crediting her with editorial and other work. Respondent Hustler Magazine, Inc., is an Ohio corporation, with its principal place of business in California. Respondent's contacts with New Hampshire consist of the sale of some 10 to 15,000 copies of *Hustler* magazine in that State each month. Petitioner claims to have been libeled in five separate issues of respondent's magazine published between September, 1975, and May, 1976.[1]

The Court of Appeals, in its opinion affirming the District Court's dismissal of petitioner's complaint, held that petitioner's lack of contacts with New Hampshire rendered the State's interest in redressing the tort of libel to petitioner too attenuated for an assertion of personal jurisdiction over respondent. The Court of Appeals observed that the "single publication rule" ordinarily applicable in multistate libel cases would require it to award petitioner "damages caused in *all* states" should she prevail in her suit, even though the bulk of petitioner's alleged injuries had been sustained outside New Hampshire. 682 F.2d, at 35.[2] The court also stressed New Hampshire's unusually long (6-year) limitations period for libel actions. New Hampshire was the only State where petitioner's suit would not have been time-barred when it was filed. Under these circumstances, the Court of Appeals concluded that it would be "unfair" to assert jurisdiction over respondent. New Hampshire has a minimal interest in applying its unusual statute of limitations to, and awarding damages for, injuries to a nonresident occurring outside the State, particularly since petitioner suffered such a small proportion of her total claimed injury within the State. *Id.,* at 35–36.

---

[1] Initially, petitioner brought suit for libel and invasion of privacy in Ohio, where the magazine was published. Her libel claim, however, was dismissed as barred by the Ohio statute of limitations, and her invasion of privacy claim was dismissed as barred by the New York statute of limitations, which the Ohio court considered to be "migratory." Petitioner then filed the present action in October, 1980.

[2] The "single publication rule" has been summarized as follows:

As to any single publication, (a) only one action for damages can be maintained; (b) all damages suffered in all jurisdictions can be recovered in the one action; and (c) a judgment for or against the plaintiff upon the merits of any action for damages bars any other action for damages between the same parties in all jurisdictions.

Restatement (Second) of Torts § 577A(4) (1977).

We conclude that the Court of Appeals erred when it affirmed the dismissal of petitioner's suit for lack of personal jurisdiction. Respondent's regular circulation of magazines in the forum State is sufficient to support an assertion of jurisdiction in a libel action based on the contents of the magazine. This is so even if New Hampshire courts, and thus the District Court under *Klaxon Co. v. Stentor Co.,* , would apply the so-called "single publication rule" to enable petitioner to recover in the New Hampshire action her damages from "publications" of the alleged libel throughout the United States.[3]

The district court found that "[t]he general course of conduct in circulating magazines throughout the state was purposefully directed at New Hampshire, and inevitably affected persons in the state." Pet., at 5a. Such regular monthly sales of thousands of magazines cannot by any stretch of the imagination be characterized as random, isolated, or fortuitous. It is, therefore, unquestionable that New Hampshire jurisdiction over a complaint based on those contacts would ordinarily satisfy the requirement of the Due Process Clause that a State's assertion of personal jurisdiction over a nonresident defendant be predicated on "minimum contacts" between the defendant and the State. See *World-Wide Volkswagen Corp. v. Woodson,*; *International Shoe Corp. v. Washington.* And, as the Court of Appeals acknowledged, New Hampshire has adopted a "long-arm" statute authorizing service of process on nonresident corporations whenever permitted by the Due Process Clause. 682 F.2d, at 33.[4] Thus, all the requisites for personal jurisdiction over Hustler Magazine, Inc., in New Hampshire are present.

We think that the three concerns advanced by the Court of Appeals, whether considered singly or together, are not sufficiently weighty to merit a different result. The "single publication rule," New Hampshire's unusually long statute of limitations, and plaintiff's lack of contacts with the forum State do not defeat jurisdiction otherwise proper under both New Hampshire law and the Due Process Clause.

In judging minimum contacts, a court properly focuses on "the relationship among the defendant, the forum, and the litigation." *Shaffer v. Heitner,* [at p. 586, *infra*]. See also *Rush v. Savchuk,* [p. 607, *infra*]. Thus, it is certainly relevant to the jurisdictional inquiry that petitioner is *seeking* to recover damages suffered in all States in this one suit. The contacts between respondent and the forum must be judged in the light of that claim, rather than a claim only for damages sustained in New Hampshire. That is, the contacts between respondent and New Hampshire must be such that it is "fair" to compel respondent to defend a multistate lawsuit in New Hampshire seeking nationwide damages for all copies of the five issues in question, even though only a small portion of those copies were distributed in New Hampshire.

---

[3] "It is the general rule that each communication of the same defamatory matter by the same defamer, whether to a new person or to the same person, is a separate and distinct publication, for which a separate cause of action arises." *Restatement (Second) of Torts* § 577A, Comment a (1971). The "single publication rule" is an exception to this general rule.

[4] Section 300:14 of the New Hampshire Revised Statutes Annotated (N.H.R.S.A.) provides in relevant part:

If a foreign corporation . . . commits a tort in whole or in part in New Hampshire, such act[] shall be deemed to be doing business in New Hampshire by such foreign corporation and shall be deemed equivalent to the appointment by such foreign corporation of the secretary of the state of New Hampshire and his successors to be its true and lawful attorney upon whom may be served all lawful process in any actions or proceedings against such foreign corporation arising from or growing out of such . . . tort.

This statute has been construed in the New Hampshire courts to extend jurisdiction over nonresident corporations to the fullest extent permitted under the federal constitution. See, e.g., *Roy v. North American Newspaper Alliance, Inc.,* 106 N.H. 92 (1964).

The Court of Appeals expressed the view that New Hampshire's "interest" in asserting jurisdiction over plaintiff's multistate claim was minimal. We agree that the "fairness" of haling respondent into a New Hampshire court depends to some extent on whether respondent's activities relating to New Hampshire are such as to give that State a legitimate interest in holding respondent answerable on a claim related to those activities. See *World-Wide Volkswagen Corp. v. Woodson, McGee v. International Life Insurance Co.* But insofar as the State's "interest" in adjudicating the dispute is a part of the Fourteenth Amendment due process equation, as a surrogate for some of the factors already mentioned, see *Insurance Corp. v. Compagnie des Bauxites,* [p. 553, note f, *infra*], we think the interest is sufficient.

The Court of Appeals acknowledged that petitioner was suing, at least in part, for damages suffered in New Hampshire. And it is beyond dispute that New Hampshire has a significant interest in redressing injuries that actually occur within the State.

> 'A state has an especial interest in exercising judicial jurisdiction over those who commit torts within its territory. This is because torts involve wrongful conduct which a state seeks to deter, and against which it attempts to afford protection, by providing that a tortfeasor shall be liable for damages which are the proximate result of his tort.'

Leeper v. Leeper, 114 N.H. 294, 298 (1974) (quoting *Restatement (Second) of Conflict of Laws* § 36, Comment c (1971)).

This interest extends to libel actions brought by nonresidents. False statements of fact harm both the subject of the falsehood *and* the readers of the statement. New Hampshire may rightly employ its libel laws to discourage the deception of its citizens. There is "no constitutional value in false statements of fact." *Gertz v. Robert Welch, Inc.,* 418 U.S. 323 (1974).

New Hampshire may also extend its concern to the injury that in-state libel causes within New Hampshire to a nonresident. The tort of libel is generally held to occur wherever the offending material is circulated. *Restatement (Second) of Torts* § 577A, Comment a (1977). The reputation of the libel victim may suffer harm even in a state in which he has hitherto been anonymous.[5] The communication of the libel may create a negative reputation among the residents of a jurisdiction where the plaintiff's previous reputation was, however small, at least unblemished.

New Hampshire has clearly expressed its interest in protecting such persons from libel, as well as in safeguarding its populace from falsehoods. Its criminal defamation statute bears no restriction to libels of which residents are the victim.[6] Moreover, in 1971 New Hampshire specifically deleted from its long-arm statute the requirement that a tort be committed "against a resident of New Hampshire."[7]

New Hampshire also has a substantial interest in cooperating with other States, through the "single publication rule," to provide a forum for efficiently litigating all issues and damage claims arising out of a libel in a unitary proceeding.[8] This rule reduces the potential serious drain of

---

[5] We do not, therefore, rely for our holding on the fact that petitioner's name appears in fine print in several places in a magazine circulating in New Hampshire.

[6] N.H.R.S.A. § 644:11(I) makes it a misdemeanor for anyone to "purposely communicate[] to *any person,* orally or in writing, any information which he knows to be false and knows will tend to expose any other living person to public hatred, contempt or ridicule." (Emphasis added.).

[7] See N.H.R.S.A. § 300:14, History.

[8] The great majority of the States now follow the "single publication rule." *Restatement (Second) of Torts* § 577A, Reporter's Note.

libel cases on judicial resources. It also serves to protect defendants from harassment resulting from multiple suits. *Restatement (Second) of Torts* § 577A, Comment *f* (1977). In sum, the combination of New Hampshire's interest in redressing injuries that occur within the State and its interest in cooperating with other States in the application of the "single publication rule" demonstrate the propriety of requiring respondent to answer to a multistate libel action in New Hampshire.[9]

The Court of Appeals also thought that there was an element of due process "unfairness" arising from the fact that the statutes of limitations in every jurisdiction except New Hampshire had run on the plaintiff's claim in this case.[10] Strictly speaking, however, any potential unfairness in applying New Hampshire's statute of limitations to all aspects of this nationwide suit has nothing to do with the jurisdiction of the Court to adjudicate the claims. "The issue is personal jurisdiction, not choice of law." *Hanson v. Denckla,* [p. 505 *supra*]). The question of the applicability of New Hampshire's statute of limitations to claims for out-of-state damages presents itself in the course of litigation only after jurisdiction over respondent is established, and we do not think that such choice of law concerns should complicate or distort the jurisdictional inquiry.

The chance duration of statutes of limitations in nonforum jurisdictions has nothing to do with the contacts among respondent, New Hampshire, and this multistate libel action. Whether Ohio's limitations period is six months or six years does not alter the jurisdictional calculus in New Hampshire. Petitioner's successful search for a State with a lengthy statute of limitations is no different from the litigation strategy of countless plaintiffs who seek a forum with favorable substantive or procedural rules or sympathetic local populations. Certainly Hustler Magazine, Inc., which chose to enter the New Hampshire market, can be charged with knowledge of its laws and no doubt would have claimed the benefit of them if it had a complaint against a subscriber, distributor, or other commercial partner.

Finally, implicit in the Court of Appeals' analysis of New Hampshire's interest is an emphasis on the extremely limited contacts of the *plaintiff* with New Hampshire. But we have not to date required a plaintiff to have "minimum contacts" with the forum State before permitting that State to assert personal jurisdiction over a nonresident defendant. On the contrary, we have upheld the assertion of jurisdiction where such contacts were entirely lacking. In *Perkins v. Benguet Mining Co.,* 342 U.S. 437 (1952), none of the parties was a resident of the forum State; indeed, neither the plaintiff nor the subject-matter of his action had any relation to that State. Jurisdiction was based solely on the fact that the defendant corporation had been carrying on in the forum

---

[9] Of course, to conclude that petitioner may properly *seek* multistate damages in this New Hampshire suit is not to conclude that such damages should, in fact, be awarded if petitioner makes out her case for libel. The actual applicability of the "single publication rule" in the peculiar circumstances of this case is a matter of substantive law, not personal jurisdiction. We conclude only that the district court has jurisdiction to *entertain* petitioner's multistate libel suit.

[10] Under traditional choice of law principles, the law of the forum State governs on matters of procedure. See *Restatement (Second) of Conflict of Laws* § 122 (1971). In New Hampshire, statutes of limitations are considered procedural. *Gordon v. Gordon,* 118 N.H. 356, 360 (1978); *Barrett v. Boston & Maine R.R.,* 104 N.H. 70 (1962). There has been considerable academic criticism of the rule that permits a forum State to apply its own statute of limitations regardless of the significance of contacts between the forum State and the litigation. See, e.g., Weintraub, *Commentary on the Conflict of Laws* § 9.2B at 517 (2d ed. 1980); Martin, *Constitutional Limitations on Choice of Law,* 61 Cornell L.Rev. 185, 221 (1976); Lorenzen, *The State of Limitations and The Conflict of Laws,* 28 Yale L.J. 492, 496–497 (1919). But we find it unnecessary to express an opinion at this time as to whether any arguable unfairness rises to the level of a due process violation.

"a continuous and systematic, but limited, part of its general business." *Id.*, at 438. In the instant case, respondent's activities in the forum may not be so substantial as to support jurisdiction over a cause of action unrelated to those activities.[11] But respondent is carrying on a "part of its general business" in New Hampshire, and that is sufficient to support jurisdiction when the cause of action arises out of the very activity being conducted, in part, in New Hampshire.

The plaintiff's residence is not, of course, completely irrelevant to the jurisdictional inquiry. As noted, that inquiry focuses on the relations among the defendant, the forum and the litigation. Plaintiff's residence may well play an important role in determining the propriety of entertaining a suit against the defendant in the forum. That is, plaintiff's residence in the forum may, because of defendant's relationship with the plaintiff, enhance defendant's contacts with the forum. Plaintiff's residence may be the focus of the activities of the defendant out of which the suit arises. See *Calder v. Jones; McGee v. International Life Ins. Co.* . But plaintiff's residence in the forum State is not a separate requirement, and lack of residence will not defeat jurisdiction established on the basis of defendant's contacts.

It is undoubtedly true that the bulk of the harm done to petitioner occurred outside New Hampshire. But that will be true in almost every libel action brought somewhere other than the plaintiff's domicile. There is no justification for restricting libel actions to the plaintiff's home forum.[12] The victim of a libel, like the victim of any other tort, may choose to bring suit in any forum with which the defendant has "certain minimum contacts . . . such that the maintenance of the suit does not offend 'traditional notions of fair play and substantial justice.' *Milliken v. Meyer,* 311 U.S. 457." *International Shoe Co. v. Washington,* 326 U.S. 310, 316 (1945).

Where, as in this case, respondent Hustler Magazine, Inc., has continuously and deliberately exploited the New Hampshire market, it must reasonably anticipate being haled into court there in a libel action based on the contents of its magazine. *World-Wide Volkswagen Corp. v. Woodson,* 444 U.S. 286, 297–298 (1980). And, since respondent can be charged with knowledge of the "single publication rule," it must anticipate that such a suit will seek nationwide damages. Respondent produces a national publication aimed at a nationwide audience. There is no unfairness in calling it to answer for the contents of that publication wherever a substantial number of copies are regularly sold and distributed.

The judgment of the Court of Appeals is reversed[13] and the cause is remanded for proceedings consistent with this opinion.

---

[11] The defendant corporation's contacts with the forum State in *Perkins* were more substantial than those of respondent with New Hampshire in this case. In *Perkins,* the corporation's mining operations, located in the Philippine Islands, were completely halted during the Japanese occupation. The president, who was also general manager and principal stockholder of the company, returned to his home in Ohio where he carried on "a continuous and systematic supervision of the necessarily limited wartime activities of the company." 342 U.S., at 448, 72 S.Ct., at 419. The company's files were kept in Ohio, several directors' meetings were held there, substantial accounts were maintained in Ohio banks, and all key business decisions were made in the State. *Ibid.* In those circumstances, Ohio was the corporation's principal, if temporary, place of business so that Ohio jurisdiction was proper even over a cause of action unrelated to the activities in the State.

[12] As noted in *Calder v. Jones,* 465 U.S. 783, at 790-791; we reject categorically the suggestion that invisible radiations from the First Amendment may defeat jurisdiction otherwise proper under the Due Process Clause.

[13] In addition to Hustler Magazine, Inc., Larry Flynt, the publisher, editor and owner of the magazine, and L.F.P., Inc., Hustler's holding company, were named as defendants in the District Court. It does not of course follow from the fact that jurisdiction may be asserted over Hustler Magazine, Inc., that jurisdiction may also be asserted over either

It is so ordered.

JUSTICE BRENNAN, concurring in the judgment.

I agree with the Court that "[r]espondent's regular circulation of magazines in the forum State is sufficient to support an assertion of jurisdiction in a libel action based on the contents of the magazine." These contacts between the respondent and the forum State are sufficiently important and sufficiently related to the underlying cause of action to foreclose any concern that the constitutional limits of the Due Process Clause are being violated. This is so, moreover, irrespective of the state's interest in enforcing its substantive libel laws or its unique statute of limitations. Indeed, as we recently explained in *Insurance Corp. v. Compagnie des Bauxites*, [p. 553 n. f., *infra*], these interests of the State should be relevant only to the extent that they bear upon the liberty interests of the respondent that are protected by the Fourteenth Amendment. "The restriction on state sovereign power described in *World-Wide Volkswagen Corp.* must be seen as ultimately a function of the individual liberty interest preserved by the Due Process Clause. That Clause is the only source of the personal jurisdiction requirement and the Clause itself makes no mention of federalism concerns." *Id.*, at 702–703 n. 10.

NOTES AND QUESTIONS

(1)(a) The accident of the Robinson family on the side of Interstate 44 in Oklahoma was real enough. The law suit as it reached the United States Supreme Court had a hidden agenda, which puzzled Justice Blackmun (p. 545) and is not apparent from reading the Court's opinion. For one thing, why would a plaintiff alleging a design defect—the gasoline tank too exposed to a rear-end impact—insist on bringing suit against the local dealer and the regional distributor, who obviously had nothing to do with the design of the car? Answer: plaintiffs wanted to remain in the District Court for Creek County, Oklahoma, rather than to try the case as a diversity action in federal court in Tulsa. The problem was that the Robinsons, though they were moving away from New York state, had not yet reached their destination in Oklahoma, and thus remained domiciliaries/citizens of New York.[a] If only the manufacturer, Audi-NSU Auto Union of Germany and the importer, Volkswagen of America, a New Jersey corporation, were defendants, the case could easily be removed to federal court;[b] with the two New York corporations—Seaway, the dealer, and World-Wide, the distributor—as parties, there would not be complete diversity[c] and the case would have to remain in Creek County.

---

of the other defendants. In *Calder v. Jones*, [465 U.S. 783 at 790], we today reject the suggestion that employees who act in their official capacity are somehow shielded from suit in their individual capacity. But jurisdiction over an employee does not automatically follow from jurisdiction over the corporation which employs him; nor does jurisdiction over a parent corporation automatically establish jurisdiction over a wholly owned subsidiary. *Consol. Textile Co. v. Gregory*, 289 U.S. 85, 88 (1933); *Peterson v. Chicago, R.I. & P. Railway Co.*, 205 U.S. 364, 391 (1907). Each defendant's contacts with the forum State must be assessed individually. See *Rush v. Savchuk*, 444 U.S. 320, 332 (1980) ("The requirements of *International Shoe* . . . must be met as to each defendant over whom a state court exercises jurisdiction.") Because the Court of Appeals concluded that jurisdiction could not be had even against Hustler Magazine, Inc., it did not inquire into the propriety of jurisdiction over the other defendants. Such inquiry is, of course, open upon remand.

[a] Recall *White v. Tennant* and *Estate of Jones*, Chapter 1, § 1.03[B], *supra*.

[b] See 28 U.S.C. § 1441, Documents Supplement, p. 13.

[c] See *Strawbridge v. Curtiss*, 7 U.S. (3 Cranch) 267 (1806).

(b) On the other side, were Seaway and World-Wide really inconvenienced—"haled into court," as Justice White put it—a continent away from their habitual surroundings? Yes, in some theoretical sense as the Supreme Court spun it out—they probably did not contemplate the chances of the Audi sold in Massena, N.Y. winding up in a wreck in Oklahoma; despite its name, World-Wide was not one step greater than Allstate Insurance Company. In fact, however, all the litigation costs were carried by Volkswagen of North America and its German principals, and the lawsuit was controlled throughout by Volkswagen's New York counsel. The principal defendants wanted removal to federal courts as badly as plaintiffs wanted to avoid it. If these motives had been made fully evident to the Supreme Court, would it change anyone's mind—assuming, that is, that certiorari had been granted and would not be reversed?

(c) In the end, the forum shopping calculations of both sides proved accurate. Once the Supreme Court decided that World-Wide and Seaway could not be sued in Oklahoma, the principal defendants (who had made a desultory motion to challenge jurisdiction in the lower Oklahoma court but had not pursued it even to the Oklahoma Supreme Court) removed the case to the U.S. Court for the Northern District of Oklahoma. Following discovery under the federal rules, the case was tried to a jury, which in January 1982 returned a verdict for defendants. Apparently, the jury believed that plaintiff's serious injuries were the result of the excessive speed (90–100 m.p.h.) of the car that struck the parked Audi, and not to defects in the design or manufacture of the car or its fuel tank.[d]

(2)(a) The preceding note may provide local color, and perhaps raise doubts about the wisdom of the Supreme Court in having accepted the *World-Wide* case for review. It does not, however, detract from the importance of the case as setting forth the Court's views both on the limits, and on the rationale, for in personam jurisdiction in the United States. What is the rationale?

(b) Conflict of laws, evidently, does not lend itself to multiple-choice questions. Just this once, however, try to complete the following sentence:

> The U.S. Supreme Court, as shown in World-Wide Volkswagen, believes the limits of state court jurisdiction are based on:
>
> (i) fair play and substantial justice;
>
> (ii) sovereignty;
>
> (iii) reasonable expectation of the parties;
>
> (iv) the burdens on the defendant;
>
> (v) fairness to both plaintiff and defendant;
>
> (vi) other;
>
> (vii) none of the above.

Now try the same game with respect to the beliefs of Justice Brennan.

(3)(a) Justice White writes that the Due Process clause requires "minimum contacts" between a nonresident defendant and the forum state in order to sustain jurisdiction. He justifies that statement by reciting two "related but distinguishable functions": protection of the defendant against the burdens of litigating in a distant or inconvenient forum; and restraint on the States

---

[d] Most of the information in this note comes from communications with counsel in the case; see also Russell J. Weintraub, *Due Process Limitations on the Personal Jurisdiction of State Courts: Time for Change,* 63 Ore. L. Rev. 485, 500, n. 98 (1984).

lest they reach out beyond their limited sovereignty in a federal system. Taking the second point first, does it suggest (i) that federal courts might reach out beyond the limits imposed on state courts; or (ii) that if the defendant were not a resident of another state of the United States, for example, if Mr. and Mrs. Robinson had bought their car just across the St. Lawrence River from Massena, N.Y., in Cornwall, Ontario, the restraint would not apply?

(b) If neither of the preceding inferences from the emphasis on state sovereignty is plausible, what do you think Justice White does have in mind?

(c) Note that the question of state sovereignty is not, in Justice White's universe, a rhetorical point. Fairness to defendants might be met by the various "even if's" on p. 535. Even so, he says, "the Due Process Clause, acting as an instrument of interstate federalism, may sometimes act to divest the State of its power to render a valid judgment." Why?

(d) Professor Weintraub, in commenting on *World-Wide Volkswagen,* writes:

> This notion that basic concepts of federalism prevent exercise of state court jurisdiction across state boundaries is the major obstacle to removal of the "minimum contacts" requirement. Federalism as a limit on state court jurisdiction may have made sense in the days of *Pennoyer v. Neff,* when exercise of jurisdiction was thought to turn on physical power over the defendant. A sister state might have objected to this exercise of power within her territory. Now, however, this federalism appendage to due process is misplaced. . . . The time has come to remove the federalism cloud from due process limitations on state court jurisdiction so that the "minimum contacts" requirement can be examined in the clear light of fairness to the defendant.[e]

Do you agree? Without the federalism/sovereignty point (not to say "cloud"), do you think *World-Wide Volkswagen* would have come out as it did?[f]

(e) Justice White (at p. 535) makes fun of the arguments concerning foreseeability. It was foreseeable, he "concedes," that Mrs. Donner would one day move to Florida, or that Mrs. Kulko, the divorced wife of a New York domiciliary,[g] would move to California. As to goods, every seller of chattels would in effect make the chattel his agent for service of process. But is there not more to foreseeability than that? It was, for instance, foreseeable in *Allstate Insurance Co. v. Hague*[h] that an insurance policy issued on a vehicle registered in Wisconsin could be the object

---

[e] Weintraub, Note d, *supra,* 63 Ore. L. Rev. at 503.

[f] In *Insurance Corporation of Ireland, Ltd. v. Compagnie des Bauxites de Guinée,* 456 U.S. 694 (1982), a case involving the authority of a court to order discovery of documents designed to aid in determining whether defendant had done sufficient business in the state to be subject to the court's jurisdiction, and, when the defendant failed to comply with discovery orders, to make a finding of jurisdiction as a sanction under Fed. R. Civ. P. 37(b)(2)(A), Justice White, writing for the Court, took back some of the statements in *World-Wide Volkswagen:*

> The personal jurisdiction requirement [of the Due Process Clause] recognizes and protects an individual liberty interest. It represents a restriction on judicial power not as a matter of sovereignty, but as a matter of individual liberty.

456 U.S. at 702.

And in a footnote to this passage, Justice White added:

> [The Due Process] clause is the only source of the personal jurisdiction requirement and the clause itself makes no mention of federalism concerns. Furthermore, if the federalism concept operated as an independent restriction on the sovereign power of the court, it would not be possible to waive the personal jurisdiction requirement.

Id. at 703 n. 10.

[g] See question 5, *infra.*

[h] Chapter 5, § 5.03.

of a suit in Minnesota, but perhaps not in Hawaii; or in *Gray v. American Radiator*[i] that a valve made in Ohio and installed in a water heater in Pennsylvania for nationwide distribution would find its way to a home in Illinois, but not in Greece. Why isn't foreseeability an important ingredient of reasonableness? Or is Justice White rejecting reasonableness as the overall principle for judicial jurisdiction?

(f) Plaintiffs sought to distinguish sale of an automobile from sale of other products, an argument that convinced the dissenters but not the majority. Isn't the expectation of a seller of a car different from that of a seller of a house or a grand piano? Or is this a sterile line of reasoning, forcing one ultimately to distinguish between an automobile and a bicycle, then between a bicycle and a tricycle, and finally between a toy sold in an airport gift shop as compared with the same toy sold in a suburban shopping center?

(g) Massena, N.Y., where the Audi was purchased, is in the Northwest corner of New York, about 20 miles from Ontario and Quebec, 100 miles from Vermont, and 200 miles from Pennsylvania, Massachusetts, and other neighboring states. If suit had been brought in any of those states, would the outcome have been different, because a crash in one of those states would be within the foreseeability that is not "wholly irrelevant," to use Justice White's words?

(4)(a) Justice Brennan, dissenting in *World-Wide Volkswagen,* thinks the majority accords too little weight to the strength of the forum state's interest in this case. He would weigh that interest against actual inconvenience to defendant. Is this putting choice of law against jurisdiction? Or is it just acknowledging what the court keeps denying, that the two issues turn on similar (if not identical) considerations?

(b) Justice Brennan says (p. 538) "*International Shoe* contemplated that the significance of the contacts necessary to support jurisdiction would diminish if some other consideration helped to establish that jurisdiction would be fair and reasonable." State interest, he suggests is such a counter-consideration; also, the less the burden on defendant, the fewer significant contacts should be required. Justice Brennan would look also at the burden of transporting witnesses or evidence, and at possible hardship to defendant. Is Justice Brennan arguing for discretionary jurisdiction, as in England under Order 11?[j]

(c) Suppose the facts of the case are altered slightly: six months after the Robinsons bought their car from Seaway, they brought it back to the dealer complaining of a rattle in the rear end. Seaway said the braces holding the fuel tank needed tightening, and that he had performed the necessary repair. Following the crash in Oklahoma, the damaged car was towed to Bill's Service Station, and plaintiffs offer to prove by testimony from Bill that the fire broke out because the braces holding the fuel tank were improperly mounted. Thus (i) the dealer is now an important party in the action; and (ii) a principal witness resides in Oklahoma, and might not testify in Massena, N.Y. Would this be a stronger case for Justice Brennan's view? Would it change Justice White's view?

(d) The most interesting portion of Justice Brennan's opinion is his suggestion that even if the case at bar is near the limits of permissible jurisdiction under *International Shoe,* that case may itself be outdated. Like Judge Friendly in *Buckley* and Justice Goodwin in *White Lumber,*[k] he questions the preference for defendant in the traditional approach to jurisdiction of courts.

---

[i] See p. 520, *supra.*

[j] See p. 496, note y, *supra.*

[k] p. 527, *supra.*

He denies that under his view all limits on personal jurisdiction would disappear. Suppose Justice Brennan had been able to persuade a majority of the Court to go along with his view of *World-Wide Volkswagen*. Draft the operative paragraph of the opinion of Justice Brennan for the Court affirming the decision of the Supreme Court of Oklahoma.

(5)(a) Both the majority and the dissent refer to *Kulko v. Superior Court of California,* 436 U.S. 84 (1978). In that case, a husband and wife had lived in New York for about ten years, and had two children; thereafter they separated pursuant to a New York separation agreement, incorporated into a Haitian divorce.[l] The agreement provided that the husband pay the wife $3000 per year in child support for the periods when the children were with her. The wife moved to California soon after the divorce and remarried. The children spent the school year in New York with their father, and vacation periods in California with the mother. Just before she was to leave for California for a vacation, the daughter told her father that she wanted to remain in California with her mother. The father bought her a one-way plane ticket, and the daughter left. Subsequently the son also moved to California, without knowledge of the father. Thereafter the wife brought suit in California, seeking full custody of the children and increased child support payments from the ex-husband. The husband moved to dismiss the action on the ground that he lacked minimum contacts with California for purposes of in personam jurisdiction. The California courts upheld the suit, holding that exercise of jurisdiction was reasonable because the father had "purposely availed himself of the benefits and protections of the laws of California" by sending his daughter to live with her mother in San Francisco.

If the effort to fit the father's conduct into the language of *Hanson v. Denckla* is strained, is the overall conclusion farfetched that a mother seeking custody of her children and the money to pay for their upkeep may bring suit at her domicile? More of this in Chapter 9.

(b) The U.S. Supreme Court reversed the California Supreme Court, and held there was no jurisdiction over the husband in these circumstances:[m]

> We cannot accept the proposition that appellant's acquiescence in [the daughter's] desire to live with her mother conferred jurisdiction over appellant in the California courts in this action. A father who agrees, in the interests of family harmony and his children's preferences, to allow them to spend more time in California than was required under a separation agreement can hardly be said to have "purposefully availed himself" of the "benefits and protections" of California's laws. . . .[n]

Justice Brennan dissented, saying that in his view the husband's connection with California was "not too attenuated under the standards of reasonableness and fairness implicit in the Due Process Clause, to require him to conduct his defense in the California courts."[o]

(c) Justice Marshall, who wrote for the Court in *Kulko,* distinguished that case in his dissent in *World-Wide Volkswagen,* by noting that *Kulko* involved individuals in a personal dispute whereas *World-Wide,* from defendant's perspective, involved a commercial activity. Is that a

---

[l] For an explanation of this arrangement, see Chapter 9, § 9.02[B].

[m] The father did not challenge the jurisdiction of the California courts to modify the custody arrangements. For a different view of this issue in the years following the *Kulko* case, see Chapter 9, § 9.03[1], *infra.*

[n] 436 U.S. at 94. Interestingly enough, Justice Marshall, who dissented in *World-Wide Volkswagen,* wrote the opinion in *Kulko;* Justice White, who wrote the Court's opinion in *World-Wide Volkswagen,* joined Justice Brennan's dissent in *Kulko.*

[o] *Id.* at 102 (Brennan, J. dissenting).

sound basis for distinction? Note that the European Convention on Jurisdiction and the Enforcement of Judgments, discussed in § 7.06, draws distinctions along these lines, for instance by special provisions for consumer contracts and insurance claims, as well as for jurisdiction at the place where the maintenance creditor (i.e., a person entitled to alimony or child support) is domiciled or habitually resides.[p]

(6)(a) Turning to *Keeton v. Hustler Magazine, Inc.,* the Supreme Court rejects the argument, which had been persuasive to the Court of Appeals, that it would be unfair to permit New Hampshire courts to hear the action because that state's period of limitations was the only one that had not expired at the time the suit was filed. In fact, as we know, plaintiff had tried to sue in Ohio, the place of incorporation of the magazine, and had failed because of that state's statute of limitations. Justice Rehnquist writes:

> The question of the applicability of New Hampshire's statute of limitations to claims for out-of-state damages presents itself in the course of litigation only after jurisdiction over respondent is established, and we do not think such choice of law concerns should complicate or distort the jurisdictional inquiry.

Is that persuasive? Could defendant argue on remand that the New Hampshire action should be dismissed, on the ground that the statute of limitations of some other state should be applied?[q] Which state? Ohio? New York? California?

(b) What about the question of damages? Is Ms. Keeton entitled only to the damages to her reputation in New Hampshire? Or is Justice Rehnquist saying, in footnote 9, that whatever the district court decides, the U.S. Supreme Court will stay out of it?

(c) Is Justice Rehnquist, by the combination of permissiveness on choice of law and exclusion of choice-of-law considerations from the jurisdictional questions, telling American lawyers to forum shop as much as they please?

(7) (a) Following the decision of the Supreme Court, the Keeton case was tried before a jury in federal district court in New Hampshire. The jury awarded $2 million to Ms. Keeton, representing harm suffered both inside and outside New Hampshire. Does that make sense, considering that New Hampshire was the only state where she could sue, and that Ms. Keeton's reputation was clearly centered elsewhere? Is this question one of tort law, choice of law, or constitutional law?

(b) The Court of Appeals for the First Circuit, hearing the case for the second time, treated the question as one of substantive law or choice of law, both matters to be decided in a diversity suit according to New Hampshire law. The Court of Appeals was unsure whether New Hampshire followed the "single publication" rule (p. 546 note 2 *supra*), and it had doubts about the applicability of the New Hampshire statute of limitations in the light of *Allstate Insurance Co.*

---

[p] European Convention, Articles 13, 8–12, and 5(2), Documents Supplement, pp. 100–104.

[q] The original action was brought in Ohio, for libel and invasion of privacy, consisting of a cartoon published in Hustler magazine in May 1976, showing Ms. Keeton, an editor of rival Penthouse magazine, with her friend, the publisher of Penthouse, and an obscene caption suggesting that she had infected him with a venereal disease. The Ohio county court dismissed the libel action as barred under Ohio's one-year statute of limitations. Ms. Keeton did not appeal dismissal of the libel action, believing she could recover substantially the same damages under the privacy count. Subsequently the Ohio court dismissed the latter claim as barred under the New York statute of limitations. This time Ms. Keeton appealed, and as soon as the dismissal in Ohio was affirmed, she filed the action in New Hampshire which led to the Supreme Court case.

v. Hague and *Phillips Petroleum v. Shutts,* Ch. 5 *supra.* Accordingly, the Court of Appeals certified two questions to the New Hampshire Supreme Court:

1. Does New Hampshire follow an interstate single publication rule in libel cases?

2. If so, does New Hampshire permit a plaintiff to recover for distribution of a libel in jurisdictions whose own statutes of limitations would bar recovery, where neither party is a New Hampshire Resident, where the only factual connection with New Hampshire is the distribution there of one percent or less of the total circulation of the material, and where the relevant statute of limitations has expired in every jurisdiction but New Hampshire?[r]

(c) The New Hampshire Supreme Court answered both questions in the affirmative.[s] New Hampshire does follow the single publication rule, and it would apply its own statute of limitations. *Sun Oil Co. v. Wortman,* Chapter 5, p. 422, *supra,* which had been decided in the interval, confirmed that there was no constitutional impediment to application of the forum state's statute of limitations, and the court held that the varied purposes that statutes of limitations are meant to serve justify application of forum law.[t] Judge Souter (as he then was) dissented, arguing that New Hampshire had no genuine interest in the enforcement of its statute of limitations, and calling the majority's characterization of the statute of limitations as procedural as "unsupportably mechanistic."[u]

(d) Coming back to the question of judicial jurisdiction, notice that the New York long-arm statute, in contrast to the New Hampshire statute, expressly excludes actions for defamation.[v] In light of the *Keeton* case, do you think New York was wise in this respect?[w]

(8)(a) Justice Brennan finally got the chance to write for the Court in a jurisdiction case, *Burger King Corporation v. Rudzewicz,* 471 U.S. 462 (1985). The case involved a dispute between Burger King, a Florida corporation, and a citizen of Michigan who had operated a Burger King fast-food restaurant in the Detroit area under a franchise. Burger King terminated the franchise for failure to make agreed payments, and when the franchisee failed to vacate the premises and return the keys, Burger King brought suit in federal district court in Florida. The district court sustained jurisdiction under Florida's long-arm statute, which extends jurisdiction to "[a]ny person, whether or not a citizen or resident of this state," who, inter alia, "[b]reach[es] a contract in this state by failing to perform acts required by the contract to be performed in this state," so long as the cause of action arises from the alleged contractual breach. The Court of Appeals reversed, saying "the circumstances of the Drayton Plains franchise and the negotiations which led to it left Rudzewicz bereft of reasonable notice and financially unprepared for the prospect of franchise

---

[r] *Keeton v. Hustler Magazine, Inc.,* 828 F.2d 64 (1st Cir. 1987).

[s] *Keeton v. Hustler Magazine, Inc.,* 131 N.H. 6, 549 A.2d 1187 (1988).

[t] 131 N.H. at 14, 549 A.2d at 1192.

[u] 131 N.H. at 25, 33, 549 A.2d at 1199, 1203.

[v] N.Y. C.P.L.R. § 302(a)(2), Documents Supplement, p. 77. Connecticut and Georgia have similar exclusions in their tort long-arm statutes.

[w] In a companion case to *Keeton v. Hustler,* the Supreme Court upheld jurisdiction of a California court in a libel action brought by a well known actress against the Enquirer newspaper, which did business in California, and also against the author and editor of the offending article, who asserted that the article had been written and edited in Florida and that they had no contacts with California. *Calder v. Jones,* 465 U.S. 783 (1984). The defendants argued that suit in California in these circumstances would have a chilling effect upon reporters and editors. The Court rejected the argument: "[T]he potential chill on protected First Amendment activity stemming from libel and defamation actions is already taken into account in the constitutional limitations on the substantive law governing such suits. . . . To reintroduce those concerns at the jurisdictional stage would be a form of double counting." 465 U.S. at 790.

litigation in Florida," and that "[j]urisdiction under these circumstances would offend the fundamental fairness which is the touchstone of due process."

The Supreme Court reversed the Court of Appeals, and reinstated the judgment of the district court. Reviewing the Supreme Court's decisions on jurisdiction since *International Shoe,* Justice Brennan wrote ". . . the constitutional touchstone remains whether the defendant purposefully established 'minimum contacts' in the forum State." Here, the franchisees had done so by signing a contract that provided for a 20-year relationship with an enterprise based primarily in Florida, which called for continuous supervision by headquarters in Florida and could "in no sense be viewed as 'random,' 'fortuitous,' or 'attenuated.' " Moreover, the contract contained a clause stating:

> This Agreement shall become valid when executed and accepted by BKC at Miami, Florida; it shall be deemed made and entered into in the State of Florida and shall be governed and construed under and in accordance with the laws of the State of Florida. The choice of law designation does not require that all suits concerning this Agreement be filed in Florida.

Rejecting the statement in *Hanson v. Denckla* about the irrelevance of choice of law considerations for jurisdiction, relied on by the Court of Appeals,[x] Justice Brennan wrote:

> This reasoning misperceives the import of the quoted proposition. The Court in *Hanson* and subsequent cases has emphasized that choice-of-law *analysis*—which focuses on all elements of a transaction, and not simply on the defendant's conduct—is distinct from minimum-contacts jurisdictional analysis—which focuses at the threshold solely on the defendant's purposeful connection to the forum. Nothing in our cases, however, suggests that a choice-of-law *provision* should be ignored in considering whether a defendant has "purposefully invoked the benefits and protections of a State's laws" for jurisdictional purposes. Although such a provision standing alone would be insufficient to confer jurisdiction, we believe that, when combined with the 20-year interdependent relationship Rudzewicz established with Burger King's Miami headquarters, it reinforced his deliberate affiliation with the forum State and the reasonable foreseeability of possible litigation there.[y]

(b) Justice Stevens dissented in an opinion in which Justice White joined:

> In my opinion there is a significant element of unfairness in requiring a franchisee to defend a case of this kind in the forum chosen by the franchisor. It is undisputed that respondent maintained no place of business in Florida, that he had no employees in that State, and that he was not licensed to do business there. Respondent did not prepare his french fries, shakes, and hamburgers in Michigan and then deliver them into the stream of commerce "with the expectation that they [would] be purchased by consumers in Florida. To the contrary, respondent did business only in Michigan, his business, property, and payroll taxes were payable in that state, and he sold all of his products there.
>
> Throughout the business relationship, respondent's principal contacts with petitioner were with its Michigan office. Notwithstanding its disclaimer, the Court seems ultimately to rely on nothing more than standard boilerplate language contained in various documents, to establish that respondent " 'purposefully availed himself of the benefits and protections of Florida's laws.' " Such a superficial analysis creates a potential for unfairness not only in

---

[x] See p. 504 and question (2)(a), p. 516, *supra.*
[y] 471 U.S. at 482-82.

§ 7.05 International Controversies

[A] General vs. Specific Jurisdiction

HELICOPTEROS NACIONALES DE COLOMBIA, S.A. v. HALL

United States Supreme Court
466 U.S. 408 (1984)

JUSTICE BLACKMUN delivered the opinion of the Court.

We granted certiorari in this case, to decide whether the Supreme Court of Texas correctly ruled that the contacts of a foreign corporation with the State of Texas were sufficient to allow a Texas state court to assert jurisdiction over the corporation in a cause of action not arising out of or related to the corporation's activities within the State.

I

Petitioner Helicopteros Nacionales de Colombia, S.A., (Helicol) is a Colombian corporation with its principal place of business in the city of Bogota in that country. It is engaged in the business of providing helicopter transportation for oil and construction companies in South America. On January 26, 1976, a helicopter owned by Helicol crashed in Peru. Four United States citizens were among those who lost their lives in the accident. Respondents are the survivors and representatives of the four decedents.

At the time of the crash, respondents' decedents were employed by Consorcio, a Peruvian consortium, and were working on a pipeline in Peru. Consorcio is the alter ego of a joint venture named Williams-Sedco-Horn (WSH).[1] The venture had its headquarters in Houston, Tex. Consorcio had been formed to enable the venturers to enter into a contract with Petro Peru, the Peruvian state-owned oil company. Consorcio was to construct a pipeline for Petro Peru running from the interior of Peru westward to the Pacific Ocean. Peruvian law forbade construction of the pipeline by any non-Peruvian entity.

Consorcio/WSH needed helicopters to move personnel, materials, and equipment into and out of the construction area. In 1974, upon request of Consorcio/WSH, the chief executive officer of Helicol, Francisco Restrepo, flew to the United States and conferred in Houston with representatives of the three joint venturers. At that meeting, there was a discussion of prices, availability, working conditions, fuel, supplies, and housing. Restrepo represented that Helicol could have the first helicopter on the job in 15 days. The Consorcio/WSH representatives decided to accept the contract proposed by Restrepo. Helicol began performing before the agreement was formally signed in Peru on November 11, 1974. The contract was written in Spanish on official government stationery and provided that the residence of all the parties would be Lima, Peru. It further stated that controversies arising out of the contract would be submitted to the

---

[z] *Id.* at 487-88 (Stevens, J. dissenting).

[1] The participants in the joint venture were Williams International Sudamericana, Ltd., a Delaware corporation; Sedco Construction Corporation, a Texas corporation; and Horn International, Inc., a Texas corporation.

jurisdiction of Peruvian courts. In addition, it provided that Consorcio/WSH would make payments to Helicol's account with the Bank of America in New York City. . . .

Aside from the negotiation session in Houston between Restrepo and the representatives of Consorcio/WSH, Helicol had other contacts with Texas. During the years 1970–1977, it purchased helicopters (approximately 80% of its fleet), spare parts, and accessories for more than $4,000,000 from Bell Helicopter Company in Fort Worth. In that period, Helicol sent prospective pilots to Fort Worth for training and to ferry the aircraft to South America. It also sent management and maintenance personnel to visit Bell Helicopter in Fort Worth during the same period in order to receive "plant familiarization" and for technical consultation. Helicol received into its New York City and Panama City, Fla., bank accounts over $5,000,000 in payments from Consorcio/WSH drawn upon First City National Bank of Houston.

Beyond the foregoing, there have been no other business contacts between Helicol and the State of Texas. Helicol never has been authorized to do business in Texas and never has had an agent for the service of process within the State. It never has performed helicopter operations in Texas or sold any product that reached Texas, never solicited business in Texas, never signed any contract in Texas, never had any employee based there, and never recruited an employee in Texas. In addition, Helicol never has owned real or personal property in Texas and never has maintained an office or establishment there. Helicol has maintained no records in Texas and has no shareholders in that State.[4] None of the respondents or their decedents were domiciled in Texas, Tr. of Oral Arg. 17, 18,[5] but all of the decedents were hired in Houston by Consorcio/WSH to work on the Petro Peru pipeline project.

Respondents instituted wrongful death actions in the District Court of Harris County, Tex., against Consorcio/WSH, Bell Helicopter Company, and Helicol. Helicol filed special appearances and moved to dismiss the actions for lack of *in personam* jurisdiction over it. The motion was denied. After a consolidated jury trial, judgment was entered against Helicol on a jury verdict of $1,141,200 in favor of respondents.[6]

The Texas Court of Civil Appeals, Houston, First District, reversed the judgment of the District Court, holding that *in personam* jurisdiction over Helicol was lacking. 616 S.W.2d 247 (Tex.1981). The Supreme Court of Texas, with three Justices dissenting, initially affirmed the judgment of the Court of Civil Appeals. Seven months later, however, on motion for rehearing, the court withdrew its prior opinions and, again with three Justices dissenting, reversed the judgment of the intermediate court. 638 S.W.2d 870 (Tex.1982). In ruling that the Texas courts had *in personam* jurisdiction, the Texas Supreme Court first held that the State's long-arm statute reaches as far as the Due Process Clause of the Fourteenth Amendment permits. *Id.,* at 872.[7]

---

[4] The Colombian national airline, Aerovias Nacionales de Colombia, owns approximately 94% of Helicol's capital stock. The remainder is held by Aerovias Corporation de Viajes and four South American individuals. See Brief for Petitioner 2, n. 2.

[5] Respondents' lack of residential or other contacts with Texas of itself does not defeat otherwise proper jurisdiction. *Keeton v. Hustler Magazine, Inc.,* [p. 546, *supra*]; *Calder v. Jones* [p. 557 note w]. We mention respondents' lack of contacts merely to show that nothing in the nature of the relationship between respondents and Helicol could possibly enhance Helicol's contacts with Texas. The harm suffered by respondents did not occur in Texas. Nor is it alleged that any negligence on the part of Helicol took place in Texas.

[6] Defendants Consorcio/WSH and Bell Helicopter Company were granted directed verdicts with respect to respondents' claims against them. Bell Helicopter was granted a directed verdict on Helicol's cross-claim against it. App. 167a. Consorcio/WSH, as cross-plaintiff in a claim against Helicol, obtained a judgment in the amount of $70,000. *Id.,* at 174a.

[7] The State's long-arm statute is Tex.Rev.Civ.Stat.Ann., Art. 2031b (Vernon 1964 & Supp. 1982–1983). It reads in relevant part:

Thus, the only question remaining for the court to decide was whether it was consistent with the Due Process Clause for Texas courts to assert *in personam* jurisdiction over Helicol. *Ibid.*

II

The Due Process Clause of the Fourteenth Amendment operates to limit the power of a State to assert *in personam* jurisdiction over a nonresident defendant. *Pennoyer v. Neff.* Due process requirements are satisfied when *in personam* jurisdiction is asserted over a nonresident corporate defendant that has "certain minimum contacts with [the forum] such that the maintenance of the suit does not offend 'traditional notions of fair play and substantial justice.' " *International Shoe Co. v. Washington,* quoting *Milliken v. Meyer,* 311 U.S. 457, 463, (1940). When a controversy is related to or "arises out of" a defendant's contacts with the forum, the Court has said that a "relationship among the defendant, the forum, and the litigation" is the essential foundation of *in personam* jurisdiction. *Shaffer v. Heitner.*

Even when the cause of action does not arise out of or relate to the foreign corporation's activities in the forum State, due process is not offended by a State's subjecting the corporation to its *in personam* jurisdiction when there are sufficient contacts between the State and the foreign corporation. *Perkins v. Benguet Consolidated Mining Co.,* 342 U.S. 437, (1952); see *Keeton v. Hustler Magazine, Inc.* . . .

All parties to the present case concede that respondents' claims against Helicol did not "arise out of," and are not related to, Helicol's activities within Texas.[10] We thus must explore the

---

"Sec. 3. Any foreign corporation . . . that engages in business in this State, irrespective of any Statute or law respecting designation or maintenance of resident agents, and does not maintain a place of regular business in this State or a designated agent upon whom service may be made upon causes of action arising out of such business done in this State, the act or acts of engaging in such business within this State shall be deemed equivalent to an appointment by such foreign corporation . . . of the Secretary of State of Texas as agent upon whom service of process may be made in any action, suit or proceedings arising out of such business done in this State, wherein such corporation . . . is a party or is to be made a party.

"Sec. 4. For the purposes of this Act, and without including other acts that may constitute doing business, any foreign corporation . . . shall be deemed doing business in this State by entering into contract by mail or otherwise with a resident of Texas to be performed in whole or in part by either party in this State, or the committing of any tort in whole or in part in this State. The act of recruiting Texas residents, directly or through an intermediary located in Texas, for employment inside or outside of Texas shall be deemed doing business in this State."

The last sentence of § 4 was added by 1979 Tex.Gen.Laws, ch. 245, § 1, and became effective Aug. 27, 1979.

The Supreme Court of Texas in its principal opinion relied upon rulings in *U-Anchor Advertising, Inc. v. Burt,* 553 S.W.2d 760 (Tex.1977); *Hoppenfeld v. Crook,* 498 S.W.2d 52 (Tex.Civ. App.1973); and *O'Brien v. Lanpar Co.,* 399 S.W.2d 340 (Tex.1966). It is not within our province, of course, to determine whether the Texas Supreme Court correctly interpreted the State's long-arm statute. We therefore accept that court's holding that the limits of the Texas statute are coextensive with those of the Due Process Clause.

[10] Because the parties have not argued any relationship between the cause of action and Helicol's contacts with the State of Texas, we, contrary to the dissent's implication, *post,* at 564, assert no "view" with respect to that issue.

The dissent suggests that we have erred in drawing no distinction between controversies that "relate to" a defendant's contacts with a forum and those that "arise out of" such contacts. This criticism is somewhat puzzling, for the dissent goes on to urge that, for purposes of determining the constitutional validity of an assertion of specific jurisdiction, there really should be no distinction between the two.

We do not address the validity or consequences of such a distinction because the issue has not been presented in this case. Respondents have made no argument that their cause of action either arose out of or is related to Helicol's contacts with the State of Texas. Absent any briefing on the issue, we decline to reach the questions (1) whether the terms "arising out of" and "related to" describe different connections between a cause of action and a defendant's

nature of Helicol's contacts with the State of Texas to determine whether they constitute the kind of continuous and systematic general business contacts the Court found to exist in *Perkins.* We hold that they do not.

It is undisputed that Helicol does not have a place of business in Texas and never has been licensed to do business in the State. Basically, Helicol's contacts with Texas consisted of sending its chief executive officer to Houston for a contract-negotiation session; accepting into its New York bank account checks drawn on a Houston bank; purchasing helicopters, equipment, and training services from Bell Helicopter for substantial sums; and sending personnel to Bell's facilities in Fort Worth for training.

The one trip to Houston by Helicol's chief executive officer for the purpose of negotiating the transportation-services contract with Consorcio/WSH cannot be described or regarded as a contact of a "continuous and systematic" nature, as *Perkins* described it, see also *International Shoe Co. v. Washington,* and thus cannot support an assertion of *in personam* jurisdiction over Helicol by a Texas court. Similarly, Helicol's acceptance from Consorcio/WSH of checks drawn on a Texas bank is of negligible significance for purposes of determining whether Helicol had sufficient contacts in Texas. There is no indication that Helicol ever requested that the checks be drawn on a Texas bank or that there was any negotiation between Helicol and Consorcio/WSH with respect to the location or identity of the bank on which checks would be drawn. Common sense and everyday experience suggest that, absent unusual circumstances, the bank on which a check is drawn is generally of little consequence to the payee and is a matter left to the discretion of the drawer. Such unilateral activity of another party or a third person is not an appropriate consideration when determining whether a defendant has sufficient contacts with a forum State to justify an assertion of jurisdiction. . . .

The Texas Supreme Court focused on the purchases and the related training trips in finding contacts sufficient to support an assertion of jurisdiction. We do not agree with that assessment, for the Court's opinion in *Rosenberg Bros. & Co. v. Curtis Brown Co.,* 260 U.S. 516, (1923) (Brandeis, J., for a unanimous tribunal), makes clear that purchases and related trips, standing alone, are not a sufficient basis for a State's assertion of jurisdiction.

The defendant in *Rosenberg* was a small retailer in Tulsa, Okla., who dealt in men's clothing and furnishings. It never had applied for a license to do business in New York, nor had it at any time authorized suit to be brought against it there. It never had an established place of business in New York and never regularly carried on business in that State. Its only connection with New York was that it purchased from New York wholesalers a large portion of the merchandise sold in its Tulsa store. The purchases sometimes were made by correspondence and sometimes through visits to New York by an officer of the defendant. The Court concluded: "Visits on such business, even if occurring at regular intervals, would not warrant the inference that the corporation was present within the jurisdiction of [New York]." *Id.,* at 518.

This Court in *International Shoe* acknowledged and did not repudiate its holding in *Rosenberg.* In accordance with *Rosenberg,* we hold that mere purchases, even if occurring at regular intervals, are not enough to warrant a State's assertion of *in personam* jurisdiction over a nonresident

---

contacts with a forum, and (2) what sort of tie between a cause of action and a defendant's contacts with a forum is necessary to a determination that either connection exists. Nor do we reach the question whether, if the two types of relationship differ, a forum's exercise of personal jurisdiction in a situation where the cause of action "relates to," but does not "arise out of," the defendant's contacts with the forum should be analyzed as an assertion of specific jurisdiction.

corporation in a cause of action not related to those purchase transactions.[12] Nor can we conclude that the fact that Helicol sent personnel into Texas for training in connection with the purchase of helicopters and equipment in that State in any way enhanced the nature of Helicol's contacts with Texas. The training was a part of the package of goods and services purchased by Helicol from Bell Helicopter. The brief presence of Helicol employees in Texas for the purpose of attending the training sessions is no more a significant contact than were the trips to New York made by the buyer for the retail store in *Rosenberg*. See also *Kulko v. California Superior Court*, 436 U.S., at 93, (basing California jurisdiction on 3-day and 1-day stopovers in that State "would make a mockery of" due process limitations on assertion of personal jurisdiction).

III

We hold that Helicol's contacts with the State of Texas were insufficient to satisfy the requirements of the Due Process Clause of the Fourteenth Amendment.[13] Accordingly, we reverse the judgment of the Supreme Court of Texas.

It is so ordered.

JUSTICE BRENNAN, dissenting.

Decisions applying the Due Process Clause of the Fourteenth Amendment to determine whether a State may constitutionally assert *in personam* jurisdiction over a particular defendant for a particular cause of action most often turn on a weighing of facts. To a large extent, today's decision follows the usual pattern. Based on essentially undisputed facts, the Court concludes that petitioner Helicol's contacts with the State of Texas were insufficient to allow the Texas state courts constitutionally to assert "general jurisdiction" over all claims filed against this foreign corporation. Although my independent weighing of the facts leads me to a different conclusion, the Court's holding on this issue is neither implausible nor unexpected.

What is troubling about the Court's opinion, however, are the implications that might be drawn from the way in which the Court approaches the constitutional issue it addresses. First, the Court limits its discussion to an assertion of general jurisdiction of the Texas courts because, in its view, the underlying cause of action does "not aris[e] out of or relat[e] to the corporation's activities within the State." Then, the Court relies on a 1923 decision in *Rosenberg Bros. & Co. v. Curtis Brown Co.*, 260 U.S. 516, without considering whether that case retains any validity after our more recent pronouncements concerning the permissible reach of a State's jurisdiction.

---

[12] This Court in *International Shoe* cited *Rosenberg* for the proposition that "the commission of some single or occasional acts of the corporate agent in a state sufficient to impose an obligation or liability on the corporation has not been thought to confer upon the state authority to enforce it." 326 U.S., at 318. Arguably, therefore, *Rosenberg* also stands for the proposition that mere purchases are not a sufficient basis for either general or specific jurisdiction. Because the case before us is one in which there has been an assertion of general jurisdiction over a foreign defendant, we need not decide the continuing validity of *Rosenberg* with respect to an assertion of specific jurisdiction, *i.e.*, where the cause of action arises out of or relates to the purchases by the defendant in the forum State.

[13] As an alternative to traditional minimum-contacts analysis, respondents suggest that the Court hold that the State of Texas had personal jurisdiction over Helicol under a doctrine of "jurisdiction by necessity." See *Shaffer v. Heitner*, [p. 589, *infra*, n. 37]. We conclude, however, that respondents failed to carry their burden of showing that all three defendants could not be sued together in a single forum. It is not clear from the record, for example, whether suit could have been brought against all three defendants in either Colombia or Peru. We decline to consider adoption of a doctrine of jurisdiction by necessity—a potentially far-reaching modification of existing law—in the absence of a more complete record.

By posing and deciding the question presented in this manner, I fear that the Court is saying more than it realizes about constitutional limitations on the potential reach of *in personam* jurisdiction. In particular, by relying on a precedent whose premises have long been discarded, and by refusing to consider any distinction between controversies that "relate to" a defendant's contacts with the forum and causes of action that "arise out of" such contacts, the Court may be placing severe limitations on the type and amount of contacts that will satisfy the constitutional minimum.

In contrast, I believe that the undisputed contacts in this case between petitioner Helicol and the State of Texas are sufficiently important, and sufficiently related to the underlying cause of action, to make it fair and reasonable for the State to assert personal jurisdiction over Helicol for the wrongful death actions filed by the respondents. Given that Helicol has purposefully availed itself of the benefits and obligations of the forum, and given the direct relationship between the underlying cause of action and Helicol's contacts with the forum, maintenance of this suit in the Texas courts "does not offend [the] 'traditional notions of fair play and substantial justice,' " that are the touchstone of jurisdictional analysis under the Due Process Clause. I therefore dissent.

. . .

The wrongful death action filed by the respondents was premised on a fatal helicopter crash that occurred in Peru. Helicol was joined as a defendant in the lawsuit because it provided transportation services, including the particular helicopter and pilot involved in the crash, to the joint venture that employed the decedents. Specifically, the respondents claimed in their original complaint that "Helicol is . . . legally responsible for its own negligence through its pilot employee." App. 6a. Viewed in light of these allegations, the contacts between Helicol and the State of Texas are directly and significantly related to the underlying claim filed by the respondents. The negotiations that took place in Texas led to the contract in which Helicol agreed to provide the precise transportation services that were being used at the time of the crash. Moreover, the helicopter involved in the crash was purchased by Helicol in Texas, and the pilot whose negligence was alleged to have caused the crash was actually trained in Texas. This is simply not a case, therefore, in which a state court has asserted jurisdiction over a nonresident defendant on the basis of wholly unrelated contacts with the forum. Rather, the contacts between Helicol and the forum are directly related to the negligence that was alleged in the respondents' original complaint. Because Helicol should have expected to be amenable to suit in the Texas courts for claims directly related to these contacts, it is fair and reasonable to allow the assertion of jurisdiction in this case.

Despite this substantial relationship between the contacts and the cause of action, the Court declines to consider whether the courts of Texas may assert specific jurisdiction over this suit. Apparently, this simply reflects a narrow interpretation of the question presented for review. See *ante,* n. 10. It is nonetheless possible that the Court's opinion may be read to imply that the specific jurisdiction of the Texas courts is inapplicable because the cause of action did not formally "arise out of" the contacts between Helicol and the forum. In my view, however, such a rule would place unjustifiable limits on the bases under which Texas may assert its jurisdictional power.

Limiting the specific jurisdiction of a forum to cases in which the cause of action formally arose out of the defendant's contacts with the State would subject constitutional standards under the Due Process Clause to the vagaries of the substantive law or pleading requirements of each

State. For example, the complaint filed against Helicol in this case alleged negligence based on pilot error. Even though the pilot was trained in Texas, the Court assumes that the Texas courts may not assert jurisdiction over the suit because the cause of action "did not 'arise out of,' and [is] not related to," that training. See *ante*, at 1872. If, however, the applicable substantive law required that negligent training of the pilot was a necessary element of a cause of action for pilot error, or if the respondents had simply added an allegation of negligence in the training provided for the Helicol pilot, then presumably the Court would concede that the specific jurisdiction of the Texas courts was applicable.

Our interpretation of the Due Process Clause has never been so dependent upon the applicable substantive law or the State's formal pleading requirements. At least since *International Shoe, supra,* the principal focus when determining whether a forum may constitutionally assert jurisdiction over a nonresident defendant has been on fairness and reasonableness to the defendant. To this extent, a court's specific jurisdiction should be applicable whenever the cause of action arises out of *or* relates to the contacts between the defendant and the forum. It is eminently fair and reasonable, in my view, to subject a defendant to suit in a forum with which it has significant contacts directly related to the underlying cause of action. Because Helicol's contacts with the State of Texas meet this standard, I would affirm the judgment of the Supreme Court of Texas.

[B] The Question of Reasonableness

ASAHI METAL INDUSTRY CO., LTD., v. SUPERIOR COURT

United States Supreme Court
480 U.S. 102 (1987)

Justice O'CONNOR announced the judgment of the Court and delivered the unanimous opinion of the Court with respect to Part I, the opinion of the Court with respect to Part II-B, in which THE CHIEF JUSTICE, Justice BRENNAN, Justice WHITE, Justice MARSHALL, Justice BLACKMUN, Justice POWELL, and Justice STEVENS join, and an opinion with respect to Parts II-A and III, in which THE CHIEF JUSTICE, Justice POWELL, and Justice SCALIA join.

This case presents the question whether the mere awareness on the part of a foreign defendant that the components it manufactured, sold, and delivered outside the United States would reach the forum State in the stream of commerce constitutes "minimum contacts" between the defendant and the forum State such that the exercise of jurisdiction "does not offend 'traditional notions of fair play and substantial justice.'" *International Shoe Co. v. Washington,* 326 U.S. 310, 316, (1945), quoting *Milliken v. Meyer,* 311 U.S. 457, 463 (1940).

I

On September 23, 1978, on Interstate Highway 80 in Solano County, California, Gary Zurcher lost control of his Honda motorcycle and collided with a tractor. Zurcher was severely injured, and his passenger and wife, Ruth Ann Moreno, was killed. In September 1979, Zurcher filed a product liability action in the Superior Court of the State of California in and for the County of Solano. Zurcher alleged that the 1978 accident was caused by a sudden loss of air and an explosion in the rear tire of the motorcycle, and alleged that the motorcycle tire, tube, and sealant were defective. Zurcher's complaint named, inter alia, Cheng Shin Rubber Industrial Co., Ltd. (Cheng Shin), the Taiwanese manufacturer of the tube. Cheng Shin in turn filed a cross-complaint seeking indemnification from its codefendants and from petitioner, Asahi Metal Industry Co., Ltd. (Asahi), the manufacturer of the tube's valve assembly. Zurcher's claims against Cheng Shin and the other defendants were eventually settled and dismissed, leaving only Cheng Shin's indemnity action against Asahi.

California's long-arm statute authorizes the exercise of jurisdiction "on any basis not inconsistent with the Constitution of this state or of the United States." Cal.Civ.Proc.Code Ann. s 410.10 (West 1973). Asahi moved to quash Cheng Shin's service of summons, arguing the State could not exert jurisdiction over it consistent with the Due Process Clause of the Fourteenth Amendment.

In relation to the motion, the following information was submitted by Asahi and Cheng Shin. Asahi is a Japanese corporation. It manufactures tire valve assemblies in Japan and sells the assemblies to Cheng Shin, and to several other tire manufacturers, for use as components in finished tire tubes. Asahi's sales to Cheng Shin took place in Taiwan. The shipments from Asahi to Cheng Shin were sent from Japan to Taiwan. Cheng Shin bought and incorporated into its tire tubes 150,000 Asahi valve assemblies in 1978; 500,000 in 1979; 500,000 in 1980; 100,000 in 1981; and 100,000 in 1982. Sales to Cheng Shin accounted for 1.24 percent of Asahi's income in 1981 and 0.44 percent in 1982. Cheng Shin alleged that approximately 20 percent of its sales in the United States are in California. Cheng Shin purchases valve assemblies from other suppliers as well, and sells finished tubes throughout the world.

In 1983 an attorney for Cheng Shin conducted an informal examination of the valve stems of the tire tubes sold in one cycle store in Solano County. The attorney declared that of the approximately 115 tire tubes in the store, 97 were purportedly manufactured in Japan or Taiwan, and of those 97, 21 valve stems were marked with the circled letter "A," apparently Asahi's trademark. Of the 21 Asahi valve stems, 12 were incorporated into Cheng Shin tire tubes. The store contained 41 other Cheng Shin tubes that incorporated the valve assemblies of other manufacturers. An affidavit of a manager of Cheng Shin whose duties included the purchasing of component parts stated: "In discussions with Asahi regarding the purchase of valve stem assemblies the fact that my Company sells tubes throughout the world and specifically the United States has been discussed. I am informed and believe that Asahi was fully aware that valve stem assemblies sold to my Company and to others would end up throughout the United States and in California." An affidavit of the president of Asahi, on the other hand, declared that Asahi "has never contemplated that its limited sales of tire valves to Cheng Shin in Taiwan would subject it to lawsuits in California." The record does not include any contract between Cheng Shin and Asahi.

Primarily on the basis of the above information, the Superior Court denied the motion to quash summons, stating: "Asahi obviously does business on an international scale. It is not unreasonable that they defend claims of defect in their product on an international scale."

The Court of Appeal of the State of California issued a peremptory writ of mandate commanding the Superior Court to quash service of summons. The court concluded that "it would be unreasonable to require Asahi to respond in California solely on the basis of ultimately realized foreseeability that the product into which its component was embodied would be sold all over the world including California."

The Supreme Court of the State of California reversed and discharged the writ issued by the Court of Appeal. The court observed: "Asahi has no offices, property or agents in California. It solicits no business in California and has made no direct sales [in California]." Moreover, "Asahi did not design or control the system of distribution that carried its valve assemblies into California." Nevertheless, the court found the exercise of jurisdiction over Asahi to be consistent with the Due Process Clause. It concluded that Asahi knew that some of the valve assemblies sold to Cheng Shin would be incorporated into tire tubes sold in California, and that Asahi benefited indirectly from the sale in California of products incorporating its components. The court considered Asahi's intentional act of placing its components into the stream of commerce—that is, by delivering the components to Cheng Shin in Taiwan—coupled with Asahi's awareness that some of the components would eventually find their way into California, sufficient to form the basis for state court jurisdiction under the Due Process Clause.

We granted certiorari, and now reverse.

II

A

4 Justices

The Due Process Clause of the Fourteenth Amendment limits the power of a state court to exert personal jurisdiction over a nonresident defendant. "[T]he constitutional touchstone" of the determination whether an exercise of personal jurisdiction comports with due process "remains whether the defendant purposefully established 'minimum contacts' in the forum State." *Burger King Corp. v. Rudzewicz,* [p. 557 *supra*], quoting *International Shoe Co. v. Washington.* Most recently we have reaffirmed the oft-quoted reasoning of *Hanson v. Denckla,* that minimum contacts must have a basis in "some act by which the defendant purposefully avails itself of the privilege of conducting activities within the forum State, thus invoking the benefits and protections of its laws." *Burger King,* 471 U.S., at 475. "Jurisdiction is proper . . . where the contacts proximately result from actions by the defendant *himself* that create a 'substantial connection' with the forum State." Ibid., quoting *McGee v. International Life Insurance Co.,* (emphasis in original).

Applying the principle that minimum contacts must be based on an act of the defendant, the Court in *World-Wide Volkswagen Corp. v. Woodson* rejected the assertion that a consumer's unilateral act of bringing the defendant's product into the forum State was a sufficient constitutional basis for personal jurisdiction over the defendant. It had been argued in World-Wide Volkswagen that because an automobile retailer and its wholesale distributor sold a product mobile by design and purpose, they could foresee being haled into court in the distant States into which their customers might drive. The Court rejected this concept of foreseeability as an insufficient basis for jurisdiction under the Due Process Clause. [p. 535 *supra*]. The Court disclaimed, however, the idea that "foreseeability is wholly irrelevant" to personal jurisdiction, concluding that "[t]he forum State does not exceed its powers under the Due Process Clause if it asserts personal jurisdiction over a corporation that delivers its products into the stream of commerce with the expectation that they will be purchased by consumers in the forum State." The Court reasoned:

"When a corporation 'purposefully avails itself of the privilege of conducting activities within the forum State,' *Hanson v. Denckla,* it has clear notice that it is subject to suit there, and can act to alleviate the risk of burdensome litigation by procuring insurance, passing the expected costs on to customers, or, if the risks are too great, severing its connection with the State. Hence if the sale of a product of a manufacturer or distributor . . . is not simply an isolated occurrence, but arises from the efforts of the manufacturer or distributor to serve, directly or indirectly, the market for its product in other States, it is not unreasonable to subject it to suit in one of those States if its allegedly defective merchandise has there been the source of injury to its owners or to others."

In *World-Wide Volkswagen* itself, the state court sought to base jurisdiction not on any act of the defendant, but on the foreseeable unilateral actions of the consumer. Since *World-Wide Volkswagen,* lower courts have been confronted with cases in which the defendant acted by placing a product in the stream of commerce, and the stream eventually swept defendant's product into the forum State, but the defendant did nothing else to purposefully avail itself of the market in the forum State. Some courts have understood the Due Process Clause, as interpreted in *World-Wide Volkswagen,* to allow an exercise of personal jurisdiction to be based on no more than the defendant's act of placing the product in the stream of commerce. Other courts have understood the Due Process Clause and the above-quoted language in *World-Wide Volkswagen* to require the action of the defendant to be more purposefully directed at the forum State than the mere act of placing a product in the stream of commerce.

The reasoning of the Supreme Court of California in the present case illustrates the former interpretation of *World-Wide Volkswagen.* The Supreme Court of California held that, because the stream of commerce eventually brought some valves Asahi sold Cheng Shin into California, Asahi's awareness that its valves would be sold in California was sufficient to permit California to exercise jurisdiction over Asahi consistent with the requirements of the Due Process Clause. The Supreme Court of California's position was consistent with those courts that have held that mere foreseeability or awareness was a constitutionally sufficient basis for personal jurisdiction if the defendant's product made its way into the forum State while still in the stream of commerce.

Other courts, however, have understood the Due Process Clause to require something more than that the defendant was aware of its product's entry into the forum State through the stream of commerce in order for the State to exert jurisdiction over the defendant. In the present case, for example, the State Court of Appeal did not read the Due Process Clause, as interpreted by *World-Wide Volkswagen,* to allow "mere foreseeability that the product will enter the forum state [to] be enough by itself to establish jurisdiction over the distributor and retailer." In *Humble v. Toyota Motor Co.,* 727 F.2d 709 (CA8 1984), an injured car passenger brought suit against Arakawa Auto Body Company, a Japanese corporation that manufactured car seats for Toyota. Arakawa did no business in the United States; it had no office, affiliate, subsidiary, or agent in the United States; it manufactured its component parts outside the United States and delivered them to Toyota Motor Company in Japan. The Court of Appeals, adopting the reasoning of the District Court in that case, noted that although it "does not doubt that Arakawa could have foreseen that its product would find its way into the United States," it would be "manifestly unjust" to require Arakawa to defend itself in the United States.

We now find this latter position to be consonant with the requirements of due process. The "substantial connection" between the defendant and the forum State necessary for a finding of minimum contacts must come about by *an action of the defendant purposefully directed toward the forum State. Burger King,* supra, 471 U.S., at 476; *Keeton v. Hustler Magazine, Inc.,* [at p. 547, *supra*]. The placement of a product into the stream of commerce, without more, is not an act of the defendant purposefully directed toward the forum State. Additional conduct of the defendant may indicate an intent or purpose to serve the market in the forum State, for example, designing the product for the market in the forum State, advertising in the forum State, establishing channels for providing regular advice to customers in the forum State, or marketing the product through a distributor who has agreed to serve as the sales agent in the forum State. But a defendant's awareness that the stream of commerce may or will sweep the product into the forum State does not convert the mere act of placing the product into the stream into an act purposefully directed toward the forum State.

Assuming, *arguendo*, that respondents have established Asahi's awareness that some of the valves sold to Cheng Shin would be incorporated into tire tubes sold in California, respondents have not demonstrated any action by Asahi to purposefully avail itself of the California market. Asahi does not do business in California. It has no office, agents, employees, or property in California. It does not advertise or otherwise solicit business in California. It did not create, control, or employ the distribution system that brought its valves to California. There is no evidence that Asahi designed its product in anticipation of sales in California. On the basis of these facts, the exertion of personal jurisdiction over Asahi by the Superior Court of California* exceeds the limits of due process.

B

The strictures of the Due Process Clause forbid a state court to exercise personal jurisdiction over Asahi under circumstances that would offend "traditional notions of fair play and substantial justice." *International Shoe Co. v. Washington,* quoting *Milliken v. Meyer.*

We have previously explained that the determination of the reasonableness of the exercise of jurisdiction in each case will depend on an evaluation of several factors. A court must consider the burden on the defendant, the interests of the forum State, and the plaintiff's interest in obtaining relief. It must also weigh in its determination "the interstate judicial system's interest in obtaining the most efficient resolution of controversies; and the shared interest of the several States in furthering fundamental substantive social policies." *World-Wide Volkswagen.*

A consideration of these factors in the present case clearly reveals the unreasonableness of the assertion of jurisdiction over Asahi, even apart from the question of the placement of goods in the stream of commerce.

Certainly the burden on the defendant in this case is severe. Asahi has been commanded by the Supreme Court of California not only to traverse the distance between Asahi's headquarters in Japan and the Superior Court of California in and for the County of Solano, but also to submit its dispute with Cheng Shin to a foreign nation's judicial system. The unique burdens placed upon one who must defend oneself in a foreign legal system should have significant weight in assessing the reasonableness of stretching the long arm of personal jurisdiction over national borders.

---

* We have no occasion here to determine whether Congress could, consistent with the Due Process Clause of the Fifth Amendment, authorize federal court personal jurisdiction over alien defendants based on the aggregate of national contacts, rather than on the contacts between the defendant and the State in which the federal court sits. See *Max Daetwyler Corp. v. R. Meyer,* 762 F.2d 290, 293-295 (CA3 1985); *DeJames v. Magnificence Carriers, Inc.,* 654 F.2d 280, 283 (CA3 1981); see also Born, *Reflections on Judicial Jurisdiction in International Cases,* to be published in 17 Ga.J. Int'l & Comp.L. 1 (1987); Lilly, *Jurisdiction Over Domestic and Alien Defendants,* 69 Va.L.Rev. 85, 127-145 (1983).

When minimum contacts have been established, often the interests of the plaintiff and the forum in the exercise of jurisdiction will justify even the serious burdens placed on the alien defendant. In the present case, however, the interests of the plaintiff and the forum in California's assertion of jurisdiction over Asahi are slight. All that remains is a claim for indemnification asserted by Cheng Shin, a Taiwanese corporation, against Asahi. The transaction on which the indemnification claim is based took place in Taiwan; Asahi's components were shipped from Japan to Taiwan. Cheng Shin has not demonstrated that it is more convenient for it to litigate its indemnification claim against Asahi in California rather than in Taiwan or Japan.

Because the plaintiff is not a California resident, California's legitimate interests in the dispute have considerably diminished. The Supreme Court of California argued that the State had an interest in "protecting its consumers by ensuring that foreign manufacturers comply with the state's safety standards." The State Supreme Court's definition of California's interest, however, was overly broad. The dispute between Cheng Shin and Asahi is primarily about indemnification rather than safety standards. Moreover, it is not at all clear at this point that California law should govern the question whether a Japanese corporation should indemnify a Taiwanese corporation on the basis of a sale made in Taiwan and a shipment of goods from Japan to Taiwan. *Phillips Petroleum Co. v. Shutts,* [p. 421 *supra*]; *Allstate Insurance Co. v. Hague,* [p. 402 *supra*]. The possibility of being haled into a California court as a result of an accident involving Asahi's components undoubtedly creates an additional deterrent to the manufacture of unsafe components; however, similar pressures will be placed on Asahi by the purchasers of its components as long as those who use Asahi components in their final products, and sell those products in California, are subject to the application of California tort law.

World-Wide Volkswagen also admonished courts to take into consideration the interests of the "several States," in addition to the forum State, in the efficient judicial resolution of the dispute and the advancement of substantive policies. In the present case, this advice calls for a court to consider the procedural and substantive policies of other nations whose interests are affected by the assertion of jurisdiction by the California court. The procedural and substantive interests of other nations in a state court's assertion of jurisdiction over an alien defendant will differ from case to case. In every case, however, those interests, as well as the Federal Government's interest in its foreign relations policies, will be best served by a careful inquiry into the reasonableness of the assertion of jurisdiction in the particular case, and an unwillingness to find the serious burdens on an alien defendant outweighed by minimal interests on the part of the plaintiff or the forum State. "Great care and reserve should be exercised when extending our notions of personal jurisdiction into the international field." *United States v. First National City Bank,* 379 U.S. 378, 404, (1965) (Harlan, J., dissenting). See Born, Reflections on Judicial Jurisdiction in International Cases, to be published in 17 Ga. J. Int'l & Comp. L. 1 (1987).

Considering the international context, the heavy burden on the alien defendant, and the slight interests of the plaintiff and the forum State, the exercise of personal jurisdiction by a California court over Asahi in this instance would be unreasonable and unfair.

III

Because the facts of this case do not establish minimum contacts such that the exercise of personal jurisdiction is consistent with fair play and substantial justice, the judgment of the Supreme Court of California is reversed, and the case is remanded for further proceedings not inconsistent with this opinion.

It is so ordered.

Justice BRENNAN, with whom Justice WHITE, Justice MARSHALL, and Justice BLACKMUN join, concurring in part and concurring in the judgment.

I do not agree with the interpretation in Part II-A of the stream-of-commerce theory, nor with the conclusion that Asahi did not "purposely avail itself of the California market." I do agree, however, with the Court's conclusion in Part II-B that the exercise of personal jurisdiction over Asahi in this case would not comport with "fair play and substantial justice," International Shoe Co. v. Washington. This is one of those rare cases in which "minimum requirements inherent in the concept of 'fair play and substantial justice' . . . defeat the reasonableness of jurisdiction even [though] the defendant has purposefully engaged in forum activities." I therefore join Parts I and II-B of the Court's opinion, and write separately to explain my disagreement with Part II-A.

Part II-A states that "a defendant's awareness that the stream of commerce may or will sweep the product into the forum State does not convert the mere act of placing the product into the stream into an act purposefully directed toward the forum State." Under this view, a plaintiff would be required to show "[a]dditional conduct" directed toward the forum before finding the exercise of jurisdiction over the defendant to be consistent with the Due Process Clause. I see no need for such a showing, however. The stream of commerce refers not to unpredictable currents or eddies, but to the regular and anticipated flow of products from manufacture to distribution to retail sale. As long as a participant in this process is aware that the final product is being marketed in the forum State, the possibility of a lawsuit there cannot come as a surprise. Nor will the litigation present a burden for which there is no corresponding benefit. A defendant who has placed goods in the stream of commerce benefits economically from the retail sale of the final product in the forum State, and indirectly benefits from the State's laws that regulate and facilitate commercial activity. These benefits accrue regardless of whether that participant directly conducts business in the forum State, or engages in additional conduct directed toward that State. Accordingly, most courts and commentators have found that jurisdiction premised on the placement of a product into the stream of commerce is consistent with the Due Process Clause, and have not required a showing of additional conduct.[1]

The endorsement in Part II-A of what appears to be the minority view among Federal Courts of Appeals represents a marked retreat from the analysis in *World-Wide Volkswagen v. Woodson.* In that case, "respondents [sought] to base jurisdiction on one, isolated occurrence and whatever inferences can be drawn therefrom: the fortuitous circumstance that a single Audi automobile, sold in New York to New York residents, happened to suffer an accident while passing through Oklahoma." The Court held that the possibility of an accident in Oklahoma, while to some extent foreseeable in light of the inherent mobility of the automobile, was not enough to establish minimum contacts between the forum State and the retailer or distributor. The Court then carefully explained:

> "[T]his is not to say, of course, that foreseeability is wholly irrelevant. But the foreseeability that is critical to due process analysis is not the mere likelihood that a product will find its way into the forum State. Rather, it is that the defendant's conduct and connection with the forum State are such that he should reasonably anticipate being haled into Court there."

---

[1] [Justice Brennan cites eight appeals court cases, as well as David Currie, Wright and Miller, and von Mehren and Trautman.]

[p. 536 *supra*]

The Court reasoned that when a corporation may reasonably anticipate litigation in a particular forum, it cannot claim that such litigation is unjust or unfair, because it "can act to alleviate the risk of burdensome litigation by procuring insurance, passing the expected costs on to consumers, or, if the risks are too great, severing its connection with the State."

To illustrate the point, the Court contrasted the foreseeability of litigation in a State to which a consumer fortuitously transports a defendant's product (insufficient contacts) with the foreseeability of litigation in a State where the defendant's product was regularly sold (sufficient contacts). The Court stated:

> "Hence if the sale of a product of a manufacturer or distributor such as Audi or Volkswagen is not simply an isolated occurrence, but arises from the efforts of the manufacturer or distributor to serve, directly or indirectly, the market for its product in other States, it is not unreasonable to subject it to suit in one of those States if its allegedly defective merchandise has there been the source of injury to its owner or to others. The forum State does not exceed its powers under the Due Process Clause if it asserts personal jurisdiction over a corporation that delivers its products into the stream of commerce *with the expectation that they will be purchased by consumers* in the forum State." (emphasis added).

The Court concluded its illustration by referring to *Gray v. American Radiator & Standard Sanitary Corp.* [p. 520 *supra*], a well-known stream-of-commerce case in which the Illinois Supreme Court applied the theory to assert jurisdiction over a component-parts manufacturer that sold no components directly in Illinois, but did sell them to a manufacturer who incorporated them into a final product that was sold in Illinois.

The Court in *World-Wide Volkswagen* thus took great care to distinguish "between a case involving goods which reach a distant State through a chain of distribution and a case involving goods which reach the same State because a consumer . . . took them there." [p. 539, *supra*] (BRENNAN, J., dissenting).[3] The California Supreme Court took note of this distinction, and correctly concluded that our holding in *World-Wide Volkswagen* preserved the stream-of-commerce theory.

In this case, the facts found by the California Supreme Court support its finding of minimum contacts. The court found that "[a]lthough Asahi did not design or control the system of distribution that carried its valve assemblies into California, Asahi was aware of the distribution system's operation, and it knew that it would benefit economically from the sale in California of products incorporating its components."[4] Accordingly, I cannot join the determination in Part II-A that Asahi's regular and extensive sales of component parts to a manufacturer it knew was making regular sales of the final product in California is insufficient to establish minimum contacts with California.

---

[3] In dissent, I argued that the distinction was without constitutional significance, because in my view the foreseeability that a customer would use a product in a distant State was a sufficient basis for jurisdiction. . . . But I do not read the decision in *World-Wide Volkswagen* to establish a per se rule against the exercise of jurisdiction where the contacts arise from a consumer's use of the product in a given State, but only a rule against jurisdiction in cases involving "one, isolated occurrence [of consumer use, amounting to] . . . the fortuitous circumstance. . . ." [p. 535 *supra*]

[4] Moreover, the Court found that "at least 18 percent of the tubes sold in a particular California motorcycle supply shop contained Asahi valve assemblies," and that Asahi had an ongoing business relationship with Cheng Shin involving average annual sales of hundreds of thousands of valve assemblies.

Justice STEVENS, with whom Justice WHITE and Justice BLACKMUN join, concurring in part and concurring in the judgment.

The judgment of the Supreme Court of California should be reversed for the reasons stated in Part II-B of the Court's opinion. While I join Parts I and II-B, I do not join Part II-A for two reasons. First, it is not necessary to the Court's decision. An examination of minimum contacts is not always necessary to determine whether a state court's assertion of personal jurisdiction is constitutional. See *Burger King Corp. v. Rudzewicz.* Part II-B establishes, after considering the factors set forth in *World-Wide Volkswagen Corp. v. Woodson,* that California's exercise of jurisdiction over Asahi in this case would be "unreasonable and unfair." This finding alone requires reversal; this case fits within the rule that "minimum requirements inherent in the concept of 'fair play and substantial justice' may defeat the reasonableness of jurisdiction even if the defendant has purposefully engaged in forum activities." Accordingly, I see no reason in this case for the plurality to articulate "purposeful direction" or any other test as the nexus between an act of a defendant and the forum State that is necessary to establish minimum contacts.

Second, even assuming that the test ought to be formulated here, Part II-A misapplies it to the facts of this case. The plurality seems to assume that an unwavering line can be drawn between "mere awareness" that a component will find its way into the forum State and "purposeful availment" of the forum's market. Ante, at 569. Over the course of its dealings with Cheng Shin, Asahi has arguably engaged in a higher quantum of conduct than "[t]he placement of a product into the stream of commerce, without more. . . ." Ibid. Whether or not this conduct rises to the level of purposeful availment requires a constitutional determination that is affected by the volume, the value, and the hazardous character of the components. In most circumstances I would be inclined to conclude that a regular course of dealing that results in deliveries of over 100,000 units annually over a period of several years would constitute "purposeful availment" even though the item delivered to the forum State was a standard product marketed throughout the world.

NOTES AND QUESTIONS

(1)(a) It is certainly worth remarking that after more than a century of hearing judicial jurisdiction cases involving parties in the United States only, the Supreme Court took up two consecutive cases in which state courts had asserted jurisdiction over parties outside the United States.[a] But do you detect a different standard for interstate and international cases? Should there be one?[b]

(b) The Court in *Helicopteros* seems to look only to the contacts of Helicol with Texas. Should it have added in the bank accounts maintained in New York and Florida, to aggregate total contacts with the USA? Note that in *Asahi* the Court raises this question (p. 569) but does not answer it.[c]

---

[a] *Insurance Company of Ireland,* p. 553, note f, *supra,* also involved a foreign party, but the decision turned only on sanctions for failure to give discovery on the issue of jurisdiction, not on jurisdiction itself.

[b] When the Texas Supreme Court, on rehearing, upheld jurisdiction, after having first rejected it, the swing vote was made up of two judges who not only stressed defendant's many contacts with Texas but indicated that they were influenced by the inability of plaintiffs to find another suitable forum in the United States if the Texas forum were not open to them. *Hall v. Helicopteros Nacionales de Colombia, S.A.,* 638 S.W.2d. 870, 875 (Campbell, J., concurring) (Tex. 1982).

[c] Recall the discussion of this question in the *West Coast Machinery* case, p. 523, note o, *supra.*

(2)(a) Notice the statement of the question by Justice Blackmun in the first paragraph of the opinion in *Helicopteros.* Is it clear that the cause of action does not arise out of, (and is not related to) Helicol's activities within Texas? Are we back to the issue of where an action arises?[d] Note that Justice Blackmun says plaintiffs' counsel conceded the point, but Justice Brennan reads the submission differently.

(b) If the action is deemed not to arise out of Helicol's activities in Texas—i.e., it is different from an action, say, by Bell Helicopter for the purchase price of a chopper—then only general jurisdiction will support this action, i.e., doing business or something like it. Consider the facts as given by the Supreme Court. Helicol bought 80 percent of its fleet from Bell in Texas over an eight-year period, expending over $4 Million; it sent its pilots to Fort Worth for training, and, subsequently, to ferry the aircraft to South America. It also sent technical personnel to Bell's plant for familiarization. And it negotiated the deal that led to the crash. Why is that not enough enough?

(c) The *Restatement (Second) of Conflict of Laws,* published in 1971, states in § 47(2):

> A state has power to exercise judicial jurisdiction over a foreign corporation which does business in the state with respect to causes of action that do not arise from the business done in the state if this business is so continuous and substantial as to make it reasonable for the state to exercise such jurisdiction.

Neither the majority nor Justice Brennan cites this section. Is it still good law after *Helicopteros*?

(3)(a) Look at Order 11 r. 1(1)(e) of the U.K. Rules of Court,[e] and Article 6(1) of the European Jurisdiction and Judgments Convention.[f] Both documents provide for jurisdiction over a non-resident defendant properly joined with defendants resident or domiciled in the forum. Here the manufacturer, Bell Helicopter, and the enterprise that hired Helicol (Consorcio/WSH) were clearly before the Texas court, but were held not liable for the crash. Is the desirability of having all proper parties before a single court not justification for bringing in a nonresident party? . . . An element to be weighed? Or is this consideration simply not relevant to the discussion of minimum contacts under the Due Process clause?

(b) The Court in *Helicopteros* resurrects a forgotten case, *Rosenberg Bros. & Co. v. Curtis Brown Co.,* dating from 1923,[g] and makes it the basis for its holding in 1984. At the time of *Rosenberg,* of course, the idea of activity-based jurisdiction at a level that did not rise to doing business was unknown in judicial decisions. *Rosenberg* itself was an action for unpaid bills on purchases made by defendant on trips to the forum state, and Justice Blackmun does not quite say that the *Rosenberg* case would come out the same way today.[h] Assuming the Court does not mean to say that Bell Helicopter could not sue Helicol for unpaid portions of the purchase price of the helicopters or the instructional services rendered, is it fair to conclude that wrongful death claims are different?

---

[d] Recall the division of the court over this point in *Mack Trucks v. Bendix-Westinghouse,* Chapter 2, p. 81, *supra,* interpreting a "borrowing statute" for limitations purposes.

[e] Documents Supplement, p. 79.

[f] Documents Supplement, p. 101.

[g] 260 U.S. 516 (1923).

[h] The opinion in *Rosenberg,* just two pages, concludes that as doing business was not found in New York, "the fact that the alleged cause of action arose in New York is immaterial." 260 U.S. at 518. For Justice Blackmun's reservation, see p. 563, n. 12, *supra.*

§ 7.05   JURISDICTION AND JUDGMENTS   □   575

(c) Turning the question around, would you support a holding that, in effect, said to aircraft operators anywhere in the world, "if you (i) buy your planes in the United States, and (ii) carry passengers domiciled in the United States, be prepared to defend accident compensation claims in the United States, regardless of where the accident occurs."?

(d) Justice Brennan, consistent with his prior opinions, would sustain jurisdiction in *Helicoptoros,* and is anxious to avoid technical questions such as whether an action arises out of, or is merely related to activity in the forum state. Professor Weintraub suggests that the distinction between general and specific jurisdiction, laboriously learned, is too sharp, and really should be replaced by a more flexible standard, something like this:

> The less the unfairness to the defendant in requiring it to defend in the forum, the less the relationship between forum contacts and the cause of action that should be required to rebut that unfairness.[i]

Do you agree? Or does it sound too much like choice of law?

(e) Speaking of choice of law, if Justice Brennan's or Professor Weintraub's view had prevailed in *Helicopteros,* what law would you expect to govern? Suppose, for example, that a limit on recoveries for wrongful death was applicable in Peru (Colombia?). Or that the relationship between the workers and Consorcio was governed by a workers' compensation regime that precluded all other claims, not only against the employer but against third parties as well.

   (i) Would the U.S. Supreme Court order application of the law of Colombia and/or Peru?

   (ii) If not, is that an argument in favor of upholding, or overruling the jurisdiction of the Texas courts?

(4)(a) In *Piper Aircraft Co. v. Reyno,* 454 U.S. 235 (1981), a product liability case resulting from an airplane accident in Scotland, the Supreme Court, reversing the Court of Appeals for the Third Circuit, granted a motion to dismiss on grounds of forum non conveniens, expressly rejecting the plaintiffs' argument that litigating in Scotland would subject them to a less favorable legal regime. The Court wrote:

> We do not hold that the possibility of an unfavorable change in law should *never* be a relevant consideration in a *forum non conveniens* inquiry. Of course, if the remedy provided by the alternative forum is so clearly inadequate or unsatisfactory that it is no remedy at all, the unfavorable change in law may be given substantial weight; the district court may conclude that dismissal would not be in the interests of justice. In these cases, however, the remedies that would be provided by the Scottish courts do not fall within this category. Although the relatives of the decedents may not be able to rely on a strict liability theory, and although their potential damages award may be smaller, there is no danger that they will be deprived of any remedy or treated unfairly.

Should the same attitude apply with respect to borderline issues of jurisdiction? Or is the question not even open in a jurisdictional inquiry governed by the Due Process clause?

(5)(a) Turning to *Asahi,* note first the sharp split between the four Justices following Justice O'Connor and the four justices following Justice Brennan on the stream of commerce theory of jurisdiction. If Justice O'Connor rejects awareness that the product may enter the American market, without more, as a basis for jurisdiction, what additional elements would satisfy her?

---

[i] Russell J. Weintraub, *Due Process Limitations on the Personal Jurisdiction of State Courts: Time for Change,* 63 Ore. L. Rev. 485 at 530 (1984). at 530.

(b) Suppose, for instance, all the facts the same as in the actual case, except that, as Asahi knew, all of Chen Shing's output was sold in the United States, so that there could be no doubt that whatever Asahi sold to Chen Shing would eventually enter the American market. Would Justice O'Connor still say there was no jurisdiction over Asahi in an American court (state or federal), because Asahi did not engage in marketing and advertising in the United States or maintain its own distribution chain?

(c) Justice Brennan, joined (among others) by Justice White, who wrote for the Court in *World-Wide Volkswagen*, writes, at p. 571, that Justice O'Connor's opinion represents a marked retreat from its analysis in *World-Wide Volkswagen*. Do you agree? Which case presents the stronger case for adjudication at the place of the accident?

(d) Why do you suppose Justice Stevens did not join Justice Brennan's concurring opinion? Is it fair to add Stevens' opinion to Brennan's and conclude that the stream of commerce doctrine is alive and well?

(6) (a) Part II-B of Justice O'Connor's opinion moves away from "minimum contacts," "purposeful availment," "foreseeability" and similar catch phrases that have not succeeded in slowing down the volume of litigation concerning judicial jurisdiction in the United States. Is "reasonableness" more useful? . . . more persuasive?

(b) Note that "reasonableness" also appears in *International Shoe*, at pp. 488–89 *supra*, and in *World-Wide Volkswagen*, at p. 533.[j] What is it in *Asahi* that makes all but one Justice agree that it would be unreasonable to subject Asahi to the jurisdiction of the California court, though the Court is sharply divided on minimum contacts, foreseeability, etc.?

(c) Is the key that Asahi is a foreign country company? If the valve maker were established in Washington state, and the tire maker in Oregon, would it be less unreasonable to subject the valve maker to the jurisdiction of the California court? Suppose the valve maker, as in the actual case, were established only in Japan, and deliveries were made in that country, but the tire maker was (i) a California, or (ii) an Oregon corporation.

(d) Or is the critical element that the claim has nothing to do with California, in that it simply involves a dispute about an indemnity? Recall that this was true also in *West Coast Machinery*, p. 522, the case about the metal press made in Japan that injured the hand of an employee of Boeing. Would that case come out the other way after *Asahi*?

(e) One major difference between the two cases is that in *West Coast Machinery* the target of the indemnity claim was the principal manufacturer, while in *Asahi* the target made only the valve for the tube for the tire of the motorcycle. Would you think that the distinction between a manufacturer of a finished product and a component maker is jurisdictionally significant in a reasonableness inquiry?

(f) A way to probe the previous questions is to change not the facts of the case, but the litigation posture. Suppose there has been no settlement with Mr. Zurcher, the accident victim, and he asserts that he needs Asahi in the case, both for purposes of evidence and in case he cannot collect from the other defendants. Does (should?) the reasonableness inquiry yield a different result from the one set forth in Part II-B of Justice O'Connor's opinion?[k]

---

[j] See also Restatement (Second) of Conflict of Laws, §24(1971); Restatement (Third) of the Foreign Relations Law of the United States §421 (1987).

[k] In the decision upholding the jurisdiction of the California court that the U.S. Supreme Court reversed, the California Supreme Court wrote that the dismissal of Mr. Zurcher from the suit had "no bearing" on the propriety of California's

§ 7.05

(7)(a) Justice O'Connor, at p. 570, distinguishes between consideration of the interests of the several *States*, and the procedural and substantive policies of other *nations*. Is this simply the answer to question 6(c), or is there a suggestion that international law plays a role here?

(b) The same paragraph speaks of the "Federal interest in its foreign relations policies." Do you suppose this is a suggestion, condensed here to a few words but spelled out over several hundred pages in the Restatement (Third) of the Foreign Relations Law of the United States,[1] that a careful inquiry into competing interests of other concerned states is the essence of reasonableness in the exercise of jurisdiction, and that reasonableness is required by international law?

(c) If the Supreme Court had denied review, or had upheld the California Supreme Court, do you think that Japan would have had any basis to complain to the United States government? If not, is there nevertheless something to the "international context," mentioned by Justice O'Connor at the end of her opinion?

(8)(a) In *Hanson v. Denckla* and *World-Wide Volkswagen*, as well as *Shaffer v. Heitner*, at p. 591 *infra*, the Court is anxious to preserve the distinction between questions of jurisdiction and questions of choice of law. That wall of separation was breached in *Burger King* (p. 557 question 8, *supra*) where a decision to sustain jurisdiction of the Florida court was supported by a clause in the contract choosing Florida law. In *Asahi*, there was no choice of law clause, and indeed no evidence in the record of a contract at all (see p. 566). Is Justice O'Connor right (p. 570) in questioning the application of California law to the indemnity dispute?

(b) Justice O'Connor's citation of *Shutts* and *Allstate v. Hague* suggests that application of California law might even be unconstitutional. Is that right? Suppose that in the settlement with Mr. Zurcher, Cheng Shin paid out $1 million, against which it secured a release from the plaintiff. Under California law, if the fault of the valve maker were proved, it would be liable for indemnity or contribution. Suppose further that under Japanese law, liability for indemnity in these circumstances arises only on the basis of a judgment. Assuming all the parties are properly before the court, would it be wrong for the California court to apply California law? Unconstitutional?

(9)(a) Many observers wondered why Justice Scalia, who agreed that the decision of the California Supreme Court should be reversed, declined to concur in Part II-B of Justice O'Connor's opinion. Do you guess he is against a distinction between national and international cases? Skeptical about interest analysis? Distrustful of emphasis on reasonableness? If the latter, is Part II-A really more precise and focused than Part II-B? Reconsider this question after reading *Burnham* in the next section.

(b) Look back, finally, at the discussion in §7.03 concerning split torts and international sales transactions. Would any of them come out differently after *Asahi*? What about the statutes in the Documents Supplement such as the 1979 amendment to New York CPLR §302 (DS-77) and variations thereof?

(c) In a recent English case that came before the House of Lords, Lord Goff indicated that the criteria for sustaining jurisdiction over a nonresident under Order 11 are essentially the same as the criteria for dismissal on grounds of forum non conveniens, except that plaintiff has the

---

exercise of jurisdiction over Asahi. *Asahi Metal Industry Co. Ltd. v. The Superior Court of Solano County*, 39 Cal.3d 35 at 52, n.9; 702 P.2d 543 at 552; 216 Cal. Rptr. 385 at 395 (1985).

[1] §§ 401-488; see especially §§ 402-403 on jurisdiction to prescribe; § 421 on jurisdiction to adjudicate. See also p. 959, *infra* and chapter 10 generally.

burden as to jurisdiction, whereas defendant has the burden as to forum non conveniens.[m] Does *Asahi* suggest the same direction, i.e., that at least at the margin, there is an element of discretion in the grant or denial of jurisdiction?

(d) Note that an affirmative answer to the previous question would cast doubt on the whole concept of judicial jurisdiction as a constitutional issue. Before you conclude that that cannot be, reread Justice Black's brief and enigmatic opinion in *International Shoe*, pp. 490-491.

§ 7.06 Property as the Basis for Judicial Jurisdiction

[A] The Rise and Fall of Quasi in Rem Jurisdiction

Pennoyer v. Neff,[a] the case that brought the Supreme Court's nineteenth century view of jurisdiction under the Due Process clause, had two branches. In the branch that led to the actual outcome, the Court held that "[t]he authority of every tribunal is necessarily restricted by the territorial limits of the State in which it is established,"[b] and therefore "no tribunal established by it can extend process beyond that territory so as to subject either persons or property to its decisions."[c] In the other branch, the court said that a court *could* exercise jurisdiction over persons or property within its territory, provided that "in an action for money or damages where a defendant does not appear in the court, and is not found within the State, and is not a resident thereof, but has property therein, the jurisdiction of the court extends only over such property. . . ."[d] In the actual case, the plaintiff[e] had levied on the defendant's property in Oregon only after securing the judgment that was ultimately held invalid.[f] The clear inference from the Supreme Court's opinion in *Pennoyer v. Neff* was that if a plaintiff subjected a person's property to the court's jurisdiction at the outset, by attachment or garnishment,[g] he could not only litigate a claim in which the property was itself the source of the controversy—e.g., a title dispute, foreclosure of a mortgage, or partition of property held jointly—but also any other claim which,

---

[m] *Spiliada Maritime Corp. v. Cansulex Ltd.*, [1987] A.C. 460, 476, 480-81.

[a] 95 U.S. 714 (1878)

[b] 95 U.S. at 720.

[c] c*Id.* at 722.

[d] *Id.* at 720.

[e] I.e., Mr. Mitchell, the Oregon lawyer suing Mr. Neff to recover a legal fee.

[f] As at least four generations of law students learned, Mitchell sued Neff, a California resident, in an Oregon court serving him by publication, and secured a default judgment. Mitchell satisfied his judgment through a sale of Neff's land, which was bought by Pennoyer. Thereafter Neff sued Pennoyer in the federal circuit court in Oregon, claiming that the judgment was invalid and therefore Pennoyer could not have acquired good title. That claim was upheld both in the circuit court and in the U.S. Supreme Court. For more on the cast of characters, one of whom was Senator and another a Governor of Oregon, see Silberman, *Shaffer v. Heitner: The End of an Era*, 53 N.Y.U. L. Rev. 33, 44, n. 53 (1978).

[g] Attachment and garnishment are conceptually interchangeable—both describing a device whereby property of a defendant is provisionally subjected to the authority of a judicial officer, such as a marshall or sheriff, pending the outcome of litigation, substitution of the attached property by a bond, or discharge of the attachment/garnishment ordered by the court. The term "garnishment" is commonly applied to service of a restraining order on third persons obligated to the defendant, as in the case of debts, wages, bank accounts, insurance policies, and the like, while "attachment" is used more commonly with respect to property held directly by the defendant, typically including land and tangible personal property. The generic term attachment is used in this section to describe all kinds of judicial restraint of property prior to judgment.

if successfully established, could be satisfied out of proceeds of the sale of the property. Justice Field, for the Court, wrote:

> [T]he State, through its tribunals, may subject property situated within its limits owned by non-residents to the payment of the demand of its own citizens against them; and the exercise of this jurisdiction in no respect infringes upon the sovereignty of the State where the owners are domiciled. . . . It is in virtue of the State's jurisdiction over the property of the non-resident situated within its limits that its tribunals can inquire into that non-resident's obligations to its own citizens, and the inquiry can then be carried only to the extent necessary to control the disposition of the property. . . .[h]

Though Justice Field was probably thinking of land, the so-called quasi-in-rem jurisdiction, where a plaintiff had no interest in the property belonging to the defendant except as a way to secure jurisdiction and to satisfy a judgment, soon was applied to all kinds of assets—defendant's bank or brokerage accounts, debts owed by residents of the forum to the defendant, wages payable to defendant by a person domiciled in the forum, such as a railroad company, and so on.[i] The high point of the imaginative use of property to secure jurisdiction was reached in *Harris v. Balk*, discussed on pp. 602–03, question 2, *infra*. For the moment it is necessary only to observe that in the era before long-arm statutes, sophisticated views of what constitutes "doing business," and other devices for securing jurisdiction over non-residents, quasi-in-rem jurisdiction was the principal relief from the rule that a plaintiff either had to catch a nonresident defendant in the forum state, or follow him to his own domicile wherever he could be found.[j] On the other hand, while no end of questions arose about the details associated with quasi-in-rem actions—what property was subject to or exempt from attachment; whether or not an intangible asset was situated within the forum; what kind of notice must be given to defendant and by whom; what kind of showing (if any) had to be made by a plaintiff in order to secure an attachment; would a bond be necessary; could a defendant contest the action without risking being served personally; and what effect as res judicata would a judgment in a quasi-in-rem action have in other states (if any)—the basic question never arose in the hundred years following the Supreme Court's decision in *Pennoyer v. Neff*: is it right and fair that the given action should be tried before this court in this state?[k]

In addition to attachment for purposes of jurisdiction over nonresidents, the law of most states provided for attachment designed to secure the payment of a judgment by a defendant over whom

---

[h] 95 U.S. at 723.

[i] Many but not all states passed laws in the late nineteenth century exempting wages from garnishment. Creditors of a railroad employee would then go to another state where the railroad operated, secure a garnishment order, and when the employee came to collect his wages at his normal place of employment, the railroad (or other employer) would say it was bound by the out-of-state garnishment. See Lowenfeld, *In Search of the Intangible: A Comment on Shaffer v. Heitner*, 53 N.Y.U. L. Rev. 102, 115–16 (1978), and sources there cited.

[j] What is here referred to simply as quasi in rem jurisdiction, is sometimes referred to as quasi in rem, type II, type I being an action concerning the *res* but not binding against all the world. See e.g. *Shaffer v. Heitner, infra*, p. 584, n. 17.

[k] Of course the statement in the text is somewhat of an overstatement—never say "never." Particularly in academic writing, the question was raised from time to time, increasingly often after the decision in *International Shoe* undermined the foundations of *Pennoyer v. Neff*. The point in the text is that the question was virtually never raised in the ordinary action begun by attachment of a non-resident defendant's property. For a more detailed description of quasi-in-rem jurisdiction as it was perceived before the events described in the following paragraphs, and of what issues engaged courts and commentators, see *Developments in the Law: State Court Jurisdiction*, 73 Harv. L. Rev. 909, 948–66 (1960).

the court had jurisdiction, but who might remove or dissipate his assets during the pendency of an action. Often, of course, the motives of obtaining jurisdiction and securing property against which a judgment could be enforced in the forum state came together. Not infrequently, also, tying up the funds or other property of a defendant was a way of bringing him to the negotiating table or inducing him to settle on terms he might not otherwise have agreed to.[1]

In some cases the security attachment was used in connection with conditional sales—actions by department stores or finance companies against consumers who had fallen behind in payments. Other devices, not strictly security or jurisdictional attachments, but like them having the characteristic of seizing property without hearing or other safeguards for the debtor, were common. As public interest and consumer law spread throughout the United States, these devices came under the scrutiny of appellate courts and eventually of the U.S. Supreme Court. In a series of cases from 1969 to 1975, the Supreme Court subjected security attachments and analogous devices to heightened requirements of fairness under the Due Process clause.[m] Though the Court in these cases expressly excluded from its holdings attachments obtained for purposes of securing quasi-in-rem jurisdiction,[n] if one kind of pre-judgment attachment had to comply with prevailing notions of due process, it was hard to see why another kind of pre-judgment attachment did not. Various law review articles raised this question,[o] and one federal judge did, in a concurring opinion.[p] Some commentators even wondered whether jurisdiction based on attachment of property could survive at all in a system of jurisdiction based on fair play and substantial justice.

SHAFFER v. HEITNER

United States Supreme Court
433 U.S. 186 (1977)

MR. JUSTICE MARSHALL delivered the opinion of the Court.

The controversy in this case concerns the constitutionality of a Delaware statute that allows a court of that State to take jurisdiction of a lawsuit by sequestering any property of the defendant that happens to be located in Delaware. Appellants contend that the sequestration statute as applied in this case violates the Due Process Clause of the Fourteenth Amendment both because it permits the state courts to exercise jurisdiction despite the absence of sufficient contacts among the defendants, the litigation, and the State of Delaware and because it authorizes the deprivation

---

[1] For example, it happened from time to time that a foreign bank against which a U.S. plaintiff had a claim found its general dollar account with a New York bank—or even at the Federal Reserve Bank of New York—tied up in connection with a lawsuit in New York, thus bringing the foreign bank's international operations to a grinding halt, if only for a few days. Negotiations usually followed very quickly, sometimes to resolve a controversy completely, sometimes to release sufficient funds to enable the foreign bank to resume its operations while restraining enough to secure plaintiff's claim, realistically viewed.

[m] See *Sniadach v. Family Finance Corp.*, 395 U.S. 337 (1969); *Fuentes v. Shevin*, 407 U.S. 67 (1972); *Mitchell v. W. T. Grant Co.*, 416 U.S. 600 (1974); *North Georgia Finishing, Inc. v. Di-Chem. Inc.*, 419 U.S. 601 (1975). For a brief summary of these cases in the present context, see Silberman, note f, *supra*, at 53–57.

[n] See, esp., *Fuentes v. Shevin*, 407 U.S. at 91, n. 23.

[o] See, e.g., Note, *Quasi in Rem Jurisdiction and Due Process Requirements*, 82 Yale L.J. 1023 (1973); also articles and notes cited in Silberman, n. f, *supra*, at 55, n. 100, 57, n. 117–18.

[p] *Jonnet v. Dollar Savings Bank*, 530 F.2d 1123, 1130 (Gibbons, J. concurring) (3d Cir. 1976).

of defendants' property without providing adequate procedural safeguards. We find it necessary to consider only the first of these contentions.

I

Appellee Heitner, a nonresident of Delaware, is the owner of one share of stock in the Greyhound Corporation, a business incorporated under the laws of Delaware with its principal place of business in Phoenix, Ariz. On May 22, 1974, he filed a shareholder's derivative suit in the Court of Chancery for New Castle County, Del., in which he named as defendants Greyhound, its wholly owned subsidiary Greyhound Lines, Inc.,[1] and 28 present or former officers or directors of one or both of the corporations. In essence, Heitner alleged that the individual defendants had violated their duties to Greyhound by causing it and its subsidiary to engage in actions that resulted in the corporations being held liable for substantial damages in a private antitrust suit[2] and a large fine in a criminal contempt action.[3] The activities which led to these penalties took place in Oregon.

Simultaneously with his complaint, Heitner filed a motion for an order of sequestration of the Delaware property of the individual defendants pursuant to 10 Del.C. § 366.[4] This motion was accompanied by a supporting affidavit of counsel which stated that the individual defendants were nonresidents of Delaware. The affidavit identified the property to be sequestered as

> common stock, 3% Second Cumulative Preferred Stock and stock unit credits of the Defendant Greyhound Corporation, a Delaware corporation, as well as all options and all

---

[1] Greyhound Lines, Inc., is incorporated in California and has its principal place of business in Phoenix, Ariz.

[2] A judgment of $13,146,090 plus attorneys' fees was entered against Greyhound in *Mt. Hood Stages, Inc. v. Greyhound Corp.*, No. 68–374, D.Ore. (filed Nov. 29, 1973), aff'd, 555 F.2d 687 (9th Cir. 1977). See *Mt. Hood Stages, Inc. v. Greyhound Corp.*, 1973–2 Trade Cas. ¶ 74,824.

[3] See *United States v. Greyhound Corp.*, 363 F.Supp. 525 (ND Ill.1973), and 370 F.Supp. 881 (ND Ill. 1973), aff'd, 508 F.2d 529 (CA7 1974). Greyhound was fined $100,000 and Greyhound Lines $500,000.

[4] 10 Del.C. § 366 provides:

"(a) If it appears in any complaint filed in the Court of Chancery that the defendant or any one or more of the defendants is a nonresident of the State, the Court may make an order directing such nonresident defendant or defendants to appear by a day certain to be designated. Such order shall be served on such nonresident defendant or defendants by mail or otherwise, if practicable, and shall be published in such manner as the Court directs, not less than once a week for 3 consecutive weeks. The Court may compel the appearance of the defendant by the seizure of all or any part of his property, which property may be sold under the order of the Court to pay the demand of the plaintiff, if the defendant does not appear, or otherwise defaults. Any defendant whose property shall have been so seized and who shall have entered a general appearance in the cause may, upon notice to the plaintiff, petition the Court for an order releasing such property or any part thereof from the seizure. The Court shall release such property unless the plaintiff shall satisfy the Court that because of other circumstances there is a reasonable possibility that such release may render it substantially less likely that plaintiff will obtain satisfaction of any judgment secured. If such petition shall not be granted, or if no such petition shall be filed, such property shall remain subject to seizure and may be sold to satisfy any judgment entered in the cause. The Court may at any time release such property or any part thereof upon the giving of sufficient security.

"(b) The Court may make all necessary rules respecting the form of process, the manner of issuance and return thereof, the release of such property from seizure and for the sale of the property so seized, and may require the plaintiff to give approved security to abide any order of the Court respecting the property.

"(c) Any transfer or assignment of the property so seized after the seizure thereof shall be void and after the sale of the property is made and confirmed, the purchaser shall be entitled to and have all the right, title and interest of the defendant in and to the property so seized and sold and such sale and confirmation shall transfer to the purchaser all the right, title and interest of the defendant in and to the property as fully as if the defendant had transferred the same to the purchaser in accordance with law."

warrants to purchase said stock issued to said individual Defendants and all contractual obligations, all rights, debts or credits due or accrued to or for the benefit of any of the said Defendants under any type of written agreement, contract or other legal instrument of any kind whatever between any of the individual Defendants and said corporation.

The requested sequestration order was signed the day the motion was filed.[5] Pursuant to that order, the sequestrator[6] "seized" approximately 82,000 shares of Greyhound common stock belonging to 19 of the defendants,[7] and options belonging to another two defendants.[8] These seizures were accomplished by placing "stop transfer" orders or their equivalents on the books of the Greyhound Corporation. So far as the record shows, none of the certificates representing the seized property was physically present in Delaware. The stock was considered to be in Delaware, and so subject to seizure, by virtue of 8 Del.C. § 169, which makes Delaware the situs of ownership of all stock in Delaware corporations.[9]

All 28 defendants were notified of the initiation of the suit by certified mail directed to their last known addresses and by publication in a New Castle County newspaper. The 21 defendants whose property was seized (hereafter referred to as appellants) responded by entering a special appearance for the purpose of moving to quash service of process and to vacate the sequestration order. They contended that the *ex parte* sequestration procedure did not accord them due process of law and that the property seized was not capable of attachment in Delaware. In addition, appellants asserted that under the rule of *International Shoe Co. v. Washington,* they did not have sufficient contacts with Delaware to sustain the jurisdiction of that State's courts.

The Court of Chancery rejected these arguments in a letter opinion which emphasized the purpose of the Delaware sequestration procedure:

> The primary purpose of "sequestration" as authorized by 10 *Del.C.* § 366 is not to secure possession of property pending a trial between resident debtors and creditors on the issue of who has the right to retain it. On the contrary, as here employed, "sequestration" is a process used to compel the personal appearance of a nonresident defendant to answer and

---

[5] As a condition of the sequestration order, both the plaintiff and the sequestrator were required to file bonds of $1,000 to assure their compliance with the orders of the court.

Following a technical amendment of the complaint, the original sequestration order was vacated and replaced by an alias sequestration order identical in its terms to the original.

[6] The sequestrator is appointed by the court to effect the sequestration. His duties appear to consist of serving the sequestration order on the named corporation, receiving from that corporation a list of the property which the order affects, and filing that list with the court. For performing those services in this case, the sequestrator received a fee of $100 under the original sequestration order and $100 under the alias order.

[7] The closing price of Greyhound stock on the day the sequestration order was issued was $14. New York Times, May 23, 1974, at 62. Thus, the value of the sequestered stock was approximately $1.2 million.

[8] Debentures, warrants, and stock unit credits belonging to some of the defendants who owned either stock or options were also sequestered. In addition, Greyhound reported that it had an employment contract with one of the defendants calling for payment of $250,000 over a 12-month period. Greyhound refused to furnish any further information on that debt on the ground that since the sums due constituted wages, their seizure would be unconstitutional. See *Sniadach v. Family Finance Corp.,* 395 U.S. 337 (1969). Heitner did not challenge this refusal.

The remaining defendants apparently owned no property subject to the sequestration order.

[9] 8 Del.C. § 169 provides:

> For all purposes of title, action, attachment, garnishment and jurisdiction of all courts held in this State, but not for the purpose of taxation, the situs of the ownership of the capital stock of all corporations existing under the laws of this State, whether organized under this chapter or otherwise, shall be regarded as in this State.

defend a suit brought against him in a court of equity. *Sands v. Lefcourt Realty Corp.,* Del.Supr., 35 Del.Ch. 340 (1955). It is accomplished by the appointment of a sequestrator by this Court to seize and hold property of the nonresident located in this State subject to further Court order. If the defendant enters a general appearance, the sequestered property is routinely released, unless the plaintiff makes special application to continue its seizure, in which event the plaintiff has the burden of proof and persuasion.

This limitation on the purpose and length of time for which sequestered property is held, the court concluded, rendered inapplicable the due process requirements enunciated in *Sniadach v. Family Finance Corp., Fuentes v. Shevin* and *Mitchell v. W. T. Grant Co.*[a] The court also found no state law or federal constitutional barrier to the sequestrator's reliance on 8 Del.C. § 169. Finally, the court held that the statutory Delaware situs of the stock provided a sufficient basis for the exercise of *quasi in rem* jurisdiction by a Delaware court.

On appeal, the Delaware Supreme Court affirmed the judgment of the court of chancery. *Greyhound Corp. v. Heitner,* 361 A.2d 225 (1976). Most of the Supreme Court's opinion was devoted to rejecting appellants' contention that the sequestration procedure is inconsistent with the due process analysis developed in the *Sniadach* line of cases. The court based its rejection of that argument in part on its agreement with the court of chancery that the purpose of the sequestration procedure is to compel the appearance of the defendant, a purpose not involved in the *Sniadach* cases. The court also relied on what it considered the ancient origins of the sequestration procedure and approval of that procedure in the opinions of this Court,[10] Delaware's interest in asserting jurisdiction to adjudicate claims of mismanagement of a Delaware corporation, and the safeguards for defendants that it found in the Delaware statute. *Id.,* at 230–236.

Appellants' claim that the Delaware courts did not have jurisdiction to adjudicate this action received much more cursory treatment. The court's analysis of the jurisdictional issue is contained in two paragraphs:

> There are significant constitutional questions at issue here but we say at once that we do not deem the rule of *International Shoe* to be one of them. . . . The reason of course, is that jurisdiction under § 366 remains . . . *quasi in rem* founded on the presence of capital stock here, not on prior contact by defendants with this forum. Under 8 Del.C. § 169 the "situs of the ownership of the capital stock of all corporations existing under the laws of this State . . . [is] in this State," and that provides the initial basis for jurisdiction. Delaware may constitutionally establish situs of such shares here, . . . it has done so and the presence thereof provides the foundation for § 366 in this case . . . On this issue we agree with

---

[a] See p. 580, note m, *supra.*

[10] The court relied, 361 A.2d, at 228, 230–231, on our decision in *Ownbey v. Morgan,* 256 U.S. 94 (1921), and references to that decision in *North Georgia Finishing, Inc. v. Di-Chem, Inc.,* (1975) (Powell, J., concurring); *Calero-Toledo v. Pearson Yacht Leasing Co.,* 416 U.S. 663, 679 n. 14 (1974); *Mitchell v. W. T. Grant Co., Fuentes v. Shevin, Sniadach v. Family Finance Corp.* The only question before the Court in *Ownbey* was the constitutionality of a requirement that a defendant whose property has been attached file a bond before entering an appearance. We do not read the recent references to *Ownbey* as necessarily suggesting that *Ownbey* is consistent with more recent decisions interpreting the Due Process Clause.

Sequestration is the equity counterpart of the process of foreign attachment in suits at law considered in *Ownbey.* Delaware's sequestration statute was modeled after its attachment statute. See *Sands v. Lefcourt Realty Corp.,* 35 Del.Ch. 340, 344–345, 117 A.2d 365, 367 (Sup.Ct.1955); Folk & Moyer, *Sequestration in Delaware: A Constitutional Analysis,* 73 Colum.L.Rev. 749, 751–754 (1973).

the analysis made and the conclusion reached by Judge Stapleton in *U. S. Industries, Inc. v. Gregg,* D.Del., 348 F.Supp. 1004 (1972).[11]

We hold that seizure of the Greyhound shares is not invalid because plaintiff has failed to meet the prior contacts tests of *International Shoe.* 361 A.2d, at 229.

II

The Delaware courts rejected appellants' jurisdictional challenge by noting that this suit was brought as a *quasi in rem* proceeding. Since *quasi in rem* jurisdiction is traditionally based on attachment or seizure of property present in the jurisdiction, not on contacts between the defendant and the State, the courts considered appellants' claimed lack of contacts with Delaware to be unimportant. This categorical analysis assumes the continued soundness of the conceptual structure founded on the century-old case of *Pennoyer v. Neff.*

[The Court summarizes the decision in *Pennoyer.*][16]

From our perspective, the importance of *Pennoyer* is not its result but the fact that its principles, and corollaries derived from them, became the basic elements of the constitutional doctrine governing state court jurisdiction. See, e. g., Hazard, *A General Theory of State-Court Jurisdiction,* 1965 Sup.Ct.Rev. 241. As we have noted, under *Pennoyer* state authority to adjudicate was based on the jurisdiction's power over either persons or property. This fundamental concept is embodied in the very vocabulary which we use to describe judgments. If a court's jurisdiction is based on its authority over the defendant's person, the action and judgment are denominated "in personam" and can impose a personal obligation on the defendant in favor of the plaintiff. If jurisdiction is based on the court's power over property within its territory, the action is called "in rem" or "quasi in rem." The effect of a judgment in such a case is limited to the property that supports jurisdiction and does not impose a personal liability on the property owner, since he is not before the court.[17] In *Pennoyer's* terms, the owner is affected only "indirectly" by an *in rem* judgment adverse to his interest in the property subject to the court's disposition.

By concluding that "[t]he authority of every tribunal is necessarily restricted by the territorial limits of the State in which it is established," 95 U.S., at 720, *Pennoyer* sharply limited the availability of *in personam* jurisdiction over defendants not resident in the forum State. If a

---

[11] The District Court judgment in *U. S. Industries* was reversed by the Court of Appeals for the Third Circuit. 540 F.2d 142 (1976), petition for cert. pending, No. 76–359. The Court of Appeals characterized the passage from the Delaware Supreme Court's opinion quoted in text as "cryptic conclusions." *Id.,* at 149.

[16] Attachment was considered essential to the state court's jurisdiction for two reasons. First, attachment combined with substituted service would provide greater assurance that the defendant would actually receive notice of the action than would publication alone. Second, since the court's jurisdiction depended on the defendant's ownership of property in the State and could be defeated if the defendant disposed of that property, attachment was necessary to assure that the court had jurisdiction when the proceedings began and continued to have jurisdiction when it entered judgment. 95 U.S., at 727–728.

[17] "A judgment *in rem* affects the interests of all persons in designated property. A judgment *quasi in rem* affects the interests of particular persons in designated property. The latter is of two types. In one the plaintiff is seeking to secure a pre-existing claim in the subject property and to extinguish or establish the nonexistence of similar interests of particular persons. In the other the plaintiff seeks to apply what he concedes to be the property of the defendant to the satisfaction of a claim against him. Restatement, Judgments, 5–9." *Hanson v. Denckla,* [p. 501, *supra,* n. 12.] As did the Court in *Hanson,* we will for convenience generally use the term "*in rem*" in place of "*in rem* and *quasi in rem.*"

nonresident defendant could not be found in a State, he could not be sued there. On the other hand, since the State in which property was located was considered to have exclusive sovereignty over that property, *in rem* actions could proceed regardless of the owner's location. Indeed, since a State's process could not reach beyond its borders, this Court held after *Pennoyer* that due process did not require any effort to give a property owner personal notice that his property was involved in an *in rem* proceeding.

The *Pennoyer* rules generally favored nonresident defendants by making them harder to sue. This advantage was reduced, however, by the ability of a resident plaintiff to satisfy a claim against a nonresident defendant by bringing into court any property of the defendant located in the plaintiff's State. See, e. g., Zammit, *Quasi-In-Rem Jurisdiction: Outmoded and Unconstitutional?,* 49 St. John's L.Rev. 668, 670 (1975). For example, in the well-known case of *Harris v. Balk,* 198 U.S. 215 (1905), Epstein, a resident of Maryland, had a claim against Balk, a resident of North Carolina. Harris, another North Carolina resident, owed money to Balk. When Harris happened to visit Maryland, Epstein garnished his debt to Balk. Harris did not contest the debt to Balk and paid it to Epstein's North Carolina attorney. When Balk later sued Harris in North Carolina, this Court held that the Full Faith and Credit Clause, U.S. Const., Art. IV, § 1, required that Harris's payment to Epstein be treated as a discharge of his debt to Balk. This Court reasoned that the debt Harris owed Balk was an intangible form of property belonging to Balk, and that the location of that property traveled with the debtor. By obtaining personal jurisdiction over Harris, Epstein had "arrested" his debt to Balk, 198 U.S., at 223, and brought it into the Maryland court. Under the structure established by *Pennoyer,* Epstein was then entitled to proceed against that debt to vindicate his claim against Balk, even though Balk himself was not subject to the jurisdiction of a Maryland tribunal. See also, e.g., *Louisville & N. R. Co. v. Deer,* 200 U.S. 176 (1906); *Steele v. G. D. Searle & Co.,* 483 F.2d 339 (CA5 1973), cert. denied, 415 U.S. 958 (1974).

Pennoyer itself recognized that its rigid categories, even as blurred by the kind of action typified by *Harris,* could not accommodate some necessary litigation. Accordingly, Justice Field's opinion carefully noted that cases involving the personal status of the plaintiff, such as divorce actions, could be adjudicated in the plaintiff's home State even though the defendant could not be served within that State. Similarly, the opinion approved the practice of considering a foreign corporation doing business in a State to have consented to being sued in that State. This basis for *in personam* jurisdiction over foreign corporations was later supplemented by the doctrine that a corporation doing business in a State could be deemed "present" in the State, and so subject to service of process under the rule of *Pennoyer.* . . .

The advent of automobiles, with the concomitant increase in the incidence of individuals causing injury in States where they were not subject to *in personam* actions under *Pennoyer,* required further moderation of the territorial limits on jurisdictional power. This modification, like the accommodation to the realities of interstate corporate activities, was accomplished by use of a legal fiction that left the conceptual structure established in *Pennoyer* theoretically unaltered. The fiction used was that the out-of-state motorist, who it was assumed could be excluded altogether from the State's highways, had by using those highways appointed a designated state official as his agent to accept process. See *Hess v. Pawloski,* 274 U.S. 352 (1927). Since the motorist's "agent" could be personally served within the State, the state courts could obtain *in personam* jurisdiction over the nonresident driver.

The motorists' consent theory was easy to administer since it required only a finding that the out-of-state driver had used the State's roads. By contrast, both the fictions of implied consent to service on the part of a foreign corporation and of corporate presence required a finding that the corporation was "doing business" in the forum State. Defining the criteria for making that finding and deciding whether they were met absorbed much judicial energy. See, e.g., *International Shoe Co. v. Washington,* [p. 486, *supra*]. While the essentially quantitative tests which emerged from these cases purported simply to identify circumstances under which presence or consent could be attributed to the corporation, it became clear that they were in fact attempting to ascertain "what dealings make it just to subject a foreign corporation to local suit." *Hutchinson v. Chase & Gilbert,* 45 F.2d 139, 141 (CA2 1930) (L. Hand, J.). In *International Shoe,* we acknowledged that fact.

The question in *International Shoe* was whether the corporation was subject to the judicial and taxing jurisdiction of Washington. Chief Justice Stone's opinion for the Court began its analysis of that question by noting that the historical basis of *in personam* jurisdiction was a court's power over the defendant's person. That power, however, was no longer the central concern:

> But now that the *capias ad respondendum* has given way to personal service of summons or other form of notice, due process requires only that in order to subject a defendant to a judgment *in personam,* if he be not present within the territory of the forum, he have certain minimum contacts with it such that the maintenance of the suit does not offend "traditional notions of fair play and substantial justice."

Thus, the inquiry into the State's jurisdiction over a foreign corporation appropriately focused not on whether the corporation was "present" but on whether there have been "such contacts of the corporation with the state of the forum as make it reasonable, in the context of our federal system of government, to require the corporation to defend the particular suit which is brought there."

Mechanical or quantitative evaluations of the defendant's activities in the forum could not resolve the question of reasonableness:

> Whether due process is satisfied must depend rather upon the quality and nature of the activity in relation to the fair and orderly administration of the laws which it was the purpose of the due process clause to insure. That clause does not contemplate that a state may make binding a judgment *in personam* against an individual or corporate defendant with which the state has no contacts, ties, or relations.

Thus, the relationship among the defendant, the forum, and the litigation, rather than the mutually exclusive sovereignty of the States on which the rules of *Pennoyer* rest, became the central concern of the inquiry into personal jurisdiction. The immediate effect of this departure from *Pennoyer's* conceptual apparatus was to increase the ability of the state courts to obtain personal jurisdiction over nonresident defendants. See, e.g., Green, *Jurisdictional Reform in California,* 21 Hastings L.J. 1219, 1231–1233 (1970); Currie, *The Growth of the Long Arm: Eight Years of Extended Jurisdiction in Illinois,* 1963 U.Ill. L.F. 533; Developments, *supra,* at 1000–1008.

No equally dramatic change has occurred in the law governing jurisdiction *in rem.* There have, however, been intimations that the collapse of the *in personam* wing of *Pennoyer* has not left that decision unweakened as a foundation for *in rem* jurisdiction. Well-reasoned lower court opinions have questioned the proposition that the presence of property in a State gives that State jurisdiction to adjudicate rights to the property regardless of the relationship of the underlying dispute and the property owner to the forum. . . . The overwhelming majority of commentators have also rejected *Pennoyer's* premise that a proceeding "against" property is not a proceeding against the owners of that property. Accordingly, they urge that the "traditional notions of fair play and substantial justice" that govern a State's power to adjudicate *in personam* should also govern its power to adjudicate personal rights to property located in the State. See, e.g., Hazard, *supra;* Von Mehren & Trautman, *Jurisdiction to Adjudicate: A Suggested Analysis,* 79 Harv.L.Rev. 1121 (1966); Traynor, *Is This Conflict Really Necessary?,* 37 Tex.L.Rev. 657 (1959); Ehrenzweig, *The Transient Rule of Personal Jurisdiction: The "Power" Myth and Forum Conveniens,* 65 Yale L.J. 289 (1956); Developments, *supra.*

Although this Court has not addressed this argument directly, we have held that property cannot be subjected to a court's judgment unless reasonable and appropriate efforts have been made to give the property owners actual notice of the action. *Schroeder v. City of New York,* 371 U.S. 208 (1962); *Walker v. City of Hutchinson,* 352 U.S. 112 (1956); *Mullane v. Central Hanover Bank & Trust Co.,* 339 U.S. 306 (1950). This conclusion recognizes, contrary to *Pennoyer,* that an adverse judgment *in rem* directly affects the property owner by divesting him of his rights in the property before the court. . . .

It is clear, therefore, that the law of state court jurisdiction no longer stands securely on the foundation established in *Pennoyer.*[21] We think that the time is ripe to consider whether the standard of fairness and substantial justice set forth in *International Shoe* should be held to govern actions *in rem* as well as *in personam.*

III

The case for applying to jurisdiction *in rem* the same test of "fair play and substantial justice" as governs assertions of jurisdiction *in personam* is simple and straightforward. It is premised on recognition that "[t]he phrase, 'judicial jurisdiction over a thing,' is a customary elliptical way of referring to jurisdiction over the interests of persons in a thing. *Restatement (Second) of Conflict of Laws* § 56, introductory note. This recognition leads to the conclusion that in order to justify an exercise of jurisdiction *in rem,* the basis for jurisdiction must be sufficient to justify exercising "jurisdiction over the interests of persons in a thing."[23] The standard for determining whether an exercise of jurisdiction over the interests of persons is consistent with the Due Process Clause is the minimum contacts standard elucidated in *International Shoe.*

This argument, of course, does not ignore the fact that the presence of property in a State may bear on the existence of jurisdiction by providing contacts among the forum State, the defendant, and the litigation. For example, when claims to the property itself are the source of the underlying controversy between the plaintiff and the defendant, it would be unusual for the State where the property is located not to have jurisdiction. In such cases, the defendant's claim to property located in the State would normally indicate that he expected to benefit from the State's protection of his interest.[26] The State's strong interests in assuring the marketability of

---

[21] Cf. *Restatement (Second) of Conflict of Laws* § 59, comment a (possible inconsistency between principle of reasonableness which underlies field of judicial jurisdiction and traditional rule of *in rem* jurisdiction based solely on land in State); § 60, comment a (same as to jurisdiction based solely on chattel in State; § 68, comment c (rule of *Harris v. Balk* "might be thought inconsistent with the basic principle of reasonableness").

[23] It is true that the potential liability of a defendant in an *in rem* action is limited by the value of the property, but that limitation does not affect the argument. The fairness of subjecting a defendant to state court jurisdiction does not depend on the size of the claim being litigated. Cf. *Fuentes v. Shevin, supra,* 407 U.S., at 88–90 (1972); n. 32, *infra.*

[26] Cf. *Hanson v. Denckla,* at [pp. 503–04, *supra*].

property within its borders and in providing a procedure for peaceful resolution of disputes about the possession of that property would also support jurisdiction, as would the likelihood that important records and witnesses will be found in the State.[28] The presence of property may also favor jurisdiction in cases such as suits for injury suffered on the land of an absentee owner, where the defendant's ownership of the property is conceded but the cause of action is otherwise related to rights and duties growing out of that ownership.[29]

It appears, therefore, that jurisdiction over many types of actions which now are or might be brought *in rem* would not be affected by a holding that any assertion of state court jurisdiction must satisfy the *International Shoe* standard.[30] For the type of *quasi in rem* action typified by *Harris v. Balk* and the present case, however, accepting the proposed analysis would result in significant change. These are cases where the property which now serves as the basis for state court jurisdiction is completely unrelated to the plaintiff's cause of action. Thus, although the presence of the defendant's property in a State might suggest the existence of other ties among the defendant, the State, and the litigation, the presence of the property alone would not support the State's jurisdiction. If those other ties did not exist, cases over which the State is now thought to have jurisdiction could not be brought in that forum.

Since acceptance of the *International Shoe* test would most affect this class of cases, we examine the arguments against adopting that standard as they relate to this category of litigation.[31] Before doing so, however, we note that this type of case also presents the clearest illustration of the argument in favor of assessing assertions of jurisdiction by a single standard. For in cases such as *Harris* and this one, the only role played by the property is to provide the basis for bringing the defendant into court.[32] Indeed, the express purpose of the Delaware sequestration procedure is to compel the defendant to enter a personal appearance.[33] In such cases, if a direct assertion of personal jurisdiction over the defendant would violate the Constitution, it would seem that an indirect assertion of that jurisdiction should be equally impermissible.

The primary rationale for treating the presence of property as a sufficient basis for jurisdiction to adjudicate claims over which the State would not have jurisdiction if *International Shoe* applied is that a wrongdoer

---

[28] We do not suggest that these illustrations include all the factors that may affect the decision, nor that the factors we have mentioned are necessarily decisive.

[29] Cf. *Dubin v. City of Philadelphia,* 34 Pa.D. & C. 61 (1938). If such an action were brought under the *in rem* jurisdiction rather than under a long arm statute, it would be a *quasi in rem* action of the second type. See n. 17, *supra*.

[30] Cf. Smit, *The Enduring Utility of In Rem Rules: A Lasting Legacy of Pennoyer v. Neff,* 48 Brooklyn L.Rev. 600 (1977). We do not suggest that jurisdictional doctrines other than those discussed in text, such as the particularized rules governing adjudications of status, are inconsistent with the standard of fairness. See, e.g., Traynor, *supra,* at 660–661.

[31] Concentrating on this category of cases is also appropriate because in the other categories, to the extent that presence of property in the State indicates the existence of sufficient contacts under *International Shoe,* there is no need to rely on the property as justifying jurisdiction regardless of the existence of those contacts.

[32] The value of the property seized does serve to limit the extent of possible liability, but that limitation does not provide support for the assertion of jurisdiction. See n. 23, *supra*. In this case, appellants' potential liability under the *in rem* jurisdiction exceeds one million dollars. See nn. 7, 8, *supra*.

[33] See [p. 583]. This purpose is emphasized by Delaware's refusal to allow any defense on the merits unless the defendant enters a general appearance, thus submitting to full *in personam* liability.

"should not be able to avoid payment of his obligations by the expedient of removing his assets to a place where he is not subject to an in personam suit." Restatement (Second) of Conflicts § 66, comment a.

This justification, however, does not explain why jurisdiction should be recognized without regard to whether the property is present in the State because of an effort to avoid the owner's obligations. Nor does it support jurisdiction to adjudicate the underlying claim. At most, it suggests that a State in which property is located should have jurisdiction to attach that property, by use of proper procedures, as security for a judgment being sought in a forum where the litigation can be maintained consistently with *International Shoe*. See, e.g., Von Mehren & Trautman, *supra,* at 1178; Hazard, *supra,* at 284–285; Beale, *supra,* at 123–124. Moreover, we know of nothing to justify the assumption that a debtor can avoid paying his obligations by removing his property to a State in which his creditor cannot obtain personal jurisdiction over him. The Full Faith and Credit Clause, after all, makes the valid *in personam* judgment of one State enforceable in all other States.[36]

It might also be suggested that allowing *in rem* jurisdiction avoids the uncertainty inherent in the *International Shoe* standard and assures a plaintiff of a forum.[37] See Folk & Moyer, *supra,* at 749, 767 (1973). We believe, however, that the fairness standard of *International Shoe* can be easily applied in the vast majority of cases. Moreover, when the existence of jurisdiction in a particular forum under *International Shoe* is unclear, the cost of simplifying the litigation by avoiding the jurisdictional question may be the sacrifice of "fair play and substantial justice." That cost is too high.

We are left, then, to consider the significance of the long history of jurisdiction based solely on the presence of property in a State. Although the theory that territorial power is both essential to and sufficient for jurisdiction has been undermined, we have never held that the presence of property in a State does not automatically confer jurisdiction over the owner's interest in that property.[38] This history must be considered as supporting the proposition that jurisdiction based

---

[36] Once it has been determined by a court of competent jurisdiction that the defendant is a debtor of the plaintiff, there would seem to be no unfairness in allowing an action to realize on that debt in a State where the defendant has property, whether or not that State would have jurisdiction to determine the existence of the debt as an original matter.

[37] This case does not raise, and we therefore do not consider, the question whether the presence of a defendant's property in a State is a sufficient basis for jurisdiction when no other forum is available to the plaintiff.

[38] To the contrary, in *Pennington v. Fourth National Bank,* 243 U.S. 269, 271, (1917), we said: "The Fourteenth Amendment did not, in guaranteeing due process of law, abridge the jurisdiction which a State possessed over property within its borders, regardless of the residence or presence of the owner. That jurisdiction extends alike to tangible and to intangible property. Indebtedness due from a resident to a non-resident—of which bank deposits are an example—is property within the State. *Chicago, Rock Island & Pacific Ry. Co. v. Sturm,* 174 U.S. 710. It is, indeed, the species of property which courts of the several States have most frequently applied in satisfaction of the obligations of absent debtors. *Harris v. Balk.* Substituted service on a non-resident by publication furnishes no legal basis for a judgment *in personam. Pennoyer v. Neff.* But garnishment or foreign attachment is a proceeding *quasi in rem. Freeman v. Alderson,* 119 U.S. 185. The thing belonging to the absent defendant is seized and applied to the satisfaction of his obligation. The Federal Constitution presents no obstacle to the full exercise of this power."

More recent decisions, however, contain no similar sweeping endorsements of jurisdiction based on property. In *Hanson v. Denckla, supra,* 357 U.S. at 246, 78 S.Ct., at 1236, we noted that a State court's *in rem* jurisdiction is "[f]ounded on physical power" and that "[t]he basis of the jurisdiction is the presence of the subject property within the territorial jurisdiction of the forum State." We found in that case, however, that the property which was the basis for the assertion of *in rem* jurisdiction was not present in the State. We therefore did not have to consider whether the presence of property in the State was sufficient to justify jurisdiction. We also held that the defendant did not have sufficient contact with the State to justify *in personam* jurisdiction.

solely on the presence of property satisfies the demands of due process, cf. *Ownbey v. Morgan, supra,* 256 U.S., at 111 (1921), but it is not decisive. "[T]raditional notions of fair play and substantial justice" can be as readily offended by the perpetuation of ancient forms that are no longer justified as by the adoption of new procedures that are inconsistent with the basic values of our constitutional heritage. Cf. *Sniadach v. Family Finance Corp., supra,* 395 U.S., at 340, *Wolf v. Colorado,* 338 U.S. 25, 27 (1949). The fiction that an assertion of jurisdiction over property is anything but an assertion of jurisdiction over the owner of the property supports an ancient form without substantial modern justification. Its continued acceptance would serve only to allow state court jurisdiction that is fundamentally unfair to the defendant.

We therefore conclude that all assertions of state court jurisdiction must be evaluated according to the standards set forth in *International Shoe* and its progeny.[39]

IV

The Delaware courts based their assertion of jurisdiction in this case solely on the statutory presence of appellants' property in Delaware. Yet that property is not the subject matter of this litigation, nor is the underlying cause of action related to the property. Appellants' holdings in Greyhound do not, therefore, provide contacts with Delaware sufficient to support the jurisdiction of that State's courts over appellants. If it exists, that jurisdiction must have some other foundation.[40]

Appellee Heitner did not allege and does not now claim that appellants have ever set foot in Delaware. Nor does he identify any act related to his cause of action as having taken place in Delaware. Nevertheless, he contends that appellants' positions as directors and officers of a corporation chartered in Delaware provide sufficient "contacts, ties, or relations," *International Shoe Co. v. Washington,* with that State to give its courts jurisdiction over appellants in this stockholder's derivative action. This argument is based primarily on what Heitner asserts to be the strong interest of Delaware in supervising the management of a Delaware corporation. That interest is said to derive from the role of Delaware law in establishing the corporation and defining the obligations owed to it by its officers and directors. In order to protect this interest, appellee concludes, Delaware's courts must have jurisdiction over corporate fiduciaries such as appellants.

This argument is undercut by the failure of the Delaware Legislature to assert the state interest appellee finds so compelling. Delaware law bases jurisdiction not on appellants' status as corporate fiduciaries, but rather on the presence of their property in the State. Although the

---

[39] It would not be fruitful for us to re-examine the facts of cases decided on the rationales of *Pennoyer* and *Harris* to determine whether jurisdiction might have been sustained under the standard we adopt today. To the extent that prior decisions are inconsistent with this standard, they are overruled.

[40] Appellants argue that our determination that the minimum contacts standard of *International Shoe* governs jurisdiction here makes unnecessary any consideration of the existence of such contacts. Brief, at 27; Reply Brief, at 9. They point out that they were never personally served with a summons, that Delaware has no long arm statute which would authorize such service, and that the Delaware Supreme Court has authoritatively held that the existence of contacts is irrelevant to jurisdiction under 10 Del.C. § 366. As part of its sequestration order, however, the Court of Chancery directed its clerk to send each appellant a copy of the summons and complaint by certified mail. The record indicates that those mailings were made and contains return receipts from at least 19 of the appellants. None of the appellants has suggested that he did not actually receive the summons which was directed to him in compliance with a Delaware statute designed to provide jurisdiction over nonresidents. In these circumstances, we will assume that the procedures followed would be sufficient to bring appellants before the Delaware courts, if minimum contacts existed.

sequestration procedure used here may be most frequently used in derivative suits against officers and directors, the authorizing statute evinces no specific concern with such actions. Sequestration can be used in any suit against a nonresident, and reaches corporate fiduciaries only if they happen to own interests in a Delaware corporation, or other property in the State. But as Heitner's failure to secure jurisdiction over seven of the defendants named in his complaint demonstrates, there is no necessary relationship between holding a position as a corporate fiduciary and owning stock or other interests in the corporation.[43] If Delaware perceived its interest in securing jurisdiction over corporate fiduciaries to be as great as Heitner suggests, we would expect it to have enacted a statute more clearly designed to protect that interest.

Moreover, even if Heitner's assessment of the importance of Delaware's interest is accepted, his argument fails to demonstrate that Delaware is a fair forum for this litigation. The interest appellee has identified may support the application of Delaware law to resolve any controversy over appellants' actions in their capacities as officers and directors.[44] But we have rejected the argument that if a State's law can properly be applied to a dispute, its courts necessarily have jurisdiction over the parties to that dispute. "[The State] does not acquire . . . jurisdiction by being the "center of gravity" of the controversy, or the most convenient location for litigation. The issue is personal jurisdiction, not choice of law. It is resolved in this case by considering the acts of the [appellants]. *Hanson v. Denckla,* [p. 505, *supra*]."[45]

Appellee suggests that by accepting positions as officers or directors of a Delaware corporation, appellants performed the acts required by *Hanson v. Denckla*. He notes that Delaware law provides substantial benefits to corporate officers and directors,[46] and that these benefits were at least in part the incentive for appellants to assume their positions. It is, he says, "only fair and just" to require appellants, in return for these benefits, to respond in the State of Delaware when they are accused of misusing their powers.

But like Heitner's first argument, this line of reasoning establishes only that it is appropriate for Delaware law to govern the obligations of appellants to Greyhound and its stockholders. It does not demonstrate that appellants have "purposefully avail[ed themselves] of the privilege of conducting activities within the forum State," *Hanson v. Denckla,* in a way that would justify bringing them before a Delaware tribunal. Appellants have simply had nothing to do with the State of Delaware. Moreover, appellants had no reason to expect to be haled before a Delaware court. Delaware, unlike some States, has not enacted a statute that treats acceptance of a directorship as consent to jurisdiction in the State. And "[i]t strains reason . . . to suggest that anyone buying securities in a corporation formed in Delaware 'impliedly consents' to subject himself to Delaware's . . . jurisdiction on any cause of action." Folk & Moyer, *supra,* at 785. Appellants, who were not required to acquire interests in Greyhound in order to hold their

---

[43] Delaware does not require directors to own stock. 8 Del.C. § 141(b).

[44] In general, the law of the State of incorporation is held to govern the liabilities of officers or directors to the corporation and its stockholders. See *Restatement (Second) of Conflict of Laws* § 309. But see Cal.Corp. Code § 2115 (West Supp.1976). The rationale for the general rule appears to be based more on the need for a uniform and certain standard to govern the internal affairs of a corporation than on the perceived interest of the state of incorporation. Cf. *Koster v. Lumbermens Mutual Casualty Co.,* 330 U.S. 518, 527–528 (1947).

[45] Justice Black, although dissenting in *Hanson,* agreed with the majority that "the question whether the law of a State can be applied to a transaction is different from the question whether the courts of that State have jurisdiction to enter a judgment. . . ." [p. 507, *supra*].

[46] See, e. g., 8 Del.C. §§ 143, 145.

positions, did not by acquiring those interests surrender their right to be brought to judgment only in States with which they had had "minimum contacts."

The Due Process Clause "does not contemplate that a state may make binding a judgment . . . against an individual or corporate defendant with which the state has no contacts, ties, or relations." *International Shoe Co. v. Washington.*

Delaware's assertion of jurisdiction over appellants in this case is inconsistent with that constitutional limitation on state power. The judgment of the Delaware Supreme Court must, therefore, be reversed.

It is so ordered.

Mr. Justice REHNQUIST took no part in the consideration or decision of this case.

Mr. Justice POWELL, concurring.

I agree that the principles of *International Shoe Co. v. Washington,* should be extended to govern assertions of *in rem* as well as *in personam* jurisdiction in state court. I also agree that neither the statutory presence of appellants' stock in Delaware nor their positions as directors and officers of a Delaware corporation can provide sufficient contacts to support the Delaware courts' assertion of jurisdiction in this case.

I would explicitly reserve judgment, however, on whether the ownership of some forms of property whose situs is indisputably and permanently located within a State may, without more, provide the contacts necessary to subject a defendant to jurisdiction within the State to the extent of the value of the property. In the case of real property, in particular, preservation of the common law concept of *quasi in rem* jurisdiction arguably would avoid the uncertainty of the general *International Shoe* standard without significant cost to ""traditional notions of fair play and substantial justice.' "

Subject to that reservation, I join the opinion of the Court.

MR. JUSTICE STEVENS, concurring in the judgment.

The Due Process Clause affords protection against "judgments without notice." *International Shoe Co. v. Washington* (opinion of Black, J.). Throughout our history the acceptable exercise of *in rem* and *quasi in rem* jurisdiction has included a procedure giving reasonable assurance that actual notice of the particular claim will be conveyed to the defendant. Thus, publication, notice by registered mail, or extraterritorial personal service has been an essential ingredient of any procedure that serves as a substitute for personal service within the jurisdiction.

The requirement of fair notice also, I believe, includes fair warning that a particular activity may subject a person to the jurisdiction of a foreign sovereign. If I visit another state, or acquire real estate or open a bank account in it, I knowingly assume some risk that the state will exercise its power over my property or my person while there. My contact with the state, though minimal, gives rise to predictable risks.

Perhaps the same consequences should flow from the purchase of stock of a corporation organized under the laws of a foreign state, because to some limited extent one's property and affairs then become subject to the laws of the state of domicile of the corporation. As a matter of international law, that suggestion might be acceptable because a foreign investment is sufficiently unusual to make it appropriate to require the investor to study the ramifications of his decision. But a purchase of securities in the domestic market is an entirely different matter.

One who purchases shares of stock on the open market can hardly be expected to know that he has thereby become subject to suit in a forum remote from his residence and unrelated to the transaction. As a practical matter, the Delaware Sequestration Statute creates an unacceptable risk of judgment without notice. Unlike the 49 other States, Delaware treats the place of incorporation as the situs of the stock, even though both the owner and the custodian of the shares are elsewhere. Moreover, Delaware denies the defendant the opportunity to defend the merits of the suit unless he subjects himself to the unlimited jurisdiction of the court. Thus, it coerces a defendant either to submit to personal jurisdiction in a forum which could not otherwise obtain such jurisdiction or to lose the securities which have been attached. If its procedure were upheld, Delaware would, in effect, impose a duty of inquiry on every purchaser of securities in the national market. For unless the purchaser ascertains both the state of incorporation of the company whose shares he is buying, and also the idiosyncrasies of its law, he may be assuming an unknown risk of litigation. I therefore agree with the Court that on the record before us no adequate basis for jurisdiction exists and that the Delaware statute is unconstitutional on its face.

How the Court's opinion may be applied in other contexts is not entirely clear to me. I agree with Mr. Justice Powell that it should not be read to invalidate *in rem* jurisdiction where real estate is involved. I would also not read it as invalidating other long accepted methods of acquiring jurisdiction over persons with adequate notice of both the particular controversy and also that their local activities might subject them to suit. My uncertainty as to the reach of the opinion, and my fear that it purports to decide a great deal more than is necessary to dispose of this case, persuade me merely to concur in the judgment.

MR. JUSTICE BRENNAN, concurring and dissenting.

I join Parts I–III of the Court's opinion. I fully agree that the minimum-contacts analysis developed in *International Shoe Co. v. Washington,* represents a far more sensible construct for the exercise of state court jurisdiction than the patchwork of legal and factual fictions that has been generated from the decision in *Pennoyer v. Neff.* It is precisely because the inquiry into minimum contacts is now of such overriding importance, however, that I must respectfully dissent from Part IV of the Court's opinion.

I

[Justice Brennan argues that since Delaware did not purport to base its jurisdiction on minimum contacts between the defendant and the state, and since no evidence on the extent of such contacts is in the record, the Supreme Court should not now rule on the sufficiency of the contacts in this case.]

II

Nonetheless, because the Court rules on the minimum-contacts question, I feel impelled to express my view. While evidence derived through discovery might satisfy me that minimum contacts are lacking in a given case, I am convinced that as a general rule a state forum has jurisdiction to adjudicate a shareholder derivative action centering on the conduct and policies of the directors and officers of a corporation chartered by that State. Unlike the Court, I therefore would not foreclose Delaware from asserting jurisdiction over appellants were it persuaded to do so on the basis of minimum contacts.

It is well settled that a derivative lawsuit as presented here does not inure primarily to the benefit of the named plaintiff. Rather, the primary beneficiaries are the corporation and its owners, the shareholders. "The cause of action which such a plaintiff brings before the court is not his own but the corporation's. . . . Such a plaintiff often may represent an important public and stockholder interest in bringing faithless managers to book." *Koster v. Lumbermen Mutual Co.,* 330 U.S. 518, 522, 524 (1947).

Viewed in this light, the chartering State has an unusually powerful interest in insuring the availability of a convenient forum for litigating claims involving a possible multiplicity of defendant fiduciaries and for vindicating the State's substantive policies regarding the management of its domestic corporations. I believe that our cases fairly establish that the States's valid substantive interests are important considerations in assessing whether it constitutionally may claim jurisdiction over a given cause of action.

In this instance, Delaware can point to at least three interrelated public policies that are furthered by its assertion of jurisdiction. First, the State has a substantial interest in providing restitution for its local corporations that allegedly have been victimized by fiduciary misconduct, even if the managerial decisions occurred outside the State. . . . Second, state courts have legitimately read their jurisdiction expansively when a cause of action centers in an area in which the forum state possesses a manifest regulatory interest. . . . Finally, a State like Delaware has a recognized interest in affording a convenient forum for supervising and overseeing the affairs of an entity that is purely the creation of that State's law. I, of course, am not suggesting that Delaware's varied interests would justify its acceptance of jurisdiction over any transaction touching upon the affairs of its domestic corporations. But a derivative action which raises allegations of abuses of the basic management of an institution whose existence is created by the State and whose powers and duties are defined by state law fundamentally implicates the public policies of that forum.

To be sure, the Court is not blind to these considerations. It notes that the State's interests "may support the application of Delaware law to resolve any controversy over appellants' actions in their capacities as officers and directors." But this, the Court argues, pertains to choice of law, not jurisdiction. I recognize that the jurisdictional and choice-of-law inquiries are not identical. *Hanson v. Denckla.* But I would not compartmentalize thinking in this area quite so rigidly as it seems to me the Court does today, for both inquiries "are often closely related and to a substantial degree depend upon similar considerations." *Id.,* at p. 507 (Black, J., dissenting). In either case an important linchpin is the extent of contacts between the controversy, the parties, and the forum state. While constitutional limitations on the choice of law are by no means settled, see, e. g., *Home Ins. Co. v. Dick,* important considerations certainly include the expectancies of the parties and the fairness of governing the defendants' acts and behavior by rules of conduct created by a given jurisdiction. See, e.g., *Restatement (Second) Choice of Law* § 6. These same factors bear upon the propriety of a State's exercising jurisdiction over a legal dispute. At the minimum, the decision that it is fair to bind a defendant by a State's laws and rules should prove to be highly relevant to the fairness of permitting that same State to accept jurisdiction for adjudicating the controversy.

Furthermore, I believe that practical considerations argue in favor of seeking to bridge the distance between the choice-of-law and jurisdictional inquiries. Even when a court would apply the law of a different forum,[3] as a general rule it will feel less knowledgeable and comfortable

---

[3] In this case the record does not inform us whether an actual conflict is likely to arise between Delaware law and that of the likely alternative forum. Pursuant to the general rule, I assume that Delaware law probably would obtain in the foreign court. *Restatement (Second) Conflicts of Law* § 309.

in interpretation, and less interested in fostering the policies of that foreign jurisdiction, than would the courts established by the State that provides the applicable law.

Obviously, such choice-of-law problems cannot entirely be avoided in a diverse legal system such as our own. Nonetheless, when a suitor seeks to lodge a suit in a State with a substantial interest in seeing its own law applied to the transaction in question, we could wisely act to minimize conflicts, confusion, and uncertainty by adopting a liberal view of jurisdiction, unless considerations of fairness or efficiency strongly point in the opposite direction.

This case is not one where, in my judgment, this preference for jurisdiction is adequately answered. Certainly nothing said by the Court persuades me that it would be unfair to subject appellants to suit in Delaware. The fact that the record does not reveal whether they "set foot" or committed "act related to [the] cause of action" in Delaware, . . . is not decisive, for jurisdiction can be based strictly on out-of-state acts having foreseeable effects in the forum state. E. g., *McGee v. International Life Ins. Co., supra; Gray v. American Radiator & Standard Sanitary Corp., supra;* Restatement (Second) Conflicts of Law § 37. I have little difficulty in applying this principle to nonresident fiduciaries whose alleged breaches of trust are said to have substantial damaging effect on the financial posture of a resident corporation.[4] Further, I cannot understand how the existence of minimum contracts in a constitutional sense is at all affected by Delaware's failure statutorily to express an interest in controlling corporate fiduciaries. . . . To me this simply demonstrates that Delaware did not elect to assert jurisdiction to the extent the Constitution would allow.[5] Nor would I view as controlling or even especially meaningful Delaware's failure to exact from appellants their consent to be sued. . . . Once we have rejected the jurisdictional framework created in *Pennoyer v. Neff,* I see no reason to rest jurisdiction on a fictional outgrowth of that system such as the existence of a consent statute, expressed or implied.[6]

I, therefore, would approach the minimum contacts analysis differently than does the Court. Crucial to me is the fact that appellants voluntarily associated themselves with the State of

---

[4] I recognize, of course, that identifying a corporation as a resident of the chartering state is to build upon a legal fiction. In many respects, however, the law acts as if state chartering of a corporation has meaning. E. g., 28 U.S.C. § 1332(c) (for diversity purposes, a corporation is a citizen of the state of incorporation). And, if anything, the propriety of treating a corporation as a resident of the incorporating state seems to me particularly appropriate in the context of a shareholder derivative suit, for the state realistically may perceive itself as having a direct interest in guaranteeing the enforcement of its corporate laws, in assuring the solvency and fair management of its domestic corporations, and in protecting from fraud those shareholders who placed their faith in that state-created institution.

[5] In fact, it is quite plausible that the Delaware Legislature never felt the need to assert direct jurisdiction over corporate managers precisely because the sequestration statute heretofore has served as a somewhat awkward but effective basis for achieving such personal jurisdiction. See, e. g., *Hughes Tool Co. v. Fawcett Publications, Inc.,* 290 A.2d 693, 695 (Del.Ch.1972): "Sequestration is most frequently resorted to in suits by stockholders against corporate directors in which recoveries are sought for the benefit of the corporation on the ground of claimed breaches of fiduciary duty on the part of directors."

[6] Admittedly, when one consents to suit in a forum, his expectation is enhanced that he may be haled into that State's courts. To this extent, I agree that consent may have bearing on the fairness of accepting jurisdiction. But whatever is the degree of personal expectation that is necessary to warrant jurisdiction should not depend on the formality of establishing a consent law. Indeed, if one's expectations are to carry such weight, then appellants here might be fairly charged with the understanding that Delaware would decide to protect its substantial interests through its own courts, for they certainly realized that in the past the sequestration law has been employed primarily as a means of securing the appearance of corporate officials in the State's courts. *Supra,* at n. 5. Even in the absence of such a statute, however, the close and special association between a state corporation and its managers should apprise the latter that the state may seek to offer a convenient forum for addressing claims of fiduciary breach of trust.

Delaware, "invoking the benefits and protections of its laws," by entering into a long term and fragile relationship with one of its domestic corporations. They thereby elected to assume powers and to undertake responsibilities wholly derived from that State's rules and regulations, and to become eligible for those benefits that Delaware law makes available to its corporations' officials. E. g., 8 Del.C. §§ 143 (interest-free loans); 145 (indemnification). While it is possible that countervailing issues of judicial efficiency and the like might clearly favor a different forum, they do not appear on the meager record before us; and, of course, we are concerned solely with "minimum" contacts, not the "best" contacts. I thus do not believe that it is unfair to insist that appellants make themselves available to suit in a competent forum that Delaware might create for vindication of its important public policies directly pertaining to appellants' fiduciary associations with the State.

INTERMEAT, INC. v. AMERICAN POULTRY INCORPORATED

United States Court of Appeals, Second Circuit
575 F.2d 1017 (1978)

GURFEIN, CIRCUIT JUDGE:

This appeal requires us to consider for the first time the effect of the constitutional rule announced in *Shaffer v. Heitner,* on the New York law authorizing *quasi-in-rem* jurisdiction over a nonresident defendant based on the attachment of a debt due to the defendant from a debtor found in New York. N.Y. C.P.L.R. §§ 6202, 5201, 314, 315.

Intermeat, Inc., a New York corporation with its office in Great Neck, New York, brought a suit in New York Supreme Court to recover damages from American Poultry Incorporated, an Ohio corporation, for wrongful rejection of a shipment of meat. After the action was removed to the United States District Court for the Eastern District of New York, the District Court (Hon. Jack B. Weinstein, Judge) held in a pre-trial order that it lacked *in personam* jurisdiction over American Poultry Incorporated ("American Poultry"). The District Court stayed its order of dismissal, however, pending disposition of a motion by Intermeat, Inc. ("Intermeat") to attach a debt in an amount exceeding the claim in suit, owed to American Poultry by the Great Atlantic & Pacific Tea Co. ("A&P"), a corporation doing business in New York. After entering an order of attachment, the District Court sitting without a jury heard the evidence and entered a judgment for Intermeat in the amount of $19,800.99 (the difference between the contract price and the amount remitted by the defendant) plus interest at the statutory rate of 6%, basing *quasi-in-rem* jurisdiction on the attachment. The court held that there were sufficient "minimum contacts" with New York to satisfy *Shaffer v. Heitner*. American Poultry, relying principally on *Shaffer v. Heitner,* contends that the District Court's assertion of jurisdiction based on the attachment of the debt was unconstitutional. It also argues that even if the District Court had jurisdiction, it should have held that the rejection of the meat by the defendant was proper. Intermeat contends that it should have been awarded its actual bank financing charges rather than interest at the statutory rate.

American Poultry has no office in New York, nor has it consented to service of process on it through the Secretary of State. Intermeat and American Poultry did, however, enter into at least five contracts for the sale of imported meat to American Poultry before January 1974. In each case, Intermeat sent to American Poultry from its office in New York a contract describing the goods sold, the price, and the delivery terms; in some instances American Poultry signed and returned a copy of the contract to the Great Neck office, while in others it apparently retained both copies without objection to the terms. Some of the contracts called for delivery to American Poultry in Cleveland, while others specified Port Newark[1] and Philadelphia. Each of the contracts, prepared on Intermeat's form contract showing its New York address, contained an arbitration clause providing for arbitration in New York in the following terms:

> Any dispute or controversy arising in or out of this contract shall be submitted to the American Arbitration Association, New York, N.Y., for arbitration in accordance with its rules and the parties hereto agree to be bound by its determination.

The District Court also found that the defendant American Poultry sells large quantities of meat to persons doing substantial business in New York, including A&P. Indeed, there was evidence that the volume of defendant's business with New York companies amounted to as much as seven million dollars a year, and that 25 to 30% of the defendant's imported meat business is with New York importers. Payments for meat purchased in this manner are made by check mailed to New York.

With this background we turn to the contract in suit. In January 1974 Intermeat and American Poultry, through the mediation of a Philadelphia broker, entered into the contract in suit, for the purchase of two loads (30 long tons) of meat by American Poultry. Intermeat sent to American Poultry one of its form contracts describing the meat as "Australian 3rd mfg. cow crops and hinds, Richardson Production," setting a price of $0.95/lb. ex-dock Philadelphia, and calling for shipment from Australia in January or early February. The standard arbitration clause appeared at the foot of the contract. As it had done in several previous transactions with Intermeat, American Poultry did not sign and return a copy of the contract to Intermeat but simply retained both copies of the contract without making any objection to its terms.

American Poultry took delivery of the meat when it arrived in Philadelphia in March 1974 and had it transported to its Cleveland plant. American Poultry notified Intermeat shortly thereafter that it was rejecting the delivery because the cartons containing the meats were marked "Tasmeats" rather than "Richardson Production." In June 1974 American Poultry sold the meat and remitted to Intermeat $44,039.01, a sum less than the original contract price by $19,800.99.[2]

I. *Jurisdiction*

The jurisdiction of a federal court over the person of a foreign corporation in a diversity action involves questions of both state and federal law. The defendant must be subject to service of process under the law of the state of the forum, a question of state law, FRCP 4, 64, and the exercise of such jurisdiction must be consistent with due process, a question of federal law. *Perkins v. Benguet Consolidated Mining Co.*, 342 U.S. 437, 440 (1952); *Arrowsmith v. United*

---

[1] Port Newark is in New Jersey, but it is under the jurisdiction of the Port of New York Authority, a bi-state agency of New York and New Jersey.

[2] Intermeat initially demanded that American Poultry arbitrate the dispute over the balance of the contract price before the American Arbitration Association in New York. American Poultry countered by filing a suit in the United States District Court for the Northern District of Ohio seeking an injunction against arbitration in New York. In reply, Intermeat filed a motion for summary judgment ordering arbitration in New York. This motion was denied, and Intermeat voluntarily withdrew its demand for arbitration. American Poultry thereupon voluntarily discontinued the Ohio action. Intermeat then filed a complaint in the Supreme Court of New York, asking money damages for breach of contract. The case was removed to the District Court resulting in the judgment previously mentioned.

Press International, 320 F.2d 219, 222–23 (2d Cir. 1963), *citing Pulson v. American Rolling Mill Co.,* 170 F.2d 193, 194–95 (1st Cir. 1948). In this case, we consider the effect of the new constitutional standard announced in *Shaffer v. Heitner, supra,* on the New York law authorizing jurisdiction based on the attachment in New York of a debt owed to a defendant foreign corporation. We are not concerned with personal service based on defendant's "doing business" in the state, N.Y. C.P.L.R. § 301, nor with activity arising out of a contract executed in New York. N.Y. C.P.L.R. § 302.

New York law provides for the attachment of any debt, "whether it was incurred within or without the state, to or from a resident or non-resident." N.Y. C.P.L.R. §§ 6202, 5201. Once a debt owed to a foreign corporation is attached in New York, the foreign corporation may be personally served with a summons outside of the state, or, in some instances, served by publication. N.Y. C.P.L.R. §§ 314, 315. These general rules, with variations of detail unimportant here, have long been part of the law of New York. . . . The Supreme Court, in *Harris v. Balk,* established the constitutionality of such jurisdiction, even where the debt attached was unrelated to the plaintiff's cause of action and the defendant had no ties to the forum state except the debt attached. The Court specifically approved the New York law of attachment under the old Civil Practice Act §§ 233, 902, and 903 in *Huron Holding Corp. v. Lincoln Mine Operating Company,* 312 U.S. 183 (1941).

As long ago as 1930, Judge Learned Hand, uncomfortable with the fiction of a corporate "presence" as the basis for jurisdiction over foreign corporations, suggested what he termed a "practical test." Stated simply, it was "whether the extent and continuity of what it has done in the state in question makes it reasonable to bring it before one of its courts." *Hutchinson v. Chase & Gilbert,* 45 F.2d 139, 141 (2d Cir. 1930). Following Judge Hand's lead, the Supreme Court reformulated the constitutional limit on *in personam* jurisdiction in *International Shoe Co. v. Washington.* . . . Though the obligation sued upon in *International Shoe* arose directly out of the corporation's limited activities within the state, the Court made it clear that the general standard it announced should be applied to test the constitutionality of any assertion of *in personam* jurisdiction. 326 U.S. at 317–19. The rejection of the "doing business" and "presence" formulations as the limits of state jurisdiction over nonresidents was confirmed in *McGee v. International Life Insurance Co.,* where the Court upheld the power of the state to subject a foreign corporation to suit in its courts on an isolated insurance contract which had "substantial connection with that state." The Court noted that "with this increasing nationalization of commerce has come a great increase in the amount of business conducted by mail across state lines. At the same time modern transportation and communication have made it less burdensome for a party sued to defend himself in a State where he engages in economic activity."

The Supreme Court's shift from the "presence" test of jurisdiction to the "minimum contacts-fairness" test in *International Shoe* did not turn on the *in personam* nature of the jurisdiction asserted in that case, however. . . .

In *Shaffer v. Heitner, supra,* decided on June 24, 1977, the Supreme Court held that the "minimum contacts" standard of due process set down for *in personam* jurisdiction in *International Shoe* should be used also to test jurisdiction based on the attachment of property. . . . In reaching its decision that the Delaware sequestration statute as applied in *Shaffer v. Heitner* violated due process requirements, the Court revised longstanding constitutional doctrine that was in the process of critical erosion. Speaking through Mr. Justice Marshall, the Court accepted the idea that a proceeding "against" property is actually a proceeding against the owner of the property. The Court made it clear that this entailed the rejection of the broad rule of *Harris v. Balk,* which held that the presence of property within a state gave that state constitutional authority to enter a valid judgment against the owner of the property to the extent of the value of the property, even though the property was unrelated to the claim sued upon and even though the defendant had no contact with the forum. The Court did not indicate total disapproval of *Harris v. Balk,* for it noted that attachment of a debt is proper wherever the debtor is found, if the attachment is authorized by the law of the state. *Shaffer v. Heitner,* [pp. 588-89, *supra.*]

The application of the "minimum contacts" standard to proceedings begun by attachment now means that the presence of the defendant's property within New York must be viewed as only one contact of the defendant with the state, to be considered along with other contacts in deciding whether the assertion of jurisdiction is consistent with "traditional notions of fair play and substantial justice." Hence, some attachments still valid under New York law, and still constituting valid bases (so far as New York law is concerned) for *quasi-in-rem* jurisdiction, will no longer satisfy the applicable due process requirement where the defendant has less than minimum contacts with New York.

The constitutional standard of due process may be met by fewer contacts, however, than those required under the more restrictive statutory test of "doing business," N.Y. C.P.L.R. § 301 . . . or the (possibly) more restrictive test of "transacting business," N.Y. C.P.L.R. § 302, since neither of these statutes governs jurisdiction based on attachment.

The difference between an *in personam* jurisdiction and a jurisdiction by attachment of a debt is that, in the former case, sitting as a New York court in a diversity case, we would have to decide the continued strength of the "doing business" concept in New York law, and hence decide whether the acts done in New York by American Poultry were enough to support such jurisdiction under N.Y. C.P.L.R. § 301, as well as enough to satisfy the test of *International Shoe.* On the other hand, in dealing with jurisdiction based upon an attachment, the test is narrower. The test is not whether the defendant is "doing business" in New York, a concept which a state, if it wishes to, is still free to assert as a minimum requirement, but whether there are sufficient minimum contacts to make it fair and just that the foreign corporation be required to come to New York to defend the action that was begun by attachment.

The "minimum contacts" test cannot be formularized. Rather, as Judge Hand suggested, such a test leaves the court to "step from tuft to tuft across the morass," *Hutchinson v. Chase & Gilbert, supra,* 45 F.2d at 142, deciding in each case whether the relationship among the plaintiff, the defendant, and the forum state make it fair and reasonable to compel the defendant to try the action in the forum state. In the case at bar, we agree with the District Court that its exercise of jurisdiction over American Poultry was consistent with due process.

We deal here with a contract which, if it was not born in New York, was at least conceived here. It was sent from the plaintiff in New York to the defendant in Ohio. The claim for relief "was based on a contract which had substantial connections with that State." *See McGee v. International Life Ins. Co.* And while we need not decide whether *in personam* jurisdiction could have attached in this case, it seems evident that the "substantial connection" of the contract with New York must be considered along with the added factor of the attachment of an intangible within the jurisdiction of the state in weighing the "minimum contacts" required for Fourteenth Amendment due process, particularly since the debtor was doing business in New York. In addition, American Poultry, a Cleveland firm, purchases a large percentage of its meat through New York importers, sometimes taking delivery of the meat at Port Newark. In the past few years it has contracted at least five times with Intermeat, a New York corporation, for such import purchases. Moreover, it twice signed and returned to Intermeat contracts committing it to arbitration in New York of disputes with Intermeat. In other transactions, American Poultry consented to arbitration in New York by retaining without objection Intermeat's form contract, which included the New York arbitration clause. N.Y. U.C.C. § 2–201(2). Consent to arbitration in New York is a consent to personal jurisdiction of the courts in New York. *Merrill Lynch, Pierce, Fenner & Smith, Inc. v. Lecopulos,* 553 F.2d 842 (2d Cir. 1977). Where a corporation located in another state is continuously involved in the commerce of New York and has repeatedly consented to arbitration in New York, we see nothing unfair or unreasonable in requiring it to defend in New York an action arising out of such commerce. Even if American Poultry was not "doing business" in New York under N.Y. C.P.L.R. § 301, it had enough "minimum contacts" with New York to satisfy the requirements of due process.

On this appeal we need not consider a possible alternative ground for upholding jurisdiction—jurisdiction by consent. It is clear that if American Poultry did agree to arbitrate this dispute in New York, and if Intermeat did not waive its right to demand arbitration before it filed suit in New York, the District Court could have exercised personal jurisdiction over American Poultry and ordered arbitration. *Merrill Lynch, Pierce, Fenner & Smith, Inc. v. Lecopulos, supra.* Because the District Court properly exercised jurisdiction under New York's attachment law, however, and because Intermeat does not appeal the District Court's refusal to order arbitration, we need not decide if an issue of fact exists whether American Poultry agreed to arbitrate the contract in suit, or whether Intermeat waived its rights under such an agreement by its conduct.

. . .

[The court affirmed the finding that the goods were wrongfully rejected, and awarded the plaintiff's actual financing charges rather than the lower statutory interest.]

The judgment is, in all other respects, affirmed.

NOTES AND QUESTIONS

(1)(a) The most important statement in *Shaffer v. Heitner,* one with which all eight of the participating Justices agree, is that from now on all types of civil actions are governed by the requirement of fair play and substantial justice. The idea that some actions could escape this requirement because they depended on power, while others demanded fairness, just doesn't go over, when stated that way. Moreover, in the context of the actual case (as in *Harris v. Balk*) the idea of seizure as a substitute for process made no sense: there was nothing to grasp but a concept—the situs of a debt or of shares of stock.

(b) In fact, plaintiffs in *Shaffer v. Heitner* did not argue to the Supreme Court that their action was not required to meet the test of due process, but rather that on the facts of the case due process was satisfied. Was it?

(c) The Supreme Court of Delaware[a] recognizing that it had a due process question before it, compared the case with the security attachment cases from *Sniadach* to *Di-Chem.*[b] While

---

[a] *Greyhound Corporation v. Heitner,* 361 A.2d 225 (Del. 1976).

[b] See p. 580, note m, *supra.*

it conceded that any procedure whereby property was seized prior to a determination of the merits "has the seeds, if not the fruits of unfairness,"[c] it concluded that the procedure for release of the attached (or sequestered) assets met the constitutional test of fairness—i.e., it fell on the right side of the line between *Mitchell v. W. T. Grant Co.* (procedure upheld) and *North Georgia Finishing Inc. v. Di-Chem, Inc.* (procedure invalidated). The U.S. Supreme Court's opinion hardly addresses that issue. Though Justice Marshall raises an eyebrow about the technique of releasing the property by making a general appearance (p. 588 and note 33, *supra*), and expresses some doubt about the situs of the shares sequestered under the Delaware procedure, one gets the impression that if Mr. Shaffer and his fellow directors had each owned a house in Delaware (other than a principal residence) and if Delaware law had made provision for a limited appearance—i.e., full ability to defend the action but no liability in excess of the property attached—the Supreme Court would still have held the quasi-in-rem action invalid, possibly with Justices Powell and Stevens dissenting rather than concurring. Assuming

    (i) notice to the defendant is proper, as has not always been the case in quasi-in-rem actions, but was true in *Shaffer v. Heitner*;

    (ii) a limited appearance is possible;

    (iii) a procedure is available for limiting the attachment to the amount of the claim;

    (iv) plaintiff is required to furnish a bond for damages caused to defendant from inability to use his property in the event judgment in the action is given for defendant; and

    (v) property subject to attachment is clearly defined, so that no unexpected assets suddenly are deemed to be situated in the forum state,

would quasi-in-rem actions still be basically unfair?

(d)(i) If your answer to the preceding question is "yes," why is it unfair? What is the missing ingredient that would render the action acceptable?

    (ii) If your answer is "it depends," what does it depend on?

(e) Until 1963, an oddity prevailed in the Federal Rules of Civil Procedure, in that no provision was made for initiating an action by attachment, but if such an action was begun in state court, it could be removed under 28 U.S.C. § 1441 and the jurisdictional attachment remained in effect.[d] Professor David Currie wrote an influential article urging that the Federal Rules be amended to provide for quasi-in-rem actions commenced in federal as well as in state courts.[e] Professor Paul Carrington, in contrast, argued that quasi-in-rem actions should be abolished altogether, on the ground that either the plaintiff didn't need jurisdiction through attachment, because some form of activity-linked jurisdiction was available, or he shouldn't be suing defendant in the given forum anyhow.[f] The Rules Committee (and of course the Supreme Court as promulgator of the Rules) cured the anomaly in favor of Currie's position, by adding Rule 4(e)(2),[g] which authorizes service and therefore jurisdiction by attachment in federal courts under the procedures in effect in the state where the district court is held. Fourteen years later, with a specific case before it, the Court seems to have adopted Carrington's position—indeed to have raised it to a constitutional

---

[c] 361 A.2d at 228.

[d] See 28 U.S.C. § 1450.

[e] D. Currie, *Attachment and Garnishment in the Federal Courts*, 59 Mich. L. Rev. 337 (1961).

[f] Carrington, *The Modern Utility of Quasi in Rem Jurisdiction*, 76 Harv. L. Rev. 302 (1962).

[g] Eff. July 1, 1963. Documents Supplement, p. 16.

command. Was this overkill—a cure for a type of jurisdiction that was open to abuse, but not fundamentally bad? Or is quasi-in-rem jurisdiction just plain unacceptable, no matter how surrounded by safeguards?

(2)(a) *Harris v. Balk,* 198 U.S. 215 (1905), the case that *Shaffer* says is overruled,[h] was a remarkable case. The bare bones of the case are summarized by Justice Marshall (p. 585). A closer look, however, is instructive:[i]

First, the underlying transaction: Epstein was an importer of general merchandise, doing business as the Baltimore Bargain House. Balk was a retailer in Washington, North Carolina, and was Epstein's regular customer. Epstein had made a series of deliveries to Balk in North Carolina on open account, net cash in 30 days; Balk had made no objection to the invoices that accompanied the deliveries, but in the period August–November 1895 had paid only $225 against invoices of $569. By today's standards, would Epstein have been entitled to pursue his claim for $344 in an in personam action in Maryland?

The cases in § 7.03[B] suggest that the answer is unclear, and may depend on whether Epstein sent a salesman to North Carolina, Balk traveled to Baltimore to make his purchases, or the purchases were made by catalogue and correspondence. *Rosenberg Bros. & Co. v. Curtis Brown,*[j] the 1923 case resurrected in *Helicopteros,* suggests that even if Balk had come to Baltimore to make his purchases, an action in Maryland for the purchase price might not succeed, though possibly there is a distinction because Balk appears to have traded as a sole proprietor, while Rosenberg ran his retail store in corporate form. At all events, in 1895 it was unlikely that Epstein could have secured in personam jurisdiction over Balk unless Balk took another trip to Baltimore. On the other hand, had Balk maintained a bank account with the Maryland Trust Company, there is little doubt that Epstein could have attached or garnished funds in that account to obtain quasi-in-rem jurisdiction over Balk. By today's standards would that have been unfair?

(b) What made the actual case so unusual was that Balk had no known assets in Maryland. But he had a friend called Harris, also a dry goods merchant in Washington, North Carolina. Harris had borrowed money from Balk on several occasions, the last $10 just before he took his fateful trip to Baltimore in August 1896. On that trip Harris took a message to Epstein from Balk saying that he would come to Baltimore soon—the implication being that when he came over he would settle his account. Somehow Epstein found out that Harris owed a total of $180 to Balk. (Harris later swore he didn't tell). There was no certificate of indebtedness, no promissory note or I.O.U., no agreed place of payment. Epstein, however, got the idea that the debt from Harris to Balk was an asset of Balk's and that it was located wherever Balk could sue Harris; so long as Harris was in Baltimore—in fact he was there only for a few days—that meant the debt (or claim) was in Baltimore, and Epstein could garnish it. And so he did, relying on the Maryland attachment statute. At Epstein's initiative, the local sheriff served Harris with an attachment order for $180. Harris did not have to give bond, and he was not detained. Harris was supposed to give notice to Balk, and he did so, either before or just after he returned to North Carolina.[k] A few days later judgment was entered against Harris in favor of Epstein in

---

[h] Page 588, *supra,* and p. 590, n. 39, *supra.*

[i] This note is adapted from Lowenfeld, *In Search of the Intangible: A Comment on Shaffer v. Heitner,* 53 N.Y.U. L. Rev. 102, 103–110 (1978). Footnote references, primarily to the record in the Supreme Court and to contemporary legislation and the lower court decisions in the controversy, can be found in that article, and are not here repeated.

[j] 260 U.S. 516 (1923).

[k] There seems to have been no requirement that Epstein give notice to Balk, though of course Balk was the real defendant in Epstein's action.

the Baltimore court for $180. Under the applicable Maryland statute, however, Balk had a year and a day in which to reopen the default and submit a defense, and Epstein had to give bond to secure Balk's possible recovery if he appeared.

At this point, is there anything unfair in the procedure by today's standards? Unfair to Harris? to Balk? or to both?

(c) Balk did not appear in the Maryland action, but instead brought suit for the $180 against Harris in county court in North Carolina. Harris, meanwhile, had paid the $180 to Epstein's lawyer, and understandably did not want to pay twice.[1] He pleaded discharge by virtue of the Maryland judgment. Should he be discharged?

(d) Balk's answer to the preceding question was no, because the Maryland judgment was void for want of jurisdiction, and thus could not be given full faith and credit. In four different sessions, the Supreme Court of North Carolina held that the Maryland judgment was void, not because it disagreed with quasi-in-rem actions as a whole, but because it found no asset of Balk's in Maryland which the courts of that state could have seized. The issue reached the U.S. Supreme Court as a full faith and credit question, not as in *McGee v. International Life Ins. Co.* with the party that had prevailed in F–1 seeking to enforce the judgment in F–2, but with the party that had suffered the judgment in F–1 seeking to use that judgment as a bar to further liability. As in *McGee,* the full faith and credit issue turned on the validity of the first judgment. That issue, in turn, depended on whether a debt had any situs, and if so where.

Where is a debt located? If A & P owes money to Mr. Jones, who lives in Boston, is the situs of the debt in Massachusetts, in Delaware, where A & P is incorporated, in New Jersey, where it has its corporate headquarters, or in every state where it operates supermarkets?

(e) Justice Peckham, speaking for the Court in *Harris v. Balk,* said the preceding question was not a meaningful one:

> We do not see the materiality of the expression "situs of the debt," when used in connection with attachment proceedings. If by *situs* is meant the place of the creation of the debt, that fact is immaterial. If it be meant that the obligation to pay the debt can only be enforced at the *situs* thus fixed, we think it is plainly untrue. The obligation of the debtor clings to and accompanies him wherever he goes. He is as much bound to pay his debt in a foreign State when therein sued upon his obligation by his creditor, as he was in the State where the debt was contracted. . . . [T]he *situs* of [the obligation] is unimportant. It is not a question of possession in the foreign State, for possession cannot be taken of a debt or of the obligation to pay for it, as tangible property might be taken possession of.[m]

It followed, said Justice Peckham, that Harris could be sued on the debt in Maryland, therefore Balk's claim against Harris could be attached there, and the payment by Harris to Epstein pursuant to the Maryland judgment in *Epstein v. Balk* was entitled to full faith and credit.

Is all that persuasive?

(f) Are *Harris v. Balk* and *Shaffer v. Heitner* distinguishable? Justice Marshall apparently thought not. If you believe they are, which has the stronger claim to jurisdiction in the attachment forum?

---

[1] Apparently, Harris paid at least in part because he found that the merchandise he had purchased in Baltimore were not being shipped; as soon as he paid, the shipments were resumed. Subsequently Epstein's lawyer became Harris' lawyer, through eight years of litigation up and down the North Carolina courts and ultimately to the U.S. Supreme Court.

[m] 198 U.S. at 222–23.

(3)(a) Coming back to *Shaffer v. Heitner,* the Supreme Court once more says that the sum of defendant's contact with the forum state—being officers and directors of a Delaware corporation—"establishes only that it is appropriate for [the state's] law to govern the obligations of [defendants]. . . . It does not demonstrate that [defendants] have purposefully availed themselves of the privilege of conducting activities within the forum State in a way that would justify bringing them before a . . . tribunal [of the state]." (p. 591). Why doesn't it? In a case such as *World-Wide Volkswagen,* it might be said that the law applicable to an accident on a state's highway may be that state's law, but that does not justify haling a far-off auto dealer into the state to defend a law suit. Unlike the English law under Order 11, U.S. concepts of jurisdiction do not normally derive jurisdiction from choice of law; but why isn't becoming a director of a Delaware corporation "availing oneself of the privileges . . ." of Delaware law?

(b) Justice Marshall makes a point of the fact that Delaware had no statute asserting an interest in holding directors of Delaware corporations as corporate fiduciaries or treating directorship in a Delaware corporation as consent to jurisdiction in the state. (p. 591). Following the decision in *Shaffer,* the Delaware legislature enacted a statute providing that any nonresident who accepts the position of director (or comparable office) of a Delaware corporation after September 1, 1977 or who serves in that capacity after June 30, 1978, is deemed to have consented to jurisdiction of the Delaware courts in any action brought by, against, or on behalf of the corporation.[n] It seems that once given, the consent is irrevocable, even if the suit is brought after the defendant has ceased to be a director, insofar as the suit relates to his service as director.

    (i) Would this statute change the result in *Shaffer*?

    (ii) Is it constitutional?[o]

If the answer to both of these questions is yes, is the actual case really about the philosophy of allocation of judicial power in a federal union, or about something more trivial?

(c) Recall that in *Pennoyer v. Neff,* the Supreme Court said the first action would have passed muster if Mitchell, the plaintiff, had caused the defendant's property to be attached before, not after he obtained a judgment; in *Shaffer,* the lesson is that Delaware should have secured the consent of Shaffer and his fellow defendant before suit was brought, not afterwards through an appearance that would release the property. Justice Brennan fails to see a constitutional infirmity in the distinction, since defendants "voluntarily associated themselves with the State of Delaware invoking the benefits and protections of its laws. . . ." (p. 595–596).

(d) Justice Brennan also urges—as he has in other cases—"seeking to bridge the distance between the choice-of-law and jurisdictional inquiries." Would you think such a movement would require stricter scrutiny of state choice-of-law decisions than the Court has been willing to undertake? Or just looser restraints on jurisdiction to adjudicate?

(e) Professor Silberman, in an important article on *Shaffer,* writes that the Court has its priorities reversed:

---

    [n] See Documents Supplement, p. 89.

    [o] The Supreme Court of Delaware held the statute was constitutional in actions alleging breach of the defendant directors' fiduciary obligations to a Delaware corporation. *Armstrong v. Pomerance,* 423 A.2d 174 (Del. 1980). However, the statute was held not to apply (and by implication to raise constitutional doubts if it were held to apply) to a director of a Delaware corporation in an action growing out of an act other than in his capacity as a director, even if that act was alleged to have harmed the corporation or its shareholders. *Hana Rauch v. Lent,* 424 A.2d 28 (Del Ch. 1980); *Istituto Bancario Italiano v. Hunter Engineering Co.,* 449 A.2d 210 (Del. 1982).

... [I]f in Shaffer, the contacts were truly sufficient for Delaware law to apply, *a fortiori* they should justify the exercise of jurisdiction by a Delaware court.[p]

Do you agree?

(f) Professor Silberman explains her statement as follows:

[Choice of forum], after all, concerns matters of convenience—of where the defendant must appear; [choice of law] crucially and dispositively affects the rights and liabilities of the parties before the court. To believe that a defendant's contacts with the forum state should be stronger under the due process clause for jurisdictional purposes than for choice of law is to believe that an accused is more concerned with where he will be hanged than whether.[q]

(4)(a) As we saw in Chapter 5, as well as in the in personam cases in this chapter, the Supreme Court has not moved as Professor Silberman suggests on either choice of law or jurisdiction. Not being prepared to restrain state courts' choice of law, it has not wanted to tie its surveillance over jurisdiction to any presumption such as Professor Silberman suggests.[r] *Allstate v. Hague* might be regarded as borderline on choice of law, problem-free on jurisdiction; *Shaffer v. Heitner* is borderline on jurisdiction, problem-free on choice of law. If a case is borderline on both counts, should the courts be more inclined to make the link between jurisdiction and choice of law in policing litigation in state and lower federal courts?

(b) Several lower court cases—both before and after the decision in *Shaffer v. Heitner*—might have been suitable for the link suggested in the preceding question, though counsel rarely pressed the linkage on the courts. Most of these cases arose out of a peculiar variation of quasi-in-rem jurisdiction, known by the first case to utilize it, *Seider v. Roth*.[s] The idea was that, say, a New York plaintiff (taking the facts of *Seider*) would bring an action in New York against a nonresident defendant (in *Seider* a resident of Quebec) arising out of an automobile accident in Vermont, by attaching the automobile liability policy that the defendant had with an insurance company that did business in New York. One might have thought that a liability policy was not a real asset, or even debt, since nothing was payable until a determination that the insured had been negligent (or otherwise responsible for the accident); and further that one could not tell the size of the obligation until plaintiff's damages had been assessed.[t] Never mind, said the courts of New York and a few other states. We will permit attachment of the policy, and give judgment quasi in rem up to the face amount of the policy. The New York Court of Appeals said there was an implied right to a limited appearance—i.e., defendant could come in to assert his freedom

---

[p] Silberman, *Shaffer v. Heitner: The End of an Era,* 53 N.Y.U. L. Rev. 33, 88 (1978). In a footnote to this passage, Professor Silberman answers the question put in paragraph (d) as follows:

I am prepared to move to a more expansive model of jurisdiction, but the necessary corollary is a control on choice of law.

Ibid, n. 286.

[q] *Ibid.*

[r] It is worth remarking that in *Home Insurance Co. v. Dick,* the leading case in which the Supreme Court held that a state could not apply its law to a transaction with no significant contacts with the forum (Chapter 5, p. 382, *supra*), jurisdiction was founded on a link that would not survive after *Shaffer v. Heitner.* Anglo-Mexicana, the Mexican company that issued the policy in suit, did not do business in Texas, but reinsured its policies, including the one issued (or assigned) to Mr. Dick, with Home Insurance Co., a New York company that did business in Texas. Thus the action was not only quasi-in-rem, but based on attachment of an intangible, and a contingent one at that.

[s] 17 N.Y.2d 111, 216 N.E.2d 312, 269 N.Y.S.2d 99 (1966).

[t] At one time, *Seider v. Roth* spawned a large number of articles. See e.g., Rosenberg, *One Procedural Genie Too Many, or Putting Seider Back in Its Bottle,* 71 Colum. L. Rev. 660 (1971).

from negligence or other defenses, without risking liability in excess of the limit of his insurance policy;[u] the federal courts in New York indicated that a judgment so obtained would not be res judicata in a later action in another forum;[v] and that the jurisdiction of the New York courts (state or federal) could be invoked in this manner only on behalf of New York residents.[w] As for choice of law, *Seider*-type courts typically applied forum law (equal, by definition to the law of the plaintiff's domicile). For more than a decade, the Supreme Court did not intervene; counsel, generally, focused their appeals and petitions on jurisdiction, and rarely stressed the interplay between jurisdiction and choice of law suggested by the law professors.[x]

(c) One case that might have tested the proposition stated in the preceding question was *Rosenthal v. Warren*, 479 F.2d 438 (2d Cir. 1973): A New York resident traveled to the New England Baptist Hospital in Boston for an operation to be performed by Dr. Warren, a famous surgeon. The patient died in the hospital shortly after the operation, and his widow sought to bring suit for malpractice against both the surgeon and the hospital in New York. For suit against the surgeon, she attached his "med-mal" insurance policy issued by the St. Paul Fire & Marine Insurance Company, a Minnesota corporation doing business in New York. Plaintiff sought more than $1 million in damages, at a time when the Massachusetts limit on damages for wrongful death was $50,000,[y] while no limit prevailed in New York. The federal Court of Appeals upheld jurisdiction via the *Seider* route, and upheld application of New York law, paying no attention in answering the second question to the means by which jurisdiction had been obtained over Dr. Warren.[z] The Supreme Court denied certiorari.[a]

(d) In another well-known case, decided shortly after *Rosenthal v. Warren,* a New York resident was employed by a New York firm to supervise construction of a shopping center in Virginia. *O'Connor v. Lee-Hy Paving Corp.*[b] While on the site near Richmond, he was struck and killed by road grading machine owned by Lee-Hy Paving, a Virginia corporation doing no business in New York. His widow brought suit against Lee-Hy in New York, attaching an insurance policy issued by a company doing business in New York. Defendant urged (i) that there could be no jurisdiction over it in the light of *Shaffer v. Heitner;* and (ii) that under Virginia law, plaintiff would be restricted to recovery under workers' compensation, and thus the claim against Lee-Hy should be barred. The district court decided both points against defendant, but on different days

---

[u] *Simpson v. Loehmann,* 21 N.Y.2d 305, 234 N.E.2d 669, 287 N.Y.S.2d 633 (1967), *motion for reargument dismissed,* 21 N.Y.2d 990, 238 N.E.2d 319, 290 N.Y.S.2d 914 (1968).

[v] *Minichiello v. Rosenberg,* 410 F.2d 106 (2d Cir. 1968), *aff'd en banc,* 410 F.2d 117 (2d Cir), *cert. denied* 396 U.S. 844 (1969).

[w] *Farrell v. Piedmont Aviation, Inc.,* 411 F.2d 812 (2d Cir. 1969). (Held, a New York administrator of non-New York passengers killed in an airplane accident in North Carolina could not invoke *Seider*-type jurisdiction.)

[x] In addition to the Silberman article cited in the preceding question, see, e.g., Martin, *Personal Jurisdiction and Choice of Law,* 78 Mich. L. Rev. 872 (1980); Reese, *Legislative Jurisdiction,* 78 Colum. L. Rev. 1587 (1978).

[y] Recall the *Kilberg* and *Pearson* cases, Chapter 3, § 3.02.

[z] An added wrinkle was that in the suit against the hospital (which had been served when one of its officers came to New York on a fund raising trip), the defense of charitable immunity under Massachusetts was raised, à la *Adams v. Berkshire,* Chapter 3, § 3.01, *supra.* Following the decision of the Court of Appeals described in the text, the district court declined to apply the Massachusetts immunity doctrine, in part because the hospital engaged in nation-wide scientific and fund-raising activities. 374 F. Supp. 522, 526 (S.D.N.Y. 1974). The choice of law aspect of this case is discussed in Chapter 3, p. 189, question (4)(b) *supra.*

[a] 414 U.S. 856 (1973).

[b] 579 F.2d 194 (2d Cir. 1978).

and in different opinions.^c On appeal, the Court of Appeals held that the decision in *Shaffer v. Heitner* and the fall of *Harris v. Balk* "does not necessarily topple *Seider.*"^d Further, the court upheld application of New York law, on the basis that the state courts would do so,^e without focusing on the connection between the two issues. In a petition for certiorari, only the jurisdiction issue was raised, and the Supreme Court denied review, with Justice Powell writing a dissent to the denial, joined by Justice Blackmun.^f

(e) Eventually the Supreme Court did take a *Seider v. Roth* type case, *Rush v. Savchuk,* 444 U.S. 320 (1980), decided on the same day as *World-Wide Volkswagen v. Woodson.* The action grew out of a one-car accident in Indiana, involving Rush, the driver, a resident of Indiana, and Savchuk, the passenger, also a resident of Indiana at the time of the accident. The car was owned by Rush's father, also a resident of Indiana, and was garaged and insured in Indiana. Indiana, at the time, had a guest statute that would have barred a claim on behalf of the passenger. Some time after the accident, Savchuk moved with his parents to Minnesota, and there commenced an action against Rush, by attaching the liability policy on the car, issued by a company that did business in Minnesota.

As in the New York cases, the Minnesota Supreme Court held in 1976 that the insurance policy was a garnishable res for purposes of obtaining quasi-in-rem jurisdiction when the cause of action arose out of state but the plaintiff was a resident of the forum at the time of suit. The Minnesota court found that considerations of fairness supported the exercise of quasi-in-rem jurisdiction, because in this kind of case the insurer controls the defense, and it was no burden on the insurance company to do so in Minnesota.

On appeal, the U.S. Supreme Court vacated the decision and remanded the case to the Minnesota Supreme Court for reconsideration in light of *Shaffer v. Heitner,* which had been decided in the meantime. The Minnesota court again found for plaintiff, holding that the Minnesota garnishment statute differed from the Delaware sequestration statute because here the garnished property was intimately related to the litigation, and the statute paralleled the manifest state interest of facilitating recoveries for resident plaintiffs.^g

On a second appeal, the Supreme Court reversed, also in an opinion by Justice Marshall. It did not pass on the presumed application by Minnesota of its own law (i.e., no guest statute). But on jurisdiction, the court held that the inquiry mandated by *Shaffer* into the relationship among the defendant, the forum, and the litigation simply did not disclose any affiliating circumstances that could support jurisdiction:

> The legal fiction that assigns a situs to a debt, for garnishment purposes, wherever the debtor is found is combined with the legal fiction that a corporation is "present," for jurisdictional purposes, wherever it does business to yield the conclusion that the obligation to defend and indemnify is located in the forum for purposes of the garnishment statute. The fictional presence of the policy obligation is deemed to give the State the power to determine the policy holder's liability for the out-of-state accident.^h

---

^c The only reported opinion, in 437 F. Supp. 994 (E.D.N.Y. 1977), deals with the jurisdiction question.

^d 579 F.2d at 199.

^e *Id.* at 202–06. See, on this point, Chapter 3, Question (4)(c), p. 189–90, *supra*.

^f *Lee-Hy Paving Corp. v. O'Connor,* 439 U.S. 1034 (1978).

^g Though the Supreme Court could not know it, the similarity between the Minnesota Court's approach in *Rush* and in *Allstate v. Hague,* both involving post-accident changes of residence and more favorable forum law, is striking.

^h 440 U.S. at 328.

Nothing doing, said the Supreme Court. The insurance company did business in all 50 states, and under plaintiff's theory "the 'debt' owed to Rush would be 'present' in each of those jurisdictions simultaneously. It is apparent that such a 'contact' can have no jurisdictional significance."[i]

It may be that the obvious law-shopping aspect of Mr. Savchuk's resort to Minnesota attachment jurisdiction helped influence the Supreme Court's condemnation of *Seider v. Roth* jurisdiction. The court's opinion, however, kept to the *Shaffer/World-Wide* definitions:

> The justifications offered in support of *Seider* jurisdiction share a common characteristic: they shift the focus of the inquiry from the relationship among the defendant, the forum, and the litigation to that among the plaintiff, the forum, the insurer, and the litigation. The insurer's contacts with the forum are attributed to the defendant because the policy was taken out in anticipation of such litigation. The State's interests in providing a forum for its residents and in regulating the activities of insurance companies are substituted for its contacts with the defendant and the cause of action. This subtle shift in focus from the defendant to the plaintiff is most evident in the decisions limiting *Seider* jurisdiction to actions by forum residents on the ground that permitting nonresidents to avail themselves of the procedure would be unconstitutional. In other words, the plaintiff's contacts with the forum are decisive in determining whether the defendant's due process rights are violated.
>
> Such an approach is forbidden by *International Shoe* and its progeny.[j]

(5)(a) *Seider v. Roth* jurisdiction, in doubt after *Shaffer v. Heitner,* seems to have been put to rest by *Rush v. Savchuk,* once and for all. Is quasi-in-rem jurisdiction, overall, relegated to history?

In fact, quasi-in-rem jurisdiction, including attachment or garnishment of debt, continues to be important in the context of enforcement of judgments, as suggested near the end of the majority opinion in *Shaffer* (pp. 589–90). Not only did the Court in *Shaffer* expressly suggest that its concerns did not apply to actions on judgments;[k] it turns out that even *Harris v. Balk* is still alive for such actions, a matter of considerable importance in the case of foreign country defendants, where long-arm jurisdiction cannot be complemented by the Full Faith and Credit clause.

Suppose, for example, Liverpool Toys, P.L.C. produces toys in England and ships them to department stores in the United States. One toy malfunctions, injuring a child in Chicago. The child and its parents bring suit in Illinois under that state's long-arm statute,[l] and recover a judgment (whether or not contested) that remains unsatisfied. As is shown in the next chapter, suit on that judgment in England would be problematical if the judgment had been contested, hopeless if defendant had defaulted or (after 1982) appeared only to challenge jurisdiction. But if Liverpool Toys continues to have a market in the United States, it will almost certainly have some kind of account receivable, debt, or letter of credit in the United States, and it may well have a bank account in the United States. Notwithstanding *Shaffer,* these assets—intangibles with no real situs but with a nexus to the United States—can serve as the object—and jurisdictional basis—for an action in the United States.

---

[i] *Id.* at 330.

[j] *Id.* at 332.

[k] See p. 589, at n. 36, *supra.*

[l] See *Gray v. American Radiator & Standard Sanitary Corp.,* p. 520, *supra.*

§ 7.06   JURISDICTION AND JUDGMENTS   □   609

(b) Is there still room for initial asset-based jurisdiction? *Intermeat v. American Poultry* suggests there may be, though the case was decided shortly after *Shaffer* and before *Rush v. Savchuk.* Do you think if *Intermeat* had been appealed to the Supreme Court, it would have passed muster? Should it?

On one level *Intermeat* not only revives quasi-in-rem jurisdiction, but indeed the wandering res à la *Harris v. Balk.* Defendant American Poultry, after all, did not own a warehouse in New York, or even have a bank account; all it had was customers, some of whom, including A & P, owed it money. Moreover, A & P, as we saw, does business in almost every state, so there was nothing to locate the debt in New York.

(c) At another level, Judge Gurfein says no, presence of defendant's property is not alone a sufficient contact, but it is an important one, and here there were other contacts—the place of contracting (?), the agreed place of arbitration, the proportion of defendant's business done with, if not in, New York. Do we now have a third threshold of contacts, lower than doing business (general jurisdiction), lower than transacting business (specific jurisdiction), but still greater than the mere presence of defendant's property? What is left out of this description?

(d) Not many quasi-in-rem cases have been reported since *Shaffer*.[m] One interesting case was *Majique Fashions Ltd. v. Warwick & Sons,*[n] decided by the intermediate appellate court in New York. Seller in Korea made a contract with buyer in New York to import apparel, payment to be made by drafts drawn by seller under a letter of credit to be opened on behalf of buyer by a New York bank in favor of seller. Under such an arrangement, seller can draw on the letter of credit—i.e., receive his purchase price, as soon as he puts the goods on board a ship, takes back a bill of lading, and tenders that document together with other documents (such as an insurance policy or proof of freight paid) on which seller and buyer agree. In order to be sure that the merchandise conforms to the contract, buyer often requires that one of the documents to be tendered when drawing on the letter of credit is a certificate of inspection issued by an inspector designated by buyer. In *Majique Fashions,* buyer designated Warwick, an inspection company doing business in Taiwan, Hong Kong, and South Korea. Seller duly tendered all the required documents, including Warwick's inspection certificate, drew against the letter of credit, and was paid. When the goods arrived, Majique claimed that they were defective, and sought to sue Warwick, the inspection company, in New York. Buyer attached a New York bank account maintained by Warwick, and sought to proceed quasi in rem, arguing that the bank account represented the proceeds of Warwick's dealings with U.S. importers, and thus was related and not unrelated property. Warwick moved to dismiss. What result?[o]

(e) The *Restatement (Second) of Judgments* (1982) attempted to sum up the current status of property based jurisdiction as follows:

   § 8. Attachment Jurisdiction

   (1) A court may exercise jurisdiction to seize property whose situs is in the state, by attachment, sequestration, or similar procedure, in an action concerning a claim against the owner of the property if:

---

[m] For a comprehensive survey, though perhaps an exaggerated title, see Michael B. Mushlin, *The New Quasi in Rem Jurisdiction: New York's Revival of a Doctrine Whose Time Has Passed,* 55 Brooklyn L. Rev. 1059 (1990).

[n] 67 A.D.2d 321, 414 N.Y.S.2d 916 (1979).

[o] The lower court dismissed; the Appellate Division reversed, saying that the New York bank account bore a relationship to the litigation, and that there was a "clear relationship between the non-resident defendant (Warwick), this State (the forum) and the litigation."

(a) The court could properly exercise jurisdiction to adjudicate the claim under the rules states in §§ 5 to 7 [in personam, in rem, or status]; or

(b) The action is to enforce a judgment against the owner of the property; or

(c) The action is properly in aid of other proceedings concerning the claim; or

(d) The exercise of such jurisdiction is otherwise reasonable.

(2) When a court undertakes to exercise jurisdiction as stated in Subsection (1), the owner of the property may make an appearance to contest the court's jurisdiction over the property without thereby submitting to the jurisdiction of the court.

Subsection (1)(d) might cover situations in which jurisdiction in personam would satisfy the Supreme Court's standards, but the local long-arm statute did not cover the situation.

[B] The Effect of *Shaffer* on Transient Jurisdiction

Many commentators thought that once all jurisdiction became subject to tests of fairness, and "power" as a basis for jurisdiction was discredited, "tag" or transient jurisdiction could not long survive.[a] The issue came before the Supreme Court in 1990—after *World-Wide Volkswagen*, *Helicopteros*, and *Asahi* had all struck down state court exercises of jurisdiction over nonresident corporations for different reasons.

BURNHAM v. SUPERIOR COURT OF CALIFORNIA

United States Supreme Court
495 U.S. 604, 110 S.Ct. 2105 (1990)

Justice SCALIA announced the judgment of the Court and delivered an opinion in which THE CHIEF JUSTICE and Justice KENNEDY join, and in which Justice WHITE joins with respect to Parts I, II-A, II-B, and II-C.

---

[a] See e.g., Daniel O. Bernstine, Shaffer v. Heitner: *A Death Warrant for the Transient Rule of In Personam Jurisdiction*, 25 Villanova L. Rev. 38 (1979); Donald J. Werner, *Dropping the other Shoe:* Shaffer v. Heitner *and the Demise of Presence Oriented Jurisdiction*, 45 Brooklyn L. Rev. 565 (1979); David H. Vernon, *Single Factor Bases of Jurisdiction of in Personam Jurisdiction: A Speculation on the Impact of* Shaffer v. Heitner, 1978 Washington U. L.Q. 319.

Comment *b* to § 28 of the 1988 Revisions of Restatement (Second) of Conflict of Laws reads:

The requirement of reasonableness.

. . . The Supreme Court held in *Shaffer v. Heitner* that the presence of a thing in a state gives that state jurisdiction to determine interests in the thing only in situations where the exercise of such jurisdiction would be reasonable. It must likewise follow that considerations of reasonableness qualify the power of a state to exercise personal jurisdiction over an individual on the basis of his physical presence within its territory. Jurisdiction will exist in such a case if the individual's relationship to the state can justly be described as significant, which would be the case if he has been present there for a substantial period of time. Jurisdiction may also exist when there is some connection between the state and the particular transaction involved. Jurisdiction will be lacking, however, when the sole basis for its exercise is the momentary presence within the state of the individual involved unless the special circumstances of the case make its exercise reasonable.

The question presented is whether the Due Process Clause of the Fourteenth Amendment denies California courts jurisdiction over a nonresident, who was personally served with process while temporarily in that State, in a suit unrelated to his activities in the State.

I

Petitioner Dennis Burnham married Francie Burnham in 1976 in West Virginia. In 1977 the couple moved to New Jersey, where their two children were born. In July 1987 the Burnhams decided to separate. They agreed that Mrs. Burnham, who intended to move to California, would take custody of the children. Shortly before Mrs. Burnham departed for California that same month, she and petitioner agreed that she would file for divorce on grounds of "irreconcilable differences."

In October 1987, petitioner filed for divorce in New Jersey state court on grounds of "desertion." Petitioner did not, however, obtain an issuance of summons against his wife and did not attempt to serve her with process. Mrs. Burnham, after unsuccessfully demanding that petitioner adhere to their prior agreement to submit to an "irreconcilable differences" divorce, brought suit for divorce in California state court in early January 1988.

In late January, petitioner visited southern California on business, after which he went north to visit his children in the San Francisco Bay area, where his wife resided. He took the older child to San Francisco for the weekend. Upon returning the child to Mrs. Burnham's home on January 24, 1988, petitioner was served with a California court summons and a copy of Mrs. Burnham's divorce petition. He then returned to New Jersey.

Later that year, petitioner made a special appearance in the California Superior Court, moving to quash the service of process on the ground that the court lacked personal jurisdiction over him because his only contacts with California were a few short visits to the State for the purposes of conducting business and visiting his children. The Superior Court denied the motion, and the California Court of Appeal denied mandamus relief, rejecting petitioner's contention that the Due Process Clause prohibited California courts from asserting jurisdiction over him because he lacked "minimum contacts" with the State. The court held it to be "a valid jurisdictional predicate for in personam jurisdiction" that the "defendant [was] present in the forum state and personally served with process." We granted certiorari.

II

A

The proposition that the judgment of a court lacking jurisdiction is void traces back to the English Year Books, see *Bowser v. Collins,* Y.B.Mich. 22 Edw. IV, f. 30, pl. 11, 145 Eng.Rep. 97 (Ex. Ch. 1482), and was made settled law by Lord Coke in *Case of the Marshalsea,* 10 Coke Rep. 68b, 77a, 77 Eng.Rep. 1027, 1041 (K.B. 1612). Traditionally that proposition was embodied in the phrase coram non judice, "before a person not a judge"—meaning, in effect, that the proceeding in question was not a judicial proceeding because lawful judicial authority was not present, and could therefore not yield a judgment. American courts invalidated, or denied recognition to, judgments that violated this common-law principle long before the Fourteenth Amendment was adopted. See, e.g., *Grumon v. Raymond,* 1 Conn. 40 (1814); *Picquet v. Swan,* 19 F.Cas. 609 (No. 11,134) (CC Mass.1828); [the Court cites four other cases decided between

1834 and 1850]. In *Pennoyer v. Neff,* we announced that the judgment of a court lacking personal jurisdiction violated the Due Process Clause of the Fourteenth Amendment as well.

To determine whether the assertion of personal jurisdiction is consistent with due process, we have long relied on the principles traditionally followed by American courts in marking out the territorial limits of each State's authority. That criterion was first announced in *Pennoyer v. Neff,* supra, in which we stated that due process "mean[s] a course of legal proceedings according to those rules and principles which have been established in our systems of jurisprudence for the protection and enforcement of private rights," including the "well-established principles of public law respecting the jurisdiction of an independent State over persons and property." In what has become the classic expression of the criterion, we said in *International Shoe Co. v. Washington,* that a state court's assertion of personal jurisdiction satisfies the Due Process Clause if it does not violate " 'traditional notions of fair play and substantial justice.' " . . . Since International Shoe, we have only been called upon to decide whether these "traditional notions" permit States to exercise jurisdiction over absent defendants in a manner that deviates from the rules of jurisdiction applied in the 19th century. We have held such deviations permissible, but only with respect to suits arising out of the absent defendant's contacts with the State. See, e.g., *Helicopteros Nacionales de Colombia v. Hall.* The question we must decide today is whether due process requires a similar connection between the litigation and the defendant's contacts with the State in cases where the defendant is physically present in the State at the time process is served upon

B

Among the most firmly established principles of personal jurisdiction in American tradition is that the courts of a State have jurisdiction over nonresidents who are physically present in the State. The view developed early that each State had the power to hale before its courts any individual who could be found within its borders, and that once having acquired jurisdiction over such a person by properly serving him with process, the State could retain jurisdiction to enter judgment against him, no matter how fleeting his visit. That view had antecedents in English common-law practice, which sometimes allowed "transitory" actions, arising out of events outside the country, to be maintained against seemingly nonresident defendants who were present in England. Justice Story believed the principle, which he traced to Roman origins, to be firmly grounded in English tradition: "[B]y the common law[,] personal actions, being transitory, may be brought in any place, where the party defendant may be found," for "every nation may . . . rightfully exercise jurisdiction over all persons within its domains." J. Story, Commentaries on the Conflict of Laws §§ 554, 543 (1846). See also id., §§ 530-538; *Picquet v. Swan,* supra, at 611-612 (Story, J.) ("Where a party is within a territory, he may justly be subjected to its process, and bound personally by the judgment pronounced, on such process, against him").

Recent scholarship has suggested that English tradition was not as clear as Story thought, see Hazard, *A General Theory of State-Court Jurisdiction,* 1965 S.Ct.Rev. 241, 253-260; Ehrenzweig, *The Transient Rule of Personal Jurisdiction: The "Power" Myth and Forum Conveniens,* 65 Yale L.J. 289 (1956). Accurate or not, however, judging by the evidence of contemporaneous or near-contemporaneous decisions, one must conclude that Story's understanding was shared by American courts at the crucial time for present purposes: 1868, when the Fourteenth Amendment was adopted. . . .

Decisions in the courts of many States in the 19th and early 20th centuries held that personal service upon a physically present defendant sufficed to confer jurisdiction, without regard to whether the defendant was only briefly in the State or whether the cause of action was related to his activities there. [Justice SCALIA cites 25 state court cases.] Particularly striking is the fact that, as far as we have been able to determine, not one American case from the period (or, for that matter, not one American case until 1978) held, or even suggested, that in-state personal service on an individual was insufficient to confer personal jurisdiction.[3]

This American jurisdictional practice is, moreover, not merely old; it is continuing. It remains the practice of, not only a substantial number of the States, but as far as we are aware all the States and the Federal Government—if one disregards (as one must for this purpose) the few opinions since 1978 that have erroneously said, on grounds similar to those that petitioner presses here, that this Court's due process decisions render the practice unconstitutional. . . . We do not know of a single state or federal statute, or a single judicial decision resting upon state law, that has abandoned in-state service as a basis of jurisdiction. Many recent cases reaffirm it. See [14 decisions between 1963 and 1989].

C

Despite this formidable body of precedent, petitioner contends, in reliance on our decisions applying the International Shoe standard, that in the absence of "continuous and systematic" contacts with the forum, a nonresident defendant can be subjected to judgment only as to matters that arise out of or relate to his contacts with the forum. This argument rests on a thorough misunderstanding of our cases.

The view of most courts in the 19th century was that a court simply could not exercise in personam jurisdiction over a nonresident who had not been personally served with process in the forum. . . . [as confirmed in *Pennoyer v. Neff*, and in dictum, set forth as a requirement of the Fourteenth Amendment.]

Later years, however, saw the weakening of the *Pennoyer* rule. In the late 19th and early 20th centuries, changes in the technology of transportation and communication, and the tremendous growth of interstate business activity, led to an "inevitable relaxation of the strict limits on state jurisdiction" over nonresident individuals and corporations. *Hanson v. Denckla* (Black, J., dissenting). States required, for example, that nonresident corporations appoint an in-state agent upon whom process could be served as a condition of transacting business within their borders, and provided in-state "substituted service" for nonresident motorists who caused injury in the State and left before personal service could be accomplished. We initially upheld these laws under the Due Process Clause on grounds that they complied with *Pennoyer's* rigid requirement of either "consent," or "presence." As many observed, however, the consent and presence were purely fictional. Our opinion in *International Shoe* cast those fictions aside and made explicit the underlying basis of these decisions: Due process does not necessarily require the States to adhere to the unbending territorial limits on jurisdiction set forth in *Pennoyer*. The validity of assertion of jurisdiction over a nonconsenting defendant who is not present in the forum depends upon whether "the quality and nature of [his] activity" in relation to the forum, renders such jurisdiction consistent with " 'traditional notions of fair play and substantial justice.' " Subsequent

---

[3] Given this striking fact, and the unanimity of both cases and commentators in supporting the in-state service rule, one can only marvel at Justice BRENNAN's assertion that the rule "was rather weakly implanted in American jurisprudence," and "did not receive wide currency until well after our decision in *Pennoyer v. Neff.*" . . .

cases have derived from the International Shoe standard the general rule that a State may dispense with in-forum personal service on nonresident defendants in suits arising out of their activities in the State. See generally *Helicopteros Nacionales de Colombia v. Hall.* As *International Shoe* suggests, the defendant's litigation-related "minimum contacts" may take the place of physical presence as the basis for jurisdiction. :

> Nothing in *International Shoe* or the cases that have followed it, however, offers support for the very different proposition petitioner seeks to establish today: that a defendant's presence in the forum is not only unnecessary to validate novel, nontraditional assertions of jurisdiction, but is itself no longer sufficient to establish jurisdiction. That proposition is unfaithful to both elementary logic and the foundations of our due process jurisprudence. The distinction between what is needed to support novel procedures and what is needed to sustain traditional ones is fundamental. . . . The short of the matter is that jurisdiction based on physical presence alone constitutes due process because it is one of the continuing traditions of our legal system that define the due process standard of "traditional notions of fair play and substantial justice." That standard was developed by analogy to "physical presence," and it would be perverse to say it could now be turned against that touchstone of jurisdiction.

D

Petitioner's strongest argument, though we ultimately reject it, relies upon our decision in *Shaffer v. Heitner.* In that case, . . . we concluded that the normal rules we had developed under *International Shoe* for jurisdiction over suits against absent defendants should apply—viz., Delaware could not hear the suit because the defendants' sole contact with the State (ownership of property there) was unrelated to the lawsuit.

It goes too far to say, as petitioner contends, that *Shaffer* compels the conclusion that a State lacks jurisdiction over an individual unless the litigation arises out of his activities in the State. *Shaffer,* like *International Shoe,* involved jurisdiction over an absent defendant, and it stands for nothing more than the proposition that when the "minimum contact" that is a substitute for physical presence consists of property ownership it must, like other minimum contacts, be related to the litigation. Petitioner wrenches out of its context our statement in *Shaffer* that "all assertions of state-court jurisdiction must be evaluated according to the standards set forth in *International Shoe* and its progeny," When read together with the two sentences that preceded it, the meaning of this statement becomes clear:

> "The fiction that an assertion of jurisdiction over property is anything but an assertion of jurisdiction over the owner of the property supports an ancient form without substantial modern justification. Its continued acceptance would serve only to allow state-court jurisdiction that is fundamentally unfair to the defendant. We therefore conclude that all assertions of state-court jurisdiction must be evaluated according to the standards set forth in *International Shoe* and its progeny."

Shaffer was saying, in other words, not that all bases for the assertion of in personam jurisdiction (including, presumably, in-state service) must be treated alike and subjected to the "minimum contacts" analysis of *International Shoe*; but rather that quasi in rem jurisdiction, that fictional "ancient form," and in personam jurisdiction, are really one and the same and must be treated alike—leading to the conclusion that quasi in rem jurisdiction, i.e., that form of in personam jurisdiction based upon a "property ownership" contact and by definition unaccompanied by personal, in-state service, must satisfy the litigation-relatedness requirement of *International Shoe.*

The logic of *Shaffer's* holding—which places all suits against absent nonresidents on the same constitutional footing, regardless of whether a separate Latin label is attached to one particular basis of contact—does not compel the conclusion that physically present defendants must be treated identically to absent ones. As we have demonstrated at length, our tradition has treated the two classes of defendants quite differently, and it is unreasonable to read *Shaffer* as casually obliterating that distinction. *International Shoe* confined its "minimum contacts" requirement to situations in which the defendant "be not present within the territory of the forum," and nothing in *Shaffer* expands that requirement beyond that.

It is fair to say, however, that while our holding today does not contradict *Shaffer,* our basic approach to the due process question is different. We have conducted no independent inquiry into the desirability or fairness of the prevailing in-state service rule, leaving that judgment to the legislatures that are free to amend it; for our purposes, its validation is its pedigree, as the phrase "traditional notions of fair play and substantial justice" makes clear. *Shaffer* did conduct such an independent inquiry, asserting that " 'traditional notions of fair play and substantial justice' can be as readily offended by the perpetuation of ancient forms that are no longer justified as by the adoption of new procedures that are inconsistent with the basic values of our constitutional heritage." Perhaps that assertion can be sustained when the "perpetuation of ancient forms" is engaged in by only a very small minority of the States. Where, however, as in the present case, a jurisdictional principle is both firmly approved by tradition and still favored, it is impossible to imagine what standard we could appeal to for the judgment that it is "no longer justified." . . . For new procedures, hitherto unknown, the Due Process Clause requires analysis to determine whether "traditional notions of fair play and substantial justice" have been offended. But a doctrine of personal jurisdiction that dates back to the adoption of the Fourteenth Amendment and is still generally observed unquestionably meets that standard.

III

A few words in response to Justice BRENNAN's opinion concurring in the judgment: It insists that we apply "contemporary notions of due process" to determine the constitutionality of California's assertion of jurisdiction. . . . [T]he concurrence's proposed standard of "contemporary notions of due process" . . . measures state-court jurisdiction not only against traditional doctrines in this country, including current state-court practice, but also against each Justice's subjective assessment of what is fair and just. Authority for that seductive standard is not to be found in any of our personal jurisdiction cases. It is, indeed, an outright break with the test of "traditional notions of fair play and substantial justice," which would have to be reformulated "our notions of fair play and substantial justice."

The subjectivity, and hence inadequacy, of this approach becomes apparent when the concurrence tries to explain why the assertion of jurisdiction in the present case meets its standard of continuing-American-tradition-plus-innate-fairness. Justice BRENNAN lists the "benefits" Mr. Burnham derived from the State of California—the fact that, during the few days he was there, "[h]is health and safety [were] guaranteed by the State's police, fire, and emergency medical services; he [was] free to travel on the State's roads and waterways; he likely enjoy[ed] the fruits of the State's economy." Three days' worth of these benefits strike us as powerfully inadequate to establish, as an abstract matter, that it is "fair" for California to decree the ownership of all Mr. Burnham's worldly goods acquired during the 10 years of his marriage, and the custody over his children. . . .

There is, we must acknowledge, one factor mentioned by Justice BRENNAN that both relates distinctively to the assertion of jurisdiction on the basis of personal in-state service and is fully persuasive—namely, the fact that a defendant voluntarily present in a particular State has a "reasonable expectatio[n]" that he is subject to suit there. By formulating it as a "reasonable expectation" Justice BRENNAN makes that seem like a "fairness" factor; but in reality, of course, it is just tradition masquerading as "fairness." The only reason for charging Mr. Burnham with the reasonable expectation of being subject to suit is that the States of the Union assert adjudicatory jurisdiction over the person, and have always asserted adjudicatory jurisdiction over the person, by serving him with process during his temporary physical presence in their territory. That continuing tradition, which anyone entering California should have known about, renders it "fair" for Mr. Burnham, who voluntarily entered California, to be sued there for divorce—at least "fair" in the limited sense that he has no one but himself to blame. Justice BRENNAN's long journey is a circular one, leaving him, at the end of the day, in complete reliance upon the very factor he sought to avoid: The existence of a continuing tradition is not enough, fairness also must be considered; fairness exists here because there is a continuing tradition.

. . . Since Justice BRENNAN's only criterion of constitutionality is "fairness," the phrase "as a rule" represents nothing more than his estimation that, usually, all the elements of "fairness" he discusses in the present case will exist. . . . [D]espite the fact that he manages to work the word "rule" into his formulation, Justice BRENNAN's approach does not establish a rule of law at all, but only a "totality of the circumstances" test, guaranteeing what traditional territorial rules of jurisdiction were designed precisely to avoid: uncertainty and litigation over the preliminary issue of the forum's competence. It may be that those evils, necessarily accompanying a freestanding "reasonableness" inquiry, must be accepted at the margins, when we evaluate nontraditional forms of jurisdiction newly adopted by the States, see, e.g., *Asahi Metal Industry Co. v. Superior Court*. But that is no reason for injecting them into the core of our American practice, exposing to such a "reasonableness" inquiry the ground of jurisdiction that has hitherto been considered the very baseline of reasonableness, physical presence.

The difference between us and Justice BRENNAN has nothing to do with whether "further progress [is] to be made" in the "evolution of our legal system." It has to do with whether changes are to be adopted as progressive by the American people or decreed as progressive by the Justices of this Court. Nothing we say today prevents individual States from limiting or entirely abandoning the in-state-service basis of jurisdiction. And nothing prevents an overwhelming majority of them from doing so, with the consequence that the "traditional notions of fairness" that this Court applies may change. But the States have overwhelmingly declined to adopt such limitation or abandonment, evidently not considering it to be progress. The question is whether, armed with no authority other than individual Justices' perceptions of fairness that conflict with both past and current practice, this Court can compel the States to make such a change on the ground that "due process" requires it. We hold that it cannot.

Affirmed.

Justice BRENNAN, with whom Justice MARSHALL, Justice BLACKMUN, and Justice O'CONNOR join, concurring in the judgment.

. . . Although I agree that history is an important factor in establishing whether a jurisdictional rule satisfies due process requirements, I cannot agree that it is the only factor such that all traditional rules of jurisdiction are, ipso facto, forever constitutional. Unlike Justice SCALIA, I would undertake an "independent inquiry into the . . . fairness of the prevailing in-state service rule." I therefore concur only in the judgment.

I

I believe that the approach adopted by Justice SCALIA's opinion today—reliance solely on historical pedigree—is foreclosed by our decisions in *International Shoe Co. v. Washington* and *Shaffer v. Heitner.* In *International Shoe,* we held that a state court's assertion of personal jurisdiction does not violate the Due Process Clause if it is consistent with " 'traditional notions of fair play and substantial justice.' "*

In *Shaffer,* we stated that "all assertions of state-court jurisdiction must be evaluated according to the standards set forth in *International Shoe* and its progeny." The critical insight of *Shaffer* is that all rules of jurisdiction, even ancient ones, must satisfy contemporary notions of due process. No longer were we content to limit our jurisdictional analysis to pronouncements that "[t]he foundation of jurisdiction is physical power," *McDonald v. Mabee,* 243 U.S. 90, 91 (1917), and that "every State possesses exclusive jurisdiction and sovereignty over persons and property within its territory." *Pennoyer v. Neff.* While acknowledging that "history must be considered as supporting the proposition that jurisdiction based solely on the presence of property satisfie[d] the demands of due process," we found that this factor could not be "decisive." We recognized that " '[t]raditional notions of fair play and substantial justice' can be as readily offended by the perpetuation of ancient forms that are no longer justified as by the adoption of new procedures that are inconsistent with the basic values of our constitutional heritage." I agree with this approach and continue to believe that "the minimum-contacts analysis developed in *International Shoe* . . . represents a far more sensible construct for the exercise of state-court jurisdiction than the patchwork of legal and factual fictions that has been generated from the decision in *Pennoyer v. Neff.*"

While our holding in *Shaffer* may have been limited to quasi in rem jurisdiction, our mode of analysis was not. Indeed, that we were willing in *Shaffer* to examine anew the appropriateness of the quasi in rem rule—until that time dutifully accepted by American courts for at least a century—demonstrates that we did not believe that the "pedigree" of a jurisdictional practice was dispositive in deciding whether it was consistent with due process. . . .

II

Tradition, though alone not dispositive, is of course relevant to the question whether the rule of transient jurisdiction is consistent with due process.[7] Tradition is salient not in the sense that

---

* Our reference in *International Shoe* to "traditional notions of fair play and substantial justice," meant simply that those concepts are indeed traditional ones, not that, as Justice SCALIA's opinion suggests, their specific content was to be determined by tradition alone. We recognized that contemporary societal norms must play a role in our analysis. See, e.g., [pp. 488-89 *supra*] (considerations of "reasonable[ness], in the context of our federal system of government").

[7] I do not propose that the "contemporary notions of due process" to be applied are no more than "each Justice's subjective assessment of what is fair and just." Rather, the inquiry is guided by our decisions beginning with *International Shoe Co. v. Washington,* and the specific factors that we have developed to ascertain whether a jurisdictional rule comports with "traditional notions of fair play and substantial justice." See, e.g., *Asahi Metal Industry Co. v. Superior Court* (noting "several factors," including "the burden on the defendant, the interests of the forum State, and the plaintiff's interest in obtaining relief"). This analysis may not be "mechanical or quantitative," *International Shoe* [p. 489 *supra*] but neither is it "freestanding," ante, at [p. 616] or dependent on personal whim. Our experience with this approach demonstrates that it is well within our competence to employ.

practices of the past are automatically reasonable today; indeed, under such a standard, the legitimacy of transient jurisdiction would be called into question because the rule's historical "pedigree" is a matter of intense debate.

Rather, I find the historical background relevant because, however murky the jurisprudential origins of transient jurisdiction, the fact that American courts have announced the rule for perhaps a century (first in dicta, more recently in holdings) provides a defendant voluntarily present in a particular State today "clear notice that [he] is subject to suit" in the forum. . . .

By visiting the forum State, a transient defendant actually "avail[s]" himself of significant benefits provided by the State. His health and safety are guaranteed by the State's police, fire, and emergency medical services; he is free to travel on the State's roads and waterways; he likely enjoys the fruits of the State's economy as well. . . . [A]ny burdens that do arise can be ameliorated by a variety of procedural devices. For these reasons, as a rule the exercise of personal jurisdiction over a defendant based on his voluntary presence in the forum will satisfy the requirements of due process.[14]

In this case, it is undisputed that petitioner was served with process while voluntarily and knowingly in the State of California. I therefore concur in the judgment.

Justice STEVENS, concurring in the judgment.

As I explained in my separate writing, I did not join the Court's opinion in Shaffer v. Heitner because I was concerned by its unnecessarily broad reach. The same concern prevents me from joining either Justice SCALIA's or Justice BRENNAN's opinion in this case. For me, it is sufficient to note that the historical evidence and consensus identified by Justice SCALIA, the considerations of fairness identified by Justice BRENNAN, and the common sense displayed by Justice WHITE, all combine to demonstrate that this is, indeed, a very easy case.[*] Accordingly, I agree that the judgment should be affirmed.

NOTES AND QUESTIONS

(1)(a) Can *Burnham* be reconciled with *Shaffer*? With *International Shoe*?

---

[14] Justice SCALIA's opinion maintains that, viewing transient jurisdiction as a contractual bargain, the rule is "unconscionabl[e]," according to contemporary conceptions of fairness. But the opinion simultaneously insists that because of its historical "pedigree," the rule is "the very baseline of reasonableness." Thus is revealed Justice SCALIA's belief that tradition alone is completely dispositive and that no showing of unfairness can ever serve to invalidate a traditional jurisdictional practice. I disagree both with this belief and with Justice SCALIA's assessment of the fairness of the transient jurisdiction bargain. I note, moreover, that the dual conclusions of Justice SCALIA's opinion create a singularly unattractive result. Justice SCALIA suggests that when and if a jurisdictional rule becomes substantively unfair or even "unconscionable," this Court is powerless to alter it. Instead, he is willing to rely on individual States to limit or abandon bases of jurisdiction that have become obsolete. This reliance is misplaced, for States have little incentive to limit rules such as transient jurisdiction that make it easier for their own citizens to sue out-of-state defendants. That States are more likely to expand their jurisdiction is illustrated by the adoption by many States of long-arm statutes extending the reach of personal jurisdiction to the limits established by the Federal Constitution. Out-of-staters do not vote in state elections or have a voice in state government. We should not assume, therefore, that States will be motivated by "notions of fairness" to curb jurisdictional rules like the one at issue here. The reasoning of Justice SCALIA's opinion today is strikingly oblivious to the raison d'etre of various constitutional doctrines designed to protect out-of-staters, such as the Art. IV Privileges and Immunities Clause and the Commerce Clause.

[*] Perhaps the adage about hard cases making bad law should be revised to cover easy cases.

(b) Do you understand the Supreme Court to say that every kind of tag jurisdiction is now acceptable in the United States, if supported by a state statute? Or would you think that in-hand service at an airport on a defendant changing planes, or at a gasoline station on an interstate highway, might still be struck down?[a] After all, it was not an accident or coincidence that brought Mr. Burnham to California.

(c) What happened to reasonableness? Could a defendant served personally in the forum state still raise, as a constitutional matter, the contention that requiring him or her to defend an action in that state would be unreasonable? Or is that contention foreclosed by the appeal to ancient tradition?

(d) Note that Justice Scalia does not carry the whole court with him, and that Justice White, for instance, might answer this question differently from Justice Scalia. Justice White does not subscribe to Part II D of Justice Scalia's opinion, concerning *Shaffer*, or Part III, p. 616 *supra*, in which Justice Scalia rejects inquiring into reasonableness in a case of physical presence of the defendant. In a one paragraph concurrence not here reproduced,[b] Justice White indicates that he is prepared to leave open cases in which the rule of physical presence would operate unfairly as applied to a particular nonresident.

(2)(a) *Burnham*, of course, was a purely domestic case. Should the holding that jurisdiction may be acquired by service on a person only transitorily present in the forum state apply equally to a person habitually resident in a foreign country?

(b) Professor Hay, in discussing *Burnham*, recalls *The Bremen v. Zapata Off-Shore Co.*, p. 294, *supra*, and in particular Chief Justice Burger's statement that it would be wrong for the United States to insist that all litigation be carried on in its courts and according to its rules.[c] Transient jurisdiction, Hay writes, presents the same problem: "The power 'myth' may do no harm—indeed it may make some sense—in the interstate context. In an international context, an unqualified, unremitting rule of transient jurisdiction seems quite intolerable, and is unfitting." Do you agree?

(c) To follow up the preceding question, suppose, for example, that the managing director of Asahi Metal Industries Ltd. had come to California to attend a convention on behalf of his company. Could service on him in California have subjected the company to jurisdiction of the California court—all other facts being the same as in the actual *Asahi* litigation? Would your answer be different if the managing director's trip to California had as its only purpose taking his family to Disneyland?[d]

---

[a] Recall *Grace v. MacArthur*, 170 F. Supp. 442 (E.D. Ark. 1959), in which jurisdiction of the Arkansas district court was upheld on the basis of service on board an airliner while it was flying over Arkansas on a non-stop flight from Memphis, Tennessee to Dallas, Texas.

[b] 495 U.S. at 628.

[c] Peter Hay, *Transient Jurisdiction, Especially over International Defendants: Critical Comments on Burnham v. Superior Court of California*, 1990 U.Ill.L.Rev. 593 at 602.

[d] For a pre-*Burnham* decision upholding tag jurisdiction over a corporate officer attending a convention in New Orleans on behalf of a German corporation, but not over the corporation that he represented, see *Amusement Equipment, Inc. v. Mordelt*, 779 F.2d 264 (5th Cir. 1985). Not many cases have addressed the question whether jurisdiction over a nonresident corporation may be obtained on the basis only of personal service on the managing agent in the forum state, that is without any finding that the corporation was doing business in the state. For a post-Burnham domestic decision upholding jurisdiction in these circumstances, see *Allied-Signal Inc. v. Purex Industries, Inc.*, 242 N.J. Super. 362, 576 A.2d 942 (1990).

(d) The Restatement (Third) of Foreign Relations Law, published after *Helicopteros* and *Asahi* but prior to *Burnham*, provides in §421(1) that

> A state may exercise jurisdiction through its courts with respect to a person or thing if the relationship of the state to the person or thing is such as to make the exercise of jurisdiction reasonable.

Section 421(2) then lists a series of contacts ((a)-(k)) that, "in general," make a state's exercise of jurisdiction to adjudicate reasonable, including defendant's nationality domicile or residence in the forum state, plus presence *other than transitory presence.* Comment e states that "tag" jurisdiction is not generally acceptable under international law. A principal source for that statement was the Brussels Convention discussed in the next section, which lists among the exorbitant bases for jurisdiction set out in Article 3[e] jurisdiction on the basis of service on the defendant during his temporary presence as known in Ireland and the United Kingdom (but not known in the other states parties to the Brussels or Lugano Conventions).

If the United States were to enter into a judgments convention, as was being actively discussed at the Hague Conference on Private International Law as this book went to press, should the *Burnham* case stand in the way? Or could the U.S. delegation agree to a convention which obligated member states to recognize and enforce judgments rendered in other member states, except for judgments rendered on the basis of service on persons temporarily in the forum state? Compare in this connection, §4(b)(6) of the Uniform Foreign Country Money-Judgments Recognition Act, drafted in the 1960's and presently in force in about half the states of the United States.[f]

§ 7.07 Judicial Jurisdiction in the European Community

As noted at the beginning of this chapter, the principle *Actor sequitur forum rei* was well established in Roman law.[a] But when that law was codified in the sixth century A.D. under the auspices of the Byzantine Emperor Justinian, provision was made for jurisdiction also for suit in tort at the place of wrongful conduct, in contract at the place of execution or performance, and in actions to vindicate property rights at the situs of the property.[b] These ideas of limited jurisdiction on the basis of contacts or liability-creating activity continued to be followed in most of the states of Western Europe that followed the civil law tradition. In addition, however, many states adopted jurisdictional bases going well beyond such limited jurisdiction, and incidentally, well beyond the jurisdiction that they would recognize when asked to recognize judgments of other states. For example, under Article 14 of the French Civil Code adopted in 1804 and (in this respect) unchanged to date, a French national can sue an alien before French courts regardless of the cause of action or the place where it arose.[c] Similar provisions were adopted in other

---

[e] Documents Supplement p. 99.

[f] Documents Supplement p. 94. For more on this Act, see Chapter VIII, § 8.03[A].

[a] See *Corpus Juris Civilis, Justinian,* Vol. XII, Book III, Title xiii, 2; Title xix, 3 (Scott. ed. 1932, repr. 1973).

[b] See Juenger, *Judicial Jurisdiction in the United States and in the European Communities: A Comparison,* 82 Mich. L. Rev. 1195, 1203–04 (1984); Juenger in turn draws on M. Kaser, *Das Römische Zivilprozessrecht* 183–84, 478–79 (1966).

[c] For discussion of the origin and applications of Article 14, see de Vries & Lowenfeld, *Jurisdiction in Personal Actions—A Comparison of Civil Law Views,* 44 Iowa L. Rev. 306, 316–30 (1959); Weser, *Bases of Judicial Jurisdiction in the Common Market Countries,* 10 Am. J. Comp. L. 323 (1961).

§ 7.07 JURISDICTION AND JUDGMENTS □ 621

states to which the Napoleonic codes spread directly or indirectly, including the Netherlands, Belgium, Luxembourg, and (with some variation) Italy. Under Article 23 of the German Code of Civil Procedure, the courts of Germany have jurisdiction in personam over persons having property in that country, not limited to the value of that property.[d] Both of these bases of jurisdiction were often criticized by commentators as exorbitant, but they were not repealed. They were, however, reexamined in the context of the effort to harmonize jurisdiction of courts, incident to the formation of the European Common Market in 1958.

As spelled out in more detail in the following chapter,[e] the original members of the European Economic Community[f] were required by the Treaty of Rome that established the Community to develop a convention on enforcement of judgments of member states of the Community. In approaching that task in the mid-1960's, they decided also to provide for a (largely) uniform law of jurisdiction within the Community, at least with respect to civil and commercial matters.[g] To that end, the framers of what became the Brussels Convention on Jurisdiction and the Enforcement of Judgments in Civil and Commercial Matters of 1968[h] adopted four basic principles.

First, and least controversial, the Convention adopted the basic principle that all persons domiciled in a member state in the Community may be sued in the courts of that state (Art. 2). *Second,* as between domiciliaries of member states, the exorbitant bases of jurisdiction, such as Article 14 of the French Civil Code and Article 23 of the German Code of Civil Procedure, were excluded (Art. 3)[i] Later, when the United Kingdom, Ireland, and Denmark joined the Community, jurisdiction based on service of a complaint or comparable document on the defendant during a temporary presence in the forum state was similarly excluded, again as between domiciliaries of member states only. *Third,* the Convention provided a series of special bases of jurisdiction, again only as between domiciliaries of contracting states, based on activity or contacts with the forum state and, generally, designed to protect the weaker party—employee, distributor, insured, accident victim, and the like—against having to follow defendants to their home ground (Art. 5–16). Interestingly, the Convention neither authorized nor required member states to adopt these special bases of jurisdiction. It simply provides that such jurisdiction exists by virtue of entry into effect of the Convention, whether or not the member states' internal law provides for such jurisdiction.[j] *Fourth,* the Convention adopted an elaborate provision on choice

---

[d] See de Vries & Lowenfeld, note c, *supra,* 330–44.

[e] See Chapter 8, § 8.03[A].

[f] Belgium, Federal Republic of Germany, France, Italy, Luxembourg, and The Netherlands.

[g] I.e., excluding not only criminal jurisdiction and administrative proceedings, but also most matters of family law, bankruptcy, wills and succession, and arbitration.

[h] Documents Supplement, p. 98. The original text is in Roman letters; amendments brought about by enlargement of the Community, and especially the entry of the United Kingdom, are shown in brackets.

[i] Member states were not required to repeal the laws authorizing the exorbitant jurisdictional bases, and could continue to apply them against persons not domiciled in a member state. For more on this point, in connection with discussion of the recognition of judgments within the Community, see Chapter 8, p. 731–732, question 5(a), *infra.*

[j] Such direct application of the Convention would be inconsistent with the constitutional system of the United Kingdom (and also Ireland), because international agreements become law only by virtue of legislation transforming them into national law. When the United Kingdom acceded to the Brussels Convention, therefore, an elaborate statute was adopted to bring the rules of jurisdiction of the Convention into effect in the UK, as among domiciliaries of member states, when the amended convention has entered into effect. UK Civil Jurisdiction and Judgments Act 1982, esp. ss. 2, 3, and 16; See also Order 11, r. 1(2) of the Rules of the Supreme Court, Documents Supplement, p. 80.

of forum clauses, on the one hand recognizing the effectiveness of such clauses as both conferring jurisdiction on the court chosen and excluding all other courts, and, on the other hand, seeking to insure that such clauses are the result of true assent and not of adhesion contracts or unilateral decision. (Art. 17)[k]

Three years after the original convention was signed, the original parties adopted a Protocol,[l] conferring jurisdiction on the Court of Justice of the European Communities to give rulings on the interpretation of the Convention, and authorizing (and in some instances requiring) courts of member states to refer questions arising under the Convention to that Court. The three decisions that follow illustrate the prevailing thought on jurisdiction within the Community—similar to, but not quite the same as, that in the United States.[m]

BIER v. MINES DE POTASSE D'ALSACE S.A.

European Court of Justice
November 30, 1976
[1976] E.C.R. 1736, [1977] 1 C.M.L.R. 284

Facts

G. J. Bier B.V. (hereinafter called Bier) of Nieuwerkerk aan de IJssel (The Netherlands), which is engaged in the business of nursery gardening, uses a water catchment area surrounding its property for its water supply and for the watering and irrigation of its seed beds. The surface waters thus used come principally from the Rhine. The high salinity of those waters causes damage to the seed beds and Bier is obliged to take expensive measures to limit it.

The Reinwater Foundation (hereinafter called Reinwater), whose registered office is at Amsterdam, exists in order to promote every possible improvement in the quality of the water in the Rhine basin, especially by opposing any deterioration in the natural quality of the water. The means whereby it seeks to achieve this purpose consist in particular in bringing legal actions so as to ensure the protection of the personal rights of all those whose environment is affected by the quality of the water of the Rhine and, in particular, of those whose livelihood is dependent upon it.

Bier and Reinwater brought an action before the Arrondissementsrechtbank (Court of first instance), Rotterdam, against the company Mines de Potasse d'Alsace, whose registered office is at Mulhouse and which works mines in Alsace. This company is alleged to discharge more than 10,000 tonnes of chlorides every twenty-four hours through a waste-flow into the Rhine, or in any event such quantities of industrial waste in the form of residuary salts that the salt content of the Rhine is thereby considerably and gravely augmented. Bier and Reinwater claimed in particular that the Netherlands court should hold that the discharge of residuary salts into the

---

[k] Documents Supplement, p. 105. This article was modified substantially when the United Kingdom acceded to the Convention, because the British insisted on a more commercially oriented and less protective provision concerning standard clauses in standard contracts.

[l] Documents Supplement, p. 123.

[m] Further cases arising under the Brussels Convention, as well as some more background, appear in Chapter 8, § 8.03[A], *infra*.

Rhine by Mines de Potasse d'Alsace is illegal and that the said company must make good the damage which they have thereby incurred or which they are liable to incur.

Mines de Potasse d'Alsace, reserving its defence as to the substance of the matter, objected that the Arrondissementsrechtbank does not have, and more generally, that the courts of the Netherlands do not have, jurisdiction in the matter by virtue of Articles 2 and 3 of the Convention of 27 September 1968 on jurisdiction and the enforcement of Judgments in Civil and Commercial Matters.

By judgment delivered on 12 May 1975, the Arrondissementsrechtbank held that it had no jurisdiction because the event that had caused the damage could only be the discharge of the residuary salts into the Rhine in France and therefore under the Convention of 1968 the case came under the jurisdiction of the French court for the area in which that discharge took place.

On 13 June 1975 Bier and Reinwater lodged an appeal against that judgment with the Gerechtshof (Appeal Court) of the Hague, and requested it to hold that it had jurisdiction to entertain their claim.

Bier and Reinwater relied on Article 5 (3) of the Convention of 27 September 1968 which provides that a defendant domiciled in a Contracting State may, in another Contracting State, be sued in matters relating to tort, delict, or quasi-delict, in the courts for the place where the harmful event occurred. The Gerechtshof, Second Chamber, felt that the proper course was to apply Article 2 (2) and Article 3 (2) of the Protocol of 3 June 1971 on the Interpretation by the Court of Justice of the Convention of 27 September 1968 on jurisdiction and the enforcement of Judgments in Civil and Commercial Matters. Accordingly, by judgment of 27 February 1976 it decided to stay the proceedings until the Court of Justice had given a preliminary ruling on the interpretation of what is meant by, "the place where the harmful event occurred" in Article 5 (3) of the Convention. In particular, it asked the Court to say whether the meaning is "the place where the damage occurred (the place where the damage took place or became apparent)" or rather "the place where the event having the damage as its sequel occurred (the place where the act was or was not performed)."

Law

. . .

Article 5 of the Convention provides: "A person domiciled in a Contracting State may, in another Contracting State, be sued: . . . (3) in matters relating to tort, delict or quasi-delict, in the courts for the place where the harmful event occurred."

That provision must be interpreted in the context of the scheme of conferment of jurisdiction which forms the subject-matter of Title II of the Convention.

That scheme is based on a general rule, laid down by Article 2, that the courts of the State in which the defendant is domiciled shall have jurisdiction.

However, Article 5 makes provision in a number of cases for a special jurisdiction, which the plaintiff may opt to choose. This freedom of choice was introduced having regard to the existence, in certain clearly defined situations, of a particularly close connecting factor between a dispute and the court which may be called upon to hear it, with a view to the efficacious conduct of the proceedings.

Thus in matters of tort, delict or quasi-delict Article 5 (3) allows the plaintiff to bring his case before the courts for "the place where the harmful event occurred."

In the context of the Convention, the meaning of that expression is unclear when the place of the event which is at the origin of the damage is situated in a State other than the one in which the place where the damage occurred is situated, as is the case inter *inter alia* with atmospheric or water pollution beyond the frontiers of a State.

The form of words "place where the harmful event occurred," used in all the language versions of the Convention, leaves open the question whether, in the situation described, it is necessary, in determining jurisdiction, to choose as the connecting factor the place of the event giving rise to the damage, or the place where the damage occurred, or to accept that the plaintiff has an option between the one and the other of those two connecting factors.

As regards this, it is well to point out that the place of the event giving rise to the damage no less than the place where the damage occurred can, depending on the case, constitute a significant connecting factor from the point of view of jurisdiction.

Liability in tort, delict or quasi-delict can only arise provided that a causal connexion can be established between the damage and the event in which that damage originates.

Taking into account the close connexion between the component parts of every sort of liability, it does not appear appropriate to opt for one of the two connecting factors mentioned to the exclusion of the other, since each of them can, depending on the circumstances, be particularly helpful from the point of view of the evidence and of the conduct of the proceedings.

To exclude one option appears all the more undesirable in that, by its comprehensive form of words, Article 5 (3) of the Convention covers a wide diversity of kinds of liability.

Thus the meaning of the expression "place where the harmful event occurred" in Article 5 (3) must be established in such a way as to acknowledge that the plaintiff has an option to commence proceedings either at the place where the damage occurred or the place of the event giving rise to it.

This conclusion is supported by the consideration, first, that to decide in favour only of the place of the event giving rise to the damage would, in an appreciable number of cases, cause confusion between the heads of jurisdiction laid down by Articles 2 and 5 (3) of the Convention, so that the latter provision would, to that extent, lose its effectiveness.

Secondly, a decision in favour only of the place where the damage occurred would, in cases where the place of the event giving rise to the damage does not coincide with the domicile of the person liable, have the effect of excluding a helpful connecting factor with the jurisdiction of a court particularly near to the cause of the damage.

Moreover, it appears from a comparison of the national legislative provisions and national case-law on the distribution of jurisdiction—both as regards internal relationships, as between courts for different areas, and in international relationships—that, albeit by differing legal techniques, a place is found for both of the two connecting factors here considered and that in several States they are accepted concurrently.

In these circumstances, the interpretation stated above has the advantage of avoiding any upheaval in the solutions worked out in the various national systems of law, since it looks to unification, in conformity with Article 5 (3) of the Convention, by way of a systematization of solutions which, as to their principle, have already been established in most of the States concerned.

Thus it should be answered that where the place of the happening of the event which may give rise to liability in tort, delict or quasi-delict and the place where that event results in damage are not identical, the expression "place where the harmful event occurred," in Article 5 (3) of the Convention, must be understood as being intended to cover both the place where the damage occurred and the place of the event giving rise to it.

The result is that the defendant may be sued, at the option of the plaintiff, either in the courts for the place where the damage occurred or in the courts for the place of the event which gives rise to and is at the origin of that damage.

. . .

On those grounds

THE COURT

In answer to the question referred to it by the Gerechtshof, The Hague, by judgment of 27 February 1976, hereby rules:

> Where the place of the happening of the event which may give rise to liability in tort, delict or quasidelict and the place where that event results in damage are not identical, the expression "place where the harmful event occurred," in Article 5 (3) of the Convention of 27 September 1968 on jurisdiction and the enforcement of Judgments in Civil and Commercial Matters, must be understood as being intended to cover both the place where the damage occurred and the place of the event giving rise to it.

> The result is that the defendant may be sued, at the option of the plaintiff, either in the courts for the place where the damage occurred or in the courts for the place of the event which gives rise to and is at the origin of that damage.

TESSILI v. DUNLOP A.G.

European Court of Justice
October 6, 1976
[1976] E.C.R. 1473, [1977] 1 C.M.L.R. 26

Facts

After the conclusion of negotiations conducted by one of its employees at the offices in Como of the company Industrie Tessili Italiana Como (hereinafter referred to as "Tessili" and after receipt of several samples, the company Dunlop A.G. (hereinafter referred to as "Dunlop"), whose registered office is in Hanau, sent an order by letter dated 29 April 1971 to Tessili for 310 women's ski suits.

Printed on Dunlop's letter were its conditions of purchase containing in particular the following clause:

"Jurisdiction: the court in Hanau am Main shall have jurisdiction to deal with disputes arising from this contract."

Tessili completed the ski suits ordered and sent them on 31 July 1971 to Dunlop through the intermediary of a transport undertaking appointed by the latter. Dunlop took delivery on 18 August 1971.

Also on 31 July 1971 Tessili made out an invoice which Dunlop received on 3 August 1971 and on the back of which Tessili's general conditions of sale were printed. These contained in particular the following clause:

"The court in Como shall have jurisdiction in any dispute which may arise and the purchaser waives his right to have the dispute decided by any other court whether by means of a consolidation order or by joinder of actions."

Dunlop considered that there were defects in the manufacture of the ski suits delivered by Tessili and on 28 June 1973, after a voluminous exchange of correspondence with Tessili brought an action before the Landgericht Hanau (Hanau Regional Court) for annulment of the contract.

Tessili argued before the Landgericht that German courts had no jurisdiction and in particular that the Landgericht Hanau had no jurisdiction *ratione loci*. Dunlop, on the other hand, claimed that the Landgericht Hanau did have jurisdiction.

By interlocutory judgment dated 10 May 1974 the Landgericht Hanau dismissed the objection to jurisdiction.

On 22 July 1974 Tessili appealed against this decision to the Oberlandesgericht Frankfurt am Main (Frankfurt am Main Higher Regional Court).

Dunlop cited Article 5 (1) of the Convention of 27 September 1968 on Jurisdiction and the Enforcement of Judgments in Civil and Commercial Matters which provides that a person domiciled in a Contracting State may, in another Contracting State, be sued in matters relating to a contract, in the courts for the place of performance of the obligation in question and the 21st Civil Senate of the Oberlandesgericht considered that the matter should be brought before the Court of Justice under Articles 2 (2) and 3 (2) of the Protocol on the Interpretation by the Court of Justice of the Convention of 27 September 1968. By order dated 14 January 1976 it stayed the proceedings until the Court had given a preliminary ruling on the interpretation of the concept of "place of performance of the obligation in question" within the meaning of Article 5 (1) of the Convention.

Law

. . .

The Convention frequently uses words and legal concepts drawn from civil, commercial and procedural law and capable of a different meaning from one Member State to another. The question therefore arises whether these words and concepts must be regarded as having their own independent meaning and as being thus common to all the Member States or as referring to substantive rules of the law applicable in each case under the rules of conflict of laws of the court before which the matter is first brought.

Neither of these two options rules out the other since the appropriate choice can only be made in respect of each of the provisions of the Convention to ensure that it is fully effective having regard to the objectives of Article 220 of the Treaty. In any event it should be stressed that the interpretation of the said words and concepts for the purpose of the Convention does not prejudge the question of the substantive rule applicable to the particular case.

The question raised by the national court

Article 5 of the Convention provides: "A person domiciled in a Contracting State may, in another Contracting State, be sued: (1) in matters relating to a contract, in the courts for the place of performance of the obligation in question." This provision must be interpreted within the framework of the system of conferment of jurisdiction under Title II of the Convention. In accordance with Article 2 the basis of this system is the general conferment of jurisdiction on the court of the defendant's domicile. Article 5 however provides for a number of cases of special jurisdiction at the option of the plaintiff.

This freedom of choice was introduced in view of the existence in certain well-defined cases of a particularly close relationship between a dispute and the court which may be most conveniently called upon to take cognizance of the matter. Thus in the case of an action relating to contractual obligations Article 5 (1) allows a plaintiff to bring the matter before the court for the place "of performance" of the obligation in question. It is for the court before which the matter is brought to establish under the Convention whether the place of performance is situate within its territorial jurisdiction. For this purpose it must determine in accordance with its own rules of conflict of laws what is the law applicable to the legal relationship in question and define in accordance with that law the place of performance of the contractual obligation in question.

Having regard to the differences obtaining between national laws of contract and to the absence at this stage of legal development of any unification in the substantive law applicable, it does not appear possible to give any more substantial guide to the interpretation of the reference made by Article 5 (1) to the "place of performance" of contractual obligations. This is all the more true since the determination of the place of performance of obligations depends on the contractual context to which these obligations belong. In these circumstances the reference in the Convention to the place of performance of contractual obligations cannot be understood otherwise than by reference to the substantive law applicable under the rules of conflict of laws of the court before which the matter is brought.

. . .

On those grounds,

THE COURT

In answer to the question referred to it by the Oberlandesgericht Frankfurt am Main by order dated 14 January 1976, hereby rules:

> The "place of performance of the obligation in question" within the meaning of Article 5 (1) of the Convention of 27 September 1968 on Jurisdiction and the Enforcement of Judgments in Civil and Commercial Matters is to be determined in accordance with the law which governs the obligations in question according to the rules of conflict of laws of the court before which the matter is brought.

IVENEL v. SCHWAB

European Court of Justice
May 26, 1982
[1982] E.C.R. 1891, [1983] 1 C.M.L.R. 538

Facts and Issues

1. On 1 September 1977 Roger Ivenel, who was living in Strasbourg (France), entered the employment of Schwab Maschinenbau, established at Oettingen (Federal Republic of Germany), as a traveller and commercial representative in France.

On 18 January 1978 Roger Ivenel brought an action against his employer before the Conseil de Prud'hommes, Strasbourg, for payment of various sums and in particular commission which allegedly had not been paid to him since 1975 and various allowances by reason of the termination of the contract of employment. As against this claim Helmut Schwab raised the objection of lack of jurisdiction both *ratione materiae* and *ratione loci,* alleging on the one hand that the plaintiff was an independent contractor and on the other that according to the Convention of Brussels of 27 September 1968 the Court having jurisdiction was that for the place of performance of the obligation in question, in this instance the place of payment of the commission, namely Oettingen.

When the action was before the Conseil de Prud'hommes Article 5 (1) of the Brussels Convention was worded as follows:

A person domiciled in a Contracting State may, in another Contracting State, be sued:

"(1) In matters relating to a contract, in the courts for the place of performance of the obligation in question."

2. By judgment of 17 April 1978 the Conseil de Prud'hommes dismissed the two objections.

When regard to the objection *ratione materiae* it found that the plaintiff was bound to the defendant by a contract of employment as a representative.

As regards the objection *ratione loci* the Conseil de Prud'hommes considered that the concept "place of performance of the obligation in question" contained in Article 5 (1) of the Brussels Convention must be understood as referring to the place of performance of the main or characteristic obligation of the contract. In the case of a contract of employment as a representative the place of performance of the work was that where the representative had his office, collated orders and attended to their execution. The court having jurisdiction under Article 5 was therefore in this case the court for the place where Roger Ivenel was ordinarily resident, namely Strasbourg.

Upon appeal by Helmut Schwab the Cour d'Appel, Colmar, by judgment of 10 October 1978 confirmed the jurisdiction *ratione materiae* of the Conseil de Prud'hommes but considered that the Conseil had no jurisdiction *ratione loci.* In that respect the Cour d'Appel considered that having regard to the judgment of the Court of Justice of 6 October 1976 in Case 14/76 *de Bloos* [1976] ECR 1497 the obligation to be taken into account was that which corresponded to the contractual right on which the plaintiff's action was based. In the case in point that was the obligation to pay the commission and allowances claimed by Ivenel from Schwab who was ordinarily resident in the Federal Republic of Germany. Since both in French and German law such a payment was due at the address of the debtor and not of the creditor the Conseil de Prud'hommes, Strasbourg, had no jurisdiction *ratione loci.*

3. Roger Ivenel thereupon appealed in cassation against the judgment of the Cour d'Appel.

In its judgment of 2 April 1981 the Cour de Cassation considered that since the proceedings related to the performance of a contract for representation involving mutual obligations, some of which at least were performed in France, the question of the place of performance of the obligation within the meaning of Article 5 (1) of the Brussels Convention raised a serious difficulty of interpretation. The Cour de Cassation therefore decided to stay the proceedings until the Court of Justice had given a ruling on this matter.

Decision

. . .

It must be observed that, as the Court of Justice has already stated, in particular in its judgment of 6 October 1976 in Case 12/76 *Tessili* [1976] ECR 1473, the "place of performance" within the meaning of Article 5 (1) of the Convention is to be determined in accordance with the law which governs the obligation in question according to the conflict rules of the court before which the matter is brought.

The question raised by the national court concerns the obligation to be taken into account for the purposes of that definition when the claim before the court is based on different obligations under a single contract for representation which has been classified by the courts concerned with the substance of the case as a contract of employment.

In its judgment of 6 October 1976 in Case 14/76 *de Bloos* [1976] ECR 1497 the Court has already stated that the obligation to be taken into account for the purposes of Article 5 (1) of the Convention in the case of a claim based on a contract granting an exclusive sales concession between two commercial undertakings is that which forms the basis of the legal proceedings. The problem raised by this case is whether the same criterion must be applied to cases of the kind described by the national court.

It is appropriate to examine that problem in the light of the objectives of the Convention and the general scheme of its provisions.

Adoption of the special rules of jurisdiction as contained in Articles 5 and 6 of the Convention is justified *inter alia* by the fact that there must be a close connecting factor between the dispute and the court with jurisdiction to resolve it. The report drawn up by the committee of experts (Official Journal 1979, C 59, p. 1) which drafted the text of the Convention stresses that connection by stating *inter alia* that the court for the place of performance of the obligation will be useful in proceedings for the recovery of fees since the creditor will have a choice between the courts of the State where the defendant is ordinarily resident by virtue of the general provisions contained in Article 2 of the Convention and the courts of another State within whose jurisdiction the services were provided, particularly where, according to the appropriate law, the obligation to pay must be performed where the services were provided.

The above-mentioned report also refers to the reasons why those drafting the Convention did not consider it appropriate to insert into the Convention a provision giving exclusive jurisdiction in contracts of employment. According to the report it is desirable as far as possible for disputes to be brought before the courts of the State whose law governs the contract whereas at the time the Convention was being drafted work was in progress to harmonize the application of the rules of employment law in the Member States of the Community. The report concludes that at present the existing provisions of the Convention, such as Article 2 stipulating the forum for the place where the defendant is ordinarily resident and Article 5 (1) the forum for the place of performance of the obligation, are likely to satisfy the relevant interests.

It should be noted that on 19 June 1980 a Convention on the law applicable to contractual obligations was opened for signature by the Member States (Official Journal 1980, L 266, p. 1). Article 6 thereof provides that a contract of employment is to be governed, in the absence of choice of the applicable law, by the law of the country in which the employee habitually carries out his work in performance of the contract unless it appears from the circumstances as a whole that the contract is more closely connected with another country.

The experts' report on the Convention on the law applicable to contractual obligations (Official Journal 1980, C 282, p. 1) explains in that respect that the adopting of a special conflict rule in relation to contracts of employment was intended to provide an appropriate arrangement for matters in which the interests of one of the contracting parties were not the same as those of the other and to secure thereby adequate protection for the party who from the socio-economic point of view was to be regarded as the weaker in the contractual relationship.

It follows from the foregoing account that in the matter of contracts Article 5 (1) of the Convention is particularly concerned to attribute jurisdiction to the court of the country which has a close connection with the case; that in the case of a contract of employment the connection lies particularly in the law applicable to the contract; and that according to the trend in the conflict rules in regard to this matter that law is determined by the obligation characterizing the contract in question and is normally the obligation to carry out work.

It emerges from an examination of the provisions of the Convention that in establishing special or even exclusive jurisdiction for insurance, instalment sales and tenancies of immovable property those provisions recognize that the rules on jurisdiction, too, are inspired by concern to afford proper protection to the party to the contract who is the weaker from the social point of view.

Those factors must be taken into account in answering the question which has been put to the Court.

In a case such as the one in point, where the national court has before it claims relating to obligations under a contract for representation, some of which concern remuneration due to the employee from an undertaking established in one State and others concern compensation based on the manner in which the work has been done in another State, it is necessary to interpret the provisions of the Convention in such a way that the national court is not compelled to find that it has jurisdiction to adjudicate upon certain claims but not on others.

Such a result would be even less compatible with the objectives and general structure of the Convention in the case of a contract of employment for which, as general rule, the law applicable contains provisions protecting the worker and is normally that of the place where the work characterizing the contract is carried out.

It follows from the foregoing considerations, taken as a whole, that the obligation to be taken into account for the purposes of the application of Article 5 (1) of the Convention in the case of claims based on different obligations arising under a contract of employment as a representative binding a worker to an undertaking is the obligation which characterizes the contract.

On those grounds,

THE COURT

In answer to the question submitted to it by the French Cour de Cassation by judgment of 2 April 1981, hereby rules:

> The obligation to be taken into account for the purposes of the application of Article 5 (1) of the Convention of 27 September 1968 on Jurisdiction and the Enforcement of Judgments in Civil and Commercial Matters in the case of claims based on different obligations arising under contract of employment as a representative binding a worker to an undertaking is the obligation which characterizes the contract.

NOTES AND QUESTIONS

(1)(a) The three cases here reproduced involve Dutch environmental interests suing a French mining enterprise in the Netherlands, a German buyer suing an Italian seller in Germany, and a French sales representative suing a German principal for his commissions in France. In each case the plaintiff prevails on the issue of jurisdiction. Would the cases have come out the same way if, say, New York were substituted for the Netherlands, Florida for France, Iowa for Italy, and Georgia for Germany?

(b) A fair answer would seem to be "yes" in the pollution case, "probably" in the case about the ski suits, and "it depends" in the traveling salesman's suit for his commission.[a] What is interesting is that the issues that would be critical for an American court—how many salesmen defendant maintained in the forum state, for instance, or where the negotiations were conducted in the sales dispute—seem not to be considered by the European court.

(2)(a) Professor Juenger, a scholar equally at home in European and American law, writes that the Brussels Convention's jurisdictional provisions "compare favorably" with American long-arm statutes.[b] Do you agree? If so, is it because the rules are more clearly set out than the sometimes shifting statements of the U.S. Supreme Court? Or because the substantive solutions are fairer?

(b) Juenger explains as follows:

> In contrast to American state legislators, who had to take into account not altogether consistent Supreme Court pronouncements, the European draftsmen could rely on their own best judgment, which helped make their work product tidier, more functional and more precise. In particular, they were able to design appropriate rules to govern multi-party practice[c] and to accord jurisdictional privileges to certain disadvantaged groups, provisions that would not pass our Supreme Court's constitutional muster. In this respect the Brussels Convention may appear persuasive to an American observer; however, it also protects enterprises against undue jurisdictional exposure.[d]

Is this persuasive? If so, does it suggest that the U.S. Supreme Court's constitutional concerns are misplaced? Recall Justice Black's cryptic opinion—neither concurrence nor dissent—in *International Shoe*.[e] Do you think that was his point?

(c) One of the most difficult aspects of the American concept of jurisdiction over non-residents is how to determine when the defendant (particularly a corporate defendant) is *doing* business in the forum state, so as to support jurisdiction on any cause of action, and when it has merely *transacted* business in the forum state, to support only actions related based on that business.[f] The Brussels Convention avoids that problem. Only related actions can be bought in the forum against a foreign corporation that is not established in the forum state, and if it is established through a branch, only actions related to activity of the branch.[g] Is that a better solution than the American one?

---

[a] Compare *International Shoe Co. v. Washington* and Question 3, p. 494, *supra*.

[b] Juenger, p. 620 note b, *supra,* at 1207.

[c] See Article 6 of the Convention, Documents Supplement, p. 101.

[d] Juenger, note b, *supra*.

[e] Page 490, *supra*.

[f] Recall the discussion in *Helicopteros* and question 2, p. 574, *supra*.

[g] See Art. 2, 5(5) and 53.

(3)(a) The issue on which *Bier v. Mines de Potasse d'Alsace* turned is a familiar one, for choice of law as well as for jurisdiction: Is the critical event in a tort case where the wrongful act was done, or where the injury took place.[h] Article 5(3) of the Brussels Convention does not resolve that question. According to the report of the drafters of the Convention, "The Committee did not think it should specify whether [the place where the harmful event occurred] is the place where the event which resulted in the damage or injury occurred, or whether it is the place where the damage or injury was sustained."[i] Whether that statement merely reflects modesty, or covers disagreement, is not clear. It is unlikely that when drafted, the formulation in the Convention was designed to leave room for development by the Court of Justice, because the decision even to provide for review by that court of questions under the Convention had not been taken.

(b) The Court of Justice employs a number of Advocates General, eight as of 1998, one of whom always makes an oral submission to the Court after all other submissions—oral and written—have been received. The opinion of the Advocate General—not linked to the interests of any private litigant, the European Commission,[j] or any member state, and containing much of the research and scholarship that seems to be missing from the opinions of the Court itself—is always published in the official Reports along with the actual judgment, and the recommendation of the Advocate General is given great weight, though of course it is not binding on the Court.

In the *Bier* case, Advocate General Caportorti summarized the law on the point in all the member states as well as in other states, citing for example, §§ 36 and 37 of the *Restatement (Second) of Conflict of Laws* (1971).[k] He concluded that Article 5(3) of the Convention should be interpreted to mean the "place where the act legally speaking is complete," i.e., the place of injury.[l] The Court here rejects the conclusion, and permits the plaintiff to elect either definition at his option. Is the Court being too permissive? . . . too pro-plaintiff?

Note that if neither of the possible definitions coincides with the defendant's domicile, plaintiff has three places to choose from for bringing his action. Forum shopping, it turns out, is not just an American pastime. Is there too much of it under the holding of *Bier v. Mines de Potasse*?

(c) Is there any indication by the Court of what law the Rotterdam court should now apply?[m]

---

[h] Recall the very first case in this book, *Alabama Great Southern R.R. v. Carroll,* Ch. 1, p. 1, *supra.*

[i] *Report on the Convention on Jurisdiction and the Enforcement of Judgments in Civil and Commercial Matters* by P. Jenard, Rapporteur of the Committee of Experts that prepared the Convention, published in 22 O.J. Eur. Comm. No. C59 p. 1, 26 (March 5, 1979) [hereafter *Jenard Report.*]

[j] I.e., the executive arm of the European Community. The role of the Commission in cases of the kind reproduced in this and the following chapter is minimal. In cases under the Treaty of Rome concerning restraints on the movement of goods, competition law, and the like, the Commission is nearly always heavily involved, often as a plaintiff against a member state or as respondent in an appeal from one of its regulations or administrative measures.

[k] Section 36, essentially, supports jurisdiction on the basis of doing an act in the forum state; § 37 supports jurisdiction on the basis of causing an effect in that state. The Advocate General might also have cited *Ohio v. Wyandotte Chemicals Corp.,* 401 U.S. 493, 500–01 (1971). In that case the Court, while denying leave to Ohio to file an original jurisdiction case, indicated that Ohio could file an action in Ohio against U.S. and Canadian companies charged with dumping mercury into streams in Canada whose courses ultimately reach Lake Erie and pollute that lake's waters.

[l] [1976] E.C.R. 1757–58.

[m] In fact, the Rotterdam court, in one of the important judgments concerning environmental law in Europe, following elaborate studies by experts of the in-and out-flow flow of the Rhine and its tributaries, applied Netherlands law as well as customary international law. It gave a substantial recovery to plaintiffs, and rejected the argument that defendant's acts were lawful where they were carried out. *Bier v. Mines de Potasse d'Alsace,* Rb. Rotterdam, Dec. 16, 1983, [1984] Nederlandse Jurisprudentie No. 341, aff'd Hoge Raad (Sup. Ct) Sept. 23, 1988, [1989] Nederlandse Jurisprudentie No. 743.

Could the Court of Justice give some suggestions, or would that be beyond the jurisdiction of the Court of Justice under the Protocol to the Convention?[n]

(4)(a) The two contract cases here reproduced again raise the question of the influence of local choice of law rules on jurisdiction of courts. Are the two cases consistent with each other?

(b) Turning first to *Tessili,* note that the issue of whether a valid choice of forum agreement was concluded, which appears in the statement of facts, does not appear in the opinion of the Court of Justice. In fact the lower German court thought that there was a valid choice of forum agreement, pointing to Hanau, in the Federal Republic; the Oberlandesgericht (appeals court) concluded that no valid agreement had been reached within the meaning of Article 17 of the Convention, but did not put that question to the Court of Justice.[o]

(c) Absent an agreement as to a forum, the question is one of interpreting Article 5(1) of the Convention. When one side undertakes to make and sell a product, and the other side undertakes to take and pay for that product, and subsequently a dispute arises, what is the place of performance? Does the answer depend on which party is the plaintiff, which the defendant? What if, as is common in disputes between buyers and sellers, there is a counterclaim?

(d) The second question posed—what if there is a counterclaim—is foreseen in the Convention itself: at least as to related counterclaims, they may be brought in the forum chosen by the plaintiff, if that forum is properly selected. (Article 6(3)). As to the first question—where is the place of performance—the Court of Justice declines to decide, but says the answer depends on the national law of the forum selected by plaintiff.

(e) The British government submitted its views in the *Tessili* case, and urged the Court not to issue a definition of the place of performance, because such a definition would, for practical purposes, determine that place for purposes of substantive law, thus changing the law in some, and perhaps all of the member states, and also inviting reference of cases involving every type of contractual relationship to the Court of Justice.[p] Thus the British submission urged the Court to do essentially what it did do, i.e., to state that jurisdiction under Article 5(1) depended on the national law, including conflict of laws, of the forum.[q]

(f) The seller in the actual case said that all obligations of sellers must be performed at their registered place of business—here Italy; the buyer argued that a uniform European law designating the place of performance of an international sales contract would go beyond the scope of the Brussels Convention. Alternatively, to give the defendant's interpretation to Article 5(1) would make that article superfluous, since suit at seller's domicile could always be brought under Article 2. Thus, buyer argued, one should look at the facts of the actual case, i.e., where delivery was to be made, title was to pass, etc. Where a warranty was involved, buyer urged, the place where the goods were located should be regarded as the place of performance.[r] Does this debate lead you to conclude that the Court was wise in its conclusion?

---

[n] Documents Supplement, p. 123.

[o] As a matter of commercial law, the consequence is that the basic sales contract is formed, because agreement has been reached on the essential terms—description of the goods, price, amount, and time of delivery; no agreement has been reached, however, on the ancillary terms, such as the place where a dispute may or must be adjudicated.

[p] [1976] E.C.R. 1479–80. Compare on the second point the arguments made in connection with *Allstate v. Hague.*

[q] On remand, the Oberlandesgericht dismissed the appeal, i.e., it confirmed that under German private international law the place of performance depended on German substantive law, which here said the place of performance was the place where the allegedly defective goods were situated.

[r] [1976] E.C.R. at 1476–77.

(5)(a) Dean Hay, an expert both in conflict of laws and in the law of the European Community, regards the decision of the Court of Justice in *Tessili v. Dunlop* as a step backward.[s] Adoption of a Community view of place of performance for purposes of the Brussels Convention would not affect substantive law, he writes, because each state would remain free to define the place of performance for substantive law purposes, including choice of law. If Community law said German courts did not take jurisdiction in *Tessili* because the place of performance was Italy, Germany's choice of law rule, of course, would be irrelevant; Italian courts, in that event, could still apply either the Italian or the German law of warranties. If, as a matter of Community law, the place of performance for jurisdictional purposes were the place of delivery or location of the goods, German courts thereafter could still decide that either German or Italian law governs the seller's obligation. The important thing, in any event, was to establish a stable criterion for jurisdiction, and the Court's response to the *Tessili* case failed to do this.

(b) Do you agree with Hay's critique? Note that in Hay's formulation, the role of the Court is quite different from that of the U.S. Supreme Court: the Supreme Court never prescribes judicial jurisdiction, it only sustains or strikes down jurisdiction assumed by lower state or federal courts. In *Tessili,* as in *Bier,* the Court of Justice assumes a similar role, throwing back to national law, or indeed to the plaintiff, a choice it refuses to make mandatory as a matter of European law.

(c) In the *Ivenel* case, denied six years after *Tessili* and *Bier,* the Court of Justice seems more inclined to establish a Community rule, and less prepared to say that each member state may determine jurisdiction on the basis of its own choice of law rules. In part this change of attitude is influenced by completion of the draft of the European Convention on the Law Applicable to Contractual Obligations,[t] but that convention had not entered into force and, as we saw, continues to engender controversy among the member of the Community.[u] More generally, the Court of Justice takes the position that the special rules of jurisdiction are designed to afford protection to the weaker party, that this is particularly true in connection with contracts of employment,[v] and that service as a traveling salesman is a type of employment contract. The Court also draw support from a concept popular among European (particularly German) writers on conflict of laws, concerning the "characteristic performance." The thought is that most contracts call for payment, so this is not a characteristic of a given contract; on the other hand, the obligation to supply a particular product, or to perform a service in a particular place, is characteristic of that contract, and should therefore supply the source of the applicable law—and here of jurisdiction.[w] Is that persuasive?

(d) If the reasoning is persuasive in the context of employment contracts, shouldn't it work in other contexts as well? For instance, going back to *Tessili,* where is the characteristic performance in that case?

---

[s] Hay, *The Case for Federalizing Rules of Civil Jurisdiction in the European Community,* 82 Mich. L. Rev. 1323, 1332–34 (1984).

[t] Documents Supplement, p. 44.

[u] See question 4, p. 276–278, *supra.* Note also that adherence to the Choice of Law Convention, in contrast to the Jurisdiction and Judgments Convention, is not a condition for membership in the Community.

[v] The drafters of the Brussels Convention were concerned with contracts of employment, and in fact an early draft contained a special provision for such contracts. The provision was dropped from the final version, in part for the reasons set out by the Court at pp. 629–30, *supra,* in part because the discussion became too involved with labor law. See *Jenard Report,* note i, *supra,* p. 24.

[w] The discussion of this approach in Europe is voluminous; for a discussion in English by a Dutch scholar, see d'Oliveira, *Characteristic Obligation in the Draft EEC Obligation Convention,* 25 Am. J. Comp. L. 303 (1977).

§ 7.07   JURISDICTION AND JUDGMENTS   □   635

(e) If some uncertainty remains concerning the application of national vs. Community law to the special jurisdiction in actions relating to a contract, note that Article 5(1) of the Convention is clear in excluding the place of contracting as an independent basis for jurisdiction, as is provided, for instance, in Order 11, r. 1(d)(i) of the United Kingdom Rules of the Supreme Court,[x] and in the law of several other member states (as well as in many American states). Is this an improvement?

(6)(a) Consider, finally, the rules of jurisdiction of the European Community (applicable only to domiciliaries of member states), alongside the rules applicable in the United States and (apart from the Community) in the United Kingdom. Granted that the survey here presented is incomplete, that there are significant differences of detail between the law in the United States, in Britain, and in the Community, and that many states have not been explored here at all, does the law as presented in this chapter support the conclusion that there is an international law standard for jurisdiction of courts?

(b) *The Restatement (Third) Foreign Relations Law* (1987) purports to set forth such an international law standard, as follows:

§ 421. Jurisdiction to Adjudicate

(1) A state may exercise jurisdiction through its courts to adjudicate with respect to a person or thing, if the relationship of the state to the person or thing is such as to make the exercise of jurisdiction reasonable.

(2) In general, a state's exercise of jurisdiction to adjudicate with respect to a person or thing is reasonable if, at the time jurisdiction is asserted:

(a) the person or thing is present in the state, other than transitorily;

(b) the person, if a natural person, is domiciled in the state;

(c) the person, if a natural person, is resident in the the state;

(d) the person, if a natural person, is a national of the state;

(e) the person, if a corporation or comparable juridical person, is organized pursuant to the law of the state;

(f) a ship, aircraft, or other vehicle to which the adjudication relates is registered under the laws of the state;

(g) the person, whether natural or juridical, has consented to the exercise of jurisdiction;

(h) the person, whether natural or juridical, regularly carries on business in the state;

(i) the person, whether natural or juridical, had carried on activity in the state, but only in respect of such activity;

(j) the person, whether natural or juridical, had carried on activity outside the state, having a substantial, direct, or foreseeable effect within the state, but only in respect of such activity; or

(k) the thing that is the subject of adjudication is owned, possessed, or used in the state, but only in respect of a claim reasonably connected with that thing.

---

[x] Documents Supplement p. 79.

(3) A defense of lack of jurisdiction is generally waived by any appearance by or on behalf of a person or thing (whether as plaintiff, defendant, or third party), if the appearance is for a purpose that does not include a challenge to the exercise of jurisdiction.

On the basis of the materials in this chapter, do you think the *Restatement* has it approximately right?

CHAPTER 8

RECOGNITION AND ENFORCEMENT OF FOREIGN JUDGMENTS

The object of litigation, of course, is to secure a judgment. Most persons pay (or otherwise carry out) civil judgments[a] even if they think they should not have been held liable, partly to maintain credit and other standing in the community, partly because they know that if they do not, their assets may be seized to satisfy the judgment. If, however, the judgment debtor resides or is established in a state other than the one where the judgment was rendered and has no assets in the judgment state, another consideration enters into the calculation. Can the judgment be enforced in the state where the judgment debtor resides and/or has assets? If the judgment creditor must bring another action to enforce his judgment, what if any issues are open to be litigated? What if the first judgment was (i) wrong; or (ii) subject to appeal; or (iii) in some way not final; or (iv) rendered upon default of the judgment debtor? What if the rendering court lacked (or may have lacked) jurisdiction? Or if the proceeding was in some other way unfair?

Each of these questions is explored in this chapter, first in the context of the American union of semi-sovereign states linked by a federal constitution; then in the context of nation-states increasingly linked by commerce, finance and communications, but not, for the most part, by formal obligations concerning recognition of judgments; and finally in the context of two treaties, one dealing with judgments, the other with arbitral awards.

§ 8.01 Recognition of Judgments Within the United States

[A] Res Judicata and Full Faith and Credit

[1] A Penny's Worth of Res Judicata

The law of *res judicata* describes the effect of a judgment secured in one litigation on a second litigation, whether in the same jurisdiction or in another one. To review this law in a nutshell: (i) If P sues D on cause *x* in one action, and loses, P cannot again sue D on that cause of action (so-called *bar*); (ii) If P sues D on a given claim and wins a judgment for $1000, (a) when P seeks to collect on the judgment D cannot again assert that he is not liable, and (b) P cannot again raise the same claim against D, asserting that D really owes $5000 (so-called *merger*).

Further, if P had two related claims against D, say a personal injury and a property claim arising out of the same accident, he usually cannot raise one of the claims and postpone the other; if he tries thus to "split his cause of action," P will be barred (putting aside some exceptions)

---

[a] We exclude for the moment judgments calling for alimony, child support, or child custody, in which the behavior patterns, as well as the legal rules are significantly different. See Chapter 9, *infra*.

from raising the second, related claim. In some but not all states, if P sues D and D has a claim against P arising out of the same transaction or event, D will be required to raise his claim in the same action, or risk being met by the defense of res judicata if he tries to raise the claim in a separate action (so-called *compulsory counterclaim*).

The narrow concept of res judicata, focused on identity of claims, applies in virtually all jurisdictions, common law, civil law, or other. In some jurisdictions, res judicata has another dimension, directed to *issues* rather than claims. Suppose, for instance, P and D are in an automobile accident, P sues D and prevails on a showing that D was negligent and P was not. Now D sues P, asserting that he, D, was not negligent and that P was. Even if no rule of compulsory counterclaims was applicable,[b] most legal systems would say the second claim fails, because the critical issues—P's and D's negligence—have already been determined.[c] (So-called *collateral estoppel* or *issue preclusion*). Some states go further, and say that even if the parties in the two actions are different, say P–2 brings suit against D arising out of the same accident, D is estopped or precluded from denying his negligence. (Of course D can raise other issues not previously litigated, such as P–2's contributory negligence, the amount of damages suffered, etc.)

[2] A First Glance at the Full Faith and Credit Clause

Everything stated in the preceding paragraphs applies whether the first and the second action were in the same state, or in a different state, usually as a result of judge-made, or "common" law.[d] What then does the Full Faith and Credit clause of the U.S. Constitution add?[e]

(a) *The Presumption of Fairness.* The first rule of recognition and enforcement of foreign judgments, quite apart from the U.S. Constitution, is that F–2 will only recognize and enforce a judgment of F–1 if F–1's legal system is viewed as basically fair. The Full Faith and Credit clause establishes a conclusive presumption in every state of the Union that the legal system or every other state is fair. A judgment debtor may be heard to say in a given case that he wasn't given notice, wasn't allowed to have counsel, or was otherwise dealt with contrary to standards of due process; he cannot, however, challenge the whole legal system of F–1 in F–2; if F–2 were to hold that F–1's system is not entitled to recognition in general (say a Massachusetts court speaking about justice in Mississippi), the U.S. Supreme Court would reverse, on the ground that F–2 had not given full faith and credit to the judicial proceedings of F–1.

(b) *No Distinction for Default Judgments.* Whereas the rules of res judicata work fairly well when the first action was contested by both (or all) parties, they might not work so well in the case of default. The Full Faith and Credit clause, however, draws no distinction between a bilateral and a default judgment; thus a defendant cannot (except on grounds of jurisdiction, [C] *infra*) defeat recognition of a judgment by refusing to participate in the action, and a state court in the position of F–2 cannot (within the United States) establish a rule such as prevails in England to the effect that it will not enforce default judgments against absent defendants.[f] Of course,

---

[b] New York State, for example, does not have any compulsory counterclaim rule, comparable to Rule 13(a) of the Federal Rules of Civil Procedure.

[c] Probably this would be true even if P's negligence was not put in issue in the first action but could have been. It would not be true if the first action had been decided upon default.

[d] See, generally *Restatement (Second) of the Law of Judgments,* esp. §§ 18–29 (1982).

[e] Article IV, § 1 of the Constitution appears in the Documents Supplement p. 4.

[f] See p. 718, question (4)(d), *infra*. The English rule does not deny enforcement to all judgments in which the defendant fails to appear or defend; but it denies enforcement if defendant was not present or otherwise submitted to the jurisdiction of the rendering court.

§ 8.01   JURISDICTION AND JUDGMENTS   □   639

as developed in the next section, it is this fact more than any other that makes long-arm jurisdiction an effective weapon in many cases.

This still leaves a good many questions open:

—What about a judgment in F–1 that could not have been obtained at all in F–2? For instance what if Ball recovered a judgment for $200,000 in New York against the Massachusetts charity, Berkshire Natural History Society, Inc., and sought to enforce it in Massachusetts, where Berkshire would not have been liable?[g]

—What about a judgment rendered in F–1 about a controversy in which F–1 had no interest, but F–2 had a great interest?

—Finally, what about a judgment of F–1 applying the law of F–2, but (according to the losing party) misapplying that law?

FAUNTLEROY v. LUM

United States Supreme Court
210 U.S. 230 (1908)

Mr. Justice Holmes delivered the opinion of the court.

This is an action upon a Missouri judgment brought in a court of Mississippi. The declaration set forth the record of the judgment. The defendant pleaded that the original cause of action arose in Mississippi out of a gambling transaction in cotton futures; that he declined to pay the loss; that the controversy was submitted to arbitration, the question as to the illegality of the transaction, however, not being included in the submission; that an award was rendered against the defendant; that thereafter, finding the defendant temporarily in Missouri, the plaintiff brought suit there upon the award; that the trial court refused to allow the defendant to show the nature of the transaction, and that by the laws of Mississippi the same was illegal and void, but directed a verdict if the jury should find that the submission and award were made, and remained unpaid; and that a verdict was rendered and the judgment in suit entered upon the same. (The plaintiff in error is an assignee of the judgment, but nothing turns upon that.) The plea was demurred to on constitutional grounds, and the demurrer was overruled subject to exception. Thereupon replications were filed, again setting up the Constitution of the United States (Art. IV, § 1), and were demurred to. The Supreme Court of Mississippi held the plea good and the replications bad, and judgment was entered for the defendant. Thereupon the case was brought here.

The main argument urged by the defendant to sustain the judgment below is addressed to the jurisdiction of the Mississippi courts.

The laws of Mississippi make dealing in futures a misdemeanor, and provide that contracts of that sort, made without intent to deliver the commodity or to pay the price, "shall not be enforced by any court." Annotated Code of 1892, §§ 1120, 1121, 2117. The defendant contends that this language deprives the Mississippi courts of jurisdiction.

. . .

---

[g] See Chapter 3, *Case 5*, p. 121, *supra*.

[The court concludes that the Mississippi statute is not jurisdictional, but more likely a way of saying that the contracts in question are not enforceable in Mississippi. But even if this conclusion is erroneous, there remains the other question:]

. . . Whether the illegality of the original cause of action in Mississippi can be relied upon there as a ground for denying a recovery upon a judgment of another State.

The doctrine laid down by Chief Justice Marshall was "that the judgment of a state court should have the same credit, validity, and effect in every other court in the United States, which it had in the State where it was pronounced, and that whatever pleas would be good to a suit thereon in such State, and none others, could be pleaded in any other court of the United States." *Hampton v. McConnel,* 3 Wheat. 234 [1818]. There is no doubt that this quotation was supposed to be an accurate statement of the law as late as *Christmas v. Russell,* 5 Wall. 290, where an attempt of Mississippi, by statute, to go behind judgments recovered in other States was declared void, and it was held that such judgments could not be impeached even for fraud.

. . .

We assume that the statement of Chief Justice Marshall is correct. It is confirmed by the Act of May 26, 1790, c. 11, 1 Stat. 122 (Rev. Stat. § 905), providing that the said records and judicial proceedings "shall have such faith and credit given to them in every court within the United States, as they have by law or usage in the courts of the State from whence the said records are or shall be taken." See further *Tilt v. Kelsey,* 207 U. S. 43, 57. Whether the award would or would not have been conclusive, and whether the ruling of the Missouri court upon that matter was right or wrong, there can be no question that the judgment was conclusive in Missouri on the validity of the cause of action. . . .

A judgment is conclusive as to all the *media concludendi,* . . . and it needs no authority to show that it cannot be impeached either in or out of the State by showing that it was based upon a mistake of law. Of course a want of jurisdiction over either the person or the subject-matter might be shown. *Andrews v. Andrews,* 188 U. S. 14; *Clarke v. Clarke,* 178 U. S. 186. But as the jurisdiction of the Missouri court is not open to dispute the judgment cannot be impeached in Mississippi even if it went upon a misapprehension of the Mississippi law. . . .

We feel no apprehensions that painful or humiliating consequences will follow upon our decision. No court would give judgment for a plaintiff unless it believed that the facts were a cause of action by the law determining their effect. Mistakes will be rare. In this case the Missouri court no doubt supposed that the award was binding by the law of Mississippi. If it was mistaken it made a natural mistake. The validity of its judgment, even in Mississippi, is, as we believe, the result of the Constitution as it always has been understood, and is not a matter to arouse the susceptibilities of the States, all of which are equally concerned in the question and equally on both sides.

Judgment reversed.

Mr. Justice White, with whom concurred Mr. Justice Harlan, Mr. Justice McKenna and Mr. Justice Day, dissenting.

Admonished that the considerations which control me are presumptively faulty, as the court holds them to be without merit, yet so strong is my belief that the decision now made unduly expands the due faith and credit clause of the Constitution, I state the reasons for my dissent.

§ 8.01 JURISDICTION AND JUDGMENTS □ 641

By law the State of Mississippi prohibited certain forms of gambling in futures, and inhibited its courts from giving effect to any contract or dealing made in violation of the prohibitive statute. In addition, it was made criminal to do any of the forbidden acts. With the statutes in force two citizens and residents of Mississippi made contracts in that State which were performed therein, and which were in violation of both the civil and criminal statutes referred to. One of the parties asserting that the other was indebted to him because of the contracts, both parties, in the State of Mississippi, submitted their differences to arbitration, and on an award being made in that State the one in whose favor it was made sued in a state court in Mississippi to recover thereon. In that suit, on the attention of the court being called to the prohibited and criminal nature of the transactions, the plaintiff dismissed the case. Subsequently, in a court of the State of Missouri, the citizen of Mississippi, in whose favor the award had been made, brought an action on the award, and succeeded in getting personal service upon the other citizen of Mississippi, the latter being temporarily in the State of Missouri. The action was put at issue. Rejecting evidence offered by the defendant to show the nature of the transactions, and that under the laws of Mississippi the same were illegal and criminal, the Missouri court submitted the cause to a jury, with an instruction to find for the plaintiff if they believed that the award had been made as alleged. A verdict and judgment went in favor of the plaintiff. Thereupon the judgment so obtained was assigned by the plaintiff to his attorney, who sued upon the same in a court of Mississippi, where the facts upon which the transaction depended were set up and the prohibitory statutes of the State were pleaded as a defense. Ultimately the case went to the Supreme Court of the State of Mississippi, where it was decided that the Missouri judgment was not required, under the due faith and credit clause, to be enforced in Mississippi, as it concerned transactions which had taken place exclusively in Mississippi, between residents of that State, which were in violation of laws embodying the public policy of that State, and to give effect to which would be enforcing transactions which the courts of Mississippi had no authority to enforce. This court now reverses on the ground that the due faith and credit clause obliged the courts of Mississippi, in consequence of the action of the Missouri court, to give efficacy to transactions in Mississippi which were criminal, and which were against the public policy of that State. Although not wishing in the slightest degree to weaken the operation of the due faith and credit clause as interpreted and applied from the beginning, it to me seems that this ruling so enlarges that clause as to cause it to obliterate all state lines, since the effect will be to endow each State with authority to overthrow the public policy and criminal statutes of the others, thereby depriving all of their lawful authority.

. . .

When the Constitution was adopted the principles of comity by which the decrees of the courts of one State were entitled to be enforced in another were generally known, but the enforcement of those principles by the several States had no absolute sanction, since they rested but in comity. Now it cannot be denied that under the rules of comity recognized at the time of the adoption of the Constitution, and which at this time universally prevail, no sovereignty was or is under the slightest moral obligation to give effect to a judgment of a court of another sovereignty, when to do so would compel the State in which the judgment was sought to be executed to enforce an illegal and prohibited contract, when both the contract and all the acts done in connection with its performance had taken place in the latter State. This seems to me conclusive of this case, since both in treatises of authoritative writers (Story, *Conflict of Law* § 609), and by repeated adjudications of this court it has been settled that the purpose of the due faith and credit clause was not to confer any new power, but simply to make obligatory that duty which, when the Constitution was adopted rested, as has been said, in comity alone.

. . .

If a judgment for a penalty in money rendered in one State may not be enforced in another, by the same principle a judgment rendered in one State, giving to the party the results of prohibited and criminal acts done in another State, is not entitled to be enforced in the State whose laws have been violated.

. . .

No special reference has been made by me to the arbitration, because that is assumed by me to be negligible. If the cause of action was open for inquiry for the purpose of deciding whether the Missouri court had jurisdiction to render a judgment entitled to be enforced in another State, the arbitration is of no consequence. The violation of law in Mississippi could not be cured by seeking to arbitrate in that State in order to fix the sum of the fruits of the illegal acts. The ancient maxims that something cannot be made out of nothing, and that which is void for reasons of public policy cannot be made valid by confirmation or acquiescence, seem to my mind decisive.

I therefore dissent.

NOTES AND QUESTIONS

(1)(a) Though decided by 5–4, with a strong dissent, *Fauntleroy v. Lum* has for close to a century been the leading case on recognition and enforcement of judgments under the Full Faith and Credit clause. The cause of action arose (if at all) in Mississippi, both parties were domiciled in Mississippi, and the transaction in question—trading in cotton futures—was contrary to the public policy and law of Mississippi.[a] The only connection of Missouri to the case was that the defendant happened to pass through that state—in other words "tag" or transient jurisdiction. Is the case correctly decided? Or is Justice White right in saying "this ruling so enlarges the [due faith and credit clause] [sic] as to cause it to obliterate all state lines. . . ."?

(b) Note that Mississippi did not say "we will not enforce judgments of the courts of other states of the United States" or ". . . of the courts of Missouri." Nor did it assert any defect in the procedures or legal system of Missouri, or challenge the jurisdiction of the Missouri court over Mr. Lum. It said "our courts have no jurisdiction to enforce gambling contracts." What is the Supreme Court's answer? How far do you think the answer would be carried, in terms of overriding Mississippi's public policy?

---

[a] In a futures transaction, seller agrees, say, to sell and buyer agrees to buy 500 lbs. of cotton in 90 days at 50£/lb. Seller may be a farmer seeking to secure the price for his crop, and buyer may be a textile manufacturer, but this need not be so. In the typical futures transaction, seller does not own the commodity and does not expect to actually make delivery, and buyer does not need the commodity or plan to take actual delivery. The contract is settled on the 90th day by comparison of the futures price with the spot price. If the spot price in the example is 52£/lb., seller will pay buyer 2£/lb. or £1,000; if the spot price is 47£/lb. buyer will pay seller 3£/lb. or £1,500; in each case the settlement price represents the gain or loss the contract party would incur if he had to go on the spot market to cover his obligation. Economists generally regard this type of transaction as smoothing out market fluctuations, and also enabling producers and users of commodities to plan (or hedge) their operations. Others, including in this case the legislature of Mississippi, have looked on futures transactions as speculation or gambling, the innuendo being that they are devices for city slickers to take advantage of farmers and other honest working folk.

§ 8.01   **JURISDICTION AND JUDGMENTS**   ☐   643

(c) Suppose before *Roe v. Wade*,[b] Mississippi made abortion a crime, and Missouri did not. Sally Brown contracts with Dr. Smith to have an abortion, the doctor performs the operation, sends his bill, and the bill is not paid. Dr. Smith sues Ms. Brown in Missouri, where she attends college and is properly served; a judgment is rendered in Dr. Smith's favor, the judgment remains unsatisfied, and he now seeks to enforce the judgment against Ms. Brown in Mississippi. What result? Would it matter if (i) Ms. Brown is a resident of Mississippi; (ii) Dr. Smith is a resident of Mississippi; (iii) the contract was made in Mississippi; or (iv) the abortion was performed in Mississippi? What if several or all of the preceding facts were true?

(2)(a) There has been a long debate, as spelled out below, about whether the Full Faith and Credit clause is self-executing, or requires implementing legislation by Congress. (Note that it says "Full Faith and Credit *shall be given* . . .," and "the Congress *may* . . . *prescribe* the Manner . . . and the Effect thereof.")[c] In fact Congress did adopt implementing legislation in the Act of May 26, 1790,[d] which, with small modifications (see question (4)(a) *infra*) remains the law,[e] but it did so rather modestly. It did not provide, for example, that judgments rendered by the courts of one state could be given to the sheriff (or comparable officer) of another state for execution;[f] it did not provide that judgments of one state could be registered in the courts of another state for purposes of recognition and enforcement;[g] and it did not create a federal cause of action to enforce judgments of one state against a judgment debtor in another state.[h] Would you, *a priori*, favor any of these proposals?

(b) It seems to have been decided early in the history of the United States that the way to enforce a judgment of another state is to bring an action, i.e., to obtain jurisdiction of the person (or property) of the judgment debtor in a court in the state where enforcement is sought. In *McElmoyle v. Cohen,* 38 U.S. (13 Pet) 312, 325 (1839), the Supreme Court said:

> By the law of 26th of May, 1790, the judgment [of a state court] is made a debt of record, not examinable upon its merits; but it does not carry with it, into another State, the efficacy of a judgment upon property or persons, to be enforced by execution. To give it the force of a judgment in another State, it must be made a judgment there; and can only be executed in the latter as its laws may permit.

---

[b] 410 U.S. 113 (1973). This was, of course, the decision of the U.S. Supreme Court holding that, within defined limits, the right of a woman to have an abortion is protected by the federal Constitution, and cannot be abridged by state laws making abortion a crime.

[c] This was, in fact, the result of a late amendment proposed by Madison; as reported by a special committee on what was then Article XVI of the draft Constitution, the text read "Full faith and credit *ought to be given* . . . and the Legislature *shall . . . prescribe* the manner . . . and the effect . . ." See 2 Farrand, *Record of the Federal Convention* 486 (Journal), 489 (Madison) (2d ed. 1966). See Nadelmann, Note m, *infra* at 192–94, 56 Mich. L. Rev. at 57–59.

[d] 1 Stat. 122 (1790), Documents Supplement p. 91.

[e] 28 U.S.C. § 1738, Documents Supplement p. 91.

[f] Madison at one time favored this suggestion, but appears not to have pushed it. See 2 Farrand *Record of the Federal Convention* 448 (Madison) Aug. 29, 1783, (2d ed. 1966).

[g] Just such a provision was adopted by Congress for registering in any federal district court final judgments rendered in any other federal district court. However, this step was not taken until 1948. 28 U.S.C. § 1963. Documents Supplement p. 94.

[h] See *Minnesota v. Northern Securities Co.,* 194 U.S. 48, 72 (1904); also 13B Wright, Miller and Cooper, *Federal Practice and Procedure* § 3563 (2d ed. 1984).

As *Fauntleroy v. Lum* shows, the judgment debtor does not have many defenses in such an action, and therefore some writers have said the need for such an action should be done away with.[i] Which defenses should be available to a judgment debtor?

(c) It seems clear that a state of the United States could not, by statute or otherwise, close the door to its courts to actions on sister-state judgments. In *Anglo-American Provision Co. v. Davis Provision Co,* 191 U.S. 373 (1903), the Court upheld a decision of the New York Court of Appeals refusing to enforce the judgment of an Illinois court, on the basis of a statute denying access to its courts to foreign corporations in suits against other foreign corporations on causes of action not arising in the state.[j] The opinion by Justice Holmes (before *Fauntleroy v. Lum*) said:

> If the plaintiff [judgment creditor] can find a court into which it has a right to come, then the effect of the judgment is fixed by the Constitution and the [implementing] act . . . But the Constitution does not require the State to provide such a court.

191 U.S. at 374.

In a later case, *Kenny v. Supreme Lodge of the World, Loyal Order of Moose,* 252 U.S. 411 (1920), also written by Justice Holmes, the holding of *Anglo-American Provision* was largely withdrawn, if not expressly overruled:

> . . . no doubt there is truth in the proposition that the Constitution does not require the State to furnish a court. But it also is true that there are limits to the power of exclusion . . .

252 U.S. at 414.

To his English friend Pollock, Justice Holmes wrote:

> I also had a case in which Illinois tried to dodge the Constitutional requirement of due faith and aids to judgments in other states by denying jurisdiction to Courts otherwise competent. They laid hold of a statement of mine in an earlier case that the Constitution did not oblige States to furnish a Court, but we said the dodge wouldn't do.[k]

When, if ever should F–2 be permitted to close its doors to an action to enforce a sister-state judgment?[l]

(3)(a)[m] It is often thought that the Full Faith and Credit clause was one of the unifying elements of the federal Constitution, in contrast with the inadequate arrangements for nation-building in the Articles of Confederation. In fact, the Articles of Confederation contained a provision very similar to the first sentence of Article IV, § 1 of the Constitution:

> Full faith and credit shall be given in each of these states to the records, acts and judicial proceedings of the courts and magistrates of every other state.[n]

---

[i] See, e.g., Cook, *The Powers of Congress under the Full Faith and Credit Clause*, 28 Yale L.J. 421 (1919), including in an Appendix the draft of a statute that would provide for registration of a state judgment in a court of like jurisdiction in every other state.

[j] Compare present N.Y. Business Corporation Law § 1314, Documents Supplement p. 56.

[k] Letter from O. W. Holmes to Sir Frederick Pollock, April 25, 1920, 2 *Holmes-Pollock Letters* 41 (2d ed. Howe 1961).

[l] Compare the related issues discussed in connection with *Hughes v. Fetter*, Chapter 5, p. 367.

[m] Much of this note is based on Nadelmann, *Full Faith and Credit to Judgments and Public Acts: A Historical-Analytical Reappraisal*, in K. Nadelmann, *Conflict of Laws: International and Interstate*, Ch. III (1972) (hereafter Nadelmann), also 56 Mich. L. Rev. 33 (1957).

[n] Articles of Confederation, Article IV, cl. 4 (1781).

§ 8.01　　　　　　　　　　JURISDICTION AND JUDGMENTS　　□　645

Indeed, as early as 1644 an amendment was introduced to the Articles of Confederation of the New England Colonies calling for "due respect" to every verdict or sentence "in any other court through the Colonies. . . ."[o]

(b) More surprising to twentieth century lawyers is that the meaning and intention of the full faith and credit clause of the Constitution remained in doubt for many years. As Professor Nadelmann has shown in a fascinating essay,[p] the constitutional provision itself could be read either as requiring the judgments of one state to be recognized and enforced in all other states of the Union, or simply as an evidentiary provision, i.e., a statement that copies of official records of one state could be authenticated so as to be admissible in evidence in the courts of other states. If the latter reading of the first sentence of Article IV, § 2 were correct, then the second sentence, authorizing the Congress to prescribe the effect of Acts, Records and Proceedings would have constituted a very substantial delegation to Congress (or postponement of the issue). Whatever the intention, the first Congress took up the offer, and adopted the Act of May 26, 1790, "to prescribe the mode in which the public acts, records, and judicial proceedings, in each State, shall be authenticated so as to take effect in every other State." The key words, of course, were

> . . . And the said records and judicial proceedings shall have such faith and credit given to them in every court of the United States, as they have by law or usage in the courts of the State from whence the said records are, or shall be taken.[q]

(c) Notwithstanding the Act of 1790, several early state and federal court decisions held that the judgment of a court of one state was only prima facie evidence of a debt, and not conclusive as to the merits.[r] Even Chief Justice Marshall, sitting as Circuit Judge, held as late as 1812 that a judgment of a Massachusetts court was not entitled to full faith and credit in North Carolina, because Congress had not in the Act of 1790 stated the effect to be given to foreign judgments.[s] Finally, in *Mills v. Duryee,* 7 Cranch (11 U.S.) 481 (1813), the Supreme Court held that judgments from other states had to be given conclusive effect. Justice Story, writing for the Court, said:

> Were the construction contended for by the [judgment debtor] to prevail, that judgments of the state Courts ought to be considered *prima facie* evidence only, this clause in the constitution would be utterly unimportant and illusory. The common law would give such judgments precisely the same effect. It is manifest however that the constitution contemplated a power in congress to give a conclusive effect to such judgments. And we can perceive no rational interpretation of the act of congress, unless it declares a judgment conclusive, when a Court of the particular state where it is rendered would pronounce the same decision.[t]

(d) The *Mills* case settled the controversy, but, interestingly enough, rested on the statute, not on the Constitution itself. Only in his *Commentaries on the Constitution,* published twenty years

---

[o] See Nadelmann at 174, 56 Mich. L. Rev. at 38.

[p] See note m, *supra.*

[q] 1 Stat. 122 (1790). The full text is reproduced in the Documents Supplement at p. 91.

[r] See e.g., *Hitchock v. Aiken,* 1 Cai. R. (N.Y.) 460 (Sup. Ct. N.Y. 1803): *Hammon and Hattaway v. Smith,* 3 S.C.L. (1 Brev.) 110 (Const'l Ct., S. Carolina 1802); *contra Armstrong v. Carson,* 1 Fed. Cas. 1140 (C.C. Pa. 1794) (No. 543).

[s] *Peck v. Williamson,* 1 Car. L. Repository 53, 1 Brunner Col. Cas. 398, 19 Fed. Cas. 85, (C.C. N.C. 1812)

[t] 7 Cranch (11 U.S.) at 485. Chief Justice Marshall voted with the majority, but did not write. Prof. Nadelmann, note t, *supra,* speculates that Marshall may in fact have been in disagreement, as it was his custom not to write dissents but to acquiesce silently in the opinion of the Court when he had "the misfortune to differ from it."

later, did Justice Story ascribe the requirement of recognition of judgments to the Constitution itself:

> The language [of the Full Faith and Credit clause] is positive, and declaratory, leaving nothing to future legislation. "Full faith and credit *shall* be given;" what then is meant by full faith and credit? Does it import no more than, that the same faith and credit are to be given to them, which, by the comity of nations, is ordinarily conceded to all foreign judgments? Or is it intended to give them a more conclusive efficiency, approaching to, if not identical with, that of domestic judgments; so that if the jurisdiction of the court be established, the judgment shall be conclusive, as to merits? The latter seems to be the true object of the clause; and, indeed, it seems difficult to assign any other adequate motive for the insertion of the clause, both in the confederation and in the constitution.[u]

Story went on to ask why the framers of the Constitution extended "so much solicitude" to judgments of other states.

> It must have been "to form a more perfect Union," and to give to each state a higher security and confidence in the others, by attributing a superior sanctity and conclusiveness to the public acts and proceedings of all.[v]

Story acknowledged the other view, that judgments of sister states were only prima facie evidence, absent action by Congress, but concluded that the question "is not, practically speaking, of such importance," because Congress had acted. Whether Congress could change the effect of the clause by repealing the Act of 1790 or its successors is thus in some doubt; Story's argument suggests that while Congress might do more under the second sentence of Article IV, § 1, it could not do less.

(4)(a) In the revision of the United States Code which enacted Title 28, effective September 1, 1948, a number of changes were made in the legislation to implement the Full Faith and Credit clause, 28 U.S.C. § 1738,[w] though the codification effort was supposed to make no changes in the substance of existing law.[x] The most striking change—which may or may not be significant—was that the word "Acts" is included in section 1738, as it is in Article IV § 1 itself, but was not in the prior statute. Some writers, including Justice Frankfurter,[y] have suggested that this change gives support to the those who urge national rules on choice of law. Professor Cheatham wrote: "There is now the same statutory basis at least for the Supreme Court taking over the unwelcome burden as to public acts which it assumed as to judgments in determining their extra-state effect."[z]

(b) If Congress had meant to move in the direction suggested, it seems highly unlikely that it would have done so without notice, and there is no indication whatever that Congress intended any change, let alone such a major one, in its codification effort. The point is interesting, however, not for what Congress did in 1948, but for what it did in 1790. Was it, one may ask, wise enough to see that there should be a difference between judicial proceedings and records on the one

---

[u] J. Story, *Commentaries on the Constitution of the United States,* p. 178 (1833).

[v] *Id.* at p. 179.

[w] Documents Supplement p. 91.

[x] See Barron, *The Judicial Code 1948 Revision,* 8 F.R.D. 439, 441 (1949).

[y] See *Carroll v. Lanza,* 349 U.S. 408, Frankfurter J. dissenting, The case is summarized in Chapter 5, question 3(e), p. 400, *supra.*

[z] Cheatham, *A Federal Nation and Conflict of Laws,* 22 Rocky Mtn. L. Rev. 109 at 114 (1950).

§ 8.01   JURISDICTION AND JUDGMENTS   □   647

hand (note neither the Constitution nor the implementing legislation says "judgments") and "public acts" on the other (assuming the Constitutional provision was not self-executing)?[a]

(c) In fact, as we saw throughout Chapter 5, the Full Faith and Credit clause has only rarely been applied to laws—i.e., to public acts—and the Supreme Court has in general rejected the "unwelcome burden," staying out of choice of law problems, and reversing lower courts that had undertaken to resolve choice of law problems by reference to the Constitution. Why should full faith and credit be so much tighter as to judgments? Coming back, after our historical excursion, to *Fauntleroy v. Lum,* we saw that interest analysis, and particularly the interest of F–2 in the controversy, plays no role when a judgment is involved. Putting the point more precisely, the only relevant interest concerning judgments within the federal union is a national interest, which overrides all else. Is that persuasive?

Reconsider your answer after reading the *Yarborough* and *Magnolia* cases in the next section, and also the cases on family law in the following chapter.

[B]   Full Faith and Credit and State Interest

YARBOROUGH v. YARBOROUGH

United States Supreme Court
290 U.S. 202 (1933)

Mr. Justice Brandeis delivered the opinion of the Court.

On August 10, 1930, Sadie Yarborough, then sixteen years of age, was living with her maternal grandfather, R. D. Blowers, at Spartanburg, South Carolina. Suing by him as guardian *ad litem,* she brought this action in a court of that State to require her father, W. A. Yarborough, a resident of Atlanta, Georgia, to make provision for her education and maintenance. She alleged "that she is now ready for college and is without funds and, unless the defendant makes provision for her, will be denied the necessities of life and an education, and will be dependent upon the charity of others."[1] Jurisdiction was obtained by attachment of defendant's property. Later he was served personally within South Carolina.

In bar of the action, W. A. Yarborough set up, among other defenses, a judgment entered in 1929 by the Superior Court of Fulton County, Georgia, in a suit for divorce brought by him against Sadie's mother. He alleged that by the judgment the amount thereafter to be paid by him for Sadie's education and maintenance had been determined; that the sum so fixed [$1,750.] had been paid; and that the judgment had been fully satisfied by him. He claimed that in Georgia the judgment was conclusive of the matter here in controversy; that having been satisfied, it relieved him, under the Georgia law, of all obligation to provide for the education and maintenance of their minor child; and that the full faith and credit clause of the Federal

---

[a] Nadelmann, who searched thoroughly, reports that there are no records of the drafting that went into the Act of 1790, possibly because the records were lost or destroyed when the Capitol was burned by the British in 1814. Nadelmann, note m, *supra* at 194, 56 Mich. L. Rev. at 60.

[1] There was no suggestion that plaintiff would be destitute or become a public charge. Indeed, her grandfather testified that he was able and willing to provide $125 a month for her education and maintenance (the amount sought by plaintiff), if her father was unable to do so.

Constitution (Art. IV, § 1) required the South Carolina court to give to that judgment the same effect in this proceeding which it has, and would have, in Georgia. The trial court denied the claim; ordered W. A. Yarborough to pay to the grandfather, as trustee, fifty dollars monthly for Sadie's education and support; and to pay $300 as fees of her counsel. It directed that the property held under the attachment be transferred to R. D. Blowers, trustee, as security for the performance of the order. The judgment was affirmed by the Supreme Court of South Carolina. A petition for rehearing was denied, with opinion. 168 S.C. 46; 166 S.E. 877. This Court granted certiorari. . . .

For sometime prior to June, 1927, W. A. Yarborough, his wife and their daughter Sadie had lived together at Atlanta, Georgia, where he then was, and ever since has been, domiciled. In that month, Sadie's mother left Atlanta for Hendersonville, N. C., where she remained during the summer. Sadie joined her there, after a short stay at a camp. In September, 1927, while they were at Hendersonville, W. A. Yarborough brought, in the Superior Court for Fulton County, at Atlanta, suit against his wife for a total divorce on the ground of mental and physical cruelty. Mrs. Yarborough filed an answer and also a cross-suit in which she prayed a total divorce, the custody of the child and "that provision for permanent alimony be made for the support of the respondent and the minor child above mentioned [Sadie], and for the education of said minor child." An order, several times modified, awarded to the wife the custody of Sadie and, as temporary alimony, sums "for the support and maintenance of herself and her minor daughter Sadie." Hearings were held from time to time at Atlanta. At some of these, Sadie (and also her grandfather) was personally present. But she was not formally made a party to the litigation; she was not served with process; and no guardian *ad litem* was appointed for her therein.

"Two concurring verdicts favoring a total divorce to plaintiff having been rendered,"[2] a decree of total divorce, with the right in each to remarry, was entered on June 7, 1929; the wife was ordered to pay the costs; and jurisdiction of the case "was retained for the purpose of further enforcement of the orders of the court theretofore passed." Among such orders, was the provision for the maintenance and education of Sadie here relied upon as *res judicata*.

W. A. Yarborough complied fully with this order.

By the law of Georgia, it is the duty of the father to provide for the maintenance and education of his child until maturity. Wilful abandonment of a minor child, leaving it in a dependent condition, is a misdemeanor. The mere loss of custody by the father does not relieve him of his obligation to provide for maintenance and education, even where the custody passes to the mother pursuant to a decree of divorce. If the father fails to make such provision, any person (including a divorced wife) who furnishes necessaries of life to his minor child, may recover from him therefor, unless precluded by the terms of the decree in the divorce suit or otherwise. In case of total divorce, the court is authorized to make, by its decree, final or permanent provision for the maintenance and education of children during minority, and thus fix the extent of the father's obligation. But even if the decree for total divorce fails to include a provision for the support of minor children, they cannot maintain in their own names, or by guardian *ad litem*, or by next friend, an independent suit for an allowance for education and maintenance.

First. . . . It is clear that Mrs. Yarborough, her husband and the court intended that this provision should absolve Sadie's father from further obligation to support her. . . .

---

[2] § 2944 of the Georgia Civil Code (1910) provides: "Divorces may be granted by the superior court and shall be of two kinds—total or from bed and board. The concurrent verdict of two juries, at different terms of the court, shall be necessary to a total divorce."

§ 8.01   JURISDICTION AND JUDGMENTS   □ 649

Second. . . . The Georgia decisions have settled that a consent decree or order fixing permanent alimony for a minor child, at whatever stage of the divorce proceedings it may have been entered, has the same effect as if based upon, and specifically mentioned in, the second verdict of a jury; and that such an order, like any other judgment, becomes unalterable after the expiration of the term.

Third. It is contended that the Georgia decree is not binding upon Sadie, because she was not a formal party to the suit, was not served with process and no guardian *ad litem* was appointed for her therein. In Georgia, as elsewhere, a property right of a minor can ordinarily be affected by legal proceedings only if these requirements are complied with. But the obligation imposed by the Georgia law upon the father to support his minor child does not vest in the child a property right. This is shown by the fact, among other things, that the minor cannot maintain in his own name, or by guardian *ad litem* or by next friend, a suit against his father to enforce the obligation. The provision which the Georgia law makes of permanent alimony for the child during minority is a legal incident of the divorce proceeding. As that suit embraces within its scope the disposition and care of minor children, jurisdiction over the parents confers *eo ipso* jurisdiction over the minor's custody and support. Hence, by the Georgia law, a consent (or other) decree in a divorce suit, fixing permanent alimony for a minor child is binding upon it, although the child was not served with process, was not made a formal party to the suit, and no guardian *ad litem* was appointed therein.

Fourth. It is contended that the order for permanent alimony is not binding upon Sadie because she was not a resident of Georgia at the time it was entered. Being a minor, Sadie's domicile was Georgia, that of her father;[16] and her domicile continued to be in Georgia until entry of the judgment in question. She was not capable by her own act of changing her domicile. Neither the temporary residence in North Carolina at the time the divorce suit was begun, nor her removal with her mother to South Carolina before entry of the judgment, effected a change of Sadie's domicile. It is true that, under the Georgia Code, a minor may acquire a domicile apart from the father if he has "voluntarily relinquished his parental authority." But the mere fact that the parents were living separately at the time the suit for divorce was brought and that Sadie was with her mother, does not establish such relinquishment. Compare *Anderson v. Watt,* 138 U.S. 694, 706. The character and extent of the father's obligation, and the status of the minor, are determined ordinarily not by the place of the minor's residence but by the law of the father's domicile. Moreover, this is not a case where the scope of the jurisdiction acquired by the Georgia court rests upon the effectiveness of service by publication upon a nonresident. Mrs. Yarborough filed a cross-bill, as well as an answer; and in the cross-bill prayed "that provision for permanent alimony be made for the" support and education of Sadie. Thus the court acquired complete jurisdiction of the marriage status and, as an incident, power to finally determine the extent of her father's obligation to support his minor child.

Fifth. The fact that Sadie has become a resident of South Carolina does not impair the finality of the judgment. South Carolina thereby acquired the jurisdiction to determine her status and the incidents of that status. Upon residents of that State it could impose duties for her benefit. Doubtless, it might have imposed upon her grandfather who was resident there a duty to support Sadie. But the mere fact of Sadie's residence in South Carolina does not give that State the power to impose such a duty upon the father who is not a resident and who long has been domiciled

---

[16] [For this and the following statements, the Court cites several sections of the Georgia Civil Code and a number of decisions of the Supreme Court of Georgia.]

in Georgia.[23] He has fulfilled the duty which he owes her by the law of his domicile and the judgment of its court. Upon that judgment he is entitled to rely. It was settled by *Sistare v. Sistare,* 218 U.S. 1, that the full faith and credit clause applies to an unalterable decree of alimony for a divorced wife. The clause applies, likewise, to an unalterable decree of alimony for a minor child. We need not consider whether South Carolina would have power to require the father, if he were domiciled there, to make further provision for the support, maintenance, or education of his daughter.

Reversed.

Mr. Justice Stone, dissenting.

I think the judgment should be affirmed.

The divorce decree of the Georgia court purported to adjudicate finally, both for the present and for the future, the right of a minor child of the marriage to support and maintenance, by directing her father to make a lump sum payment for that purpose. More than two years later, after the minor had become a domiciled resident of South Carolina, and after the sum paid had been exhausted, a court of that State, on the basis of her need as then shown, has rendered a judgment directing further payments for her support out of property of the father in South Carolina, in addition to that already commanded by the Georgia judgment.

For present purposes we may take it that the Georgia decree, as the statutes and decisions of the State declare, is unalterable and, as pronounced, is effective to govern the rights of the parties in Georgia. But there is nothing in the decree itself, or in the history of the proceedings which led to it, to suggest that it was rendered with any purpose or intent to regulate or control the relationship of parent and child, or the duties which flow from it, in places outside the State of Georgia where they might later come to reside. It would hardly be thought that Georgia, by judgment of its courts more than by its statutes, would attempt to regulate the relationship of parents and child domiciled outside of the State at the very time the decree was rendered; and, in the face of constitutional doubts that arise here, it is far from clear that its decree is to be interpreted as attempting to do more than to regulate that relationship while the infant continued to be domiciled within the State. But if we are to read the decree as though it contained a clause, in terms, restricting the power of any other state, in which the minor might come to reside, to make provision for her support, then, in the absence of some law of Congress requiring it, I am not persuaded that the full faith and credit clause gives sanction to such control by one state of the internal affairs of another.

Congress has said that the public records and the judicial proceedings of each state are to be given such faith and credit in other states as is accorded to them in the state "from which they are taken." But this broad language has never been applied without limitations. See *McElmoyle v. Cohen,* 13 Pet. 312. Between the prohibition of the due process clause, acting upon the courts of the state from which such proceedings may be taken, and the mandate of the full faith and credit clause, acting upon the state to which they may be taken, there is an area which federal authority has not occupied. As this Court has often recognized, there are many judgments which need not be given the same force and effect abroad which they have at home, and there are some, though valid in the state where rendered, to which the full faith and credit

---

[23] It appeared that W. A. Yarborough, having married again, invited Sadie to his home in Atlanta and offered to maintain her there. She refused.

clause gives no force elsewhere. In the assertion of rights, defined by a judgment of one state, within the territory of another, there is often an inescapable conflict of interest of the two states, and there comes a point beyond which the imposition of the will of one state beyond its own borders involves a forbidden infringement of some legitimate domestic interest of the other. That point may vary with the circumstances of the case; and in the absence of provisions more specific than the general terms of the congressional enactment.[2] this Court must determine for itself the extent to which one state may qualify or deny rights claimed under proceedings or records of other states.

More than once this Court has approved the doctrine that a state need give no effect to judgments for conviction of crime or for penalties, procured in a sister state, see *Wisconsin v. Pelican Insurance Co.,* 127 U.S. 265; *Huntington v. Attrill,* 146 U.S. 657; *Finney v. Guy,* 189 U.S. 335; see also *Martin v. Hunter's Lessee,* 1 Wheat. 304, 330, 337. And the intervention of a sister state's judgment will not overcome a local policy against allowing to foreign corporations the use of local courts in settling foreign disputes. *Anglo-American Provision Co. v. Davis Provision Co.,* 191 U.S. 373; compare *Kenny v. Supreme Lodge of Moose,* 252 U.S. 411. The state of matrimonial domicile may preserve to its own resident his rights in the marriage status where another state has sought to terminate it without acquiring jurisdiction of his person, *Haddock v. Haddock,* 201 U.S. 562, even though terminated within the other state, cf. *Maynard v. Hill,* 125 U.S. 190. The full faith and credit clause does not require one state, at the behest of the courts of another, to surrender its powers to decide what criminal penalties it shall impose, to circumscribe, within limits, the classes of disputes to which its courts must give ear, or to protect its residents from undue interference with the marriage relationship.

A statute, record or judgment of one state, establishing the right of an illegitimate or adopted child to inherit from his putative parent, may be given extra-state effect for many purposes, but it does not establish his right to inherit land in another state. See *Hood v. McGehee,* 237 U.S. 611; *Olmsted v. Olmsted,* 216 U.S. 386. Parties who have, in one state, litigated the proper construction of a will disposing of realty are not, by the judgment there, concluded in another state where the testator's realty is located. Cf. *Clarke v. Clarke,* 178 U.S. 186. Nor will a divorce decree seeking to apportion the rights of the parties to realty be conclusive with respect to land outside the state. *Fall v. Eastin,* 215 U.S. 1. The interest of a state in controlling all the legal incidents of real property located within its boundaries is deemed so complete and so vital to the exercise of its sovereign powers of government within its own territory as to exclude any control over them by the statutes or judgments of other states.

---

[2] The mandatory force of the full faith and credit clause as defined by this Court may be, in some degree not yet fully defined, expanded or contracted by Congress. Much of the confusion and procedural deficiencies which the constitutional provision alone has not avoided may be remedied by legislation. Cook, *Powers of Congress under the Full Faith and Credit Clause,* 28 Yale Law Journal, 421; Corwin, *The "Full Faith and Credit"* Clause, 81 University of Pennsylvania Law Rev. 371; cf. 33 Columbia Law Rev. 854, 866. The constitutional provision giving Congress power to prescribe the effect to be given to acts, records and proceedings would have been quite unnecessary had it not been intended that Congress should have a latitude broader than that given the courts by the full faith and credit clause alone. It was remarked on the floor of the Constitutional Convention that without the extention of power in the legislature, the provision "would amount to nothing more than what now takes place among all Independent Nations." Hunt and Scott, *Madison's Reports of the Debates in the Federal Convention of 1787,* p. 503. The play which has been afforded for the recognition of local public policy in cases where there is called in question only a statute of another state, as to the effect of which Congress has not legislated, compared with the more restricted scope for local policy where there is a judicial proceeding, as to which Congress has legislated, suggests the Congressional power.

It would be going farther than this Court has been willing to go in any decision to say that the power of a state to pass judgment upon the sanity of its own citizen could be foreclosed by an earlier judgment of the court of some other state dealing with the same subject matter. Cf. *Gasquet v. Fenner,* 247 U.S. 16.

Similarly, it has been almost uniformly recognized that a divorce decree which by its terms, or by operation of law, forbids remarriage of one or both of the parties, can have no effect outside of the state which rendered it. Jurisdictional requirements being satisfied, the decree is effective to end the marriage for all states, but enforcement of its prohibition against remarriage in another state, even though the parties do not take up their residence there, would infringe upon the interest which every state has to maintain the stability of a union entered into according to the laws of the place of celebration.

Whatever view may be held of the particular restrictions upon the operation of the full faith and credit clause in these cases, the validity of the principle upon which they rest has never been denied. Its validity is likewise recognized in those cases where this Court has held that the Fourteenth Amendment denies to a state the power of unduly extending its authority beyond its own borders, by the mere expedient of rendering a judgment against one of whose person or property it has acquired jurisdiction. *New York Life Ins. Co. v. Head,* 234 U.S. 149; *Home Insurance Co. v. Dick,* 281 U.S. 397. Just as due process of law will not permit a state, by its judgment, to inflict parties "with a perpetual contractual paralysis" which will prevent them from altering outside of the state their contracts or ordinary business relations entered into within it, *New York Life Ins. Co. v. Head, supra,* 161, so full faith and credit does not command that the obligations attached to a status, because once appropriately imposed by one state, shall be forever placed beyond the control of every other state, without regard to the interest in it and the power of control which the other may later acquire. See *Bradford Elec. Light Co. v. Clapper,* 286 U.S. 145, 157, n. 7. Whatever difference there may be between holding that a judgment is invalid under the Fourteenth Amendment because it is "extra-territorial," and in holding that it is not entitled to full faith and credit although it does not infringe the Fourteenth Amendment, is one of degree, or of a difference in circumstances which may prevent the operation of the latter provision of the Constitution. The Georgia judgment with which we are now concerned does not infringe the Fourteenth Amendment, for Georgia had "jurisdiction" of the parties and subject matter at the time its judgment was rendered. The possibility of conflict of the Georgia judgment with the interest of South Carolina first arose when the minor transferred her domicile to South Carolina, long after the Georgia judgment was given.

The question presented here is whether the support and maintenance of a minor child, domiciled in South Carolina, is so peculiarly a subject of domestic concern that Georgia law can not impair South Carolina's authority. The subject matter of the judgment in each state is the duty which government may impose on a parent to support a minor child. The maintenance and support of children domiciled within a state, like their education and custody, is a subject in which government itself is deemed to have a peculiar interest and concern. Their tender years, their inability to provide for themselves, the importance to the state that its future citizens should be clothed, nourished and suitably educated, are considerations which lead all civilized countries to assume some control over the maintenance of minors.[12] The states very generally make some

---

[12] This control is particularly important in the case of the children of divorced couples. They are usually young; in Maryland over 60% are under ten years of age when divorce occurs. Divorces are often not contested and the intervention of a disinterested judge is frequently nominal. Allowances for children in the divorce court are typically small. Marshall and May, *The Divorce Court,* 31, 79–80, 82, 226–231, 323.

provision from their own resources for the maintenance and support of orphans or destitute children, but in order that children may not become public charges the duty of maintenance is one imposed primarily upon the parents, according to the needs of the child and their ability to meet those needs. This is usually accomplished by suit brought directly by some public officer, by the child by guardian or next friend, or by the mother, against the father for maintenance and support. The measure of the duty is the needs of the child and the ability of the parent to meet those needs at the very time when performance of the duty is invoked. Hence, it is no answer in such a suit that at some earlier time provision was made for the child, which is no longer available or suitable because of his greater needs, or because of the increased financial ability of the parent to provide for them, or that the child may be maintained from other sources.

In view of the universality of these principles it comes as a surprise that any state, merely because it has made some provision for the support of a child, should, either by statute or judicial decree, so tie its own hands as to foreclose all future inquiry into the duty of maintenance however affected by changed conditions.[17]

Even though the Constitution does not deny to Georgia the power to indulge in such a policy for itself, it by no means follows that it gives to Georgia the privilege of prescribing that policy for other states in which the child comes to live. South Carolina has adopted a different policy. It imposes on the father or his property located within the state the duty to support his minor child domiciled there. It enforces the duty by criminal prosecution and also permits suit by the minor child maintained by guardian *ad litem.* The measure of the duty is the present need of the child and the ability of the parent to provide for it. In this case the suit was begun by attachment of the father's property in South Carolina and by personal service of process upon him there. The court found that the lump sum paid for support of the child under the Georgia decree had been expended; that she was justifiably residing with her mother in South Carolina rather than with her father in Georgia; that she was then without financial resources and that, considering her station in life and the circumstances of her father, an allowance for the future of $50.00 a month for her education, maintenance and support would be fair and just; and this amount was ordered to be paid for that purpose from the attached property.

The opinion of this Court leaves it uncertain whether it is thought that the Constitution commands that the duty of support prescribed by Georgia, the domicile of the father, shall be dominant over that enjoined by South Carolina, the domicile of the child, in any event, or only after the duty has been defined by a judgment of Georgia. It is attested by eminent authority that the Fourteenth Amendment, at least, does not prevent the state of the child's domicile from imposing the duty, *Restatement of Conflict of Laws,* § 498A,[22] a view confirmed by the uniform rulings that the father is liable to the criminal process of the state of the child's residence, though before, and at all times during his failure to conform to the duty demanded by that state, he has been domiciled elsewhere. . . .

---

[17] Georgia seems to be the only state to do so. II Vernier, *Family Laws,* 196 ff. A similar attempt by the courts of another state has been held null and void and subject to collateral attack. See *Walder v. Walder,* 159 La. 231; 105 So. 300.

[22] "A state may impose upon one person a duty to support another person if:

1. The person to be supported is domiciled within the state, and the person to support is within the jurisdiction of the state; . . .

[This reference appears to be to Draft No. 34 of the first *Restatement* (1930), which, with some changes, became § 457 in the final version of the first *Restatement* (1934). There is no comparable version in the second *Restatement,* published in 1971.]

The Fourteenth Amendment does not enable a father, by the expedient of choosing a domicile other than the state where the child is rightfully domiciled, to avoid the duty which that state may impose for support of his child. The reason seems plain. The locality of the child's residence must see to his welfare. While it might be more convenient for creditors of the father to look to the law of his residence as fixing all his obligations, it would seem that the compelling interest in the welfare of children, to which performance of the duties of parentage is a necessary incident, outweighs commercial convenience; the more so where, as in this case, the obligation is to be satisfied from the father's property within the state of the child's domicile.

The conclusion must be the same when the issue is that of the credit to be given the prior Georgia judgment. Whatever may be said of the local interest which was deemed controlling in those cases in which this Court has denied to a state judgment the same force and effect outside the state as is given to it at home, it would not seem open to serious question that every state has an interest in securing the maintenance and support of minor children residing within its own territory so complete and so vital to the performance of its functions as a government, that no other state could set limits upon it. Of that interest, South Carolina is the sole mistress within her own territory. . . . Even though we might appraise it more lightly than does South Carolina, it is not for us to say that a state is not free, within constitutional limitations, to regard that interest as fully as important and as completely within the realm of state power as the legal incidents of land located within its boundaries, or of a marriage relationship, wherever entered into but of which it is the domicile, or its power to pass upon the sanity of its own residents, notwithstanding the earlier pronouncements of the courts of other states.

* * *

Here the Georgia decree did not end the relationship of parent and child, as a decree of divorce may end the marriage relationship. Had the infant continued to reside in Georgia, and had she sought in the courts of South Carolina to compel the application of property of her father, found there, to her further maintenance and support, full faith and credit to the Georgia decree applied to its own domiciled resident might have required the denial of any relief. . . .

But when she became a domiciled resident of South Carolina, a new interest came into being,— the interest of the State of South Carolina as a measure of self-preservation to secure the adequate protection and maintenance of helpless members of its own community and its prospective citizens. That interest was distinct from any which Georgia could conclusively regulate or control by its judgment, even though rendered while the child was domiciled in Georgia. The present decision extends the operation of the full faith and credit clause beyond its proper function of affording protection to the domestic interests of Georgia and makes it an instrument for encroachment by Georgia upon the domestic concerns of South Carolina.

Mr. Justice Cardozo concurs in this opinion.

MAGNOLIA PETROLEUM CO. v. HUNT

United States Supreme Court
320 U.S. 430 (1943)

Mr. Chief Justice Stone delivered the opinion of the Court.

The question for decision is whether, under the full faith and credit clause, Art. IV, § 1 of the Constitution of the United States, an award of compensation for personal injury under the Texas Workmen's Compensation Law, bars a further recovery of compensation for the same injury under the Louisiana Workmen's Compensation Law.

Magnolia Petroleum Company, petitioner here, employed respondent in Louisiana as a laborer in connection with the drilling of oil wells. In the course of his employment respondent, a Louisiana resident, went from Louisiana to Texas, and while working there for petitioner on an oil well, he was injured by a falling drill stem. He sought and procured in Texas an award of compensation for his injury under its Workmen's Compensation Law, and petitioner's insurer made payments of compensation as required by the statute and the award. The award became final in accordance with the terms of the Texas statute.[2]

Respondent then brought the present proceeding in the Louisiana District Court to recover compensation for his injury under the Louisiana Workmen's Compensation Law. Petitioner filed exceptions to respondent's petition on the ground that the recovery sought was barred as res judicata by the Texas award which, by virtue of the constitutional command, was entitled in the Louisiana courts to full faith and credit. The District Court overruled the exceptions and gave judgment for the amount of the compensation fixed by the Louisiana statute, after deducting the amount of the Texas payments. The Louisiana Court of Appeal affirmed, and the Supreme Court of Louisiana refused writs of certiorari and review for the reason that it found "no error of law in the judgment complained of." We granted certiorari, because of the importance of the constitutional question presented. . . .

In Texas a compensation award against the employer's insurer (with exceptions not here applicable, is explicitly made by statute in lieu of any other recovery for injury) to the employee. . . . A compensation award which has become final "is entitled to the same faith and credit as a judgment of a court."

---

[2] Respondent filed with the Texas Industrial Accident Board a claim for compensation for his injury under the Texas Workmen's Compensation Law, as is the usual method of instituting a proceeding before the Board. Without awaiting an award on respondent's claim petitioner's insurer paid respondent compensation for his injury at the statutory maximum rate for seventy-three weeks. A dispute as to the proper prognosis of respondent's injury, a request for advice made by respondent to the Board, and a suspension by the insurer of further compensation payments to respondent, on the ground that his total disability had terminated, all prompted the Board to set the case for a hearing on his pending claim. Respondent received notice of the hearing and was requested to furnish medical evidence of his continued disability. Upon his failure to do this, the Board entered on December 3, 1940, as the full compensation for his injury, an award of a lump sum for total disability for 75 weeks and of weekly payments for partial disability for a further period of 125 weeks, and directed that payments already made by the insurer be credited upon the award. Respondent was notified as to the appeal he was required to take if he was dissatisfied with the award. No appeal was taken, and the award became final. Respondent has refused payments which have been tendered to him subsequent to the making of the Texas award. On December 18, 1940, he began the present suit in Louisiana.

. . .

The Louisiana Court of Appeal recognized that Texas had jurisdiction to award compensation to respondent for the injury received while working for petitioner within the state, and that the award has the same force and effect in Texas as a judgment rendered by a court of competent jurisdiction in that state. But it thought that full faith and credit did not require the Louisiana courts to give effect to the judgment as res judicata because Louisiana, despite the command of the full faith and credit clause, was entitled to give effect to its own statute prescribing compensation for resident employees of a resident employer even though the injury occurred outside the state.

It does not appear, nor is it contended, that Louisiana more than Texas allows in its own courts a second recovery of compensation for a single injury. The contention is that since Louisiana is better satisfied with the measure of recovery allowed by its own laws, it may deny full faith and credit to the Texas award, which respondent has procured by his election to pursue his remedy in that state. In thus refusing, on the basis of state law and policy, to give effect to the Texas award as a final adjudication of respondent's claim for compensation for his injury suffered in Texas, the Louisiana court ignored the distinction, long recognized and applied by this Court, and recently emphasized in *Williams v. North Carolina,* [p. 749 *infra*], between the faith and credit required to be given to judgments and that to which local common and statutory law is entitled under the Constitution and laws of the United States.

In the case of local law, since each of the states of the Union has constitutional authority to make its own law with respect to persons and events within its borders, the full faith and credit clause does not ordinarily require it to substitute for its own law the conflicting law of another state, even though that law is of controlling force in the courts of that state with respect to the same persons and events. It was for this reason that we held that the state of the employer and employee is free to apply its own compensation law to the injury of the employee rather than the law of another state where the injury occurred. *Alaska Packers Assn. v. Industrial Accident Comm'n,* [p. 386, *supra*]. And for like reasons we held also that the state of the place of injury is free to apply its own law to the exclusion of the law of the state of the employer and employee. *Pacific Employers Ins. Co. v. Industrial Accident Comm'n,* [p. 389, *supra*].

But it does not follow that the employee who has sought and recovered an award of compensation in either state may then have recourse to the laws and courts of the other to recover a second or additional award for the same injury. Where a court must make choice of one of two conflicting statutes of different states and apply it to a cause of action which has not been previously litigated, there can be no plea of res judicata. But when the employee who has recovered compensation for his injury in one state seeks a second recovery in another he may be met by the plea that full faith and credit requires that his demand, which has become res judicata in one state, must be recognized as such in every other.

The full faith and credit clause and the Act of Congress implementing it have, for most purposes, placed a judgment on a different footing from a statute of one state, judicial recognition of which is sought in another. . . .

From the beginning this Court has held that these provisions have made that which has been adjudicated in one state res judicata to the same extent in every other. . . .

Even though we assume for present purposes that the command of the Constitution and the statute is not all-embracing, and that there may be exceptional cases in which the judgment of one state may not override the laws and policy of another, this Court is the final arbiter of the extent of the exceptions.

We are aware of no such exception in the case of a money judgment rendered in a civil suit. Nor are we aware of any considerations of local policy or law which could rightly be deemed to impair the force and effect which the full faith and credit clause and the Act of Congress require to be given to such a judgment outside the state of its rendition. . . .

The constitutional command requires a state to enforce a judgment of a sister state for its taxes, *Milwaukee County v. White Co.,* [p. 673, question (9)(d), *infra*], or for a gambling debt, *Fauntleroy v. Lum,* [p. 639, *supra*], or for damages for wrongful death, *Kenney v. Supreme Lodge,* [252 U.S. 411 (1920)] although the suit in which the judgment was obtained could not have been maintained under the laws and policy of the forum to which the judgment is brought. It compels enforcement of a judgment in that forum, even though a suit upon the original cause of action was barred there by limitations before the judgment was procured, *Christmas v. Russell,* [72 U.S.290 (1866)]; Roche v. McDonald, 275 U. S. 449. It demands recognition of it even though the statute on which the judgment was founded need not be applied in the state of the forum because in conflict with the laws and policy of that state. . . .

These consequences flow from the clear purpose of the full faith and credit clause to establish throughout the federal system the salutary principle of the common law that a litigation once pursued to judgment shall be as conclusive of the rights of the parties in every other court as in that where the judgment was rendered, so that a cause of action merged in a judgment in one state is likewise merged in every other. The full faith and credit clause like the commerce clause thus became a nationally unifying force. It altered the status of the several states as independent foreign sovereignties, each free to ignore rights and obligations created under the laws or established by the judicial proceedings of the others, by making each an integral part of a single nation, in which rights judicially established in any part are given nation-wide application. . . . Because there is a full faith and credit clause a defendant may not a second time challenge the validity of the plaintiff's right which has ripened into a judgment and a plaintiff may not for his single cause of action secure a second or a greater recovery.

Here both Texas and Louisiana have undertaken to adjudicate the rights of the same parties arising from a single injury sustained in the course of employment under the same contract. Each state has awarded to respondent compensation for that injury. But whether the Texas award purported also to adjudicate the rights and duties of the parties under the Louisiana law or to control persons and courts in Louisiana is irrelevant to our present inquiry. For Texas is without power to give extraterritorial effect to its laws. See . . . *Home Insurance Co. v. Dick,* [p. 382, *supra*]. The significant question in this case is whether the full faith and credit clause has deprived Louisiana of the power to deny that the Texas award has the same binding effect on the parties in Louisiana as it has in Texas.

It is not, as the state court thought, a sufficient answer to the bar of the Texas award to assert that Louisiana has a recognized interest in awarding compensation to Louisiana employees who are injured out of the state, see *Alaska Packers Assn. v. Industrial Accident Comm'n, supra,* for Texas, the state in which the injury occurred, has a like interest in making an award, see *Pacific Employers Ins. Co. v. Industrial Accident Comm'n, supra.* And in each of the cases we have cited, the state to which the judgment was brought had an interest in the subject matter of the suit and a public policy contrary to that of the state in which the judgment was obtained. No convincing reason is advanced for saying that Louisiana has a greater interest in awarding compensation for an injury suffered in an industrial accident, than North Carolina had in determining the marital status of its domiciliary against whom a divorce decree had been rendered in another state, *Williams v. North Carolina,* or Mississippi in stamping out gambling within its borders, *Fauntleroy v. Lum,* or South Carolina in requiring a parent to support his child who was domiciled within that state, *Yarborough v. Yarborough.*

In each of these cases the words and purpose of the full faith and credit clause were thought to demand that the interest of the state in which the judgment was obtained and was res judicata, should override the laws and policy of the forum to which the judgment was taken. And we can perceive no tenable ground for saying that a compensation award need not be given the same effect as res judicata in another state as it has in the state where rendered.

. . .

Respondent was free to pursue his remedy in either state but, having chosen to seek it in Texas, where the award was res judicata, the full faith and credit clause precludes him from again seeking a remedy in Louisiana upon the same grounds. The fact that a suitor has been denied a remedy by one state because it does not afford a remedy for the particular wrong alleged, may not bar recovery in another state which does provide a remedy. . . .

But . . . it is a very different matter to say that recovery can be had in every state which affords a remedy.

The suggestion that there is a second and different cause of action in Louisiana, merely because Louisiana law authorizes compensation, and in a different measure than does Texas, or because the jurisdiction of the court of one state depends on the place of the injury and that of the other on the place of the employment contract, would if accepted prove too much. . . .

If an employee employed in one state but injured in another has a different cause of action for compensation in each state because each has its own compensation statute, it could as well be argued in any case where plaintiff has recovered a judgment in one state, and seeks a second recovery in a second state for the same injury, that he is suing upon a second and different cause of action. But it has never been thought that an actionable personal injury gives rise to as many causes of action as there are states whose laws will permit a suit to recover for the injury or that despite the full faith and credit clause the injured person, more than one entitled to recover for breach of contract, could go from state to state to recover in each damages or compensation for his injury. A judgment in tort or in contract is not immune from the requirement of full faith and credit because the successful plaintiff could have maintained his suit under the law of other states and have secured a larger recovery in some, or because the jurisdiction of the court in one state to hear the cause may depend upon some facts different from the facts necessary to sustain the jurisdiction in another. . . .

And we cannot say that a workmen's compensation award for injury stands on any different footing. . . .

Reversed.

[JUSTICE JACKSON concurs on the strength of *Williams I,* [*infra,* p. 749] though if the Court were to reconsider that case, in which he dissented, he would join the dissent here.]

MR. JUSTICE DOUGLAS, dissenting.

. . .

[Justice Douglas, who wrote for the Court in *Williams I*, says that case is quite different from this one, because in *Williams* the question was whether a divorce granted in Nevada must be given full faith and credit—a situation wholly incompatible with a bigamy prosecution in another state, whereas here additional payment under Louisiana law is not incompatible with payment under the Texas award.]

If the claim under the Texas Act had been denied because of statutory defenses accorded the employer, I do not suppose that the requirements of full faith and credit would bar the subsequent claim under a Louisiana statute which did not recognize such defenses. . . .

If the full faith and credit clause would not prevent a recovery under the Louisiana Act where an award under the Texas Act had been denied, I do not see how Louisiana can be prevented from granting a recovery after Texas has made an award. . . .

If the Texas award had undertaken to adjudicate the rights and duties of the parties under the Louisiana contract of employment, which we are told carries the right to compensation under the Louisiana Act (10 So. 2d 109, 112), the result would be quite different. Then the judgment, like the divorce decree in the *Williams* case, would undertake to regulate the relationship of the parties, or their rights and duties which flow from it, as respects their undertakings in another State. And since Texas would have had jurisdiction over the parties its decree would be a bar to the present action in Louisiana. But there is nothing in the Texas proceeding or in the Texas award to indicate that that was either intended or done. . . .

Here the Texas award is not only a limited one. The employee is domiciled in Louisiana, the employer is authorized to do business in Louisiana. The employment contract is a Louisiana contract. Louisiana has such a considerable interest at stake that I would allow its policy to be obliterated or subordinated only in case what took place in Texas is irreconcilable with what Louisiana now seeks to do. I do not think it is.

. . .

Mr. Justice Murphy joins in this dissent.

Mr. Justice Black, dissenting.

. . .

As I see it, this case properly involves two separate legal questions: (1) Did Texas intend the award of its Industrial Accident Board against the insurer to bar the right granted the employee by the Louisiana Workmen's Compensation Law to collect from his employer for the same injury the difference between the compensation allowed by Texas and the more generous compensation allowed by Louisiana? (2) Assuming the Texas award was intended to constitute such a bar, does the interest of Louisiana in regulating the employment contracts of its residents nevertheless permit it to grant that larger measure of compensation which as a matter of local policy it believes necessary? The decision of the Court on both of these issues appears to me to be wrong.

. . .

The proceeding in this case before the Texas Board was against the insurer only and the award entered, by its express terms, was limited to a release of the insurance company from further liability. The liability of the employer under Louisiana law was not in issue before the Board and could not have been put in issue. The employer was not a party to that proceeding; nor was there "privity" between the insurer and the employer since the insurer's liability did not extend to rights which the employee might have against his employer under Louisiana law.

Moreover the jurisdiction of the Accident Board is limited to administration of the Texas Workmen's Compensation Act; even if the issues of liability under Louisiana law had been raised they could not have been decided by that Board. The decision of this Court today, therefore, is tantamount to holding that Texas intended to extinguish a claim against the employer in a proceeding in which the employer was not a party and the issue of its liability under Louisiana law was not allowed to be raised. I cannot impute such an intention to Texas.

. . .

In the absence of compelling language this Court should not construe the statutes of Texas in such a manner that grave questions of their constitutionality are raised. . . .

It is extremely doubtful whether Texas has the power, by any legal device, to preclude a sister state from granting to its own residents employed within its own borders that measure of compensation for occupational injuries which it deems advisable. . . .

The practical result of the decision here is to hold that Texas has power to nullify a Louisiana statute which gives the beneficial protection of workmen's compensation to an injured workman who is a resident of Louisiana and made his contract of employment there. I "am not persuaded that the full faith and credit clause gives sanction to such control by one state of the internal affairs of another." *Yarborough v. Yarborough.*

II.

It is apparently conceded that Louisiana would not have been required to apply the Texas statute had there not been a judgment in the particular case by the Texas tribunal . . . *Alaska Packers Assn. v. Industrial Accident Comm'n,* 294 U. S. 532, 541–543, 549; cf. *Pacific Employers Ins. Co. v. Industrial Accident Comm'n,* 306 U. S. 493, 503. . . . The argument of state interest is hardly less compelling when Louisiana chooses to reject as decisive of the issues of the case a foreign judgment than when it rejects a foreign statute.

The interest of Texas in providing compensation for an injured employee who like respondent was only temporarily employed in the state is not the same as that of Louisiana where the respondent was domiciled and where the contract of employment was made. Someone has to take care of an individual who has received, as has respondent, an injury which permanently disables him from performance of his work. If employers or the consumers of their goods do not shoulder this responsibility, the general public of a state must. Neither state merely vindicates a private wrong growing out of tortious conduct. . . . The Louisiana Act was passed in the interest of the general welfare of the people of Louisiana. If it chooses to be more generous to injured workmen than Texas, no Constitutional issue is presented.

. . .

The Court seems in some parts of its opinion to adopt a wholly new and far reaching policy relating to the power of states to allow complete indemnification for a personal injury by permitting more than one suit against the wrongdoer, and to engraft this policy on to the full faith and credit clause. Courts schooled in the common law have long objected to what has been designated "splitting a cause of action." They have phrased this policy objection in many common law concepts, one of which has been the doctrine of "election of remedies." This predilection of common law judges in favor of compelling the aggregation of all possible elements of damage into one law suit is here apparently elevated to a position of Constitutional impregnability in the full faith and credit clause. The Court now seems to interpret that clause to prohibit a recovery of full compensation for a personal injury in more than one suit even if one or more states think full compensation can best be accorded in this manner. The practical result of this drastic new Constitutional doctrine is that State B must give *more* faith and credit to State A's judgment for damages for personal injury than State A itself intended the judgment should be given. State A's and State B's judgments are said to be mutually exclusive, not because either state made them so, but apparently on the ground that the full faith and credit clause imposes a rule of substantive law which requires this result. This doctrine would accord to the full faith and credit clause a meaning which it would have had if its authors had stated, "Full Faith and Credit shall be given in each State to the . . . judicial Proceedings of every other State, *and in addition two recoveries shall never be allowed by separate states for losses resulting from a single personal injury."* When the authors of the Constitution desired to prohibit two criminal prosecutions for the same offense, they had no difficulty in expressing their views. Had they wished to hobble the states in their efforts to provide more than one remedy in order to accomplish full justice in civil cases, I think they could and would have expressed themselves with equal clarity and emphasis.

The effect of the decision of this Court today is to strike down as unconstitutional an important provision of the workmen's compensation laws of at least eleven states. For more than half a century the power of the states to regulate their domestic economic affairs has been narrowly restricted by judicial interpretation of the federal Constitution. The chief weapon in the arsenal of restriction, only recently falling into disrepute because of overuse, is the due process clause. The full faith and credit clause, used today to serve the same purposes, is no better suited to control the freedom of the states. The practical question now before us can be decided by the states in many ways and most of the states which have expressed themselves seem ready to dispose of the problem as has Louisiana. Our notions of policy should not permit the Constitution to become a barrier to free experimentation by the states with the problems of workmen's compensation.

Mr. Justice Douglas, Mr. Justice Murphy, and Mr. Justice Rutledge concur in this opinion.

The split among the Justices, and the striking difference between the *Alaska Packers/Pacific Employers* line of cases and the result in *Magnolia*—i.e. between choice of law on the one hand and a judgment growing out of a workers compensation claim on the other—did not last long. Oddly enough, considering the text of the Full Faith and Credit clause and the implementing statute, subsequent cases focused on the question raised by Justice Black (p. 659). Did F-1 intend the award of its Accident Board against the insurer to bar the employee from collecting for the same injury under another state's workers compensation law?

INDUSTRIAL COMMISSION OF WISCONSIN v. McCARTIN

United States Supreme Court
330 U.S. 622 (1947)

Mr. Justice Murphy delivered the opinion of the Court.

[An Illinois worker, Leo Kopp, employed by an Illinois contractor, McCartin, was injured on a construction job in Wisconsin. Kopp first filed a claim with the Industrial Commission of

Wisconsin, but when the insurance carrier entered an objection to that commission's jurisdiction, he filed his claim with the Illinois commission. The Wisconsin commission wrote to the insurance carrier that so far as it was concerned, Kopp could claim under the Illinois Workmen's Compensation Act, and thereafter claim under the Wisconsin act, with credit to be given for the amount awarded under the Illinois act.

Kopp and the employer entered into a settlement, approved by the Illinois commission. The settlement contract stated that "This settlement does not affect any rights that applicant may have under the Workmen's Compensation Act of the State of Wisconsin."]

In the meantime, on December 20, 1943, this Court's decision in *Magnolia Petroleum Co. v. Hunt* was rendered. The Wisconsin Commission then held a hearing on February 20, 1944, on Kopp's application before it. McCartin and the insurance carrier filed an amended answer, contending that under the full faith and credit clause the Wisconsin proceedings were barred by the award and payment under the Illinois Act; reliance was placed upon the *Magnolia Petroleum Co.* case. The Commission overruled this objection and ordered the payment to Kopp of certain benefits, after giving credit for the sums paid under the Illinois Act.

The Circuit Court for Dane County, Wisconsin, set aside the Wisconsin Commission's order on the authority of the *Magnolia Petroleum Co.* case. On appeal, the Supreme Court of Wisconsin affirmed the lower court's judgment on the same authority. We granted certiorari to determine the applicability of the full faith and credit clause, as interpreted in the *Magnolia Petroleum Co.* case, to the facts of this case.

If it were apparent that the Illinois award was intended to be final and conclusive of all the employee's rights against the employer and the insurer growing out of the injury, the decision in the *Magnolia Petroleum Co.* case would be controlling here. . . . But we do not believe that the same situation exists in this case, the Illinois award being different in its nature and effect from the Texas award in the *Magnolia* case.

The Illinois Workmen's Compensation Act was concededly applicable under the circumstances of this case. Section 3 of that Act provides that it shall apply automatically and without election to all employers and employees engaged in businesses or enterprises such as those involving the erection or construction of any structure.

. . .

[I]n situations to which the Act applies, the right of action against the employer under the Illinois common law or under the Illinois Personal Injuries Act has been abolished. To that extent, the Act provides an exclusive remedy.

But there is nothing in the statute or in the decisions thereunder to indicate that it is completely exclusive, that it is designed to preclude any recovery by proceedings brought in another state for injuries received there in the course of an Illinois employment. . . .

And in light of the rule that workmen's compensation laws are to be liberally construed in furtherance of the purpose for which they were enacted, . . . we should not readily interpret such a statute so as to cut off an employee's right to sue under other legislation passed for his benefit. Only some unmistakable language by a state legislature or judiciary would warrant our accepting such a construction. Especially is this true where the rights affected are those arising under legislation of another state and where the full faith and credit provision of the United States Constitution is brought into play. . . .

We need not rest our decision, however, solely upon the absence of any provision or construction of the Illinois Workmen's Compensation Act forbidding an employee from seeking alternative or additional relief under the laws of another state. There is additional evidence that the employee is free to ask for additional compensation in Wisconsin. That evidence is in the Illinois award itself, an award which is acknowledged to have been made in compliance with the Illinois statute.

Here the employer and the employee entered into a settlement contract fixing the amount of compensation to which the employee was entitled under the Illinois statute, thereby avoiding the expense and delay of litigating the matter. This contract, together with the employee's petition for a lump sum payment, was approved by one of the Commissioners of the Illinois Industrial Commission. By that approval, the agreement became "in legal effect an award." . . .

One of the provisions in the settlement contract which became the award was the statement that "This settlement does not affect any rights that applicant may have under the Workmen's Compensation Act of the State of Wisconsin." . . . The Commissioner confessed that he did not know the meaning of this provision, but he did not order it stricken. Rather he approved it for whatever it was worth.

This contract provision saving the rights of the employee in Wisconsin thus became part of the Illinois award, an award which has achieved finality in the absence of a timely appeal. This provision means more than might be implied in the case of an ordinary judgment or decree. Any party, of course, has the right to seek another judgment or decree, however inconsistent or futile such an attempt might be; and it takes no reservation in the original judgment or decree to give him that right. But when the reservation in this award is read against the background of the Illinois Workmen's Compensation Act, it becomes clear that the reservation spells out what we believe to be implicit in that Act—namely, that an Illinois workmen's compensation award of the type here involved does not foreclose an additional award under the laws of another state. And in the setting of this case, that fact is of decisive significance.

Since this Illinois award is final and conclusive only as to rights arising in Illinois, Wisconsin is free under the full faith and credit clause to grant an award of compensation in accord with its own laws. *Magnolia Petroleum Co. v. Hunt* thus does not control this case.

Reversed.

Thomas v. Washington Gas Light Co., 448 U.S. 261 (1980).

Thomas, a resident of the District of Columbia, was injured while working in one of the suburbs of Washington, located in Virginia. He made a claim under the Workmen's Compensation Act of Virginia, and received an award from the Virginia Industrial Commission. Three years later, Thomas made a claim under the District of Columbia Workmen's Compensation Act. The employer opposed the claim, primarily on the ground that since, as a matter of Virginia law, the Virginia award excluded any other recovery "at common law or otherwise" on account of the injury in Virginia, the District of Columbia's obligation to give that award full faith and credit precluded a second, supplemental award in the District.

Thomas prevailed before the District of Columbia authorities, but the Court of Appeals reversed, holding that a "second and separate proceeding in another jurisdiction upon the same injury after a prior recovery in another State [is] precluded by the Full Faith and Credit Clause."

The Supreme Court, reviewing *Magnolia* and *McCartin*, focused on the statement in *McCartin* that "[O]nly some unmistakable language by a state legislature or judiciary would warrant our accepting . . . a construction" that a workmen's compensation statute "is designed to preclude any recovery by proceedings brought in another state." Justice Stevens, on behalf of a plurality, wrote:

> The Virginia Workmen's Compensation Act's exclusive remedy provision, is not exactly the same as Illinois'; but it contains no "unmistakable language" directed at precluding a supplemental compensation award in another State that was not also in the Illinois Act. Consequently, *McCartin* by its terms, rather than the earlier *Magnolia* decision, is controlling as between the two precedents. Nevertheless, the fact that we find ourselves comparing the language of two state statutes, neither of which has been construed by the highest court of either State, in an attempt to resolve an issue arising under the Full Faith and Credit Clause makes us pause to inquire whether there is a fundamental flaw in our analysis of this federal question.
>
> We cannot fail to observe that, in the Court's haste to retreat from *Magnolia,* it fashioned a rule that clashes with normally accepted full faith and credit principles. It has long been the law that "the judgment of a state court should have the same credit, validity, and effect, in every other court in the United States, which it had in the state where it was pronounced." *Hampton v. McConnel*, 3 Wheat. 234, 235 (Marshall, C. J.,). See also *Mills v. Duryee,* 7 Cranch 481, 484 (Story, J.). This rule, if not compelled by the Full Faith and Credit Clause itself, is surely required by 28 U. S. C. § 1738, which provides that the "Acts, records and judicial proceedings . . . [of any State] shall have the same full faith and credit in every court within the United States . . . as they have by law or usage in the courts of [the] State . . . from which they are taken." Thus, in effect, by virtue of the full faith and credit obligations of the several States, a State is permitted to determine the extraterritorial effect of its judgments; but it may only do so indirectly, by prescribing the effect of its judgments within the State.
>
> The *McCartin* rule, however, focusing as it does on the extraterritorial intent of the rendering State, is fundamentally different. It authorizes a State, by drafting or construing its legislation in "unmistakable language," directly to determine the extraterritorial effect of its workmen's compensation awards. An authorization to a state legislature of this character is inconsistent with the rule established in *Pacific Employers Ins. Co. v. Industrial Accident Comm'n,* [p. 391, *supra*]:
>
>> This Court must determine for itself how far the full faith and credit clause compels the qualification or denial of rights asserted under the laws of one state, that of the forum, by the statute of another state.
>
> It follows inescapably that the *McCartin* "unmistakable language" rule represents an unwarranted delegation to the States of this Court's responsibility for the final arbitration of full faith and credit questions. . . .
>
> To vest the power of determining the extraterritorial effect of a State's own laws and judgments in the State itself risks the very kind of parochial entrenchment on the interests of other States that it was the purpose of the Full Faith and Credit Clause and other provisions of Art. IV of the Constitution to prevent. . . .
>
> Thus, a re-examination of *McCartin*'s "unmistakable language" test reinforces our tentative conclusion that it does not provide an acceptable basis on which to distinguish

§ 8.01   JURISDICTION AND JUDGMENTS   □ 665

Magnolia. But if we reject that test, we must decide whether to overrule either *Magnolia* or *McCartin*. In making this kind of decision, we must take into account both the practical values served by the doctrine of *stare decisis* and the principles that inform the Full Faith and Credit Clause.

After an analysis of the aims of *stare decisis*, Justice Stevens concluded that it was *Magnolia* that had to give way:

> A final judgment entered by a court of general jurisdiction normally establishes not only the measure of the plaintiff's rights but also the limits of the defendant's liability. A traditional application of res judicata principles enables either party to claim the benefit of the judgment insofar as it resolved issues the court had jurisdiction to decide. Although a Virginia court is free to recognize the perhaps paramount interests of another State by choosing to apply that State's law in a particular case, the Industrial Commission of Virginia does not have that power. Its jurisdiction is limited to questions arising under the Virginia Workmen's Compensation Act. Typically, a workmen's compensation tribunal may only apply its own State's law. In this case, the Virginia Commission could and did establish the full measure of petitioner's rights under Virginia law, but it neither could nor purported to determine his rights under the law of the District of Columbia. Full faith and credit must be given to the determination that the Virginia Commission had the authority to make; but by a parity of reasoning, full faith and credit need not be given to determinations that it had no power to make. Since it was not requested, and had no authority, to pass on petitioner's rights under District of Columbia law, there can be no constitutional objection to a fresh adjudication of those rights.
>
> It is true, of course, that after Virginia entered its award, that State had an interest in preserving the integrity of what it had done. . . . Thus, Virginia had an interest in having respondent pay petitioner the amounts specified in its award. Allowing a supplementary recovery in the District does not conflict with that interest.
>
> As we have already noted, Virginia also has a separate interest in placing a ceiling on the potential liability of companies that transact business within the State. But past cases have established that that interest is not strong enough to prevent other States with overlapping jurisdiction over particular injuries from giving effect to their more generous compensation policies when the employee selects the most favorable forum in the first instance.
>
> . . . .
>
> We therefore would hold that a State has no legitimate interest within the context of our federal system in preventing another State from granting a supplemental compensation award when that second State would have had the power to apply its workmen's compensation law in the first instance. The Full Faith and Credit Clause should not be construed to preclude successive workmen's compensation awards. Accordingly, *Magnolia Petroleum Co. v. Hunt* should be overruled.

Justice White, joined by Justices Burger and Powell, agreed with the result, but pointed out that relying on the limited powers of the Virginia Industrial Commission could not be the entire basis of the decision, since all an employer concerned about a second claim in another state need do under that theory would be to seek judicial review of a decision of the commission. If a judicial decision upholding the award were preclusive, Justice Stevens' rationale would not hold up. "But if such a judicial decision is not preclusive in the second forum, then it appears that the plurality's rationale is not limited in its effect to judgments of administrative tribunals." However, Justice White concluded:

> Although I find *McCartin* to rest on questionable foundations, I am not now prepared to overrule it. And I agree with the plurality that *McCartin,* rather than *Magnolia,* is controlling as between the two precedents since the Virginia Workmen's Compensation Act lacks the "unmistakable language" which *McCartin* requires if a workmen's compensation award is to preclude a subsequent award in another State.

Justice Rehnquist, joined by Justice Thurgood Marshall, dissented:

> This is clearly a case where the whole is less than the sum of its parts. In choosing between two admittedly inconsistent precedents, *Magnolia Petroleum Co. v. Hunt,* and *Industrial Comm'n of Wisconsin v. McCartin,* six of us agree that the latter decision, *McCartin,* is analytically indefensible. . . .
>
> The remaining three Members of the Court concede that it "rest[s] on questionable foundations." . . . Nevertheless, when the smoke clears, it is *Magnolia* rather than *McCartin* that the plurality suggests should be overruled. . . . Because I believe that *Magnolia* was correctly decided, and because I fear that the rule proposed by the plurality is both ill-considered and ill-defined, I dissent.
>
> . . . .
>
> I suspect that my Brethren's insistence on ratifying *McCartin's* result despite condemnation of its rationale is grounded in no small part upon their concern that injured workers are often coerced or maneuvered into filing their claims in jurisdictions amenable to their employers. There is, however, absolutely no evidence of such overreaching in the present case.
>
> . . . .
>
> I fear that the plurality, in its zeal to remedy a perceived imbalance in bargaining power, would badly distort an important constitutional tenet. Its "interest analysis," once removed from the statutory choice-of-law context considered by the Court in *Alaska Packers* and *Pacific Employers,* knows no metes or bounds. Given the modern proliferation of quasi-judicial methods for resolving disputes and of various tribunals of limited jurisdiction, such a rule could only lead to confusion. I find such uncertainty unacceptable, and prefer the rule originally announced in *Magnolia Petroleum Co. v. Hunt,* a rule whose analytical validity is, even yet, unchallenged.
>
> The Full Faith and Credit Clause did not allot to this Court the task of "balancing" interests where the "public Acts, Records, and judicial Proceedings" of a State were involved. It simply directed that they be given the "Full Faith and Credit" that the Court today denies to those of Virginia. I would affirm the judgment of the court below.

NOTES AND QUESTIONS

(1)(a) Which outcome for the *Yarborough* case is the more attractive—the one reached by the Supreme Court of South Carolina and favored by Justice Stone, or the one reached by the majority in the U.S. Supreme Court? Does your answer depend on compassion for Sadie, as weighed against an enlightened view of federalism? Or is that the wrong way to put the question?

(b) Could you write a more persuasive opinion for either side?

(c) Is it possible that Justice Stone's opinion is consistent with the Full Faith and Credit clause of the Constitution, but not with the implementing legislation? If so, should the implementing legislation be amended? Notice Justice Stone's suggestion to this effect in *Yarborough* at p. 651, note 2.

(2)(a) Justice Brandeis seems to be troubled by the fact that Sadie Yarborough was not a party to the Georgia proceeding. One might think there is something odd about the idea of a child being a party to her parents' divorce. But apart from such thoughts, why is Justice Brandeis even worried about the point? If the constitutional mandate is to treat the judgment in the same way as it would be treated in Georgia, and Sadie would be barred from attacking the judgment in Georgia, why is it relevant whether she was a party?[a]

(b) Justice Brandeis is also concerned about the fact that Sadie was not a resident of Georgia at the time the decree was issued, but he resolves that concern with a rather formalistic conclusion that her domicile was that of her father until the decree was entered. Again, why is this relevant?

(c) The most puzzling of Justice Brandeis' concerns appears in the last sentence of the majority opinion (p. 650) analogous to the statement in *Home Insurance v. Dick* (also by Justice Brandeis) reserving on the question of how the case would come out if the Mexican insurance company had been doing business in Texas (p. 385, *supra*). What difference does it make to the analysis of res judicata and full faith and credit where Mr. Yarborough chooses to reside after his marriage breaks up? Isn't Justice Brandeis playing into the hands of Justice Stone and comparative interest analysis?

(3)(a) Justice Stone says there is nothing in the Georgia decree to suggest that it was intended to regulate or control the relationship of parent and child outside Georgia. Assuming it were possible to discern such intent, why is it relevant? Isn't such intent implicit in the Full Faith and Credit clause and the implementing legislation, which requires the same full faith and credit in every court in the United States as in the rendering court? Note how the intent of F–1—"We really mean it" vs. "We don't care what else you may do" comes back in *McCartin* and *Thomas*.

(b) Justice Stone goes on to say (p. 650) that even if the decree of the Georgia court could be read to be intended to apply outside Georgia, "I am not persuaded that the full faith and credit clause give sanction to such control by one state to the internal affairs of another." Is *Yarborough* different from *Fauntleroy v. Lum*? Or would his opinion, if it commanded a majority, require overruling *Fauntleroy*?

(c) Suppose Justice Stone's view had prevailed, Mr. Yarborough had been ordered to pay additional sums to support Sadie's education, but he had failed to comply fully. Would the South Carolina judgment have been enforceable in Georgia?

(d) Speaking of enforcement, suppose Mr. Yarborough had failed to pay the original $1750 pursuant to order of the Georgia court. Would there be any doubt that the judgment could be enforced against Mr. Yarborough in South Carolina? Why then should the standard for recognition be different when the same judgment is sought to be used defensively?

---

[a] Reconsider this question in connection with *Johnson v. Muelberger,* Chapter 9, p. 775-76, question 3, *infra.*

(4)(a) Perhaps the most interesting passage in Justice Stone's opinion is the statement (p. 650) that "between the prohibition of the due process clause . . . and the mandate of the full faith and credit clause, . . . there is an area which federal authority has not occupied." Some of this repeats (actually antedates) Justice Stone's opinions for the Court in *Alaska Packers* and *Pacific Employers*.[b] The inference seems to be that in this gray area, F–2 may, but need not, give full faith and credit to a judgment of F–1. Is this, or should it be, true for judgments as well as for laws?

(b) Section 103 of the *Restatement (Second) of Conflict of Laws,* reads:

> A judgment rendered in one State of the United States need not be recognized or enforced in a sister State if such recognition or enforcement is not required by the national policy of full faith and credit because it would involve an improper interference with important interests of the sister State.

The Reporter's Note says that ". . . the rule is based primarily upon the views expressed by Mr. Justice Stone in his dissenting opinion in *Yarborough* and in his majority opinions in *Milwaukee County v. M. E. White Co.* [question (9)(d) below] and *Magnolia Petroleum Co. v. Hunt.*" Assuming § 103 is a correct statement of constitutional law,[c] —by no means certain[d] —what interest of South Carolina would be interfered with by recognizing the Georgia judgment, when paid, as a discharge? Couldn't South Carolina give Sadie a scholarship to the state university—or for that matter to Wellesley?[e]

(4)(c) One problem with the *Yarborough* case may have been that in contrast to support orders in most states, the Georgia judgment was apparently not subject to modification. But what if it had been modifiable upon appropriate showing, say, that Sadie's needs and Mr. Yarborough's means were both greater than was apparent when the original judgment was rendered? Should Sadie be required to apply to the rendering court in Georgia for a modification? Or should she be permitted to seek modification in South Carolina, assuming a court in that state had jurisdiction over her father? If your answer is that a South Carolina court should be able to modify, what law should govern?[f] More of this problem in the next chapter.[g]

(5)(a) Turning to *Magnolia Petroleum Co. v. Hunt,* this time Justice Stone (by now Chief Justice) writes for the majority, and sounds rather different. "[W]hether the Texas award purported also to adjudicate the rights and duties of the parties under Louisiana law," he writes (p. 657) "or to control persons and courts in Louisiana is irrelevant to our present inquiry." And, further, "It lends no support to the decision of the Louisiana court in this case to say that Louisiana

---

[b] § 5.02[B].

[c] Comment *a* to § 103 says the rule there stated "has an extremely narrow scope of application," and Comment *b* says "Almost invariably, the federal policy of full faith and credit will outweigh any interest that a State may have in not recognizing or enforcing a sister State judgment."

[d] Professor Ehrenzweig, commenting on § 103 in a draft form, wrote "There is . . . no authority whatsoever for the startling proposition [contained in what became § 103]." Ehrenzweig, *The Second Conflicts Restatement: A Last Appeal for Its Withdrawal,* 113 U. Pa. L. Rev. 1230, 1240 (1965).

[e] Justice Stone makes just such a point in *Magnolia,* in a passage not here reproduced, suggesting that Louisiana could be generous to Mr. Hunt out of the general funds of its Treasury, 320 U.S. at 442.

[f] While generally the substantive law of support is similar (and vague) in most states, such questions as the effect of remarriage of one spouse, or the age of majority for a child, do vary from state to state and may make considerable difference in controversies over support.

[g] See *Worthley v. Worthley,* p. 804, question (2)(d) *infra.*

has chosen to be more generous with an employee than Texas has . . . ." Has Justice Stone seen the light? Bowed to precedent?[h] Or are *Yarborough* and *Magnolia* distinguishable in a way that favors local interests in one case, national interests in the other?[i]

(b) We know from *Pacific Employers*[j] that Texas can apply its law to the accident that occurred in Texas, and we know from *Alaska Packers*[k] that Louisiana can apply its law to an accident arising from employment contracted for in Louisiana. No one argued that the employee could get two complete recoveries; the question was whether, having secured one award, he could get a second, higher, award, crediting against the second award the payments received pursuant to the first one. Quite apart from the contours of the Full Faith and Credit clause, is there something fishy about Mr. Hunt's efforts here? Is it double dipping? Or is it like collecting for an accidental death both under an accident and under a life insurance policy?

(c) Justice Stone repeats his statement in *Yarborough* about exceptions to Full Faith and Credit, but he says a judgment for a sum of money is not one of them. Clearly an injured party could not bring a common law action in Texas against a tortfeasor, recover, say, $10,000, and then sue the same defendant on the same claim in Louisiana, asserting that his injuries were really worth $30,000. To Justice Stone, changing the action from one in tort to one for workers' compensation does not change the basic principle. Is he right?

(d) Justice Douglas turns Justice Stone's example around: Suppose, he suggests, the claimant had lost in Texas, say because he was injured following an intermediate stop on the way to his lodgings from work, which would have disqualified him under Texas law, but Louisiana law would have considered every injury while he was employed away from home as work-related.[l] Could Mr. Hunt still apply for Workers' Compensation in Louisiana? If the answer is that losing in Texas would not bar him, why should winning do so?

(e) The last question highlights what may be a significant difference between a tort or contract action, and a proceeding for workers' compensation. In an action at law, a court can apply the law of another jurisdiction, and at least in theory the court goes through the choice of law process; industrial accident commissions, as Justice Black points out, generally (and in the present case,) administer only a single statute or group of related statutes of the state where they sit. Does that make any difference?[m]

(6) Several points in Justice Black's opinion in *Magnolia* are worth reflecting upon in the context of Full Faith and Credit.

(a) If Chief Justice Stone is correct, at p. 657, in saying that the clear purpose of the Full Faith and Credit clause is to establish the common law of res judicata throughout the federal system, how much baggage does the common law bring along? Is the doctrine of election of remedies, for instance, also now subject to constitutional control? Also splitting causes of action?

---

[h] Note how Justice Black, dissenting in *Magnolia*, throws Justice Stone's words from *Yarborough* (question 3(b) above) back at him.

[i] For an interesting discussion of *Yarborough* and *Magnolia*, see Freund, *Chief Justice Stone and the Conflict of Laws*, 59 Harv. L. Rev. 1210, 1225–30 (1946).

[j] Page 389, *supra.*

[k] Page 386, *supra.*

[l] See, generally Arthur Larson, *The Law of Workmen's Compensation* Vol. 1, ch. IV (1952 and Supps.).

[m] This point is stressed in Reese and Johnson, *The Scope of Full Faith and Credit to Judgments,* 49 Colum. L. Rev. 153, 171–77 (1949).

What about compulsory counterclaims in F–1, but not in F–2? Would Chief Justice Stone seek to exercise Supreme Court vigilance over such issues as well?

(b) Note Justice Black, twenty years before *Babcock v. Jackson,* talking not only of state interests, but weighing the respective interests—not surprisingly in favor of the state of domicile of the injured person.

(c) Justice Black again brings up the intent of F–1—either of the legislature or of the Industrial Accident Board, as Justice Stone did in *Yarborough* (question (3)(a) above). If full faith and credit is designed to do favors for states in the position of F–1, it is easy to see the point of an argument that says don't do favors that aren't asked for; but if the clause has a national, unifying, purpose, doesn't the question lose meaning?

(7)(a) The question of intent becomes decisive in *McCartin,* a 9–0 judgment of the Supreme Court again involving a worker hired in one state, but injured on the job in another, though this time the first award was made in the state of employment (Illinois). In contrast to the Texas Industrial Accident Board, which probably never thought of the issue, the Industrial Commission of Illinois approved a settlement that said expressly that it was without prejudice to what the Wisconsin Commission might award. Could the Illinois court in an automobile accident case say "Whatever we award to the plaintiff in this case is without prejudice to what he may collect in any other court"? If not, why is this case different?[n]

(b) Justice Stevens in *Thomas* says *McCartin* "clashes with normally accepted full faith and credit principles" (p. 664) and "represents an unwarranted delegation to the States of this Court's responsibility. . . ." Why then does he vote to reverse the decision of the Court of Appeals which respected the F–1 award?

(c) Justice Stevens asks which interests of F–1 (Virginia) would be impaired by permitting a second proceeding in F–2 (District of Columbia), and concludes that the only relevant interest of F–1 that would be impaired by permitting a second claim is its interest in the integrity of its judgments. What happened to the national interest?

(d) The improbable combination of Justices Rehnquist and Marshall says this case is less than the sum of its parts. Justice Rehnquist also suggests that sympathy for a coerced employee, such as Justice Black expressed in *Magnolia,* played a role in the peculiar outcome of the *Thomas* case. Is he right in saying (p. 666) that interest analysis, once removed from the choice-of-law context "knows no metes or bounds."?

(8) The tension between full faith and credit and public policy appeared in a novel setting in *Baker v. General Motors Corp.*, 118 S. Ct. 657 (Jan. 13, 1998).

(a) The case grew out of a fatal automobile accident involving a 1985 Chevrolet S-10 Blazer, which caught fire after colliding with another vehicle. The children of the deceased passenger brought suit in Missouri against General Motors, alleging that the fire was caused by a defective fuel pump which continued to pump gasoline to the engine instead of shutting down after the collision. GM, having removed the action to federal court, denied that the fuel pump was defective, and asserted that the deaths were caused by the collision, not the fire. To establish their claim of product defect, plaintiffs sought to call a former member of GM's engineering analysis staff, Ronald Elwell, and GM objected.

(b) It turned out that Mr. Elwell had been discharged by GM after some 30 years as a GM employee, and that he had sued GM for wrongful discharge in state court in Michigan. GM had

---

[n] Note that Chief Justice Stone died before argument of the *McCartin* case.

§ 8.01   JURISDICTION AND JUDGMENTS   □   671

counterclaimed, alleging that Elwell had divulged privileged information in testifying in various product liability actions against GM. The litigation between Elwell and GM was eventually settled. As part of that settlement, Elwell consented to entry of an injunction issued by the Michigan Court that precluded him from testifying against GM in product liability cases, unless ordered to do so by a court.

(c) When plaintiffs in the Missouri action called Elwell as witness, GM objected, contending that the Michigan injunction was entitled to full faith and credit. Plaintiffs argued that the injunction was not entitled to full faith and credit, and that even if it were, the settlement agreement would permit the witness to testify if the Missouri Court so ordered. The district court permitted plaintiffs to take Mr. Elwell's deposition and allowed him to testify at the trial, on the basis that a public policy exception to full faith and credit was applicable, apparently based on the value of "whistleblowers." Is such a public policy exception to full faith and credit persuasive?

(d) The Court of Appeals thought not.º Assuming, the court wrote, that a public policy exception exists to the command of the full faith and credit clause, the district court erred by not honoring Missouri's equally strong public policy favoring full faith and credit. Is that how you would have phrased a reversal? Isn't it a federal policy—indeed a federal Constitutional command—that is involved?

(e) The district court had another basis for its holding: since the injunction was modifiable in Michigan, it could be modified by the court in Missouri as well. Is that persuasive? Why should modifiability make any difference in the courts of another state?ᵖ

(f) Again the Court of Appeals thought the district court had gotten it wrong. "The full faith and credit clause," it wrote, "is not so weak that it can be evaded by mere mention of the word 'modification.' ."ᑫ [citation omitted]. What kind of showing might the Michigan court require before granting a request permitting Mr. Elwell to testify in Missouri? Turning the question around, should GM have moved in Michigan for a contempt order against Mr. Elwell as soon as it learned that he had agreed (for a fee) to testify in the Missouri action?

(g) Plaintiffs, facing a retrial without their star witness, applied for certiorari. Plaintiffs reframed the question, however, as follows:

> The question presented is whether the court below erred in holding that petitioners, who were not parties to the state proceeding or in privity with any party, could be precluded from obtaining the witness's testimony on the basis of an obligation to give Full Faith and Credit to state court judgments.

º Baker v. General Motors, 86 F.3d 811 (1996).

ᵖ For more on this question in the context of spouse and child support, see Chapter 9, §9.03[A], *infra*.

ᑫ As the Court of Appeals noted, the 1988 Revisions to the Restatement (Second) of Conflict of Laws states, in black letter:

§109. Modifiable Judgment

A court will recognize or enforce a judgment rendered in a State of the United States that remains subject to modification in the State of rendition.

The original (1971) version of §109 provided that a modifiable judgment of a sister state need not be recognized or enforced, but that the second State "is free to recognize or enforce [such] a judgment." Note that the current version says a court "will recognize. . ."; it does not say "must" and does not speak in terms of Constitutional command.

(h) The Supreme Court granted certiorari and reversed unanimously, though with three different opinions. Justice Ginsburg, for the majority, was careful to emphasize that the Full Faith and Credit Clause makes no distinction between law and equity, that the clause imposes an "exacting obligation" to recognize sister-state judgments, as contrasted with laws, and that there is no local public policy exception to the requirement of full faith and credit. Having thus confirmed the law of full faith and credit, however, the Court held that "[e]nforcement measures do not travel with the sister state judgment as preclusive effects do;" thus, the Michigan judgment could not reach beyond the controversy between Elwell and General Motors, and could not require the courts in other states to refrain from ordering Elwell to testify. Since the Michigan judgment had included an exception for orders of other courts, Justice Ginsburg pointed out that Elwell would not be in contempt of the Michigan court if he testified pursuant to a lawful order of the federal court in Missouri. It seems that the result would be the same, however, even if the Michigan judgment had contained no such exception, and even if General Motors had returned to the Michigan court and had secured an injunction against testimony by Elwell in the Missouri suit.

(9)(a) The gray area between due process and full faith and credit described by Justice Stone in several opinions has had its ups and downs. At one time certain divorces were valid but not entitled to full faith and credit. See *Haddock v. Haddock,* 201 U.S. 562 (1906).[r] Support and custody decrees have also been subject to differing levels of enforceability, though usually the reason given had to do with lack of finality, or modifiability, or jurisdiction. All of these issues are discussed in the next chapter, devoted to family law. Judgments concerning interests in land outside the rendering state were often stated not to be entitled to full faith and credit, the reason being that the court that issued the judgment, even if it had all the parties before it, lacked jurisdiction over the subject matter. See *Clarke v. Clarke* and *Fall v. Eastin,* discussed in the following section.

(b) As regards final, non-modifiable judgments rendered by a court with clear jurisdiction over the subject matter and the parties, the principal gray area seems to cover penal and revenue judgments, in each case apparently reflecting a famous (and perhaps misunderstood) one-line quotation: Lord Mansfield's statement that "no country ever takes notice of the revenue laws of another,"[s] and Chief Justice Marshall's statement that "The Courts of no country execute the penal laws of another."[t] Neither of these statements was given in a case involving a judgment, and both are clearly overstatements if taken literally, though they do reflect a continuing reluctance to become involved in controversies between a foreign state and a private person, even within a federal union. Is there good reason for such reluctance? Can it be squared with the Full Faith and Credit clause?

(c) Judgments rendered by criminal courts in one state of the United States are still generally not *enforced* in other states, though they are recognized, for example in interstate extradition,[u] and also in connection with sentencing, grant of bail, and comparable procedures in which the

---

[r] See p. 750 and p. 765, question (6)(a), *infra.*

[s] *Holman v. Johnson,* 1 Cowp. 341, 98 Eng. Rep. 1120 (1775), reproduced in Ch. 10 at page 893. The quotation appears in the first paragraph of the opinion, p. 894.

[t] *The Antelope,* 23 U.S. (10 Wheat.) 66, 123 (1825), Chapter I, § question 1, p. 38. *supra.*

[u] Note that section 2 of Article IV of the Constitution, following the Full Faith and Credit clause, Documents Supplement p. 4, contains the interstate extradition clause. That clause is implemented both through federal legislation, 18 U.S.C. § 3182, and through state law, for all but two states the Uniform Criminal Extradition Act, 11 U.L.A. 51.

§ 8.01   JURISDICTION AND JUDGMENTS   □   673

prior record of an accused or convicted person is relevant. Some courts have declined to enforce civil judgments with penal elements—e.g., with damages exceeding the injury found. However, the U.S. Supreme Court, relying in part on a decision of the Privy Council on appeal from the courts of Canada,ᵛ held that a New York statute imposing liability on directors of a corporation to its creditors was not "penal in the international sense;" accordingly, a New York judgment based on that statute was entitled to full faith and credit when sued on in Maryland. *Huntington v. Attrill,* 146 U.S. 657 (1892).

(d) Until 1935, it was thought that states of the United States were not required to recognize judgments for taxes rendered in other states.ʷ In *Milwaukee County v. M. E. White Co.,* 296 U.S. 268 (1935), again per Justice Stone, the Supreme Court put that belief to rest:

> Such exception as there may be to [the] all-inclusive command [of the full faith and credit clause and the implementing legislation] is one which is implied from the nature of our dual system of government, and recognizes that consistently with the full-faith and credit clause there may be limits to the extent to which the policy of one state, in many respects sovereign, may be subordinated to the policy of another. . . . Without attempting to say what their limits may be, we . . . direct our inquiry to the question whether a state to which a judgment for taxes is taken may have a policy against its enforcement meriting recognition as a permissible limitation upon the full-faith and credit clause. Of that question this court is the final arbiter . . . .
>
> . . . .
>
> We can perceive no greater possibility of embarrassment in litigating the validity of a judgment for taxes and enforcing it than any for the payment of money. The very purpose of the full faith and credit clause was to alter the status of the several states as independent foreign sovereignties, . . . and to make them integral parts of a single nation throughout which a remedy upon a just obligation might be demanded as of right, irrespective of the state of its origin. That purpose ought not lightly to be set aside out of a deference to a local policy which, if it exists, would seem to be too trivial to merit serious consideration when weighed against the policy of the constitutional provision and the interest of the state whose judgment is challenged. In the circumstances here disclosed [a judgment entered in a Wisconsin court for corporate income tax due, sought to be enforced in an Illinois court against an Illinois corporation] no state can be said to have a legitimate policy against payment of its neighbor's taxes the obligation of which has been judicially established by courts to whose judgments in practically every other instance it must give full faith and credit. Compare *Fauntleroy v. Lum.*

296 U.S. at 273–74, 276–77

(e) In *Milwaukee County v. White,* Justice Stone was careful to distinguish enforcement of a judgment for taxes from a suit on a tax claim not reduced to judgment, which the opinion expressly left open.ˣ If the State of Washington, for example, had sought to enforce its tax claim against the International Shoe Company by suit at its headquarters in Missouri,ʸ there was no

---

ᵛ *Huntington v. Attrill,* [1893] A.C. 150 (P.C.).

ʷ See *Restatement of the Law of Conflict of Laws* § 443 (1934).

ˣ 296 U.S. at 275.

ʸ See *International Shoe Co. v. State of Washington,* 326 U.S. 310 (1945), reproduced in Chapter 7, at p. 486, *supra.*

assurance that such a suit could have been entertained. In fact the Missouri Court of Appeals, in the very next year after the U.S. Supreme Court upheld Washington's resort to its own courts, upheld a suit by Oklahoma on a claim for income tax incurred by defendants (now residents of Missouri) when they were residents of Oklahoma. *State ex rel. Oklahoma Tax Commission v. Rodgers,* 238 Mo. App. 1115, 193 S.W.2d 919 (Mo. App. 1946), and somewhat more than half the states in the Union now entertain such suits, either by statute or by court decision.[z] But the Supreme Court has not required this result, even when the obligation sued on has been determined by an administrative decision,[aa] thus again illustrating the unique quality of a sister-state judgment in the American system of federalism.

[C] Full Faith and Credit and Jurisdiction of the Rendering Court

As one moves from clear to marginal bases for exercise of judicial jurisdiction, it is apparent that the prospect for enforcement of any judgment that might result become critical. If plaintiff's counsel is debating whether to bring his client's claim in F–1, where he feels most comfortable, where plaintiff is at home, and where he thinks the law (including choice of law) is favorable, but with which defendant's contacts are borderline, or alternatively to sue in F–2, where defendant is established and no issue of jurisdiction can arise, he will need to consider the risks and costs of enforcing a default judgment. If plaintiff does bring suit in F–1, defendant's counsel will need to make an immediate decision: Should the action be defended in F–1, or should he default? Of course, if defendant has or expects to have substantial assets in F–1 (including bank accounts, accounts receivable and even debtors who do business in F–1),[a] he may have little choice but to defend. If he has no assets at risk, defendant may elect to default, and if plaintiff secures a judgment, defendant may then challenge the jurisdictional basis of that judgment when plaintiff seeks to enforce the judgment in F–2. That, for example, was the strategy by the insurance company in *McGee v. International Insurance Co.,*[b] and by the trust companies in *Hanson v. Denckla.*[c] The difficulty with this strategy is that if the challenge to jurisdiction fails in F–2, there is no further opportunity to raise a substantive defense to the action. The judgment rendered in F–1, in other words, will be enforced.

A different strategy would be to challenge the jurisdiction of the F–1 court in F–1, which can now be joined in all states in the United States (and most other countries) with a defense to the merits.[d] Thus if defendant's motion to dismiss for lack of jurisdiction succeeds (whether

---

[z] See Greenberg, *Extrastate Enforcement of Tax Claims and Administrative Tax Determinations under the Full Faith and Credit Clause,* 43 Brooklyn L. Rev. 630 (1977).

[aa] See, e.g. *City of Philadelphia v. Cohen,* 11 N.Y.2d 401, 230 N.Y.S.2d 188, 184 N.E.2d 167 (1962), *cert. denied,* 371 U.S. 934 (1962). New York promptly enacted a statute reversing the effect of the *Cohen* case, on the basis of reciprocity, but not its holding on the requirements for full faith and credit. N.Y. Tax Law § 902.

[a] See *Intermeat Inc. v. American Poultry Co.,* Chapter 7, p. 596, *supra.*

[b] p. 491, *supra.*

[c] p. 498, *supra.*

[d] Provided the challenge to jurisdiction is raised in the first response (whether by answer or motion) to the complaint. See, e.g., Fed. R. Civ. Pro. Rule 12(b) and 12(h); N.Y. Civil Practice Law and Rules, R. 3211(a)(8) and R. 320(b). For description of the prior practice, in which it was often necessary to choose between a challenge to jurisdiction and a defense to the merits, see Note *Developments in the Law: State Court Jurisdiction,* 73 Harv. L. Rev. 909, 991–98 (1960).

in the court of first instance or on appeal), defendant prevails; if he loses on jurisdiction but plaintiff fails to establish his claim, defendant also prevails. But what if defendant loses his challenge to jurisdiction in F–1, and thereafter either withdraws from the action or loses on the merits, so that a judgment against him is rendered in F–1? If plaintiff now seeks to enforce his judgment in F–2, should defendant be able to there challenge the jurisdiction of the F–1 court? What if the challenge to jurisdiction of the F–1 court is directed to subject matter, rather than to personal jurisdiction?

BALDWIN v. IOWA STATE TRAVELING MEN'S ASSOCIATION

United States Supreme Court
283 U.S. 522 (1931)

MR. JUSTICE ROBERTS delivered the opinion of the Court.

[Plaintiff brought suit in state court in Missouri against defendant, an Iowa corporation. The corporation removed the action to the federal district court for the Western District of Missouri, and thereafter moved to dismiss for lack of jurisdiction over it. After a hearing in which both sides appeared, the district court in Missouri sustained jurisdiction. Thereafter the corporation did not appear further in the action, and judgment was entered against it.

When the judgment was not paid, plaintiff filed suit thereon in the U.S. District Court for the Southern District of Iowa. The corporation defended on the ground there had been no jurisdiction over it in the action in Missouri, and therefore there could be no action on the judgment of the Missouri district court. The Iowa district court and the Court of Appeals for the Eighth Circuit held for defendant, and plaintiff applied for certiorari]:

The substantial matter for determination is whether the judgment amounts to *res judicata* on the question of the jurisdiction of the court which rendered it over the person of the respondent. It is of no moment that the appearance was a special one expressly saving any submission to such jurisdiction. That fact would be important upon appeal from the judgment, and would save the question of the propriety of the court's decision on the matter even though after the motion had been overruled the respondent had proceeded, subject to a reserved objection and exception, to a trial on the merits. . . . The special appearance gives point to the fact that the respondent entered the Missouri court for the very purpose of litigating the question of jurisdiction over its person. It had the election not to appear at all. If, in the absence of appearance, the court had proceeded to judgment and the present suit had been brought thereon, respondent could have raised and tried out the issue in the present action, because it would never have had its day in court with respect to jurisdiction. *Thompson v. Whitman,* 18 Wall. 457; *Pennoyer v. Neff,* 95 U. S. 714; . . .

It had also the right to appeal from the decision of the Missouri District Court, as is shown by *Harkness v. Hyde* [98 U. S. 476], and the other authorities cited. It elected to follow neither of those courses, but, after having been defeated upon full hearing in its contention as to jurisdiction, it took no further steps, and the judgment in question resulted.

Public policy dictates that there be an end of litigation; that those who have contested an issue shall be bound by the result of the contest, and that matters once tried shall be considered forever settled as between the parties. We see no reason why this doctrine should not apply in every case where one voluntarily appears, presents his case and is fully heard, and why he should not, in the absence of fraud, be thereafter concluded by the judgment of the tribunal to which he has submitted his cause.

While this Court has never been called upon to determine the specific question here raised, several federal courts have held the judgment *res judicata* in like circumstances. . . . And we are in accord with this view.

. . .

The judgment is reversed and the cause remanded for further proceedings in conformity with this opinion.

DURFEE v. DUKE

United States Supreme Court
375 U.S. 106 (1963)

Mr. Justice Stewart delivered the opinion of the Court.

The United States Constitution requires that "Full Faith and Credit shall be given in each State to the . . . judicial Proceedings of every other State." The case before us presents questions arising under this constitutional provision and under the federal statute enacted to implement it.

In 1956 the petitioners brought an action against the respondent in a Nebraska court to quiet title to certain bottom land situated on the Missouri River. The main channel of that river forms the boundary between the States of Nebraska and Missouri. The Nebraska court had jurisdiction over the subject matter of the controversy only if the land in question was in Nebraska. Whether the land was Nebraska land depended entirely upon a factual question—whether a shift in the river's course had been caused by avulsion or accretion. The respondent appeared in the Nebraska court and through counsel fully litigated the issues, explicitly contesting the court's jurisdiction over the subject matter of the controversy. After a hearing the court found the issues in favor of the petitioners and ordered that title to the land be quieted in them. The respondent appealed, and the Supreme Court of Nebraska affirmed the judgment after a trial *de novo* on the record made in the lower court. The State Supreme Court specifically found that the rule of avulsion was applicable, that the land in question was in Nebraska, that the Nebraska courts therefore had jurisdiction of the subject matter of the litigation, and that title to the land was in the petitioners. *Durfee v. Keiffer,* 168 Neb. 272, 95 N. W. 2d 618. The respondent did not petition this Court for a writ of certiorari to review that judgment.

Two months later the respondent filed a suit against the petitioners in a Missouri court to quiet title to the same land. Her complaint alleged that the land was in Missouri. The suit was removed to a Federal District Court by reason of diversity of citizenship. The District Court after hearing evidence expressed the view that the land was in Missouri, but held that all the issues had been adjudicated and determined in the Nebraska litigation, and that the judgment of the Nebraska Supreme Court was *res judicata* and "is now binding upon this court." The Court of Appeals reversed, holding that the District Court was not required to give full faith and credit to the Nebraska judgment, and that normal *res judicata* principles were not applicable because the controversy involved land and a court in Missouri was therefore free to retry the question of the Nebraska court's jurisdiction over the subject matter. 308 F. 2d 209. We granted certiorari to consider a question important to the administration of justice in our federal system. . . . For the reasons that follow, we reverse the judgment before us.

The constitutional command of full faith and credit, as implemented by Congress, requires that "judicial proceedings . . . shall have the same full faith and credit in every court within the United States . . . as they have by law or usage in the courts of such State . . . from which they are taken." Full faith and credit thus generally requires every State to give to a judgment at least the *res judicata* effect which the judgment would be accorded in the State which rendered it. "By the Constitutional provision for full faith and credit the local doctrines of *res judicata*, speaking generally, become a part of national jurisprudence, and therefore federal questions cognizable here." Riley v. New York Trust Co., 315 U. S. 343, 349.

It is not questioned that the Nebraska courts would give full *res judicata* effect to the Nebraska judgment quieting title in the petitioners. It is the respondent's position, however, that whatever effect the Nebraska courts might give to the Nebraska judgment, the federal court in Missouri was free independently to determine whether the Nebraska court in fact had jurisdiction over the subject matter, *i. e.,* whether the land in question was actually in Nebraska.

In support of this position the respondent relies upon the many decisions of this Court which have held that a judgment of a court in one State is conclusive upon the merits in a court in another State only if the court in the first State had power to pass on the merits—had jurisdiction, that is, to render the judgment. . . . The principle has been restated and applied in a variety of contexts.

However, while it is established that a court in one State, when asked to give effect to the judgment of a court in another State, may constitutionally inquire into the foreign court's jurisdiction to render that judgment, the modern decisions of this Court have carefully delineated the permissible scope of such an inquiry. From these decisions there emerges the general rule that a judgment is entitled to full faith and credit—even as to questions of jurisdiction—when the second court's inquiry discloses that those questions have been fully and fairly litigated and finally decided in the court which rendered the original judgment.

With respect to questions of jurisdiction over the person,[8] this principle was unambiguously established in *Baldwin v. Iowa State Traveling Men's Assn.* There it was held that a federal court in Iowa must give binding effect to the judgment of a federal court in Missouri despite the claim that the original court did not have jurisdiction over the defendant's person, once it was shown to the court in Iowa that that question had been fully litigated in the Missouri forum. "Public policy," said the Court, "dictates that there be an end of litigation; that those who have contested an issue shall be bound by the result of the contest, and that matters once tried shall be considered forever settled as between the parties. We see no reason why this doctrine should not apply in every case where one voluntarily appears, presents his case and is fully heard, and why he should not, in the absence of fraud, be thereafter concluded by the judgment of the tribunal to which he has submitted his cause."

Following the *Baldwin* case, this Court soon made clear in a series of decisions that the general rule is no different when the claim is made that the original forum did not have jurisdiction over the subject matter. *Davis v. Davis,* 305 U. S. 32; *Stoll v. Gottlieb,* 305 U. S. 165; *Treinies v.*

---

[8] It is not disputed in the present case that the Nebraska courts had jurisdiction over the respondent's person. She entered a general appearance in the trial court, and initiated the appeal to the Nebraska Supreme Court.

Sunshine Mining Co., 308 U. S. 66; *Sherrer v. Sherrer,* 334 U. S. 343. In each of these cases the claim was made that a court, when asked to enforce the judgment of another forum, was free to retry the question of that forum's jurisdiction over the subject matter. In each case this Court held that since the question of subject-matter jurisdiction had been fully litigated in the original forum, the issue could not be retried in a subsequent action between the parties.

. . .

While this Court has not before had occasion to consider the applicability of the rule of *Davis, Stoll, Treinies,* and *Sherrer* to a case involving real property, we can discern no reason why the rule should not be fully applicable.

It is argued that an exception to this rule of jurisdictional finality should be made with respect to cases involving real property because of this Court's emphatic expressions of the doctrine that courts of one State are completely without jurisdiction directly to affect title to land in other States. This argument is wide of the mark. Courts of one State are equally without jurisdiction to dissolve the marriages of those domiciled in other States. But the location of land, like the domicile of a party to a divorce action, is a matter "to be resolved by judicial determination." *Sherrer v. Sherrer,* 334 U. S., at 349. The question remains whether, once the matter has been fully litigated and judicially determined, it can be retried in another State in litigation between the same parties. Upon the reason and authority of the cases we have discussed, it is clear that the answer must be in the negative.

It is to be emphasized that all that was ultimately determined in the Nebraska litigation was title to the land in question as between the parties to the litigation there. Nothing there decided, and nothing that could be decided in litigation between the same parties or their privies in Missouri, could bind either Missouri or Nebraska with respect to any controversy they might have, now or in the future, as to the location of the boundary between them, or as to their respective sovereignty over the land in question. . . .

Either State may at any time protect its interest by initiating independent judicial proceedings here. Cf. *Missouri v. Nebraska,* 196 U. S. 23.[15]

For the reasons stated, we hold in this case that the federal court in Missouri had the power and, upon proper averments, the duty to inquire into the jurisdiction of the Nebraska courts to render the decree quieting title to the land in the petitioners. We further hold that when that inquiry disclosed, as it did, that the jurisdictional issues had been fully and fairly litigated by the parties and finally determined in the Nebraska courts, the federal court in Missouri was correct in ruling that further inquiry was precluded. Accordingly the judgment of the Court of Appeals is reversed, and that of the District Court is affirmed.

It is so ordered.

Mr. Justice Black, concurring.

. . .

I concur in today's reversal of the Court of Appeals' judgment, but with the understanding that we are not deciding the question whether the respondent would continue to be bound by the Nebraska judgment should it later be authoritatively decided, either in an original proceeding

---

[15] The alternative of a negotiated settlement of any dispute between the States over the location of the boundary would also always be available. See U. S. Const., Art. I, § 10.

between the States in this Court or by a compact between the two States under Art. I, § 10, that the disputed tract is in Missouri.

NOTES AND QUESTIONS

(1)(a) Is the *Baldwin* case correctly decided?

(b) The Court says that public policy dictates that there be an end of litigation—the basic rationale for the doctrine of res judicata. Do you read the decision as made under the Full Faith and Credit clause? Compelled by the clause?[a] Note that this is not just an academic question: if it is based on a fundamental principle, it should apply equally to the judgment of a foreign court; if it is based on constitutional command, a different rule may be applied with respect to foreign country judgments. See the *Somportex* case, p. 708, *infra*.[b]

(2)(a) There is no way to tell from the opinion of the Supreme Court in *Baldwin* what the basis was for defendant's challenge to the jurisdiction of the Missouri court. Should it matter whether the controversy was a factual one—e.g., was X the defendant's agent in Missouri, or how many representatives did defendant have in the state, or a legal one—e.g., does an undisputed level of activity or representation constitute "doing business"?[c]

(b) Suppose the question of whether defendant participated in the F–1 action is itself in dispute. For instance, as happens not infrequently, an out-of-state defendant retains a lawyer in the forum state shortly before expiration of the time to respond to the complaint, the lawyer is tied up on other matters, and so he moves to extend the time in which to answer. When defendant subsequently moves to dismiss for lack of jurisdiction, he is met with a decision that the motion for more time constituted a general appearance, thus rendering the issue of jurisdiction moot. Thereafter defendant does not participate further, a judgment is rendered in plaintiff's favor, and enforcement is sought in F–2. Defendant says (i) the rendering court did not have jurisdiction; and (ii) he was unfairly denied an opportunity to raise the issue in F–1. Plaintiff (judgment creditor) says the judgment is entitled to the same faith and credit in F–2 as it has in F–1, and under F–1's law the issue of jurisdiction was waived. What result?

(c) Carrying the preceding example one stage further, suppose the F–2 court holds that the F–1 rule about appearance by motion to extend the time to answer violates due process, and therefore it will treat the F–1 judgment as a default judgment, permitting defendant to raise his challenge to F–1's jurisdiction. In ruling on that challenge, the F–2 court decides in defendant's favor. Plaintiff now seeks review in the Supreme Court asserting violation of the Full Faith and Credit clause. Should the answer depend on the Supreme Court's view of the fairness of the F–1 rule? Or would a principled response read something like the following?

---

[a] Though both Article IV § 1 of the Constitution and the implementing legislation read in terms of judicial proceedings of any *state*, it has long been clear that judgments of federal courts are entitled to the same full faith and credit as judgments of state courts. See, e.g., *Stoll v. Gottlieb*, 305 U.S. 165 (1938), 18 C. Wright, A. Miller, E. Cooper, *Federal Practice and Procedure* §§ 4468–69 (1981). The reverse question—credit in federal courts to state court judgments—does not arise, because the Constitution says "in each State" and the implementing legislation says "in every court within the United States."

[b] See also question (2)(c) for application of the question in an interstate context.

[c] In fact one question was whether a person on whom service was made was the Iowa Association's agent; the other was whether solicitation of insurance policies in Missouri by correspondence from Iowa constituted doing business. See *Baldwin v. Iowa State Traveling Men's Association*, 40 F.2d 357 (8th Cir. 1930).

Though we have grave doubts about the fairness in this case of F–1's rule depriving defendant of his opportunity to challenge the jurisdiction of the courts of F–1, and though that state's jurisdiction was questionable under the applicable precedents of this Court, Defendant's remedy was to appeal through the F–1 courts, if necessary to this Court. Having failed to do this, he cannot now avoid the consequences of the judgment rendered against him by resort to the processes of F–2. *Baldwin v. Iowa State Traveling Men's Association;* see also *Harris v. Balk.*

Reversed and judgment ordered enforced.

(3)(a) *Durfee v. Duke* requires some explanation. First, the question of jurisdiction itself. The Supreme Court has held in numerous cases that the common law rule that actions concerning land, including trespass, suits to quiet title, and proceedings concerning succession upon death, must be heard where the land is situated is (or at least informs) constitutional law. If this is true, it seems, a judgment of state *A* concerning land in state *B* is a judgment rendered without jurisdiction and therefore not entitled to full faith and credit.

Is this proposition drawn into question by *Durfee v. Duke*? Overruled?

(b) An interesting, though somewhat complicated example of the proposition stated came before the U.S. Supreme Court in *Clarke v. Clarke,* 178 U.S. 186 (1900). Mrs. Henry Clarke, a wealthy heiress and granddaughter of P. T. Barnum, died domiciled in South Carolina, leaving real and personal property in that state and real property (among other places) in Connecticut. According to her will, her property wherever situated was to be divided one third to her husband Henry, the other two thirds to Henry in trust for each of her children—Nancy, aged 5, and Julia, aged two months—until they reached 25, and then outright to the children. Julia died shortly after her mother, and the question was who would succeed to her share.

Henry, as executor and trustee brought an action in South Carolina seeking instructions as to how to carry out his duties. The South Carolina court held that the will of Mrs. Clarke worked an equitable conversion, with the effect of bringing the land under the jurisdiction of the South Carolina court.[d] As to Julia's share, it would pass under South Carolina's law of intestate succession, one half to Henry, her father, the other half to Nancy, her sister.

Henry thereupon commenced a proceeding in the probate court in Connecticut to enable him to carry out his duties, and was appointed administrator of Julia's estate. The Connecticut court held that no equitable conversion had taken place and that under Connecticut law, the entire estate of Julia must pass to her sister Nancy as Julia's sole heir. The Connecticut court rejected the contention that the decision of the South Carolina court with respect to equitable conversion was binding on it. Henry appealed to the U.S. Supreme Court, which affirmed:

> The proposition [advanced on behalf of Henry], when truly comprehended, amounts but to the contention that the laws of the respective States controlling the transmission of real property by will, or in case of intestacy, are operative only so long as there does not exist in a foreign jurisdiction a judgment or decree which in legal effect has changed the law of the situs of the real estate. This is but to contend that what cannot be done directly can

---

[d] Usually equitable conversion in a will case requires an express "direction to sell" in the will. South Carolina, but not Connecticut, inferred such a direction from the blending of real and personal property and instructions to "pay over the whole sum." See Hancock, *Full Faith and Credit to Foreign Laws and Judgments in Real Property Litigation: The Supreme Court and the Land Taboo,* 18 Stan. L. Rev. 1299, 1305–10 (1966).

§ 8.01   JURISDICTION AND JUDGMENTS   □   681

be accomplished by indirection, and that the fundamental principle which gives to a sovereignty an exclusive jurisdiction over the land within its borders is in legal effect dependent upon the non-existence of a decree of a court of another sovereignty determining the status of such land. Manifestly, however, an authority cannot be said to be exclusive, or even to exist at all, where its existence may be frustrated at any time.

. . . .

When, therefore, Henry P. Clarke, as administrator, applied to the Connecticut probate court to determine who was entitled to the "real estate" owned by the intestate . . . [that court's] power . . . was not limited by the fact that in order to determine who owned the real estate, it was necessary for the court to construe the will of the mother of the intestate. . . . Having a right to decide these questions, it was not constrained to adopt the construction of the will which had been announced by the court of South Carolina. . . . [I]t follows that because the court of Connecticut applied the law of that State in determining the devolution of the title to real estate there situated, thereby no violation of the constitutional requirement that full faith and credit must be given in one State to the judgments and decrees of the courts of another State, was brought about, as the decree of the South Carolina court, in the particular under consideration, was not entitled to be followed by the courts of Connecticut, by reason of a want of jurisdiction in the court of South Carolina over the particular subject matter which was sought to be concluded in Connecticut by such decree.

178 U.S. at 191–92,195.

Is this convincing? Is it inconsistent with *Durfee v. Duke*? Recall that in *Estate of Barrie*[e] the Supreme Court of Iowa (writing before *Durfee*) operated on the same assumptions as are reflected in *Clarke*.[f]

(c) Second, in order to understand *Durfee,* it is necessary to know the difference between *avulsion,* a sudden removal of land to another's estate, as by flood or earthquake, and *accretion,* a gradual increase of land, as by deposit of sand or mud caused by flowing water. Everyone agreed that the boundary between Durfee's property and Duke's property was marked by the riverbed, and that the riverbed shifted course. The Nebraska Supreme Court, on the basis of earlier precedents, had held that when a riverbed that forms a boundary changes gradually (i.e., by accretion), the boundary shifts along with the river; when the riverbed shifts suddenly, however (i.e., by avulsion), the prior boundary continues in effect. See *Durfee v. Keiffer,* 168 Neb. 272, 95 N.W.2d 618 (1959). The peculiar combination of fact and law that gave rise to the controversy was that the title dispute between Durfee and Duke depended on the same issue that determined whether Nebraska or Missouri had "subject matter jurisdiction." If the Nebraska court had found that the shift in the riverbed was due to accretion over time, it might have given judgment for Mrs. Duke, but more likely would have dismissed the action for lack of jurisdiction. In the actual case, the Nebraska court found the opposite: the river's shift was due to avulsion, the Nebraska court had jurisdiction, and the property belonged to Mr. Durfee.

(d) When Mrs. Duke now filed suit in Missouri, Mr. Durfee quite properly said (i) this controversy has been litigated, i.e., it is res judicata; and (ii) the judgment of the Nebraska court

---

[e] Chapter 1, page 20, *supra.*

[f] See also, e.g., *Fall v. Eastin,* 215 U.S. 1 (1909), in which a deed issued by a court in Washington in a divorce action in which both husband and wife participated was held ineffective to pass title to land in Nebraska.

is entitled to full faith and credit. Sure, there was a jurisdictional dispute, and it might have been decided incorrectly, but it was decided after full participation by both sides. The case, says Durfee, is governed by *Baldwin v. Iowa State Traveling Men's Association.* Is that right? Is there any persuasive argument the other way?[g]

(e) Suppose in the *Clarke* case summarized in (b) above, there had been a controversy about whether the property in Connecticut was or wasn't real property—say an apartment in a cooperative or condominium, or "shared time" in a resort complex—and the South Carolina court had held that Mrs. Clarke's interest was personalty. Instead of depending on a peculiar fiction,[h] in other words, the decision of the South Carolina court depended on a factual determination made after an evidentiary hearing. After *Durfee v. Duke,* would the variation on *Clarke* come out differently? What about the actual case?[i]

(4)(a) Suppose Smith, a citizen of Nebraska, sues Jones in federal district court in Nebraska for breach of contract, alleging diversity of citizenship. Jones says he is also a citizen of Nebraska and moves to dismiss for lack of diversity of citizenship. Following a hearing, the Nebraska court determines that Jones' house in Nebraska is only a vacation house and that he is really a citizen of Missouri. Accordingly, the action goes forward in Nebraska and judgment is entered for Smith on the contract claim. Smith now seeks to enforce the judgment in Missouri. Can Jones resist enforcement with the assertion that he is in fact a citizen of Nebraska, so that the federal court in Nebraska had no subject matter jurisdiction?[j]

(b) Does the answer differ if the action to enforce in Missouri is brought in federal court?

(c) Note, finally, that both the majority in *Durfee v. Duke* and Justice Black emphasize that no decision has been rendered that would be binding on Missouri and Nebraska themselves. The states were, evidently, not parties to the litigation and did not even file briefs as amici curiae. What is the difference between the position of the majority and Justice Black? Whose position is more persuasive?

(5)(a) The law of res judicata, and of full faith and credit, often distinguishes between judgments "on the merits" and judgments not on the merits. The *Restatement (Second) of Conflict of Laws,* for instance, says, in § 110:

> A judgment for the defendant that is not on the merits will be recognized in other states only as to issues actually decided.

Often, however, it is not clear whether a judgment is on the merits or not, and whether that determination is made by F–1, F–2, or national standards.

To take an easy case first, if P sues D in state *A,* and D successfully moves to dismiss because of defective service, it is clear that P can try to serve D again in *A,* or can sue him on the same

---

[g] It is interesting that the unanimous opinion of the Court of Appeals, holding that neither full faith and credit nor res judicata applied, was written by then Judge Harry Blackmun.

[h] See *Hancock,* Note d, *supra.*

[i] In *Underwriters National Assurance Co. v. North Carolina Life & Accident & Health Insurance Guaranty Ass'n.,* 455 U.S. 691 (1982), not involving land but involving jurisdiction by an Indiana court over a trust fund in North Carolina, the Supreme Court applied the principle of *Baldwin* and *Durfee* in striking down a North Carolina judgment concerning the trust fund which had disregarded the Indiana decision as lacking subject matter jurisdiction, without inquiring whether the issue had been "fully considered and finally determined" in the Indiana proceedings.

[j] Recall *Capron v. Van Noorden,* 6 U.S. (2 Cranch) 126 (1804), holding that the judgment of a federal court in a diversity case where diversity had not been established could be set aside, even on appeal by the original plaintiff who had lost the action on the merits.

cause of action in *B*. No determination has been made concerning D's liability to P. If, however, the service was held defective because X was determined not to be D's agent, that issue has been determined against P and he cannot attempt again to acquire jurisdiction over D by service on X.

(b) What about the effect of a dismissal in state *A* on the basis that the law of that state does not recognize the cause of action on which the claim is based, or that such a claim is contrary to its public policy? Recall the opinion of Judge Reese in *Case 3* of the *Adams v. Knickerbocker Nature Study Society* series,[k] when Mr. Adams sought to invoke the "outlaw on the highway" law of Massachusetts in his action in New York. Judge Reese (but none of his colleagues) wanted to dismiss on the grounds of "sound public policy," but to do so "without prejudice," i.e., without precluding Mr. Adams from bringing the same claim in Massachusetts or Vermont. Does that make sense? Is it consistent with full faith and credit?[l]

(c) Recall again the question put in Chapter 2 concerning *Mertz v. Mertz*.[m] After the New York court rejects Mrs. Mertz' action against her husband arising out of an automobile accident in Connecticut because under New York law (as it then stood) spouses could not sue each other in tort, can she bring an action in Connecticut based on the same accident? Was the decision of the New York court, in other words, "on the merits"?

(d) Suppose P sues D on a tort claim in State *A* and D defends successfully on the ground that *A*'s two-year statute of limitations has run. Assuming there is no applicable borrowing statute,[n] may P now sue D on the same claim in State *B*, which has a four-year statute?

(e) The Supreme Court has not passed on the question raised in the preceding paragraph, and there are not many decisions of other courts on the point. In one well known case, *Warner v. Buffalo Drydock Co.*, 67 F.2d 540 (2d Cir. 1933), the owners of a ship brought suit in federal court in Ohio for damage to their ship caused by defendant's alleged negligence; defendant pleaded the Ohio statute of limitations, and the court gave judgment for defendants. Thereafter, plaintiffs brought suit on the same claim in federal court in New York. The district court dismissed on the ground that the court in Ohio had rendered a judgment on the merits for defendant. The Court of Appeals, in an opinion by Judge Augustus N. Hand, reversed, stating:

> A decision that the Ohio statute of limitations barred the remedy was not res judicata in an action to assert plaintiff's rights in another forum. If the Ohio statute had extinguished the plaintiff's right, as in case of adverse possession of real property beyond the statutory period of limitation, the situation would be different.
>
> . . .
>
> All the court in Ohio decided was that the remedy was barred there because of laches. If another action had been brought in that court, the Ohio decree would have been a bar, for it determined the applicability of the Ohio statute of limitations which would necessarily have been involved in any jurisdiction where that statute operated. . . .
>
> The Ohio decree does not fail to bar the remedy in the present action because it is not res judicata as to everything which it decided, but because it did not decide that the plaintiffs'

---

[k] Chapter 3, p. 114, *supra*.

[l] Compare question (1)(a), p. 642, *supra*.

[m] Chapter 2, p. 65, question (6)(a).

[n] See Chapter 2, § 2.03.

claim was extinguished, but only that they could not sue in Ohio on account of the local statute of limitations.

. . .

In our opinion, the dismissal of the libel by the Ohio court was not a bar to the present action.

67 F.2d at 541–43.

The Supreme Court denied certiorari.[o]

Clearly this decision is inconsistent with a policy (if there is one) against forum shopping. Is it consistent with the Full Faith and Credit clause? On the basis of his opinion in *Yarborough*, how do you think Justice Brandeis would have come out if the *Buffalo Drydock* case had been heard by the Supreme Court?[p]

---

§ 8.02 Recognition of Foreign Country Judgments

[A] Comity

HILTON v. GUYOT

United States Supreme Court
159 U.S. 113 (1895)

THE first of these two cases was an action at law, brought December 18, 1885, in the Circuit Court of the United States for the Southern District of New York, by Gustave Bertin Guyot, as official liquidator of the firm of Charles Fortin & Co., and by the surviving members of that firm, all aliens and citizens of the Republic of France, against Henry Hilton and William Libbey, citizens of the United States and of the State of New York, and trading as copartners, in the cities of New York and Paris and elsewhere, under the firm name of A. T. Stewart & Co. The action was upon a judgment recovered in a French court at Paris in the Republic of France by the firm of Charles Fortin & Co., all whose members were French citizens, against Hilton and Libbey, trading as copartners as aforesaid, and citizens of the United States and of the State of New York.

The complaint alleged that in 1886, and since, during the time of all the transactions included in the judgment sued on, Hilton and Libbey, as successors to Alexander T. Stewart and Libbey, under the firm of A. T. Stewart & Co., carried on a general business as merchants in the cities of New York and Paris and elsewhere, and maintained a regular store and place of business at Paris; that during the same time Charles Fortin & Co. carried on the manufacture and sale of gloves at Paris, and the two firms had there large dealings in that business, and controversies arose in the adjustment of accounts between them.

---

[o] 291 U.S. 678 (1934). Note that this case was decided before *Erie R. Co. v. Tompkins*, and that the first (but apparently not the second) action was in admiralty. To the extent the case presents an issue under the Full Faith and Credit clause, of course, it is a federal question not affected by *Erie*; to the extent it is a question of common law res judicata, a federal court sitting in a diversity action would be required to follow state law.

[p] For an indication that the holding in *Buffalo Drydock* is still viewed as current law, see *Keeton v. Hustler*, Chapter 7, p. 546 and p. 556, question (6)(a).

. . .

The defendants, in their answer, set forth in detail the original contracts and transactions in France between the parties, and the subsequent dealings between them, modifying those contracts; and alleged that the plaintiffs had no just claim against the defendants, but that, on the contrary, the defendants, upon a just settlement of the accounts, were entitled to recover large sums from the plaintiffs.

The answer admitted the proceedings and judgments in the French courts; and that the defendants gave up their business in France before the judgment on appeal, and had no property within the jurisdiction of France, out of which that judgment could be collected.

. . .

The answer further alleged that, without any fault or negligence on the part of the defendants, there was not a full and fair trial of the controversies before the arbitrator, in that no witness was sworn or affirmed; in that Charles Fortin was permitted to make, and did make, statements not under oath, containing many falsehoods; in that the privilege of cross-examination of Fortin and other persons who made statements before the arbitrator was denied to the defendants; and in that extracts from printed newspapers, the knowledge of which was not brought home to the defendants, and letters and other communications in writing between Fortin & Co. and third persons, to which the defendants were neither privy nor party, were received by the arbitrator; that without such improper evidence the judgment would not have been obtained; and that the arbitrator was deceived and misled by the false and fraudulent accounts introduced by Fortin & Co., and by the hearsay testimony given without the solemnity of an oath and without cross-examination, and by the fraudulent suppression of the books and papers.

The answer further alleged that Fortin & Co. made up their statements and accounts falsely and fraudulently, and with intent to deceive the defendants and the arbitrator and the said courts of France, and those courts were deceived and misled thereby; that, owing to the fraudulent suppression of the books and papers of Fortin & Co., upon the trial, and the false statements of Fortin regarding matters involved in the controversy, the arbitrator and the courts of France "were deceived and misled in regard to the merits of the controversies pending before them and wrongfully decided against said Stewart & Co. as hereinbefore stated; that said judgment hereinbefore mentioned is fraudulent, and based upon false and fraudulent accounts and statements, and is erroneous, in fact and in law, and is void; that the trial hereinbefore mentioned was not conducted according to the usages and practice of the common law, and the allegations and proofs given by said Fortin & Co., upon which said judgment is founded, would not be competent or admissible in any court or tribunal of the United States in any suit between the same parties involving the same subject-matter; and it is contrary to natural justice and public policy that the said judgment should be enforced against a citizen of the United States; and that, if there had been a full and fair trial upon the merits of the controversies so pending before said tribunals, no judgment would have been obtained against said Stewart & Co.

Defendants, further answering, allege that it is contrary to natural justice, that the judgment hereinbefore mentioned should be enforced without an examination of the merits thereof; that by the laws of the Republic of France, to wit, article 181 [121] of the Royal Ordinance of June 15, 1629, it is provided, namely:

> Judgments rendered, contracts or obligations recognized, in foreign kingdoms and sovereignties, for any cause whatever, shall give rise to no lien or execution in our kingdom.

Thus the contracts shall stand for simple promises, and notwithstanding such judgments our subjects against whom they have been rendered may contest their rights anew before our own judges.

. . .

And it is further provided by the laws of France, . . . that no comity is displayed toward the judgments of tribunals of foreign countries against the citizens of France, when sued upon in said courts of France, and the merits of the controversies upon which the said judgments are based are examined anew, unless a treaty to the contrary effect exists between the said Republic of France and the country in which such judgment is obtained; that no treaty exists between the said Republic of France and the United States, by the terms or effect of which the judgments of either country are prevented from being examined anew upon the merits, when sued upon in the courts of the country other than that in which it is obtained; that the tribunals of the Republic of France give no force and effect, within the jurisdiction of the said country, to the duly rendered judgments of the courts of competent jurisdiction of the United States against citizens of France after proper personal service of the process of said courts is made thereon in this country.

. . .

The records of the judgments of the French courts, put in evidence by the plaintiffs, showed that all the matters now relied on to show fraud were contested in and considered by those courts.

The plaintiffs objected to all the evidence offered by the defendants, on the grounds that the matters offered to be proved were irrelevant, immaterial, and incompetent; that, in respect to them, the defendants were concluded by the judgment sued on and given in evidence; and that none of those matters, if proved, would be a defence to this action upon that judgment.

The [Circuit] court declined to admit any of the evidence so offered by the defendants, and directed a verdict for the plaintiffs in the sum of $277,775.44, being the amount of the French judgment and interest. The defendants, having duly excepted to the rulings and direction of the court, sued out a writ of error.

MR. JUSTICE GRAY, after stating the case, delivered the opinion of the court.

These two cases, the one at law and the other in equity, of *Hilton v. Guyot,* and the case of *Ritchie v. McMullen* which has been under advisement at the same time, present important questions relating to the force and effect of foreign judgments, not hitherto adjudicated by this court, which have been argued with great learning and ability, and which require for their satisfactory determination a full consideration of the authorities. To avoid confusion in indicating the parties, it will be convenient first to take the case at law of *Hilton v. Guyot.*

International law, in its widest and most comprehensive sense—including not only questions of right between nations, governed by what has been appropriately called the law of nations; but also questions arising under what is usually called private international law, or the conflict of laws, and concerning the rights of persons within the territory and dominion of one nation, by reason of acts, private or public, done within the dominions of another nation—is part of our law, and must be ascertained and administered by the courts of justice, as often as such questions are presented in litigation between man and man, duly submitted to their determination.

The most certain guide, no doubt, for the decision of such questions is a treaty or a statute of this country. But when, as is the case here, there is no written law upon the subject, the duty still rests upon the judicial tribunals of ascertaining and declaring what the law is, whenever it becomes necessary to do so, in order to determine the rights of parties to suits regularly brought before them. In doing this, the courts must obtain such aid as they can from judicial decisions, from the works of jurists and commentators, and from the acts and usages of civilized nations.

No law has any effect, of its own force, beyond the limits of the sovereignty from which its authority is derived. The extent to which the law of one nation, as put in force within its territory, whether by executive order, by legislative act, or by judicial decree, shall be allowed to operate within the dominion of another nation, depends upon what our greatest jurists have been content to call "the comity of nations." Although the phrase has been often criticised, no satisfactory substitute has been suggested.

"Comity," in the legal sense, is neither a matter of absolute obligation, on the one hand, nor of mere courtesy and good will, upon the other. But it is the recognition which one nation allows within its territory to the legislative, executive or judicial acts of another nation, having due regard both to international duty and convenience, and to the rights of its own citizens or of other persons who are under the protection of its laws.

. . .

A judgment *in rem,* adjudicating the title to a ship or other movable property within the custody of the court, is treated as valid everywhere. . . .

A judgment affecting the status of persons, such as a decree confirming or dissolving a marriage, is recognized as valid in every country, unless contrary to the policy of its own law.

. . .

Other judgments, not strictly *in rem,* under which a person has been compelled to pay money, are so far conclusive that the justice of the payment cannot be impeached in another country, so as to compel him to pay it again. For instance, a judgment in foreign attachment is conclusive, as between the parties, of the right to the property or money attached. *Story on Conflict of Laws,* (2d ed.) § 592 *a.* . . .

. . .

The extraterritorial effect of judgments *in personam,* at law or in equity, may differ, according to the parties to the cause. A judgment of that kind between two citizens or residents of the country, and thereby subject to the jurisdiction, in which it is rendered, may be held conclusive as between them everywhere. So, if a foreigner invokes the jurisdiction by bringing an action against a citizen, both may be held bound by a judgment in favor of either. And if a citizen sues a foreigner, and judgment is rendered in favor of the latter, both may be held equally bound.

The effect to which a judgment, purely executory, rendered in favor of a citizen or resident of the country, in a suit there brought by him against a foreigner, may be entitled in an action thereon against the latter in his own country—as is the case now before us—presents a more difficult question, upon which there has been some diversity of opinion.

Early in the last century, it was settled in England that a foreign judgment on a debt was considered not, like a judgment of a domestic court of record, as a record or a specialty, a lawful consideration for which was conclusively presumed; but as a simple contract only.

. . .

The law upon this subject, as understood in the United States, at the time of their separation from the mother country, was clearly set forth by Chief Justice Parsons, speaking for the Supreme

Judicial Court of Massachusetts, in 1813, and by Mr. Justice Story, in his Commentaries on the Constitution of the United States, published in 1833. Both those eminent jurists declared that by the law of England the general rule was that foreign judgments were only *prima facie* evidence of the matter which they purported to decide; and that by the common law, before the American Revolution, all the courts of the several Colonies and States were deemed foreign to each other, and consequently judgments rendered by any one of them were considered as foreign judgments, and their merits reëxaminable in another Colony, not only as to the jurisdiction of the court which pronounced them, but also as to the merits of the controversy, to the extent to which they were understood to be reëxaminable in England.

. . .

It was because of that condition of the law, as between the American Colonies and States, that the United States, at the very beginning of their existence as a nation, ordained that full faith and credit should be given to the judgments of one of the States of the Union in the courts of another of those States.

By the Articles of Confederation of 1777, art. 4, § 3, "Full faith and credit shall be given, in each of these States, to the records, acts and judicial proceedings of the courts and magistrates of every other State." 1 Stat. 4. By the Constitution of the United States, art. 4, § 1, "Full faith and credit shall be given in each State to the public acts, records and judicial proceedings of every other State; and the Congress may by general laws prescribe the manner in which such acts, such faith and credit given to them in every court within the United States, as they have by law or usage in the courts of the State from whence the said records are or shall be taken." Act of May 26, 1790, c. 11, 1 Stat. 122; Rev. Stat. § 905.

. . .

The decisions of this court have clearly recognized that judgments of a foreign state are *prima facie* evidence only, and that, but for these constitutional and legislative provisions, judgments of a State of the Union, when sued upon in another State, would have no greater effect.

. . .

In view of all the authorities upon the subject, and of the trend of judicial opinion in this country and in England, following the lead of Kent and Story, we are satisfied that, where there has been opportunity for a full and fair trial abroad before a court of competent jurisdiction, conducting the trial upon regular proceedings, after due citation or voluntary appearance of the defendant, and under a system of jurisprudence likely to secure an impartial administration of justice between the citizens of its own country and those of other countries, and there is nothing to show either prejudice in the court, or in the system of laws under which it was sitting, or fraud in procuring the judgment, or any other special reason why the comity of this nation should not allow it full effect, the merits of the case should not, in an action brought in this country upon the judgment, be tried afresh, as on a new trial or an appeal, upon the mere assertion of the party that the judgment was erroneous in law or in fact. The defendants, therefore, cannot be permitted, upon that general ground, to contest the validity or the effect of the judgment sued on.

But they have sought to impeach that judgment upon several other grounds, which require separate consideration.

It is objected that the appearance and litigation of the defendants in the French tribunals were not voluntary, but by legal compulsion, and therefore that the French courts never acquired such jurisdiction over the defendants, that they should be held bound by the judgment.

Upon the question what should be considered such a voluntary appearance, as to amount to a submission to the jurisdiction of a foreign court, there has been some difference of opinion in England.

. . .

But it is now settled in England that, while an appearance by the defendant in a court of a foreign country, for the purpose of protecting his property already in the possession of that court, may not be deemed a voluntary appearance, yet an appearance solely for the purpose of protecting other property in that country from seizure is considered as a voluntary appearance.

The present case is not one of a person travelling through or casually found in a foreign country. The defendants, although they were not citizens or residents of France, but were citizens and residents of the State of New York, and their principal place of business was in the city of New York, yet had a storehouse and an agent in Paris, and were accustomed to purchase large quantities of goods there, although they did not make sales in France. Under such circumstances, evidence that their sole object in appearing and carrying on the litigation in the French courts was to prevent property, in their storehouse at Paris, belonging to them, and within the jurisdiction, but not in the custody, of those courts, from being taken in satisfaction of any judgment that might be recovered against them, would not, according to our law, show that those courts did not acquire jurisdiction of the persons of the defendants.

It is next objected that in those courts one of the plaintiffs was permitted to testify not under oath, and was not subjected to cross-examination by the opposite party, and that the defendants were, therefore, deprived of safeguards which are by our law considered essential to secure honesty and to detect fraud in a witness; and also that documents and papers were admitted in evidence, with which the defendants had no connection, and which would not be admissible under our own system of jurisprudence. But it having been shown by the plaintiffs, and hardly denied by the defendants, that the practice followed and the method of examining witnesses were according to the laws of France, we are not prepared to hold that the fact that the procedure in these respects differed from that of our own courts is, of itself, a sufficient ground for impeaching the foreign judgment.

It is also contended that a part of the plaintiffs' claim is affected by one of the contracts between the parties having been made in violation of the revenue laws of the United States, requiring goods to be invoiced at their actual market value. Rev. Stat. § 2854. It may be assumed that, as the courts of a country will not enforce contracts made abroad in evasion or fraud of its own laws, so they will not enforce a foreign judgment upon such a contract. But as this point does not affect the whole claim in this case, it is sufficient, for present purposes, to say that there does not appear to have been any distinct offer to prove that the invoice value of any of the goods sold by the plaintiffs to the defendants was agreed between them to be, or was, in fact, lower than the actual market value of the goods.

It must, however, always be kept in mind that it is the paramount duty of the court, before which any suit is brought, to see to it that the parties have had a fair and impartial trial, before a final decision is rendered against either party.

When an action is brought in a court of this country, by a citizen of a foreign country against one of our own citizens, to recover a sum of money adjudged by a court of that country to be due from the defendant to the plaintiff, and the foreign judgment appears to have been rendered by a competent court, having jurisdiction of the cause and of the parties, and upon due allegations and proofs, and opportunity to defend against them, and its proceedings are according to the course of a civilized jurisprudence, and are stated in a clear and formal record, the judgment is *prima facie* evidence, at least, of the truth of the matter adjudged; and it should be held conclusive upon the merits tried in the foreign court, unless some special ground is shown for impeaching the judgment, as by showing that it was affected by fraud or prejudice, or that, by the principles of international law, and by the comity of our own country, it should not be given full credit and effect.

There is no doubt that both in this country, as appears by the authorities already cited, and in England, a foreign judgment may be impeached for fraud.

. . .

Under what circumstances this may be done does not appear to have ever been the subject of judicial investigation in this country.

. . .

In the case at bar, the defendants offered to prove, in much detail, that the plaintiffs presented to the French court of first instance and to the arbitrator appointed by that court, and upon whose report its judgment was largely based, false and fraudulent statements and accounts against the defendants, by which the arbitrator and the French courts were deceived and misled, and their judgments were based upon such false and fraudulent statements and accounts. This offer, if satisfactorily proved, would, according to the decisions of the English Court of Appeal . . . be a sufficient ground for impeaching the foreign judgment, and examining into the merits of the original claim.

But whether those decisions can be followed in regard to foreign judgments, consistently with our own decisions as to impeaching domestic judgments for fraud, it is unnecessary in this case to determine, because there is a distinct and independent ground upon which we are satisfied that the comity of our nation does not require us to give conclusive effect to the judgments of the courts of France; and that ground is, the want of reciprocity, on the part of France, as to the effect to be given to the judgments of this and other foreign countries.

In France, the Royal Ordinance of June 15, 1629, art. 121, provided as follows: "Judgments rendered, contracts or obligations recognized, in foreign kingdoms and sovereignties, for any cause whatever, shall have no lien or execution in our kingdom. Thus the contracts shall stand for simple promises; and, notwithstanding the judgments, our subjects against whom they have been rendered may contest their rights anew before our judges." Touillier, Droit Civil, lib. 3, tit. 3, c. 6, sect. 3, no. 77.

By the French Code of Civil Procedure, art. 546, "Judgments rendered by foreign tribunals, and acts acknowledged before foreign officers, shall not be capable of execution in France, except in the manner and in the cases provided by articles 2123 and 2128 of the Civil Code," which are as follows: By article 2123, "A lien cannot arise from judgments rendered in a foreign country, except as far as they have been declared executory by a French tribunal; without prejudice to provisions to the contrary which may exist in public laws and treaties." By article 2128, "Contracts entered into in a foreign country cannot give a lien upon property in France, if there are no provisions contrary to this principle in public laws or in treaties." Touillier, *ub. sup.* no. 84.

The defendants, in their answer, cited the above provisions of the statutes of France, and alleged, and at the trial offered to prove, that, by the construction given to these statutes by the judicial tribunals of France, when the judgments of tribunals of foreign countries against the

§ 8.02   **JURISDICTION AND JUDGMENTS**   ☐   **691**

citizens of France are sued upon in the courts of France, the merits of the controversies upon which those judgments are based are examined anew, unless a treaty to the contrary effect exists between the Republic of France and the country in which such judgment is obtained, (which is not the case between the Republic of France and the United States,) and that the tribunals of the Republic of France give no force and effect, within the jurisdiction of that country, to the judgments duly rendered by courts of competent jurisdiction of the United States against citizens of France after proper personal service of the process of those courts has been made thereon in this country. We are of opinion that this evidence should have been admitted.

[The Court cites numerous decisions and authors of treatises on international law, including the following:]

Mr. Justice Story said: "If a civilized nation seeks to have the sentences of its own courts held of any validity elsewhere, they ought to have a just regard to the rights and usages of other civilized nations, and the principles of public and national law in the administration of justice." *Bradstreet v. Neptune Ins. Co.,* 3 Sumner, 600, 608.

Mr. Justice Woodbury said that judgments *in personam,* rendered under a foreign government, "are, *ex comitate,* treated with respect, according to the nature of the judgment, and the character of the tribunal which rendered it, and the reciprocal mode, if any, in which that government treats our judgments;" and added, "Nor can much comity be asked for the judgments of another nation, which, like France, pays no respect to those of other countries." *Burnham v. Webster,* 1 Woodb. & Min. 172, 175, 179.

Mr. Justice Cooley said, "True comity is equality; we should demand nothing more, and concede nothing less." *McEwan v. Zimmer,* 38 Michigan, 765, 769.

Mr. Wheaton said: "There is no obligation, recognized by legislators, public authorities, and publicists, to regard foreign laws; but their application is admitted only from considerations of utility and the mutual convenience of States—*ex comitate, ob reciprocam utilitatem."* "The general comity, utility and convenience of nations have, however, established a usage among most civilized States, by which the final judgments of foreign courts of competent jurisdiction are reciprocally carried into execution." *Wheaton's International Law,* (8th ed.) §§ 79, 147.

Since Story, Kent and Wheaton wrote their commentaries, many books and essays have been published upon the subject of the effect to be allowed by the courts of one country to the judgments of another, with references to the statutes and decisions in various countries. Among the principal ones are Foelix, *Droit International Privé,* (4th ed. by Demangeat, 1866) lib. 2, tits. 7, 8; Moreau, *Effets Internationaux des Jugements* (1884); *Piggott, on Foreign Judgments* (2d ed. 1884); Constant, *de l'Exécution des Jugements Étrangers* (2d ed. 1890), giving the text of the articles of most of the modern codes upon the subject, and of French treaties with Italian, German and Swiss States; and numerous papers in Clunet's *Journal de Droit International Privé,* established in 1874, and continued to the present time. For the reasons stated at the outset of this opinion, we have not thought it important to state the conflicting theories of continental commentators and essayists as to what each may think the law ought to be; but have referred to their works only for evidence of authoritative declarations, legislative or judicial, of what the law is.

By the law of France, settled by a series of uniform decisions of the Court of Cassation, the highest judicial tribunal, for more than half a century, no foreign judgment can be rendered executory in France without a review of the judgment *au fond*—to the bottom, including the whole merits of the cause of action on which the judgment rests.

[The Court summarizes a leading French case in which the judgment of an American court was denied enforcement, and reviews the enforcement practice of more than twenty other states.]

It appears, therefore, that there is hardly a civilized nation on either continent, which, by its general law, allows conclusive effect to an executory foreign judgment for the recovery of money. In France, and in a few smaller States—Norway, Portugal, Greece, Monaco, and Haiti—the merits of the controversy are reviewed, as of course, allowing to the foreign judgment, at the most, no more effect than of being *prima facie* evidence of the justice of the claim. In the great majority of the countries on the continent of Europe—in Belgium, Holland, Denmark, Sweden, Germany, in many cantons of Switzerland, in Russia and Poland, in Roumania, in Austria and Hungary, (perhaps in Italy,) and in Spain—as well as in Egypt, in Mexico, and in a great part of South America, the judgment rendered in a foreign country is allowed the same effect only as the courts of that country allow to the judgments of the country in which the judgment in question is sought to be executed.

The prediction of Mr. Justice Story (in § 618 of his *Commentaries on the Conflict of Laws,* already cited), has thus been fulfilled, and the rule of reciprocity has worked itself firmly into the structure of international jurisprudence.

The reasonable, if not the necessary, conclusion appears to us to be that judgments rendered in France, or in any other foreign country, by the laws of which our own judgments are reviewable upon the merits, are not entitled to full credit and conclusive effect when sued upon in this country, but are *prima facie* evidence only of the justice of the plaintiffs' claim.

In holding such a judgment, for want of reciprocity, not to be conclusive evidence of the merits of the claim, we do not proceed upon any theory of retaliation upon one person by reason of injustice done to another; but upon the broad ground that international law is founded upon mutuality and reciprocity, and that by the principles of international law recognized in most civilized nations, and by the comity of our own country, which it is our judicial duty to know and to declare, the judgment is not entitled to be considered conclusive.

. . .

MR. CHIEF JUSTICE FULLER, with whom concurred MR. JUSTICE HARLAN, MR. JUSTICE BREWER, and MR. JUSTICE JACKSON, dissenting.

Plaintiffs brought their action on a judgment recovered by them against the defendants in the courts of France, which courts had jurisdiction over person and subject-matter, and in respect of which judgment no fraud was alleged, except in particulars contested in and considered by the French courts. The question is whether under these circumstances, and in the absence of a treaty or act of Congress, the judgment is reëxaminable upon the merits. This question I regard as one to be determined by the ordinary and settled rule in respect of allowing a party, who has had an opportunity to prove his case in a competent court, to retry it on the merits, and it seems to me that the doctrine of *res judicata* applicable to domestic judgments should be applied to foreign judgments as well, and rests on the same general ground of public policy that there should be an end of litigation.

This application of the doctrine is in accordance with our own jurisprudence, and it is not necessary that we should hold it to be required by some rule of international law. The fundamental principle concerning judgments is that disputes are finally determined by them, and I am unable to perceive why a judgment *in personam* which is not open to question on the ground of want of jurisdiction, either intrinsically or over the parties, or of fraud, or on any other recognized ground of impeachment, should not be held *inter partes,* though recovered abroad, conclusive on the merits.

Judgments are executory while unpaid, but in this country execution is not given upon a foreign judgment as such, it being enforced through a new judgment obtained in an action brought for that purpose.

The principle that requires litigation to be treated as terminated by final judgment properly rendered, is as applicable to a judgment proceeded on in such an action, as to any other, and forbids the allowance to the judgment debtor of a retrial of the original cause of action, as of right, in disregard of the obligation to pay arising on the judgment and of the rights acquired by the judgment creditor thereby.

That any other conclusion is inadmissible is forcibly illustrated by the case in hand. Plaintiffs in error were trading copartners in Paris as well as in New York, and had a place of business in Paris at the time of these transactions and of the commencement of the suit against them in France. The subjects of the suit were commercial transactions, having their origin, and partly performed, in France under a contract there made, and alleged to be modified by the dealings of the parties there; and one of the claims against them was for goods sold to them there. They appeared generally in the case, without protest, and by counterclaims relating to the same general course of business, a part of them only connected with the claims against them, became actors in the suit and submitted to the courts their own claims for affirmative relief, as well as the claims against them. The courts were competent and they took the chances of a decision in their favor. As traders in France they were under the protection of its laws and were bound by its laws, its commercial usages and its rules of procedure. The fact that they were Americans and the opposite parties were citizens of France is immaterial, and there is no suggestion on the record that those courts proceeded on any other ground than that all litigants, whatever their nationality, were entitled to equal justice therein. If plaintiffs in error had succeeded in their cross suit and recovered judgment against defendants in error, and had sued them here on that judgment, defendants in error would not have been permitted to say that the judgment in France was not conclusive against them. As it was, defendants in error recovered, and I think plaintiffs in error are not entitled to try their fortune anew before the courts of this country on the same matters voluntarily submitted by them to the decision of the foreign tribunal. We are dealing with the judgment of a court of a civilized country, whose laws and system of justice recognize the general rules in respect to property and rights between man and man prevailing among all civilized peoples. Obviously the last persons who should be heard to complain are those who identified themselves with the business of that country, knowing that all their transactions there would be subject to the local laws and modes of doing business. The French courts appear to have acted "judicially, honestly, and with the intention to arrive at the right conclusion;" and a result thus reached ought not to be disturbed.

. . .

In any aspect, it is difficult to see why rights acquired under foreign judgments do not belong to the category of private rights acquired under foreign laws. Now the rule is universal in this country that private rights acquired under the laws of foreign states will be respected and enforced in our courts unless contrary to the policy or prejudicial to the interests of the state where this is sought to be done; and although the source of this rule may have been the comity characterizing the intercourse between nations, it prevails to-day by its own strength, and the right to the application of the law to which the particular transaction is subject is a juridical right.

And, without going into the refinements of the publicists on the subject, it appears to me that that law finds authoritative expression in the judgments of courts of competent jurisdiction over parties and subject-matter.

It is held by the majority of the court that defendants cannot be permitted to contest the validity and effect of this judgment on the general ground that it was erroneous in law or in fact; and the special grounds relied on are *seriatim* rejected. In respect of the last of these, that of fraud, it is said that it is unnecessary in this case to decide whether certain decisions cited in regard to impeaching foreign judgments for fraud could be followed consistently with our own decisions as to impeaching domestic judgments for that reason, "because there is a distinct and independent ground upon which we are satisfied that the comity of our nation does not require us to give conclusive effect to the judgments of the courts of France, and that ground is the want of reciprocity on the part of France as to the effect to be given to the judgments of this and other foreign countries." And the conclusion is announced to be "that judgments rendered in France or in any other foreign country, by the laws of which our own judgments are reviewable upon the merits, are not entitled to full credit and conclusive effect when sued upon in this country, but are *prima facie* evidence only of the justice of the plaintiff's claim." In other words, that although no special ground exists for impeaching the original justice of a judgment, such as want of jurisdiction or fraud, the right to retry the merits of the original cause at large, defendant being put upon proving those merits, should be accorded in every suit on judgments recovered in countries where our own judgments are not given full effect, on that ground merely.

I cannot yield my assent to the proposition that because by legislation and judicial decision in France that effect is not there given to judgments recovered in this country which, according to our jurisprudence, we think should be given to judgments wherever recovered, (subject, of course, to the recognized exceptions), therefore we should pursue the same line of conduct as respects the judgments of French tribunals. The application of the doctrine of *res judicata* does not rest in discretion; and it is for the government, and not for its courts, to adopt the principle of retorsion, if deemed under any circumstances desirable or necessary.

As the court expressly abstains from deciding whether the judgment is impeachable on the ground of fraud, I refrain from any observations on that branch of the case.

JOHNSTON v. COMPAGNIE GENERALE TRANSATLANTIQUE

New York Court of Appeals
242 N.Y. 381, 152 N.E. 121 (1926)

POUND, J.

The controversy arises over an alleged wrongful delivery of goods by the defendant, a steamship carrier, which is a foreign corporation organized under the laws of the Republic of France. Plaintiff is the assignee of triplicate bills of lading issued in New York, under which one Frank E. Webb shipped the goods from New York to Havre. Defendant delivered the goods to other parties upon presentation of a non-negotiable copy of the bill of lading which Webb retained as an office copy not used for presentation to secure the delivery of the goods.

Defendant set up as a defense an adjudication of the Tribunal of Commerce at Paris in favor of defendant upon the same cause of action, in an action brought by plaintiff thereon and established on the trial that the French judgment was the final judgment on the merits of a court of competent jurisdiction. No attempt was made to impeach it for fraud.

The courts below refused to give effect to the French judgment on the authority of *Hilton v. Guyot,* decided in 1895, for the reason that by the law of France no foreign judgment can be rendered executory in France without a review of the judgment *au fond,* that is, of the whole merits of the cause of action on which the judgment rests; that for want of reciprocity the courts of this State are not bound by the judgment but will, in their discretion, examine the rights of the parties as fully and absolutely as if the matter had never been submitted to the French court; and that on the merits the French judgment was contrary to the principles of our law and should be disregarded.

The New York rule was stated in *Dunstan v. Higgins* (138 N. Y. 70), decided in 1893, as follows:

> It is the settled law of this State that a foreign judgment is conclusive upon the merits. It can be impeached only by proof that the court in which it was rendered had not jurisdiction of the subject matter of the action or of the person of the defendant, or that it was procured by means of fraud. . . .

No case has previously arisen in this State which necessarily involved the consideration of *Hilton v. Guyot.* The question here presented may be regarded as an open one in this court. . . .

To what extent is this court bound by *Hilton v. Guyot*? It is argued with some force that questions of international relations and the comity of nations are to be determined by the Supreme Court of the United States; that there is no such thing as comity of nations between the State of New York and the Republic of France and that the decision in *Hilton v. Guyot* is controlling as a statement of the law. But the question is one of private rather than public international law, of private right rather than public relations and our courts will recognize private rights acquired under foreign laws and the sufficiency of the evidence establishing such rights. A right acquired under a foreign judgment may be established in this State without reference to the rules of evidence laid down by the courts of the United States. Comity is not a rule of law, but it is a rule of "practice, convenience and expediency. It is something more than mere courtesy, which implies only deference to the opinion of others, since it has a substantial value in securing uniformity of decision, and discouraging repeated litigation of the same question." (BROWN, J., in *Mast, Foos & Co. v. Stover Mfg. Co.,* 177 U. S. 485, 488.) It, therefore, rests, not on the basis of reciprocity, but rather upon the persuasiveness of the foreign judgment. (*Loucks v. Standard Oil Co.,* 224 N. Y. 99, 111.) When the whole of the facts appear to have been inquired into by the French courts, judicially, honestly and with full jurisdiction and with the intention to arrive at the right conclusion, and when they have heard the facts and come to a conclusion, it should no longer be open to the party invoking the foreign court against a resident of France to ask the American court to sit as a court of appeal from that which gave the judgment. I reach the conclusion that this court is not bound to follow the *Hilton* case and reverse its previous rulings.

The reasoning of the learned justice who wrote the prevailing opinion is, however, entitled to most respectful consideration. Nor need we disregard the authority of the *Hilton* case. We may limit it to the questions actually decided. Mr. Justice GRAY says: "In England, and in the Colonies subject to the law of England, the fraud alleged in its [the French judgment] procurement would be a sufficient ground for disregarding it." As this State has always permitted foreign judgments to be impeached for fraud, the preceding fifty-four pages of the opinion may be regarded as magnificent dictum, entitled to the utmost respect, but not determinative of the question.

Furthermore, the learned justice limits his discussion to the effect which a judgment, purely executory, rendered in favor of a citizen or resident of France in a suit there brought by him against a citizen of the United States may be entitled to in an action thereon in the United States. Here the plaintiff was the actor in the French court. After having sought the jurisdiction of the foreign tribunal, brought the defendant into that court and litigated the question there, he now seeks to impeach the judgment rendered against him. The principles of comity should give conclusiveness to such a judgment as a bar to the present action. *Dicey on Conflict of Laws* (3d ed. p. 455) states separately the rule as to foreign judgments pleaded as a defense, as follows: "A valid foreign judgment *in personam* if it is final and conclusive on the merits (but not otherwise) is a good defense to an action for the same matter when either (1) the judgment was in favor of defendant or (2) the judgment in favor of the plaintiff has been satisfied." The law of the State of New York remains unchanged and the French judgment should be given full faith and credit.

The judgments should be reversed and the complaint dismissed, with costs in all courts.

NOTES AND QUESTIONS

(1)(a) All discussion of recognition or enforcement of foreign judgments in the United States begins with *Hilton v. Guyot,* both for the defenses that it rejects and for the defense it upholds. Note first the arguments of the judgment debtor that might have some appeal, but that the Court firmly (and apparently unanimously) rejects:

> 1. Defendant says he did not appear in the French action voluntarily. But Mr. Hilton and his partner were not making what today would be called a limited appearance, just to protect property that had been subjected to judicial attachment. Here Hilton and Libbey were engaged in business in France; the fact that the object of contesting the action in France was (at least in part) to prevent their property from being seized to satisfy a judgment that might be rendered against them does not turn their participation in the action into a limited appearance, or render the exercise of judicial jurisdiction over them unfair.
>
> 2. Next, defendant attempts to cast doubt on the fairness of the procedure in the French court:
>
>> (i) plaintiff was permitted to testify not under oath;
>>
>> (ii) there was no proper cross-examination;
>>
>> (iii) documents were admitted that would have been excluded "under our own system of jurisprudence."

In perhaps the most important sentence in *Hilton v. Guyot,*[a] the court says:

> [I]t having been shown . . . that the practice followed and the method of examining witnesses were according to the laws of France, we are not prepared to hold that the fact

---

[a] The full opinion runs to 74 pages in the official reports, plus 40 pages of summary of the argument of counsel, and 6 pages for the dissenting opinion.

that the procedure in these respects differed from that of our own courts is, of itself, a sufficient ground for impeaching the foreign judgment.[b]

Had the defendants shown some personal bias against themselves in the practice of the court (or perhaps against all Americans or all foreigners), the result might have been different.

(b) Note the slap—one might say the gratuitous slap—by the Supreme Court against transient or "tag" jurisdiction. This was not a case, says the Court (p. 689), of a person travelling through or casually found in a foreign country. If Hilton had just been passing through France, it seems, the jurisdiction of the rendering court might well be questioned. Here, however, the French court clearly had jurisdiction by American standards.[c]

(c) A harder question concerns the assertion by defendants that the judgment sought to be enforced was based on fraud. In fact the Court avoids deciding the issue. Why should there be any doubt about the proposition that judgments procured by fraud are not entitled to recognition?

(d) The answer to the preceding question, generally applicable for domestic as well as for foreign judgments, is based on the distinction between so-called "extrinsic fraud," i.e., action taken by the prevailing party that deprived the losing party of adequate opportunity to present its case, and "intrinsic fraud," i.e, action that affected the result in the actual litigation. An example of extrinsic fraud would be a lack of notice or service, coupled with a false statement by a process-server that the court papers had been duly placed in the hands of defendant; an example of intrinsic fraud would be an allegation that the testimony before the rendering court was perjured, or that falsified documents had been submitted to the court. Ordinarily extrinsic fraud would, but intrinsic fraud would not, lead to rejection of a foreign judgment, on the ground that the latter allegation should be submitted to the rendering court.[d] In *Hilton*, the Court did not pass on the defense or draw the distinction made here, because it thought it had a more persuasive ground for denying recognition. The dissenting justices, it seems, would have focused on this issue, but it is not clear how they would have decided it.

(2)(a) The decision in *Hilton v. Guyot* ultimately turns on the issue of *reciprocity*, which in turn seems related to *comity*.

Quite apart from recognition of foreign judgments, what is reciprocity?

(i) Is it doing to B what B does to you? Or expecting B to do for you what you have done for him?

---

[b] 159 U.S. at 205, p. 689, *supra*.

[c] It seems that appraisal of the foreign court's jurisdiction by U.S. criteria applies even if the stated basis of jurisdiction would not pass muster under U.S. standards. For example, Article 14 of the French Civil Code reads:

An alien, though not residing in France, can be cited before the French court, for the performance of obligations contracted by him in France with a Frenchman; he can be brought before French courts for obligations contracted by him in a foreign country toward Frenchmen.

At least the second half of Article 14 is generally considered exorbitant, for it may subject persons with neither domicile nor presence nor property in France to the courts of France. But if the obligation on which the claim is based arises out of a business conducted in France, the U.S. standard would probably be satisfied, even if the asserted basis of jurisdiction was a provision of the Code that in other circumstances would not be accepted. For a survey of case law under Article 14 in France, see de Vries and Lowenfeld, *Jurisdiction in Personal Actions—A Comparison of Civil Law Views*, 44 Iowa L. Rev. 306 (1959).

[d] A court asked to recognize and enforce a foreign judgment may grant a stay to the judgment debtor for a period sufficient to give him opportunity to set aside the first judgment, subject, in appropriate cases, to the giving of security.

(ii) Could you, in the name of reciprocity, say "I won't do *B* a favor unless I am sure he would do (or has done) the same favor for me."? Or alternatively, "I will treat *B* as well as I treat everyone, unless and until it is shown to me that *B* would not grant me comparable treatment."?[e]

(b) Moving to the subject of international relations, it is easy to understand a treaty in which state *A* says we grant, say, most-favored-nation tariff treatment only to states that have made the same commitment, for example by participating in a multilateral agreement. It is understood that each party is prepared to grant certain benefits, and can enjoy certain benefits, and a reciprocal agreement is a normal and plausible way to achieve the desired result, whether in a bilateral or multilateral context. But does it make sense in a private (or public/private) context? Is it sensible to punish M. Guyot for the fact that the French legislature has not seen fit to repeal an ordinance of Louis XIII?

(c) Suppose it is true that under French law judgments of foreign states are not enforced against citizens of France except pursuant to treaty. Would any interest of the United States, or any self-respect, be impaired if a court in the United States recognized and enforced the judgment of a French court?

(d) In Germany, the rule seems to be like that enunciated in the *Hilton* case. Judgments rendered in foreign states will be recognized and enforced only on the basis of reciprocity.[f] Apart from treaty, can two states with this posture ever recognize each other's judgments? Is this not, as Chief Justice Fuller suggests, a case of two wrongs not making a right?

(e) Incidentally, we briefly raised the question of reciprocity at the beginning of this book with respect to choice of law (p. 11, question (1)(b), but neither courts nor writers showed much enthusiasm for the idea. Why should reciprocity be more persuasive in connection with recognition of judgments?

(3)(a) It is sometimes stated that *Hilton v. Guyot* stands for the proposition that a U.S. court will not recognize a foreign judgment except upon a showing that the courts of the state where the judgment was rendered would recognize judgments of U.S. courts. Postponing for the moment consideration of later developments,[g] notice that this is not a precise statement of the holding in Hilton. Though the penultimate paragraph in the portion of the majority's opinion here reproduced (p. 692) does not make the point, the statement at p. 689–90 makes clear that the holding of the case is addressed only to the case of a suit brought in France by a French national against a U.S. national. If the U.S. national had been the plaintiff, or had prevailed in the action, or the action had been between two French parties (and perhaps between a Frenchman and, say, an Italian), it seems that the Supreme Court would have enforced the judgment. The dissenting opinion, at p. 692–93 confirms this conclusion.

(b) On the same day that *Hilton v. Guyot* was decided, the court also rendered a decision in *Ritchie v. McMullen*,[h] the second case mentioned by Justice Gray at the beginning of his opinion.

---

[e] This is so called *conditional* most-favored nation treatment (MFN), applicable in connection with customs tariffs and related trade practices, for example under the General Agreement on Tariffs and Trade (GATT). The United States has had a policy since at least 1934 of *unconditional* MFN, i.e., it grants the most favorable tariff treatment to products of all countries (with some exceptions), whether or not they reciprocate. See 19 U.S.C. § 2136.

[f] Federal Republic of Germany, Code of Civil Procedure (ZPO) § 328(5).

[g] See question (5)(a) below.

[h] 159 U.S. 235 (1895).

§ 8.02　　　　　　　　JURISDICTION AND JUDGMENTS　　□　699

Ritchie involved an action by a citizen of Illinois and a citizen of Canada, upon a money judgment of the High Court of Justice of Ontario. The defendant claimed the judgment was void because he had had no hearing, and because the contract sued on was not meant to create a legally enforceable obligation. Plaintiffs objected that these assertions did not constitute a defense, and the U.S. Supreme Court agreed:

> By the law of England, prevailing in Canada, a judgment rendered by an American court under like circumstances, would be allowed full and conclusive effect. Upon principle, therefore, as well as upon authority [quoting *Hilton*] comity requires that the judgment sued on should be held conclusive of the matter adjudged.[i]

(c) France maintained the rule that led to the judgment in *Hilton v. Guyot* until 1964. In that year the Supreme Court of France reversed the rule, and in the famous case of *Munzer v. Munzer-Jacoby*[j] set forth the current French law on recognition of foreign judgments. Foreign judgments are entitled to recognition or enforcement in France, provided they meet five conditions:

(i)　the rendering court had jurisdiction, and French courts did not, by French standards, have exclusive jurisdiction;

(ii)　the procedure was regular;

(iii)　the foreign court applied the law that would have beeen applicable under French conflict of laws rules or reached a substantially equivalent result;

(iv)　the foreign judgment does not offend French public policy; and

(v)　there was no evasion of mandatory rules of law (e.g., exchange controls).

> policy defense is sometimes used to raise defects in notice or opportunity to be heard that would raise issues of due process in U.S. practice.

Would you think that an American court that still adheres to the reciprocity rule, such as a court in Massachusetts,[k] would treat a judgment of a French court since *Munzer* in favor of a French national against an American as entitled to recognition? Or should the Massachusetts court inquire into the choice of law adopted by the French court?

(4)(a) In evaluating the result in *Hilton,* as well as later developments, it is worth asking again why foreign judgments are enforced at all. Within the American federal union, it is rarely necessary to ask that question: the short answer is that judgments are enforced because the Constitution requires it, and the more thoughtful answer usually stops with the observation that the drafters of the Constitution viewed full faith and credit as an important instrument for unifying the disparate states.[l] Some of the same thinking may have been behind the European Convention on Jurisdiction and the Enforcement of Judgments in Civil and Commercial Matters, discussed in § 8.03[A] *infra*. But there is no serious drive to unify the United States and France, or England and Switzerland, etc. The reason for recognizing foreign judgments must be found elsewhere.

(b) The Supreme Court in *Hilton* speaks of *comity* (p. 687), and explains that term as somewhere between courtesy and obligation, with perhaps a suggestion of foreign relations thrown in. Others, including the dissenters in *Hilton v. Guyot* (p. 693), have justified recognition

---

[i] 159 U.S. at 242–43.

[j] Cass. Civ. Jan 7, 1964, [1964] Semaine Juridique II, 13590.

[k] See the Massachusetts version of the Uniform Foreign Money Judgments Act, Mass. Gen. L. ch. 235, § 23A, adding a reciprocity requirement to section (4)(b) of the Uniform Act, Documents Supplement p. 93.

[l] See the Nadelmann article discussed at p. 644 question (3)(a)*supra*.

of foreign judgments in terms of legal obligations or *vested rights;* thus a judgment creates a fixed relation between private parties, quite unrelated to foreign relations or interests of states. A third rationale, proposed for example by Professor Reese, is that "public policy dictates that there be an end to litigation," i.e., that the principles behind *res judicata* apply to foreign as well as to domestic judgments.[m]

Do the various rationales suggest different answers to the questions concerning reciprocity? About other issues, such as comparison of different systems of procedure, or the consequence of allegations of fraud?

(5)(a) *Hilton v. Guyot* came to the U.S. Supreme Court from a lower federal court, where the action had been brought on the basis of diversity of citizenship. The Supreme Court, considering the issue to be one drawn from the law of nations, did not address the state/federal implications of its decision. But under *Swift v. Tyson,* if (i) the rule of *Hilton v. Guyot* were one of national law (i.e., international law as interpreted by highest judicial organ of the nation), it would be binding on the states under Supremacy Clause of the Constitution;[n] on the other hand, if (ii) the rule were simply a matter of general common law, like rules about res judicata or consideration or holders in due course, then state courts could well apply different rules. Furthermore, if (i) were correct, the shift from *Swift* to *Erie R. Co. v. Tompkins* would make no difference to this issue; if (ii) were correct, federal courts after 1938 would have to follow the rule of the state where they sat in considering foreign judgments.

Which is it?

(b) In *Johnston v. Compagnie Generale Transatlantique,* decided twelve years before *Erie,* Judge Pound addresses this question, and answers it by saying that the law of nations or public international law has to do with relations between states, while enforcement of judgments is a matter of private international law: While it is true that comity (whatever that term means) exists between France and the United States, not France and New York or Pennsylvania, the issue before the court is one of obligations and rights of private parties; thus the state court is not bound by the national Supreme Court. (Compare the discussion in question 4(b), *supra.*) Is Judge Pound persuasive?

(c) Would your answer to the preceding question be the same if the dissent in *Hilton* had prevailed, so that reciprocity was rejected as a defense by the U.S. Supreme Court, while a majority of the New York Court of Appeals favored the view espoused by Justice Gray?

(d) Note that *Johnston* is in two respects different from *Hilton.* First, the judgment of the French court is sought to be used defensively, not offensively; second, the American citizen was plaintiff in the action in France, i.e., it was he who first chose the French forum. Thus as Judge Pound himself acknowledges, the *Johnston* case did not literally come within the *Hilton* rule, and he could have reached the same result as he did without departing from *Hilton.* But partly because the lower court had relied on *Hilton* and partly because the New York Court of Appeals seems to have wanted to declare its independence in this regard, the opinion stresses the private

---

[m] See Reese, *The Status in this Country of Judgments Rendered Abroad,* 50 Colum. L. Rev. 783 at 784 (1950). See also *Restatement (Second) of Conflict of Laws* § 98, (1971), Comment *b:*

> Judgments rendered in a foreign nation are not entitled to the protection of full faith and credit, [but] in most respects such judgments . . . will be accorded the same degree of recognition to which sister State judgments are entitled. This is because public policy requires that there be an end of litigation. [citing *Baldwin v. Iowa Traveling Men's Association,* p. 675, *supra.*]

[n] Article VI, § 2, Documents Supplement p. 5.

§ 8.02   JURISDICTION AND JUDGMENTS   ☐   701

international law character of the issue, thus answering the question in paragraph (a), *supra* as under alternative (ii).

(e) In the year following the decision in *Johnston v. Compagnie Generale Transatlantique*, New York's intermediate appellate court took *Johnston* one step further. In *Cowans v. Ticonderoga Pulp and Paper Co.*,° a citizen of Canada sought to enforce a money judgment rendered in Quebec against a New York corporation; defendant showed that under Quebec law an action to enforce a foreign judgment would have been subject to defenses on the merits. The Appellate Division enforced the judgment, rejecting the argument based on reciprocity:

> The force and effect which is to be given to a foreign judgment is for each sovereign power to determine for itself. . . . The general rule in this State is settled as follows: A judgment recovered in a foreign country, when sued upon in the courts of this State, is conclusive so far as to preclude a retrial of the merits of the case, subject, however, to certain well-recognized exceptions, namely, where the judgment is tainted with fraud, or with an offense against the public policy of the State, or the foreign court had not jurisdiction. . . .The respondent does not question the general rule as above stated, but urges that the denial of reciprocity in the Province of Quebec furnishes a further exception to the general rule. It rests its contention confidently on the decision in *Hilton v. Guyot.* ;. . .
>
> The Court of Appeals in its latest utterance has not accepted the decision in the *Hilton* case as controlling authority in this State upon this question. [The court summarizes *Johnston v. Compagnie Generale Transatlantique.*]
>
> . . . .
>
> Of course comity adds nothing to the strength, worth, or, as Judge Pound calls it, "persuasiveness" of the foreign judgment. The same persuasiveness is present with or without comity, or with or without reciprocity; and, without reciprocity, the United States Supreme Court still gives the foreign judgment recognition. It is to be received in evidence as *prima facie* proof of the cause of action. If no defense on the merits is made it is sufficient proof on which to render judgment. Still, if there is want of reciprocity between the two countries, that court would deny to the foreign judgment the persuasiveness it really possesses. Our Court of Appeals has we think definitely refused to accept that holding as the policy of this State; and without reciprocity, would give to the foreign judgment the full effect to which its persuasiveness entitles it. The decision in the *Hilton* case would deprive a party of the private rights he has acquired by reason of a foreign judgment because the country in whose courts that judgment was rendered has a rule of evidence different from that which we have and does not give the same effect as this State gives to a foreign judgment.
>
> We think the general rule as above stated must be applied to this case, and that the proposition which the respondent would maintain is in conflict with the policy and law of this State.

219 App. Div. at 121, 219 N.Y.S. at 286.

The Court of Appeals affirmed on the opinion of the Appellate Division.ᴾ

(f) Thus prior to 1938, if the New York courts were right, the judgment of a French court (or court of other states whose law on enforcement of foreign judgments was not able to withstand

---

° 219 App. Div. 120, 219 N.Y.S. 284 (1927).

ᴾ 246 N.Y. 603, 159 N.E. 669 (1927).

the test of reciprocity) would be treated differently in a state court of the United States (at least in New York), than in a federal court. If the holder of a foreign judgment carefully sued his judgment debtor only in the state of which the latter was a citizen,[q] he could avoid the *Hilton* rule in those states that answered the question in paragraph (a) as the New York courts did and also took the same position as New York on the substance of the reciprocity issue.

After 1938, if the New York courts were right on the national/state issue, it would not matter whether an action to enforce a foreign judgment were heard in state or federal court, as the federal court would be required to follow not the prior Supreme Court holding but the current law of the state where it sat.[r] This conclusion is reflected in the *Somportex* case that follows, as well as in the Uniform Foreign Money-Judgments Recognition Act,[s] which has been adopted by about half of the fifty states of the United States and contains no provision on reciprocity.[t]

(6) One final point. If a foreign judgment is not recognized because the rendering court was without jurisdiction, because the procedures were fundamentally unfair, or because the judgment was affected by fraud, it is treated in the second state as a nullity. If it is not recognized for reasons such as lack of reciprocity, as in *Hilton v. Guyot*, it is not a nullity. The judgment debtor is permitted to put in his defense, but the judgment creditor need not establish his claim from square one. "[J]udgments rendered in France . . . are not entitled to full credit and conclusive effect when sued upon in this country, but are prima facie evidence . . . of the justice of the plaintiffs' claim."[u]

[B] Foreign Country Judgments and the Question of Jurisdiction

Hilton, Johnston, and *Cowans* all involved judgments rendered after full litigation by both parties. What if one side (a) does not participate at all? or (b) participates to some extent, as by challenging the jurisdiction of the court or applying for a stay, but then withdraws from the litigation?

In exploring the enforcement of judgments within the United States, we saw (i) that default judgments are not treated differently from bilateral judgments for purposes of recognition and enforcement,[v] and (ii) that res judicata applies to determinations by the first forum of challenges to its jurisdiction, as well as to determinations of the merits of the controversy.[w] The combination of these two rules, of course, is critical to the effectiveness of the expanded bases of judicial jurisdiction seen in the preceding chapter, as well as to the objective of unification inherent in

---

[q] Note that from 1887 on, a citizen of the state where an action was commenced could not remove to federal court if the action was brought under the diversity of citizenship jurisdiction. See 28 U.S.C. § 1441(b), Documents Supplement p. 10.

[r] At least if the jurisdiction of the federal court were based on diversity of citizenship. If the federal action were in admiralty, or in a bankruptcy proceeding, the analysis might be questioned.

[s] Documents Supplement p. 93. See also *Restatement (Third) of the Foreign Relations Law of the United States* §481 and Comment *d and Reporters' Note 1 (1987).*

[t] As pointed out in note k, *supra,* Massachusetts added a reciprocity clause to section 4 of the Uniform Act.

[u] *Hilton v. Guyot* at p. 684, *supra.* The word "only" is omitted from the final clause quoted in order to emphasize the affirmative effect of the foreign judgment, as is picked up in the opinion in *Cowans.*

[v] I.e., leaving aside the consequences of default judgments for purposes of collateral estoppel or issue preclusion.

[w] Recall *Baldwin v. Iowa State Traveling Men's Association, Durfee v. Duke,* pp. 675, 676, *supra.*

the Full Faith and Credit Clause. The question raised in the following cases is whether these rules apply, or should apply, in an international setting as well.

SOMPORTEX, LTD. v. PHILADELPHIA CHEWING GUM CORPORATION

Court of Appeal (U.K.)
3 All E.R. 26 (1968)

Lord Denning, M.R..

Somportex, Ltd. is an English company. They had dealings with an American company called Philadelphia Chewing Gum Corporation which supplies chewing gum. There had been dealings between them apparently since early 1964. Then at the end of 1966 and the beginning of 1967 there were negotiations between these two companies for a projected agency, if I may use that word, in England for a new chewing gum which was going to be brought out called Tarzan chewing gum. In pursuance of those negotiations, the English company opened an irrevocable letter of credit for over one hundred thousand dollars in favour of the American company or their agents. At some stage or other it is said by the English company that a contract was made. It was made, they say, in a telephone conversation on Dec. 17, 1966. Early in 1967 difficulties arose and the American company declined to go on any further. They said they were still in the stage of negotiations; whereas the English company said there was a concluded contract.

Thereupon the English company sought to claim damages against the American company for breach of contract. They issued a writ against the American company in the High Court here in London. It was simply endorsed "Damages for breach of an agreement made between the [English company] and the [American company] on or about Dec. 17, 1966." They applied for leave to serve notice of that writ out of the jurisdiction. They made the usual affidavit in support, alleging that the contract was either made within the jurisdiction or was to be governed by English law. They said that on all their official orders there was a clause saying that disputes were to be decided according to English law.

In pursuance of that application, on May 10, 1967, the master gave leave to serve notice of the writ out of the jurisdiction. On May 15, 1967, the writ was issued. Notice of it was given the same day to the American company.

The alternatives then open to the American company were these: first, they need not have entered an appearance at all. If so, judgment might go against them in England, but if the English company sought to enforce that judgment in the courts of Pennsylvania (where the American company was incorporated) it could not be enforced there, because the American company would not have submitted to the jurisdiction of the English courts. The second alternative was to enter a conditional appearance to this writ and contend that the English courts had no jurisdiction in the matter and apply to set aside the writ. That was the course they took. On Aug. 9, 1967, their lawyers, Clifford-Turner & Co., entered a conditional appearance here for the Philadelphia Chewing Gum Corporation without prejudice to an application to set aside the writ. The memorandum of conditional appearance was stamped with the usual formula:

> This appearance is to stand as unconditional unless the defendant applies within fourteen days to set aside the writ and service thereof and obtains an order to that effect.

The defendants, the American company, did within those fourteen days take out a summons to set it aside. On Aug. 18, 1967, they applied to set it aside on the ground that there was no agreement between the parties: alternatively, it was not within the jurisdiction of the English courts or not to be governed by English law. That was all quite in order. It was vacation time, however, so the hearing of the summons was delayed. It did not come before the master until Nov. 13, 1967. By that time the American company had had second thoughts: they had decided not to proceed with this application to set aside the writ. They wished to go back to the the first alternative and not recognise the jurisdiction of the English courts at all. They wished to withdraw their appearance altogether. They asked leave to withdraw it under R.S.C., Ord. 21, r. 1, which says: "A party who has entered an appearance in an action may withdraw the appearance at any time with the leave of the court." The reason why they wanted to withdraw their appearance was simply this: they wanted to be quite sure that they had not submitted to the jurisdiction of the English courts.

The first summons to come before the master was the summons by the American company to set aside the writ. On Nov. 13, 1967, the master dismissed that summons. He directed, however, that the order of dismissal should not be drawn up for seven days. He allowed them those seven days so as to enable them to apply for leave to withdraw their appearance. Within those seven days, on Nov. 17, 1967, they did so apply: and the master on Nov. 27, 1967, gave them leave to withdraw their appearance. The English company appealed to the judge in chambers. He dismissed the appeal but gave leave to appeal. Then the English company appealed to this court, which that day consisted of only two members. They differed in their views. So it has been argued afresh before a court of three.

It is indeed a difficult point. No doubt in a proper case this court can give leave to withdraw an appearance. It would do so, for instance, if a solicitor entered an appearance without proper authority, or if some mistake had been made which rendered it just to allow the appearance to be withdrawn. It was submitted to us that this was a case of mistake—a mistake by the Pennsylvanian lawyers advising the American company—because they did not understand the effect of a conditional appearance in England. Mr. Guth,[1] who made an affidavit, says:

> It was my understanding that the conditional appearance would be entered on a tentative basis solely to preserve my client's right to contest the jurisdiction of the court in England if my firm deemed such action desirable after reviewing the facts more fully. It was further my understanding that the conditional appearance could be withdrawn at any time before the question of jurisdiction was litigated.

He added:

> I believed "conditional" meant that the appearance was fully conditional and I now realise that I was misled by this phrase when Clifford-Turner & Co. were instructed to enter a conditional appearance on behalf of Philadelphia Chewing Gum Corporation.

In order to decide the point, I think that one has to put oneself in the position of the American company and their advisers when faced with this notice of the writ. They could have not entered an appearance at all, in which case by the law of Pennsylvania they would not be bound by any judgment. Instead of doing that, however, after consultation with a distinguished firm of lawyers in the city of London they decided to enter a conditional appearance. That was a very

---

[1] Mr. P. D. Guth, attorney and a partner in the firm acting for the American company. His affidavit was sworn on Nov. 22, 1967.

important step for them to take (especially if they had assets in England or were likely to bring assets into England) because it was an essential way of defending their own position. After all, if they did not enter an appearance at all, and in consequence the English courts gave judgment against them in default of appearance, that judgment could be executed against them in England in respect of assets in England. In order to guard against that eventuality, they had first to enter a conditional appearance here, then argue whether it was within the jurisdiction of the court or not. If it was outside the jurisdiction, all well and good. The writ would be set aside. They would go away free. If it was within the jurisdiction, however, their appearance became unconditional and they could fight out the case on the merits. In these circumstances it seems to me that they were very wise to enter a conditional appearance. It was a step which would be advised by any competent lawyer if there was a likelihood that assets would then or afterwards come into England.

We have, therefore, a wise course of action deliberately decided on by eminent firms in England and the United States after consultation, and I do not think that they they should be allowed now to go back on it. It must be remembered that, on the faith of this entry of appearance, the English company have altered their position. They have not gone to the United States, as they might have done, and taken steps there against the American company. They have remained in this country and pursued the action here—on the faith that there was a conditional appearance entered which would become unconditional unless it was duly set aside. In the circumstances, I do not think that we should give leave to withdraw the appearance.

I know that this is a matter in the ordinary way for the discretion of the master and the judge. But the judge gave leave to appeal, thus inviting a review of his discretion. In these circumstances, even though the case is so nicely balanced, this court should come to its own decision on the matter. I think that no mistake has been shown such as to warrant our allowing this appearance to be withdrawn.

I would, therefore, allow the appeal. The appearance will stand. So will the original order which was made by the master on Nov. 13 dismissing the application to set aside. The writ therefore will stand. On the other hand, if the American company would wish to to appeal from the order of Nov. 13, I see no reason why the time should not be extended and they can argue that matter out at a later stage if they should so wish.

SALMON, L.J.

I agree and add a word only because we are differing from the conclusion of the judge. According to the case for the plaintiffs, the English company, on or about Dec. 17, 1966, they entered into a contract with the defendants, the American company in Philadelphia, to buy goods to the value of some $112,000. The contract was made partly over the transatlantic telephone and partly by documents passing between the parties. According to the English company, these documents contained a clause that the contract should be governed by English law and that any dispute between the parties arising out of the contract should be litigated in the English courts. Again, according to the English company (and their evidence at the moment is entirely uncontradicted) they had done a large volume of business with the American sellers since 1964 on the basis of documents in the same form. Therefore, according to the English company, the English courts clearly would have jurisdiction to decide any dispute that might arise between the parties under the contract, just as the courts of Philadelphia mutatis mutandis would have had jurisdiction to decide any such disputes if the contract had provided that they should be litigated in the U.S.A.

The alleged contract contained a term that the English company should give a confirmed letter of credit for some $112,000. This they did. It was acknowledged by the American company who said that it was entirely in order, or words to that effect. Later it became difficult or inconvenient, however, for the American company to carry out what the English company said was the contract. At any rate, they certainly did not do so. The English company then went to the master and obtained an order under R.S.C., Ord. 11, for leave to serve notice of the writ, claiming damages for breach of contract, on the defendants in Pennsylvania. On the now contradicted evidence before the master, that was clearly a proper order for him to make and he made it. That notice was duly served. The American company, when they were served with the notice, had, as their counsel has submitted, several courses open to them. First, they might do nothing. Secondly, they could move by originating motion to have the service set aside on the ground that the English courts had no jurisdiction. Thirdly, they could enter a conditional appearance and apply by a summons in the action to have the writ set aside on the same grounds. Fourthly, they could enter an unconditional appearance. There is no doubt that the American company were extremely anxious that the matter should not be litigated in the English courts, and, therefore, there was no question of their taking the fourth course. If they had taken the first course, judgment would have been entered against them in default of appearance. If they had taken the second course and had been successful on their originating motion, the action would have been killed stone-dead. Had they failed on the originating motion (and there seems to be a distinct possibility that they might have done so), judgment would have been entered against them in default of appearance. Of course, they could have contemplated judgment being entered against them in default of appearance with perfect equanimity if they had no assets here and no intention of bringing assets here for, according to the law of Pennsylvania, the English company could not then have executed that judgment in Pennsylvania since the American company would have done nothing to submit to the jurisdiction of the English courts. Had the American company taken the third course of entering a conditional appearance, and succeeded in persuading the master or the judge or the Court of Appeal or the House of Lords that the English courts had no jurisdiction, the action would also have been stone-dead. If they had failed, however, the conditional appearance would now become unconditional. The advantage for the American company in taking the third course would be that they would have preserved their position in the event of failing on the summons to have the writ set aside. In such an event, they would be safeguarded against judgment being entered against them in default of appearance. This advantage would, however, be of no practical value unless they had assets here or intended to bring assets here. Nor in any event would it be of any value unless they had some chance of succeeding in the action. On the other hand, if the summons to set aside the writ failed, the conditional appearance then becoming unconditional, it would in law amount to a submission to the jurisdiction of the English courts. This would enable the English company to execute any judgment which they might obtain against the American company in the U.S.A.

The American company had the courses open to them to which I have referred. I do not suppose (as Mr. Guth[2] says in his affidavit) that they knew much about procedure in England, but they took the very sensible course of going to one of the most eminent firms of solicitors in the city of London for advice. No-one suggests that the partner in that firm who was dealing with the matter was under any sort of illusion as to what courses were open to his American clients or that he has made any mistake. He advised them, no doubt sensibly, to enter a conditional appearance. If there was any sort of merit in their objection to the jurisdiction of the English

---

[2] See footnote (1), [p. 704, *supra*].

courts, that is to say, if they had not by their conduct unequivocally agreed to the English courts being the arbiter of any dispute arising out of this contract, then the writ would have been set aside and the end which they desired would have been achieved.

On the advice of that partner, which they accepted, they instructed him to enter a conditional appearance on their behalf, and he did so. For my part I am entirely unable to understand how it can be said in those circumstances that the conditional appearance was entered by mistake. Of course, it is quite plain under R.S.C., Ord. 21 that if an appearance, whether it be conditional or unconditional, is entered by mistake, the judge may order it to be set aside. It is true that Ord. 21 says nothing expressly about mistake, but that order is based on the old practice. For example, if a solicitor, who has no instructions and no authority, by mistake enters an appearance on behalf of his client, then under Ord. 21 that appearance will be set aside. If a lay client—I am merely giving another example—thinking he is entering an appearance in one action, enters it in a different action by mistake, that appearance will be set aside. No-one has suggested that the defendants' English solicitors made any mistake. I have no doubt that if they had made a mistake, they would have been the first to say so. There is no affidavit from them. It seems to me that their knowledge on matters of this sort was the knowledge of their clients.

Mr. Guth's affidavit, which I am sure was perfectly candid, is somewhat economic in the information which it gives. He says it was his understanding that the conditional appearance could be withdrawn at any time before the question of jurisdiction was litigated. Well, it is quite true that it could be, by consent of the court. One cannot help wondering what he knew about withdrawing a conditional appearance in England, unless he had acquired that knowledge from the English firm of solicitors; and if this had been discussed with them, there being no evidence to the contrary, it is a fair assumption, particularly with a firm of this eminence, that they would have given the right advice.

The learned judge founded his judgment on mistake. I am afraid that I am quite unable to find any sort of mistake here on which the American company can rely. Having elected to take a certain course, the combined effect of R.S.C., Ord. 12, r. 7 and r. 8, is this, that unless steps are taken within fourteen days to obtain an order setting the writ aside and unless such an order is made, the conditional appearance becomes an unconditional appearance.

The American company's solicitors indicated to the English company's solicitors that they intended to take out a summons to have the writ set aside and asked for an extension of time. The matter had already then been hanging about for considerable while and the English company's solicitors replied that on their instructions they could not allow it to hang about any longer; the American company's solicitors then took out a summons within fourteen days to have the writ set aside. This was in August. They applied, together with the English company's solicitors, for an appointment before the master to hear the summons. An appointment could not be had until Nov. 13: so there was a delay as the result of this procedure for some three months. I think that if a party, who has had the best professional advice, elects to take a course of this kind, acts on it and that action has the effect of postponing the proceedings for three months, he should not subsequently be able to say that he resiles from what he has done and would now rather elect one of the other courses which had been open to him.

I do not accept that this view will entail any hardship whatsoever for the American company if they have any merits. As LORD DENNING, M.R., has said, if they apply for an extension of time and they persuade the court that it has no jurisdiction to try this action, the writ will be set aside. If, however, they cannot so persuade the court because they themselves have agreed that this very court shall decide the dispute between the parties, they can hardly complain that it is a hardship that they are being held to their word.

I agree that this appeal should be allowed.

Edmund Davies, L.J..

I desire to add but very few words. In my judgment, there is a notable and crucial gap in the material on which this court is asked to hold that it was solely by reason of a mistake that the American company authorised their eminent London solicitors to enter a conditional appearance. I refer to the complete absence of any affidavit from those London solicitors regarding the advice they rendered their clients. Had it been available, a failure in communications might have been disclosed and thereby the basis and origin of some mistake laid bare. On the exiguous material before us, however, I fail to see that any mistake has been shown such as would entitle the American company to withdraw their appearance.

Contrary to and with all respect to the submission made by counsel for the American company, for my part I do not consider that this case turns on the discretion of the judge and therefore is one in which we ought not to differ from him unless we are convinced that he exercised his discretion on wrong principles. On the contrary, it involves the straight question: was there or was there not here such a mistake as, in the light of the decided cases, ought to have the effect for which the American company now contend? Agreeing as I do entirely with both judgments already delivered by my lords, I think that that question demands a negative answer.

I, therefore, concur in holding that this appeal should be allowed.

Appeal allowed. Order that the appearance herein do stand unconditional, restored. Leave to appeal to the House of Lords refused.

SOMPORTEX LIMITED v. PHILADELPHIA CHEWING GUM CORPORATION

United States Court of Appeals, Third Circuit
453 F.2d 435 (1971)
Cert. denied, 405 U.S. 1017 (1972)

Aldisert, Circuit Judge.

Several interesting questions are presented in this appeal from the district court's order, 318 F.Supp 161, granting summary judgment to enforce a default judgment entered by an English court. To resolve them, a complete recitation of the procedural history of this case is necessary.

This case has its genesis in a transaction between appellant, Philadelphia Chewing Gum Corporation, and Somportex Limited, a British corporation, which was to merchandise appellant's wares in Great Britain under the trade name "Tarzan Bubble Gum." According to the facts as alleged by appellant, there was a proposal which involved the participation of Brewster Leeds and Co., Inc., and M. S. International, Inc., third-party defendants in the court below. Brewster made certain arrangements with Somportex to furnish gum manufactured by Philadelphia; M. S. International, as agent for the licensor of the trade name "Tarzan," was to furnish the African name to the American gum to be sold in England. For reasons not relevant to our limited inquiry, the transaction never reached fruition.

Somportex filed an action against Philadelphia for breach of contract in the Queen's Bench Division of the High Court of England. Notice of the issuance of a Writ of Summons was served, in accordance with the rules and with the leave of the High Court, upon Philadelphia at its registered address in Havertown, Pennsylvania, on May 15, 1967. The extraterritorial service was based on the English version of long-arm statutes utilized by many American states.[1] Philadelphia then consulted a firm of English solicitors, who, by letter of July 14, 1967, advised its Pennsylvania lawyers:

> I have arranged with the Solicitors for Somportex Limited that they will let me have a copy of their Affidavit and exhibits to that Affidavit which supported their application to serve out of the Jurisdiction. Subject to the contents of the Affidavit, and any further information that can be provided by Philadelphia Chewing Gum Corporation after we have had the opportunity of seeing the Affidavit, it may be possible to make an application to the Court for an Order setting the Writ aside. But for such an application to be successful we will have to show that on the facts the matter does not fall within the provision of (f) and (g) [of the long-arm statute, note 1, *supra*] referred to above.
>
> In the meantime we will enter a conditional Appearance to the Writ in behalf of Philadelphia Chewing Gum Corporation in order to preserve the status quo.

On August 9, 1967, the English solicitors entered a "conditional appearance to the Writ" and filed a motion to set aside the Writ of Summons.[2] At a hearing before a Master on November

---

[1] The English Statute provides:

(f) if the action begun by the Writ is brought against a Defendant not domiciled or ordinarily resident in Scotland to enforce, rescind, dissolve, annul or otherwise affect a contract, or to recover damages or obtain other relief in respect of the breach of a contract, being (in either case) a contract which—

(i) was made within the jurisdiction, or

(ii) was made by or through an Agent trading or residing within the Jurisdiction on behalf of a principal trading or residing out of the jurisdiction, or

(iii) is by the terms, or by implication, governed by the English law;

(g) If the action begun by the Writ is brought against a Defendant not domiciled or ordinarily resident in Scotland or Northern Ireland, in respect of a breach committed within the Jurisdiction of a contract made within or out of Jurisdiction, and irrespective of the fact, if such be the case, that the breach was preceded or accompanied by a breach committed out of the Jurisdiction that rendered impossible the performance of so much of the Contract as ought to have been performed within the Jurisdiction;

Cf., the Pennsylvania Statute authorizing service on a foreign corporation, which provides:

For the purpose of determining jurisdiction of courts within this Commonwealth, the doing by any corporation in this Commonwealth of a series of similar acts for the purpose of thereby realizing pecuniary benefit or otherwise accomplishing an object, or doing a single act in this Commonwealth for such purpose, with the intention of thereby initiating a series of such acts, shall constitute "doing business." For the purposes of this subsection the shipping of merchandise directly or indirectly into or through this Commonwealth shall be considered the doing of such an act in this Commonwealth.

15 Pa.Stat.Ann. § 2011, subd. C.

Pennsylvania decisional law has generously interpreted its long-arm statute. See state cases summarized in *Siders v. Upper Mississippi Towing Corp.,* 423 F.2d 535 (3rd Cir. 1970).

[2] The memorandum of conditional appearance was stamped with this formula: "This appearance is to stand as unconditional unless the defendant applies within fourteen days to set aside the writ and service thereof and obtains an order to that effect."

The motion alleged:

(1) that there was no agreement made between the Plaintiffs and Defendants on or about 17th December 1966;

(2) alternatively that if there was such an agreement:—

13, 1967, the solicitors appeared and disclosed that Philadelphia had elected not to proceed with the summons or to contest the jurisdiction of the English Court, but instead intended to obtain leave of court to withdraw appearance of counsel. The Master then dismissed Philadelphia's summons to set aside plaintiff's Writ of Summons. Four days later, the solicitors sought to withdraw their appearance as counsel for Philadelphia, contending that it was a conditional appearance only. On November 27, 1967, after a Master granted the motion, Somportex appealed. The appeal was denied after hearing before a single judge, but the Court of Appeal, reversing the decision of the Master, held that the appearance was unconditional and that the submission to the jurisdiction by Philadelphia was, therefore, effective.[3] But the court let stand "the original order which was made by the master on Nov. 13 dismissing the application to set aside. The writ therefore will stand. On the other hand, if the American company would wish to appeal from the order of Nov. 13, I see no reason why the time should not be extended and they can argue that matter out at a later stage if they should so wish."[4]

Thereafter, Philadelphia made a calculated decision: it decided to do nothing. It neither asked for an extension of time nor attempted in any way to proceed with an appeal from the Master's order dismissing its application to set aside the Writ. Instead, it directed its English solicitors to withdraw from the case. There being no appeal, the Master's order became final.

Somportex then filed a Statement of Claim which was duly served in accordance with English Court rules. In addition, by separate letter, it informed Philadelphia of the significance and effect of the pleading, the procedural posture of the case, and its intended course of action.[5]

Philadelphia persisted in its course of inaction; it failed to file a defense. Somportex obtained a default judgment against it in the Queen's Bench Division of the High Court of Justice in

---

(a) it was not made within the jurisdiction of this honourable Court; or

(b) it was not made by or through an agent trading or residing within the jurisdiction on behalf of the Defendants a principal trading or residing out of the jurisdiction; or

(c) it was not by its terms or by implication to be governed by English law;

(3) in the further alternative that if there was such an agreement there has been no breach of the said agreement committed within the jurisdiction of this honourable court; . . .

[3] [The court quotes from the opinion of Lord Denning, *supra,* concerning the options available to the defendants]

[4] *Ibid.*

[5] . . .

Accompanying this letter is the Plaintiff's Statement of Claim the service of which upon yourselves is the next step in the action after the entry of your appearance. You will observe that it contains in numbered paragraphs the material facts relied on by our Clients in support of their claim against you. Under the Rules of the Supreme Court in England, you may serve upon us as Solicitors for the Plaintiffs your Defence (should you consider that you have one) in writing within 14 days from the date of service upon you of the Statement of Claim. In view of the fact that Messrs. Clifford-Turner & Company no longer appear to be acting on your behalf, we recognise that you may have some difficulty in preparing and serving your Defence within that time. Accordingly, we are prepared voluntarily to give you an extension of time for the service of your Defence, namely a further 14 days, so that you may have 28 days in all for this purpose. Should you fail to serve your Defence before the expiry of this extended period, the Plaintiffs will proceed to obtain judgment against you in default of Defence. If however you do enter a Defence, the action will then proceed to a trial at which you will have an opportunity of contesting fully and fairly the merits of the Plaintiff's claim.

We have thought it right to draw your attention to the points mentioned above so that you may fully understand your present position in relation to the action now being prosecuted against you. Further we feel bound to inform you that in the event of judgment being obtained against you, the Plaintiffs will seek to enforce the judgment against you through the appropriate Court in Pennsylvania.

England for the sum of £39,562.10.10 (approximately $94,000.00). The award reflected some $45,000.00 for loss of profit; $46,000.00 for loss of good will and $2,500.00 for costs, including attorneys' fees.

Thereafter, Somportex filed a diversity action in the court below, seeking to enforce the foreign judgment, and attached to the complaint a certified transcript of the English proceeding. The district court granted plaintiff's motion for summary judgment, F.R.C.P. 56(a).

Appellant presents a cluster of contentions supporting its major thesis that we should not extend hospitality to the English judgment. First, it contends, and we agree, that because our jurisdiction is based solely on diversity, "the law to be applied . . . is the law of the state," in this case, Pennsylvania law. *Erie R. Co. v. Tompkins,* 304 U.S. 64 (1938); *Svenska Handelsbanken v. Carlson,* 258 F.Supp. 448 (D.Mass. 1966).

Pennsylvania distinguishes between judgments obtained in the courts of her sister states, which are entitled to full faith and credit, and those of foreign courts, which are subject to principles of comity. *In re Christoff's Estate,* 411 Pa. 419, 192 A.2d 737, *cert. denied,* 375 U.S. 965 (1964).

Comity is a recognition which one nation extends within its own territory to the legislative, executive, or judicial acts of another. It is not a rule of law, but one of practice, convenience, and expediency. Although more than mere courtesy and accommodation, comity does not achieve the force of an imperative or obligation. Rather, it is a nation's expression of understanding which demonstrates due regard both to international duty and convenience and to the rights of persons protected by its own laws. Comity should be withheld only when its acceptance would be contrary or prejudicial to the interest of the nation called upon to give it effect.[8]

Thus, the court in *Christoff, supra,* 192 A.2d at 739, acknowledged the governing standard enunciated in *Hilton v. Guyot,* [p. 689-90, *supra*]:

> When an action is brought in a court of this country by a citizen of a foreign country against one of our own citizens . . . and the foreign judgment appears to have been rendered by a competent court, having jurisdiction of the cause and of the parties and upon due allegations and proofs, and opportunity to defend against them, and its proceedings are according to the course of a civilized jurisprudence, and are stated in a clear and formal record, the judgment is prima facie evidence, at least, of the truth of the matter adjudged; and it should be held conclusive upon the merits tried in the foreign court, unless some special ground is shown for impeaching the judgment, as by showing that it was affected by fraud or prejudice, or that by the principles of international law, and by the comity of our own country, it should not be given full credit and effect.

---

[8] In *Hilton v. Guyot,* the Supreme Court spoke of the likelihood of reciprocity as a condition precedent to the recognition of comity. The doctrine has received no more than desultory acknowledgement. *Direction der Disconto-Gesellschaft v. United States Steel Corp.,* 300 F. 741, 747 (S.D.N.Y.1921); see also, *Banco Nacional de Cuba v. Sabbatino,* [p. 982, *infra*] (dictum). It has been rejected by the courts of New York, *Johnston v. Compagnie Generale Transatlantique,* and by statute in California. See Reese, *The Status in this Country of Judgments Rendered Abroad,* 50 Col.L.Rev. 783, 790–93 (1950).

We agree with the district court that this issue of the enforceability of foreign judgments has not frequently been litigated in Pennsylvania, and the Court has not been cited to, nor has independent examination revealed any Pennsylvania cases which even intimate that a finding of reciprocity is an essential precondition to their enforcing a foreign judgment.

Somportex Limited v. Philadelphia Chewing Gum Corp., 318 F.Supp. 161, 168 (E.D.Pa.1970).

It is by this standard, therefore, that appellant's arguments must be measured.

Appellant's contention that the district court failed to make an independent examination of the factual and legal basis of the jurisdiction of the English Court at once argues too much and says too little. The reality is that the court did examine the legal basis of asserted jurisdiction and decided the issue adversely to appellant.

Indeed, we do not believe it was necessary for the court below to reach the question of whether the factual complex of the contractual dispute permitted extraterritorial service under the English long-arm statute. In its opinion denying leave of defense counsel to withdraw, the Court of Appeal specifically gave Philadelphia the opportunity to have the factual issue tested before the courts; moreover, Philadelphia was allocated additional time to do just that. Lord Denning said: ". . . They can argue that matter out at a later stage if they should so wish." Three months went by with no activity forthcoming and then, as described by the district court, "[d]uring this three month period, defendant changed its strategy and, not wishing to do anything which might result in its submitting to the English Court's jurisdiction, decided to withdraw its appearance altogether." Under these circumstances, we hold that defendant cannot choose its forum to test the factual basis of jurisdiction. It was given, and it waived, the opportunity of making the adequate presentation in the English Court.

Additionally, appellant attacks the English practice wherein a conditional appearance attacking jurisdiction may, by court decision, be converted into an unconditional one. It cannot effectively argue that this practice constitutes "some special ground . . . for impeaching the judgment," as to render the English judgment unwelcome in Pennsylvania under principles of international law and comity because it was obtained by procedures contrary or prejudicial to the host state. The English practice in this respect is identical to that set forth in both the Federal and Pennsylvania rules of civil procedure. F.R.C.P. 12(b) (2) provides the vehicle for attacking jurisdiction over the person, and, in *Orange Theatre Corp. v. Rayherstz Amusement Corp.*, 139 F.2d 871, 874 (3d Cir. 1944), we said that Rule 12 "has abolished for the federal courts the age-old distinction between general and special appearances." Similarly, a conditional or *"de bene esse"* appearance no longer exists in Pennsylvania. *Monaco v. Montgomery Cab Co.*, 417 Pa. 135, 208 A.2d 252 (1965), Pa.R.C.P. 1451(a) (7). A challenge to jurisdiction must be asserted there by a preliminary objection raising a question of jurisdiction. Pa.R.C.P. 1017(b) (1).

Thus, we will not disturb the English Court's adjudication. That the English judgment was obtained by appellant's default instead of through an adversary proceeding does not dilute its efficacy. In the absence of fraud or collusion, a default judgment is as conclusive an adjudication between the parties as when rendered after answer and complete contest in the open courtroom.

The polestar is whether a reasonable method of notification is employed and reasonable opportunity to be heard is afforded to the person affected. *Restatement (Second) Conflict of Laws*, § 92.

English law permits recovery, as compensatory damages in breach of contract, of items reflecting loss of good will and costs, including attorneys' fees. These two items formed substantial portions of the English judgment. Because they are not recoverable under Pennsylvania law, appellant would have the foreign judgment declared unenforceable because it constitutes an ". . . action on the foreign claim [which] could not have been maintained because contrary

§ 8.02   JURISDICTION AND JUDGMENTS   □   713

to the public policy of the forum," citing *Restatement, Conflict of Laws,* § 445.[15] We are satisfied with the district court's disposition of this argument:

> The Court finds that . . . while Pennsylvania may not agree that these elements should be included in damages for breach of contract, the variance with Pennsylvania law is not such that the enforcement "tends clearly to injure the public health, the public morals, the public confidence in the purity of the administration of the law, or to undermine that sense of security for individual rights, whether of personal liberty or of private property, which any citizen ought to feel, is against public policy." *Goodyear v. Brown,* 155 Pa. 514, 518, 26 A. 665, 666 (1893).

Somportex Limited v. Philadelphia Chewing Gum Corp., 318 F.Supp. 161, 169 (E.D. Pa.1970).

Finally, appellant contends that since "it maintains no office or employee in England and transacts no business within the country" there were no insufficient contacts there to meet the due process tests of *International Shoe Co. v. Washington,* 326 U.S. 310, 66 S.Ct. 154, 90 L.Ed. 95 (1965). It argues that, at best, "the only contact Philadelphia had with England was the negotiations allegedly conducted by an independent New York exporter by letter, telephone and telegram to sell Philadelphia's products in England." In *Hanson v. Denckla,* 357 U.S. 235, 253, 78 S.Ct. 1228, 1240, 2 L.Ed.2d 1283 (1958), Chief Justice Warren said: "The application of [the requirement of contact] rule will vary with the quality and nature of the defendant's activity, but it is essential in each case that there be some act by which the defendant purposely avails itself of the privilege of conducting business within the forum State, thus invoking the benefits and protection of its laws." We have concluded that whether the New York exporter was an independent contractor or Philadelphia's agent was a matter to be resolved by the English Court. For the purpose of the constitutional argument, we must assume the proper agency relationship. So construed, we find his activity would constitute the "quality and nature of the defendant's activity" similar to that of the defendant in *McGee v. International Life Ins. Co.,* 355 U.S. 220, 78 S.Ct. 199, 2 L.Ed.2d 223 (1957), there held to satisfy due process requirements.

For the reasons heretofore rehearsed we will not disturb the English Court's adjudication of jurisdiction; we have deemed as irrelevant the default nature of the judgment; we have concluded that the English compensatory damage items do not offend Pennsylvania public policy; and hold that the English procedure comports with our standards of due process.

In sum, we find that the English proceedings met all the tests enunciated in *Christoff, supra.* We are not persuaded that appellant met its burden of showing that the British "decree is so palpably tainted by fraud or prejudice as to outrage our sense of justice, or [that] the process of the foreign tribunal was invoked to achieve a result contrary to our laws of public policy or to circumvent our laws or public policy." *Christoff, supra,* 192 A.2d at 739.

The judgment of the district court will be affirmed.

---

[15] The limited scope of public policy as a controlling principle of Pennsylvania jurisprudence was underscored by Justice Stern in *Mamlin v. Genoe,* 340 Pa. 320, 325, 17 A.2d 407, 409 (1941):

> It is only when a given policy is so obviously for or against the public health, safety, morals or welfare that there is a virtual unanimity of opinion in regard to it, that a court may constitute itself the voice of the community in so declaring. . . . Familiar illustrations are those involving unreasonable restraints of marriage or of trade, collusive arrangements for obtaining divorces, suppression of bids for public contracts, interference with freedom of conscience or religion. . . . Only in the clearest cases, therefore, may a court make an alleged public policy the basis of judicial decision.

NOTES AND QUESTIONS

(1) The *Somportex* litigation is interesting in a number of respects, both in its English and in its American phase.

(a) Looking first at the English case, is there anything basically unfair about the decision of the Court of Appeal? Essentially what the court holds is that once a defendant raises his hand, he cannot put it down again. Philadelphia did not waive, and did not consent to, jurisdiction. Nor did it forfeit its opportunity to challenge the jurisdiction of the court. Lord Denning expressly says that if after the decision of the Court of Appeal Philadelphia wants more time to appeal from the master's order dismissing its challenge to jurisdiction (technically dismissing Philadelphia's summons to set aside the writ issued pursuant to Order 11), it may have it. All Philadelphia did by first entering a conditional appearance and then being unsuccessful in its attempt to withdraw that appearance was to avoid having a judgment in default of appearance entered against it by the English court. Is that unfair?

(b) A conditional appearance, under the English practice until 1980, was similar to, but not the same as, a special appearance in (former) U.S. practice. The purpose of a conditional appearance was to enable the defendant to prevent a default judgment from being entered against him, while preserving the right to object to the jurisdiction of the court. If defendant failed to apply within the time specified (usually 14 days) for an order to set aside the writ, or if he so applied but the application was unsuccessful, the appearance automatically became unconditional. If the application to set aside succeeded, the action came to an end. What happened in this case was that Philadelphia made its conditional appearance, moved to set aside, and when that motion was denied, the appearance stood as unconditional, subject to appeal.[a]

(c) Lord Denning is not correct in saying (at p. 703) that if Philadelphia had done nothing whatever, the resulting judgment could not have been enforced in the courts of Pennsylvania. That indeed is the English rule,[b] but it is not the American rule. "In the absence of fraud or collusion," as Judge Aldisert wrote for the Third Circuit, (p. 712) "a default judgment is as conclusive an adjudication between the parties as when rendered after answer and complete contest in the open courtroom." What then is the consequence of the decision of the English court for the American action?

(d) The jurisdictional question before the English court (actually the master) can be pieced together by reading both decisions. Somportex said there was a contract between it and Philadelphia, and that it was either made within England,[c] or even if not, that it was to be governed by English law.[d] Philadelphia said that at the time it decided to break off negotiation, no contract had been concluded. There was no assertion by Somportex that Brewster Leeds was doing

---

[a] The provision for conditional appearance, Order 12, r.8, was replaced in 1980 by new Order 12, r.7 and 8, which calls simply for an acknowledgment of service and an application for setting aside the writ, and states expressly that a defendant who makes such an application "shall not be treated as having submitted to the jurisdiction of the court by reason of having given notice to defend." Order 12, r.8(b).

[b] Codified, since 1982 in the Civil Jurisdiction and Judgments Act, 1982, ss. 32(1)(c) and 33(1), Documents Supplement p. 96. Not all default judgments are denied enforcement in England; the statement in the text would not apply if the judgment debtor had been in the first forum at the time of the judgment or had submitted to the jurisdiction, for example by contract.

[c] See Order 11, r.1(d)(i), (formerly r.1(f)(i)), Documents Supplement p. 79.

[d] See Order 11, r.1(d)(iii) (formerly r.1(f)(iii)).

business in England,[e] but BL's role in accepting an offer on behalf of Philadelphia with or without authority to do so may have been an issue.[f] Philadelphia's motion to the master[g] said simply that there was no contract, but if there was one it wasn't concluded in England, made through an agent trading in England, or governed by English law. As is often the case in international transactions, the issue of jurisdiction and liability overlapped: if there was no contract there could be neither jurisdiction nor liability; if there was a contract—i.e., some form of acceptance of Somportex's order, it may well have included the choice of English law contained in the order form, which could be a basis of jurisdiction under English law.[h] Assuming relitigation of the determination by the master is precluded, is the underlying basis for exercise of jurisdiction acceptable? As a basis for addressing this question, see the Uniform Foreign Country Money-Judgments Recognition Act, § 5(a)(2), (3) and (b)[i]

(2)(a) Coming then to the action to enforce the judgment, Philadelphia asserts that the lower (U.S.) court did not make an examination of the factual and legal basis of the jurisdiction of the English court. The Court of Appeals replies (p. 712) that the district court did make an examination of the legal basis, and it affirms the result of that examination. Is the Third Circuit saying that this case is just like *Baldwin v. Iowa State Traveling Men's Association?* Is it?

(b) Does the Court of Appeals answer the question put at (1)(d) above? Or is it only passing on the fairness of the conditional appearance/withdrawal question? What is the meaning of the statement "For the purpose of the constitutional argument, we must assume the proper agency relationship [between BL and Philadelphia]."?

(c) Philadelphia also objects to the award of compensation for loss of good will, which it says an American court would not award, and of attorney's fees, which certainly would not be awarded in the United States in these circumstances. Is there anything to this argument? Look again at the Uniform Foreign Country Money-Judgments Recognition Act. Quite apart from the fact that what the English court did doesn't seem repugnant to fundamental moral values, notice that section 4(b)(3) speaks about the *cause of action,* not the measure of damages.[j]

(d) Philadelphia's lawyers, who do not distinguish themselves in any part of this litigation, seem not quite to have known what to do with *Hilton v. Guyot,* except to say it was still good law. Should they have argued that English courts would not recognize a U.S. judgment if the facts were reversed? See qu. (3). Or would that have made no difference?

(e) Speaking of *Hilton,* the Third Circuit disposes of that case rather lightly, saying it is sitting in diversity, and under *Erie,* it must follow the Pennsylvania practice. It thus decides question

---

[e] Philadelphia's version of the facts was that the negotiations between it and Somportex were contingent upon securing a license for the use of the trademark "Tarzan." Since that license had not been obtained, it contended that Brewster Leeds, which was conducting the negotiations, could not have accepted Somportex's purchase order.

[f] See Order 11, r.1(d)(ii), formerly (f)(iv).

[g] Reproduced in note 2, p. 709, to the opinion of the Third Circuit.

[h] Whether choice of English law, by itself, is by American standards an acceptable basis for jurisdiction of an English court, is doubtful. The point is not picked up by the Third Circuit, however, probably because it did not appear as the sole ground of decision by the master, whose decision could have been, but was not, appealed.

[i] Documents Supplement p. 93. Pennsylvania had not adopted the Uniform Act, but one could fairly state that the Act reflected current American views of acceptable bases for jurisdiction of foreign courts. See also *Restatement (Third) of Foreign Relations Law,* Part IV, chapter 8, Introductory Note, as well as § 482(b) and § 421 (1987).

[j] In contrast, the British Protection of Trading Interests Act, Documents Supplement p. 206, which was adopted in response to perceived excesses of U.S. antitrust litigation, provides that a judgment for multiple damages shall not be enforced in any court in the U.K. (s.5) and may be subject to "clawback" (s.6(2)).

(5)(a) on p. 700 in favor of solution (ii), but with hardly any discussion of a far from simple problem. Should the Supreme Court have granted certiorari to resolve this important issue? If the issue had been duly raised,[k] how do you think the Supreme Court would have resolved it about eighty years after *Hilton,* thirty-five years after *Erie,* and a decade after *Sabbatino*?[l]

(3) The issue of reciprocity as a condition for enforcement of foreign judgments can take several forms, as illustrated by a well known English case, *Société Cooperative Sidmetal v. Titan International Limited,* [1966] 1 Q.B. 828.

(a) An English steel company, Titan, had agreed to sell 400 tons of a specified type of steel to a Belgian company, Sidmetal, for delivery to an Italian company which had purchased the steel from Sidmetal. When the steel arrived in Italy, the Italian company was dissatisfied with the quality of the shipment, and brought suit against Sidmetal in the Commercial Court in Brussels. Sidmetal brought a third party proceeding against Titan, serving Titan in England. Titan did not answer or appear in the Belgian proceeding, and a judgment was rendered against it by the Belgian court. Thereafter, Sidmetal sought to enforce the judgment against Titan in England.

(b) The case was complicated because of a controversy about application of a Foreign Judgments (Reciprocal Enforcement) Act, 1933, and a U.K.-Belgian treaty, both of which the English court found not to be applicable. The Belgian judgment creditor argued, however, that the Act was not the exclusive vehicle for enforcement, and that the "comity of nations" called for enforcement in this case. Counsel for the Belgian company argued

> (i) that the courts of England ought to recognize a judgment of the Belgian court if the courts of England would claim equivalent jurisdiction for themselves if the position of the two countries had been reversed.

Alternatively, counsel for the Belgian company argued

> (ii) that the courts of England ought to recognize a judgment of the Belgian court if the Belgian court would have recognized the judgment of the English court had the position of the two countries been reversed.

Assuming that some kind of reciprocity exists between the United Kingdom and Belgium (all this, of course, before the UK joins the European Community), is either of these arguments persuasive? Note that alternative (ii) would have satisfied the Supreme Court in *Hilton v. Guyot*; alternative (i) would not.

---

[k] In fact, Philadelphia's petition for certiorari asserted that the Third Circuit had misconstrued the doctrine of comity, and that Pennsylvania courts continue to rely upon *Hilton v. Guyot.* Somportex, opposing review by the Supreme Court, said that the petition raised no substantial federal question, and was "to a large extent based on . . . unique facts . . . and therefore has no universal significance."

[l] *Banco Nacional de Cuba v. Sabbatino,* 376 U.S. 398 (1964) reproduced in Ch. 10 at p. 982. See esp. the discussion at pp. 986–87, holding that the issue of the effect to be given to a foreign act of state is an issue of national law. In 1981, the Court of Appeals for the D.C. Circuit, holding that the issue of the effect to be given to a foreign act of state is an issue of federal law, wrote:

> The logical rule would seem to be that, in the absence of an action by the legislature, the courts should refrain from creating or resurrecting a reciprocity doctrine. The issue of how best to respond to a foreign nations's scrutinization of an American judgment is, after all, a political one. Moreover, notwithstanding *Erie Railroad Co. v. Tompkins,* the issue seems to be national rather than state.

Tahan v. Hodgson, 662 F.2d 862, 868 (D.C. Cir. 1981).

For an argument that recognition and enforcement of foreign country judgments should be a question of national law, see A. Lowenfeld, *Nationalizing International Law: Essay in Honor of Louis Henkin,* 36 Colum. J. Transnat'l L. 121 (1997).

§ 8.02   JURISDICTION AND JUDGMENTS   □   717

(4)(a) In *Vogel v. Kohnstamm Ltd.,* [1973] 1 Q.B. 133, another borderline case of enforcement of a foreign judgment came before the English High Court, but this time counsel for the judgment creditor had to rely solely on the common law, not on any bilateral treaty that would bring into play the 1933 Act that had proved unhelpful in *Sidmetal v. Titan.* Kohnstamm, an English leather manufacturer, arranged with a Mr. Kornbluth, a resident of Israel, to show its products and solicit inquiries and orders in that country. Kornbluth was not permitted to quote prices or accept orders, but he could communicate about these matters with interested persons in Israel, and help to facilitate negotiations. Payment for goods sold would be made directly to the English company or through banks, but not through Mr. Kornbluth. The English company paid commissions to Kornbluth on orders he had procured, but did not guarantee a minimum commission or contribute to maintenance of Kornbluth's office in Tel Aviv. Kornbluth also handled merchandise for other foreign companies in Israel.

After this arrangement had continued for some time, a controversy over quality of merchandise shipped arose between Kohnstamm and one of the customers that Kornbluth had procured. The buyer brought suit against the English manufacturer in the District Court of Tel Aviv, serving defendant in England with leave of the court. Kohnstamm's English solicitors wrote to the court that "our clients do not admit that your court has any jurisdiction in this matter. . . . [T]his letter is not to be taken as any appearance in these proceedings at all." Eventually the Tel Aviv court rendered judgment for the buyer, jurisdiction being based on the fact that the manufacturer had done business in Israel through Mr. Kornbluth, its agent, and that judgment was sued on in England. How should this case be decided? Is the question whether Kornbluth was an agent under Israeli law, or under English law?[m]

(b) Though it is fairly clear that English courts are reluctant to enforce judgments rendered upon default against non-resident defendants, the question whether a judgment is one of default or the defendant has subjected himself to the jurisdiction of the rendering court—i.e., the question in *Somportex v. Philadelphia Chewing Gum Corporation*—has come before the English courts as well.

Henry v. Geoprosco International Ltd., [1976] Q.B. 726 (C.A.), arose out of an employment contract signed in Calgary, Alberta between Geoprosco, an English oil service company and Mr. Henry, a resident of Calgary, for work in the Trucial States on the Arabian peninsula. Mr. Henry took up his job and went to the Trucial States, but was summarily discharged a few months later. Henry returned to Alberta and there brought suit against the oil company. The Alberta court, operating under rules of practice substantially in conformity with Order 11 of the U.K. Supreme Court Rules, gave leave to serve Geoprosco at its home office, on the basis that the contract had been made within the jurisdiction.[n]

Geoprosco first attempted to get the plaintiff to withdraw its suit in virtue of an arbitration clause in the employment contract, but plaintiff refused. Geoprosco thereupon moved to set aside service on the ground (inter alia) of forum non conveniens, and in the alternative for a stay pending arbitration. The Alberta judge denied the motion, Geoprosco appealed, and the Court of Appeal dismissed the appeal. Thereafter, Geoprosco took no further part in the proceedings.

Judgment was subsequently entered for plaintiff, and he sought to enforce the judgment by an action in London. Geoprosco contended that the action was upon a default judgment not

---

[m] The English court, in a lengthy opinion, compared the facts with various English precedents concerning presence or agency, and denied enforcement. It made no effort to inquire into Israeli law.

[n] Compare Order 11, r.1(d)(i). Documents Supplement p. 79.

entitled to enforcement; Henry asserted that by the steps it had taken in Alberta, Geoprosco had submitted to the jurisdiction of the rendering court. How should this case be decided?

(c) The English Court of Appeal, reversing the High Court, held (i) that the issue should be decided not by the law of Alberta, but by reference to English principles of conflict of laws; and (ii) that under these principles, even though it had never participated in litigation on the merits, Geoprosco had voluntarily submitted to the jurisdiction of the Alberta court by calling upon that court, in its discretion, to dismiss the case.

(d) The decision in *Henry v. Geoprosco* provoked strong criticism in England.º When legislation was being prepared to implement the United Kingdom's accession to the Brussels Convention on Jurisdiction and the Enforcement of Judgments in Civil and Commercial Matters, (§ 8.03[A]), the critics succeeded in securing reversal of the *Geoprosco* rule. Section 33 of the U.K. Civil Jurisdiction and Judgments Act 1982,ᵖ (not applicable to judgments coming under the Convention), says that for purpose of recognition or enforcement of a foreign judgment

> the person against whom the judgment was given shall not be regarded as having submitted to the jurisdiction of the Court by reason only of the fact that he appeared . . .
>
> (a) to contest the jurisdiction of the court
>
> (b) to ask the court to dismiss or stay the proceedings on the ground that the dispute . . . should be submitted to arbitration or to the determination of the courts of another country.
>
> (c) to protect property seized or threatened with seizure in the proceedings.

Moreover, section 32(3) makes clear that a court in the United Kingdom will not be bound by any determinations of the foreign court on jurisdictional issues.

Would you have voted for such legislation? Note that since it is quite contrary to the Brussels Convention discussed in the next section, it means that judgments of, say, courts in the United States are treated much less favorably than judgments of member states of the European Community.

§ 8.03 Recognition of Judgments and Awards by Treaty

[A] The European Convention on Jurisdiction and Judgments

When the architects of the European Community set out to draft what became the Treaty of Rome Establishing the European Economic Community (1957), they concentrated on the free movement of persons and goods among the member states, the establishment of a common external tariff, development of a common agricultural policy, and creation of the Community's institutions—the Commission, the Council, the Court of Justice, and the European Parliament. They believed, however, that creation of a customs union and some common institutions would not, in the long run, suffice to create the unified Europe to which they aspired, and they committed the member states to negotiate on a number of other matters. Article 220 of the Treaty of Rome says:

º See, e. g. Collins, *Harris v. Taylor Revived*. 92 L.Q. Rev. 268, 280–87 (1976). Mr. Collins was one of the editors, and since 1985 has been editor-in-chief, of Dicey and Morris, *Conflict of Laws*.

ᵖ Documents Supplement pp. 96–97.

Member States shall, so far as is necessary, enter into negotiations with each other with a view to receiving for the benefit of their nationals:

. . . .

—the simplification of formalities governing the reciprocal recognition and enforcement of judgments of courts or tribunals and of arbitration awards.

The Treaty of Rome entered into force among the original six member states[a] on January 1, 1958. Less than two years later, the Commission (i.e., the executive arm of the Community) formally invited the member states to commence negotiations on a judgments convention.[b] Shortly thereafter, the member states established a committee of experts, which worked over a period of four and a half years to prepare a preliminary convention. Following comments by governments as well by various bar associations and business groups, the committee of experts adopted a final text in July 1966. The Convention on Jurisdiction and the Enforcement of Judgments in Civil and Commercial Matters was formally signed by the Six in Brussels on September 27, 1968, and entered into force on February 1, 1973.

According to Article 63 of the Brussels Convention, any state that might subsequently become a member of the EEC—notably the United Kingdom, which had at first declined to join the Common Market, then applied and been vetoed by President De Gaulle of France, and was likely to reapply—"shall be required to accept this Convention as a basis for negotiations . . . to ensure implementation of the last paragraph of Article 220 of the Treaty [of Rome]," and this was confirmed in the so-called Act of Accession whereby the Six approved the entry of the United Kingdom, Ireland, and Denmark into the Community.[c] In fact a number of changes in the Brussels Convention were negotiated following the entry of the new states into the European Community in 1973, and some further changes have been made each time a new state or group of states joined the Community.[d]

Two major issues came before the drafters of the Convention at the outset, comparable to the issues that came before the drafters of the United States Constitution. *First,* given the overriding principle that judgments of the other states could be enforced only if they were rendered by a court having jurisdiction, should the Convention set forth rules on jurisdiction as well as on judgments? *Second,* should the Convention rely solely on the courts of member states, or should it be subject to supervision by the European Court of Justice? Unlike the founding fathers in Philadelphia in the eighteenth century, the twentieth century experts in Brussels answered the first question in the affirmative. As discussed in the preceding chapter,[e] they agreed

---

[a] Belgium, France, Federal Republic of Germany, France, Italy, and Luxembourg.

[b] Commission of EEC, Note of 22 October, 1959.

The Note pointed out that a true internal market between the six States will be achieved only if adequate legal protection can be secured. The economic life of the Community may be subject to disturbances and difficulties unless it is possible, where necessary by judicial means, to ensure the recognition and enforcement of the various rights arising from the existence of a multiplicity of legal relationships. As jurisdiction in both civil and commercial matters is derived from the sovereignty of Member States, and since the effect of judicial acts is confined to each national territory, legal protection and, hence, legal certainty in the common market are essentially dependent on the adoption by the Member States of a satisfactory solution to the problem of recognition and enforcement of judgments.

[c] Act concerning the conditions of the Accession of the United Kingdom, Ireland, and Denmark . . . Art. 3(2). The accession documents are collected in O. J. Eur. Comm. Spec. Ed., 27 March 1972.

[d] The Convention as amended through the accession of Spain and Portugal is reproduced in the Documents Supplement at pp. 98–127.

[e] See Chapter 7, § 7.07, *supra.*

on a basic principle of jurisdiction of courts, focused on the domicile of the defendant,[f] and also agreed on a number of special bases of jurisdiction, linked (and limited) to particular causes of action.[g] Further, they expressly excluded, as between persons domiciled in a Contracting State, certain bases of jurisdiction regarded as exorbitant, including jurisdiction on the basis of the nationality of the plaintiff (France, Belgium, Luxembourg and Netherlands), jurisdiction on the basis of property in the forum state (Germany and (later) Denmark), and (later) jurisdiction on the basis of "tag" (United Kingdom and Ireland).[h] What started out as a convention on judgments thus became a convention on jurisdiction as well.[i]

As to the second question, agreement could not be reached in the original negotiations, but at the time of signing the Brussels Convention, the six governments issued a Joint Declaration that they were ready to "examine the possibility of conferring jurisdiction in certain matters on the Court of Justice . . . and, if necessary, to negotiate an agreement to this effect."[j] In 1971 the Six agreed on a Protocol[k] conferring jurisdiction on the Court of Justice to give rulings on the interpretation of the Convention and authorizing the highest courts of the member states, as well as specified appellate courts and other authorities, to request the Court of Justice to give such rulings.[l]

It is instructive to compare the judgments provisions of the Brussels Convention with the law developed pursuant to the Full Faith and Credit clause of the U.S. Constitution. The style, of course, is quite different; consider, however, in what ways you might wish to follow, or vary, the outcome of full faith and credit in the United States if you were drafting a judgments convention for use first by six fairly homogeneous states, and later by many more states with substantial differences in both political and legal tradition.[m]

---

[f] Brussels Convention, Article 2.

[g] Id. Articles 5, 8–12, 13–15, 16.

[h] Id. Article 3. Note that the Convention does not just preclude recognition and enforcement of judgments based on exorbitant jurisdiction, but directly prohibits exercise of jurisdiction on such basis. For illustration of how the exorbitant French and German bases of jurisdiction worked, see, e.g., de Vries and Lowenfeld, *Jurisdiction in Personal Actions—A Comparison of Civil Law Views*, 44 Iowa L. Rev. 306, 316–330, 332–44 (1959). It should be noted that jurisdiction on the basis of presence of defendant's property, as under Article 23 of the German Code of Civil Procedure (ZPO) is not what Americans have called quasi in rem jurisdiction, limited to the value of the property, but purports to be general jurisdiction over the defendant.

[i] The drafters had some, but not too much misgiving in proposing a convention based on *domicile,* though Article 220 of the Rome Treaty spoke of "benefit of *nationals.*"

[j] Joint Declaration of the Six on Signing the Convention on Jurisdiction and Enforcement of Judgments . . . 27 September 1968, Art. 1.

It is worth remarking that the founding fathers in Philadelphia not only did not make provision for supervision of the Full Faith and Credit clause by the Supreme Court, but said nothing at all about review by the Supreme Court of decisions of state courts. That gap was filled by § 25 of the Judiciary Act of 1789, 1 Stat. 73, 85, and upheld in *Martin v. Hunter's Lessee,* 14 U.S. (1 Wheat.) 304 (1816).

[k] Documents Supplement p. 123.

[l] The formula for seeking rulings from the Court of Justice is drawn from Article 177 of the Treaty of Rome, which provides for references from national courts to the Court of Justice when questions arise under the Treaty of Rome. However, in order to preclude defendants or judgment debtors from making excessive use of the review procedure, the phrase "any court" in Article 177 of the Treaty of Rome is replaced by authority in appellate courts, plus the enforcing courts specified in Article 37 of the Convention. Note also the difference between "shall, if . . ." in Article 3(1) of the Protocol, referring to the member states' highest courts, and "may . . ." in Article 3(2), referring to other courts authorized to refer questions to the Court of Justice.

[m] The Report on the Convention by the Committee of Experts which prepared it (1966) (the Jenard Report) together with the reports on the 1971 Protocol and the 1978 Accession Convention are conveniently collected in O.J. Eur. Comm. No. C59, (5 March 1979).

Note first the exclusions from the Convention (Art. 1). As the Report of the Committee of Experts makes clear, ideally all civil and commercial litigation would have been covered, but "the Committee did not feel free to adopt this approach, and limited the scope of the Convention to matters relating to property rights, . . . the main reason being the difficulties resulting from the absence of any overall solution to the problem of conflict of laws."[n] There is, of course, no comparable exclusion in the U.S. Full Faith and Credit clause, but the developments concerning judgments involving land, penal judgments, workers' compensation, and family law (see Chapter 9) suggest the difference is not as great as might appear at first glance.[o]

In order for a judgment of one Contracting State (F–1) to be enforced in another Contracting State (F–2), it must be enforceable in F–1 (Art. 31), and it must have been rendered by a court with jurisdiction according to the standards set forth in the Convention (Art. 28). Recognition is automatic, without any special procedure (Art. 26); *enforcement* requires application to a court in F–2 in accordance with the law of F–2 (Art. 31–33), but the application is *ex parte,* and it is up to the judgment debtor to initiate a proceeding to set aside enforcement (Art. 34–36). Recognition (and enforcement) may be denied only for specified grounds (Art. 27–28, 34), and a judgment of F–1 may "under no circumstances" be reviewed as to its substance. (Art. 29, 34). The Report on the Convention[p] (but not the Convention itself) says "Recognition must have the result of conferring on judgments the authority and effectiveness accorded to them in the State in which they were given,"—almost a verbatim repetition of the legislation implementing Article IV § 1 of the U.S. Constitution.

As we saw in discussing the United States,[q] an important test of the effectiveness of a system of enforcing judgments rendered in different jurisdictions is how it deals with default judgments. Read the provisions on choice of forum clauses (Art. 17); on proof of service (Art. 27(2), 46(2), 48); on appearance (Art. 18); and on jurisdictional determinations and their effect (Art. 20, 28). Is a defendant domiciled in one state in the Community sued in another member state faced with the same choice as in the United States?[r] Or are the calculations different?

Two decisions rendered by the European Court of Justice, decided within a few months of each other, supply a partial answer to the preceding question, as well as a further idea of how the Court of Justice addresses questions put to it.

ELEFANTEN SCHUH GmbH v. JACQMAIN

European Court of Justice
24 June 1981
[1981] E.C.R. 1671, [1982] 3 C.M.L.R. 1

By judgment dated 9 June 1980 which was received at the Court on 24 June 1980 the Cour de Cassation [Supreme Court] of Belgium referred to the Court for a preliminary ruling under

---

[n] Report on Convention, note m, *supra,* Ch. III (iv).

[o] Note that while actions affecting status are excluded, actions for maintenance and judgments thereon are included. Article 5(2) was substantially changed at the time of the 1978 Accession Convention, both to include the maintenance aspect of an action for divorce or custody, and to include jurisdiction at the domicile of the maintenance creditor (e.g., the deserted wife), except where that jurisdiction is based solely on the nationality of one of the parties.

[p] Note m, *supra.*

[q] See § 8.01[C], *supra.*

[r] See p. 674, *supra.*

the Protocol of 3 June 1971 on the Interpretation by the Court of Justice of the Convention of 27 September 1968 on Jurisdiction and the Enforcement of Judgments in Civil and Commercial Matters several questions as to the interpretation of Articles 17, 18 and 22 of that Convention.

Those questions were put in the context of an appeal in cassation against a judgment of the Arbeidshof Antwerpen [Labour Court, Antwerp] ordering Elefanten Schuh GmbH, a company incorporated under German law, and Elefant NV, a company incorporated under Belgian law, to pay jointly the sum of BFR 3,120,597 together with interest to Mr Pierre Jacqmain for having *inter alia* dismissed Mr. Jacqmain without notice.

It appears from the papers placed before the Court that in 1970 Mr. Jacqmain was employed as a sales agent by the German company Hoffmann GmbH which subsequently adopted the name Elefanten Schuh GmbH; however, he actually worked in Belgium, in particular in the provinces of Antwerp, Brabant and Limburg, on instructions which he received from the Belgian subsidiary of that undertaking, Elefant NV. The main action arose as a result of difficulties which occurred in 1975 between Mr. Jacqmain and the two companies concerning details of the transfer of the contract of employment from the German company to the Belgian company.

Mr. Jacqmain brought an action in the Arbeidsrechtbank Antwerpen [Labour Tribunal, Antwerp] against the two companies. The defendant companies appeared before that court and by their first submissions they contested the substance of the applications lodged against them. In further submissions lodged nine months later the German company claimed that the Arbeidsrechtbank did not have jurisdiction on the ground that the contract of employment contained a clause stipulating that the court at Kleve in the Federal Republic of Germany was to have exclusive jurisdiction in the event of any dispute. The Arbeidsrechtbank dismissed that objection. It took the view that such a clause could not derogate from Article 627 of the Belgian Judicial Code which in disputes of this kind provides that the court of the place where the occupation is pursued is to have jurisdiction.

The Arbeidshof Antwerpen, to which an appeal from the judgment of the Arbeidsrechtbank was made, considered that pursuant to Article 17 of the Brussels Convention of 27 September 1968 the parties to the contract of employment could confer territorial jurisdiction on the court of Kleve by agreeing in writing to derogate from the rules on territorial jurisdiction contained in the Belgian Judicial Code. However, the Arbeidshof held that the German company could not rely on the jurisdiction clause on the ground that the contract of employment had to be written in Dutch by virtue of Article 10 of the Decree of 19 July 1973 governing the use of languages in relations between employers and employees, adopted by the Cultuurraad voor Nederlandse Cultuurgemeenschap [Culture Council for the Netherlands Cultural Community]. The Arbeidshof took the view that Article 10, which provides that any act or document not written in Dutch is null and void, applies to documents drawn up before the decree entered into force. Consequently the contract of employment, drawn up in German, was null and void and the clause conferring jurisdiction contained therein was invalid.

The appeal in cassation lodged against the judgment of the Arbeidshof by the Belgian company was declared inadmissible by the [Cour de Cassation]. As the appeal in cassation lodged by the German company concerned the validity of the jurisdiction clause in particular the Hof van Cassatie decided in view of Article 17 of the Brussels Convention to put three questions to the Court of Justice.

Question 1 is worded as follows:

1. (a) Is Article 18 of the Brussels Convention applicable if parties have agreed to confer jurisdiction on a court within the meaning of Article 17?

(b) Is the rule on jurisdiction contained in Article 18 applicable if the defendant has not only contested jurisdiction but has in addition made submissions on the action itself?

(c) If it is, must jurisdiction then be contested *in limine litis?* [at the outset of the action].

Articles 17 and 18 form Section 6 of Title II of the Convention which deals with prorogation of jurisdiction; Article 17 concerns jurisdiction by consent and Article 18 jurisdiction implied from submission as a result of the defendant's appearance. The first part of the question seeks to determine the relationship between those two types of prorogation.

In the first sentence, Article 18 of the convention lays down the rule that a court of a Contracting State before whom a defendant enters an appearance is to have jurisdiction and in the second sentence it provides that that rule is not to apply where appearance was entered solely in order to contest the jurisdiction, or where another court has exclusive jurisdiction by virtue of Article 16 of the Convention.

The case envisaged in Article 17 is not therefore one of the exceptions which Article 18 allows to the rule which it lays down. Moreover neither the general scheme nor the objectives of the Convention provide grounds for the view that the parties to an agreement conferring jurisdiction within the meaning of Article 17 are prevented from voluntarily submitting their dispute to a court other than that stipulated in the agreement.

It follows that Article 18 of the Convention applies even where the parties have by agreement designated a court which is to have jurisdiction within the meaning of Article 17.

The second and third parts of the question envisage the case in which the defendant has appeared before a court within the meaning of Article 18 but contests the jurisdiction of that court.

The Hof van Cassatie first asks if Article 18 has application where the defendant makes submissions as to the jurisdiction of the court as well as on the substance of the action.

Although differences between the different language versions of Article 18 of the Convention appear when it is sought to determine whether, in order to exclude the jurisdiction of the court seised, a defendant must confine himself to contesting that jurisdiction, or whether he may on the contrary still achieve the same purpose by contesting the jurisdiction of the court as well as the substance of the claim, the second interpretation is more in keeping with the objectives and spirit of the Convention. In fact under the law of civil procedure of certain Contracting States a defendant who raises the issue of jurisdiction and no other might be barred from making his submissions as to the substance if the court rejects his plea that it has no jurisdiction. An interpretation of Article 18 which enabled such a result to be arrived at would be contrary to the right of the defendant to defend himself in the original proceedings, which is one of the aims of the Convention.

However, the challenge to jurisdiction may have the result attributed to it by Article 18 only if the plaintiff and the court seised of the matter are able to ascertain from the time of the defendant's first defence that it is intended to contest the jurisdiction of the court.

The Hof van Cassatie asks in this regard whether jurisdiction must be contested *in limine litis.* For the purposes of interpreting the Convention that concept is difficult to apply in view of the appreciable differences existing between the legislation of the Contracting States with regard to bringing actions before courts of law, the appearance of defendants and the way in which the parties to an action must formulate their submissions. However, it follows from the aim of Article 18 that if the challenge to jurisdiction is not preliminary to any defence as to the substance it may not in any event occur after the making of the submissions which under national procedural law are considered to be the first defence addressed to the court seised.

Therefore the answer to the second and third parts of Question 1 should be that Article 18 of the Convention must be interpreted as meaning that the rule on jurisdiction which that provision lays down does not apply where the defendant not only contests the court's jurisdiction but also makes submissions on the substance of the action, provided that, if the challenge to jurisdiction is not preliminary to any defence as to the substance, it does not occur after the making of the submissions which under national procedural law are considered to be the first defence addressed to the court seised.

Question 2 is as follows:

> 2(a) In application of Article 22 of the Convention, can related actions which, had they been brought separately, would have had to be brought before courts of different Contracting States, be brought simultaneously before one of those courts, provided that the law of that court permits the consolidation of related actions and that court has jurisdiction over both actions?
>
> (b) Is that also the case if the parties to one of the disputes which have given rise to the actions have agreed, in accordance with Article 17 of the Convention, that a court of another Contracting State is to have jurisdiction to settle that dispute?

Article 22 of the Convention is intended to establish how related actions which have been brought before courts of different Member States are to be dealt with. It does not confer jurisdiction; in particular, it does not accord jurisdiction to a court of a Contracting State to try an action which is related to another action of which that court is seised pursuant to the rules of the Convention.

The answer to Question 2 should therefore be that Article 22 of the Convention applies only where related actions are brought before courts of two or more Contracting States.

The final question is worded as follows:

> 3. Does it conflict with Article 17 of the Convention to rule that an agreement conferring jurisdiction on a court is void if the document in which the agreement is contained is not drawn up in the language which is prescribed by the law of a Contracting State upon penalty of nullity and if the court of the State before which the agreement is relied upon is bound by that law to declare the document to be void of its own motion?

From that wording it appears that the Hof van Cassatie is solely concerned with the validity of an agreement conferring jurisdiction which is rendered void by the national legislation of the court seised as having been written in a language other than that prescribed by that legislation.

Article 17 stipulates that the agreement conferring jurisdiction must take the form of an agreement in writing or an oral agreement evidenced in writing.

According to the Report on the Convention submitted to the Governments of the Contracting States at the same time as the draft Convention those formal requirements were inserted out of the concern not to impede commercial practice, yet at the same time to cancel out the effects of clauses in contracts which might go unread, such as clauses in printed forms for business correspondence or in invoices, if they were not agreed to by the party against whom they operate. For those reasons jurisdiction clauses should be taken into consideration only if they are the subject of a written agreement, and that implies the consent of all the parties. Furthermore, the draftsmen of Article 17 were of the opinion that, in order to ensure legal certainty, the formal requirements applicable to agreements conferring jurisdiction should be expressly prescribed.

Article 17 is thus intended to lay down itself the formal requirements which agreements conferring jurisdiction must meet; the purpose is to ensure legal certainty and that the parties have given their consent.

Consequently Contracting States are not free to lay down formal requirements other than those contained in the Convention. That is confirmed by the fact that the second paragraph of Article 1 of the Protocol annexed to the Convention expressly prescribes special requirements of form with regard to persons domiciled in Luxembourg.

When those rules are applied to provisions concerning the language to be used in an agreement conferring jurisdiction they imply that the legislation of a Contracting State may not allow the validity of such an agreement to be called in question solely on the ground that the language used is not that prescribed by that legislation.

Moreover, any different interpretation would run counter to Article 17 of the Convention the very purpose of which is to enable a court of a Contracting State to be chosen by agreement where that court, if not so chosen, would not normally have jurisdiction. That choice must therefore be respected by the courts of all the Contracting States.

Consequently, the answer to Question 3 must be that Article 17 of the Convention must be interpreted as meaning that the legislation of a Contracting State may not allow the validity of an agreement conferring jurisdiction to be called in question solely on the ground that the language used is not that prescribed by that legislation.

. . .

On those grounds,

THE COURT,

in answer to the questions referred to it by the Hof van Cassatie by judgment of 9 June 1980, hereby rules:

> 1. Article 18 of the Convention of 27 September 1968 on Jurisdiction and the Enforcement of Judgments in Civil and Commercial Matters applies even where the parties have by agreement designated a court which is to have jurisdiction within the meaning of Article 17 of that Convention.
>
> 2. Article 18 of the Convention of 27 September 1968 must be interpreted as meaning that the rule on jurisdiction which that provision lays down does not apply where the defendant not only contests the court's jurisdiction but also makes submissions on the substance of the action, provided that, if the challenge to jurisdiction is not preliminary to any defence as to the substance, it does not occur after the making of the submissions which under national procedural law are considered to be the first defence addressed to the court seised.
>
> 3. Article 22 of the Convention of 27 September 1968 applies only where related actions are brought before courts of two or more Contracting States.

4. Article 17 of the Convention of 27 September 1968 must be interpreted as meaning that the legislation of a Contracting State may not allow the validity of an agreement conferring jurisdiction to be called in question solely on the ground that the language used is not that prescribed by that legislation.

ETABLISSEMENTS ROHR S.A. v. OSSBERGER

European Court of Justice
22 October 1981
[1981] E.C.R. 2431, [1982] 3 C.M.L.R. 29

Facts and Issues

The facts of the case, the course of the procedure and the observations submitted under Article 20 of the Protocol on the Statute of the Court of Justice of the EEC may be summarized as follows:

I—Facts and procedure

1. The undertaking Ossberger Turbinenfabrik (hereinafter referred to as "Ossberger"), Weissenburg, Bavaria, Federal Republic of Germany, has for some years supplied water turbines to the Établissements Rohr Société Anonyme (hereinafter referred to as "Rohr"), Sarcelles, Val d'Oise, France, which sold them under its own name to customers in France.

Ossberger, founding on a clause conferring jurisdiction in its general conditions of sale, instituted proceedings against Rohr before the Landgericht [Regional Court] Ansbach, within whose jurisdiction Weissenburg is situated, for in all to DM 120,216, together with interest. Before the Landgericht Rohr argued that that court had no jurisdiction *ratione loci* but did not submit any defence as to the substance.

By a provisionally enforceable final judgment of 15 December 1978 the Landgericht Ansbach considered that the clause in question conferring jurisdiction was valid under Article 17 of the Brussels Convention of 27 September 1968 and, having regard to the fact that Rohr failed to defend the substance of the claim, ordered it to pay Ossberger the principal sum of DM 120,216 with interest and to pay the costs. The costs were taxed at DM 4,742.24 with interest by an order of the Landgericht Ansbach of 5 February 1979.

Rohr appealed to the Oberlandesgericht Nürnberg [Higher Regional Court, Nuremberg]. In the course of the appellate procedure Rohr merely relied upon the objection of lack of jurisdiction and did not submit any defence as to the substance. The Oberlandesgericht Nürnberg, since it considered that the Landgericht Ansbach had jurisdiction under the provisions of the Brussels Convention and since Rohr had still failed to submit a defence as to the substance in the course of the appellate procedure, dismissed the appeal by a judgment of 13 June 1979. A further appeal on a point of law by Rohr to the Bundesgerichtshof [Federal Supreme Court] was dismissed as inadmissible by an order of 19 March 1980 because the grounds for the appeal were not stated within the prescribed time-limits.

2. Even before the judgment of the Landgericht Ansbach of 15 December 1978 had become final Ossberger requested the President of the Tribunal de Grande Instance [Regional Court], Pontoise, to declare enforceable in France that judgment together with the taxing order of the

Landgericht Ansbach of 5 February 1979. The court acceded to that request by an order of 5 June 1979.

Rohr lodged an appeal against that order with the Cour d'Appel, Versailles, claiming in particular that pursuant to Article 18 of the Brussels Convention it was impossible to lodge a defence as to the substance before the German courts since the right to raise the objection of lack of jurisdiction would thereby be lost. The fact that the German courts did not restrict themselves to giving a ruling on jurisdiction but also gave judgment on the substance of the case constitutes a manifest infringement of the rights of the defence and is accordingly contrary to public policy within the meaning of Article 27 (1) of the Brussels Convention, which infringement precludes recognition of that judgment in France.

Ossberger contended before the Cour d'Appel, Versailles, that Article 18 of the Brussels Convention, like Articles 74 and 76 of the French Nouveau Code de Procédure Civile [New Code of Civil Procedure] and Article 39 of the German Zivilprozess Ordnung [Code of Civil Procedure], does not prohibit the submission of a defence as to the substance in the alternative and subject to the objection of lack of jurisdiction but that Rohr voluntarily refrained from pursuing the appropriate procedures. The judgment obtained in Germany is accordingly enforceable in France under the provisions of the Brussels Convention.

Since the Cour d'Appel, Versailles, considered that the outcome of this case depended upon a question of the interpretation of the Brussels Convention it decided, in a judgment of 26 November 1980, to stay the proceedings and requested the Court of Justice to give a ruling, under the Protocol of 3 June 1971 on the Interpretation by the Court of Justice of the Brussels Convention, on the following preliminary question:

> Must it be held with regard to all the versions of the Convention of 27 September 1968 which are drawn up in the Dutch, French, German and Italian languages in accordance with Article 68 of the Convention either that Article 18 thereof prohibits the simultaneous submission in the alternative of a defence concerning the substance of the case where an objection contesting jurisdiction as allowed by that provision has been raised, in order that a final decision on jurisdiction must be reached before any argument on the substance of the action, or that the said Article 18 permits, although it does not say so expressly, the objection contesting jurisdiction for which it makes provision to be submitted at the same time as a defence in the alternative regarding the substance of the action in order to permit the court before which the action is brought to give a decision in a single judgment, if that is appropriate, on both the objection and the substance of the action on the pattern of the express provisions of Article 76 of the Nouveau Code de Procédure Civile [New Code of Civil Procedure] together with the detailed procedures for the protection of rights of the defence?

Decision

. . .

The Court of Justice has had occasion to give a preliminary ruling on a similar question in *Elefanten Schuh GmbH v. Jacqmain*. In that judgment the Court declared:

> Although differences between the different language versions of Article 18 of the Convention appear when it is sought to determine whether, in order to exclude the jurisdiction of the court seised, a defendant must confine himself to contesting that

jurisdiction, or whether he may on the contrary still achieve the same purpose by contesting the jurisdiction of the court as well as the substance of the claim, the second interpretation is more in keeping with the objectives and spirit of the Convention. In fact under the law of civil procedure of certain Contracting States a defendant who raises the issue of jurisdiction and no other might be barred from making his submissions as to the substance if the court rejects his plea that it has no jurisdiction. An interpretation of Article 18 which enabled such a result to be arrived at would be contrary to the right of the defendant to defend himself in the original proceedings, which is one of the aims of the Convention.

This case has disclosed no factor of such a kind as to affect these findings. Accordingly the answer to the question submitted must be that Article 18 of the Convention of 27 September 1968 must be interpreted as meaning that it allows the defendant not only to contest the jurisdiction but to submit at the same time in the alternative a defence on the substance of the action without, however, losing his right to raise an objection of lack of jurisdiction.

On those grounds,

THE COURT (Third Chamber)

in answer to the question referred to it by the Cour d'Appel, Versailles, by judgment of 26 November 1980, hereby rules:

> Article 18 of the Convention of 27 September 1968 must be interpreted as meaning that it allows the defendant not only to contest the jurisdiction but to submit at the same time in the alternative a defence on the substance of the action without, however, losing his right to raise an objection of lack of jurisdiction.

NOTES AND QUESTIONS

(1)(a) Consider again the questions put at p. 721 about the calculation to be made by a person domiciled in one member state of the Community who is sued in another member state. Do the two cases reproduced change the conclusion you reached from just reading the Convention itself?

(b) Note that the two cases illustrate the two ways that jurisdictional issues can come up. In *Elefanten Schuh v. Jacqmain,* the issue is raised in a reference from F–1 (compare *International Shoe Co. v. Washington*);[a] in *Rohr v. Ossberger,* the issue is raised in a reference from F–2 (Compare *McGee v. International Life Insurance Co.*)[b]

(c) It is evident that within the Community the preference is to have the jurisdictional determination made in F–1, and to limit the opportunity of defendant to challenge that determination in F–2. Compared to the American system,[c] (i) which is the sounder in terms of judicial administration; (ii) is there an appreciable difference in terms of fairness to the parties?

(d) In part the preference in the Community for determination of jurisdiction in F–1 by the courts of F–1 stems from the fact that the rules for jurisdiction are clearly spelled out in the

---

[a] Ch. 7, p. 486, *supra.*

[b] Ch. 7, p. 491, *supra.* Note, however, that in *McGee,* the F–2 court in Texas refused to give full faith and credit; in *Rohr,* the F–2 court in France did believe that the judgment should be enforced, but the appellate court was not sure and accordingly put the question to the Court of Justice.

[c] See § 8.01[C], *supra.*

Convention, whereas no comparable rules appear in the U.S. Constitution or federal statutes. On the other hand, at least since *Pennoyer v. Neff,* [d] it has been clear that jurisdiction in the United States is subject to consitutional standards, and at least since *Baldwin* and *Durfee,* [e] it has been clear that jurisdictional determinations, if made after challenge, are binding on F–2. Would you favor greater deference to determinations in F–1 for the United States, coupled with a requirement of specific findings by the F–1 court?[f] Could Congress legislate such a change?

(2)(a) Article 18 of the Brussels Convention, which is relevant to both cases here reproduced, seems to provide for what in American practice would be called a special appearance, i.e., an appearance only to challenge the jurisdiction. The Advocate General in the *Elefanten Schuh* case, a former Judge of the English High Court of Justice, urged the Court of Justice not to be too literal in construing Article 18:

> It would seem to be contrary to the spirit and intention of the Convention to place difficulties in the way of litigants. . . . It would seem an unattractive result that a defendant who desires to contest the jurisdiction should be barred from raising a point which could be speedily dealt with if he failed on jurisdiction. . . .[g]

Essentially the Court accepted this argument of the Advocate General, and held the defendant not precluded from joining its jurisdictional challenge to a defense on the merits. The result is thus comparable to the general rule in the United States.[h]

(b) This still left the question whether defendant's jurisdictional objection was valid. The contract sued on had a choice of forum clause designating Germany as the exclusive forum, and it seemed to violate none of the several provisions of the Convention excluding the effectiveness of such clauses—for consumer contracts (Art. 15), for many contracts of insurance (Art. 12),[i] and for contracts that do not clearly evidence consent to be bound by such a clause (Art. 17, second sentence).[j] But the contract was in German, not Dutch, as required by the local law. Looking again at the aim of the Convention, which was to contribute to the unification of the Community and the free movement of persons and goods, the Court strikes down this impediment to uniformity, rather along the same lines as the decision of the U.S. Supreme Court in overriding

---

[d] 95 U.S. 714 (1878).

[e] Pages 678, 679 *supra*. See also *Sherrer v. Sherrer,* ch. 9, p. 768, *infra*.

[f] Reconsider the question after reading *Williams v. North Carolina* I and II, Chapter 9, pp. 749, 758, *infra*.

[g] [1981] E.C.R. at 1694, [1982] 3 C.M.L.R. at 10–11.

[h] See e.g., Fed. R. Civ. Pro. R. 12(h). Documents Supplement p. 25. In the actual case on remand, the Belgian court held that by having asserted that it was not liable as employer on a contract signed by its parent, the Belgian defendant had submitted to the jurisdiction of the court and lost its opportunity to make the defense based on the choice of forum clause.

[i] Article 12(4) and (5) as well as Article 12A were not in the original Brussels Convention, but were added at the insistence of the British insurance industry.

[j] In two leading cases, the Court of Justice held that a jurisdiction clause as part of "General Conditions of Sale" on a standard purchase order form, even if signed by the other party, does not meet this requirement, nor does a contract that incorporates a longer form with such a clause—for instance an exchange of telexes making reference to a trade association form contract. *Estasis Salotti . . . v. RUWA,* Dec. of 14 Dec. 1976, Case 24/76, [1976] E.C.R. 1831, [1977], 1 C.M.L.R. 345, *Galeries Segoura SPRL v. Bonakdarian,* Dec. of 14 Dec. 1976, Case 25/76, [1976] E.C.R. 1851, [1977], 1 C.M.L.R. 361. Note that the alternative to a writing, providing for a form which accords with practices in international trade or commerce, was also added by the Accession Treaty at the insistence of the British, who thought the needs of commerce more important than protection of social interests. See the still critical article by one of England's leading commercial judges, Sir Michael Kerr, *The EEC Judgments Convention: Some Repercussions beyond the EEC,* in 15 Europarecht 352 (Oct.–Dec. 1980).

the Puerto Rico Dealers' Contract Act in upholding the arbitration clause in *Mitsubishi Motors Corp. v. Soler Chrysler-Plymouth, Inc.*[k]

(3)(a) *Rohr v. Ossberger* again involved the effectiveness of a choice of forum clause. Evidently Rohr, the French buyer, relying on the two cases cited at note b, had asserted that its assent to the general conditions of sale on the back of the order confirmation supplied by Ossberger, the German seller, did not consitute the degree of consent required under Article 17 to confer jurisdiction on the German court designated on the form. That issue, however, did not come before the Court of Justice. The problem before the Court is that Rohr submitted only an article 17 defense, fearing that if it also introduced a substantive defense—e.g., the turbines were defective or arrived late—it would be deemed to have abandoned its jurisdictional defense. Though the case came before the Court of Justice shortly after *Elefanten Schuh,* Rohr had had to make its decision in response to the action in Ansbach three years earlier. Given that the German law on the question was unclear,[l] how should the case have been decided?

(b) Note the technique of the Court of Justice in *Rohr.* The relevant provision of the Convention, Article 18, said—at least in German ("nur"), Italian ("solo"), and Dutch ("uitsluitend") as well as English—that an appearance does not constitute submission to jurisdiction where appearance was entered *solely* to contest the jurisdiction. The defendant said he was deprived of his right to present a defense, by having to choose between a challenge to jurisdiction and a defense on the merits, and contended that this was unfair, and therefore contrary to Article 27 (1) concerning the public law of F–2.

The Court implies that defendant might have had a point: if it had attempted to put in a defense on the merits after, or together with, its challenge to jurisdiction and the German court had held that the jurisdictional challenge had been abandoned, the European Court would have overturned the result, citing *Elefanten Schuh.* But the Court would not presume that the German court would so construe its own law. The defendant should have submitted both his jurisdictional and his substantive defense, and having failed to do so cannot now complain that he was deprived of due process. In the process, the message comes through clearly: (i) Courts of member states may not require a defendant to choose between submitting a jurisdictional and a substantive defense; (ii) Article 18 of the Brussels Convention is to be read sensibly, not literally.

(4)(a) As a result of the way it disposed of the case, the Court in *Rohr* did not need to address a point made by the Advocate General, that the last paragraph of Article 28 of the Convention expressly precludes applying the test of public policy to a jurisdictional objection, with exceptions not here relevant.[m] Prior to the Convention, public policy had often been used as justification for refusal to enforce a foreign judgment, sometimes when the objection went to the choice of law applied by F–1 court, sometimes as a substitute for what Americans would call a due process objection. An objection to the choice of law by F–1 is limited by Article 27(4) to "preliminary questions" relating to family law or succession, and otherwise precluded.[n] Due process objections,

---

[k] Ch. 4, p. 322 *supra.*

[l] See Code of Civil Procedure (ZPO) § 39, amended in 1974. 1 Bülow-Böckstiegel, Internationaler Rechtsverkehr, p. 606-56 (1977 & Supp.).

[m] The exceptions go to matters of insurance, consumer contracts and matters covered by Article 16 which might be classified as "local" actions committed exclusively to one state. For the reference to Article 59, see question 5(b) below.

[n] This has to be implied from the text of the Convention itself, but is stated explicitly in the Jenard Report, p. 720, note m, *supra,* at p. 44.

i.e., questions going to service, notice, and an opportunity to present a defense, are supposed to be dealt with in Article 27(2), which, it turns out, does give the court in F–2 the right (and perhaps duty) to reexamine the basis for jurisdiction in F–1.

(b) In Case 228/81, *Pendy Plastic Products B.V. v. Pluspunkt Handelsgesellschaft m.b.H.,*[o] decided by the Court of Justice some nine months after *Rohr v. Ossberger,* a Dutch firm had brought an action before a Dutch court against a German company, serving the summons and complaint on a Dutch judicial officer with instructions to serve them on the defendant at its last known address in Germany. The request to serve defendant was carried out in accordance with the Hague Service Convention of 1965,[p] which was applicable both in The Netherlands and in the Federal Republic of Germany, but the defendant was not found at the address stated. Plaintiff furnished the court with an extract of the commercial register of the German town, listing the address of defendant at the place where service had been attempted. The court in The Netherlands ruled that plaintiff had demonstrated that it had taken all the necessary steps to locate the person on whom the documents were to be served, and thereafter issued a judgment for about 30,000 guilders plus interest and costs. Plaintiff sought to enforce the judgment in Germany. Should the judgment be enforced?

(c) The German courts rejected enforcement under Articles 34 and 27(2) of the Brussels Convention, because they had not been able to verify that defendant had been served. Plaintiff appealed to the Bundesgerichtshof (Supreme Court), contending that the Dutch court had made the determination called for by Article 20 of the Convention, which could not now be reexamined. The Bundesgerichtshof believed that it had a duty to verify whether service had been properly effected, but put the question to the Court of Justice.[q] The Court of Justice held that

> in accordance with the objective of Article 27 of the Convention, the court of the State in which enforcement is sought must examine the question posed by paragraph (2) of that Article, notwithstanding the decision given by the court of the original State on the basis of the second and third paragraph of Article 20.

The court did not base its holding on public policy, but rather on the objective of Article 27 and the reassuring fact that the prohibition of Article 34—review as to substance—had not been breached.

(d) Think back to the *Somportex* litigation,[r] and assume (i) instead of Philadelphia Chewing Gum Co. the purveyor of Tarzan Gum had been Frankfurt Kaugummi, AG; and (ii) the Brussels Convention had been in full effect in the United Kingdom. The events in London take place as in the actual case, and now Somportex seeks to enforce the judgment in the German court. What result would you expect?

(5)(a) One other aspect of the Brussels Convention is worth noting. Article 3, as we saw, prohibits adjudication on the basis of exorbitant jurisdiction, such as the nationality of the plaintiff

---

[o] Dec. of 15 July 1982, [1983] E.C.R. 2723, [1983] 1 C.M.R. 665.

[p] Convention on the Service Abroad of Judicial and Extrajudicial Documents in Civil or Commercial Matters done at The Hague, Nov. 15, 1965, 20 U.S.T.361, T.I.A.S. No. 6638, 658 U.N.T.S. 163. The Convention is reproduced in 28 U.S.C.A. following Fed. R. Civ. P. 4, and explained in *Restatement (Third) of the Foreign Relations Law of the United States* § 471 (1987).

[q] It appears that the defendant had moved from the address stated in the Commercial Register to another address in the same town, but had not changed its listing in the Register. Whether there was an obligation to change the listing is not clear. The Court of Justice suggests that the process server might have tried harder.

[r] § 8.02[B], *supra.*

or the presence of property of the defendant, but only against persons domiciled in a contracting state. Article 34, however, says that *all* final judgments of Contracting States must be enforced, subject only to the defenses stated in Articles 27 and 28, which focus on conflict with some of the special bases of jurisdiction but say nothing about the exorbitant bases of jurisdiction listed in Article 3. It is thus possible that a person not domiciled in the Community could be sued in one member state on a basis that other member states would normally regard as contrary to international law, but that a judgment resulting from such an action would be required to be enforced in all member states where the defendant might have some property. For example, a French national might bring suit in France against an American company on the basis of the famous Article 14 of the *Code Civil,* which requires only that plaintiff be a French national; if the American company kept funds in a bank account in London, it seems that (once the Convention were effective in England), English courts would have to enforce a judgment of the French court, including a default judgment, against the defendant's English assets. Is that fair?

(b) The drafters of the Brussels Convention understood that this situation might give rise to concern, not only in third countries, such as the United States, but also in countries, such as the United Kingdom, which enjoy their role as financial centers for multinational enterprises. Accordingly, the drafters provided in Article 59 of the Convention[s] that any member state may enter into a bilateral or multilateral convention on the recognition and enforcement of judgments with non-member states which provides that the member state shall not recognize judgments against defendants domiciled in the non-member state that it would not recognize if the defendant were its own domiciliary.

Thus, for example, the United Kingdom could agree with the United States (i) that each other's judgments in civil or commercial matters would be recognized and enforced, subject to stated conditions; and (ii) that judgments rendered on the basis of specified exorbitant jurisdiction in third countries against their domiciliaries would not be recognized or enforced. Assuming such a treaty could be negotiated, if a French judgment against an American defendant founded on Article 14 were presented to an English court for enforcement, the English court would be obligated to the United States not to enforce the judgment, and would not be in violation of the Brussels Convention if it refused enforcement.

(c) In fact, the United States and Britain did conduct negotiations looking to a judgments convention, commencing shortly after Britain joined the Common Market, and well before conclusion of the negotiations on accession of the UK (and the other states) to the Brussels Convention. The hope on the part of the British was that legislation to bring the Brussels Convention into effect, to make other reforms in the law of judgments,[t] and to implement the U.S.–U.K. judgments convention could all be submitted to Parliament in one package. For the United States, which initiated the effort, the negotiation with the United Kingdom appears to have been the first effort to negotiate a treaty on recognition and enforcement of judgments; the British, as we saw, had previously been party to numerous judgments conventions, both within the Commonwealth and with other states, such as the treaty with Belgium involved in the *Sidmetal* case.[u] The expectation was that if the two major common law states could reach agreement, linked to the Common Market convention, such an agreement might serve as a model for other

---

[s] Documents Supplement p. 119.

[t] See p. 718, question (4)(d), *supra.*

[u] See p. 716, question (3), *supra.*

agreements, both to improve the recognition and enforcement of judgments and to reduce the application of exorbitant jurisdiction.

(d) After three years of negotiations (1974–76), the delegates of the two states initialled the text of a draft convention, and thereafter the draft was published by the British government.ᵛ The reaction in Britain was slow in coming, but when it came it was overwhelmingly negative. The provision to take advantage of Article 59 of the Brussels Convention was not objectionable. But the idea that all judgments of courts in the United States would be required to be enforced, including "excessive" jury verdicts, treble damage antitrust judgments, class actions, and judgments rendered on the basis of long-arm jurisdiction, American style, all sent shivers down the spines of the English bar, and particularly the insurance industry.ʷ By September 1978, the British delegation made it clear that without major revisions, the treaty stood no chance of approval by Parliament. For another year, attempts were made to write exclusions into the treaty to make it palatable to the British. Class actions might be excluded, and possibly the trebled part of antitrust damages or even all civil damages given in antitrust actions. But the suggestion that judgments in tort be excluded, or that enforcement of such judgments be made discretionary with the courts where enforcement was sought, proved to be more than the United States could accept. Why have a judgments convention at all if so important a part of civil litigation were not included?

(e) A last effort to keep the negotiations alive centered around a proposed Article 8A, reading as follows:

> Where respondent established that the amount awarded by the court of origin is greatly in excess of the amount, including costs, that would have been awarded on the basis of the findings of law and fact established in the court of origin, had the assessment of that amount been a matter for the court addressed that court may, to the extent then permitted by the law generally applicable in that court to the recognition and enforcement of foreign judgments, recognize and enforce the judgment in a lesser amount.

Should either the United States, or the United Kingdom, favor such a provision? Or would a proceeding to enforce a judgment turn into a *de novo* trial on what the F–2 court would award in comparable circumstances? Could one build a kind of choice of law provision into such a provision, so that, for example the F–2 (say English) court should make its determination not on the basis of an English construction worker's salary but on the salary of the actual injured plaintiff in F–1 (say in Chicago)?

(f) In the spring of 1980, the United Kingdom formally notified the U.S. State Department of what everyone involved in the project already knew. Negotiations of a U.S.-U.K. Judgments Convention were suspended indefinitely.

No further bilateral negotiations of a judgments convention were undertaken by the United States. However, the Hague Conference on Private International Law launched a project in the mid-1990's looking to a multilateral Convention on the Recognition and Enforcement of Judgments, and as of year-end 1997, that project was well underway, with the United States

---

ᵛ Proposed Convention between the United Kingdom and the United States for the Reciprocal Recognition and Enforcement of Judgments in Civil Matters, Cmnd. 6771 (1977). The text is reproduced also in 16 Int'l Leg. Mat. 71 (1977).

ʷ England, of course, also has long-arm jurisdiction under Order 11, as we saw in Chapter 7. What worried the British most, however, was the so-called split tort—where the product was manufactured, say, in England, but the injury occurred in Illinois, and the Illinois court not only took jurisdiction but applied its version of strict liability.

among its principal proponents. It is fair to add that while a number of judgments originating in the United States were denied enforcement in Europe and elsewhere,[x] the original impetus for negotiating a judgments convention with a Common Market country remained theoretical: No case has been reported of the kind suggested in paragraph (a), where a judgment rendered against a third country domiciliary in one member state of the European Community on the basis of exorbitant jurisdiction was sought to be enforced against defendant's assets located in another member state.

[B] The United Nations Convention on Recognition and Enforcement of Foreign Arbitral Awards

As we saw in Chapter 4, many international commercial transactions, including transactions involving a governmental party, are carried on through contracts that contain a provision for arbitration.[a] Typically, arbitration is held at a "neutral" forum, i.e., in neither party's home state. While an agreement to arbitrate nearly always avoids problems of jurisdiction, an arbitration in a state where neither party is domiciled obviously raises questions of enforcement.

One way to enforce arbitral awards in the past was to convert the arbitral award into a judgment (sometimes called "confirming the award"); if the losing party did not pay the award, the resulting judgment could then be enforced like any other judgment, both at the situs and in other states. However, this process was uncertain and time consuming, and as early as the 1920's the states of Western Europe (but not the United States) joined two conventions designed to facilitate enforcement both of agreements to arbitrate and arbitral awards. In 1958, after years of effort spurred by the International Chamber of Commerce but conducted largely under auspices of the United Nations, a conference held in New York produced a Convention on the Recognition and Enforcement of Foreign Arbitral Awards.[b]

At first the United States was reluctant to adhere to the New York Convention, but in 1970—more than ten years after the Convention had entered into force—the Senate gave its advice and consent to U.S. participation, and at the same time Congress adopted implementing legislation in the form of title II of the Federal Arbitration Act, 9 U.S.C. §§ 201–208. The United Kingdom, which had also been reluctant, joined in 1975, and by 1980 all the major commercial states, most of the states of Eastern Europe (including the Soviet Union), and a respectable number of developing countries had become parties to the Convention.[c]

---

[x] See A. Lowenfeld, *International Litigation and Arbitration*, pp. 476-92 (2d ed. 2002).

[a] The law of sovereign immunity is well beyond the scope of this volume. It is pertinent here, however, to point out that an agreement to arbitrate entered into by a state instrumentality is a convenient middle position between submission to jurisdiction of another state's courts, and insisting on an immunity which is hard to sustain and would in many instances lead to no deal at all. Usually an agreement to arbitrate is considered to include consent to jurisdiction to compel arbitration, and to enforce the award, at least at the place chosen as situs of the arbitration. See, generally, *Restatement (Third) of Foreign Relations Law* § 487–88 (1987).

[b] Documents Supplement p. 128.

[c] As of year-end 1997, well over 100 states were parties to the New York Convention, including Russia and most of the former members of the Soviet Union, China, and most of the states of Latin America that had long resisted international arbitration.

§ 8.03 JURISDICTION AND JUDGMENTS 735

Without here pursuing a detailed exploration of the New York Convention,[d] a brief description of the Convention's provision for recognition and enforcement of awards is instructive, both for the comparison with enforcement of judgments of courts, and for its treatment of choice of law.

(1) All Contracting States are required to recognize and enforce arbitral awards to which the Convention applies, without need for resort to the courts of the state where the award was rendered (Art. III), subject only to very limited defenses (Art. V).

(2) For some states, the Convention applies to all arbitral awards considered foreign regardless of where the award was rendered (Art. I(1)); the majority of state parties, however, have made the first reservation provided for in Article I(3), so that the Convention applies only to awards made in another Contracting State. The nationality or domicile of the parties to an arbitration, however, is not significant, nor is the place of performance of the contract subject of the arbitration or the applicable law: an award rendered in an arbitration held in Geneva between a Libyan and a Brazilian party, for example, will be enforceable in the United States, the United Kingdom, France, etc., because those states are parties to the Convention and so is Switzerland.[e]

(3) Arbitrators in international commercial disputes are generally required to decide according to law,[f] but unless the contract in question or the agreement to arbitrate specifies the law to be applied, they seem to be able to decide on the basis of any law they choose. Some arbitrators choose the law applicable where the arbitration is held, some choose the law to which the conflict of laws rule of the situs of the arbitration points, some choose according to their own views on choice of law, and some try to avoid the choice of law question by determining, for example, that whether seller's or buyer's law is chosen, the solution to the problem (e.g., consequence of non-conformity of the merchandise with the specifications) would be the same.[g] At all events, whatever law the arbitrators apply and however they reach the their decision (absent corruption), error in choice of law or in interpreting the law chosen is not a ground for refusing enforcement of the award.

(4) The New York Convention draws no distinction between contested proceedings and awards rendered on default. Even if one party fails to appoint an arbitrator,[h] or fails to participate in the proceedings, an award can be made effective and enforceable, provided proper notice was given and the arbitrators did not exceed the authority conferred on them by the agreement to arbitrate (Article V (1)).

Some idea of the scope of the Convention, and of differing interpretations particularly of the question of arbitrability and public policy (Art. V (2)) can be seen in the two cases that follow, one American, the other Belgian.

---

[d] For a book-length analysis, see A. Van den Berg, *The New York Arbitration Convention* (1981). See also the Quigley and Aksen articles cited in the *Parsons v. Whittemore* case, pp. 738, 740 *infra;* A. Lowenfeld, *International Litigation and Arbitration,* ch. IV (1993).

[e] Arbitration always depends on an agreement to arbitrate, either contained in a contract concluded in advance of any dispute or made after a dispute arises. An agreement to arbitrate normally makes provision for the situs of the arbitration or for choosing that situs, as well as for choosing the arbitrator.

[f] Unless they are expressly authorized in the agreement to arbitrate to act as *amiable compositeurs* or to decide *ex aequo et bono.*

[g] For a discussion of these and other options as well as citation to the copious literature on the subject, see A. Lowenfeld, *The Two-Way Mirror: International Arbitration as Comparative Procedure,* 7 Michigan Yearbook of International Legal Studies 163 (1986).

[h] Many international arbitration agreements call for each side to appoint an arbitrator, and then (i) for the two arbitrators so chosen to appoint the chairman; or (ii) for an institution, such as the International Chamber of Commerce, the American Arbitration Association, the Society of Maritime Arbitrators, etc. to appoint the chairman.

PARSONS & WHITTEMORE OVERSEAS CO., INC. v. SOCIETE GENERALE DE L'INDUSTRIE DU PAPIER (RAKTA)

United States Court of Appeals, Second Circuit
508 F.2d 969 (1974)

J. JOSEPH SMITH, CIRCUIT JUDGE.

Parsons & Whittemore Overseas Co., Inc., (Overseas), an American corporation, appeals from the entry of summary judgment on February 25, 1974, by Judge Lloyd F. MacMahon of the Southern District of New York on the counterclaim by Société Générale de L'Industrie du Papier (RAKTA), an Egyptian corporation, to confirm a foreign arbitral award holding Overseas liable to RAKTA for breach of contract. RAKTA in turn challenges the court's concurrent order granting summary judgment on Overseas' complaint, which sought a declaratory judgment denying RAKTA's entitlement to recover the amount of a letter of credit issued by Bank of America[1] in RAKTA's favor at Overseas' request. Jurisdiction is based on 9 U.S.C. § 203, which empowers federal district courts to hear cases to recognize and enforce foreign arbitral awards, and 9 U.S.C. § 205, which authorizes the removal of such cases from state courts, as was accomplished in this instance.[2] We affirm the district court's confirmation of the foreign award.

In November 1962, Overseas consented by written agreement with RAKTA to construct, start up and, for one year, manage and supervise a paperboard mill in Alexandria, Egypt. The Agency for International Development (AID), a branch of the United States State Department, would finance the project by supplying RAKTA with funds with which to purchase letters of credit in Overseas' favor. Among the contract's terms was an arbitration clause, which provided a means to settle differences arising in the course of performance, and a "force majeure" clause, which excused delay in performance due to causes beyond Overseas' reasonable capacity to control.

Work proceeded as planned until May, 1967. Then, with the Arab-Israeli Six Day War on the horizon, recurrent expressions of Egyptian hostility to Americans—nationals of the principal ally of the Israeli enemy—caused the majority of the Overseas work crew to leave Egypt. On June 6, the Egyptian government broke diplomatic ties with the United States and ordered all Americans expelled from Egypt except those who would apply and qualify for a special visa.

Having abandoned the project for the present with the construction phase near completion, Overseas notified RAKTA that it regarded this postponement as excused by the force majeure clause. RAKTA disagreed and sought damages for breach of contract. Overseas refused to settle and RAKTA, already at work on completing the performance promised by Overseas, invoked the arbitration clause. Overseas responded by calling into play the clause's option to bring a dispute directly to a three-man arbitral board governed by the rules of the International Chamber of Commerce. After several sessions in 1970, the tribunal issued a preliminary award, which recognized Overseas' force majeure defense as good only during the period from May 28 to June 30, 1967. In so limiting Overseas' defense, the arbitration court emphasized that Overseas had made no more than a perfunctory effort to secure special visas and that AID's notification

---

[1] Bank of America assumes the position of an innocent stakeholder and awaits this court's direction on the letter of credit claim.

[2] Overseas initiated suit in New York Supreme Court and the case was removed to federal court on RAKTA's petition.

that it was withdrawing financial backing did not justify Overseas' unilateral decision to abandon the project.[3] After further hearings in 1972, the tribunal made its final award in March, 1973: Overseas was held liable to RAKTA for $312,507.45 in damages for breach of contract and $30,000 for RAKTA's costs; additionally, the arbitrators' compensation was set at $49,000, with Overseas responsible for three-fourths of the sum.

Subsequent to the final award, Overseas in the action here under review sought a declaratory judgment to prevent RAKTA from collecting the award out of a letter of credit issued in RAKTA's favor by Bank of America at Overseas' request. The letter was drawn to satisfy any "penalties" which an arbitral tribunal might assess against Overseas in the future for breach of contract. RAKTA contended that the arbitral award for damages met the letter's requirement of "penalties" and counterclaimed to confirm and enter judgment upon the foreign arbitral award. Overseas' defenses to this counterclaim, all rejected by the district court, form the principal issues for review on this appeal. Four of these defenses are derived from the express language of the applicable United Nations Convention on the Recognition and Enforcement of Foreign Arbitral Awards (Convention), 330 U.N.T.S. 38, and a fifth is arguably implicit in the Convention. These include: enforcement of the award would violate the public policy of the United States, the award represents an arbitration of matters not appropriately decided by arbitration; the tribunal denied Overseas an adequate opportunity to present its case; the award is predicated upon a resolution of issues outside the scope of the contractual agreement to submit to arbitration; and the award is in manifest disregard of law. In addition to disputing the district court's rejection of its position on the letter of credit, RAKTA seeks on appeal modification of the court's order to correct for an arithmetical error in the sum entered for judgment, as well as an assessment of damages and double costs against Overseas for pursuing a frivolous appeal.

I. OVERSEAS' DEFENSES AGAINST ENFORCEMENT

In 1958 the Convention was adopted by 26 of the 45 states participating in the United Nations Conference on Commercial Arbitration held in New York. For the signatory states, the New York Convention superseded the Geneva Convention of 1927, 92 League of Nations Treaty Ser. 302. The 1958 Convention's basic thrust was to liberalize procedures for enforcing foreign arbitral awards: While the Geneva Convention placed the burden of proof on the party seeking enforcement of a foreign arbitral award and did not circumscribe the range of available defenses to those enumerated in the convention, the 1958 Convention clearly shifted the burden of proof to the party defending against enforcement and limited his defenses to seven set forth in Article V. *See* Contini, International Commercial Arbitration, 8 Am.J. Comp.L. 283, 299 (1959). Not a signatory to any prior multilateral agreement on enforcement of arbitral awards, the United States declined to sign the 1958 Convention at the outset. The United States ultimately acceded to the Convention, however, in 1970, [1970] 3 U.S.T. 2517, T.I.A.S. No. 6997, and implemented its accession with 9 U.S.C. §§ 201–208. Under 9 U.S.C. § 208, the existing Federal Arbitration Act, 9 U.S.C. §§ 1–14, applies to the enforcement of foreign awards except to the extent to which the latter may conflict with the Convention. *See generally,* Comment, International Commercial Arbitration under the United Nations Convention and the Amended Federal Arbitration Statute, 47 Wash.L.Rev. 441 (1972).

A. *Public Policy*

---

[3] RAKTA represented to the tribunal that it was prepared to finance the project without AID's assistance.

Article V(2)(b) of the Convention allows the court in which enforcement of a foreign arbitral award is sought to refuse enforcement, on the defendant's motion or *sua sponte,* if "enforcement of the award would be contrary to the public policy of [the forum] country." The legislative history of the provision offers no certain guidelines to its construction. Its precursors in the Geneva Convention and the 1958 Convention's ad hoc committee draft extended the public policy exception to, respectively, awards contrary to "principles of the law" and awards violative of "fundamental principles of the law." In one commentator's view, the Convention's failure to include similar language signifies a narrowing of the defense. Contini, *supra,* 8 Am.J. Comp.L. 283 at 304. On the other hand, another noted authority in the field has seized upon this omission as indicative of an intention to broaden the defense. Quigley, Accession by the United States to the United Nations Convention on the Recognition and Enforcement of Foreign Arbitral Awards, 70 Yale L.J. 1049, 1070–71 (1961).

Perhaps more probative, however, are the inferences to be drawn from the history of the Convention as a whole. The general pro-enforcement bias informing the Convention and explaining its supersession of the Geneva Convention points toward a narrow reading of the public policy defense. An expansive construction of this defense would vitiate the Convention's basic effort to remove preexisting obstacles to enforcement. *See* Straus, Arbitration of Disputes between Multinational Corporations, in New Strategies for Peaceful Resolution of International Business Disputes 114–15 (1971); Digest of Proceedings of International Business Disputes Conference, April 14, 1971, in *id.* at 191 (remarks of Professor W. Reese). Additionally, considerations of reciprocity—considerations given express recognition in the Convention itself[4]—counsel courts to invoke the public policy defense with caution lest foreign courts frequently accept it as a defense to enforcement of arbitral awards rendered in the United States.

We conclude, therefore, that the Convention's public policy defense should be construed narrowly. Enforcement of foreign arbitral awards may be denied on this basis only where enforcement would violate the forum state's most basic notions of morality and justice. *Cf.* 1 Restatement Second of the Conflict of Laws § 117, comment c, at 340 (1971); *Loucks v. Standard Oil Co.,* 224 N.Y. 99, 111, 120 N.E. 198 (1918).

Under this view of the public policy provision in the Convention, Overseas' public policy defense may easily be dismissed. Overseas argues that various actions by United States officials subsequent to the severance of American-Egyptian relations—most particularly, AID's withdrawal of financial support for the Overseas-RAKTA contract—required Overseas, as a loyal American citizen, to abandon the project. Enforcement of an award predicated on the feasibility of Overseas' returning to work in defiance of these expressions of national policy would therefore allegedly contravene United States public policy. In equating "national" policy with United States "public" policy, the appellant quite plainly misses the mark. To read the public policy defense as a parochial device protective of national political interests would seriously undermine the Convention's utility. This provision was not meant to enshrine the vagaries of international polities under the rubric of "public policy." Rather, a circumscribed public policy doctrine was

---

[4] A Contracting State shall not be entitled to avail itself of the present Convention against other Contracting States except to the extent that it is itself bound to apply the Convention.

Article XIV. *Cf.* Comment, *supra,* 47 Wash.L.Rev. 441 at 486–87:

> [I]n a system based upon reciprocity any tendency to take an overly narrow view of foreign arbitral awards will be balanced by a desire to obtain the widest acceptance of America's awards among the courts of other signatory states, which also have the public policy loophole available to them.

contemplated by the Convention's framers and every indication is that the United States, in acceding to the Convention, meant to subscribe to this supranational emphasis. *Cf. Scherk v. Alberto-Culver Co.,* 417 U.S. 506, 94 S.Ct. 2449, 41 L.Ed.2d 270 (1974).[5]

To deny enforcement of this award largely because of the United States' falling out with Egypt in recent years would mean converting a defense intended to be of narrow scope into a major loophole in the Convention's mechanism for enforcement. We have little hesitation, therefore, in disallowing Overseas' proposed public policy defense.

B. *Non-Arbitrability*

Article V(2)(a) authorizes a court to deny enforcement, on a defendant's or its own motion, of a foreign arbitral award when "[t]he subject matter of the difference is not capable of settlement by arbitration under the law of that [the forum] country." Under this provision, a court sitting in the United States might, for example, be expected to decline enforcement of an award involving arbitration of an antitrust claim in view of domestic arbitration cases which have held that antitrust matters are entrusted to the exclusive competence of the judiciary. *See, e. g., American Safety Equipment Corp. v. J. P. Maguire & Co.,* 391 F.2d 821 (2d Cir. 1968). On the other hand, it may well be that the special considerations and policies underlying a "truly international agreement," *Scherk v. Alberto-Culver Co., supra,* 417 U.S. 506 at 515, 94 S.Ct. 2449, call for a narrower view of non-arbitrability in the international than the domestic context. *Compare id. with Wilko v. Swan,* 346 U.S. 427, 74 S.Ct. 182, 98 L.Ed. 168 (1953) (enforcement of international, but not domestic, agreement to arbitrate claim based on alleged Securities Act violations.)

Resolution of Overseas' non-arbitrability argument, however, does not require us to reach such difficult distinctions between domestic and foreign awards. For Overseas' argument, that "United States foreign policy issues can hardly be placed at the mercy of foreign arbitrators 'who are charged with the execution of no public trust' and whose loyalties are to foreign interests," Brief for Appellant at 23, plainly fails to raise so substantial an issue of arbitrability. The mere fact that an issue of national interest may incidentally figure into the resolution of a breach of contract claim does not make the dispute not arbitrable. Rather, certain *categories* of claims may be non-arbitrable because of the special national interest vested in their resolution. *Cf. American Safety Equipment Corp., supra,* 391 F.2d 821 at 826–827. Furthermore, even were the test for non-arbitrability of an ad hoc nature, Overseas' situation would almost certainly not meet the standard, for Overseas grossly exaggerates the magnitude of the national interest involved in the resolution of its particular claim. Simply because acts of the United States are somehow implicated in a case one cannot conclude that the United States is vitally interested in its outcome. Finally, the Supreme Court's decision in favor of arbitrability in a case far more prominently displaying public features than the instant one, Scherk v. Alberto-Culver Co., *supra,* compels by analogy the conclusion that the foreign award against Overseas dealt with a subject arbitrable under United States law.

The court below was correct in denying relief to Overseas under the Convention's non-arbitrability defense to enforcement of foreign arbitral awards. There is no special national interest in judicial, rather than arbitral, resolution of the breach of contract claim underlying the award in this case.

---

[5] Moreover, the facts here fail to demonstrate that considered government policy forbids completion of the contract itself by a private party.

C. *Inadequate Opportunity to Present Defense*

Under Article V(1)(b) of the Convention, enforcement of a foreign arbitral award may be denied if the defendant can prove that he was "not given proper notice . . . or was otherwise unable to present his case." This provision essentially sanctions the application of the forum state's standards of due process. See, Quigley, *supra,* 70 Yale L.J. 1049 at 1067 n. 81; Quigley, *Convention on Foreign Arbitral Awards,* 58 A.B. A.J. 821, 825 (1972); Aksen, *American Arbitration Accession Arrives in the Age of Aquarius,* in New Strategies, *supra,* at 48.

Overseas seeks relief under this provision for the arbitration court's refusal to delay proceedings in order to accommodate the speaking schedule of one of Overseas' witnesses, David Nes, the United States Chargé d'Affaires in Egypt at the time of the Six Day War. This attempt to state a due process claim fails for several reasons. First, inability to produce one's witnesses before an arbitral tribunal is a risk inherent in an agreement to submit to arbitration. By agreeing to submit disputes to arbitration, a party relinquishes his courtroom rights—including that to subpoena witnesses—in favor of arbitration "with all of its well known advantages and drawbacks." Secondly, the logistical problems of scheduling hearing dates convenient to parties, counsel and arbitrators scattered about the globe argues against deviating from an initially mutually agreeable time plan unless a scheduling change is truly unavoidable. In this instance, Overseas' allegedly key witness was kept from attending the hearing due to a prior commitment to lecture at an American university—hardly the type of obstacle to his presence which would require the arbitral tribunal to postpone the hearing as a matter of fundamental fairness to Overseas. Finally, Overseas cannot complain that the tribunal decided the case without considering evidence critical to its defense and within only Mr. Nes' ability to produce. In fact, the tribunal did have before it an affidavit by Mr. Nes in which he furnished, by his own account, "a good deal of the information to which I would have testified." Appendix to Brief of Appellant at 184a. Moreover, had Mr. Nes wished to furnish *all* the information to which he would have testified, there is every reason to believe that the arbitration tribunal would have considered that as well.

The arbitration tribunal acted within its discretion in declining to reschedule a hearing for the convenience of an Overseas witness. Overseas' due process rights under American law, rights entitled to full force under the Convention as a defense to enforcement, were in no way infringed by the tribunal's decision.

D. *Arbitration in Excess of Jurisdiction*

Under Article V(1)(c), one defending against enforcement of an arbitral award may prevail by proving that:

> The award deals with a difference not contemplated by or not falling within the terms of the submission to arbitration, or it contains decisions on matters beyond the scope of the submission to arbitration. . . .

This provision tracks in more detailed form § 10(d) of the Federal Arbitration Act, 9 U.S.C. § 10(d), which authorizes vacating an award "[w]here the arbitrators exceeded their powers." Both provisions basically allow a party to attack an award predicated upon arbitration of a subject matter not within the agreement to submit to arbitration. This defense to enforcement of a foreign award, like the others already discussed, should be construed narrowly. Once again a narrow construction would comport with the enforcement-facilitating thrust of the Convention. In addition, the case law under the similar provision of the Federal Arbitration Act strongly supports a strict reading.

§ 8.03   JURISDICTION AND JUDGMENTS   □   741

In making this defense as to three components of the award, Overseas must therefore overcome a powerful presumption that the arbitral body acted within its powers. Overseas principally directs its challenge at the $185,000 awarded for loss of production. Its jurisdictional claim focuses on the provision of the contract reciting that "[n]either party shall have any liability for loss of production." The tribunal cannot properly be charged, however, with simply ignoring this alleged limitation on the subject matter over which its decision-making powers extended. Rather, the arbitration court interpreted the provision not to preclude jurisdiction on this matter. As in *United Steelworkers of America v. Enterprise Wheel & Car Corp., supra,* the court may be satisfied that the arbitrator premised the award on a construction of the contract and that it is "not apparent," 363 U.S. 593 at 598, that the scope of the submission to arbitration has been exceeded.

The appellant's attack on the $60,000 awarded for start-up expenses and $30,000 in costs cannot withstand the most cursory scrutiny. In characterizing the $60,000 as "consequential damages" (and thus proscribed by the arbitration agreement), Overseas is again attempting to secure a reconstruction in this court of the contract—an activity wholly inconsistent with the deference due arbitral decisions on law and fact. See generally, *Bernhardt v. Polygraphic Company of America, Inc.,* 350 U.S. 198, 203 & n. 4, (1956). The $30,000 in costs is equally unassailable, for the appellant's contention that this portion of the award is inconsistent with guidelines set by the International Chamber of Commerce is twice removed from reality. First of all, contrary to Overseas' representations, these guidelines (contained in the Guide to ICC Arbitration and reproduced in relevant part in Appendix to Brief of Appellant at 408a) do not require, as a pre-condition to an award of expenses, express authority for such an award in the arbitration clause. The arbitration agreement's silence on this matter, therefore, is not determinative in the case under review. Secondly, since the parties in fact complied with the *Guide's* advice to reach agreement on this matter prior to arbitration—*i. e.,* the request by each for such an award for expenses amounts to tacit agreement on this point—any claim of fatal deviation from the *Guide* is disingenuous to say the least.

Although the Convention recognizes that an award may not be enforced where predicated on a subject matter outside the arbitrator's jurisdiction, it does not sanction second-guessing the arbitrator's construction of the parties' agreement. The appellant's attempt to invoke this defense, however, calls upon the court to ignore this limitation on its decision-making powers and usurp the arbitrator's role. The district court took a proper view of its own jurisdiction in refusing to grant relief on this ground.

E. *Award in "Manifest Disregard" of Law*

Both the legislative history of Article V, *see supra,* and the statute enacted to implement the United States' accession to the Convention[6] are strong authority for treating as exclusive the bases set forth in the Convention for vacating an award. On the other hand, the Federal Arbitration Act, specifically 9 U.S.C. § 10, has been read to include an implied defense to enforcement where the award is in "manifest disregard" of the law. *Wilko v. Swan,* 346 U.S. 427, 436.

This case does not require us to decide, however, whether this defense stemming from dictum in *Wilko, supra,* obtains in the international arbitration context. For even assuming that the "manifest disregard" defense applies under the Convention, we would have no difficulty rejecting

---

[6] . . . The court shall confirm the award unless it finds one of the grounds for refusal or deferral of recognition or enforcement specified in the said Convention.
9 U.S.C. § 207.

the appellant's contention that such "manifest disregard" is in evidence here. Overseas in effect asks this court to read this defense as a license to review the record of arbitral proceedings for errors of fact or law—a role which we have emphatically declined to assume in the past and reject once again. "[E]xtensive judicial review frustrates the basic purpose of arbitration, which is to dispose of disputes quickly and avoid the expense and delay of extended court proceedings."

Insofar as this defense to enforcement of awards in "manifest disregard" of law may be cognizable under the Convention, it, like the other defenses raised by the appellant, fails to provide a sound basis for vacating the foreign arbitral award. We therefore affirm the district court's confirmation of the award.

SOC. AUDI-NSU AUTO UNION, A.G. v. S. A. ADELIN PETIT

Cour de Cassation (Supreme Ct.) Belgium
June 28, 1979
[1979] 1 Pasicrisie Belge 1260.[i]

[Petit held an exclusive franchise for distribution of Audi automobiles in Belgium and Luxembourg, pursuant to a contract entered into in 1950, and renewed several times, most recently until December 31, 1973. By letter of December 9, 1972, Audi notified Petit that its distributorship would be terminated effective December 31, 1973, and when Petit protested, Audi commenced arbitration proceedings in Zurich, pursuant to an arbitration clause in the contract. An arbitral panel was convened in Zurich, but Petit appeared solely to challenge the jurisdiction of the arbitrators. The arbitral tribunal held in a preliminary award that it did have jurisdiction, and the District Court of Zurich confirmed the tribunal's jurisdiction.

On December 6, 1975, the arbitral tribunal held that the exclusive franchise had been validly terminated effective December 31, 1973, and that no damages were due to Petit. Meanwhile, Petit had begun an action before the Commercial Court of Liège, Belgium, seeking compensation and damages. Audi challenged the jurisdiction of the Belgian court, and counterclaimed for recognition and enforcement of the arbitral awards. The Commercial Court, as well as the Court of Appeal (citing a decision of the European Court of Justice[j]) held that the Belgian courts had jurisdiction, and that the arbitration clause in the franchise agreement was invalid under Belgian law, because it conflicted with a Law of July 27, 1961 concerning Unilateral Termination of Exclusive Distributorship Contracts]:

THE COURT

. . .

Considering that the recognition of foreign arbitral awards by Belgian courts is, in principle, subject to the condition that the controversy be arbitrable according to Belgian law and can therefore be withdrawn from the jurisdiction of courts;

Considering that the Swiss-Belgian Convention on the Recognition and Enforcement of Judgments and Arbitral Awards of 1959 . . . does not derogate from this rule, which is in any event applicable even if not expressly stated in an international treaty;

---

[i] Translated from the French and edited by the present author; the statement of facts is based on the report of the decision of the Court of Appeal, [1977] Journal des Tribunaux 710: See also 4 Yb. Com'l Arb. 254 (1979).

[j] *Ets. A. de Bloos, S.P.R.L. v. Bouyer,* Dec. of 6 Oct. 1976, [1976] E.C.R. 1497, [1977] 1 C.M.L.R. 60.

Considering that this rule is confirmed by Article 5(2) of the New York Convention on Recognition and Enforcement of Arbitral Awards, which both Switzerland and Belgium have ratified . . .;

. . .

Considering that the Law of July 27, 1961, as amended, provides in Article 4 that if the termination of a sales franchise produces effects in whole or in part in Belgian territory, the injured holder of the franchise can bring suit against the grantor of the franchise in Belgium, in the court either of his own domicile or of the registered office of the grantor, and . . . that that court will exclusively apply Belgian law.

Considering that under Article 6 of the same law, its provisions are applicable notwithstanding any agreement to the contrary concluded prior to the expiration of the contract granting the franchise;

Considering that these mandatory provisions are designed to safeguard for the franchise holder in every case the right to invoke the protection of Belgian law, except if he has renounced that right by an agreement concluded after the expiration of the contract granting the franchise;

Considering that a proceeding concerning the termination of an exclusive sales franchise with effect in whole or in part in Belgian territory is, accordingly, not capable of being settled by an arbitration agreed on prior to the expiration of the contract and having the purpose and effect of applying foreign law;

Considering that, as found by the lower court the exclusive distribution contract contains in Article 16 an arbitration clause conferring jurisdiction on an arbitral tribunal sitting in Zurich, and that Article 15 of the contract provides for the application of the law of the Federal Republic of Germany;

Considering that the court below found, moreover, that the same Article 15 of the contract provides that the place of performance of the contract is at the principal place of business (siège social) of the plaintiff, in Germany; that the court of appeal considers that in this respect, the clause is inconsistent with the real state of affairs, since the franchise was to be carried out in Belgium, and thus is only an artifice motivated by the wish to avoid application of Belgian law, as is shown also by a letter from plaintiff, and that the court of appeal held that this clause can only be considered as consituting an abuse of law (fraude à la loi);

Considering that, in light of the above, the decision appealed from was correct in refusing recognition of the arbitral awards or according them the effect of *res judicata,* because the controversy was not, under Belgian law, capable of settlement by arbitration.[k]

. . .

For these reasons, the appeal is dismissed.

---

[k] The Cour de Cassation also rejects a challenge to the jurisdiction of the Belgian court over the German company, holding that that jurisdiction is consistent with Article 5(1) of the Brussels Convention (Documents Supplement p. 100), and (again) that the attempt in the contract to provide that the place of performance is Germany fails.

NOTES AND QUESTIONS

(1)(a) At least where the United States is involved as either F–1 or F–2, it is apparent that arbitral awards are much easier to enforce than judgments of foreign courts. Is that as it should be?

(b) Consider that judgments of courts are based on a wide variety of jurisdictional bases, only one of which depends on the consent of the judgment debtor; arbitral awards, in contrast, are virtually always based on consent to jurisdiction, given either in advance by contract, or once the dispute arises by a special agreement. Is this difference an adequate explanation of the different treatment of foreign judgments and awards?

(c) Arbitral awards are, generally, final when rendered—i.e., they are usually not appealable and efforts to set them aside are confined to such issues as corruption of the arbitrators or violation of basic procedural norms. Errors of law, mistaken findings of fact, and rulings on discovery or evidence are typically not a basis for setting arbitral awards aside where rendered.[a] Which way does this cut on the question of enforceability?

(2)(a) The *Parsons & Whittemore* case is a fairly comprehensive summary of the obligations inherent in the New York Convention, and of the narrow scope of the defenses available to the party resisting enforcement of an award. Does the statement on p. 738, concerning the public policy defense seem persuasive to you? Should it be applied to enforcement of foreign judgments as well as to foreign arbitral awards? Or is it uniquely dependent on the New York Convention?[b]

(b) Consider the elements of public policy invoked by Overseas. It has agreed with an Egyptian company to construct and manage a paper mill in Egypt, with financing by A.I.D., the United States foreign assistance agency. As tension rises in the Middle East just before the Six-Day War of 1967, the U.S. nationals working for Overseas leave Egypt; thereafter Egypt and the United States break diplomatic relations and restrictions are imposed by the State Department on travel to Egypt by U.S. citizens.

Overseas says we regard the project as abandoned, and our obligation discharged by force majeure. RAKTA, the Egyptian company, disagrees, and the issue is submitted to arbitration in Sweden.[c] The arbitral tribunal says the excuse of force majeure is good only for about five weeks; the fact that AID financing is withdrawn did not, in the arbitrators' view, justify Overseas in pulling out of the project. Is this a case where a defense based on public policy should have prevailed?

(c) What if

(i) the U.S. State Department had requested Overseas not to resume work on the paper mill; or

---

[a] Given the many countries in the world, the statement in the text is obviously oversimplified; it does, however, represent the typical situation in most states where international arbitration is commonly conducted—e.g., France, Switzerland, Sweden, The Netherlands, the United States, Japan, and even the United Kingdom since 1979.

[b] Note that Judge Smith cites to *Loucks v. Standard Oil Co.*, Ch. 1, p. 34, *supra*, which contains Judge Cardozo's classic formulation of the use of public policy in choice of law.

[c] The arbitrators were a U.S. citizen, an Egyptian, and as chairman Judge Lagergren of Sweden, who later became the first President of the Iran-U.S. Claims Tribunal sitting at The Hague. Both party-appointed arbitrators dissented, for different reasons, and thus the award was essentially Judge Lagergren's alone.

(ii) the State Department had notified the court that it regarded the award in favor of RAKTA as contrary to U.S. public policy.

Would either element change the binding character of the award?

(3)(a) Note that Article V(2) of the New York Convention contains two main grounds for refusal to enforce a foreign arbitral award, both discretionary with the court in F–2. Paragraph (a) speaks to the arbitrability under the law of F–2, and paragraph (b) speaks to the public policy of F–2. Which is involved in *Petit v. Audi*?

(b) One way to try to separate the two clauses is to vary the facts of the *Audi* case. Suppose the arbitrators in Zurich had found that Audi was not justified in terminating the distributorship, and had awarded damages to Petit. He then seeks to enforce the award in Belgium, and Audi defends on the ground that under Belgian law disputes between distributors and dealers with effect in Belgium are not capable of settlement by arbitration. Would the Belgian court deny enforcement under Article V(2)(a), even though Article V(2)(b) is clearly not involved?

(c) In many ways the *Audi* case is similar to *Mitsubishi v. Soler Chrysler-Plymouth*,[d] decided by the U.S. Supreme Court some six years later, except of course that *Audi* involved recognition of an award, whereas *Mitsubishi* involved only the agreement to arbitrate. Nevertheless, one gets the impression that the two Supreme Courts weigh somewhat differently the values of the international convention, set against the local protective legislation. Which approach do you prefer?[e]

(d) Note that both in *Audi* and in *Mitsubishi* the manufacturer includes a choice of law clause designed (at least in part) to avoid local protective laws. Audi adds a provision that offends the Belgian court, stating that the contract is deemed to be performed in Germany. An English court might well regard such a clause more favorably, but at least some American courts would agree with the Belgian court.[f] Could one then draft a contract providing for arbitration in Zurich but without any choice of law clause, or even with a clause providing for Belgian law to be applied? Do you think such a clause would have changed the result in *Petit v. Audi,* either in Zurich or in Liège?

(4)(a) The drafters of the Brussels Convention considered but eventually rejected including arbitral awards within the scope of the Convention.[g] Does the *Audi* case suggest this was a wise decision?

(b) Suppose there had been no arbitration clause in the contract between Petit and Audi, but instead a choice of forum clause pointing to a German court, as in *Elefanten Schuh*. Suppose, further, that the contract was written in all the necessary languages and duly assented to by Petit. The contract is terminated, Petit protests, Audi brings suit in Germany, relying on Article 17 of the Brussels Convention, and the German court renders a judgment in favor of Audi. That judgment comes up for recognition in Belgium, and Petit pleads Article 27(1) of the Brussels Convention. Would you expect the same result as in the actual case? Remember that in the actual

---

[d] Ch. 4, p. 322, *supra.*

[e] The *Audi* case was cited in the dissenting opinion in *Mitsubishi,* for the proposition that the New York Convention does permit exceptions for subjects the forum regards as non-arbitrable.

[f] Recall *Southern International Sales v. Potter & Brumfield Div.,* Ch. 4, p. 272, *supra.*

[g] Note that Article 220 of the Treaty of Rome, p. 718–19, *supra,* speaks both of judgments of courts and of arbitration awards.

case, the judgment of the Belgian Cour de Cassation is the last word; in the hypothetical case, the Belgian court might (or might have to?) ask for a ruling from the European Court of Justice.

(c) The last hypothetical brings up a basic difference between the New York Arbitration Convention and the European Judgments Convention. The former aims at universality, but leaves implementation to the courts (and statutes) of member states; the latter is limited to a group of states linked to one another in a variety of ways, and (since the 1971 Protocol) provides for supervision by a single Court of Justice, similar in function to the U.S. Supreme Court.

CHAPTER 9

CONFLICT OF LAWS AND FAMILY LAW

INTRODUCTION: The State's Interest in Marriage—Two Thousand Years of History

Contrary to common belief,[a] it is not true that marriage was always subject to control of government. In ancient Rome, for example, the marriage relation was deemed to be wholly a matter of personal concern. Marriage was based entirely on the will of the parties, and was freely terminable. While there were certain customary ceremonies, neither state nor church took any part. The early Christian Church accepted this situation, even after the rise of the Christian emperors (ca. 300 A.D.); as late as the time of Justinian (ca. 550 A.D.), there had been no legislation concerning marriage, no requirement of religious blessing, and an attempt to restrict divorce and remarriage failed.[b]

As more and more of the life of the people came under influence of the Christian church, marriage too became the subject of a religious service, and gradually a bridal mass became customary in Western Europe, including England. But apparently the religious service had nothing to do with the legality or validity of the marriage. To the extent there was civil legislation concerning marriage, it provided that in specified circumstances—for instance the adultery of the wife—the guilty party was to be handed over to the bishop for judgment. When William the Conqueror definitively separated spiritual from temporal tribunals, the whole of marriage law was assigned to the Church. If matrimonial questions became important in civil litigation, the king's courts would look to the ecclesiastical courts. By the late middle ages (ca. 1200–1500) the Church had developed elaborate matrimonial law, including rules concerning prohibited degrees of consanguinity, requirements that a priest be present at all weddings, and eventually, that marriage was a sacrament. Divorce was not possible, but a variety of diriments, impediments, and dispensations made annulments possible, at least for those able to pay.

The uncertainty and apparent arbitrariness of the Church's law on marriage and divorce became, in England and in Germany, one of the factors contributing to the Reformation.[c] In England, of course, the ecclesiastical marriage law became a direct precipitant of the Reformation, when

---

[a] "Marriage, as creating the most important relation in life, as having more to do with morals and civilization of a people than any other institution, has always been subject to the control of the legislature." Field, J. in *Maynard v. Hill,* 125 U.S. 190, 205 (1888). Similar statements appear in the cases in this chapter and many other cases and debates.

[b] See, e.g., Bryce, *Marriage and Divorce Under Roman and English Law,* in *Studies in History and Jurisprudence* 782, 798–99 (1901).

[c] "Ein lauter Narrenspiel," Luther called it—"a pure fool's game." Von Ehesachen (1530) in 30(3) *Luther's Werke* 209, 211 (Weimar 1910).

it collided with the personal wishes of King Henry VIII.[d] What Henry did was to cut the ties between the "English" Church and the Papacy, and to "enact establish and ordain That all Causes Testamentary, Causes of Matrimony and Divorce . . . shall be from henceforth heard . . . finally and definitively adjudged and determined within the King's jurisdiction and Authority, and not elsewhere."[e] The archbishops of Canterbury and York were given supreme appellate jurisdiction over matrimonial causes; Cranmer, Henry's supporter, became Archbishop of Canterbury, granted Henry his annulment, and Henry was free to marry again. In the process, what had been ecclesiastical law not connected to the state, became English law, though committed to special courts. With minor changes, that law—now the law of England, remained unchanged until 1857. When English settlers came to America, this was one of the two principal sources of American family law.

The other principal source was more clearly Protestant. It flourished only briefly in England in the seventeenth century, but it manifested an intellectual tradition antecedent to much of the thought of the New England colonies—anti-establishment, anti-clerical, and dedicated to the proposition that it was the people through their elected secular representatives who would make the laws, and conduct the ceremonies, concerned with marriage. John Milton wrote, "As for marriages, that ministers should meddle with them, as not sanctified or legitimate without their celebration, I find no ground in scripture, either of precept or example."[f] In the New England colonies, legislation concerning marriage was a way of protecting the settlers against the English crown. Gradually, the legislation took on more substantive content, about divorce, support, permitted and forbidden marriage, and so on, as well as dower and similar economic incidents of marriage. Unlike the Catholic/Anglican tradition, the Puritans considered marriage a contract, subject to regulation by civil law. Of course, to the Puritans, legislating morality came naturally.

After independence, the two strands came together in the United States, as ecclesiastical courts in the southern states disappeared, and separation of church and state spread throughout the growing country. The substance of the law varied widely, but the idea that marriage and divorce were proper subjects for state action came to be accepted. Where legislatures acted,[g] courts were not far behind. In an era before Human Services Administrations, Social Security, and similar institutions, courts were available to apply the law and resolve disputes.

Interestingly enough, neither the jurisdiction of the courts, nor their ability to choose the law to be applied, seem to have been thought through with care. While the substance of the law

---

[d] One can get an appreciation of the intricacies of medieval canon law by examining Henry's case itself. Strictly speaking, the King did not seek a divorce, but a declaration that he had never been legally married to Catherine of Aragon. There was some substance to the claim, as Catherine had been previously married to Henry's deceased brother, Arthur. Henry's marriage to Catherine had been pursuant to a dispensation by a previous pope, but now Henry sought an annulment by reason of affinity. The annulment might well have been granted; the same pope had a few years earlier granted an annulment on far weaker grounds to Henry's sister, Margaret of Scotland. The crisis came because Pope Clement VII, following the sack of Rome, found himself in 1530 in the power of the Emperor Charles V, the nephew and protector of Catherine of Aragon.

[e] 24 Henry 8, c. 12 (1532).

[f] Similar statements were made on the European continent by the leaders of the Reformation, notably by Luther, who rebelled against (among other things) the prohibition of marriage by clergy.

[g] For instance, Pennsylvania adopted a general divorce law in 1785, Massachusetts in 1786, and all of the New England states and New York had divorce laws before 1800. In New York, the only ground for divorce under the law of 1787 was adultery; Vermont in 1798 adopted a law permitting divorce for impotence, adultery, intolerable severity, three years' willful desertion, and long absence with presumption of death; Rhode Island allowed divorce for "gross misbehaviour and wickedness in either of the parties, repugnant to and in violation of the marriage covenant," and so on. See N. Blake, *The Road to Reno, A History of Divorce in the United States,* 50 (1962).

varied widely once one got past prohibitions against bigamy and incest, a common thread was that a divorce could be granted only by a court and that it required cause—grounds was the usual term—i.e., one party had to allege that the other party was at fault and that she (or he) was not. Divorce by consent was contrary to public policy—i.e., contrary to the interest of the state—and some courts were especially attentive to the danger of collusion. Moreover, an action for divorce was not like any other action, in which one sued the defendant where he could be found; for divorce, the court's jurisdiction had to be based on some relation between the forum and the parties, usually the domicile of the plaintiff, rather than of the defendant.[h] This made sense when the deserted wife sought freedom from the husband whose whereabouts were unknown. What would happen, however, if the plaintiff established a domicile other than where he had lived with his/her wife/husband? This is the problem of the *Williams* case.

§ 9.01 Ex Parte Divorce: Jurisdiction and the Full Faith and Credit Clause

WILLIAMS v. NORTH CAROLINA (I)

United States Supreme Court
317 U.S. 287 (1942)

Mr. Justice Douglas delivered the opinion of the Court.

Petitioners were tried and convicted of bigamous cohabitation under § 4342 of the North Carolina Code, 1939, and each was sentenced for a term of years to a state prison. The judgment of conviction was affirmed by the Supreme Court of North Carolina. 220 N. C. 445, 17 S. E. 2d 769. The case is here on certiorari.

Petitioner Williams was married to Carrie Wyke in 1916 in North Carolina and lived with her there until May, 1940. Petitioner Hendrix was married to Thomas Hendrix in 1920 in North Carolina and lived with him there until May, 1940. At that time petitioners went to Las Vegas, Nevada, and on June 26, 1940, each filed a divorce action in the Nevada court. The defendants in those divorce actions entered no appearance nor were they served with process in Nevada. In the case of defendant Thomas Hendrix, service by publication was had by publication of the summons in a Las Vegas newspaper and by mailing a copy of the summons and complaint to his last post-office address. In the case of defendant Carrie Williams, a North Carolina sheriff delivered to her in North Carolina a copy of the summons and complaint. A decree of divorce was granted petitioner Williams by the Nevada court on August 26, 1940, on the ground of extreme cruelty, the court finding that "the plaintiff has been and now is a *bona fide* and continuous resident of the County of Clark, State of Nevada, and had been such resident for more than six weeks immediately preceding the commencement of this action in the manner prescribed by law." The Nevada court granted petitioner Hendrix a divorce on October 4, 1940, on the grounds of wilful neglect and extreme cruelty, and made the same finding as to this petitioner's *bona fide* residence in Nevada as it made in the case of Williams. Petitioners were

---

[h] For the suggestion that Story is the true author of the rule that divorce jurisdiction rests on domicile, see Cook, *Is Haddock v. Haddock Overruled?* 18 Ind. L.J. 165, 166 (1943), citing J. Story, *Commentaries on the Conflict of Laws* § § 228–30. (1st ed. 1834). Story in turn relies on early Massachusetts cases based on a statute of 1795 vesting jurisdiction to grant divorce in the courts of the county "where the parties live."

married to each other in Nevada on October 4, 1940. Thereafter they returned to North Carolina where they lived together until the indictment was returned. Petitioners pleaded not guilty and offered in evidence exemplified copies of the Nevada proceedings, contending that the divorce decrees and the Nevada marriage were valid in North Carolina as well as in Nevada. The State contended that since neither of the defendants in the Nevada actions was served in Nevada nor entered an appearance there, the Nevada decrees would not be recognized as valid in North Carolina. On this issue the court charged the jury in substance that a Nevada divorce decree based on substituted service where the defendant made no appearance would not be recognized in North Carolina. . . . The State further contended that petitioners went to Nevada not to establish a *bona fide* residence but solely for the purpose of taking advantage of the laws of that State to obtain a divorce through fraud upon that court. On that issue the court charged the jury that, . . . the defendants had the burden of satisfying the jury, but not beyond a reasonable doubt, of the *bona fides* of their residence in Nevada for the required time. Petitioners excepted to these charges. The Supreme Court of North Carolina in affirming the judgment held that North Carolina was not required to recognize the Nevada decrees under the full faith and credit clause of the Constitution (Art. IV, § 1) by reason of *Haddock v. Haddock,* 201 U. S. 562 [1906]. The intimation in the majority opinion (220 N. C. pp. 460–464) that the Nevada divorces were collusive suggests that the second theory on which the State tried the case may have been an alternative ground for the decision below, adequate to sustain the judgment under the rule of *Bell v. Bell,* 181 U. S. 175—a case in which this Court held that a decree of divorce was not entitled to full faith and credit when it had been granted on constructive service by the courts of a state in which neither spouse was domiciled. But there are two reasons why we do not reach that issue in this case. In the first place, North Carolina does not seek to sustain the judgment below on that ground. Moreover it admits that there probably is enough evidence in the record to require that petitioners be considered "to have been actually domiciled in Nevada." In the second place, the verdict against petitioners was a general one. Hence, even though the doctrine of *Bell v. Bell, supra,* were to be deemed applicable here, we cannot determine on this record that petitioners were not convicted on the other theory on which the case was tried and submitted, *viz.* the invalidity of the Nevada decrees because of Nevada's lack of jurisdiction over the defendants in the divorce suits. That is to say, the verdict of the jury for all we know may have been rendered on that ground alone, since it did not specify the basis on which it rested. It therefore follows here as in *Stromberg v. California,* 283 U. S. 359, 368, that if one of the grounds for conviction is invalid under the Federal Constitution, the judgment cannot be sustained. . . .

. . . Accordingly, we cannot avoid meeting the *Haddock v. Haddock* issue in this case by saying that the petitioners acquired no *bona fide* domicil in Nevada. . . . [W]e cannot evade the constitutional issue in this case on the easy assumption that petitioners' domicil in Nevada was a sham and a fraud. Rather, we must treat the present case for the purpose of the limited issue before us precisely the same as if petitioners had resided in Nevada for a term of years and had long ago acquired a permanent abode there. In other words, we would reach the question whether North Carolina could refuse to recognize the Nevada decrees because, in its view and contrary to the findings of the Nevada court, petitioners had no actual, *bona fide* domicil in Nevada, if and only if we concluded that *Haddock v. Haddock* was correctly decided. But we do not think it was.

The *Haddock* case involved a suit for separation and alimony, brought in New York by the wife on personal service of the husband. The husband pleaded in defense a divorce decree obtained by him in Connecticut where he had established a separate domicil. This Court held that New York, the matrimonial domicil where the wife still resided, need not give full faith and credit to the Connecticut decree, since it was obtained by the husband who wrongfully left his wife in the matrimonial domicil, service on her having been obtained by publication and she not having entered an appearance in the action. But we do not agree with the theory of the *Haddock* case that, so far as the marital status of the parties is concerned, a decree of divorce granted under such circumstances by one state need not be given full faith and credit in another.

. . . .

This Court only recently stated that Art. IV, § 1 and the Act of May 26, 1790 require that "not some, but full" faith and credit be given judgments of a state court. *Davis* v. *Davis,* 305 U. S. 32, 40. Thus, even though the cause of action could not be entertained in the state of the forum, either because it had been barred by the local statute of limitations or contravened local policy, the judgment thereon obtained in a sister state is entitled to full faith and credit. . . . So far as *judgments* are concerned, the decisions, as distinguished from dicta, show that the actual exceptions have been few and far between, apart from *Haddock v. Haddock.* For this Court has been reluctant to admit exceptions in case of *judgments* rendered by the courts of a sister state, since the "very purpose" of Art. IV, § 1 was "to alter the status of the several states as independent foreign sovereignties, each free to ignore obligations created under the laws or by the judicial proceedings of the others, and to make them integral parts of a single nation . . . ."[quoting from *Milwaukee County v. White Co.,* p. 673, *supra.*]

This Court, to be sure, has recognized that in case of *statutes,* "the extra-state effect of which Congress has not prescribed," some "accommodation of the conflicting interests of the two states" is necessary. *Alaska Packers Assn. v. Industrial Accident Comm'n* [p. 386, *supra*]. But that principle would come into play only in case the Nevada decrees were assailed on the ground that Nevada must give full faith and credit in its divorce proceedings to the divorce statutes of North Carolina. Even then, it would be of no avail here. For as stated in the *Alaska Packers* case, *"Prima facie* every state is entitled to enforce in its own courts its own statutes, lawfully enacted. One who challenges that right, because of the force given to a conflicting statute of another state by the full faith and credit clause, assumes the burden of showing, upon some rational basis, that of the conflicting interests involved those of the foreign state are superior to those of the forum . . . ." It is difficult to perceive how North Carolina could be said to have an interest in Nevada's domiciliaries superior to the interest of Nevada. Nor is there any authority which lends support to the view that the full faith and credit clause compels the courts of one state to subordinate the local policy of that state, as respects its domiciliaries, to the statutes of any other state. Certainly *Bradford Electric Co. v. Clapper* [p. 385, *supra*], did not so hold. Indeed, the recent case of *Pacific Employers Ins. Co. v. Industrial Accident Comm'n* [p. 389, *supra*], held that in the case of statutes "the full faith and credit clause does not require one state to substitute for its own statute, applicable to persons and events within it, the conflicting statute of another state, even though that statute is of controlling force in the courts of the state of its enactment with respect to the same persons and events."

Moreover, *Haddock v. Haddock* is not based on the contrary theory. Nor did it hold that a decree of divorce granted by the courts of one state need not be given full faith and credit in another if the grounds for the divorce would not be recognized by the courts of the forum. . . .

The historical view that a proceeding for a divorce was a proceeding *in rem* (2 Bishop, Marriage & Divorce, 4th ed., § 164) was rejected by the *Haddock* case. We likewise agree that it does not aid in the solution of the problem presented by this case to label these proceedings as proceedings *in rem.* Such a suit, however, is not a mere *in personam* action. Domicil of the plaintiff, immaterial to jurisdiction in a personal action, is recognized in the *Haddock* case and elsewhere (Beale, Conflict of Laws, § 110.1) as essential in order to give the court jurisdiction which will entitle the divorce decree to extraterritorial effect, at least when the defendant has neither been personally served nor entered an appearance. The findings made in the divorce decrees in the instant case must be treated on the issue before us as meeting those requirements. For it seems clear that the provision of the Nevada statute that a plaintiff in this type of case must "reside" in the State for the required period requires him to have a domicil, as distinguished from a mere residence, in the state. . . . Hence, the decrees in this case, like other divorce decrees, are more than *in personam* judgments. They involve the marital status of the parties. Domicil creates a relationship to the state which is adequate for numerous exercises of state power. . . . Each state as a sovereign has a rightful and legitimate concern in the marital status of persons domiciled within its borders. The marriage relation creates problems of large social importance. Protection of offspring, property interests, and the enforcement of marital responsibilities are but a few of commanding problems in the field of domestic relations with which the state must deal. Thus it is plain that each state, by virtue of its command over its domiciliaries and its large interest in the institution of marriage, can alter within its own borders the marriage status of the spouse domiciled there, even though the other spouse is absent. There is no constitutional barrier if the form and nature of the substituted service . . . meet the requirements of due process. . . . Accordingly, it was admitted in the *Haddock* case that the divorce decree, though not recognized in New York, was binding on both spouses in Connecticut where granted. . . . It therefore follows that, if the Nevada decrees are taken at their full face value (as they must be on the phase of the case with which we are presently concerned), they were wholly effective to change in that state the marital status of the petitioners and each of the other spouses by the North Carolina marriages. Apart from the requirements of procedural due process . . . not challenged here by North Carolina, no reason based on the Federal Constitution has been advanced for the contrary conclusion. But the concession that the decrees were effective in Nevada makes more compelling the reasons for rejection of the theory and result of the *Haddock* case.

This Court stated in *Atherton v. Atherton* [181 U.S. 155 (1901)] that "A husband without a wife, or a wife without a husband, is unknown to the law." But if one is lawfully divorced and remarried in Nevada and still married to the first spouse in North Carolina, an even more complicated and serious condition would be realized. . . . Under the circumstances of this case, a man would have two wives, a wife two husbands. The reality of a sentence to prison proves that that is no mere play on words. Each would be a bigamist for living in one state with the only one with whom the other state would permit him lawfully to live. Children of the second marriage would be bastards in one state but legitimate in the other. And all that would flow from the legalistic notion that where one spouse is wrongfully deserted he retains power over the matrimonial domicil so that the domicil of the other spouse follows him wherever he may go, while, if he is to blame, he retains no such power. But such considerations are inapposite. As stated by Mr. Justice Holmes in his dissent in the *Haddock* case (201 U. S. p. 630), they constitute a "pure fiction, and fiction always is a poor ground for changing substantial rights." Furthermore, the fault or wrong of one spouse in leaving the other becomes under that view a jurisdictional fact on which this Court would ultimately have to pass. Whatever may be said as to the practical effect which such a rule would have in clouding divorce decrees, the question as to where the fault lies has no relevancy to the existence of state power in such circumstances. . . . The existence of the power of a state to alter the marital status of its domiciliaries, as distinguished from the wisdom of its exercise, is not dependent on the underlying causes of the domestic rift. As we have said, it is dependent on the relationship which domicil creates and the pervasive control which a state has over marriage and divorce within its own borders. . . . As stated above, we see no reason, and none has here been advanced, for making the existence of state power depend on an inquiry as to where the fault in each domestic dispute lies. And it is difficult to prick out any such line of distinction in the generality of the words of the full faith and credit clause. Moreover, so far as state power is concerned, no distinction between a matrimonial domicil and a domicil later acquired has been suggested or is apparent. . . . It is one thing to say as a matter of state law that jurisdiction to grant a divorce from an absent spouse should depend on whether by consent or by conduct the latter has subjected his interest in the marriage status to the law of the separate domicil acquired by the other spouse. Beale, Conflict of Laws, § 113.11; Restatement, Conflict of Laws, § 113. But where a state adopts, as it has the power to do, a less strict rule, it is quite another thing to say that its decrees affecting the marital status of its domiciliaries are not entitled to full faith and credit in sister states. Certainly if decrees of a state altering the marital status of its domiciliaries are not valid throughout the Union even though the requirements of procedural due process are wholly met, a rule would be fostered which could not help but bring "considerable disaster to innocent persons" and "bastardize children hitherto supposed to be the offspring of lawful marriage" . . . These intensely practical considerations emphasize for us the essential function of the full faith and credit clause in substituting a command for the former principles of comity. . . .

It is objected, however, that if such divorce decrees must be given full faith and credit, a substantial dilution of the sovereignty of other states will be effected. For it is pointed out that under such a rule one state's policy of strict control over the institution of marriage could be thwarted by the decree of a more lax state. But such an objection goes to the application of the full faith and credit clause to many situations. It is an objection in varying degrees of intensity to the enforcement of a judgment of a sister state based on a cause of action which could not be enforced in the state of the forum. Mississippi's policy against gambling transactions was over-ridden in *Fauntleroy v. Lum,* [p. 639, *supra*], when a Missouri judgment based on such a Mississippi contract was enforced by this Court. Such is part of the price of our federal system.

This Court, of course, is the final arbiter when the question is raised as to what is a permissible limitation on the full faith and credit clause. . . . But the question for us is a limited one. In the first place, we repeat that in this case we must assume that petitioners had a *bona fide* domicil in Nevada, not that the Nevada domicil was a sham. We thus have no question on the present record whether a divorce decree granted by the courts of one state to a resident, as distinguished from a domiciliary, is entitled to full faith and credit in another state. Nor do we reach here the question as to the power of North Carolina to refuse full faith and credit to Nevada divorce decrees because, contrary to the findings of the Nevada court, North Carolina finds that no *bona fide* domicil was acquired in Nevada. In the second place, the question as to what is a permissible limitation on the full faith and credit clause does not involve a decision on our part as to which state policy on divorce is the most desirable one. It does not involve selection of a rule which will encourage on the one hand or discourage on the other the practice of divorce. That choice in the realm of morals and religion rests with the legislatures of the states. Our own views as to the marriage institution and the avenues of escape which some states have created are immaterial. It is a Constitution which we are expounding—a Constitution which in no small measure brings separate sovereign states into an integrated whole through the medium of the full faith and credit clause. Within the limits of her political power North Carolina may, of course, enforce her own policy regarding the marriage relation—an institution more basic in our civilization than any other. But society also has an interest in the avoidance of polygamous marriages . . . and in the protection of innocent offspring of marriages deemed legitimate in other jurisdictions. And other states have an equally legitimate concern in the status of persons domiciled there as respects the institution of marriage. So, when a court of one state acting in accord with the requirements of procedural due process alters the marital status of one domiciled in that state by granting him a divorce from his absent spouse, we cannot say its decree should be excepted from the full faith and credit clause merely because its enforcement or recognition in another state would conflict with the policy of the latter. Whether Congress has the power to create exceptions . . . is a question on which we express no view. It is sufficient here to note that Congress, in its sweeping requirement that judgments of the courts of one state be given full faith and credit in the courts of another, has not done so. And the considerable interests involved, and the substantial and far-reaching effects which the allowance of an exception would have on innocent persons, indicate that the purpose of the full faith and credit clause and of the supporting legislation would be thwarted to a substantial degree if the rule of *Haddock v. Haddock* were perpetuated.

Haddock v. Haddock is overruled. The judgment is reversed and the cause is remanded to the Supreme Court of North Carolina for proceedings not inconsistent with this opinion.

MR. JUSTICE FRANKFURTER, concurring:

I join in the opinion of the Court but think it appropriate to add a few words.

Article 91 of the British North America Act (1867) gives the Parliament of Canada exclusive legislative authority to deal with marriage and divorce. Similarly, Article 51 of the Australia Constitution Act (1900) empowers the Commonwealth Parliament to make laws with respect to marriage and divorce. The Constitution of the United States, however, reserves authority over marriage and divorce to each of the forty-eight states. That is our starting-point. In a country like ours where each state has the constitutional power to translate into law its own notions of policy concerning the family institution, and where citizens pass freely from one state to another, tangled marital situations, like the one immediately before us, inevitably arise. They arose before and after the decision in the *Haddock* case, 201 U.S. 562, and will, I daresay, continue to arise no matter what we do today. For these complications cannot be removed by any decisions this Court can make—neither the crudest nor the subtlest juggling of legal concepts could enable us to bring forth a uniform national law of marriage and divorce.

We are not authorized nor are we qualified to formulate a national code of domestic relations. We cannot, by making "jurisdiction" depend upon a determination of who is the deserter and who the deserted, or upon the shifting notions of policy concealed by the cloudy abstraction of "matrimonial domicile," turn this into a divorce and probate court for the United States. There may be some who think our modern social life is such that there is today a need, as there was not when the Constitution was framed, for vesting national authority over marriage and divorce in Congress, just as the national legislatures of Canada and Australia have been vested with such powers. Beginning in 1884, numerous proposals to amend the Constitution to confer such authority have been introduced in Congress. But those whose business it is to amend the Constitution have not seen fit to amend it in this way. . . . This Court should abstain from trying to reach the same end by indirection. We should not feel challenged by a task that is not ours, even though it is difficult. Judicial attempts to solve problems that are intrinsically legislative—because their elements do not lend themselves to judicial judgment or because the necessary remedies are of a sort which judges cannot prescribe—are apt to be as futile in their achievement as they are presumptuous in their undertaking.

There is but one respect in which this Court can, within its traditional authority and professional competence, contribute uniformity to the law of marriage and divorce, and that is to enforce respect for the judgment of a state by its sister states when the judgment was rendered in accordance with settled procedural standards. As the Court's opinion shows, it is clearly settled that if a judgment is binding in the state where it was rendered, it is equally binding in every other state. This rule of law was not created by the federal courts. It comes from the Constitution and the Act of May 26, 1790, c. 11, 1 Stat. 122. Congress has not exercised its power under the Full Faith and Credit Clause to meet the special problems raised by divorce decrees. There will be time enough to consider the scope of its power in this regard when Congress chooses to exercise it.

. . . .

For all but a very small fraction of the community the niceties of resolving such conflicts among the laws of the states are, in all likelihood, matters of complete indifference. Our occasional pronouncements upon the requirements of the Full Faith and Credit Clause doubtless have little effect upon divorces. Be this as it may, a court is likely to lose its way if it strays outside the modest bounds of its own special competence and turns the duty of adjudicating only the legal phases of a broad social problem into an opportunity for formulating judgments of social policy quite beyond its competence as well as its authority.

. . . .

Mr. Justice Jackson, dissenting:

I cannot join in exerting the judicial power of the Federal Government to compel the State of North Carolina to subordinate its own law to the Nevada divorce decrees. The Court's decision to do so reaches far beyond the immediate case. It subjects matrimonial laws of each state to important limitations and exceptions that it must recognize within its own borders and as to its own permanent population. It nullifies the power of each state to protect its own citizens against dissolution of their marriages by the courts of other states which have an easier system of divorce. It subjects every marriage to a new infirmity, in that one dissatisfied spouse may choose a state of easy divorce, in which neither party has ever lived, and there commence proceedings without personal service of process. The spouse remaining within the state of domicile need never know of the proceedings. Or, if they come to one's knowledge, the choice is between equally useless alternatives: one is to ignore the foreign proceedings, in which case the marriage is quite certain to be dissolved; the other is to follow the complaining spouse to the state of his choice and there defend under the laws which grant the dissolution on relatively trivial grounds. To declare that a state is powerless to protect either its own policy or the family rights of its people against such consequences has serious constitutional implications. It is not an exaggeration to say that this decision repeals the divorce laws of all the states and substitutes the law of Nevada as to all marriages one of the parties to which can afford a short trip there. The significance of this decision is best appraised by orienting its facts with reference to the States involved, for the court approves this concrete case as a pattern which anybody in any state may henceforth follow under the protection of the federal courts.

From the viewpoint of North Carolina, this is the situation: The Williamses, North Carolina people, were married in North Carolina, lived there twenty-five years, and have four children. The Hendrixes were also married in North Carolina and resided there some twenty years. In May of 1940, Mr. Williams and Mrs. Hendrix left their homes and respective spouses, departed the state, but after an absence of a few weeks reappeared and set up housekeeping as husband and wife. North Carolina then had on its hands three marriages among four people in the form of two broken families, and one going concern. What problems were thereby created as to property or support and maintenance, we do not know. North Carolina, for good or ill, has a strict policy as to divorce. The situation is contrary to its laws, and it has attempted to vindicate its own law by convicting the parties of bigamy.

The petitioners assert that North Carolina is made powerless in the matter, however, because of proceedings carried on in Nevada during their brief absence from North Carolina. We turn to Nevada for that part of the episode.

Williams and Mrs. Hendrix appear in the State of Nevada on May 15, 1940. For barely six weeks they made their residences at the Alamo Auto Court on the Las Vegas-Los Angeles Road. On June 26, 1940, both filed bills of complaint for divorce through the same lawyer, and alleging almost identical grounds. No personal service was made on the home-staying spouse in either case; and service was had only by publication and substituted service. Both obtained divorce decrees. The Nevada policy of divorce is reflected in Mrs. Hendrix's case. Her grounds were "extreme mental cruelty." She sustained them by testifying that her husband was "moody;" did not talk or speak to her "often;" when she spoke to him he answered most of the time by a nod or shake of the head and "there was nothing cheerful about him at all." The latter of the two divorces was granted on October 4, 1940, and on that day in Nevada they had benefit of clergy and emerged as man and wife. Nevada having served its purpose in their affairs, they at once returned to North Carolina to live.

The question is whether this court will now prohibit North Carolina from enforcing its own policy within that State against these North Carolinians on the ground that the law of Nevada under which they lived a few weeks is in some way projected into North Carolina to give them immunity.

There is confided to the Court only the power to resolve constitutional questions raised by these divorce procedures, and not moral, religious, or social questions as to divorce itself. I do not know with any certainty whether in the long run strict or easy divorce is best for society or whether either has much effect on moral conduct. It is enough for judicial purposes that to each state is reserved constitutional power to determine its own divorce policy. It follows that a federal court should uphold impartially the right of Nevada to adopt easy divorce laws and the right of North Carolina to enact severe ones. No difficulties arise so long as each state applies its laws to its own permanent inhabitants. The complications begin when one state opens its courts and extends the privileges of its laws to persons who never were domiciled there and attempts to visit disadvantages therefrom upon persons who have never lived there, have never submitted to the jurisdiction of its courts, and have never been lawfully summoned by personal service of process. This strikes at the orderly functioning of our federal constitutional system, and raises questions for us.

. . . .

The effect of the Court's decision today—that we must give extraterritorial effect to any judgment that a state honors for its own purposes—is to deprive this Court of control over the operation of the full faith and credit and the due process clauses of the Federal Constitution in cases of contested jurisdiction and to vest it in the first state to pass on the facts necessary to jurisdiction. It is for this Court, I think, not for state courts, to implement these great but general clauses by defining those judgments which are to be forced upon other states.

Conflict between policies, laws, and judgments of constituent states of our federal system is an old, persistent, and increasingly complex problem. The right of each state to experiment with rules of its own choice for governing matrimonial and social life is greatly impaired if its own authority is overlapped and its own policy is overridden by judgments of other states forced on it by the power of this Federal Court. If we are to extend protection to the orderly exercise of the right of each state to make its own policy, we must find some way of confining each state's authority to matters and persons that are by some standard its own.

The framers of the Constitution did not lay down rules to guide us in selecting which of two conflicting state judgments or public acts would receive federal aid in its extraterritorial enforcement. Nor was it necessary. There was, and is, an adequate body of law, if we do not reject it, by which to test jurisdiction or power to render the judgments in question so far as faith and credit by federal command is concerned. By the application of well established rules these judgments fail to merit enforcement for two reasons.

. . . .

The opinion concedes that Nevada's judgment could not be forced upon North Carolina in absence of personal service if a divorce proceeding were an action *in personam*. In other words, settled family relationships may be destroyed by a procedure that we would not recognize if the suit were one to collect a grocery bill.

We have been told that this is because divorce is a proceeding *in rem*. The marriage relation is to be reified and treated as a *res*. Then it seems that this *res* follows a fugitive from matrimony into a state of easy divorce, although the other party to it remains at home where the *res* was contracted and where years of cohabitation would seem to give it local situs. . . .

I doubt that it promotes clarity of thinking to deal with marriage in terms of a *res,* like a piece of land or a chattel. It might be more helpful to think of marriage as just marriage—a relationship out of which spring duties to both spouse and society and from which are derived rights—such as the right to society and services and to conjugal love and affection—rights which generally prove to be either priceless or worthless, but which none the less the law sometimes attempts to evaluate in terms of money when one is deprived of them by the negligence or design of a third party.

It does not seem consistent with our legal system that one who has these continuing rights should be deprived of them without a hearing. Neither does it seem that he or she should be summoned by mail, publication, or otherwise to a remote jurisdiction chosen by the other party and there be obliged to submit marital rights to adjudication under a state policy at odds with that of the state under which the marriage was contracted and the matrimonial domicile was established.

Marriage is often dealt with as a contract. Of course a personal judgment could not be rendered against an absent party on a cause of action arising out of an ordinary commercial contract, without personal service of process. I see no reason why the marriage contract, if such it be considered, should be discriminated against, nor why a party to a marriage contract should be more vulnerable to a foreign judgment without process than a party to any other contract. I agree that the marriage contract is different, but I should think the difference would be in its favor.

The Court thinks the difference is the other way: we are told that divorce is not a "mere *in personam* action" since *Haddock v. Haddock, supra,* held that domicile is necessary to jurisdiction for divorce. But to hold that a state cannot have divorce jurisdiction unless it is the domicile is not to hold that it must have such jurisdiction if it is the domicile, as *Haddock v. Haddock* itself demonstrates. . . .

Although the Court concedes that its present decision would be insupportable if divorce were a "mere *in personam* action," it relies for support on opinions that the state where one is domiciled has the power to enter valid criminal, tax, and simple money judgments *against*—not *for*—him. Those opinions are wholly inapposite unless they mean that Nevada has jurisdiction to nullify contract rights of a person never in the state or to declare that he is not liable for the commission of crime, payment of taxes, or the breach of a contract, in another state; and I am sure that nobody has ever supposed they meant that.

To hold that the Nevada judgments were not binding in North Carolina because they were rendered without jurisdiction over the North Carolina spouses, it is not necessary to hold that they were without any conceivable validity. It may be, and probably is, true that Nevada has sufficient interest in the lives of those who sojourn there to free them and their spouses to take new spouses without incurring criminal penalties under Nevada law. I know of nothing in our Constitution that requires Nevada to adhere to traditional concepts of bigamous unions or the legitimacy of the fruit thereof. And the control of a state over property within its borders is so complete that I suppose that Nevada could effectively deal with it in the name of divorce as completely as in any other. But it is quite a different thing to say that Nevada can dissolve the marriages of North Carolinians and dictate the incidence of the bigamy statutes of North Carolina by which North Carolina has sought to protect her own interests as well as theirs. In this case there is no conceivable basis of jurisdiction in the Nevada court over the absent spouses, and, *a fortiori,* over North Carolina herself. I cannot but think that in its preoccupation with the full faith and credit clause the Court has slighted the due process clause. . . .

. . . .

WILLIAMS v. NORTH CAROLINA (II)

United States Supreme Court
325 U.S. 226 (1945)

MR. JUSTICE FRANKFURTER delivered the opinion of the Court.

This case is here to review judgments of the Supreme Court of North Carolina, affirming convictions for bigamous cohabitation, assailed on the ground that full faith and credit, as required by the Constitution of the United States, was not accorded divorces decreed by one of the courts of Nevada. *Williams v. North Carolina,* 317 U. S. 287, decided an earlier aspect of the controversy. It was there held that a divorce granted by Nevada, on a finding that one spouse was domiciled in Nevada, must be respected in North Carolina, where Nevada's finding of domicil was not questioned, though the other spouse had neither appeared nor been served with process in Nevada and though recognition of such a divorce offended the policy of North Carolina. The record then before us did not present the question whether North Carolina had the power "to refuse full faith and credit to Nevada divorce decrees because, contrary to the findings of the Nevada court, North Carolina finds that no *bona fide* domicil was acquired in Nevada." This is the precise issue which has emerged after retrial of the cause following our reversal. Its obvious importance brought the case here.

. . . .

Under our system of law, judicial power to grant a divorce—jurisdiction, strictly speaking—is founded on domicil. *Bell v. Bell,* 181 U. S. 175; *Andrews v. Andrews,* 188 U. S. 14. The framers of the Constitution were familiar with this jurisdictional prerequisite, and since 1789 neither this Court nor any other court in the English-speaking world has questioned it. Domicil implies a nexus between person and place of such permanence as to control the creation of legal relations and responsibilities of the utmost significance. The domicil of one spouse within a State gives power to that State, we have held, to dissolve a marriage wheresoever contracted. In view of *Williams v. North Carolina* [I], the jurisdictional requirement of domicil is freed from confusing refinements about "matrimonial domicil." Divorce, like marriage, is of concern not merely to the immediate parties. It affects personal rights of the deepest significance. It also touches basic interests of society. Since divorce, like marriage, creates a new status, every consideration of policy makes it desirable that the effect should be the same wherever the question arises.

It is one thing to reopen an issue that has been settled after appropriate opportunity to present their contentions has been afforded to all who had an interest in its adjudication. This applies also to jurisdictional questions. After a contest these cannot be relitigated as between the parties. . . . But those not parties to a litigation ought not to be foreclosed by the interested actions of others; especially not a State which is concerned with the vindication of its own social policy and has no means, certainly no effective means, to protect that interest against the selfish action of those outside its borders. The State of domiciliary origin should not be bound by an unfounded, even if not collusive, recital in the record of a court of another State. As to the truth or existence of a fact, like that of domicil, upon which depends the power to exert judicial authority, a State not a party to the exertion of such judicial authority in another State but seriously affected by it has a right, when asserting its own unquestioned authority, to ascertain the truth or existence of that crucial fact.

These considerations of policy are equally applicable whether power was assumed by the court of the first State or claimed after inquiry. This may lead, no doubt, to conflicting determinations of what judicial power is founded upon. . . . If a finding by the court of one State that domicil in another State has been abandoned were conclusive upon the old domiciliary State, the policy of each State in matters of most intimate concern could be subverted by the policy of every other State.

Although it is now settled that a suit for divorce is not an ordinary adversary proceeding, it does not promote analysis, as was recently pointed out, to label divorce proceedings as actions *in rem. Williams v. North Carolina, supra,* at [pp. 751–52]. But insofar as a divorce decree partakes of some of the characteristics of a decree *in rem,* it is misleading to say that all the world is party to a proceeding *in rem.* . . . All the world is not party to a divorce proceeding. What is true is that all the world need not be present before a court granting the decree and yet it must be respected by the other forty-seven States provided—and it is a big proviso—the conditions for the exercise of power by the divorce-decreeing court are validly established whenever that judgment is elsewhere called into question. In short, the decree of divorce is a conclusive adjudication of everything except the jurisdictional facts upon which it is founded, and domicil is a jurisdictional fact. To permit the necessary finding of domicil by one State to foreclose all States in the protection of their social institutions would be intolerable.

But to endow each State with controlling authority to nullify the power of a sister State to grant a divorce based upon a finding that one spouse had acquired a new domicil within the divorcing State would, in the proper functioning of our federal system, be equally indefensible. No State court can assume comprehensive attention to the various and potentially conflicting interests that several States may have in the institutional aspects of marriage. The necessary accommodation between the right of one State to safeguard its interest in the family relation of its own people and the power of another State to grant divorces can be left to neither State.

The problem is to reconcile the reciprocal respect to be accorded by the members of the Union to their adjudications with due regard for another most important aspect of our federalism whereby "the domestic relations of husband and wife . . . were matters reserved to the States, . . . and do not belong to the United States. . . ." The rights that belong to all the States and the obligations which membership in the Union imposes upon all, are made effective because this Court is open to consider claims, such as this case presents, that the courts of one State have not given the full faith and credit to the judgment of a sister State that is required by Art. IV, § 1 of the Constitution.

But the discharge of this duty does not make of this Court a court of probate and divorce. Neither a rational system of law nor hard practicality calls for our independent determination, in reviewing the judgment of a State court, of that rather elusive relation between person and place which establishes domicil. "It is not for us to retry the facts," as was held in a case in which, like the present, the jurisdiction underlying a sister-State judgment was dependent on domicil. *Burbank v. Ernst,* 232 U. S. 162, 164. The challenged judgment must, however, satisfy our scrutiny that the reciprocal duty of respect owed by the States to one another's adjudications has been fairly discharged, and has not been evaded under the guise of finding an absence of domicil and therefore a want of power in the court rendering the judgment.

What is immediately before us is the judgment of the Supreme Court of North Carolina. We have authority to upset it only if there is want of foundation for the conclusion that that Court reached. The conclusion it reached turns on its finding that the spouses who obtained the Nevada decrees were not domiciled there. The fact that the Nevada court found that they were domiciled there is entitled to respect, and more. The burden of undermining the verity which the Nevada decrees import rests heavily upon the assailant. But simply because the Nevada court found that it had power to award a divorce decree cannot, we have seen, foreclose reexamination by another State. Otherwise, as was pointed out long ago, a court's record would establish its power and the power would be proved by the record. Such circular reasoning would give one State a control over all the other States which the Full Faith and Credit Clause certainly did not confer. *Thompson v. Whitman,* [85 U.S. (18 Wall.) 457 (1874)]. If this Court finds that proper weight was accorded to the claims of power by the court of one State in rendering a judgment the validity of which is pleaded in defense in another State, that the burden of overcoming such respect by disproof of the substratum of fact—here domicil—on which such power alone can rest was properly charged against the party challenging the legitimacy of the judgment, that such issue of fact was left for fair determination by appropriate procedure, and that a finding adverse to the necessary foundation for any valid sister-State judgment was amply supported in evidence, we cannot upset the judgment before us. And we cannot do so even if we also found in the record of the court of original judgment warrant for its finding that it had jurisdiction. If it is a matter turning on local law, great deference is owed by the courts of one State to what a court of another State has done. . . . But when we are dealing as here with an historic notion common to all English-speaking courts, that of domicil, we should not find a want of deference to a sister State on the part of a court of another State which finds an absence of domicil where such a conclusion is warranted by the record.

When this case was first here, North Carolina did not challenge the finding of the Nevada court that petitioners had acquired domicils in Nevada. . . . Upon retrial, however, the existence of domicil in Nevada became the decisive issue. The judgments of conviction now under review bring before us a record which may be fairly summarized by saying that the petitioners left North Carolina for the purpose of getting divorces from their respective spouses in Nevada and as soon as each had done so and married one another they left Nevada and returned to North Carolina to live there together as man and wife. Against the charge of bigamous cohabitation under § 14-183 of the North Carolina General Statutes, petitioners stood on their Nevada divorces and offered exemplified copies of the Nevada proceedings. The trial judge charged that the State had the burden of proving beyond a reasonable doubt that (1) each petitioner was lawfully married to one person; (2) thereafter each petitioner contracted a second marriage with another person outside North Carolina; (3) the spouses of petitioners were living at the time of this second marriage; (4) petitioners cohabited with one another in North Carolina after the second marriage. The burden, it was charged, then devolved upon petitioners "to satisfy the trial jury, not beyond a reasonable doubt nor by the greater weight of the evidence, but simply to satisfy" the jury from all the evidence, that petitioners were domiciled in Nevada at the time they obtained their divorces. The court further charged that "the recitation" of *bona fide* domicil in the Nevada decree was "prima facie evidence" sufficient to warrant a finding of domicil in Nevada but not compelling "such an inference." If the jury found, as they were told, that petitioners had domicils in North Carolina and went to Nevada "simply and solely for the purpose of obtaining" divorces, intending to return to North Carolina on obtaining them, they never lost their North Carolina domicils nor acquired new domicils in Nevada. Domicil, the jury was instructed, was that place where a person "has voluntarily fixed his abode . . . not for a mere special or temporary purpose, but with a present intention of making it his home, either permanently or for an indefinite or unlimited length of time."

The scales of justice must not be unfairly weighted by a State when full faith and credit is claimed for a sister-State judgment. But North Carolina has not so dealt with the Nevada decrees. She has not raised unfair barriers to their recognition. North Carolina did not fail in appreciation or application of federal standards of full faith and credit. Appropriate weight was given to the finding of domicil in the Nevada decrees, and that finding was allowed to be overturned only by relevant standards of proof. There is nothing to suggest that the issue was not fairly submitted to the jury and that it was not fairly assessed on cogent evidence. . . . It would be highly unreasonable to assert that a jury could not reasonably find that the evidence demonstrated that petitioners went to Nevada solely for the purpose of obtaining a divorce and intended all along to return to North Carolina.

. . . .

. . . The legitimate finding of the North Carolina Supreme Court that the petitioners were not in truth domiciled in Nevada was not a contingency against which the petitioners were protected by anything in the Constitution of the United States. . . .

We conclude that North Carolina was not required to yield her State policy because a Nevada court found that petitioners were domiciled in Nevada when it granted them decrees of divorce. North Carolina was entitled to find, as she did, that they did not acquire domicils in Nevada and that the Nevada court was therefore without power to liberate the petitioners from amenability to the laws of North Carolina governing domestic relations. And, as was said in connection with another aspect of the Full Faith and Credit Clause, our conclusion "is not a matter to arouse the susceptibilities of the States, all of which are equally concerned in the question and equally on both sides." *Fauntleroy v. Lum,* [p. 640 *supra*].

As for the suggestion that *Williams v. North Carolina* [I], foreclosed the Supreme Court of North Carolina from ordering a second trial upon the issue of domicil, it suffices to refer to our opinion in the earlier case.

Affirmed.

Mr. Justice Rutledge, dissenting.

Once again the ghost of "unitary domicil" returns on its perpetual round, in the guise of "jurisdictional fact," to upset judgments, marriages, divorces, undermine the relations founded upon them, and make this Court the unwilling and uncertain arbiter between the concededly valid laws and decrees of sister states. . . .

. . . .

Stripped of its common-law gloss, the basic constitutional issue inherent in the problem is whether the states shall have power to adopt so-called "liberal" divorce policies and grant divorces to persons coming from other states while there transiently or for only short periods not sufficient in themselves, absent other objective criteria, to establish more than casual relations with the community. One could understand and apply, without decades of confusion, a ruling that transient divorces, founded on fly-by-night "residence," are invalid where rendered as well as elsewhere; in other words, that a decent respect for sister states and their interests requires that each, to validly decree divorce, do so only after the person seeking it has established connections which give evidence substantially and objectively that he has become more than casually affiliated with the community. Until then the newcomer would be treated as retaining his roots, for this purpose, as so often happens for others, at his former place of residence. One equally could understand and apply with fair certainty an opposite policy frankly conceding state power to grant transient or short-term divorces, provided due process requirements for giving notice to the other spouse were complied with.

. . . But either choice would be preferable to the prevailing attempt at compromise founded upon the "unitary domicil-jurisdictional fact-permissible inference" rule.

That compromise gives effect to neither policy. It vitiates both; and does so in a manner wholly capricious alike for the institutional and the individual aspects of the problem. The element of caprice lies in the substantive domiciliary concept itself and also in the mode of its application.

. . . .

Domicil . . . combines the essentially contradictory elements of permanence and instantaneous change. No legal conception, save possibly "jurisdiction," of which it is an elusive substratum, affords such possibilities for uncertain application. The only thing certain about it, beyond its uncertainty, is that one must travel to change his domicil. But he may travel without changing it, even remain for a lifetime in his new place of abode without doing so. Apart from the necessity for travel, hardly evidentiary of stabilized relationship in a transient age, the criterion comes down to a purely subjective mental state, related to remaining for a length of time never yet defined with clarity.

With the crux of power fixed in such a variable, small wonder that the states vacilate in applying it and this Court ceaselessly seeks without finding a solution for its quandary. . . .

. . . .

. . . I think escape should be forthright and direct. It can be so only if the attempt to compromise what will not yield to compromise is forsworn, with the ancient gloss that serves only to conceal in familiar formula its essentially capricious and therefore nullifying character. This discarded, choice then would be forced between the ideas of transiency with due process safeguards and some minimal establishment of more than casual or transitory relations in the new community, giving the newcomer something of objective substance identifying him with its life.

. . . .

[JUSTICE BLACK wrote a separate dissenting opinion in which JUSTICE DOUGLAS joined.]

NOTES AND QUESTIONS

(1)(a) The brief and obviously incomplete summary in the Introduction to this Chapter of how the state came to play a role in the matter of marriage and divorce is designed only to raise doubt in the face of repeated declarations "From time immemorial. . . ." But what is the state's interest in marriage?

(b) In part, the answer may be secretarial. Marriages are recorded, as are births, deaths, adoptions, and other events in persons' lives, and these records are clearly useful. They are also, on the whole, value-free. If John and Mary are over the age of consent[a] (and are not too closely related), the state would not suggest that they do not belong together, or should wait until they finish their education, or undergo psychological testing. All of these suggestions may be wise in the circumstances, but they are not thought to be appropriate for governmental intervention, whether by legislature, official, or judge. Is divorce somehow different?

(c) If there is a state interest in marriage and divorce, is it a genuine one, like the state's interest, for example, in prosecuting and punishing crime or collecting taxes? Or is it closer to the kind of state interest that we saw in the tort cases, such as New York's interest in *Babcock* or Wisconsin's interest in *Hague*? Note that in this context, the interest of a state is used not in contrast with the interest of another state, but in contrast with saying that the subject matter is a private one for the persons concerned.

(d) Finally, if the state has an interest, and if that interest is vindicated through courts, what should be the basis of the courts' jurisdiction?

(2)(a) Judging by the *Williams* cases, the answer to the question of jurisdiction seems to be both wider and narrower than jurisdiction over other kinds of actions. Why?

---

[a] Usually 18 for the man, 16 to 18 for the woman, in either case younger with parental permission.

(b) Who are the parties to a divorce? If it takes two to tango, and to marry, how can divorce be unilateral or *ex parte*?

(c) The origin of ex parte divorces seems to be in the situation of the deserted wife; if she can only secure a divorce when she finds her husband, and he is not to be found, she is doomed to enjoy the benefits neither of matrimony nor of freedom.[b] In the late twentieth century one might base jurisdiction in such cases on a long-arm statute, on the theory that each spouse engaged in liability–creating activity at the marital domicile, i.e., the place where they lived together.[c] The deserted wife, of course, appeared long before non-resident motorists or far-away design defects caused compensable injuries in forum states.

(d) Should "marital domicile" in the preceding paragraph be changed to "either party's domicile" or "plaintiff's domicile"?

(e) Should this progression be confined to actions based on desertion, abandonment, or similar liability-creating activity? Or is the basis for the cause of action—grounds in the parlance of family law—irrelevant to the question of jurisdiction?

3(a) With this background, we are ready to turn to the *Williams* cases. Do they undercut what we have seen about jurisdiction, judgments, and domicile in other chapters of the book? What about choice of law?

(b) Justice Douglas in *Williams I* says (at p. 752, *supra*) that the marriage relation "creates problems of large social importance" including protection of children, property interests, and enforcement of marital responsibilities. Judged by *Williams,* does he mean it?

(c) Justice Douglas also says, (at p. 751, *supra*) "It is difficult to perceive how North Carolina could be said to have an interest in Nevada's domiciliaries superior to the interest of Nevada." Is that a serious statement, as applied to this case? Even assuming Mr. Williams and Mrs. Hendrix have in mind remaining indefinitely in Nevada (i.e., don't hold return tickets, haven't kept their houses in Granite Falls, N.C., have given up their jobs, etc.), isn't it still true that Mr. Williams and his (first) wife lived in North Carolina for twenty-five years, and raised four children there, and that Mrs. Hendrix and her (first) husband lived in North Carolina almost as long? Or are these points, made by Justice Jackson, not relevant under any conceivable view of the case?

(4)(a) Carrie Williams is sitting in her living room in Granite Falls, N.C. (population, according to the 1940 census, 1,873), when the sheriff of Caldwell County (population 35,795) knocks on the door and delivers a letter. The letter is from some lawyer in Las Vegas, Nevada, notifying her that her husband has filed for a divorce under Nevada law § 000. While her marriage is clearly not what it once was, she does not look forward to living in Granite Falls as a divorcée; moreover, she certainly wouldn't want "That Hendrix woman" to end up with *her* husband. Should she

(i) Throw the notice in the waste basket;

---

[b] For evidence that this concern is neither farfetched nor ancient, see *Garthwaite v. Garthwaite,* [1964] P. 356, 370 (U.K. Ct. App.). *H* and *W* were married in 1950 in England, where both were domiciled. In 1956 *H* obtained a divorce decree in Nevada, then moved to New York. *W* petitioned for a declaration that the marriage remained valid and subsisting. The Court of Appeal, reversing the lower court, held that if *W* was still married to *H,* she would have no domicile but his, and therefore the court would not have jurisdiction; if she were not married to *H,* the court would have jurisdiction, but could not grant her the relief sought, i.e., a declaration that the marriage was subsisting.

[c] Compare New York C.P.L.R. § 302(b), Documents Supplement p. 77.

(ii) Retain a North Carolina lawyer to try to stop the divorce action from going forward;

(iii) Retain a Nevada lawyer to contest the divorce?

(b) If she follows course (iii), what should her Nevada lawyer do?

(i) Argue that the Nevada court has no jurisdiction;

(ii) Urge that the law of North Carolina be applied, and that under that law, Mr. Williams has failed to state a cause of action?

(c) We saw in Chapter 8, *supra,* particularly in *Baldwin v. Iowa Traveling Men's Ass'n,*[d] that if a defendant challenges the jurisdiction in F–1, he cannot challenge it again in F–2. Of course an argument on substance without challenging jurisdiction of the Nevada court would be deemed a waiver of any jurisdictional defect. In any other context, it might be wise strategy not to take part in the Las Vegas proceeding, and rely on challenge in F–2 (North Carolina). Whether for strategic or other reasons, we know Carrie in fact did nothing. Why is she deprived of the option that any other defendant in a far away court has?

(d) Suppose Carrie Williams and Tom Hendrix had not been notified of the actions in Nevada at all. Would the divorces still have been valid? Is the Court saying, in other words, that the out-of-state defendants in a divorce action have no due process rights at all, or just that notice not amounting to personal service is sufficient?

(e) Here the scandal was caused by the immediate return of the newly-divorced, newly-wed couple to North Carolina, not far from Granite Falls.[e] Would the scandal be any less if the couple had moved to Chicago or New York or Philadelphia? Or if the whole scenario had taken place in one of those cities?

(5)(a) The Supreme Court in the first *Williams* case criticizes the prosecution for mixing up two issues so that one cannot tell which one was decisive. Is that fair?

(b) The prosecution said O. B. Williams and Lillie Shaver Hendrix were living as man and wife while each was married to another. The defense depended on a divorce that the prosecution said was not valid because

(i) it was rendered without jurisdiction over the other spouse; and

(ii) even assuming there could be jurisdiction without presence of the respondent spouse if the plaintiff spouse was domiciled in the forum state, that was not true in *Williams v. Williams* or *Hendrix v. Hendrix.*

If O. B. Williams and Lillian Hendrix seek to establish the validity of their divorces and remarriage, why isn't the burden on them, as proponents of the Nevada judgments, to establish both points? Is this a question of full faith and credit, or is it a question of the burden of proof in a criminal trial?

(6)(a) On the assumption that Mr. Williams and Mrs. Hendrix were domiciled in Nevada at the time of their actions for divorce, Justice Douglas goes to great length to repudiate *Haddock v. Haddock.*[f] In that case the husband had moved from New York to Connecticut and secured

---

[d] p. 675, *supra.*

[e] In fact Mr. Williams was a storekeeper in Granite Falls, and Mr. Hendrix worked as a clerk in Mr. Williams' store, when the latter ran off with his clerk's wife. On their return, they moved a few miles west of Granite Falls to Pineola, in neighboring Avery County. See, for these details, Powell, *And Repent at Leisure,* 58 Harv. L. Rev. 930, 932 (1945).

[f] 201 U.S. 562 (1906).

a divorce, ex parte. Thereafter the wife brought an action in New York for separation and alimony, and the husband defended on the ground that they were divorced. The Supreme Court (by 5–4) upheld the New York court, which had declined to recognize the Connecticut judgment, because Connecticut was not the marital domicile and the husband had acquired a domicile there after wrongful abandonment of the wife. In contrast, in *Atherton v. Atherton*,[g] decided a few years before *Haddock,* an ex parte divorce granted to the husband in the state of marital domicile was held entitled to full faith and credit, and thus to constitute a bar to an action for separation brought by the wife in another state. Does the *Haddock/Atherton* combination, which does not deny recognition to all ex parte divorces but seems to limit recognition to those obtained in the state of the marital domicile, not make sense, viewed from the point of view of the state's interest in marriage? Or is the inquiry into fault as a basis of jurisdiction doomed to failure?

(b) Could the Supreme Court in *Haddock* have

(i) required the Connecticut court to apply New York law; or

(ii) at least held that if the Connecticut court did not do so, its judgment would not be entitled to full faith and credit?

Note the Court's reliance in *Williams I* on *Alaska Packers*[h] in addressing this question (p. 751, *supra*)

(7)(a) Justice Frankfurter in *Williams I* makes some straightforward points about the Full Faith and Credit clause, but also makes some interesting suggestions. Congress, he points out, has no authority to legislate over marriage and divorce, and the Court should not attempt to do so by indirection. But should the Constitution be amended to give Congress such authority?

(b) Justice Frankfurter also suggests that some special legislation under the Full Faith and Credit clause might address the problem of divorce. What might such legislation say? Compare in this connection the Parental Kidnaping Prevention Act of 1980,[i] in which custody orders issued on specified bases of jurisdiction, but no others, were required to be granted recognition by other states. Would such a proposal work for divorce? What might the bases be?

(c) Justice Jackson, in a part of his dissent not reproduced in the text, argued that on the record before it—six weeks at the Alamo Auto Court—the court could not get around the issue of domicile. "If Nevada may prescribe six weeks of indefinite-permanent abode in a motor court as constituting domicile," he wrote, "she may as readily prescribe six days."[j] Does the majority have an answer?

(d) In answer to the Court's "intensely practical considerations" in support of the decision (p. 753), Justice Jackson writes

> I agree that it is serious if a Nevada court without jurisdiction for divorce purports to say that the sojourn of two spouses gives four spouses rights to acquire four more, but I think it is far more serious to force North Carolina to acquiesce in any such proposition.[k]

---

[g] 181 U.S. 155 (1901).

[h] Chapter 5, p. 386, *supra*.

[i] Documents Supplement, p. 180, and § 9.04, *infra*. See also the discussion of the Defense of Marriage Act, § 9.05[B], and esp. pp. 864–65, questions 3-5, *infra*.

[j] 317 U.S. at 321 (Jackson, J. dissenting).

[k] *Id.* at 324.

If that seems persuasive, does it follow that the divorce should be void for all purposes? Or could the divorce be valid in Nevada as consistent with due process, but still not required to be given full faith and credit by other states? Is that the result of *Williams II*?

(8)(a) Turning then to the second prosecution, there is no double jeopardy, since the accused were convicted the first time, and the conviction was reversed on appeal. But what is different in the second case?

(b) The answer, of course, is that this time the prosecutor was more careful, and the jury expressly found that the defendants had not been domiciled in Nevada at the time of their purported divorce. By what standard is domicile to be judged for this purpose?

(i) a North Carolina standard;

(ii) a Nevada standard;

(iii) a national standard?

If the answer is (iii), is it a Constitutional standard?

(c) Justice Frankfurter says. "Under our system of law, judicial power to grant a divorce—jurisdiction, strictly speaking—is founded on domicil." Putting aside some questionable history, Frankfurter makes a powerful case (p. 759). Divorce affects personal rights of the deepest significance; it also touches basic interests of society. Non-parties ought not to be foreclosed, he goes on, by the interested actions of others—including the first Mrs. Williams, and the State of North Carolina. Why couldn't all of this have been said in *Williams I*? Has the court changed its mind?

(d) Justice Frankfurter goes on to say that a court cannot by itself conclusively establish its own jurisdiction. "To permit the necessary finding of domicil by one State to foreclose all States in the protection of their social institutions would be intolerable." The Supreme Court, he continues, must function as the umpire, to achieve the "necessary accommodation" between the right of one state and the power of the other. (p. 760).

(9)(a) The fact that the Nevada court found that the parties were domiciled in that state, the Court says, "is entitled to respect, and more." What does that mean?

(b) Further on, Justice Frankfurter talks about the scales of justice not being unfairly weighted. Has domicile now become just a factual question, with the burden on the party contesting the initial finding?

(c) Justice Rutledge wrote a lengthy dissent, questioning the whole concept of domicile as a jurisdictional foundation for domicile but not really proposing an alternative. Could you propose a different standard that the parties in *Williams* have met? Should divorce become a transitory action?

(10) Following the two *Williams* cases, how should an attorney advise someone who desires a divorce but cannot meet the criteria, or afford to wait the required time, of his/her home state?[1] Should the client still be sent to Nevada? Would it make any difference if the other spouse agreed?

---

[1] New York, for example, had only a single ground for divorce until the mid-1960s—adultery.

§ 9.02 Bilateral Divorce: Res Judicata and Full Faith and Credit

Suppose, going back to question 4, p. 764, *supra,* but changing the basic assumption, Carrie Williams shared her husband's longing for a divorce. Under North Carolina's law as it read at the time, Mr. and Mrs. Williams could have secured a divorce by living apart for two years,[a] but perhaps they did not want to wait that long. Could she strengthen the effectiveness of Mr. Williams' effort in Nevada by filing an appearance? If so, should she admit her husband's domicile in Nevada? Or should she contest domicile, and be content to lose? Would any of these avenues affect the interest of North Carolina, asserted, as we saw, in two prosecutions taken all the way to the U.S. Supreme Court?

[A] Within the United States

SHERRER v. SHERRER

United States Supreme Court
334 U.S. 343 (1948)

Mr. Chief Justice Vinson delivered the opinion of the Court.

. . . .

Petitioner Margaret E. Sherrer and the respondent, Edward C. Sherrer, were married in New Jersey in 1930, and from 1932 until April 3, 1944, lived together in Monterey, Massachusetts. Following a long period of marital discord, petitioner, accompanied by the two children of the marriage, left Massachusetts on the latter date, ostensibly for the purpose of spending a vacation in the State of Florida. Shortly after her arrival in Florida, however, petitioner informed her husband that she did not intend to return to him. Petitioner obtained housing accommodations in Florida, placed her older child in school, and secured employment for herself.

On July 6, 1944, a bill of complaint for divorce was filed at petitioner's direction in the Circuit Court of the Sixth Judicial Circuit of the State of Florida. The bill alleged extreme cruelty as grounds for divorce and also alleged that petitioner was a "bona fide legal resident of the State of Florida."[3] The respondent received notice by mail of the pendency of the divorce proceedings. He retained Florida counsel who entered a general appearance and filed an answer denying the allegations of petitioner's complaint, including the allegation as to petitioner's Florida residence.

---

[a] See N.C. Code § 1659(a), quoted in *State v. Williams I,* 220 N.C. 445, 457, 17 S.E. 2d 769, 777 (1939). In addition, a divorce could be obtained for adultery, impotence, pregnancy by the wife at the time of marriage with another man's child, and "the abominable and detestable crime against nature, with mankind or beast." See N.C. Code of 1935 and 1937 Supp.

[3] Section 65.02 of Florida Stat. Ann. provides: "In order to obtain a divorce the complainant must have resided ninety days in the State of Florida before the filing of the bill of complaint." The Florida courts have construed the statutory requirement of residence to be that of domicile. Respondent does not contend nor do we find any evidence that the requirements of "domicile" as defined by the Florida cases are other than those generally applied or differ from the tests employed by the Massachusetts courts. *Wade v. Wade,* 93 Fla. 1004, 113 So. 374 (1927); *Evans v. Evans,* 141 Fla. 860, 194 So. 215 (1940); *Fowler v. Fowler,* 156 Fla. 316, 22 So. 2d 817 (1945).

On November 14, 1944, hearings were held in the divorce proceedings. Respondent appeared personally to testify with respect to a stipulation entered into by the parties relating to the custody of the children. Throughout the entire proceedings respondent was represented by counsel. Petitioner introduced evidence to establish her Florida residence and testified generally to the allegations of her complaint. Counsel for respondent failed to cross-examine or to introduce evidence in rebuttal.

The Florida court on November 29, 1944, entered a decree of divorce after specifically finding that petitioner "is a bona fide resident of the State of Florida, and that this court has jurisdiction of the parties and the subject matter in said cause; . . ." Respondent failed to challenge the decree by appeal to the Florida Supreme Court.

On December 1, 1944, petitioner was married in Florida to one Henry A. Phelps, whom petitioner had known while both were residing in Massachusetts and who had come to Florida shortly after petitioner's arrival in that State. Phelps and petitioner lived together as husband and wife in Florida, where they were both employed, until February 5, 1945, when they returned to Massachusetts.

In June, 1945, respondent instituted an action in the Probate Court of Berkshire County, Massachusetts, which has given rise to the issues of this case. Respondent alleged that he is the lawful husband of petitioner, that the Florida decree of divorce is invalid, and that petitioner's subsequent marriage is void. Respondent prayed that he might be permitted to convey his real estate as if he were sole and that the court declare that he was living apart from his wife for justifiable cause. Petitioner joined issue on respondent's allegations.

In the proceedings which followed, petitioner gave testimony in defense of the validity of the Florida divorce decree. The Probate Court, however, resolved the issues of fact adversely to petitioner's contentions, found that she was never domiciled in Florida, and granted respondent the relief he had requested. The Supreme Judicial Court of Massachusetts affirmed the decree on the grounds that it was supported by the evidence and that the requirements of full faith and credit did not preclude the Massachusetts courts from reexamining the finding of domicile made by the Florida court.

. . . .

That the jurisdiction of the Florida court to enter a valid decree of divorce was dependent upon petitioner's domicile in that State is not disputed. This requirement was recognized by the Florida court which rendered the divorce decree, and the principle has been given frequent application in decisions of the State Supreme Court. But whether or not petitioner was domiciled in Florida at the time the divorce was granted was a matter to be resolved by judicial determination. Here, unlike the situation presented in *Williams v. North Carolina [II]*, the finding of the requisite jurisdictional facts was made in proceedings in which the defendant appeared and participated. The question with which we are confronted, therefore, is whether such a finding made under the circumstances presented by this case may, consistent with the requirements of full faith and credit, be subjected to collateral attack in the courts of a sister State in a suit brought by the defendant in the original proceedings.

The question of what effect is to be given to an adjudication by a court that it possesses requisite jurisdiction in a case, where the judgment of that court is subsequently subjected to collateral attack on jurisdictional grounds, has been given frequent consideration by this Court over a period of many years. Insofar as cases originating in the federal courts are concerned, the rule has evolved that the doctrine of *res judicata* applies to adjudications relating either to jurisdiction of the person or of the subject matter where such adjudications have been made in proceedings in which those questions were in issue and in which the parties were given full opportunity to litigate. The reasons for this doctrine have frequently been stated. Thus in *Stoll v. Gottlieb,* 305 U. S. 165, 172 (1938), it was said: "Courts to determine the rights of parties are an integral part of our system of government. It is just as important that there should be a place to end as that there should be a place to begin litigation. After a party has his day in court, with opportunity to present his evidence and his view of the law, a collateral attack upon the decision as to jurisdiction there rendered merely retries the issue previously determined. There is no reason to expect that the second decision will be more satisfactory than the first."

This Court has also held that the doctrine of *res judicata* must be applied to questions of jurisdiction in cases arising in state courts involving the application of the full faith and credit clause where, under the law of the state in which the original judgment was rendered, such adjudications are not susceptible to collateral attack.

In *Davis v. Davis,* 305 U. S. 32 (1938), the courts of the District of Columbia had refused to give effect to a decree of absolute divorce rendered in Virginia, on the ground that the Virginia court had lacked jurisdiction despite the fact that the defendant had appeared in the Virginia proceedings and had fully litigated the issue of the plaintiff's domicile. This Court held that in failing to give recognition to the Virginia decree, the courts of the District had failed to accord the full faith and credit required by the Constitution. During the course of the opinion, this Court stated: "As to petitioner's domicil for divorce and his standing to invoke jurisdiction of the Virginia court, its finding that he was a bona fide resident of that State for the required time is binding upon respondent in the courts of the District. She may not say that he was not entitled to sue for divorce in the state court, for she appeared there and by plea put in issue his allegation as to domicil, introduced evidence to show it false, took exceptions to the commissioner's report, and sought to have the court sustain them and uphold her plea. Plainly, the determination of the decree upon that point is effective for all purposes in this litigation."

We believe that the decision of this Court in the *Davis* case and those in related situations are clearly indicative of the result to be reached here. Those cases stand for the proposition that the requirements of full faith and credit bar a defendant from collaterally attacking a divorce decree on jurisdictional grounds in the courts of a sister State where there has been participation by the defendant in the divorce proceedings, where the defendant has been accorded full opportunity to contest the jurisdictional issues, and where the decree is not susceptible to such collateral attack in the courts of the State which rendered the decree.

Applying these principles to this case, we hold that the Massachusetts courts erred in permitting the Florida divorce decree to be subjected to attack on the ground that petitioner was not domiciled in Florida at the time the decree was entered. Respondent participated in the Florida proceedings by entering a general appearance, filing pleadings placing in issue the very matters he sought subsequently to contest in the Massachusetts courts, personally appearing before the Florida court and giving testimony in the case, and by retaining attorneys who represented him throughout the entire proceedings. It has not been contended that respondent was given less than a full opportunity to contest the issue of petitioner's domicile or any other issue relevant to the litigation. . . . If respondent failed to take advantage of the opportunities afforded him, the responsibility is his own. We do not believe that the dereliction of a defendant under such circumstances should be permitted to provide a basis for subsequent attack in the courts of a sister State on a decree valid in the State in which it was rendered.

. . . .

It is urged further, however, that because we are dealing with litigation involving the dissolution of the marital relation, a different result is demanded from that which might properly be reached if this case were concerned with other types of litigation. It is pointed out that under the Constitution the regulation and control of marital and family relationships are reserved to the States. It is urged, and properly so, that the regulation of the incidents of the marital relation involves the exercise by the States of powers of the most vital importance. Finally, it is contended that a recognition of the importance to the States of such powers demands that the requirements of full faith and credit be viewed in such a light as to permit an attack upon a divorce decree granted by a court of a sister State under the circumstances of this case even where the attack is initiated in a suit brought by the defendant in the original proceedings.

But the recognition of the importance of a State's power to determine the incidents of basic social relationships into which its domiciliaries enter does not resolve the issues of this case. This is not a situation in which a State has merely sought to exert such power over a domiciliary. This is, rather, a case involving inconsistent assertions of power by courts of two States of the Federal Union and thus presents considerations which go beyond the interests of local policy, however vital. In resolving the issues here presented, we do not conceive it to be a part of our function to weigh the relative merits of the policies of Florida and Massachusetts with respect to divorce and related matters. Nor do we understand the decisions of this Court to support the proposition that the obligation imposed by Article IV, § 1 of the Constitution and the Act of Congress passed thereunder amounts to something less than the duty to accord *full* faith and credit to decrees of divorce entered by courts of sister States. The full faith and credit clause is one of the provisions incorporated into the Constitution by its framers for the purpose of transforming an aggregation of independent, sovereign States into a nation. If in its application local policy must at times be required to give way, such "is part of the price of our federal system." *Williams v. North Carolina [I]* [p. 753 *supra*].[25]

This is not to say that in no case may an area be recognized in which reasonable accommodations of interest may properly be made. But as this Court has heretofore made clear, that area is of limited extent. We believe that in permitting an attack on the Florida divorce decree which again put in issue petitioner's Florida domicile and in refusing to recognize the validity of that decree, the Massachusetts courts have asserted a power which cannot be reconciled with the requirements of due faith and credit. We believe that assurances that such a power will be exercised sparingly and wisely render it no less repugnant to the constitutional commands.

It is one thing to recognize as permissible the judicial reexamination of findings of jurisdictional fact where such findings have been made by a court of a sister State which has entered a divorce decree in *ex parte* proceedings. It is quite another thing to hold that the vital rights and interests involved in divorce litigation may be held in suspense pending the scrutiny by courts of sister States of findings of jurisdictional fact made by a competent court in proceedings conducted in a manner consistent with the highest requirements of due process and in which the defendant has participated. We do not conceive it to be in accord with the purposes of the full faith and credit requirement to hold that a judgment rendered under the circumstances of this case may

---

[25] But we may well doubt that the judgment which we herein announce will amount to substantial interference with state policy with respect to divorce. Many States which have had occasion to consider the matter have already recognized the impropriety of permitting a collateral attack on an out-of-state divorce decree where the defendant appeared and participated in the divorce proceedings. . . .

be required to run the gantlet of such collateral attack in the courts of sister States before its validity outside of the State which rendered it is established or rejected. That vital interests are involved in divorce litigation indicates to us that it is a matter of greater rather than lesser importance that there should be a place to end such litigation. And where a decree of divorce is rendered by a competent court under the circumstances of this case, the obligation of full faith and credit requires that such litigation should end in the courts of the State in which the judgment was rendered.

Reversed.

MR. JUSTICE FRANKFURTER, with whom MR. JUSTICE MURPHY concurs, dissenting.

What Mr. Justice Holmes said of the ill-starred *Haddock v. Haddock* may equally be said here: "I do not suppose that civilization will come to an end whichever way this case is decided." 201 U. S. 562, 628. But, believing as I do that the decision just announced is calculated, however unwittingly, to promote perjury without otherwise appreciably affecting the existing disharmonies among the forty-eight States in relation to divorce, I deem it appropriate to state my views.

Not only is today's decision fraught with the likelihood of untoward consequences. It disregards a law that for a century has expressed the social policy of Massachusetts, and latterly of other States, in a domain which under our Constitution is peculiarly the concern of the States and not of the Nation.

. . . .

If the marriage contract were no different from a contract to sell an automobile, the parties thereto might well be permitted to bargain away all interests involved, in or out of court. But the State has an interest in the family relations of its citizens vastly different from the interest it has in an ordinary commercial transaction. That interest cannot be bartered or bargained away by the immediate parties to the controversy by a default or an arranged contest in a proceeding for divorce in a State to which the parties are strangers. Therefore, the constitutional power of a State to determine the marriage status of two of its citizens should not be deemed foreclosed by a proceeding between the parties in another State, even though in other types of controversy considerations making it desirable to put an end to litigation might foreclose the parties themselves from reopening the dispute. I cannot agree that the Constitution forbids a State from insisting that it is not bound by any such proceedings in a distant State wanting in the power that domicile alone gives, and that its courts need not honor such an intrinsically sham proceeding, no matter who brings the issue to their attention.

That society has a vital interest in the domestic relations of its members will be almost impatiently conceded. But it is not enough to pay lip-service to the commonplace as an abstraction. Its implications must be respected. They define our problems. Nowhere in the United States, not even in the States which grant divorces most freely, may a husband and wife rescind their marriage at will as they might a commercial contract. Even if one thought that such a view of the institution of marriage was socially desirable, it could scarcely be held that such a personal view was incorporated into the Constitution or into the law for the enforcement of the Full Faith and Credit Clause, enacted by the First Congress.

. . . .

Massachusetts has seen fit to subject its citizens to the following law:

"A divorce decreed in another jurisdiction according to the laws thereof by a court having jurisdiction of the cause and of both the parties shall be valid and effectual in this commonwealth; but if an inhabitant of this commonwealth goes into another jurisdiction to obtain a divorce for a cause occurring here while the parties resided here, or for a cause which would not authorize a divorce by the laws of this commonwealth, a divorce so obtained shall be of no force or effect in this commonwealth." Mass. Gen. Laws c. 208, § 39 (1932).

. . . .

Massachusetts says through this statute that a person who enjoys its other institutions but is irked by its laws concerning the severance of the marriage tie, must either move his home to some other State with more congenial laws, or remain and abide by the laws of Massachusetts. He cannot play ducks and drakes with the State, by leaving it just long enough to take advantage of a proceeding elsewhere, devised in the interests of a quick divorce, intending all the time to retain Massachusetts as his home, and then return there, resume taking advantage of such of its institutions as he finds congenial but assert his freedom from the restraints of its policies concerning severance of the marriage tie. Massachusetts has a right to define the terms on which it will grant divorces, and to refuse to recognize divorces granted by other States to parties who at the time are still Massachusetts domiciliaries. Has it not also the right to frustrate evasion of its policies by those of its permanent residents who leave the State to change their spouses rather than to change their homes, merely because they go through a lukewarm or feigned contest over jurisdiction?

The nub of the *Williams* decision was that the State of domicile has an independent interest in the marital status of its citizens that neither they nor any other State with which they may have a transitory connection may abrogate against its will. Its interest is not less because both parties to the marital relationship instead of one sought to evade its laws. In the *Williams* case, it was not the interest of Mrs. Williams, or that of Mr. Hendrix, that North Carolina asserted. It was the interest of the people of North Carolina. The same is true here of the interest of Massachusetts. While the State's interest may be expressed in criminal prosecutions, with itself formally a party as in the *Williams* case, the State also expresses its sovereign power when it speaks through its courts in a civil litigation between private parties. Cf. *Shelley v. Kraemer,* 334 U. S. 1.

. . . .

Today's decision may stir hope of contributing toward greater certainty of status of those divorced. But when people choose to avail themselves of laws laxer than those of the State in which they permanently abide, and where, barring only the interlude necessary to get a divorce, they choose to continue to abide, doubts and conflicts are inevitable, so long as the divorce laws of the forty-eight States remain diverse, and so long as we respect the law that a judgment without jurisdictional foundation is not constitutionally entitled to recognition everywhere. . . .

. . . .

. . . The only way in which this Court can achieve uniformity, in the absence of Congressional action or constitutional amendment, is by permitting the States with the laxest divorce laws to impose their policies upon all other States. We cannot as judges be ignorant of that which is common knowledge to all men. We cannot close our eyes to the fact that certain States make an industry of their easy divorce laws, and encourage inhabitants of other States to obtain "quickie" divorces which their home States deny them. To permit such States to bind all others to their decrees would endow with constitutional sanctity a Gresham's Law of domestic relations.

Fortunately, today's decision does not go that far. But its practical result will be to offer new inducements for conduct by parties and counsel, which, in any other type of litigation, would be regarded as perjury, but which is not so regarded where divorce is involved because ladies and gentlemen indulge in it. . . .

. . . The essence of the matter is that through the device of a consent decree a policy of vital concern to States should not be allowed to be defied with the sanction of this Court. If perchance the Court leaves open the right of a State to prove fraud in the ordinary sense—namely, that a mock contest was won by prearrangement—the claim falls that today's decision will substantially restrict the area of uncertainty as to the validity of divorces. If the Court seeks to avoid this result by holding that a party to a feigned legal contest cannot question in his home State the good faith behind an adjudication of domicile in another State, such holding is bound to encourage fraud and collusion still further.

. . . .

Even to a believer in the desirability of easier divorce—an issue that is not our concern—this decision should bring little solace. It offers a way out only to that small portion of those unhappily married who are sufficiently wealthy to be able to afford a trip to Nevada or Florida, and a six-week or three-month stay there.[18]

. . . .

. . . [T]he crux of today's decision is that regardless of how overwhelming the evidence may have been that the asserted domicile in the State offering bargain-counter divorces was a sham, the home State of the parties is not permitted to question the matter if the form of a controversy has been gone through. To such a proposition I cannot assent. Decisions of this Court that have not stood the test of time have been due not to want of foresight by the prescient Framers of the Constitution, but to misconceptions regarding its requirements. I cannot bring myself to believe that the Full Faith and Credit Clause gave to the few States which offer bargain-counter divorces constitutional power to control the social policy governing domestic relations of the many States which do not.

NOTES AND QUESTIONS

(1)(a) Given the premises of the state's interest in marriage and divorce of its citizens, is *Sherrer v. Sherrer* correctly decided?

(b) If the answer to the preceding question is no, does that suggest that the case is wrongly decided, or that the premises are wrong?

(c) What is the rationale for the Supreme Court's holding? Is it waiver? Estoppel? Res judicata? Full faith and credit? Could the result be changed by Congress, for example by conditioning full faith and credit on specific periods of residence or indicia of domicile? Or is the result in *Sherrer* now a constitutional command?

---

[18] The easier it is made for those who through affluence are able to exercise disproportionately large influence on legislation, to obtain migratory divorces, the less likely it is that the divorce laws of their home States will be liberalized, insofar as that is deemed desirable, so as to affect all. See Groves, *Migratory Divorces,* 2 Law & Contemp. Prob. 293, 298. For comparable instances, in the past, of discrimination against the poor in the actual application of divorce laws, cf. Dickens, *Hard Times,* c. 11; Hankins, *Divorce,* 5 Encyc. Soc. Sci. 177, 179.

§ 9.02 JURISDICTION AND JUDGMENTS □ 775

(d) In *Williams II,* the Supreme Court said:

[T]he decree of divorce is a conclusive adjudication of everything except the jurisdictional facts upon which it is founded, and domicil is a jurisdictional fact. To permit the necessary finding of domicil by one State to foreclose all States in the protection of their social institutions would be intolerable.[b]

Why is this not equally true in *Sherrer?*

(e) If Edward Sherrer has done something that precludes him from contesting a fact or conclusion, that can certainly not be said for the Commonwealth of Massachusetts. Could the District Attorney of Berkshire County, Mass. bring a bigamy prosecution against Mr. and Mrs. Phelps?

(2)(a) Justice Frankfurter, who concurred in *Williams I* but wrote for the majority in *Williams II,* here dissents, essentially on the ground that the parties cannot bargain away the interests of the state. A person who enjoys the other institutions of Massachusetts, he says, cannot "play ducks and drakes" with the state when it comes to its divorce law. Is that persuasive?

(b) Five decades after the event, and without any knowledge of what really went on between Mr. and Mrs. Sherrer, Justice Frankfurter's argument sounds somewhat abstract. Suppose some other facts not disclosed in the opinions, either of the Massachusetts court[c] or the Supreme Court: Mrs. Sherrer calls her husband and says, "I don't want to come back to live with you, I love Phelps, and I want to marry him as soon as possible. If you agree to appear in the Florida proceeding and follow my lawyer's directions, I will let you have the children." Alternatively, the deal is proposed by Mr. Sherrer, and Margaret, torn between her children and her love of Phelps, makes the deal, on advice of counsel that without Edward's agreement her Florida divorce would be too vulnerable. Has the children's welfare not been made the subject of a bargain that no court, or even social agency, has scrutinized?[d]

(c) One of the elements of *Sherrer* that is hard to understand from reading only the Supreme Court's opinion is just what Mr. Sherrer was suing about. Under Massachusetts law as it then read, Mr. Sherrer could not convey his homestead free of dower if he had been the guilty party in a divorce action. What the Massachusetts court said, in effect, was that it did not believe that that law, designed to protect Massachusetts wives in furtherance of the state's interest in the family, should protect the ex-Mrs. Sherrer in these circumstances. The result of the Supreme Court's decision is to force Massachusetts to protect Margaret, by giving full faith and credit to a judgment in which Florida asserted its interest (however transient) in the Sherrer family. Does that make sense?

(d) Note that in the Florida action, Mr. Sherrer denied (i) Margaret's Florida domicile; and (ii) the allegation of cruelty. If he had admitted either or both of these allegations, would the case have come out differently?

(3)(a) After the two *Williams* cases and *Sherrer,* it appears that an ex parte migratory divorce is valid (*Williams I*) but vulnerable (*Williams II*); divorces in which both parties participate and the rendering court makes a finding that at least one party is domiciled in the rendering state

---

[b] See p. 760, *supra.*

[c] *Sherrer v. Sherrer,* 320 Mass. 351, 69 N.E.2d 801 (1946).

[d] A stipulation relating to custody of the children was in fact submitted to the Florida court (p. 769, *supra*). The arrangement, as appears from the record before the Massachusetts courts, provided that Edward would have custody of the children during the school year, and Margaret would have custody during the children's vacations.

are valid, and (at least relatively) invulnerable. How far does this invulnerablility extend? Would it apply to third parties affected by a divorce?

(b) Bruce Johnson was a resident of New York, married with one daughter. When his first wife died, he married Madoline, and continued to live with her in New York. Subsequently, Madoline traveled to Florida, filed for divorce (although she had not spent the required 90 days in the Sunshine State). Bruce appeared by counsel, and the Florida court granted the divorce. Thereafter Bruce married Genevieve. When Bruce died, he left a will giving his entire estate to his daughter Eleanor. Genevieve filed notice of election against the will as surviving spouse under N.Y. Decedent Estate Law 18.[e] Eleanor opposed the election on the ground that her father's divorce from Madoline had been invalid, and therefore Genevieve was never lawfully married to him. What result?

(c) The New York Surrogate held that because the Florida divorce had been contested it was not subject to attack in New York. The New York Court of Appeals reversed, holding that the Florida judgment bound only the parties themselves, and not a third party, such as the daughter.[f] The U.S. Supreme Court reversed, *Johnson v. Muelberger,* 340 U.S. 581 (1951). The Court could not find any Florida case concerning the right of a child to contest the divorce of its parent in circumstances where the parent could not himself challenge the divorce. But whatever was the Florida law, Eleanor was out of luck:

> If the laws of Florida should be that a surviving child is in privity with its parent as to that parent's estate, surely the Florida doctrine of *res judicata* would apply to the child's collateral attack as it would to the father's. If, on the other hand, Florida holds, as New York does in this case, that the child of a former marriage is a stranger to the divorce proceedings, late opinions of Florida indicate that the child would not be permitted to attack the divorce, since the child had a mere expectancy at the time of the divorce.[g]

Thus, concluding that Florida would not permit Eleanor to attack the divorce between her father and stepmother, the Court held that under the Full Faith and Credit clause New York could not permit such attack either. Is this a sound result? Do you think it would come out the same way if the divorce between Bruce and Madoline had been *ex parte,* but the time to challenge it had expired in Florida? What if Bruce had been the plaintiff?

(d) Note again the irony of the Supreme Court compelling states to apply family protective legislation in favor of persons whom the state does not want to protect. New York does not, of course, have to protect surviving spouses; since it does so, however, it must protect Genevieve, notwithstanding New York's view that she is not such a spouse, and the testator's wish to favor his daughter.

(4)(a) Thus far all the cases in this chapter have said that domicile of the plaintiff is a requirement for jurisdiction to divorce, or at least for a divorce entitled to recognition under the Full Faith and Credit clause. The debate has been about whether a finding of domicile is conclusive or subject to challenge, with everyone understanding that domicile for divorce purposes did not really require a long-term commitment to the forum, just a mild form of perjury.[h]

---

[e] Presently N.Y. E.P.T.L. § 5–1.1. Recall the discussion of D.E.L. § 18 in *Estate of Clark,* Chapter 4, p. 348, and question (1)(d), p. 359, *supra.*

[f] *Matter of Johnson,* 301 N.Y. 13, 92 N.E.2d 44 (1950).

[g] 340 U.S. at 588.

[h] For the testimony of Mrs. Hendrix in the Nevada proceeding about her intention to establish an "indefinite permanent residence," see Powell, *And Repent at Lesiure,* 58 Harv. L. Rev. 930, 945 n.36 (1945).

§ 9.02   JURISDICTION AND JUDGMENTS   □   777

Could a state adopt a divorce law that did not require either party's domicile at all? The Court in *Williams II* seems to say no, but as Justice Rutledge pointed out in his dissent, "The Court is careful not to say that Nevada's judgment is not valid in Nevada."[i] How would the Court rule in a case unencumbered by issues of res judicata, full faith and credit, estoppel, or bigamy prosecutions?

(b) In 1953, the legislature of the U.S. Virgin Islands, amended its divorce law to provide as follows:

> . . . if the plaintiff is within the district at the time of the filing of the complaint and has been continuously for six weeks immediately prior thereto, this shall be prima facie evidence of domicile, and where the defendant has been personally served within the district or enters a general appearance in the action, then the Court shall have jurisdiction of the action and of the parties thereto without further reference to domicile or to the place where the marriage was solemnized or the cause of action arose.

Is such a statute constitutional?

(c) In the first case to raise this question, Sonia Alton of West Hartford, Connecticut arrived in the Virgin Islands on February 10, 1953; six weeks and a day later, on March 25, 1953, she filed for divorce, alleging "incompatibility of temperament" with her husband, David. The husband entered an appearance by counsel, waived service, and did not contest the allegations. The judge, however, asked for proof of domicile, and when none was furnished, dismissed the action. The wife appealed to the U.S. Court of Appeals for the Third Circuit. That court, sitting en banc, divided 4–3, with the majority upholding the district judge, i.e., striking down the statute. *Alton v. Alton,* 207 F. 667 (3d Cir. 1953). Judge Goodrich, writing for the majority, said both the presumption of domicile and authority to grant divorce without reference to domicile were constitutionally defective:

> A six-week's sojourn without proof of the intent with which one makes it, we think, tends to establish nothing but the fact of six weeks' physical presence. . . . If domicile is really the basis for a divorce jurisdiction . . . then six weeks' physical presence without more is not a reasonable way to prove it.[j]

Conceding that the statutory presumption "will doubtless eliminate the temptation to . . . perjury," the court nevertheless regarded the statute "as an attempt by the legislature to convert the suit for divorce into what is in fact a transitory action masquerading under a fiction of domiciliary jurisdiction.[k]

(d) As to the second part of the statute, dispensing with domicile altogether if both sides participate in the action, the court rejected it outright:

> We think that the premise that divorce jurisdiction is founded on domicile is still the law.[l]

Accordingly,

> a state where the party is not domiciled is, in rendering him a divorce, attempting to create an interest where it has no jurisdiction. Its attempt to do so is an invalid attempt, and contrary to the due process clause.[m]

---

[i] *Williams v. North Carolina II,* 325 U.S. 226 at 246 (Rutledge, J. dissenting).
[j] 207 F.2d at 671, 672.
[k] *Id.* at 673.
[l] *Id.* at 676.
[m] Ibid.

(e) In both aspects of its criticism of the Virgin Islands statute, the court based its ruling on the Due Process Clause of the Fifth Amendment, citing among other cases, *Home Insurance Co. v. Dick*.[n] In dissent, Judge Hastie asked "whose due process has been denied?," pointing out that the Constitution reads "No *person* shall . . . be deprived of life, liberty, or property without due process of law. . . ."

As to divorce without domicile, Judge Hastie asked

> . . . what is it that raises this judicial rule of self-restraint to the status of an invariable Constitutional principle?

He answered his own question quite differently from Justice Frankfurter:

> I can find nothing in the history of the present judge-made rule which entitles it to Constitutional sanction. . . .

> My conclusion [from a survey of English and early American practice] is that, on such evidence as is at hand, the limitation of the divorce power to the domiciliary state has no such ancient roots as to suggest its entitlement to perpetuation as a Constitutional requirement.[o]

Further,

> in selecting the alternative of personal jurisdiction over both parties, the [Virgin Islands] legislature has obviated that very disregard of interests on the defendant's side which is the great weakness of the domiciliary rule. In this action I can find nothing arbitrary or unfair; hence, nothing inconsistent with the Fifth Amendment.[p]

Is this persuasive? Or has Judge Hastie short-changed the interest of the state?

(f) Judge Hastie was conscious of this problem, and made another suggestion:

> . . . once the power to decide the case is based merely upon personal jurisdiction a court must decide as a separate question upon what basis, if any, the local substantive law of divorce can properly be applied. . . . In this case, if it should appear that Mr. and Mrs. Alton were both domiciled in Connecticut at the time of suit in the Virgin Islands and that their estrangement had resulted from conduct in the matrimonial home state, it may well be that under correct application of conflict of laws doctrine, and even under the due process clause, it is encumbent upon the Virgin Islands, lacking connection with the subject matter, to apply the divorce law of some state that has such connection, here Connecticut.[q]

Is this a useful suggestion? If so, is it equally pertinent to the *Williams I* and *Sherrer* situations as well?

Would you favor a federal statute that said:

> In order for a divorce granted by one state or territory of the United States to be entitled to recognition in any other state, the court granting the divorce must (i) make a finding concerning the last state where the parties lived together as man and wife; and (ii) apply the law of that state in granting or denying a divorce.

---

[n] See Chapter 5, p. 382, *supra*.

[o] 207 F.2d at 681, (Hastie, J. dissenting).

[p] *Id.* at 683.

[q] *Id.* at 685.

§ 9.02   JURISDICTION AND JUDGMENTS   □   779

What difficulties would you foresee in applying such a statute? Could the same result be achieved by decision of the Supreme Court?

(g) Speaking of the Supreme Court, it first granted certiorari in *Alton,*[r] then dismissed the case as moot when the husband secured a divorce in Connecticut.[s] A second case, commenced in the Virgin Islands almost simultaneously on virtually identical facts, was decided by the district and circuit courts on the strength of *Alton,* and the Supreme Court granted review. *Granville-Smith v. Granville-Smith,* 349 U.S. 1 (1955). However, the case proved to be an anticlimax; on the basis of an elaborate examination of the grant of legislative authority to the Island legislature, the Court concluded (5–3) that the legislature's authority extended only to acts of "local application." The statistics concerning divorce in the Virgin Islands—343 divorces and only 237 marriages in 1952—led to "controlling doubts of the 'local' application of [the 1953 amendment.]" Thus migratory divorce in the Virgin Islands came to an end, but the issues debated in *Alton* were left unresolved by the Supreme Court.[t]

(h) As of year-end 1997, the Supreme Court had not again returned to the subject of migratory divorce, except to hold that there was no constitutional right to such relief. In *Sosna v. Iowa,* 419 U.S. 393 (1975), the wife, who had resided in New York with her husband and also for a year after they separated, moved to Iowa with her children, and within a month petitioned the local Iowa court for a divorce. The husband, who had been personally served in Iowa when he came to visit the children, appeared specially to contest the jurisdiction of the Iowa court. The court dismissed the action, on the basis of a statute requiring either that the petitioner had resided in the state for a year prior to the action, or that the respondent be a resident of the state and be personally served.

Rather than appeal the dismissal, the wife challenged the durational residence requirement before a three-judge federal district court, which upheld the statute. On appeal, the Supreme Court affirmed. While durational residence requirements are unconstitutional as a qualification for welfare payments, voting, and medical care, "Iowa's divorce residency requirement is of a different stripe." Not only are consequences of great moment riding on a divorce decree which justify Iowa in insisting on the "modicum of attachment" required here:

> Such a requirement additionally furthers the State's parallel interests in both avoiding officious intermeddling in matters in which another State has a paramount interest, and in minimizing the susceptibility of its own divorce decrees to collateral attack. A State such as Iowa may quite reasonably decide that it does not wish to become a divorce mill. . . .

419 U.S. at 407.

[B]   Foreign Country Divorce

If *Sherrer v. Sherrer* was based on the Full Faith and Credit clause, it could have no application to a divorce rendered outside the United States; if on the other hand, the rationale were some

---

[r] 347 U.S. 911 (1954).

[s] 347 U.S. 610 (1954). (Justice Black dissented.)

[t] Justice Clark dissented, saying "There are limits to which the Courts should not run to escape a constitutional adjudication." He added:

> . . . I see no sense in striking down the Islands' law. There is no virtue in a state of the law the only practical effect of which would be to make New Yorkers fly 2,400 miles over land to Reno instead of 1,450 miles over water to the Virgin Islands.

349 U.S. at 26, 28 (Clark, J. dissenting).

combination of waiver, estoppel, and res judicata, these concepts might be applicable to judicial proceedings in foreign countries as well. Surely no provision of the United States Constitution could prescribe the jurisdictional basis for divorce granted by a foreign country. On the other hand, as we saw in Chapter 8, the recognition of foreign country judgments in the United States has generally been considered a matter for individual states, not raising constitutional or other federal questions. In fact, different states responded differently to situations in which persons like Mrs. Alton traveled not to the Virgin Islands, but to Mexico, Haiti, or the Dominican Republic.

ROSENSTIEL v. ROSENSTIEL

New York Court of Appeals
16 N.Y.2d 64, 262 N.Y.S.2d 86, 209 N.E.2d 709 (1965)
cert. denied, 384 U.S. 971 (1966)

BERGAN, J.

The defendant wife's former husband Felix Ernest Kaufman in 1954 obtained a divorce from her in a district court at Juarez in Chihuahua, Mexico. Plaintiff and defendant were married in New York in 1956 and this action by the husband seeks to annul that marriage on the ground the 1954 divorce is invalid and that, therefore, the defendant wife was incompetent in 1956 to contract a marriage.

In seeking the divorce in Mexico Mr. Kaufman went to El Paso, Texas, where he registered at a motel and the next day crossed the international boundary to Juarez. There he signed the Municipal Register, an official book of residents of the city, and filed with the district court a certificate showing such registration and a petition for divorce based on incompatibility and ill treatment between the spouses.

After about an hour devoted to these formalities, Mr. Kaufman returned to El Paso. The following day his wife, the present defendant, appeared in the Mexican court by an attorney duly authorized to act for her and filed an answer in which she submitted to the jurisdiction of the court and admitted the allegations of her husband's complaint. The decree of divorce was made the same day. The judgment is recognized as valid by the Republic of Mexico.

The Divorce Law of the State of Chihuahua provides that the court may exercise jurisdiction either on the basis of residence or of submission. Article 22 provides that the Judge "competent to take cognizance of a contested divorce" is the Judge "of the place of residence of the plaintiff" and of a divorce "by mutual consent," the Judge "of the residence of either of the spouses."

For the purposes of article 22, the statute further provides that the residence "shall be proven" by the "certificate of the Municipal Register" of the place (art. 24). . . .

After a trial at Special Term in the present husband's action for annulment, the court, holding that New York would not recognize the Mexican decree, granted judgment for the plaintiff and annulled the marriage; the Appellate Division reversed this judgment and dismissed the complaint.

In the background of this problem is a long series of decisions over a period of a quarter of a century in the New York Supreme Court at Appellate Division and at Special Term recognizing the validity of bilateral Mexican divorces which we consider has some relevancy to the question before us. No New York decision has refused to recognize such a bilateral Mexican divorce.

It has been estimated that many thousands of persons have been affected in their family and property status by these decisions. . . . In this respect the problem in New York differs somewhat from that in New Mexico, New Jersey and Ohio which have as a matter of their own public policy refused to accept as valid such Mexican divorces (*Golden v. Golden,* 41 N. M. 356; *Warrender v. Warrender,* 42 N. J. 287; *Bobala v. Bobala,* 68 Ohio App. 63).

There is squarely presented to this court now for the first time the question whether recognition is to be given by New York to a matrimonial judgment of a foreign country based on grounds not accepted in New York, where personal jurisdiction of one party to the marriage has been acquired by physical presence before the foreign court; and jurisdiction of the other has been acquired by appearance and pleading through an authorized attorney although no domicile of either party is shown within that jurisdiction; and "residence" has been acquired by one party through a statutory formality based on brief contact.

In cases where a divorce has been obtained without any personal contact with the jurisdiction by either party or by physical submission to the jurisdiction by one, with no personal service of process within the foreign jurisdiction upon, and no appearance or submission by, the other, decision has been against the validity of the foreign decree (*Caldwell v. Caldwell,* 298 N. Y. 146 [1948]; *Rosenbaum v. Rosenbaum,* 309 N. Y. 371 [1955]).

Although the grounds for divorce found acceptable according to Mexican law are inadmissible in New York, and the physical contact with the Mexican jurisdiction was ephemeral, there are some incidents in the Mexican proceedings which are common characteristics of the exercise of judicial power.

The former husband was physically in the jurisdiction, personally before the court, with the usual incidents and the implicit consequences of voluntary submission to foreign sovereignty. Although he had no intention of making his domicile there, he did what the domestic law of the place required he do to establish a "residence" of a kind which was set up as a statutory prerequisite to institute an action for divorce. This is not our own view in New York of what a bona fide residence is or should be, but it is that which the local law of Mexico prescribes.

Since he was one party to the two-party contract of marriage he carried with him legal incidents of the marriage itself, considered as an entity, which came before the court when he personally appeared and presented his petition. In a highly mobile era such as ours, it is needful on pragmatic grounds to regard the marriage itself as moving from place to place with either spouse, a concept which underlies the decision in *Williams v. North Carolina I.* (See, especially, Justice FRANKFURTER'S concurrence.).

The voluntary appearance of the other spouse in the foreign court by attorney would tend to give further support to an acquired jurisdiction there over the marriage as a legal entity. In theory jurisdiction is an imposition of sovereign power over the person. It is usually exerted by symbolic and rarely by actual force, e.g., the summons as a symbol of force; the attachment and the civil arrest, as exerting actual force.

But almost universally jurisdiction is acquired by physical and personal submission to judicial authority and in legal theory there seems to be ground to admit that the Mexican court at Juarez acquired jurisdiction over the former marriage of the defendant.

It is true that in attempting to reconcile the conflict of laws and of State interests in matrimonial judgments entered in States of the United States, where the Constitution compels each to give full faith and credit to the judgments of the others, a considerable emphasis has been placed on domicile as a prerequisite to that compulsory recognition. . . . But domicile is not intrinsically an indispensable prerequisite to jurisdiction. . . .

The duration of domicile in sister States providing by statute for a minimal time to acquire domicile as necessary to matrimonial action jurisdiction is in actual practice complied with by a mere formal gesture having no more relation to the actual situs of the marriage or to true domicile than the formality of signing the Juarez city register. The difference in time is not truly significant of a difference in intent or purpose or in effect.

The State or country of true domicile has the closest real public interest in a marriage but, where a New York spouse goes elsewhere to establish a synthetic domicile to meet technical acceptance of a matrimonial suit, our public interest is not affected differently by a formality of one day than by a formality of six weeks.

Nevada gets no closer to the real public concern with the marriage than Chihuahua. New York itself will take jurisdiction of a matrimonial action without regard to domicile or residence if it happened, by mere fortuity, that the marriage was contracted here, even between people entirely foreign to our jurisdiction (Domestic Relations Law, § 170, subd. 2. . . .)

A leading New York decision on the recognition of a divorce granted in a foreign nation where we are under no constitutional compulsion to give full faith and credit is *Gould v. Gould* (235 N. Y. 14 [1923]) and there the court sustained a judgment of divorce in France between parties not domiciled in France at a time when the husband, who instituted the French action, was domiciled in New York. Indeed, the New York law was applied by the French court because "the plaintiff Gould" was a resident of New York.

. . . .

The opinion in *Caldwell v. Caldwell* . . . dealing with divorces obtained on no personal presence or submission by either party in Mexico, the "mail-order decree," discusses domicile, but the question was not decisive of that case (cf. dissenting opinion, CONWAY, J., *Matter of Rathscheck,* 300 N. Y. 346, 355).

A balanced public policy now requires that recognition of the bilateral Mexican divorce be given rather than withheld and such recognition as a matter of comity offends no public policy of this State.

The order should be affirmed, with costs.

Chief Judge DESMOND (concurring in part).

Although for reasons hereafter stated I would not void past-granted Chihuahua divorces, I emphatically reject the proposition that New York State must continue to recognize these one-day decrees awarded to our residents in manner and on theories repugnant to our basic ideas.

There is no justification in positive law, public policy, natural justice or morals for a validation by this court of the practice of some of the citizens of our State of going to Mexico for divorces of the sort attacked on these appeals. My vote against recognizing them for the future is based on these self-evident propositions:

1. Divorce decrees rendered in foreign countries and purporting to dissolve New York marriages are entitled to recognition and effect in New York State only when such recognition

is consistent with the public policy of our State.... The *Gould* case is illustrative. There the New York courts upheld a divorce granted in France but only because the parties had actually lived for years in their Paris home and the decree was granted after an actual court contest without collusion and on a ground recognized in New York, that is, adultery.

2. Mexican "bilateral" divorces where one party crosses a bridge from El Paso, Texas, spends a day in Juarez and, by arrangement, the other appears by attorney, followed by a *pro forma* one-hour court appearance with no real hearing, or persuasive evidence or independent judicial determination lack almost all the elements which New York State considers requisites for a valid divorce. The residence requirements of the State of Chihuahua are minimal and inadequate to form a recognizable domiciliary jurisdictional base since in Mexico and contrary to our views neither spouse need have a true or real domicile in Mexico.... Domicile as the law uses the term means a fixed, permanent and principal home to which a person wherever temporarily located always intends to return (Black's Law Dictionary, 4th ed.).

3. No attention is paid in Juarez divorces to the principle, fundamental with us, that marriage is an institution in which the public as a third party has a vital interest.... The Mexican State does not concern itself with maintenance of the marriage or reasons for its dissolution. In these latter respects the one-day judgments here attacked differ in no essential respect from the mail-order writs described in *Caldwell v. Caldwell* (298 N. Y. 146).

4. Such decrees are blatantly and obviously the fruit of consensual divorce arrangements and as such are forbidden by New York public policy statute....

5. Although there is a line of lower court decisions in the State upholding these "Chihuahua" decrees ... they are, so we are told and so it would seem, refused recognition everywhere else.... Approval of these lower court decisions puts our State in the uneasy and inappropriate position of sole acceptor of Mexican "quickie" divorces. The suggestion in the majority opinion that these trial court and Appellate Division decisions, together with the fact that Mexico has issued numerous divorces to New Yorkers, plus the fact of advices by New York attorneys to their clients, force this court into a totally wrong public policy is a suggestion that answers itself. We are forgetting that the public policy of this State as to divorce "exists to promote the permanency of the marriage contracts and the morality of the citizens of the state." ...

Of course, it is in the modern manner to shrug off all this, to ask what is the difference between a one-day "domicile" in Juarez and a six weeks' "domicile" in Reno, to pile scorn and ridicule on New York's one-ground divorce law as archaic, cruel or worse. The approach is too facile. For 160 years New York as a State has recognized one cause only for divorce and has refused to approve the practice of its domiciliaries going to other jurisdictions to evade our laws by obtaining divorces after short sojourns and on grounds not cognizable here (*Jackson v. Jackson*, 1 Johns. 424 [1806]). This official position of our State stands not on mere parochialism but on some of the oldest and deepest-felt sentiments of humanity. As Lord MANSFIELD wrote long ago: "Matrimony was one of the first commands given by God to mankind after the Creation, repeated again after the Deluge, and ever since echoed by the voice of nature to all mankind."[u]

---

[u] The quotation comes from *Low v. Peers*, S.C. Burr. 2225, 97 Eng. Rep. 138 at 141 (Exchequer Chamber 1770), actually in a decision by Lord Chief Justice Wilmot, on appeal from a decision of Lord Mansfield setting aside a jury verdict. The case involved an allegation by plaintiff that defendant had promised he would not marry anyone but her, and that if he married anyone else, he would pay her £1,000. Defendant did marry someone else, and did not pay her the £1,000. Her suit upon the promise failed, on the ground that it was not a promise to marry, but rather a restraint upon marriage that the courts should not enforce.

Seventy-seven years ago in *Maynard v. Hill* (125 U. S. 190, 205, *supra*) the United States Supreme Court referred to marriage as creating the most important relation in life and as having more to do with the morals of a civilized people than any institution, and pointed out that while marriage is in a sense a contract, it "partakes more of the character of an institution controlled by public authority, upon principles of public policy, for the benefit of the community" . . . No court is licensed to write a new State policy, however attractive or convenient. As to divorces gotten in other States of the Union we are constrained to recognition by modern constructions of the Federal full faith and credit clause. But when asked to recognize divorces rendered in foreign countries we as a court have neither right nor need to look beyond our own declared and unmistakable State policy. . . .

As to analogizing the one-day Mexican divorce to the six weeks' Nevada decree, the first and ready answer is that judgments from other States are given faith and credit here because the Federal Constitution so commands. The second answer is a substitution of the true analogy, that is, between one-day foreign divorces and post-card foreign divorces, as between which there is no logical or real difference at all. . . .

It is suggested, too, that a Juarez divorce is some sort of official "act of State" of a sovereign foreign power and, as such, safe from our scrutiny or ban. That might be so as to Mexico divorcing her own citizens. But our recognition of any foreign judgments is a mere act of official courtesy, implying no surrender of our own sovereignty. There is no compulsion. Were we to give credit to these Mexican judgments we would as a court be turning our backs on New York's restrictive divorce policy and allowing the divorce of our own citizen-residents by a foreign government having no interest in the marriage *res*.

For these reasons I vote for a declaration that such divorces are void, but I am not bound to and do not vote to give this ruling any more than prospective effect. I cannot shut my eyes to the realities. Tens of thousands of such purported divorces have been granted to New Yorkers who acted on advice of attorneys who relied on 25 years of decisions by the New York lower courts. No social or moral purpose would now be served by ruling that marriages long ago dissolved are still in existence, and the result would be destructive to the present homes, marriage and lives of those who remarried on the strength of Juarez decrees. This court has a clear right to give our ruling prospective effect only.

. . . .

[Judge SCILEPPI dissents, essentially for the same reasons given by Chief Judge DESMOND in his concurrence. He would also not apply his view retroactively but would apply it to the present case.]

THE CARIBBEAN CAPER

HISPANIOLA'S THE NAME OF THE ISLAND, AND DIVORCE IS THE NAME OF THE GAME*

The New York Times, Sunday, February 13, 1972
By Pam Pollock Bruns

Barbra Streisand and Elliott Gould took "the Dominican route" last July and early this month George C. Scott of "Patton" fame and his actress-wife Colleen Dewhurst did the same. Both couples took advantage of recently liberalized divorce laws that have made the Dominican Republic one of the two new "divorce capitals" of the Western Hemisphere—the other being Haiti, its neighbor on the island of Hispaniola.

In the Streisand-Gould divorce, Gould flew to Santo Domingo, the Dominican capital, and within 24 hours had a mutual consent decree. In the Dewhurst-Scott action, the actress was the partner appearing, getting a decree virtually overnight. In between, more than 1,700 other couples have dissolved their marriages on the island—in the quickie fashion of those former Mexican divorces.

Mexico, the former divorce "capital"—anxious to shed that image—passed reform legislation last March shutting down the divorce mills of Juarez and Caliente. Into the breach—at the persistent prodding of several Juarez-wise lawyers—stepped first Haiti (in February) and then the Dominican Republic (in June). Tourist-shy, they hoped to snare what is reported to have been a $50-million-a-year "industry" in Mexico that drew some 18,000 Americans annually. About 75,000 Americans, all told, had terminated marriages in Mexico—among them Elizabeth Taylor, Mia Farrow, Lauren Bacall, Sheila MacRae, Rod Steiger, Franklin Roosevelt Jr. and Huntington Hartford.

Up and Coming

Even with the Gould-Streisand names to garner attention, the Dominican Republic and Haiti, which share the island of Hispaniola, have a long way to go to do the kind of business Mexico did. True, by the end of 1971 Haiti had already handled about 1,000 divorce cases and the Dominican Republic about 700, but luring the divorce "tourist" down is one thing; getting him or her to stay a while to sample the sun and beaches and rum punches, I discovered on a recent visit to both countries, is quite another.

I visited the Dominican Republic and Haiti not to get a divorce myself but to find out how the quickie divorce package works and what one does or can do for fun outside the courtroom. The preliminaries are taken care of by your stateside lawyer, and when you and your spouse consent to the final action (usually on grounds of mutual incompatibility), he places you in the hands of a representative either in the Dominican Republic or Haiti. One of the parties must fly down for the court hearing, paying his or her own round-trip plane fare (about $200) and accommodations (about $25 a day).

Among the busiest representatives in the Dominican Republic is Manuel Espinosa. Formerly based in Juarez, Espinosa handles at least 75 per cent of the American divorces in Santo Domingo,

---

* Copyright © 1972 by the New York Times Company. Reprinted by permission.

the Dominican capital. Even with that corner on the market, he cannot match his lucrative days in Juarez. "My biggest day so far was 20 clients," he says, "but my obsession is to get up to 60 a day—like when I was in Juarez."

Dapper in one of his many sportcoats and shiny silk ties, Manny Espinosa leans back in his office chair and picks up the phone. It's long distance from New York, a call from one of the lawyers for whom Espinosa handles divorce cases in the Dominican Republic. (Espinosa charges about $400, which covers court appearances, taxes, copies of the final decree and translations.)

"Sure I can handle it, as soon as you want" . . . pause . . . "Fine, we'll expect him tomorrow."

Espinosa hangs up, jots a name down on a list and calls for Nancy Jettman, his official hostess for incoming clients. Nancy, a loquacious, sun-tanned blonde from Brooklyn, enters from the outer office and is handed tomorrow's list of arrivals. There will be only five, which, until Hispaniola divorces catch on, is about average. (December turned out to be the slowest month; it seems divorces are postponed until joint tax returns are filed.)

Santo Domingo has a sparkling new airport, and the next day Nancy Jettman moves quickly through the expansive lobby to take her position to greet Espinosa's clients. The first flight from New York, Pan Am No. 233, arrives at 12:20, too late to get the people into court before it closes at 1 P.M. As the passengers file through passport control, then immigration, Nancy reads over her list and reminds the policeman who collects tourist cards to flash them so she can identify her customers. Behind the glass partition the new arrivals mix with guards, a merengue band and a hostess serving welcoming drinks of Dominican rum.

"After a while it's easy to spot them," says Nancy as she cranes her neck to get a better look. "Mainly because most of the passengers are Dominicans, and an American sticks out. There's one now—that paunchy guy with the wrinkled business suit. And there, too, that nervous lady trying to look calm."

Suddenly the policeman waves a tourist card for a girl from Queens, an Italian-American whom Nancy has pegged as a Dominican. Nancy hurries to the door just as the girl passes through.

Helping Hand

"Hi, I'm Nancy, Mr. Espinosa's representative. I'm here to help you with baggage check and to get you into town." The girl is openly relieved to be met, but surprised to hear a Brooklyn accent.

"Are you nervous?" Nancy asks.

"Oh, yes. I didn't think I would be. And I'm so hot. Mother insisted I wear these warm clothes and bring this coat," which she tossed down on a lounge chair in the 85-degree heat. "You know how mothers are!"

About an hour later, her clients cleared through customs, Nancy loads them into waiting cabs for the ride into town. It's a 45-minute trip along a highway lined with swaying palms and offering a spectacular view of the azure Caribbean.

"It's so beautiful," says Mary, a thirtyish housewife from outside Boston. "I wish I didn't have to rush back to the kids to relieve the babysitter." The Italian-American girl chimes in, "Yes, I have to get back to my little baby, too." John, a husky blond fellow from Yonkers, who has the look of a Norwegian gun-runner, grins and says, "I have to get back to my baby, too. Only she's the older type."

The scenic ride along the Caribbean and through about 10 minutes of downtown Santo Domingo is the only sightseeing most of the clients will do in their 24-hour stay here. Espinosa believes in "service," and he keeps things well organized and uncomplicated. His office is in the lobby of the luxurious Embajador Hotel, outside the mainstream of the town, and all his clients spend the night there. And with restaurants, a bar, a casino and a swimming pool at hand in the hotel, most clients—largely inexperienced travelers—seem pleased not to have to venture out.

As Nancy's clients check into the hotel, small overnight bags in hand, invitations go around, and everyone ends up having drinks and lunch together out by the pool. The group is of mixed ages and backgrounds, but their common purpose for being in Santo Domingo soon has them on a first-name basis and chatting openly about how they decided to get a quickie divorce.

Lunch stretches through the afternoon and by the time they retire for the night, after dinner and more drinks, they will have discussed each other's failed marriages and separation problems and compared their stateside lawyers' fees. Nancy chuckles over this. "You can't imagine how ticked-off they get when they hear how much their lawyer charged them in comparison with someone else."

Most of the clients remain sequestered in the hotel during their stay, but there are exceptions, of course. Some clients bring future spouses, lawyers, mothers or fathers, and occasionally even the kids, and make a vacation out of it.

Whether they've been out on the town or remained at the hotel, the next morning at 8:30 sharp all of Espinosa's clients report to his office. Manny shepherds them to his waiting cars and whisks them to the courthouse, a five-minute ride through an upper-class suburb of wide, quiet streets and big comfortable homes. The Hall of Justice is a modern, well-maintained building, and as the clients file up the stairs after Espinosa, the chatter dies down. The big moment is approaching.

The courtroom is a large airy room, with two long walls of open-louvered windows. There are seats for about 200, but the Espinosa party has the courtroom to itself. With everyone seated in the front row, Espinosa clasps his hands reverently in front of him and addresses his audience. He draws attention to the crucifix which stands on the judge's bench, reminds his clients to stand when the judge enters, and concludes by listing all the questions the judge will ask: "Name, nationality, residence, and whether you would like to proceed with this divorce. Please, if you are going to say no to *that,* tell me now!"

Several minutes go by, with no one saying a word. Finally the silence is broken by the entrance of the brisk-moving, black-robed judge, the secretary of the court and the bailiff. Almost before the clients are seated again, Carol, the woman from Queens, hears her name being read off. She walks to the bench and Espinosa translates the judge's four questions from Spanish to English. After the final question is answered "yes," lawyer and divorcee return to their seats. Then a local Dominican lawyer reads the grounds and terms of the divorce in Spanish, the judge raps his gavel and the next case is ready to be heard. No more than two minutes have elapsed. Carol is smiling so broadly that there is a twitter of suppressed laughter from those waiting their turn.

Fifteen minutes later, as they all clamber down the stairs. Manny is invited for drinks by his happy clients. "I'm free at last after 13 years in prison," rejoices the man in the rumpled suit.

"Now I can really celebrate." His companions nod and laugh with nervous relief as they climb into two waiting cars, and settle back with their new-found freedom. One of the men loosens his tie in the sultry heat and mumbles, "If I had known it was going to be this easy, I would have done it years ago."

By 10 A.M. they are all toasting each other with rum punches. Shortly afterward, as his clients prepare to leave the hotel for the airport, Espinosa's round, smiling face turns serious. He has a final word: "Please call your lawyers when you get back home and tell them how it went. They always want to know." This is as close as he will get to advertising.

Two hours after court, back at the same airport where they had all arrived as strangers the day before, the newly independent Santo Domingo Five cluster together like old friends, merrily chatting away as their bags are checked in. At the other end of the airport, Nancy Jettman is looking over her new list of charges and reminding the policeman to please flash their tourist cards.

As far as the Dominican Republic tourist office is concerned, the newly divorced are leaving too soon. Officials had been led to believe that anyone traveling all the way from New York or Chicago would stay at least a week, bolstering the tourist trade by visiting Dominican resorts—Constanza, Puerta Plata, Sosua or the new development of La Romana—as well as Santo Domingo. Those were the trumpetings of the law's proponents. Yet, even so, the divorce legislation met with strong opposition from the Roman Catholic Church. President Joaquin Balaguer vetoed the first enabling bill (a bill helped along when Manuel Espinosa incorporated a dozen legislators and government officials into his firm to insure their support), but his veto was overridden.

Perhaps a "let's get in on it, too" mentality was working, because Haiti had passed similar legislation several months before (legislation purposely patterned after the Mexican law to enhance its acceptability by U.S. courts). In Haiti, under President-for-Life François (Papa Doc) Duvalier, who died last spring, such matters could be handled expeditiously. His approval of what promised to be a lucrative business removed any roadblocks to passage of the quickie divorce law.

Subsequently, IBO Tours, a travel agency whose chief owner is Luckner Cambronne, the powerful minister of Interior and National Defense, was given a monopoly on the divorce business. Although several lawyers handle the legal end of divorce proceedings, arrangements must be made through IBO Tours.

A key operative in the divorce business in Port-au-Prince, the Haitian capital, is Donald McKay, an Alabama lawyer who was once based in Juarez. He handles an estimated 80 per cent of the divorce cases in Haiti. Relaxing at his home, which was formerly the Guatemalan Embassy, McKay swirls his drink as he explains his business. "We'll divorce'em in the morning and, if they want, marry'em in the afternoon," he drawls.

. . . .

McKay and his wife and daughter, Honey, split up the task of greeting clients at the airport and taking them to their hotel. He favors Castle Haiti, which is tour-group oriented and lacks the quaintness and charm of such other hotels as the Sans Souci and the Oloffson (around which the movie "The Comedians" was set).

McKay's office is in the crowded downtown section, and the trip to the courthouse can take a good 20 minutes through Haitian-style traffic jams of donkeys, people pushing carts, and assorted versions of automobiles.

Divorce court in Haiti is in harmony with the rest of the country—not quite on time and like an unrestored historical landmark. McKay has six clients this particular sultry morning, and as they wait in the civil courtroom they chuckle at the performance of a lawyer in a tattered black robe, gesturing dramatically toward a withered, sleepy judge who nods occasionally, oblivious to Haiti's answer to William Jennings Bryan. Barking dogs (one bounding into the courtroom), playing children, the milling about of local men, all add to the confusion—and color.

McKay, still in shirtsleeves, finally ushers in his clients one by one to a small, dingy room adjoining the civil courtroom. The judge is already seated, wearing a business suit and a loosened tie, with an open briefcase beside him.

The same basic procedures take place as in Santo Domingo, and after only two or three minutes the "court appearance" is over. The last client is a trembling young lady who has flown in from Ireland in particularly complicated circumstances, and her future mother-in-law wrings her hands in anguish. But moments later the girl rushes out of the adjoining room and embraces the woman, tears streaming down her face. "At last, at last," she cries.

Al Seitz, the manager of the Oloffson, watches the comings and goings of his divorce clientele with a certain bemusement. Sitting out on his hotel's front porch, he chomps on his cigar and says, "You should have met the American lady from Egypt last week. She had bracelets from her elbows to her wrists. Her Moslem husband wanted to take on a new wife or two and she didn't want to stay around for that." Holding his worked-over cigar, he continued, "She wanted to spend her spare time getting her fortune read. So I set her up with some *great* voodoo priests."

Seitz looked over the balcony as a young, sunburned man came trudging up the stairs lugging two bulging straw bags of assorted Haitian bargains—wood carvings, straw hats, leather goods and a painting. "The guy got his divorce," says Seitz, "and is staying on for a week, while he buys out Port-au-Prince."

. . . .

Whether they will ever come—and stay awhile—as the result of the new divorce laws is difficult to predict. Most of those coming now to shed a mate make it a fast trip. But they are coming, many who would not otherwise visit Hispaniola. So far the overwhelming majority have come from the northeastern United States, but some have traveled from as far as the Philippines, Singapore and Australia. And one recent client of McKay's was a woman who came all the way from Italy—and she was 81.

FURTHER NOTES AND QUESTIONS

(5)(a) Consider the facts in *Rosenstiel*:

> Susan is married to Felix, and both reside in New York; Felix flies to El Paso, Texas, then takes a taxi to Juarez, Chihuahua, Mexico. Susan appears in the court in Juarez by attorney; the court grants a divorce. Two years later, Susan marries Lewis Rosenstiel. Now Lewis seeks an annulment, asserting that the divorce between Susan and Felix was invalid.

Has Lewis done something that should estop him from challenging the divorce between his present wife and her prior husband? Is his position like that of the daughter in *Johnson v. Muelberger*?[a]

---

[a] Question (3), p. 775-76, *supra*.

(b) The New York Court of Appeals does not speak of estoppel, but says rather that "domicile is not intrinsically an indispensable prerequisite to jurisdiction" to grant a divorce. That statement is, of course, directly contrary to the statement of the majority in *Alton*,[b] and arguably contrary to the statement of the Supreme Court in *Williams II*. Is there a constitutional infirmity to the *Rosenstiel* case? Or is the *Williams-Alton* outlook limited to the English-speaking peoples?

(c) Realistically speaking, Judge Bergan writes (p. 782), "Nevada gets no closer to the real public concern with the marriage than Chihuahua." Isn't that correct? But what follows? Isn't Chief Judge Desmond also correct in saying (at p. 783) that the divorce in *Rosenstiel* (or rather *Kaufman*) differs in no essential respect from *Caldwell v. Caldwell*,[c] in which *both* parties appeared by attorney only and the divorce was held invalid.[d]

(d) Judge Bergan says (at p. 781) that "although the grounds for divorce found acceptable according to Mexican law are inadmissible in New York, and the physical contact with the Mexican jurisdiction was ephemeral, there are some incidents in the Mexican proceedings which are common characteristics of the exercise of judicial power." What do you suppose he has in mind? Putting the question in more practical terms, when Mexico tires of the image of a divorce mill, what does Mr. Espinosa tell his new hosts they must do to pass scrutiny by New York's highest court?

(e) Suppose Mr. Kaufman had notified Mrs. Kaufman in due time (and could prove that) but she had not appeared in Juarez either in person or by attorney. Would Judge Bergan still recognize the divorce?

(f) Many persons for many years had criticized New York's divorce law as it stood up to 1966, which excluded divorce by consent and recognized only adultery as a ground for divorce.[e] But is there any basis for the court's statement at the close of the majority opinion that recognition of Mexico's one-day, no ground divorce "offends no public policy of this State"?

(g) Judge SCILEPPI, in a dissent not here reproduced, essentially agreed with Judge DESMOND, except on the question of retroactivity. To Judge Bergan's point that Nevada gets no closer to real public concerns than Mexico, Judge Scileppi gave a candid answer:

> in the case of a sister State we are *compelled* to give full faith and credit to its decrees. In the case of a foreign country we are not compelled to do so and should not voluntarily recognize its decrees.[f]

Could New York, or any other state in the United States, change the outcome of *Sherrer* by statute?

(6)(a) Shortly after *Rosenstiel* was decided, the New York legislature adopted a general reform of its domestic relations law, including for the first time several fault grounds and living apart for two or more years. As part of the complicated maneuvering that led to passage of the Divorce

---

[b] See question 4, pp. 776–77, *supra*.

[c] 298 N.Y. 146, 81 N.E.2d 60 (1948).

[d] Prof. David Currie wrote, "I think the reason the court did not distinguish *Caldwell* was that it was indistinguishable." D. Currie, *Suitcase Divorce in the Conflict of Laws: Simons, Rosenstiel, and Borax*, 34 U. Chi. L. Rev. 26, at 60 (1966).

[e] See N.Y. Domestic Relations Law § 170 as it read (under different headings and in slightly different wording) from 1787 to 1966. For a history of efforts to change the law in the nineteenth century, see N. Blake, *The Road to Reno*, 64–79 (1962).

[f] 16 N.Y.2d at 85, 262 N.Y.S.2d at 100–01, 209 N.E.2d at 720. (Scileppi, J. dissenting).

Reform Law,[g] the legislature enacted section 250 of the Domestic Relations Law, designed to ensure, if possible, that the carefully drawn compromises would not immediately be flouted by trips to Nevada, Florida, or Mexico.[h] Would you support the section (Documents Supplement p. 133)?

(b) In part, § 250 was a reaction to the *Rosentiel* case, which had received great publicity while going through the New York courts, and which was decided by the Court of Appeals just as the debate over divorce reform was reaching a climax.[i] The legislature seems to have understood § 250 as a reversal of the *Rosenstiel* case, though some observers pointed out that the section spoke in terms of domicile, while the Court of Appeals had said domicile was not required. Others thought that if it was meant to apply only to Mexican (or other foreign-country) divorces, it might be effective, but that it could not pass muster under the Constitution if applied to sister-state divorces. Do you agree? Note that § 250 is drawn from the Uniform Divorce Recognition Act, but New York, unlike California, did not adopt section 1.[j]

(c) Is the constitutional question the same for a bilateral divorce, à la *Sherrer,* as for an ex parte divorce, à la *Williams*?

(d) The New York legislature repealed § 250 in 1973 before it received any significant test.[k] Had it been tested, and had the New York courts denied recognition to a Nevada or Florida divorce in which both parties participated, even as they had their return tickets to New York in their pockets,—say on the basis of fraud on the court—it is conceivable that the Supreme Court would have reexamined the whole sequence of cases from *Williams I* on. Consider how a different approach might have rearranged the status of ex parte and bilateral, interstate and international divorce.[l]

(7)(a) It is interesting that Mexico came to regard Juarez divorces as somehow demeaning—playing with sovereignty, as it were—and put pressure on Chihuahua to eliminate its "quickie" divorces.[m] But as the article from the New York Times—in the travel section—points out, the

---

[g] New York Laws 1966, ch. 254, effective (with some exceptions) Sept. 1, 1967.

[h] For a brief history of § 250, see Foster, *Recognition of Migratory Divorces: Rosenstiel v. Section 250,* 43 N.Y.U. L. Rev. 429, 439–440 (1968). Professor Foster writes that section 250 and establishment of a Conciliation Bureau were the prices paid for the expansion of divorce grounds in New York.

[i] Mr. Rosenstiel was a prominent businessman, chairman of the board of Schenley Industries, and a man often in the news in New York and elsewhere. Both his lawyer, Roy Cohn, and Susan's Lawyer, Louis Nizer, were skilled in drawing the press into their professional activities.

[j] Section 5001 in the California version reproduced in the Documents Supplement at p. 133. Sections 5003 and 5004 as adopted in California were not in the original version as promulgated by the Commissioners on Uniform State Laws in 1948, largely in response to the Supreme Court's decision in *Williams I.*

[k] N.Y. Laws 1973, ch. 67. For the thinking behind repeal, see *Kraham v. Kraham,* 73 Misc. 2d 977, 980, 342 N.Y.S.2d 943, 947 (Sup. Ct. Nassau Cty. 1973).

[l] The Uniform Divorce Recognition Act remains in effect in California (and a few other states) as of year-end 1997, but no major test of its impact in the interstate setting has been reported.

[m] In an earlier period, roughly 1922–28, France was for a time the favorite place divorce forum for Americans. This ended when the French government insisted on strict application of French law, as well as disciplinary measures against American lawyers practicing in Paris. See Nelson Blake, *The Road to Reno,* 159–61 (1962). For the development of Mexico's divorce business, see Blake 161–65 and sources there cited, including several Congressional inquiries as well as contemporary newspaper accounts. Divorce in Mexico was a matter of state and not federal law, but the national government ended divorce in Chihuaha and a few other states for non-residents by establishing rules for the acquisition of domicile in the Republic, and prohibiting all courts from processing divorce or annulment actions involving aliens who were not in possession of a certificate of legal residence issued by the Ministry of Interior. Decree of Feb. 3, 1971, "Amendments to Art. 35 and Additions to Art. 39 of the Law of Nationality and Naturalization," Diario Oficial Feb. 20, 1971, p. 18.

practice did not end, it just changed venue. Even with much liberalized divorce, including in nearly every state some form of divorce without fault-grounds, it turns out that parties who cannot or do not want to wait for the required length of time—one year in New York as of 1998—make the trip to the Dominican Republic or Haiti. The majority of states in the United States that have passed on the question have denied recognition to such divorces, even when both parties are represented.[n] A few states, led by New York but including also Connecticut, Tennessee, and the Virgin Islands, have upheld such divorces.[o]

(b) Given that there is no compulsion of the Constitution or the Supreme Court, should such foreign country suitcase divorces be recognized? Is your view based on your attitude to the family or divorce? Or does it come from your understanding of conflict of laws?

(c) Suppose a married couple domiciled in New York secure a divorce in Santo Domingo, with Robert making the trip and his wife Barbara appearing by attorney. Thereafter Barbara moves to Pennsylvania, and wishes to remarry. Should Pennsylvania recognize her divorce from Robert?[p]

(8) Consider finally the following roughly contemporaneous views of migratory divorce, the first by an expert on conflict of laws, the second by an expert in family law:

David Currie:

. . . In a federal system with such extreme variations among states as we have, on a subject of such intense concern as divorce, the situation is one big mess. . . . [T]he law of migratory divorce inhabits a looking-glass world in which the usual conflicts principles are distorted beyond recognition. Jurisdiction over the defendant seems to be neither necessary nor sufficient to empower a court to hear a divorce case. Foreign law is never considered, much less applied. A foreign judgment may be collaterally attacked on the issue of domicile, which ordinarily relates to choice of law. Jurisdiction is sustained every day on the basis of testimony that nobody begins to believe. . . . The Constitution is lost in the shuffle, and the law is held up to disrespect.[q]

Henry Foster, Jr.:

. . . [T]he fact remains that there is little practical good to be attained by the imposition of restrictive rules upon willing subjects where those rules are not backed up by a consensus. The conflict of laws rules as to recognition of divorce decrees, no less than the substantive grounds for divorce, must therefore be responsive to current values concerning marriage and divorce. The sterile conceptualism of the dogma of domicile is obsolete. It has no place in a modern domestic relations law.[r]

---

[n] See, e.g., *Warrender v. Warrender,* 79 N.J. Super, 114, 190 A.2d 684 (App. Div. 1963), aff'd 42 N.J. 287, 200 A.2d 123 (1964); *Weber v. Weber,* 200 Neb. 659, 265 N.W.2d 436 (1978); Annotation, 13 A.L.R.3d 1419 (1967 & Supp.).

[o] See 13 A.L.R.3d 1419, note n *supra*. For affirmation of the rule in New York, see *Greschler v. Greschler,* 51 N.Y.2d 368, 434 N.Y.S.2d 194, 414 N.E.2d 694 (1980).

[p] For an affirmative answer, see *Restatement (Third) of Foreign Relations Law* § 484(3) and Reporters' Note 4 (1987). See also Note, *New York-approved Mexican Divorces: Are They Valid in Other States?,* 114 U. Pa. L. Rev. 771, 777 (1966). For the parallel rule in Great Britain, see *Armitage v. Attorney General,* [1906] p. 135, recognizing a South Dakota divorce procured by the English wife, on the basis of a showing that it would be upheld in New York, the domicile of the husband.

[q] D. Currie, note d, *supra* at 26–27.

[r] Foster, note h, *supra* at 430.

Can you decide between these views? Or would you want first to consider the economic and child care aspects of divorce, as explored briefly in the succeeding sections of this chapter?

"It couldn't have been a nicer holiday. The weather was perfect, the food was delicious, and that cute little judge who granted us the divorce was right out of a storybook."

Cosmopolitan May 1984. Reprinted by permission.

§ 9.03 Economic Incidents of Divorce

Though all the opinions reproduced in this chapter speak of the state's interest in terms of property and children as well as status, thus far the cases have involved only the validity of the divorce itself. As divorce in the United States (and elsewhere) has become easier, with "grounds" giving way to the concept of marital breakdown, the battleground has shifted to the incidents and consequences of marital breakdown—support or lack thereof, and struggles over children.

The first case in this section illustrates an odd aspect of the understanding of the Full Faith and Credit clause. Only final judgments, it seems, are regarded as "enforceable" in other states, and judgments for alimony or child support tend not to be final for this purpose because they are modifiable. The second and third cases in this section go back to *Williams I* and raise the question of whether and to what extent jurisdiction based on domicile only of the plaintiff can affect economic benefits of the defendant associated with the marital relationship.

[A] The "Non-final" Judgment

LYNDE v. LYNDE

United States Supreme Court
181 U.S. 183 (1901)

This was an action brought May 26, 1898, in the Supreme Court for the county and State of New York, on a decree of the Court of Chancery of New Jersey of December 28, 1897, by which it was ordered that the plaintiff was entitled to recover of the defendant the sum of $7840 for alimony at the rate of $80 per week from February 11, 1896, to the date of the decree, and the further sum of $80 per week permanent alimony from the date of the decree, the said weekly payments to be valid liens on the defendant's real estate. . . . The record showed the following material facts:

On November 18, 1892, the plaintiff in this action filed her bill for a divorce in the Court of Chancery of New Jersey, setting forth her marriage with the present defendant on March 25, 1884, in New Jersey, where she has since resided; and praying for a divorce from the bond of matrimony for desertion for two years, and for reasonable alimony. The defendant was not served with process other than by publication, and did not appear or answer the bill. On August 7, 1893, a decree of divorce was entered, not mentioning alimony.

On February 10, 1896, the plaintiff, alleging that this decree was incomplete through the neglect of her counsel, filed a petition in that court, praying for an opening and amendment of the decree by allowing reasonable alimony. Upon this petition, a rule to show cause was entered, and it was ordered that copies of the petition and affidavits accompanying it be served on the defendant.

In answer to the rule, the defendant appeared generally, and filed an affidavit, declaring that he was a resident of New York, "that this defendant was by the decree of this court divorced from said petitioner" on August 7, 1893, "and since that time has been married again to another woman," "that the decree for divorce in said cause was purposely drawn without providing for or reserving any alimony;" and "that he is financially unable to pay alimony."

On October 26, 1896, the Court of Chancery of New Jersey amended the decree of August 7, 1893, by ordering that the petitioner "have the right to apply to this court at any time hereafter, at the foot of this decree, for reasonable alimony, and for such other relief in the premises touching alimony as may be equitable and just; and this court reserves the power to make such order or decree as may be necessary to allow and compel the payment of alimony to the petitioner by defendant, or to refuse to allow alimony." 6 Dickinson (54 N. J. Eq.) 473. On appeal this order was affirmed by the New Jersey Court of Errors and Appeals. 10 Dickinson (55 N. J. Eq.) 591. Thereupon an order of reference, based on all prior proceedings, and on notice to the solicitor for the defendant, was made by the Court of Chancery to a master to find the amount of alimony, if any, due to the plaintiff. Neither the defendant nor his solicitor appeared at the hearing before the master; and on December 28, 1897, the Court of Chancery, confirming the master's report, made the decree now sued on.

That court, on its being made to appear that a certified copy of this decree was personally served on the defendant, and that he refused to comply with said decree, ordered that a receiver be appointed to take possession of all the defendant's real and personal property in New Jersey to apply it to the payment of the plaintiff's claim. The receiver, however, was "unable to obtain

§ 9.03   JURISDICTION AND JUDGMENTS   □   795

possession of any property or assets of said defendant in the State of New Jersey;" nor had the defendant "complied with said decree in any respect."

The Supreme Court of New York decreed that the plaintiff was "entitled to a judgment against the defendant, enforcing against said defendant the decree of the Court of Chancery of New Jersey, dated December 28, 1897," and the order appointing a receiver, and enjoining the defendant from transferring his property; also that the plaintiff was entitled to judgment that the defendant pay her $8976.07, "being alimony, counsel fee and costs, due under said decree," and interest thereon from its date; also the "sum of $4400, being the amount of weekly alimony which has accrued since said decree in accordance with the terms thereof," and interest thereon; also $80 a week from the date of this decision "as and for permanent alimony," bearing interest until paid; that he give bond "in the sum of $100,000 to secure payment of the several sums of money aforesaid;" and that, if the defendant fail to comply with this decision, "a receiver be appointed, ancillary to the receiver heretofore appointed by the Court of Chancery of New Jersey as aforesaid, of the real and personal property of the defendant within the State of New York."

On appeal by the defendant to the Appellate Division, the decree was modified so as to allow the plaintiff to recover only $8840 alimony, the amount declared by the New Jersey court as due and payable at the date of its decree. Thus modified, the judgment of the Supreme Court was affirmed. 41 N. Y. App. Div. 280.

From the judgment of the Appellate Division both parties appealed to the Court of Appeals, which affirmed the judgment of the Appellate Division. 162 N. Y. 405. Each party sued out a writ of error from this court.

MR. JUSTICE GRAY, after stating the case as above, delivered the opinion of the court.

The husband, as the record shows, having appeared generally in answer to the petition for alimony in the Court of Chancery in New Jersey, the decree of that court for alimony was binding upon him. *Laing v. Rigney,* 160 U. S. 531. The court of New York having so ruled, thereby deciding in favor of the full faith and credit claimed for that decree under the Constitution and laws of the United States, its judgment on that question cannot be reviewed by this court on writ of error. *Gordon v. Caldcleugh,* 3 Cranch, 268; *Missouri v. Andriano,* 138 U. S. 496. The husband having appeared and been heard in the proceeding for alimony, there is no color for his present contention that he was deprived of his property without due process of law. Nor does he appear to have made any such contention in the courts of the State. His writ of error, therefore, must be dismissed.

By the Constitution and the act of Congress, requiring the faith and credit to be given to a judgment of the court of another State that it has in the State where it was rendered, it was long ago declared by this court: "The judgment is made a debt of record, not examinable upon its merits; but it does not carry with it, into another State, the efficacy of a judgment upon property or persons, to be enforced by execution. To give it the force of a judgment in another State, it must be made a judgment there; and can only be executed in the latter as its laws may permit." *McElmoyle v. Cohen,* 13 Pet. 312, 325; *Thompson v. Whitman,* 18 Wall. 457, 463; *Wisconsin v. Pelican Ins. Co.,* 127 U. S. 265, 292; *Bullock v. Bullock,* 6 Dickinson (51 N. J. Eq.) 444, and 7 Dickinson (52 N. J. Eq.) 561.

The decree of the Court of Chancery of New Jersey, on which this suit is brought, provides, first, for the payment of $7840 for alimony already due, and $1000 counsel fee; second, for the payment of alimony since the date of the decree at the rate of $80 per week; and third, for the giving of a bond to secure the payment of these sums, and, on default of payment or of giving bond, for leave to apply for a writ of sequestration, or a receiver and injunction.

The decree for the payment of $8840 was for a fixed sum already due, and the judgment of the court below was properly restricted to that. The provision of the payment for alimony in the future was subject to the discretion of the Court of Chancery of New Jersey, which might at any time alter it, and was not a final judgment for a fixed sum. The provisions for bond, sequestration, receiver and injunction, being in the nature of execution, and not of judgment, could have no extraterritorial operation; but the action of the courts of New York in these respects depended on the local statutes and practice of the State, and involved no Federal question.

On the writ of error of the wife, therefore,

The judgment is affirmed.

[B] "Divisible Divorce"

ESTIN v. ESTIN

United States Supreme Court
334 U.S. 541 (1948)

Opinion of the Court by MR. JUSTICE DOUGLAS, announced by MR. JUSTICE REED.

This case, here on certiorari to the Court of Appeals of New York, presents an important question under the Full Faith and Credit Clause of the Constitution. Article IV, § 1. It is whether a New York decree awarding respondent $180 per month for her maintenance and support in a separation proceeding survived a Nevada divorce decree which subsequently was granted petitioner.

The parties were married in 1937 and lived together in New York until 1942 when the husband left the wife. There was no issue of the marriage. In 1943 she brought an action against him for a separation. He entered a general appearance. The court, finding that he had abandoned her, granted her a decree of separation and awarded her $180 per month as permanent alimony. In January 1944 he went to Nevada where in 1945 he instituted an action for divorce. She was notified of the action by constructive service but entered no appearance in it. In May, 1945, the Nevada court, finding that petitioner had been a bona fide resident of Nevada since January 30, 1944, granted him an absolute divorce "on the ground of three years continual separation, without cohabitation." The Nevada decree made no provision for alimony, though the Nevada court had been advised of the New York decree.

Prior to that time petitioner had made payments of alimony under the New York decree. After entry of the Nevada decree he ceased paying. Thereupon respondent sued in New York for a supplementary judgment for the amount of the arrears. Petitioner appeared in the action and moved to eliminate the alimony provisions of the separation decree by reason of the Nevada decree. The Supreme Court denied the motion and granted respondent judgment for the arrears. . . . The judgment was affirmed by the Appellate Division, . . . and then by the Court of Appeals. . . .

We held in *Williams v. North Carolina* [I and II], (1) that a divorce decree granted by a State to one of its domiciliaries is entitled to full faith and credit in a bigamy prosecution brought in another State, even though the other spouse was given notice of the divorce proceeding only through constructive service; and (2) that while the finding of domicile by the court that granted the decree is entitled to *prima facie* weight, it is not conclusive in a sister State but might be relitigated there. . . . The latter course was followed in this case, as a consequence of which the Supreme Court of New York found, in accord with the Nevada court, that petitioner "is now and since January, 1944, has been a bona fide resident of the State of Nevada."

Petitioner's argument therefore is that the tail must go with the hide—that since by the Nevada decree, recognized in New York, he and respondent are no longer husband and wife, no legal incidence of the marriage remains. We are given a detailed analysis of New York law to show that the New York courts have no power either by statute or by common law to compel a man to support his ex-wife, that alimony is payable only so long as the relation of husband and wife exists, and that in New York, as in some other states, . . . a support order does not survive divorce.

The difficulty with that argument is that the highest court in New York has held in this case that a support order can survive divorce and that this one has survived petitioner's divorce. That conclusion is binding on us, except as it conflicts with the Full Faith and Credit Clause. . . .

We can put to one side the case where the wife was personally served or where she appeared in the divorce proceedings. . . . The only service on her in this case was by publication and she made no appearance in the Nevada proceeding. The requirements of procedural due process were satisfied and the domicile of the husband in Nevada was foundation for a decree effecting a change in the marital capacity of both parties in all the other States of the Union, as well as in Nevada. *Williams v. North Carolina* [I]. But the fact that marital capacity was changed does not mean that every other legal incidence of the marriage was necessarily affected.

. . . .

An absolutist might . . . demand a rule that once a divorce is granted, the whole of the marriage relation is dissolved, leaving no roots or tendrils of any kind. But there are few areas of the law in black and white. The greys are dominant and even among them the shades are innumerable. For the eternal problem of the law is one of making accommodations between conflicting interests. This is why most legal problems end as questions of degree. That is true of the present problem under the Full Faith and Credit Clause. The question involves important considerations both of law and of policy which it is essential to state.

The situations where a judgment of one State has been denied full faith and credit in another State, because its enforcement would contravene the latter's policy, have been few and far between. . . . The fact that the requirements of full faith and credit, so far as judgments are concerned, are exacting, if not inexorable . . . does not mean, however, that the State of the domicile of one spouse may, through the use of constructive service, enter a decree that changes every legal incidence of the marriage relationship.

Marital status involves the regularity and integrity of the marriage relation. It affects the legitimacy of the offspring of marriage. It is the basis of criminal laws, as the bigamy prosecution in *Williams v. North Carolina* dramatically illustrates. The State has a considerable interest in preventing bigamous marriages and in protecting the offspring of marriages from being bastardized. The interest of the State extends to its domiciliaries. The State should have the power to guard its interest in them by changing or altering their marital status and by protecting them in that changed status throughout the farthest reaches of the nation. For a person domiciled in one State should not be allowed to suffer the penalties of bigamy for living outside the State with the only one which the State of his domicile recognizes as his lawful wife. And children born of the only marriage which is lawful in the State of his domicile should not carry the stigma of bastardy when they move elsewhere. These are matters of legitimate concern to the State of the domicile. They entitle the State of the domicile to bring in the absent spouse through constructive service. In no other way could the State of the domicile have and maintain effective control of the marital status of its domiciliaries.

Those are the considerations that have long permitted the State of the matrimonial domicile to change the marital status of the parties by an *ex parte* divorce proceeding, . . . But those considerations have little relevancy here. In this case New York evinced a concern with this broken marriage when both parties were domiciled in New York and before Nevada had any concern with it. New York was rightly concerned lest the abandoned spouse be left impoverished and perhaps become a public charge. The problem of her livelihood and support is plainly a matter in which her community had a legitimate interest. The New York court, having jurisdiction over both parties, undertook to protect her by granting her a judgment of permanent alimony. Nevada, however, apparently follows the rule that dissolution of the marriage puts an end to a support order. . . . But the question is whether Nevada could under any circumstances adjudicate rights of respondent under the New York judgment when she was not personally served or did not appear in the proceeding.

Bassett v. Bassett, 141 F. 2d 954, held that Nevada could not. We agree with that view.

The New York judgment is a property interest of respondent, created by New York in a proceeding in which both parties were present. It imposed obligations on petitioner and granted rights to respondent. The property interest which it created was an intangible, jurisdiction over which cannot be exerted through control over a physical thing. Jurisdiction over an intangible can indeed only arise from control or power over the persons whose relationships are the source of the rights and obligations. . . .

Jurisdiction over a debtor is sufficient to give the State of his domicile some control over the debt which he owes. . . . But we are aware of no power which the State of domicile of the debtor has to determine the personal rights of the creditor in the intangible unless the creditor has been personally served or appears in the proceeding. The existence of any such power has been repeatedly denied. *Pennoyer v. Neff,* 95 U. S. 714; *Hart v. Sansom,* 110 U. S. 151; *New York Life Ins. Co. v. Dunlevy,* 241 U. S. 518.

We know of no source of power which would take the present case out of that category. The Nevada decree that is said to wipe out respondent's claim for alimony under the New York judgment is nothing less than an attempt by Nevada to restrain respondent from asserting her claim under that judgment. That is an attempt to exercise an *in personam* jurisdiction over a person not before the court. That may not be done. Since Nevada had no power to adjudicate respondent's rights in the New York judgment, New York need not give full faith and credit to that phase of Nevada's judgment. A judgment of a court having no jurisdiction to render it is not entitled to the full faith and credit which the Constitution and statute of the United States demand. . . .

The result in this situation is to make the divorce divisible—to give effect to the Nevada decree insofar as it affects marital status and to make it ineffective on the issue of alimony. It accommodates the interests of both Nevada and New York in this broken marriage by restricting each State to the matters of her dominant concern.

Since Nevada had no jurisdiction to alter respondent's rights in the New York judgment, we do not reach the further question whether in any event that judgment would be entitled to full faith and credit in Nevada. See *Sistare v. Sistare,* 218 U. S. 1; *Barber v. Barber,* 323 U. S. 77; *Griffin v. Griffin,* 327 U. S. 220. And it will be time enough to consider the effect of any discrimination shown to out-of-state *ex parte* divorces when a State makes that its policy.

Affirmed.

Mr. Justice Frankfurter, dissenting.

. . . .

Nevada did not purport, so far as the record discloses, to rule on the survival of the New York separate maintenance decree. Nevada merely established a change in status. It was for New York to determine the effect, with reference to its own law, of that change in status. If it was the law of New York that divorce put an end to its separate maintenance decree, the respondent's decree would have been terminated not by the Nevada divorce but by the consequences, under the New York law, of a change in status, even though brought about by Nevada. Similarly, Nevada could not adjudicate rights in New York realty, but, if New York law provided for dower, a Nevada divorce might or might not terminate a dower interest in New York realty depending on whether or not New York treated dower rights as extinguished by divorce.

If the Nevada decree, insofar as it affected the New York separate maintenance decree, were violative of due process, New York of course would not have to give effect to it. It could not do so even if it wished. If the Nevada decree involved a violation of due process, there is an end of the matter and other complicated issues need not be considered! It would not matter whether New York had a special interest in preventing its residents from becoming public charges, or whether New York treated maintenance decrees as surviving a valid divorce.

Accordingly, the crucial issue, as I see it, is whether New York has held that *no* "ex parte" divorce decree could terminate a prior New York separate maintenance decree, or whether it has decided merely that no "ex parte" divorce decree of another State could. The opinion of the Court of Appeals leaves this crucial issue in doubt. The prior decisions of the New York courts do not dispel my doubts. Neither do the cases cited in the Court of Appeals' opinion, which, with the exception of *Wagster v. Wagster,* 193 Ark. 902, do not involve "ex parte" domestic divorces. New York may legitimately decline to allow any "ex parte" divorce to dissolve its prior separate maintenance decree, but it may not, consistently with *Williams v. North Carolina* [I], discriminate against a Nevada decree granted to one there domiciled, and afford it less effect than it gives to a decree of its own with similar jurisdictional foundation. I cannot be sure which it has done.

I am reinforced in these views by Mr. Justice Jackson's dissent. As a New York lawyer and the Justice assigned to the Second Circuit, he is presumably not without knowledge of New York law. The Court's opinion is written in a spirit of certitude that the New York law is contrary to that which Mr. Justice Jackson assumes it to be. Thus, on the issue that I deem decisive of the question whether New York has given full faith and credit to the Nevada decree—namely, whether under New York's law divorce decrees based on publication terminate support—her law has thus far not spoken with ascertainable clarity. I would therefore remand the case to the New York Court of Appeals for clarification of its rationale. . . .

MR. JUSTICE JACKSON, dissenting.

If there is one thing that the people are entitled to expect from their lawmakers, it is rules of law that will enable individuals to tell whether they are married and, if so, to whom. Today many people who have simply lived in more than one state do not know, and the most learned lawyer cannot advise them with any confidence. The uncertainties that result are not merely technical, nor are they trivial; they affect fundamental rights and relations such as the lawfulness of their cohabitation, their children's legitimacy, their title to property, and even whether they are law-abiding persons or criminals. In a society as mobile and nomadic as ours, such uncertainties affect large numbers of people and create a social problem of some magnitude. It is therefore important that, whatever we do, we shall not add to the confusion. I think that this decision does just that.

. . . .

The Court reaches the Solomon-like conclusion that the Nevada decree is half good and half bad under the full faith and credit clause. It is good to free the husband from the marriage; it is not good to free him from its incidental obligations. Assuming the judgment to be one which the Constitution requires to be recognized at all, I do not see how we can square this decision with the command that it be given *full* faith and credit. For reasons which I stated in dissenting in *Williams v. North Carolina* [I], I would not give standing under the clause to constructive service divorces obtained on short residence. But if we are to hold this divorce good, I do not see how it can be less good than a divorce would be if rendered by the courts of New York.

As I understand New York law, if, after a decree of separation and alimony, the husband had obtained a New York divorce against his wife, it would terminate her right to alimony. If the Nevada judgment is to have *full* faith and credit, I think it must have the same effect that a similar New York decree would have. I do not see how we can hold that it must be accepted for some purposes and not for others, that he is free of his former marriage but still may be jailed as he may in New York, for not paying the maintenance of a woman whom the Court is compelled to consider as no longer his wife.

SIMONS v. MIAMI BEACH FIRST NATIONAL BANK

United States Supreme Court
381 U.S. 81 (1965)

MR. JUSTICE BRENNAN delivered the opinion of the Court.

The question to be decided in this case is whether a husband's valid Florida divorce, obtained in a proceeding wherein his nonresident wife was served by publication only and did not make a personal appearance, unconstitutionally extinguished her dower right in his Florida estate.

The petitioner and Sol Simons were domiciled in New York when, in 1946, she obtained a New York separation decree that included an award of monthly alimony. Sol Simons moved to Florida in 1951 and, a year later, obtained there a divorce in an action of which petitioner had valid constructive notice but in which she did not enter a personal appearance.[1] After Sol Simons' death in Florida in 1960, respondent, the executor of his estate, offered his will for probate in the Probate Court of Dade County, Florida. Petitioner appeared in the proceeding and

---

[1] Petitioner was served by publication while still living in New York and received copies of the order for publication and the divorce complaint. She did not enter an appearance in the Florida proceeding on advice of counsel.

filed an election to take dower under Florida law, rather than have her rights in the estate governed by the terms of the will, which made no provision for her.[2] The respondent opposed the dower claim, asserting that since Sol Simons had divorced petitioner she had not been his wife at his death, and consequently was not entitled to dower under Florida law. Petitioner thereupon brought the instant action in the Circuit Court for Dade County in order to set aside the divorce decree and to obtain a declaration that the divorce, even if valid to alter her marital status, did not destroy or impair her claim to dower. The action was dismissed after trial, and the Florida District Court of Appeal for the Third District affirmed. . . . The Supreme Court of Florida declined to review the case. . . . We granted certiorari. . . . We affirm.

. . . .

. . . We . . . proceed to the decision of the question whether the Florida courts unconstitutionally denied petitioner's dower claim.

Petitioner argues that since she had not appeared in the Florida divorce action the Florida divorce court had no power to extinguish any right which she had acquired under the New York decree. She invokes the principle of *Estin v. Estin,* where this Court decided that a Nevada divorce court, which had no personal jurisdiction over the wife, had no power to terminate a husband's obligation to provide the wife support as required by a pre-existing New York separation decree. As this was so, we there ruled that New York, in giving continued effect to the maintenance provisions of its separation decree, did not deny full faith and credit to the Nevada decree. The application of the *Estin* principle to the instant case, petitioner contends, dictates that we hold the Florida courts to their constitutional duty to give effect to the New York decree, inherent in which is a preservation of her dower right.

The short answer to this contention is that the only obligation imposed on Sol Simons by the New York decree, and the only rights granted petitioner under it, concerned monthly alimony for petitioner's support. Unlike the ex-husband in *Estin,* Sol Simons made the support payments called for by the separate maintenance decree notwithstanding his *ex parte* divorce. In making these payments until his death he complied with the full measure of the New York decree; when he died there was consequently nothing left of the New York decree for Florida to dishonor.

This conclusion embodies our judgment that there is nothing in the New York decree itself that can be construed as creating or preserving any interest in the nature of or in lieu of dower in any property of the decedent, wherever located. Petitioner refers us to no New York law that treats such a decree as having that effect, or, for that matter, to any New York law that has such an effect irrespective of the existence of the decree. . . . It follows that insofar as petitioner's argument rests on rights created by the New York decree or by New York law, the denial of her dower by the Florida courts was not a violation of the Full Faith and Credit Clause. . . .

Insofar as petitioner argues that since she was not subject to the jurisdiction of the Florida divorce court its decree could not extinguish any dower right existing under Florida law,

---

[2] 21 Fla. Stat. Ann. 1964, § 731.34 provides as follows:

"Whenever the widow of any decedent shall not be satisfied with the portion of the estate of her husband to which she is entitled under the law of descent and distribution or under the will of her husband, or both, she may elect in the manner provided by law to take dower, which dower shall be one third in fee simple of the real property which was owned by her husband at the time of his death or which he had before conveyed, whereof she had not relinquished her right of dower as provided by law, and one third part absolutely of the personal property owned by her husband at the time of his death. . . ."

Vanderbilt v. Vanderbilt, 354 U. S. 416, 418, the answer is that under Florida law no dower right survived the decree. The Supreme Court of Florida has said that dower rights in Florida property, being inchoate, are extinguished by a divorce decree predicated upon substituted or constructive service. . . .

It follows that the Florida courts transgressed no constitutional bounds in denying petitioner dower in her ex-husband's Florida estate.

Affirmed.

Mr. Justice Harlan, concurring.

I am happy to join the opinion of the Court because it makes a partial retreat from *Vanderbilt v. Vanderbilt,* 354 U. S. 416, a decision which I believe must eventually be rerationalized, if not entirely overruled.

The *Vanderbilt* case was this. The Vanderbilt couple was domiciled in California. Mr. Vanderbilt went to Nevada, established a new domicile, and obtained an *ex parte* divorce decree which did not provide for alimony payments to Mrs. Vanderbilt. In the meantime Mrs. Vanderbilt went to New York. After the Nevada decree had become final, she sued in New York for support under New York law, sequestering Mr. Vanderbilt's property located there. New York ordered support payments, rejecting full-faith-and-credit arguments based on the Nevada decree. Over dissents by Mr. Justice Frankfurter and myself (354 U. S., at 419, 428) the Court affirmed the New York award, holding that because the Nevada court had no personal jurisdiction over Mrs. Vanderbilt, "the Nevada decree, to the extent it purported to affect the wife's right to support, was void. . . ."

Two rules emerged from the case, neither of which, I suggest with deference, commends itself: (1) an *ex parte* divorce can have no effect on property rights; (2) a State in which a wife subsequently establishes domicile can award support to her regardless of her connection with that State at the time of the *ex parte* divorce and regardless of the law in her former State of domicile.

The first rule slips unobtrusively into oblivion in today's decision, for Florida is allowed to turn property rights on its *ex parte* decree. A concurrence disputes this, but I do not understand how the Court's language in this case can be read as anything less. If I may paraphrase only slightly, the Court says, "Insofar as petitioner argues that since she was not subject to the jurisdiction of the Florida divorce court, its decree could not extinguish any dower right existing under Florida law, *Vanderbilt v. Vanderbilt,* 354 U. S. 416, 418, the answer is that the Florida decree extinguished petitioner's dower rights. . . ." The Court goes on to state and accept the Florida law that an *ex parte* divorce extinguishes dower rights. I do not see how a withdrawal from the due process phase of *Vanderbilt* could be clearer.

Because New York was petitioner's State of domicile at all times relevant to this case and did not purport to invest her with any rights to property beyond those she received from her husband, the second rule is not involved here. My hope is that its time will come too. I continue to believe that the views expressed in my *Vanderbilt* dissent embody a more satisfactory and workable approach to the law of "divisible divorce" (*Estin v. Estin,* 334 U. S. 541) than can be distilled from existing Court opinions.

MR. JUSTICE BLACK, with whom MR. JUSTICE DOUGLAS joins, concurring.

I agree completely with the Court's judgment and opinion, and add these few words only in reply to the suggestion of my Brother HARLAN that the Court here is making "a partial retreat from *Vanderbilt v. Vanderbilt.*" I do not think that today's decision marks any "retreat" at all from the opinion or holding in *Vanderbilt,* and I do not understand the Court so to regard it. *Vanderbilt* held that a wife's right to support could not be cut off by an *ex parte* divorce. In the case before us, Mrs. Simons' Florida dower was not terminated by the *ex parte* divorce. It simply never came into existence. No one disputes that the *ex parte* divorce was effective to end the marriage, so that after it Mrs. Simons was no longer Mr. Simons' wife. Florida law, as the Court's opinion shows, grants dower only to a woman who is the legal wife of the husband when he dies. Mrs. Simons therefore had no property rights cut off by the divorce. She simply had her marriage ended by it, and for that reason was not a "widow" within the meaning of the Florida law. Unless this Court were to make the novel declaration that Florida cannot limit dower rights to widows, I see no possible way in which the *Vanderbilt* case, which dealt with rights which a State did give to divorced wives, could be thought to apply. . . .

[Mr. Justice Stewart and Mr. Justice Goldberg filed a dissenting opinion stating that certiorari had been improvidently granted in the case since only issues of state law were involved.]

NOTES AND QUESTIONS

(1)(a) *Lynde* sets forth, without any discussion, the proposition that because the New Jersey judgment, as to alimony, (i) called for periodic rather than lump sum payments, and (ii) was subject to the continuing discretion of the court, it "could have no extraterritorial operation," or in other words, it could not be required to be given full faith and credit under the U.S. Constitution. Why not? Where does it say anything about "final" or "unmodifiable" judgments in the Full Faith and Credit clause—or indeed about judgments at all?[a]

(b) It generally makes sense for a court that issues a judgment for alimony and child support to retain jurisdiction, because circumstances are likely to change: The husband remarries and has a second family; the wife remarries, children grow up and move out of the house; someone becomes ill, or inherits money, loses a job, gains a promotion, and so on. But why should this sensible attitude in F–1[b] weaken the effectiveness of the judgment in F–2?

(c) If the New Jersey court, with personal jurisdiction over Mr. Lynde, orders him to pay $80 per week to his ex-wife, why shouldn't the New York court issue a corresponding order, unless Mr. Lynde establishes to the New Jersey court that the order is no longer appropriate?

(d) In the actual case, the lower New York court did what is suggested in paragraph (c), but the appellate courts reversed. If the New York Court of Appeals had reinstated the order of the lower court, could Mr. Lynde have appealed successfully to the U.S. Supreme Court? Or is this one of the cases where the state court in F–2 has discretion to go either way in recognizing an F–1 judgment?

---

[a] Note that Justice Jackson asks the same question in *Barber,* question (2)(c), *infra.*

[b] Recall the different approach of Georgia in *Yarborough,* Chapter 8, p. 647, *supra.*

(e) Could the New York court modify the New Jersey judgment?

(2)(a) In *Barber v. Barber,* 323 U.S. 77 (1944), the wife had secured a judgment of separation in North Carolina in 1920, together with an order directing the husband to pay her $160 per month. The husband stopped paying in 1932, and at some point moved to Tennessee. In 1940, the wife went back to the original rendering court and secured a judgment of $19,700 for accrued and unpaid alimony. She then brought suit in Tennessee against the husband to recover on the North Carolina judgment. The husband defended on the ground that the judgment was not final because it was modifiable, as he claimed, both as to past and as to future payments. The wife prevailed in the lower Tennessee court, but the Tennessee Supreme Court reversed, on the ground that the North Carolina judgment was without the finality entitling it to credit under the Full Faith and Credit clause of the Constitution. The wife appealed to the Supreme Court. How should this case be decided?

(b) The majority of the U.S. Supreme Court reaffirmed the doctrine of the *Lynde* case:[c] Thus if the North Carolina judgment was indeed still modifiable, it would not have to be enforced by the Tennessee court. However, the Supreme Court was not bound by the Tennessee court's interpretation of the North Carolina judgment, and after elaborate investigation, Chief Justice Stone, for the Court, concluded that that judgment was not now modifiable as to accrued alimony payments, and therefore did have to be enforced.

(c) Justice Jackson thought that the judgment of the North Carolina court was entitled to faith and credit in Tennessee even if it was not a final one:

> Neither the full faith and credit clause of the Constitution [he wrote], nor the Act of Congress implementing it says anything about final judgments or, for that matter, about any judgments. . . . Of course, if a judgment by its terms reserves power to modify or states conditions, a judgment entered upon it could appropriately make like reservations or conditions. . . . Any application for such relief should be addressed to the North Carolina court and not to the Tennessee court nor to this one. The purpose of the full faith and credit clause is to lengthen the arm of the state court and to eliminate state lines as a shelter from judicial proceedings. This is defeated by entertaining a plea to review the support in state law for the judgment as it has been rendered, which is a delaying inquiry as has been shown in this case.[d]

Do you prefer Justice Jackson's approach to Justice Stone's? Could the first part of Jackson's approach stand without the second, so that, for instance, Mr. Barber could ask the Tennessee court to modify the North Carolina judgment, say if Mrs. Barber had inherited a substantial sum while he had had financial reverses?

(d) In *Worthley v. Worthley,* 49 Cal. 2d 465, 283 P.2d 19 (1955), a New Jersey wife brought suit in California, where her ex-husband now lived, to enforce a judgment of support issued by a court in New Jersey. She sought both a judgment for arrearages and an order to establish the obligation to make weekly payments to her as a California decree. The Supreme Court of California, by 4–3, with Chief Justice Traynor writing for the majority, observed that under *Lynde* and *Barber,* there was no constitutional requirement that the New Jersey judgment be enforced in California, but neither was there a constitutional impediment to doing so. Furthermore,

---

[c] As well as of a later case substantially the same as *Lynde, Sistare v. Sistare,* 218 U.S. 1 (1910).

[d] 323 U.S. at 87–88 (Jackson, J., dissenting).

overruling an earlier decision of the California Supreme Court, the court now held that the issue of modification could be tried in California without requiring either party to return to New Jersey.[e]

Is this sound?[f] What law should a California court apply in considering modification of a New Jersey judgment?[g]

(3)(a) *Estin v. Estin* is in several respects an odd case, as the opening sentence in Justice Jackson's dissent makes emphatically clear. Does *Estin* show that *Williams I* was wrongly decided, as Jackson, among others, argued? Or is the case, rather, a further realistic accommodation of the interests of the two states concerned, following logically from the *Williams/Sherrer* series?

(b) The substantive law involved in *Estin*—the effect of a divorce on a prior support order—seems to vary from state to state. Prima facie (putting aside all issues of different jurisdictions) an order of support incident to a legal separation is terminated by (or merged in) a divorce, so that if the obligee (typically the wife) intends to seek support payments after divorce, she should demand them in the divorce proceeding. Where the states seem to differ, as shown in the discussion in *Estin* itself, is whether this basic rule is applied in case of an ex parte divorce. The majority opinion seems to say, and Justice Frankfurter's concurrence confirms, that in New York a domestic ex parte divorce would not have the effect of terminating a prior support obligation. Accordingly, says the Court, New York need not give effect to the Nevada judgment so as to terminate the support obligation. Is this the right way to state the question?

If the Court is saying that New York must give the same faith and credit (but no more) to Nevada's decree as it would give to its own comparable decrees, isn't that the reverse of what the Full Faith and Credit clause requires? Is it possible that an ex parte Nevada divorce decree has one effect on support obligations in New York, another in Pennsylvania?

(c) Alternatively, is the Court saying that a divorce decree rendered without personal jurisdiction over the respondent can never deprive the latter of economic benefits?[h]

(d) What if, say, H and W are domiciled in State *A*, H abandons W and leaves for parts unknown, W files for divorce, and seeks support or alimony. Could a court in state *A* order H to make support payments which would be enforceable (i) against H's property in *A*; (ii) against H himself when he is later located in *B*?

---

[e] The text simplifies the story somewhat. In fact Mr. Worthley had made the support payments ordered by the New Jersey court in its separation decree until he obtained an ex parte Nevada divorce. The wife was suing to enforce the pre-existing support order, in reliance on *Estin v. Estin.*

[f] For similar decisions in other state courts, see, e.g., *Light v. Light,* 12 Ill.2d 502, 147 N.E.2d 34 (1958); *Walzer v. Walzer,* 173 Conn. 62, 376 A.2d 414 (1977). In recognition of these and similar cases, the 1988 Revisions of the Restatement (Second) of Conflict of Laws changed § 109 on Modifiable Judgments to read:

> A court will recognize or enforce a judgment rendered in a State of the United States that remains subject to modification in the State of rendition.

The prior version had said that such a judgment "need not be recognized or enforced. . . .", but that a court is free to do so.

[g] In general, modification of a support order will depend on factual determinations concerning need on one side, ability to pay on the other. However, different rules may apply from state to state on such matters as the effect of remarriage of the wife and the age of majority of the children.

[h] In *Rodda v. Rodda,* 185 Or. 140, 200 P.2d 616 (1949), the Oregon Supreme Court held (4–3) that as a matter of Oregon law a Nevada ex parte divorce obtained by the husband did terminate the wife's rights under a prior Oregon decree of separate maintenance. The U.S. Supreme Court denied certiorari. 337 U.S. 946 (1949).

(e) About half the states of the United States have a special long-arm statute for matrimonial and related actions, designed to make sure the preceding question is answered in the affirmative.[i] Granted that *Estin* was decided in 1948, after *International Shoe* but prior to *McGee v. International Life Ins. Co.* and the many other cases reproduced or summarized in Chapter 7, are the statements in the paragraph on p. 798, beginning "Jurisdiction over a debtor . . ." and ending with citation to *Pennoyer v. Neff* supportable today? If not, is the decision nevertheless correct?

(f) One might distinguish *Estin* from cases brought under state long-arm statutes on the basis that in those cases the plaintiff is the stay-at-home spouse, and that the wandering spouse should not be able to deprive the court at the marital domicile of jurisdiction. But suppose Mrs. Estin had traveled to Nevada to procure a divorce, ex parte, while Mr. Estin remained in New York. Could she (i) secure an order for alimony from the Nevada court that was enforceable in New York; (ii) continue to enforce in New York her prior support order?

(4)(a) *Estin* might be read as referring only to the situation where the respondent spouse is the creditor under a preexisting judgment.[j] But *Vanderbilt v. Vanderbilt*, 354 U.S. 416 (1957), shows either that this was not the basis of the decision in *Estin* or that the Court moved another half step in the nine years between the two cases. In *Vanderbilt*, summarized by Justice Harlan, concurring in *Simons* (p. 802, *supra*), the parties had lived as a married couple in California until 1952, when they separated. In February 1953, the wife moved to New York; in March of the same year the husband filed for divorce in Nevada, which was granted, ex parte, in June 1953. In April 1954 Mrs. Vanderbilt brought suit for support in New York, on the theory that the support obligation attached as soon as Mrs. Vanderbilt set foot in New York with intent to remain.[k] "The factor which distinguishes the present case from *Estin*," Justice Black wrote for the Court, "is that here the wife's right to support had not been reduced to judgment prior to the husband's *ex parte* divorce. In our opinion this difference is not material on the question before us."[l]

(b) Assuming *Estin* is correctly decided, does *Vanderbilt* go one step too far in compensating the absent spouse, (in Justice Frankfurter's phrase) for the subordination of her interests in the marital relation, as the result of *Williams I*?[m]

What if Mrs. Vanderbilt had not acquired her New York domicile until July 1953, after the Nevada divorce was granted? Could New York still say (i) we don't recognize the Nevada divorce for economic purposes; and (ii) therefore we consider the [ex]-husband has an obligation under New York law to support the [ex]-wife who is a New York domiciliary?[n]

(c) Incidentally, the action in New York against Mr. Cornelius Vanderbilt, Jr. was begun as a quasi-in-rem action, by attaching some of his considerable assets in that state. Do you think

---

[i] See Walker & Elrod, *Family Law in the Fifty States: An Overview*, 26 Fam. L. Q. 319, 401 (table) (1993). For one such statute, see New York C.P.L.R. § 302(b), Documents Supplement p. 77.

[j] Note that in the last paragraph of the majority opinion, the court raises but does not decide the question whether Nevada should have given full faith and credit to the New York support order.

[k] Recall *White v. Tennant*, Chapter 1, p. 25, *supra*.

[l] 354 U.S. at 418.

[m] See 354 U.S. at 422 (Frankfurter, J. dissenting).

[n] The New York Court of Appeals has held that in these circumstances New York law did not afford the ex-wife a cause of action for support, and the Supreme Court denied certiorari. *Loeb v. Loeb*, 4 N.Y.2d 542, 176 N.Y.S.2d 590, 152 N.E.2d 36 (1958), *cert. denied* 359 U.S. 913 (1959). It is not clear what the Supreme Court would have held had the New York court found for Mrs. Loeb.

that such an action, not based on a prior judgment, would stand up after *Shaffer v. Heitner*?°
Should it?

(d) Look in this connection at New York CPLR § 302(b), the provision of New York's long-arm statute addressed to matrimonial actions. Note that § 302(b) does not cover Mrs. Vanderbilt's situation, since she was not domiciled or resident in New York at the time of her demand, and New York was not the matrimonial domicile. It would, however, cover the situation of persons like the first Mrs. Williams, who was a resident of the forum state at all time, and had lived there with her [ex-] husband. Did the New York legislature get it right?

(e) Suppose an ex-wife in the position of Mrs. Williams brings an action for support, alimony, and division of property, asserting jurisdiction over the ex-husband under § 302(b). The ex-husband, who obtained an ex parte Nevada divorce, now lives in Los Angeles, and is served there. May the New York court grant a money judgment against him? Would such a judgment be enforceable in California? Could it be enforced against property of the ex-husband in New York?

(5)(a) Justice Harlan is pleased that *Vanderbilt* is overruled in *Simons v. First National Bank*. Justice Black, and apparently the majority of the Court, think that conclusion is quite wrong. Are *Estin, Vanderbilt,* and *Simons* consistent or inconsistent with each other? Note that *Estin* and *Vanderbilt* were appeals from F–2 judgments in favor of the ex-wife, while *Simons* was an appeal from an F–1 judgment that denied the wife any recovery.

(b) Consider a person in the position of Lucy Simons. She is separated from her husband, but he is making regular support payments to her pursuant to a New York judgment. She receives notice of divorce proceedings in Florida, and consults her lawyer. In the actual case, her lawyer advised her not to appear in the Florida action, apparently because he was afraid that the Florida court might modify the existing support order. Would she have been better advised to appear and raise her economic concerns before the Florida court? Could she have secured some right to her husband's estate in the divorce proceeding?

(c) Professor David Currie finds the decision in *Simons* wholly unfair.ᴾ Even if Mrs. Simons' claim to dower was inchoate, in the sense that she could not presently assign it and that it would not survive if she died before Mr. Simons, it was not without value. As a result of the Supreme Court's decision, Currie says, she is a third of a million dollars poorer. How might a decision the other way have been drafted? Suppose, for example, that Mr. Simons had married again, and when Lucy came to claim her dower rights, she was met by Nancy, who asserted that *she* was the only one entitled to dower?

(d) If Mr. Simons had failed to make monthly payments under the New York support order once he obtained his divorce, could Mrs. Simons have enforced that obligation in Florida? Would a Florida court have been required to give full faith and credit to the New York judgment?ᵠ Could she have recovered accrued and unpaid amounts from Mr. Simons' estate?

(e) Suppose Mr. Simons left property in New York, which is being administered by an ancillary administrator with the will attached. Could Mrs. Simons elect against Mr. Simons' will (i) in the actual case, in which Mr. Simons appears to have remained domiciled in Florida; (ii) if Mr.

° See Chapter 7, p. 580, *supra*.

ᴾ D. Currie, *Suitcase Divorce in the Conflict of Laws: Simons, Rosenstiel, and Borax*, 34 U. Chi. L. Rev. 26, at 34–35 (1966).

ᵠ Recall that the Supreme Court avoided this question in *Estin*. See note j, *supra*.

Simons, having secured his divorce in Florida, had returned to New York?[r] See New York E.P.T.L. § § 5–1.2(a)(1); 5–1.1(d)(7).[s] In the first case, would it matter if the New York assets included real property?

[C] Equitable Distribution

In the last third of the twentieth century, major changes took place in family law throughout the United States. The concept that divorce was a remedy granted by the court to the innocent partner in the marriage because of the fault of the guilty partner—adultery, cruelty, desertion, etc.—was replaced in nearly all states by the concept of marital breakdown, regardless of fault. The implementation of this concept still differed among the states, particularly with respect to waiting periods and residence requirements. But consensual divorce, which had long been rejected because it failed to take account of the state's interest in marriage, came to be seen as the normal basis for dissolution of a marriage.[a]

In part as the result of the changed approach to divorce, and in part as the result of demonstration that alimony tended to be inadequate even when paid and often was not paid, most states in the United States adopted some form of property division between spouses, usually on the basis of *equitable distribution*.

In some respects, the concept of equitable distribution is similar to community property (though the word "equitable" is not necessarily a synonym of "equal");[b] but whereas community property is supposed to govern property rights during the marriage, succession upon death, and division upon divorce, equitable distribution is directed only to division upon divorce. Moreover, equitable distribution is supposed to focus not on legal title, nor on when a given asset was acquired, but rather on the court's assessment of fairness between the parties.

The many aspects of equitable distribution are well beyond the scope of this volume.[c] Inevitably, however, questions arise that call for conflict of laws analysis, as married persons change their domiciles, and own property—movable and immovable—in different states. We saw in chapter IV, § 4.03, some of the complications concerning marital property when one spouse dies domiciled in one state or nation, leaving property in another. In *Crichton*[d] and *Clark*,[e] the

---

[r] In the lower court proceedings in Florida, Mrs. Simons introduced evidence designed to show that Mr. Simons had kept his New York domicile throughout. This claim seems to have been abandoned in the Supreme Court.

[s] Documents Supplement, pp. 42, 35.

[a] California led the way in 1969; as of year-end 1997, every state in the Union had adopted some kind of no-fault divorce. In some states no-fault was the only kind of divorce, in some no-fault divorce existed alongside divorce based on marital misconduct; in some states divorce could be granted on a unilateral demonstration of marital breakdown, in others no-fault divorce was available only when both parties consented. See, e.g., Herbert Jacob, *The Silent Revolution: The Transformation of Divorce Law in the United States* (1988), and for an annual state-by-state survey, Linda D. Elrod and Robert Spector, "A Review of the Year in Family Law," 30 Family L. Q. 765 (1997).

[b] Community property never became part of the law of those states of the United States that were settled from England, or by persons from those states. Many of the states of the United States that were formerly ruled from Spain, France, or Mexico retained their community property regimes when they became part of the United States—Arizona, California, Louisiana, Nevada, New Mexico, Texas—plus Idaho and Washington. Wisconsin adopted community property by statute, effective in 1986.

[c] For a book-length treatment, see e.g., Brett R. Turner, *Equitable Distribution of Property* (2d.ed. 1994).

[d] P. 359, *supra*.

[e] P. 346 *supra*.

New York Court of Appeals looked to the law of the spouses' domicile rather than the situs of the assets, which in *Crichton* led to application of New York law despite the fact that the bulk of the assets were located in Louisiana, a community property state. In *Wyatt v. Fulrath*,[f] the joint bank account case, the same court looked to the situs, on the basis of a not wholly convincing finding of intent. A priori, should distribution of property between divorcing spouses be subject to the same choice of law analysis as distribution upon death? Or would you think the considerations are sufficiently different so that the analyses developed in connection with trusts and estates should be rejected as a point of departure for distribution of property upon divorce?[g]

The *Restatement (Second) of Conflict of Laws*, published in 1971, addresses marital property in the context of community property, and (except for real property) generally looks to the marital domicile at the time of acquisition of the asset in question.[h] Thus if an asset was acquired by the husband while the spouses were living in a separate property state and they subsequently moved to a community property state, the asset would not be regarded as community property. Conversely, if the spouses lived in a community property state when the asset was acquired, it would remain community property even after they moved to a separate property state.[i] If the asset was converted into another asset, for instance if shares of stock acquired as separate property were sold and the proceeds were used to purchase land in a community property state, the character of the property would not change, even if the land was situated in a community property state where the couple were now domiciled.[j]

The following cases illustrate how equitable division works and how the teaching of conflict of laws is or is not useful in this field.

---

[f] Page 338 *supra*.

[g] It is interesting that the leading American treatise on conflict of laws urges that similar choice of law considerations should apply in regard to both issues. Eugene F. Scoles and Peter Hay, *Conflict of Laws* p. 469 (2d ed. 1992), while the leading treatise on equitable distribution urges rejection of both traditional and current choice of law rules. Turner, note c, *supra* p. 71.

[h] § 258. **Interests in Movables Acquired during Marriage**

(1) The interest of a spouse in a movable acquired by the other spouse during the marriage is determined by the local law of the state which, with respect to the particular issue, has the most significant relationship to the spouses and the movable under the principles stated in § 6.

(2) In the absence of an effective choice of law by the spouses, greater weight will usually be given to the state where the spouses were domiciled at the time the movable was acquired than to any other contact in determining the state of the applicable law.

The first Restatement, published in 1934, provided in § 290;

Interests of one spouse in movables acquired by the other during the marriage are determined by the law of the domicil of the parties when the movables are acquired.

Sections 292 and 293 added that movables held by spouses in community continue to be held in community when taken into a non-community state, and interests held separately by either spouse remain separate interests although the movables are taken into a community property state.

[i] For the same rule under English law, see *Dicey and Morris on the Conflict of Laws*, Rule 152 (12th ed. Collins 1993).

[j] For critique of this approach and illustration of what he calls the "appalling mess" created by these rules, see Russell J. Weintraub, *Commentary on the Conflict of Laws*, § 8.14 (3d ed. 1986).

In re the MARRIAGE OF WHELCHEL

Court of Appeals of Iowa
476 N.W.2d 104 (1991)

DONIELSON, Judge.

Beth and Leon Whelchel were married in Texas in 1975. They moved to Iowa from Texas in 1986. They have three children, girls born in January 1977 and December 1980 and a boy born in August 1986. The dissolution decree placed the children in joint legal custody and in Beth's primary physical care. These custody provisions are not challenged in this appeal.

Leon, fifty years old at trial, is employed as a pilot earning a net income of slightly over $2,800 per month. From 1965 to 1983 he was employed as a pilot by Continental Airlines. In 1983 Continental filed for bankruptcy protection, and Leon's employment was terminated. He later received a lump sum retirement benefit of $154,794.11 for his service with Continental.

Beth has not been employed outside the home during the marriage. She now plans to complete her college education and obtain a teaching certificate. She testified this would probably take three years.

The parties had substantial assets including a Merrill Lynch cash management account acquired while the parties were married and living in Texas. Leon started this account with $20,000 in proceeds from the sale of real estate he owned before the marriage. He also placed his lump sum retirement benefit of $154,794.11 in this account. Beth contributed $20,000 in gifts and inheritances from her family to the account. The parties have continued to maintain the account in Texas, despite their move to Iowa. The court valued the account at $214,758.

In dividing the Merrill Lynch account between the parties, the district court first set aside to Leon the sum of $85,996.72. The court found this amount constituted the portion of Leon's lump sum retirement benefit which had accrued prior to the marriage. The court then set aside to Leon the $20,000 with which he had started the account. Next, the court set aside to Beth the $20,000 she had contributed to the account from gifts and inheritances. These set-asides left a balance of $88,761.28; the court directed that this balance be divided evenly between the parties. In total, Leon received $150,377.36, and Beth received $64,380.64.

The court awarded the parties' house, valued at $55,000, to Beth, but gave Leon a $10,000 lien against the house. The lien, bearing interest of seven percent per year, is payable when the last of the parties' children becomes emancipated or dies.

In addition to these assets, Beth was awarded a car, household goods, and savings of about $17,600. Leon was awarded a car, household goods, savings of about $9,450, two antique airplanes of uncertain value, and an airplane hangar valued at $16,000.

The court directed Leon to pay Beth child support of $1,220 per month while all three children are eligible for support, $813.33 per month when two children remain eligible for support, and $406.66 per month when only one child remains eligible for support.

The decree also directed Leon to pay Beth rehabilitative alimony of $400 per month for thirty-six months or until she dies or remarries. Neither the alimony nor the child support are to cease upon Leon's death, but are to be a lien against his estate.

Beth has appealed from the dissolution decree. In this equity action, our review is de novo. . . . We give weight to the fact findings of the trial court, but are not bound by them.

I. *Property Division.* Beth, first, challenges the division of the Merrill Lynch cash management account. She contends she should receive half the account, after a setaside to Leon for the $20,000 in premarital property with which he started the account. She contends this result should be reached under the principles of community property because the account was acquired and kept in Texas. In the alternative, she contends the same result should be reached under Iowa's equitable distribution principles, even if Texas law is inapplicable.

The first question presented is one of choice of law. That is, whether Texas or Iowa law should be applied in dividing the corpus of the Merrill Lynch cash management account and to what stages of the analysis should it be applied. To answer this question, we must examine the property characterization and division schemes of the two states to determine whether there is an actual conflict.

A. *Iowa Law.* Iowa is an equitable distribution state. Under Iowa law the partners in the marriage are "entitled to a just and equitable share of the property accumulated through their joint efforts." The distribution of the property of the parties should be that which is equitable under the circumstances after consideration of the criteria codified in Iowa Code section 598.21(1). Section 598.21(1) of the 1989 Iowa Code provides in relevant part:

> The court shall divide all property, except inherited property or gifts received by one party, equitably between the parties after considering all of the following:
>
> a. The length of the marriage.
>
> b. The property brought to the marriage by each party.
>
> c. The contribution of each party to the marriage, giving appropriate economic value to each party's contribution in homemaking and child care services.
>
> d. The age and physical and emotional health of the parties.
>
> e. The contribution by one party to the education, training or increased earning power of the other.
>
> f. The earning capacity of each party, including educational background, training, employment skills, work experience, length of absence from the job market, custodial responsibilities for children and the time and expense necessary to acquire sufficient education or training to enable the party to become self-supporting at a standard of living reasonably comparable to that enjoyed during the marriage.
>
> g. The desirability of awarding the family home or the right to live in the family home for a reasonable period to the party having custody of the children, or if the parties have joint legal custody, to the party having physical care of the children.
>
> h. The amount and duration of an order granting support payments to either party pursuant to subsection 3 and whether the property division should be in lieu of such payments.
>
> i. Other economic circumstances of each party, including pension benefits, vested or unvested, and future interests.
>
> j. The tax consequences to each party.
>
> k. Any written agreement made by the parties concerning property distribution.
>
> l. The provisions of an antenuptial agreement.
>
> m. Other factors the court may determine to be relevant in an individual case.

Pension benefits are treated as marital property in Iowa and are subject to equitable distribution.

B. *Texas Law.* Texas is a community property state. The general theory behind the community property scheme is that "husband and wife should share equally in property acquired by their joint efforts during marriage. . . ." Texas law characterizes the spouses' property in the following manner:

> (a) A spouse's separate property consists of: (1) the property owned or claimed by the spouse before marriage; (2) the property acquired by the spouse during marriage by gift, devise, or descent; and (3) the recovery for personal injuries sustained by the spouse during marriage, except any recovery for loss of earning capacity during marriage.
>
> (b) Community property consists of the property, other than separate property, acquired by either spouse during marriage.

Guiding the division of the spouses' property, section 3.63(a) of the Texas Family Code Annotated states:

> In a decree of divorce or annulment the court shall order a division of the estate of the parties in a manner that the court deems just and right, having due regard for the rights of each party and children of the marriage.

C. *Conflict of Laws.* A technical conflict does exist between the characterizations placed on the property by Texas and Iowa law. Under the Texas community property system, any property brought into the marriage by one spouse is that spouse's separate property. See Tex.Fam.Code Ann. § 5.01(a)(1) (Vernon Supp.1990). In Iowa, the concept of marital property does not automatically exclude this property; but rather, directs the dissolution court to take such property into consideration in making an equitable distribution of the marital property. See Iowa Code § 598.21(1)(i) (1989).

Leon had worked for Continental, earning a portion of his pension, prior to the marriage. Texas law characterizes that portion of the pension earned before the marriage as separate property. Therefore, it seems Texas law prohibits the division of that portion of Leon's pension. Iowa law does not.

Beth argues the lump sum pension was deposited along with other funds in the account and such commingling causes all portions of the pension to lose their separate character. Therefore, according to her argument, no conflict exists because the entire pension is subject to division as it would be under Iowa law.

Texas law, by constitution, statute, and case law, establishes a strong presumption that all property held at the time of dissolution is community property. See Tex. Const. art. XVI, § 15; Tex.Fam.Code Ann. § 5.02 (Vernon Supp.1990). To rebut this presumption, the spouse challenging the community character of the property must demonstrate its separate character. The court took judicial notice of Texas Family Code Annotated section 5.02, the statute codifying this presumption. The party with the burden must demonstrate the separate character of the property with clear and satisfactory evidence.

From an examination of the record, we find that Leon adequately demonstrated the separate character of a portion of the pension. The court correctly determined the sum. There is a conflict between the two states' prescription for the characterization of the property.

D. *Choice of Law in Characterizing the Property Interests.* "When marriage is ended by divorce . . . there are frequent problems in determining the marital property rights of the spouses. These problems are compounded if there is doubt as to which state's law will define those rights." Weintraub, Obstacles to Sensible Choice of Law for Determining Marital Property Rights on Divorce or in Probate: Hanau and the Situs Rule, 25 Hous.L.Rev. 1113, 1113 (1988). "Family law, in particular, presents some rather unique problems in the field of conflicts of law." Comment, Conflicts of Law in Divorce Litigation: A Looking-Glass World?, 10 Campbell L.Rev. 145, 145 (1987). "The Restatement (Second) of Conflict of Laws was published in 1971, and drafted before many states had departed from rigid lex loci choice-of-law rules." Id. at 1125. Iowa had changed its position before 1971.).

The Restatement of Conflict of Laws sections 258, 289-90 (1934) provided that "the law of the state in which the spouses are domiciled governs dissolution of their marriage and their interests in movable property." The Restatement rule, while providing a degree of predictability and uniformity, was simply too inflexible, failing to consider relevant policy issues. Flexibility was added by the Restatement (Second) of Conflict of Laws, published in 1971.

> The Restatement (Second) of Conflicts drops the territorial location of vested rights approach in favor of applying the laws of the state with the most significant relationship to the parties, property or issue. Although principles espoused by the first Restatement, such as choosing the law of the state of domicile, situs, or aquisition, are incorporated in the second Restatement's approach, they are relegated to the status of factors instead of rules used in choosing the correct law. The second Restatement is much more flexible in that it guides a court to the choice of the correct law by means of "Choice-of-Law Principles" instead of hard and fast rules of choice.
>
> As applied to the interests of a spouse in movables aquired by the other spouse during marriage, this approach refers a court to the local law of the state with the most significant relationship to the spouses and the movable, with the greatest weight being given to the law of the state of the spouses' domicile at the time of acquisition. [quoting from Note: 22 J. Family Law 311 at 325 (1983-84)].

The Iowa courts have not determined the choice of law rule applicable in deciding which state's law applies to issues of property characterization and distribution in divorce actions involving parties who own personal property in a community property state. In other areas of the law, Iowa has adopted, as choice of law doctrine, the "most significant relationship" rule espoused by the Restatement (Second) of Conflict of Laws. . . . [The court quotes § 258, and numerous cases in which the Restatement has been followed in other areas]. We adopt this provision as our choice of law rule in determining whether Iowa or Texas law should be applied in characterizing and distributing the corpus of the parties cash management account in Texas.

. . .

Guided by these principles, together with the fact that the parties acquired this account shortly after being married in Texas, we find that Texas has the most significant relationship to the issue of characterizing the corpus of the account. Therefore, Texas law governs the parties' rights in the account and should have been applied in characterizing the property. It is not clear which state's law the district court applied. The outcome reached by the district court is consistent with the application of community property or marital property principles.

E. *Choice of Law in Dividing the Property.* However, once the property was characterized, the trial court should have applied Iowa law in dividing the property. Under the circumstances of this case, the two states' laws are not in apparent conflict on the issue of property division.

Once the property has been characterized as marital or community property, both states' laws provide for equitable distribution of the property. Furthermore, the Texas property division statute, Texas Family Code Annotated section 3.63 (Vernon Supp.1990), was not pleaded or proved. We, therefore, must treat the Texas law as though it were identical to Iowa law.

Under Iowa law the spouses are "entitled to a just and equitable share of the property accumulated through their joint efforts." In light of these considerations, we find the division of the Merrill Lynch cash management account to be just and equitable, and we affirm the district court on this issue.

II. *Judicial Lien and Rehabilitative Alimony.* Beth also contends that the appellate court should either (1) eliminate Leon's $10,000 lien on the house awarded to her, or (2) increase her three-year rehabilitation alimony award from $400 per month to $800 per month.

We consider property division and alimony together in evaluating their individual sufficiency.

The partners in a marriage are "entitled to a just and equitable share of the property accumulated through their joint efforts." Alimony is not an absolute right; an award depends upon the circumstances of each particular case. The discretionary award of alimony is made after considering those factors listed in Iowa Code section 598.21(3).

We find the $10,000 lien awarded to Leon and the $400 per month alimony award granted to Beth to be just and equitable. We affirm the district court's division of the property and award of alimony.

For all the reasons stated, the district court's judgment is *affirmed.*

MICHELLE M. DAY v. JOHN V. DAY

Court of Appeals of Oregon
137 Ore. App. 264; 904 P.2d 171 (1995)

ARMSTRONG, J.

Wife appeals from a dissolution judgment, contending that the trial court erred in its distribution of the parties' property and in its award of spousal support and attorney fees. . . .

The parties began living together in June 1984 and were married in California on May 4, 1985. During the early years of the marriage, both parties held jobs, but husband's work as an engineer was the primary source of family income. Wife worked at a yarn store purchased by the parties, which proved unprofitable and was closed. Wife stopped working outside the home in January 1990, and has remained unemployed since that time.

In June 1990, husband received an inheritance of approximately $500,000. He quit his job as an engineer shortly thereafter. He used $200,000 of the inheritance to pay off the mortgage on the family home in Scotts Valley, California. The remainder of the inheritance was placed in stocks. In November 1990, husband began to manage full time the stock portfolio that contained the proceeds of his inheritance. Since then, the parties' source of income has been the principal and earnings from the stock.

In August 1992, husband moved to Klamath Falls [Oregon] and purchased a house. Wife and the parties' two minor children joined him there.

The parties separated in December 1992. Husband traveled to California where he filed for separation. Wife remained in Oregon where she filed for separation. Wife filed a petition for dissolution in November 1993. After appropriate proceedings to resolve which state had jurisdiction, the Oregon court proceeded to determine the issues in the dissolution.

The trial court considered California law in making the property distribution. The effect of that was to reimburse husband for the $200,000 from his inheritance that was used to pay off the Scotts Valley mortgage.[1] The trial court then divided the remainder of the parties' property, including the stock portfolio, approximately equally, with the Klamath Falls house going to wife, and the Scotts Valley house going to husband. The court's distribution was based on the finding that "[wife] is not in a position to begin earning a viable living. She has been absent from the work force for a longer period than [husband], and has custody of two small children. [Husband] would have substantial assets to begin a new life, and would be debt free."

Under the distribution, wife's post-dissolution assets are worth approximately $167,100, and husband's post-dissolution assets are worth approximately $332,263.

Wife contends that the trial court erred by reimbursing husband for the $200,000 from his inheritance that was used to pay off the mortgage on the Scotts Valley house. Wife also assigns error to the amount and duration of spousal support, and to the denial of her request for additional attorney fees. We write only to address the property division.

Wife does not contest the characterization of husband's inheritance as his separate property, nor that $200,000 of the equity in the Scotts Valley house was acquired using husband's inheritance. Rather, wife assigns error to the trial court's application of California law to the distribution of the equity in the Scotts Valley house, which resulted in $200,000 of that equity being carved out of the marital estate.

ORS 107.105 provides, in part:

> (1) Whenever the court grants a decree of marital annulment, dissolution or separation, it has power further to decree as follows:
>
> * * * * *
>
> (f) For the division or other disposition between the parties of the real or personal property, or both, of either or both of the parties as may be just and proper in all the circumstances. * * * The court shall consider the contribution of a spouse as a homemaker as a contribution to the acquisition of marital assets. There is a rebuttable presumption that both spouses have contributed equally to the acquisition of property during the marriage, whether such property is jointly or separately held.

The term "the real or personal property, or both, of either or both of the parties," describes all of the property that is within the dispositional authority of the court in a dissolution. ORS 107.105(1)(f) also uses the term "marital assets," which describes any real or personal property,

---

[1] The trial court concluded that husband's inheritance is separate property under California Family Code § 770, which provides, in part:

   (a) Separate property of a married person includes all of the following:

       . . .

       (2) All property acquired by the person after marriage by gift, bequest, devise or descent.

The trial court then applied California Family Code § 2640, which recognizes the right of a party making a separate-property contribution to the acquisition of real property to be reimbursed on dissolution for that contribution, to the extent the contribution can be traced. . . .

or both, acquired by either of the spouses, or both, during the marriage. Marital assets, a subset of the total property over which the court has dispositional authority, are subject to a statutory rebuttable presumption of equal contribution. That presumption may be overcome by a finding that the property was acquired by one spouse uninfluenced directly or indirectly by the other spouse, that is, that the other spouse did not contribute economically or otherwise to the acquisition of the property.

In this case, because the Scotts Valley house was acquired during the marriage, it is a marital asset, subject to the presumption of equal contribution. Husband argues, however, that the trial court correctly applied California law to distribute the equity in the Scotts Valley house, because the property at issue is real property, and the law of the situs of such property should apply to resolve any issue about it.

That argument might have force if the California law at issue dealt with the ownership of the property, because, in appropriate cases, the law of the situs can be used to determine the ownership of such property. However, the California law at issue does not address the ownership of the Scotts Valley house. Rather, it determines how the equity in the house should be distributed on dissolution. In an Oregon dissolution case, that issue is governed by Oregon law, specifically ORS 107.105(1)(f), and not by California law. Hence, the trial court erred in applying California law and carving out a portion of the equity in the house from the marital estate. Having determined that Oregon's statutory presumption of equal contribution applies to the Scotts Valley house, we turn to whether husband rebutted that presumption.

. . .

In this case, the Scotts Valley house has a total equity of $300,000, $200,000 of which was acquired using husband's inheritance. The fact that husband's inheritance was the source of funds used to obtain a portion of the equity in the house, without more, does not rebut the presumption of equal contribution by both parties to the acquisition of that house. Furthermore, the extent to which the parties' commingled their funds weighs in favor of applying the presumption. Husband testified that he used a portion of his inheritance to pay off the mortgage on the Scotts Valley house so that he would be able to stop paying the monthly mortgage:

> "I did it as an investment. It was an easy way to stop paying an $1,800 mortgage bill every month * * *. My mortgage each year was costing me $24,000. I took $200,000 of my inheritance, paid off the mortgage and I was essentially earning $24,000 a year."

In this case, the contribution from husband's inheritance allowed the parties to stop making monthly mortgage payments and to put to other family needs and desires the interest and principal from the stock portfolio. Husband gives no compelling reason to treat the proceeds of the inheritance as segregated for the purpose of distribution. Husband has not rebutted the presumption of equal contribution with regard to the Scotts Valley house.[3]

We now turn to distribution of the marital estate. ORS 107.105(1)(f) requires courts to distribute the spouses' property, including separate property, "as may be just and proper in all the circumstances." Among the goals we may seek to achieve in dividing property in a dissolution proceeding are to enable the parties to preserve assets and to begin post-marital life with a degree of economic self-sufficiency.

---

[3] The trial court divided the remainder of the proceeds of husband's inheritance, that is, the parties' stock portfolio, equally. Husband does not argue here that the presumption of equal contribution has been rebutted with regard to those proceeds.

It will be necessary for both parties to re-enter the employment market because their investments no longer can support them. Husband's earning capacity, on re-entering the employment market as an engineer, is approximately $4,166 per month. Wife's earning capacity is approximately $823 per month, which may be impaired while she attends school to obtain a bachelor's degree in business, a course of study she was pursuing at the time of separation. Of the parties' two houses, the Klamath Falls house has a $75,000 mortgage, with monthly payments of $895. The Scotts Valley house is owned free and clear and has an attached apartment that rents for $600 per month.

To enable the parties to preserve assets and to begin post-marital life with some degree of economic self-sufficiency, we award the Scotts Valley house to wife. We award to husband the Klamath Falls house, the entire stock portfolio and the tax credit of $15,000. To equalize the distribution, we also award to husband a $65,000 judgment against wife, payable in four years.[5] The $65,000 judgment shall be secured by a lien on the Scotts Valley house, the form of which shall be determined by the trial court. The remainder of the marital property is to be distributed in accordance with the disposition of the trial court.

NOTES AND QUESTIONS

(1) As we saw, proponents of equitable distribution as the way to resolve controversies connected with the break-up of a marriage argue that since the only focus is what is fair here and now, the law of the forum should be applied in all cases, regardless of where the assets of the two spouses are located, when they were acquired, or whether they consist of personal property, real property, or such interests as retirement benefits or pensions.[k] On the basis of the two cases here reproduced, do you agree?

(2)(a) Looking first at the *Whelchel* case, we know that Beth and Leon were married for about 15 years. Though the marriage has broken up, they seem not to be hostile toward one another, since they have accepted joint custody over their three children. They are not rich, but neither are they poor, and they have an account at Merrill Lynch of more than $200,000. Should that amount simply be split evenly—$107,379 to each party? Or would that be contrary to Iowa law?

(b) The Iowa statute, as quoted in the court's opinion, lists a great many factors, plus (m) "other factors the court may determine to be relevant. . . ." But the statute gives no guidance as to how the factors are to be evaluated. For instance, under (f), if the husband has greater earning capacity than the wife, does that suggest that he should receive a greater share of the pool, because he has contributed more, or less, because the wife needs more? Focusing on the issue before the court, the statute gives no guidance concerning the property brought to the marriage by each party, except (b) that this is a factor to be considered by the court. And of course the statute says nothing about out-of-state property or change of domicile by one or both parties.[l] The court tells us, however, that under Iowa law pension benefits are to be treated as marital property.

---

[5] Under that distribution, wife's post-dissolution assets will have a net value of approximately $249,600 and husband's post-dissolution assets will have a net value of approximately $249,763.

[k] See note g, *supra*.

[l] "Of course" is meant ironically. Some states, notably California, have in fact adopted statutes that address out-of-state property or change of domicile. See Russell J. Weintraub, *Commentary on the Conflict of Laws* § 8.14 and sources there cited (3d ed. 1986 and 1991 Supp.)

(c) The Texas statute, not focused primarily on divorce, is more specific. Property that each spouse owned prior to the marriage remains separate property. In particular, it appears that retirement benefits are deemed to accrue as they are earned, and since Leon earned more than half of his retirement benefit before he was married, that amount would not be community property under Texas law and not subject to division if Texas law were applied. It follows, the Iowa court holds, that since both parties resided in Texas when the retirement benefits accrued, it is Texas that has the most significant relationship with the issue before the court. Iowa courts have applied the Restatement in other contexts, and so its approach should be applied here. Is all this persuasive?

(d) Some years earlier in a divorce action between spouses domiciled in Texas, the Texas Supreme Court had held that property acquired during marriage that would have been community property if the parties had been domiciled in Texas when the property was acquired would be treated as community property for purposes of division upon divorce.[m] Should counsel for the wife have urged the Iowa court to take the same approach, i.e., that property that would have been treated as marital property for purposes of equitable distribution had the parties been domiciled in Iowa when it was acquired (or accrued) will be so treated now that the divorcing parties are domiciled in Iowa? Or would that be an improper use of reciprocity?

(e) Alternatively, could not the Iowa court simply have held that it is up to Iowa to characterize the property in question, and that the Texas rules of characterization have no relevance?

(3)(a) Essentially this is what the Oregon court does in *Day*. Under the law of California (like Texas a community property state), the husband's inheritance would be excluded from community property, and if it was commingled with marital property, for example to purchase real property, he would be entitled to reimbursement upon dissolution of the marriage. The Oregon court says that may well be correct for California, but it does not concern us. Even the fact that the inheritance was used to acquire real estate in California (or pay off the mortgage), does not sway the court: it is not concerned with title to the Scottsdale property, only with establishing the value of the assets from which the wife's share will be calculated.

(b) Does the decision in *Day* reach the better result? Does it sacrifice choice of law theory for a vague standard of "just and proper in all the circumstances"?

(4)(a) Speaking of choice of law theory, we have seen that in the mid-1980's, portions of the Restatement (Second) of Conflict of Laws were revised and updated, to take account of developments in such areas as quasi-in-rem jurisdiction, forum selection clauses, statutes of limitation, and recognition of modifiable judgments. Section 258, concerned with marital property,[n] was not reconsidered. Should it have been?

(b) Assuming an affirmative answer to the preceding question, try your hand at drafting a replacement section.

(c) One way to approach this task would be to leave § 258 as it stands for succession upon death, and to draft a separate provision for division of property in connection with divorce. Are the considerations different? Or is § 258 persuasive/unpersuasive on both issues?

---

[m] *Cameron v. Cameron*, 641 S.W.2d (Tex. 1982). For a different result in the context of succession upon death, see *Estate of Hanau v. Hanau*, 730 S.W.2d 663 (Tex. 1987), criticized by Prof. Weintraub in the article cited by the Iowa Court (p. 813), Russell J. Weintraub, *Obstacles to Sensible Choice of Law for Determining Marital Property Rights on Divorce or in Probate:* Hanau *and the Situs Rule*, 25 Houston L. Rev. 1113 (1988).

[n] Note h *supra*.

(d) At the same time that the Restatement (Second) of Conflict of Laws was published, the National Conference of Commissioners on Uniform State Laws came out with a Uniform Disposition of Community Property Rights at Death Act.º As of 1997 this act had been adopted by 14 states, including New York, Michigan, and—more to the point of the *Day* case—Oregon. The idea of the proponents of the Act is that when spouses move from a state where a community property regime prevails to a state that has no such system, the move should not deprive the spouses of any existing property rights. Thus, the Act provides that upon the death of a married person fitting this pattern, one half of the property to which the Act applies—i.e., personal property acquired as community property under the law of another state (or with the proceeds of such property)—is the property of the surviving spouse and is not subject to testamentary disposition of the decedent or to distribution under the laws of intestate succession of the enacting state. The other half is treated as property of the decedent and passes by his/her will or under the rules of intestate succession, except that the surviving spouse has no rights of election against the will. Thus, suppose H and W resided together in California. They held $300,000 in property, all in H's name but acquired as community property. H and W move to Oregon, then H dies without leaving a will. W is entitled to $150,000 as "her" property; she is also entitled to one third of "his" property under the intestate succession law of Oregon, i.e., another $50,000.

Should Oregon adopt a similar regime for dissolution of marriage other than by death? Or would that undercut the purposes of equitable distribution? Note that the result in the *Whelchel* case in Iowa is very much like the result that would be achieved by adapting the Uniform Community Property Rights at Death Act to divorce.

[D] Family Support as a National Problem

As early as 1909, the Uniform Law movement in the United States studied the subject of non-support for children and spouses—within the states of the Union and across state lines. The early efforts, including a Uniform Desertion and Non-Support Act promulgated in 1910 and adopted by 24 states, looked to the criminal law in enforcing support orders, which rarely worked when fathers/husbands moved to another state, and was usually of small comfort to the beneficiaries even when the delinquent obligor was caught and punished.

In 1950, the Commissioners on Uniform State Laws adopted the Uniform Reciprocal Enforcement of Support Act (URESA) which (in one of several versions) was adopted by every state in the United States. Under URESA, an action for support could be started in state *A* to secure an order of support from an obligor residing in state *B*, and the court in state *A* could make a preliminary finding as to whether the petitioner had shown that support was owed and that the obligor resided in state *B*. If the finding was affirmative, the file would be transmitted to a designated agency or court in state *B*, which was supposed to find the obligor, serve him, and (usually through the local district attorney) seek a judgment from the court in *B*. However, the obligor could present defenses in *B*, for instance that his earnings had decreased or his obligations to a second wife were too burdensome, or that the petitioner had other means of support than those recited in the petition.

By all accounts, use of the courts to enforce support obligations was largely unsuccessful, even within a given state. The two-state procedure provided for in URESA rarely worked well,

---

º 8A Uniform Laws Annotated 191 (1993 and Supp.)

particularly when it depended (as it generally did with poor people) on the assistance of the district attorney in state *B*, who often had priorities other than pursuing a citizen of *B* for the benefit of citizens of *A*. More and more, the failure of enforcement of support obligations came to be seen as a burden on the welfare system, and thus as a burden on federal taxpayers.

In 1975 Congress adopted the Child Enforcement Support Act, which added Title IV-D to the Social Security Act.[a] Title IV-D required states to establish a federally supported program for enforcement of child and spousal enforcement orders, according to guidelines set by the Federal Department of Health and Human Services, including maintenance of a parent locator service. If the support creditor (typically the wife, ex-wife, or unwed mother) received welfare payments, she was required to assign to the state her right to receive support payments from the obligor (typically the husband, ex-husband/father). Thus if litigation against the obligor was undertaken, the state (or its relevant agency) would be the plaintiff—whether in state *A* or in state *B*. The beneficiary (spouse or mother) was, however, required to cooperate with the state in the enforcement proceeding, including help in finding the husband/father and, if the issue was in dispute, help in establishing paternity.[b]

Title IV-D was not addressed particularly to the problem of interstate enforcement, but it largely replaced resort to URESA, and also led to acceptance of federal involvement in the details of a field that traditionally had been left to the states, including passage in 1992 of a federal Child Support Recovery Act,[c] and in 1994 of the federal Full Faith and Credit for Child Support Orders Act discussed below.[d]

In 1988 Congress created a Commission on Interstate Child Support; one of the Commission's findings concerning the difficulty of enforcing support orders across state lines was that such orders were not, under prevailing law, entitled to full faith and credit.[e] The response was two-fold. As had happened with regard to child custody a decade earlier (§ 9.04 *infra*), both the National Commissioners on Uniform State Laws and Congress adopted legislation to change the teaching of *Lynde, Sistare, Barber* and similar cases, which had held that because support orders were modifiable they could not be regarded as final, and because such orders were not final they need not be recognized and enforced pursuant to the Full Faith and Credit clause. First, in 1992 the National Conference of Commissioners on Uniform State Laws adopted a Uniform Interstate Family Support Act (UIFSA) designed to supersede URESA.[f] Two years later Congress, legislating under the second sentence of the Full Faith and Credit clause of the Constitution adopted a Full Faith and Credit for Child Support Orders Act, codified as 28 U.S.C. § 1738B.[g]

---

[a] Pub. L. No. 93-647, 88 Stat. 2337 (1975), codified as 42 U.S.C. § 651 et seq.

[b] If a support obligee was not receiving welfare payments, she was not required to participate in the IV-D program, but could do so for a fee.

[c] Pub. L. 102-521, 106 Stat. 340, § 2(a), codified as 18 U.S.C. § 228. Note that this Act appears in Title 18, the federal criminal code; the thrust of the statute is to make it a federal crime for a parent to willfully fail to make support payments with respect to a child who resides in another state. Upon conviction, the statute provides for fines, imprisonment and restitution of past due support obligations.

[d] It is estimated that 60 percent or more of all child support cases in the United States are now in the IV-D collection system. This number includes all cases in which the custodial parent receives welfare or Medicaid payments, as well as other cases in which the support creditor requests the assistance of the system. See Paul K. Legler, "The Coming Revolution in Child Support Policy: Implications of the 1996 Welfare Act," 30 Family L. Q. 519 at 522 (1996).

[e] See U.S. Commission on Interstate Child Support, *Supporting Our Children: A Blueprint for Reform* (1992).

[f] The Act, as amended in 1996, appears in the Documents Supplement at pp. 146–66.

[g] Documents Supplement p. 167. The original legislation implementing the Full Faith and Credit clause, adopted

The Uniform Act, looking to passage by state legislatures, deals both with jurisdiction—initial and continuing—and with enforcement of judgments; the federal act, adopted within the limited legislative jurisdiction of the national government, deals only with recognition and enforcement of orders rendered in other states. Also, the federal act is focused only on child support, whereas the Uniform Act treats spousal support as well.

In the Findings introducing the operative portions of the Federal Act, Congress expressed the frustrations of the interplay of the federal system, the ease and freedom of travel, and the traditional interpretation of the Full Faith and Credit clause:

(1)there is a large and growing number of child support cases annually involving disputes between parents who reside in different States;

(2)the laws by which the courts of different jurisdictions determine their authority to establish child support orders are not uniform;

(3)those laws, along with the limits imposed by the Federal system on the authority of each State to take certain actions outside its own boundaries—

(A)encourage noncustodial parents to relocate outside the States where their children and the custodial parents reside to avoid the jurisdiction of the courts of such States, resulting in an increase in the amount of interstate travel and communication required to establish and collect on child support orders and a burden on custodial parents that is expensive, time consuming, and disruptive of occupations and commercial activity;

(B) contribute to the pressing problem of relatively low levels of child support payments in interstate cases and to inequities in child support payments levels that are based solely on the noncustodial parent's choice of residence;

(C) encourage a disregard of court orders resulting in massive arrearages nationwide;

(D) allow noncustodial parents to avoid the payment of regularly scheduled child support payments for extensive periods of time, resulting in substantial hardship for the children for whom support is due and for their custodians; and

(E) lead to the excessive relitigation of cases and to the establishment of conflicting orders by the courts of various jurisdictions, resulting in confusion, waste of judicial resources, disrespect for the courts, and a diminution of public confidence in the rule of law;. . .[h]

The solution—or at least the objective adopted by both the state and the federal acts—was to be "one order at a time." Only one state order should govern a given obligation of support; if there is occasion to modify the order, for instance if one party or the other remarries, or his/her economic situation changes, an application for modification should be addressed to the issuing court, which retains *continuing exclusive jurisdiction*, so long as the obligor, the individual obligee, or the child remains a resident of the state where the original order was issued.[i]

---

in 1790 and slightly amended in 1948, is codified as 28 U.S.C. § 1738. The Parental Kidnapping Prevention Act of 1980, discussed in § 9.04 *infra*, is codified as § 1738A. A third recent statute, the Defense of Marriage Act, 1996 (§ 9.05 *infra*) is codified as § 1738C.

[h] Pub. L. 103-383, 108 Stat 4064, Oct. 22, 1994 § 2(a).

[i] UIFSA § § 205, 206; § 1738B(d). Note that under UIFSA § 205(f), "continuing, exclusive jurisdiction" applies to spousal support orders as well, without the conditions on residence of one of the parties applicable to child support orders. The official comment to § 205 states that interstate modification of pure spousal support was relatively rare under the prior uniform act; further, that avoiding conflict of law problems is almost impossible if spousal support orders are subject to modification in a second state. Moreover, the comment says that in most jurisdictions a dramatic

One may wonder why both federal and state remedies were used to address the same problem at roughly the same time. It seems that the political pressures to "do something" were brought at both state and federal level, and the proponents did not want to give up either opportunity. In particular, when Congress adopted its act, it was not clear that all states would adopt UIFSA (see finding (2) supra). Congress addressed that problem directly two years later in connection with the comprehensive reform of the welfare system, by including a provision requiring all states to adopt UIFSA by January 1, 1998 in order to remain eligible for federal funding of child support enforcement.[j]

NOTES AND QUESTIONS ABOUT UIFSA[k]

(1) Consider first the paradigm case, and then some variations.[l]

(a) Suppose a husband (H), wife (W) and child reside in state *A*. H and W separate, H moves to state *B*, and W remains with the child in state *A*. W now seeks spousal and child support from H. She brings suit in *A*, and serves H in state *B* in accordance with the law of *B*. H makes no appearance in *A*. Can the court of *A* issue a monetary judgment against H? Or would such a judgment violate due process, as understood from *Pennoyer v. Neff* through *Estin* and *Kulko*?

(b) According to § 201(3) of UIFSA the court of *A* has jurisdiction over H in respect of the claim for child support, because H resided with the child in state *A*. Is there any constitutional objection to assertion on this basis of long-arm jurisdiction? Note that this case differs from *Kulko*,[m] in that here H, W, and the child resided together in the forum state, whereas in *Kulko* plaintiff wife moved to California, the forum state, after the parties separated.

(c) Where does the federal act fit in? See § 1738B(c)(1)(B).

(2)(a) Assume the court in *A* takes jurisdiction, and after hearing, orders H to pay $800 per month to W as child support. W could register that order in state *B* under UIFSA § 601 and § 602. Then what? See § § 606-607. But see also subsection (a)(1) of the federal act, which seems not to allow any defenses, in stating that *B* shall enforce a child support order of another state "in accordance with its terms." Does subsection (h)(1) of the federal act solve this conundrum?[n]

(b) Note that § 607 of UIFSA limits the defenses available to H essentially to matters of procedure. An important change from URESA and its amendments is that H cannot seek a

---

improvement in the obligor's economic circumstances will have little or no relevance in an action seeking an upward modification of spousal support, but might well be the basis for an increase in child support. The difference is based on the policy choice that post-divorce success of an obligor-parent should benefit the obligor's child, not the ex-spouse.

As noted above, the federal act does not address spousal support at all.

[j] Personal Responsibility and Work Opportunity Reconciliation Act of 1996, Pub. L. 104-193 § 321, 110 Stat. 2221, codified as 42 U.S.C. § 666(f).

[k] The Act is reproduced in the Documents Supplement at pp. 146–66.

[l] For a larger selection of hypothetical cases, from which the following examples are adapted, see Patricia Wick Hatamyar, "Critical Applications and Proposals for Improvement of the Uniform Interstate Family Support Act and the Full Faith and Credit for Child Support Orders Act," 71 St.John's L. Rev. 1 (1997).

[m] Chapter 7, p. 555 question 5, *supra*.

[n] Prof. Hatamyar, note 1 *supra*, at p. 35, suggests an affirmative answer, on the ground that § 607 fits within the definition of the forum state's law.

modification of the order in State *B* on economic grounds. Any application on the merits of the order issued in state *A* must be brought in *A*.

(c) If H does not contest the registered order, or the contest is unsuccessful, the order is confirmed in state *B*, and takes effect as a judgment of *B*.

(d) Both UIFSA in § 604(a), and the Full Faith and Credit for Child Support Orders Act, in § 1738B(h)(2), require that the law of state *A* be applied to define the obligation. Thus if the order states that H is to pay $800 per month until the child reaches majority, the law of *A* and not of *B* determines when that occurs.°

(3) Suppose H and W have more than one child. The first child was born while H and W lived in state *A*; subsequently the family moved to state *B*, where a second child was born. Thereafter, the marriage broke up, and W returned to state *A* with both children. As in the first case, W seeks an order of child support from the court of *A*, and H, after due service, makes no appearance.

(a) It seems that jurisdiction over H could not be founded on UIFSA § 201(3) with respect to the second child, because H did not reside with her in state *A*. Does that make sense?

(b) Is the result suggested in question (a) the inevitable result of the American federal system and constitutional constraints on personal jurisdiction?ᵖ Or could jurisdiction in this context be sustained under § 201(8), once it has been established that the court of *A* has jurisdiction over H with respect to support for the first child? Recall that in *Asahi v. Superior Court*, Chapter 7, § 7.05[B], the Supreme Court seemed to add a reasonableness inquiry to the inquiry concerning minimum contacts. The Court gave no indication whether the exercise of jurisdiction might be reasonable, and therefore constitutional, even if minimum contacts between the defendant and the forum had not been established. Might this be such an instance?ᑫ

(c) Suppose after the marriage breaks up, W moves to state *C*, where neither she nor the children ever resided with H. That, as mentioned above, was the situation in *Kulko*. If W meets the residency requirements of state *C*, she can secure a divorce in *C*, and under the Uniform Child Custody Jurisdiction Act discussed in the next section, W can probably secure an order granting her custody.ʳ But jurisdiction to secure monetary support will require some activity both in state *C*, where W and the children now reside, and in state *B* where H resides. Given the dissatisfaction with URESA in the 40 years preceding adoption of UIFSA how should this be worked out to

---

° Note also that as to statutes of limitation, UIFSA § 604(b) says either the statute of the forum state or the statute of the issuing state applies, whichever is longer. Thus for support obligations, the drafters adopt a preference generally rejected in other contexts.

ᵖ Contrast Article 5(2) of the Brussels Convention on Jurisdiction and the Enforcement of Judgments, Documents Supplement p. 100, which provides for jurisdiction in matters relating to maintenance in the courts for the place where the maintenance creditor is domiciled or habitually resident.

ᑫ For a decision declining to order support in respect to the second child in this context (though sustaining jurisdiction for purposes of a custody order), see *Abu-Dalbouh v. Abu-Dalbouh*, 547 N.W.2d 700 at 705 (Minn. Ct. App. 1996).

ʳ The word "probably" is used because generally under UCCJA § § 2(5) and 3(a)(1)(i), W and the children must have resided in state *C* for at least 6 months prior to initiating the action, subject to certain exceptions. The residence requirements for divorce jurisdiction vary state by state, from zero to six weeks, 60 days, 90 days, 6 months and 1 year. See Linda D. Elrod and Robert G. Spector, "A Review of the Year in Family Law," 30 Family L.Q. 765, Appendix, Table 4 (1997).

provide the maximum chances for W (or the state as welfare provider) to secure support from H?[s]

(4)(a) For the situation where long-arm jurisdiction over H is thought not to be possible in W's state of residence, UIFSA still requires a two-state procedure. W (or *C's* IV-D agency, acting on her behalf) must secure a preliminary finding of existence of a support obligation from the court in *C* (the initiating tribunal), for forwarding to the court in *B* (the responding tribunal) (§ § 301(c), 304, 305). If no prior order is in effect, the responding tribunal in *B* will then issue an order of support (§ 401), which may include an order to H's employer to garnish wages, or be otherwise enforceable in *B*.

(b) Section 303 provides that the issuing tribunal (the court in *B* in our case) will apply the law of *this state*, i.e., the law of the forum. But UIFSA removes one common issue from the field of choice of law, by providing, in § 305(d), that a responding tribunal may not condition the payment of a support order upon compliance with provisions for visitation. A rationale for this exclusion is that in the interstate context, the support creditor, typically W, is generally not before the tribunal in *B*, and conflicts over visitation ought not to be adjudicated without her.[t] Beyond this, the drafters evidently believed that conflicts where H says "if you won't let me see the children, I'll cut off your allowance," or where W says "if you don't pay the support you owe promptly, I won't let you see the children" ought to be minimized as far as possible. Is there any inconsistency between § 604 and § 303?

(5) As noted in the text, the problem of modification, which had led to the difficulties under the Full Faith and Credit clause, was to be dealt with through a system of "one order at a time." Even when, as in the case discussed in question (4), the procedure for securing a support order still requires participation by courts in two states, no court other than the one that issued the order may modify that order or issue another one. Continuing exclusive jurisdiction is to be retained by the issuing court, unless all affiliating factors with the state in which that court is located have been lost, i.e., neither H, nor W, nor the child remains a resident of the state (UIFSA § 205(a), Federal Act § 1738B(d)), or all the individual parties consent in writing to assumption of continuing exclusive jurisdiction by the tribunal of another state.[u]

(b) What problems do you foresee in the regime of "continuing exclusive jurisdiction"? Suppose, for instance, W secures a support order in state *A*, in the paradigm case discussed in question (1). H stops paying, and W resorts to the enforcement procedure discussed in question (2). As pointed out in that question, H cannot seek modification of the support order except in the state that issued it. But suppose W seeks not only enforcement of the existing order but also an upward modification, on the ground, say, that it costs more to support a teen-ager than a toddler, or on the ground that H's earnings have substantially increased from the time the initial order was issued. Should W consent to exercise of jurisdiction by a tribunal of *B* pursuant to UIFSA § 205(a)(2) and § 1738B(e)(2)B? Would she not then lose the benefit of exclusive jurisdiction in the court of her domicile? Note that this question cannot arise with respect to an order of spousal support or alimony, because the consent provisions of UIFSA § 205(a)(2)

---

[s] Note that the same questions would arise if, in place of the hypothetical posed in the text. H remains in state *A*, the marital domicile, and W and the children move to state *B*. Either way, the jurisdiction of the state where W and the children reside lacks jurisdiction over H under § 201.

[t] See UIFSA, Official Comment to § 305.

[u] Note that even if the residence contacts no longer apply, the existing order is still in effect and required to be enforced unless and until it is modified.

are not applicable.[v] Thus if she wanted increased alimony as well, she would have to go back to the issuing tribunal in any event.

(c) Take the reverse example. H has lost his job, is only working part-time, and seeks a downward modification of his support obligation. Or H claims that W has inherited money from an aunt, and no longer requires support from him. As UIFSA and § 1738B are written, H cannot seek modification except in the state of the original issuing tribunal. Overall, this seems to be a sound response to the continuing problem of the "run-away pappy." In the individual case, it may result in hardship.[w]

---

§ 9.04 Child Custody: Jurisdiction, Modification, and Recognition of Judgments

Even more than issues of support, alimony, or division of property, conflicts over custody of children give rise to bitter controversies. Couples who agree, more or less, that their marriage has broken down and that divorce is the best solution, continue their quarrels in battles over the children.[a] The rights involved are so personal and intimate, so mixed up with love and guilt, that in many instances perfectly law-abiding persons conclude that disobedience to a judgment is a lesser evil than abandoning their child to the custody of another. A recurring phenomenon, occurring in the United States more than 100,000 times a year, is child-snatching—sometimes literally kidnapping, more often deliberate failure by a non-custodial parent to release or return a child who has been on an agreed or court-ordered visit. In many cases, of course, divorced couples come to reside in different states quite apart from disputes about custody; in many other cases, the non-custodial parent believes that the best way to overcome a custody decree in favor of the ex-spouse is to move to another state and secure a determination in his/her favor there.

The question of jurisdiction to adjudicate issues of custody (either separately or in connection with an action for divorce or separation) has been a difficult one for American courts. Is an action for custody like an action for divorce, which can be founded on domicile of the plaintiff, or is it more like an action affecting economic rights, which requires "personal jurisdiction" over the respondent spouse? Even more difficult, are custody decrees entitled to full faith and credit in other states, or, since they are nearly always modifiable, are they subject to the same infirmity that we saw with respect to support orders in *Lynde v. Lynde* and *Barber v. Barber*? Finally, what about modification? Can a custody decree be modified only by the rendering court, or could (should?) the suggestion of Justice Traynor in *Worthley*[b] in connection with support orders be applied to custody decrees as well?

All of these issues have troubled courts and legislatures in the United States. The first part of this section reproduces the leading decision of the U.S. Supreme Court on custody, rendered in 1953. Since that time, two major legislative efforts, one a uniform state law, the other a federal statute, have substantially changed the situation with respect to interstate custody, as illustrated in the second part of this section. The third part of this section introduces the international

---

[v] See UIFSA § 205(f) and note i *supra*.

[w] For other situations either not considered by the drafters or imperfectly resolved, see Hatamyar, note 1 supra, pp. 48 et seq.

[a] See Bodenheimer, *The Uniform Child Custody Jurisdiction Act,* 4 Fam. L. Q. 304, 305 (1970).

[b] Question (2)(d), p. 804, *supra*.

dimension, and an international convention designed to address the problem when one parent takes the child or children to another country.

[A] The Traditional View

MAY v. ANDERSON

United States Supreme Court
345 U.S. 528 (1953)

Mr. Justice Burton delivered the opinion of the Court.

The question presented is whether, in a habeas corpus proceeding attacking the right of a mother to retain possession of her minor children, an Ohio court must give full faith and credit to a Wisconsin decree awarding custody of the children to their father when that decree is obtained by the father in an *ex parte* divorce action in a Wisconsin court which had no personal jurisdiction over the mother. For the reasons hereafter stated, our answer is no.

This proceeding began July 5, 1951, when Owen Anderson, here called the appellee, filed a petition for a writ of habeas corpus in the Probate Court of Columbiana County, Ohio. He alleged that his former wife, Leona Anderson May, here called the appellant, was illegally restraining the liberty of their children, Ronald, Sandra and James, aged, respectively, 12, 8 and 5, by refusing to deliver them to him in response to a decree issued by the County Court of Waukesha County, Wisconsin, February 5, 1947. With both parties and their children before it, the Probate Court ordered that, until this matter be finally determined, the children remain with their mother subject to their father's right to visit them at reasonable times.

After a hearing "on the petition, the stipulation of counsel for the parties as to the agreed statement of facts, and the testimony," the Probate Court decided that it was obliged by the Full Faith and Credit Clause of the Constitution of the United States to accept the Wisconsin decree as binding upon the mother.

. . . .

The parties were married in Wisconsin and, until 1947, both were domiciled there. After marital troubles developed, they agreed in December, 1946, that appellant should take their children to Lisbon, Columbiana County, Ohio, and there think over her future course. By New Year's Day, she had decided not to return to Wisconsin and, by telephone, she informed her husband of that decision.

Within a few days he filed suit in Wisconsin, seeking both an absolute divorce and custody of the children. The only service of process upon appellant consisted of the delivery to her personally, in Ohio, of a copy of the Wisconsin summons and petition. Such service is authorized by a Wisconsin statute for use in an action for a divorce but that statute makes no mention of its availability in a proceeding for the custody of children. Appellant entered no appearance and took no part in this Wisconsin proceeding which produced not only a decree divorcing the parties from the bonds of matrimony but a decree purporting to award the custody of the children to their father, subject to a right of their mother to visit them at reasonable times. Appellant contests only the validity of the decree as to custody. . . .

Armed with a copy of the decree and accompanied by a local police officer, appellee, in Lisbon, Ohio, demanded and obtained the children from their mother. The record does not disclose what took place between 1947 and 1951, except that the children remained with their father in Wisconsin until July 1, 1951. He then brought them back to Lisbon and permitted them to visit their mother. This time, when he demanded their return, she refused to surrender them.

Relying upon the Wisconsin decree, he promptly filed in the Probate Court of Columbiana County, Ohio, the petition for a writ of habeas corpus now before us. Under Ohio procedure that writ tests only the immediate right to possession of the children. It does not open the door for the modification of any prior award of custody on a showing of changed circumstances. Nor is it available as a procedure for settling the future custody of children in the first instance.

. . . .

The narrow issue thus presented was noted but not decided in *Halvey v. Halvey,* 330 U. S. 610, 615–616. There a mother instituted a suit for divorce in Florida. She obtained service on her absent husband by publication and he entered no appearance. The Florida court granted her a divorce and also awarded her the custody of their child. There was, therefore, inherent in that decree the question "whether in absence of personal service the Florida decree of custody had any binding effect on the husband; . . ." *Id.,* at 615. We were not compelled to answer it there and a decision on it was expressly reserved.

Separated as our issue is from that of the future interests of the children, we have before us the elemental question whether a court of a state, where a mother is neither domiciled, resident nor present, may cut off her immediate right to the care, custody, management and companionship of her minor children without having jurisdiction over her *in personam*. Rights far more precious to appellant than property rights will be cut off if she is to be bound by the Wisconsin award of custody.

> "[I]t is now too well settled to be open to further dispute that the "full faith and credit' clause and the act of Congress passed pursuant to it do not entitle a judgment *in personam* to extra-territorial effect if it be made to appear that it was rendered without jurisdiction over the person sought to be bound." *Baker v. Baker, Eccles & Co.,* 242 U. S. 394, 401, and see 403; *Thompson v. Whitman,* 18 Wall. 457; *D'Arcy v. Ketchum,* 11 How. 165.

In *Estin v. Estin* . . . this Court upheld the validity of a Nevada divorce obtained *ex parte* by a husband, resident in Nevada, insofar as it dissolved the bonds of matrimony. At the same time, we held Nevada powerless to cut off, in that proceeding, a spouse's right to financial support under the prior decree of another state. In the instant case, we recognize that a mother's right to custody of her children is a personal right entitled to at least as much protection as her right to alimony.

In the instant case, the Ohio courts gave weight to appellee's contention that the Wisconsin award of custody binds appellant because, at the time it was issued, her children had a technical domicile in Wisconsin, although they were neither resident nor present there.[7] We find it unnecessary to determine the children's legal domicile because, even if it be with their father,

---

[7] By stipulation, the parties recognized her domicile in Ohio. . . .

For the general rule that in cases of the separation of parents, apart from any award of custody of the children, the domicile of the children is that of the parent with whom they live and that only the state of that domicile may award their custody, see Restatement, Conflict of Laws (1934), §§ 32 and 146, Illustrations 1 and 2.

that does not give Wisconsin, certainly as against Ohio, the personal jurisdiction that it must have in order to deprive their mother of her personal right to their immediate possession.[8]

The judgment of the Supreme Court of Ohio, accordingly, is reversed and the cause is remanded to it for further proceedings not inconsistent with this opinion.

Mr. Justice Clark, not having heard oral argument, took no part in the consideration or decision of this case.

Mr. Justice Frankfurter, concurring.

The views expressed by my brother Jackson make it important that I state, in joining the Court's opinion, what I understand the Court to be deciding and what it is not deciding in this case.

What is decided—the only thing the Court decides—is that the Full Faith and Credit Clause does not require Ohio, in disposing of the custody of children in Ohio, to accept, in the circumstances before us, the disposition made by Wisconsin. The Ohio Supreme Court felt itself so bound. This Court does not decide that Ohio would be precluded from recognizing, as a matter of local law, the disposition made by the Wisconsin court. For Ohio to give respect to the Wisconsin decree would not offend the Due Process Clause. Ohio is no more precluded from doing so than a court of Ontario or Manitoba would be, were the mother to bring the children into one of these provinces.

Property, personal claims, and even the marriage status (see, *e. g., Sherrer v. Sherrer,* [p. 768, *supra*], generally give rise to interests different from those relevant to the discharge of a State's continuing responsibility to children within her borders. Children have a very special place in life which law should reflect. Legal theories and their phrasing in other cases readily lead to fallacious reasoning if uncritically transferred to determination of a State's duty towards children. There are, of course, adjudications other than those pertaining to children, as for instance decrees of alimony, which may not be definitive even in the decreeing State, let alone binding under the Full Faith and Credit Clause. Interests of a State other than its duty towards children may also prevail over the interest of national unity that underlies the Full Faith and Credit Clause. But the child's welfare in a custody case has such a claim upon the State that its responsibility is obviously not to be foreclosed by a prior adjudication reflecting another State's discharge of its responsibility at another time. Reliance on opinions regarding out-of-State adjudications of property rights, personal claims or the marital status is bound to confuse analysis when a claim to the custody of children before the courts of one State is based on an award previously made by another State. Whatever light may be had from such opinions, they cannot give conclusive answers.

---

[8] ". . . the weight of authority is in favor of confining the jurisdiction of the court in an action for divorce, where the defendant is a non-resident and does not appear, and process upon the defendant is by substituted service only, to a determination of the *status* of the parties. . . . This rule of law extends to children who are not within the jurisdiction of the court when the decree is rendered, where the defendant is not a resident of the state of the seat of the court, and has neither been personally served with process nor appeared to the action. . . . [Citing cases.]

"By the authority of the cases *supra*, a decree of the custody of a minor child under the circumstances stated is void." . . .

The instant case does not present the special considerations that arise where a parent, with or without minor children, leaves a jurisdiction for the purpose of escaping process or otherwise evading jurisdiction, and we do not have here the considerations that arise when children are unlawfully or surreptitiously taken by one parent from the other.

MR. JUSTICE JACKSON, whom MR. JUSTICE REED joins, dissenting.

The Court apparently is holding that the Federal Constitution prohibits Ohio from recognizing the validity of this Wisconsin divorce decree insofar as it settles custody of the couple's children. In the light of settled and unchallenged precedents of this Court, such a decision can only rest upon the proposition that Wisconsin's courts had no jurisdiction to make such a decree binding upon appellant. *Baker v. Baker, Eccles & Co.,* 242 U. S. 394, 401; *Esenwein v. Commonwealth,* 325 U. S. 279, 281.

. . . .

The Ohio courts reasoned that although personal jurisdiction over the wife was lacking, domicile of the children in Wisconsin was a sufficient jurisdictional basis to enable Wisconsin to bind all parties interested in their custody. This determination that the children were domiciled in Wisconsin has not been contested either at our bar or below. Therefore, under our precedents, it is conclusive. *Williams v. North Carolina,* 317 U. S. 287, 302. The husband, plaintiff in the case, was at all times domiciled in Wisconsin; the defendant-wife was a Wisconsin native, was married there and both were domiciled in that State until her move in December 1946, when the parties stipulate that she acquired an Ohio domicile. The children were born in Wisconsin, were always domiciled there, and were physically resident in Wisconsin at all times until December 1946, when their mother took them to Ohio with her. But the Ohio court specifically found that she brought the children to Ohio with the understanding that if she decided not to go back to Wisconsin the children were to be returned to that State. In spite of the fact that she did decide not to return, she kept the children in Ohio. It was under these circumstances that the Wisconsin decree was rendered in February 1947, less than two months after the wife had given up her physical residence in Wisconsin and held the children out of the State in breach of her agreement.

The husband subsequently went to Ohio, retrieved the children and took them back to Wisconsin, where they remained with him for four years. Then he voluntarily brought them to Ohio for a visit with their mother, whereupon she refused to surrender them, and he sought habeas corpus in the Ohio courts. In this situation Wisconsin was no meddler reaching out to draw to its courts controversies that arose in and concerned other legal communities. If ever domicile of the children plus that of one spouse is sufficient to support a custody decree binding all interested parties, it should be in this case. Cf. *Yarborough v. Yarborough,* [p. 647 at 649, *supra.*]

I am quite aware that in recent times this Court has been chipping away at the concept of domicile as a connecting factor between the state and the individual to determine rights and obligations. We are a mobile people, historically on the move, and perhaps the rigid concept of domicile derived by common law from feudal attachment to the land is too rigid for a society so restless as ours. But if our federal system is to maintain separate legal communities, as the Full Faith and Credit Clause evidently contemplates, there must be some test for determining to which of these a person belongs. If, for this purpose, there is a better concept than domicile, we have not yet hit upon it. Abandonment of this ancient doctrine would leave partial vacuums in many branches of the law. It seems to be abandoned here.

The Court's decision holds that the state in which a child and one parent are domiciled and which is primarily concerned about his welfare cannot constitutionally adjudicate controversies as to his guardianship. The state's power here is defeated by the absence of the other parent for a period of two months. The convenience of a leave-taking parent is placed above the welfare of the child, but neither party is greatly aided in obtaining a decision. The Wisconsin courts cannot bind the mother, and the Ohio courts cannot bind the father. A state of the law such as this, where possession apparently is not merely nine points of the law but all of them and self-help the ultimate authority, has little to commend it in legal logic or as a principle of order in a federal system.

Nor can I agree on principle with the Court's treatment of the question of personal jurisdiction of the wife. I agree with its conclusion and that of the Ohio courts that Wisconsin never obtained jurisdiction of the person of the appellant in this action and therefore the jurisdiction must be rested on domicile of the husband and children. . . .

In spite of the fact that judges and law writers long have recognized the similarity between the jurisdictional requirements for divorce and for custody, this decision appears to equate the jurisdictional requirements for a custody decree to those for an *in personam* money judgment. One reads the opinion in vain to discover reasons for this choice, unless it is found in the remark that for the wife "rights far more precious . . . than property will be cut off" in the custody proceeding. The force of this cardiac consideration is self-evident, but it seems to me to reflect a misapprehension as to the nature of a custody proceeding or a revision of the views that have heretofore prevailed. When courts deal with inanimate property by the conventional *in rem* proceeding, their principal concern is the distribution of rights in that property, rather than with the welfare of the property apart from its ownership claims. But even where dealing solely with property rights, where concern with the *"res"* is minimal and concern with the claimants is paramount, courts may exercise jurisdiction *in rem* over the property without having personal jurisdiction over all of the claimants. Only when they seek to render a party liable to some personal performance must they acquire personal jurisdiction.

The difference between a proceeding involving the status, custody and support of children and one involving adjudication of property rights is too apparent to require elaboration. In the former, courts are no longer concerned primarily with the proprietary claims of the contestants for the *"res"* before the court, but with the welfare of the *"res"* itself. Custody is viewed not with the idea of adjudicating rights *in* the children, as if they were chattels, but rather with the idea of making the best disposition possible for the welfare of the children. To speak of a court's "cutting off" a mother's right to custody of her children, as if it raised problems similar to those involved in "cutting off" her rights in a plot of ground, is to obliterate these obvious distinctions. Personal jurisdiction of all parties to be affected by a proceeding is highly desirable, to make certain that they have had valid notice and opportunity to be heard. But the assumption that it overrides all other considerations and in its absence a state is constitutionally impotent to resolve questions of custody flies in the face of our own cases. The wife's marital ties may be dissolved without personal jurisdiction over her by a state where the husband has a genuine domicile because the concern of that state with the welfare and marital status of its domiciliary is felt to be sufficiently urgent. Certainly the claim of the domiciled parent to relief for himself from the leave-taking parent does not exhaust the power of the state. The claim of children as well as the home-keeping parent to have their status determined with reasonable certainty, and to be free from an incessant tug of war between squabbling parents, is equally urgent.

The mother in this case would in all probability not be permanently precluded from attempting to redetermine the custody of the children. If the Wisconsin courts would allow modification of the decree upon a showing of changed circumstances, such modification could be accomplished by another state which acquired jurisdiction over the parties. . . .

I fear this decision will author new confusions. The interpretative concurrence, if it be a true interpretation, seems to reduce the law of custody to a rule of seize-and-run. I would affirm the decision of the Ohio courts that they should respect the judgment of the Wisconsin court, until it or some other court with equal or better claims to jurisdiction shall modify it.

Mr. Justice Minton, dissenting.

The opinion of the Court and the dissent of Mr. Justice Jackson deal with a jurisdictional question not raised on the record.

As I understand the law of Ohio, "parents are the legal and natural custodians of their minor children and each parent has an equal right to their custody in the absence of an order, judgment, or decree of a court of competent jurisdiction fixing their custody. Section 8032, General Code. It is well settled that *habeas corpus* is not the proper or appropriate action to determine, as between parents, who is entitled to the custody of their minor children." *In re Corey,* 145 Ohio St. 413, 418, 61 N. E.2d 892, 894–895.

. . . .

The only question before the Ohio court was whether that court should give full faith and credit to the Wisconsin decree. That unappealed decree was valid on its face, and its validity was not attacked by any pleading. . . . Since appellant failed to challenge its validity by any pleading, the decree was entitled to full faith and credit in Ohio under Art. IV, § 1 of the United States Constitution. . . .

I would therefore affirm.

NOTES AND QUESTIONS

(1)(a) The majority opinion in *May v. Anderson,* rehearsing some of the phrases from the *Williams* cases, speaks of "rights far more precious . . . than property rights." Citing *Estin,* the Court says these rights cannot be cut off without personal jurisdiction over the respondent—here the ex-wife. Is that sound? Does it not subordinate the best interests of the children to the rights of the defendant?

(b) Justice Frankfurter says the Supreme Court is not holding that Ohio may not recognize the Wisconsin judgment, but only that the Ohio court erred in assuming that it was required to do so by the Full Faith and Credit clause. Justice Jackson says this can't be, since giving full faith and credit to a judgment rendered without jurisdiction would be a denial of due process. Who is right? Has Frankfurter redefined the majority's opinion?

(c) Would Frankfurter's point apply only in a case such as the actual one, where one parent was not before the court? Or is the argument equally applicable to custody orders in which there can be no doubt about the jurisdiction of the court that issues the initial custody order? Recall Justice Stone's suggestion in *Yarborough*[c] about a gray area between the prohibition of the due process clause and the mandate of full faith and credit.

(d) Justice Jackson asks why the Wisconsin court here does not have jurisdiction to issue a custody decree. Writing after *International Shoe* but before the general rise of long-arm statutes, Jackson agrees that the Wisconsin court did not have *personal* jurisdiction over the wife;[d] but

---

[c] Chapter 8, p. 650, *supra.*

[d] Contrast N.Y. C.P.L.R. § 302(b), adopted in 1974, Documents Supplement, p. 77.

he argues that it was not necessary when one parent and the children were domiciled in the forum state, particularly as this was also the marital domicile. Putting aside the analogy to in rem actions, which, as he concedes himself is unsatisfactory, is Jackson not right in terms of a fair and rational system of allocation of judicial authority?

(2)(a) Justice Frankfurter writes that

> . . . the child's welfare in a custody case has such a claim upon the State that its responsibility is obviously not to be foreclosed by a prior adjudication reflecting another State's discharge of its responsibility at another time.

If the word "obviously" seems exaggerated, there is nevertheless a good deal of appeal to the position stated. Indeed the statement goes beyond the decision in the *Halvey* case, quoted in the majority opinion, which held that since a custody decree given ex parte in Florida was modifiable under Florida law, it could be modified by a New York court as well, when that court had jurisdiction over all the parties. Justice Frankfurter's formulation here seems not to depend on modifiability of the initial custody decree, though doubtless Frankfurter assumed that such decrees would usually be subject to modification. Is child custody sufficiently different from other subjects of judicial jurisdiction so that the interests in finality and in reducing the consequences of state lines that inform the Full Faith and Credit clause should be subordinated to more compelling concerns?[e]

[B] Legislative Change: UCCJA and PKPA

In the years following the decision in *May v. Anderson,* Justice Frankfurter's concurrence rather than the majority opinion reflected the prevailing view in the United States, both with respect to jurisdiction and with respect to recognition and modification.[f] Courts felt free to take jurisdiction on the basis of domicile of one parent plus (usually) the presence of the child, both to render initial decrees and to modify existing ones. If there had been a prior custody decree in another state, courts in the position of F–2 faced with a petition to modify usually saw their task as determining the best interests of the child as of the time of the hearing, rather than inquiring into jurisdictional (or indeed other) aspects of the first decree. The fact that the petitioning parent in F–2 had brought the child to the new state (or failed to return it) contrary to the orders of the court in F–1 was rarely disqualifying in the second state. Thus in a great many cases the result was just as Justice Jackson had predicted—the law of custody became a rule of seize and run or, at a minimum, a search for a favorable forum.

Gradually the perception changed: best interests of children might not necessarily be what the last judge to hear the case thought, until the next judge came along. What was most necessary

---

[e] In addition to his concurrence in *May v. Anderson,* see Justice Frankfurter concurring in *New York ex rel Halvey v. Halvey,* 330 U.S. 610, 616–17 (1947):

> The constitutional policy formulated by the Full Faith and Credit Clause cannot be fitted into tight little categories or too abstract generalities. . . . Thus, in judgments affecting domestic relations technical questions of "finality" as to alimony and custody seem to me irrelevant in deciding the respect to be accorded by a State to a valid prior judgment touching custody and alimony rendered by another State. . . .
>
> The child's welfare must be the controlling consideration whenever a court which can actually lay hold of a child is appealed to on behalf of the child.

[f] See, e.g., *Restatement (Second) of Conflict of Laws,* § 79 and Comments *a* and *c* (1971). That section is completely changed in the 1988 Revisions, to take account of the developments described hereafter.

for healthy, normal development of children was a stable home environment, and constancy and continuity of personal attachments. Frequent moves were bad for children, and recurring contests and inconsistent results often disastrous. The state of conflicts/constitutional law in this area was fundamentally unsound. As Professor Brigitte Bodenheimer, one of the leaders in the reform movement, put it:

> The doctrine that custody decisions must always remain open to change for the child's benefit is often employed in the interest not of the child, but of his feuding parents or relatives. The child loses his home, not because of any urgent necessity from the standpoint of the care he receives, but to satisfy the urge to continue the marital discord at its most vulnerable point, which is the competition for the affection and control of the children. While this is a problem in intrastate cases when the same court, perhaps the same judge, is asked for a modification of the decree, the situation is greatly aggravated when a reopening and change of the custody decision is applied for in another state. Competition between courts is then added to competition between custody claimants, and partiality for the local petitioner may be shown.[g]

The solution, as developed by Professor Bodenheimer and others,[h] was to seek to change by legislation both the jurisdictional foundation of custody decrees and their recognition and enforcement in other states: (1) Jurisdiction to issue custody orders should be exercised only by a state that had a significant connection with the child, preferably the home state, as that term would be defined. Thus jurisdiction on the basis of "presence" or "best interests" of the child would be eliminated, except for true emergencies; and (2) full faith and credit should be given to custody decrees issued in other states by courts with jurisdiction as under (1), so that a parent who had been awarded custody in F–1 but whose child had been taken to F–2 could bring suit in the latter state to enforce the F–1 decree. As far as possible, the courts of F–2 would be precluded from litigating the merits of a custody dispute: if one party sought modification, he or she would be referred to F–1.[i]

By the late 1960's, most scholars concerned with the problem of child custody in the United States were in agreement in favoring reform along these lines, though with various differences of detail. There was disagreement, however, about the way to bring about the reforms. Some thought the solution lay in federal legislation pursuant to the second sentence of the Full Faith and Credit clause of the Constitution; others thought the reform should come from the states, by means of a Uniform Act. Eventually both approaches were adopted, and both succeeded: The Commissioners on Uniform State Laws promulgated the Uniform Child Custody Jurisdiction Act in 1968, and in the period 1973–84 every state in the Union adopted it.[j] In 1977, at a time when only 19 states had adopted the UCCJA, a drive led by Senator Wallop of Wyoming began in the United States Senate for a federal Parental Kidnapping Prevention Act, which was eventually signed into law by President Carter in December 1980, including a new 28 U.S.C. § 1738A.[k]

---

[g] B. Bodenheimer, *The Uniform Child Custody Jurisdiction Act,* 3 Fam. L. Q. 304, 305 (1969).

[h] Professor Juenger, in paying tribute to Professor Bodenheimer when she died, said, "Of all the people concerned with conflict of laws, Brigitte is the only one in recent years who actually did something to make things better." Quoted in 14 Fam. L.Q. No. 4, viii (1981).

[i] Note that this approach, similar to the approach of the Uniform Interstate Family Support Act described in § 9.03[D], antedates that law by more than two decades. Indeed, it is clear that the UCCJA, described in this section, served as the model for UIFSA.

[j] The UCCJA appears in the Documents Supplement, pp. 170–79.

[k] Documents Supplement, pp. 180–83. Note that § 1738, Documents Supplement p. 91, is essentially the Act of 1790 (slightly amended), implementing the Full Faith and Credit clause with respect to judgments generally.

Both statutes essentially follow the plan outlined above, but the UCCJA deals with jurisdiction as well as judgments, while the PKPA deals only with recognition. Also, as the *Glanzner* case reproduced below illustrates, the UCCJA makes provision for at least two bases of jurisdiction that can operate concurrently, while the PKPA has a strict order of preference, with the effect that if the "home state," as defined, exercises jurisdiction, that state's decree, and no other, is entitled to recognition and enforcement in other states.[1]

Before starting on the cases that follow, read the UCCJA, and particularly §§ 1, 3, 8, 13, and 14, as well as § 1738A of the PKPA.

BROCK v. DISTRICT COURT OF COUNTY OF BOULDER

Supreme Court of Colorado
620 P.2d 11 (1980)

QUINN, JUSTICE.

In this original proceeding Karen Lane Brock (petitioner) seeks relief in the nature of prohibition against the respondent district court in connection with its exercise of child-custody jurisdiction under the Uniform Child Custody Jurisdiction Act (UCCJA). We issued a rule to show cause and now make the rule absolute.

The petitioner is the mother of an eight-year old son born as issue of her marriage to John Lane (father). On May 27, 1976, the Superior Court of Floyd County, Georgia, entered a decree of divorce and awarded permanent custody of the minor child to petitioner with visitation rights to the father. After the divorce the petitioner remained with her minor child in Georgia and the father moved to Colorado. In June 1980 the child came to Boulder, Colorado, to visit his father for one month. At the conclusion of the visitation period the father refused to allow the child to return to his mother in Georgia and he filed with the respondent court a petition for an order awarding temporary and permanent custody to him.

The father invoked jurisdiction of the respondent court under [UCCJA § 3(a)], claiming that an emergency existed with respect to the return of the child to Georgia. The petitioner traveled to Boulder and filed a motion to dismiss the father's petition on the grounds that Georgia still retained jurisdiction over this matter and the respondent court lacked jurisdiction under the UCCJA. Prior to the court's determination of the motion to dismiss the father submitted psychiatric and psychological reports that indicated the child was hyperactive and was experiencing a childhood adjustment disorder. The court denied the petitioner's motion to dismiss and awarded temporary custody to the father. It held (1) that Georgia no longer had jurisdiction over custody in this case, (2) Colorado did have jurisdiction under [UCCJA § 3(a)], and (3) the father's showing of an emergency justified the court's award of temporary custody to him. Original proceedings followed in this court. We conclude that the respondent court's exercise of jurisdiction was invalid and prohibition is in order.

---

[1] For analyses of the differences between the two acts, see Foster, *Child Custody Jurisdiction: UCCJA and PKPA*, 27 N.Y.L. Sch. L. Rev. 297 (1981); Coombs, *Interstate Child Custody: Jurisdiction, Recognition, and Enforcement*, 66 Minn. L. Rev. 711 (1982).

I.

Georgia, like Colorado, has enacted the provisions of the UCCJA. The objectives of that act, as pertinent here, were recently summarized in *Roberts v. District Court,* 198 Colo. 79, 596 P.2d 65, 68 (1979):

> First, we seek to avoid conflict with the courts of other states concerning custody determination. [UCCJA § 1(a)(1)]. Second, we seek to deter the unilateral action of a parent in contravention of an existing child custody decree in order to obtain a different custody decree. [UCCJA § 1(a)(5)]. Lastly, we seek to promote cooperation with the courts of other states in order to ensure that the determination of custody is made by the court which can best decide the case in the interest of the child. [UCCJA § 1(a)(2)].

[UCCJA § 3(a)(3)] does authorize Colorado courts to exercise jurisdiction over custody matters in emergency situations when the child is physically present in the state and is threatened with mistreatment, abuse, or is otherwise neglected or dependent. However, that section neither grants the courts of this state the right, nor imposes upon them the duty, to modify out-of-state custody decrees under any and all circumstances merely because of a claimed emergency and a threshold showing that some form of judicial intervention might be appropriate. In order to effectuate the general purposes of the UCCJA and to deter "jurisdictional fishing with children as bait," [UCCJA § 3(a)] must be read in conjunction with other provisions of the act.

[UCCJA § 13] requires Colorado courts to recognize and enforce a custody decree of another state when the rendering court "assumed jurisdiction under statutory provisions substantially in accordance with this article" or when that court entered the decree "under factual circumstances meeting the jurisdictional standards" of the UCCJA. Similarly, [UCCJA § 14(a)] prohibits Colorado courts from modifying the custody decree of another state unless it appears that the rendering state "does not now have jurisdiction under jurisdictional prerequisites substantially in accordance with this article or has declined to assume jurisdiction to modify the decree. . . ." See *Woodhouse v. District Court,* 196 Colo. 558, 587 P.2d 1199 (1978).

Neither the petitioner nor the father questions the Georgia court's jurisdiction to enter the original custody decree nor the validity of that decree. The central inquiry in this proceeding, therefore, is whether Georgia presently has jurisdiction in this matter. If the Georgia courts have continuing jurisdiction over custody and have not declined to exercise that jurisdiction, then the respondent court is precluded by [UCCJA §§ 13 and 14], from exercising jurisdiction in this case, at least in the absence of a grave emergency.

Georgia statutory law clearly vests their courts with jurisdiction to modify the custody decree in this case. [The court quotes § 3 of the UCCJA, Documents Supplement at p. 171.]

Because Georgia courts have jurisdiction at this time to hear and determine any request for modification of the initial Georgia custody decree, the respondent court clearly exceeded its jurisdiction under the UCCJA in assuming plenary subject-matter jurisdiction over the issue of custody.

II.

The respondent court asserts that even if Georgia has jurisdiction to modify the custody decree, a Colorado court should be able to exercise jurisdiction under the circumstances of this case under the doctrine of *parens patriae.* We do not agree.

In *Wilson v. Wilson,* 172 Colo. 566, 474 P.2d 789 (1970), we noted that where an emergency exists affecting the immediate needs and welfare of the child, a Colorado court may enter appropriate orders for the protection of the child even if its orders contravene those of a sister state that still retains jurisdiction over custody. An "emergency," however, is not a talisman which, by its mere inclusion in a modification-petition, removes those salutary impediments to jurisdictional competition and conflict established by the UCCJA. The exercise of *parens patriae* jurisdiction should be limited to those cases where there is substantial evidence of a grave emergency affecting the immediate welfare of the child. Generally, judicial relief in such cases should not extend beyond the issuance of temporary protective orders pending the application to the court of the rendering state for appropriate modification of the custody decree. Only when there are compelling reasons, articulated in the record, that render such out-of-state application impractical, should a Colorado court grant anything but temporary relief under its *parens patriae* jurisdiction. . . .

The circumstances of this case do not involve the type of compelling emergency that justifies the extraordinary relief granted by the respondent court. The father's claim of emergency is based on a condition of hyperactivity and a childhood adjustment disorder, neither of which is particularly unusual for an eight year old whose life has been disrupted by a broken home and parental discord. There is no evidence of physical abuse or imminent physical or emotional danger to the child upon his return to Georgia. Where, as here, no compelling reason exists for the exercise of *parens patriae* jurisdiction, and the child has been retained in this state by the non-custodial parent after the term of visitation has expired, the respondent court has no basis in fact or law to grant the non-custodial parent temporary custody of the minor child. *See* [UCCJA § 8(b)].

The rule to show cause is made absolute and the cause is remanded to the district court with directions to order the immediate return of the child to the custody of the petitioner and to dismiss the father's petition for a modification of custody.

KEITH GLANZNER v. STATE OF MISSOURI, DEPARTMENT OF SOCIAL SERVICES, DIVISION OF CHILD SUPPORT ENFORCEMENT, IN RE CUSTODY OF BRADLEY CARL GLANZNER.

Missouri Court of Appeals,
835 S.W.2d 386 (1992)

GRIMM, Judge.

In this case of first impression, we are called upon to resolve conflicting child custody decrees from California and Missouri. The California decree granted custody to mother; a later Missouri decree granted custody to father. Under the federal Parental Kidnapping Prevention Act (PKPA), we are required to hold that the California decree is not entitled to interstate enforcement because Missouri was the child's "home state." We therefore deny mother's petition for writ of habeas corpus and quash our temporary order.

This court consolidated a companion case which was pending on appeal. In that case, the State appeals from the trial court's judgment reversing a decision of the Department of Social Services which ordered father to pay spousal and child support arrearage of $11,118.00. We affirm the child support order and reverse the spousal support order.

I. Background

Suzanne E. Glanzner and Keith W. Glanzner are the mother and father of Bradley Carl Glanzner. Gary and Paula Glanzner are Bradley's paternal grandparents.

Mother and father were married in Illinois on September 5, 1981. Father was then in military service and the parties lived in Tennessee. Bradley was born in St. Louis on August 13, 1982.

Mother and, after his birth, child, lived with paternal grandparents in St. Louis from June, 1982, to November, 1983; father was stationed in Okinawa during that time.

From November, 1983, to January, 1985, mother, father, and child all lived in California where father was stationed. Mother had lived in California for seven years prior to her marriage.

In January, 1985, mother, father, and child came to Missouri. All three of them resided in Missouri until mother and child returned to California on October 29, 1985.

On December 18, 1985, mother filed a petition for legal separation and custody[1] in California. Father was personally served January 13, 1986. He filed a motion to quash service on the grounds that California should not exercise jurisdiction over the child custody issue.

In the meantime, on January 10, 1986, father filed a petition for dissolution in St. Louis County. Mother was apparently served on July 17, 1986.

Proceedings continued in California. On June 4, 1986, the California court conducted a hearing on father's motion to quash. The hearing included a phone consultation with a judge in St. Louis County.

On June 18, 1986, the California court found that "[t]he state in which the minor child resided for 6 consecutive months prior to the filing of the petition was Missouri." However, the court noted the child had now resided in California for 7 months. Although child had family members in both states, the court found "California has the most significant contacts with the minor child." As a result, the court held that under the Uniform Child Custody Jurisdiction Act (UCCJA), California was the proper jurisdiction in which to adjudicate the claim. A formal order incorporating that finding was entered July 2, 1986.

On August 12, 1986, following a hearing, the California court granted custody of child to mother "pending trial or until further order of this court." Father was ordered to pay $253 per month child support, as well as $151 per month spousal support, commencing August 15, 1986. Father was given reasonable visitation rights with child within California.

On November 3, 1986, the California court dissolved the marriage of the parties. Mother was granted custody of the child, and father was granted reasonable visitation rights in California. In addition, father was ordered to pay child support and spousal support.

In the St. Louis County action filed January 10, 1986, mother filed a special appearance and objection to jurisdiction about August 15, 1986. She attached a copy of the June 4, 1986 order wherein the California court assumed jurisdiction over the child custody issue. On September 5, 1986, the St. Louis County court overruled mother's objections to jurisdiction. A default decree

---

[1] On July 7, 1986, the petition was amended to seek a dissolution of marriage.

of dissolution was granted on September 26, 1986; the decree gave custody of child to father, and reasonable visitation rights to mother.

From October 29, 1985, until the summer of 1991, mother had continuous physical custody of child. Father admits he has not visited the child since that date. However, he claims he has attempted to exercise his rights, but mother has interfered with his efforts by "frequently moving, changing her address and not apprising [him] as to the whereabouts of the minor child."

In the spring of 1991, paternal grandparents visited mother and child in California. After returning to Missouri, grandmother phoned mother and asked if child could come to Missouri for a visit during the summer vacation. After receiving assurances from grandparents they would return the child, mother consented. Grandparents purchased a round trip airline ticket for child and sent it to mother. Child flew from California to St. Louis on July 27, 1991; he was to return on September 1, 1991.

Child did not return on September 1. On September 13, mother filed a petition for writ of habeas corpus with this court. Following a brief hearing, this court ordered custody of child returned to mother until further order. Our order was conditioned on mother filing a bond, which she filed.

In addition, we consolidated the appeal of the Division of Child Support Enforcement. That appeal involves the trial court's order finding the California court lacked jurisdiction to enter the custody and support order.

II. Dissolution Proceedings

In his answer to the petition for writ of habeas corpus, father claims he is entitled to custody of child pursuant to the St. Louis County decree of dissolution granted September 26, 1986. He contends the California orders "were contrary to the Uniform Child Custody Jurisdiction Act and the Parental Kidnapping Prevention Act."

. . .

Under the California and Missouri versions of the UCCJA, a court has jurisdiction to make a child custody determination if two conditions are met. First, the child and at least one parent has a significant connection with the state; second, substantial evidence concerning the child's present or future care, protection, training, and personal relationships is available in the state. In the summer of 1986, the California court determined it had jurisdiction because mother, child, and maternal grandmother were in California, as well as "neutral third parties from the school" who could testify.

The PKPA does not grant or deny initial jurisdiction to a state. Rather, it governs only the enforcement and modification of foreign decrees and the treatment of concurrent proceedings. Coombs, *Interstate Child Custody: Jurisdiction, Recognition, and Enforcement*, 66 Minn.L.Rev. 711, 765 (1982).Thus, the PKPA did not prevent California from exercising jurisdiction.

Further, the prohibition against simultaneous proceedings applies only to the state in which proceedings are subsequently commenced; the petition in California was filed before the petition in Missouri. Thus, California was not prohibited from hearing mother's case.

Also, father contends the California court did not have personal jurisdiction over him. Mother disagrees: father was personally served and he does not contest that fact. Father's California attorney, however, did file a motion to quash service; a copy of that motion was not furnished us.

§ 9.04   JURISDICTION AND JUDGMENTS   □   839

On June 4, 1986, the court conducted a hearing on the motion to quash. Father's California attorney was present. Following the hearing, mother's attorney was directed to prepare a proposed order reflecting the June 4 proceedings. The proposed order was submitted to father's attorney for examination. On June 26, 1986, father's attorney "approved [the proposed order] as conforming to the order of the court." In the order signed July 2, 1986, the court indicates the grounds of the motion to quash were "that California should not exercise jurisdiction over the issue of custody of the minor child." Nothing before us indicates father's appearance was a "special or limited" appearance or that he challenged personal jurisdiction.

Under California procedure, a general appearance "is equivalent to personal service of summons on such party.". . . If a defendant wishes to object that the court does not have "jurisdiction over his person, he must specially appear for that purpose only;" otherwise, he waives any objection to jurisdiction. . . .Thus, from the record, it appears that father waived any objections to jurisdiction.

However, as we explain below, under the PKPA, it is immaterial to the child custody question whether California had personal jurisdiction over father. This is because Missouri was the child's home state under both the California and Missouri versions of the UCCJA, as well as the PKPA.

Missouri defines "home state" as "the state in which, immediately preceding the filing of custody proceeding, the child lived with his parents, [or] a parent . . . for at least six consecutive months; . . ." [UCCJA § 2(5).] California has a similar definition. A Missouri court has jurisdiction if Missouri is the child's home state or had been the child's home state within six months before the commencement of the proceeding. [UCCJA § 3(a)(1)(ii)]. Mother, father, and child lived in Missouri for approximately nine months from January, 1985, until mother and child moved to California on October 29, 1985. Since child had been in California approximately 51 days when mother filed her petition December 18, 1985, California was not the child's home state. Father filed his petition on January 10, 1986. Since child had been in Missouri for approximately nine months and was absent from the state only for approximately 74 days before father filed, Missouri "[h]ad been the child's home state within six months before commencement of the proceeding." [UCCJA § 3(a)(1)(ii); see also 28 U.S.C.A. 1738A(b)(4)]. Thus, the Missouri court had jurisdiction.

Mother contends the Missouri court was without jurisdiction because (1) only personal service on her was attempted, (2) the return of service was defective, and (3) the only appearance mother made was a "special appearance and objection to jurisdiction." Father admits because the return of service was defective, "such service was not sufficient to confer personal jurisdiction."

However, the parties agree that in personam jurisdiction is not necessary to dissolve a marriage or determine child custody. Mother was served with the summons and petition on July 17, 1986. Although she entered a special appearance, she did not object that the service or return of service was insufficient. The notice given mother was sufficient to satisfy the requirements of [UCCJA § 5(c)]

The question then becomes which decree is entitled to be enforced. Under the PKPA, any decree "made consistently with the provisions of [the PKPA shall be enforced] by a court of another State." § 1738A(a).

[The court quotes PKPA Sections (c) and (d).]

Section 1738A(c) imposes two conditions in order to make a court's child custody determination consistent with the PKPA, and therefore entitled to full faith and credit. First, the court must have jurisdiction under the law of the state. The California court explicitly and the Missouri court implicitly, each held it met this condition under the UCCJA; California reached this conclusion through the "significant connection" test, Missouri through the "home state" test.

Second, one of the conditions enumerated in § 1738A(c)(2) must be met. If the petition is filed in the child's home state, the second condition is satisfied. Because Missouri had been child's home state within six months of filing, the Missouri petition satisfied § 1738A(c)(2)(A).

As previously noted, California did not meet the home state requirements. Thus, we consider whether California met any other requirements for acting consistently with the PKPA as enumerated in § 1738A(c)(2).

Section 1738A(c) provides that a state's child custody determination is consistent with this section if "it appears that no other State would have jurisdiction under [the home state provisions of paragraph (A)]." California did not meet this requirement because the child had a home state—Missouri. Thus, § 1738A(c)(2)(B) is not applicable.

The third condition in this section of the PKPA applies only if the child has been (1) abandoned or (2) subjected to or threatened with mistreatment or abuse. § 1738A(c)(2)(C). Neither is applicable here.

Likewise, the fourth and fifth conditions do not apply. The fourth condition applies if "it appears that no other State would have jurisdiction under [the other subparagraphs] or another State has declined to exercise jurisdiction." § 1738A(c)(2)(D). Missouri had jurisdiction and did not decline to exercise it.

The fifth condition applies if "the court has continuing jurisdiction pursuant to subsection (d)." § 1738A(c)(2)(E). Subsection (d) applies only if the child custody determination was made consistently with the PKPA. Here, the California court had not entered a decree consistently with the requirements of the PKPA.

The PKPA requires a state to give full faith and credit only to those child custody determinations made consistently with its provisions. Under the PKPA, California would be required to give full faith and credit to the Missouri decree because the Missouri proceedings comply with the PKPA. On the other hand, the PKPA precludes Missouri and other states from giving full faith and credit to the California decree because it did not meet any of the enumerated conditions in § 1738A(c)(2).

Our conclusion is supported by decisions in other jurisdictions. [The court cites to decisions in New York, Texas, and Louisiana.]

Implicit in our holding is recognition that the PKPA preempts conflicting state law in interstate custody matters. "Congressional enactments which do not expressly exclude state legislation in the field nevertheless override state laws with which they conflict. U.S. Const. art. 1, § 8. In deciding whether state and federal laws are so inconsistent that state law must give way, we must 'determine whether, under the circumstances of this particular case [the state's] law stands as an obstacle to the accomplishment and execution of the full purposes and objectives of Congress.' " (citations omitted).

Section 1738A does not expressly exclude state legislation. However, Congress enacted the PKPA in part to avoid jurisdictional competition and to facilitate the enforcement of custody decrees in sister states. Both exist under the UCCJA. As a result, numerous states have recognized that the PKPA preempts conflicting portions of the UCCJA. . . . We recognize the preemption of the PKPA where it conflicts with our state law. To do otherwise would frustrate the sound purposes of the PKPA.

Here, Missouri was the only state which could enter a decree consistent with the PKPA unless Missouri declined to exercise jurisdiction. Missouri did not decline and its decree is enforceable throughout the United States. No other state's decree would be. To hold otherwise would result in a decree which was subject to the same problems as those entered pre-PKPA, a system Congress found was inadequate.

Mother contends, however, that [UCCJA § 6(a)] precluded the Missouri court from exercising jurisdiction. This section directs Missouri courts not to exercise jurisdiction "if, at the time of filing the petition, a proceeding concerning the custody of the child was pending in a court of another state exercising jurisdiction substantially in conformity" with the UCCJA. As a result, mother argues that Missouri was required to recognize and enforce the California decree.

Mother's contention might be tenable if we looked only at the California and Missouri UCCJA provisions, and not at the PKPA. However, some would argue that even under the UCCJA, preference to home state jurisdiction should be given. . . . Under this interpretation, California may not have been exercising jurisdiction substantially in conformity with the UCCJA.

More importantly, one of the reasons Congress adopted the PKPA was "to establish national standards under which the courts of such jurisdictions will determine . . . the effect to be given by each such jurisdiction to such decisions by the courts of other such jurisdictions." § 1738A historical and statutory notes. The national standard which Congress established requires states to give full faith and credit to child custody orders which are "consistent with the provisions" of the PKPA. The California order is not.

Mother's final argument relies on a hypothetical situation taken from Coombs' article, 66 Minn.L.Rev. at 787. The hypothetical situation has some similarity to the facts here, and Coombs says that the non-home state could "decide the child's custody without violating the federal or, presumedly, the state statute." We agree.

However, the issue before us is not whether the initial California decree violated the UCCJA or PKPA when entered. Rather, the question is whether that decree is entitled to be enforced. Under the PKPA, it is not. As Coombs says on page 788, "Although possessing jurisdiction under its own law, a court in which an initial custody proceeding is filed may consider whether the exercise of that jurisdiction would be consistent with section 1738A. *The resulting decree would be entitled under the federal statute to interstate enforcement only if made consistently with section 1738A.*" Id. at 788 (emphasis supplied).

Mother's petition for a writ of habeas corpus is denied, and we quash our temporary order.

III. Child Support Obligation

We turn now to the State's appeal. It appeals the trial court's judgment reversing a decision of the Department of Social Services. The Department ordered father to pay support arrearage of $11,118.00. The trial court found the Department's decision was "not supported by competent and substantial evidence upon the whole record [because] the decision is based upon a custody and support Order entered by a California Court without jurisdiction under the provisions of the [PKPA] and there was a lack of minimum contacts by [father] with the State of California for the California Court to obtain personal jurisdiction over [father]."

On appeal, the State urges two points. First, the trial court erred in failing to enforce the California child custody and support orders because they complied with the UCCJA. Second, the trial court erred in finding that father had a lack of minimum contacts with the State of California for the California Court to obtain personal jurisdiction over him. We consider these points together.

The PKPA precludes the enforcement of the California child custody order. Because that child custody order cannot be enforced, it follows that a child support award based on that child support order also fails. It would be incongruous for a Missouri court to enforce a California child support award when the Missouri court is prohibited from enforcing the California child custody order. Thus, that portion of the trial court's order reversing the Department of Social Services decision as it pertains to child support is affirmed.

A portion of the Department's order, however, concerned spousal support of $2,642.50. The PKPA is applicable to child custody orders; nothing in that act addresses spousal support.

We again observe that the record before us reflects father did not object in the California trial court to California's jurisdiction over him. Rather, he challenged only its jurisdiction as it pertained to child custody. As such, he waived any right he had under California law to claim that jurisdiction had not been obtained.

The Due Process Clause "does not contemplate that a state may make binding a judgment in personam against an individual . . . with which the state has no contacts, ties, or relations." *International Shoe Co. v. Washington.* Here, however, father had sufficient contacts with California.

Father and mother lived in lawful marriage with their child in California from November, 1983, to January, 1985. Mother filed her petition on October 29, 1985, and father was personally served January 13, 1986, about one year after he left California. Cf. *Kulko v. Superior Court* [p. 555, supra.]

The trial court's judgment reversing the Department's order concerning spousal support of $2,642.50 is reversed. Costs are assessed equally to father and mother.

FURTHER NOTES AND QUESTIONS

(1) Before analyzing the cases reproduced in the preceeding pages, consider again the facts of *May v. Anderson,* on the assumption that the UCCJA had been in effect in both Wisconsin and Ohio at the relevant time.

(a)

(i) The Wisconsin court would clearly have had jurisdiction in 1947 (§ 3(a)(1)(i)), provided the mother were duly notified in accordance with §§ 4 and 5;

(ii) The Ohio court would be required to recognize and enforce the Wisconsin decree, and if necessary, order the mother to surrender the children to the father (§ 13).[a]

Would this be a better result than the outcome in the actual case?

---

[a] Accord: PKPA § 1738A(a).

(b) Given the split on the Supreme Court in *May v. Anderson,* the uncertainty of the various positions, and the developments in other aspects of the law of jurisdiction and judgments, the drafters of the UCCJA evidently thought that if a case under the Act were reviewed by the Supreme Court the Act would be sustained.[b] Do you think that judgment is essentially sound? Could you regard the UCCJA, in the circumstances of the *Anderson* case, as essentially a long-arm statute?

(c) What about the modifiability aspect of the Wisconsin decree, not discussed by the majority, but stressed by Justice Frankfurter? Is there any Constitutional problem with UCCJA § 14? . . . with § 8?[c]

(d) Suppose instead of the actual facts, Mrs. Anderson (May) had taken the children to Ohio in advance of any judgment in Wisconsin, and had put them in school in Ohio. Mrs. Anderson could not (in contrast to prior law) apply for custody until six months had passed. (See §§ 3(a)(1)(i) and 2(5)). What advice would you give the father in these circumstances? See §§ 3(c) and 6(a).

(2)(a) *Brock v. District Court* is a typical case showing the effect of the UCCJA on interstate custody cases in the United States. The mother is awarded custody, with a month in the summer to be spent with the father; the father moves to a second state, and when the time for the visit is up, he declines to return the child. Either the mother seeks to enforce the decree in her favor in the second state and the father counterclaims for modification, or, as in *Brock,* the father moves first, seeking modification in his favor in the best interests of the child. Before passage of the UCCJA, F–2, where the father is domiciled, would probably have taken jurisdiction, and might well have modified the earlier award.[d] Under the UCCJA the Colorado court (F–2) did not have authority to modify the Georgia decree (§ 14), since Georgia still had jurisdiction under § 3 and had not declined to exercise it. Correspondingly, if Mrs. Brock had brought suit in Colorado for return of the child, the court could not, under § 13, have declined to exercise jurisdiction to enforce the Georgia decree.[e]

(b) Varying the facts of *Brock,* suppose that shortly after the issuance of the Georgia decree, the mother moves with her child to Tennessee. The other facts remain the same. The son spends a month in the summer in Colorado with his father, who declines to return him. Does Colorado now have an obligation to enforce the Georgia decree? . . . jurisdiction to modify?

(c) What if there were no Georgia decree, either on the facts of the actual case or the variation in (b)? How should the Colorado court deal with the father's petition for custody?

(d) Suppose as in (b), the mother moves to Tennessee with her child, shortly after the issuance of the Georgia decree granting her custody, but the father remains in Georgia. A year later the mother seeks a modification of the custody decree, for example to change the summer visitation provisions. Under the UCCJA, can she now petition the court in Tennessee for such modification? See § 3(a)(2)(i) and § 14. If your answer so far is yes, what about the PKPA? See § 1738A(f)(2) and (d). Is it clear that the federal act trumps? Is the federal solution the sounder one?

---

[b] But notice § 25, just in case.

[c] In 1980 the Supreme Court granted certiorari in a case that might have shed light on this question, but the Court dismissed the case after having granted certiorari, on the ground that the federal claim under the Full Faith and Credit Clause had not been properly raised. *Webb v. Webb,* 451 U.S. 493 (1981).

[d] See, e.g. *New York ex Rel. Halvey v. Halvey,* 330 U.S. 310 (1947), discussed in *May v. Anderson* at p. 827, *supra.*

[e] Again, accord under the PKPA, § 1738A, (a), (c)(1) and (2)(A).

(e) Incidentally, if State *B* in the preceding example exercises jurisdiction, has it violated the due process rights of the father? Or would you agree with Professor Bodenheimer that §§ 4 and 5 of the UCCJA meet the due process requirements of fairness without the need for minimum contacts of the defendant with state *B*?[f] Notice the difference between this hypothetical and *May v. Anderson*.

(3) (a) Unlike the *Brock* case, in which the upper court in Colorado saw to it that inconsistent decrees would not be issued, *Glanzner* does present just such a case. The California court conceded that the "home state" of the child, as defined, was Missouri. But by the time it came to hear the case (as contrasted with the date of filing), the California court concluded, not implausibly, that California had the most significant connection with the child, and thus that it had jurisdiction to make a custody determination under UCCJA § 3(a)(ii). Meanwhile the father had filed in Missouri, and the court there took jurisdiction as the "home state" under UCCJA § 3(a)(i). If one state must give way, and a "first to file" rule is unattractive, which one should it be?

(b) The Missouri court concludes that because the federal law prevails under the Supremacy Clause, "significant connection" gives way, and "home state" trumps. That seems to be the correct answer under the PKPA. As best you can tell from the printed record, does it yield the right result for Bradley Carl Glanzner? Is linking the definition of "home state" to the period immediately before filing for custody too rigid?

(c) The father claims that California did not have personal jurisdiction over him. That contention seems unsound, because after moving to quash service he made a general appearance in the California proceeding. Anyhow, the court says (p. 840), that question is immaterial. Is that right?

Is the Missouri court agreeing with Professor Bodenheimer, question (2)(e) *supra*? Or is the point that since California violates the Full Faith and Credit clause as implemented by the PKPA, its jurisdiction is void to begin with—at least for custody purposes? Or just that custody is like divorce—in personam jurisdiction is not necessary? The issue comes back with respect to child and spousal support, as discussed below.

(d) The mother makes the same contention in Missouri, and the father admits that service on her was not sufficient to confer personal jurisdiction.[g] Again, however, in personam jurisdiction is not necessary, as long as the notice to her satisfied UCCJA § 5(c).

(e) The Missouri court says (p. 841) that the PKPA precludes it from giving full faith and credit to the California decree. The PKPA does not say that in so many words. Is it nevertheless a correct inference? Recall Justice Frankfurter in *May v. Anderson*, arguing that F-2 (Ohio) was not required to give full faith and credit to the decree of F-1 (Wisconsin), but was not prohibited from doing so.[h]

(f) What is wrong with the mother's argument under UCCJA § 6(a), designed to prevent parallel proceedings?

---

[f] See Bodenheimer & Neely-Kvarme, *Jurisdiction over Child Custody after Shaffer and Kulko*, 12 U.C. Davis L. Rev. 229, at 240 (1979). *Accord: In re Marriage of Leonard*, 122 Cal. App. 3d 443, 459, 175 Cal. Rptr. 903, 912 (1981); *contra: Pasqualone v. Pasqualone*, 63 Ohio St. 2d 96, 406 N.E.2d 1121 (1980).

[g] Compare *Burnham v. Superior Court*, Chapter 7, p. 610, *supra*.

[h] But see also p. 831, question (1)(b), pointing out Justice Jackson's disagreement with Frankfurter on this point.

(4) The *Glanzner* case illustrates also the interplay of proceedings for divorce, child custody, child support, and spousal support, in the context where the parties are in different states.

(a) Missouri clearly has jurisdiction over the father, a resident of the state. But rather than making its own determination concerning support, the Missouri IV-D agency[i] ordered enforcement of the California support order. Is that the right thing to do in a two-state situation?

(b) The court says that because the California child custody order cannot be enforced, it follows that a child support order based on that custody order also fails. Is that persuasive? Note that the order of the Department of Social Services relates to arrearages—evidently for a period when the child lived with his mother.

(c) Though it rejects enforcement of the California child support order, the Missouri court does enforce so much of the order as relates to spousal support. What is the basis of this distinction? Has full faith and credit been transmuted into due process? or subject matter jurisdiction? or something else still?

(d) The *Glanzner* case was decided before the Uniform Interstate Family Support Act entered into effect. How would the support aspects of the *Glanzner* case come out if both California and Missouri had adopted UIFSA? See § 201(1) and (2), § 204(a), § 205(a)(1), and § 603.[j]

(5) As this book went to press (year-end 1997), the National Conference of Commissioners on Uniform State Laws was finishing up a revision of the UCCJA, to be known as the Uniform Child Custody Jurisdiction and Enforcement Act (UCCJEA). The jurisdictional provisions of the new act are designed to eliminate the differences betwen the state laws and the PKPA, establishing priority for "home state" jurisdiction, with jurisdiction based on "significant connection" available only in the absence of a home state. If there is no home state and two states have significant connection jurisdiction, the state where the action is first filed would have jurisdiction, and the other state would be required to decline jurisdiction. Do you agree with these proposed revisions?[k]

[C] The International Dimension

1. *Under the UCCJA*

Custody problems, do not, of course, respect national frontiers any more than they respect state frontiers. Particularly with regard to American servicemen who married women from nations where they were stationed, and also with regard to foreign students in the United States who married Americans, and with regard to the continental neighbors of the United States, international problems of the same kind illustrated in the cases here reproduced have been quite common. The PKPA, drafted as legislation in implementation of the Full Faith and Credit clause, could not, of course, address the question of foreign custody orders. The UCCJA, however, does address the issue. Section 23[a] states that the provisions of the Act apply to foreign custody decrees (and

---

[i] See p. 820, *supra*.

[j] Documents Supplement pp. 148–49, 160.

[k] The UCCJEA makes a number of other revisions, both with respect to foreign country custody orders (see below), and with respect to relief available for enforcement of orders, including orders to produce a child on 24 hours' notice, make-up visitation, and fees and costs to the prevailing party. Also, the new act introduces the concept of continuing exclusive jurisdiction and provides for registration of inter-state custody orders in both respects, drawing on precedents in UIFSA.

[a] Documents Supplement, p. 178.

similar orders), provided they are rendered by appropriate authorities of other nations and reasonable notice and opportunity to be heard were given. Unlike the Uniform Foreign Country Money-Judgments Act, which is by its terms applicable only in about half of the states of the Union, the UCCJA, as we saw, is applicable in all 50 states and the District of Columbia.[b] What problems do you foresee in this approach?

(b) In fact, a number of courts in the United States have applied the UCCJA, and have either declined to modify, or have enforced, foreign custody awards, even against the argument that a child born in the United States was being denied the opportunity to grow up as an American citizen.[c] Where both parents have emigrated from the nation where courts issued the initial custody order, courts in the United States have been prepared to modify foreign custody orders in application of UCCJA §§ 14(a)(1) and 3.

(c) Under the proposed revision of the UCCJA, (p. 845, question (5) *supra*), the discretion under § 23 would be replaced by a requirement that foreign custody decrees be respected.

2. *The Hague Child Abduction Convention*

The Hague Conference on Private International Law is an organization established in 1893 which has for many years conducted studies and prepared multilateral treaties and uniform laws concerned with judicial cooperation. The United States has been a member since 1964, and has, for instance, become a party to the Hague Service Convention and the Hague Evidence Convention.[d] In the mid-1970's, the Hague Conference began to address the problem of international child abduction, and in 1980 proposed a Convention on the Civil Aspects of International Child Abduction.[e] The United States became a party to that convention in 1988, following advice and consent of the Senate and passage by both Houses of Congress of implementing legislation.[f]

The Convention is somewhat different in approach from the UCCJA and PKPA, in that it focuses on custody rights, whether or not these rights have been subject to adjudication in the state of the child's habitual residence. (Art. 3 and 5). The Convention requires member states to establish a central authority to help locate an abducted child and secure its return, if possible through voluntary procedures but if necessary with the assistance of the courts. The fact that a custody order has been issued in the requested state does not, by itself, constitute a ground for refusing to return a child as required by the Convention, but, in applying the Convention, the court may take account of the reasons for the prior decision. (Art. 17).

---

[b] See also *Restatement (Third) of the Foreign Relations Law of the United States* § 485 (1987), essentially restating the UCCJA as part of the American law of recognition of foreign judgments.

[c] See, e.g. *Miller v. Superior Court of Los Angeles County,* 22 Cal. 3d 923, 987 P.2d 723 (1978); *In re Marriage of Ben Yehoshua,* 91 Cal. App. 3d 259, 154 Cal. Rptr. 80 (1979); *Taylor v. Taylor,* 278 Pa. Super. 339, 420 A.2d 570 (1980), *cert. denied* 454 U.S. 1151 (1982). See also cases cited in *Restatement of Foreign Relations Law* § 485, Reporters' Notes 4–6, as well as in 20 A.L.R.4th 677 (1983 and Supp.).

[d] Convention on the Service Abroad of Judicial and Extrajudicial Documents in Civil or Commercial Matters, Done at The Hague Nov. 15, 1965, 20 U.S.T 361, TIAS 6638, 658 UNTS 163; Convention on the Taking of Evidence Abroad in Civil or Commercial Matters, Done at The Hague March 18, 1970, 23 U.S.T. 2555, TIAS 7444, 847 UNTS 231. For exploration of these conventions, see, e.g., A. Lowenfeld, *International Litigation and Arbitration*, pp. 226-29, 809-58 (1993).

[e] T.I.A.S. No 11670, entered in force for United States July 1, 1988. Documents Supplement, pp. 184–96.

[f] The implementing legislation, as amended, is codified in 42 U.S.C. § § 11601-11610. For a thorough discussion, see Linda Silberman, *Hague International Child Abduction Convention: A Progress Report*, 57 Law & Contemp. Probs. 209 (1994).

§ 9.04   JURISDICTION AND JUDGMENTS   □   847

Since the Hague Child Abduction Convention is a treaty of the United States, an action pursuant to the Convention may be brought in federal court.[g] An idea of how the Hague Convention works may gained from the following decision of the Court of Appeals for the Sixth Circuit.

EMANUEL FRIEDRICH v. JEANA MICHELE FRIEDRICH

United States Court of Appeals
Sixth Circuit
78 F.3d 1060 (1996)

BOGGS, Circuit Judge.

For the second time, we address the application of the Hague Convention on the Civil Aspects of International Child Abduction ("the Convention") and its implementing legislation, the International Child Abduction Remedies Act ("the Act"), 42 U.S.C. § § 11601-11610, to the life of Thomas Friedrich, now age six. We affirm the district court's order that Thomas was wrongfully removed from Germany and should be returned.

I

Thomas was born in Bad Aibling, Germany, to Jeana Friedrich, an American servicewoman stationed there, and her husband, Emanuel Friedrich, a German citizen. When Thomas was two years old, his parents separated after an argument on July 27, 1991. Less than a week later, in the early morning of August 2, 1991, Mrs. Friedrich took Thomas from Germany to her family home in Ironton, Ohio, without informing Mr. Friedrich. Mr. Friedrich sought return of the child in German Family Court, obtaining an order awarding him custody on August 22. He then filed this action for the return of his son in the United States District Court for the Southern District of Ohio on September 23.

We first heard this case three years ago. *Friedrich v. Friedrich*, 983 F.2d 1396 (6th Cir. 1993) ("*Friedrich I*"). At that time, we reversed the district court's denial of Mr. Friedrich's claim for the return of his son to Germany pursuant to the Convention. We outlined the relevant law on what was then an issue of first impression in the federal appellate courts, and remanded with instructions that the district court determine whether, as a matter of German law, Mr. Friedrich was exercising custody rights to Thomas at the time of removal. We also asked the district court to decide if Mrs. Friedrich could prove any of the four affirmative defenses provided by the Convention and the Act. Thomas, meanwhile, remained with his mother and his mother's parents in Ohio.

On remand, the district court allowed additional discovery and held a new hearing. The court eventually determined that, at the time of Thomas's removal on August 1, 1991, Mr. Friedrich was exercising custody rights to Thomas under German law, or would have been exercising such rights but for the removal. The court then held that Mrs. Friedrich had not established any of the affirmative defenses available to her under the Convention. The court ordered Mrs. Friedrich

---

[g] This is confirmed by the International Child Abduction Remedies Act, note f supra, 42 U.S.C. § 11603(a). The jurisdiction is concurrent with that of the state court in the place where the child is located.

to return Thomas to Germany "forthwith," but later stayed the order, upon the posting of a bond by Mrs. Friedrich, pending the resolution of this appeal.[1]

Mrs. Friedrich's appeal raises two issues that are central to the young jurisprudence of the Hague Convention. First, what does it mean to "exercise" custody rights? Second, when can a court refuse to return a child who has been wrongfully removed from a country because return of the abducted child would result in a "grave" risk of harm?

In answering both these questions, we keep in mind two general principles inherent in the Convention and the Act, expressed in *Friedrich I*, and subsequently embraced by unanimous federal authority. First, a court in the abducted-to nation has jurisdiction to decide the merits of an abduction claim, but not the merits of the underlying custody dispute. Hague Convention, Article 19; 42 U.S.C. § 11601(b)(4); *Friedrich I*, 983 F.2d at 1400;. . . . Second, the Hague Convention is generally intended to restore the pre-abduction status quo and to deter parents from crossing borders in search of a more sympathetic court.

II

The removal of a child from the country of its habitual residence is "wrongful" under the Hague Convention if a person in that country is, or would otherwise be, exercising custody rights to the child under that country's law at the moment of removal. Hague Convention, Article 3. The plaintiff in an action for return of the child has the burden of proving the exercise of custody rights by a preponderance of the evidence. We review the district court's findings of fact for clear error and review its conclusions about American, foreign, and international law *de novo*. See Fed. R. Civ. P. 44.1 (a district court's determination of foreign law should be reviewed as a ruling on a question of law).

The district court held that a preponderance of the evidence in the record established that Mr. Friedrich was exercising custody rights over Thomas at the time of Thomas's removal. Mrs. Friedrich alleges that the district court improperly applied German law. Reviewing *de novo*, we find no error in the court's legal analysis. Custody rights "may arise in particular by operation of law or by reason of a judicial or administrative decision, or by reason of an agreement having legal effect under the law of the State." Hague Convention, Article 3. German law gives both parents equal *de jure* custody of the child, German Civil Code § 1626(1), and, with a few exceptions, this *de jure* custody continues until a competent court says otherwise. See *Currier v. Currier*, 845 F. Supp. 916, 920 (D.N.H. 1994) ("under German law both parents retain joint rights of custody until a decree has been entered limiting one parent's rights").

Mrs. Friedrich argues that Mr. Friedrich "terminated" his custody rights under German law because, during the argument on the evening of July 27, 1991, he placed Thomas's belongings and hers in the hallway outside of their apartment. The district court properly rejected the claim that these actions could end parental rights as a matter of German law. We agree. After examining the record, we are uncertain as to exactly what happened on the evening of July 27, but we do know that the events of that night were not a judicial abrogation of custody rights. Nor are we persuaded by Mrs. Friedrich's attempts to read the German Civil Code provisions stipulated

---

[1] The stay of the judge's order pending appeal, hotly contested below, is not now challenged by Mr. Friedrich. It may have been improvident. Staying the return of a child in an action under the Convention should hardly be a matter of course. The aim of the Convention is to secure prompt return of the child to the correct jurisdiction, and any unnecessary delay renders the subsequent return more difficult for the child, and subsequent adjudication more difficult for the foreign court.

to by the parties in such a way as to create the ability of one parent to terminate his or her custody rights extrajudicially.[2]

Mrs. Friedrich also argues that, even if Mr. Friedrich had custody rights under German law, he was not exercising those custody rights as contemplated by the Hague Convention. She argues that, since custody rights include the care for the person and property of the child, Mr. Friedrich was not exercising custody rights because he was not paying for or taking care of the child during the brief period of separation in Germany.

The Hague Convention does not define "exercise." As judges in a common law country, we can easily imagine doing so ourselves. One might look to the law of the foreign country to determine if custody rights existed de jure, and then develop a test under the general principles of the Hague Convention to determine what activities—financial support, visitation—constitute sufficient exercise of de jure rights. The question in our immediate case would then be: "was Mr. Friedrich's single visit with Thomas and plans for future visits with Thomas sufficient exercise of custodial rights for us to justify calling the removal of Thomas wrongful?" One might even approach a distinction between the exercise of "custody" rights and the exercise of "access" or "visitation" rights. If Mr. Friedrich, who has *de jure* custody, was not exercising sufficient *de facto* custody, Thomas's removal would not be wrongful.[3]

We think it unwise to attempt any such project. Enforcement of the Convention should not to be made dependent on the creation of a common law definition of "exercise." The only acceptable solution, in the absence of a ruling from a court in the country of habitual residence, is to liberally find "exercise" whenever a parent with *de jure* custody rights keeps, or seeks to keep, any sort of regular contact with his or her child.

We see three reasons for this broad definition of "exercise." First, American courts are not well suited to determine the consequences of parental behavior under the law of a foreign country. It is fairly easy for the courts of one country to determine whether a person has custody rights under the law of another country. It is also quite possible for a court to determine if an order by a foreign court awards someone "custody" rights, as opposed to rights of "access." Far more difficult is the task of deciding, prior to a ruling by a court in the abducted-from country, if a parent's custody rights should be ignored because he or she was not acting sufficiently like a custodial parent. A foreign court, if at all possible, should refrain from making such policy-oriented decisions concerning the application of German law to a child whose habitual residence is, or was, Germany.

Second, an American decision about the adequacy of one parent's exercise of custody rights is dangerously close to forbidden territory: the merits of the custody dispute. The German court in this case is perfectly capable of taking into account Mr. Friedrich's behavior during the August

---

[2] Mrs. Friedrich cites German Civil Code § 1629, which says that a parent who exercises parental care alone can also represent the child in legal matters alone. Obviously, the ability of one parent to "represent" the child does not imply that the other parent has no custody rights. Mrs. Friedrich also cites German Civil Code § 1631, which says that the Family Court, if petitioned, can assist the parents in providing parental care. We have no idea how this provision, which is essentially no more than a grant of jurisdiction to appoint and direct a family services officer, can support Mrs. Friedrich's claim that "a German parent can certainly relinquish custody or parental rights absent a judicial determination."

[3] Article 21 of the Hague Convention instructs signatory countries to protect the "rights of access" of non-custodial parents to their children. Courts have yet to address the question whether Article 21 implies that a custodial parent can remove a child from its country of habitual residence without the permission of a parent whose rights that country's courts have expressly limited to "visitation."

1991 separation, and the German court presumably will tailor its custody order accordingly. A decision by an American court to deny return to Germany because Mr. Friedrich did not show sufficient attention or concern for Thomas's welfare would preclude the German court from addressing these issues—and the German court may well resolve them differently.

Third, the confusing dynamics of quarrels and informal separations make it difficult to assess adequately the acts and motivations of a parent. An occasional visit may be all that is available to someone left, by the vagaries of marital discord, temporarily without the child. Often the child may be avoided, not out of a desire to relinquish custody, but out of anger, pride, embarrassment, or fear, vis-à-vis the other parent.[5] Reading too much into a parent's behavior during these difficult times could be inaccurate and unfair. Although there may be situations when a long period of unexplainable neglect of the child could constitute non-exercise of otherwise valid custody rights under the Convention, as a general rule, any attempt to maintain a somewhat regular relationship with the child should constitute "exercise." This rule leaves the full resolution of custody issues, as the Convention and common sense indicate, to the courts of the country of habitual residence.

We are well aware that our approach requires a parent, in the event of a separation or custody dispute, to seek permission from the other parent or from the courts before taking a child out of the country of its habitual residence. Any other approach allows a parent to pick a "home court" for the custody dispute *ex parte*, defeating a primary purpose of the Convention. We believe that, where the reason for removal is legitimate, it will not usually be difficult to obtain approval from either the other parent or a foreign court. Furthermore, as the case for removal of the child in the custody of one parent becomes more compelling, approval (at least the approval of a foreign court) should become easier to secure.

Mrs. Friedrich argues that our approach cannot adequately cope with emergency situations that require the child and parent to leave the country. In her case, for example, Mrs. Friedrich claims that removal of Thomas to Ohio was necessary because she could no longer afford to have the child stay at the army base, and Mr. Friedrich refused to provide it shelter. Examining the record, we seriously doubt that Mr. Friedrich would have refused to lodge Thomas at his expense in Germany. In any event, even if an emergency forces a parent to take a child to a foreign country, any such emergency cannot excuse the parent from returning the child to the jurisdiction once return of the child becomes safe. Nor can an emergency justify a parent's refusal to submit the child to the authority of the foreign court for resolution of custody matters, including the question of the appropriate temporary residence of the child.

We therefore hold that, if a person has valid custody rights to a child under the law of the country of the child's habitual residence, that person cannot fail to "exercise" those custody rights under the Hague Convention short of acts that constitute clear and unequivocal abandonment of the child.[6] Once it determines that the parent exercised custody rights in any manner, the

---

[5] When Mrs. Friedrich took Thomas and her belongings from the family apartment on the morning of July 28, she was accompanied by some friends from work: soldiers of the United States Army. Mr. Friedrich testified that he was "intimidated" by the presence of the soldiers, and discouraged from making a stronger objection to the removal of his child.

[6] The situation would be different if the country of habitual residence had a legal rule regarding the exercise of custody rights clearly tied to the Hague concept of international removal. If, for example, Germany had a law stating that, for the purposes of the Convention, mere visitation without financial support during a period of informal separation does not constitute the "exercise" of custody rights, we would, of course, be bound to apply that law in this case.

court should stop—completely avoiding the question whether the parent exercised the custody rights well or badly. These matters go to the merits of the custody dispute and are, therefore, beyond the subject matter jurisdiction of the federal courts.

In this case, German law gave Mr. Friedrich custody rights to Thomas. The facts before us clearly indicate that he attempted to exercise these rights during the separation from his wife. Mr. and Mrs. Friedrich argued during the evening of July 27, 1991, and separated on the morning of July 28. Mrs. Friedrich left with her belongings and Thomas. She stayed on the army base with the child for four days. Mr. Friedrich telephoned Mrs. Friedrich on July 29 to arrange a visit with Thomas, and spent the afternoon of that day with his son. Mr. and Mrs. Friedrich met on August 1 to talk about Thomas and their separation. The parties dispute the upshot of this conversation. Mrs. Friedrich says that Mr. Friedrich expressed a general willingness that Thomas move to America with his mother. Mr. Friedrich denies this. It is clear, however, that the parties did agree to immediate visitations of Thomas by Mr. Friedrich, scheduling the first such visit for August 3. Shortly after midnight on August 2, Mrs. Friedrich took her son and, without informing her husband,[7] left for America by airplane.

Because Mr. Friedrich had custody rights to Thomas as a matter of German law, and did not clearly abandon those rights prior to August 1, the removal of Thomas without his consent was wrongful under the Convention, regardless of any other considerations about Mr. Friedrich's behavior during the family's separation in Germany.

III

Once a plaintiff establishes that removal was wrongful, the child must be returned unless the defendant can establish one of four defenses. Two of these defenses can be established by a preponderance of the evidence: the proceeding was commenced more than one year after the removal of the child and the child has become settled in his or her new environment, Hague Convention, Article 12; or, the person seeking return of the child consented to or subsequently acquiesced in the removal or retention, Hague Convention, Article 13a. The other two defenses must be shown by clear and convincing evidence: there is a grave risk that the return of the child would expose it to physical or psychological harm, Hague Convention, Article 13b; or, the return of the child "would not be permitted by the fundamental principles of the requested State relating to the protection of human rights and fundamental freedoms," Hague Convention, Article 20.[8]

All four of these exceptions are "narrow." They are not a basis for avoiding return of a child merely because an American court believes it can better or more quickly resolve a dispute. In fact, a federal court retains, and should use when appropriate, the discretion to return a child, despite the existence of a defense, if return would further the aims of the Convention.

---

[7] Q. You didn't call your husband, Mrs. Friedrich, because you didn't want him to know you were leaving; isn't that the reason?

A. Yes it is.

Transcript of October 16, 1991, Proceedings at 36.

[8] The situation changes somewhat when the child is older. The Hague Convention allows a court in the abducted-to country to "refuse to order the return of the child if it finds that the child objects to being returned and has attained an age and degree of maturity at which it is appropriate to take account of its views." Hague Convention, Article 13.

Mrs. Friedrich alleges that she proved by clear and convincing evidence in the proceedings below that the return of Thomas to Germany would cause him grave psychological harm. Mrs. Friedrich testified that Thomas has grown attached to family and friends in Ohio. She also hired an expert psychologist who testified that returning Thomas to Germany would be traumatic and difficult for the child, who was currently happy and healthy in America with his mother.

> [Thomas] definitely would experience the loss of his mother . . . if he were to be removed to Germany. That would be a considerable loss. And there then would be the probabilities of anger both towards his mother, who it might appear that she has abandoned him [sic], and towards the father for creating that abandonment. [These feelings] could be plenty enough springboard for other developmental or emotional restrictions which could include nightmares, antisocial behavior, a whole host of anxious-type behavior.

Blaske Deposition at 28-29.

If we are to take the international obligations of American courts with any degree of seriousness, the exception to the Hague Convention for grave harm to the child requires far more than the evidence that Mrs. Friedrich provides. Mrs. Friedrich alleges nothing more than adjustment problems that would attend the relocation of most children. There is no allegation that Mr. Friedrich has ever abused Thomas. The district court found that the home that Mr. Friedrich has prepared for Thomas in Germany appears adequate to the needs of any young child. The father does not work long hours, and the child's German grandmother is ready to care for the child when the father cannot. There is nothing in the record to indicate that life in Germany would result in any permanent harm or unhappiness.

Furthermore, even if the home of Mr. Friedrich were a grim place to raise a child in comparison to the pretty, peaceful streets of Ironton, Ohio, that fact would be irrelevant to a federal court's obligation under the Convention. We are not to debate the relevant virtues of Batman and Max und Moritz, Wheaties and Milchreis. The exception for grave harm to the child is not license for a court in the abducted-to country to speculate on where the child would be happiest. That decision is a custody matter, and reserved to the court in the country of habitual residence.

Mrs. Friedrich advocates a wide interpretation of the grave risk of harm exception that would reward her for violating the Convention. A removing parent must not be allowed to abduct a child and then—when brought to court—complain that the child has grown used to the surroundings to which they were abducted.[9] Under the logic of the Convention, it is the abduction that causes the pangs of subsequent return. The disruption of the usual sense of attachment that arises during most long stays in a single place with a single parent should not be a "grave" risk of harm for the purposes of the Convention.

In thinking about these problems, we acknowledge that courts in the abducted-from country are as ready and able as we are to protect children. If return to a country, or to the custody of a parent in that country, is dangerous, we can expect that country's courts to respond accordingly. And if Germany really is a poor place for young Thomas to grow up, as Mrs. Friedrich contends, we can expect the German courts to recognize that and award her custody in America. When we trust the court system in the abducted-from country, the vast majority of claims of harm—those that do not rise to the level of gravity required by the Convention—evaporate.

---

[9] We forgo the temptation to compare this behavior to the standard definition of "chutzpah." See A. Kozinski & E. Volokh, *Lawsuit, Shmawsuit*, 103 Yale L.J. 463, 467 (1993).

The international precedent available supports our restrictive reading of the grave harm exception. In *Thomson v. Thomson*, 119 D.L.R. 4th 253 (Can. 1994), the Supreme Court of Canada held that the exception applies only to harm "that also amounts to an intolerable situation." Id. at 286. The Court of Appeal of the United Kingdom has held that the harm required is "something greater than would normally be expected on taking a child away from one parent and passing him to another." *In re A.*, 1 F.L.R. 365, 372 (Eng. C.A. 1988). And other circuit courts in America have followed this reasoning in cases decided since *Friedrich I.* . . . Finally, we are instructed by the following observation by the United States Department of State concerning the grave risk of harm exception.

> This provision was not intended to be used by defendants as a vehicle to litigate (or relitigate) the child's best interests. Only evidence directly establishing the existence of a grave risk that would expose the child to physical or emotional harm or otherwise place the child in an *intolerable* situation is material to the court's determination. The person opposing the child's return must show that the risk to the child is grave, not merely serious.

A review of deliberations on the Convention reveals that "intolerable situation" was not intended to encompass return to a home where money is in short supply, or where educational or other opportunities are more limited than in the requested State. An example of an "intolerable situation" is one in which a custodial parent sexually abuses the child. If the other parent removes or retains the child to safeguard it against further victimization, and the abusive parent then petitions for the child's return under the Convention, the court may deny the petition. Such action would protect the child from being returned to an "intolerable situation" and subjected to a grave risk of psychological harm.

Public Notice 957, 51 FR 10494, 10510 (March 26, 1986) (emphasis added).

For all of these reasons, we hold that the district court did not err by holding that "the record in the instant case does not demonstrate by clear and convincing evidence that Thomas will be exposed to a grave risk of harm." Although it is not necessary to resolve the present appeal, we believe that a grave risk of harm for the purposes of the Convention can exist in only two situations. First, there is a grave risk of harm when return of the child puts the child in imminent danger prior to the resolution of the custody dispute—e.g., returning the child to a zone of war, famine, or disease.

Second, there is a grave risk of harm in cases of serious abuse or neglect, or extraordinary emotional dependence, when the court in the country of habitual residence, for whatever reason, may be incapable or unwilling to give the child adequate protection. Psychological evidence of the sort Mrs. Friedrich introduced in the proceeding below is only relevant if it helps prove the existence of one of these two situations.

IV

Mrs. Friedrich also claims that the district court erred in ordering Thomas's return because Mrs. Friedrich proved by a preponderance of the evidence that Mr. Friedrich (i) consented to, and (ii) subsequently acquiesced in, the removal of Thomas to America.

Mrs. Friedrich bases her claim of consent to removal on statements that she claims Mr. Friedrich made to her during their separation. Mr. Friedrich flatly denies that he made these statements. The district court was faced with a choice as to whom it found more believable in a factual dispute. There is nothing in the record to suggest that the court's decision to believe

Mr. Friedrich, and hold that he "did not exhibit an intention or a willingness to terminate his parental rights," was clearly erroneous. In fact, Mr. Friedrich's testimony is strongly supported by the circumstances of the removal of Thomas—most notably the fact that Mrs. Friedrich did not inform Mr. Friedrich that she was departing. Supra n.7. The deliberately secretive nature of her actions is extremely strong evidence that Mr. Friedrich would not have consented to the removal of Thomas. For these reasons, we hold that the district court did not abuse its discretion in finding that Mrs. Friedrich took Thomas to America without Mr. Friedrich's consent.

Mrs. Friedrich bases her claim of subsequent acquiescence on a statement made by Mr. Friedrich to one of her commanding officers, Captain Michael Farley, at a cocktail party on the military base after Mrs. Friedrich had left with Thomas. Captain Farley, who cannot date the conversation exactly, testified that:

> During the conversation, Mr. Friedrich indicated that he was not seeking custody of the child, because he didn't have the means to take care of the child.

Farley Deposition at 13. Mr. Friedrich denies that he made this statement. The district court made no specific finding regarding this fact. We believe that the statement to Captain Farley, even if it was made, is insufficient evidence of subsequent acquiesence. Subsequent acquiescence requires more than an isolated statement to a third-party. Each of the words and actions of a parent during the separation are not to be scrutinized for a possible waiver of custody rights. Although we must decide the matter without guidance from previous appellate court decisions, we believe that acquiescence under the convention requires either: an act or statement with the requisite formality, such as testimony in a judicial proceeding; a convincing written renunciation of rights; or a consistent attitude of acquiescence over a significant period of time.

By August 22, 1991, twenty-one days after the abduction, Mr. Friedrich had secured a German court order awarding him custody of Thomas. He has resolutely sought custody of his son since that time. It is by these acts, not his casual statements to third parties, that we will determine whether or not he acquiesced to the retention of his son in America. Since Mrs. Friedrich has not introduced evidence of a formal renunciation or a consistent attitude of acquiesence over a significant period of time, the judgment of the district court on this matter was not erroneous.

V

The district court's order that Thomas be immediately returned to Germany is AFFIRMED, and the district court's stay of that order pending appeal is VACATED.

Because Thomas's return to Germany is already long-overdue, we order, pursuant to Fed. R. App. P. 41(a), that our mandate issue forthwith.

---

§ 9.05 Marriage, Public Policy and Conflict of Laws

In a sense the presentation in this chapter has been backwards, in focusing first on divorce, rather than on marriage. That is because divorce involves judgments or decrees, and often questions of judicial jurisdiction, whereas marriage is typically a consensual transaction in which the state has only a recording, and not an adjudicating function. Of course the *Williams, Sherrer* and *Rosenstiel* cases, among others, involved attacks on marriages, but in each of these cases the vulnerability of the marriage depended on a challenge to a prior divorce. What about a challenge to the marriage itself, independent of any prior marriage?

The classical cases of this type involved challenges based on the age of one or both parties or on their blood relationship. Recently a new type of marriage, and fierce response thereto, have occupied courts, the Congress and the press—marriage between persons of the same sex.

A full discussion of these issues would go well beyond the scope and focus of this volume. But a brief look affords an opportunity for a somewhat different view of public policy from the views of that elusive concept up to now.

[A] Capacity to Marry

One of the least controversial principles of conflict of laws is that the validity of a marriage is governed by the place of celebration. For centuries, English couples have gotten married in Gretna Green, just over the border in Scotland; German couples have gone to Tonder, just across the border in Denmark, and American couples to Elkton, Maryland, a few miles from the borders with Pennsylvania, Delaware, and New Jersey, and not far from New York and the New England states.

Generally, "forum selection" in this context has been upheld, but not always. Should it matter whether the challenge in state *A* of a marriage in state *B* is raised soon after the celebration of the marriage or many years later? Whether the challenge is to the marriage itself, as contrasted with a question of inheritance, or, say, social security benefits?

In re MAY'S ESTATE.

New York Court of Appeals
305 N.Y. 486, 114 N.E.2d 4 (1953)

LEWIS, Chief Judge.

In this proceeding, involving the administration of the estate of Fannie May, deceased, we are to determine whether the marriage in 1913 between the respondent Sam May and the decedent, who was his niece by the half blood—which marriage was celebrated in Rhode Island, where concededly such marriage is valid—is to be given legal effect in New York where statute law declares incestuous and void a marriage between uncle and niece.

The question thus presented arises from proof of the following facts: The petitioner Alice May Greenberg, one of six children born of the Rhode Island marriage of Sam and Fannie May, petitioned in 1951 for letters of administration of the estate of her mother Fannie May, who had died in 1945. Thereupon, the respondent Sam May, who asserts the validity of his marriage to the decedent, filed an objection to the issuance to petitioner of such letters of administration upon the ground that he is the surviving husband of the decedent and accordingly, under section 118 of the Surrogate's Court Act, he has the paramount right to administer her estate. Contemporaneously with, and in support of the objection filed by Sam May, his daughter Sirel Lenrow and his sons Harry May and Morris B. May who are children of the challenged marriage filed objections to the issuance of letters of administration to their sister, the petitioner, and by such objections consented that letters of administration be issued to their father Sam May.

The petitioner, supported by her sisters Ruth Weisbrout and Evelyn May, contended throughout this proceeding that her father is not the surviving spouse of her mother because, although their marriage was valid in Rhode Island, the marriage never had validity in New York where they were then resident and where they retained their residence until the decedent's death.

The record shows that . . . the respondent Sam May . . . came to New York in December, 1912, and within a month thereafter he and the decedent—both of whom were adherents of the Jewish faith—went to Providence, Rhode Island, where, on January 21, 1913, they entered into a ceremonial marriage performed by and at the home of a Jewish rabbi. The certificate issued upon that marriage gave the age of each party as twenty-six years and the residence of each as "New York, N. Y." Two weeks after their marriage in Rhode Island the respondent May and the decedent returned to Ulster County New York, where they lived as man and wife for thirty-two years until the decedent's death in 1945. Meantime the six children were born who are parties to this proceeding.

A further significant item of proof to which more particular reference will be made was the fact that in Rhode Island on January 21, 1913, the date of the marriage here involved, there were effective statutes which prohibited, the marriage of an uncle and a niece, excluding, however, those instances of which the present case is one where the marriage solemnized is between persons of the Jewish faith within the degrees of affinity and consanguinity allowed by their religion.

In Surrogate's Court, where letters of administration were granted to the petitioner, the Surrogate ruled that although the marriage of Sam May and the decedent in Rhode Island in 1913 was valid in that State, such marriage was not only void in New York as opposed to natural law but is contrary to the provisions of subdivision 3 of section 5 of the Domestic Relations Law. Accordingly the Surrogate concluded that Sam May did not qualify in this jurisdiction for letters of administration as the surviving spouse of the decedent.

At the Appellate Division the order of the Surrogate was reversed on the law. . . . The case comes to us upon appeal as of right by the petitioner and her two sisters Ruth Weisbrout and Evelyn May.

We regard the law as settled that, subject to two exceptions presently to be considered, and in the absence of a statute expressly regulating within the domiciliary State marriages solemnized abroad, the legality of a marriage between persons sui juris is to be determined by the law of the place where it is celebrated.

The statute of New York upon which the appellants rely is subdivision 3 of section 5 of the Domestic Relations Law which, insofar as relevant to our problem, provides:

§ 5. *Incestuous and void marriages*

A marriage is incestuous and void whether the relatives are legitimate or illegitimate between either:

. . .

3. An uncle and niece or an aunt and nephew.

If a marriage prohibited by the foregoing provisions of this section be solemnized it shall be void, and the parties thereto shall each be fined not less than fifty nor more than one hundred dollars and may, in the discretion of the court in addition to said fine, be imprisoned for a term not exceeding six months. Any person who shall knowingly and wilfully solemnize such marriage, or procure or aid in the solemnization of the same, shall be deemed guilty of a misdemeanor and shall be fined or imprisoned in like manner.

Although the New York statute quoted above declares to be incestuous and void a marriage between an uncle and a niece and imposes penal measures upon the parties thereto, it is important to note that the statute does not by express terms regulate a marriage solemnized in another State where, as in our present case, the marriage was concededly legal. . . .

As section 5 of the New York Domestic Relations Law does not expressly declare void a marriage of its domiciliaries solemnized in a foreign State where such marriage is valid, the statute's scope should not be extended by judicial construction. Indeed, had the Legislature been so disposed it could have declared by appropriate enactment that marriages contracted in another State which if entered into here would be void shall have no force in this State. Although examples of such legislation are not wanting, we find none in New York which serve to give subdivision 3 of section 5 of the Domestic Relations Law extraterritorial effectiveness. Accordingly, as to the first exception to the general rule that a marriage valid where performed is valid everywhere, we conclude that, absent any New York statute expressing clearly the Legislature's intent to regulate within this State marriages of its domiciliaries solemnized abroad, there is no "positive law" in this jurisdiction which serves to interdict the 1913 marriage in Rhode Island of the respondent Sam May and the decedent.

As to the application of the second exception to the marriage here involved between persons of the Jewish faith whose kinship was not in the direct ascending or descending line of consanguinity and who were not brother and sister we conclude that such marriage, solemnized, as it was, in accord with the ritual of the Jewish faith in a State whose legislative body has declared such a marriage to be "good and valid in law," was not offensive to the public sense of morality to a degree regarded generally with abhorrence and thus was not within the inhibitions of natural law.

DESMOND, Judge (dissenting).

It is fundamental that every State has the right to determine the marital status of its own citizens. Exercising that right, New York has declared in section 5 of the Domestic Relations Law that a marriage between uncle and niece is incestuous, void and criminal. Such marriages, while not within the Levitical forbidden degrees of the Old Testament, have been condemned by public opinion for centuries (see 1 Bishop on Marriage, Divorce and Separation, § 738), and are void, by statute in (it would seem) forty-seven of the States of the Union (all except Georgia, and except, also, that Rhode Island, one of the forty-seven, exempts from its local statute "any marriage which shall be solemnized among the Jews, within the degrees of affinity or consanguinity allowed by their religion.") It is undisputed here that this uncle and niece were both domiciled in New York in 1913, when they left New York for the sole purpose of going to Rhode Island to be married there, and that they were married in that State conformably to its laws. . .and immediately returned to New York and ever afterwards resided in this State. That Rhode Island marriage, between two New York residents, was, in New York, absolutely void for any and all purposes, by positive New York law which declares a strong public policy of this State. See Penal Law, § 1110.[a]

The general rule that "a marriage valid where solemnized is valid everywhere" (see Restatement [First], Conflict of Laws, § 121) does not apply. To that rule there is a proviso or exception, recognized, it would seem, by all the States, as follows: "unless contrary to the prohibitions of natural law or the express prohibitions of a statute." Section 132 of the Restatement of Conflict

---

[a] Present N.Y. Penal Law § 255.25, *Incest*.

of Laws states the rule apparently followed throughout America: "A marriage which is against the law of the state of domicil of either party, though the requirements of the law of the state of celebration have been complied with, will be invalid everywhere in the following cases: . . . (b) incestuous marriage between persons so closely related that their marriage is contrary to a strong public policy of the domicil". . . .

. . . Section 5 of the Domestic Relations Law, the one we are concerned with here, lists the marriages which are 'incestuous and void' in New York, as being those between parent and child, brother and sister, uncle and niece, and aunt and nephew. All such misalliances are incestuous, and all, equally, are void. The policy, language, meaning and validity of the statute are beyond dispute. It should be enforced by the courts.

CONWAY, DYE, FULD and FROESSEL, JJ., concur with LEWIS, C.J.

DESMOND, J., dissents in opinion.

WILKINS v. ZELICHOWSKI

Supreme Court of New Jersey.
26 N.J. 370, 140 A.2d 65 (1958)

JACOBS, J.

. . . [P]laintiff's complaint . . . sought an annulment of her marriage to the defendant. . . .

The plaintiff and the defendant were domiciled in New Jersey as were their respective parents. They ran away from New Jersey to marry and they chose Indiana because they believed "it was the quickest place." The Indiana statutes provide that "females of the age of sixteen" are capable of marriage. . . . After their marriage in Indiana on April 23, 1954 the plaintiff and defendant returned immediately to New Jersey where they set up their home. On February 22, 1955 the plaintiff bore the defendant's child. On April 22, 1955 the defendant, having been convicted on several independent charges of automobile theft, was sent to Bordentown Reformatory where he was still confined at the time of the hearing in the Chancery Division. On January 4, 1956 the plaintiff filed her annulment complaint under [the statute] which provides that a judgment of nullity may be rendered on the wife's application upon a showing that she was under the age of 18 years at the time of her marriage and that the marriage has not been "confirmed by her after arriving at such age;" the statute also provides that where a child has been born there shall be no judgment of nullity unless the court is of the opinion that the judgment "will not be against the best interests of the child." Although the defendant was duly served he did not file any answer and he chose not to contest the plaintiff's proceeding.

The plaintiff's evidence adequately established that she was 16 years of age when she was married and that she did not confirm her marriage after she had reached 18 years of age and the Chancery Division expressly found that an annulment would be "for the best interests of the child;" nevertheless it declined to grant the relief sought by the plaintiff on the ground that the marriage was valid in Indiana and should therefore, under principles of the conflict of laws, not be nullified by a New Jersey court because of the plaintiff's nonage. In reaching the same result the Appellate Division recognized that the Chancery Division had ample power to nullify the Indiana marriage of the New Jersey domiciliaries, but expressed the view that comity dictated that it should not take such action unless there was an imperative New Jersey policy (which it did not find) against marriages of 16-year-old females.

. . .

The vigor of New Jersey's policy against marriages by persons under the prescribed age is evidenced not only by the breadth of the statutory language but also by the judicial decisions. . . .

It is undisputed that if the marriage between the plaintiff and the defendant had taken place here, the public policy of New Jersey would be applicable and the plaintiff would be entitled to the annulment; and it seems clear to us that if New Jersey's public policy is to remain at all meaningful it must be considered equally applicable though their marriage took place in Indiana. While that State was interested in the formal ceremonial requirements of the marriage it had no interest whatever in that marital status of the parties. Indeed, New Jersey was the only State having any interest in that status, for both parties were domiciled in New Jersey before and after the marriage and their matrimonial domicile was established here. The purpose in having the ceremony take place in Indiana was to evade New Jersey's marriage policy and we see no just or compelling reason for permitting it to succeed.

We are not here concerned with a collateral attack on an Indiana marriage or with a direct attack on an Indiana marriage between domiciliaries of Indiana or some state other than New Jersey. We are concerned only with a direct and timely proceeding, authorized by the New Jersey statute by an underage wife for annulment of an Indiana marriage between parties who have at all times been domiciled in New Jersey. We are satisfied that at least in this situation the strong public policy of New Jersey requires that the annulment be granted. The annulment will not render the plaintiff's child illegitimate and, as the Chancery Division found, it will be for his best interests. The annulment will also serve the plaintiff's best interests for it will tend to reduce the tragic consequences of her immature conduct and unfortunate marriage. The Legislature has clearly fixed the State's policy in her favor and has granted her the right to apply for a judgment nullifying her marriage; we know of no considerations of equity or justice or overriding principles of the law which would lead us to deprive her of the relief she seeks under the circumstances she presents.

Reversed.

In re DALIP SINGH BIR'S ESTATE.

*District Court of Appeal, Third District, California.
83 Cal.App.2d 256, 188 P.2d 499 (1948)*

ADAMS, Presiding Justice.

Dalip Singh Bir, a native of India, died intestate in San Joaquin County on April 18, 1945. . . . On April 4, 1947, two women named Harnam Kaur and Jiwi, both residents of India, joined in a petition to determine heirship, alleging in their petition:

'That your petitioners were, at the time of the death of the deceased herein, the legally wedded wives of said deceased, having lawfully married said deceased in the Punjab over 50 years ago whilst all parties were domiciled in Punjab Province, British India, according to the law and manner of the Jat community, in which province and community said marriages are lawful and valid. As said widows of deceased, petitioners are entitled to distribution of his estate.'

Their petition further alleged that the residue of the estate consists of approximately $1,450 in cash and that in India petitioners would be entitled to share equally in the estate.

The trial court found that decedent, while domiciled in the Punjab Province of India, there married and was possessed of two wives, the petitioners above named, and that petitioners were legal spouses of decedent under the laws of the Punjab Province of India; that thereafter decedent emigrated to the United States and established residence in California, and that the money belonging to his estate was community property; that neither of said marriages had been dissolved prior to decedent's death but that no satisfactory proof was introduced as to which of the marriages was first performed.

Upon these findings of fact the trial court concluded that under the laws of California and the public policy thereof, only the first wife of decedent can be recognized as his legal widow. It therefore entered an order continuing the matter awaiting proof as to which of the marriages was first performed and which of the two petitioners was the initial wife of decedent. From that order the two wives have appealed.

Appellants rely on the provisions of section 63 of the Civil Code which reads:

> All marriages contracted without this state, which would be valid by the laws of the country in which the same were contracted are valid in this state.

[The court reviews American, Canadian, and British cases and scholarly writing.]

The decision of the trial court was influenced by the rule of "public policy;" but that rule, it would seem, would apply only if decedent had attempted to cohabit with his two wives in California. Where only the question of descent of property is involved, "public policy" is not affected. It was so held in the *Succession of Caballero,* [24 La. Ann. 573 (1872)]. On the authority of Beale on Conflict of Laws [vol. II, p. 666 (1935)], *Yew v. Attorney General of British Columbia* [1 D.L.R. 1166 (B.C. Ct. App. 1923)], and *Succession of Caballero, supra*, the two wives of decedent should share equally in the money in question. No case has been found that is opposed to those authorities. True, there are cases holding invalid polygamous marriages entered into in places where such marriages are legal, but in each such case found, all the parties were living and no question of succession to property was considered. Therefore, it would seem that the above cited authorities which actually considered the right of succession and granted such succession in cases growing out of marriages legal where entered into but illegal in the place where probate proceedings are being had, are controlling. 'Public policy" would not be affected by dividing the money equally between the two wives, particularly since there is no contest between them and they are the only interested parties.

The order appealed from is therefore reversed with directions to the trial court to enter a decree in accordance with the views herein expressed.

NOTES AND QUESTIONS

(1)(a) In the tort and contract cases in chapters 1, 3 and 4, "public policy" was often, as Paulsen and Sovern wrote,[b] a substitute for analysis. Does public policy acquire more meaning in the context of marriage?[c]

(b) What about "state interest"? "Significant contacts"? "Reasonable expectations"?

(c) Professor Willis Reese, the Reporter of the Restatement (Second) of Conflict of Laws (and model for one of the protagonists in the Adams v. Knickerbocker series) wrote:

> The traditional view . . . is that a marriage is either good or bad for all purposes. The rule for selecting the law governing validity is heavily weighted in favor of validation and in many respects is flexible in operation. It is commonly assumed, however, that the rule should be applied without regard to the issue involved. To do otherwise would be inconsistent with the notions that marriage is a status and that the question of a marriage's validity should be determined independently of any other issue. To do so, on the other hand, would be inconsistent with the modern American view that at least in many areas, such as torts and contracts, choice of the applicable law should be made in the light of the particular issue. . . .[d]

Reese approves of the decision in all three cases here reproduced. Do you agree?

(2)(a) Both *May* and *Zelichowski* accept the principle that a marriage valid under the law of the state of celebration is valid elsewhere except . . . . Is the public policy against under-age marriage stronger than the policy against incest? Or is the critical issue simply that the court in *Zelichowski* is looking to the future while the court in *May* is looking to the past?

(b) Suppose we turn the cases around. Fannie May, six months after the Rhode Island wedding, applies for annulment in New York; Shirley Wilkins remains married to Stephen Zelichowski for 32 years, then dies, and a dispute arises between Stephen and one of their children about who should administer her estate. Do both cases come out the other way?

(3)(a) The court in *Dalip Singh Bir* quotes with approval the following illustration from the first Restatement:

> A, domiciled in state X, validly marries B and C in X. By the law of Y, a polygamous marriage is void. A brings B and C to state Y; Y may refuse to permit him to cohabit with them. A and B die. Y may grant a widow's allowance to C.[e]

Is that persuasive?

(b) Does it follow, as in the actual case, that if only A dies, B and C split whatever benefits are derived from A's death?

---

[b] Ch. 1, p. 39 question (4).

[c] Recall the discussion in *Lilienthal v. Kaufman*, the spendthrift trust case (Ch. 4, p. 232 at p. 236), in which the Oregon Supreme Court reports that it did not invalidate an out-of-state marriage by a spendthrift concluded without his guardian's consent, but did invalidate an out-of-state marriage concluded before the expiration of the no-remarriage period made part of an Oregon decree of divorce.

[d] Willis L.M. Reese, General Course on Private International Law, 150 Recueil des Cours, Hague Academy Int'l Law 1 at 165 (1976-II).

[e] ALI, *Restatement (First) of Conflict of Laws*, § 134, Illustration 1 (1934).

(c) Note that the report in the *Dalip Singh Bir* case does not make clear whether the wives remained in India or accompanied their husband to California. Should that make any difference? What if one wife came along and the other did not?

(4)(a) Coming back to choice of law in New York, Judge Desmond, in his dissent in *May's Estate,* is remarkably consistent with other opinions of his that we have seen in the emphasis on domicile, family law, and public policy. Compare, in particular, his dissent in *Wyatt v. Fulrath,* § 4.03 *supra,* in which he would have applied Spanish law to the rights of the Spanish duke and duchess, and his "concurrence" in *Rosenstiel,* p. 782 *supra,* in which he would have rejected the Mexican divorce granted to domiciliaries of New York. More generally, Judge Desmond was willing to apply New York's public policy in favor of a New York domiciliary in *Kilberg,* § 3.02, as well as in *Dym v. Gordon* and (it seems) in *Macey v. Rozbicki* (§ 3.04).

(b) What about Judge Fuld, whose approach (not to say philosophy) we have followed throughout chapters 3 and 4? Judge Fuld does not write in *May's Estate,* but he accepts the approach of the majority. Is that approach not contrary to Fuld's emphasis on common domicile in the tort cases from *Babcock* to *Neumeier*? Or is that an unfair question, reaching for an analogy where none should be drawn?

[B] Same-Sex Marriages and the Federal System

Beginning in the 1970's, as homosexual orientation became increasingly open and accepted in the United States, efforts were launched to authorize same-sex marriages, and to abolish laws that restricted marriage to persons of opposite sex. Primarily, these efforts were part of the general initiative to achieve recognition for homosexuals as entitled to equal rights and freedom from discrimination; in addition, proponents pointed out that many economic benefits flowed from the status of marriage, including health insurance, workers' compensation and social security benefits, community property (in some states), standing to sue in wrongful death actions, right to file joint tax returns, and so on.

The initiative gained nation-wide attention in 1993, when the Supreme Court of Hawaii rendered a decision holding that the refusal of the state Department of Health to issue marriage licenses to three same-sex couples constituted discrimination on the basis of sex, which could be upheld only on the basis of "compelling state interests." *Baehr v. Lewin*, 74 Haw. 530, 852 P.2d 44 (1993). The decision of the Hawaii Supreme Court set off frantic discussion throughout the United States, even before Hawaii itself had sorted out the consequences of the decision.[f]

---

[f] The Supreme Court of Hawaii remanded the case for trial, but before the trial took place, the state legislature amended the marriage act to provide explicitly that a valid marriage contract can exist only between a man and a woman. The trial court, however, held that the State had failed to meet the test of compelling state interest, and thus that the amended statute violated Hawaii's constitution.

Thereafter, Hawaii's legislature adopted a proposed amendment to the state constitution, providing "The legislature shall have the power to reserve marriage to opposite-sex couples." The amendment was to be placed before the voters in 1998. As part of the compromise necessary to achieve the required two thirds vote in both Houses of the state legislature, the legislature adopted a Reciprocal Beneficiaries Law, 1997 Hi. Act 383, 1977 Hi. HB 118, approved July 8, 1997, extending certain benefits previously available only to married couples to other couples, including brother-sister, uncle-niece, widowed mother and son, as well as persons of the same sex. Among the benefits available to a "designated beneficiary" are inheritance rights, health insurance, and hospital visitation. At the same time the statute restates the legislative finding "that the people of Hawaii choose to preserve the tradition of marriage as a unique social institution based upon the committed union of one man and one woman."

Would Hawaii now become the Nevada of homosexual couples from all 50 states, their marriages entitled to recognition everywhere by virtue of the Full Faith and Credit Clause of the Federal Constitution? Many persons thought so, including both advocates and opponents of single-sex marriage.

Eighteen states enacted laws "designed to protect against the impending assault upon their marriage laws;"[g] Congressional committees held urgent hearings, and organizations dedicated to "traditional values" gave the alarm.

NOTES AND QUESTIONS

(1)(a) In the light of the cases reproduced in chapters 5, 8 and the preceding sections of this chapter, would you agree that single-sex marriages entered into in Hawaii by non-domiciliaries of that state would be required to be recognized in other states?

(b) If not, is it because a marriage is not a "judgment"? Or because states could treat the issue as one of choice of law and decline on public policy grounds to give effect to the act of a Hawaii official?

(c) What if a single-sex marriage were incorporated in a judgment, for instance in a divorce, or in a tort judgment awarding damages for wrongful death to the surviving spouse?

(2)(a) In a letter responding to an editorial warning of ominous challenge to the nation's federal system if some states did not give full faith and credit to Hawaii single-sex marriages,[h] Professor Linda Silberman wrote:

> A marriage ceremony is not a "judicial proceeding." Therefore, a sister state may look to its own interests in deciding what law to apply when an issue about the validity of a marriage is raised.[i]

However you feel about single sex marriage, and simply from the point of view of conflict of laws analysis, do you agree?

(b) Professor Silberman went on to urge:

> If Hawaii authorizes same sex marriages, it should not try to impose its laws on a sister state when the same-sex couple lives in that other state. A "quickie" trip to Hawaii and a formal marriage ceremony thus should not change the balance.[j]

If that advice makes good sense,[k] can it be linked to a legal principle? See, e.g., *Williams v. North Carolina II*, (p. 758, *supra*).

The statute also provides that "the right if any, of the surviving spouse or the Reciprocal Beneficiary of a decedent who dies domiciled outside this State to take an elective share in property in this state, is governed by the law of the decedent's domicile at death." Id. § 12(d)

[g] In sixteen other states such legislation was defeated, withdrawn, or vetoed. See House Report, note p *infra* at 10, 1996 U.S. Cong. & Ad. News at 2914.

[h] Editorial, New York Times, April 7, 1996, § 4, p. 10, col. 1.

[i] Silberman, Letter to Editor, New York Times, April 11, 1996, § A, p. 24, col. 4.

[j] Id.

[k] Contra, Note: *In Sickness and in Health, in Hawaii and Where Else?, Conflict of Laws and Recognition of Same-Sex Marriages*, 109 Harv. L. Rev. 2038 (1996), arguing for strict adherence of the rule of *lex celebrationis*.

(c) If Hawaii in the end makes single-sex marriages lawful,[l] should it also enact the following provision, adapted from the laws of Wyoming?

> Unless there is an order to waive the requirements of this section by a judge of a court of record . . . the clerk shall refuse to issue a [marriage] license if:
>
> > (i) Either of the parties is legally incompetent to enter into a marriage contract according to the law of this state; or
> >
> > (ii) there is any legal impediment to the parties entering into the marriage contract according to the laws of the state of their residence.[m]

Could such a provision be confined to single-sex marriages, so as to leave room for persons with other impediments not applicable in Hawaii, such as consanguinity, minority, or orders attendant on a divorce?

(3)(a) The U.S. Congress was not persuaded that states would be free to deny recognition single-sex marriages, and was worried about the effort of gay rights organizations to take advantage of the expected legitimization of single-sex marriage. It responded with a "Defense of Marriage Act" (DOMA), codified as 28 U.S.C. § 1738C, that is as part of the section of the Judiciary Code adopted in implementation of the second sentence of article IV, section 1 of the Constitution:[n]

> No State, territory, or possession of the United States, or Indian tribe, shall be required to give effect to any public act, record or judicial proceeding of any other State, territory, possession, or tribe respecting a relationship between persons of the same sex that is treated as a marriage under the laws of such other State, territory, possession or tribe, or a right or claim arising from such relationship.[o]

Again, putting aside your feelings about same-sex marriage, and granting that different states, judges, legislators, and voters may have different views on this issue, should the President have signed this bill? Could he have vetoed it on constitutional grounds?

(b) The "effects" clause of Article IV, section 1 of the Constitution seems to contemplate implementing, not limiting the reach of the Full Faith and Credit clause. The House Report on DOMA, while agreeing with this statement, says that nevertheless "Congress retains a discretionary power to carve out such exceptions as it deems appropriate."[p] Is that a persuasive reading of the Full Faith and Credit Clause?[q]

---

[l] See note f *supra*.

[m] Wyo. Stat § 20-1-103(b) and (c) (1977), referred to also in Linda Silberman, "Can the Island of Hawaii Bind the World?" A Comment on Same-Sex Marriage and Federalism Values," 16 Quinnipiac L. Rev. 189 (1997)

[n] Documents Supplement p. 4.

[o] Publ. L. No. 104-199, § 2(a), 110 Stat. 2419 (1996). The bill also contained another section, defining "marriage" and "spouse":

> In determining the meaning of any Act of Congress, or of any ruling, regulation, or interpretation of the various administrative bureaus and agencies of the United States, the word 'marriage' means only a legal union between one man and one woman as husband and wife, and the word 'spouse' refers only to a person of the opposite sex who is a husband or a wife.

[p] *Defense of Marriage Act*, Report of House Comm. on Judiciary on H.R. 3396, H.R. Rept. No. 104-664 at p. 26, 1996 U.S. Cong. & Ad. News 2930.

[q] See pp. 645-46, question 3(d), *supra*.

(c) As we saw, § § 1738A and 1738B, recently enacted to provide for recognition of child custody and child support orders,[r] expanded the reach of the Full Faith and Credit clause to require recognition and enforcement of orders previously thought not to be required to be enforced because they were modifiable.[s] § 1738C, the Defense of Marriage Act, is the reverse.

(4) Could Congress have written the bill to read "No State . . . *shall give effect*. . . ." instead of "No state . . . *shall be required to give effect*. . . ."? Or would such a bill have intruded impermissibly into the reserved powers of the states to deal with family matters?

(5) If the Defense of Marriage Act is constitutional, could its approach be used as well in respect of quickie divorces? For instance, how about a bill providing:

> No State . . . shall be required to give effect to a decree of divorce rendered by the court of a State in which at least one party has not resided for a minimum period of [six] months with intent to remain in that State.

Note that if such a bill ever became law, the option granted to the several states would lead precisely to the disuniformity that the Full Faith and Credit clause sought to avoid.

* * *

Looking back over this whole chapter, do you conclude that somehow family law does not fit into the regime of conflict of laws—unruly as that regime is—as illustrated in the rest of this book?

---

[r] § § 9.03[D], 9.04 *supra*.

[s] See e.g., *Lynde v. Lynde*, § 9.03[A] *supra*.

PART IV

INTERNATIONAL LAW AND CONFLICT OF LAWS

CHAPTER 10

CONFLICT OF LAWS ON THE INTERNATIONAL STAGE

Introduction

In the eighteenth and early nineteenth centuries, conflict of laws was seen both in Europe and in the Anglo-American tradition as a branch of the law of nations. As the United States spread over a continent and the dream of the "common," i.e., the unified, law faded, conflict of laws in the United States turned inward, with only occasional reference (typically in maritime matters) to foreign nation law.[a] In Europe, the tendency was the reverse, with national codes unifying previously local and customary law, first in France, then in the Low Countries, and later in Germany, Switzerland and Italy. Thus outside the United States, conflict of laws became more and more inter-, as contrasted with intra-, national law, and indeed was usually called "private international law."[b]

Some scholars and institutions tried to keep public and private international law together,[c] but by and large that effort failed. Private international law or conflict of laws was concerned with contracts, with inheritance, with marriage and divorce, and later with injuries and accidents (as well as with a variety of problems of jurisdiction and recognition of judgments), while public international law was concerned with recognition and succession of states, with various kinds of immunities, with treaties, with the law of the sea, and with the rules of war.[d] Not only were the subjects of the two disciplines different, but the techniques, vocabulary, and particularly the decision-makers grew apart. Private international law or conflict of laws was for ordinary courts,

---

[a] The statement in the text is somewhat of an exaggeration, especially if Canada is seen as a foreign nation. In fact, as we have seen, e.g. in *Babcock v. Jackson, Macey v. Rozbicki* and *Neumeier v. Kuehner,* the Canadian provinces were treated for choice of law purposes just like other states of the United States, so that, say, the Ontario guest statute and the Colorado guest statute would be viewed by New York courts without distinction, and without any suggestion that international relations might be involved in the former, and constitutional considerations in the latter.

[b] The term seems to have been introduced by Story in his treatise, published in 1834, but he did not use it for his title and the term did not catch on in the United States. See Story, *Commentaries on the Conflict of Laws,* p. 9, (1st. Ed. 1834); Juenger, *A Page of History,* 35 Mercer L. Rev. 419, 420, 444 (1984). Story wrote:

> The jurisprudence . . . arising from the conflict of laws of different nations in their application to modern commerce and intercourse, is a most interesting and important branch of public law . . . This branch of public law may be fitly denominated private international law, since it is chiefly seen and felt in its application to the common business of private persons, and rarely rises to the dignity of national negotiations, or national controversies.

[c] Notably the Institut de Droit International, founded in 1873 under non-governmental auspices, by scholars interested in both the private and public side of international law, i.e., in subjects ranging from marine insurance and enforcement of foreign judgments to the rules of war and rules governing international treaties.

[d] After World War II, of course, restraints on the use of force, human rights, and international economic law replaced the earlier concerns to some extent.

typically without the aid of either national legislation or international treaties.[e] Public international law, in contrast, rarely came before national courts, except in prize cases or in connection with sovereign and diplomatic immunities, and was developed largely through custom and practice of states, i.e., actions and declarations of governments taken from a sense of legal obligation. There were a few international arbitrations, typically about the consequences of war for neutrals,[f] and after World War I a World Court to which only states had access and jurisdiction depended on consent.

Public international law, in other words, did not concern private persons; conversely, private international law seemed not to pay attention to public international law, and indeed to public law generally, except to exclude it. Certainly a (public) law derived from (or at least based on) sovereignty, could not, it was thought, be the subject of choice of law, either by parties or by courts, and could not be anything but territorial and vertical. Public law—i.e., the whole gamut of regulation from workers' compensation and seamen's relief to antitrust and tax and securities regulation to banking secrecy to protection and expropriation of private investment—was viewed as beyond the scope of conflict of laws. Some viewed this as a consequence, indeed a rule of international law itself: public law simply was not international, any more than criminal law was; and any attempt to apply a state's public law beyond that state's borders was "extraterritorial" and in violation of international law. Others said that if people and ships and planes and goods and bank deposits could move around, it made no sense to pretend that law—including government regulation—stopped at each nation's frontier. Furthermore, the proposition that public international law concerned only the conduct of states vis-à-vis other states seemed inconsistent with the increasing impact of public law on persons, natural and juridical.

On the one hand, individuals and corporations began to seek out national courts for redress of violations of international law; on the other hand, the suggestion was made that international law imposed restraints on the reach of national courts, and more important, on the reach of national laws and regulations. In both of these aspects, courts, legislatures, and writers began to use the vocabulary, and the analyses, of the conflict of laws: contacts, state interest, justified expectations, and fairness. "Jurisdiction," the favorite term of conflict of laws (with a multiplicity of meanings), and "sovereignty," the building block of modern public international law, began to intrude into each other's domain. As in American conflict of laws, there was much talk, in the context of application of domestic law to transnational transactions, of the intent of the legislature; generally it was presumed that the legislature could not have wanted to violate international law,[g] but the content of that law was not always clear.

Thus even as conflict of laws was undergoing revolution (especially, but not exclusively in the United States[h]) and public international law was (not for the first time) plunged into self-doubt and disillusion, the public and private strands of international law seemed once again to come

---

[e] The German Civil Code of 1900 had an Introductory Law devoted to conflict of laws. The Italian Civil Code also contained preliminary articles devoted to Conflict of Laws, but the French Civil Code, and the codes of most of the countries that followed the French model, either have no conflicts statute at all or have a very recent one.

[f] For example the famous *Alabama Claims* arbitration between the United States and Great Britain following the American Civil War. See, e.g., W. Bishop, *International Law, Cases and Materials,* 1023 (3d ed. 1971).

[g] Compare Chief Justice Marshall's famous statement that "an act of Congress ought never to be construed to violate the law of nations, if any other possible construction remains . . ." *Murray v. The Charming Betsy,* 6 U.S. (2 Cranch) 64, 118 (1804), cited in *Lauritzen v. Larsen,* at p. 873, *infra.*

[h] See, e.g., Symposium: *The Influence of Modern American Conflicts Theories on European Law,* 30 Am. J. Comp. L. 1 (1982).

§ 10.01 Conflict of Laws on the International Stage

LAURITZEN v. LARSEN

United States Supreme Court
345 U.S. 571 (1953)

Mr. Justice Jackson delivered the opinion of the Court.

The key issue in this case is whether statutes of the United States should be applied to this claim of maritime tort. Larsen, a Danish seaman, while temporarily in New York joined the crew of the *Randa,* a ship of Danish flag and registry, owned by petitioner, a Danish citizen. Larsen signed ship's articles, written in Danish, providing that the rights of crew members would be governed by Danish law and by the employer's contract with the Danish Seamen's Union, of which Larsen was a member. He was negligently injured aboard the *Randa* in the course of employment, while in Havana harbor.

Respondent brought suit under the Jones Act[1] on the law side of the District Court for the Southern District of New York and demanded a jury. Petitioner contended that Danish law was applicable and that, under it, respondent had received all of the compensation to which he was entitled. He also contested the court's jurisdiction. Entertaining the cause, the court ruled that American rather than Danish law applied, and the jury rendered a verdict of $4,267.50. The Court of Appeals, Second Circuit, affirmed. . . .

The question of jurisdiction is shortly answered. A suit to recover damages under the Jones Act is *in personam* against the ship's owner and not one *in rem* against the ship itself. The defendant appeared generally, answered and tendered no objection to jurisdiction of his person. As frequently happens, a contention that there is some barrier to granting plaintiff's claim is cast in terms of an exception to jurisdiction of subject matter. A cause of action under our law was asserted here, and the court had power to determine whether it was or was not well founded in law and in fact. . . .

Denmark has enacted a comprehensive code to govern the relations of her shipowners to her seagoing labor which by its terms and intentions controls this claim. Though it is not for us to decide, it is plausibly contended that all obligations of the owner growing out of Danish law have been performed or tendered to this seaman. The shipowner, supported here by the Danish

---

[i] For an elaboration of these thoughts by the present author, see Lowenfeld, *Public Law in the International Arena: Conflict of Laws, International Law, and Some Suggestions for their Interaction,* 163 Recueil des Cours 311 (Hague Acad. Int'l L. 1979).

[1] Any seaman who shall suffer personal injury in the course of his employment may, at his election, maintain an action for damages at law, with the right of trial by jury, and in such action all statutes of the United States modifying or extending the common-law right or remedy in cases of personal injury to railway employees shall apply. . . . 46 U. S. C. § 688.

Government, asserts that the Danish law supplies the full measure of his obligation and that maritime usage and international law as accepted by the United States exclude the application of our incompatible statute.

That allowance of an additional remedy under our Jones Act would sharply conflict with the policy and letter of Danish law is plain from a general comparison of the two systems of dealing with shipboard accidents. Both assure the ill or injured seafaring worker the conventional maintenance and cure at the shipowner's cost, regardless of fault or negligence on the part of anyone. But, while we limit this to the period within which maximum possible cure can be effected, *Farrell v. United States,* 336 U. S. 511, the Danish law limits it to a fixed period of twelve weeks, and the monetary measurement is different. The two systems are in sharpest conflict as to treatment of claims for disability, partial or complete, which are permanent, or which outlast the liability for maintenance and cure, to which class this claim belongs. Such injuries Danish law relieves under a state-operated plan similar to our workmen's compensation systems. Claims for such disability are not made against the owner but against the state's Directorate of Insurance Against the Consequences of Accidents. They may be presented directly or through any Danish Consulate. They are allowed by administrative action, not by litigation, and depend not upon fault or negligence but only on the fact of injury and the extent of disability. Our own law, apart from indemnity for injury caused by the ship's unseaworthiness, makes no such compensation for such disability in the absence of fault or negligence. But, when such fault or negligence is established by litigation, it allows recovery for elements such as pain and suffering not compensated under Danish law and lets the damages be fixed by jury. In this case, since negligence was found, United States law permits a larger recovery than Danish law. If the same injury were sustained but negligence was absent or not provable, the Danish law would appear to provide compensation where ours would not.

Respondent does not deny that Danish law is applicable to his case. The contention as stated in his brief is rather that "A claimant may select whatever forum he desires and receive the benefits resulting from such choice" and "A ship owner is liable under the laws of the forum where he does business as well as in his own country." This contention that the Jones Act provides an optional cumulative remedy is not based on any explicit terms of the Act, which makes no provision for cases in which remedies have been obtained or are obtainable under foreign law. Rather he relies upon the literal catholicity of its terminology. If read literally, Congress has conferred an American right of action which requires nothing more than that plaintiff be "any seaman who shall suffer personal injury in the course of his employment." It makes no explicit requirement that either the seaman, the employment or the injury have the slightest connection with the United States. Unless some relationship of one or more of these to our national interest is implied, Congress has extended our law and opened our courts to all alien seafaring men injured anywhere in the world in service of watercraft of every foreign nation—a hand on a Chinese junk, never outside Chinese waters, would not be beyond its literal wording.

But Congress in 1920 wrote these all-comprehending words, not on a clean slate, but as a postscript to a long series of enactments governing shipping. All were enacted with regard to a seasoned body of maritime law developed by the experience of American courts long accustomed to dealing with admiralty problems in reconciling our own with foreign interests and in accommodating the reach of our own laws to those of other maritime nations.

The shipping laws of the United States, set forth in Title 46 of the United States Code, comprise a patchwork of separate enactments, some tracing far back in our history and many designed for particular emergencies. While some have been specific in application to foreign shipping and others in being confined to American shipping, many give no evidence that Congress addressed itself to their foreign application and are in general terms which leave their application to be judicially determined from context and circumstance. By usage as old as the Nation, such statutes have been construed to apply only to areas and transactions in which American law would be considered operative under prevalent doctrines of international law. Thus, in *United States v. Palmer,* 3 Wheat. 610, this Court was called upon to interpret a statute of 1790 (1 Stat. 115) punishing certain acts when committed on the high seas by "any person or persons," terms which, as Mr. Chief Justice Marshall observed, are "broad enough to comprehend every human being." But the Court determined that the literal universality of the prohibition "must not only be limited to cases within the jurisdiction of the state, but also to those objects to which the legislature intended to apply them" (p. 631) and therefore would not reach a person performing the proscribed acts aboard the ship of a foreign state on the high seas.

This doctrine of construction is in accord with the long-heeded admonition of Mr. Chief Justice Marshall that "an act of congress ought never to be construed to violate the law of nations if any other possible construction remains. . . ." *The Charming Betsy,* 2 Cranch 64, 118. And it has long been accepted in maritime jurisprudence that ". . . if any construction otherwise be possible, an Act will not be construed as applying to foreigners in respect to acts done by them outside the dominions of the sovereign power enacting. That is a rule based on international law by which one sovereign power is bound to respect the subjects and the rights of all other sovereign powers outside its own territory." Lord Russell of Killowen in *The Queen v. Jameson,* [1896] 2 Q. B. 425, 430. This is not, as sometimes is implied, any impairment of our own sovereignty, or limitation of the power of Congress. "The law of the sea," we have had occasion to observe, "is in a peculiar sense an international law, but application of its specific rules depends upon acceptance by the United States." *Farrell v. United States,* 336 U. S. 511, 517. On the contrary, we are simply dealing with a problem of statutory construction rather commonplace in a federal system by which courts often have to decide whether "any" or "every" reaches to the limits of the enacting authority's usual scope or is to be applied to foreign events or transactions.

. . .

[The Court summarizes the history of the Jones Act and its predecessor statute.]

Congress could not have been unaware of the necessity of construction imposed upon courts by such generality of language and was well warned that in the absence of more definite directions than are contained in the Jones Act it would be applied by the courts to foreign events, foreign ships and foreign seamen only in accordance with the usual doctrine and practices of maritime law.

Respondent places great stress upon the assertion that petitioner's commerce and contacts with the ports of the United States are frequent and regular, as the basis for applying our statutes to incidents aboard his ships. But the virtue and utility of sea-borne commerce lies in its frequent and important contacts with more than one country. If, to serve some immediate interest, the courts of each were to exploit every such contact to the limit of its power, it is not difficult to see that a multiplicity of conflicting and overlapping burdens would blight international carriage by sea. Hence, courts of this and other commercial nations have generally deferred to a non-national or international maritime law of impressive maturity and universality.[12] It has the force of law, not from extraterritorial reach of national laws, nor from abdication of its sovereign powers by any nation, but from acceptance by common consent of civilized communities of rules designed to foster amicable and workable commercial relations.

International or maritime law in such matters as this does not seek uniformity and does not purport to restrict any nation from making and altering its laws to govern its own shipping and territory. However, it aims at stability and order through usages which considerations of comity, reciprocity and long-range interest have developed to define the domain which each nation will claim as its own. Maritime law, like our municipal law, has attempted to avoid or resolve conflicts between competing laws by ascertaining and valuing points of contact between the transaction and the states or governments whose competing laws are involved. The criteria, in general, appear to be arrived at from weighing of the significance of one or more connecting factors between the shipping transaction regulated and the national interest served by the assertion of authority. It would not be candid to claim that our courts have arrived at satisfactory standards or apply those that they profess with perfect consistency. But in dealing with international commerce we cannot be unmindful of the necessity for mutual forbearance if retaliations are to be avoided; nor should we forget that any contact which we hold sufficient to warrant application of our law to a foreign transaction will logically be as strong a warrant for a foreign country to apply its law to an American transaction.

In the case before us, two foreign nations can claim some connecting factor with this tort—Denmark, because, among other reasons, the ship and the seaman were Danish nationals; Cuba, because the tortious conduct occurred and caused injury in Cuban waters. The United States may also claim contacts because the seaman had been hired in and was returned to the United States, which also is the state of the forum. We therefore review the several factors which, alone or in combination, are generally conceded to influence choice of law to govern a tort claim, particularly a maritime tort claim, and the weight and significance accorded them.

1. *Place of the Wrongful Act.*—The solution most commonly accepted as to torts in our municipal and in international law is to apply the law of the place where the acts giving rise to the liability occurred, the *lex loci delicti commissi.* This rule of locality, often applied to maritime torts, would indicate application of the law of Cuba, in whose domain the actionable wrong took place. The test of location of the wrongful act or omission, however sufficient for torts ashore, is of limited application to shipboard torts, because of the varieties of legal authority over waters she may navigate. . . .

We have sometimes uncompromisingly asserted territorial rights. . . . But the territorial standard is so unfitted to an enterprise conducted under many territorial rules and under none that it usually is modified by the more constant law of the flag. . . . The locality test, for what it is worth, affords no support for the application of American law in this case and probably refers us to Danish in preference to Cuban law, though this point we need not decide, for neither party urges Cuban law as controlling.

2. *Law of the Flag.*—Perhaps the most venerable and universal rule of maritime law relevant to our problem is that which gives cardinal importance to the law of the flag. Each state under

---

[12] See the famous opinion of Mr. Justice Story in *De Lovio v. Boit,* Fed. Cas. No. 3,776, 2 Gall. 398; *The Sally,* 8 Cranch 382 and 2 Cranch 406; *The Scotia,* 14 Wall. 170; Dickinson, *The Law of Nations as Part of the National Law of the United States,* 101 U. of Pa. L. Rev. 26, 28–29, 792, 803–816.

§ 10.01   INTERNATIONAL LAW AND CONFLICT OF LAWS   □   875

international law may determine for itself the conditions on which it will grant its nationality to a merchant ship, thereby accepting responsibility for it and acquiring authority over it.

. . .

It is significant to us here that the weight given to the ensign overbears most other connecting events in determining applicable law. As this Court held in *United States v. Flores, supra,* at 158, and iterated in *Cunard Steamship Co. v. Mellon, supra,* at 123:

> And so by comity it came to be generally understood among civilized nations that all matters of discipline and all things done on board which affected only the vessel or those belonging to her, and did not involve the peace or dignity of the country, or the tranquillity of the port, should be left by the local government to be dealt with by the authorities of the nation to which the vessel belonged as the laws of that nation or the interests of its commerce should require. . . .

This was but a repetition of settled American doctrine.

These considerations are of such weight in favor of Danish and against American law in this case that it must prevail unless some heavy counterweight appears.

3. *Allegiance or Domicile of the Injured.*—Until recent times there was little occasion for conflict between the law of the flag and the law of the state of which the seafarer was a subject, for the long-standing rule, as pronounced by this Court after exhaustive review of authority, was that the nationality of the vessel for jurisdictional purposes was attributed to all her crew. *In re Ross,* 140 U. S. 453, 472. Surely during service under a foreign flag some duty of allegiance is due. But, also, each nation has a legitimate interest that its nationals and permanent inhabitants be not maimed or disabled from self-support. In some later American cases, courts have been prompted to apply the Jones Act by the fact that the wrongful act or omission alleged caused injury to an American citizen or domiciliary. We need not, however, weigh the seaman's nationality against that of the ship, for here the two coincide without resort to fiction. Admittedly, respondent is neither citizen nor resident of the United States. While on direct examination he answered leading questions that he was living in New York when he joined the *Randa,* the articles which he signed recited, and on cross-examination he admitted, that his home was Silkeburg, Denmark. His presence in New York was transitory and created no such national interest in, or duty toward, him as to justify intervention of the law of one state on the shipboard of another.

4. *Allegiance of the Defendant Shipowner.*—... Until recent times this factor was not a frequent occasion of conflict, for the nationality of the ship was that of its owners.[22] But it is common knowledge that in recent years a practice has grown, particularly among American shipowners, to avoid stringent shipping laws by seeking foreign registration eagerly offered by some countries. Confronted with such operations, our courts on occasion have pressed beyond the formalities of more or less nominal foreign registration to enforce against American shipowners the obligations which our law places upon them. But here again the utmost liberality in disregard of formality does not support the application of American law in this case, for it appears beyond doubt that this owner is a Dane by nationality and domicile.

5. *Place of Contract.*—Place of contract, which was New York, is the factor on which respondent chiefly relies to invoke American law. It is one which often has significance in choice

---

[22] Many nations (including both the United States and Denmark) still allow only those ships wholly or predominantly owned by its nationals to register under its flag. See 46 U.S.C. §§ 11, 808; Denmark, Maritime Law of May 7, 1937, § 1.

of law in a contract action. But a Jones Act suit is for tort, in which respect it differs from one to enforce liability for maintenance and cure. . . .

The place of contracting in this instance, as is usual to such contracts, was fortuitous. A seaman takes his employment, like his fun, where he finds it; a ship takes on crew in any port where it needs them. The practical effect of making the *lex loci contractus* govern all tort claims during the service would be to subject a ship to a multitude of systems of law, to put some of the crew in a more advantageous position than others, and not unlikely in the long run to diminish hirings in ports of countries that take best care of their seamen.

But if contract law is nonetheless to be considered, we face the fact that this contract was explicit that the Danish law and the contract with the Danish union were to control. Except as forbidden by some public policy, the tendency of the law is to apply in contract matters the law which the parties intended to apply.[25] We are aware of no public policy that would prevent the parties to this contract, which contemplates performance in a multitude of territorial jurisdictions and on the high seas, from so settling upon the law of the flag-state as their governing code. This arrangement is so natural and compatible with the policy of the law that even in the absence of an express provision it would probably have been implied. We think a quite different result would follow if the contract attempted to avoid applicable law, for example, so as to apply foreign law to an American ship.

. . . .

We do not think the place of contract is a substantial influence in the choice between competing laws to govern a maritime tort.

6. *Inaccessibility of Foreign Forum.*—It is argued, and particularly stressed by an *amicus* brief, that justice requires adjudication under American law to save seamen expense and loss of time in returning to a foreign forum. This might be a persuasive argument for exercising a discretionary jurisdiction to adjudge a controversy; but it is not persuasive as to the law by which it shall be judged. . . .

Confining ourselves to the case in hand, we do not find this seaman disadvantaged in obtaining his remedy under Danish law from being in New York instead of Denmark. The Danish compensation system does not necessitate delayed, prolonged, expensive and uncertain litigation. It is stipulated in this case that claims may be made through the Danish Consulate. There is not the slightest showing that to obtain any relief to which he is entitled under Danish law would require his presence in Denmark or necessitate his leaving New York. And, even if it were so, the record indicates that he was offered and declined free transportation to Denmark by petitioner.

7. *The Law of the Forum.*—It is urged that, since an American forum has perfected its jurisdiction over the parties and defendant does more or less frequent and regular business within the forum state, it should apply its own law to the controversy between them. The "doing business" which is enough to warrant service of process may fall quite short of the considerations necessary to bring extraterritorial torts to judgment under our law. Under respondent's contention, all that is necessary to bring a foreign transaction between foreigners in foreign ports under American law is to be able to serve American process on the defendant. We have held it a denial of due process of law when a state of the Union attempts to draw into control of its law otherwise foreign controversies, on slight connections, because it is a forum state. *Hartford Accident & Indemnity Co. v. Delta & Pine Land Co.,* 292 U. S. 143; *Home Insurance Co. v. Dick,* 281 U.

---

[25] See Yntema, *"Autonomy" in Choice of Law,* 1 Am. J. Comp. L. 341.

S. 397. The purpose of a conflict-of-laws doctrine is to assure that a case will be treated in the same way under the appropriate law regardless of the fortuitous circumstances which often determine the forum. Jurisdiction of maritime cases in all countries is so wide and the nature of its subject matter so far-flung that there would be no justification for altering the law of a controversy just because local jurisdiction of the parties is obtainable.

It is pointed out that our statute on limitation of shipowner's liability which formerly applied in terms to "any vessel" was applied by our courts to foreign causes.[26] Hence, it is argued by analogy that "any seaman" should be construed so to apply. But the situation is inverted. The limitation-of-liability statute was construed to thus apply only against those who had chosen to sue in our courts on foreign transactions. Because a law of the forum is applied to plaintiffs who voluntarily submit themselves to it is no argument for imposing the law of the forum upon those who do not. Furthermore, this application of the limitation on liability brought our practice into harmony with that of all other maritime nations,[28] while the application of the Jones Act here advocated would bring us into conflict with the maritime world.

This review of the connecting factors which either maritime law or our municipal law of conflicts regards as significant in determining the law applicable to a claim of actionable wrong shows an overwhelming preponderance in favor of Danish law. The parties are both Danish subjects, the events took place on a Danish ship, not within our territorial waters. Against these considerations is only the fact that the defendant was served here with process and that the plaintiff signed on in New York, where the defendant was engaged in our foreign commerce. The latter event is offset by provision of his contract that the law of Denmark should govern. We do not question the power of Congress to condition access to our ports by foreign-owned vessels upon submission to any liabilities it may consider good American policy to exact. But we can find no justification for interpreting the Jones Act to intervene between foreigners and their own law because of acts on a foreign ship not in our waters.

In apparent recognition of the weakness of the legal argument, a candid and brash appeal is made by respondent and by *amicus* briefs to extend the law to this situation as a means of benefiting seamen and enhancing the costs of foreign ship operation for the competitive advantage of our own. We are not sure that the interest of this foreign seaman, who is able to prove negligence, is the interest of all seamen or that his interest is that of the United States. Nor do we stop to inquire which law does whom the greater or the lesser good. The argument is misaddressed. It would be within the proprieties if addressed to Congress. Counsel familiar with the traditional attitude of this Court in maritime matters could not have intended it for us.[29]

The judgment below is reversed and the cause remanded to District Court for proceedings consistent herewith.

Mr. Justice Black agrees with the Court of Appeals and would affirm its judgment.

---

[26] *The Scotland,* 105 U. S. 24; *The Titanic,* 233 U. S. 718. At the time these cases were decided the statute purported to apply to "any vessel." In 1936 it was amended so as expressly to apply to foreign, as well as domestic, vessels. 49 Stat. 1479.

[28] Limitation of liability has been an essential part of the maritime law of every maritime nation since the *Grand Ordonnance* of Louis XIV in 1681. See discussion in the opinion of Mr. Justice Brown in *The Main v. Williams,* 152 U. S. 122.

[29] Cf. *The Peterhoff,* 5 Wall. 28, 57:

In cases such as that now in judgment, we administer the public law of nations, and are not at liberty to inquire what is for the particular advantage or disadvantage of our own or another country.

ROMERO v. INTERNATIONAL TERMINAL OPERATING CO.

United States Supreme Court
358 U.S. 354 (1959)

MR. JUSTICE FRANKFURTER delivered the opinion of the Court.

Petitioner Francisco Romero, a Spanish subject, signed on as a member of the crew of the S. S. *Guadalupe* for a voyage beginning about October 10, 1953. The *Guadalupe* was of Spanish registry, sailed under the Spanish flag and was owned by respondent Compania Trasatlantica (also known as Spanish Line), a Spanish corporation. At the completion of the voyage for which he signed, Romero continued uninterruptedly to work on the *Guadalupe.* Thereby, under the law of Spain, the terms and conditions of the original contract of hire remained in force. Subsequently the S. S. *Guadalupe* departed from the port of Bilbao in northern Spain, touched briefly at other Spanish ports, and sailed to the port of New York at Hoboken. From here the ship made a brief trip to the ports of Vera Cruz and Havana returning to Hoboken where, on May 12, 1954, Romero was seriously injured when struck by a cable on the deck of the *Guadalupe.* Thereupon petitioner filed suit on the law side of the District Court for the Southern District of New York.

The amended complaint claimed damages from four separate corporate defendants. . . .

Following a pre-trial hearing the District Court dismissed the complaint. . . . The court held that the action under the Jones Act against Compania Trasatlantica must be dismissed for lack of jurisdiction since that Act provided no right of action for an alien seaman against a foreign shipowner under the circumstances detailed above. The claims under the general maritime law against Compania also were dismissed since the parties were not of diverse citizenship and 28 U. S. C. § 1331 did not confer jurisdiction on the federal law courts over claims rooted in federal maritime law. The District Court dismissed the Jones Act claim against Garcia & Diaz, Inc., pursuant to its finding that Garcia was not the employer of Romero nor, as a husbanding agent for Compania, did it have the operation and control of the vessel. The remaining claims, including those against the other respondents, were dismissed because of lack of the requisite complete diversity under the rule of *Strawbridge v. Curtiss,* 3 Cranch 267. Upon examination of the Spanish law the district judge also declined jurisdiction "even in admiralty as a matter of discretion." 142 F. Supp., at 574. The Spanish law provides Romero with a lifetime pension of 35% to 55% of his seaman's wages which may be increased by one-half if the negligence of the shipowner is established; it also allows the recovery of the Spanish counterpart of maintenance and cure. These rights under the Spanish law may be enforced through the Spanish consul in New York.

The Court of Appeals affirmed the dismissal of the complaint, 244 F. 2d 409. We granted certiorari, . . . because of the conflict among Courts of Appeals as to the proper construction of the relevant provision of the Judiciary Act of 1875 (now 28 U. S. C. § 1331) and because of questions raised regarding the applicability of *Lauritzen v. Larsen* to the situation before us. . . .

I. JURISDICTION.

(a) *Jurisdiction under the Jones Act.*—The District Court dismissed petitioner's Jones Act claims for lack of jurisdiction. . . . Petitioner asserts a substantial claim that the Jones Act affords him a right of recovery for the negligence of his employer. Such assertion alone is sufficient to empower the District Court to assume jurisdiction over the case and determine whether, in fact, the Act does provide the claimed rights. . . .

(b) *Jurisdiction under 28 U. S. C. § 1331.*—Petitioner, a Spanish subject, asserts claims under the general maritime law against Compania Trasatlantica, a Spanish corporation. The jurisdiction of the Federal District Court, sitting as a court of law, was invoked under the provisions of the Judiciary Act of 1875 which granted jurisdiction to the lower federal courts "of all suits of a civil nature at common law or in equity, . . . arising under the Constitution or laws of the United States, ..." (now 28 U. S. C. § 1331).

. . .

[The Court holds, after a 21-page analysis, that suits on the law side of the federal courts based on general maritime law are grounded in state law and do not "arise under" the Constitution or laws of the United States. Accordingly such a suit can be maintained in federal courts only if there is complete diversity of citizenship between the parties, not including alien v. alien. If a Jones Act complaint can be sustained, pendent jurisdiction against Compania may be possible; general maritime claims may proceed against the U.S. citizen parties.]

II. THE CLAIMS AGAINST COMPANIA TRASATLANTICA—THE CHOICE-OF-LAW PROBLEM.

We now turn to the claims against Compania Trasatlantica under the Jones Act and the general maritime law. In light of our recent decision in *Lauritzen v. Larsen,* these claims present the narrow issue, whether the maritime law of the United States may be applied in an action involving an injury sustained in an American port by a foreign seaman on board a foreign vessel in the course of a voyage beginning and ending in a foreign country.

While *Lauritzen v. Larsen* involved claims asserted under the Jones Act, the principles on which it was decided did not derive from the terms of that statute. . . . The broad principles of choice of law and the applicable criteria of selection set forth in *Lauritzen* were intended to guide courts in the application of maritime law generally. Of course, due regard must be had for the differing interests advanced by varied aspects of maritime law. But the similarity in purpose and function of the Jones Act and the general maritime principles of compensation for personal injury, admit of no rational differentiation of treatment for choice of law purposes. Thus the reasoning of *Lauritzen v. Larsen* governs all claims here.

We are not here dealing with the sovereign power of the United States to apply its law to situations involving one or more foreign contacts. But in the absence of a contrary congressional direction, we must apply those principles of choice of law that are consonant with the needs of a general federal maritime law and with due recognition of our self-regarding respect for the relevant interests of foreign nations in the regulation of maritime commerce as part of the legitimate concern of the international community. These principles do not depend upon a mechanical application of a doctrine like that of *lex loci delicti commissi.* The controlling considerations are the interacting interests of the United States and of foreign countries, and in assessing them we must move with the circumspection appropriate when this Court is adjudicating issues inevitably entangled in the conduct of our international relations. We need not repeat the exposition of the problem which we gave in *Lauritzen v. Larsen.* Due regard for the relevant factors we there enumerated, and the weight we indicated to be given to each, preclude application of American law to the claims here asserted.

In this case, as in *Lauritzen v. Larsen,* the ship is of foreign registry and sails under a foreign flag. Both the injured seaman and the owner of the ship have a Spanish status: Romero is a Spanish subject and Compania Trasatlantica a Spanish corporation. Unlike the contract in

Lauritzen, Romero's agreement of hire was entered into in Spain. By noting this fact, we do not mean to qualify our earlier view that the place of contracting is largely fortuitous and of little importance in determining the applicable law in an action of marine tort. Here, as in *Lauritzen,* the foreign law provides a remedy for the injury, and claims under that law may be conveniently asserted before the Spanish consul in New York.

In *Lauritzen v. Larsen* the injury occurred in the port of Havana and the action was brought in New York. Romero was injured while temporarily in American territorial waters. This difference does not call for a difference in result. Discussing the significance of the place of the wrongful act, we pointed out in *Lauritzen* that "[t]he test of location of the wrongful act or omission, however sufficient for torts ashore, is of limited application to shipboard torts, because of the varieties of legal authority over waters she may navigate. . . . the territorial standard is so unfitted to an enterprise conducted under many territorial rules and under none that it usually is modified by the more constant law of the flag." Although the place of injury has often been deemed determinative of the choice of law in municipal conflict of laws, such a rule does not fit the accommodations that become relevant in fair and prudent regard for the interests of foreign nations in the regulation of their own ships and their own nationals, and the effect upon our interests of our treatment of the legitimate interests of foreign nations. To impose on ships the duty of shifting from one standard of compensation to another as the vessel passes the boundaries of territorial waters would be not only an onerous but also an unduly speculative burden, disruptive of international commerce and without basis in the expressed policies of this country. The amount and type of recovery which a foreign seaman may receive from his foreign employer while sailing on a foreign ship should not depend on the wholly fortuitous circumstance of the place of injury.

Thus we hold that the considerations found in *Lauritzen v. Larsen* to preclude the assertion of a claim under the Jones Act apply equally here, and affirm the dismissal of petitioner's claims against Compania Trasatlantica.

. . .

Mr. Justice Black, dissenting.

. . . This Court in *Lauritzen v. Larsen,* held that the words "any seaman" did not include foreign seamen sailing foreign ships and injured in foreign waters. I dissented from that holding. It was based I thought, on the Court's concepts of what would be good or bad for the country internationally rather than on an actual interpretation of the language of the Jones Act. Thus, it seemed to me that the *Lauritzen* holding rested on notions of what Congress should have said, not on what it did say. Such notions, weak enough in *Lauritzen,* seem much weaker still in this case where the tort involved occurred in our own waters. I cannot but feel that, at least as to torts occurring within the United States, Congress knew what it was doing when it said "any seaman" and I must dissent from today's further and, I believe, unjustifiable reduction in the scope of the Jones Act. Moreover since the tort occurred in the navigable waters of the United States, I think the complaint against Compania Trasatlantica stated a good cause of action under general maritime law whether jurisdiction of the cause is based, as I believe, on 28 U. S. C. § 1331, or, as the Court assumes, on some theory of "pendent jurisdiction."

Mr. Justice Douglas joins in the first paragraph of this opinion. He believes that *Lauritzen v. Larsen* is inapposite to the present case, because of the numerous incidents connecting this transaction with the United States. He therefore agrees with Mr. Justice Black that the District Court should take jurisdiction over petitioner's claim against Compania Trasatlantica.

§ 10.01   INTERNATIONAL LAW AND CONFLICT OF LAWS   □   881

Mr. Justice Brennan, [dissenting in part and concurring in part, filed a 25-page dissent on the issue of jurisdiction, arguing that federal courts have long heard claims under general maritime law, with or without a statute. He concurs with the Court's decision on choice of law.]

McCULLOCH v. SOCIEDAD NACIONAL DE MARINEROS DE HONDURAS

United States Supreme Court
372 U.S. 10 (1963)

Mr. Justice Clark delivered the opinion of the Court.

. . .

I.

The National Maritime Union of America, AFL–CIO, filed a petition in 1959 with the National Labor Relations Board seeking certification under § 9 (c) of the Act, 29 U. S. C. § 159 (c), as the representative of the unlicensed seamen employed upon certain Honduran-flag vessels owned by Empresa Hondurena de Vapores, S. A., a Honduran corporation. The petition was filed against United Fruit Company, a New Jersey corporation which was alleged to be the owner of the majority of Empresa's stock. Empresa intervened and on hearing it was shown that United Fruit owns all of its stock and elects its directors, though no officer or director of Empresa is an officer or director of United Fruit and all are residents of Honduras. In turn the proof was that United Fruit is owned by citizens of the United States and maintains its principal office at Boston. Its business was shown to be the cultivation, gathering, transporting and sale of bananas, sugar, cacao and other tropical produce raised in Central and South American countries and sold in the United States.

United Fruit maintains a fleet of cargo vessels which it utilizes in this trade. A portion of the fleet consists of 13 Honduran-registered vessels operated by Empresa and time chartered to United Fruit, which vessels were included in National Maritime Union's representation proceeding. The crews on these vessels are recruited by Empresa in Honduras. They are Honduran citizens (save one Jamaican) and claim that country as their residence and home port. The crew are required to sign Honduran shipping articles, and their wages, terms and condition of employment, discipline, etc., are controlled by a bargaining agreement between Empresa and a Honduran union, Sociedad Nacional de Marineros de Honduras. Under the Honduran Labor Code only a union whose "juridic personality" is recognized by Honduras and which is composed of at least 90% of Honduran citizens can represent the seamen on Honduran-registered ships. The N. M. U. fulfils neither requirement. Further, under Honduran law recognition of Sociedad as the bargaining agent compels Empresa to deal exclusively with it on all matters covered by the contract. The current agreement in addition to recognition of Sociedad provides for a union shop, with a no-strike-or-lockout provision, and sets up wage scales, special allowances, maintenance and cure provisions, hours of work, vacation time, holidays, overtime, accident prevention, and other details of employment as well.

United Fruit, however, determines the ports of call of the vessels, their cargoes and sailings, integrating the same into its fleet organization. While the voyages are for the most part between Central and South American ports and those of the United States, the vessels each call at regular intervals at Honduran ports for the purpose of taking on and discharging cargo and, where necessary, renewing the ship's articles.

II.

The Board concluded from these facts that United Fruit operated a single, integrated maritime operation within which were the Empresa vessels, reasoning that United Fruit was a joint employer with Empresa of the seamen covered by N. M. U.'s petition. Citing its own *West India Fruit & Steamship Co.* opinion, 130 N. L. R. B. 343 (1961), it concluded that the maritime operations involved substantial United States contacts, outweighing the numerous foreign contacts present. The Board held that Empresa was engaged in "commerce" within the meaning of § 2 (6) of the Act[3] and that the maritime operations "affected commerce" within § 2 (7), meeting the jurisdictional requirement of § 9 (c)(1). It therefore ordered an election to be held among the seamen signed on Empresa's vessels to determine whether they wished N. M. U., Sindicato Maritime Nacional de Honduras,[6] or no union to represent them.

. . .[The U.S. District Court for the District of Columbia enjoined enforcement of the Board's order. The Supreme Court granted certiorari before judgment.]

III.

Since the parties all agree that the Congress has constitutional power to apply the National Labor Relations Act to the crews working foreign-flag ships, at least while they are in American waters, *The Exchange,* 7 Cranch 116, 143 (1812); *Wildenhus's Case,* 120 U. S. 1, 11 (1887); *Benz v. Compania Naviera Hidalgo,* 353 U. S. 138, 142 (1957), we go directly to the question whether Congress exercised that power. Our decision on this point being dispositive of the case, we do not reach the other questions raised by the parties and the *amici curiae.*

The question of application of the laws of the United States to foreign-flag ships and their crews has arisen often and in various contexts. As to the application of the National Labor Relations Act and its amendments, the Board has evolved a test relying on the relative weight of a ship's foreign as compared with its American contacts. That test led the Board to conclude here, as in *West India Fruit & Steamship Co., supra,* that the foreign-flag ships' activities affected "commerce" and brought them within the coverage of the Act. Where the balancing of the vessel's contacts has resulted in a contrary finding, the Board has concluded that the Act does not apply.

Six years ago this Court considered the question of the application of the Taft-Hartley amendments to the Act in a suit for damages "resulting from the picketing of a foreign ship operated entirely by foreign seamen under foreign articles while the vessel [was] temporarily in an American port." *Benz v. Compania Naviera Hidalgo, supra,* at 139. We held that the Act did not apply, searching the language and the legislative history and concluding that the latter

---

[3] 29 U. S. C. § 152 (6):

The term "commerce" means trade, traffic, commerce, transportation, or communication among the several States, or between the District of Columbia or any Territory of the United States and any State or other Territory, or between any foreign country and any State, Territory, or the District of Columbia, or within the District of Columbia or any Territory, or between points in the same State but through any other State or any Territory or the District of Columbia or any foreign country.

[6] Sindicato, a Honduran union, had intervened in the proceeding. Sociedad was invited to intervene but declined to do so.

"inescapably describes the boundaries of the Act as including only the workingmen of our own country and its possessions." *Id.,* at 144. . . .

It is contended that this case is . . . distinguishable from *Benz* in two respects. First, here there is a fleet of vessels not temporarily in United States waters but operating in a regular course of trade between foreign ports and those of the United States; and, second, the foreign owner of the ships is in turn owned by an American corporation. We note that both of these points rely on additional American contacts and therefore necessarily presume the validity of the "balancing of contacts" theory of the Board. But to follow such a suggested procedure to the ultimate might require that the Board inquire into the internal discipline and order of all foreign vessels calling at American ports. Such activity would raise considerable disturbance not only in the field of maritime law but in our international relations as well. In addition, enforcement of Board orders would project the courts into application of the sanctions of the Act to foreign-flag ships on a purely *ad hoc* weighing of contacts basis.[9] This would inevitably lead to embarrassment in foreign affairs and be entirely infeasible in actual practice. The question, therefore, appears to us more basic; namely, whether the Act as written was intended to have any application to foreign registered vessels employing alien seamen.

Petitioners say that the language of the Act may be read literally as including foreign-flag vessels within its coverage. But, as in *Benz,* they have been unable to point to any specific language in the Act itself or in its extensive legislative history that reflects such a congressional intent. Indeed, the opposite is true as we found in *Benz,* where we pointed to the language of Chairman Hartley characterizing the Act as "a bill of rights both for *American* workingmen and for their employers." 353 U. S., at 144. We continue to believe that if the sponsors of the original Act or of its amendments conceived of the application now sought by the Board they failed to translate such thoughts into describing the boundaries of the Act as including foreign-flag vessels manned by alien crews. Therefore, we find no basis for a construction which would exert United States jurisdiction over and apply its laws to the internal management and affairs of the vessels here flying the Honduran flag, contrary to the recognition long afforded them not only by our State Department[11] but also by the Congress.[12] In addition, our attention is called to the well-established rule of international law that the law of the flag state ordinarily governs the internal affairs of a ship. See *Wildenhus's Case, supra,* at 12; Colombos, *The International Law of the Sea* (3d rev. ed. 1954), 222–223. The possibility of international discord cannot therefore be gainsaid. Especially is this true on account of the concurrent application of the Act and the Honduran Labor Code that would result with our approval of jurisdiction. Sociedad, currently the exclusive bargaining agent of Empresa under Honduran law, would have a head-on collision with N. M. U. should it become the exclusive bargaining agent under the Act. This would be

---

[9] Our conclusion does not foreclose such a procedure in different contexts, such as the Jones Act, 46 U. S. C. § 688, where the pervasive regulation of the internal order of a ship may not be present. As regards application of the Jones Act to maritime torts on foreign ships, however, the Court has stated that "[p]erhaps the most venerable and universal rule of maritime law relevant to our problem is that which gives cardinal importance to the law of the flag." *Lauritzen v. Larsen,* 345 U. S. 571, 584 (1953); see *Romero v. International Terminal Operating Co.,* 358 U. S. 354, 381–384 (1959). . . .

[11] State Department regulations provide that a foreign vessel includes "any vessel regardless of ownership, which is documented under the laws of a foreign country." 22 CFR § 81.1 (f).

[12] Article X of the Treaty of Friendship, Commerce and Consular Rights between Honduras and the United States, 45 Stat. 2618 (1927), provides that merchant vessels flying the flags and having the papers of either country "shall, both within the territorial waters of the other High Contracting Party and on the high seas, be deemed to be the vessels of the Party whose flag is flown."

aggravated by the fact that under Honduran law N. M. U. is prohibited from representing the seamen on Honduran-flag ships even in the absence of a recognized bargaining agent. Thus even though Sociedad withdrew from such an intramural labor fight—a highly unlikely circumstance—questions of such international import would remain as to invite retaliatory action from other nations as well as Honduras.

The presence of such highly charged international circumstances brings to mind the admonition of Mr. Chief Justice Marshall in *The Charming Betsy,* 2 Cranch 64, 118 (1804), that "an act of congress ought never to be construed to violate the law of nations if any other possible construction remains. . . ." We therefore conclude, as we did in *Benz,* that for us to sanction the exercise of local sovereignty under such conditions in this "delicate field of international relations there must be present the affirmative intention of the Congress clearly expressed." 353 U. S., at 147. Since neither we nor the parties are able to find any such clear expression, we hold that the Board was without jurisdiction to order the election. This is not to imply, however, "any impairment of our own sovereignty, or limitation of the power of Congress" in this field. *Lauritzen v. Larsen,* 345 U. S. 571, 578 (1953). In fact, just as we directed the parties in *Benz* to the Congress, which "alone has the facilities necessary to make fairly such an important policy decision," 353 U. S., at 147, we conclude here that the arguments should be directed to the Congress rather than to us. Cf. *Lauritzen v. Larsen, supra,* at 593.[j]

. . .

HELLENIC LINES LTD. v. RHODITIS

United States Supreme Court
398 U.S. 306 (1970)

Mr. Justice Douglas delivered the opinion of the Court.

This is a suit under the Jones Act by a seaman who was injured aboard the ship *Hellenic Hero* in the Port of New Orleans. The District Court, sitting without a jury, rendered judgment for the seaman. . . . The Court of Appeals affirmed.

Petitioner Hellenic Lines Ltd. is a Greek corporation that has its largest office in New York and another office in New Orleans. More than 95% of its stock is owned by a United States domiciliary who is a Greek citizen—Pericles G. Callimanopoulos (whom we call Pericles). He lives in Connecticut and manages the corporation out of New York. He has lived in this country since 1945. The ship *Hellenic Hero* is engaged in regularly scheduled runs between various ports of the United States and the Middle East, Pakistan, and India. The District Court found that its entire income is from cargo either originating or terminating in the United States.

Respondent, the seaman, signed on in Greece, and he is a Greek citizen. His contract of employment provides that Greek law and a Greek collective-bargaining agreement apply between the employer and the seaman and that all claims arising out of the employment contract are to be adjudicated by a Greek court. And it seems to be conceded that respondent could obtain relief through Greek courts, if he desired.

---

[j] Justice Goldberg, who had participated in the government's formulation of its position as Secretary of Labor, took no part in consideration of these cases; Justice Douglas filed a brief concurring opinion.

The Jones Act speaks only of "the defendant employer" without any qualifications. In *Lauritzen v. Larsen,* however, we listed seven factors to be considered in determining whether a particular shipowner should be held to be an "employer" for Jones Act purposes:

> (1) the place of the wrongful act; (2) the law of the flag; (3) the allegiance or domicile of the injured seaman; (4) allegiance of the defendant shipowner; (5) the place where the contract of employment was made; (6) the inaccessibility of a foreign forum; and (7) the law of the forum.

Of these seven factors it is urged that four are in favor of the shipowner and against jurisdiction: the ship's flag is Greek; the injured seaman is Greek; the employment contract is Greek; and there is a foreign forum available to the injured seaman.

The *Lauritzen* test, however, is not a mechanical one. We indicated that the flag that a ship flies may, at times, alone be sufficient. The significance of one or more factors must be considered in light of the national interest served by the assertion of Jones Act jurisdiction. Moreover, the list of seven factors in *Lauritzen* was not intended as exhaustive. As held in *Pavlou v. Ocean Traders Marine Corp.,* 211 F. Supp. 320, 325, and approved by the Court of Appeals in the present case, 412 F. 2d, at 923 n. 7, the shipowner's *base of operations* is another factor of importance in determining whether the Jones Act is applicable; and there well may be others.

In *Lauritzen* the injured seaman had been hired in and was returned to the United States, and the shipowner was served here. Those were the only contacts of that shipping operation with this country.

The present case is quite different.

Pericles became a lawful permanent resident alien in 1952. We extend to such an alien the same constitutional protections of due process that we accord citizens. *Kwong Hai Chew v. Colding,* 344 U. S. 590, 596. The injury occurred here. The forum is a United States court. Pericles' base of operations is New York. The *Hellenic Hero* was not a casual visitor; rather, it and many of its sister ships were earning income from cargo originating or terminating here. We see no reason whatsoever to give the Jones Act a strained construction so that this alien owner, engaged in an extensive business operation in this country, may have an advantage over citizens engaged in the same business by allowing him to escape the obligations and responsibility of a Jones Act "employer." The flag, the nationality of the seaman, the fact that his employment contract was Greek, and that he might be compensated there are in the totality of the circumstances of this case minor weights in the scales compared with the substantial and continuing contacts that this alien owner has with this country. If, as stated in *Bartholomew v. Universe Tankships Inc.,* 263 F. 2d 437, the liberal purposes of the Jones Act are to be effectuated, the facade of the operation must be considered as minor, compared with the real nature of the operation and a cold objective look at the actual operational contacts that this ship and this owner have with the United States. By that test the Court of Appeals was clearly right in holding that petitioner Hellenic Lines was an "employer" under the Jones Act.

Affirmed.

Mr. Justice Harlan, with whom The Chief Justice and Mr. Justice Stewart join, dissenting.

I dissent from today's decision holding that a Greek seaman who signs articles in Greece for employment on a Greek-owned, Greek-flag vessel may recover under the Jones Act for shipboard injuries sustained while the vessel was in American territorial waters. This result is supported neither by precedent, nor realistic policy, and in my opinion is far removed from any intention that can reasonably be ascribed to Congress.

. . .

A

[The majority departs from the principle that Congress legislates against a background of international and maritime law, and cannot be presumed to have intended to go as far as the lengths to which the literal terms of its acts might reach. This principle was stated in *Lauritzen* and reiterated in *Romero* and *McCulloch*.]

The only justification that I can see for extending extraterritorially a remedial type provision like § 688 is that the injured seaman is an individual whose well-being is a concern of this country. It was for this reason that *Lauritzen* recognized the residence of the plaintiff as a factor that should properly be considered in deciding who is a "seaman" as Congress employed that term in § 688. See D. Cavers, *The Choice-of-Law Process* 96–97 (1965). . . .

In the early decisions involving citizen and resident alien seamen serving on foreign vessels, some additional factor, such as the vessel's presence in American waters or beneficial American ownership, was considered to be an element justifying recovery. . . . *Lauritzen* in enumerating these factors ("contacts") as independent considerations, was attempting to focus analysis on those factors that are the necessary ingredients for a statutory cause of action: first, as a matter of statutory construction, is plaintiff within that class of seamen that Congress intended to cover by the statute? and, second, is there a sufficient nexus between the defendant and this country so as to justify the assertion of legislative jurisdiction? In other words the Court must define "seaman" and "employer" as those words are used in § 688. In this regard the *situs* of the accident or the vessel's contacts with this country by virtue of its beneficial ownership or the frequency of calls at our ports simply serves as an adequate nexus between this country and defendant to assert jurisdiction in a case where congressional policy is otherwise furthered. But no matter how qualitatively substantial or numerous these kinds of contacts may be, they have no bearing in themselves on whether Jones Act recovery is appropriate in a given instance. For transactions occurring aboard foreign-flag vessels that question should be answered by reference to the plaintiff's relationship to this country. . . . [T]oday's decision and decisions of several lower courts that have taken the phenomenon of "convenient" foreign registry as a wedge for displacing the law of the flag, . . . have, I believe, misconstrued these basic premises on which *Lauritzen* was founded. . . . presupposed or construed legislative purpose to be furthered by reaching across the border.

The *Lauritzen* statement, lifted out of context, has acquired a dynamism and become the justification for recovery by foreign seamen simply on the ground that convenient "registry" somehow circumvents an obligation that Congress desired to impose on all owners within its jurisdiction.

This underlies today's decision which relies on the fact that Hellenic Lines is an American-based operation and its vessels would be accorded a competitive advantage over American-flag vessels were we to permit petitioners to avoid responsibility under the Jones Act. Liability is only one factor that contributes to the higher cost of operating an American-flag vessel. Indeed, recognizing the insurance factor, it is doubtful that this factor is a significant contribution to the competitive advantage of foreign-flag ships, especially given the higher crew wages (see 46 U. S. C. § 1132 requiring American crews) and construction costs for American-flag ships, which must be built in American yards if they are to participate in the congressional programs specifically designed to offset the higher costs that the Court today takes as justification for displacing settled international principles of choice of law. See, *e. g.,* 46 U. S. C. § 883 (coastwise trade); 46 U. S. C. § 1180 (subsidy). See generally S. Lawrence, *United States Merchant Shipping Policies and Politics* 61–67 (1966).

Even were Jones Act liability a significant uncompensated cost in the operation of an American ship, I could not regard this as a reason for extending Jones Act recovery to foreign seamen when the underlying concern of the legislation before us is the adjustment of the risk of loss between individuals and not the regulation of commerce or competition.

B

Today's decision suggests that courts have become mesmerized by contacts, and notwithstanding the purported eschewal of a mechanical application of the *Lauritzen* test, they have lost sight of the primary purpose of *Lauritzen* which, as I conceive it, was to reconcile the all-embracing language of the Jones Act with those principles of comity embodied in international and maritime law that are designed to "foster amicable and workable commercial relations." 345 U. S., at 582. *Lauritzen,* properly understood, should, I submit, be taken to focus the judicial inquiry on the purpose of Congress and the presence or absence of an adequate basis for the assertion of American jurisdiction, when that purpose may be furthered by application of the statute in the circumstances presented.

Where, as in the case before us, the injured plaintiff has no American ties, the inquiry should be directed toward determining what jurisdiction is primarily concerned with plaintiff's welfare and whether that jurisdiction's rule may, consistent with those notions of due process that determine the presence of legislative jurisdiction, govern recovery. In the case before us, there is no reason to disregard either the law of the flag or plaintiff's contractual undertaking to accept Greek law as controlling, thereby in effect assuming that he signed articles under conditions that would justify disregarding the contractual choice of law. Rhoditis is a Greek national who resides in Greece. Under these circumstances Greek law provides the appropriate rule.

I would reverse the judgment of the Court of Appeals, and hold that the Jones Act affords no redress to this seaman.

NOTES AND QUESTIONS

(1)(a) Before analyzing the four seamen's cases in detail, it is worth remembering that here the U.S. Supreme Court is acting not as an arbitrator of interstate conflicts within a constitutional federation, as in the cases in Chapter 5, but as a domestic forum asked by one side to apply the law of the forum, and by the other side to dismiss because that law does not govern the activity in question. Thus the Supreme Court in these cases is in a posture analogous to that of the New York Court of Appeals in the *Kilberg/Babcock* series, Chapter 3, *supra,* and in some ways the *Lauritzen* series resembles the *Babcock* series, though it starts a full decade earlier.

(b) One might be tempted to draw out the analogy, and suggest that the role of the Constitution in the New York cases be compared to the role of the law of nations in the international cases.

In fact, as we saw, the role of the Constitution in state choice of law cases was not very great.[k] The role of international law in these, and succeeding cases, remains to be explored.

(c) A third feature of this series of cases, replicated in all the American cases in this chapter, is that the Court feels free to fashion choice of law rules on its own from a combination of federal common law, international law, and presumptions about the intent of Congress, with no reference to the law of the states, or to *Erie, Klaxon,* or comparable restraints on law-making by federal courts.[l]

(2)(a) Turning to *Lauritzen v. Larsen,* note first that Justice Jackson quickly disposes of a contention that confused lawyers in numerous cases with transnational aspects, particularly in the antitrust area.[m] The issue is not one of jurisdiction, in the sense of due process, either of the person of the defendant or of the subject matter, because there are "minimum contacts" with the United States. What is at issue is choice of law. If, for instance, Danish law gave no protection to the disabled seaman, it seems likely that the Court would have permitted him to recover under the Jones Act, because there would have been no *conflict* of laws; the court would certainly not have dismissed for want of subject matter jurisdiction.[n]

(b) The best argument for Mr. Larsen is that the Jones Act read *"Any seaman . . . may,* at his election, maintain an action for damages [under the Act]." If Congress had wanted to say, "Any seaman holding U.S. citizenship . . .," or, "Any seaman aboard a U.S.-flag vessel . . .," it could have said so. What is the answer to this argument?

(c) By invoking the traditions of international and maritime law, is Justice Jackson imputing an intent to Congress, not writing on a clean slate, as he says, or is he saying that Congress could not have covered Mr. Larsen's accident on a Danish ship in Cuban waters even if it wanted to?

(d) Suppose the Jones Act had read, or was interpreted to read:

> Any seaman, regardless of his citizenship and regardless of the flag of the vessel on which he is employed, may bring an action under this Act, provided the vessel regularly calls at ports in the United States or its owner regularly engages in business in the United States.

Would such a statute be contrary to international law? Ineffective as U.S. law?[o]

(3)(a) Notice Justice Jackson's characterization of the international customary law relevant to the controversy before the Court—"a non-national or international maritime law of impressive maturity and universality":

---

[k] Recall *Pearson v. Northeast Airlines,* p. 135, and *Allstate Insurance Co. v. Hague,* p. 402, *supra.*

[l] For prior evidence of this attitude to cases having a maritime flavor, recall *Bournias,* p. 75 and *Siegelman,* p. 259, *supra.*

[m] See § 10.03, *infra.*

[n] For more on that term, see § 10.04, *infra.*

[o] The ALI *Restatement (Third) of the Foreign Relations Law of the United States* (1987) says:

> § 114. Where fairly possible, a United States statute is to be construed so as not to conflict with international law or with an international agreement of the United States.

> § 115(1)(a). An act of Congress supersedes an earlier rule of international law or a provision of an international agreement as law of the United States if the purpose of the act to supersede the earlier rule or provision is clear or if the Act and the earlier rule or provision cannot be fairly reconciled.

Section 115(1)(b) goes on to make clear that effectiveness of the statute as domestic law does not relieve the United States of its international obligation or of the consequences of violation of that obligation.

It has the force of law, not from extraterritorial reach of national laws, nor from abdication of its sovereign powers by any nation, but from acceptance by common consent of civilized communities designed to foster amicable and workable commercial relations (p. 874).

(b) Justice Jackson goes on to say:

The criteria [for resolving conflicts between competing laws] appear to be arrived at from weighing of the significance of one or more connecting factors between the shipping transaction regulated and the national interest served by the assertion of authority. . . .

He concedes that the courts have not arrived at satisfactory standards and do not apply the standards that they do profess with perfect consistency.

But in dealing with international commerce we cannot be unmindful of the necessity for mutual forbearance if retaliations are to be avoided. . . .

(c) Do these observations resolve the case of the injured seaman?

(d) Having placed the case in an international law setting, Justice Jackson goes on to catalogue possible contacts, mostly as in a tort case—place of wrongful act, domicile of plaintiff, domicile of defendants, the law of the forum, place of contract (since plaintiff is an employee of defendant)—partly with reference points unique to maritime actions, notably the flag of the vessel. Thus the case comes out both as a conflicts or private international law decision and as a decision sounding in public international law. Each approach fortifies the other, and both fortify the conclusion about the intent of Congress.

(4)(a) In *Lauritzen,* the accident took place in Cuba, the parties' domicile and the vessel's flag were Danish; only the place of contracting and the forum were in the United States, and the place of contracting was at least partially offset by the choice-of-Danish-law clause. In *Romero,* the contract was signed in Spain, but the accident, which cost the plaintiff his left leg, took place in the United States. Under traditional American conflicts law, apart from international or maritime considerations, that would have pointed to application of U.S. law, and had the case been put to the drafters of the Act in 1920, they might well have said the Act should apply. But Justice Frankfurter, writing several years before the conflicts revolution, says, "we must apply . . . principles of choice of law that . . . do not depend upon a mechanical application of a doctrine like that of *lex loci delicti commissi"* (p. 879), evidently because of the pull of international law.

(b) Note the source of the principles of international law on which Justice Frankfurter draws. They do not come from treaty, or from decisions of the World Court, but from custom, and from "recognition of our self-regarding respect for the relevant interests of foreign nations in the regulation of maritime commerce as part of the legitimate concern of the international community" and "the interacting interests of the United States and of foreign countries." The opinion also speaks of "the circumspection appropriate when this Court is adjudicating issues inevitably entangled in the conduct of our international relations."

(c) Justice Black, nearly always the champion of injured workers, dissents in *Romero.* He argues that what is good or bad for the country is not the proper basis of the Court's decision of a particular law suit; if the proponents of the Act had been asked in 1920 whether they wanted to include foreign seamen injured in the United States, "I cannot but feel" that they would have said yes. If he is right about what Congress would have thought had it thought about the point at all, does that undermine the majority's position? Or is the right rule the one stated by Justice

Marshall[p] and by § 114 of the *Foreign Relations Restatement,* that the burden is on those who would construe the intent of the legislature as derogating from general international law?

(d) In *Lauritzen* and *Romero* there was little controversy about the proposition that general maritime or international law looks predominantly to the law of the flag of the vessel. As consensus on the substance of a given rule of international law becomes weaker, would you expect the principle of construing the legislature's intent to be consistent with international law to become weaker as well? Reconsider this point in the light of *Alcoa,* p. 909, *infra.*

(5)(a) Professor Brainerd Currie, in a major article about the *Romero* case, wrote:

> The only way to begin discussion of the conflict-of-laws aspect of the *Romero* case is with a word of fervent thanksgiving for the Court's adherence to the basic methodology of *Lauritzen* v. *Larsen.* As in *Lauritzen,* there is no mechanical approach to the question of the applicability of American law. There is no preclusive "characterization" of the case as one of contract or of tort; there is no slavish submission to the law of the place of contracting, nor of the place of injury, nor of the flag. There is no territorial dogma . . .. A prime advantage of [the approach of "reconciling our own with foreign interests and . . . accommodating the reach of our own laws to those of other nations"] over traditional conflict of laws methodology is that, while inquiring specifically into the governmental policies and interests involved, it explicitly recognizes the power of the legislative branch to determine what domestic policy is and when domestic interests require application of that policy, so that legislative rectification of any interpretation that does not serve the public interest is positively invited . . .[q]

Is that persuasive? Is it what you would expect from Currie?

(b) Currie went on to say that while the method employed by the Court in the two cases was admirably constructive, in *Romero* insufficient consideration might have been given to legitimately applicable American policy, because Romero had incurred heavy medical and related expenses in the United States. But the suggestion referred to in the last full paragraph of *Lauritzen,* that plaintiff should be entitled to enjoy the benefits of the Jones Act in order to equalize the costs of foreign and domestic shipment, earns Currie's rebuke as it did that of the Court, because such a policy "was so collateral to the obvious policy of the Jones Act . . . and so predatory that no grounds existed for inferring it, even if the Court had been so inclined."[r]

(6)(a) *Lauritzen* and *Romero* basically read like conflict of laws decisions informed by international law. *McCulloch* reads more like affirmation of a "well established rule of international law," which Congress could violate in exercise of U.S. sovereignty (pp. 882–83), but which is not subject to the techniques of counting or weighing contacts and interests. Is the issue clearer in *McCulloch,* the union organizing case, than in the seamen's injury cases?

(b) The thrust of the Supreme Court's decision in *McCulloch* is made clearer by comparing it to the opinion of the Court of Appeals for the Second Circuit.[s] Judge Friendly, writing for

---

[p] In the excerpt from *The Charming Betsy* quoted at p. 873, *supra.*

[q] Currie, *The Silver Oar and All That: A Study of the Romero Case,* 27 U. Chi. L. Rev. 1, 65–66, (1959), reprinted in abridged version in B. Currie, *Selected Essays on the Conflict of Laws* 361, 364–65 (1963).

[r] 27 U. Chi. L. Rev. at 68, Currie, *Selected Essays* at 367.

[s] In response to certification of a union election by the National Labor Relations Board, Empresa Hondurena, the shipowner, applied for an injunction in New York against the regional director of the NLRB, while Sociedad Nacional de Marineros, the Honduran union, applied for an injunction in the District of Columbia against the Chairman of the NLRB. Eventually the two proceedings were consolidated for argument and decision in the Supreme Court.

the Second Circuit in reversing the District Court's refusal to enjoin the election, was not prepared to establish an absolute preference for the law of the flag, but would weigh competing interests of the concerned states:

> The [Labor] Board is right in saying the scope of its power in respect of the [crew of the Honduran-flag vessel] is not to be determined by the simple notion that a Honduran registered ship is a floating piece of Honduran territory . . .
>
> [Quoting *Lauritzen* at p. 874 about the "cardinal importance given to the law of the flag"], how "cardinal" the importance is, and how much "weight" should be given must depend, in the absence of clear expression by Congress, on what other factors of foreign and United States interest are present, and on the nature of the United States statute sought to be applied, taking particular account of the danger that an attempt to apply our law may result in collision with the foreign sovereign. . . . Here, application of [stated sections] of the National Labor Relations Act would involve the risk of continuous conflict between the United States and Honduras. . . .
>
> The case made by [Empresa Hondurena's] complaint goes far beyond the flying of the Honduran flag, important as *Lauritzen* teaches that to be. In this case there is also the Honduran citizenship of the crews, the employment of the crews in Honduras under Honduran articles, the vessels' regular visits to Honduras, the Honduran corporate identity—admittedly not fictitious—of the owner, the long recognition of and contract with the Honduran union, and the provisions of Honduran law regulating labor matters . . .. The only United States contacts not matched by Honduran ones are United Fruit's ownership and its direction and use of the voyages; these are substantially outweighed, for the purpose here at issue, by Honduras' interests.[t]

(7)(a) Returning to injured seamen, the essential facts in *Rhoditis* seem to be the same as in the other cases—alien crew on foreign-flag vessel, with a choice of Greek law in the contract of employment. Yet the outcome is different. Why?

(b) If the answer is the beneficial ownership of the vessel by a U.S. resident, isn't that true of *McCulloch* as well? After *Rhoditis,* should the American labor unions make another effort to organize flag-of-convenience vessels beneficially owned by and chartered to American companies?[u]

(c) Would you think the piercing of the corporate veil in *Rhoditis* is itself subject to scrutiny under international law standards? Reconsider this question after reading the *Fruehauf* and *Pipeline* cases, § 10.05, *infra.*

(8)(a) It is easy to vary the facts of *Rhoditis* slightly to explore what is and what is not critical in the opinion:

  (i) Suppose Pericles, as the Court calls him, had arrived in the United States two years, instead of 25 years, before the accident;

---

[t] *Empresa Hondurena de Vapores, S.A. v. McLeod,* 300 F.2d 222 at 234 (2d Cir. 1962).

[u] No such development occurred in the United States. However, attempts to change the governing international law have been made in the United Nations Conference on Trade and Development (UNCTAD), generally over the opposition of the industrial states, including the United States. See Osieke, *Flags of Convenience Vessels: Recent Developments,* 73 Am. J. Int'l L. 604 (1979); Juda, *World Shipping, UNCTAD, and the New International Economic Order,* 35 Int'l Org. 493 (1981); proposed *UN Convention on Conditions for Registration of Ships,* UN Doc. TD/RS/CONF/23 (1986).

(ii) Suppose he owned 40 percent of the shares of Hellenic Lines, while ownership of the other shares was distributed among many citizens and residents of Greece;

(iii) Or suppose Pericles owned 40 percent and one other Greek citizen and resident owned the other 60 percent;

(iv) Suppose Pericles owned only a small quantity of shares, but nevertheless the company was managed from New York and was engaged predominantly in carriage to and from the United States;

(v) Suppose the accident had occurred on the high seas; . . . in Greece; . . . in Spain.

Would any of these variations (alone or in combination) change the result?

(b) If, to take Justice Harlan's approach, the Court had focused on the plaintiff, and it had turned out that though he was a Greek citizen, he had resided for many years in the United States, the Court might well have concluded that Mr. Rhoditis was one of those whom Congress intended to protect when it adopted the Jones Act. Why should the residence of the principal shareholder of the employer matter?

(c) Congress did not take up the suggestion in the last full paragraph of *Lauritzen* to change the coverage of the Jones Act. Is the inference from *Rhoditis* that the role of "settled principles of international law" in construing the intent of Congress is diminished? That the "'principles of comity embodied in international and maritime law that are designed to foster amicable and workable commercial relations' " (to quote Harlan quoting Jackson) are of diminished relevance in the eyes of the Supreme Court? Other cases that we have seen—e.g., *Zapata* and *Scherck*[v] —suggest that such an inference is inconsistent with the Court's perspective on international commercial relations generally. Can you account for the shift from *Lauritzen* to *Rhoditis* in some other way?

(9)(a) It was suggested in Question (1)(a), *supra,* that the series of cases from *Larsen* to *Rhoditis* is analogous to the *Babcock* series in New York and similar developments in other states of the United States, in that the court is searching for reasons to apply or not to apply forum law to an interstate/international transaction. Can the Supreme Court's shift be explained by a shift from contacts to interest analysis paralleling the domestic developments? Or to principles of preference?

(b) How would you expect Judge Cavers to decide the *Rhoditis* case?[w]

(c) *Romero* raises the question, albeit in a context confused by the debate about jurisdiction of the federal courts, whether the issue is really one of construing an act of Congress, or simply one of choosing the applicable law. Suppose Messrs. Larsen, Romero, and Rhoditis simply preferred the American common law of torts to the regimes of accident compensation available in Denmark, Spain, or Greece. Would the cases all come out just as they actually did? Or is there something special about the vaguely focused act of Congress? Putting the question another way, is the presumption about not construing domestic law contrary to the traditions of

---

[v] See Chapter 4, pp. 294, 315, *supra.*

[w] Professor Cavers, in the book from which the *Adams v. Knickerbocker* series is taken, cites *Lauritzen v. Larsen* as a good example of the process of construing the intent of the legislature by reference to the general objectives of the legislation in question, rather than focusing on particular words such as "Any seaman . . ." Cavers, *The Choice of Law Process,* 97 (1965).

(customary) international law equally valid with respect to common as to statutory law? Should it be?[x]

§ 10.02 Public Policy in an International Context

HOLMAN v. JOHNSON

King's Bench
1 Cowp. 341, 98 Eng. Rep. 1120 (1775)

Assumpsit for goods sold and delivered: plea non assumpsit and verdict for the plaintiff. Upon a rule to shew cause why a new trial should not be granted, Lord Mansfield reported the case, which was shortly this: the plaintiff who was resident at, and an inhabitant of, Dunkirk, together with his partner, a native of that place, sold and delivered a quantity of tea, for the price of which the action was brought, to the order of the defendant, knowing it was intended to be smuggled by him into England: they had, however, no concern in the smuggling scheme itself, but merely sold this tea to him, as they would have done to any other person in the common and ordinary course of their trade.

Mr. Mansfield, [on behalf of defendant], insisted, that the contract for the sale of this tea being founded upon an intention to make an illicit use of it, which intention and purpose was with the privity and knowledge of the plaintiff, he was not entitled to the assistance of the laws of this country to recover the value of it. He cited Huberus 2 vol. 538, 539, and *Robinson v. Bland,* to shew that the contract must be judged of by the laws of this country, and consequently that an action for the price of the tea could not be supported here.

Mr. Dunning, Mr. Davenport, and Mr. Buller, contra, for the plaintiff, contended, that the contract being complete by the delivery of the goods at Dunkirk, where the plaintiff might lawfully sell, and the defendant lawfully buy, it could neither directly nor indirectly be said to be done in violation of the laws of this country; consequently it was a good and valid contract, and the plaintiff entitled to recover. It was of no moment or concern to the plaintiff what the defendant meant to do with the tea, nor had he any interest in the event. If he had, or if the contract had been that the plaintiff should deliver the tea in England, it would have been a different question; but there was no such undertaking on his part. They pressed the argument ab inconvenienti, and cited several cases. MSS. at Ni. Pri. before Lord Mansfield, sittings in London—An action brought by the plaintiffs, who were lacemerchants in Paris, for laces (which were contraband in this country) sold and delivered to the defendant's order at Calais. The question made was, whether the vendor of contraband goods at Paris was not bound to run the risk of their being smuggled into this country? But Lord Mansfield held, that as the contract on the part of the plaintiff was complete by his delivering the laces at Calais, he was clearly entitled to recover, and the jury found a verdict accordingly.—*Faikney v. Reynous and Richardson,* East, 7 Geo. 3, B. R. since reported in 4 Bur. 2069, & 1 Black. 633, where one partner in a stock-jobbing contract lent the other 1500 &. to pay his moiety of the differences on the recounter day; and though this was pleaded to the bond, the Court upon demurrer over-ruled the plea, and held the plaintiff was

---

[x] For discussion of these and subsequent lower court cases in an admiralty context, see Gilmore & Black, *The Law of Admiralty* 471–84 (2d ed. 1975).

entitled to recover. *Bruston v. Clifford,* in Chan. before Lord Camden, 4th December, 1767. *Alsibrook v. Hall* in C. B. where money paid for the defendant for a gaming debt was held recoverable by the plaintiff.

LORD MANSFIELD.

There can be no doubt, but that every action tried here must be tried by the law of England; but the law of England says, that in a variety of circumstances, with regard to contracts legally made abroad, the laws of the country where the cause of action arose shall govern.—There are a great many cases which every country says shall be determined by the laws of foreign countries where they arise. But I do not see how the principles on which that doctrine obtains are applicable to the present case. For no country ever takes notice of the revenue laws of another.

The objection, that a contract is immoral or illegal as between plaintiff and defendant, sounds at all times very ill in the mouth of the defendant. It is not for his sake, however, that the objection is ever allowed; but it is founded in general principles of policy, which the defendant has the advantage of, contrary to the real justice, as between him and the plaintiff, by accident, if I may so say. The principle of public policy is this; *ex dolo malo non oritur actio.* No Court will lend its aid to a man who founds his cause of action upon an immoral or an illegal act. If, from the plaintiff's own stating or otherwise, the cause of action appears to arise *ex turpi causâ,* or the transgression of a positive law of this country, there the Court says he has no right to be assisted. It is upon that ground the Court goes; not for the sake of the defendant, but because they will not lend their aid to such a plaintiff. So if the plaintiff and defendant were to change sides, and the defendant was to bring his action against the plaintiff, the latter would then have the advantage of it; for where both are equally in fault, *potior est conditio defendentis.*

The question therefore, is whether, in this case, the plaintiff's demand is founded upon the ground of any immoral act or contract, or upon the ground of his being guilty of any thing which is prohibited by a positive law of this country.—An immoral contract it certainly is not; for the revenue laws themselves, as well as the offences against them, are all positivi juris. What then is the contract of the plaintiff? It is this: being a resident and inhabitant of Dunkirk, together with his partner, who was born there, he sells a quantity of tea to the defendant, and delivers it at Dunkirk to the defendant's order, to be paid for in ready money there, or by bills drawn personally upon him in England. This is an action brought merely for goods sold and delivered at Dunkirk. Where then, or in what respect is the plaintiff guilty of any crime? Is there any law of England transgressed by a person making a complete sale of a parcel of goods at Dunkirk, and giving credit for them? The contract is complete, and nothing is left to be done. The seller, indeed, knows what the buyer is going to do with the goods, but has no concern in the transaction itself. It is not a bargain to be paid in case the vendee should succeed in landing the goods; but the interest of the vendor is totally at an end, and his contract complete by the delivery of the goods at Dunkirk.

To what a dangerous extent would this go if it were to be held a crime. If contraband clothes are bought in France, and brought home hither; or if glass bought abroad, which ought to pay a great duty, is run into England; shall the French taylor or the glass-manufacturer stand to the risk or loss attending their being run into England? Clearly not. Debt follows the person, and may be recovered in England, let the contract of debt be made where it will; and the law allows a fiction for the sake of expediting the remedy. Therefore, I am clearly of opinion, that the vendors of these goods are not guilty of any offence, nor have they transgressed against the provisions of any Act of Parliament.

I am very glad the old books have been looked into. The doctrine Huberus lays down, is founded in good sense, and upon general principles of justice. I entirely agree with him. He puts the general case in question, thus: Tit. *De Conflictu Legum, vol 2, pag. 539.* "*In certo loco merces quaedam prohibitae sunt. Si vendantur ibi, contractus est nullus. Verum, si merx eadem alibi sit vendita, ubi non erat interdicta, emptor condemnabitur, quia, contractus inde ab initio validus fuit.*" Translated, it might be rendered thus: In England, tea, which has not paid duty, is prohibited; and if sold there the contract is null and void. But if sold and delivered at a place where it is not prohibited, as at Dunkirk, and an action is brought for the price of it in England, the buyer shall be condemned to pay the price; because the original contract was good and valid.—He goes on thus: "*Verum si merces venditae in altero loco, ubi prohibitae sunt essent tradendae, jam non fieret condemnatio, quia repugnaret hoc juri et commodo reipublicae quae merces prohibuit.*" Apply this in the same manner.—But if the goods sold were to be delivered in England, where they are prohibited; the contract is void, and the buyer shall not be liable in an action for the price, because it would be an inconvenience and prejudice to the State if such an action could be maintained.

The gist of the whole turns upon this; that the conclusive delivery was at Dunkirk. If the defendant had bespoke the tea at Dunkirk to be sent to England at a certain price; and the plaintiff had undertaken to send it into England, or had had any concern in the running it into England, he would have been an offender against the laws of this country. But upon the facts of the case, from the first to the last, he clearly has offended against no law of England. Therefore, let the rule for a new trial be discharged.

The three other Judges concurred.

GOVERNMENT OF INDIA v. TAYLOR

House of Lords
[1955] A.C. 491

The facts, stated by Viscount Simonds, were as follows: The respondents to this appeal were the liquidators in the voluntary winding up of an English company, the Delhi Electric Supply & Traction Co. Ld., which was in the year 1906 incorporated for the purpose of operating an electricity supply undertaking and tramway undertakings under a licence and order granted by the Municipality of Delhi. The appellant was the Government of India, a sovereign independent republic which acknowledged Her Majesty as head of the British Commonwealth. The question for decision was whether Vaisey J. and the Court of Appeal were right in rejecting the appellant's claim to prove in the liquidation of the company in respect of an amount of income tax due from the company to the appellant under Indian income tax law.

The company having carried on its undertakings in India until the year 1947, in that year sold the whole of them to the Government of India as from March 2, 1947, for the sum of Rs.82,11,580. The greater part of that sum was paid to the company in India on March 1, 1947, and was remitted to England a few days later. The balance was paid to the company in India in September, 1948, and remitted to England shortly afterwards.

On April 18, 1947, the Indian Income Tax and Excess Profits Tax (Amendment) Act, 1947, was passed, and by section 6 thereof section 12B was inserted in the Indian Income Tax Act, 1922. The opening words of section 12B were as follows:

> The tax shall be payable by an assessee under the head "Capital gains" in respect of any profits or gains arising from the sale, exchange or transfer of a capital asset effected after March 31, 1946; and such profits and gains shall be deemed to be income of the previous year in which the sale, exchange or transfer took place.

This amendment was deemed by section 1 (2) of the Act of 1947 to have come into force on March 31, 1947.

On May 25, 1949, the company went into voluntary liquidation by special resolution and the respondent Taylor and one Lovering were appointed joint liquidators. They had previously as directors of the company made a statutory declaration as to the solvency of the company and later in their statement as to the position of the liquidation of the company they referred to the liability for special taxation in India. They also in March, 1951, inserted a notice in the Gazette of India calling upon all creditors to prove their debts or claims and acceded to a request by the Commissioner of Income Tax at Delhi to stay the liquidation proceedings to enable his Department to prove their claim.

On October 24, 1951, the Commissioner of Income Tax served a demand notice under section 29 of the Indian Income Tax Act, 1922, for the year 1948–49 calling on the company to pay Rs.16,54,945.11.0 of tax, which consisted mainly of a sum of Rs.15,62,817.3.0 representing tax on the surplus on the sale of the company's undertakings. Various steps were taken in India, appeals against the assessment, payment of a sum on account out of assets which were still in India, re-assessment of the amounts claimed to be due under the head "capital gains" and further demands which culminated in a claim upon the surviving liquidator Taylor in February, 1953 (Lovering having in the meantime died), for sums of Rs.15,62,817.3.0 and Rs.13,001.10.0. The quantum of those assessments was still a matter of appeal in India, but that there was some liability in India in respect of tax for capital gains was beyond doubt, and there appeared to be also an ascertained liability in respect of ordinary income tax which was not under appeal.

It was in those circumstances that the respondent Taylor in April and May, 1953, rejected the appellant's claims, stating that no part of the company's assets (all of which were then in England) could properly be applied in payment of any claim for taxes by a foreign Government. Thereupon the appellant applied to the High Court in England for an order reversing the rejection of its claim and on July 30, 1953 (the respondent Hume having in the meantime been appointed joint liquidator with the respondent Taylor), Vaisey J. made an order refusing the appellant's application. From that order the appellant appealed to the Court of Appeal (Evershed M.R., Jenkins and Morris L.JJ.) and that court unanimously dismissed the appeal.

VISCOUNT SIMONDS

. . .

My Lords, I will admit that I was greatly surprised to hear it suggested that the courts of this country would and should entertain a suit by a foreign State to recover a tax. For at any time since I have had any acquaintance with the law I should have said as Rowlatt J. said in the *King of the Hellenes v. Brostron*[1] :

> It is perfectly elementary that a foreign government cannot come here—nor will the courts of other countries allow our Government to go there—and sue a person found in that jurisdiction for taxes levied and which he is declared to be liable to in the country to which he belongs.

---

[1] (1923) 16 Ll.L. Rep. 190, 193.

. . .

My Lords, the history and origin of the rule, if it be a rule, are not easy to ascertain and there is on the whole remarkably little authority upon the subject. I am inclined to agree with the Court of Appeal that the early cases of *Attorney-General v. Lutwydge*[4] and *Boucher v. Lawson,*[5] to which some reference was made, do not give much help. It is otherwise when we advance a few years to the age of Lord Mansfield C.J. That great judge in a series of cases repeated the formula "For no country ever takes notice of the revenue laws of another."[6]

. . . Where Lord Mansfield led, Lord Kenyon C.J. followed, though he was not a judge who followed blindly. . . . Here, my Lords, is a formidable array of authority.

The matter is carried one step further by the fact that the rule appears to have been recognized by Parliament. For I see no other reason for the exclusion from the advantages of the Foreign Judgments (Reciprocal Enforcement) Act, 1933, of a judgment for "a sum payable in respect of taxes or other charges of a like nature or in respect of a fine or other penalty" (section 1 (2) (*b*)), except that it was regarded as axiomatic that the courts of one country do not have regard to the revenue laws of another and therefore will not allow judgments for foreign taxes to be enforced.

It may well be asked, then, upon what grounds this appeal is founded. I think that counsel relied upon two main grounds, first that Lord Mansfield's proposition, which I have more than once quoted, extended to revenue law a doctrine properly applicable only to penal law and (I think it must be faced) that Lord Mansfield was wrong in so extending it and everyone who has since followed him was wrong: and secondly that, whatever may have been the rule in the past, there ought to be and is a trend towards a mitigation of the rule, particularly as between States which are united by the bonds of federal union or by such looser ties as bind the British Commonwealth of nations.

My Lords, these seem to me frail weapons with which to attack a strong fortress.

. . .

I would dismiss this appeal with costs.

Lord Keith of Avonholm.

One explanation of the rule . . . may be thought to be that enforcement of a claim for taxes is but an extension of the sovereign power which imposed the taxes, and that an assertion of sovereign authority by one State within the territory of another, as distinct from a patrimonial claim by a foreign sovereign, is (treaty or convention apart) contrary to all concepts of independent sovereignties. Another explanation has been given by an eminent American judge, Judge Learned Hand, in the case of *Moore v. Mitchell,*[24] in a passage, quoted also by Kingsmill Moore J. in the case of *Peter Buchanan Ld.* as follows:

> While the origin of the exception in the case of penal liabilities does not appear in the books, a sound basis for it exists, in my judgment, which includes liabilities for taxes as well. Even in the case of ordinary municipal liabilities, a court will not recognize those arising in a

---

[4] (1729) Bunb. 280

[5] (1735–6) Cunning. 144

[6] See *Planché v. Fletcher,* (1779) 1 Doug. 251, 253. *Holman v. Johnson,* (1775) 1 Cowp. 341, 343. *Lever v. Fletcher,* (1780) Unrep.

[24] (1929) 30 F. (2d) 600, 604.

foreign State, if they run counter to the "settled public policy" of its own. Thus a scrutiny of the liability is necessarily always in reserve, and the possibility that it will be found not to accord with the policy of the domestic State. This is not a troublesome or delicate inquiry when the question arises between private persons, but it takes on quite another face when it concerns the relations between the foreign State and its own citizens or even those who may be temporarily within its borders. To pass upon the provisions for the public order of another State is, or at any rate should be, beyond the powers of the court; it involves the relations between the States themselves, with which courts are incompetent to deal, and which are intrusted to other authorities. It may commit the domestic State to a position which would seriously embarrass its neighbour. Revenue laws fall within the same reasoning; they affect a State in matters as vital to its existence as its criminal laws. No court ought to undertake an inquiry which it cannot prosecute without determining whether those laws are consonant with its own notions of what is proper.

On either of the explanations which I have just stated I find a solid basis of principle for a rule which has long been recognized and which has been applied by a consistent train of decisions. It may be possible to find reasons for modifying the rule as between States of a federal union. But that consideration, in my opinion, has no relevance to this case.

I agree the appeal should be dismissed.

LORD SOMERVELL OF HARROW.

The first issue in the present appeal is whether a foreign State can use the courts of this country for the collection of its taxes. The statement by Lord Mansfield in *Holman v. Johnson:* "For no country ever takes notice of the revenue laws of another," may include the present issue but goes beyond it and is, I think, directed to a different problem. The plaintiff claimed the price of tea delivered in Dunkirk. The defendant intended, as the plaintiff knew, to smuggle the tea into England. Lord Mansfield uses the words cited in considering the lex loci contractus. He is stating that the courts there would in no circumstances have regard to any illegality arising under the revenue laws of this or any other country. He then proceeds to consider the alleged illegality under our law: The question whether today our courts would as between parties enforce a contract to break the revenue laws of another country has little if any relevance to the issue which we have to decide. In *Ralli Brothers v. Compania Naviera Sota y Aznar*[32] Scrutton L.J., in a passage cited by the Master of the Rolls, reserved that issue for consideration should it arise. What I desire to make clear is that I am not dealing with that issue.

There is no decision binding on your Lordships' House and the matter therefore falls to be considered in principle. If one State could collect its taxes through the courts of another, it would have arisen through what is described, vaguely perhaps, as comity or the general practice of nations inter se. The appellant was therefore in a difficulty from the outset in that after considerable research no case of any country could be found in which taxes due to State A had been enforced in the courts of State B. Apart from the comparatively recent English, Scotch and Irish cases there is no authority. There are, however, many propositions for which no express authority can be found because they have been regarded as self-evident to all concerned. There must have been many potential defendants.

Tax gathering is an administrative act, though in settling the quantum as well as in the final act of collection judicial process may be involved. Our courts will apply foreign law if it is the

---

[32] [1920] 2 K.B. 287, 300; sub nom. *Sota y Aznar v. Ralli Brothers,* 36 T.L.R. 456.

proper law of a contract, the subject of a suit. Tax gathering is not a matter of contract but of authority and administration as between the State and those within its jurisdiction. If one considers the initial stages of the process, which may, as the records of your Lordships' House show, be intricate and prolonged, it would be remarkable comity if State B allowed the time of its courts to be expended in assisting in this regard the tax gatherers of State A. Once a judgment has been obtained and it is a question only of its enforcement the factor of time and expense will normally have disappeared. The principle remains. The claim is one for a tax.

. . .

The appellant is asking the English courts to do what the courts of no other country have done. In some fields this might commend the argument but here, for the reason which I stated at the outset, it is fatal.

Appeal dismissed.

REGAZZONI v. K. C. SETHIA (1944) LTD.

House of Lords
[1958] A.C. 301

The facts as stated by Viscount Simonds were as follows: The appellant, who resided in Switzerland, brought the action out of which this appeal arose against the respondents claiming damages for breach of contract. He alleged that the respondents had agreed to sell and deliver to him September/October, 1948, c.i.f. Genoa 500,000 jute bags of the quality and standard known in the trade as new B twills and that they had wrongfully repudiated the agreement. The respondents defended the action on numerous grounds, with only one of which the House of Lords were now concerned, namely, that "the said contract, if any, was to the [appellant's] knowledge an illegal contract and/or was void and unenforceable in that it had for its purpose an object which was illegal and/or contrary to public policy, namely, the taking and shipment of jute goods from India where the ultimate destination was the Union of South Africa, in breach of" a certain Act of the Indian Parliament and Regulations made thereunder.

The Act in question was the Sea Customs Act, 1878, which (as modified up to December 1, 1950) provided by section 19 that the Central Government might "from time to time by notification in the [Official Gazette] prohibit or restrict the bringing or taking by sea or by land goods of any specified description into or out of [the States across any customs frontier as defined by the Central Government]," and by section 134 that the Central Government might from time to time by similar notification "prohibit at any specified port or at all ports, the transhipment of any specified class of goods, generally or when destined for any specified ports." By section 138 of the Act provision was made for security for the due shipment, export and landing of goods and by section 167 for the punishment of offences. The prescribed penalties were severe. It was provided that if any goods, the importation or exportation of which was prohibited or restricted by or under the Act, should be imported into or exported from India contrary to such prohibition or restriction, or if any attempt should be made so to import or export any such goods, the goods themselves should be liable to confiscation, and any person concerned in any such offence should be liable to a penalty not exceeding three times the value of the goods or not exceeding 1,000 rupees.

In exercise of the powers conferred by this Act on July 17, 1946, the Central Government of India duly made an order prohibiting the taking

> by sea or by land out of British India of goods from whatever place arriving which are destined for any port or place in the Union of South Africa or in respect of which the Chief Customs Officer is satisfied that the goods although destined for a port or place outside the Union of South Africa are intended to be taken to the Union of South Africa.

VISCOUNT SIMONDS stated the claim and the defence and the Indian legislation and continued: my Lords, I do not think it necessary to state at length the facts of the case. They have been found by Sellers J. and his findings were accepted by the Court of Appeal. No other conclusion was, in my opinion, possible than that (in the words of the learned judge)

> both parties . . . contemplated and intended that the contract goods would be shipped from India and be made available in Genoa so that the plaintiff might make a resale or fulfil a bargain of resale to the South African buying agency.

Nor is it to be doubted that both parties were well aware of the restrictions imposed by the order of July 17, 1946. A strenuous attempt was made to persuade your Lordships that the contract did not infringe Indian law, and this was vouched by a Mr. Nissim, whose qualification to give expert evidence was not challenged. But I must say, with all respect to him, that I find his testimony confused and unconvincing. It may well be that an Indian shipper would not be subject to any penalty if he could prove that he was unaware of the ultimate destination of the goods. But it is not possible for parties whose common intention it is to procure the shipment of goods from India directly or indirectly to the Union of South Africa to plead the innocence of the transaction on the ground that the Indian shipper may be deceived or even that the Chief Customs Officer may be satisfied (contrary to the fact) that the ultimate destination is not the Union of South Africa. On the contrary, it must be assumed that the Chief Customs Officer would not be so satisfied: if so, the shipment inevitably falls within the prohibition and could only be carried out in violation of Indian law.

The question then arises—and it is, as I say, the only question for your Lordships' consideration—whether the respondents were justified in repudiating the contract. They claim to be justified on the ground that I have already stated. Their broad proposition is that whether or not the proper law of the contract is English law, an English court will not enforce a contract, or award damages for its breach, if its performance will involve the doing of an act in a foreign and friendly State which violates the law of that State. For this they cite the authority of the well-known case of *Foster v. Driscoll*,[2] and much of the debate in this House has been whether that case was rightly decided, and if so, whether it is distinguishable from the present case. The appellant contends that it was not rightly decided, and further invokes a familiar principle which he states in these wide but questionable terms, "An English court will not have regard to a foreign law of a penal, revenue, or political character," and claims that the Indian law here in question is of such a character.

My Lords, in the consideration of this matter I deem it of the utmost importance to bear in mind that we are not here concerned with a suit by a foreign State to enforce its laws. The recent case in this House of *Government of India v. Taylor* shows beyond all doubt that an English court will not enforce the penal or revenue laws of another country at the suit of that country.

---

[2] [1929] 1 K.B. 470; [In this case the English court refused to enforce a contract made in England by English nationals and residents for the importation of whiskey into the United States during Prohibition.]

That proposition was there exhaustively examined and nothing remains to be said about it except that there is still a question how far, if at all, the doctrine extends to laws which are described as having a "political" or "public" character. It is clear at least, as Denning L.J. said in this case, that "these courts do not sit to collect taxes for another country or to inflict punishments for it." But, as I say, we are not concerned with such a case, but with a very different question, viz., *whether* in a suit between private persons the court will enforce a contract which involves the doing in a foreign country of an act which is illegal by, and violates, the law of that country. When I say "foreign country" I mean a foreign and friendly country and will not repeat the phrase. In the statement of the question I call particular attention to the words "the doing in a foreign country," for it may well be that different considerations will arise and a different conclusion will be reached if the law of the contract is English and the contract can be wholly performed in England, or at least in some other country than that whose law makes the act illegal. . . . There are points at which the two questions appear to touch each other, and sometimes the one proposition has been treated as an exception on the other. But there is, I think, a fundamental difference. It can hardly be regarded as a matter of comity that the courts of this country will not entertain a suit by a foreign State to enforce its revenue laws. It is, on the other hand, nothing else than comity which has influenced our courts to refuse as a matter of public policy to enforce, or to award damages for the breach of, a contract which involves the violation of foreign law on foreign soil, and it is the limits of this principle that we have to examine. If the principle is, as I think it clearly is, based on public policy, your Lordships will not hesitate, while disclaiming any intention to create any new head of public policy, to apply an old principle to new circumstances.

Just as public policy avoids contracts which offend against our own law, so it will avoid at least some contracts which violate the laws of a foreign State, and it will do so because public policy demands that deference to international comity. The question is what contracts? . . . the principle being based on public policy, exceptions to it must be similarly based. It would, therefore, not be surprising if a contract, in one age, falls within the proposition, in another, without it. This observation has particular relevance to the first case that I shall cite. In *Boucher v. Lawson*, the trade of exporting gold from Portugal being prohibited by the law of that country, Lord Hardwicke, then Lord Chief Justice, nevertheless upheld a contract which involved the violation of that law, observing that

> if it should be laid down, that because goods are prohibited to be exported by the laws of any foreign country from whence they are brought, therefore the parties should have no remedy or action here, it would cut off all benefit of such trade from this kingdom, which would be of very bad consequence to the principal and most beneficial branches of our trade; nor does it ever seem to have been admitted.

I must admit to some doubt whether, if this case had come before the court two hundred years later, so robust an assertion in favour of national interest to the prejudice of international comity would have been made. But, at any rate, in what might be regarded as purely revenue laws the same idea persisted.

. . . It does not follow from the fact that today the court will not enforce a revenue law at the suit of a foreign State that today it will enforce a contract which requires the doing of an act in a foreign country which violates the revenue law of that country. The two things are not complementary or co-extensive. This may be seen if for revenue law penal law is substituted. For an English court will not enforce a penal law at the suit of a foreign State, yet it would be surprising if it would enforce a contract which required the commission of a crime in that State. It is sufficient, however, for the purposes of the present appeal to say that, whether or not an exception must still be made in regard to the breach of a revenue law in deference to old authority, there is no ground for making an exception in regard to any other law. I should myself have said—and this is, I think, the only point upon which I do not agree with the Court of Appeal—that the present case was precisely covered by the decision in *Ralli Brothers.* For when the fact is found that the very thing which the parties intended to do was to export the jute bags from India in order that they might go via Genoa to the Union of South Africa, it appears to me irrelevant that upon the face of the documents that wrongful intention was not disclosed. But, whether this is so or not, it is clearly covered by *Foster v. Driscoll,* a decision the correctness of which is not to be doubted. . . . The appeal should, in my opinion, be dismissed with costs.

LORD REID. . . .

To my mind, the question whether this contract is enforceable by English courts is not, properly speaking, a question of international law. The real question is one of public policy in English law: but in considering this question we must have in mind the background of international law and international relationships often referred to as the comity of nations. This is not a case of a contract being made in good faith but one party thereafter finding that he cannot perform his part of the contract without committing a breach of foreign law in the territory of the foreign country. If this contract is held to be unenforceable, it should, in my opinion, be because from the beginning the contract was tainted so that the courts of this country will not assist either party to enforce it.

I do not wish to express any opinion about a case where parties agree to deal with goods which they both know have already been smuggled out of a foreign country, or about a case where the seller knows that the buyer intends to use the goods for an illegal purpose or to smuggle them into a foreign country. Such cases may raise difficult questions. The crucial fact in this case appears to me to be that both parties knew that the contract could not be performed without the respondents procuring a breach of the law of India within the territory of that country.

On that question I do not get very much assistance from the older cases. Most of them do not deal with that point and, further, it must, I think, be borne in mind that they date from a time when international relationships were somewhat different and when theories of political economy now outmoded were generally accepted. Many dealt with revenue laws or penal laws, which have always been regarded as being in a special position, and I do not wish on this occasion to say more than that probably some re-examination of some of these cases may in future be necessary. The Indian law prohibiting exports to South Africa does not appear to me to be a revenue or penal law any more than was the law of exchange control considered by this House in *Kahler v. Midland Bank Ltd.*

Further, this case does not, in my view, involve the enforcement of Indian law in England. In fact, no breach of Indian law in the execution of this contract was ever committed or attempted because the contract came to an end by its repudiation by the respondents within a few days after it was made.

Finally, it was argued that, even if there be a general rule that our courts will take notice of foreign laws so that agreements to break them are unenforceable, that rule must be subject to exceptions and this Indian law is one of which we ought not to take notice. It may be that there are exceptions. I can imagine a foreign law involving persecution of such a character that we would regard an agreement to break it as meritorious. But this Indian law is very far removed from anything of that kind. It was argued that this prohibition of exports to South Africa was a hostile act against a Commonwealth country with which we have close relations, that such a prohibition is contrary to international usage, and that we cannot recognize it without taking sides in the dispute between India and South Africa.

My Lords, it is quite impossible for a court in this country to set itself up as a judge of the rights and wrongs of a controversy between two friendly countries, we cannot judge the motives or the justifications of governments of other countries in these matters and, if we tried to do so, the consequences might seriously prejudice international relations. By recognizing this Indian law so that an agreement which involves a breach of that law within Indian territory is unenforceable we express no opinion whatever, either favourable or adverse, as to the policy which caused its enactment. In my judgment this appeal should be dismissed.

Lord Cohen. My Lords, I concur.

Lord Keith of Avonholm. My Lords, on the only question of fact in this case I agree that the contracting parties knew that the contract could only be carried out, and intended that it should be carried out in circumstances which, if all the facts were known to the Indian shipper, would be a violation of Indian law.

It is accepted that the proper law of the contract is English law, and the only other question is whether the contract is one which the English courts will enforce. I am clear that it is not.

. . .

In the present case I see no escape from the view that to recognize the contract between the appellant and the respondent as an enforceable contract would give a just cause for complaint by the Government of India and should be regarded as contrary to conceptions of international comity. On grounds of public policy, therefore, this is a contract which our courts ought not to recognize. It is said that the Indian legislation is discriminatory legislation against a country which is a member of the Commonwealth and with which this country is on friendly terms. But that, in my opinion, is irrelevant. The English courts cannot be called on to adjudicate upon political issues between India and South Africa. The Indian law is not a law repugnant to English conceptions of what may be regarded as within the ordinary field of legislation or administrative order even in this country. It is the illegality under the foreign law that is to be considered and not the effect of the foreign law on another country.

. . .

I would dismiss the appeal.

Lord Somervell of Harrow. . . .

It seems to me impossible to suggest that our courts would enforce an agreement to commit in country A a crime such as murder, arson or burglary. Is there any justification for drawing a line between what are evils generally and acts prohibited by the foreign State, no doubt because they are regarded as local evils?

The statements in the old cases support the view that it is the illegality under the foreign law which is the test and one does not have to distinguish or attempt to distinguish between what is "wrong" from what is prohibited. Your Lordships were invited to make an exception to the principle on the ground that the law in question was directed against the Union of South Africa arising out of a dispute between the two States. I do not think this would justify taking the case out of the rule.

The statement that in this field one country takes no notice of the revenue laws of another seems to have been based on the principle that smuggling and freedom "gang thegither." . . .

. . . It was submitted that the prohibition in the present case of export to a particular destination was a revenue law, and one can imagine such a prohibition being a revenue law. On the evidence in the present case it would seem not to fall within the ordinary meaning of the phrase, but in any event I myself think that the courts of this country should not today enforce a contract to smuggle goods into or out of a foreign and friendly State.

There may, of course, be laws the enforcement of which would be against "morals." In such a case an exception might be made to the general principle. The point can be dealt with if it arises.

I would dismiss the appeal.

Appeal dismissed.

NOTES AND QUESTIONS

(1)(a) Is there anything to *Holman v. Johnson* other than a simple contract action, decided according to the law of the place of performance?

(b) The possibility seems to have been raised, at least in the mind of Lord Mansfield, that the case called for the application of renvoi,—i.e., that the English court would decide the case as a French court would decide it, and that if France would regard the transaction as unlawful because it was contrary to the law of England, then French courts would not permit the plaintiff to recover his purchase price and neither should the English courts. But that possibility is rejected by the great judge, "For no country ever takes notice of the *revenue* laws of another." Thus France's presumed application of its own law is what is upheld, and plaintiff seller wins.

(c) Lord Mansfield says the objection that the contract is immoral sounds very ill in the mouth of the buyer, who has participated in the transaction, and, it appears, received the tea. Had the sale concerned heroin (or whatever was the eighteenth century equivalent), it would have been a different story—a transaction *ex turpi causa*. But here "an immoral act it certainly is not." What follows from this distinction?

(d) If the act had been immoral, it seems, the English court would not have engaged in choice of law at all, but would simply have dismissed the action; since it was not immoral, the English court puts itself in position of the French court, which, as we saw, leads to application of French law.

(e) Lord Mansfield, of course, is famous for one-liners, as was Holmes a century later. "Debt follows the person," for instance (p. 894, *supra*), as well as the line quoted in the subsequent cases. He is also a scholar, and like Story, looks to Huber for advice on conflict of laws, here for support for the distinction based on the place of delivery. If the contract called for delivery in England, no action could have been brought thereon, even if the tea had in fact been delivered. Is that sound? Would the result be the same if suit were brought in France? Note that if the distinction is a territorial one—i.e., the lawfulness of the transaction depends wholly on the place of delivery, then the statement that no country ever takes notice of the revenue laws of another is quite unnecessary to decision of the case—a dictum in every sense of the word.

(2)(a) Apart from its intrinsic interest, *Holman v. Johnson* is known primarily for the so-called revenue rule—"a strong fortress," in the words of Viscount Simonds in *Taylor,* against which such questions as "why?" are "frail weapons." Why indeed should an English court not hear a tax claim by India, apart from the fact that the noble Lords were "greatly surprised"? If international law is built on respect for other nations—and surely every major nation collects taxes—why should a tax judgment not be cognizable in the courts of another state? Note that India here is not asking that its judgment be enforced without scrutiny, but is simply asking for the right to prove its claim in a liquidation proceeding.

(b) Lord Keith wonders about this question, too. He puts forward, first, a theory based on "all concepts of independent sovereignties;" since that does not totally convince, he advances another suggestion, borrowed from Learned Hand in an interstate context:[a] (i) We don't want to enforce a foreign tax without looking at it; and (ii) if we look we may not like what we see and that might give offense; ergo, (iii) we will not enforce any tax claim at all. Is that sensible? After all, the Government of India came to the court as plaintiff, and invited scrutiny of the tax on which its claim was based.

(c) Lord Somervell finally concedes that the emperor wears no clothes. Whatever Lord Mansfield meant, *Holman* "has little if any relevance to the issue which we have to decide." But then he, too, is stopped by the lack of precedent; "The appellant is asking the English courts to do what the courts of no other country have done. . . ."

(d) The rule in the United States used to be the same as that reflected in *Government of India v. Taylor,* even among states in the Union. Not until 1935 was it overturned as to tax judgments rendered in one state of the United States and sought to be enforced in another state, *Milwaukee County v. M. E. White & Co.,* 296 U.S. 268 (1935), and the Court said in that case that it was an "open question" whether one state must enforce an unadjudicated tax claim of another state[b]

In a recent decision arising out of a claim by tax authorities of British Columbia against American citizens who had engaged in logging operations in that province and had left without paying a logging tax, the U.S. Court of Appeals for the Ninth Circuit declined to enforce the tax, though liability had been adjudicated in British Columbia with participation of the defendants and had in fact been reduced in amount from the original assessment. *Her Majesty the Queen in Right of the Province of British Columbia v. Gilbertson,* 597 F.2d 1161 (9th Cir. 1979). The court cited *Holman v. Johnson* as well as *Moore v. Mitchell* to show that the revenue rule had continued validity. "Additionally," the court said, "if the court below was compelled to recognize the tax judgment from a foreign nation, it would have the effect of furthering the governmental interests of a foreign country, something which our courts customarily refuse to do."[c] Does that sound like comity?

(e) In *British Columbia v. Gilbertson,* the court also referred to the requirements of reciprocity, which "would itself be a sufficient basis for denying British claim," because sixteen years earlier the courts of British Columbia had refused to give effect to a judgment for taxes of an American court, and that refusal had been affirmed by the Supreme Court of Canada, *United States v.*

---

[a] *Moore v. Mitchell,* 30 F.2d 600, 604 (2d Cir. 1929), Concurring opinion, affirmed *on other grounds,* 281 U.S. 18 (1930).

[b] 296 U.S. at 275. For excerpts from that case as well as discussion of enforcement of interstate tax claims not reduced to judgment, see Chapter 8, pp. 673–74, questions 9(d) and (e), *supra.*

[c] 597 F.2d at 1165.

Harden, [1963] S.C.R. 366, 41 D.L.R.2d 721 (1963).[d] Is there any way out of a rule like this if each side insists on reciprocity? Wouldn't a more enlightened use of comity be to say "we will give effect to your judgment for a tax liability, and we fully expect that when tables are reversed you will do the same for us"?

(f) The *Restatement (Third) of Foreign Relations Law* (1987), surveying the case law and also criticism of these cases, says, in § 483:

> Courts in the United States are not required to recognize or to enforce judgments for the collection of taxes, fines, or penalties rendered by courts of other states.

The first Comment is entitled "Non-recognition not required but permitted," and states that "no rule of United States law or international law would be violated if a court in the United States enforced a judgment of a foreign court for payment of taxes or comparable assessments," assuming the other conditions for recognition of foreign judgments were met.[e]

(3) The most interesting of the cases in this section is *Regazzoni,* decided three years after *Government of India v. Taylor* and with participation of all the Law Lords who wrote in *Taylor* plus Lord Reid.

(a) Plaintiff in *Regazzoni* argued that his case was governed by *Taylor,* that the English court should not take note of India's revenue rule, and that therefore he should prevail on his breach of contract claim. The House of Lords did not repudiate *Taylor,* but rejected plaintiff's argument. Are the two cases reconcilable? If not, which is the more persuasive?

(b) Viscount Simonds refers to *Boucher v. Lawson,* decided in 1734,[f] when England and English courts didn't mind that an export of gold from Portugal was contrary to Portuguese law, and Lord Somervell recalls the principle that smuggling and freedom "gang thegither." But both Lords conclude that times have changed. National interest cannot be so robustly asserted, Simonds says, to the prejudice of international comity.

(c) Would India's national interest be prejudiced if the contract were enforced here? After all, as Lord Reid remarks, no breach of Indian law was committed and the jute bags never left India.

(d) Lord Reid (who did not sit in *India v. Taylor*) emphasizes that both parties to the contract knew that it was illegal to export Indian goods to South Africa. Would the case come out the other way if the seller, but not the buyer, knew about the embargo?

(4)(a) Is *Regazzoni* a choice of law case? Lord Keith, who had doubts about the result in *Taylor,* says the proper law of the contract is English, though as appears from the lower court reports, it was made by an exchange of telegrams between buyer in Switzerland and Seller's agent in Germany;[g] why then is English law, which puts no restraints on trade with South Africa, not applied?

(b) Two possible explanations may be offered in response to the preceding question, though neither one emerges clearly from the speeches of the Law Lords. One explanation would be that

---

[d] Discussed in 77 Harv. L. Rev. 1327 (1964).

[e] Id. Comment *a.*

[f] Ca. t. H. 85, 95 Eng. Rep. 53 (1734).

[g] Apparently it was agreed that the parties intended to refer to the United Kingdom Jute Trade Association's form contract, which provided for English law. See *Regazzoni v. K. C. Sethia (1944) Ltd.,* [1956] 2 W.L.R. 204, [1955] 2 Lloyd's Rep. 766 at 774. (Q.B.).

certain kinds of public law, sometimes called "mandatory rules," cannot be avoided by choice of law clauses—express or implied. Export controls (including embargoes) would be an obvious candidate for such a rule—certainly if the forum is in the country imposing the controls, possibly in other fora as well.

Alternatively, by choosing English law the parties chose the whole law of England, and here English law looks to Indian law. Which of the two explanations seems closer to what Lord Keith has in mind?

(c) Lord Somervell resumes the discussion begun briefly by Lord Mansfield in *Holman v. Johnson:* Of course our courts would not enforce an agreement to commit murder or arson; but is the prohibited act here *ex turpi causa,* in Mansfield's words, or merely a statutory prohibition, or indeed akin to a "revenue law"? Lord Somervell says one does not have to distinguish. Would it be different if instead of a prohibition on exports destined for South Africa, the law prohibited exports of goods without payment of an export tax, and the contract was designed to avoid payment of the tax? What about a transaction designed to defeat a requirement that all foreign exchange earned from exports be turned in to the Reserve Bank of India, in exchange for rupees at an official rate?[h]

(d) Several of the Law Lords emphasize that English courts cannot be called on to adjudicate upon political issues between India and South Africa, as Lord Keith puts it. Lord Reid, making the same point, concedes that there may be exceptions to the rule that agreements to break foreign laws are unenforceable. (pp. 902–903) Substitute Saudi Arabia for India and Israel for South Africa. Is the Unified Law on the Boycott of Israel "of such a character that we would regard an agreement to break it as meritorious"?

(e) How do you suppose (i) the actual case, or (ii) the Saudi Arabia/Israel variation, would be decided in the United States?

(f) Before moving too far into political speculation, could one develop some non-political principles applicable to cases of this kind? For example:

  (i) the law of the place of export will be given effect unless . . .; alternatively

  (ii) preference will be given to the law that gives effect to the transaction.

Is either of these a neutral principle? Does either have a public international law component?

(5) Some additional questions on *Regazzoni* come to mind:

(a) How would Lord Mansfield have decided the case? Note that *Regazzoni* presents neither the same fact pattern as *Holman* nor the hypothetical variation posed by Mansfield in his opinion.

(b) Suppose instead of getting cold feet as in the actual case, the seller ships, buyer fails to pay for the goods, and now seller is the plaintiff and buyer pleads illegality. What result? Do the principles you developed in response to Question 4(f) solve this variation?

(c) Suppose neither party knew about the prohibition, or more realistically, the prohibition was imposed between the time of contracting and the time set for delivery. Is the seller

---

[h] For a case that represented roughly that situation, involving exports of coffee from Brazil to the United States, see *Banco do Brasil, S.A. v. A.C. Israel Commodity Co., Inc.,* 12 N.Y.2d 371, 239 N.Y.S.2d 872, 190 N.E.2d 235 (1963), *cert. denied,* 376 U.S. 906 (1964). The New York Court of Appeals held (4–3) that the complaint by the Brazilian bank to recover damages for a conspiracy to defraud the Government of Brazil did not state a cause of action under New York law.

discharged? Or is this, too, a choice of law question? Reconsider this issue after reading the *Pipeline* case, § 10.05, *infra*.

(6) Finally, though there is some talk of comity in the opinions, there is no discussion of international law.

(a) Would India have a complaint against Great Britain if *Regazzoni* had been decided the other way? If so, why doesn't it have a complaint about *Taylor,* which actually cost India money?

(b) Do you see a gap between private and public international law searching for a conflict of laws principle? Consider how the state of the law revealed by these cases should impact on the problems revealed in the succeeding sections of this chapter.

§ 10.03 Jurisdiction to Prescribe

Jurisdiction to prescribe, also known as regulatory or legislative jurisdiction, is defined as the authority of a state to make law for, or apply its law to, persons, activities or things. To the extent a state's legislation is applied in its own territory to its own citizens, the issue of jurisdiction to prescribe does not arise, except in construing the intent of the legislature to delegate rule-making authority to an agency or executive department. When the state's legislation is applied to activity outside its territory, or to activity by non-citizens, the question arises whether that exercise of jurisdiction is within or beyond its authority. The limits of that authority are controversial, and indeed in the case of *The S.S. Lotus (France v. Turkey)*, [1927] P.C.I.J. Ser. A. No. 10, the inter-war World Court declined to set down any limits on the exercise of jurisdiction outside a state's territory.[a] The prevailing view, however, is that international law does set limits on the application by a state (including but not limited to its courts) of its law to activities with transnational aspects. What those limits are and who should decide on them is the focus of this section.

Note that in a number of the cases, the American courts speak of "subject matter jurisdiction," a term borrowed, it seems from the constitutional battles in the 1920's and thirties in the United States over the permissible scope of federal legislation, against claims that such legislation fell outside the powers delegated to the national government by the states of the Union. In these debates, eventually won (with a few exceptions) by the national authority, resort was often had to constitutional "hooks"—use of the mails, crossing of state lines, failure to report income on a Federal return—giving federal regulators and law enforcement officials "subject matter

---

[a] The *Lotus* case concerned a collision at sea between a French and a Turkish ship. When the French ship subsequently put in to Constantinople, Turkey arrested and tried the French officer who had been on duty at the time of the collision, and France claimed that Turkey's action was contrary to international law. The Court (by the President's casting vote) rejected the claim:

> . . . [T]he first and foremost restriction imposed by international law upon a State is that . . . it may not exercise its power in any form in the territory of another State. . . . It does not, however, follow that international law prohibits a state from exercising jurisdiction in its own territory, in respect of any case which relates to acts which have taken place abroad, and in which it cannot rely on some permissive rule of international law. Such a view would only be tenable if international law contained a general prohibition to States to extend the application of their laws and the jurisdiction of their courts to persons, property, and acts outside their territory, and if, as an exception to this general prohibition, it allowed States to do so in certain specific cases. But this is certainly not the case under international law as it stands at present. . . .

[1927] P.C.I.J. Ser. A, No. 10 at 18–19.

jurisdiction," even when the contract or hook in question was only peripherally related to the activity or regulation in question. In reading the succeeding cases, consider whether the process of resolving the question of jurisdiction to prescribe is not more analogous to the choice of law process as we have seen it illustrated throughout this book than to the yes/no process pertinent to the constitutional scrutiny of child labor or agricultural adjustment laws under the heading of subject matter jurisdiction.[b]

UNITED STATES v. ALUMINUM CO. OF AMERICA

United States Court of Appeals, Second Circuit
148 F.2d 416, 443–45 (1945)

[In 1928, Aluminium, Limited ("Limited") was incorporated in Canada to take over properties located outside the United States and owned by Aluminum Company of America ("Alcoa"), a Pennsylvania corporation. Alcoa's shareholders received Limited's common stock in exchange for those properties. A major administrative office of Limited was established in New York.

In 1931, Limited and a group of British, French, German, and Swiss corporations formed a cartel to restrict aluminum production. In 1936, they (the "shareholders") agreed that any member producing in excess of a specific quota was to pay a royalty that would be divided among the other members. The shareholders agreed that imports into the United States would be included in the quotas.

On the basis of those acts, Alcoa and Limited were charged with violating § 1 of the Sherman Act. Section 1 provides:

> Every contract, combination in the form of trust or otherwise, or conspiracy, in restraint of trade or commerce among the several States, or with foreign nations, is hereby declared to be illegal.[3]

The district court dismissed the action, and the United States appealed directly to the Supreme Court. That Court was unable to muster a quorum to hear the case and referred it to the Court of Appeals for the Second Circuit.[4] That court was thus sitting as a court of last resort.

In an opinion by Judge Learned Hand, the court sustained the lower court's finding that Alcoa was not a party to the cartel and had not participated in its formation. Further, the court held, the fact that the shareholders controlling Alcoa also controlled Limited was not a sufficient basis for charging Alcoa with participation in the cartel. (Two United States families and the officers and directors of Alcoa owned 48.9 per cent of Alcoa's stock and 48.5 per cent of Limited's stock.) Accordingly, the court affirmed the dismissal of the claim that Alcoa had violated § 1 by conspiring to restrict United States imports.

Judge Hand then turned to the question whether Limited had violated § 1.]

---

[b] This point is spelled out at somewhat greater length by the present author in Lowenfeld, *Antitrust, Interest Analysis, and the New Conflict of Laws,* Review of Atwood and Brewster, *Antitrust and American Business Abroad* (2d Ed. 1981), 95 Harv. L. Rev. 1976, 1978–84 (1982).

[3] 15 U.S.C. § 1.

[4] See the Act of June 9, 1944, c. 239, 58 Stat. 272 (now 28 U.S.C. § 2109).

Did either the agreement of 1931 or that of 1936 violate § 1 of the Act? The answer does not depend upon whether we shall recognize as a source of liability a liability imposed by another state. On the contrary we are concerned only with whether Congress chose to attach liability to the conduct outside the United States of persons not in allegiance to it. That being so, the only question open is whether Congress intended to impose the liability, and whether our own Constitution permitted it to do so: as a court of the United States, we cannot look beyond our own law. Nevertheless, it is quite true that we are not to read general words, such as those in this Act, without regard to the limitations customarily observed by nations upon the exercise of their powers; limitations which generally correspond to those fixed by the "Conflict of Laws." We should not impute to Congress an intent to punish all whom its courts can catch, for conduct which has no consequences within the United States. . . . On the other hand, it is settled law—as "Limited" itself agrees—that any state may impose liabilities, even upon persons not within its allegiance, for conduct outside its borders that has consequences within its borders which the state reprehends; and these liabilities other states will ordinarily recognize. . . . It may be argued that this Act extends further. Two situations are possible. There may be agreements made beyond our borders not intended to affect imports, which do affect them or which affect exports. Almost any limitation of the supply of goods in Europe, for example, or in South America, may have repercussions in the United States if there is trade between the two. Yet when one considers the international complications likely to arise from an effort in this country to treat such agreements as unlawful, it is safe to assume that Congress certainly did not intend the Act to cover them. Such agreements may on the other hand intend to include imports into the United States, and yet it may appear that they have had no effect upon them. That situation might be thought to fall within the doctrine that intent may be a substitute for performance in the case of a contract made within the United States; or it might be thought to fall within the doctrine that a statute should not be interpreted to cover acts abroad which have no consequence here. We shall not choose between these alternatives; but for argument we shall assume that the Act does not cover agreements, even though intended to affect imports or exports, unless its performance is shown actually to have had some effect upon them. . . .

Both agreements would clearly have been unlawful, had they been made within the United States; and it follows from what we have just said that both were unlawful, though made abroad, if they were intended to affect imports and did affect them. . . . The judge found that it was not the purpose of the agreement to "suppress or restrain the exportation of aluminum to the United States for sale in competition with 'Alcoa.' " By that we understand that he meant that the agreement was not specifically directed to "Alcoa," because it only applied generally to the production of the shareholders. If he meant that it was not expected that general restriction upon production would have an effect upon imports, we cannot agree, for the change made in 1936 was deliberate and was expressly made to accomplish just that. . . . The first of the conditions which we mentioned was therefore satisfied; the intent was to set up a quota system for imports.

The judge also found that the 1936 agreement did not "materially affect the . . . foreign trade or commerce of the United States;" apparently because the imported ingot was greater in 1936 and 1937 than in earlier years. We cannot accept this finding, based as it was upon the fact that, in 1936, 1937 and the first quarter of 1938, the gross imports of ingot increased. It by no means follows from such an increase that the agreement did not restrict imports; and incidentally it so happens that in those years such inference as is possible at all, leads to the opposite conclusion. . . . We do not mean to infer from this that the quota system of 1936 did in fact restrain imports, as these figures might suggest; but we do mean that nothing is to be inferred from the gross increase of imports. We shall dispose of the matter therefore upon the assumption that, although the shareholders intended to restrict imports, it does not appear whether in fact they did so. Upon our hypothesis the plaintiff would therefore fail, if it carried the burden of proof upon this issue as upon others. We think, however, that, after the intent to affect imports was proved, the burden of proof shifted to "Limited." In the first place a depressant upon production which applies generally may be assumed, ceteris paribus, to distribute its effect evenly upon all markets. Again, when the parties took the trouble specifically to make the depressant apply to a given market, there is reason to suppose that they expected that it would have some effect, which it could have only by lessening what would otherwise have been imported. If the motive they introduced was over-balanced in all instances by motives which induced the shareholders to import, if the United States market became so attractive that the royalties did not count at all and their expectations were in fact defeated, they to whom the facts were more accessible than to the plaintiff ought to prove it, for a prima facie case had been made. Moreover, there is an especial propriety in demanding this of "Limited," because it was "Limited" which procured the inclusion in the agreement of 1936 of imports in the quotas.

There remains only the question whether this assumed restriction had any influence upon prices. . . . [A]n agreement to withdraw any substantial part of the supply from a market would, if carried out, have some effect upon prices, and was as unlawful as an agreement expressly to fix prices. The underlying doctrine was that all factors which contribute to determine prices must be kept free to operate unhampered by agreements. For these reasons we think that the agreement of 1936 violated § 1 of the Act.

. . .

Judgment reversed, and cause remanded for further proceedings not inconsistent with the foregoing.

UNITED STATES v. IMPERIAL CHEMICAL INDUSTRIES, LTD.

United States District Court, Southern District of New York
105 F. Supp. 215 (1952)

[Imperial Chemical Industries, Ltd. ("ICI") was organized under United Kingdom laws and had its principal place of business in London. In *United States v. Imperial Chemical Industries, Ltd.*, 100 F. Supp. 504 (S.D.N.Y. 1951), the court held that ICI and E.I. duPont deNemours & Co. ("duPont") had violated § 1 of the Sherman Act by dividing the world markets in certain nylon and other products and by other arrangements in restraint of trade. In the opinion on relief excerpted below, the court required ICI and duPont to license, on a reasonable royalty basis, United States patents used to further their unlawful activities.]

RYAN, District Judge. We now approach the task of formulating a final decree designed to prevent and restrain the violations of law which we have found. 15 U.S.C.A. § 4.

Our objective is to fashion, in the terms of a decree, means by which the agreement found to exist is terminated, its revival prevented and its effects destroyed by the reestablishment of competitive conditions insofar as they pertain to United States exports and imports. The decree must be based upon the facts as we have found them, and designed to be carried out with a minimum of judicial supervision and control of the future activities of the defendants. . . .

Where competition has been eliminated, it must be restored. Only those provisions reasonably necessary to accomplish correction and adjustment of a dislocated competitive situation may be applied.

The essence of the violation found was the unlawful agreement to divide world territories. It was this enduring and basic understanding which was fundamental to all of the dealings of the conspirators. It was to accomplish this purpose and end that the various means were adopted.

. . .

The Government does not seek a decree directing ICI to grant compulsory licenses of its British patents. The Government requests that ICI be required to grant immunity under its foreign patents which correspond to the United States patents which we have made subject to compulsory licensing. Such a provision was included in paragraph "7" of the final decree in *National Lead,* 63 F. Supp., 495, 534, and left undisturbed by the Supreme Court. We have had testimony offered on behalf of ICI by an expert in British law that a provision for granting immunities is contrary to British public policy and that a British court will not enforce such a provision in the judgment of a court of a foreign jurisdiction. As to this, we observe that, acting on the basis of our jurisdiction in personam, we are merely directing ICI to refrain from asserting rights which it may have in Britain, since the enforcement of those rights will serve to continue the effects of wrongful acts it has committed within the United States affecting the foreign trade of the United States.

We are not unmindful that under British law there are restrictions upon exports from the United States by reason of the existence of the British patents owned by ICI. The exclusion of unlicensed imports and the prohibition of unlicensed sales is enforceable because of the legal rights which attach to a British patent.

We accept as correct the statements in the brief of ICI that: . . . "In the British Empire the law is even more stringent [than in the United States]. The owner of a British patent may bar the importation of any product patented in Great Britain and also any product made by any process where the process is patented under British law. It is clear that a patent on a process essential to the production of a product is infringed by sale of an imported product made abroad by that process. . . ."

. . .

. . . [A]s we have heretofore observed . . . lawful rights were employed as means to accomplish the unlawful purpose of their underlying agreement.

While it is true that these rights exist independent of any provision in the patents and processes agreements, they were granted to ICI by the disclosure or assignment of inventions by duPont pursuant to the terms of these agreements. Inventions were also licensed by ICI to duPont for its exclusive use and exploitation in the United States in accordance with the agreements. In the first instance the patents were employed to restrain duPont's exports to Great Britain, in plain violation of American antitrust laws; in the second instance the patents were used as a means to prevent ICI exports to the United States and placed a restraint upon the foreign trade of Great Britain, in violation of her declared policy, if not her laws. It does not seem presumptuous for this court to make a direction to a foreign defendant corporation over which it has jurisdiction to take steps to remedy and correct a situation which is unlawful both here and in the foreign jurisdiction in which it is domiciled. Two evils have resulted from the one understanding of ICI and duPont—restraints upon the foreign trade and commerce of the United States as well as on that of Great Britain. It is not an intrusion on the authority of a foreign sovereign for this court to direct that steps be taken to remove the harmful effects on the trade of the United States.

. . .

The history of the basic British nylon patents reveals a studied and continued purpose on the part of ICI and duPont to remove these patents from within the scope of any decree which might ultimately be made by this court. . . . These British patents were issued to duPont. By the agreement of March 30, 1939, ICI received an exclusive license under them; in January, 1940, ICI granted irrevocable and exclusive rights to make nylon yarn from nylon polymer (which is manufactured by ICI) to British Nylon Spinners, Ltd. (BNS). ICI has a stock interest of 50% in BNS, the remaining 50% is held by Courtaulds, Inc. BNS is in the business of manufacturing and distributing nylon yarn. Not content with this arrangement and with the deliberate purpose to "materially reduce the risk of any loss of rights" as a result of this suit . . ., duPont pursuant to the nylon agreement of 1946 assigned the basic British nylon patents to ICI. It is now urged that we may not decree with reference to these British patents so as to direct ICI to remove restrictions on imports into Great Britain of nylon polymer or nylon yarn from the United States. It is argued that the sum total of all these agreements is not to create by itself any restrictions against American imports, and that those which exist arise from the right to be free from competition which is inherent in the British patents and cannot possibly be repugnant to the American antitrust laws.

BNS is not before this court; although they were knowing participants in acts designed to thwart the granting of full relief, we may not direct our decree to them. The lack of majority stock ownership in ICI likewise prevents control of the future acts of BNS by this means; however, we are not without some remedy still available.

Objection is raised by ICI that we are without power to decree that the British nylon patents may not be asserted to prevent the importation of nylon polymer and nylon yarn into Great Britain because BNS has rights which exist independent of those possessed by ICI. This overlooks the circumstances under which BNS acquired its rights to these patents by licenses from ICI.

. . .

The nylon agreement between duPont and ICI of December 31, 1946, provides . . . for the assignment of patents and patent applications. . . . By this writing, ICI became the owner of the British patents, in which its interest up to that time had been that of a licensee. Throughout all these negotiations it appears that BNS was advised of the dealings between ICI and duPont concerning the British nylon patents. Both ICI and duPont are parties to the instant suit; they were advised in fact and realized that the further use and control of the rights pertaining to the British nylon patents were subject to a decree of this court to be entered in this suit. We find that in fact Courtaulds and BNS were also fully advised of this situation. The first, or "manufacturing sub-license" which BNS received granted to it no greater rights than had been acquired by ICI; it was subject to the same infirmities as existed against ICI. The second license granted after the assignment of the patents to ICI did not come to BNS as an innocent party. BNS, again, knew exactly what it was receiving; its rights are wholly subject to the inherent vices of the agreements through which they were acquired. We have found them to be tainted with the illegality of the unlawful conspiracy; of this probability BNS was informed. The circumstances surrounding the execution of the assignment to ICI in December, 1946, makes this clear. . . .

We do not hesitate therefore to decree that the British nylon patents may not be asserted by ICI to prevent the importation of nylon polymer and of nylon yarn into Great Britain. What credit may be given to such an injunctive provision by the courts of Great Britain in a suit brought by BNS to restrain such importations we do not venture to predict. We feel that the possibility that the English courts in an equity suit will not give effect to such a provision in our decree should not deter us from including it.

BRITISH NYLON SPINNERS, LTD. v. IMPERIAL CHEMICAL INDUSTRIES, LTD.

High Court of Justice (U.K.)
Chancery Division
[1955] 1 Ch. 37

DANCKWERTS J.

This is an action brought by British Nylon Spinners Ld. against Imperial Chemical Industries Ld. Each of the parties is an English corporation formed under the provisions of the Companies Acts. The object of the action is to compel the defendant company to grant licences in respect of certain British patents, relating (amongst other things) to nylon yarn, which are now owned by the defendant company. The contract which it is sought to enforce is a contract made by a letter written on behalf of the defendant company and dated March 5, 1947, by which an earlier agreement in writing between the parties and dated January 5, 1940, was modified or superseded. The parties, therefore, are both English corporations and the contract on which their rights depend is a contract made in England and regulated by English law, as the proper law of that contract.

The plaintiff company was incorporated on January 1, 1940, for the purpose of carrying out a joint venture of the defendant company, Imperial Chemical Industries Ld., and another English company, Courtaulds Ld. These two companies, under the provisions of the articles of the plaintiff company, were to own the share capital in equal shares; of the board of directors, five were to be nominees of each of the two companies, I.C.I. and Courtaulds. By modifications made at a later date, three additional directors were appointed, who were to be the nominees of I.C.I. and Courtaulds jointly. So long, therefore, as they acted in agreement, I.C.I. and Courtaulds, together, could control the plaintiff company absolutely, but neither of them alone could control the affairs of the company. I.C.I. alone could not force its will upon the plaintiff company. In case of dispute, in effect, the three neutral directors would have to exercise their functions in the interests of the plaintiff company only. The business of the plaintiff company is (as its name suggests) that of producers of and dealers in multifilament yarns and staple fibres, threads and sewing threads, derived from nylon polymers and similar substances.

The patents, which are now the property of I.C.I., were previously the property of a corporation, formed under the laws of Delaware in the United States of America, called E. I. du Pont de Nemours & Co., and between the I.C.I. and this American corporation there has been a great measure of co-operation in the development of these important inventions, to which the patents relate. Co-operation, though beneficial in many respects, may, from another aspect, be regarded as tending to produce a monopoly. At any rate, proceedings were taken in the United States Federal Court for the Southern District of New York against I.C.I. and du Pont and a number of other corporations and their officers under the Sherman anti-trust law of the United States of America, in which an illegal conspiracy between those corporations and individuals was alleged, which resulted in an order of his Honour Judge Sylvester Ryan on July 30, 1952.

The difficulties which exist in the present case arise out of that order, and these have already been the subject of interlocutory proceedings in this action, in which an injunction designed to prevent frustration of the relevant contract was granted against I.C.I. by Upjohn J. on August 13, 1952, and his decision was affirmed by the Court of Appeal on October 16, 1952[a] . . .

The defendant company, I.C.I., have in fact no wish to break their contract with the plaintiff company, but they are apprehensive that, if they carry it out, they will be guilty of a disregard of the terms of the order of the United States court, and may be involved in penal proceedings of some kind in the United States of America. They have been put in an even more embarrassing position by the desire of the United States court that they should fully and fairly present in this action all the facts on which the judgment of the United States court was founded, and which appear to have included matters of evidence which would not be admissible as evidence against the plaintiff company, except possibly in proceedings in which a claim of conspiracy was formulated against the plaintiff company and others. Sir Andrew Clark[b] did his best to carry out the moral obligation cast on his clients in this way (no actual order or direction was made in the United States court in this respect), but he found great difficulty in supporting the admission in this action of evidence consisting largely of internal communications between the directors or officers of I.C.I., and I was unable to allow such evidence to be admitted. It should be made clear that, while I.C.I. were effectually joined as a party in the proceedings in the United States Federal Court, the plaintiff company were not a party in those proceedings and are in no way bound by the order of the United States court.

It is now necessary for me to go into the facts and the history of the case in more detail. By an agreement in writing dated March 30, 1939, between du Pont and I.C.I., du Pont granted to I.C.I. licences in respect of the patents which were exclusive for the countries in the British Commonwealth (except Canada and Newfoundland) and in the Irish Free State, Egypt, Palestine, Iran and Irak and their colonies, protectorates and mandated territories, and were non-exclusive for certain other countries. By an agreement in writing dated January 5, 1940, between I.C.I. and the plaintiff company (in which the material parts of the above-mentioned agreement of March 30, 1939, the "du Pont nylon agreement," were scheduled, and it was recited that I.C.I. had agreed to grant to the plaintiff company

> a manufacturing sub-licence under such of the du Pont inventions comprised in the du Pont Nylon agreement as related to the production treatment or use of multifilament yarns and staple fibres made from nylon polymers)

I.C.I. granted to the plaintiff company "a manufacturing sub-licence as defined in article II of the du Pont Nylon agreement" (which was to be exclusive and non-exclusive for the respective territories already mentioned) "to exercise and practise such inventions" within the defined field of the agreement and

> with the free and unrestricted right to grant sub-licenses to its customers under any inventions in the sub-licence field in so far as they relate to the use or treatment of multifilament yarns or staple fibres in a commercially finished form.

---

[a] *British Nylon Spinners, Ltd. v. Imperial Chemical Industries, Ltd.*, [1953] Ch. 19.
[b] Counsel for ICI.

By article II of the du Pont Nylon agreement of 1939 du Pont had granted to I.C.I. a licence "to exercise and practise" the inventions, and the article contained a provision that I.C.I. should have the free and unrestricted right to grant sub-licences to its customers within the I.C.I.'s licensed territory and that the said sub-licences should be referred to as "customers' sub-licences." I.C.I. was to have the right to grant other sub-licences only on prior written approval of du Pont, which approval du Pont agreed it would not unreasonably withhold, and it was stated that such other sublicences should thereinafter be referred to as "manufacturing sub-licences."

. . .

There was also a tripartite agreement of January 5, 1940, between I.C.I., Courtaulds and the plaintiff company, which dealt with the issue of shares in the capital of the plaintiff company and certain other matters which might be material in the event of the manufacture of nylon yarns being undertaken in countries other than the United Kingdom.

On January 6, 1944, the proceedings were instituted under the Sherman Anti-Trust Act of 1890 in the United States District Court for the Southern District of New York. The proceedings went to trial on April 3, 1950, and the trial concluded on June 30, 1950. The issues were finally submitted to the court for determination in November, 1950. His Honour Judge Sylvester Ryan delivered an opinion on the facts on September 28, 1951, an opinion on remedies on May 16, 1952, and a final judgment on July 30, 1952, which was modified by him subsequently in certain minor respects.

Meanwhile, I.C.I. and du Pont, who were both defendants in those proceedings, naturally suffered anxiety as to the result of the proceedings in regard to their agreements and co-operation. No doubt as a result of this those two corporations entered into a further agreement in writing on December 31, 1946. By this agreement the agreement of March 30, 1939, was cancelled and terminated; du Pont assigned to I.C.I. the entire right, title and interest in and to the patents which were the subject of the licences regulated by the former agreement; the provisions of the previous agreement for the exchange of information and knowledge were brought to an end, and the basis and rates of the royalties were varied. Thus the position of I.C.I. in regard to the patents was substantially changed. I.C.I., instead of being simply licensees, now became the owner of the patents, and, accordingly, the plaintiff company were no longer sub-licensees, and the agreement of 1939 by reference to which their rights had been largely regulated had come to an end. Some fresh arrangement between I.C.I. and the plaintiff company was necessary.

The plaintiff company were not a party in the United States proceedings and they were not a party to the discussions and arrangements which took place between du Pont and I.C.I. Certain of the directors of I.C.I. were also directors of the plaintiff company, but under English law, at any rate, knowledge acquired by them as directors of I.C.I. cannot be treated as the knowledge of the plaintiff company. Naturally, the directors of the plaintiff company, however, had some knowledge of the proceedings in the United States, and on June 3, 1946, a letter was written on behalf of the plaintiff company to I.C.I. inquiring as to the effect of the proceedings on the relation between du Pont and I.C.I. On June 27, 1946, Mr. Lutyens replied on behalf of I.C.I., enclosing a letter from the legal department of I.C.I., in which the view is expressed that, if the American proceedings resulted in a decree, by consent or otherwise, some modification of the nylon licence rights might be necessary, though the fact that the plaintiff company had sub-licence rights and were not before the court would involve the court in difficulty in settling a decree which could be effectively observed.

. . .

§ 10.03 INTERNATIONAL LAW AND CONFLICT OF LAWS □ 917

The agreement of December 31, 1946, apparently was concluded between du Pont and I.C.I. without further communication to the plaintiff company. On March 5, 1947, a letter was written to the plaintiff company by Mr. Ridsdale, the head of the legal department of I.C.I., in which he said:

> Now that the new Nylon Agreement has been concluded between du Pont and I.C.I., I am able to advise you of certain changes which will affect the licence agreement dated January 5, 1940, between I.C.I. and B.N.S., and also the co-operation agreement of the same date between I.C.I., Courtaulds and B.N.S. In due course it will be necessary to enter into formal agreements covering these alterations but as these agreements will take a little time to prepare I am writing you now to let you know the position. As regards the licence agreement I think it is easier to deal with the changes in the following way. 1. You are aware, I think, that I.C.I. have acquired by assignment from du Pont a large range of patent rights, including those the subject of the licence agreement. This will mean that instead of holding a sub-licence from I.C.I. under these patent rights you will be entitled to a direct licence from I.C.I. who are now the owners of the rights in question.

. . . The terms of this letter were never expressly accepted in writing, but it is common ground that it was acted on and accepted by conduct on behalf of the plaintiff company, and this is the contract which I am asked to enforce. Draft documents were prepared but were never finally agreed in view of the difficulties felt by I.C.I. as a result of the United States proceedings. But in June, 1952, the plaintiff company required licences to be granted by I.C.I., so that they could be registered in respect of the patents, and on July 24, 1952, the writ in this action was issued, six days before the effective judgment given by the Federal District judge in New York on July 30, 1952.

Now, though this case involves some difficult questions of jurisdiction and possibilities of conflict between this court and the United States court in New York, it is natural and proper that each court should recognize the difficulties of the judge of the other jurisdiction in dealing with matters which involve the nationals or legal creations of another sovereign State and the application of different laws in a situation which is not precisely the same, therefore, in its circumstances. His Honour Judge Sylvester Ryan has been exceedingly moderate and courteous in his references to the possible courses which might be adopted by the English court in dealing with the subject-matter of the agreements between the parties, and if I appear to reach different results and different conclusions from those which he has reached, or those which would be the most convenient for the carrying out of the decree which he has felt bound to make, this is not due to my unwillingness to co-operate, and the divergence is caused by the differences in the legal situation in our respective jurisdictions.

The judge was applying an enactment of Congress, which has no application to the United Kingdom, of course, and I am dealing with a contract between two British corporations in regard to British property, that is, the patents, and involving solely matters which are to be carried out in the United Kingdom. With these observations in mind, it is necessary to consider the details of the United States judge's findings and directions.

In his opinion on the facts of September 28, 1951, the judge decided that documents tendered on behalf of the United States were admissible. He said:

> If a conspiracy has been shown prima facie by evidence aliunde, declarations of co-conspirators in furtherance of the conspiracy are admissible against all. Since we have found that a conspiracy has been so proven, the sole issue is whether the challenged documents

are declarations in furtherance of the conspiracy. Because of the nature of the conspiracy, and of its participants, we conclude that they are.

The plaintiff company were not a party in those proceedings, and in the present action there is no issue of conspiracy, and it is clear, therefore, that I should not be justified in admitting the evidence admitted in the United States case which related to the declarations or internal dealings of the parties in the United States proceedings. Nor can I accept any conspiracy as being proved by such evidence for the purpose of the present action. The judge stated his conclusion as to the 1939 agreements thus:

> We find that the nylon agreement of 1939 stands condemned as within the patents and processes agreements. We find that the nylon agreement of 1939 was illegal because it was part of a licensing scheme, accomplished by concerted action of du Pont and I.C.I. for allocation of territories and pooling of patents embracing the whole of the nylon manufacturing industry and the whole of the nylon technology.

In reference to the agreement of December 31, 1946, the judge said:

> We find that du Pont, desiring to minimize the possibility of nylon being included in any decree that might be entered in this suit because of the questionable legality of some provisions of the earlier nylon agreement under the anti-trust laws of the United States, sought and secured from I.C.I. a new nylon agreement.

It seems to me, however, that such a course might be regarded not so much as an attempt to evade the effect of the Anti-Trust Act as an intention to rearrange the affairs of the corporations so as to secure compliance with the principles of the same statute, and so avoid offending against the law. I should add that Sir Andrew Clark referred me to those passages in support of the argument which he felt bound to advance, that this court ought not to give any relief in respect of an agreement which was part of a concerted plan to carry out some transaction contrary to the laws of a friendly State.

In his opinion on remedies, given on May 16, 1952, the judge expressed his purpose as follows:

> The Government does not seek a decree directing I.C.I. to grant compulsory licences of its British patents. The Government requests that I.C.I. be required to grant immunity under its foreign patents which correspond to the United States patents which we have made subject to compulsory licensing. Such a provision was included in paragraph 7 of the final decree in *National Lead* (63 Federal Supplement, 495, 534), and left undisturbed by the Supreme Court. We have had testimony offered on behalf of I.C.I. by an expert in British law that a provision for granting immunities is contrary to British public policy and that a British court will not enforce such a provision in the judgment of a court of a foreign jurisdiction. As to this, we observe that acting on the basis of our jurisdiction in personam, we are merely directing I.C.I. to refrain from asserting rights which it may have in Britain, since the enforcement of those rights will serve to continue the effects of wrongful acts it has committed within the United States affecting the foreign trade of the United States." Later the judge observed: "Our power so to regulate is limited and depends upon jurisdiction in personam; the effectiveness of the exercise of that power depends upon the recognition which will be given to our judgment as a matter of comity by the courts of the foreign sovereign which has granted the patents in question.

On page 25 he said:

British Nylon Spinners is not before this court; although they were knowing participants in acts designed to thwart the granting of full relief, we may not direct our decree to them. The lack of majority stock ownership in I.C.I. likewise prevents control of the future acts of British Nylon Spinners by this means; however, we are not without some remedy still available.

I must observe that so far as the evidence admissible in this court is concerned, there is no evidence of any participation by British Nylon Spinners in acts designed to thwart the granting of full relief. On the contrary, it appears that they accepted a situation which was presented to them as an accomplished fact after it had been arranged by du Pont and I.C.I. Courtaulds, the other shareholder, interested equally with I.C.I. in British Nylon Spinners, also were not before the United States court or amenable to a decree of that court. The statement by the learned judge that "throughout all these negotiations it appears that B.N.S. was advised of the dealings between I.C.I. and du Pont concerning the British Nylon patents" is not supported by the evidence before me. The whole of the learned judge's observations on that page is based on an assumption that B.N.S. were party to a conspiracy to evade some law of the United States and were not an innocent party. The learned judge then said:

> We do not hesitate therefore to decree that the British nylon patents may not be asserted by I.C.I. to prevent the importation of nylon polymer and of nylon yarn into Great Britain. What credit may be given to such an injunctive provision by the courts of Great Britain in a suit brought by B.N.S. to restrain such importations we do not venture to predict. We feel that the possibility that the English courts in an equity suit will not give effect to such a provision in our decree should not deter us from including it. In any event it appears that B.N.S. would have the right under section 63 of the Patent Act of 1949, as the exclusive licensee, to bring suit for infringement against an importer of yarn and staple fibre. There would then be a speedy determination of the effectiveness of the immunity provision of the decree with reference to these products. If the British courts were not to give credit to this provision, no injury would have been done; if the holding of the British courts were to the contrary, a remedy available would not have been needlessly abandoned. Specifically, with relation to nylon, the judgment shall provide that the agreement between du Pont and I.C.I. concerning the British nylon patents shall be cancelled; a new agreement may be executed by the parties granting a non-exclusive licence, providing for the payment of royalties and removing all contractual barriers to exportation.

It is evident that the learned judge was far from certain that the English courts would accept the validity of his order, and recognized that these provisions in his order would be entirely without effect unless they were accepted and enforced by the English court.

The learned judge's final judgment was not given until July 30, 1952, and by article XIV of it it was provided that the judgment should become effective forthwith. . . .

. . .

In article IV, para. 3, there appears this curiously expressed provision (the effect of which will be discussed later):

> 3. No provision of this judgment shall operate against I.C.I. for action taken in compliance with any law of the United States Government, or of any foreign government or instrumentality thereof, to which I.C.I. is at the time being subject, and concerning matters over which, under the law of the United States, such foreign government or instrumentality thereof has jurisdiction.

. . .

Article VII, which is entitled "Cancellation of agreements," by para. 1 provides as follows:

> 1. The contracts and agreements listed in Schedule A of this judgment are adjudged to be unlawful under section 1 of the Sherman Act and are hereby cancelled and terminated. Except as otherwise provided in articles VIII and XI of this judgment, defendants shall not further perform or enforce any of the provisions of the contracts and agreements, and of any amendatory or supplemental contracts and agreements.

The du Pont Nylon Agreement of March 30, 1939, is included among the agreements listed in Schedule A, but the agreement of December 31, 1946, is not among them. It is, however, referred to in para. 5 of the same article, which is in these terms:

> 5. The Nylon Agreement between du Pont and I.C.I., dated December 31, 1946, is hereby cancelled and terminated and neither du Pont nor I.C.I. shall further perform, enforce or claim any right under any of the provisions thereof.

. . .

The question, therefore, is whether this judgment of the United States Federal Court provides a defence for I.C.I. in this action for specific performance, and whether by reason of that judgment I should refuse to grant specific performance of the contract which has admittedly been made between the plaintiffs and the defendants.

It was argued on behalf of the defendants that this court would not enforce a contract which involved the deliberate violation of the laws of a friendly country, and I was referred to Dicey's Conflict of Laws, 6th ed., p. 607, and *Foster v. Driscoll*,[4] which was a case of a contract, the object of which was the illegal importation of whisky into the United States of America. There is no evidence before me that the object of the contract of March 5, 1947, was to do anything contrary to the law of the United States of America and no evidence that the plaintiff company was party to or had knowledge of any conspiracy contrary to the law of the United States when that contract was entered into. It is impossible for me to accept the conclusions of the United States court as findings of fact binding in this action against the plaintiff company who were not a party to the American proceedings. Consequently, it seems to me that *Foster v. Driscoll* is in no way applicable to the present case, and I should apply the principle laid down by the Court of Appeal in *Kleinwort's* case.[5]

There are, however, further considerations which also lead to the same result. I had the advantage of the evidence of Mr. Marshall Konopak Skadden, a member of the Bar of the State of New York, practising in the relevant United States courts. His evidence was that the British court would be accepted under the law of the United States as an appropriate court having jurisdiction for the enforcement of the contract under consideration in the present case; further, his evidence was that, if I.C.I., though prohibited from doing so by a judgment of a court in the United States, complied with an order of a British court and executed a licence, this would not be treated by an American court as a contempt of court; and Mr. Skadden referred to a number

---

[4] [1929] 1 K.B. 470, [cited in *Regazzoni v. Sethia* and summarized in note 2, p. 900, *supra*.]

[5] [1939] 2 K.B. 678. In this case an English bank extended credit in London to a Hungarian firm. When the time for repayment came, the borrower refused to pay on the ground that under Hungarian law it was illegal to remit money abroad, to acquire British currency, or dispose of assets abroad. The court held that Hungarian law was no defense, since English law was the proper law of the contract, and Hungarian law could not affect the legality of a promise neither governed by Hungarian law nor to be performed in Hungary.

of decisions of American courts in support of these propositions. This evidence indicates to me that the American courts would not regard a judgment of this court in the present circumstances enforcing against I.C.I. the contract of March 5, 1947, as in any way inappropriate, and there does not appear, therefore, to be any difficulty in regard to comity between the courts of the two countries in this case.

Furthermore, it would appear that the judgments of his Honour Judge Sylvester Ryan recognized this principle and were intended to provide for and limit his own judgment in this very respect. This appears to be the intention of article IV, para. 3, of the judgment of July 30, 1952: [quoted above]

. . .

. . . [H]is Honour Judge Ryan has been careful so to limit his judgment that neither his judgment, nor any judgment of mine which the law of England requires me to give, will disturb the comity which the courts of the United States and the courts of England are so anxious and careful to observe.

I would only add that Sir Andrew Clark, as counsel for the defendants, I.C.I., fully carried out to the best of his ability, in somewhat difficult circumstances, the desire expressed by his Honour Judge Ryan that the considerations which led the American court to reach the conclusions and make the order that it did should be before this court.

In the result, my conclusion is that, notwithstanding the judgment of the United States court of July 30, 1952, the defendants, I.C.I., are bound by English law to carry out their agreement of March 5, 1947, and I ought to make the declaration which is asked by the amended statement of claim, and grant specific performance of the contract. The order will, therefore, be for specific performance—an order that they shall execute these licenses; and an injunction restraining them from doing anything to the contrary until the exclusive licenses have been registered in the appropriate registry.

Declaration accordingly.

AN ENGLISH COMMENTATOR ON THE NYLON PATENT CASES

Kahn-Freund, *English Contracts and American Anti-Trust Law—The Nylon Patent Case*

18 Modern L. Rev. 65 (1955)

. . .

At first sight the case looks unproblematical. The licensing agreement between I.C.I. and Nylon was a contract made in England between two English companies carrying on business here, referring mainly to United Kingdom patents, and to be performed in England, *i.e.*, it was clearly an English contract. Danckwerts J. (at p. 914) had no hesitation in saying that English law was the proper law of the entire contract, and the Master of the Rolls emphasised (at p. 26) that Nylon's right, *i.e.*, the right which related to all the patents, whether granted in the United Kingdom or elsewhere in the Commonwealth, was a right under "an English contract made between English nationals and to be performed in England." It was an English contract which mainly, though not entirely, concerned a "species of English property," *viz.*, United Kingdom patents, choses in action "situated" here. How could American law, how could an American judgment applying American law possibly vary the rights and obligations created by an English contract to be performed outside the United States? There was nothing, from the point of view of the conflict of laws, to connect the licensing agreement between the parties with the United States. The proposition that American law should be able to compel an English company in England to break its English contract with another English company is plainly absurd. . . .

So much for the contractual aspect of the case. Its far deeper significance lies in the question whether the judgment of the Federal District Court does not constitute a violation of public international law and whether for that reason alone it should not be regarded as incapable of having any effect outside the United States.

The jurisdiction of the Federal Courts under the Anti-Trust laws is a penal jurisdiction, no matter whether it is exercised in criminal or in equitable proceedings. It was held by the Supreme Court and emphasised by Mr. Justice Holmes in *American Banana Co. v. United Fruit Co.* (1909) 213 U.S. 347, at p. 356 that, whatever form it takes, this jurisdiction cannot be exercised beyond the limits set to criminal prosecutions by international law, *i.e.,* that it cannot be exercised against non-Americans with regard to acts done outside the United States. This does not seem to have been doubted in America, but a novel interpretation has been given in a number of recent American decisions to the concept of *locus delicti*. This new conception that anything which "affects" or "concerns" American trade is deemed to have been done inside the United States is reflected in the judgment of Judge Ryan. . . . Whether this new conception has become part of American law is not clear, but even if it has, it certainly has not become part of international law. The assertion of this jurisdiction cannot be justified from the international point of view, and, for that reason alone, it is submitted, the American judgment should in the instant case have been regarded as invalid so far as it purported to regulate the conduct of an English company outside the United States.

NOTES AND QUESTIONS

(1)(a) It is generally agreed that the basic foundations of jurisdiction to prescribe are territoriality and nationality. Does *Alcoa* fit under either category?

(b) Judge Hand says that "any state may impose liabilities, even upon persons not within its allegiance, for conduct outside its borders that has consequences within its borders which the state reprehends." Putting aside the question of whether this is indeed "settled law" (compare Kahn-Freund *supra*), is jurisdiction on this basis—often called the "effects doctrine"—a new category, or is it an aspect of jurisdiction based on territoriality?[c] Does anything turn on the answer to this question?

(c) Note that Judge Hand is careful not to put the issue of U.S. jurisdiction over the foreign-based cartel in terms of power, or in terms of derivation from judicial jurisdiction over the participants. "We should not impute to Congress," he writes, "an intent to punish all whom its courts can catch." Like Justice Jackson a few years later in *Lauritzen* and Justice Marshall in

---

[c] The *Restatement (Third) of Foreign Relations Law (1987)*, in § 402(1)(c) classifies jurisdiction over conduct outside the state's territory which has or is intended to have substantial effect within its territory as an aspect of territorial jurisdiction, but then makes authority to exercise such jurisdiction depend on further factors. See pp. 959–60, question 3, *infra*. Others have given a different answer to this question.

The Charming Betsy, Judge Hand would construe the intent of Congress in light of "the limitations customarily observed by nations upon the exercise of their powers," and he characterizes these limitations as generally corresponding to "those fixed by the Conflict of Laws." How does conflict of laws help here? If *Alcoa* (i.e., the international aspect here reproduced) is a choice of law case, is it like *Regazzoni*? Or *Lauritzen*? Or *Kilberg*? If none of these cases (all of which, of course, were decided after *Alcoa*) leap out as analogous, is the comparison nevertheless persuasive?

(d) The excerpts from the opinion in *Alcoa* quoted in the preceding paragraph suggest both that international law/conflict of laws imposes limits on the application of U.S. law to foreign events and that the intent of Congress will be construed to uphold this principle. But in the immediately preceding passage, Hand says, "we are concerned only with whether Congress chose to attach liability . . . and whether our own Constitution permitted it to do so . . . .." How can these two thoughts be reconciled? Is the choice of law process to be conducted under the fiction of plumbing for the intent of Congress?

(2)(a) Judge Hand says that two constituent links to the United States are necessary to support jurisdiction to prescribe and apply U.S. law to foreign conduct by non-nationals—intent and effect. Unintended or incidental effect of a foreign act or activity is not enough; and intent that does not have actual effect is also not enough. But he adds that if intent is shown, the burden of proof that there was no effect in the United States is on the person resisting application of U.S. law. Do these seem to be the correct tests? Do they sound in conflict of laws, as Judge Hand says?

(b) Suppose an Italian labor union has a dispute with a trucking company and calls a strike. A glove manufacturer in Florence, despite warning by the union, continues to deal with the trucking company, and thereupon the union throws a picket line around the glove factory. As a result, it becomes impossible for the glove manufacturer to meet his obligations to customers; prices rise and shortages result in the United States. If all the events described had taken place in the United States, the union would probably be guilty of a secondary boycott, an unfair labor practice under the National Labor Relations Act.[d] Would you think the National Labor Relations Act should apply, or to put it differently, that the jurisdiction of the United States to prescribe should be held to apply to the actions of the Italian labor union?

(c) Nearly everyone would say "no" to the preceding question, but the explanations are not always the same. Some would point to the possibility of *international complications,* as Judge Hand does; others would say it would not be *reasonable* to apply U.S. labor law to labor disputes in Italy, and that if the exercise of jurisdiction would not be reasonable, it would not be lawful.[e] Still others have urged a modification of the *Alcoa* test, to provide that the effect in the territory of the state applying its law must be substantial, direct, and foreseeable, and/or that the activity must be of the kind that is generally recognized as a crime or tort by states with reasonably developed legal systems.[f]

---

[d] See § 8(b)(4) of the Act, 29 U.S.C. § 158(b)(4).

[e] This essentially, is the approach of the *Restatement (Third) of Foreign Relations Law, §§ 402 and 403.* See question 3, pp. 959–60, *infra.*

[f] The first part of this formulation was adopted by Congress in the Foreign Trade Antitrust Improvements Act of 1982, Title IV of Pub. L. 97–290, adopting 15 U.S.C. §§ 6a, 45(a)(3), which extend however only to antitrust jurisdiction and within that only to application of the Sherman and FTC Acts to export transactions from the United States.

Both parts of the formulation (linked by "or") are embodied in § 18(b) of the *Restatement (Second) of Foreign Relations Law,* published in 1965. See p. 947, note 18.

(d) Without completely modifying the *Alcoa* test, might you balance Judge Hand's two elements, so that if the intent was specific but, say, a conspiracy was nipped in the bud and the effect was slight, jurisdiction would attach, but if the intent was marginal or unfocused the actual effect must be substantial? Alternatively, could you reverse Judge Hand's burdens of proof, so that instead of inferring effect from intent, you would infer intent from effect?

(e) Are all these questions limited to jurisdiction to apply the antitrust laws? Or would you think they apply to jurisdiction to prescribe generally? Keep this question in mind in pursuing the topic in the context of the succeeding cases.

(3)(a) Turning to the *Nylon* case, there is no doubt—at least on the American side—that the cartel itself was unlawful, in that it restricted imports into the United States and exports from the United States. All that had been previously decided. The opinion here reproduced concerns only the remedy, and in particular the application of that remedy abroad. Note first that though exercise of jurisdiction to prescribe is usually thought of as legislative activity, in contrast to adjudication, which is carried out by courts, here it is the U.S. district court that is exercising jurisdiction to prescribe, as Judge Ryan seeks to devise an equitable decree containing specific directions and prohibitions as to future conduct.

(b) The essence of the violation, as established after lengthy trial, was a worldwide territorial division of the market for nylon. The basic invention had been made in the United States, but patents covering the product and the related manufacturing processes had been issued to du Pont by various states, including Great Britain and members of the Commonwealth. Du Pont had first licensed ICI under the patent, and subsequently, as we saw, assigned the patent itself to ICI, in implementation, as the court found, of the unlawful conspiracy. Thus as Judge Ryan sees it, the center of gravity of the nylon cartel is in the United States.

(c) The United States government, as plaintiff, had sought cancellation of the nylon patents, but Judge Ryan thought that would be going too far. Instead he decreed compulsory licensing, i.e., an offer by du Pont to license any qualified manufacturer under the patents for a reasonable royalty; any dispute about what was a reasonable royalty could be brought back to the court if necessary. In so far as the British patents were concerned, it appears that the assignment from du Pont to ICI would be cancelled, and that ICI would be treated as having a non-exclusive license, which might entitle ICI to grant a sublicense, but would not support an action to exclude imports from the United States or third countries into Great Britain. As a way of attempting to remedy the consequences of an unlawful global cartel—two evils resulting from one understanding, as Judge Ryan puts it—is the decree not reasonable? Is it, as Judge Ryan himself asks, "an instrusion on the authority of a foreign sovereign"?

(d) Judge Ryan acknowledges testimony on behalf of ICI that a provision for granting immunities—i.e., a non-exclusive license—is contrary to British public policy, but he says he is entitled to direct ICI, a person before his court, to refrain from asserting rights which it may have under British law. As a choice of law matter, is Judge Ryan correct?

(4) Consider now how Judge Ryan's judgment looks from England.

(a) First, is Judge Ryan's decree not entitled to recognition as a foreign judgment? Suppose a child in the United States wears a pajama made of ICI's nylon and the pajama catches fire, injuring the child. Suit is brought in the United States on behalf of the child, ICI defends on the merits, and judgment is given in favor of the child. The judgment remains unsatisfied, and suit is brought on the judgment in England. Is there any doubt that the judgment would be enforced in England? That argument about evidence admitted or excluded in the American action would be irrelevant? And that an assertion that in England ICI might have prevailed on a defense such as lack of privity or a statute of limitations would likewise be dismissed? If all this is true, why is the actual case, *United States v. ICI,* different?

(b) Speaking of evidence, how can Judge Danckwerts make the statement, p. 920, that

there is no evidence before me that the object of the contract [between ICI and BNS] was to do anything contrary to the law of the United States of America and no evidence that [BNS] was party to or had knowledge of any conspiracy contrary to the law of the United States . . .?

Literally, the statement may have been true, since evidence of internal communications among officers of ICI was excluded, and neither BNS nor ICI had reason to give evidence of a conspiracy to Judge Danckwerts. But there was not only evidence, but a detailed finding on the point by Judge Ryan. Can the British judge simply disregard the American judgment on this point?

(c) Judge Danckwerts writes "It is impossible for me to accept the conclusions of the United States court as findings of fact binding in this action, against the plaintiff company who were not a party to the American proceedings." Is he suggesting that BNS is some kind of bona fide purchaser, whose rights are greater than those of its grantor?

(d) Mr. Skadden, the American lawyer testifying in the English action, assures Judge Danckwerts that if ICI is ordered to perform its contract with BNS, it will not be found in contempt of the U.S. court. In fact no effort was made to hold ICI in contempt, and the order of the British court, entered after a good faith defense on behalf of ICI (the role of Sir Andrew Clark), was treated de facto as an excuse. Is that as it should be? If the opposite were true, i.e., if the British judge were persuaded that ICI would be subjected to contempt sanctions in the United States if it obeyed the British judgment, should he then decline to find for BNS?[g]

(5)(a) Lord Evershed, M.R., who delivered the principal opinion in the interlocutory British judgment, conceded that

it is competent for the court of a particular country, in a suit between persons who are . . . subject to its jurisdiction, to make orders in personam against one such party—directing it . . . to do something or to refrain from doing something in another country affecting either party to the action.[h]

"But the plaintiffs in this case," he continues (unlike ICI), "are neither subjects nor nationals of the United States, nor were they parties to the proceedings before his Honour, nor are they otherwise subject to his jurisdiction."[i] Though he entertains at least some doubt about the independence of BNS from ICI,[j] he treats BNS as an independent English company. He then treats the action between BNS and ICI as:

---

[g] Analogous situations arose several times in the 1980's in connection with subpoenas issued to banks in the United States demanding records located in Britain and other countries where the court was prepared to enjoin disclosure but only if the bank would not be punished in the United States for obeying the British injunction. See e.g., *X A.G. v. A Bank,* [1983] 2 All. E.R. 464 (Q.B.). For an instance when the U.S. court would not accept the foreign injunction as an excuse, see *Garpeg, Ltd. v. United States,* 583 F. Supp. 789 (S.D.N.Y. 1984).

[h] *British Nylon Spinners, Ltd. v. Imperial Chem. Indus. Ltd.,* [1953] Ch. 19 at 25.

[i] *Ibid.*

[j] So much so that he expressly disclaims any intention of doing so. *Id.* at 25–26.

an English contract made between English nationals, and to be performed in England . . ..[k] Is that the long and short of it?

(b) Is Lord Evershed saying, as Prof. Kahn-Freund said, that "There was nothing, from the point of view of the conflict of laws, to connect the licensing agreement between the parties with the United States"? How would you reply to Kahn-Freund on this point? Could you say this was a contract about an invention made in the United States, designed to limit exports from the United States and to further a conspiracy entered into in the United States? Or is all of the choice of law discussion overtaken by the fact that the English court has a judgment to deal with?

(c) There is at least some suggestion that the U.S. judgment is without jurisdiction, because it concerns a British patent, something like a judgment concerning land in another state.[l] But Judge Ryan is not really adjudicating the validity of the British patent; moreover, it seems that the case would not come out differently if it concerned merely a web of exclusive distributorships and agreements not to compete in each other's territories, not linked to a patent or group of patents.

(d) With so much of the discussion about whether BNS was a party or had knowledge, and about where the contract is centered, it is easy to lose sight of what is, after all, a clash of sovereignties about the scope of jurisdiction to prescribe. Consider the following variations (all other facts being the same):

(i) du Pont had retained ownership of the British patents and ICI had been the licensee, as under the original arrangements; or

(ii) ICI had retained full title to the British patents, rather than agreeing to license BNS; or

(iii) BNS had been amenable to suit in New York.

Would any of these variations have led to a different result?

(6)(a) Look, finally, at Kahn-Freund's major point, that not only Judge Ryan, but the effects doctrine as enunciated by Learned Hand in *Alcoa,* are contrary to international law. It is fair to point out that neither Judge Danckwerts nor the justices who spoke in the first phase of the English litigation made this argument, and indeed they acknowledge Judge Ryan's rather deferential attitude. But Kahn-Freund was one of England's leading experts in conflict of laws (and a Consulting Editor of several editions of Dicey), and his view cannot be lightly disregarded. Assuming that as of the early 1950's the law of nations on this point was not firmly settled, should it develop in the direction Kahn-Freund suggests? Or would you think the more flexible techniques of conflict of laws are more promising?

(b) To be more specific, Judge Ryan recognizes the possibility of conflict, but hopes the other side will do so as well, and will be persuaded by the weight of his argument. If Kahn-Freund is right, it seems, there is little if any room for persuasion.

(c) Note that the British government made no appearance in the *Nylon* case, either in the United States or in Great Britain, whereas the United States government threw major resources into a decade-long investigation and litigation. Does this suggest that from the point of view of interest

---

[k] *Id.* at 26.

[l] See *Clarke v. Clarke,* Chapter 8, pp. 680–81, *supra.*

analysis the United States had the stronger interest? If so, does that argue for the American position on the nylon cartel? Or against the use of interest analysis?

§ 10.04 More on "Subject Matter Jurisdiction," Jurisdiction to Prescribe, and Conflict of Laws

Not all the controversy concerning so-called "exterritorial jurisdiction" involved antitrust cases. A related series of cases involved U.S. securities legislation, and two of the leading cases in that series are reproduced here, with subsequent decisions discussed in the Notes and Questions. The securities cases are followed by two more landmark antitrust cases, both brought on private, not governmental, initiative, in which the appellate courts reconsider *Alcoa* and *ICI,* and attempt to develop some guidelines to determine when it is and when it is not appropriate to apply U.S. law to activity having links both in the United States and abroad. In 1993, in the *Insurance Antitrust* case, the U.S. Supreme Court addressed the issues here discussed, and the relevant portions of the majority and dissenting opinions in that case are reproduced in the final portion of this section, followed by further notes and questions.

SCHOENBAUM v. FIRSTBROOK

United States Court of Appeals, Second Circuit
405 F.2d 200, rehearing en banc 405 F.2d 215 (1968)
cert. denied sub nom., Manley v. Schoenbaum, 395 U.S. 906 (1968)

LUMBARD, Chief Judge:

Plaintiff, an American shareholder of Banff Oil Ltd., a Canadian corporation, brought this shareholder derivative action to recover under Section 10(b) of the Securities Exchange Act of 1934, 15 U.S.C. 78j(b) and Rule 10b–5, 17 CFR § 240.10b–5 (1967), for damages to the corporation resulting from the sales, in Canada, of Banff treasury stock to defendants Aquitaine of Canada, Ltd., and Paribas Corporation. Plaintiff alleged that the defendant corporations and Banff's directors, who are the individual defendants in this action, conspired to defraud Banff by making Banff sell treasury shares at the market price which the defendants, who had inside information not yet disclosed to the public, knew did not represent the true value of the shares.

Defendants moved pursuant to Rules 12(c) and 56, Fed.R.Civ.P., for summary judgment, and under Rule 12(b) to dismiss the complaint on the ground that the Court lacked jurisdiction over the subject matter. Judge Cooper, refusing to permit plaintiff to carry out a program of discovery, entered judgment for defendants, holding that the Court lacked jurisdiction because the Securities and Exchange Act does not have extraterritorial application, and that plaintiff failed to state a cause of action under § 10(b) and Rule 10b–5. 268 F.Supp. 385 (SDNY 1967).

. . .

The Facts

Banff is a Canadian corporation and conducts all of its operations within Canada. Its common stock is registered with the SEC and traded upon both the American Stock Exchange and the

Toronto Stock Exchange. In February 1964, Aquitaine Company of Canada, Ltd., acquired control of Banff through a tender offer to Banff shareholders in the United States and Canada. Aquitaine is a wholly owned subsidiary of a French corporation, Société Nationale des Petroles d'Aquitaine, which in turn is a subsidiary of Enterprises for Research and Activities in Petroleum (ERAP), a French governmental oil agency.

In March 1964, Banff and Aquitaine entered into an agreement to conduct joint oil explorations. In October 1964, Banff entered into a "farmout agreement" with Socony Mobil under which Banff and Aquitaine would receive a 50% interest in 160,000 acres in the Rainbow Lake area of Alberta, Canada, in return for paying the total cost of drilling two exploratory wells. The Rainbow, area is a desolate wilderness region over 100 miles from the nearest all-weather road or railway. At least sixteen wells had previously been drilled in the general vicinity by six different oil companies, and all had been abandoned as failures. Because of the difficulty of conducting explorations in this region and the highly speculative prospects for success Socony Mobil was willing to give up a half interest merely for drilling two test wells.

Banff received a 5% interest and Aquitaine received a 45% interest, pursuant to their joint exploration agreement, with the drilling costs to be paid 10% by Banff and 90% by Aquitaine. On December 11, 1964 Banff's Board of Directors, the three Aquitaine representatives abstaining, voted to offer to sell 500,000 shares of Banff treasury stock to Aquitaine at the current market price allegedly for the purpose of financing Banff's share of the exploration expenses. On January 5, 1965, Aquitaine's president wrote to Banff that "our Chairman and Managing Director . . . has agreed to your . . . proposal." On January 26, Banff issued a press release announcing that Aquitaine "intended to purchase" 500,000 shares of common stock at the price of $1.35 per share, the closing price on the Toronto Stock Exchange on December 11, 1964. Actual delivery of the shares took place March 16, 1965.

Exploration in the Rainbow area commenced toward the end of 1964. On February 6, 1965, the test well flowed oil to the surface on a drillstem test. This information was released to the public on February 8. The well reached total depth on March 17, 1965, the day after delivery on the Aquitaine purchase. On March 18, Banff issued a press release indicating that the discovery well was completed and that no further information would be disclosed in the immediate future. A further release on April 20 explained that the company was taking advantage of the Alberta law permitting it to withold information on its discovery for one year to reduce competition from other companies in bidding on government oil lands in the discovery area. The release stated "The Board feels that this discovery is of great significance to the company but it is too early to have any idea of the areal extent."

After the discovery, further exploration activity was undertaken. In September 1965, a press release announced the formation of a company, in which Banff has a 3% interest and Aquitaine has a 30% interest, to build a pipeline into the area. To finance its activities, Banff's Board of Directors authorized negotiation of sales of treasury shares of common stock at $6.75 per share or more. Paribas Corporation—a Delaware corporation doing business in New York and a wholly owned subsidiary of Banque de Paris et des Pays-Bas, a French banking institution—negotiated a purchase of 270,000 shares of Banff Common at $7.30 per share, the current price on the Toronto Stock Exchange, on behalf of Banque de Paris et des Pays-Bas pour le Grand Duché de Luxembourg, another subsidiary of Banque de Paris. The issue was to be placed with "ten European professional investors." A verbal offer was made by Paribas on November 19, 1965. A written offer was mailed by Paribas from New York and was accepted by Banff in Canada on November 22. Payment and delivery took place in Canada January 24, 1966.

§ 10.04   INTERNATIONAL LAW AND CONFLICT OF LAWS   □   929

The Allegations in the Complaint

The complaint alleged that "For some time prior to February 6, 1965, Aquitaine and the other defendants knew Banff had exceptionally valuable oil properties located in the Rainbow Lake area in Alberta, Canada." It alleged that the Aquitaine purchase of 500,000 treasury shares at $1.35 per share took place March 15, 1965, and that the Paribas purchase of 270,000 shares at $7.30 on January 24, 1966 was on behalf of "affiliates, business associates and friends" of Aquitaine and its parent companies, and that defendants withheld information until March 16, 1966 in order to purchase the treasury shares at an artificially low market price, paying to Banff about $10,000,000 less than the stock's fair market value.[1]

The individual defendants are all of Banff's directors. They allegedly conspired with the corporate defendants and approved of, participated in or acquiesced in the transactions with the corporate defendants.

Subject Matter Jurisdiction

Plaintiff predicated subject matter jurisdiction upon Section 27 of the Securities and Exchange Act, 15 U.S.C. § 78aa, which gives the district courts exclusive jurisdiction over all "actions at law brought to enforce any liability or duty created by this title or the rules and regulations thereunder." The district court concluded that the Act has no extraterritorial application, and that therefore no liability arose under the Act with regard to the sales in question, which took place in Canada between foreign buyers and sellers. The court found nothing to rebut the presumption that the Act was intended to apply only to transactions within the territorial limits of the United States. It also stated that the presumption was reinforced by the "specific mandate" of Section 30(b), 15 U.S.C. § 78dd(b), which provides that the Act does not apply "to any person insofar as he transacts a business in securities without the jurisdiction of the United States. . . ."

We disagree with the district court's conclusion. We believe that Congress intended the Exchange Act to have extraterritorial application in order to protect domestic investors who have purchased foreign securities on American exchanges and to protect the domestic securities market from the effects of improper foreign transactions in American securities. In our view, neither the usual presumption against extraterritorial application of legislation nor the specific language of Section 30(b) show Congressional intent to preclude application of the Exchange Act to transactions regarding stocks traded in the United States which are effected outside the United States, when extraterritorial application of the Act is necessary to protect American investors.

Section 2 of the Exchange Act, 15 U.S.C. § 78b, states that because transactions in securities are affected with "a national public interest" it is "necessary to provide for regulation and control of such transactions and of practices and matters related thereto, . . . necessary to make such regulation and control reasonably . . . complete in order to protect interstate commerce and to insure the maintenance of fair and honest markets in such transactions."

The Act seeks to regulate the stock exchanges and the relationships of the investing public to corporations which invite public investment by listing on such exchanges. . . .

Banff common stock is registered and traded on the American Stock Exchange. To protect United States shareholders of Banff common stock, Banff is required to comply with the provisions of the Securities Exchange Act concerning financial reports to the SEC, § 13, 15 U.S.C.

---

[1] Banff common stock traded at prices as high as $18 per share in 1966.

§ 78m; proxy solicitation, § 14, 15 U.S.C. § 78n, and reports of insider holdings, § 16, 15 U.S.C. § 78p. Similarly, the anti-fraud provision of § 10(b), which enables the Commission to prescribe rules "necessary or appropriate in the public interest or for the protection of investors" reaches beyond the territorial limits of the United States and applies when a violation of the Rules is injurious to United States investors.

. . .

The Commission has recognized the broad extraterritorial applicability of the Act and has specifically exempted certain foreign issuers from the operation of Sections 14 and 16 of the Act, when enforcement would be impractical.

. . .

Although it has the power to grant exemptions from rules under § 10(b), . . . the Commission has not promulgated a rule exempting foreign transactions from Rule 10b–5.[2]

. . .

We hold that the district court has subject matter jurisdiction over violations of the Securities Exchange Act although the transactions which are alleged to violate the Act take place outside the United States, at least when the transactions involve stock registered and listed on a national securities exchange, and are detrimental to the interests of American investors. See . . . *United States v. Aluminum Company of America*, 148 F.2d 416, 443–444 (2d Cir. 1945).

However, the district court found that the only harm alleged was to the foreign corporation on whose behalf plaintiff brought the action. We do not agree. A fraud upon a corporation which has the effect of depriving it of fair compensation for the issuance of its stock would necessarily have the effect of reducing the equity of the corporation's shareholders and this reduction in equity would be reflected in lower prices bid for the shares on the domestic stock market. This impairment of the value of American investments by sales by the issuer in a foreign country, allegedly in violation of the Act, has in our view, a sufficiently serious effect upon United States commerce to warrant assertion of jurisdiction for the protection of American investors and consideration of the merits of plaintiff's claim.

[The court first holds, with Judge Hays dissenting, that plaintiff has not made out his claim against the purchasers of Banff's stock under Rule 10b–5, since all of Banff's directors knew the facts. At most there might be a claim against the directors for a breach of their fiduciary duty to the corporation. On rehearing en banc, 405 F.2d 215 (1968), the grant of summary judgment in favor of defendants is reversed, and the court holds that the complaint states a triable claim under § 10b and Rule 10b–5 against all but one of the defendants.]

LEASCO DATA PROCESSING EQUIPMENT CORPORATION v. MAXWELL

United States Court of Appeals, Second Circuit
468 F.2d 1326 (1972)

FRIENDLY, Chief Judge:

---

[2] However, a transaction conducted entirely outside of the United States would not violate § 10(b) since the requisite use of interstate commerce or the mails would be lacking. See discussion, *infra*.

§ 10.04   INTERNATIONAL LAW AND CONFLICT OF LAWS   □   931

[In this case the plaintiffs, collectively referred to as Leasco, seek large damages allegedly resulting from the purchase of shares of a British company on the London Stock Exchange. The case comes to the Court of Appeals after denial of all motions to dismiss but before any factual determination. The court relies at this stage on affidavits submitted on behalf of Leasco.]

. . .

I. *The Facts Claimed by Leasco*

The gist of the complaint is that the defendants conspired to cause Leasco to buy stock of Pergamon Press Limited ("Pergamon"), a British corporation controlled by defendant Robert Maxwell, a British citizen, at prices in excess of its true value, in violation of § 10(b) of the Securities Exchange Act and the SEC's sufficiently known Rule 10b–5. According to Leasco, and—as we shall not always repeat—we here state only Leasco's version, the first contact occurred early in 1969 when Maxwell came to Great Neck, N. Y., where Leasco then had its principal office, and proposed to Saul Steinberg, Chairman of Leasco, that Pergamon and Leasco engage in a joint venture in Europe. Maxwell falsely told Steinberg that Pergamon had a computerized typesetting plant in Ireland and gave Steinberg the most recent Pergamon annual report, which contained untruthful and misleading statements of Pergamon's affairs. Steinberg telephoned Maxwell in London to decline the joint venture; Maxwell invited him to come there to discuss areas of possible cooperation.

Steinberg and Robert Hodes, a director of Leasco, met Maxwell at the latter's London office in late April, 1969; Maxwell made various false or exaggerated statements of Pergamon's performance and prospects. When he suggested that Pergamon could acquire Leasco's European operations, Steinberg responded that Leasco would be interested only in acquiring Pergamon and its related companies. Clark, a director of Pergamon, entered the room, Maxwell having left for a short time, and whetted Leasco's interest by falsely touting the profitability of International Learning Systems Company (ILSC). Pergamon was a 50% owner and had an option to acquire the other 50% of ILSC. When Maxwell rejoined the group, he told Steinberg and Hodes that Ladislaus Majhtenyi, an official of Pergamon Press, Inc., an American subsidiary whose stock was traded on the American Stock Exchange, would provide Leasco with all financial data necessary to evaluate the worth of Pergamon and the Maxwell-related companies.

In late April or early May, Michael Gibbs, Leasco's director of corporate planning, met in New York with Majhtenyi. The latter said that the Pergamon and Maxwell operations were very profitable. He added that Pergamon was in the process of acquiring MSI Publishers, Inc. (MSI) and falsely spoke in glowing terms of the profitability of that company's operations in selling Pergamon back issues in Canada, Mexico and South America. This was followed by telephone calls between Maxwell and Steinberg; in some (or perhaps all) of the calls, one (or perhaps both) of the participants were in the United States. Maxwell reported enthusiastically, and falsely, about sales of ILSC encyclopedias in Australia. Expressing surprise at the paucity of information Majhtenyi had given to Gibbs, he said he would meet Steinberg in New York City.

The meeting occurred at a hotel in early May; Maxwell, with Majhtenyi present, made various misrepresentations about the sales and earnings of Pergamon and ILSC. Around May 17 Maxwell mailed a letter from London to Leasco in New York enclosing a dozen documents. Among these were a false report of ILSC's profits; a draft of the 1968 Pergamon annual report, certified by defendant Chalmers, Impey & Co., containing false reports of profits; and a misleading report on Pergamon's affairs, prepared by Whinney, Murray & Co., accountants retained by defendant

Robert Fleming & Co. Ltd. (Fleming Ltd.), a London banking firm whose clients were large holders of Pergamon stock and which also acted as financial adviser to Pergamon. Late in the month Maxwell, in London, called Steinberg, in New York; he said that any contract for the takeover would have to be signed before the Pergamon annual meeting on or about June 19. As a result, Gibbs and Schwartz went to London around May 30 and met for four days with Maxwell, Clark, Kerman (a director of Pergamon and Pergamon Press, Inc. and senior partner of a large London firm of solicitors which represented Pergamon and the Maxwell family interests), and others. Many further misrepresentations with respect to Pergamon and ILSC were allegedly made by Maxwell. The meetings were followed by telephone conversations between Maxwell in London and Steinberg in New York, in the course of which Maxwell is claimed to have made further false statements, especially with respect to Pergamon's profits from the sale of back issues. Around the same time Richard Fleming, chairman of Fleming Ltd., and Lawrence Banks, president of its American subsidiary, Robert Fleming, Incorporated (Fleming, Inc.), visited Leasco's offices in New York and told Schwartz and Hodes that Pergamon was far more valuable than the price Leasco was proposing to pay; in effect they also vouched for the correctness of the Whinney Murray & Co. report.

Later Maxwell telephoned from London that the contract would have to be signed on or before June 17. He and Paul DiBiase, a member of Kerman's firm, arrived in New York shortly thereafter. In the course of a series of meetings, he told Leasco that the condition of Pergamon and its related companies could accurately be determined by relying on the public financial statements certified by Chalmers, Impey & Co. Allegedly these statements misrepresented the profits of Pergamon and ILSC and included a false statement with respect to a large payment from MSI. Other oral misrepresentations were made. Banks, who was present during some of the meetings, repeated that the proposed price was too low and that Fleming Ltd. might oppose the offer if Leasco did not agree to terms satisfactory to Fleming. The upshot was an agreement between Leasco and Maxwell signed in New York on June 17, 1969. This provided that, subject to certain conditions, Leasco would offer to acquire each outstanding share of Pergamon for 37 shillings in cash or Leasco debentures plus, in respect of each 10 Pergamon shares tendered, a 5-year warrant to acquire from Leasco one Pergamon share for 42 shillings. Among the conditions were acceptance by not less than 51% of the Pergamon shares and the obtaining of all necessary United Kingdom exchange control permits. The tender offer was to comply with the Code on Take-Overs and Mergers of the City of London and the regulations of the London Stock Exchange. Maxwell agreed to accept the offer and procure the assent of "the Maxwell interests," to recommend acceptance by the Pergamon shareholders, and to use his best efforts to obtain a similar recommendation by the Pergamon board of directors. The closing was to be had at the office of Fleming Ltd. in London, unless otherwise agreed. Leasco was permitted to cause the offer to be made by a wholly-owned subsidiary (or a wholly-owned subsidiary of such subsidiary), providing Leasco remained responsible for the due performance of its obligations.

Apparently Steinberg and Hodes accompanied Maxwell back to England. There he told them, on June 18, that it would be in Leasco's interest to purchase Pergamon stock on the open market as soon as possible. At a press conference Maxwell stated that Pergamon's overdraft was less than $500,000, whereas in fact it was approximately $2,500,000. Later in June, Maxwell, from London, called Steinberg, in New York,[1] and said that there were rumors of a counter-takeover

---

[1] Defendant Maxwell contends it was impossible that the call was made to New York since Steinberg could not have returned there sufficiently in advance of the initial open-market purchase.

bid and that it would be in Leasco's interests to purchase Pergamon stock to prevent this. Leasco claims that if there were any such rumor, the defendants instigated it. On June 20 Leasco, acting through the London banking firm of N. M. Rothschild & Sons ("Rothschild") began buying Pergamon shares on the London Stock Exchange. By July 24 it purchased 5,206,210 such shares, expending some $22,000,000; later it learned that some 600,000 of these shares had been secretly sold by one or more of the defendants. The stock was paid for with cash furnished by a wholly-owned subsidiary, Leasco International N. V. (Leasco N. V.), a Netherlands Antilles corporation, which had recently sold to a group headed by two United States underwriters $40,000,000 of 5% debentures and $20,000,000 of 7% notes for offering only outside the United States and to persons not nationals or citizens thereof or resident or normally resident therein. Both the debentures and the notes were unconditionally guaranteed by Leasco, and the debentures were convertible into its common stock.

Investigation of Pergamon's affairs by Leasco, authorized by the June 17 agreement, caused Leasco's representatives to make further inquiries of Maxwell in England; many of his responses are alleged to have been false and misleading. In early August, Leasco's representatives met with Maxwell, Majhtenyi and others in Elmsford, N. Y.; Leasco was provided with data indicating that previous representations on the subject of sales of back issues had been misleading. As a result of this and other information, Leasco declined to go forward with the tender offer. However, it was left with the $22,000,000 of Pergamon stock acquired on the London Stock Exchange. Leasco seeks damages in that amount, together with exemplary damages.

We shall reserve the statement of further facts relevant to the issue of personal jurisdiction over those defendants who raise that issue until we have disposed of the question of subject matter jurisdiction.

II. *Subject Matter Jurisdiction*

One of the few points on which all parties are in accord is that subject matter jurisdiction depends on the applicability of the Securities Exchange Act. Leasco's principal place of business is in New York. Defendants Isthmus Enterprises, Inc., Maxwell Scientific International, Inc., and MSI Publishers, Inc. appear to have their principal offices in New York, and this is stated to be true of defendant Robert Fleming, Inc. Plaintiff Leasco World Trade Company (U.K.) Limited, the reason for whose joinder is not apparent, is a British corporation, and most of the defendants are British citizens or corporations. There is thus no jurisdiction under 28 U.S.C. § 1332(a). However, § 27 of the Securities Exchange Act vests the district court with jurisdiction over an action "to enforce any liability created by this title or the rules and regulations thereunder. . . ." Section 10(b) makes it unlawful, *inter alia,* for any person

> by the use of any means or instrumentality of interstate commerce or of the mails. . . .
>
> . . . .
>
> To use or employ, in connection with the purchase or sale of any security registered on a national securities exchange or any security not so registered, any manipulative or deceptive device or contrivance in contravention of such rules and regulations as the Commission may prescribe as necessary or appropriate in the public interest or for the protection of investors.

We see no need for quoting Rule 10b–5, since this does not affect the question of subject matter jurisdiction; Leasco plainly alleged enough to show a violation of the Rule if the statute is applicable.[2]

It will be useful at the outset to differentiate the problem here presented from the point decided in *Schoenbaum v. Firstbrook,* [p. 927, *supra*]. *Schoenbaum* held § 10(b) to be applicable, *even when the fraudulent acts were all committed outside the United States* and the security was that of a foreign company doing no business in the United States, in a case where "the transactions involve stock registered and listed on a national securities exchange, and are detrimental to the interests of American investors." 405 F.2d at 208. If we treat the matter in terms of the distinctions drawn in the *Restatement (Second) of Foreign Relations Law of the United States* (1965), *Schoenbaum* raised the problem, considered in § 18, of the circumstances in which "[a] state has jurisdiction to prescribe a rule of law attaching legal consequences to conduct that occurs outside its territory and causes an effect within its territory . . ." and consequently may be thought to have meant to do so. If all the misrepresentations here alleged had occurred in England, we would entertain most serious doubt whether, despite *United States v. Aluminum Co. of America,* 148 F.2d 416, 443–444 (2 Cir. 1954), and *Schoenbaum,* § 10(b) would be applicable simply because of the adverse effect of the fraudulently induced purchases in England of securities of an English corporation, not traded in an organized American securities market, upon an American corporation whose stock is listed on the New York Stock Exchange and its shareholders. It is true, as Judge L. Hand pointed out in the *Aluminum* case, that if Congress has expressly prescribed a rule with respect to conduct outside the United States, even one going beyond the scope recognized by foreign relations law, a United States court would be bound to follow the Congressional direction unless this would violate the due process clause of the Fifth Amendment. However, the language of § 10(b) of the Securities Exchange Act is much too inconclusive to lead us to believe that Congress meant to impose rules governing conduct throughout the world in every instance where an American company bought or sold a security. When no fraud has been practiced in this country and the purchase or sale has not been made here, we would be hard pressed to find justification for going beyond *Schoenbaum.*

On plaintiffs' version of the facts, that issue does not here arise. The instant case deals rather with the problem considered in the Restatement's § 17, "Jurisdiction to Prescribe with Respect to Conduct, Thing, Status, or other Interest within Territory." While the black letter seems to require that, in a case like this, not only there should be conduct within the territory but also the conduct relate "to a thing located, or a status or other interest localized, in its territory," Comment A and Illustrations 1 and 2, the latter of which[3] is quite pertinent here, appear to be satisfied if there has been conduct within the territory. Conduct within the territory alone would seem sufficient from the standpoint of *jurisdiction* to prescribe a rule. It follows that when, as here, there has been significant conduct within the territory, a statute cannot properly be held inapplicable simply on the ground that, absent the clearest language, Congress will not be assumed to have meant to go beyond the limits recognized by foreign relations law. Defendants' reliance on the principle stated in *Foley Bros. v. Filardo,* 336 U.S. 281 (1949), that regulatory statutes

---

[2] Section 3(a)(17) defines "interstate commerce" to include transportation or communication "between any foreign country and any State."

[3] X and Y are in state A. X makes a misrepresentation to Y. X and Y go to State B. Solely because of the prior misrepresentations, Y delivers money to X. A has jurisdiction to prescribe a criminal penalty for obtaining money by false pretenses.

Restatement (Second) of the Foreign Relations Law of the United States 45.

§ 10.04

will generally not be construed as applying to conduct wholly outside the United States, is thus misplaced. However, it would be equally erroneous to assume that the legislature always means to go to the full extent permitted. This is a question of the interpretation of the particular statute, which we will consider below with specific reference to § 10(b).

We would not wish defendants to think that in thus defining the issue we have failed to consider their argument that the critical misrepresentations, if such they were, were made in England during the four days of meetings in early June and in the interval between the signing of the agreement in New York and the beginning and continuation of the purchases on the London Stock Exchange. Even limiting ourselves to plaintiff's answers to defendants' interrogatories, as defendant Maxwell suggests, there were abundant misrepresentations in the United States. Maxwell's initial misrepresentations were made here, although then in a context of seeking to interest Steinberg in a joint venture. Further misrepresentations were made by Majhtenyi in late April or early May. These were elaborated by Maxwell and Majhtenyi at the hotel meeting in early May. There was the visit by Fleming and Banks in late May.[4] Finally, there were the meetings preceding the signature of the June 17 contract. Beyond this we see no reason why, for purposes of jurisdiction to impose a rule, making telephone calls and sending mail to the United States should not be deemed to constitute conduct within it. On what is now before us it is impossible to say that conduct in the United States was not "an essential link," in leading Leasco into the contract of June 17, 1969. And that contract, signed in the United States, was "an essential link" in inducing Leasco to make the open-market purchases, whether these were triggered by a call from London to New York, as Leasco contends, or by a conversation in England, as defendants assert. Putting the matter in another way, if defendants' fraudulent acts in the United States significantly whetted Leasco's interest in acquiring Pergamon shares, it would be immaterial, from the standpoint of foreign relations law, that the damage resulted, not from the contract whose execution Maxwell procured in this country, but from interrelated action which he induced in England or, for that matter, which Leasco took there on its own. . . .

Up to this point we have established only that, because of the extensive acts alleged to have been performed in the United States, considerations of foreign relations law do not preclude our reading § 10(b) as applicable here. The question remains whether we should. Appellants have three lines of defense: they claim (1) that § 10(b) has no application to transactions in foreign securities not on an organized American market; (2) that if it does, it has no application when such transactions occur outside the United States; and (3) that in any event it can have no application when the purchaser is not a citizen of the United States.

[The court holds that Congress did not intend to limit 10 (b) of the Securities Exchange Act of 1934 to trades on U.S. markets.]

Since Congress thus meant § 10(b) to protect against fraud in the sale or purchase of securities whether or not these were traded on organized United States markets, we cannot perceive any reason why it should have wished to limit the protection to securities of American issuers. The New Yorker who is the object of fraudulent misrepresentations in New York is as much injured if the securities are of a mine in Saskatchewan as in Nevada. Defendants have pointed to nothing in the legislative history which would indicate an intention that the language of § 10(b) should be narrowed so as not to protect him.

---

[4] Fleming's visit in May does not appear in plaintiffs' answers to interrogatories, but is not contested by defendants and, indeed, appears in Fleming's own affidavit.

We likewise cannot see any sound reason for believing that, in a case like that just put, Congress would have wished protection to be withdrawn merely because the fraudulent promoter of the Saskatchewan mining security took the buyer's check back to Canada and mailed the certificate from there. In the somewhat different yet closely related context of choice of law, the mechanical test that, in determining the *locus delicti,* "The place of wrong is in the state where the last event necessary to make an actor liable for an alleged tort takes place," *Restatement of the Conflict of Laws* § 377 (1934), has given way, in the case of fraud and misrepresentation, to a more extensive and sophisticated analysis. See *Restatement (Second) of the Conflict of Laws* § 148 (1971).

Our case, however, is not the simple one thus hypothesized. In that instance not only the fraudulent misrepresentation but the issuance of the check and the receipt of the securities occurred in the United States, although the check was deposited and the security mailed in Canada. Here it was understood from the outset that all the transactions would be executed in England. Still we must ask ourselves whether, if Congress had thought about the point, it would not have wished to protect an American investor if a foreigner comes to the United States and fraudulently induces him to purchase foreign securities abroad—a purpose which its words can fairly be held to embrace. While, as earlier stated, we doubt that impact on an American company and its shareholders would suffice to make the statute applicable if the misconduct had occurred solely in England, we think it tips the scales in favor of applicability when substantial misrepresentations were made in the United States.

. . .

Before leaving subject-matter jurisdiction, we should say a word in answer to the defendants' argument that since choice of law principles would select the law of England as the rule governing liability, application of § 10(b) of the Securities Exchange Act would violate international law. *Cf. Lauritzen v. Larsen,* [p. 871, *supra.*] At first blush the contention that the courts of the forum transgress their jurisdiction if they apply the forum's own law when correct choice of law doctrines would require them to apply the law of another state as the normative principle would scarcely seem to warrant discussion, particularly in a case like this where the full faith and credit clause of the Constitution can have no application. However, the argument is more subtle. Defendants concede that a New York court or a federal court if diversity jurisdiction existed, seized of an action by plaintiffs for common law fraud, would not transgress international law if, after due consideration, it erroneously chose New York rather than English law; the difficulty alleged to exist here is that a federal court will feel constrained to apply § 10(b) of the Securities Exchange Act rather than the law of England. We are not as certain as the defendants that, under the principles stated in § 148 of the *Restatement of Conflicts Second,* English law would necessarily govern an action in New York for common law fraud.[7] But if it would, the conclusion asserted by defendants would not follow. For, as we have already demonstrated, in the circumstances described in § 17 of the Restatement of Foreign Relations Law, under which this case fits, the nation where the conduct has occurred has jurisdiction to displace foreign law and to direct its courts to apply its own.

We therefore hold that the motions to dismiss for lack of subject matter jurisdiction were properly denied.

---

[7] Professor Ehrenzweig contends that "no 'conflicts' case [of fraud] can be found in which the court would have decided differently had all elements of the case been entirely domestic" and that the rule "is this simple: the court in a fraud case involving foreign elements will apply its own law." *Conflict of Laws* 558–59 (1962).

III. *Jurisdiction over the Person*

Jurisdiction over the person is challenged, thus far unsuccessfully, by defendants Fleming Ltd., and Chalmers, Impey & Co. and, thus far successfully, by defendant Kerman. Plaintiffs assert personal jurisdiction on the basis of § 27 of the Securities Exchange Act. Alternatively they claim personal jurisdiction with respect to Fleming Ltd. under New York CPLR 301 and 302(a)(1) and (2) with respect to Kerman under New York CPLR 302(a)(1) and (3). Since we hold that Congress meant § 27 to extend personal jurisdiction to the full reach permitted by the due process clause, it is unnecessary to discuss the applicability of the New York statutes, which could reach no further.

[The court reviews the latest developments concerning personal jurisdiction, particularly *McGee v. International Life Ins. Co.* and *Hanson v. Denckla.* It sustains jurisdiction over Fleming Ltd., Maxwell's banker, whose managing director accompanied Maxwell to several meetings in the United States and allegedly made misrepresentations concerning the value of Pergamon. It denies jurisdiction over Chalmers, Impey & Co., the accountants, who had done no act in the United States related to the present cause of action. The court states that the issue with respect to Kerman, the London solicitor who was a director and allegedly a shareholder of Pergamon, is close. The question is remanded to the district court for decision after Kerman answers plaintiff's interrogatories concerning ownership of shares and participation in the Maxwell scheme. As to forum non conveniens, the court says:]

Despite plaintiffs' contrary arguments, there is little doubt that, viewed simply as a matter of trial convenience and apart from plaintiffs' desire to have whatever advantages may come from Rule 10b–5, which an English court might not apply, the balance of convenience would favor a trial in England. But that is not enough to justify a district court in dismissing the complaint of an American citizen, much less to warrant an appellate court's requiring it to do so.

NOTES AND QUESTIONS

(1)(a) *Schoenbaum v. Firstbrook* involved the purchase in Canada by one Canadian corporation of shares in another Canadian corporation, both corporations being engaged in the oil business in Canada. What possible business is this of the United States?

(b) Think back to Learned Hand's test in *Alcoa.* Is there any evidence that Acquitaine or its directors had the intention to affect U.S. commerce? The court cites *Alcoa,* and makes a plausible case for effect in the United States, in that the minority shareholders are deprived of a portion of the gain in the value of Banff shares. Is the fact that shares of the acquired company, Banff, are traded on a U.S. stock exchange, as the defendants certainly knew, an adequate substitute for intent, even though the actual transaction was not on the exchange?

(c) The district judge argued for dismissal as follows:

> We recognize in choice of law principles strong reasoning why the transaction is governed by Canadian law. The complaint essentially alleges a breach of the directors' fiduciary duty. . . . The determination of a director's fiduciary duty to the corporation and its shareholders is governed by the law of the State of incorporation. . . .
>
> The only exception to this principle that has developed are those cases which found the corporation to be foreign in name only . . . The reason for this rule is the legitimate interest

of all in the certainty of governing relationships *inter sese* of the corporation, directors, and shareholders by a single law. . . . In this way, the reasonable expectations of the shareholders are protected.[a]

Is this not persuasive?

(d) Judge Cooper continued, however, by saying "We recognize that choice of law principles are not determinative as to whether Congress intended the Exchange Act to have extraterritorial effect," and it was on the issue of the intent of Congress that the Court of Appeals reversed. Judge Lombard did not so much explore the intent of Congress as consider the objective of the legislation, i.e., to protect the interests of American investors and in particular the integrity of the stock market. Does applying U.S. law to the purchase of Banff shares in this case meet that objective? Is it sound interest analysis?[b]

(e) No one seems to have raised Canadian or Alberta law. Isn't Canadian law the "proper law," in the English terminology, or the place of the most significant relationship, in American conflicts terms?

Suppose it were shown (i) that under Canadian law, there would be no liability in the circumstances of this case; or (ii) that an action by the minority shareholders in Alberta might well succeed. Would either showing help defendants in New York? Which is the stronger argument?

(2)(a) *Leasco* is different from *Schoenbaum* in several respects. First, no U.S. market is involved, and second, a formal securities market of another country becomes the locus of most of the injury charged. On the other hand, some, though probably not a majority of the representations alleged to be false were made in the United States. Should U.S. law apply here?

(b) The agreement between Leasco and Maxwell calling for purchase of the Pergamon shares states (at p. 932) that it is subject to clearance by the U.K. exchange control and subject to the Code on Take-Overs and Mergers of the City of London, and the regulations of the London Stock Exchange. Isn't that a choice of law clause, electing English law?[c]

(c) Apart from the choice of law clause, if one were to analogize the action to a tort claim, the first part of Leasco's claim, based on allegedly false representations and records, might be thought to be sufficiently related to the United States to support application of U.S. law of the United States—the place of the acts and injury. But the major wrong, and the major injury, resulted from the rumor of a counter-takeover bid and Leasco's purchases of outstanding shares of Pergamon—in London. Why shouldn't this suit (i) be brought in England; and (ii) even if it is brought in New York, be governed by English law?

(d) Judge Friendly begins by comparing *Leasco* to *Schoenbaum*. "If all the misrepresentations here alleged had occurred in England," he says, "we would entertain most serious doubt whether, despite *Alcoa* and *Schoenbaum*, § 10(b) would be applicable simply because of the adverse effect . . . upon an American corporation . . . and its shareholders." Here, however, the question is not the reach of the effects doctrine, i.e., liability for action taken abroad, but of jurisdiction based on territoriality, i.e., liability for action taken here. Once "jurisdiction attaches" on this

---

[a] *Schoenbaum v. Firstbrook*, 268 F. Supp. 385 at 392 (S.D.N.Y. 1967).

[b] The Securities and Exchange Commission, which was not in the case originally, came into the case as *amicus curiae* on rehearing, urging application of U.S. law.

[c] Note how Judge Friendly returns to this question at the end of his opinion, p. 936, *supra*.

basis, it seems, the rest of the scheme is subject to U.S. law as well, without need to sort out which statement or misstatement was made where.

(e) "Up to this point," Judge Friendly continues, "we have established only that . . . considerations of foreign relations law do not preclude our reading § 10(b) as applicable here. The question remains whether we should." Should he? What goes into answering the question?

(f) Judge Friendly reviews the development of the 1933 and 1934 Securities Acts, and says he cannot perceive any reason why Congress should have wished to limit the protection against fraud in the sale or purchase of securities to securities of American issuers: "The New Yorker who is the object of fraudulent misrepresentations in New York is as much injured if the securities are of a mine in Saskatchewan as in Nevada [or presumably of a printing company in England.]" Ergo the United States has the required interest, and one must assume that had Congress thought about the question, it would have wanted to protect that interest. Is this satisfactory? Or would you, rather, say that if Judge Friendly has answered the question of "could" without transgressing international law, the question of "should" remains doubtful? Would an inquiry into the expectations of the parties here have been helpful?

(g) Consider finally, the professionals who are made subject to U.S. law according to the *Leasco* case. If the chartered accountants made the inquiries and prepared the reports required by English accounting practices, is it fair to hold them to American standards in these circumstances? What about the lawyers?

(3)(a) In the *Schoenbaum* case there was no conduct in the United States, but the critical link, as the court found, was the potential effect on shares traded on a U.S. exchange. In *Leasco,* there was no effect on a U.S. market, but the court found the combination of impact on an American company and its shareholders and substantial misrepresentations in the United States sufficient to sustain application of U.S. law. Suppose one of these two elements—conduct and effect—is absent. In what circumstances should U.S. law nevertheless apply?

(b) In one important case decided a few years after *Leasco,* meetings were held at lawyers' offices and hotel rooms in New York concerning construction and financing of a pulp and paper complex in Manitoba, Canada. Subsequently the Canadian lender alleged that representations by the European promoters at those meetings had been misleading, and that credit had been extended in reliance on those representations. It seems clear under *Alcoa* and related cases that Canadian (or Manitoba) law could be applied to this situation. But should U.S. law, in particular § 10(b) of the Securities Exchange Act, be applied? Is the case for application of U.S. law—or "subject matter jurisdiction under the Exchange Act"—stronger if the plaintiff is the SEC itself? Should the SEC assert a U.S. interest in this kind of a case? Is the case for application of U.S. law stronger or weaker if Canadian (or Manitoba) law would not support liability—for example because *omission* of a material fact (as contrasted with an affirmative false statement) would not be considered actionable? What if under Manitoba law there would be no liability because the representations were made outside the province?

(c) In the actual case, *SEC v. Kasser,* 548 F.2d 109 (3d Cir.), *cert. denied,* 431 U.S. 938 (1977), the party alleging injury, an agency of the Manitoba government, sought assistance from the SEC, and the Commission brought suit under U.S. law. The District Court dismissed, on the grounds that the transactions on which the complaint was based were essentially foreign to the United States, "having no significant impact on either the domestic investing public or on the domestic securities markets."[c] The Court of Appeals reversed, accepting the Commission's

---

[c] *SEC v. Kasser,* 391 F. Supp. 1167 at 1172–73 (D.N.J. 1975).

argument that "by reviving the complaint in this case, this Court will enhance the ability of the SEC to police vigorously the conduct of securities dealings within the United States. . . . Such a result would appear to comport with the basic purposes of the federal statutes."[d] Thus even though there was no effect in the United States, the jurisdiction of the Commission to apply U.S. law was upheld. Is this persuasive?

(d) Note one important difference between this case and some of the prior cases in this section. Here the government of Canada, on behalf of Manitoba, was urging application of U.S. law. In *Schoenbaum,* the Canadian government appears to have been indifferent; in *ICI,* the British government seems to have had an interest contrary to that of the United States. Thus if the issue is one of balancing genuine interests of states, *Kasser* presents little problem. But if the issue is accurate choice of law rules, including recognition of the justified expectations of the parties, the case is troubling, and seems to go at least half a step beyond *Leasco.*

(4)(a) In *Kook v. Crang,* 182 F. Supp. 388 (S.D.N.Y. 1960), a Canadian brokerage firm sold stock in Canadian mining companies to a New York customer on margin. The firm told its client that if he wanted to purchase these shares he would have to come to Toronto, and he did so, giving his check for the portion of the purchase price required by the Toronto Stock Exchange's margin requirements. Subsequently, the investments went sour, and following various margin calls, the broker sold the stock, leaving the New York buyer out $20,000. It turned out that the broker had an office in New York that dealt with financial institutions but not with individual clients. The broker, in other words, was "doing business" for purposes of judicial jurisdiction; possibly there were sufficient "minimum contacts" for "subject matter jurisdiction." But when the client brought suit in New York on the ground that the broker had not complied with U.S. law in extending him credit, the court threw out the case. Judge Ryan (who had sat in *United States v. ICI*) held that Congress did not intend to make the Securities Acts applicable to these transactions. Conceding that Congress probably gave no thought whatever to the issue raised by this case, do you have any quarrel with the result?

(b) Suppose the same facts as in the actual case, but the broker had conducted an advertising campaign in the United States, and offered free hotel rooms to Americans who came to its offices in Toronto to buy Canadian mining stock. Does the case come out the other way?

(c) Take the same facts as in (b), but add misrepresentations by the broker within the meaning of the U.S. securities laws, but made in Toronto. What do you think Judge Friendly would say? What would you say?

(5)(a) Another case raising some of the questions suggested in the preceding question came before the Court of Appeals for the Second Circuit, and again Judge Friendly wrote for the court. *Bersch v. Drexel Firestone, Inc.* 519 F.2d 974 (2d Cir. 1975), *cert. denied,* 423 U.S. 1018 (1975), was one of many cases that grew out of the world-wide operations and later demise of the IOS/Cornfield/Fund of Funds group of companies. Investors Overseas Services, based in Geneva, sold stock and mutual funds outside of the United States, essentially using American techniques of merchandising without the supervision of the SEC. In 1969, the stock of IOS itself was offered to the public, accompanied by prospectuses stating that the shares were being sold outside the United States and only to nonresidents of the United States. None of the offerings had been registered with the SEC under U.S. law. Eventually, however, some of the shares found their way into the hands of 22 U.S. citizens residing in the United States, all of whom had had some

---

[d] 548 F.2d at 116.

prior relations with the IOS group. When the stock collapsed, these purchasers brought a class action in New York against the underwriters whose overseas branches or subsidiaries had distributed the stock, and against the accountants who had certified the financial statements in the prospectuses, alleging violations of U.S. securities law. The defendants moved to dismiss for lack of subject matter jurisdiction. The court, however, saw the issue in the terms suggested here—essentially as a question of choice of law. Just on the facts stated thus far, and in light of the discussion of the *Schoenbaum, Leasco,* and *Kasser* cases, should U.S. securities law apply?

(b) Plaintiffs had a number of arguments to support their claim to U.S. jurisdiction. *First,* certain activities such as meetings with underwriters, lawyers, and accountants, had taken place in New York. The court stepped back somewhat from *Schoenbaum* and *Leasco*:

> We have no doubt [Judge Friendly wrote] that the activities within the United States . . . were sufficient to authorize the United States to impose a rule with respect to consequences flowing from them wherever they might appear. . . . But it would be erroneous to assume that the legislature always means to go to the full extent permitted. When, as here, a court is confronted with transactions that on any view are predominantly foreign, it must seek to determine whether Congress would have wished the precious resources of United States courts and law enforcement agencies to be devoted to them rather than leave the problem to foreign countries.[e]

On the first question, the answer was no.

(c) *Second,* plaintiffs offered expert testimony that the collapse of IOS shares had had a detrimental effect on world-wide confidence in the American stock market, because IOS was identified as American in the public's mind, and the underwriters and accountants were largely U.S.-based firms. This, of course, was an effort to come within the "effects doctrine" as set out in *Alcoa*.[f] Should the effects doctrine support application of U.S. law in these circumstances?[g]

(d) *Third,* plaintiffs asserted that despite the warnings in the prospectus, the defendants must have known that *some* shares would be bought by residents of the United States. Should this factor—the reasonable expectations of defendants—here tip the scales?[h]

(e) Thus far, plaintiffs' contentions were all founded on the territorial basis of jurisdiction. Their final contention tried the other basis—nationality. Many of the purchasers of IOS shares, they said, were U.S. citizens residing abroad—both civilian and military. These U.S. citizens, said plaintiffs, were within the ambit of protection provided by the U.S. securities laws. Again the court thought there was some basis for the contention, but not enough:

> Congress surely did not mean the securities laws to protect the many thousands of American residing in foreign countries against securities frauds by foreigners acting there and we see no sufficient reason to believe it would have intended otherwise simply because an American participated, so long as he had done nothing in the United States.[i]

---

[e] 519 F.2d at 985.

[f] Plaintiff also relied on § 18 of the *Restatement (Second) of Foreign Relations Law* (1965), which accepted the *Alcoa* approach in somewhat modified form. See p. 934, *supra.*

[g] The court thought that while there might well be some truth to the plaintiff's theory, it was hard to base jurisdiction in an anti-fraud action on so generalized a concept, even when combined with the alleged activities in the United States.

[h] The court thought not, though again it believed that the plaintiff's assumption was probably correct.

[i] 519 F.2d at 992.

(f) Putting aside the ritual reference to the presumed intent of Congress, hasn't the Second Circuit gone to a conflict of laws analysis?

(6)(a) Judge Friendly summed up in *Bersch* as follows:

We have thus concluded that the anti-fraud provisions of the securities laws:

(1) Apply to losses from sales of securities to Americans resident in the United States whether or not acts (or culpable failures to act) of material importance occurred in this country [i.e., if the victims are U.S. citizens *and* U.S. residents];

(2) Apply to losses from sales of securities to Americans resident abroad if, but only if, acts (or culpable failures to act) of material importance in the United States have contributed thereto [i.e., if the victims are U.S. citizens and important activity occurred in the United States];

(3) Do not apply to losses from sales of securities to foreigners outside the United States unless acts (or culpable failures to act) within the United States directly caused such losses [i.e., if the victims are non-resident aliens, the activity in the United States must be the direct cause of the harm.]

519 F.2d at 993. Is this beginning to sound like Judge Fuld's principles in *Neumeier v. Kuehner*?[j]

(b) In the actual case, Judge Friendly's principles led to dismissal of the claims of all purchasers except residents or citizens of the United States. The original 22 plaintiffs were in category (1); the activity in the United States was not so central as to sustain the action under category (3); as for the middle category—U.S. citizens residing abroad, the case would be remanded to see whether the links to the United States were strong enough to justify application of U.S. law.

(c) The present author, while praising Judge Friendly for adopting a conflict of laws rather than a minimum contacts "jurisdiction" approach, criticized the judge for relying too much on contacts or hooks, rather than on other approaches of modern conflict of laws—governmental interests, expectations of the parties, center of gravity of the transaction, or the gravity of the offense.[k] Do you agree?

(d) Category (3) of Judge Friendly's formula, not applicable in *Bersch* itself, became the foundation of another case arising out of the collapse of the IOS empire, decided on the same day as *Bersch*. In *IIT v. Vencap,* 519 F.2d 1001 (2d Cir. 1975), the Luxembourg liquidator of IIT, formerly part of the IOS group, was permitted to bring suit against Vencap, a Bahamian corporation apparently engaged in a looting operation, on the ground that substantial planning, including legal drafting, had been carried out in New York. "We do not think," Judge Friendly wrote, "Congress intended to allow the United States to be used as a base for manufacturing fraudulent security devices for export, even when they are peddled only to foreigners." (519 F.2d at 1017.)

(e) In *Vencap* (but not in *Bersch*) the SEC participated as amicus curiae, urging the court to hear the case. In none of the securities cases, in contrast to some of the antitrust cases (as well as the economic boycott cases discussed in § 10.05, *infra*) did any other country express an interest. Thus while these cases test the reach of U.S. jurisdiction to prescribe, they seem not to call for balancing of competing state interests or resolution of actual conflicts.

---

[j] Page 181 at 184.

[k] Lowenfeld, *Public Law in the International Arena: Conflict of Laws, International Law, and some Suggestions for their Interaction,* 163 Recueil des Cours 311, at 363. (Hague Acad. Int'l L., 1979).

(7) As the number of American cases involving jurisdiction over activity with transnational elements kept increasing, the suggestion grew up that a checklist of factors or criteria might be useful in assessing when it was, and when it was not suitable to apply United States law. The first suggestion along these lines was made by Professor Kingman Brewster in the later 1950's.[1] Subsequently other authors, the *Restatement of Foreign Relations Law,* and a number of courts took up the suggestion. The two most prominent judicial decisions proposing guidelines for the exercise of jurisdiction in transnational cases are reproduced in the pages that follow. Consider, as you read these decisions, as well as alternative formulations reproduced in the succeeding Notes and Questions, what is the source of the proposals. Is it wisdom and prudence, conflict of laws doctrine, "comity," international law, or a blend of all of these?

TIMBERLANE LUMBER CO. v. BANK OF AMERICA, N.T. & S.A.

United States Court of Appeals, Ninth Circuit
549 F.2d 597 (1976)

CHOY, Circuit Judge:

Four separate actions, arising from the same series of events, were dismissed by the same district court and are consolidated here on appeal. The principal action is *Timberlane Lumber Co. v. Bank of America* (Timberlane action), an antitrust suit alleging violations of sections 1 and 2 of the Sherman Act (15 U.S.C. §§ 1, 2) and the Wilson Tariff Act (15 U.S.C. § 8). This action raises important questions concerning the application of American antitrust laws to activities in another country, including actions of foreign government officials. The district court dismissed the action under the act of state doctrine and for lack of subject matter jurisdiction.

. . .

The basic allegation of the Timberlane plaintiffs is that officials of the Bank of America and others located in both the United States and Honduras conspired to prevent Timberlane, through its Honduras subsidiaries, from milling lumber in Honduras and exporting it to the United States, thus maintaining control of the Honduran lumber export business in the hands of a few select individuals financed and controlled by the Bank. The intent and result of the conspiracy, they contend, was to interfere with the exportation to the United States, including Puerto Rico, of Honduran lumber for sale or use there by the plaintiffs, thus directly and substantially affecting the foreign commerce of the United States. . . .

Cast of Characters

There are three affiliated plaintiffs in the Timberlane action. Timberlane Lumber Company is an Oregon partnership principally involved in the purchase and distribution of lumber at wholesale in the United States and the importation of lumber into the United States for sale and use. Danli Industrial, S.A., and Maya Lumber Company, S. de R.L., are both Honduras corporations, incorporated and principally owned by the general partners of Timberlane. Danli held contracts to purchase timber in Honduras, and Maya was to conduct the milling operations to produce the lumber for export. (Timberlane, Danli, and Maya will be collectively referred to as "Timberlane.")

---

[1] K. Brewster, *Antitrust and American Business Abroad,* (1958). See especially Ch. 15.

The primary defendants are Bank of America Corporation (Bank), a California corporation, and its wholly-owned subsidiary, Bank of America National Trust and Savings Association, which operates a branch in Tegucigalpa, Honduras. Several employees of the Bank have also been named and served as defendants. . . .

Facts as Alleged

The conspiracy sketched by Timberlane actually started before the plaintiffs entered the scene. The Lima family operated a lumber mill in Honduras, competing with Lamas and Casanova, in both of which the Bank had significant financial interests. The Lima enterprise was also indebted to the Bank. By 1971, however, the Lima business was in financial trouble. Timberlane alleges that driving Lima under was the first step in the conspiracy which eventually crippled Timberlane's efforts, but the particulars do not matter for this appeal. What does matter is that various interests in the Lima assets, including its milling plant, passed to Lima's creditors: Casanova, the Bank, and the group of Lima employees who had not been paid the wages and severance pay due them. Under Honduran law, the employees' claim had priority.

Enter Timberlane, with a long history in the lumber business, in search of alternative sources of lumber for delivery to its distribution system on the East Coast of the United States. After study, it decided to try Honduras. In 1971, Danli was formed, tracts of forest land were acquired, plans for a modern log-processing plant were prepared, and equipment was purchased and assembled for shipment from the United States to Danli in Honduras. Timberlane became aware that the Lima plant might be available and began negotiating for its acquisition. Maya was formed, purchased the Lima employees' interest in the machinery and equipment in January 1972, despite opposition from the conspirators, and re-activated the Lima mill.

Realizing that they were faced with better-financed and more vigorous competition from Timberlane and its Honduran subsidiaries, the defendants and others extended the anti-Lima conspiracy to disrupt Timberlane's efforts. The primary weapons employed by the conspirators were the claim still held by the Bank in the remaining assets of the Lima enterprise under the all-inclusive mortgage Lima had been forced to sign and another claim held by Casanova. Maya made a substantial cash offer for the Bank's interest in an effort to clear its title, but the Bank refused to sell. Instead, the Bank surreptitiously conveyed the mortgage to Casanova for questionable consideration, Casanova paying nothing and agreeing only to pay the Bank a portion of what it collected. Casanova immediately assigned the Bank's claim and its own on similar terms to Caminals, who promptly set out to disrupt the Timberlane operation.

Caminals is characterized as the "front man" in the campaign to drive Timberlane out of Honduras, with the Bank and other defendants intending and carrying responsibility for his actions. Having acquired the claims of Casanova and the Bank, Caminals went to court to enforce them, ignoring throughout Timberlane's offers to purchase or settle them. Under the laws of Honduras, an "embargo" on property is a court-ordered attachment, registered with the Public Registry, which precludes the sale of that property without a court order. Honduran law provides, upon embargo, that the court appoint a judicial officer, called an "interventor" to ensure against any diminution in the value of the property. In order to paralyze the Timberlane operation, Caminals obtained embargoes against Maya and Danli. Acting through the interventor, since accused of being on the payroll of the Bank, guards and troops were used to cripple and, for a time, completely shut down Timberlane's milling operation. The harassment took other forms as well: the conspirators caused the manager of Timberlane's Honduras operations, Gordon Sloan

Smith, to be falsely arrested and imprisoned and were responsible for the publication of several defamatory articles about Timberlane in the Honduran press.

As a result of the conspiracy, Timberlane's complaint claimed damages then estimated in excess of $5,000,000. Plaintiffs also allege that there has been a direct and substantial effect on United States foreign commerce, and that defendants intended the results of the conspiracy, including the impact on United States commerce.

Act of State

The classic enunciation of the act of state doctrine is found in *Underhill v. Hernandez*, 168 U.S. 250, 252 (1897):

> Every sovereign State is bound to respect the independence of every other sovereign State, and the courts of one county will not sit in judgment on the acts of the government of another done within its own territory.

From the beginning, this principle has been applied in foreign trade antitrust cases. In *American Banana Co. v. United Fruit Co.*, 213 U.S. 347, 29 S.Ct. 511, 53 L.Ed. 826 (1909), the first such case of significance, the American owner of a banana plantation caught in a border dispute between Panama and Costa Rica claimed that a competitor violated the Sherman Act by persuading the Costa Rican government to seize his lands. The act complained of would have required an adjudication of the legality of the Costa Rican seizure, an action which the Supreme Court said our courts could not challenge. . . .

The defendants argue—as the district court apparently held—that the injuries allegedly suffered by Timberlane resulted from acts of the Honduran government, principally in connection with the enforcement of the security interests in the Maya plant, which American courts cannot review. Such an application of the act of state doctrine seems to us to be erroneous. Even if the *coup de grace* to Timberlane's enterprise in Honduras was applied by official authorities, we do not agree that the doctrine necessarily shelters these defendants or requires dismissal of the Timberlane action.

[The court summarizes the *Sabbatino* case, p. 982, *infra*, as well as post-Sabbatino developments.]

A corollary to the act of state doctrine in the foreign trade antitrust field is the often-recognized principle that corporate conduct which is compelled by a foreign sovereign is also protected from antitrust liability, as if it were an act of the state itself. . . .

On the other hand, mere governmental approval or foreign governmental involvement which the defendants had arranged does not necessarily provide a defense. . . .

The touchstone of *Sabbatino*—the potential for interference with our foreign relations—is the crucial element in determining whether deference should be accorded in any given case. We wish to avoid "passing on the validity" of foreign acts. *Sabbatino*, 376 U.S. at 423. . . .

. . .

Here, the allegedly "sovereign" acts of Honduras consisted of judicial proceedings which were initiated by Caminals, a private party and one of the alleged co-conspirators, not by the Honduran government itself. Timberlane does not seek to name Honduras or any Honduran officer as a defendant or co-conspirator, nor does it challenge Honduran policy or sovereignty in any fashion that appears on its face to hold any threat to relations between Honduras and the United States.

In fact, there is no indication that the actions of the Honduran court and authorities reflected a sovereign decision that Timberlane's efforts should be crippled or that trade with the United States should be restrained. Moreover, . . . plaintiffs here apparently complain of additional agreements and actions which are totally unrelated to the Honduran government. These separate activities would clearly be unprotected even if procurement of a Honduran act of state were one part of defendants' overall scheme.

Under these circumstances, it is clear that the "act of state" doctrine does not require dismissal of the Timberlane action.

Extraterritorial Reach of the United States Antitrust Laws

There is no doubt that American antitrust laws extend over some conduct in other nations. There was language in the first Supreme Court case in point, *American Banana Co. v. United Fruit Co.,* 213 U.S. 347 (1909), casting doubt on the extension of the Sherman Act to acts outside United States territory. But subsequent cases have limited *American Banana* to its particular facts, and the Sherman Act—and with it other antitrust laws—has been applied to extraterritorial conduct. *See, e. g., Continental Ore Co. v. Union Carbide & Carbon Corp.,* 370 U.S. 690 (1962); *United States v. Sisal Sales Corp.,* 274 U.S. 268 (1927); *United States v. Aluminum Co. of America,* (the *"Alcoa"* case). The act may encompass the foreign activities of aliens as well as American citizens. *Alcoa, supra; Swiss Watch,* 1963 Trade Cases ¶ 70,600; *United States v. General Electric Co.,* 82 F.Supp. 753 (D.N.J.1949), *judgment implementing decree,* 115 F.Supp. 835 (D.N.J.1953).

That American law covers some conduct beyond this nation's borders does not mean that it embraces all, however. Extraterritorial application is understandably a matter of concern for the other countries involved. Those nations have sometimes resented and protested, as excessive intrusions into their own spheres, broad assertions of authority by American courts. Our courts have recognized this concern and have, at times responded to it, even if not always enough to satisfy all the foreign critics. *See Alcoa,* 148 F.2d at 443; *Swiss Watch,* 1965 Trade Cases ¶ 71,352 (modification of order); *General Electric,* 115 F.Supp. at 878 (implementation of decree). In any event, it is evident that at some point the interests of the United States are too weak and the foreign harmony incentive for restraint too strong to justify an extraterritorial assertion of jurisdiction.

What that point is or how it is determined is not defined by international law. Miller, *Extraterritorial Effects of Trade Regulation,* 111 U.Pa.L.Rev. 1092, 1094 (1963). Nor does the Sherman Act limit itself. In the domestic field the Sherman Act extends to the full reach of the commerce power. To define it somewhat more modestly in the foreign commerce area courts have generally, and logically, fallen back on a narrower construction of congressional intent, such as expressed in Judge Learned Hand's oft-cited opinion in *Alcoa.*

It is the effect on American foreign commerce which is usually cited to support extraterritorial jurisdiction. *Alcoa* set the course, when Judge Hand declared, *id.*:

> [I]t is settled law . . . that any state may impose liabilities, even upon persons not within its allegiance, for conduct outside its borders that has consequences within its borders which the state reprehends; and these liabilities other states will ordinarily recognize.

Despite its description as "settled law," *Alcoa's* assertion has been roundly disputed by many foreign commentators as being in conflict with international law, comity, and good judgment.

Nonetheless, American courts have firmly concluded that there is some extraterritorial jurisdiction under the Sherman Act.

Even among American courts and commentators, however, there is no consensus on how far the jurisdiction should extend. The district court here concluded that a "direct and substantial effect" on United States foreign commerce was a prerequisite, without stating whether other factors were relevant or considered. The same formula was employed, to some extent, by the district courts in the *Swiss Watch* case, 1963 Trade Cases ¶ 70,600, in *United States v. R. P. Oldham Co.,* 152 F.Supp. 818, 822 (N.D.Cal.1957), and in *General Electric,* 82 F.Supp. at 891. It has been identified and advocated by several commentators. *See, e. g., Restatement (Second) of Foreign Relations Law of the United States* § 18.[18]

. . .

Other courts have used different expressions, however. *See, e. g., Thomsen v. Cayser,* 243 U.S. 66, 88 (1917) ("the combination affected the foreign commerce of this country"); *Alcoa,* 148 F.2d at 444 ("intended to affect imports and exports [and] . . . is shown actually to have had some effect on them"); *United States v. Imperial Chemical Industries, Ltd.,* 100 F.Supp. 504, 592 (S.D.N.Y.1951) ("a conspiracy . . . which affects American commerce"); *United States v. Timken Roller Bearing Co.,* 83 F.Supp. 284, 309 (N.D.Ohio 1949), *modified and affirmed,* 341 U.S. 593 (1951) ("a direct and influencing effect on trade").

Different standards have been urged by other commentators. . . .

Few cases have discussed the nature of the effect required for jurisdiction, perhaps because most of the litigated cases have involved relatively obvious offenses and rather significant and apparent effects on competition within the United States. . . . It is probably in part because the standard has not often been put to a real test that it seems so poorly defined.

The effects test by itself is incomplete because it fails to consider other nations' interests. Nor does it expressly take into account the full nature of the relationship between the actors and this country. Whether the alleged offender is an American citizen, for instance, may make a big difference; applying American laws to American citizens raises fewer problems than application to foreigners.

. . .

American courts have, in fact, often displayed a regard for comity and the prerogatives of other nations and considered their interests as well as other parts of the factual circumstances, even when professing to apply an effects test. To some degree, the requirement for a "substantial"

---

[18] *Restatement* § 18 reads:

A state has jurisdiction to prescribe a rule of law attaching legal consequences to conduct that occurs outside its territory and causes an effect within its territory, if either

    (a) the conduct and its effect are generally recognized as constituent elements of a crime or tort under the law of states that have reasonably developed legal systems, or

    (b)(i) the conduct and its effect are constituent elements of activity to which the rule applies; (ii) the effect within the territory is substantial; (iii) it occurs as a direct and foreseeable result of the conduct outside the territory; and (iv) the rule is not inconsistent with the principles of justice generally recognized by states that have reasonably developed legal systems.

The "direct" and "substantial" requirements come from (b)(ii) and (iii). Comment *a* to this section specifically indicates, however, that this rule applies only to aliens, since United States citizens may be bound by nationality, and governs only where there has been no significant conduct within the United States, since otherwise territorial jurisdiction could be asserted.

effect may silently incorporate these additional considerations, with "substantial" as a flexible standard that varies with other factors. The intent requirement suggested by *Alcoa,* is one example of an attempt to broaden the court's perspective, as is drawing a distinction between American citizens and non-citizens.

The failure to articulate these other elements in addition to the standard effects analysis is costly, however, for it is more likely that they will be overlooked or slighted in interpretating past decisions and reaching new ones. Placing emphasis on the qualification that effects be "substantial" is also risky, for the term has a meaning in the interstate antitrust context which does not encompass all the factors relevant to the foreign trade case.

Indeed, that "substantial effects" element of interstate antitrust analysis may well be responsible for the use of an effects test for foreign commerce. The Sherman Act reaches restraints directly intended to limit the flow of interstate trade or whose sole impact is on interstate commerce, but it also reaches "wholly local business restraints" if the particular restraint "substantially and adversely affects interstate commerce." Such a test is necessary in the interstate context to separate the restraints which fall within the federal ambit under the interstate commerce clause from those which, as purely intrastate burdens, remain the province of the states. Since, however, no comparable constitutional problem exists in defining the scope of congressional power to regulate *foreign* commerce, it may be unwise blindly to apply the "substantiality" test to the international setting. Only respect for the role of the executive and for international notions of comity and fairness limit that constitutional grant.

A tripartite analysis seems to be indicated. As acknowledged above, the antitrust laws require in the first instance that there be *some* effect—actual or intended—on American foreign commerce before the federal courts may legitimately exercise subject matter jurisdiction under those statutes. Second, a greater showing of burden or restraint may be necessary to demonstrate that the effect is sufficiently large to present a cognizable injury to the plaintiffs and, therefore, a civil *violation* of the antitrust laws. Third, there is the additional question which is unique to the international setting of whether the interests of, and links to, the United States—including the magnitude of the effect on American foreign commerce—are sufficiently strong, vis-à-vis those of other nations, to justify an assertion of extraterritorial authority.

It is this final issue which is both obscured by undue reliance on the "substantiality" test and complicated to resolve. An effect on United States commerce, although necessary to the exercise of jurisdiction under the antitrust laws, is alone not a sufficient basis on which to determine whether American authority *should* be asserted in a given case as a matter of international comity and fairness. In some cases, the application of the direct and substantial test in the international context might open the door too widely by sanctioning jurisdiction over an action when these considerations would indicate dismissal. At other times, it may fail in the other direction, dismissing a case for which comity and fairness do not require forebearance, thus closing the jurisdictional door too tightly—for the Sherman Act does reach some restraints which do not have both a direct and substantial effect on the foreign commerce of the United States. A more comprehensive inquiry is necessary. We believe that the field of conflict of laws presents the proper approach, as was suggested, if not specifically employed, in *Alcoa.* The same idea is reflected in *Restatement (Second) of Foreign Relations Law of the United States* § 40:

> Where two states have jurisdiction to prescribe and enforce rules of law and the rules they may prescribe require inconsistent conduct upon the part of a person, each state is required

by international law to consider, in good faith, moderating the exercise of its enforcement jurisdiction . . .

The act of state doctrine discussed earlier demonstrates that the judiciary is sometimes cognizant of the possible foreign implications of its action. Similar awareness should be extended to the general problems of extraterritoriality. Such acuity is especially required in private suits, like this one, for in these cases there is no opportunity for the executive branch to weigh the foreign relations impact, nor any statement implicit in the filing of the suit that that consideration has been outweighed.

What we prefer is an evaluation and balancing of the relevant considerations in each case—in the words of Kingman Brewster, a "jurisdictional rule of reason."

. . .

The elements to be weighed include the degree of conflict with foreign law or policy, the nationality or allegiance of the parties and the locations or principal places of business of corporations, the extent to which enforcement by either state can be expected to achieve compliance, the relative significance of effects on the United States as compared with those elsewhere, the extent to which there is explicit purpose to harm or affect American commerce, the foreseeability of such effect, and the relative importance to the violations charged of conduct within the United States as compared with conduct abroad.[31] A court evaluating these factors should identify the potential degree of conflict if American authority is asserted. A difference in law or policy is one likely sore spot, though one which may not always be present.[32] Nationality is another; though foreign governments may have some concern for the treatment of American citizens and business residing there, they primarily care about their own nationals.[33] Having assessed the conflict, the court should then determine whether in the face of it the contacts and interests of the United States are sufficient to support the exercise of extraterritorial jurisdiction.[34]

---

[31] *Restatement (Second) of Foreign Relations Law of the United States* § 40 states that a court should act in the light of such factors as

    (a) vital national interests of each of the states,

    (b) the extent and the nature of the hardship that inconsistent enforcement actions would impose upon the person,

    (c) the extent to which the required conduct is to take place in the territory of the other state,

    (d) the nationality of the person, and

    (e) the extent to which enforcement by action of either state can reasonably be expected to achieve compliance with the rule prescribed by that state.

President (then Professor) Brewster lists these variables:

(a) the relative significance to the violations charged of conduct within the United States as compared with conduct abroad; (b) the extent to which there is explicit purpose to harm or affect American consumers or Americans' business opportunities; (c) the relative seriousness of effects on the United States compared with those abroad; (d) the nationality or allegiance of the parties or in the case of business associations, their corporate location, and the fairness of applying our law to them; (e) the degree of conflict with foreign laws and policies, and (f) the extent to which conflict can be avoided without serious impairment of the interests of the United States or the foreign country.

K. Brewster, *supra* at 446.

[32] Particularly in the field of trade regulation, American laws may not be duplicated by the other nation. That does not necessarily indicate a "conflict," however, since non-prohibition does not always mean affirmative approval.

[33] Some argue that a defendant's American citizenship might be enough by itself to support jurisdiction. *See Restatement (Second) of Foreign Relations Law of the United States* § 30.

[34] In requiring district courts to assess the conflicting contacts and interests of those nations involved, we do not thereby assign them the same task which the "act of state" doctrine prohibits them from undertaking. . . .

We conclude, then, that the problem should be approached in three parts: Does the alleged restraint affect, or was it intended to affect, the foreign commerce of the United States? Is it of such a type and magnitude so as to be cognizable as a violation of the Sherman Act? As a matter of international comity and fairness, should the extraterritorial jurisdiction of the United States be asserted to cover it? The district court's judgment found only that the restraint involved in the instant suit did not produce a direct and substantial effect on American foreign commerce. That holding does not satisfy any of these inquiries.

. . .

We, therefore, vacate the dismissal and remand the Timberlane action.

MANNINGTON MILLS, INC. v. CONGOLEUM CORP.

United States Court of Appeals, Third Circuit
595 F.2d 1287 (1979)

WEIS, CIRCUIT JUDGE.

Alleging that foreign patents were secured by fraud, which if perpetrated in securing a domestic patent would lead to antitrust liability, plaintiff seeks treble damages and injunctive relief. The district court dismissed the complaint, relying primarily upon the act of state doctrine. We conclude that in this instance that ground does not bar consideration of plaintiff's claim. Because we determine, however, that in deciding whether jurisdiction should be exercised the district court should weigh the enforcement of the antitrust laws against the interests of comity and international relations, we remand for the development of an adequate record.

Congoleum Corporation holds American patents for the manufacture of chemically embossed vinyl floor covering and owns corresponding patents in some 26 foreign countries. Mannington Mills, Inc., too, is in the business of manufacturing flooring and is licensed to use the Congoleum patents in this country. Although Mannington claimed to have similar rights under the foreign patents, that contention was decided adversely in companion litigation, *Mannington Mills, Inc. v. Congoleum Industries, Inc.,* 197 U.S.Pat.Q. 145 (D.N.J.1977), and Congoleum has instituted infringement suits against Mannington in New Zealand, Canada, Australia, and Japan.

In 1974, Mannington filed suit in the district court of New Jersey alleging, *inter alia,* that Congoleum's licensing practices in the overseas markets violated § 2 of the Sherman Antitrust Act, 15 U.S.C. § 2. Summary judgment on the antitrust claim was entered in favor of the defendant and the case is presently on appeal. Mannington had sought to amend its complaint in that suit by adding allegations of Congoleum's fraud in securing its foreign patents. The district court denied leave to amend the complaint as to this specific contention. Thereafter, Mannington filed the present action based on essentially the same grounds. The district court dismissed the

---

[T]here is an important distinction between examining the validity of the "public interests" which are involved in a sovereign policy decision amounting to an "act of state" and evaluating the relative "interests" which each state may have "in providing the means of adjudicating disputes or claims that arise within its territory." Our "jurisdictional rule of reason" does not in any way require the court to question the "validity" of "foreign law or policy." Rather, the legitimacy of each nation's interests is assumed. It is merely the relative involvement and concern of each state with the suit at hand that is to be evaluated in determining whether extraterritorial jurisdiction should be exercised by American courts as a matter of comity and fairness.

complaint for failure to state a claim and also declined to exercise jurisdiction in a pendent state unfair competition count.

Mannington's complaint alleges that Congoleum made fraudulent representations to various foreign patent offices in the following general categories:

    1. False statements about the reactions and performance of some of the chemical components of the vinyl flooring;

    2. Misrepresentation of test data;

    3. Suppression of information critical to the practice of the invention;

    4. Misleading statements about the status and contents of the United States patent applications.

The complaint charges that Congoleum enforced the foreign patents by bringing and threatening the institution of infringements suits in foreign countries. This activity allegedly restrained the export trade of the United States by restricting the foreign business of Mannington and other American competitors in addition to demonstrating an intent to monopolize. Mannington asserts further that Congoleum's false claims of priority dates were in violation of the Paris Convention of March 20, 1883, *as amended,* [1962] 13 U.S.T. 1, and the Pan-American Convention of August 20, 1910, 38 Stat. 1811.

The district court held that since no private right of action was set out in the treaties no relief could be granted. The antitrust count was dismissed on the grounds that the validity of the foreign patents was to be determined by the courts of the respective issuing nations and there was no necessity for American firms to apply for foreign patents in any way other than as established by the respective nations. The court stated that to enjoin Congoleum from enforcing its foreign patents in other nations against Mannington would violate the act of state doctrine.

Mannington emphasizes that it is not challenging the right of a foreign government to confer patents under its own requirements and indeed does not seek to have the patents at issue adjudged invalid. Rather, its claims are said to arise out of breach of standards imposed by American law and thus are properly determinable in the district court. Mannington argues that use of the United States courts to resolve antitrust claims stemming from fraud in the procurement of patents abroad is consistent with the extraterritorial jurisdiction of the Sherman Act, and litigation in a single forum furthers judicial efficiency. Congoleum contends, however, that Mannington's theory for antitrust relief is barred by the act of state doctrine, and subjecting a putative patentee to United States standards for foreign patent procurement is an unwarranted extension of the antitrust laws.

I

JURISDICTION

We turn first to the question of jurisdiction. Both parties are subject to service of process in New Jersey and in personam jurisdiction is concededly present. What is at issue, however, is subject matter jurisdiction.

The challenge here is to conduct by an American corporation in a foreign country, arguably legal there, and the issue is whether that activity is answerable in the courts of the United States under the Sherman Act's broad and potentially far-reaching language. The extraterritorial application of the Act to "trade or commerce . . . with foreign nations" has been and continues to be the subject of lively controversy. *See, e.g.,* Kintner & Griffin, *Jurisdiction Over Foreign*

Commerce Under the Sherman Antitrust Act, 18 B.C.Ind. & Com.L.Rev. 199 (1977). Neither the Act nor its legislative history gives any clear indication of the scope of the extraterritorial jurisdiction conferred, leaving such determination to the courts. *Id.* at 200–19; *see* Ongman, *"Be No Longer a Chaos:" Constructing a Normative Theory of the Sherman Act's Extraterritorial Jurisdictional Scope,* 71 Nw. U.L. Rev. 733, 735–41 (1977).

Justice Holmes's opinion in *American Banana Co. v. United Fruit Co.,* 213 U.S. 347 (1909), cast doubt on the intent of Congress to extend the Sherman Act to action perpetrated beyond United States territory. Since then, however, the Supreme Court has made it clear that "foreign commerce" applies to importing, exporting, and other commercial transactions, as well as transportation and communication between the United States and a foreign country. Acts and agreements occurring outside the territorial boundaries of the United States that adversely and materially affect American trade are not necessarily immune from United States antitrust laws.

In oft-quoted language, Judge Learned Hand in *United States v. Aluminum Co. of America* concluded that although Congress did not intend the Sherman Act to prohibit conduct having no effect in the United States, it did intend the Act to reach conduct having consequences within this country—even where the parties concerned had no allegiance to the United States—if the conduct is intended to and actually does have an effect upon United States imports or exports. This wide-reaching "intended effects" test has been cited with approval by the Supreme Court. *See, e.g., Continental Ore Co. v. Union Carbide & Carbon Corp.,* 370 U.S. 690, 705, (1962). *See also Restatement (Second) of the Foreign Relations Law of the United States* § 18 (1965).

It can no longer be doubted that practices of an American citizen abroad having a substantial effect on American foreign commerce are subject to the Sherman Act. . . . This view has been criticized because its failure to abide by the basic tenet that a nation's legislation is valid only in the territory it governs leads to unnecessary international friction. Nevertheless, when two American litigants are contesting alleged antitrust activity abroad that results in harm to the export business of one, a federal court does have subject matter jurisdiction. *Zenith Radio Corp. v. Hazeltine Research, Inc.,* 395 U.S. 100, (1969). Therefore, we are satisfied that the district court did have jurisdiction in this case.

II

ACT OF STATE

[The court summarizes the act of state doctrine, discussed in § 10.06, *infra.*]

. . .

The defendant here contends that, whether valid or invalid, the grants of foreign patents could be accomplished only by affirmative governmental actions and therefore are acts of state which American courts are not free to examine. We are unable to accept the proposition that the mere issuance of patents by a foreign power constitutes either an act of state, as that term has developed under case law, or an example of governments' compulsion.

There is no allegation of collusion with foreign governments in securing the patents, nor was the defendant compelled to refuse a license to the plaintiff. Thus, by issuance of the patents per se, the foreign governments did not force the defendant to exclude the plaintiff from the foreign markets and the defense of compulsion is not available.

The case *sub judice* also fails to fall within the more traditional applications of the act of state doctrine.

. . .

The grant of patents for floor coverings is not the type of sovereign activity that would be of substantial concern to the executive branch in its conduct of international affairs. Although enforcement of a decree in the present litigation may possibly present problems of international relations, as will be discussed *infra,* the granting of the patents per se, in substance ministerial activity, is not the kind of governmental action contemplated by the act of state doctrine or its correlative, foreign compulsion. We conclude, therefore, that the asserted act of state defense does not support dismissal of plaintiff's complaint and it does not apply to the patents issued in the foreign countries.

III
COMITY, ABSTENTION AND INTERNATIONAL REPERCUSSIONS

Having concluded that the act of state doctrine is not applicable in these circumstances and that there is subject matter jurisdiction, the question remains whether jurisdiction should be exercised.

Some analysis of the plaintiff's position is helpful in identifying the considerations bearing on this issue. . . .

Mannington . . . is not attacking Congoleum's American patents but only its corresponding ones abroad. Mannington asserts that it need not prove the invalidity of the foreign patents under the issuing countries' laws. It argues that they were obtained by conduct considered fraudulent under American law and would expose Congoleum to antitrust liability in this country if domestic patents were at issue. Therefore, says Mannington, it is not necessary to examine the patent law of 26 foreign countries to determine if the Congoleum patents are valid there. . . . Mannington urges that a patent, even though valid under the law of a foreign nation, cannot act as an exemption for antitrust liability if procured by conduct unacceptable by American standards. Mannington would hold Congoleum liable for its activity abroad that impaired plaintiff's foreign business or barred it from competition in a nation altogether.

. . .

In addition to treble damages, Mannington asks that Congoleum be enjoined from enforcing these hypothetically valid patents in the foreign jurisdictions. Obviously, some potential for conflict with the policy of foreign nations is present in both forms of relief.

A judgment against Congoleum in this country would have direct and ripple effects abroad. It is not unusual for other nations to condition the issuance of patents upon certain requirements, *e.g.,* that the article be manufactured in that country; that it be actively "worked;" or that licenses be restricted in various ways, or at the other extreme, be compulsory. It may be also that some nations might require that the patent be enforced. Nationals may be preferred over foreigners or patent laws may have been designed to develop the technical know-how of an underdeveloped country. *See* Wayman, *Patent Protection in International Business Transactions,* 45 Den. L.J. 64 (1968). Many of these policies could be frustrated by a decree of an American court which, in effect, declares the foreign patent invalid both by American standards and as it may affect American commerce.

This may, indeed, be a situation where the consequences to the American economy and policy permit no alternative to firm judicial action enforcing our antitrust laws abroad. But before that step is taken, there should be a weighing of competing interests.

The antitrust statutes enacted by Congress commit this country to the free enterprise system and the exercise of open competition. If an American company is excluded from competition in a foreign country by fraudulent conduct on the part of another American company, then our national interests are adversely affected. In a purely domestic situation, the right to a remedy would be clear. When foreign nations are involved, however, it is unwise to ignore the fact that foreign policy, reciprocity, comity, and limitations of judicial power are considerations that should have a bearing on the decision to exercise or decline jurisdiction.[6]

Some decisions of American courts have been criticized for failure to adequately assess these concerns. . . .

In other cases, orders by American courts directed to foreign countries to produce their records in this country have provoked protest and specific prohibitory legislation from those nations.

Some courts have exhibited a greater sensitivity to principles of international comity. For example, in *United States v. General Electric Co.,* 82 F.Supp. 753 (D.N.J.1949), *opinion on remedies,* 115 F.Supp. 835 (D.N.J.1953), then District Judge Forman inserted a savings clause in his order so as not to place the defendant in violation of laws in foreign countries where it carried on business.

In eschewing a provincial approach, these latter cases, in our view, best reflect the realities of international commerce. Courts should not shrink from their duty because of an inability by the affected parties to reach a consensus. Enough has been said, however, to demonstrate the appropriateness of a recent commentary made in another context: "Perhaps the one point that deserves to be stressed for the future is that the substantive antitrust analysis must not be applied mechanically where foreign contacts are involved—not even in the so called per se area. More subtlety is required. . . ." 1 P. Areeda & D. Turner, *Antitrust Law* § 240 at 278 (1978).

In *Timberlane Lumber Co. v. Bank of America,* the Court of Appeals for the Ninth Circuit adopted a balancing process in determining whether extraterritorial jurisdiction should be exercised, an approach with which we find ourselves in substantial agreement. The factors we believe should be considered include:

1. Degree of conflict with foreign law or policy;
2. Nationality of the parties;
3. Relative importance of the alleged violation of conduct here compared to that abroad;
4. Availability of a remedy abroad and the pendency of litigation there;
5. Existence of intent to harm or affect American commerce and its foreseeability;
6. Possible effect upon foreign relations if the court exercises jurisdiction and grants relief;
7. If relief is granted, whether a party will be placed in the position of being forced to perform an act illegal in either country or be under conflicting requirements by both countries;
8. Whether the court can make its order effective;

---

[6] The [Department of Justice] Antitrust Guide [For International Operations] takes the position that:

[C]onsiderations of jurisdiction, enforcement policy, and comity often, but not always, lead to the same conclusion: the United States antitrust laws should be applied to an overseas transaction when there is a substantial and foreseeable effect on the United States commerce; and, consistent with these ends, it should avoid unnecessary interference with the sovereign interests of foreign nations.

Antitrust Guide, *supra* at 6–7, (1977).

9. Whether an order for relief would be acceptable in this country if made by the foreign nation under similar circumstances;

10. Whether a treaty with the affected nations has addressed the issue.

The record in this case is not adequate to allow a reasoned decision on these highly complex issues even if only one foreign nation were involved rather than 26. Moreover, we do not believe that the extensive inquiry required must yield the same answer in each instance. The legislation and policy of each nation is not likely to be the same, nor is it probable that the effect upon commerce in each instance will be as substantial as others. Although the plaintiff would prefer to have the matter resolved as a unitary one, that cannot be done when the individual interests and policies of each of the foreign nations differ and must be balanced against our nation's legitimate interest in regulating anticompetitive activity.

We conclude, therefore, that it was error to dismiss the plaintiff's complaint without preparation of a record which will allow an evaluation of the factors counseling for or against the exercise of jurisdiction.

ADAMS, CIRCUIT JUDGE, concurring.

My differences with the majority regarding Mannington's basic claim are threefold. First, I believe that . . . Mannington's complaint has set forth a claim upon which relief can be granted. Second, I do not agree that a court may conclude that it is invested with subject-matter jurisdiction under the Sherman Act but may nonetheless abstain from exercising such jurisdiction in deference to considerations of international comity; rather, it seems that those considerations are properly to be weighed at the outset when the court determines whether jurisdiction vel non exists, or in fashioning the decree. Third, it appears evident that notwithstanding the foreign elements involved, jurisdiction exists in the present case, and that possible repercussions abroad should be examined by the court when and if it formulates a remedy.

. . .

Mannington's complaint should be analyzed, as I view it, by engaging in a dual inquiry into first, whether the challenged conduct affects "commerce . . . with foreign nations" so as to be within the jurisdictional scope of the Sherman Act, and second, whether there is a monopolization or attempted monopolization of trade or commerce so as to be violative of the Act. Although these are separate questions, courts have generally recognized, albeit in other contexts, that a final determination as to the existence of subject-matter jurisdiction must often await some clarification of the substantive offense. This interrelationship between the jurisdictional and substantive issues seems to be borne out in the present case, where an understanding of the substantive offense sheds light on whether jurisdiction exists.

[Judge Adams concludes that the allegation of monopolization through fraudulent procurement of foreign patents states a cause of action under § 2 of the Sherman Act.]

With this understanding of the substantive offense charged, we may now turn to the question whether there is a monopolization of "trade or commerce . . . with foreign nations" so as to invest the federal courts with subject-matter jurisdiction. Although the test for subject-matter jurisdiction has traditionally been framed in terms of whether there is an actual or intended effect upon foreign commerce, it has also been recognized that "anything that affects the external trade and commerce of the United States also affects the trade and commerce of other nations, and may have far greater consequences for others than for the United States."

[Judge Adams quotes from *Alcoa* and *Timberlane,* as well as § 40 of the *Restatement (Second) of Foreign Relations Law.*]

It is important to note, however, that this concern for international comity does not require that the Sherman Act, or any other statute, not be enforced extraterritorially whenever a party's conduct is also subject to regulation by a foreign government. It is only when foreign law requires conduct *inconsistent* with that mandated by the Sherman Act that problems of international comity become significant. And even in such circumstances, it is recognized that extraterritorial jurisdiction may be asserted if the relevant factors, some of which are enumerated in the majority opinion, weigh in favor of the exercise of jurisdiction.

Relating this jurisdictional test to the present case, it is manifest that jurisdiction exists because there is no indication that Congoleum was conforming to a rule of conduct prescribed by foreign law when it allegedly undertook a scheme to monopolize trade with purchasers in twenty-six foreign nations by fraudulently procuring patents in those nations. Nor has it been suggested that Congoleum was compelled by foreign law to make materially false representations in connection with its patent applications. The dictate of the Sherman Act that Congoleum refrain from monopolizing foreign commerce is thus not at variance in this regard with the commands of any foreign nation. In addition, Congoleum is an American company and is alleged to have masterminded and directed its monopolization scheme from its headquarters in Kearney, New Jersey, with the intention of affecting its American competitors' export markets. Given these alleged facts, there appears to be no reason why Congoleum should not be held accountable in the courts of the United States for monopolizing trade with foreign nations.

Problems may, of course, arise regarding the formulation of relief, but they do not appear to constitute a threshold jurisdictional barrier. Instead, they are matters that can be dealt with, if need be, at a subsequent stage of the litigation. Indeed, it would appear that there would not be any interference with the policies of foreign nations if relief were limited to treble damages, and the public interest in enforcing the antitrust laws, as well as the private interest of Mannington in obtaining a remedy, may be satisfied in large measure through such an award.

FURTHER NOTES AND QUESTIONS

(1)(a) Apart from detailed focus on links and contacts, consider whether the allegations in *Timberlane* seem suitable for application of the United States antitrust laws. It seems that two groups were competing for the dominant position in the Honduran lumber industry; the Timberlane group consisted of one U.S. and two Honduran companies; and the Caminals group consisted of Hondurans but was backed, according to the complaint, by the Bank of America. Both groups aimed to supply the United States market. As a choice of law matter—whether approached from the point of view of the parties' expectations, the center of gravity of the transactions, or the interests of the United States—should U.S. law apply to this case?

(b) Of course the question put in the preceding paragraph is not the question traditionally put in the context of antitrust cases having international elements, including *Alcoa* and *ICI*. The traditional question—is the activity in (or does it have effect on) the commerce of the United States—is fairly easily answered in the affirmative. There is thus, in the traditional formulation, "subject matter jurisdiction." But Judge Choy, having reversed the lower court's dismissal on

§ 10.04   INTERNATIONAL LAW AND CONFLICT OF LAWS   □   957

act of state grounds,[m] attempts to sort out the arguments for and against exercise of jurisdistion through a process of balancing similar to what we have seen in numerous choice of law cases involving "private law." "The effects test," Judge Choy says, "is incomplete because it fails to consider other nations' interests." "Nor," he goes on, "does it expressly take into account the full nature of the relationship between the actors and [the forum state]." (p. 947, *supra*). In part, he suggests, the addition of the word "substantial" before the word "effects" may well have reflected a regard for comity and the prerogatives and interests of other nations. Furthermore, he says, the intent requirement of *Alcoa* itself reflects an attempt to broaden the court's perspective, as does drawing a distinction between American citizens and non-citizens. But the factors that go into implied inquiries—the factors to be weighed, as Judge Choy puts it—have not been clearly articulated in the decided cases. *Timberlane,* he believes, presents a useful opportunity to spell out the relevant factors.

(c) Judge Choy proposes a three-part inquiry: *First,* is there a minimum contact, an effect (or intended effect) upon the commerce of the United States; *Second,* is the alleged restraint of the type and magnitude so as to be cognizable under the antitrust laws of the United States; and *Third,* should the jurisdiction of the United States be asserted to cover the restraint? Postponing for the moment the criteria proposed for answering the third question, are the questions correctly stated? Are they stated in the right order?

(d) Note that Judge Choy first lists a series of factors to answer his third question that sound much like traditional conflict of laws doctrine, or rather like American conflict of laws doctrine since *Babcock v. Jackson* and the *Second Restatement*. Then there is a second inquiry concerning the likelihood of conflict if American authority is asserted. Thus the same set of facts in, say, Great Britain, might give rise to a different conclusion from the actual facts in Honduras, if Great Britain asserts an active interest and Honduras does not. The suggestion is similar, though not identical, to the distinction between false and true conflicts emphasized by Currie and Cavers. In Judge Choy's view, the interest of the United States ought to be substantial before U.S. jurisdiction is asserted in a true conflicts situation.[n]

(2)(a) *Mannington Mills,* decided three years after *Timberlane,* essentially accepts Judge Choy's approach, though the list of criteria is somewhat different. Mannington, facing infringement suits from Congoleum in 26 countries, alleges in a U.S. court that Congoleum has procured the foreign patents by fraud and in violation of U.S. antitrust laws. Congoleum says that an American court

---

[m] For discussion of this subject, see § 10.06, *infra*.

[n] In the actual case on remand, the District Court (with a different judge sitting) again came out for the defendant, following discovery. Though the complaint passed the first test of the Court of Appeals' three-step approach, it failed the second and third tests:

> [We] would strain U.S. antitrust law beyond credibility by applying it to these facts. . . . We deem Honduran law clearly superior by which to judge defendants' conduct, and to provide plaintiffs with any remedies appropriate. Although plaintiffs have brought the action styled with U.S. citizens on both sides, we look through the formal pleadings into the substance of the action. The true nature of the complaint is an action in tort and contract by [Honduran citizens] against certain personnel of the Bank's branch in Honduras . . . Were this simply a straightforward tort complaint, the only legitimate choice of law would be Honduran; in this event, we would clearly dismiss for *forum non conveniens*. . . . Unlike the first prong of the *Timberlane* test, in this inquiry the weight, as opposed to the mere existence of the commerce is significant. . . . Were we to apply either the traditional territorial, most significant relationship, or comparative interest analysis tests of conflicts of law we would select Honduran law for application.

Timberlane Lumber Co. v. Bank of America, 574 F.Supp. 1453, 1469–70 (N.D.Cal. 1983), *aff'd,* 749 F.2d 1378 (9th Cir. 1984), *cert. denied,* 105 S.Ct. 3514 (1985).

may not adjudicate the validity or use of foreign patents, but Mannington says it is not challenging the patents themselves but only Congoleum's breach of standards imposed by U.S. law. The court is unanimous in concluding that there is sufficient effect on the foreign commerce of the United States to support "subject matter jurisdiction," and for Judge Adams that is enough. He rejects balancing or a conflict of laws approach, and thinks "comity" may be invoked only in the case of actual conflict:

> I do not agree [Judge Adams writes] that a court may conclude that it is invested with subject matter jurisdiction under the Sherman Act but may nonetheless abstain from exercising such jurisdiction in deference to international comity; rather it seems that those considerations are properly to be weighed at the outset when the court determines whether jurisdiction vel non exists, or in fashioning the decree. (p. 955).

Judge Weis, for the majority, thinks otherwise:

> This may, indeed be a situation [Judge Weis writes] where the consequences to the American economy and policy permit no alternative to firm judicial action enforcing our antitrust laws abroad. But before that step is taken, there should be a weighing of competing interests. (p. 953).

Such weighing, the majority says, need not await a determination of actual conflict, but should take place in every case, or at least in every doubtful case.

(b) *Mannington Mills,* like *ICI,* involved foreign patents and raised the possibility, as the court says (p. 953), that the policies of some foreign countries "could be frustrated by a decree of an American court which in effect declares the foreign patent invalid . . . by American standards." The court reverses the district court's dismissal, however, since there may be consequences to the American economy and policy that "permit no alternative to firm judicial action enforcing our antitrust laws abroad." Thus the court is led to balancing along the lines suggested by *Timberlane.* Would the checklist developed by Judge Weis have helped Judge Ryan in *ICI*? Would it have changed the result?

(c) More important, suppose Judge Ryan, using the *Timberlane* or *Mannington Mills* guidelines, had reached the same result that he did reach; would his judgment have been more likely to win recognition from the British courts?

(d) Some U.S. courts have declined to follow the approach suggested by the *Timberlane* and *Mannington Mills* cases, not because they disagreed with the specific criteria, but because they regard balancing as beyond the capacity of courts, at least when there is an actual conflict. For example, in an opinion involving discovery of documents located abroad and sought in an international cartel case, Judge Prentice Marshall wrote:

> Several defendants . . . rely on broad notions of "international comity" for the proposition that we should balance the vital national interests of the United States and the foreign countries to determine which interests predominate. Aside from the fact that the judiciary has little expertise or even authority, to evaluate the economic and social policies of a foreign country such a balancing test is inherently unworkable in this case [because] [t]he competing interests here display an irreconcilable conflict on precisely the same plane of national policy. . . . It is simply impossible to judicially "balance" these totally contradictory and mutually negating actions.

In re Uranium Antitrust Litigation, 480 F.Supp. 1138, 1148 (N.D. Ill. 1979.)°

° See also *Laker Airways Limited v. Sabena, Belgian World Airlines,* 731 F.2d 909, 951–53 (D.C. Cir. 1984)

Even if you could not resolve true conflicts, would the balancing technique not be useful in separating true from false conflicts? Could you develop principles of preference in situations of true conflicts?

(3)(a) In the early 1980's the American Law Institute undertook a new project of restating the Foreign Relations Law of the United States, and as the project evolved, a substantial effort was devoted to defining the scope of a state's jurisdiction to prescribe. *The Restatement (Third)* proposed a two-step approach. *First,* it said, jurisdiction to prescribe must be based on either territoriality or nationality, i.e., the activity being regulated was either conducted in (or impacted directly on) the territory of the state exercising jurisdiction, or was carried on by nationals of that state.[p] *Second,* even if one of these bases of jurisdiction were present, jurisdiction could (not *should*) be exercised only if it were not unreasonable in the circumstances to do so. To determine whether exercise of jurisdiction would be reasonable or unreasonable the *Restatement* proposed its own list of factors, similar to those of Brewster, *Timberlane,* and *Mannington Mills,* and drawing also on § 6 of the *Restatement (Second) of Conflict of Laws,* but not precisely the same as any of these antecedents.

§ 403. Limitations on Jurisdiction to Prescribe

. . .

(2) Whether exercise of jurisdiction over a person or activity is unreasonable, is determined by evaluating all relevant factors, including, where appropriate:

(a) the link of the activity to the territory of the regulating state, i.e., the extent to which the activity takes place within the territory or has substantial, direct, and foreseeable effect upon or in the territory;

(b) the connections, such as nationality, residence, or economic activity, between the regulating state and the persons principally responsible for the activity to be regulated, or between that state and those whom the law or regulation is designed to protect;

(c) the character of the activity to be regulated, the importance of regulation to the regulating state, the extent to which other states regulate such activities, and the degree to which the desirability of such regulation is generally accepted;

(d) the existence of justified expectations that might be protected or hurt by the regulation;

(e) the importance of the regulation to the international political, legal or economic system;

(f) the extent to which such regulation is consistent with the traditions of the international system;

(g) the extent to which another state may have an interest in regulating the activity; and

(h) the likelihood of conflict with regulation by another state.

(b) Consider how these factors might have been applied in deciding *Alcoa, ICI, Schoenbaum, Leasco, Bersch, Timberlane,* or *Mannington Mills.* Would any of them have come out differently?

---

[p] *Restatement (Third) of Foreign Relations Law § 402 (1987).* The discussion here omits certain auxiliary bases of jurisdiction directed to universal crimes such as slavery, and jurisdiction based on the so-called "protective principle," such as over counterfeiting of national currency.

(c) Only *ICI,* of the cases mentioned, presented an actual conflict, and even that was not clear at the time of the decision of the district court. For actual conflicts, such as the one faced by Judge Marshall in the *Uranium* case,[q] the *Restatement* first proposed the following resolution:

> § 403 (3) An exercise of jurisdiction which is not unreasonable according to the criteria indicated in Subsection (2) may nevertheless be unreasonable if it requires a person to take action that would violate a regulation of another state which is not unreasonable under those criteria. Preference between conflicting exercises of jurisdiction is determined by evaluating the respective interests of the regulating states in light of the factors listed in Subsection (2).[r]

This formulation was criticized by some as involving circular reasoning, and by others as not reflecting the decided cases. In its revised formulation, the *Restatement* says:

> (3) When it would not be unreasonable for each of two states to exercise jurisdiction over a person or activity, but the prescriptions by the two states are in conflict, each state has an obligation to evaluate its own as well as the other state's interest in exercising jurisdiction in light of all the relevant factors, including those set out in Subsection (2); a state should defer to the other state if that state's interest is clearly greater.[s]

Thus the intellectual exercise of balancing competing interests is required, but deferring to the law of the state with the stronger basis for exercising jurisdiction is stated as an objective that *should* be followed. Is this a sounder formulation? How does it compare to the principles of preference you developed in response to question (2)(d), *supra*?

(4) The *Restatement* factors came before the Supreme Court in the *Insurance Antitrust Case*, reproduced in pertinent part below. Both the majority and the dissent accepted the *Restatement* as a source for their respective opinions, yet reached sharply different results. Consider whether this outcome validates, or invalidates, the *Restatement*'s effort to articulate principles of general application concerning the limits placed by international law on the exercise by a state of prescriptive jurisdiction over activity carried on outside the state.

The *Insurance Antitrust* Case

The background of the case was a perception widely (but not universally) shared that there was an insurance crisis in the United States, compelling a variety of facilities to shut down because they could not obtain insurance;[a] the reason that they could not obtain insurance, so the theory went, was that potential insurers could not obtain adequate reinsurance.

Plaintiffs in the action, brought in the federal district court in San Francisco in 1988, were the Attorneys General of 19 states of the United States, plus a number of private plaintiffs, led by the Attorney General of California.[b] The basic charge was that the defendants had

---

[q] A discovery request involving documents located in Canada to which the plaintiff was entitled under U.S. law, but whose disclosure was prohibited under applicable Canadian regulations.

[r] *Restatement of Foreign Relations Law (Revised)*, Tent. Draft No. 2 (1981).

[s] *Restatement (Third)*, final version, 1987.

[a] For contrasting views on this point, see e.g., "Symposium: Perspectives on the Insurance Crisis," 5 Yale J. on Regulation 367 (1988); also George L. Priest, "The Current Insurance Issues and Modern Tort Law." 96 Yale L.J. 1521 (1987).

[b] Interestingly, it was the attorneys general and not the insurance commissioners who filed the action; in many

agreed—unlawfully agreed—(1) to eliminate occurrence-based or "long-tail" coverage in favor of exclusive issuance of claims-made policies, and (2) to eliminate "sudden and accidental" pollution from liability policies.[c] The defendants were four major domestic insurance companies, several domestic reinsurance companies, brokers, and insurance associations—plus a number of foreign reinsurers and their principals, in particular a number of underwriting agencies at Lloyd's.

For students of conflict of laws and international law, the significant claim was that the London defendants had violated United States antitrust law by refusing, in England, to offer reinsurance to American companies except on terms to which the London defendants had jointly agreed, thus harming parties for whom the state attorneys general acted as *parentes patriae*. The English defendants did not deny that their actions had effects in the United States—indeed direct and substantial effects. They argued, however, that their conduct was legal in the state where it took place, that they operated in full compliance with a regime of regulation and self-regulation as prescribed by the British parliament. Accordingly, under principles of international law and comity, as spelled out particularly in *Timberlane* and *Mannington Mills*, as well as two generations of Restatements of the Foreign Relations Law of the United States, jurisdiction to apply U.S. law should not be exercised in this case.

The Federal District Court in San Francisco and the Court of Appeals for the Ninth Circuit both considered the international aspect of the case in the light of *Timberlane*, and in particular in the light of the list of factors set out in that case by Judge Choy. Judge Schwarzer in the District Court dismissed the action, on the basis that "the *conflict* with English law and policy which could result from the extraterritorial application of the [U.S.] antitrust laws in this case is not outweighed by other factors."[d] Judge Noonan, for the Court of Appeals, going through the same factors, acknowledged the "significant conflict" with English law and policy,[e] but held that the conflict was outweighed by the "significance of the effects on American commerce, their foreseeability and their purposefulness."[f] Accordingly, the Court of Appeals reinstated the action. Thus when the Supreme Court granted review, much of the argument on the international aspect of the case focused on the relative importance under *Timberlane* of conduct—clearly in England, versus effect—largely in the United States. Since both lower courts had accepted that there was a conflict between United States and English law, not much argument focused on defining the conflict.[g] In the Supreme Court, however, it was precisely the existence or non-existence of conflict that divided the majority and the dissent.

---

instances, the state insurance commissioners were opposed to bringing of the suit. But since the action was brought under federal law and no allegations were made of violation of state law, the insurance commissioners were not responsible for the decisions to file or join the suit.

[c] An insurance policy based on occurrence during the effective period of the policy has the effect that the issuer cannot close its books on policies written for a given period until long after the end of the term of the policy. In the 1980's insurers and reinsurers that had written occurrence-based policies for the United States found themselves confronted with massive claims arising out of the use of asbestos in the construction of buildings, and also with claims arising out of underground chemical pollution. Defendants contended that whatever they had done was intended only to stanch the losses arising as a result of such claims. Plaintiffs asserted that nevertheless the agreements were unlawful under U.S. antitrust law.

[d] *In re Insurance Antitrust Litigation*, 723 F.Supp. 464 at 490 (N.D. Cal. 1989).

[e] *In re Insurance Antitrust Litigation*, 938 F.2d 919 at 933 (9th. Cir. 1991).

[f] Id. at 934.

[g] The U.S. government, which had declined to become involved in the case earlier, submitted a brief amicus curiae on behalf of the plaintiffs, primarily devoted to the domestic aspects of the case. The brief of the Solicitor General

HARTFORD FIRE INSURANCE CO. v. CALIFORNIA

United States Supreme Court
509 U.S. 764 (1993)

Justice SOUTER delivered the opinion of the Court with respect to Parts I, II-A, III, and IV:

. . .

III

Finally, we take up the question whether certain claims against the London reinsurers should have been dismissed as improper applications of the Sherman Act to foreign conduct. The Fifth Claim for Relief in the California Complaint alleges a violation of § 1 of the Sherman Act by certain London reinsurers who conspired to coerce primary insurers in the United States to offer CGL coverage on a claims-made basis, thereby making "occurrence CGL coverage . . . unavailable in the State of California for many risks." The Sixth Claim for Relief in the California Complaint alleges that the London reinsurers violated § 1 by a conspiracy to limit coverage of pollution risks in North America, thereby rendering "pollution liability coverage . . . almost entirely unavailable for the vast majority of casualty insurance purchasers in the State of California." The Eighth Claim for Relief in the California Complaint alleges a further § 1 violation by the London reinsurers who, along with domestic retrocessional reinsurers, conspired to limit coverage of seepage, pollution, and property contamination risks in North America, thereby eliminating such coverage in the State of California.

At the outset, we note that the District Court undoubtedly had jurisdiction of these Sherman Act claims, as the London reinsurers apparently concede. See Tr. of Oral Arg. 37 ("Our position is not that the Sherman Act does not apply in the sense that a minimal basis for the exercise of jurisdiction doesn't exist here. Our position is that there are certain circumstances, and that this is one of them, in which the interests of another State are sufficient that the exercise of that jurisdiction should be restrained"). Although the proposition was perhaps not always free from doubt, see *American Banana Co. v. United Fruit Co.*, 213 U.S. 347, (1909), it is well established by now that the Sherman Act applies to foreign conduct that was meant to produce and did in fact produce some substantial effect in the United States. See *Matsushita Elec. Industrial Co. v. Zenith Radio Corp.*, 475 U.S. 574, 582, n. 6, (1986); *United States v. Aluminum Co. of America*, 148 F.2d 416, 444 (CA2 1945) (L. Hand, J.); Restatement (Third) of Foreign Relations Law of the United States § 415, and Reporters' Note 3 (1987) (hereinafter Restatement (Third) Foreign Relations Law); 1 P. Areeda & D. Turner, Antitrust Law ¶ 236 (1978); cf. *Continental Ore Co. v. Union Carbide & Carbon Corp.*, 370 U.S. 690, 704, 82 S.Ct. 1404, 1413, (1962); *Steele v. Bulova Watch Co.*, 344 U.S. 280, 288, 73 S.Ct. 252, 256, (1952); *United States v. Sisal Sales Corp.*, 274 U.S. 268, 275-276, 47 S.Ct. 592, 593-594, (1927).[22] Such is the conduct

---

also argued, however, that application of U.S. law should be stayed only in case of a direct conflict, defined as existing only if

(1) the foreign government has directed the defendants to engage in the challenged conduct, or

2) the defendants would have frustrated clearly articulated policies of the foreign government if they had not engaged in the disputed conduct.

[22] Justice SCALIA believes that what is at issue in this litigation is prescriptive, as opposed to subject-matter, jurisdiction. The parties do not question prescriptive jurisdiction, however, and for good reason: it is well established that Congress has exercised such jurisdiction under the Sherman Act. See G. Born & D. Westin, International Civil Litigation in United States Courts 542, n. 5 (2d ed. 1992) (Sherman Act is a "prime exampl[e] of the simultaneous exercise of prescriptive jurisdiction and grant of subject matter jurisdiction").

alleged here: that the London reinsurers engaged in unlawful conspiracies to affect the market for insurance in the United States and that their conduct in fact produced substantial effect.[23]

According to the London reinsurers, the District Court should have declined to exercise such jurisdiction under the principle of international comity.[24] The Court of Appeals agreed that courts should look to that principle in deciding whether to exercise jurisdiction under the Sherman Act. This availed the London reinsurers nothing, however. To be sure, the Court of Appeals believed that "application of [American] antitrust laws to the London reinsurance market 'would lead to significant conflict with English law and policy,' " and that "[s]uch a conflict, unless outweighed by other factors, would by itself be reason to decline exercise of jurisdiction." But other factors, in the court's view, including the London reinsurers' express purpose to affect United States commerce and the substantial nature of the effect produced, outweighed the supposed conflict and required the exercise of jurisdiction in this litigation.

When it enacted the FTAIA, Congress expressed no view on the question whether a court with Sherman Act jurisdiction should ever decline to exercise such jurisdiction on grounds of international comity. See H.R.Rep. No. 97-686, p. 13 (1982) ("If a court determines that the requirements for subject matter jurisdiction are met, [the FTAIA] would have no effect on the court['s] ability to employ notions of comity . . . or otherwise to take account of the international character of the transaction") (citing Timberlane). We need not decide that question here, however, for even assuming that in a proper case a court may decline to exercise Sherman Act jurisdiction over foreign conduct (or, as Justice SCALIA would put it, may conclude by the employment of comity analysis in the first instance that there is no jurisdiction), international comity would not counsel against exercising jurisdiction in the circumstances alleged here.

The only substantial question in this litigation is whether "there is in fact a true conflict between domestic and foreign law." *Societe Nationale Industrielle Aerospatiale v. United States Dist. Court for Southern Dist. of Iowa,* 482 U.S. 522, 555 (1987) (BLACKMUN, J., concurring in part and dissenting in part). The London reinsurers contend that applying the Act to their conduct would conflict significantly with British law, and the British Government, appearing before us

---

[23] Under § 402 of the Foreign Trade Antitrust Improvements Act of 1982 (FTAIA), 96 Stat. 1246, 15 U.S.C. § 6a, the Sherman Act does not apply to conduct involving foreign trade or commerce, other than import trade or import commerce, unless "such conduct has a direct, substantial, and reasonably foreseeable effect" on domestic or import commerce. § 6a(1)(A). The FTAIA was intended to exempt from the Sherman Act export transactions that did not injure the United States economy, see H.R.Rep. No. 97-686, pp. 2-3, 9-10 (1982); P. Areeda & H. Hovenkamp, Antitrust Law ¶ 236a, pp. 296-297 (Supp.1992), and it is unclear how it might apply to the conduct alleged here. Also unclear is whether the Act's "direct, substantial, and reasonably foreseeable effect" standard amends existing law or merely codifies it. See id., ¶ 236a, p. 297. We need not address these questions here. Assuming that the FTAIA's standard affects this litigation, and assuming further that that standard differs from the prior law, the conduct alleged plainly meets its requirements.

[24] Justice SCALIA contends that comity concerns figure into the prior analysis whether jurisdiction exists under the Sherman Act. This contention is inconsistent with the general understanding that the Sherman Act covers foreign conduct producing a substantial intended effect in the United States, and that concerns of comity come into play, if at all, only after a court has determined that the acts complained of are subject to Sherman Act jurisdiction. See *United States v. Aluminum Co. of America* [p. 910 *supra*] ("[I]t follows from what we have . . . said that [the agreements at issue] were unlawful [under the Sherman Act], though made abroad, if they were intended to affect imports and did affect them"); *Mannington Mills, Inc. v. Congoleum Corp.,* [p. 950] (once court determines that jurisdiction exists under the Sherman Act, question remains whether comity precludes its exercise); H.R.Rep. No. 97-686, supra, at 13. But cf. *Timberlane Lumber Co. v. Bank of America, N.T. & S.A.,* [p. 943]; 1 J. Atwood & K. Brewster, Antitrust and American Business Abroad 166 (1981). In any event, the parties conceded jurisdiction at oral argument, and we see no need to address this contention here.

as amicus curiae, concurs. They assert that Parliament has established a comprehensive regulatory regime over the London reinsurance market and that the conduct alleged here was perfectly consistent with British law and policy. But this is not to state a conflict. "[T]he fact that conduct is lawful in the state in which it took place will not, of itself, bar application of the United States antitrust laws," even where the foreign state has a strong policy to permit or encourage such conduct. Restatement (Third) Foreign Relations Law § 415, Comment j; see Continental Ore Co., supra, 370 U.S., at 706-707, 82 S.Ct., at 1414-1415. No conflict exists, for these purposes, "where a person subject to regulation by two states can comply with the laws of both." Restatement (Third) Foreign Relations Law § 403, Comment e.[25] Since the London reinsurers do not argue that British law requires them to act in some fashion prohibited by the law of the United States, see Reply Brief for [the London reinsurers] or claim that their compliance with the laws of both countries is otherwise impossible, we see no conflict with British law. See Restatement (Third) Foreign Relations Law § 403, Comment e, § 415, Comment j. We have no need in this litigation to address other considerations that might inform a decision to refrain from the exercise of jurisdiction on grounds of international comity.

IV

The judgment of the Court of Appeals is affirmed in part and reversed in part, and the cases are remanded for further proceedings consistent with this opinion.

It is so ordered.

Justice SCALIA delivered the opinion of the Court with respect to Part I, and delivered a dissenting opinion with respect to Part II, in which Justice O'CONNOR, Justice KENNEDY, and Justice THOMAS have joined.

. . .

II

Petitioners in No. 91-1128, various British corporations and other British subjects, argue that certain of the claims against them constitute an inappropriate extraterritorial application of the Sherman Act. It is important to distinguish two distinct questions raised by this petition: whether the District Court had jurisdiction, and whether the Sherman Act reaches the extraterritorial conduct alleged here. On the first question, I believe that the District Court had subject-matter jurisdiction over the Sherman Act claims against all the defendants (personal jurisdiction is not contested). Respondents asserted nonfrivolous claims under the Sherman Act, and 28 U.S.C. § 1331 vests district courts with subject-matter jurisdiction over cases "arising under" federal statutes. As precedents such as *Lauritzen v. Larsen,* [p. 871 *supra*], make clear, that is sufficient to establish the District Court's jurisdiction over these claims. Lauritzen involved a Jones Act claim brought by a foreign sailor against a foreign shipowner. The shipowner contested the District Court's jurisdiction, apparently on the grounds that the Jones Act did not govern the dispute between the foreign parties to the action. Though ultimately agreeing with the shipowner that the Jones Act did not apply, the Court held that the District Court had jurisdiction.

---

[25] Justice SCALIA says that we put the cart before the horse in citing this authority, for he argues it may be apposite only after a determination that jurisdiction over the foreign acts is reasonable. But whatever the order of cart and horse, conflict in this sense is the only substantial issue before the Court.

"As frequently happens, a contention that there is some barrier to granting plaintiff's claim is cast in terms of an exception to jurisdiction of subject matter. A cause of action under our law was asserted here, and the court had power to determine whether it was or was not well founded in law and in fact." [p. 871, *supra*].

See also *Romero v. International Terminal Operating Co.,* [p. 878, *supra*].

The second question—the extraterritorial reach of the Sherman Act—has nothing to do with the jurisdiction of the courts. It is a question of substantive law turning on whether, in enacting the Sherman Act, Congress asserted regulatory power over the challenged conduct. See *EEOC v. Arabian American Oil Co.,* [499 U.S. 244 (1991) ("It is our task to determine whether Congress intended the protections of Title VII to apply to United States citizens employed by American employers outside of the United States"). If a plaintiff fails to prevail on this issue, the court does not dismiss the claim for want of subject-matter jurisdiction—want of power to adjudicate; rather, it decides the claim, ruling on the merits that the plaintiff has failed to state a cause of action under the relevant statute. See *Romero,* supra, (holding no claim available under the Jones Act); *American Banana Co. v. United Fruit Co.,* (holding that complaint based upon foreign conduct "alleges no case under the [Sherman Act]").

There is, however, a type of "jurisdiction" relevant to determining the extraterritorial reach of a statute; it is known as "legislative jurisdiction," *Aramco,* supra; Restatement (First) Conflict of Laws § 60 (1934), or "jurisdiction to prescribe," 1 Restatement (Third) of Foreign Relations Law of the United States [p.] 235 (1987) (hereinafter Restatement (Third)). This refers to "the authority of a state to make its law applicable to persons or activities," and is quite a separate matter from "jurisdiction to adjudicate," see id., at [p.] 231. There is no doubt, of course, that Congress possesses legislative jurisdiction over the acts alleged in this complaint: Congress has broad power under Article I, § 8, cl. 3, "[t]o regulate Commerce with foreign Nations," and this Court has repeatedly upheld its power to make laws applicable to persons or activities beyond our territorial boundaries where United States interests are affected. But the question in this litigation is whether, and to what extent, Congress has exercised that undoubted legislative jurisdiction in enacting the Sherman Act.

Two canons of statutory construction are relevant in this inquiry. The first is the "longstanding principle of American law 'that legislation of Congress, unless a contrary intent appears, is meant to apply only within the territorial jurisdiction of the United States.' " *Aramco,* supra, (quoting *Foley Bros., Inc. v. Filardo,* 336 U.S. 281, 285, 1949)). Applying that canon in *Aramco,* we held that the version of Title VII of the Civil Rights Act of 1964 then in force, did not extend outside the territory of the United States even though the statute contained broad provisions extending its prohibitions to, for example, " 'any activity, business, or industry in commerce.' " We held such "boilerplate language" to be an insufficient indication to override the presumption against extraterritoriality. The Sherman Act contains similar "boilerplate language," and if the question were not governed by precedent, it would be worth considering whether that presumption controls the outcome here. We have, however, found the presumption to be overcome with respect to our antitrust laws; it is now well established that the Sherman Act applies extraterritorially.

But if the presumption against extraterritoriality has been overcome or is otherwise inapplicable, a second canon of statutory construction becomes relevant: "[A]n act of congress ought never to be construed to violate the law of nations if any other possible construction remains." *Murray v. Schooner Charming Betsy,* 2 Cranch 64, 118, (1804) (Marshall, C.J.). This canon is "wholly independent" of the presumption against extraterritoriality. *Aramco*. It is relevant to determining the substantive reach of a statute because "the law of nations," or customary international law, includes limitations on a nation's exercise of its jurisdiction to prescribe. See Restatement (Third) §§ 401-416. Though it clearly has constitutional authority to do so, Congress is generally presumed not to have exceeded those customary international-law limits on jurisdiction to prescribe.

Consistent with that presumption, this and other courts have frequently recognized that, even where the presumption against extraterritoriality does not apply, statutes should not be interpreted to regulate foreign persons or conduct if that regulation would conflict with principles of international law. For example, in *Romero v. International Terminal Operating Co.,* the plaintiff, a Spanish sailor who had been injured while working aboard a Spanish-flag and Spanish-owned vessel, filed a Jones Act claim against his Spanish employer. The presumption against extraterritorial application of federal statutes was inapplicable to the case, as the actionable tort had occurred in American waters. The Court nonetheless stated that, "in the absence of a contrary congressional direction," it would apply "principles of choice of law that are consonant with the needs of a general federal maritime law and with due recognition of our self-regarding respect for the relevant interests of foreign nations in the regulation of maritime commerce as part of the legitimate concern of the international community." "The controlling considerations" in this choice-of-law analysis were "the interacting interests of the United States and of foreign countries."

Romero referred to, and followed, the choice-of-law analysis set forth in *Lauritzen v. Larsen.* As previously mentioned, *Lauritzen* also involved a Jones Act claim brought by a foreign sailor against a foreign employer. The *Lauritzen* Court recognized the basic problem: "If [the Jones Act were] read literally, Congress has conferred an American right of action which requires nothing more than that plaintiff be 'any seaman who shall suffer personal injury in the course of his employment.' " The solution it adopted was to construe the statute "to apply only to areas and transactions in which *American law would be considered operative under prevalent doctrines of international law.*" (emphasis added). To support application of international law to limit the facial breadth of the statute, the Court relied upon—of course—Chief Justice Marshall's statement in *Schooner Charming Betsy,* quoted *supra.* It then set forth "several factors which, alone or in combination, are generally conceded to influence choice of law to govern a tort claim." (discussing factors). See also *McCulloch v. Sociedad Nacional de Marineros de Honduras,* [p. 881, *supra*] (applying *Schooner Charming Betsy* principle to restrict application of National Labor Relations Act to foreign-flag vessels).

Lauritzen, Romero, and *McCulloch* were maritime cases, but we have recognized the principle that the scope of generally worded statutes must be construed in light of international law in other areas as well. See, e.g., *Sale v. Haitian Centers Council, Inc.,* 509 U.S. 155, 178, n. 35, (1993); *Weinberger v. Rossi,* 456 U.S. 25, 32, (1982). More specifically, the principle was expressed in *United States v. Aluminum Co. of America,* the decision that established the extraterritorial reach of the Sherman Act. In his opinion for the court, Judge Learned Hand cautioned "we are not to read general words, such as those in [the Sherman] Act, without regard to the limitations customarily observed by nations upon the exercise of their powers; limitations which generally correspond to those fixed by the 'Conflict of Laws.' "

More recent lower court precedent has also tempered the extraterritorial application of the Sherman Act with considerations of "international comity." See *Timberlane Lumber Co. v. Bank of America, N.T. & S.A.; Mannington Mills, Inc. v. Congoleum Corp.; Montreal Trading Ltd.*

v. Amax Inc., 661 F.2d 864, 869-871 (CA10 1981); *Laker Airways Limited v. Sabena, Belgian World Airlines,* 731 F.2d 909, 938 and n. 109. The "comity" they refer to is not the comity of courts, whereby judges decline to exercise jurisdiction over matters more appropriately adjudged elsewhere, but rather what might be termed "prescriptive comity": the respect sovereign nations afford each other by limiting the reach of their laws. That comity is exercised by legislatures when they enact laws, and courts assume it has been exercised when they come to interpreting the scope of laws their legislatures have enacted. It is a traditional component of choice-of-law theory. See J. Story, Commentaries on the Conflict of Laws § 38 (1834) (distinguishing between the "comity of the courts" and the "comity of nations," and defining the latter as "the true foundation and extent of the obligation of the laws of one nation within the territories of another"). Comity in this sense includes the choice-of-law principles that, "in the absence of contrary congressional direction," are assumed to be incorporated into our substantive laws having extraterritorial reach. Considering comity in this way is just part of determining whether the Sherman Act prohibits the conduct at issue.[9]

In sum, the practice of using international law to limit the extraterritorial reach of statutes is firmly established in our jurisprudence. In proceeding to apply that practice to the present cases, I shall rely on the Restatement (Third) for the relevant principles of international law. Its standards appear fairly supported in the decisions of this Court construing international choice-of-law principles (*Lauritzen, Romero,* and *McCulloch*) and in the decisions of other federal courts, especially *Timberlane*. Whether the Restatement precisely reflects international law in every detail matters little here, as I believe this litigation would be resolved the same way under virtually any conceivable test that takes account of foreign regulatory interests.

Under the Restatement, a nation having some "basis" for jurisdiction to prescribe law should nonetheless refrain from exercising that jurisdiction "with respect to a person or activity having connections with another state when the exercise of such jurisdiction is unreasonable." Restatement (Third) § 403(1). The "reasonableness" inquiry turns on a number of factors including, but not limited to: "the extent to which the activity takes place within the territory [of the regulating state]," id., § 403(2)(a); "the connections, such as nationality, residence, or economic activity, between the regulating state and the person principally responsible for the activity to be regulated," id., § 403(2)(b); "the character of the activity to be regulated, the importance of regulation to the regulating state, the extent to which other states regulate such activities, and the degree to which the desirability of such regulation is generally accepted," id., § 403(2)(c); "the extent to which another state may have an interest in regulating the activity," id., § 403(2)(g); and "the likelihood of conflict with regulation by another state," id., § 403(2)(h). Rarely would these factors point more clearly against application of United States law. The activity relevant to the counts at issue here took place primarily in the United Kingdom, and the defendants in these counts are British corporations and British subjects having their principal place of business or residence outside the United States.[10] Great Britain has established a

---

[9] Some antitrust courts, including the Court of Appeals in the present cases, have mistaken the comity at issue here for the "comity of courts," which has led them to characterize the question presented as one of "abstention," that is, whether they should "exercise or decline jurisdiction." *Mannington Mills, Inc. v. Congoleum Corp.,* [p. 950, *supra*]; see also *In re Insurance Antitrust Litigation,* 938 F.2d 919, 932 (CA9 1991). As I shall discuss, that seems to be the error the Court has fallen into today. Because courts are generally reluctant to refuse the exercise of conferred jurisdiction, confusion on this seemingly theoretical point can have the very practical consequence of greatly expanding the extraterritorial reach of the Sherman Act.

[10] Some of the British corporations are subsidiaries of American corporations, and the Court of Appeals held that "[t]he interests of Britain are at least diminished where the parties are subsidiaries of American corporations." In effect, the Court of Appeals pierced the corporate veil in weighing the interests at stake. I do not think that was proper.

comprehensive regulatory scheme governing the London reinsurance markets, and clearly has a heavy "interest in regulating the activity," id., § 403(2)(g). See [Cb. at 116]; *In re Insurance Antitrust Litigation,* 723 F.Supp. 464, 487-488 (ND Cal.1989); see also J. Butler & R. Merkin, Reinsurance Law A.1.1-02 (1992). Finally, § 2(b) of the McCarran-Ferguson Act allows state regulatory statutes to override the Sherman Act in the insurance field, subject only to the narrow "boycott" exception set forth in § 3(b)—suggesting that "the importance of regulation to the [United States]," Restatement (Third) § 403(2)(c), is slight. Considering these factors, I think it unimaginable that an assertion of legislative jurisdiction by the United States would be considered reasonable, and therefore it is inappropriate to assume, in the absence of statutory indication to the contrary, that Congress has made such an assertion.

It is evident from what I have said that the Court's comity analysis, which proceeds as though the issue is whether the courts should "decline to exercise . . . jurisdiction," rather than whether the Sherman Act covers this conduct, is simply misdirected. I do not at all agree, moreover, with the Court's conclusion that the issue of the substantive scope of the Sherman Act is not in the cases. To be sure, the parties did not make a clear distinction between adjudicative jurisdiction and the scope of the statute. Parties often do not, as we have observed (and have declined to punish with procedural default) before. . . . It is not realistic, and also not helpful, to pretend that the only really relevant issue in this litigation is not before us. In any event, if one erroneously chooses, as the Court does, to make adjudicative jurisdiction (or, more precisely, abstention) the vehicle for taking account of the needs of prescriptive comity, the Court still gets it wrong. It concludes that no "true conflict" counseling nonapplication of United States law (or rather, as it thinks, United States judicial jurisdiction) exists unless compliance with United States law would constitute a violation of another country's law. That breathtakingly broad proposition, which contradicts the many cases discussed earlier, will bring the Sherman Act and other laws into sharp and unnecessary conflict with the legitimate interests of other countries—particularly our closest trading partners.

In the sense in which the term "conflic[t]" was used in *Lauritzen,* and is generally understood in the field of conflicts of laws, there is clearly a conflict in this litigation. The petitioners here, like the defendant in *Lauritzen,* were not compelled by any foreign law to take their allegedly wrongful actions, but that no more precludes a conflict-of-laws analysis here than it did there. (detailing the differences between foreign and United States law). Where applicable foreign and domestic law provide different substantive rules of decision to govern the parties' dispute, a conflict-of-laws analysis is necessary. See generally R. Weintraub, Commentary on Conflict of Laws 2-3 (1980); Restatement (First) of Conflict of Laws § 1, Comment c and Illustrations (1934).

Literally the only support that the Court adduces for its position is § 403 of the Restatement (Third)—or more precisely Comment e to that provision, which states:

> "Subsection (3) [which says that a State should defer to another state if that State's interest is clearly greater] applies only when one state requires what another prohibits, or where compliance with the regulations of two states exercising jurisdiction consistently with this section is otherwise impossible. It does not apply where a person subject to regulation by two states can comply with the laws of both. . . ."

The Court has completely misinterpreted this provision. Subsection (3) of § 403 (requiring one State to defer to another in the limited circumstances just described) comes into play only after subsection (1) of § 403 has been complied with—i.e., after it has been determined that the exercise of jurisdiction by both of the two States is not "unreasonable." That prior question is answered by applying the factors (inter alia) set forth in subsection (2) of s 403, that is, precisely the factors that I have discussed in text and that the Court rejects.[11]

* * *

I would reverse the judgment of the Court of Appeals on this issue, and remand to the District Court with instructions to dismiss for failure to state a claim on the three counts at issue in [the appeal of the London reinsurers].

NOTES AND QUESTIONS ON THE INSURANCE ANTITRUST CASE

(1)(a) Justice Souter writes that the only substantial question in this case is whether there is in fact a true conflict between domestic and foreign law (p. 963). Is that correct?

(b) "True conflict," as we have seen throughout this volume, is understood in modern approaches to conflict of laws as a condition when two states have a genuine interest in resolution of a legal dispute. That is evidently not Justice Souter's understanding of the term. He says that if the defendants can comply with U.S. law without violating British law, "no conflict exists." Isn't Justice Souter confusing conflict with compulsion?[h]

(c) It seems that Justice Souter, and the majority in the Supreme Court, would have deferred to the British interest if the British government had ordered the London reinsurers to use only the amended form. Could any lesser degree of expression of British interest have swayed the Court? Suppose for instance, (i) British law required any agreement among members of the reinsurance market to be submitted to the relevant minister for approval, and the minister had approved the agreement being challenged. What if (ii) British law required only that an agreement be submitted to the minister, and that it would enter into effect within 30 days unless the minister disapproved? Is the Court telling the British government how to express its interest in the management of a London market?

(d) Justice Souter quotes a portion of Comment e to §403 of the Restatement [at p. 964], which states that subsection (3) of §403 (p. 960) applies only when the subject of a regulation cannot comply with a regulation of both concerned states. But as Justice Scalia points out, subsection (3) only applies when the regulations in conflict are not unreasonable according to the factors listed in §403(2) (p. 959, *supra*). Does application of the Sherman Act to the London reinsurers of American risks pass this test?

(2)(a) Justice Scalia's dissenting opinion relies heavily on the three maritime cases reproduced in §10.01 above—*Lauritzen, Romero*, and *McCulloch*,—to illustrate the presumption against extraterritorial application of U.S. statutes in conflict with principles of international law, and to assert (p. 967) that in the sense in which the term "conflict" was used in these cases, *Hartford*

---

[11] The Court skips directly to subsection (3) of § 403, apparently on the authority of Comment *j* to § 415 of the Restatement (Third). But the preceding commentary to § 415 makes clear that "[a]ny exercise of [legislative] jurisdiction under this section is subject to the requirement of reasonableness" set forth in § 403(2). Restatement (Third) § 415, Comment *a*. Comment j refers back to the conflict analysis set forth in § 403(3), which, as noted above, comes after the reasonableness analysis of § 403(2).

[h] The present author gave an affirmative reply to this question. See A. Lowenfeld, *Conflict, Balancing of Interests, and the Exercise of Jurisdiction to Prescribe: Reflections on the Insurance Antitrust Case*, 89 Am. J. Int'l L. 42 (1995).

Fire Insurance Co. v. California clearly presented a conflict. Justice Scalia, in other words, understands conflict to mean "inconsistent with." Is that more persuasive?

(b) Justice Scalia also relies heavily on *Equal Employment Opportunity Commission v. Arabian American Oil Co. (Aramco)*, 499 U.S. 244 (1991), a case not cited by the majority, though it had been decided just two years earlier. The *Aramco* case involved a claim under title VII of the U.S. Civil Rights Act of 1964[i] by a U.S. citizen of Lebanese origin, who had been hired by Aramco to work in Saudi Arabia, and had subsequently been discharged. The plaintiff claimed that he had been the victim of discrimination because of his race, religion and national origin. Aramco, a Delaware corporation with its principal place of business in Saudi Arabia plus offices in several states of the United States, denied the charge of discrimination, but contended that in any event, Title VII did not apply to conduct abroad. It followed, according to Aramco's submission, that U.S. courts lacked jurisdiction over the action.

(c) The District and Circuit Courts agreed, and dismissed the action. The Supreme Court, by 6-3, affirmed the dismissal. Chief Justice Rehnquist, for the majority, agreed that Congress had the authority to enforce its laws beyond the territorial boundaries of the United States, but wrote that it is "a long-standing principle of American law that legislation of Congress, unless a contrary intent appears, is meant to apply only within the territorial jurisdiction of the United States."[j] Putting aside a detailed debate about the intent of Congress to be inferred from text, legislative history, and amendments of the Civil Rights Act,[k] would you think the arguments for applying U.S. law are stronger in *Aramco* or in *Hartford*? Can you think of a principled basis for distinguishing between the two outcomes?

(d) Note that in *Aramco* the defendant (as well as the plaintiff) were U.S. citizens, whereas the London reinsurers in *Hartford* were all British citizens or corporations. Judged by the Restatement criteria, were both cases wrongly decided?

(e) In *Hartford*, the majority found that there was no conflict, as the Court defined the term. In *Aramco*, the Court inferred the intent of Congress in part from the difference between Title VII of the Civil Rights Act and the Age Discrimination in Employment Act (ADEA),[l] which Congress had recently amended to make it applicable abroad, subject to the proviso that it is not unlawful for an employer to take any action prohibited by the ADEA "where compliance with the ADEA would cause such employer to violate the laws of the country in which such workplace is located."[m] "It is . . . reasonable to conclude," the Chief Justice wrote, "that had Congress intended Title VII to apply overseas, it would have addressed the subject of conflicts with foreign laws and procedures."[n] Could that not have been said with respect to the Sherman Act as well?

(f) Professor Kramer criticizes Justice Souter in *Hartford* for not mentioning the *Aramco* case, even after he had presumably seen a draft of Justice Scalia's dissent.[o] Kramer states that the

---

[i] 42 U.S.C. § 2000e et seq.

[j] 499 U.S. at 248, citing *Foley Bros., Inc. v. Filarto*, 336 U.S. 281, 284-85 (1949), cited also by Justice Scalia in *Hartford*.

[k] See 499 U.S. at 248-50, 253-59 (majority), and 499 U.S. at 265-75 (dissent by Marshall, with Blackmun and Stevens).

[l] 29 U.S.C. § 621 et seq.

[m] 29 U.S.C. § 623(f)(1).

[n] 499 U.S. at 256.

[o] Larry Kramer, *Extraterritorial Application of American Law after the Insurance Antitrust Case: A Reply to Professors Lowenfeld and Trimble*, 89 Am. J. Int'l L. 750 (1995).

two cases stand in considerable tension. Do you agree? Or are civil rights laws and competition laws sufficiently different to make the solution of one case irrelevant for the other? Note that in *Hartford,* it was conceded that the challenged action was intended to take effect in the United States; *Aramco,* in contrast involved, at least potentially, imposition of American social values in a foreign, and very different country.

(g) Further, Professor Kramer wonders how to advise persons who may (or may not) be subject to other U.S. statutes, for instance the federal securities laws. He writes that there is enough space between *Hartford* and *Aramco* to make both positions tenable as a matter of precedent, but goes on to argue that *Aramco* was a "very misguided decision," and looks to *Hartford* to limit *Aramco* and restore "a more sensible, policy-oriented approach to defining the extraterritorial reach of American law."[p] What policies do you think Professor Kramer had in mind? Does his approach suggest that U.S. policy is generally superior to that of the other country? Or that U.S. courts should apply forum law when there is any forum interest, along the lines of Currie's approach to choice of law in interstate controversies?[q]

(3) Apart from the antitrust and securities cases that have come before courts—and more recently discrimination cases as well, the exercise of regulatory jurisdiction by governments may result in controversies that do not come before courts at all, or where the courts play only a subordinate role. The Restatement criteria, set out at p. 959, are addressed not only to courts, but to governments more generally. The following section describes two *causes célèbres* in circumstances where there could be no doubt about existence of conflict, or about the existence of genuine national interests on both sides. Consider as you read the next section whether the Restatement is useful—or could be useful if governments were prepared to follow its methodology—in weighing state A's national interests against the national interests of state B, and yielding to the stronger interest.

§ 10.05 True Conflicts in International Relations

[A] The Fruehauf Case

[1] Background

In the fall of 1964, the United States and the People's Republic of China had virtually no relations—economic, political, or otherwise. Since mainland China had joined the Korean War on the North Korean side in December 1950, the United States had maintained a total embargo on trade and other economic relations with China (as well as North Korea, and later North Vietnam and Cuba). The embargo was instituted pursuant to a statute known as the Trading with the Enemy Act, adopted in 1917, amended during World War II, but applicable also during any period of national emergency, such as one proclaimed by President Truman in 1950 and never rescinded. Transactions by "persons subject to the jurisdiction of the United States" were prohibited unless licensed by the U.S. Treasury, whether or not they involved goods originating in the United States. Licenses were virtually never granted for commercial undertakings. Under

---

[p] 89 Am. J. Int'l L. at 754.

[q] Following the decision in *Aramco,* Congress amended Title VII to provide expressly "with respect to employment in a foreign country, [the term 'employee'] includes an individual who is a citizen of the United States." 42 U.S.C. § 2000e(f).

the so-called Foreign Assets Control Regulations of the U.S. Treasury, persons subject to the jurisdiction of the United States included:

(1) Any person, wheresoever located, who is a citizen or resident of the United States;

(2) Any person actually within the United States;

(3) Any corporation organized under the laws of the United States or any state, territory, district or possession of the United States;

(4) Any partnership, association, corporation or other association, wheresoever organized or doing business, which is owned or controlled by persons specified in subparagraph (1), (2), or (3) of this paragraph.[a]

Category (4) of the definition of "Person subject to the Jurisdiction of the United States" would, it seems, take in subsidiaries of U.S.-based corporations—surely if they were 100 percent-owned by the parent company, and probably even with lesser, but controlling shareholding. Category (4) made no exception for companies incorporated under the laws of a foreign state.

S.A. Fruehauf-France fit into the latter category. Seventy percent of its shares were owned by Fruehauf Corporation of Detroit, a major manufacturer of truck-trailers since 1918. Fruehauf-France had a plant about 15 miles south of Paris, a board made up of five directors appointed by Detroit, and three appointed by the minority French group, which included the President, Raoul Massardy. In the fall of 1964, Berliet, a French truck manufacturer, invited bids on a large export transaction of tractor-trailers, and Fruehauf-France was the successful bidder. It signed a contract with Berliet in December 1964, with delivery to begin in February 1965. In January 1965, the U.S. Treasury learned of this transaction, and discovered that the tractor trailers were destined for mainland China. The U.S. Treasury called in the senior management of the Fruehauf Corporation in Detroit, and instructed them to cause Fruehauf-France to cancel the contract with Berliet forthwith, as execution of the contract would be a violation of the Foreign Assets Control Regulations, punishable by heavy criminal penalties. Following several weeks of meetings and telephone calls, Fruehauf Detroit complied with the order of the U.S. Treasury, and formally instructed Fruehauf-France to cancel the contract and to seek to minimize damages vis-à-vis Berliet. Berliet refused to release Fruehauf-France and threatened suit. The government of France issued vigorous protests, both publicly and through diplomatic channels. Massardy resigned as president of Fruehauf-France, and the three French directors petitioned the local commercial court for the appointment of a temporary administrator who would manage the company and carry out the contract. The court granted the petition on February 16, 1965. The corporation, on the basis of a resolution adopted by the five American directors, appealed.

---

[a] 31 C.F.R. § 500.329 (1950–86).

[2] Fruehauf Corporation v. Massardy, (1965)

FRUEHAUF CORPORATION v. MASSARDY

Court of Appeal Paris
May 22, 1965
(1968) D.S. Jur. 147, (1965) J.C.P. II 1427 bis, (1965) Gaz. Pal. 86

This is an appeal taken by William Grace, Alex Aranyos, Société Anonyme Fruehauf Corporation, Richard Cronan and R. D. Rowan from a provisional order rendered on February 16, 1965 by the President of the Commercial Court of Corbeil-Essones. The Court has also heard argument from the appellees, Raoul Massardy, Georges Massardy and Paul Godbille, as well as from S.A. Automobiles Berliet, Intervenor, and Solvet, Judicial Administrator, as second Intervenor.

Considering that S.A. Fruehauf-France, founded in 1946 with a seat at Ris-Orangis, has as its object the building in France and exportation of trailers, semi-trailers, and materials of the "Fruehauf" mark; considering that its current capital, fixed at 7,500,000 francs, is divided into 150,000 shares belonging two-thirds to one group of shareholders residing in the United States of America and one-third to a group of French shareholders; considering that its Board of Directors had, until recently, a parallel composition, in that, under the Chairmanship of Raoul Massardy, General Manager, it consisted on the one hand of the five Appellants, including the Fruehauf Corp. (Detroit) represented by its permanent Representative, Richard Cronan, and on the other hand of the three French Appellees.

Considering that on December 24, 1964, the automobile company, Berliet, ordered from Fruehauf-France, for a price of 1,785,310 francs, 60 Fruehauf semi-trailers of 25 and 45 tons and 60 couplers, which were to be delivered beginning February 15, 1965 and were destined for exportation to the People's Republic of China; considering that on January 12, 1965, Alex Aranyos, President of the company "Fruehauf-International," which seems to coordinate the activities of the various Fruehauf companies, notified François Godbille, Deputy General Manager of Fruehauf-France, that the United States authorities had undertaken an investigation on the subject of this sale, which was contrary to the regulations of the United States, adding "We have been ordered to suspend the execution of the contract in the absence of a license from the Department of the Treasury which, as we have been told, would not be consistent with present policy;" considering that François Godbille stated that the future of Fruehauf-France would be compromised by cancellation of such an important order concerning goods designed and fabricated in France, whose financing was provided by a special credit of French origin, and which could equally well have been supplied by competing firms; but considering that on January 28, a telegram was addressed to François Godbille containing the following sentence: "We hereby formally instruct you to cancel the contract and reduce the possible losses to a minimum."

Considering that on February 11, 1965, Raoul Massardy asked Paul Berliet if it would be possible for him to consent to cancellation of the contract, given that the material and moral damages which would result from its execution would be "for our American friends;" considering that on the following day Berliet replied that it would not consider in any way accepting such a cancellation and that it would hold Fruehauf-France fully responsible for any direct and indirect injury which might be caused by its default.

Considering that on February 13, 1965, Raoul Massardy drafted a letter of resignation of his functions as President-General Manager because of the difficulties which the majority of the Board of Directors were making for him and because of the seriousness of this situation for Fruehauf-France; considering that the three French members of the Board immediately appeared before the President of the Commercial Court of Corbeil, who authorized them to summon before him the five American Directors for February 16, with a view to appointment of an Agent of the Court charged with managing the company for a fixed period, executing its current orders, and calling a shareholder's meeting at an appropriate time; considering that this summons was delivered on February 15 to the Appellants who, on the same day, convoked the Board with a view to nominating a [new] Director, President-General Manager, and Deputy General Manager.

Considering that on February 16, 1965, the President of the Commercial Court, holding essentially that Fruehauf-France was deprived of its organ of legal direction and that the non-performance of its obligations would put its existence in peril, named Solvet Temporary Administrator for a period of three months or until otherwise ordered, with the mission of running said company, and, in particular, executing its current orders; considering finally that on February 18, 1965, the Board of Directors, meeting in the absence of Appellees, took note of the resignation of Raoul Massardy, nominated Pierre Cheret as Director and President-General Manager, and maintained François Godbille in his capacity as Deputy General Manager.

Considering that on March 4, 1965, the Appellees summoned the Appellants before the Commercial Court of Corbeil with a view to securing a declaration of nullity of the resolution [of February 18]; considering that the American Directors maintain on this appeal that the court below had no jurisdiction in the absence of emergency and because it could not, without prejudicing the company itself, interfere with the management of a corporation to impose on the majority of the shareholders and Directors the views of the minority; considering that the Appellees, who argue for the affirmance of the order, have joined as intervenor S.A. Automobiles Berliet, which is prepared to abide by a decision of the Court, asking only that it be protected against non-delivery of the order on its due date in accordance with the contract, and Solvet, who asks the Court to decide however it sees fit on the merits of the appeal and to notify him of its decision.

Considering that it does not in principle belong to the jurisdiction of the magistrates to substitute even temporarily an Agent of the Court for the administrative organs of a company; considering that this rule would be bent only in exceptional circumstances when, for example, the normal function of the company is no longer assured, the company is threatened with ruin, or its management is manifestly prevented from acting by grave dissension among its members; considering that, thus, the emergency that might justify the court's jurisdiction cannot be decided without an examination of the underlying merits of the relief requested; considering that in this case the court below wrongly found absence of management of S.A. Fruehauf-France; that in fact the company was provided with a complete and regularly named Board of Directors qualified to replace the resigned President-General Manager, who was effectively replaced from February 18, 1965, only five days after his resignation, regardless of the criticism of that replacement raised today before this court by the Appellees; but considering that the documents submitted to this court show without serious doubt not only the evident interest for S.A. Fruehauf-France in the faithful execution of the contract with its principal customer, Berliet, which accounts for approximately 40% of its exports, but above all the catastrophic consequences which would have followed from the cancellation of this contract on the eve of the promised delivery date and which would still follow today since the buyer would apparently have been entitled to claim from its supplier complete reparation for its commercial loss, estimated at more than 5,000,000 francs, resulting from the breaking of its agreements with China.

Considering that these consequences, for which neither Fruehauf Corporation [Detroit] nor Fruehauf-International has agreed to assume liability, would be such as to definitively ruin the financial equilibrium and credit of Fruehauf-France and to bring about its disappearance and the laying off of more than 600 workers; that these circumstances establish sufficiently the emergency and the justification of the conservatory measure taken, it being noted that in naming a Temporary Administrator the Judge must be governed by social interests in preference to the personal interests of certain members, even though they be in the majority; and, moreover, considering that it is by no means certain that this nomination was contrary to the real interests of the Appellants.

Considering, nevertheless, that the general mandate conferred on the Court-appointed administrator must not lead him to compel the execution of orders, the opportuneness of which for the company in each particular case he alone is in a position to appreciate; considering that in the absence of appeal by the administrator the court cannot in this case prolong the mission of Solvet beyond the time set by the court below, nor can it contemplate convocation of a general meeting of shareholders:

For these reasons, the Court admits the appeal and the interventions; holds the appeal unfounded and the interventions well founded; grants to the intervenors the documents requested; confirms the decree of February 16, 1965, in which Solvet was nominated Temporary Administrator of S.A. Fruehauf-France with the mission of managing the said company; and charges Grace, Aranyos, Fruehauf Corporation, Cronan and Rowan with the costs of proceedings below, the appeal and the interventions.

NOTES AND QUESTIONS

(1)(a) The United States had several interests in the Fruehauf contract with Berliet. For one thing, it had maintained, with a high degree of success, the integrity of its embargo, at considerable cost in friction with Canada and other countries. To let the Fruehauf-France project go through might, it was thought, literally let a truck be driven through the embargo, with the prospect that in all other countries where subsidiaries of U.S. companies were operating, demands would become irresistible to modify the reach of the embargo.

(b) Perhaps equally important, the united front of the western Allies against the People's Republic was beginning to crumble; permitting this deal to go forward would, it was believed, "send the wrong signal" to Peking, just when China might be considering how deeply to become involved—on the enemy's side—in the Vietnam war.

(c) The United States itself was not yet heavily involved in the Vietnam war—at least as far as troops were concerned—but Administration officials were concerned that it might be "permitting" trailer trucks to be sent to China which would soon be ferrying troops and weapons down the Ho Chi Minh trail to kill American boys.

(d) One need not agree with any of these views to acknowledge that they were real, and deeply felt. In contrast to worrying about New York's interest in Ms. Babcock or Ms. Tooker, which was probably made up to fit into a conflict of laws theory, the interest of the United States here was a genuine, public, and in the minds of the Administration, vital national interest.

(e) France too had serious interests. Not only was there the part legal, part political insistence that a French company in France takes orders only from the French Republic. In addition, President de Gaulle had recently returned from Peking—the first important western leader to make such a journey. He believed in realism in international politics, and he wanted to follow up the visit with trade relations. The Berliet deal was the first important contract to come out of the new "opening to China" policy, and he certainly wanted to avoid frustration of that contract.

(f) If, then, this was a genuine "true conflict," do the teachings of conflict of laws help to resolve it? What about the *Restatement* criteria set out at p. 959-60?

(2)(a) The Court of Appeal seems not to address the concerns of national policy mentioned in the preceding paragraph, but for the most part treats the case as a problem in corporate law. To the extent state interest is involved at all, it is the "social interests"—i.e., employment or lay-off for 600 workers, the credit of Fruehauf-France, and (it seems) the financing supplied by the French state. If Fruehauf-France had been 100 percent owned by Fruehauf Detroit, wouldn't these interests be just as real? Could the court have appointed an intervener or temporary administrator even in that case?

(b)[b] Speaking of corporation law, the court was anxious not to bend that law more than necessary. In the leading French case on judicial intervention in corporate affairs prior to 1965, the Supreme Court of France (Cour de Cassation), reversing two lower courts, had declined to compel payment of a dividend demanded by the minority but opposed by the majority. It had not been proved, the Supreme Court said, that "the shareholder resolution in question had been taken contrary to the general interest of the corporation and with the sole intention to favor the members of the majority to the deteriment of the minority."[c] How is the Fruehauf case different?

(3)(a) After the decision by the Court of Appeal of Paris, the United States government took the position that since the parent corporation did not *control* Fruehauf-France (at least for the time being), Fruchauf-France was not a U.S. person for purpose of the regulations. Thus on the one hand it did not issue a license permitting the contract with Berliet to go forward, and on the other hand it did not seek to impose sanctions on Fruehauf-Detroit, though of course Detroit still *owned* 70 percent of the shares of Fruehauf-France. Is that just politics, or is there a legal lesson to be drawn from this outcome?

(b) An attempt—ultimately unsuccessful—was launched within the U.S. government to draw some lessons from the *Fruehauf* episode, which would enable the U.S. government to evaluate—or at least recognize—its own and other states' interests in situations where it was regulating on the basis of nationality (or the analogy of corporate parenthood), while State *B* was exercising jurisdiction on the basis of territoriality. If total abandonment by the United States of jurisdiction in these circumstances was not in the cards, could you develop some presumption or principles of preference to avoid collisions such as the one in *Fruehauf*?[d]

---

[b] This paragraph is adapted from Craig, *Application of the Trading with the Enemy Act to Foreign Corporations Owned by Americans: Reflections on Fruehauf v. Massardy,* 83 Harv. L. Rev. 579, 582 (1970).

[c] *Soc. Anciens Etabl. Picquarad et Durey-Sohy v. Schumann,* [1961] D. Jur. 661, [1961] J.C.P. II 12, 164 (Cass. Civ. Com.). For citations to the lower court decisions in this case and comments on the case, see Craig, note b, *supra*, at 582, notes 13–14.

[d] For more detailed treatment of the *Fruehauf* case, including its relation to prior programs of export controls and embargoes, see A. Lowenfeld, *Trade Controls for Political Ends,* pp. 90–105 (2d ed. 1983).

[B] The Siberia-Western Europe Pipeline

[1] Background[e]

The world's largest untapped proven reserves of natural gas—long known but not exploited—lay below the frozen tundra near Urengoy, where Western Siberia fronts on the Arctic Circle. In the early 1970's, discussions had been held between gas companies and the Soviet Union looking to a gigantic project to build a liquefaction plant at Murmansk, and to transport the liquefied gas in specially built cryogenic (i.e., super-refrigerated) tankers to the United States. That project had come to naught as detente lost appeal both in Washington and Moscow. In the late 1970's the Soviet Union revived the project, but sought its partners in Western Europe. The idea was to build a large-diameter pipeline from the Yamal peninsula on the Arctic Circle to a place in West Germany, from which smaller pipelines would feed the gas to utilities in Holland, Belgium, France, Austria and Italy, as well as West Germany. The Western European countries would lend the Soviets some $10–15 billion to cover all the external costs of construction of the pipeline, with the understanding that the pipe, compressor stations, and pipelaying equipment would be procured as far as possible in the states making the loans; the Soviet Union would commit itself to sell and deliver stated quantities of natural gas to Western Europe, and to repay the loans out of the proceeds of these sales. For the West European states, the pipeline project was seen as a way to reduce their dependence on the unstable Middle East for their energy supplies, and also as a way to employ unemployed steel workers in productive tasks.

By fall 1981 most of the arrangements for the pipeline had been completed, and construction of components was proceeding. Because the United States, which had recently completed the trans-Alaska pipeline, had certain technical capabilities difficult to duplicate in Western Europe, several companies in France, Great Britain, Italy, West Germany, and the Netherlands that had contracted with the Soviet Union to build portions of the pipeline had contracts to purchase components, equipment, or technology for the pipeline from U.S. companies, such as General Electric, Caterpillar Tractor, and others. Also, a number of European subsidiaries of U.S. companies were engaged in pieces of the immense project. The U.S. government, both under President Carter and under President Reagan, was opposed to the project, believing that Western Europe might become too dependent on the Soviet Union, and also that the loans to the U.S.S.R. for the project represented an unwarranted subsidy to that country. However, until the events described below, no legal impediments were placed in the way of American firms supplying goods or technology for use in the pipeline project.

Even as the pipeline project was occupying the leaders of the Western Europe, another development was in progress in Poland, with potentially more far-reaching consequences for all of Eastern Europe. In Poland a labor union at a shipyard in Gdansk (formerly Danzig) had gone on strike in August 1980 and had seized the shipyard. Within a few days the strike had spread—first to some 120,000 workers in northern Poland, then to 200,000 coal miners in Silesia, and eventually throughout the nation. A new popular leader, Lech Walesa, had emerged from the shipyards, and a new movement was born, *Solidarity*.

The story of Solidarity is beyond the scope of these pages. Suffice it to say that first one and then a second First Secretary of the United Workers [Communist] Party resigned, Solidarity

---

[e] Abridged from A. Lowenfeld, *Trade Controls for Political Ends,* pp. 268–270, 273–76 (2d ed. 1983).

reached a membership of close to 10 million persons, a related movement, Rural Solidarity, arose among Poland's farmers, and even the Communist Party's central committee held free elections by secret ballot, with the result that only one tenth of the membership was re-elected. All the world—East and West—was watching in fascination to see whether Poland could really become something like a free country.

For sixteen months freedom in Poland seemed to grow day by day. At midnight, Saturday, December 12, 1981, however, everything changed. Warsaw was ringed by tanks, soldiers manned check-points on all major roads, guards stood outside major buildings, bayonets fixed. At 6 a.m. Sunday, December 13, martial law and a national emergency were proclaimed. All public gatherings were forbidden, Solidarity's leaders were arrested, telephone lines were cut, and a total news blackout was imposed. The tanks and soldiers running Poland were Polish, not Russian; in Washington, however, the perception was that the Soviet Union must be behind the crackdown.

[2] A Clash of Wills

In Western Europe, the political leaders deplored the situation in Poland, but (with minor exceptions) imposed no sanctions. President Reagan, in contrast, responded to martial law in Poland by saying, "We're not going to let them get away with it."[f] Within two weeks, he put in place a program of export controls as well as related economic sanctions, both against Poland and against the Soviet Union. The most important sanction concerned the Pipeline: all exports from the United States designed to be used for the pipeline, regardless of country of destination or level of technology, would henceforth require a license, and no licenses would be issued. As with other export controls, penalties for violation would include denial of "export privileges," i.e., a firm found by the Department of Commerce to have violated the controls would be prohibited from engaging in any export transaction (or in export transactions specified in the denial order) for such period as the Department prescribed. A denial order could apply to a firm anywhere in the world, and any person that knowingly engaged in a transaction with a person on the denial list risked being placed on the list itself.[g]

The announcement of this sanction brought about some grumbling, especially from firms in Great Britain, West Germany, France, and Italy that were contractually obligated to deliver compressors to the Soviet Union that contained components built in the United States. As for the governments of Western Europe, there were complaints about lack of consultation in the alliance, and about lack of consistency in American policy,[h] but no vehement protests, and no assertions that the United States had transgressed any legal standards. It seemed understood that as a matter of international law, the United States had the right to control exports of products made in the United States.

By spring of 1982, it had become clear that efforts by the United States government to persuade the countries of Western Europe to adopt a comparable program of sanctions had failed. On the

---

[f] President Reagan's News Conference of December 17, 1981, 17 Weekly Comp. Pres. Docs. 1379, 1381 (Dec. 21, 1979).

[g] See Export Administration Act of 1979, 50 U.S.C. App. § 2371 et seq. For more precise and detailed summaries, see, e.g., A. Lowenfeld, *Trade Controls for Political Ends* Ch. I–II, (2d ed. 1983); Berman & Garson, *United States Export Controls—Past, Present, and Future,* 67 Colum. L. Rev. 791 (1969).

[h] This charge stemmed from the repeal by the Reagan Administration of the grain embargo imposed by President Carter after the Soviet Union invaded Afghanistan in 1979.

other hand, there was no sign that the situation in Poland was improving. In June, 1982, following an Economic Summit in Versailles, President Reagan tightened the screws:

> I have reviewed the sanctions on the export of oil and gas equipment to the Soviet Union imposed on December 30, 1981, and have decided to extend these sanctions through adoption of new regulations to include equipment produced by subsidiaries of U.S. companies abroad, as well as equipment produced abroad under licenses issued by U.S. companies.
>
> . . . .
>
> The decision taken today will, we believe, advance our objective of reconciliation in Poland.[i]

Thus (1) the assertion of jurisdiction that produced the *Fruehauf* case would be repeated, but on a far wider scale; and (2) a new basis of jurisdiction would be asserted, based on the link of technology licenses previously issued by American firms to firms in Europe.

The reaction in Europe was quick, and all negative. The Foreign Ministers of the European Community met within a few days, and declared:

> This action, taken without consultation with the Community, implies an extraterritorial extension of U.S. jurisdiction, which in the circumstances, is contrary to international law.[j]

More than that, the governments of Great Britain, France, and West Germany not only denounced the decision, but ordered companies organized in their territories (both locally owned and subsidiaries of American firms) to carry out their contractual obligations with respect to the pipeline, notwithstanding the U.S. ban. For its part, the U.S. Department of Commerce proceeded to secure "temporary denial orders" against six European companies that were continuing to supply the pipeline. Arguments about deference or comity seemed to be succeeding neither in Europe nor in America. As for the alliance, the French foreign minister told a television interviewer, "We no longer speak the same language."[k]

FURTHER NOTES AND QUESTIONS

(1)(a) In *Fruehauf,* only one company and one country were involved, and as we saw the corporation itself had a minority shareholder. In *Pipeline,* all the countries of the European Community were involved, not initially as antagonists of the United States but, as they viewed it, as victims of an American response to events in Eastern Europe which they did not agree with. Put in legal terms, the Europeans saw the United States applying its law to persons and activities that should have been governed by the laws of France, England, Italy, etc. How should the United States respond?

(b) Part of the problem of the U.S. action was that the jurisdictional links were perceived to be inadequate. Had the United States purported only to regulate activities of U.S. individual citizens, for example, or of branches (as contrasted to subsidiaries) of U.S. companies, the reaction would certainly have been less intense. And even the effort to regulate activities of subsidiaries

---

[i] Statement of the President on Extension of U.S. Sanctions, June 18, 1982, 18 Weekly Comp. Pres. Doc. 820 (June 21, 1982).

[j] Statement of the Foreign Ministers of the European Community, June 23, 1982, *New York Times,* June 24, 1982, p. 1, col. 5.

[k] *New York Times,* July 23, 1982, p. 1, col. 6.

of U.S. companies might have been less provocative than the link of contractual arrangements with U.S. firms, which was both unprecedented and retroactive, in that it placed restraints on the execution of contracts previously (and lawfully) made. Thus on two counts the exercise of jurisdiction by the United States did not correspond to justified expectations or to the traditions of the international legal system.

(c) Look back to the other factors listed in § 403 of the *Restatement of Foreign Relations Law*.[l] Can the June 1982 regulations pass muster under any of the factors? If not, does that suggest that the factors are wrong? Or that the U.S. action was unreasonable? . . . And therefore unlawful?

(2)(a) Dresser (France), S.A. among others, applied to the U.S. District Court in Washington, D.C. for an order restraining the Department of Commerce from imposing sanctions against it if it obeyed the order of the French government. Should this application be granted?

(b) The District Court, in a series of orders, postponed decision on the merits, on the ground that Dresser (France), a wholly-owned subsidiary of Dresser Industries, a U.S. company, had not exhausted its administrative remedies, and that it would not favor Dresser's private interests against the strong public (i.e., foreign policy) interests of the United States.[m] In the proceedings in the Commerce Department, Dresser lost at each step; on review of the decision of the Hearing Examiner, the Assistant Secretary of Commerce for Trade Administration ruled

> Appellant has failed to establish that the issuance of the [Temporary Denial Order] was not in compliance with the pertinent regulations [of the Department], that the December and June regulations were not in compliance with the Export Administration Act under which they were issued, or that the implementation of the regulations in this case . . . was in violation of the Due Process clause of the Fifth Amendment. Thus the appeal of Dresser-France and Dresser Industries from the . . . initial decision of the Hearing Commissioner . . . is denied.[n]

As to the contention that the June regulations were contrary to international law, the Assistant Secretary wrote, "such a challenge is not within the purview of my jurisdiction."[o] A court would presumably not make the last statement. But should it (can it) override the President on an issue of this kind? In other words, if the Assistant Secretary is right that the regulations authorize the sanctions and the Act authorizes the regulations, is the application of U.S. law nevertheless subject to restraints of international law?

(c) Dresser argued forcefully in Washington that it should be excused from compliance with the U.S. regulation by the defense of foreign government compulsion. If that argument has merit in Washington, why should it not be equally persuasive in France, in resisting the order of the French government to continue to manufacture and deliver equipment for the Pipeline?

(d) The Netherlands subsidiary of a U.S.-based company had a contract with a French company to supply geological sensing equipment to be used in construction of the Pipeline. On orders

---

[l] See pp. 959, *supra*.

[m] Several decisions were issued by the District Court to this effect, only one of which was published, *Dresser Industries, Inc. v. Baldrige*, 549 F. Supp. 108 (D. D.C. 1982). For excerpts from the related decisions, see Lowenfeld, note g, *supra*, p. 298–300.

[n] Dresser (France) S.A., *Decision and Orders of Asst. Secy. for Trade Administration of Nov. 1, 1982*, 47 Fed. Reg. 51463 (Nov. 15, 1982).

[o] *Id.* at 51467.

from the parent company, the Netherlands subsidiary notified its French customer that it would be unable to perform its obligations under the contract. The French company brought suit in the Netherlands seeking performance of the contract. How should this action be decided?[p]

(3) In the fall of 1982, the United States position on the Pipeline sanctions became increasingly untenable. Not only, as we saw, was the controversy over the U.S. actions diverting attention away from the repression in Poland, and creating a persistent and highly visible irritant in relations between the United States and Western Europe, but the American business community was chafing under the restraints, seeing contracts lost and long-term business relationships threatened. The House Foreign Affairs Committee approved a bill to terminate the controls,[q] and the bill failed on the floor of the House of Representatives by only three votes, 206–203.[r] Secretary of State Shultz, who came into office just after the June regulations were issued, looked for a formula to rescind the controls, and by November 1982, he had found one. The Western allies, it was announced, had agreed on a joint program to control high technology exports to the Soviet Union, and a new study was being undertaken of energy alternatives for the West. In return, the United States would revoke the pipeline regulations, and rescind the denial orders that had been issued to firms that had violated the regulations in the period June–November 1982.[s]

Held . . . ?

(4) A detailed examination of U.S. trade controls is not only beyond the scope of this volume, but would call for exploration of history, politics, economics, and technology. The suggestion, however, is that a significant ingredient in such an exploration would be conflict of laws.

(a) Do the *Fruehauf* and *Pipeline* cases, taken together, not represent a contribution to conflict of laws, an illustration of true conflicts of true state interests?

(b) Is it possible to draw on the techniques of conflict of laws to resolve such conflicts, or to prevent them from happening?

§ 10.06 The Act of State Doctrine

Sections 10.03–10.05, have dealt in various configurations with the applications by State *A* of its law to activities with some links to *A* but arguably greater links to some other state. In this final section the pattern is reversed. It is State *B* that has taken some action within its own territory, and there is no doubt about *B*'s jurisdiction. The issue here is whether *B*'s action is subject to external legal restraints, and whether *B*'s compliance or non-compliance with those restraints may be reviewed in the courts of *A*.

---

[p] The District Court in The Hague gave judgment for plaintiff, ordering delivery of the equipment contracted for by a stated date, on penalty of 10,000 guilder fine per day of default after that date. The court held that the contract was valid and that the United States had no jurisdiction over either the contract or the company organized under Netherlands law. *Compagnie Européenne des Petroles, S.A. v. Sensor Nederland, B.V.,* Dist. Ct. The Hague, Sept. 17, 1982, 36 Rechtspraak van de Week-Kort Geding 167 (1982), reprinted in English in 22 Int'l Leg. Mat. 66 (1983).

[q] H.R. 6838, 97th Cong., 2d. Sess. (1982).

[r] 128 Cong. Rec. H 7929 (Daily Ed. Sept. 29, 1982). For a description of the legislative maneuvers designed to put pressure on the President without embarrassing him too much, see 40 Congressional Quarterly 2467 (Oct. 2, 1982).

[s] See *New York Times,* Nov. 14, 1982, p. 1, col. 6, Radio Address of President Reagan of Nov. 13, 1982, 18 Weekly Comp. Pres. Docs. 1475 (1982). The formal orders revoking the regulations appear in 47 Fed. Reg. 51858 (Nov. 18, 1982) and the orders rescinding sanctions against the individual companies such as Dresser appear in 47 Fed. Reg. 52489–91 (Nov. 22, 1982).

One way to look at these cases—though by no means the only way—to ask (i) what law should be applied to the actions in question according to the conflict of laws rules of the forum; and (ii) whether there is a persuasive reason to depart from those rules. What the act of state doctrine does is to say that if the answer to (i) points to State *B* and the action was taken by the government of *B* in its sovereign capacity, question (ii) may not be asked. Critics of the doctrine agree with step (i), but see no reason (absent overriding considerations of foreign relations) to depart from step (ii), and indeed look to a step (iii) to enunciate the international law standard which they say should be applied to the acts of State *B*.

BANCO NACIONAL DE CUBA v. SABBATINO

United States Supreme Court
376 U.S. 398 (1964)

Mr. Justice Harlan delivered the opinion of the Court.

The question which brought this case here, and is now found to be the dispositive issue, is whether the so-called act of state doctrine serves to sustain petitioner's claims in this litigation. Such claims are ultimately founded on a decree of the Government of Cuba expropriating certain property, the right to the proceeds of which is here in controversy. The act of state doctrine in its traditional formulation precludes the courts of this country from inquiring into the validity of the public acts a recognized foreign sovereign power committed within its own territory.

I.

In February and July of 1960, respondent Farr, Whitlock & Co., an American commodity broker, contracted to purchase Cuban sugar, free alongside the steamer, from a wholly owned subsidiary of Compania Azucarera Vertientes-Camaguey de Cuba (C. A. V.), a corporation organized under Cuban law whose capital stock was owned principally by United States residents. Farr, Whitlock agreed to pay for the sugar in New York upon presentation of the shipping documents and a sight draft.

On July 6, 1960, the Congress of the United States amended the Sugar Act of 1948 to permit a presidentially directed reduction of the sugar quota for Cuba. On the same day President Eisenhower exercised the granted power. The day of the congressional enactment, the Cuban Council of Ministers adopted "Law No. 851," which characterized this reduction in the Cuban sugar quota as an act of "aggression, for political purposes" on the part of the United States, justifying the taking of countermeasures by Cuba. The law gave the Cuban President and Prime Minister discretionary power to nationalize by forced expropriation property or enterprises in which American nationals had an interest. Although a system of compensation was formally provided, the possibility of payment under it may well be deemed illusory. Our State Department has described the Cuban law as "manifestly in violation of those principles of international law which have long been accepted by the free countries of the West. It is in its essence discriminatory, arbitrary and confiscatory."

Between August 6 and August 9, 1960, the sugar covered by the contract between Farr, Whitlock and C. A. V.[6] was loaded, destined for Morocco, onto the S. S. *Hornfels,* which was

---

[6] The parties have treated the interest of the wholly owned subsidiary as if it were identical with that of C. A. V.; hence no distinction between the two companies will be drawn in the remainder of this opinion.

standing offshore at the Cuban port of Jucaro (Santa Maria). On the day loading commenced, the Cuban President and Prime Minister, acting pursuant to Law No. 851, issued Executive Power Resolution No. 1. It provided for the compulsory expropriation of all property and enterprises, and of rights and interests arising therefrom, of certain listed companies, including C. A. V., wholly or principally owned by American nationals. The preamble reiterated the alleged injustice of the American reduction of the Cuban sugar quota and emphasized the importance of Cuba's serving as an example for other countries to follow "in their struggle to free themselves from the brutal claws of Imperialism." In consequence of the resolution, the consent of the Cuban Government was necessary before a ship carrying sugar of a named company could leave Cuban waters. In order to obtain this consent, Farr, Whitlock, on August 11, entered into contracts, identical to those it had made with C. A. V., with the Banco Para el Comercio Exterior de Cuba, an instrumentality of the Cuban Government. The S. S. *Hornfels* sailed for Morocco on August 12.

Banco Exterior assigned the bills of lading to petitioner, also an instrumentality of the Cuban Government, which instructed its agent in New York, Societe Generale, to deliver the bills and a sight draft in the sum of $175,250.69 to Farr, Whitlock in return for payment. Societe Generale's initial tender of the documents was refused by Farr, Whitlock, which on the same day was notified of C. A. V.'s claim that as rightful owner of the sugar it was entitled to the proceeds. In return for a promise not to turn the funds over to petitioner or its agent, C. A. V. agreed to indemnify Farr, Whitlock for any loss.[8] Farr, Whitlock subsequently accepted the shipping documents, negotiated the bills of lading to its customer, and received payment for the sugar. It refused, however, to hand over the proceeds to Societe Generale. Shortly thereafter, Farr, Whitlock was served with an order of the New York Supreme Court, which had appointed Sabbatino as Temporary Receiver of C. A. V.'s New York assets, enjoining it from taking any action in regard to the money claimed by C. A. V. that might result in its removal from the State. Following this, Farr, Whitlock, pursuant to court order, transferred the funds to Sabbatino, to abide the event of a judicial determination as to their ownership.

Petitioner then instituted this action in the Federal District Court for the Southern District of New York. Alleging conversion of the bills of lading, it sought to recover the proceeds thereof from Farr, Whitlock and to enjoin the receiver from exercising any dominion over such proceeds. Upon motions to dismiss and for summary judgment, the District Court, 193 F. Supp. 375, sustained federal *in personam* jurisdiction despite state control of the funds. It found that the sugar was located within Cuban territory at the time of expropriation and determined that under merchant law common to civilized countries Farr, Whitlock could not have asserted ownership of the sugar against C. A. V. before making payment. It concluded that C. A. V. had a property interest in the sugar subject to the territorial jurisdiction of Cuba. The court then dealt with the question of Cuba's title to the sugar, on which rested petitioner's claim of conversion. While acknowledging the continuing vitality of the act of state doctrine, the court believed it inapplicable when the questioned foreign act is in violation of international law. Proceeding on the basis that a taking invalid under international law does not convey good title, the District Court found the Cuban expropriation decree to violate such law in three separate respects: it was motivated by a retaliatory and not a public purpose; it discriminated against American nationals; and it failed to provide adequate compensation. Summary judgment against petitioner was accordingly granted.

---

[8] C. A. V. also agreed to pay Farr, Whitlock 10% of the $175,000 if C. A. V. ever obtained that sum. 307 F. 2d, at 851.

The Court of Appeals, 307 F. 2d 845, affirming the decision on similar grounds, relied on two letters (not before the District Court) written by State Department officers which it took as evidence that the Executive Branch had no objection to a judicial testing of the Cuban decree's validity. The court was unwilling to declare that any one of the infirmities found by the District Court rendered the taking invalid under international law, but was satisfied that in combination they had that effect. We granted certiorari because the issues involved bear importantly on the conduct of the country's foreign relations and more particularly on the proper role of the Judicial Branch in this sensitive area. 372 U. S. 905. For reasons to follow we decide that the judgment below must be reversed.

Before considering the holding below with respect to the act of state doctrine, we must deal with narrower grounds urged for dismissal of the action or for a judgment on the merits in favor of respondents.

II.

It is first contended that this petitioner, an instrumentality of the Cuban Government, should be denied access to American courts because Cuba is an unfriendly power and does not permit nationals of this country to obtain relief in its courts.

Under principles of comity governing this country's relations with other nations, sovereign states are allowed to sue in the courts of the United States. . . .

Respondents, pointing to the severance of diplomatic relations, commercial embargo, and freezing of Cuban assets in this country, contend that relations between the United States and Cuba manifest such animosity that unfriendliness is clear, and that the courts should be closed to the Cuban Government. We do not agree. This Court would hardly be competent to undertake assessments of varying degrees of friendliness or its absence, and, lacking some definite touchstone for determination, we are constrained to consider any relationship, short of war, with a recognized sovereign power as embracing the privilege of resorting to United States courts. . . .

. . .

Respondents further urge that reciprocity of treatment is an essential ingredient of comity generally, and, therefore, of the privilege of foreign states to bring suit here. Although *Hilton v. Guyot*, [p. 684, *supra*] contains some broad language about the relationship of reciprocity to comity, the case in fact imposed a requirement of reciprocity only in regard to conclusiveness of judgments, and even then only in limited circumstances. . . .

There are good reasons for declining to extend the principle to the question of standing of sovereign states to sue. Whether a foreign sovereign will be permitted to sue involves a problem more sensitive politically than whether the judgments of its courts may be re-examined, and the possibility of embarrassment to the Executive Branch in handling foreign relations is substantially more acute. . . .

. . .

We hold that this petitioner is not barred from access to the federal courts.

III.

Respondents claimed in the lower courts that Cuba had expropriated merely contractual rights the situs of which was in New York, and that the propriety of the taking was, therefore, governed by New York law. The District Court rejected this contention on the basis of the right of ownership possessed by C. A. V. against Farr, Whitlock prior to payment for the sugar. That the sugar itself was expropriated rather than a contractual claim is further supported by Cuba's refusal to let the S. S. *Hornfels* sail until a new contract had been signed. Had the Cuban decree represented only an attempt to expropriate a contractual right of C. A. V., the forced delay of shipment and Farr, Whitlock's subsequent contract with petitioner's assignor would have been meaningless. Neither the District Court's finding concerning the location of the S. S. *Hornfels* nor its conclusion that Cuba had territorial jurisdiction to expropriate the sugar, acquiesced in by the Court of Appeals, is seriously challenged here. Respondents' limited view of the expropriation must be rejected.

Respondents further contend that if the expropriation was of the sugar itself, this suit then becomes one to enforce the public law of a foreign state and as such is not cognizable in the courts of this country. They rely on the principle enunciated in federal and state cases that a court need not give effect to the penal or revenue laws of foreign countries or sister states.

The extent to which this doctrine may apply to other kinds of public laws, though perhaps still an open question, need not be decided in this case. For we have been referred to no authority which suggests that the doctrine reaches a public law which, as here, has been fully executed within the foreign state. Cuba's restraint of the S. S. *Hornfels* must be regarded for these purposes to have constituted an effective taking of the sugar, vesting in Cuba C. A. V.'s property right in it. Farr, Whitlock's contract with the Cuban bank, however compelled to sign Farr, Whitlock may have felt, represented indeed a recognition of Cuba's dominion over the property.

In these circumstances the question whether the rights acquired by Cuba are enforceable in our courts depends not upon the doctrine here invoked but upon the act of state doctrine discussed in the succeeding sections of this opinion.

IV.

The classic American statement of the act of state doctrine, which appears to have taken root in England as early as 1674, *Blad v. Bamfield,* 3 Swans. 604, 36 Eng. Rep. 992, and began to emerge in the jurisprudence of this country in the late eighteenth and early nineteenth centuries is found in *Underhill v. Hernandez,* 168 U. S. 250, where Chief Justice Fuller said for a unanimous Court (p. 252):

> Every sovereign State is bound to respect the independence of every other sovereign State, and the courts of one country will not sit in judgment on the acts of the government of another done within its own territory. Redress of grievances by reason of such acts must be obtained through the means open to be availed of by sovereign powers as between themselves.

Following this precept the Court in that case refused to inquire into acts of Hernandez, a revolutionary Venezuelan military commander whose government had been later recognized by the United States, which were made the basis of a damage action in this country by Underhill, an American citizen, who claimed that he had been unlawfully assaulted, coerced, and detained in Venezuela by Hernandez.

None of this Court's subsequent cases in which the act of state doctrine was directly or peripherally involved manifest any retreat from *Underhill.* See *American Banana Co. v. United Fruit Co.,* 213 U. S. 347; *Oetjen v. Central Leather Co.,* 246 U. S. 297; *Ricaud v. American*

Metal Co., 246 U. S. 304; *Shapleigh v. Mier*, 299 U. S. 468; *United States v. Belmont*, 301 U. S. 324; *United States v. Pink*, 315 U. S. 203. On the contrary in two of these cases, *Oetjen* and *Ricaud*, the doctrine as announced in *Underhill* was reaffirmed in unequivocal terms.

. . .

In deciding the present case the Court of Appeals relied in part upon an exception to the unqualified teachings of *Underhill, Oetjen,* and *Ricaud* which that court had earlier indicated.

[The Court describes the so-called *Bernstein* exception, according to which the act of state doctrine does not apply if the executive branch advises the court that it has no objection to adjudication of the claim. Whatever the merits of the exception, the Court holds that it is not applicable in the present case, because the State Department said only that it did not wish to make any statement on the litigation.]

The outcome of this case, therefore, turns upon whether any of the contentions urged by respondents against the application of the act of state doctrine in the premises is acceptable: (1) that the doctrine does not apply to acts of state which violate international law, as is claimed to be the case here; (2) that the doctrine is inapplicable unless the Executive specifically interposes it in a particular case; and (3) that, in any event, the doctrine may not be invoked by a foreign government plaintiff in our courts.

V.

Preliminarily, we discuss the foundations on which we deem the act of state doctrine to rest, and more particularly the question of whether state or federal law governs its application in a federal diversity case.[20]

We do not believe that this doctrine is compelled either by the inherent nature of sovereign authority, as some of the earlier decisions seem to imply, or by some principle of international law. If a transaction takes place in one jurisdiction and the forum is in another, the forum does not by dismissing an action or by applying its own law purport to divest the first jurisdiction of its territorial sovereignty; it merely declines to adjudicate or makes applicable its own law to parties or property before it. The refusal of one country to enforce the penal laws of another is a typical example of an instance when a court will not entertain a cause of action arising in another jurisdiction. While historic notions of sovereign authority do bear upon the wisdom of employing the act of state doctrine, they do not dictate its existence.

That international law does not require application of the doctrine is evidenced by the practice of nations. Most of the countries rendering decisions on the subject fail to follow the rule rigidly. No international arbitral or judicial decision discovered suggests that international law prescribes recognition of sovereign acts of foreign governments, see 1 Oppenheim's *International Law,* § 115aa (Lauterpacht, 8th ed. 1955), and apparently no claim has ever been raised before an international tribunal that failure to apply the act of state doctrine constitutes a breach of international obligation. If international law does not prescribe use of the doctrine, neither does it forbid application of the rule even if it is claimed that the act of state in question violated international law. The traditional view of international law is that it establishes substantive principles for determining whether one country has wronged another. Because of its peculiar

---

[20] Although the complaint in this case alleged both diversity and federal question jurisdiction, the Court of Appeals reached jurisdiction only on the former ground, 307 F. 2d, at 852. We need not decide, for reasons appearing hereafter, whether federal question jurisdiction also existed.

nation-to-nation character the usual method for an individual to seek relief is to exhaust local remedies and then repair to the executive authorities of his own state to persuade them to champion his claim in diplomacy or before an international tribunal.

Despite the broad statement in *Oetjen* that "The conduct of the foreign relations of our Government is committed by the Constitution to the Executive and Legislative . . . Departments," 246 U. S., at 302, it cannot of course be thought that "every case or controversy which touches foreign relations lies beyond judicial cognizance." *Baker v. Carr,* 369 U. S. 186, 211. The text of the Constitution does not require the act of state doctrine; it does not irrevocably remove from the judiciary the capacity to review the validity of foreign acts of state.

The act of state doctrine does, however, have "constitutional" underpinnings. It arises out of the basic relationships between branches of government in a system of separation of powers. It concerns the competency of dissimilar institutions to make and implement particular kinds of decisions in the area of international relations. The doctrine as formulated in past decisions expresses the strong sense of the Judicial Branch that its engagement in the task of passing on the validity of foreign acts of state may hinder rather than further this country's pursuit of goals both for itself and for the community of nations as a whole in the international sphere. Many commentators disagree with this view; they have striven by means of distinguishing and limiting past decisions and by advancing various considerations of policy to stimulate a narrowing of the apparent scope of the rule. Whatever considerations are thought to predominate, it is plain that the problems involved are uniquely federal in nature. If federal authority, in this instance this Court, orders the field of judicial competence in this area for the federal courts, and the state courts are left free to formulate their own rules, the purposes behind the doctrine could be as effectively undermined as if there had been no federal pronouncement on the subject.

We could perhaps in this diversity action avoid the question of deciding whether federal or state law is applicable to this aspect of the litigation. New York has enunciated the act of state doctrine in terms that echo those of federal decisions decided during the reign of *Swift v. Tyson,* 16 Pet. 1.

. . .

However, we are constrained to make it clear that an issue concerned with a basic choice regarding the competence and function of the Judiciary and the National Executive in ordering our relationships with other members of the international community must be treated exclusively as an aspect of federal law.[23] It seems fair to assume that the Court did not have rules like the act of state doctrine in mind when it decided *Erie R. Co. v. Tompkins.* Soon thereafter, Professor Philip C. Jessup, now a judge of the International Court of Justice, recognized the potential dangers were *Erie* extended to legal problems affecting international relations.[24] He cautioned that rules of international law should not be left to divergent and perhaps parochial state interpretations. His basic rationale is equally applicable to the act of state doctrine.

. . .

We conclude that the scope of the act of state doctrine must be determined according to federal law.

---

[23] At least this is true when the Court limits the scope of judicial inquiry. We need not now consider whether a state court might, in certain circumstances, adhere to a more restrictive view concerning the scope of examination of foreign acts than that required by this Court.

[24] *The Doctrine of Erie Railroad v. Tompkins Applied to International Law,* 33 Am. J. Int'l L. 740 (1939).

VI.

If the act of state doctrine is a principle of decision binding on federal and state courts alike but compelled by neither international law nor the Constitution, its continuing vitality depends on its capacity to reflect the proper distribution of functions between the judicial and political branches of the Government on matters bearing upon foreign affairs. It should be apparent that the greater the degree of codification or consensus concerning a particular area of international law, the more appropriate it is for the judiciary to render decisions regarding it, since the courts can then focus on the application of an agreed principle to circumstances of fact rather than on the sensitive task of establishing a principle not inconsistent with the national interest or with international justice. It is also evident that some aspects of international law touch much more sharply on national nerves than do others; the less important the implications of an issue are for our foreign relations, the weaker the justification for exclusivity in the political branches. The balance of relevant considerations may also be shifted if the government which perpetrated the challenged act of state is no longer in existence, as in the *Bernstein* case, for the political interest of this country may, as a result, be measurably altered. Therefore, rather than laying down or reaffirming an inflexible and all-encompassing rule in this case, we decide only that the Judicial Branch will not examine the validity of a taking of property within its own territory by a foreign sovereign government, extant and recognized by this country at the time of suit, in the absence of a treaty or other unambiguous agreement regarding controlling legal principles, even if the complaint alleges that the taking violates customary international law.

There are few if any issues in international law today on which opinion seems to be so divided as the limitations on a state's power to expropriate the property of aliens. There is, of course, authority, in international judicial and arbitral decisions, in the expressions of national governments, and among commentators for the view that a taking is improper under international law if it is not for a public purpose, is discriminatory, or is without provision for prompt, adequate, and effective compensation. However, Communist countries, although they have in fact provided a degree of compensation after diplomatic efforts, commonly recognize no obligation on the part of the taking country. Certain representatives of the newly independent and underdeveloped countries have questioned whether rules of state responsibility toward aliens can bind nations that have not consented to them and it is argued that the traditionally articulated standards governing expropriation of property reflect "imperialist" interests and are inappropriate to the circumstances of emergent states.

The disagreement as to relevant international law standards reflects an even more basic divergence between the national interests of capital importing and capital exporting nations and between the social ideologies of those countries that favor state control of a considerable portion of the means of production and those that adhere to a free enterprise system. It is difficult to imagine the courts of this country embarking on adjudication in an area which touches more sensitively the practical and ideological goals of the various members of the community of nations.[34]

When we consider the prospect of the courts characterizing foreign expropriations, however justifiably, as invalid under international law and ineffective to pass title, the wisdom of the

---

[34] There are, of course, areas of international law in which consensus as to standards is greater and which do not represent a battleground for conflicting ideologies. This decision in no way intimates that the courts of this country are broadly foreclosed from considering questions of international law.

precedents is confirmed. While each of the leading cases in this Court may be argued to be distinguishable on its facts from this one—*Underhill* because sovereign immunity provided an independent ground and *Oetjen, Ricaud,* and *Shapleigh* because there was actually no violation of international law—the plain implication of all these opinions, and the import of express statements in *Oetjen,* 246 U. S., at 304, and *Shapleigh,* 299 U. S., at 471, is that the act of state doctrine is applicable even if international law has been violated. . . .

The possible adverse consequences of a conclusion to the contrary of that implicit in these cases is highlighted by contrasting the practices of the political branch with the limitations of the judicial process in matters of this kind. Following an expropriation of any significance, the Executive engages in diplomacy aimed to assure that United States citizens who are harmed are compensated fairly. Representing all claimants of this country, it will often be able, either by bilateral or multilateral talks, by submission to the United Nations, or by the employment of economic and political sanctions, to achieve some degree of general redress. Judicial determinations of invalidity of title can, on the other hand, have only an occasional impact, since they depend on the fortuitous circumstance of the property in question being brought into this country. Such decisions would, if the acts involved were declared invalid, often be likely to give offense to the expropriating country; since the concept of territorial sovereignty is so deep seated, any state may resent the refusal of the courts of another sovereign to accord validity to acts within its territorial borders. Piecemeal dispositions of this sort involving the probability of affront to another state could seriously interfere with negotiations being carried on by the Executive Branch and might prevent or render less favorable the terms of an agreement that could otherwise be reached. Relations with third countries which have engaged in similar expropriations would not be immune from effect.

The dangers of such adjudication are present regardless of whether the State Department has, as it did in this case, asserted that the relevant act violated international law. If the Executive Branch has undertaken negotiations with an expropriating country, but has refrained from claims of violation of the law of nations, a determination to that effect by a court might be regarded as a serious insult, while a finding of compliance with international law would greatly strengthen the bargaining hand of the other state with consequent detriment to American interests.

Even if the State Department has proclaimed the impropriety of the expropriation, the stamp of approval of its view by a judicial tribunal, however impartial, might increase any affront and the judicial decision might occur at a time, almost always well after the taking, when such an impact would be contrary to our national interest. Considerably more serious and far-reaching consequences would flow from a judicial finding that international law standards had been met if that determination flew in the face of a State Department proclamation to the contrary. When articulating principles of international law in its relations with other states, the Executive Branch speaks not only as an interpreter of generally accepted and traditional rules, as would the courts, but also as an advocate of standards it believes desirable for the community of nations and protective of national concerns. In short, whatever way the matter is cut, the possibility of conflict between the Judicial and Executive Branches could hardly be avoided.

Respondents contend that, even if there is not agreement regarding general standards for determining the validity of expropriations, the alleged combination of retaliation, discrimination, and inadequate compensation makes it patently clear that this particular expropriation was in violation of international law.[37] If this view is accurate, it would still be unwise for the courts so to determine. Such a decision now would require the drawing of more difficult lines in subsequent cases and these would involve the possibility of conflict with the Executive view. Even if the courts avoided this course, either by presuming the validity of an act of state whenever the international law standard was thought unclear or by following the State Department declaration in such a situation, the very expression of judicial uncertainty might provide embarrassment to the Executive Branch.

Another serious consequence of the exception pressed by respondents would be to render uncertain titles in foreign commerce, with the possible consequence of altering the flow of international trade.[38] If the attitude of the United States courts were unclear, one buying expropriated goods would not know if he could safely import them into this country. Even were takings known to be invalid, one would have difficulty determining after goods had changed hands several times whether the particular articles in question were the product of an ineffective state act.[39]

Against the force of such considerations, we find respondents' countervailing arguments quite unpersuasive. Their basic contention is that United States courts could make a significant contribution to the growth of international law, a contribution whose importance, it is said, would be magnified by the relative paucity of decisional law by international bodies. But given the fluidity of present world conditions, the effectiveness of such a patchwork approach toward the formulation of an acceptable body of law concerning state responsibility for expropriations is, to say the least, highly conjectural. Moreover, it rests upon the sanguine presupposition that the decisions of the courts of the world's major capital exporting country and principal exponent of the free enterprise system would be accepted as disinterested expressions of sound legal principle by those adhering to widely different ideologies.

It is contended that regardless of the fortuitous circumstances necessary for United States jurisdiction over a case involving a foreign act of state and the resultant isolated application to any expropriation program taken as a whole, it is the function of the courts to justly decide individual disputes before them. Perhaps the most typical act of state case involves the original owner or his assignee suing one not in association with the expropriating state who has had "title" transferred to him. But it is difficult to regard the claim of the original owner, who otherwise

---

[37] Of course, to assist respondents in this suit such a determination would have to include a decision that for the purpose of judging this expropriation under international law C. A. V. is not to be regarded as Cuban and an acceptance of the principle that international law provides other remedies for breaches of international standards of expropriation than suits for damages before international tribunals. See 307 F. 2d, at 861, 868 for discussion of these questions by the Court of Appeals.

[38] This possibility is consistent with the view that the deterrent effect of court invalidations would not ordinarily be great. If the expropriating country could find other buyers for its products at roughly the same price, the deterrent effect might be minimal although patterns of trade would be significantly changed.

[39] Were respondents' position adopted, the courts might be engaged in the difficult tasks of ascertaining the origin of fungible goods, of considering the effect of improvements made in a third country on expropriated raw materials, and of determining the title to commodities subsequently grown on expropriated land or produced with expropriated machinery.

By discouraging import to this country by traders certain or apprehensive of nonrecognition of ownership, judicial findings of invalidity of title might limit competition among sellers; if the excluded goods constituted a significant portion of the market, prices for United States purchasers might rise with a consequent economic burden on United States consumers. Balancing the undesirability of such a result against the likelihood of furthering other national concerns is plainly a function best left in the hands of the political branches.

may be recompensed through diplomatic channels, as more demanding of judicial cognizance than the claim of title by the innocent third party purchaser, who, if the property is taken from him, is without any remedy.

Respondents claim that the economic pressure resulting from the proposed exception to the act of state doctrine will materially add to the protection of United States investors. We are not convinced, even assuming the relevance of this contention. Expropriations take place for a variety of reasons, political and ideological as well as economic. When one considers the variety of means possessed by this country to make secure foreign investment, the persuasive or coercive effect of judicial invalidation of acts of expropriation dwindles in comparison. The newly independent states are in need of continuing foreign investment; the creation of a climate unfavorable to such investment by wholesale confiscations may well work to their long-run economic disadvantage. Foreign aid given to many of these countries provides a powerful lever in the hands of the political branches to ensure fair treatment of United States nationals. Ultimately the sanctions of economic embargo and the freezing of assets in this country may be employed. Any country willing to brave any or all of these consequences is unlikely to be deterred by sporadic judicial decisions directly affecting only property brought to our shores. If the political branches are unwilling to exercise their ample powers to effect compensation, this reflects a judgment of the national interest which the judiciary would be ill-advised to undermine indirectly.

It is suggested that if the act of state doctrine is applicable to violations of international law, it should only be so when the Executive Branch expressly stipulates that it does not wish the courts to pass on the question of validity. See Association of the Bar of the City of New York, Committee on International Law, *A Reconsideration of the Act of State Doctrine in United States Courts* (1959). We should be slow to reject the representations of the Government that such a reversal of the *Bernstein* principle would work serious inroads on the maximum effectiveness of United States diplomacy. Often the State Department will wish to refrain from taking an official position, particularly at a moment that would be dictated by the development of private litigation but might be inopportune diplomatically. Adverse domestic consequences might flow from an official stand which could be assuaged, if at all, only by revealing matters best kept secret. Of course, a relevant consideration for the State Department would be the position contemplated in the court to hear the case. It is highly questionable whether the examination of validity by the judiciary should depend on an educated guess by the Executive as to probable result and, at any rate, should a prediction be wrong, the Executive might be embarrassed in its dealings with other countries. We do not now pass on the *Bernstein* exception, but even if it were deemed valid, its suggested extension is unwarranted.

However offensive to the public policy of this country and its constituent States an expropriation of this kind may be, we conclude that both the national interest and progress toward the goal of establishing the rule of law among nations are best served by maintaining intact the act of state doctrine in this realm of its application.

VII.

Finally, we must determine whether Cuba's status as a plaintiff in this case dictates a result at variance with the conclusions reached above. If the Court were to distinguish between suits brought by sovereign states and those of assignees, the rule would have little effect unless a careful examination were made in each case to determine if the private party suing had taken property in good faith. Such an inquiry would be exceptionally difficult, since the relevant transaction would almost invariably have occurred outside our borders. If such an investigation were deemed irrelevant, a state could always assign its claim.

. . .

Certainly the distinction proposed would sanction self-help remedies, something hardly conducive to a peaceful international order. Had Farr, Whitlock not converted the bills of lading, or alternatively breached its contract, Cuba could have relied on the act of state doctrine in defense of a claim brought by C. A. V. for the proceeds. It would be anomalous to preclude reliance on the act of state doctrine because of Farr, Whitlock's unilateral action, however justified such action may have been under the circumstances.

Respondents offer another theory for treating the case differently because of Cuba's participation. It is claimed that the forum should simply apply its own law to all the relevant transactions. An analogy is drawn to the area of sovereign immunity, *National City Bank v. Republic of China,* 348 U. S. 356, in which, if a foreign country seeks redress in our courts, counterclaims are permissible. But immunity relates to the prerogative right not to have sovereign property subject to suit; fairness has been thought to require that when the sovereign seeks recovery, it be subject to legitimate counterclaims against it. The act of state doctrine, however, although it shares with the immunity doctrine a respect for sovereign states, concerns the limits for determining the validity of an otherwise applicable rule of law. It is plain that if a recognized government sued on a contract with a United States citizen, concededly legitimate by the locus of its making, performance, and most significant contacts, the forum would not apply its own substantive law of contracts. Since the act of state doctrine reflects the desirability of presuming the relevant transaction valid, the same result follows; the forum may not apply its local law regarding foreign expropriations.

Since the act of state doctrine proscribes a challenge to the validity of the Cuban expropriation decree in this case, any counterclaim based on asserted invalidity must fail. Whether a theory of conversion or breach of contract is the proper cause of action under New York law, the presumed validity of the expropriation is unaffected. Although we discern no remaining litigable issues of fact in this case, the District Court may hear and decide them if they develop.

The judgment of the Court of Appeals is reversed and the case is remanded to the District Court for proceedings consistent with this opinion.

MR. JUSTICE WHITE, dissenting.

I am dismayed that the Court has, with one broad stroke, declared the ascertainment and application to international law beyond the competence of the courts of the United States in a large and important category of cases. I am also disappointed in the Court's declaration that the acts of a sovereign state with regard to the property of aliens within its borders are beyond the reach of international law in the courts of this country. However clearly established that law may be, a sovereign may violate it with impunity, except insofar as the political branches of the government may provide a remedy. This backward-looking doctrine, never before declared in this Court, is carried a disconcerting step further: not only are the courts powerless to question acts of state proscribed by international law but they are likewise powerless to refuse to adjudicate the claim founded upon a foreign law; they must render judgment and thereby validate the lawless act. Since the Court expressly extends its ruling to all acts of state expropriating property, however clearly inconsistent with the international community, all discriminatory expropriations of the property of aliens, as for example the taking of properties of persons belonging to certain races, religions or nationalities, are entitled to automatic validation in the courts of the United States. No other civilized country has found such a rigid rule necessary for the survival of the executive branch of its government; the executive of no other government seems to require such insulation from international law adjudications in its courts; and no other judiciary is apparently so incompetent to ascertain and apply international law.

I do not believe that the act of state doctrine, as judicially fashioned in this Court, and the reasons underlying it, require American courts to decide cases in disregard of international law and of the rights of litigants to a full determination on the merits.

[JUSTICE WHITE'S 20-page dissent, in so far as here relevant, is summarized in Question 2, pp. 1001-02, *infra.*]

SOCIEDAD MINERA EL TENIENTE S.A. v. A.G. NORDDEUTSCHE AFFINERIE

District Court of Hamburg (January 23, 1973)
12 International Legal Materials 251 (1973)

FACTS

A. The petitioner submits claim in its character as split company of the former corporation under Chilean law, the SOCIEDAD MINERA EL TENIENTE S.A. (SMETSA). The defendant is a German copper-processing company with registered office in Hamburg.

A shipment of copper from Chile was judicially attached on its arrival in Germany at the behest of Kennecott Copper Corporation. The copper came from the El Teniente mine, owned until 1967 by Kennecott, and from 1967 to 1971 by Soc. Min. El Teniente, S.A., a joint venture of Kennecott and the state-owned Chilean Copper Corporation (CODELCO). Kennecott asserted that its interest had been lawfully expropriated by the Allende government, which took office in Chile in September 1970.[a]

The petitioner asks that the injunction issued by Decision of January 5, 1973, be maintained in force. . . .[b]

The defendant filed opposition against the Decision of January 5, 1973 pursuant to Sec. 924 of the Code of Civil Procedure; the CORPORATION DEL COBRE (CODELCO), Santiago de Chile, intervened the action on the side of the defendant. No objections to its intervention were made by the parties. Since CODELCO has credibly shown its legal interest in the dispute, its intervention is permissible.

B. The dispute is based on the following facts:

In 1904 "The Rancagua Mines Co." was founded in Maine, U.S.A.; its firm name was changed shortly thereafter to "BRADEN COPPER COMPANY" (hereinafter called BRADEN).

In April 1915, the "KENNECOTT COPPER CORPORATION" (hereinafter called KENNECOTT) was formed in the State of New York. It acquired the entire capital stock of BRADEN, which is thus

---

[a] The El Teniente mine is the world's largest underground copper mine. For a detailed account of the events giving rise to this action, see A. Lowenfeld, *International Private Investment,* Ch. II (2d ed. 1983).

[b] On January 5, 1973, the same court had ordered that the copper be sequestered by the court against DM 200,000 security given by Kennecott, pending full hearing of the petition.

a 100% subsidiary of KENNECOTT. In 1905, Braden acquired the mining rights to the El Teniente mine located in the district of Rancagua in Chile, which mine was enlarged during the course of time by further acquisitions.

In 1967 BRADEN employed about 9,000 Chilean and 20 non-Chilean employees there.

The mining of the copper is carried out as follows:

After the excavation of the ore, it is treated in the metallurgical plant which forms part of the mine. One ton of crude ore contains about 10 kg. or copper. The so-called blister copper obtained after the treatment contains about 990 kg. of copper per ton. This blister copper is then refined in other companies, for instance at the defendant's plant, in order to obtain pure copper.

On September 16, 1966, the SOCIEDAD MINERA EL TENIENTE S.A. (SMETSA) was established as a company under Chilean law. By Presidential decree No. 2,167 of October 1, 1966, it was confirmed that the company has juridical personality. By agreements of September 16, 1966, and March 21, 1967, BRADEN agreed to transfer all rights in the mine, including the treasures of the earth located there, the excavating rights and the plants, to SMETSA, in exchange for a transfer of all shares of the new company.

On April 13, 1967, again in accordance with an agreement, 51% of said shares were transferred to a Chilean State Company, the CORPORACION DEL COBRE (CODELCO) at an agreed price of $80 million to be paid to BRADEN in installments and relent by BRADEN to SMETSA. In addition, BRADEN lent to SMETSA the sum of U.S. $12,743.000, representing the interest due until December 31, 1971. Management remained with BRADEN, pursuant to a Management Agreement of April 13, 1967. By a further agreement of the same date, sales and marketing were delegated to the KENNECOTT SALES CORPORATION.

The purpose of the reorganization was among other things, to increase the production of the mine from about 180,000 tons to 280,000 tons of copper per year. In August 1970, an official inauguration of the operations which had been expanded for this purpose took place.

In December 1970, the new Allende Government submitted a bill for the nationalization of major copper mining enterprises. While this bill was still being considered, CODELCO, on the basis of Authorization Law No. 16,624, appointed "supervisory organs" for SMETSA, thus excluding BRADEN from management of the mining operation.

By Law No. 17,450 of July 11, 1971, amending the Constitution, all major copper mining enterprises in Chile, including SMETSA, were nationalized. In accordance with Art. 1 of said law, the State has the unrestricted, exclusive, and inalienable right of ownership of all mines.

In order to wind up the previous company assets, the mining right was divided into two categories, namely "rights to excavate the treasures of the earth" and "rights of ownership in mining equipment."

For the first category no indemnification was provided, while for the second group the indemnification was to be calculated on basis of the liquidation book value on December 31, 1971. Furthermore, this book value was to be reduced so that all investments made after December 31, 1964, were to be disregarded. Finally, deductions were ordered if the equipment taken over was classified as being in defective condition. In addition, the indemnification calculated in this manner was to be paid out only after deduction of an "excess profit compensation tax," the amount of which was to be established by the President.

The book value of the plant as of December 31, 1970, was fixed at about U.S. $319 million. For defects in the equipment and for investments during the period after 1965 which were not to be taken into consideration, deductions were made in the amount of about $230 million. Finally, by Presidential Decree No. 92 of September 28, 1971, the excess profit tax was established in such a manner that no amount was paid out as indemnification for the expropriation, and the accounting was terminated with a negative balance of about U.S. $310 million for the petitioner.

BRADEN, as a party concerned, filed an appeal from this accounting with a "Special Copper Tribunal" established for this purpose pursuant to Law No. 17,450; this court renders its decisions in accordance with its own procedural rules and held that for each sheet of paper which was filed by BRADEN in said proceedings, a stamp tax of about U.S. $4,000 had to be paid.

The appeal was dismissed in August 1972; the Special Copper Tribunal declared that it lacked jurisdiction to examine into the excess profit tax which was determined solely and finally by the President.

In the meantime, the following had happened:

Following passage of the Expropriation Law No. 17,450 of July 11, 1971, the President issued a Decree of July 16, 1971 on the basis of which the State, with immediate effect, took possession, property, and management of SMETSA. Up until July 1972, possession, property, and management were in the hands of the State.

By Presidential Decree of July 7, 1972 (in effect from July 15, 1972), a new company was founded "SOCIEDAD MINERA EL TENIENTE" (hereinafter called SMET II). CODELCO received 95% of the shares of this company, while another State trading organization, the "EMPRESA NACIONAL DE MINERIA" (ENAMI) received 5%. The new company was not a corporation but a company of persons provided with juridical personality of its own. This company is a new creation and is not identical to SMETSA.

Insofar as the deliveries of copper to the defendant are concerned, the following—which was not known to the Court when rendering its [preliminary] Decision of January 5, 1973—may be stated.

In January 1969, SMETSA, through the BRADEN COPPER COMPANY as its New York agent, had executed with the defendant a work contract extending over the period from 1970 to and including 1973 for the refining of an amount of copper of 18,000 tons in 1970 and 24,000 tons per year in 1971–1973.

. . .

In June 1971, SMETSA advised the defendant that as from July 1, 1971, CODELCO would take over all rights and obligations arising from the contract. Deliveries of copper to the defendant continued thereafter without change.

After the entire copper export had been transferred to CODELCO by Decree No. 57 of October 9/24, 1972 of the Chilean Minister of Mining, all shipping documents were made out in the name of CODELCO as shipper, issuer of the invoice, and exporter.

By form letter of September 7, 1972, . . . KENNECOTT COPPER CORPORATION warned the defendant against acquiring the copper in view of the existing rights of KENNECOTT (BRADEN).

Pursuant to the 1969 contract and in accordance with shipping documents submitted, CODELCO, as exporter, during November 1972 shipped from the port of San Antonio—where only copper of the EL TENIENTE mine is loaded—about 3,000 tons of copper with port of destination Hamburg, which tonnage was unloaded in Hamburg from January 5 to 7, 1973.

On basis of an agreement made between the parties after the [preliminary] Decision of January 5, 1973, the copper has been stored in trust with the defendant, pending outcome of this proceeding.

The above facts, being the results of the hearing of January 18, 1973, are not disputed by the parties.

C. The petitioner is of the opinion that the granting of the mining rights to BRADEN and the transfer thereof to SMETSA has the effect that SMETSA is the owner of all minerals present in the copper mine. It claims that it did not lose its ownership as the result of the expropriation of 1971, since that expropriation was invalid, in that it was in violation of international law and also of the rules of German public policy, since it was effected without actual indemnification, and since the parties affected were denied a legal hearing. In accordance with the rules on split companies recognized in Germany, it claims that it is the legal holder of the company property not covered by the expropriation, since it is acknowledged that a split or residual company formed from the original members of the expropriated company has the right to make disposition of assets located abroad.

Aside from the copper at issue, petitioner claims that it also has other assets in the Federal Republic of Germany in the form of trademarks registered and protected here. . . . It declares that it bases its claim against the defendant for surrender of the copper on German law (Sec. 985 of the German Civil Code[c]) as the lex rei sitae. Further, petitioner asserts that on basis of the German-American Treaty of Friendship,[d] it is entitled to be treated in Germany in the same way as though a German citizen had been affected by the expropriation.

The petitioner requests:
That the injunction of January 5, 1973 be affirmed; . . .

The defendant requests:
That the injunction be set aside and the ancillary petitions be dismissed.

The intervening party:
Joins in the defendant's pleading.

The defendant and the intervening party allege:

(i) That the expropriation is not illegal and in particular that payment of indemnification was provided for.

(ii) That SMET II, is presently the legal owner of the ores mined. Even if the opinion of the petitioner as to the invalidity of the expropriation were accepted, it lost the ownership of the ore, under the applicable Chilean law, by the processing thereof, which was carried out in the metallurgical plant of the new SMET II; and

(iii) That Chilean law provides a claim for replevin against an unjustified miner of ore only if the minerals are still in the possession of the invading party (Art. 110 of the Mining Code); that this is not true here.

---

[c] Art. 985 of the German Civil Code reads:

The owner may demand the return of his property from the person in possession.

[d] Treaty of Friendship, Commerce and Navigation between the United States and the Federal Republic of Germany, signed October 29, 1954, 7 U.S.T. 1839; T.I.A.S. 3593; 273 UNTS 3. Article VI(1) reads (in pertinent part):

Nationals and companies of either Party shall be accorded national treatment with respect to access to the court of justice . . . in the territories of the other Party, both in pursuit and in defense of their rights. It is understood that companies of either Party not engaged in activities within the territory of the other Party shall enjoy such access therein without any requirement of registration or domestication.

GROUNDS OF DECISION

In accordance with the results of the hearing and proceedings for the taking of proof and evidence held on January 18, 1973, the injunction of January 5, 1973, cannot be maintained in force since a claim of a right of disposition of the copper has not been credibly shown.

I.

The Court has international and local jurisdiction.

German international procedural law governs the international competence indirectly via the provisions concerning local competence (Sections 12 et seq. of the Code of Civil Procedure).

In accordance with Secs. 937 and 17 of the Code of Civil Procedure, the Landgericht (Superior Court) of Hamburg is a proper venue since the defendant has its registered office here. International jurisdiction is thus also present.

II.

(1) The question as to whether the parties and the intervening party are proper parties and authorized to appear as such are to be decided in accordance with the procedural law of Germany.

(2) Pursuant to Section 50–52 of the Code of Civil Procedure, there is no doubt the defendant, which is a juridical person under German law, is a proper party.

(3) The qualification as party of the petitioner depends upon whether it is a legally competent a proper party in accordance with the law of its home country. . . .

. . .

The fact that the split company has not established any registered office of its own does not prevent the possibility of protecting rights, since it would be illogical to consider that its registered office has continued to exist in a country which does not recognize the existence or legal rights of the juridical person. Therefore, the company which has been expropriated in Chile may assert its rights in the Federal Republic of Germany, regardless of whether it has established a registered office outside of Chile. . . . The petitioner is therefore a proper party and competent to bring the action

(4) Since it has been credibly shown that the intervening party [CODELCO] is a juridical person under Chilean law, there are also no doubts as to its being a proper party and competent to appear in court.

III.

(1) Doubts as to the admissibility of the proceedings could possibly be based on the contention that a decision might infringe against the principle of separation of powers, since it "in impermissible fashion invades the freedom of political decision" and decides on international questions "which can never be up to the courts to regulate if only because the data necessary for decision is unavailable to them." . . .

In the Decision of the U.S. Supreme Court of 3/23/1964 in the matter of *Banco Nacional de Cuba v. Sabbatino,* reference was made to the difficulties in making decisions in a field which "concerns primarily the practical and ideological goals of the members of the international community." [p. 982, *supra*]

The court by no means fails to recognize these difficulties and knows that by its decision, serious questions of international financial relations as well as of politics are affected, the final settlement of which cannot be effected by court decision. Nevertheless, the court, in accordance with the principles of German procedural law, cannot refuse to render a decision, since its decision will violate neither the principle of separation of powers nor any Constitutional or substantive rights of the parties. For similar reasons, the Hanseatic Court of Appeals of Bremen, in the so-called *Indonesian Tobacco Case*,[e] likewise held that the Court has jurisdiction over the subject matter of a foreign expropriation.

IV.

As right of disposition, the petitioner alleges a right to the return of ownership. First, there arises in this connection the question as to the law pursuant to which this right is to be judged. German private international law contains no statutory provisions concerning property law. Under customary law, the *lex rei sitae* applies to personal and real property. This law determines the coming into existence, transfer and loss of rights in rem. . . . Whether ownership was acquired upon the mining of the copper in Chile, or whether the ownership relationships change with the processing in Chile or with the delivery of the blister copper to CODELCO as State export company therefore depends on Chilean law, since the facts are to be judged in accordance with the time when they occurred. . . . An interest which has come into existence under the law of the first state will, after the change in situs, be recognized also by the law of the second state. Thus in accordance with German private international law, ownership [of the copper in question] is determined on the basis of Chilean substantive law. The petitioner would have rights of action for surrender only if, under Chilean law, it became on the one hand the owner of the blister copper and on the other hand had not lost its ownership.

V.

(1) Whether the petitioner is vested with the ownership or co-ownership of the copper at issue which is now located in Germany depends, accordingly, on whether the German Court must recognize the expropriation pronounced against SMETSA in Chile.

The legal evaluation of such foreign expropriation is as a rule—as is also true in connection with Chile—not covered by international treaty or national law. The foreign act of expropriation must therefore be judged in accordance with the principles of international administrative law, the law of nations, and private international law. Here the Court adopts the opinion now prevailing in the Federal Republic of Germany that an expropriation which has been effected abroad must in principle be recognized as being formally valid, since in accordance with the internationally recognized principle of territoriality, measures of expropriation cover without limitation the property which was subject to the sovereignty of the expropriating state at the time of the expropriation. This means that an expropriation effected in the course of nationalization or socialization measures remains an internal matter of the foreign state as long as it does not apply to property located outside of its boundaries. . . .

In modern international law there is no generally recognized principle that the foreign court is obligated to consider as a priori null and void a foreign sovereign act which is in violation

---

[e] For an account of this case, see Domke, *Indonesian Nationalization Measures before Foreign Courts*, 54 Am. J. Int'l L. 305 (1960).

of international law; nor does international law provide that either the recognition of foreign acts which are in violation of international law or the recognition of a claim for restitution by a former owner would violate international law. Even if an appropriation was effected under circumstances of discrimination or was pronounced without indemnification, it remains valid if an item of property which was in the expropriating country at the time of the expropriation has subsequently come into a foreign country. Any other position would lead to impossible complications of a political and economic nature and would interfere with international order. Nor is the principle of territoriality thereby violated, since said principle is intended to prevent expropriation extending to property which is abroad at the time of the act of expropriation. However, we are not confronted by such a case here.

(2) Nevertheless, an expropriation would not be recognized in the Federal Republic of Germany if recognition of the foreign act were to violate basic principles of German public policy.

(a) The German court must, therefore, ask itself whether in our view the foreign procedure violates public policy or the purpose of a German law at the time of rendering of the decision, and it is necessary further to determine whether there exists a sufficient relationship to this country to justify the application of the exception contained in Article 30 of the Introductory Law to the German Civil Code.[f]

In the opinion of this court, the consideration of the foreign law can here in fact lead to finding a violation of public policy within the meaning of Article 30 of the Introductory Law to the German Civil Code. In any event, this viewpoint is justifiable within the scope of summary proceedings in which exhaustive examination of the problem is not possible, if only for reasons of time available. In this connection, in the opinion of this court, the events which led to the expropriation of SMETSA are to be considered not in their individual aspects, but as a whole; the expropriation was effected for all practical purposes without indemnification, it was effected under discriminatory conditions, and legal channels have been closed to the parties concerned.

There is principle of international law which is confirmed in particular by United Nations Resolution No. 1,803 (XVII) of December 14, 1962 [on Permanent Sovereignty over Natural Resources] that every expropriation or nationalization must provide for a reasonable indemnification . . . Violation of international law would be material through Article 25 of the Constitution[g] within the scope of Article 30 of the Introductory Law to the German Civil Code.

A reasonable indemnification was, in fact, not granted the petitioner. To be sure, the Chilean Expropriation Law of 1971 provides for indemnification for the expropriation of the mining equipment proper, but the law, with one stroke and at the same time as granting indemnification, creates a new and peculiar provision for the nonpayment of the indemnification; this—in combination with the excess profit tax stipulated in the same law—leads, in effect, by way of a negative indemnification, to a taxing of the expropriated party.

However, even if this form of "equalization" were considered a "reasonable" indemnification, there would still be other considerations which establish a violation of German principles of law.

---

[f] Article 30 of the Introductory Law to the Civil Code reads:

The application of foreign laws is excluded if such application would be contrary to good morals or the purpose of a German law.

[g] Article 25 of the German Constitution reads:

The general rules of international law are a part of national law. They have priority over laws, and create rights and obligations directly for the residents of the national territory.

As has not been denied by the defendant or the intervening party, the expropriation was intended primarily for nationalization. An expropriation which is directed specifically against foreigners is to be considered discriminatory and thus an act which is not to be approved in accordance with the principles of public policy. . . . Even though it may be understandable for a State to wish to free itself from the position of economic domination of foreign companies which control particularly important portions of its economy, on the other hand the principle of contractual loyalty which governs every legal system should not be violated.

As the petitioner has credibly shown, the formation of SMETSA with the cooperation and approval of the former President of Chile, Mr. Frei, was effected specifically in view of the special economic conditions of Chile. Under these circumstances, the petitioner had to be able to rely on the fact that a few years later it would not be expropriated at short notice by the Chilean government, since a majority participation had already been granted to the State of Chile. Here it was to be expected that Chile would either grant the petitioner an effective indemnification reasonable with respect to the consequences of loss of property, or that it would grant the company a reasonable period of transition, as has recently become customary in the case of investment contracts with developing countries by a promise not to expropriate investment assets before the expiration of a stipulated period of time, and as would also be in accord with the sense of a Decision of the Chilean Supreme Court handed down in 1964 on the obligation of the Government to comply with a long-term tax promise despite the introduction of a new, more onerous tax law.

Since none of this has been taken into account, we are confronted with substantial discrimination, in which connection it is unnecessary to take up the question whether the amount of the stamp tax stipulated by the Special Copper Tribunal is to be considered a further act of discrimination.

The Court in this connection accords particular weight to the following:

The petitioner has credibly shown that the imposition of the excess profit tax which is in an insoluble relationship to the expropriation proceedings, is effected by the President of the country at his own free discretion. This act of discretion, which is not subject to any restriction, is not subject to review by the courts, as the Copper Tribunal itself stated in the grounds of its Decision. This means that legal channels are closed, and the party concerned is denied a legal hearing. Thus, a fundamental principle of German law is violated, which—even though in this case a German citizen is not involved—is so severe that it must be found to be a violation of German public policy.

In any event, this combination of acts of violation appears so serious as to be entirely unbearable under our view of legality and morality.

. . .

(b) This conclusion, however, is not sufficient for the application of Art. 30 of the Introductory Law to the German Civil Code, since every clause providing for a reservation is a disturbing factor in international legal life. Only if the German legal system is substantially affected by the violation of public policy, and thus a close relationship between what has been done and German interests is created, is Art. 30 of the Introductory Law to the German Civil Code applicable.

A close relationship to German interests could possibly be found to exist if—as the Court assumed in its Decision of January 5, 1973—the defendant had been the purchaser of the lot of copper and on basis of the petitioner's circular of September 7, 1972, had to run the risk of having to pay the purchase price again to the petitioner because of acquisition from the nonjustified party.

A relationship to German interests which is material from a legal standpoint in this sense, however, does not exist when the copper is supplied to the German defendant merely for the carrying out of a processing contract. There is no question whatsoever in this connection of any ownership relationship on the part of the defendant.

The proposition that the mere bringing of articles which have been expropriated without indemnification into Germany does not constitute any essential relationship to German interests has been repeatedly confirmed by the decided cases. . . .

. . .

(3) Since neither international law nor German public policy in the given situation compels the German courts to deny recognition to the expropriation of SMETSA carried out in Chile, even with respect to assets which have arrived in other countries, the petitioner has not credibly shown its right of disposition, namely its ownership.

Injunction dissolved.

NOTES AND QUESTIONS

(1)(a) Note first that Justice Harlan emphasizes the national character of the act of state doctrine. The doctrine is not required by the Constitution, but it has constitutional underpinnings, derived in part from the separation of powers within the United States, and in part from the role of the United States (as contrasted with the states of the Union) as a member of the family of nations. Thus the power of the federal court does not depend on a grant from the states, *Erie R. Co. v. Tompkins* is not applicable, and failure of a state court to give effect to the act of state doctrine would raise a federal question.[h]

(b) Justice Harlan does not speak of conflict of laws, and Justice White does so only briefly. Seen in conflict of laws terms, however, *Sabbatino* is in a sense analogous to the *Lauritzen, Romero, McCulloch, Rhoditis* series,[i] in that the Supreme Court is in the position of a forum deciding whether to apply the law of its own [nation-]state, or of another state. However, whereas in *Lauritzen* and successor cases the Court uses international law to limit the scope of a U.S. statute, here the very authority of foreign law is challenged as conflicting with international law. In *Sabbatino,* the Supreme Court rejects that challenge. In the various attempts to limit the act of state doctrine, the challenge is renewed.

(2) Justice White, while not rejecting the act of state doctrine altogether, makes several arguments calling for rejection of the doctrine in the circumstances of the *Sabbatino* case.

(a) Though he would not generally entertain a challenge to the validity of a foreign law on the "ordinary conflicts ground" of repugnancy to the public policy of the forum, he says that

---

[h] Note that Justice Harlan reserves, in footnote 23, on the question of a state adhering to a more restrictive view of the scope of examination of foreign states' acts than is required by the Supreme Court.

[i] § 10.01, *supra.*

principle should not be applied to acts in clear violation of international law. Does Justice Harlan answer this point adequately?

(b) Further, Justice White says that the Court's job is to determine controversies on the merits, and that this includes administering international law. How does Justice Harlan answer this point? Is he persuasive?

(c) Justice White goes on to point out that the Court applies international law to several aspects of the case—the basic concept of territorial sovereignty, for instance, and also the determination that the sugar situated off the Cuban mainland was within Cuba's territorial waters. Why then is the issue of taking of alien property different?

(d) Justice White says that refusal by the Court to inquire into the question of whether norms of the international community have been contravened by the act of state under review "would seem to deny the existence . . . of such norms"? Is that fair?

(e) Justice White concedes, as he must, that Cuba has violated no treaty; at most what Cuba has violated is customary international law. Though he suggests that the lack of consensus to which Justice Harlan refers [p. 988, *supra*] may not be as clear as the majority believes, Justice White regards the role of the U.S. Supreme Court as law giver to be important whether there is consensus or not. Justice Harlan does not address this point directly, but it is at least plausible to suggest that he was thinking of the *Swift-Erie* analogy. Where White [Story] would find a general common law of nations reflecting eternal verities (*et apud omnes gentes, et omni tempore*), Harlan, like Brandeis, can find no "transcendental body of law outside of any particular [nation-]state but obligatory within it." Who has the better of this argument? Is it simply an argument over what the world will think about narrow parochialism? Or is it an argument about the philosophy of law? Or about international political theory?

(f) As we saw in the discussion of *Government of India v. Taylor*[j] and *British Columbia v. Gilbertson*,[k] efforts by foreign states to secure recognition and enforcement in other states of judgments involving public law matters have generally been unsuccessful, apparently because the courts in the second forum did not consider it right to scrutinize the public acts of foreign governments, but were not prepared to grant recognition to judgments concerning such acts without scrutiny. In the act of state context, the reluctance or refusal to scrutinize the acts of the foreign state is equally prevalent, but the result is the reverse, in that (if none of the exceptions apply) the foreign act of state is, in effect, granted recognition without review. How do you account for this difference? Is there a good reason why executive and legislative acts of general application should be accorded greater deference than judgments of courts in particular cases?

(3)(a) In the key paragraph of the majority's opinion (p. 988), Justice Harlan wrote:

> [R]ather than laying down or reaffirming an inflexible and all-encompassing rule in this case, we decide only that the Judicial Branch will not examine the validity of [i] a taking of property [ii] within its own territory by a foreign sovereign government, [iii] extant and recognized by this country at the time of suit, [iv] in the absence of a treaty or other unambiguous agreement regarding controlling legal principles, even if the complaint alleges that the taking violates customary international law.

The *Sabbatino* case involved property taken by the government of a recognized state within its own territory, and the legal challenge to the taking was founded on customary law, not on a

---

[j] P. 895, *supra*.

[k] Question (2)(d), p. 905, *supra*.

§ 10.06   INTERNATIONAL LAW AND CONFLICT OF LAWS   □   1003

treaty or other international agreement. Thus there is no way of knowing how Justice Harlan would have decided a case in which one or more of these conditions was absent, or which reservations were necessary to mobilize the 8–1 majority for the *Sabbatino* decision. Which of the conditions would you think are so critical to the doctrine that without them the doctrine should not be applied? Which of the several rationales advanced for the act of doctrine by Justice Harlan emerges from peeling off the conditions one by one?

(b) Perhaps the most interesting possible exception (though probably not the most important one in terms of number of applications) is the one based on existence of a treaty. Of course if a treaty to which the United States is a party provides:

> Nationals of either high contracting party may bring claims of violation of this treaty before the courts of either high contracting party

such a provision would be binding on the courts of the United States, as well as of Patria. But there are no such treaties, at least not in the areas such as protection of transnational investment around which the act of state debate turns. The argument for a treaty exception, rather, stresses that the doctrine is based on the absence of controlling legal principles by which to judge a foreign state's actions, and that that gap is filled when a treaty contains standards by which to judge the acts of the foreign state. Is this persuasive? Note again the analogy to the Story–Brandeis, common law–statute law, inquiries into the source of law and the role of courts.[l]

(c) Putting aside the treaty point, should the act of state doctrine be limited to the taking of property? Or should it cover all claims that would require the courts of *A* to scrutinize the actions of the government of *B*? For example, suppose one oil company sues a second oil company, claiming it has unlawfully conspired to induce the government of *B* to terminate the first company's concession. The second company pleads the act of state doctrine. Should the claim be dismissed?[m]

(d) The *Sabbatino* decision was unpopular in large segments of the business community (generally excluding the major banks and insurance companies). As a result Congress adopted an amendment to the Foreign Assistance Act, known as the Sabbatino Amendment or the second Hickenlooper Amendment, designed to reverse the decision of the Supreme Court.[n] After a confusing debate over two sessions of Congress, the final version of the amendment read, in pertinent part:

---

[l] One court of appeals, reversing a district court, held there was a treaty exception to the act of state doctrine, and therefore sustained justiciability of a claim by an American investor against the government of Ethiopia based on the latter's taking of shares in an Ethiopian company. The court held that the conduct of Ethiopia could be measured against a Treaty of Friendship, Commerce and Navigation containing a provision that:

> Property of nationals and companies of either High Contracting Party . . . shall not be taken except for a public purpose, nor shall it be taken without prompt payment of just and effective compensation.

Kalamazoo Spice Extraction Co. v. Government of Socialist Ethiopia, 729 F.2d 422 (6th Cir. 1984).

[m] Several Courts of Appeals in the United States have said yes to this question. *Occidental Petroleum Corporation v. Buttes Gas & Oil Co.,* 331 F. Supp. 92 (C.D. Cal. 1971), *aff'd,* 461 F.2d 1261 (9th Cir.), *cert. denied,* 409 U.S. 950 (1972); *Hunt v. Mobil Oil Corporation,* 550 F.2d 68 (2d Cir.), *cert. denied,* 434 U.S. 984 (1977); *Occidental of Umm al Qaywayn, Inc. v. A Certain Cargo of Petroleum,* 577 F.2d 1196 (5th Cir. 1978), *cert. denied,* 442 U.S. 928 (1979.) But when defendants' conduct could be judged without scrutiny of the acts or motives of the foreign government, the act of state doctrine has not been applied. *Timberlane Lumber Co. v. Bank of America Nat'l Trust & Savings Ass'n,* p. 943 at 945–46. See also the decision of the House of Lords in *Buttes Gas & Oil Co. v. Hammer,* [1982] A.C. 888 (H.L. (E.)), also declining to become involved in scrutinizing the actions of a foreign sovereign.

[n] Section 620(e)(2) of the Foreign Assistance Act of 1961 as amended, 22 U.S.C. § 2370(e)(2).

[N]o court in the United States shall decline on the ground of the federal act of state doctrine to make determination on the merits giving effect to the principles of international law in a case in which a claim of title or other right to property is asserted by any party . . . based upon (or traced through) a confiscation or other taking after January 1, 1959 by an act of that state in violation of the principles of international law [except with respect to certain letters of credit and when the President has determined that application of the act of state doctrine is required in a particular case.][o]

Courts in the United States have almost uniformly interpreted the amendment not to effect a basic reversal of the doctrine, but to create an exception for property actually before the court, such as an American-owned ship seized by the government of Patria which subsequently comes into a U.S. port.[p] Thus, as construed, the Sabbatino Amendment became a special aspect of the territorial compromise discussed in the following question.

(4)(a) Other aspects of the continuing debate about the act of state doctrine—for example about the role of the executive branch,[q] about an exception for counterclaims,[r] and about an exception for commercial (as contrasted with "sovereign") acts[s] —go well beyond the conflict of laws.[t] But perhaps the most significant limitation on the act of state doctrine is the territorial limitation, which must be based on, or at least reflect, conflict of laws thinking. If, for example Patria expropriates the ABC Company, a Patrian company, and ABC has a bank account or a trade mark in the United States, as well as assets in Patria, the act of state doctrine will preclude review by U.S. courts of the lawfulness of the taking of ABC's assets in Patria, but not of the New York bank account or the U.S. trademark.[u] Why should this be so?

(b) If S.A. XYZ a company incorporated in France, has assets in the United States, and ownership of XYZ is transferred by merger or inheritance, a contest over ownership of XYZ, Inc., the U.S. subsidiary, or of S.A. XYZ's New York bank account, would be decided according to French law. Why is the result different if the ownership of S.A. XYZ passes by expropriation without compensation?

---

[o] The complete text of § 620(e) appears in the Documents Supplement at pp. 201–02.

[p] See, e.g., *French v. Banco Nacional de Cuba*, 23 N.Y.2d 46, 295, N.Y.S.2d 433, 242 N.E.2d 704 (1968); *Banco Nacional de Cuba v. First National City Bank of New York*, 431 F.2d 394, 399–402 (2d Cir. 1970), *reversed on other grounds*, 406 U.S. 759 (1979); *Hunt v. Coastal States Gas Producing Co*, 583 S.W.2d 322 (Tex. 1979).

[q] See *Banco Nacional de Cuba v. First National City Bank of New York*, 406 U.S. 759 (1982); Lowenfeld, *Act of State and Department of State First National City Bank v. Banco Nacional de Cuba*, 66 Am. J. Int'l L. 795 (1972).

[r] See *Banco Nacional de Cuba v. First National City Bank of New York*, Note p, *supra*; *Banco Nacional de Cuba v. Chase Manhattan Bank*, 658 F.2d 875, 884 (2d Cir. 1981); *First National City Bank v. Banco Para El Comercio Exterior de Cuba*, 462 U.S. 611 (1983).

[s] See *Alfred Dunhill of London, Inc. v. Republic of Cuba*, 425 U.S. 682 (1976).

[t] Point (iii) of Justice Harlan's conditions, focusing on recognition of the government in question, was necessary in *Sabbatino* itself to distinguish between "recognition" and maintenance of diplomatic relations, which had been broken between the United States and Cuba at the close of the Eisenhower administration. The condition might have been important in the 1960's, as neither the People's Republic of China nor the German Democratic Republic were then recognized by the United States. However, as of year-end 1997, no case since *Sabbatino* involving an act of an unrecognized government had come up in a U.S. court.

[u] Numerous cases, before and after *Sabbatino*, support the statement in the text. See e.g., *Zwack v. Kraus Bros. & Co.*, 237 F.2d 255 (2d Cir. 1956) (U.S. trademark not included in seizure of Hungarian wine business by Hungarian People's Republic); *Republic of Iraq v. First National City Bank*, 353 F.2d 47 (2d Cir. 1965), *cert. denied*, 382 U.S. 1027 (1966) (act of state doctrine not applied to U.S. assets confiscated by foreign state contrary to policy and law of the United States.)

(c) No fully articulated explanation of the territorial limitation on the act of state doctrine has appeared. The opponents of the doctrine support all limitations, and the supporters have been willing to concede that it is confined not only to acts of a state within its own territory but to effects of such acts within that territory. One explanation would be that the territorial limitation reflects a compromise between those who would subject all sovereign acts of foreign states to scrutiny of domestic courts (at least in the case of plausible allegations of breach of international law), and those who would keep U.S. courts out of the business of engaging in review of the sovereign acts of foreign states. Another way to look at the territorial limitation is to say that an investor who puts his assets into Patria expects (or should expect) his ownership of those assets to be governed by Patrian law; the same expectation does not attach to a bank account in New York, even if it is owned by the Patrian enterprise. Still another explanation is that the act of state doctrine is a special illustration of the territorial preference which we have seen in connection with exercise of jurisdiction to prescribe and foreign compulsion, and indeed throughout conflict of laws generally.

(d) The territorial limitation on the act of state doctrine inevitably raises the question of the situs of intangible assets: (i) Suppose a Cuban company has an account with a New York bank. What is the situs of the money in the account? Does it matter whether the account was opened with the Havana branch of the bank, rather than with the head office in New York? (ii) How about goods sold by a Cuban company to a New York buyer on credit? Is the obligation to pay the purchase price a debt of the New York buyer, located in New York, or is it an asset—i.e., a receivable—of the company in Cuba and thus subject to expropriation by the Cuban state along with real estate, machinery, and inventory located in Cuba?[v]

(e) The *Restatement of Foreign Relations Law* says in a Reporters' Note on this question:

> In principle, it might be preferable to approach the question of the applicability of the act of state doctrine to intangible assets not by searching for an imaginary situs for property that has no real situs, but by determining how the act of the foreign state in the particular circumstances fits within the reasons for the act of state doctrine and for the territorial limitation.[w]

Is that persuasive? Does it solve the problem of bank deposits, foreign trade marks, or accounts receivable? How about a trust maintained in Patria, whose assets are shares of corporations organized in other countries?

(5) Finally, one could view the debate about the act of state doctrine as, at bottom, a debate about state interest—not U.S.A. or Cuba or Patria, but what the true U.S. interest is in separating politics from adjudication, in limiting the judiciary to subjects for which it has a mandate, or in vindicating the rights of U.S. investors (and perhaps others) who have been harmed by actions of foreign states.

Suppose a U.S. court had before it a controversy between a German investor and the government of Patria or those claiming under it. Suppose, for instance, the El Teniente mine in Chile had been previously owned or controlled by Metallgesellschaft, A.G., a major West German producer and refiner of non-ferrous metals, and a ship carrying copper from that mine

---

[v] This, in essence, was the problem in *Alfred Dunhill of London, Inc. v. Republic of Cuba*, 425 U.S. 682 (1976). See Lowenfeld, *In Search of the Intangible: A Comment on Shaffer v. Heitner*, 53 N.Y.U. L. Rev. 102, 111–122 (1978).

[w] *Restatement (Third) of the Foreign Relations Law of the United States* § 443, Reporters' Note 4 (1987).

had put into Baltimore harbor. The succeeding events took place as in Hamburg, and eventually the case reached the U.S. Supreme Court. If the United States were a "disinterested forum," would you expect Justice Harlan and White to be on the same side? Which side?

(6)(a) Turning then to the *S.M. El Teniente* case, note first the preliminary questions faced by the Hamburg court: Can Kennecott sue at all—whether in its own name or that of SMETSA? After all, the copper belonged to SMETSA, and KENNECOTT owned only 49 percent of SMETSA.[x] Is the court on sound ground in its resolution of this question? What law governs the question? Do you think it would come out the same way in a U.S. court?

(b) Having passed the initial hurdle, the Hamburg court is faced with the question of whether or not to conduct a review of Chile's actions. It cites the *Sabbatino* case, but rejects the idea of abstaining from a review of Chile's acts, because it is required by German law to render a decision, and because it sees no interference with the principle of separation of powers. The court says (p. 998–999) that international law neither requires nor prohibits it to declare a foreign state's act null and void if that act is in violation of international law. Further, the court says that the transfer of title must be judged according to the law of Chile. Thus the court rejects international law as a basis for declining to review the acts of the Chilean government, though when it does conduct its review, international law comes back through Article 25 of the Constitution of the Federal Republic.

(c) The basis for reviewing Chile's action, it turns out, is not international law but the public policy of the forum—the reverse of the position taken by Justice White in *Sabbatino*.

(7)(a) Once it gets to reviewing Chile's action toward Kennecott, the Hamburg court has little difficulty in finding that Kennecott's property was taken without compensation, and that Kennecott (or SMETSA) was the victim of discrimination, ex post facto legislation, and breach of contractual arrangements. Taken together, Chile's transgression "appears so serious as to be entirely unbearable under our view of legality and morality." (p. 1000). Is this conclusion more persuasive than the comparable statement of Justice White in *Sabbatino*[y] just because it isn't "home town justice"?

(b) Or is all of the Hamburg court's opinion made irrelevant by the final paragraphs—an elaborate dictum of no practical or jurisprudential value? If so, would the court have been wiser

---

[x] The El Teniente mine had been developed at the beginning of the century by the Guggenheim and Braden interests that became Kennecott, and had been wholly-owned by Kennecott until the mid-1960's. As stated by the Hamburg court (p. 994, *supra*), Kennecott had entered into what was in effect a joint venture arrangement with the government of Chile under President Frei (1964–70), whereby (simplifying somewhat) (i) a new enterprise Soc. Minera El Teniente, S.A. (SMETSA) was established to hold Kennecott's Chilean assets; (ii) Kennecott sold 51 percent of the shares in SMETSA to Chile (Codelco); (iii) Chile drastically reduced the tax rate applicable to the mining enterprise; (iv) Kennecott re-lent the proceeds of the purchase price for the 51 percent to SMETSA; (v) SMETSA entered into sales and management contracts with Kennecott; and (vi) The United States Ex-Im Bank made a major development loan to SMETSA.

[y] See, e.g., the following excerpt from Justice White's dissent:

Where a clear violation of international law is not demonstrated, I would agree that principles of comity underlying the act of state doctrine warrant recognition and enforcement of the foreign act. But none of these considerations relieve a court of the obligation to make an inquiry into the validity of the foreign act, none of them warrant a flat rule of no inquiry at all. The vice of the act of state doctrine as formulated by the Court and applied in this case, where the decree is alleged not only to be confiscatory but also retaliatory and discriminatory and has been found by two courts to be a flagrant violation of international law, is that it precludes any such examination and proscribes any decision on whether Cuban Law No. 851 contravenes an accepted principle of international law.

376 U.S. at 458–59 (White, J. dissenting).

to have followed the example of the *Sabbatino* case, and simply ruled that the actions of the government of Chile were not subject to its review?

(c) Consider again the hypothetical case posed in question (5), in which the investor in Chile's copper industry was not Kennecott but Metallgesellschaft, but this time the case comes before the German court in Hamburg. It seems that the analysis would have proceeded as in the actual case up to the paragraph stating that Chile's actions are "entirely unbearable," but the final paragraphs would not have been written and plaintiff would have prevailed. Is this distinction sound? Or is it just the kind of thinking Justice Harlan had in mind when he warned (at p. 990) against "a patchwork approach towards the formulation of an acceptable body of law concerning state responsibility for expropriations," and expressed his doubt that decisions of U.S. courts against Cuba would be accepted as "disinterested expressions of sound legal principle by those adhering to widely different ideologies"?

(8) This chapter began with the assertion that in contrast to governmental interest analysis applied to guest statutes, workers' compensation claims, or limits on recovery for wrongful death, in the international arena conflict of laws was much more often played out in the context of genuine conflicts of state interest. That conflict certainly shows up in this final section in assessing the interests of Cuba or Chile. But notice what happens to interest analysis in the United States and Germany: in *Sabbatino,* the forum clearly has an interest (however defined), but the Supreme Court rejects favoring that interest à la Currie, and prefers to abstain. In *El Teniente,* the court is fully prepared to apply the public policy of the forum, but concludes that the forum has no interest in the controversy. In neither case is the forum's view of how alien investors should be treated translated into a holding that the property before the court belongs to the former owner, and that title derived from the expropriation is invalid. At this frontier between public and private international law, the fortress of territoriality remains strong, if not always impregnable.

TABLE OF CASES

[References are to page numbers. Discussion of principal cases in the succeeding notes and questions is not separately listed.]

A

Adams v. Knickerbocker Nature Study Soc'y *104*
Abu-Dalbouh v. Abu-Dalbouh 823
Air Crash Disaster at Boston, In re . . . 465
Air Crash Disaster Near Chicago, In re . . . 467
Alabama Great Southern R.R. v. Carroll . . . *1*
Alaska Packers Ass'n v. Industrial Accident Comm'n *386*
Alfred Dunhill v. Republic of Cuba . . 1004, 1005
Allied-Signal, Inc. v. Purex Industries, Inc. 619
Allstate Insurance Co. v. Hague *402*
Alton v. Alton 777
Aluminum Co. of America, United States v. *909*
American Banana Co. v. United Fruit Co. . . 155, 945
American Safety Equip. Corp. v. J.P. McGuire & Co. 324
Amusement Equipment, Inc. v. Mordelt . . . 619
Angel v. Bullington 454
Anglo-American Provision Co. v. Davis Provision Co 644
Annesley, In re *41*
Antelope, The *35, 38*
Armstrong v. Carson 645
Armstrong v. Pomerance 604
Arrowsmith v. United Press Int'l 485
Asahi Metal Industry Co. v. Superior Ct. (S.Ct.) *565*
Asahi Metal Industry Co. v. Superior Ct. (Cal.) 577
Atherton v. Atherton 752
Audi-NSU Auto Union v. Adelin Petit . . *742*
Auten v. Auten *146, 246*

B

Babcock v. Jackson *145, 153, 156*
Baehr v. Lewin 862
Baker v. Bolton 132, 380
Baker v. General Motors Corporation . . 670
Baldwin v. Iowa State Traveling Men's Ass'n *675*, 700
Baltimore & Ohio R.R. v. Baugh . . 438, 440
Banco de Brasil, S.A. v. A.C. Israel Com. Co., ... 907
Banco Nac'l de Cuba v. Chase Manhattan Bank 1004

Banco Nac'l de Cuba v. First Nat. City Bank 1004
Banco Nacional de Cuba v. Sabbatino . . *982*
Barber v. Barber 804
Barrie, In re Estate of *20*
Bauer, Matter of *356*, 515
Baxter v. Sturm Ruger & Co (2d Cir.) . . . *92, 98*
Baxter v. Sturm Ruger & Co. (Conn.) . . . *95*
Ben Yehoshua, In Re Marriage 846
Benn v. Linden Crane Co *523*
Bernkrant v. Fowler *239*
Bersch v. Drexel Firestone, Inc. 940
Bier v. Mines de Potasse d'Alsace S.A. (Eur.Ct.Just.) *622*
Bier v. Mines de Potasse d'Alsace (Neth.) . . . 632
Bing v. Thunig 104, 213
Bisso v. Inland Waterways Corp. . . 296, 309
Black & White Taxi v. Brown & Yellow Taxi 437, 441
Boucher v. Lawson 906
Bournias v. Atlantic Maritime Co *75*
Bradford Elec. Light Co. v. Clapper . . . 385, 400
Bremen, The v. Zapata Off-Shore Co. . . . *294*
British Columbia v. Gilbertson 905
British Nylon Spinners, v. Imp. Chem. Indus. *914, 925*
Brock v. District Court of County of Boulder *834*
Brewster v. Boston Herald-Traveler Corp. . . . 116
Buckeye v. Buckeye 53
Buckley v. New York Post Corp. 527
Burger King Corp. v. Rudzewicz 557
Burr v. Beckler *47*
Burnham v. Superior Ct *610*
Bushkin Assocs. v. Raytheon Co. 254
Buttes Gas & Oil Co. v. Hammer 1003
Byrd v. Blue Ridge Rural Elec. Coop . . 455

C

Calder v. Jones 550, 557
Caldwell v. Caldwell 782, 790
Cameron v. Cameron 818
Canadian Northern Ry. v. Eggen 90
Capron v. Van Noorden 682
Carbon Black Export, Inc. v. The Monrosa . . . 295
Cardillo v. Liberty Mut. Ins. Co. 406
Carnival Cruise Lines, Inc., v. Shute . . 337
Carroll v. Lanza 400
Carvalho v. Hull, Blyth (Angola) Ltd. . . . *302*

[References are to page numbers. Discussion of principal cases in the succeeding notes and questions is not separately listed.]

Charming Betsy, The 873, 890, 923
Cherniack v. Home National Bank & Trust Co. 345
Chila v. Owens 189
Christoff's Estate, In re 711
Cie. Europeénne des Petroles, v. Sensor Nederland 981
Cie. Tunis. de Navig. v. Cie. D'Armement Mar. 282, 332
Cipolla v. Shaposka 190, 192
Clark, Estate of 346, 808
Clark v. Clark 196, 465
Clarke v. Clarke 680
Clay v. Sun Insurance Office, Ltd. 395
Coast Lines, Ltd. v. Hudig & Veder Chartering N.V. 509
Cohen v. Beneficial Indus. Loan Corp. 455
Cohn, In re 71
Conklin v. Canadian-Colonial Airways 131, 134
Cook, In re 361
Cooney v. Osgood Machinery, Inc. 225
Cort v. Steen 68, 69, 70
Coster v. Coster 54, 134
Cousins v. Instrument Flyers, Inc. 188, 213
Cowans v. Ticonderoga Pulp & Paper Co. 701
Crichton, Estate of 349, 359, 808

D

Daetwyler Corp v. Meyer 569
Dalip Singh Bir's Estate, in re 859
Davenport v. Webb 142
Davis v. Davis 770
Davis v. Mills 77
Day v. Day 814
Day & Zimmerman v. Challoner 454
DeBloos v. Volkswagen A.G. 629
DeJames v. Magnificence Carriers, Inc. 569
Delagi v. Volkswagen A.G. 495
Deutsch v. West Coast Machinery Co. ... 522
Dixilyn Drilling Corp. v. Crescent Towing & Salv. 296
Dole v. Dow Chemical Co. .. 216, 227, 229
Dresser Indus., Inc. v. Baldridge 980
Duggan v. Bay State St. Ry. 66, 74
Duncan v. Cessna Aircraft Co. 231
Dunstan v. Higgins 695
Durfee v. Duke 676
Dym v. Gordon 152

E

EEOC v. Aramco 965, 970
Edwards v. Elliott 480
Elefanten Schuh v. Jacqmain 721
El Teniente, S.M. v. A. G. Norddeutsche Affinerie 993

Emery v. Burbank 244
Emery v. Emery 54
Empresa Hondurena de Vapores v. McLeod 891
Erie R. Co. v. Tompkins 435, 700
Estasis Salotti v. RUWA 729
Estin v. Estin 796
Etab. Rohr S.A. v. Ossberger 726

F

Fall v. Eastin 681
Farber v. Smolack 165
Farrell v. Piedmont Aviation, Inc. 606
Fauntleroy v. Lum 639
Feathers v. McLucas 521
Ferens v. John Deere & Co 463
First Nat'l Bank of Chicago v. United Air Lines 371
First Nat'l City Bank v. Banco Para El Com. Ext. de Cuba 1004
Fitzpatrick v. Int'l Ry. 134
Foley Bros. v. Filardo 965, 970
Forbes v. Forbes 55
Forgo, Heirs of 44
Foster v. Driscoll 900, 920
Foster v. Leggett 192
French v. Banco Nacional deCuba ... 1004
Friedrich v. Friedrich 847
Fruehauf Corp. v. Massardy 973
Fuentes v. Shevin 580

G

G S.A. v. U S.p.A (Swiss Fed'l Ct.) 336
Galeries Segoura SPRL v. Bonakdarian ... 729
Galgay v. Bulletin Co. 525
General Electric Co., United States v. 954
Garpeg Ltd. v. United States 925
Garthwaite v. Garthwaite 764
Gasperini v. Center for Humanities, Inc. 471
George v. Douglas Aircraft Co., Inc. 85
Gerli & Co. v. Cunard S.S. Co. 256, 301
Gienar v. Meyer 256
Gilbert v. Burnstine 313
Glanzner v. Missouri Dept of Social Services 836
Gordon v. Parker 192
Gore v. Northeast Airlines 167
Grant v. McAuliffe 67
Granville-Smith v. Granville-Smith ... 779
Gray v. Am. Radiator & Standard Sanitary Corp. 520
Green v. Hudson River R.R. 132
Greschler v. Greschler 792
Greyhound Corp. v. Heitner 600
Griffith v. United Air Lines ... 82, 190, 464
Guaranty Trust Co. v. York 455

[References are to page numbers. Discussion of principal cases in the succeeding notes and questions is not separately listed.]

Gulf Oil Co. v. Gilbert 295, 461

H

Haag v. Barnes 249
Haddock v. Haddock 750, 765
Hall v. Helicoopteros Nac. de Colombia (Tex.) 573
Halvey, New York ex rel. v. Halvey . . . 827, 832
Hammon and Hattaway v. Smith 645
Hana Rauch v. Lent 604
Hanau, Estate of v. Hanau 818
Hanna v. Plumer 456
Hanson v. Denckla 498
Harbour Assurance v. Kansa Gen'l Int'l Assurance 332
Harden, United States v. 905
Harris v. Balk 398, 585, 602
Harrisburg, The 76
Hartford Acc. & Indem. v. Delta & Pine Land 398, 404
Hartford Fire Ins. Co. v. California . . . 962
Haumschild v. Continental Casualty Co. . . . 52
Helicopteros Nac. de Colombia v. Hall (S.Ct.) 559
Hellenic Lines Ltd. v. Rhoditis 884
Henry v. Geoprosco Int'l Ltd. 717
Hilton v. Guyot 684
Hitchcock v. Aiken 645
Holman v. Johnson 893
Holzer v. Deutsche Reichsbahn-Gesellschaft 39
Home Ins. Co. v. Dick 382
Hoopeston Canning Co. v. Cullen 398
Horn v. North British Ry. Co. 6
Hughes v. Fetter 140, 367
Hunt v. Coastal States Gas Producing Co. . . . 1004
Hunt v. Mobil Oil Corp. 1003
Hutchinson v. Chase & Gilbert . . . 488, 494, 586
Hutchison v. Ross 340

I

IIT v. Vencap 942
Imperial Chem. Indus., United States v. . . . 911
India, Government of v. Taylor 895
Indussa Corp. v. S.S. Ranborg 309
Industrial Comm'n of Wisc. v. McCartin . . . 661
Insurance Antitrust Case, The 960
Ins. Corp. of Ireland v. Comp. des Bauxites de Guineé 553
Intercontinental Planning, Ltd. v. Daystrom, Inc. 254
Intercontinental Hotels Corp. v. Golden 177

Intercontinental Planning, Ltd. V. Daystrom, Inc. 254
Intermeat, Inc. v. American Poultry, Inc. . . . 596
International Shoe Co. v. Washington (Wash.) 493
International Shoe Co. v. Washington (S. Ct.) 486
Iraq, Republic of v. First Nat'l City Bank . . . 1004
Istituto Bancario Italiano v. Hunter Engineering Co. 604
Ivenel v. Schwab 627

J

John Hancock Mut. Life Ins. Co. v. Yates . . 395, 405, 417
Johnson, Matter of 776
Johnson v. Hassett 418
Johnson v. Muelberger 776
Johnston v. Compagnie Generale Transatlantique 694
Jones, In re Estate of 28
Jonnett v. Dollar Sav. Bank 580

K

Kalmazoo Spice Extr. Co. v. Gov't of Ethiopia 1003
Kansai Iron Works Ltd. v. Marbeni-Iida . . . 522
Kaufman v. American Youth Hostels . . 134
Keeton v. Hustler Magazine, Inc. 546
Kell v. Henderson 160
Kenny v. Supr. Lodge of World Order of Moose 644
Kilberg v. Northeast Airlines 129, 146
Klaxon Co. v. Stentor Elec. Mfg. Co. . . . 136, 449
Kleinwort v. Benson 920
Kook v. Crang 940
Kotam Electr. Inc. v. JBL Consumer Prod., Inc. 337
Kramer v. Vogl 525
Krause v. Krause 346
Kryger v. Wilson 374, 397
Kulko v. Superior Court of California . . 541, 555
Kulukundis Shipping v. Amtorg Trading . . . 309, 328
Kurent v. Farmers Ins. of Columbus, Inc. . . 221

L

Labree v. Major 193
Laker Airways v. Sabena Airlines 958
Lanari Estate 351
Lauritzen v. Larsen 871
Leasco Data Processing Equip. Corp. v. Maxwell 930

[References are to page numbers. Discussion of principal cases in the succeeding notes and questions is not separately listed.]

Leonard, In re Marriage of 844
Levy v. Daniels' U-Drive Auto Renting Co. . . . 61
Levy v. Steiger 66, 444, 447
Light v. Light 805
Lilienthal v. Kaufman 232
Lillegraven v. Tengs 114
Livingston v. Jefferson 378
Loeb v. Loeb 806
Long v. Pan Amer. World Airways, Inc. . . . 167
Lotus Case (France v. Turkey) 908
Loucks v. Standard Oil Co. 34
Low v. Peers 783
Lynde v. Lynde 794

M

Maccoun / Watts v. Lanari / Meyer 351
Macey v. Rozbicki 162
Mackender v. Feldia 496
Mack Trucks v. Bendix Westinghouse Auto. Air Brake 81
Magnolia Petroleum v. Hunt 655
Majique Fashions Ltd. v. Warwick & Sons . . . 609
Mannington Mills, Inc. v. Congoleum Corp. 950
Marie v. Garrison 115, 116
May v. Anderson 826
Maynard v. Hill 784
May's Estate, In re 855
McCulloch v. Soc. Nac. de Mari. de Honduras 881
McDonnell Douglas v. Islamic Repub. of Iran 310
McElmoyle v. Cohen 374, 422, 643
McGee v. International Life Ins. Co. 491
McLean v. Pettigrew 149
Mertz v. Mertz 58, 683
Mesa y Hernandez, Matter of 342
Milkovich v. Saari 194
Miller v. Miller 171
Miller v. Superior Court of Los Angeles County 846
Milliken v. Pratt 14
Mills v. Duryee 645
Milwaukee County v. M. E. White Co. 673, 905
Minichiello v. Rosenberg 606
Minneapolis & St. Louis R.R. Co. v. Bombolis 480
Minnesota v. Northern Securities Co. . . 643
Mitchell v. W.T. Grant Co. 580
Mitsubishi Motors v. Soler Chrysler-Plymouth 322
Moore v. Mitchell 897
Moragne v. States Marine Lines 380
Mullane v. Central Hanover Trust Co. 508, 541
Muller, Wm. H. & Co. v. Swedish Am. Lines 295, 309

Munzer v. Munzer-Jacoby 699
Mutual Life Ins. Co. of N.Y. v. Liebing 397

N

National Equip. Rental, Ltd. v. Szukhent . . . 297
National Shawmut Bank v. Cumming . . 343
Nelson v. Employers Mut. Casualty Co. 408
Neumeier v. Kuehner 181
Nevada v. Hall 404
Newman v. Dore 346
New Amsterdam Casualty Co. v. Stecker . . . 65
New York Life Ins. Co. v. Dodge 397
New York Life Ins. Co. v. Head 398
Nghiem v. NEC Electronics, Inc. 337
North Georgia Finishing, Inc. v. DiChem. Inc. 580

O

Occidental of Umm al Qaywayn v. Certain Cargo 1003
Occidental Petrol. v. Buttes Gas & Oil Co. . . . 1003
O'Connor v. Lee-Hy Paving Corp . . 189, 606
Ohio v. Wyandotte Chemicals Corp. . . . 539, 632
Oklahoma Tax Commission, State ex rel. v. Rodgers 674
Oltarsh v. Aetna Casualty Inc. Co. . . . 177, 401

P

Pacific Employers Ins. v. Indus. Acc. Comm'n 389
Palmer v. Hoffman 455
Paris Air Crash, In re 466
Parsons & Whittemore v. Soc. Gen. de L'Industrie 736
Pasqualone v. Pasqualone 844
Paul v. National Life 202
Pearson v. Northeast Airlines 135
Peck v. Williamson 645
Pendy Plastic v. Pluspunkt Handelsgesellschaft 731
Pennoyer v. Neff 495, 578, 729
Philadelphia, City of v. Cohen 674
Phillips v. Eyre 149
Phillips Petroleum Co. v. Shutts 421
Piper Aircraft Co v. Reyno 575
Pisacane v. Italia Soc. Per Azioni di Navigazione 271
Prima Paint v. Flood & Conklin Mfg. . . . 319, 326, 332
Pritchard v. Norton 381

[References are to page numbers. Discussion of principal cases in the succeeding notes and questions is not separately listed.]

R

Ragan v. Merchants Transfer & Warehouse Co. ... 454
Reasor-Hill Corp. v. Harrison ... 378
Regazzoni v. K. C. Sethia (1944) Ltd. ... 899
Reich v. Purcell ... 244
Renard, Estate of ... 361
Republic of Iraq v. First Nat'l City Bank ... 1004
Rhodes, Matter of Estate of ... 363
Richards v. United States ... 138, 376
Richardson v. C.I.R. ... 453
Ritchie v. McMullen ... 698
Rockwell Int'l Systems v. Citibank ... 310
Rodda v. Rodda ... 805
Rodriguez de Quijas v. Shearson/American Exp. ... 337
Rohr, Etablissements v. Ossbserger ... 726
Romero v. International Terminal Operating Co. ... 878
Roorda v. Volkswagenwerk, A.G. ... 495
Rosenberg Bros. v. Curtis Brown Co. ... 489, 562, 574
Rosenstiel v. Rosenstiel ... 780
Rosenthal v. Warren ... 189, 606
Rubin v. Irving Trust Co. ... 245
Rush v. Savchuk ... 607

S

Sampson v. Channell ... 444
Scheer v. Rockne Motors Corp. ... 115, 116
Scherk v. Alberto-Culver Co ... 315
Schneider's Estate, In re ... 48
Schoenbaum v. Firstbrook ... 927
Schultz v. Boy Scouts of America ... 205
Schulze v. Illinois Highway Transportation Co. ... 218
Scott v. Lord Seymour ... 9
Sea-Land Services v. Gaudet ... 467
SEC v. Kasser ... 939
Seider v. Roth ... 398, 605
Shaffer v. Heitner ... 580
Shannon v. Irving Trust Co. ... 130, 131
Shearson/American Express, Inc. v. McMahon ... 337
Sherrer v. Sherrer ... 768
Shutts v. Phillips Petroleum Co. (Kan.) ... 422
Sibbach v. Wilson ... 455
Sidmetal, Soc. Coop. v. Titan International Ltd. ... 716
Siegelman v. Cunard White Star ... 259
Silvestri v. Slatowski ... 74
Simons v. Miami Beach First Nat'l Bank ... 800
Simpson v. Loehmann ... 606
Sistare v. Sistare ... 804
Slater v. Mexican Nat'l R.R. Co. ... 116, 117, 131, 376

Smith, Valentine & Smith, Inc. v. Superior Court ... 311
Sniadach v. Family Finance Corp. ... 580
Soc. Anc. Etabl. Picquarad v. Schumann ... 976
Soc. Audi-NSU Auto Union v. S.A. Adelin Petit ... 742
Soc. Cooperative Sidmetal v. Titan International ... 716
Soc. Minera El Teniente v. A.G. Norddeutsche ... 993
Somportex v. Philadelphia Chewing Gum Corp. (U.K.) ... 703
Somportex v. Philadelphia Chewing Gum Corp. (U.S.) ... 708
Sosna v. Iowa ... 779
Soulie´Case ... 44
Southern Int'l Sales v. Potter & Brumfield Div. ... 272
Spiliada Maritime Corp. v. Cansulex Ltd. ... 578
Stanat Mfg. Co. v. Imperial Metals Finishing Co. ... 525
State (N.C.) v. Williams ... 768
Stewart Organization, Inc. v. Ricoh ... 311
Stoll v. Gottlieb ... 679, 770
Strawbridge v. Curtiss ... 551
Sun Oil v. Wortman (S.Ct.) ... 422, 557
Swift V. Tyson ... 432, 700

T

Tahan v. Hodgson ... 716
Taylor v. Taylor ... 846
Tessili v. Dunlop A.G. ... 625
Thomas v. Washington Gas Light Co. ... 663
Thompson v. Whitman ... 760
Timberlane Lumber Co. v. Bank of America ... 943
Toledo Society for Crippled Children v. Hickok ... 337
Tooker v. Lopez ... 173
Totten, In re ... 343
Towley v. King Arthur Rings ... 188
Trauth v. Northeast Airlines ... 144
Tzortzis and Sykias v. Monark Line ... 279, 332

U

Underwriters Nat. v. N.C. Life & Acc. & Health Ins. ... 682
United States v. Aluminum Co. of America ... 909
United States v. Harden ... 905
United States v. Imperial Chem. Indus., Ltd. ... 911
University of Chicago v. Dater ... 46
Unterweser Reederei G.m.b.H v. Zapata Off-Shore Co. ... 290
Uranium Antitrust Litigation, In re ... 958

[References are to page numbers. Discussion of principal cases in the succeeding notes and questions is not separately listed.]

V

Vanderbilt v. Vanderbilt 802, 806
Van Dusen v. Barrack 457
Vimar Seguros y Reaseguros v. MV Sky Reefer 337
Vita Food Products, Inc. v. Unus Shipping Co. 256, 309
Vogel v. Kohnstamm Ltd. 717

W

Walker v. Armco Steel Corp. 454
Walker v. Sauvinet 475
Walzer v. Walzer 805
Warner v. Buffalo Drydock Co. 683
Warrender v. Warrender 792
Watson v. Employers Liability Assurance Corp. *392*
Watts v. Swiss Bank Corp. 354
Webb v. Webb 843
Weber v. Weber 792
Wells v. Simonds Abrasive Co. . . . 137, *374*
Wessling v. Paris 192
West v. Theis 79
West Coast Machinery 522
Whelchel, In re the Marriage of 810
White v. Tennant 25
White Lumber Sales v. Sulmonetti, State ex. rel. 526
Wilkins v. Zelichowski *858*
Wilko v. Swan 316, 327
Williams v. North Carolina (I) 749
Williams v. North Carolina (II) 758
Williamson v. Massachusetts Bonding & Ins. Co. 65
Wood & Selick v. Cie. Generale Transatlantique 77
Wooden v. Western N.Y. & Pa. R.R. Co. 131
Woods v. Interstate Realty Co. 454
World-Wide Volkswagen Corp. v. Woodson *531*
Worthley v. Worthley 804
Wortman v. Sun Oil Co. (Kan.) 422
Wyatt & Fulrath 338, 809

X

X A.G. v. A Bank 925

Y

Yarborough v. Yarborough 647

Z

Zwack v. Kraus Bros. 1004

INDEX

[References are to pages.]

A

ACT OF STATE DOCTRINE
Conflict of law and . . . 945, 952, 981
Sabbatino Amendment . . . 1003
Sabbatino case . . . 982

AIR CRASH LITIGATION
Choice of law and . . . 129
Erie doctrine and . . . 465

ANTITRUST LAWS
Effects doctrine . . . 909, 911, 946, 956
Transnational transactions . . . 911, 962

APPELLATE REVIEW
Jury verdicts . . . 470

ARBITRATION
Agreements to arbitrate . . . 312
Awards, recognition of . . . 734
Choice of forum clause, as . . . 279, 282, 312
New York Convention . . . 319, 325, 734
Public law and . . . 315, 331

ATTACHMENT (See QUASI IN REM ACTIONS)

B

BEALE, JOSEPH HENRY
Choice of law clauses . . . 256
Contracts . . . 19
Real property . . . 21
Torts . . . 103
Vested rights theory . . . 146

BERNSTINE, DANIEL O.
Transient jurisdiction . . . 610

BODENHEIMER, BRIGITTE
Child custody . . . 825, 833, 844

BRANDEIS, JUSTICE LOUIS
Erie Case . . . 435, 440
Federal Rules of Civil Procedure . . . 454

BREITEL, JUDGE CHARLES D.
Choice of law . . . 172, 179, 185, 187

BREWSTER, KINGMAN
Transnational transactions and jurisdiction to prescribe . . . 943, 949

BRUSSELS CONVENTION
Choice of forum clauses (See CHOICE OF FORUM CLAUSES)
European Court of Justice . . . 622
Judgments, enforcement of . . . 718
Jurisdiction of courts . . . 620
Nonmember states . . . 732

BUTLER, JUSTICE PIERCE
Erie Case . . . 442

C

CARDOZO, JUDGE BENJAMIN
Public policy . . . 34, 38

CARRINGTON, PAUL
Quasi in rem actions . . . 601

CAVERS, DAVID F.
Choice of Law . . . 103, 142, 144, 169, 170, 192, 200, 243, 245, 892
Eric and Choice of law . . . 452
Guest statutes . . . 169, 174, 195
Imaginary cases . . . 104

CENTER OF GRAVITY
Auten v. Auten . . . 247
Babcock v. Jackson . . . 145

CHARACTERIZATION
Erie Doctrine . . . 444
Escape device, as . . . 52

CHAYES, ABRAM
Erie Doctrine . . . 462

CHEATHAM ELLIOT E.
Choice of Law and Full Faith and Credit . . . 646

CHILD ABDUCTION
Hague Convention . . . 847
Parental Kidnapping Prevention Act (PKPA) . . 833, 838

CHILD CUSTODY
International aspects . . . 845
Modifiability . . . 832, 843
Parental Kidnapping Prevention Act (PKPA) . . 833, 838
Traditional view . . . 827, 832
Uniform Child Custody Jurisdiction Act (UCCJA) . . 833
Uniform Child Custody Jurisdiction and Enforcement Act (UCCJEA) . . . 845

CHILD SUPPORT
Congressional action . . . 819
Uniform Interstate Family Support Act (UIFSA) . . . 820, 822
Uniform Reciprocal Enforcement of Support Act (URESA) . . . 819

CHOICE OF FORUM CLAUSES
Brussels Convention . . . 621, 625, 721, 726, 729
Conferring and ousting jurisdiction . . . 290
Implying choice of law . . . 278, 306
Overcome . . . 302, 310

I–1

[References are to pages.]

CHOICE OF LAW
Contracts (See CONTRACTS)
Due process and . . . 381, 401, 421
Federal courts and . . . 428, 444, 465
Full faith and credit . . . 367, 385, 398, 419
Governmental interest analysis . . . 109, 119, 122, 200
Guest statutes . . . 145, 168, 173, 190
Party autonomy . . . 256, 346, 361
Torts . . . 103
Wills and trusts . . . 231

CHOICE OF LAW CLAUSES
Jurisdiction of courts and . . . 557, 577

CHOICE OF LAW THEORIES
Beale, Joseph Henry . . . 146
Cavers, David F. . . . 104
Currie, Brainerd . . . 104
Griswald, Erwin N. . . . 104
Grouping of contacts . . . 145, 246, 253
Leflar, Robert A. . . . 196, 403, 465
Reese, Willis . . . 104
Rheinstein, Max . . . 104

COMITY
Judgments, enforcement of . . . 684, 697
Jurisdiction to prescribe . . . 953, 962
Reciprocity . . . 697

CONSTITUTION (U.S.)
Choice of law and . . . 367
Contract clause . . . 392, 397
Due process and choice of law . . . 381, 401, 421
Due process and jurisdiction of courts 486, 515, 531, 578
Erie case and . . . 438, 442
Forum
    Law of . . . 392
    Obligation to provide . . . 367
Full faith and credit clause . . . 638, 642
Out-of-state contracts . . . 392
Privileges and immunities clause . . . 90
Transitory actions . . . 367

CONTRACTS
American rule . . . 14
Capacity to contract . . . 14, 46
Choice of forum clauses . . . 278, 290
Choice of law . . . 231
Contracts of adhesion . . . 259, 337
English rule (traditional) . . . 17
Governmental interests . . . 232
Insurance contracts . . . 382, 392, 402, 960
Interstate contracts . . . 232
Most significant relationship . . . 246
Out-of-state contracts . . . 392
Party autonomy . . . 256, 621
Place of contract . . . 14
"Proper law" . . . 17

COOK, WALTER WHEELER
Capacity to sue . . . 53
Enforcement of Judgments . . . 644

CURRIE, BRAINERD
Constitution and Choice of Law . . . 379
Governmental interest analysis . . . 109, 119, 122, 200
Romero case, on . . . 890

CURRIE, DAVID
Long-arm statutes . . . 527
Migratory divorce . . . 792
Quasi in rem actions . . . 601

CUSTODY (See CHILD CUSTODY)

D

DAMAGES, LIMITATION ON
Choice of law . . . 129
Public policy . . . 34, 129, 142

DECEDENT ESTATES
Choice of law . . . 337
Domicile . . . 25, 34, 41, 346
Interest analysis . . . 346, 359
Party autonomy . . . 346, 361

DESMOND, JUDGE CHARLES S.
Choice of law . . . 129, 159, 162
Marriage and public policy . . . 857, 862
Succession and domicile . . . 340, 344

DE VRIES, HENRY P.
Civil law views on jurisdiction . . . 621

DISCOVERY RULE
Statue of limitations . . . 91

DIVERSITY JURISDICTION
Appellate review of jury verdicts . . . 470
Erie doctrine . . . 431
Multidistrict litigation . . . 464
Transfer of venue . . . 457, 462

DIVORCE
Bilateral divorce and full faith and credit . . 768, 774
Economic incidents . . . 793
Equitable distribution . . . 808
Ex parte divorce . . . 749
Foreign country divorce . . . 779
Full faith and credit . . . 749, 796
History . . . 747, 808
Jurisdiction . . . 748, 749
Migratory divorce . . . 749
Non-final judgments . . . 794

DOMICILE
Common domicile and choice of law . . . 145, 152, 184
Definition . . . 25, 34, 188
Divorce cases . . . 758, 767
Renvoi . . . 41

DOMINICAN REPUBLIC
Migratory divorce . . . 785

DONATIVE TRANSFERS
Choice of law . . . 337
Inter vivos transfers . . . 338
Party autonomy . . . 346

[References are to pages.]

DONATIVE TRANSFERS—Cont.
State interests . . . 346
Testamentary transfers . . . 338

DUE PROCESS
Choice of law . . . 381, 401, 421
Jurisdiction of courts . . . 486, 515, 531, 578

E

ECONOMIC SANCTIONS
U.S. measures abroad, effect of . . . 971

EHRENZWEIG, ALBERT
Adhesion contracts . . . 267
Choice of law . . . 198
Full faith and credit . . . 668

ELY, JOHN HART
Erie Doctrine . . . 454, 462

ENGLAND (See UNITED KINGDOM)

EQUITABLE DOCTRINE (See DIVORCE)

***ERIE* DOCTRINE**
Appellate review of jury verdicts . . . 470
Choice of law . . . 444
Development of . . . 454
Federal Rules of Civil Procedure . . . 454
Swift v. Tyson, contrasted to . . . 441
Transfer of venue and . . . 457, 462

ESTATES, POWERS AND TRUSTS LAW (N.Y.)
Choice of law provisions . . . 344, 363
Election by spouses . . . 346, 359
Party autonomy . . . 345
Testamentary substitutes . . . 346

EUROPEAN CONVENTION ON JURISDICTION AND ENFORCEMENT OF JUDGMENTS (See BRUSSELS CONVENTION)

EUROPEAN CONVENTION ON LAW APPLICABLE TO CONTRACTUAL OBLIGATIONS (See ROME CONVENTION)

F

FAMILY LAW
See also CHILD CUSTODY, CHILD SUPPORT, DIVORCE, MARRIAGE
Conflict of law and . . . 747

FEDERAL COURTS
Choice of law . . . 869
Erie doctrine . . . 444
Multidistrict litigation . . . 469
Transfer of venue . . . 457, 462

FEDERAL RULES OF CIVIL PROCEDURE
Erie doctrine . . . 454, 456
Quasi in rem actions . . . 601

FIELD, JUSTICE STEPHEN J.
Quasi in rem actions . . . 579

FORCED HEIRSHIP
Civil and common law contrasted . . . 41, 48, 351, 361

FORD, ALAN
Interspousal immunity . . . 53

FOSTER, HENRY, JR.
Migratory divorce . . . 792

FRANK, JUDGE JEROME
Choice of Law clauses . . . 264

FRANKFURTER, JUSTICE FELIX
Arbitration . . . 317
Child custody . . . 828
Choice of law and full faith and credit . . . 646
Choice of law and international law . . . 879, 889
Erie doctrine . . . 455

FREUD, PAUL A.
Conflict of law . . . 138

FRIENDLY, JUDGE HENRY
Choice of law and the Constitution . . . 139
Erie doctrine . . . 442
International law and choice of law . . . 930, 940
Jurisdiction of courts . . . 527
Jurisdiction to prescribe . . . 941

FULD, JUDGE STANLEY H.
Choice of law . . . 132, 145, 156, 168, 177, 181
Decedent estates . . . 346, 357, 359, 364
Jurisdiction of courts . . . 521

FULLER, CHIEF JUSTICE MELVILLE
Act of state doctrine . . . 985
Enforcement of foreign judgments . . . 692

FULL FAITH AND CREDIT
Choice of law . . . 367, 385, 398, 419
Divorce . . . 749, 796
Enforcement of judgments . . . 637
Probate . . . 21, 680
Same sex marriage . . . 862
State interests . . . 647

FULL FAITH AND CREDIT FOR CHILD SUPPORT ORDERS ACT
Findings . . . 821
Passage by Congress . . . 820
UIFSA and Federal Act . . . 821, 823

G

GOVERNMENTAL INTERESTS
Choice of law approach . . . 109, 119, 122, 200
Contracts . . . 232
International relations . . . 971

GRISWOLD, ERWIN N.
Choice of law . . . 105
Renvoi . . . 49, 56, 63

GUEST STATUTES
Choice of Law . . . 145, 168, 173, 190

H

HAGUE CONVENTION ON CIVIL ASPECTS OF INTERNATIONAL CHILD ABDUCTION (See CHILD ABDUCTION)

HAITI
Migratory divorce . . . 785

HAND, JUDGE LEARNED
Choice of law clauses . . . 256
Jurisdiction of courts . . . 494
Jurisdiction to prescribe . . . 909, 946, 952
Revenue rule . . . 897

HARLAN, JUSTICE JOHN
Act of state doctrine . . . 982, 1001
Choice of law clauses . . . 259
Statute of limitations . . . 75

HAY, PETER
Brussels Convention . . . 634

HEISER, WALTER W.
Forum selection clauses . . . 337

HENRY, PATRICK
Federal courts and choice of law . . . 428

HILL, ALFRED
Allstate v. Hague . . . 419
Interest analysis . . . 236

HOLMES, JUSTICE OLIVER WENDELL
Antitrust laws . . . 922, 952
Choice of law . . . 117, 244
Full faith and credit . . . 644
Swift v. Tyson . . . 438, 441

I

INTEREST ANALYSIS (See GOVERNMENTAL INTERESTS)

INTERNATIONAL LAW
Act of state . . . 981
Choice of law . . . 869
Jurisdiction to prescribe . . . 908, 960
Public policy . . . 893
True conflicts . . . 971

J

JAPAN
Enforcement of U.S. judgment . . . 523

JESSUP, PHILIP C.
Erie applied to international law . . . 987

JUDGMENTS
Brussels Convention . . . 718
Comity . . . 355, 684, 697, 711
Divorce decrees . . . 794
Enforcement quasi in rem . . . 589, 608
English rules . . . 716
Foreign-country judgments . . . 355, 684

JUDGMENTS—Cont.
Full faith and credit . . . 124, 491, 498, 637
Hague Conference on Private Int'l Law . . . 733
Jurisdictional questions . . . 674, 702, 718
Res judicata . . . 355, 637, 674, 694, 768
Sister-state judgments . . . 639
U.S.-U.K. Convention (Proposed) . . . 732
Workers' compensation . . . 655, 668

JUENGER, FRIEDRICH
Brigitte Bodenheimer . . . 834
Jurisdiction of courts . . . 620, 631
Supreme Court and choice of law . . . 419

JURISDICTION OF COURTS
Generally . . . 485
Activity by non-resident as basis for jurisdiction . . . 519
Brussels Convention . . . 620
Choice of law and . . . 504, 557, 575, 577, 591, 604
Diversity of jurisdiction (See DIVERSITY JURISDICTION)
English rules . . . 496, 509, 574, 703, 714
European Community . . . 620
General and specific jurisdiction contrasted . . . 559, 573
International controversies . . . 559
Long-arm jurisdiction . . . 493
Minimum contacts . . . 488, 503, 522, 536, 567, 570
Prescribe, to (See JURISDICTION TO PRESCRIBE)
Property as basis for jurisdiction . . . 578
Quasi in rem actions . . . 398, 501, 578, 600
Reasonableness . . . 488, 565, 576, 635
Sales contracts . . . 524
Split torts . . . 520
Tag jurisdiction . . . 610
Transient jurisdiction . . . 610

JURISDICTION TO PRESCRIBE
Antitrust actions . . . 908, 943
Comity . . . 953, 962
Effects test . . . 909, 921, 946, 953, 956
Extraterritorial jurisdiction . . . 908, 971
Securities transactions . . . 927
Transnational activities . . . 960

JURY VERDICTS
Appellate review of . . . 470

K

KAHN-FREUND, OTTO
Effects doctrine and international law . . . 921, 926

KORN, HAROLD L.
Choice of law in New York . . . 151, 205

KRAMER, LARRY
Extraterritorial jurisdiction . . . 970
Renvoi . . . 63

KURLAND, PHILIP
Personal jurisdiction . . . 486, 494, 529

L

LAND (See REAL PROPERTY)

LEFLAR, ROBERT A.
Choice of law considerations . . . 196, 403, 465

LEGISLATIVE JURISDICTION (See JURISDICTION TO PRESCRIBE)

LONG-ARM JURISDICTION (See JURISDICTION OF COURTS)

LORENZEN, ERNEST G.
Contracts, choice of law in . . . 234

LOWENFELD, ANDREAS F.
American and European approaches contrasted 204
Arbitration of public law issues . . . 335
Choice of law and the Constitution . . . 420
Civil law views on jurisdiction . . . 621
Insurance Antitrust case . . . 969
Quasi in rem actions . . . 602
Securities regulations and jurisdiction to prescribe . . . 942
Wills and trusts . . . 343

M

MANSFIELD, WILLIAM MURRY, LORD
Revenue rule . . . 894, 904

MARRIAGE
Bigamy . . . 859, 861
Capacity to marry . . . 855
Incest and . . . 855
Public policy . . . 854
Same sex . . . 862
State interest in . . . 747, 763
Under-age marriage . . . 858

MARSHALL, CHIEF JUSTICE JOHN
Federal courts and choice of law . . . 428
Law of nations and U.S. law . . . 873
Public policy . . . 38

MEXICO
Migratory divorce . . . 791

MUSHLIN, MICHAEL B.
Quasi in rem jurisdiction . . . 609

N

NADELMAN, KURT H.
Full faith and credit . . . 645, 647

NEW YORK
Tort cases . . . 152

NEW YORK CONVENTION
Agreements to arbitrate . . . 315, 333, 742
Enforcement of arbitral awards . . . 734
Public policy . . . 738, 742, 744

P

PARENTAL KIDNAPPING PREVENTION ACT (PKPA)
Congress, passed by . . . 833
UCCJA compared . . . 832, 836

PARTY AUTONOMY
Agreements to arbitrate . . . 312
Contracts . . . 256, 621
Donative transfers . . . 346
Forum selection (See CHOICE OF FORUM CLAUSES)
Wills and trusts . . . 346, 361

PAULSEN, MONRAD G.
Public policy and conflict of laws . . . 39

PERSONAL JURISDICTION (See JURISDICTION OF COURTS)

POWERS OF APPOINTMENT
Choice of law . . . 356, 363, 498, 516

PRODUCT LIABILITY
Jurisdiction of courts . . . 521, 531, 565, 575
Reformation of law . . . 520

PROPERTY
Jurisdiction, basis for . . . 578
Real property (See REAL PROPERTY)

PUBLIC POLICY
Arbitral awards, enforcement of . . . 736
Choice of law and . . . 39, 114, 156, 235
Damages, limitation on . . . 34, 129, 142
Interspousal immunity . . . 58
Marriage and . . . 855

Q

QUASI IN REM ACTIONS
Attachment . . . 578
Enforcement of judgments . . . 589, 608
Federal Rules of Civil Procedure . . . 601
Garnishment . . . 602
Insurance policies . . . 398, 607
Jurisdiction of courts . . . 398, 501, 578, 600

R

RABEL, ERNST
Capacity to sue . . . 53
Party autonomy . . . 257

REAL PROPERTY
Choice of law and succession . . . 20
Domicile, role of . . . 25
Jurisdiction and enforcement of foreign judgments . . . 578, 676, 680
Situs of real property . . . 20

RECIPROCITY
Choice of law . . . 12
Enforcement of foreign judgments . . . 684, 697, 716

[References are to pages.]

REED, JUSTICE STANLEY F.
Erie case . . . 442

REESE, WILLIS L.M.
Allstate v. Hague . . . 420
Choice of forum . . . 297
Choice of law . . . 104, 182, 195
Enforcement of foreign judgments . . . 700

REGULATORY JURISDICTION (See JURISDICTION TO PRESCRIBE)

RENVOI
American cases . . . 46, 56, 57
Analysis . . . 62
English use . . . 41

RES JUDICATA (See JUDGMENTS)

RESTATEMENT OF CONFLICT OF LAWS (FIRST)
Capacity to contract . . . 234, 242
Contracts . . . 19, 249, 266
Domicile . . . 34
Foreign rights . . . 59
Party autonomy . . . 256
Public policy . . . 60
Real property . . . 21
Substance/procedure . . . 68, 72, 76
Title to land . . . 50
Torts . . . 103, 129, 145, 520, 936
Vested rights . . . 145

RESTATEMENT OF CONFLICT OF LAWS (SECOND)
Choice of forum clauses . . . 278, 297, 311
Choice of law clauses . . . 258
Contracts . . . 234, 242, 258, 274, 275, 276
Damages . . . 141
Domicile . . . 34
Full faith and credit . . . 668, 682
Interspousal immunity . . . 55
Jurisdiction of courts . . . 574, 587, 589, 632
Party autonomy . . . 258, 278
Statute of limitations . . . 100
Substance/procedure . . . 73
Torts . . . 108, 110, 126, 146, 178, 181, 936

RESTATEMENT OF FOREIGN RELATIONS LAW (SECOND)
Jurisdiction to prescribe . . . 923, 934, 941, 943, 947

RESTATEMENT OF FOREIGN RELATIONS LAW (THIRD)
Act of state doctrine . . . 1005
Foreign judgments . . . 715
Insurance Antitrust case . . . 962, 965
Jurisdiction of courts . . . 635
Jurisdiction to prescribe . . . 922, 959, 980

RESTATEMENT OF JUDGMENTS (SECOND)
Quasi in rem actions . . . 610
Res judicata . . . 638

RHEINSTEIN, MAX
Capacity to sue . . . 53
Choice of law . . . 104, 125

RHEINSTEIN, MAX—Cont.
Personal jurisdiction . . . 529

ROME CONVENTION
Generally . . . 277
Compared with American developments . . . 277
United Kingdom and . . . 17

ROSENBERG, MAURICE
Kell v. Henderson . . . 170

S

SAWAKI, TAKAO
West Coast Machinery case . . . 524

SCOTT, AUSTIN W.
Hanson v. Denckla . . . 516

SECURITIES REGULATION
Arbitration . . . 315
Transnational transactions . . . 927

SILBERMAN, LINDA
Choice of law and jurisdiction of courts . . . 605
Choice of law and the Constitution . . . 420
Hague Child Abduction Convention . . . 846
Same sex marriage and full faith and credit . . . 863

SMIT, HANS
Quasi in rem jurisdiction . . . 588

SOVERN, MICHAEL I.
Public policy and conflict of laws . . . 39

STATUTE OF LIMITATIONS
Generally . . . 75
Access to courts . . . 374
Borrowing statutes . . . 79, 89
Choice of law and the Constitution . . . 422
Discovery rule . . . 91
Foreign Limitation Periods Act (U.K.) . . . 99
Statutes of repose . . . 91
Substance/procedure . . . 422
Tolling statutes . . . 79, 89
Uniform Conflict of Laws Limitation Act . . . 100

STONE, CHIEF JUSTICE HARLAN F.
Choice of law and the Constitution . . . 386, 389
Full faith and credit to judgments . . . 650, 655

STORY, JUSTICE JOSEPH
Capacity to contract . . . 16
Domicile . . . 30
Enforcement of foreign country judgments . . 687, 691
Full faith and credit . . . 645
Private international law . . . 869
Real property . . . 21
Swift v. Tyson . . . 432, 439

STUMBERG, GEORGE WILFRED
Contracts, choice of law in . . . 234

SUBJECT MATTER JURISDICTION
Jurisdiction to prescribe . . . 908, 927, 960, 965

[References are to pages.]

SUBSTANCE/PROCEDURE
Choice of law . . . 66
Erie doctrine . . . 444, 451
Evidence . . . 71, 74
Statute of limitations . . . 75, 99, 422
Survival of actions . . . 67, 73

SUPREME COURT (U.S.)
Act of state doctrine . . . 981, 1001
Choice of law and the Constitution . . . 367, 401
Choice of law in international setting . . . 871
Jurisdiction of courts . . . 486, 515, 531
Jurisdiction to prescribe . . . 871, 962

SWIFT v. TYSON
Abuse of . . . 437, 440
Doctrine explored . . . 436, 439

T

TAXES
Foreign-country judgments, enforcement of . . . 895, 905
Sister-state judgments, enforcement of . . . 673

TORTS
Choice of law . . . 103
Jurisdiction of courts . . . 1, 531
Mass disaster actions . . . 465
New York cases . . . 152
No-fault compensation . . . 217
Place of injury rule
    Generally . . . 1
    Move away from . . . 129
Survival statutes . . . 67
Uninsured motorist statutes . . . 216, 402
Workers compensation . . . 216

TOTTEN TRUSTS
Testamentary substitute . . . 343, 346

TRAUTMAN, DONALD T.
Guest statutes . . . 168
Jurisdiction of courts . . . 530, 571, 587, 589

TRAYNOR, JUSTICE ROGER J.
Conflict of laws . . . 233
Substance/procedure . . . 67, 73

TRUSTS
Choice of law . . . 339, 343, 356, 498, 515
Inter vivos vs. testamentary transfers . . . 349
Testamentary substitutes . . . 346
Totten trusts . . . 343, 346

U

U.N. CONVENTION ON RECOGNITION AND ENFORCEMENT OF ARBITRAL AWARDS (See NEW YORK CONVENTION)

UNIFORM CHILD CUSTODY JURISDICTION ACT (UCCJA) (See CHILD CUSTODY)

UNIFORM CONFLICT OF LAWS LIMITATION ACT (See STATUTE OF LIMITATIONS)

UNIFORM RECIPROCAL ENFORCEMENT OF SUPPORT ACT (URESA) (See CHILD SUPPORT)

UNITED KINGDOM
Choice of law clauses . . . 256
Choice of law in contract . . . 17
Enforcement of judgments . . . 716
Enforcement of judgments convention . . . 732
Foreign Limitation Periods Act . . . 99
Jurisdiction over nonresidents . . . 496, 574
Lord Campbell's Act . . . 6

V

VENUE
Transfer of . . . 457, 462

VIRGIN ISLANDS
Migratory divorce . . . 777

VITTA, EDOARDO
Choice of law; European view . . . 204

VON MEHREN, ARTHUR
Jurisdiction of courts . . . 530, 587, 589

W

WEINSTEIN, JUDGE JACK
Erie and the federal rules . . . 454

WEINTRAUB, RUSSELL, J.
Marital property . . . 809, 817
Personal jurisdiction . . . 575

WORKER'S COMPENSATION
Choice of law . . . 216, 225, 385, 398
Recognition of out-of-state awards . . . 655

WRIGHT, BARON ROBERT A.
Party autonomy in choice of law . . . 257